ENVIRONMENTAL LAW

By Arnold W. Reitze, Jr.

Professor of Law and Director of the Environmental Law Program
of The National Law Center of The George Washington University

Second Edition

NORTH AMERICAN INTERNATIONAL
Publishers of Quality Books from Around the World

ABOUT THIS BOOK

THE PAPER which comprises this book was made to order for North American International during the week of April 24-28, 1972, at the Fitchburg Paper Company in Fitchburg, Massachusetts. The formula, which includes just over 50% post-industrial-use waste paper, had never previously been manufactured, although the firm had made similar papers with a 25% waste paper content.

TYPE for this book is in several faces, but the basic text is in Times Roman, a face developed from the modern Scotch family of Roman faces for the Times of London. Setting was largely by Automatic Composition of Washington, D.C.

PLATE-MAKING and PRINTING were by the Vinmar Lithographing Company of Lutherville-Timonium, Maryland, which used a 70-by-45-inch sheet-fed perfecting press.

CLOTH for the cover was manufactured to order by Joanna Western Mills of Chicago, Illinois. It is buckram, a cloth once much-favored by book-makers because of its great strength & bold texture, but now seldom used because of its relatively high cost. It is impregnated with Pyroxylin, a plastic, to resist dirt.

BINDING was by L. H. Jenkins, Inc., of Richmond, Virginia. The signatures were sewn together by the Smyth process, in which front and back signatures are double-sewn, for extra strength.

Copies of this book are available from North American International, P.O. Box 28278, Washington, D.C. 20005, for $19.95. The set of two volumes (the second to be available late in 1972) will be available for $35.20. Bulk rates are available for classroom use. Your comments will be welcomed by both author and publisher.

International Standard Book Number (this volume): 0-88265-001-7
ISBN (two-volume set): 0-88265-003-3

Library of Congress Card Number: 73-183226

Second Edition

Published by North American International
P.O. Box 28278 Central Station 20005
1609 Connecticut Ave., N.W. 20009
Washington, D.C.

ACKNOWLEDGEMENTS

This book has been made possible by the combined efforts of those who are working to improve our environment. Without their efforts, environmental law would not exist. In this vein, I must pay tribute to Dean (now President) Louis A. Toepfer of Case Western Reserve University, who encouraged and supported my research and teaching in this field before it became a major national concern. I also gratefully acknowledge the support that the Environmental Law Program at The National Law Center has received from the faculty, from Dean Robert Kramer, Associate Dean Ralph C. Nash, Jr., and The Ford Foundation.

Perhaps the most frustrating (as well as most challenging) aspect of environmental law is the speed with which it changes, abetted by voluminous outpourings from administrative agencies. Many of my students during the past several years assisted me in keeping up with this material. Among the student assistants who aided me in this effort have been David B. Kenyon, Myra G. Kovey, Bruce Lubman, Alan R. Spirer, and James Spensley. Mr. Spensley wrote the first draft of the evaluation of the National Environmental Policy Act which appears in Chapter One.

My two major assistants in this project have been Mrs. Lynda Spikell, who has typed the manuscripts and aided in the many preparatory tasks necessary in putting words to paper. Mr. Dennis P. Koehler, of the class of '72, worked with me during the summer and fall of 1971, when the notes and class materials developed over the past several years were developed into this book. His assistance has been invaluable.

My brother, Glenn Reitze, has been my editor. I do not believe an editor could give more assistance to an author than he has provided. In addition, he researched and wrote most of the material on recycling in Chapter Two.

The completion of this first volume merely points to the need for renewed effort to improve and keep this material up-to-date in subsequent editions. While I have usually taken a position on the issues discussed in the text, no claim of omniscience is made. Suggestions and criticisms will be appreciated.

ADDITIONAL ACKNOWLEDGEMENTS FOR THE SECOND EDITION

There is nothing, as you know by experience, that takes more time than filling in the little gaps one has left in his work.

—Friedrich Schiller in a letter to Goethe, 1799

In January 1972 the first edition of this text was published. During the spring semester the book was used as a text in my Environmental Law course. The experience of using the book as a classroom text together with continued research has been utilized to produce an expanded and updated second edition.

I have been assisted in this project by Mr. Dennis Koehler, of the class of '72, Mr. John Zimmerman, of the class of '73 and Mr. Alan Spirer, of the class of '71, LL.M. '72, who has been a graduate fellow in environmental law. Ms. Lynda Spikell has typed the manuscripts and helped keep the project moving.

In addition to their general assistance, Mr. Spirer has had the major responsibility for the material dealing with the National Environmental Policy Act and wrote much of the discussion. Mr. Zimmerman has had the major responsibility for editing the material on noise pollution. Mr. Koehler together with Mr. Jeffrey Howard, '72, prepared the material on waste oil in Chapter Two. Mr. Charles Shipley, LL.M. in Environmental Law '72, wrote the article on deep well disposal found in Chapter Three. Mr. Alexander Whitaker of the class of '72 wrote a legislative history of the proposed water pollution legislation. Mr. Gregory Ghen worked on proofreading and helped prepare the index.

TABLE OF CONTENTS
Volume One

APPENDIX—Chapter Three

SUB-CHAPTER THREE-B: Noise

CHAPTER FOUR: WATER POLLUTION

APPENDIX—Chapter Four

CHAPTER FIVE: PRIVATE REMEDIES

APPENDIX—Chapter Five

FOREWORD: *The Ethics of Ecosystems*

All of Mankind's institutions are shaped by its views of nature.

Our legal system is a method of social control that seeks to achieve goals by securing obedience to a formal system of regulation. The goals and the formal means used to seek these goals are dependent on the philosophy of those who promulgate the laws. For most subdivisions of our legal system, the philosophy underlying the legal rules is so thoroughly accepted that it is rarely mentioned; we commonly question the means and the ends, but we seldom question the questions that we pose for our legal system to solve.*

Legal change is normally a process of continuing modification, rather than abrupt change, and it rarely includes any challenge to the underlying philosophic assumptions. The powerful, at least, do not question the need for public sector financing through taxation, and federal financing through a progressive income tax has become almost completely accepted. A right to private ownership of property is also accepted with little opposition, and it becomes a philosophical issue only when such rights conflict with other accepted rights. Such a conflict often occurs in the criminal law area, when a balancing of interests is required to protect both property and personal rights (freedom).

When dealing with attitudes toward the earth's ecosystem, however, we must recognize the absence of a commonly accepted philosophical base for the development of an environmental law system. As a nation we have no controlling ethical relationship with our natural environment; some persons wish to exploit, others to preserve, and most are in between. As a result, the basic framework of an environmental law system develops slowly, often with inconsistent rules on the same subject. And this development of law occurs in a political environment that is often acrimonious, for the basic values of some members of our society are challenged by the new rules dealing with the environment.

But as national attitudes change, so does the law. For example, wilderness in biblical references was the antithesis of a garden, and gardens were created by man overcoming nature. To the Puritans, wilderness was a hostile environment, a last refuge for sinners. Wilderness in eighteenth and nineteenth century western literature had an evil connotation. Often the phrase "howling wilderness" was used. Today, we have a Wilderness Act, Wilderness Areas, a Wilderness Society, and wilderness conferences—all more or less in praise of wilderness. Other concepts relating to the environment have been subject to similar changes of attitude.

*Put another way, this old sawhorse runs that it is always more important to formulate the question than to supply an answer. This need not be mere verbalizing: acts speak louder. For instance, the promulgation of war poses a question to youths who may reply by entering the military, leaving the country, etc. But obviously the promulgators of the question, even if they were in turn merely "answering" other questions, had relatively far greater power than their answerers. Power is posing unignorable questions.

An example of these attitudes can be seen in what we today generally regard as a national treasure—the Grand Canyon. Yet the first western man to see the canyon, *don* López Cárdenas, did not even write of his journey. The first report, by Pedro de Castañeda, gives a vivid account of the difficulties of the descent into the canyon, but not a word of its beauty or grandure. Three hundred years later, U.S. Army Lt. Joseph Ives explored the canyon. He concluded that the Colorado River at the canyon's bottom would be an economical avenue for the transport of supplies, but that the area was a profitless locality which would forever be unvisited and undisturbed.

Ten years later, John Wesley Powell, the first man to follow the river through the entire canyon, described it as the "Grand Canyon." In 1903 Theodore Roosevelt called the canyon a natural wonder unparalleled throughout the world, and sought to protect it. In the 1960's the U.S. Bureau of Reclamation sought to dam the river in the National Park to provide electricity. The sale of this power would have produced profits which would have been used to subsidize agriculture in the Southwest.

Thus the history of the Grand Canyon is an example of the changing attitudes of man to nature. Yet this recent controversy concerning it demonstrates the lack of a consistent national philosophy toward its natural resources.

Nature was once thought to be the enemy against whom man struggled to survive. Later nature became the source of exploitive wealth. In recent time we have begun to appreciate the unity of man with nature, and man's dependence on the rest of nature. This "newer" theory, which was not exactly unknown among some primitive groups, calls for man to utilize nature's bounty, but to exist so that the dynamic natural system survives. However, many people, often those with political and economic power, operate with an atavistic philosophy that threatens to destroy the natural environment and with it: man.

The historical development of environmental law parallels the changing philosophical view of nature. Prior to the beginning of the 20th Century, the legal system was used to encourage the development and exploitation of our natural environment. The government encouraged canal building, and gave away millions of acres of public lands to those who would exploit them. Beginning in the late 19th Century, the concept of conservation became popular, and this resulted in legislation in the early part of this century to conserve some of our natural resources.

But conservation means many things to many people, and shortly after the conservation movement began, it split into two camps or schools of thought—a development that to some extent continues today. John Muir led the protectionist or nonexploitation conservationists, while Gifford Pinchott was the leader of the "careful extraction" or "wise-use" school of conservation.

Today, most conservation proponents avoid the easily labeled positions of these earlier conservationists, but the philosophical bent of each lives on. Environmental law moves forward under such labels as: planning, multiple-use, total planning, etc., but this jargon is used with equal facility by those representing the most extreme 19th Century exploitation mentality.

Because the words commonly used to define conservation can be so easily distorted through misuse, it is probably wiser for the seeker of truth to look for basic principles, rather than to cling to iron rules that may be easily turned around. The basic principle of conservation has been expressed in many hundreds of ways, most long before conservation became popular. Some aspects of the ages-old nature religions were conservationist at heart; others caused vast ecological destruction in the worship of nature. For example, the Teotihuacán people of Mexico's Classic period destroyed the forests, very likely to make lime for stuccoing their huge "City of the Gods," contributing to a drop in the water table and the drying of their corn fields—all while worshipping various nature gods and goddesses, including the goddess of water. Such destruction of the environment has been exceedingly common wherever man has multiplied to the point where his actions could strongly affect the environment. The basic attitude, therefore, that man is a part of nature and that his well being depends on the survival of the natural environment is not enough. There must also be understanding; for this today we use science.

Conservation is the doctrine that aims to preserve the well being of our habitat—the planet earth. It recognizes the rights of future generations to live. To quote Juenger, "There can be no talk of riches produced by technology. What really happens is rather a steady, forever growing consumption. It is ruthless destruction, the like of which the earth has never before seen. A more and more ruthless destruction of resources is the characteristic of our technology."

One need only pick up a popular magazine or watch television for a short time to see numerous examples of commercial exploitations encouraging people to consume, use up, or enjoy the convenience of the throw-away society. But there is no place left to throw anything away, and the natural values which are lost to provide material and energy for our destructive society are gone forever. The ethic of conservation recognizes that the supply of nonrenewable resources, including minerals, fossil fuels and other substances such as salt in deposits and sulfur is finite, and therefore should be used carefully.

To conserve these nonrenewable resources requires also the conservation of energy, for vast quantities of the hydrocarbons which stored energy over millions of years are consumed daily to release energy.

The renewable resources, forests, grasslands, wildlife, should be managed to sustain a continuous yield with the health of the soil—a primary provider of these resources—a consideration basic to all resource planning. An ethical as well as biological honesty would recognize the value of all life and attempt to protect and encourage the diversity of living resources. The flow resources, including water and air, which have a capacity, though limited, to absorb man's wastes, should be protected. No one should use these resources so as to diminish their quality. Where such diminution is necessary to produce a product valued by society more than the biodestruction it causes, certainly the decision to produce the product should not be that of the producer motivated by the desire for monetary gain.

Conservation is a way of life. Needless to say, few people are willing to subscribe to the return to nature plea. But it should be made clear that living in harmony with nature need not require the giving up of many of the advances that a thousand years of applied science and technology have provided. Much of our environmental destruction is carried on to benefit a small number of people who profit from a particular technological slant. From any rational view, the large American automobile is most unsatisfactory for transporting people in urban areas. Yet our transportation system is geared almost entirely to serving automobiles and not people. Building expensive and environmentally destructive dams to irrigate desert land to provide agriculture crops while rural counties in other parts of the nation are economically depressed and losing population would seem unwise, but some people find this system very profitable.

One of the proponents of humanizing technology to serve human needs is Admiral Rickover. We must, he says, understand the dangerous qualities of our technology and direct it to humane ends. He distinguishes between science and technology. Science has to do with discovering true facts and relationships, but technology cannot claim the authority of science. Science requires the exclusion of the human factor to discover truth, and is the antithesis of humanism. But the discoveries are thoughts and ideas which in themselves harm no one. Technology is the action which, unless adopted to human needs, creates harm. Technology can have no legitimate purpose but to serve mankind. Thus, human society must govern technology to achieve what, in their wisdom and experience, is just and fair. He questions whether man is really wise enough to upset beneficially the balance of nature:

> "These are complicated matters for ordinary citizens to evaluate and decide. How to make wiser use of technology in the future is perhaps the paramount public issue facing electorates in all industrial democracies. A free society centers on man. It gives paramount consideration to human rights, interest and needs. But once ordinary citizens come to feel that public issues are beyond their comprehension, a pattern of life may develop where technology, not man, would become central to the purpose of society. If we permit this to happen, the human liberties for which mankind has fought, at so great a cost of effort and sacrifice, will be extinguished."

Other writers recognize the impact of technology on our environment, but focus more directly on the role of those who control these technologies. Murray Bookchin sees the notion that man must dominate nature as emerging directly from the domination of man by man. Modern capitalism, in his view, pits humans against one another. "Growth," "industrial society" and "urban blight" are euphemisms for man's domination of his fellow man. Needs are tailored by the mass media to create a public demand for unneeded commodities which require the plundering of the earth. The role of the consumer in the mass market has been documented by Professor Kenneth Galbraith in *The New Industrial State,* but Bookchin recognizes the environmental problem of trying to survive this economic system. The irony is that the technology which could remove man from material scarcity could destroy his biological habitat. Bookchin calls on man to master his technology in order to live, but says this requires a social reconstruction.

This theme is carried on by Charles Reich in *The Greening of America,* where he finds youth in the state of Consciousness III, recognizing the social relationship necessary to end environmental and social abuses. The environmental destructiveness of our society requires an ever-willing group of consumers who are ready to accept whatever the corporate state delivers. It also requires a docile work force willing to work at boring and unsatisfying jobs to produce unneeded or even socially or environmentally destructive products. The solution, according to Reich, it to not play the game. If a sizable portion of the citizenry opts for flowers instead of astroturf, or bicycles instead of 300-horsepower automobiles, the destructive consumption cycle can be broken, Reich believes.

Another writer, with a similar desire for environmental sanity, but with a somewhat different emphasis, is Professor Earl Murphy, who emphasizes the compatibility of an urban-industrial society within a living and thriving environment. This can be done only by an appreciation of the fact that man must exist as part of nature. This in turn requires a great deal more basic information as to how the natural system functions. His system would formulate a body of regulations which attempt to translate this information as rapidly as possible into a law for life. Jurisdictions such as air sheds, river basins, and fish protection zones, would attempt to prevent the disruption of natural equilibriums or, failing that, deal effectively in a biological sense with any new balances created.

It is clear that the personal gains that can be obtained by exploitation of our environment are vast, and this makes the development and implementation of a body of law designed to protect our 'Babbittat' an extremely difficult task. A potential side effect is the capacity of such legal protection to limit further our freedom, and inject the state into many aspects of our lives heretofore considered immune from governmental interference. Therefore, such governmental change must be considered carefully.

A common thread running through the writing of all of these critics of unbridled technology, regardless of the solution they propose or the villians they identify, is the need to return the decision-making process to the citizenry. Power to the people is the cry of those who see runaway technology destroying our environment. Professor Murphy would further emphasize the need for fiscal resources at the local level to solve the problems. But we should ask the further question of whether we have the ability to accomplish such changes without breaking up the national and international economic blocks whose control of capital shape government decisions and whose control of the mass media limit substantially the meaning of the First Amendment (freedom of speech, religion, and assembly) to the United States Constitution.

The philosopy of natural resources management is rarely labeled as such, but the aims, attitudes, and goals of government are the embodiment of the philosophy of the nation. Furthermore, the kind of planning engaged in by a nation is determined by its view of the ethical relation of man to his environment.

In our nation that absence of any strong recognition of the values offered by a natural environment make legal protection difficult—though recent developments of national concern for such values may allow for meaningful protection to evolve.

Until very recently, conservationists were nearly all white, middle class, and comparatively well schooled. Generally their interests were issue-oriented, and their participation in social problems was limited to conservation issues—a position that limited the ability of their groups to combine with other groups to be effective politically.

In the past few years another sort of environmentalist has appeared, sometimes simply by conversion. These environmentalists are actively interested in the abolition of war (or at least the Vietnam war), and in obtaining justice for blacks, women, and others. Often they have a concern for worldwide economic quality improvement, and they give frequent emphasis to providing a plurality of choices in order to release more human intellectually creative resources.

These idealistic views often seem simplistic. Yet those who deal with conservation in a vacuum, believing that national parks can be created and pesticide use curtailed without reference to economic and political realities, appear equally naive. As long as diseases carried by organisms controlled by pesticides are a major world problem, and as long as developed nations use large war budgets to keep poor nations under control (so that raw materials flow to those developed nations), then a sanely protected environment, social justice, and peace will be difficult to obtain, and these problems will remain intertwined.

Selective bibliography

Books

Ethics, history & general works

BALDWIN and PAGE, eds., *Law and the Environment, Walker and Co., New York 1970*

BROWN, Harrison Scott; *The Challenge of Man's Future, an Inquire Concerning the Condition of Man during the Years that Lie Ahead;* New York, Viking Press, 1954

CLEPPER, Henry Edward, ed. *Origins or American Conservation,* New York, Ronald Press, 1966

COMMONER, Barry, *The Closing Circle,* Knopf, 1971

COYLE, David Cushman, *Conservation*, New Brunswick, J.J. Rutgers University Press, 1957

DASMANN, Raymond F., *A Different Kind of Country,* New York, Macmillan, 1968

DOUGLAS, William, O., *A Wilderness Bill of Rights,* Boston, Little, Brown, 1965 paper

EKIRCH, Arthur A., Jr., *Man and Nature in America,* New York, Columbia University Press, 1963

ELLUL, Jacques, *The Technological Society,* New York, Vintage Books, 1964 paper

HARDIN, *The Tragedy of the Commons, from The Environmental Handbook,* ed. Garrett De Bell !970

HAYS, Samuel P., *Conservation and the Gospel of Efficiency: The Progressive Conservation Movement, 1890-1920,* Cambridge-Harvard Univ. Press, 1959

HELFRICH, Harold W., ed., *The Environmental Crisis: Man's Struggle to Live with Himself,* New Haven, Yale University Press, 1970 paper

JARRETT, Henry, ed., *Perspective on Conservation,* Baltimore, The Johns Hopkins Press, 1958 paper

JUENGER, Frederick, *The Failure of Technology,* Hinsdale, Ill., Henry Regnery Co., 1949 (written 1939)

KERR, Robert S., *Land, Wood, and Water,* N. Y., Fleet Publishing Co., (No Year) pp. 380

KING, Judson, *The Conservation Fight: From Theodore Roosevelt to the Tennessee Valley Authority,* Washington, D.C., Public Affairs Press, 1959

MAYDA, *Environment and Resources,* the University of Puerto Rico 1968 paper

NASH, Roderick, *Wilderness and the American Mind,* New Haven, Yale Univ. Press, 1967

NASH, Roderick, *The American Environment: Readings in the History of Conservation,* Reading, Mass., Addison-Wesley Publishing Co., 1968 paper

Ethics, history & general works

NELSON, Richard R., *Technology, Economic Growth, and Public Policy,* Washington, Brookings Institution, 1967

OSBORN, Fairfield, *Our Plundered Planet,* New York, Pyramid Books, 1948, reprint 1968 paper

RICHARDSON, Elmo R., *The Politics of Conservation: Crusades and Controversies, 1897–1913,* Berkeley, University of California Press, 1962

SMITH, Frank E., *The Politics of Conservation,* New York, Pantheon Books, 1966

SWAIN, Donald C., *Federal Conservation Policy, 1921–1933,* Berkeley, University of California Press, 1963

SWIFT, Ernest F., *A Conservation Saga,* Washington, D.C., National Wildlife Federation, 1967

TUNNARD, Christopher, *Man-Made America: Chaos or Control?,* New Haven, Yale University Press, 1966

WARD, Barbara, *Space Ship Earth,* New York, Columbia University Press, 1966 paper

Articles

Beazley, K., Conservation Decision Making: A Rationalization, 7 Nat. Res. J. 345 (July 1967).

Bibliography of Recent Books & Periodicals, 3 Nat. Res. Law. 357, May 1970.

Callester, E. G., & Hayse, R. F., Legal Muscle for the Fight Against Pollution, 9 Washburn L.J. 342 (Sept. 1970)

Environmental Policy: New Directions in Federal Action: A Symposium, 28 Pub. Admin. Rev. 30 (July-Aug. 1968).

Fox, I. K., New Horizons in Water Resources Administration, 26 Pub. Admin. Rev. 61 (March 1965).

Freeman, O. L., Towards a National Policy on Balanced Communities, 53 Minn. L. Rev. 1163 (Dec. 1969).

Hamell, L., Process of Making Good Decisions about the Use of the Environment of Man, 8 Nat. Rex. J., 279 (April 1968).

Henning, A Selected Bibliography on Public Environmental Policy and Administration, 11 Nat. Res. J. 201 (Jan. 1971).

Hutchinson, S. B., Bringing Resource Conservation Into the Mainstream of American Thought, 9 Nat. Res. J., 518 (October 1969).

Krutch, *The Eye of the Beholder,* 4 *The American West* 18 (May 1967)

Literature—Books, 2 Nat. Res. Law., 64 (June 1969).

Mantz, C. O., Role of Government in Public Resource Management, 15 Rocky Mt. ML Institute, 1, 1969.

Mayela, J., Conservation, "New Conservation" & Economic Management, 1969 Wisc. L. Rev. 788 (1969).

Moses, R. J., What Happened to Multi-Purpose Resource Development—A Plea for Reasonableness, 3 Land & Water L. Rev., 435 (1968).

Muskie, E. S., Environmental Jurisdiction in the Congress and the Executive, 22 Maine L. Rev., 171 (1970).

Role of the Judiciary in the Confrontation with the Problems of Environmental Quality, 17 UCLA L. Rev., 1070 (May 1970).

Sax, J. L., Public Trust Doctrine in Nat. Resources Law: Effective Judicial Intervention, 68 Mich L. Rev., 473 (June 1970).

INTRODUCTION

a. Ecology for planners

Ecology is a science that encompasses major aspects of the other physical and life sciences. To discuss adequately this subject is clearly beyond the capabilities of a text on law; yet certain ecological principles should be grasped, for these must be the basis for social regulation if such legislation is to work. The classic text in this field is Odum, Eugene, *Fundamentals of Ecology,* 2d.ed., 1959. Other materials are listed in the bibliography at the end of this section.

To understand ecology—and the present dilemma that man has created for himself—one must first understand the concept of "ecosystem." An ecosystem is the sum total of all of the living and nonliving parts that support a chain of life within a selected area. The four primary links in the chain:

NONLIVING MATTER: the sunlight, water, oxygen, carbon dioxide, organic compounds and other nutrients used by plants for their growth.
THE PLANTS: ranging in size from the microscopic phytoplankton in water up through grass and shrubs to trees, these organisms convert carbon dioxide and water, in a process called photosynthesis, into carbohydrates required both by themselves and other organisms in the ecosystem.
THE CONSUMERS: those higher organisms that feed on the producers. Herbivores, such as cows and sheep, are primary consumers. Carnivorous man and such animals as the wolf feed upon the herbivores and are secondary consumers.
THE DECOMPOSERS: these tiny creatures—bacteria, fungi and insect—close the circle of the ecosystem when they break down the dead producers and consumers and return their chemical compounds to the ecosystem for reuse by the plants.

Although growth and decay are going on simultaneously and continuously in an ecosystem, they tend to balance each other over the long run—and thus the chain is said to be in equilibrium. Non-human environments have a remarkable resiliency; as many as 25 or even 50 percent of a certain fish or rodent population might be lost in a habitat during a plague or disaster, yet the species will recover its original strength within one or two years. It is man-made interference—or pollution—that can profoundly disturb the ecosystem and its equilibrium.

Four elements make up the major portion of living things in the environment: carbon, oxygen, hydrogen, and nitrogen. Green plants convert carbon dioxide into food, fiber, and fuel and at the same time produce oxygen. Plants also convert inorganic nitrogen into protein. A myriad of microorganisms, about which we know very little, keeps the cycle of biological interactions going,which is necessary to have pure air and water and fertile soil. Evaporation of water in turn regulates our weather. Thus our biosphere is a complex living machine. This machine is our biologic capital without which we can have no productivity, yet it is this machine that our technology threatens to destroy. The most disquieting aspect of this destruction is that it is part of, not a by-product, of our technology. The challenge is to make the extreme and fundamental adjustments in our production system that threatens to destroy our biologic life support system. The hidden social costs of most production results in the deterioration of our health and environment.The ways in which these biological insults appear make political and legal remedies difficult to achieve.

basics of ecology

terms defined

The person dealing with environmental concepts should develop a basic understanding of the commonly used terms. Some of these are:

ECOLOGY The study of the interrelationships of organisms to one another and to the environment.

ECOSYSTEM a community of all organisms within an environment forming an interacting system. (Also called biosystem)

BIOTA All of the species of plants and animals occurring within a certain area or region.

BIOSPHERE The portion of the earth and its atmosphere that is capable of supporting life.

BIOLOGICAL-EQUILIBRIUM or **BIOTIC BALANCE** The state of more or less self-regulation of the numbers of plants and animals in a community, brought about by interactions within and between species and by the effects of environmental conditions. cf. Life-cycle, Balance of nature.

10 easy lessons

Below are ten brief lessons in ecology that the environmentally protective non-scientist would do well to learn.

The testing of our technologies can create irrevocable harm as our ability to develop and use new products exceeds our understanding of their effects. Examples of this problem are legion. They range from nuclear testing, to the development of military biological weapons. Even household detergents fall in this category.

Environmental health hazards develop slowly. Decades can elapse before injury becomes manifest and thus it may be very difficult to relate cause and effect. The controversy over the relationship between cigarettes and cancer is a good example. Often only statistical comparisons of large groups can show injury; a problem that complicates legal proof. The medical costs to society of pollution become deferred future costs.

Environmental damage occurs so slowly that its benefits are not missed. Clear skies, brilliant stars at night, and clean air are no longer something to which most Americans are normally exposed. Local fishing and swimming holes and natural recreation sites, a short walk from home, are no longer a part of our "affluent society". Much environmental damage thus destroys the quality of life.

The harm may be removed in time and distance from the cause. For example, inorganic fertilizer, especially nitrogen, alters the porosity of soil to oxygen and thus reduces the efficiency of the utilization of the fertilizer by the crops. This unused fertilizer runs off into waterways and causes the over-growth of green plants which in decomposing rob the water of its dissolved oxygen and thus its ability to assimilate other organic waste. In the Midwest and California, the increase in nitrate level of drinking water is another health hazard. The use of artificial fertilizer is in turn due to many factors including th availability of cheap electric power, favorable freight rates, and the absence of water pollution control requirements for agricultural lands.

Man can become accustomed to pollution but he cannot adapt to it. Adaption takes many generations and requires genetic changes. Therefore the danger is that pollution levels at or below nuisance levels can cause much pathological damage.

ecology

Use of environmentally destructive techniques can become a self-destructive cycle. For example, the use of pesticides can kill the natural insect enemies. Thus ever increasing doses are necessary. The target insect often has the greatest ability to reestablish itself—particularly as its natural enemies are destroyed. Thus, continuously more toxic and more broadly destructive pesticides are developed and used.

Those who suffer most from pollution are those that society has already rejected as social outcasts. The aged, especially those suffering from cardiovascular diseases are most affected by air pollution. The poor and minority groups often live in the areas of highest pollution. The health problems of these groups are only exacerbated by the addition of pollution-related maladies.

The substitution of artificial environments for natural environments decreases diversity and increases the danger of major biological upheaval from disease, or insects or other pestilence. The much-touted "green revolution" may, by inducing widespread use of small variety of high-yield grains with a very short heredity and an unknown genetic strength, result in increased problems and could even lead to widespread famine.

Conserving genetic information is threatened by the widespread altering of ecosystems and extinction of species. For example, Representative Garmatz of Maryland proposed a $10 million plan to eliminate the stinging jelly-fish while Dr. Frank Johnson of Princeton was discovering in jelly-fish a substance that can be used to determine calcium levels in the human bloodstream and thus indicate the presence of parathyroid disorders.

The solutions to pollution problems often increase or create other pollution problems. For example, to lower the air pollution from automobiles from carbon monoxide and hydrocarbons requires more complete combustion. However improved high-compression engines operate at higher temperatures and create air pollution by nitrogen oxides. Another example is the increased use of modern municipal waste water treatment facitlities to break the waste into nitrate, phosphate, and carbon dioxide that can trigger algae growth and lower water oxygen levels.

Wind-blown soil buries farm machinery and automobile in barn lot, Gregory County, S. Dak., 1936.

The following discussion is excerpted from The National Water Commission's Interim Report No. 1 of December 31, 1969 at 56:

the complexity of ecosystems

Each ecosystem is complex and still incompletely understood. It is, however, generally accepted that each ecosystem possesses feedback mechanisms which determine and control the relative size of the populations of its various species. Energy is fixed and transferred throughout the ecosystem in many ways through various levels of organization, called trophic levels (i.e., primary producers, herbivores, and carnivores). At the base of the food web in the ecosystem is the production of organic material by plant populations. Plant production must be maintained not only for food but also because the process of photosynthesis is essential to maintain the oxygen content of our atmosphere upon which all animal life depends. At the apex of the food web are the predators, including man. Many of our populations of predatory birds are now endangered by the indiscriminate use of persistent pesticides and, unless other predators fill the gap, the American farmer may lose more of his crop to rodents than he would have lost to the insects. The explosive population growth of the European Hare which was introduced into Australia almost completely destroyed Australian agriculture because there were no natural predators. This problem was alleviated by the introduction of a disease which attacked the rabbits, but it is a perfect example of how thoughtless tampering with our environment can have disastrous results. Other examples could be given to illustrate that the elimination or the introduction of a single species into an ecosystem can have a profound effect. Neither of these activities should be tolerated without careful consideration of the ecological effects. Certainly, the elimination of an entire trophic level would have disastrous results. Probably all of man's activities and technological developments can be accomplished, however, without creating these problems if proper ecological considerations are taken into account in the early planning stages.

Strip mining in Washington State. Acid formed by water-mineral contact following surface mining is a key water pollutant in some areas. The soil is also destroyed as a viable part of the ecosystem. Surface mining is discussed in Volume Two.

It should also be emphasized that some water resources problems have international, some even global importance. The Secretary General of the United Nations issued a report entitled "Problems of the Human Environment" (E/4667 26 May 1969) in which global problems were discussed. He makes the following statement:

> Water pollution may also be a global problem as may the release of radioactive isotopes, the discharge of toxic materials, excessive nutrients, or heated water into estuaries or coastal waters on which the productivity of the ocean is dependent. The agricultural regions of the world are the source of many pollutants which affect the entire world.

Impoundments of waters either for irrigation or for human use may increase the incidence of schistosomiasis, particularly in tropical areas. Migratory birds make their migrations without regard to national boundaries, and the widespread distribution of many aquatic organisms has been attributed to transport by waterfowl.

A few general principles of ecology should be mentioned because they are applicable to the problems of the National Water Commission. It is obvious that such a list cannot be complete in a brief report.

Given the availability of energy, the productivity of the landscape is largely a function of the amount of water available providing other factors are not limiting. Civilization has evolved in a situation in which natural resources, including water, minerals, and living things were in abundance. Within the past few decades, these resources have become limited in terms of the demands put upon them by civilization. Many of the resources of the earth are a product of the evolution of living things and the hydrologic cycle is an intimate part of this. The characteristics of ecological systems which must be considered when using natural resources include, among many, the following:

1. A natural ecosystem tends to recycle its resources, especially resources in short supply.
2. The effectiveness of recycling tends to be proportional to the biological diversity of the ecosystem.
3. Maximum species diversity (the number of species present) tends to produce stability of an ecosystem.
4. Diversity tends to increase with available water, provided sufficient energy and minerals are available to support growth.
5. When a resource, such as water, becomes limiting, species diversity is reduced and often the ecosystem becomes less stable and more vulnerable to damage by use.

Man has traditionally managed the landscape for maximum agricultural productivity by reducing diversity and creating an ecosystem highly vulnerable to climate, to pests, or to impact by other forces. Man also has refused to abide by the basic laws of nature, such as the recycling of resources. He exploits mineral resources, wastes water, and pollutes the air, the streams, the lakes and the oceans. By these actions, many ecosystems with which he comes in contact are degraded, tend to diminish in diversity and become less stable. The following are examples of man's activities undertaken without regard for these principles, or of ecosystems in which they are especially important.

A. Large monoculture (single or few species) tends toward instability or vulnerability. This is the inverse of the third principle listed.

1. Agricultural areas of wheat only or corn only are particularly vulnerable to insect infestation and to climatic extremes. Recycling of nutrients is essential in order to avoid pollution of water resources.

2. Urban-industrial areas are concentrations of large numbers of people creating large demands for water of high quality. If polluted upstream the costs of purification are increased.

B. Semi-arid regions, such as the Southwestern United States, have relatively sparse vegetative cover because water is a limiting factor, and, as a result, are considered to be fragile regions or ones that are easily disturbed by use, such as grazing or recreation.

C. An excess of nutrients in a lake or stream will reduce species diversity, reduce competition among species, increase the productivity of a few adventitious but generally obnoxious species, and result in eutrophication of the water.

basics of ecosystems

The resources of the earth, including its air, water, land and many minerals have been modified to produce their present qualities as a direct result of the evolution of living systems. These systems, moreover, continue to play important roles in maintaining certain qualities of the environment that are essential for survival, including the hydrologic cycle. We might call these systems the "life support systems" of the biosphere (a term which includes all living organisms on earth).

The evolution of natural ecosystems has progressed in such a way as to provide for an appropriate degree of species diversity in each environment, but the diversity varies depending upon the degree of environmental variation. For example, diversity is generally greater in the tropics than in polar regions. Increased diversity increases the stability of the system with respect to numbers of individuals of any species, microclimate, water conservation, and other factors. Diversity tends to increase with available water, unless other factors are limiting. Disturbance, including drought or other abrupt changes in environment, usually reduces diversity, making the system less stable and more vulnerable to damage by further disturbance.

man's effect on the earth

Civilization has, thus, developed in a world dominated by natural ecosystems, which have evolved continuously toward greater and greater diversity with all of the implications for the structure and function of the biosphere. While these natural ecosystems dominated the earth, the resources that have been built and maintained over geologic time were large in proportion to human needs. Until the industrial revolution man had little more impact on the environment than any other large predatory animal. Within the last century or so, however, man's demands on natural resources, and his vastly increased ability to modify the environment have reached the point where the natural ecosystems themselves are threatened world-wide. Most of the earth's natural ecosystems have already been affected in important ways through pollution of air and water and the accumulation of toxic substances, many of which are transported in water. It is no longer possible for civilization to continue expanding, relying on dilution to render innocuous all of its wastes. Man-made systems must recycle resources, especially water and nutrients so essential to life. The panel strongly recommends that the Commission give detailed consideration to the general problem of recycling, not only of water but also of nutrients and toxic wastes that may affect living systems far from their point of release. There is abundant evidence that manipulation of natural and man-made ecosystems to provide adequate recycling is possible, although at present poorly exploited. This is fundamentally an ecological problem to which engineers have not yet devoted adequate attention.

End, excerpt from National Water Commission report.

Selected Bibliography: Ecology

BENARDE, Melvin, *Our Precarious Habitat,* New York, W.W. Norton & Co., Inc.

CALLISON, Charles, *America's Natural Resources, New York, The Ronald Press, Co., 1967*

COMMONER, Barry, *Science & Survival,* The Viking Press, New York, 1963, paper

DARLING, F. Fraser and Milton, John P., eds., *Future Environments of North America: Transformation of A Continent,* Garden City, New York—The Natural History Press—1966

DASMANN, Raymond F., *Environmental Conservation,* 2d ed., New York, Wiley, 1968

DUBOS, Rene, *Man Adapting,* New Haven, Yale Univ. Press, 1965 paper
So Human an Animal, New York, Scribner, 1968 paper

FARB, Peter and The Editors of Life, *Ecology,* New York, Time, Inc., 1963

FARB, Peter, *Face of North America,* New York, Harper & Row 1963, 1968 paper ed. *Living Earth,* New York, Harper & Row, 1959, paper ed. 1968

HANSON, Herbert C., *Dictionary of Ecology,* Philosophical Library, Inc., New York, 1962

MILNE, Lorus & Margery, *Water and Life,* Athenum Press, New York, 1966

MILNE, Lorus Jr., *The Balance of Nature,* N.Y., Alfred E. Knopf, 1969

ODUM, Eugene, *Fundamentals of Ecology,* 2d ed. Philadelphia, W. B. Saunders Co., 1959

SMITH, Guy-Harold, Ed., *Conservation of Natural Resources,* John Wiley & Sons, Inc., New York, 1965

The Fitness of Man's Environment, Smithsonian Institution Press, Washington, 1968

b. Population

On June 2, 1972, the U.S. National Center for Health Statistics of the Department of Health Education and Welfare announced that the U.S. birthrate had dropped to an all-time low: 15.8 births per 1,000 persons in the first quarter of 1972, down by 1.8 per 1,000 from the corresponding period in 1971. This meant that the estimated number of children for women in the child-bearing age declined to 2.145 in that quarter compared with 2.284 for the average of 1971.

Population specialists from the Center estimate that if women have an average of 2.11 children during their lifetimes, the nation will reach zero population growth within 40 to 50 years, excluding immigration. In 1970, the average family had about 2.4 children, well above the figure needed for zero population growth.

What have been the causes of this declining birthrate in the United States? The Government specialists speculated that economic factors were a prime cause, since during the 1969-70 slowdown, many normally well-off persons were unemployed. New attitudes by women, who preferred to postpone marriages or having children in order to pursue careers, was also believed to be a factor.

people as a problem

An additional possibility that to the author's knowledge has not been mentioned previously in print, is that a very gradual poisoning of the U.S. population—particularly by lead from automobile fuels (both in the air and in drinking water), pesticides, herbicides, and the chemicals known as plasticizers—may be having some effect on fertility. There seem to be no studies on this possibility, and it seems difficult to imagine how such studies would be made. However, various heavy metals and chemicals now found in increasingly higher levels in persons in virtually all technologically advanced nations have been shown to affect fertility in animals, and full lead poisoning definitely affects human fertility. Obviously, however, this possibility is purely speculation at this time.

Does the falling birthrate mean that the United States does not have a population problem—or that it at least does not have to worry about overpopulation? No. First, a huge number of women born in the post-war "baby boom" have recently entered their fertile years, and are expected to push up the birth rate. In addition, the problems of population are far too complex to be solved by a "zero population growth" alone. Proportionally stable age distribution is also needed for a stable population, while geographical distribution is another important factor.

World-wide, the population explosion continues, with a birth rate averaging about twice that of the United States. Although we are well sheltered in most of the U.S. from the realities of much of the world, other countries are experiencing deaths by the tens of thousands from starvation, and hundreds of millions are greatly undernourished. Because this book is centered on the problems of the U.S., little mention will be made of the rest of the world. But it should be remembered that in this small world, sooner or later the problems of our neighbors will affect us.

Modern medicine and public health measures reduced the world death rate dramatically in the past fifty years. The resulting rate of population growth, now about two percent a year, would, if started by the 12 apostles and their wives, have produced a present population of over 300 billion, or nearly 100 times the present world population. Clearly such growth cannot continue. We are rapidly destroying our habitat. Increased deaths from air pollution are found in the rich countries, starvation in the poor nations. Everywhere the quality of life deteriorates.

However, the concept that the principles of wildlife biology apply to human population seems not to occur to politicians. If wildlife herds increase beyond their habitat's carrying capacity, the habitat is destroyed, and all or nearly all the animals perish.

population control the natural way

Humanitarian remedies such as predator control, or artificial feeding delay the destruction for but a short time. To protect a population you must protect its range. Since range improvement or external aid programs can at best increase arithmetically they cannot keep up with a population increasing exponentially. A population that doubles and then doubles again and again will either die off in large numbers or stop reproducing. Birth control or death control are the only choice. What the optimum population is certainly is questionable. But two-thirds of the world are hungry now, and at least three and a half million persons will starve to death this year.

Nearly everyone agrees that trying to provide for this population is not possible. Some people claim God will provide, but his methods are drastic, and are the same as used with other wildlife species. To stave off a disaster beyond any that has ever occurred on this planet requires a zero population growth, though better yet would be a negative population growth.

The cyclone in November of 1970 in over-crowded East Bengal killed an estimated 500,000 people. But the Gangetic delta is just above sea level, and several thousand people are killed each year in ordinary storms. This habitat is chosen only because there is no other to be chosen. Nevertheless, to emphasize the need for death control, the Pakistan parents replaced the half million loss of life in 40 days.

Even the United States, which consumes 40 percent of the total raw material resource output of the free world, and creates 70 percent of the world's solid wastes, has had to provide for nearly 100 million Americans in just over fifty years.

The Census Bureau's preliminary count, the first of many reports to come from the data acquired during the 19th decennial census, found 200,263,721 residents of the United States. When the count is completed, it is expected to show about 204 million Americans, an increase of 25 million people in ten years, and still increasing by one person every 15½ seconds. The rate of population growth decreased from 18.5 percent in the decade of the 50's to about 14 percent in the 60's, though the birth rate moved up again in 1969.

Controlling this growth, if that is desired, will be a difficult task, for it requires dealing with strong emotional, religious, ethical, and political attitudes. Compounding the problem is the fact that our population growth is due primarily to the activities of middle-class families, who use some type of contraception and who normally have only those children they want. Approximately two-thirds of the 3.5 million babies born each year in this country are from families that cannot be considered poor.

A complicating factor is the inability to provide meaningful roles for women outside the family. In the United States the most babies are produced by girls of 19. Like many environmental problems, the solution to the population problem is tied to the larger issues of social justice for all.

It was not until 1964 that the Supreme Court in *Griswold v. Connecticut* [381 U.S. 479] held a law forbidding the use of contraceptives or for clinics to prescribe contraceptives to be unconstitutional. In that case the defendants had been providing contraceptives to a married couple. In *Baird v. Eisenstadt,* 92 U.S. 1029 (1972), 40 USLW 4303, the Supreme Court upheld a First Circuit Court of Appeals decision that reversed the conviction of a defendant who supplied contraceptives to an unmarried woman. The Court held that inherent in the right of privacy enunciated in *Griswold* is the right of the individual, whether married or unmarried, to be free from unwarranted governmental intrusion into matters so fundamentally affecting a person as the decision of whether to bear a child.

But research has yet to provide a completely satisfactory method of birth control, and the efforts in this respect have been woefully inadequate. Furthermore, information and services are not universally available in this country. The worldwide problems are horrendous.

abortion

All U.S. states permit abortion if the mother's life is in danger, but prior to 1970, only 14 states allowed abortions for reasons other than saving the life of the mother. Of these 14, nearly all permitted abortions in the case of rape (forcible or statutory) or incest, while a few also permitted it in cases of fetal deformity, or when the physical or mental health of the mother was endangered.

By 1972, four additional states had passed liberalized abortion statutes, although that of New York, especially, came under heavy legislative attack in an attempt to repeal the law. A detailed examination of these laws is beyond the scope of this book. One group that specializes in information in this field is the Association for the Study of Abortion, Inc., 120 West 57th Street, New York City.

In the courts, the New York State abortion law was upheld 5-2 by that State's supreme court early in July of 1972 on a case brought by Fordham Professor Robert M. Byrn.

In the U.S. Supreme Court, Chief Justice Warren E. Burger stirred considerable controversy by delaying rulings that reportedly would have struck down the anti-abortion laws of Georgia and Texas. The cases, argued in December of 1971, were to be reheard with the Court enlarged by new Justices Lewis F. Powell, Jr. and William H. Rehnquist. *See* a New York Times News Service article in *The* (Washington, D.C.) *Evening Star;* July 5, 1972 at F7, and *Time* magazine, July 10, 1972 at 40.

Meanwhile the old anti-abortion laws have been challenged in court and found invalid. *People v. Belous* (Cal. Sup. Ct.), 458 P.2d 194 (1969)
U.S. v. Vuitch (D.C. Dis. Ct.), 305 F.Supp. 1032 (1969)
Babbitz v. McCann (Wis.), 310 F.Supp. 293 (1970)

The fight continues on many fronts, complicated by the fact that many people want children even though the combined effect of such decisions is social disaster. Such decisions are eased by the fact that society absorbs many of the costs, both economic and non-economic. The general public pays for schools. This costs nearly $1,000 a year per pupil in better school systems, and thus an average earner with four children will never pay sufficient taxes to pay for the family "hobby."

In a message to Congress during the summer of 1969 [Doc. No. 91-139, July 21], President Nixon called for the creation of a commission on population growth and the American future, for additional research on population problems, and for a clearer commitment to family planning. Within a year and a half Congress responded favorably to the President's message, passing two acts incorporating the proposals. These two acts were Public Law 91-213 (March 16, 1970) "To establish a Commission on Population Growth and the American Future," and Public Law 91-572 (Dec. 24, 1970), titled the "Family Planning Services and Population Research Act of 1970." The former set up a commission for 26 months to study population problems; the latter authorized grants for additional population and family planning research, and expanded the government's family planning assistance activities.

Spurred by the two 1970 Acts, Federal expenditures for population stabilization have increased quite substantially, though they still are quite small compared with the seriousness of the problem. Federal outlays for population research will increase in Fiscal Year 1972 to an estimated $44 million from $33 million in FY 1971. Overall Federal support of family planning programs, including research, will increase to an estimated $189 million in FY 1972 from about $135 million in FY 1971, although the figures that contribute to this sum vary by a couple of million dollars, depending upon which page of the Federal budget you happen to be reading. To provide better coordination, an Office of Deputy Assistant Secretary for Population Affairs has been established in the Department of Health, Education and Welfare. The main center for population control activities will be the Center for Population Research, and the National Center for Family Planning Services. However, many other agencies within HEW and elsewhere deal with population matters. These agencies include the National Institutes of Health, the Office of Economic Opportunity, and the Food and Drug Administration.

The following is excerpted from *Population and the American Future,* the report of the Commission on Population Growth and the American Future, submitted March 27, 1972. In addition to the version from the Government Printing Office, at least one commercial publisher, Signet, has issued the report (paperback).

The tremendous growth in the world's population is a recent development in the history of mankind. In pre-industrial times, birthrates were high; but hunger, ignorance, and disease combined to stack the odds against an infant surviving to the age of parenthood. Societies required high birthrates simply to keep themselves going.

In modern times, the reductions in mortality have given the average person a longer, healthier life and have inaugurated a phase of rapid population growth. The world's population grew from one-half billion around 1650, to about 1½ billion by 1900, to 2½ billion in 1950, and had already surpassed 3½ billion by 1970. The world's total has doubled during the last 50 years.

From the beginning of the Christian era to 1650, mankind increased by an average of 150,000 persons a year. Today, the world total is increasing by about 78 million persons annually. If current rates of growth continue for another 50 years, the world's population will number some 10 billion.

Even a cursory examination of the data reveals that, since 1900, the United States has undergone something of a demographic revolution. (See table) In terms of total numbers, our population has increased from about 76 million in 1900 to almost 205 million in 1970. This represents an additional 129 million people that our society has been called upon to accommodate over the past 70 years. By mid-1972, our country will have about 209 million people.

The growth of population is sustained only as long as the yearly number of new entrants (births and immigrants) exceeds the number required to replace those who die or emigrate. Although the United States has always been a growing population, the rapid growth rates characterizing our early years began to taper off in the 19th century.

In the 20th century, we have seen substantial changes in all three components of population growth—fertility, mortality, and migration. First, consider the birthrate. It is important to understand that this measure simply indicates the average level of yearly births in the population. Although it obscures a considerable amount of variation associated with such factors as age and socioeconomic status, it is nevertheless a useful measure of the contribution of births to population growth. The birthrate was about 32 births per 1,000 population in 1900, and declined fairly steadily to about 18 per 1,000 in the depths of the Depression. Just when the experts had become convinced—some even concerned—that our level of fertility would soon dip below the level required for replacement of the population, couples began increasing their rates of childbearing. This aberration in the history of American fertility, of which we will have more to say shortly, came to be called the "baby boom." By 1947, the birthrate stood at 27 per 1,000, and it remained at around 25 per 1,000 for a decade before resuming its long-term decline. By the early 1960's, the boom had run its course, and our birthrate today is below pre-World War II levels. (See chart)

Demographic Perspective of 20th Century United States

	Around 1900	Around 1970
Population	76 million	205 million
Life expectancy	47 years	70 years
Median age	23 years	28 years
Births per 1000 population	32	18
Deaths per 1000 population	17	9
Immigrants per 1000 population	8	2
Annual growth	1¾ million	2¼ million
Growth rate	2.3 percent	1.1 percent

SOURCES: U. S. Bureau of the Census, *Historical Statistics of the United States, Colonial Times to 1957,* 1961. U. S. National Center for Health Statistics, *Vital Statistics of the United States,* Volume II Section 5, *Life Tables,* 1968. Irene B. Taeuber, "Growth of the Population of the United States in the Twentieth Century" (prepared for the Commission, 1972).

TOTAL FERTILITY RATE

CHILDREN PER WOMAN

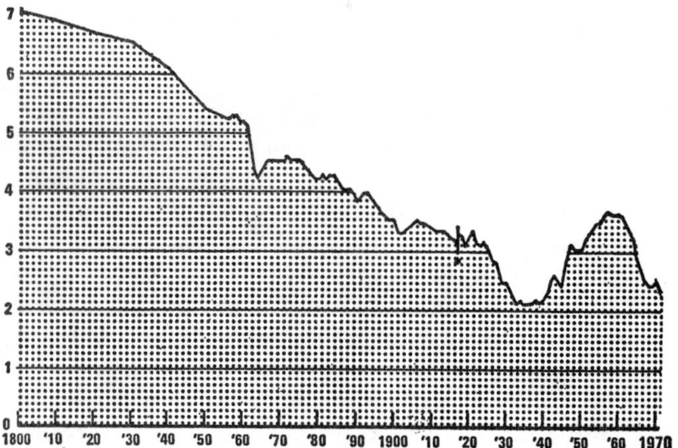

*Prior to 1917 data available only for white population; after 1917, for total population.

Annual births expressed in terms of implied completed family size, declined until the 1930's, rose, and fell again.

SOURCES: Prior to 1917—Ansley J. Coale and Melvin Zelnik, *New Estimates of Fertility and Population in the United States,* (Princeton: Princeton University Press) 1963. 1917 to 1968—U. S. National Center for Health Statistics, *Natality Statistics Analysis,* Series 21, Number 19, 1970. 1969 to 1971—U. S. Bureau of the Census, *Current Population Reports,* Series P-23, No. 36, "Fertility Indicators: 1970," 1971. The figure for 1971 is based on an unpublished Census staff estimate.

A second basic determinant of how fast a nation grows is the degree to which it succeeds in preserving and extending the lives of its people. We have seen dramatic progress toward reducing the threat of early death. The death rate has fallen from about 17 per 1,000 population at the turn of the century, to its present level of about nine per 1,000. The average life expectancy today is about 70 years, or 23 years longer than in 1900. Most of these declines in mortality were achieved prior to 1960, and all segments of our population have gained some, though not equal, benefits in terms of increased longevity.

In the United States, mortality during the early years of life is already so low that any substantial further improvements in life expectancy will have to come primarily among persons over the age of 50. Since this segment of the population is generally beyond childbearing, the extension of their life span would not result in any significant increase in births. Consequently, further additions to the duration of life in this country would simply result in somewhat larger numbers of people at the older ages, where they still can be quite productive members of society.

The third factor associated with growth is, of course, immigration. Only the Indians, who numbered less than one million when the first English colonists settled in Massachusetts and Virginia, can rightfully claim original status. Our population is comprised primarily of immigrants and their descendants. Since 1900 alone, 20 million more people have moved into this country than out of it. Approximately 40 percent of the population growth in the first decade of this century was attributable to immigration. During the 1930's, the number of immigrants was slightly lower than the number of people leaving the country. Immigration once again increased following World War II, and during the 1960's, it accounted for about 16 percent of our national growth.

When all of these demographic credits and debits are tallied, we are left with either net population growth or net decline. The United States has had a long history of diminishing growth rates. Our annual rate of growth dropped from about 3.3 percent in the second decade of the 19th century to 2.1 percent by the first decade of this century, to an average of around 0.7 percent during the 1930's. It then rose to about 1.9 percent during the fifties, before falling to its present level of 1.1 percent. However, the size of our population is now so large that even our low current rate of growth translates into about 2¼ million people added to our society each year—more than enough to fill a city the size of Philadelphia.

We cannot predict how fast our population will grow in the years ahead, but we can be sure that, barring some unforeseen catastrophe, substantial additions to our numbers lie ahead. Our population has a potential for further growth greater than that of almost any other advanced country. The reasons for this are a pattern of early and nearly universal marriage and childbearing, fertility levels above those required to replace the parental generation, and a preponderance of youth in the population. The youngsters born during the baby boom are reaching adulthood today and beginning to do many of the things their parents and grandparents did before them—finishing school, seeking jobs, developing careers, getting married, and having children of their own.

THE "BIRTH DEARTH"

In the summer of 1971, the news media spread a report that, because women were having fewer babies than had been expected, we were in the midst of a "baby bust." That story was based on data for the first six months of 1971, which showed a drop in birthrates at a time when most of the experts had expected them to rise again as the baby-boom generation reached adulthood. These expectations seemed to be realized when the birthrate, after reaching a new low of 17.5 in 1968, moved up to about 18.2 in 1970. But, instead of continuing upward in 1971, the rate dropped back to about 17.3, and so was born the idea of the "birth dearth."

This phenomenon is notable because birthrates are showing declines at a time when everyone was expecting them to increase. It had long been assumed that birthrates would rise during the 1970's as potential parents who were born during the baby-boom years came of age. If general fertility (the rate of childbearing among women aged 15 to 44) remained constant, there would be an unavoidable "echo boom" in the birthrate of the total population, as larger and larger numbers of potential parents reached childbearing age. The increase in the number of people entering the childbearing ages is, however, presently being offset by a decline in the level of general fertility.

Two factors seem to account for this recent decline. One is temporary; the other may or may not be permanent. The first element arises from the fact that we are now in a period of gradually rising age at childbearing. This means that, in any given year, some fraction of the births is, in effect, postponed to a later year. The effect is temporary because the age at childbearing will not rise indefinitely; when it stabilizes, the postponement will stop and the birthrate will rise again.

The other and more important element is that today's young people expect to have far fewer children than people a few years their senior. On the average, women now in their late thirties already have more than three children. According to a 1971 Census Bureau survey, married women 18 to 24 say that they expect to have an average of 2.4 children before they complete their families. Not everyone will marry, so the total for this generation could ultimately be lower. On the other hand, experience with similar surveys in the past indicates that women usually end up having more children than they estimated when they were young. The baby-bust phenomenon is significant and somewhat surprising, but it would be premature to say that we are on the verge of a fertility level that would ultimately stabilize the population.

The baby-bust psychology may give rise to unwarranted complacency born of the notion that all of the problems associated with population growth are somehow behind us. Our population growth has developed its own momentum which makes it very difficult to stop, no matter how hard the brakes are applied. Even if immigration from abroad ceased and couples had only two children on the average—just enough to replace themselves—our population would continue to grow for about 70 years. (See charts) Our past rapid growth has given us so many young couples that, to bring population growth to an immediate halt, the birthrate would have to drop by almost 50 percent, and today's young generation of parents would have to limit themselves to an average of about one child. That is just not going to happen.

IMPLICATIONS OF GROWTH

If families in the United States have only two children on the average and immigration continues at current levels, our population would grow to 271 million by the end of the century. If, however, families should have an average of three children, the population would reach 322 million by the year 2000. One hundred years from now, the 2-child family would result in a population of about 350 million persons, whereas, the 3-child family would produce a total of nearly a billion. (See chart on page 19.) Thus, a difference of only one extra child per family would result in an additional 51 million people over the next three decades, and if extended over a century, an additional two-thirds of a billion people.

When we speak of 2- or 3-child families, we are talking about averages which can be made up by many possible combinations of family sizes, ranging from childless couples to those with many children.

The total size of our future population is not our sole concern. Perhaps just as important are the changes which lie ahead in the size of various age categories that play an important role in the demands placed on our society.

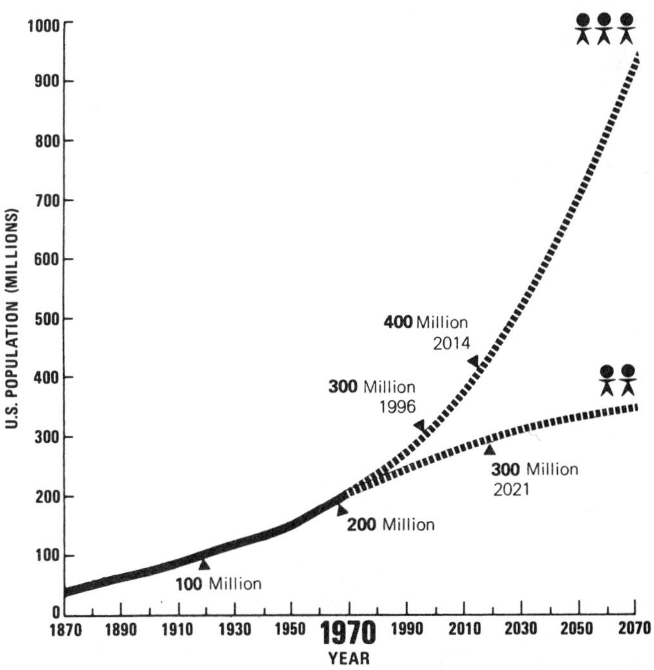

If families average three children, we can expect to find about 46 percent more young people of elementary and secondary school age (5 to 17 years), and 36 percent more persons of college age (18 to 21 years) in the year 2000, than would be the case if families average only two children. (See table on page 20.) Thus, a difference of only one child per family will have important consequences for the magnitude of the load on our educational system.

The burden placed on those in the economically active segment of the population, traditionally considered to be those aged 18 to 64, will also be influenced by future family size. The dependency burden is determined chiefly by the proportion of the population in the childhood and adolescent years. Projections indicate that the number of persons in the dependent ages under 18 in the year 2000 would be 52 percent greater if families average three children than if the 2-child average prevails. The size of the population 65 and over in the year 2000 would be unaffected by changes in the average number of children, since everyone who will be over the age of 30 at the end of this century is already born. Consequently, the numbers in the dependent ages, relative to persons of working age, would be about one-third larger under the 3-child than under the 2-child projection.

In sum, it should be evident that, even if the recent unexpected drop in the birthrate should develop into a sustained trend, there is little cause for complacency. Whether we see it or not—whether we like it or not—we are in for a long period of growth, and we had best prepare for it.

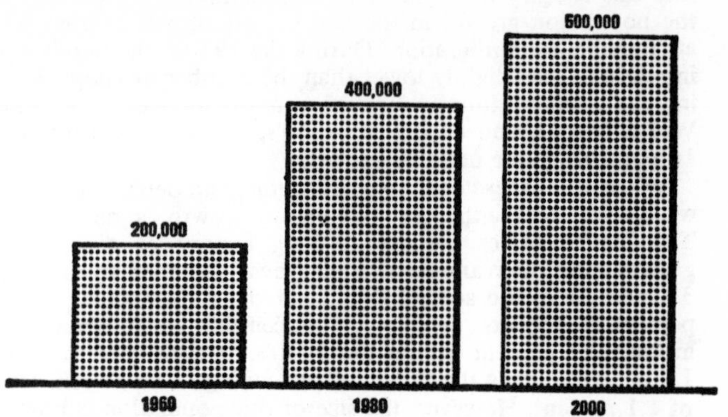

The territory of urban regions is doubling in the period 1960 to 1980. By the year 2000, urban regions will encompass one-sixth of the United States land area (excl. Alaska and Hawaii).

SOURCE: Jerome P. Pickard, "U. S. Metropolitan Growth and Expansion, 1970-2000, With Population Projections" (prepared for the Commission, 1972).

AN AVERAGE OF 2 CHILDREN PER FAMILY WOULD SLOW POPULATION GROWTH, BUT WOULD NOT STOP IT SOON BECAUSE THE NUMBER OF PEOPLE OF CHILDBEARING AGE IS INCREASING...

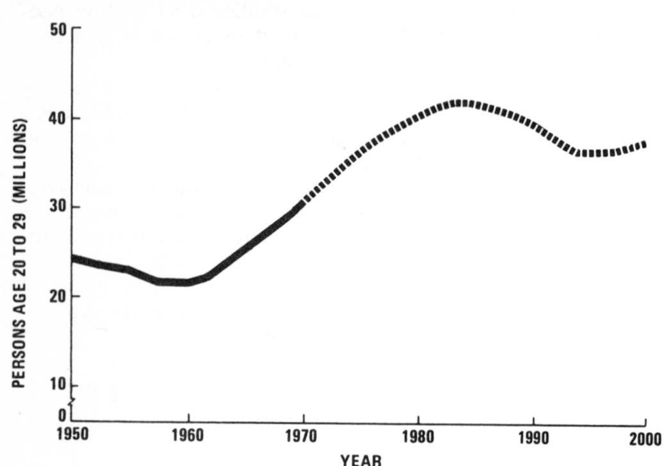

...THE RESULTING BIRTHS WILL CONTINUE TO EXCEED DEATHS FOR THE REST OF THIS CENTURY...

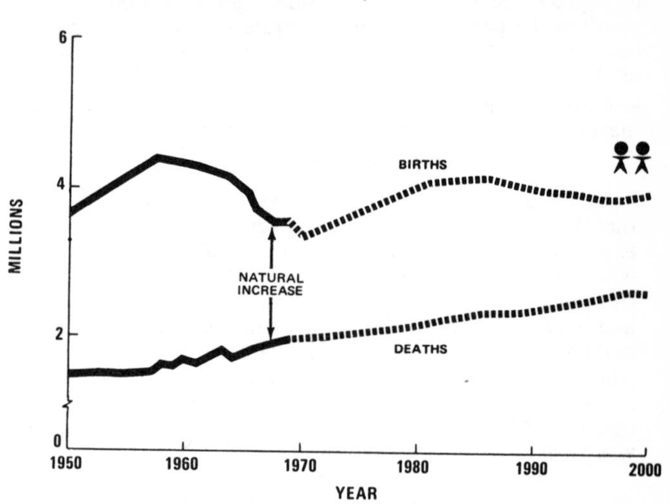

...SO EVEN IF FAMILY SIZE DROPS TO A 2-CHILD AVERAGE...

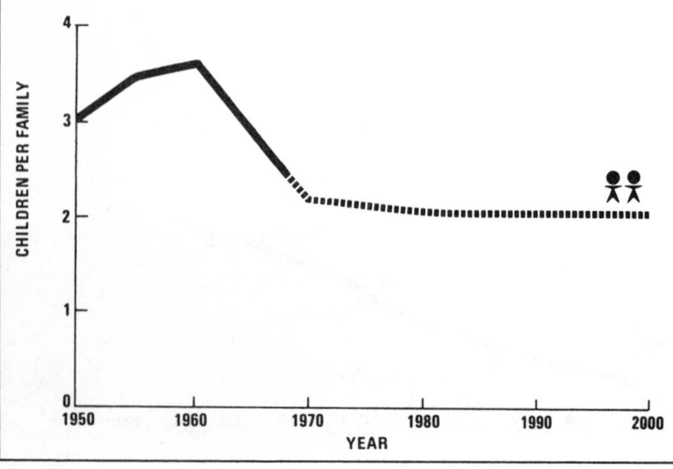

...SO THE POPULATION WILL STILL BE GROWING IN THE YEAR 2000, BUT AT A DECREASING RATE.

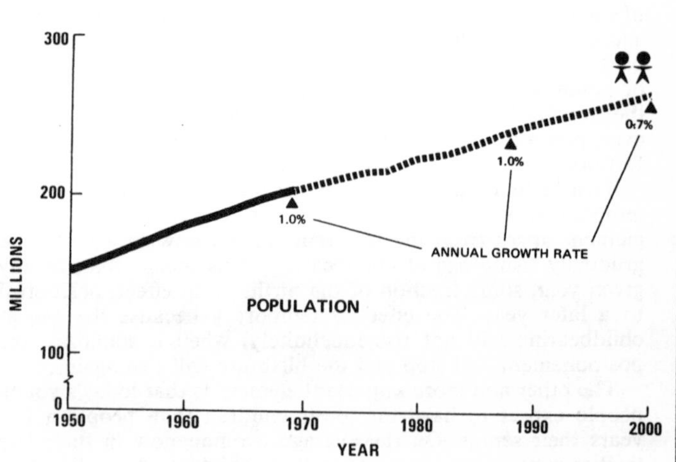

1. Metropolitan Belt
   1.a. Atlantic Seabord
   1.b. Lower Great Lakes
2. California Region
3. Florida Peninsula
4. Gulf Coast
5. East Central Texas—Red River
6. Southern Piedmont
7. North Georgia—South East Tennessee
8. Puget Sound
9. Twin Cities Region
10. Colorado Piedmont
11. Saint Louis
12. Metropolitan Arizona
13. Willamette Valley
14. Central Oklahoma—Arkansas Valley
15. Missouri—Kau Valley
16. North Alabama
17. Blue Grass
18. Southern Coastal Plain
19. Salt Lake Valley
20. Central Illinois
21. Nashville Region
22. East Tennessee
23. Oahu Island
24. Memphis
25. El Paso—Ciudad Juarez

Based on 2-child family projection

SOURCE: Jerome P. Pickard, "U. S. Metropolitan Growth and Expansion, 1970-2000, With Population Projections" (prepared for the Commission, 1972).

UNITED STATES POPULATION, 1970 AND 2000

(Numbers in Millions)

	1970	2000	
		2-child average	3-child average
All Ages	205	271	322
Under 5	17	20	34
5 to 17	53	55	80
18 to 21	15	17	24
under 18	70	75	114
18 to 64	115	167	179
65 and over	20	29	29
Dependency Ratio[a]	78	62	80

[a]Number of persons 65 and over plus persons under 18 per 100 persons aged 18 to 64.

These data are based on the Census Bureau's *Current Population Reports*, Series P-25, No. 470, "Projections of the Population of the United States by Age and Sex: 1970 to 2000." These projections served as the basis for much of the research reported in this volume. We examined how the population would grow between now and the year 2000 under the 2-child family projection (Census Series E) and under the 3-child projection (Census Series B).

Series B assumes that in the future, women will be giving birth at an "ultimate" rate averaging out to 3.1 children per woman over her lifetime. The transition from the 1969 rate of 2.4 to the "ultimate" future rate is not instantaneous in the projections, but most of the change is assumed to occur by 1980. The 3.1 figure is an average for all women, regardless of marital status. In the United States today, almost all women (95 percent) marry at some time in their lives, so the Series B rate of childbearing represents a reasonable approximation to an average family of 3 children.

Series E assumes an ultimate rate of childbearing that works out to an average of 2.1 children per woman over a lifetime. This is the rate at which the parental generation would exactly replace itself. The extra 0.1 allows for mortality between birth and the average age of mothers at childbearing, and for the fact that boy babies slightly outnumber girl babies.

Different generations born in the 20th century have reproduced at widely varying average levels, some exceeding three children (as did the women born from 1930 to 1935) and some approaching two (as did women who were born from 1905 to 1910). The fact that major groups in our modern history have reproduced at each of these levels lends credibility to projections based on either of these averages.

It is assumed in both projections that future reductions in mortality will be slight. The net flow of immigrants into the United States is assumed, in the projections, to continue at the present level of about 400,000 persons annually.

WATER

Water requirements already exceed available flow in the southwestern United States. Our research shows that growing population and economic activity will cause the area of water shortage to spread eastward and northward across the country in the decades ahead. Such deficits will spread faster if population growth follows the 3-child projection than if it follows the 2-child projection. (See bar graph and map.) This will occur despite large expenditures on water treatment, dams, and reservoirs during the next 50 years. Population growth will be more important than economic growth in causing these growing problems.

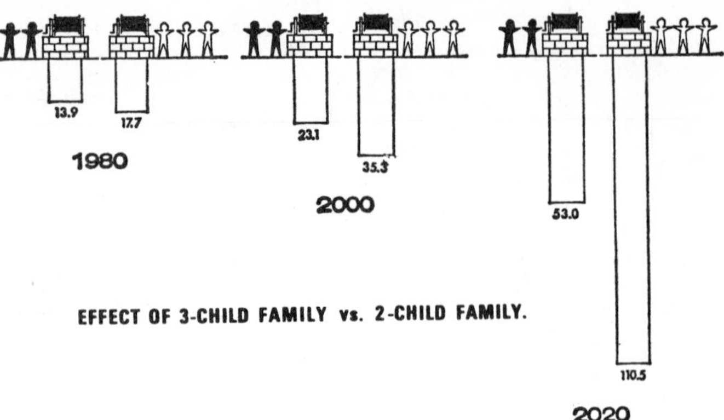

Our national abundance of water does not change this picture significantly. If water could be shipped across the country like oil, coal, or manufactured goods, there would be no problems of water shortage. But distances are so long and the amounts of water used so huge, that it would be prohibitively expensive to solve these regional problems by transfers of water from surplus to deficit areas. Nor is there scope for sufficiently large relocation of water users—people and industries—to regions where water is plentiful. An inexpensive method of taking the salt out of seawater could solve the problem, but such technology is not now available. Similarly, artificial control of rain is not advanced enough to be used to any significant extent. While little is known about the extent of groundwater reserves, most experts do not consider the mining of such reserves an adequate alternative.

On the other hand, there is wide scope for reducing use through rationing and the adoption of water-conserving technology. Even today, most water is used virtually free of cost or is distributed on a fee basis that provides no incentives for conservation; and free use of water bodies as waste dumping grounds is more the rule than the exception. If the cost of utilizing water for these purposes were raised to more appropriate levels, factories and power plants would install techniques of production that save water instead of wasting it; farmers would modify their irrigation practices or otherwise adjust by changing location or shifting to crops using less water; and households would eventually adjust by reducing lawns and shrubbery.

Sooner or later we will have to deal with water as a scarce resource. The sooner this is done, the fewer water crises will emerge in the years ahead. However, doing this will not be easy technically or politically—most water supplies are run by local governments. And few will like the austerity created by the need to conserve on something as fundamental as water. The rate of national population growth will largely determine how rapidly we must accomplish these changes.

WATER DEFICIT REGIONS: 3-CHILD FAMILY

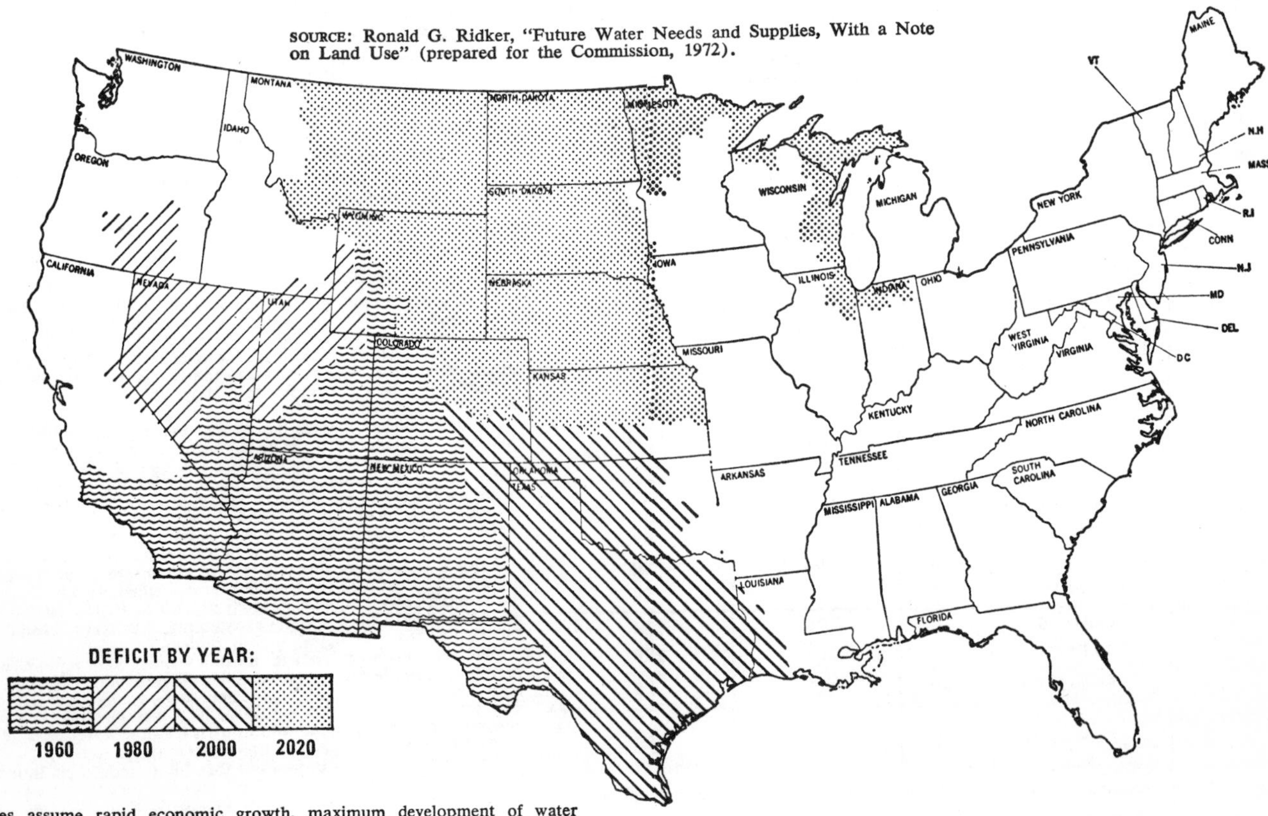

SOURCE: Ronald G. Ridker, "Future Water Needs and Supplies, With a Note on Land Use" (prepared for the Commission, 1972).

Estimates assume rapid economic growth, maximum development of water storage facilities, and tertiary treatment. Alaska and Hawaii not shown: Commission's data did not include these states.

POLLUTION

As the gross national product goes up, so does the production of pollutants. An irony of economic measurement is that the value of goods and services represented by GNP includes the cost of producing the pollutants as well as expenditures for cleaning up afterward. We may fill our tank with gasoline, but due to engine inefficiency, some portion of that ends up in the atmosphere as air pollution. Such pollutants are not free—we had to pay good money to put them in the air. Yet the cost of putting them there is included in our principal measure of national economic well-being.

If we clean up the pollutants, the cost of the cleanup effort is also added to GNP. But many of the costs, such as poorer health and deteriorated surroundings, are never counted at all. It is an indictment of our ignorance and indifference toward what we do to the environment, that in our national economic accounts we count so few of the "bads," and that even when we do count them, we count them as "goods."

To understand the contribution of population to pollution, we have to distinguish two broad classes of pollutants. The first class includes the major products of combustion—carbon monoxide, carbon dioxide, oxides of nitrogen, oxides of sulfur, hydrocarbons, and particulates—and several measures of water pollution, including biochemical demand for oxygen and suspended and dissolved solids. The pollutants in this group, once produced, endure in the environment for a relatively short time—short enough so that long-term accumulations are not a problem. This group contains the more massive and commonly discussed pollutants, and enough information exists about them so that we can link them to economic activity and population.

The second class of pollutants includes those which endure longer—radiation and pesticides, plus a wide variety of ever-changing chemicals emitted by our high technology industries. Most such chemicals are emitted in small, often highly poisonous amounts. For many of these pollutants, future developments depend more heavily on changes in technology than on changes in population and economic growth. In any case, they are very difficult to link to population and economic growth in a simple and quantitative fashion. For this reason, the results we present here are for the first class of pollutants, although this does not minimize the environmental damage done by the others.

In the next 30 years, most of these pollutants can be eliminated by enforcing treatment standards for pollution emissions. Slower population and economic growth would help; but over this period, by far the biggest reduction in pollution can be achieved by a head-on attack. This is illustrated in the figure showing hydrocarbons —a major component of auto exhaust and other combustion. In this example, the treatment standard is the Environmental Protection Agency's 1975 standard for emissions into the air. Even if this standard were not met on schedule, it certainly will be met by the year 2000; indeed, by that time, we are likely to have much tighter standards.

The relationships shown in the figure hold generally for the other pollutants we examined. The reason for the spectacular results from enforcing standards is that we have imposed so little control in the past. The results do not assume any big new technological breakthroughs. It is just that we have only now begun to fight. Many of the required changes could be implemented today. Soap could be used instead of detergent; natural-colored paper could replace heavily bleached paper in many uses; returnable bottles could be used; the horsepower of auto engines could be reduced. It is not difficult to find answers when one begins to look.

Whatever we assume about future treatment policy, pollution emissions in the year 2000 would be less with the 2-child than with the 3-child rate of population growth—from five to 12 percent less, depending on the pollutant. If population were one percent less than projected in the year 2000, pollution emissions would be 0.3 to 0.6 percent less. If GNP per capita were one percent less than projected, emissions would be 0.2 to 0.9 percent less.

Once we achieve control over the emissions from each source, pollution will once again rise in response to economic and population growth. We can already see this process at work in rapidly growing parts of the country. At our Los Angeles public hearing, meteorologist James D. Edinger described the successful efforts in Los Angeles to control air pollution from stationary sources—power plants, heavy industry, home heating—and the beginnings of the program to control pollution from motor vehicles. But, he said, in recent years:

> . . . a close race has been run between increasing numbers of sources and decreasing emissions per source. But as emission levels per source are trimmed lower and lower the effort required to achieve each new increment of improvement gets more and more difficult. The increase in the number of sources, on the other hand, is projected to rise steadily. If the race for acceptable air quality is to be won, the heroic emission control programs, present and anticipated in Los Angeles, must soon be joined by a leveling off, if not a reduction, in the number of sources.

Our own research on air pollution indicates that such worries are well founded. The standard for concentrations of nitrogen oxides used by the Environmental Protection Agency is 100 micrograms per cubic meter. In 1970, the air in 36 urban areas had concentrations above this level. An active abatement policy would eliminate the problem in most areas. But if our projections of economic and population growth come anywhere close to the truth, Los Angeles and San Diego in the year 2000 will still have a problem. In Los Angeles, we estimate that even with an active abatement policy, concentrations of nitrogen oxides will still be at least 50 percent above standard, and probably well above that. In this region of the country, clearly something must give: the rate of population growth, the use of the internal combustion engine—especially for personal transport—or the standard itself.

As the case of air quality in Los Angeles illustrates, problems of environmental quality are often worse in metropolitan areas that are larger and in regions that are more densely populated. This is clearly true for air pollution (and associated respiratory disease), noise, traffic congestion, and time spent getting to work. Other factors are less clear. Our research shows that sewage and water treatment costs per person decline as city size increases to about 100,000; above that, engineering data suggest that costs should be the same for conventional facilities, but the actual observed costs appear to rise. If large cities have to change their sewage facilities, costs per person will be much higher. Similarly, solid waste disposal costs either follow a U-shaped curve or increase with city size and density. There is also evidence that large cities change local climate—wind, cloudiness, temperature, and precipitation; we really do not know whether or not such changes are bad. The inner city has all these environmental problems but to a heightened degree.

Yet the underlying cause of poor environmental quality in the larger urban centers may often not be size. Most of our largest centers are the old cities of the north; their problems may arise more from urban forms and transportation systems appropriate to an earlier era, old and uncoordinated facilities, multiple governmental jurisdictions, and the injustices that lead to inadequate financing and high proportions of minority groups and poor in central cities. In new cities as well as old, environmental quality suffers from inadequate pricing of public facilities and common property resources like space and waste disposal media, such as rivers and air. The historical evidence relating environmental quality to metropolitan size may not be applicable to the building of new cities and the refitting of older cities; indeed, many such problems would remain wherever people live.

The total volume of pollutants in the United States reponds, as we have seen, to the size of the national economy, which in turn depends heavily on the size of the national population. People consume resources wherever they live. Whether in New York City or a small town in the midwest, people still drive an automobile made of steel using coal mined in West Virginia. In the process, the air in cities is fouled by smoke and the scenery and the streams of West Virginia are spoiled by strip mining. Wherever Americans live, they make huge demands on the nation's and the world's resources and environment.

AGRICULTURAL LAND AND FOOD PRICES

At a time when the federal government pays farmers to hold land out of production, it seems absurd to be looking forward to a scarcity of good agricultural land and rising food prices. Yet these are the prospects indicated by our analysis of what rapid United States population growth implies.

This picture emerges when we combine the requirements for feeding a rapidly growing population with a sound environmental policy which restricts the use of pesticides and chemical fertilizers. There are a number of reasons for believing that the nation will wish to limit application of these chemicals. But to do so will retard improvements in per acre productivity. This means that, to produce a given quantity of food, more acres must be brought into production. It is likely that, with such restrictions, all the high quality land will have been returned to production by the year 2000. Consequently, the task of feeding the more rapidly growing population would force us to bring an additional 50 million acres of relatively low-quality land into production.

This is an expensive undertaking requiring heavy investment in equipment, fertilizer, and manpower, for which farmers must be compensated. The result is that 50 years from now the population resulting from the 3-child average could find itself having to pay farm food prices some 40 to 50 percent higher than they would be otherwise. The needs of the population at the lower growth rate could be met with practically no price increase.

The larger population could avoid the price rise by shifting away from consumption of animal livestock towards vegetables and synthetic meats. Perhaps it would shift to a closed system of agriculture—food from factories. One way or another, a solution can be found. The problem for a growing population is to survey the possible solutions and select the ones it dislikes least.

End, excerpts from *Population and the American Future.* In summary, these were the Commission's recommendations:

population recommendations

1) Schools should be assisted in programs of population and sex education, and that such information should also be provided through the media and responsible community organizations. Such information dissemination should also strive to improve the quality of education for parenthood.
2) Discrimination based on sex should be fought through passage of the proposed Equal Rights (for men and women) amendment to the Constitution. In addition, adequate child-care arrangements should be provided for parents who wish to use them.
3) Eliminate discrimination against children born out of wedlock, and reform adoption laws.
4) Increase investment to improve means by which individuals may control their own fertility.
5) Liberalize access to abortion services, with the admonition that abortion not be considered a primary means of fertility control.
6) Extend and improve health services related to fertility, including prenatal and pediatric care, contraceptive services, voluntary sterilization, abortion, and the treatment of infertility, through public and private financing mechanisms.
7) Permit no increase in present levels of legal immigration, and stop illegal immigration.
8) To ease problems created by poor population distribution, develop programs for human resource development and assistance in relocating.
9) Use comprehensive planning on a metropolitan and regional scale, executing this through greater public control over land use.
10) Promote genuine freedom of choice of housing within metropolitan areas for minorities.
11) Create a National Institute of Population Sciences within the National Institutes of Health, and an Office of Population Growth and Distribution within the Executive branch.

President Nixon, although saying that, "I do not plan to comment extensively on the contents and recommendations" of the above Commission's report, thanked the Commission for the report, but immediately rejected the main recommendations, and supported none of them. He said that liberalizing abortion laws "would demean human life," and that he wished "to make it clear that I do not support the unrestricted distribution of family planning services and devices to minors. Such measures would do nothing to preserve and strengthen close family relationships." (*Washington Post,* May 6, 1972 at 1.)

population
& resources

Below we quote from the statement of Dr. Preston E. Cloud, Jr. at hearings September 15, 1969, before the Conservation and Natural Resources Subcommittee of the Committee on Government Operations, House of Representatives. Dr. Cloud, Professor of Biology at the University of California at Santa Barbara, was chairman of the National Academy of Sciences Committee on Resources and Man, which had just completed (and was about to publish) an extensive report titled *Resources and Man.*

The Subcommittee's hearings, "Effects of Population Growth on Natural Resources and the Environment," are among the most informative materials in this field (35-506 GPO, 1969, $1.00 paper) Testimony of Dr. Cloud:

Let me state my conclusions at the outset and then give you some of the reasons for them. I define an optimum population as one that is large enough to provide the diversity, leisure, and substance whereby the creative genius of man can focus on the satisfactory management of his ecosystem, but not so large as to strain the capabilities of the earth to provide adequate diet, industrial raw materials, pure air and water, and attractive living and recreational space for all men, everywhere, into the indefinite future. I take it as self-evident under this definition that there is an optimum population, or at least optimal limits.

I believe, moreover, that the present world population of more than 3.5 billion substantially exceeds this optimum and that the present U.S. population of more than 200 million is beyond the optimum for our own country. Inasmuch, therefore, as the number of births needed to maintain the population at its present level is about 2.3 per fertile female, the number of children that couples ought to want—for the good of these children and the society in which they will live—is, at least until populations show signs of stabilizing, no more than two.

Unfortunately, the populations of the Nation and the world are going to get larger before they level off or become smaller, no matter what we do short of nuclear, chemical, or biological warfare, and no matter how fast we do it. This follows from the age structure of existing populations and the inadequate understanding that most people still have of the dimensions of the problem or what to do about it. That is all the more reason for thinking hard and carefully about what might be done and for getting on with it as rapidly as possible.

Now let me outline the reasons for these views.

The resources of the earth as an abode for man are large, but they are not infinite. No matter how discrepant or how large informed estimates of these resources may be, they must all agree that there is some annual harvest of food that cannot be exceeded on a sustained basis, some maximal quantity of each mineral and chemical resource that can be extracted and kept in circulation.

Technology and economies of scale result in the situation that these maximal quantities differ for different models of industrial civilization although the models that give the largest ultimate quantities also consume them at higher rates.

Thus it is possible to think of man in relation to his renewable resources of food, water, and breathable air as limited in numbers by the sustainable annual crop. His nonrenewable resources—metals, petrochemicals, mineral fuels, et cetera—can be thought of as some quantity which may be used up at different rates, but for which the quantity beneath the curve of cumulative total consumption from first use to exhaustion does not, in the final analysis, vary significantly.

In other words, the depletion curve of a given nonrenewable raw material, or of that class of resources, may rise and decline steeply over a relatively short time—as seems to be the case with petroleum, mercury, and helium—or it may be a flatter curve that lasts for a longer time. This is a choice that civilized industrialized man expresses, consciously or unconsciously, whenever his collective judgment takes form in a given density of population and per capita rate of consumption.

The Committee on Resources and Man studied the ultimate capability of an efficiently managed world to produce food, given the cultivation of all potentially arable and marginal lands and an optimal expression of scientific and technological innovations, both on land and in the sea. Its results imply that world food supplies might eventually

population & Resources

be increased to as much as nine times the present, provided that sources of protein were essentially restricted to plants, and to seafood mostly from a position lower in the marine food chain than is now customarily harvested—and provided metal resources and mineral fertilizers are equal to the task.

Given equitable distribution, such an ultimate level of productivity might sustain a world population of 30 billion, at a level of chronic malnutrition for the great majority. That places a maximal limit on world populations, at a figure that would be reached by about the year 2075 at present rates of increase—by which time, given concerted effort and luck, the maximal sustainable level of food production might have been reached.

Many students of the problem do not believe that it is possible to sustain 30 billion people, and I have no dispute with them. Here I seek simply to establish some theoretical outside limit based on relatively optimistic assumptions, both about what could be possible and what we may do about it. More important attributes than a starvation diet would be sacrificed by a world that full.

Similarly optimistic assumptions about demographic balances that might ensue from the present wave of concern, however, led the Committee on Resources and Man to judge it likely that world population might level off at around 10 billion by about the year 2050. Yet, in my view, even such a leveling off would still result in a world population of about 3 billion more than might eventually—and temporarily—be supported at a general level of living comparable to that enjoyed by developed nations at a modest state of affluence. That is the number of people—7 billion—that continuation of current rates of population increase would place on earth by the end of this century.

Granting the far from established assumption that such a population can be nourished adequately, and accepting the often-expressed American goal of development for all now underdeveloped countries, what would it take to bring a world population of 7 billion to an average level of living comparable to that of the United States in 1969?

It can be calculated that this would require keeping in circulation more than 60 billion tons of iron, about a billion tons of lead, around 700 million tons of zinc, and more than 50 million tons of tin—about 200 to 400 times the present annual world production of these commodities. Assuming these metals were placed in circulation, efficiently recycled, and demand stabilized, it would still take large quantities of new metals annually merely to replace those lost by unavoidable oxidation and friction—about 400,000 tons of new iron a year, for example. The needed quantities of lead, zinc, and tin, moreover, not to mention other metals, greatly exceed informed estimates of eventually recoverable quantities—that of tin, for instance, by at least two and one-half times.

program suggestions

COPING WITH THE PROBLEM OF OVERPOPULATION: SUGGESTIONS TO THE HOUSE SUBCOMMITTEE ON CONSERVATION AND NATURAL RESOURCES, BY PRESTON CLOUD, DEPARTMENT OF GEOLOGY, UNIVERSITY OF CALIFORNIA, SANTA BARBARA

As has been rightly and repeatedly pointed out, the problem of overpopulation is not one of numbers of births alone. It is one of births minus deaths multiplied by per capita consumption of resources and amenities. Where overpopulation exists or threatens we can bring things into balance by changing either or all of these variables. That is, we can increase the death rate, decrease the per capita consumption of resources, or decrease the birth rate—although under any rate of utilization of resources there are ultimate limits to supportable populations that cannot be exceeded.

If the choice as to how to balance this demographic equation were put to a vote in these terms, there can be little doubt that the decision would be overwhelmingly in favor of decreasing the birth rate; that is, of population control. While the concept of an optimum density of population is valid, however, just what the optimum might be depends so much on time, place, and circumstances that its estimation may vary widely and change with time and person. But population control must come everywhere in a world where death control is desired, even should coercive measures be necessary to achieve it. The best way to avoid the ultimate necessity of coercion is to devise and apply noncoercive measures and incentives as soon as possible. It is essential that whatever measures are adopted not discriminate against children who are born, whether wanted or not.

Specific steps that might at this time be taken toward the goal of eventual population control follow. Most are not original, but they deserve emphasis.

1. Enact a bipartisan joint declaration by the Congress and the President as to the desirability of limiting families to two children until population does come into balance. This might not do any good, but it can hardly do any harm, and it might help.

2. Repeal compulsory pregnancy (as Garrett Hardin so aptly calls it)—that is, legalize abortion for any female desiring it, free to those who cannot pay.

3. Repeal legal restraints to homosexual unions between consenting adults.

4. Repeal tax laws and other incentives that encourage the bearing of children.
5. Further revise welfare laws along lines that neither encourage the bearing of children nor penalize those who are born. A guaranteed annual income will be necessary—the sooner the better, but one that does not increase beyond the second child.
6. Where welfare parents improvidently have more than two children, preschool clinics and free school meals, books, and services should be available to help the children without putting money additional to their guaranteed income in the pockets of irresponsible parents.
7. Increase Federal support of higher education. Available records show that the number of children desired by and born to people decreases with the amount of education they have. Moreover, ever higher levels of education will be necessary for gainful employment.
8. Support education of all segments of the population in relevant aspects of sex, family life, pregnancy prevention and termination, and the inevitables of the demographic equation.
9. Authorize and appropriate funds for birth control clinics where information, devices, and services will be free to all comers without question.
10. Study the various proposals that have been made for population control (summarized by Bernard Berelson, 1969, *Science*, v. 163, pp. 533–543) and enact whatever further legislation seems most likely to achieve both public acceptance and promotion of the desired control.

population program suggestions

Other legislative measures which I believe might help to balance the demographic equation are:

1. Enact a new national law that has the effect of equating property taxes with actual instead of potential use of land. Cities would not gobble up suburban land so fast if the farms engulfed were taxed according to their productivity as farms and not according to the going prices of adjacent land for residential or commercial construction.
2. Create 120 new urban grant universities dispersed throughout the country and charged with the nucleation of 120 new cities. The initial grant to such universities might consist of from 2,000 up to as much as 5,000 acres each of attractive but peripheral public land, plus a construction and recruiting fund. Each university would be expected to reserve some part of its land for a campus and lease the remainder for income. The idea would be to attract light industry, research labs, and State and Federal activities around which a planned city would grow, marginal to the public lands which would serve as a permanent green belt and limited recreation area. Done right, such university-nucleated cities could serve as magnets to draw threatening population increases away from existing cities to more attractive surroundings, obtain a better distribution of population in relation to resources, and provide models for existing cities to emulate. Of course, there will be many details to work out, but none insurmountable to a country aware of its growing complex of educational, urban, and resource crises and determined to master them.
3. Enact such legislation and appropriate such funds as may be needed to implement the recommendations of the National Academy of Sciences' Committee on Resources and Man.

End, quote from hearings.

Unwanted Fertility in the United States, 1970[a]

Race and Education	Most Likely Number of Births per Woman	Percent of Births 1966-70 Unwanted	Percent of Births 1966-70 Unplanned[b]	Theoretical Births per Woman without Unwanted Births
All Women	3.0	15	44	2.7
College 4+	2.5	7	32	2.4
College 1-3	2.8	11	39	2.6
High School 4	2.8	14	44	2.6
High School 1-3	3.4	20	48	2.9
Less	3.9	31	56	3.0
White Women	2.9	13	42	2.6
College 4+	2.5	7	32	2.4
College 1-3	2.8	10	39	2.6
High School 4	2.8	13	42	2.6
High School 1-3	3.2	18	44	2.8
Less	3.5	25	53	2.9
Black Women	3.7	27	61	2.9
College 4+	2.3	3	21	2.2
College 1-3	2.6	21	46	2.3
High School 4	3.3	19	62	2.8
High School 1-3	4.2	31	66	3.2
Less	5.2	55	68	3.1

[a] Based on data from the 1970 National Fertility Study for currently married women under 45 years of age.

[b] Unplanned births include unwanted births.

The Total Cost of a Child, 1969

	Discounted	Undiscounted[a]
Cost of giving birth	$ 1,534	$ 1,534
Cost of raising a child	17,576	32,830
Cost of college education	1,244	5,560
Total direct cost	20,354	39,924
Opportunity costs for the average woman[b]	39,273	58,437
Total costs of a first child	$59,627	$98,361

[a] Discounted and undiscounted costs—spending $1,000 today costs more than spending $1,000 over a 10-year period because of the nine years of potential interest on the latter. This fact is allowed for in the discounted figures by assuming interest earned annually on money not spent in the first year. True costs are not accurately reflected in the undiscounted estimates, for these are simply accumulations of total outlays without regard to the year in which they must be made.

[b] Depending on the educational background of the mother, the opportunity costs (earnings foregone by not working) could be higher or lower.

SOURCE: Ritchie H. Reed and Susan McIntosh, "Costs of Children" (prepared for the Commission, 1972).

SOURCE of both tables: *Report of the Commission on Population and the American Future,* 1972.

Selected Bibliography: Population

For an excellent short discussion of the current status of abortion laws, *see* "Legal Abortion: How safe? How costly?", *Consumer Reports;* July 1972 at 466.

HARDIN, Garret, *ed., Population, Evolution, and Birth Control,* 2d. ed., W. H. Freeman & Co., San Francisco, 1969

EHRLICH, Paul R. & Anne H., *Population, Resources, Environment, Issues in* #10, *Human Ecology,* W. H. Freeman & Co., San Francisco, 1970

HOWARD, *Man's Population-Environment Crisis,* 4 Nat. Res. Law 99 Jan. 1971

PERELMAN, *Second Thoughts on the Green Revolution,* The New Republic, July 17, 1971 at 21

CLAXTON, *Population and Law,* 4 Nat. Res. Law 113 Jan. 1971

YOUNG, Louise B., ed., *Population in Perspective,* Oxford University Press, New York, 1968 paper

STOCKWELL, Edward G., *Population and People,* Quadrangle Books, Chicago, 1968

DAY, Lincoln, and DAY, Alice, *Too Many Americans,* Houghton-Mifflin Co., Boston, 1964

GROSSWIRTH, Marvin, "Who's Afraid of Vasectomy?" *Saturday Review* June 10, 1972 at 38 (from 1973 book, *The Truth About Vasectomy,* Prentice-Hall).

McCORMACK, Arthur, *The Population Problem* 1970

STRANGELAND, Charles E., *Pre-Malthusian Doctrines of Population,* (1904) 1966

APPLEMAN, Philip, *The Silent Explosion,* Beacon Press, Boston, 1965 paper

EHRLICH, Paul, *The Population Bomb,* Ballantine Books, New York, 1968 paper

LEACH, Gerald,, *The Biocrats,* McGraw-Hill Book Co., New York, 1970

SHEPARD, P., & McKinley, D., eds., *Essays Toward an Ecology of Man,* Houghton Mifflin Co., Boston, 1969

National Goals Research Staff Report, *Toward Balanced Growth: Quantity With Quality,* Supt. of Doc., Washington, D.C., July 1970

Hearings before the U.S. Senate Subcommittee on Foreign Aid Expenditures, *Population Crisis,* Socio-Dynamics Publications, Washington, D.C., 1970

Department of Health, Education, and Welfare Report on Population and Family Planning Activities (Report to the House Committee on Appropriations, March 1971)

U.S. Dept. of Health, Education, and Welfare, *Family Planning Services Project Grants to the National Center for Family Planning Services, Policies and Guidelines for Applicants* (February 1971)

HOW MANY BIRTHS ARE UNWANTED?

ONE FIFTH OF ALL U.S. BIRTHS, 1960-65, WERE UNWANTED.

Data on unwanted childbearing are from L. Bumpass and C. F. Westoff, "The 'Perfect Contraceptive' Population," *Science*, 169: 1177-1182, September 1970.

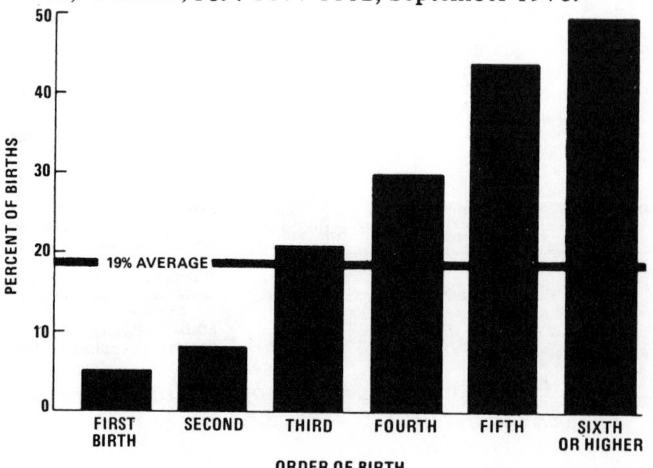

c. Substipollution & Social Factors

It has been said that pollution is the result of the related factors of population size, per capita consumption, and an "environmental impact" index that measures, in part, how wisely we apply the technology that goes with consumption.[1] Multiplying the population size by the per capita consumption equals the total quantity of goods consumed, which, discounting exports, imports, etc., roughly approximates total production. Multiplying the latter by the environmental impact (pollution per unit of production) then produces the level of pollution. This equation may be expressed as:

population size× per capita consumption × environmental impact per unit of production= level of pollution.

An analysis of each of the first two factors in the above equation reveals their inadequacy, by themselves, to explain the increase in the level of pollution estimated by some authorities to be from 200 to 1000 percent.[2] The Bureau of the Census indicates that U.S. population has risen 43 percent for the period 1946-68,[3] while pollution levels have increased at a much greater rate.

The rise in the second factor, per capita consumption, is also insufficient to explain the pollution level increases, as recent Department of Commerce figures for the same period indicate a rise in Gross National Product (GNP) per capita of approximately 59 percent.[4]

pollution by 'progress'

A study of the types of products manufactured or consumed over the 1946-68 period reveals the heart of the pollution increase problem. American technology has been substituting new, environmentally-degrading products for older, less polluting ones on a scale massive enough to permanently tip our environmental balance. Growth in the utilization of one product is counterbalanced by the reduction in use of similar ones; plastics have been substituted for lumber; detergents for soap; air and truck shipment for railroad freight; nonreturnable cans and bottles for returnable ones, etc. The following table[5] shows these changes in production or consumption per capita. (The zero increase in fish consumption, for example, represents an absolute increase of 43%, which matches exactly the population increase for the same period, and so the relative percentage increase is zero):

Item	Period	% Increase
Mercury for chlorine and sodium hydroxide products	1946–68	2,150
Noncellulosic synthetic fiber (consumption)	1950–68	1,792
Plastics	1946–68	1,024
Air freight—ton-miles	1950–68	593
Nitrogen fertilizer	1946–68	534
Synthetic organic chemicals	1946–68	495
Chlorine gas	1946–68	410
Aluminum	1946–68	317
Detergents	1952–68	300
Electric power	1946–68	276
Pesticides	1950–68	217
Total horsepower	1950–68	178
Wood pulp	1946–68	152
Motor vehicle registration	1946–68	110
Motor fuel (consumption)	1946–68	100
Cement	1946–68	74
Truck freight—ton-miles	1950–68	74
Total mercury (consumption)	1946–68	70
Cheese (consumption)	1946–68	58
Poultry (consumption)	1946–68	49
Steel	1946–68	39
Total freight—ton-miles	1950–68	28
Total fuel energy (consumption)	1946–68	25

Newspaper advertisements (space)	1950–68	22
Newsprint (consumption)	1950–68	19
Meat (consumption)	1946–68	19
New copper	1946–68	15
Newspaper news (space)	1950–68	10
All fibers (consumption)	1950–68	6
Beer (consumption)	1950–68	4
Fish (consumption)	1946–68	0
Hosiery	1946–68	–1
Returnable pop bottles	1946–69	–4
Calorie (consumption)	1946–68	–4
Protein (consumption)	1946–68	–5
Cellulosic synthetic fiber (consumption)	1950–68	–5
Railroad freight—ton-miles	1950–68	–7
Shoes	1946–68	–15
Egg (consumption)	1946–68	–15
Grain (consumption)	1946–68	–22
Lumber	1946–68	–23
Cotton fiber (consumption)	1950–68	–33
Milk and cream (consumption)	1946–68	–34
Butter	1946–68	–47
Railroad horsepower	1950–68	–60
Wool fiber (consumption)	1950–68	–61
Returnable beer bottles	1946–69	–64
Saponifiable fat (for soap products)	1944–64	–71
Work animal horsepower	1950–68	–84

substipollution

Nor can production of the so-called "necessities of life" (food, clothing, and shelter) be blamed for the increase in overall pollution levels. Increases in per capita food consumption, clothing production, and housing unit production have generally kept pace with the population increase, and in one case (food consumption), have even declined somewhat, from 3,390 calories per person per day to 3,250 per person per day in 1968.[6]

As evidenced above, the sharpest increases in per capita production have been in the following areas:

(1) synthetic organic chemicals and products made from them, i.e. pesticides, plastics, synthetic fibers, etc.
(2) wood pulp and paper products
(3) energy production
(4) total horsepower of engines produced
(5) petroleum and petroleum products
(6) cement
(7) mercury
(8) aluminum

---

1. Ehrlich & Holdren, "The People Problem," The Saturday Review, July 4, 1970, p. 2.
2. Commoner, "The Causes of Pollution," 13 Environment 2 (April 1971).
3. Bureau of the Census, *Statistical Abstract of the United States,* U.S. Govt. Print. Off. (Washington, D.C., 1970) p. 5.
4. Department of Commerce *The National Income and Products Accounts of the United States,* 1929–1965, U.S. Govt. Print. Off. (Washington, D.C., 1966), pp. 4–5.
5. This table, appearing in the Commoner article, *op-cit.,* derives from the following reports:

   Bureau of the Census, *Statistical Abstract,* U.S. Government Printing Office, Washington, D.C., 1949: pp. 511, 512, 526, 741, 746, 773, 775, 797, 961, 963, 964, 968, 973; 1953: pp. 92, 93, 821; 1955: p. 830; 1969: p. 509; 1970: pp. 83, 84, 498, 505, 506, 507, 535, 544, 548, 590, 638, 637, 658, 661, 666, 712, 713, 717, 718, 719, 722. Bureau of the Census, "Glass Containers," *Current Industrial Reports,* M32G (69)-13, Washington, D.C., 1970. Department of Agriculture, *Agriculture Statistics 1955,* U.S. Government Printing Office, Washington, D.C., 1956, p. 486. Bureau of Mines, *Minerals Yearbook,* U.S. Government Printing Office, Washington, D.C., 1947: p. 772; 1968, Volume 1: p. 695. *Statistical Abstract, op. cit.,* 1970, pp. 535, 548, 554, 555.
6. Bureau of the Census, *Statistical Abstract,* 1953: pp. 92–93; 1970: pp. 83–84.

The rises in per capita production in each of these areas range from 100 to 1000 percent, increases which parallel the earlier estimates of the increase in general pollution. A brief examination of each of these classes reveals that this relationship is probably cause-and-effect, for paper mills, chemical companies, and cement plants are infamous water and air pollutors, and most air pollution in the U.S. is caused by the internal combustion engine and by electric power generation. Modern agricultural production, intensified by new technologies such as feedlots and fertilizers, causes increased (and obvious) pollution, despite the fact that per capita food consumption has not risen. Most of the synthetic "improvements" which American technology has substituted for the older, natural-origin products fit into the natural ecosystems either poorly or not at all. Well-known examples of this are plastics and pesticides.

Perhaps more important, however, than the final impact on the environment of these new products is the environmental pollution caused by their production. The difference in energy required to produce a pound of cotton and a corresponding pound of synthetic fiber is tremendous, as the photosynthetic process of natural cotton production is virtually pollution-free compared with the multitude of complex, energy-requiring and polluting processes such as distillation and evaporation involved in producing a synthetic such as nylon. This type of comparison holds across-the-board, as the production of synthetic detergents, artificial rubber and plastics inevitably involves more environmental pollution, weight-for-weight, than the production of soap, natural rubber, or wood.

substipollution

Aluminum, which is rapidly replacing steel as a food/beverage container, requires approximately 6.5 times the energy used to produce an identical quantity of steel.[7] The environmental cost of aluminum production in one area alone—air pollution due to electric power production and fossil fuel consumption—seems to demand a reevaluation of its continued expansion. To keep pace with the American substitution technology, the production of electric power has accelerated rapidly, increasing by 662 percent between 1946-68.[8] Much of urban air pollution is caused by the electric power companies' use of fossil fuels, and radioactive pollution results from nuclear power production. Because all electric power ultimately results in heat, thermal pollution of the air and cooling waters is increasing at a pace concomitant with the power increase.

However, the focus on technology as the major factor in America's pollution problem does not allow for simplistic solutions. For example, nylon may seem to create more pollution in its manufacture than cotton. But to meet our fiber needs through cotton would result in the use of more pesticides and inorganic fertilizers, perhaps new irrigated acreage would be needed. Thus, men such as Barry Commoner who have pioneered in this work point to the need for a great deal of additional study to provide the information necessary if we are to know the environmental impacts of various alternative courses of action that are open to us.

At the same time we cannot ignore the population and consumption factors in the equation, for each of the elements multiplies the effect of the others. Furthermore, they are interrelated. Population and consumptive pressure may force us to adopt more damaging technologies. Cheap, though destructive technologies, may encourage an increase in consumption.

In less-developed nations, the population factor may be the most important. In our own nation, a reduction in the population would reduce the impact of the consumption and technology factor. Nevertheless, technology as a factor in polluting our nation is of prime importance.[9]

---

7. Bureau of the Census, *Census of Manufacturing 1963,* U.S. Govt. Print. Off. (Washington, D.C.) pp. 33A-44, 33C-41. Statistical Abstract, *op-cit.*, 1966: pp. 737, 810.

8. Statistical Abstract, *op-cit.*, 1948: p. 493; 1970: p. 507.

9. Recently an unfortunately acrimonious controversy has developed. On one side is Paul Ehrlich and John Holdren, who are exponents of population control as the most important measure for environmental control. On the other side is Barry Commoner, who considers technology the major United States problem. Their charges and counter charges can be found in *Environment,* Vol. 14, No. 3, April 1972 at 24.

'Social value' factor

There may be a fourth factor of such importance that it should be added to the equation. This would be a "social value" factor. While the effect of this factor is implicit in Commoner's study, it deserves more careful scrutiny. The purpose of the equation is to simplify the understanding of the problem so as to be able to deal more effectively with it. Therefore we must consider that for any given level of population, consumption and technology, various levels of environmental impact are possible. Pollution control equipment may or may not be purchased. If purchased, it may or may not be properly used. Environmental protection laws may be strong or weak. They may be enforced or unenforced.

Thus, a major factor in determining how much environmental impact occurs is the political-economic-social context in which man's activities take place. A few generalizations can be made to indicate that solving the environmental problem requires dealing with society as a whole.

Pollution shifts a cost-of-doing-business onto the general public. Economic and health costs are absorbed by the public, but pollution is profitable for the pollutor. (The production orientation of other economic systems brings similar results.)

In an economic system in which demand is molded by large advertising expenditures and consumer choices are limited, the environmentally destructive practices are built into the system, with change threatening the well-being of the economy. An example would be the large expenditures for roads and corresponding failure to provide mass transit. Thus, the automobile is the only viable means of transportation for most people, and the economy depends upon continued production of automobiles and related products and services.

In an economic system in which most production is in the hands of a small number of large corporations, the structure of these corporations is a major factor in determining environmental impact. The size of these corporations and their political power means that unwanted change comes slowly if at all. An example would be the automobile manufacturers' resistance to air pollution controls, or the electric utilities which continue to advertise to increase consumption in the face of brownouts. Corporations are very willing to substitute technology for employees, and thus the environmental impact is increased, but the social problems of unemployment results. An example would be coal mining. The underground mining of coal is not without its environmental impact, but technology has produced the equipment for the much-more-destructive strip mining. Unemployment as well as environmental destruction follows.

We live in a political system that requires large expenditures to run for election. These funds are obtained primarily from large economic interests that wish to be protected from undesired regulation. The costs of pollution control equipment means that it is often cheaper to buy politicians than to clean up. The committee system common in our legislatures makes such purchases easier and cheaper.

While other writers have recognized the social-political-economic aspects of our technology, the use of any technology has social decisional components that can be examined separately. Cotton for example can be produced using different kinds of fertilizers and pesticides. But the decision to produce cotton is made after considering Department of Agriculture policies, the Internal Revenue Code, transportation costs (Based on I.C.C. rates), etc. Changing these factors means dealing with Congress, some of whose members receive considerable amounts of money under the existing system, although perhaps the most pathetic thing is just how cheaply men will often sell-out their country. Scattered campaign contributions not even reaching into the hundreds of thousands of dollars affect votes meaning billions of dollars.

Detergent pollution depends upon massive advertising campaigns. Nuclear power development requires hundreds of millions of dollars of federal funds. The list can go on, but the point is obvious. The environmental impact of our actions are intertwined in our social structure.

d. Planning & Evaluation

To understand the role of the government in destroying our environment requires an appreciation of the degree to which governmental decisions determine the use and allocation of our natural resources.

When the first colonists reached our shores, all natural resources were available for the taking. Thus, resources were held in common, though individuals could reduce these resources to private ownership by capture—that is, by possession—or, in some cases, by notifying their neighbors that specific resources were now to be considered private property.

As long as the supply of a resource exceeds any demand made upon it by consumers, such ownership creates little friction within the human community. When demand exceeds supply, one of two developments can take place. The resource can continue to be treated as a common resource, in which case most users will seek to use or capture as much as possible, since, if they do not, their neighbors will. The alternative course is management of resources.

Following the first course (of self interest or Adam Smith's "invisible hand") leads either to elimination of the resource or to its reduction to the point where further exploitation is uneconomical. Such an economic pattern has resulted in the stripping of our forests, the overgrazing of our grasslands and consequent loss of soil, and now it threatens to destroy our ocean fisheries.

The alternative is limiting the availability of the resource. As with the practice of holding resources in common without limitations on use, this can be for the benefit of the few (e.g. the King's deer or Republic Steel's Cuyahoga River poisons' disposal system [consumption]), or for the many (the Queen's swans or the West German national forests [conservation for 1, esthetic pleasures; 2, long-term sustained use and yield]).

for few
or for many

Obviously the first alternative is not worthy of *homo sapiens*. And the second alternative requires planning if it is to significantly be better than the first.

In societies with governments, governments must do the planning, at least from the action standpoint. If they don't, no one else can. Government in our society must therefore plan and control the exploitation of natural resources so as to sustain their yields or, if the resource is nonrenewable, limit the rate of its consumption or extraction and promulgate its reuse.

The recognition of the need for planning (and control) is an admission that traditional laissez-faire ideas were nothing more than a denial of the one basic justification for government: that of limiting violence of one man on another (in this case through destruction of his habitat). Because of the threat to these values, there are those who maintain that we have no natural resource planning.

In truth, we have a great deal: but not of the best sort. The Federal Communications Commission rules a sector of the electromagnetic spectrum, deciding who will control what it is that members of the American public can see and hear at a distance. The Interstate Commerce Commission decides who can use up all sorts of resources by engaging in commercial land transportation, and has a strong hand in deciding what type of transportation shall be furnished. The Department of the Interior leases public lands for mining, and grants timber contracts which result in swift no-tree, no-soil land for many thousands of acres. We have oil import quotas, protective tax policies, and tariffs (including President Nixon's latest surcharge [August 15, 1971] to, in effect, increase domestic resource consumption and lower foreign natural resource consumption for the purpose of offsetting war-caused inflation). And we have a massive governmental effort to aid a small percentage of the possessors of active or former farmland.

As even the most cursory examination of the careers of many of our political leaders will demonstrate, the difference between poverty and great abundance very often depends on how successful a person is in obtaining boons from federal planning agencies. To fail in our system results in the welfare check or worse—to be eliminated from the economic system. To succeed is to receive $100,000 for not growing a non-salable crop, or not making a workable military tank after contracting to do so. Yet for the bulk of Americans between these extremes, their welfare too depends greatly on policy decisions formulated very largely in secret within administrative agencies.

Such an economic system is not necessarily bad, and certainly is not the worst possible, nor even the most illogical: the Northwestern Indian tribes that practiced potlatch came close in their methods of status-gaining destruction to matching the Throw-away Society in materialistic lunacy; though of course they lacked the tremendous capacity of, for instance, the Peabody Coal Company to destroy much more valuable things (top soil). Indeed, the present system basically may be the only viable alternative at present to the economic chaos and resource destruction of the "common goods" philosophy. In an over-populated, complex, interdependent community, some kind of planning is mandatory. However, the goals of such planning should be thought-out clearly, preferably commonly agreed upon, and based on an attempt to exist harmoniously with our biological habitat.

role of our governments

A very different state of affairs generally is present in government planning. Goals commonly are defined in amorphous terms such as "the public interest," "the common good," "multiple use," and other misty terms that could not be used meaningfully even by philosopher-kings. Especially dangerous is the concept that decisions can be made independent of the private values of the decision-makers. The result is the allocation by government agencies of scarce natural resources for the benefit of some of the people, usually at the expense of most of the people. Meanwhile, great efforts are expended to convince innocent students and voters that the rule of law will achieve justice and prevent improper distribution of wealth. To contort the carved quotation on the crumbling Hudson County Courthouse in Jersey City: "Precedent makes law; if you stand ill, don't stand still."

Congress ratifies these injustices both through its direct actions and its inactions that leave vast powers to the administrative agencies. The courts, by overturning administrative decisions only for extremely arbitrary administrative action, encourage the shift of government to the "headless" branch. Policy-making there involves only a narrow range of the affected interests: the policy-makers all too often champion the economic interests they regulate. Discretion is exercised to benefit the powerful. Abuses of democratic processes are the accepted practice. Agency decision making is a secret process. Often the public is unaware a decision affecting their lives is being made. Information, even if legally available, is often not available in fact; and the complexity of the information that is available further complicates citizen participation in the decisions of government.

The result of these planning powers is a government with the ability to make citizens—in theory its bosses—kings or paupers at its whim. Even the air and the water are slowly losing their "free goods" status, and are available only on terms made by government agencies. It is therefore becoming of immense importance that public decisions concerning resource allocation represent a broader spectrum of interest than has been the practice. The first step is to destroy the myth that unbridled discretion in granting valuable resources is either democratic or a wise method of protecting the values of our society.

planning against 'progress'

Perhaps the most interesting aspect of planning is that advocated by Raymond Dasmann in his book, *A Different Kind of Country* (1968). He advocates planning against progress. Planning creates or has been involved in some of our worst blunders. City planning requires new values. Irreplaceable qualities of the environment must be preserved and growth must be controlled. Yellowstone, and many of our unique priceless environments were protected when little political opposition could develop. Such is not the situation today. But to destroy the habitat of endangered wildlife destroys the wildlife. A highway ends wilderness, and dams end a wild river. There is only one Everglade. Yet politically powerful economic interests press to destroy the rarest commodity—these unique environments.

Planning must, therefore, include as its primary purpose the protection of these environments and the encouragement of diversity. Conflicts that threaten these primary values should recognize the highest value is to be placed on these environments, for they cannot be replaced. Moreover, the challenge is to protect small areas. Except in Alaska, the opportunity for new Yellowstone National Parks is gone. Some new parks can and should be quickly created, though the total cost—perhaps equal to one year of the Army's ammunition budget—may make such acquisitions beyond the financial means of our nation. But it is the small natural areas that add diversity, beauty, and contact with nature to the daily life of Americans that need immediate protection by each level of government and its citizenry.

Coast land, small marshes, pockets of virgin timber, sand dunes, natural islands, are the targets of developers and must be the concern of the planners against progress. Often these lands are held by private owners interested in their protection. But tax policies, condemnation power held by utilities, and pollution can destroy them. We should, therefore, plan on the basis that open space is fixed and all other land uses are flexible. Furthermore, each community should have a size and population beyond which further growth is discouraged. And each community should strive for its own distinctive character in order to preserve urban diversity. It means that city planning should seek to minimize private transportation; it means protecting agriculture lands from development. A basic problem, however, is that creating the Garden of Eden is expensive. It takes public sector effort and generally public sector money, though some progress can be made by channeling or encouraging private expenditures. It means foregoing or changing the means for private economic gain. Optimism for the continued existence of irreplaceable environments is therefore difficult to maintain.

Loss of Coastal Wetlands, 1954–64

(In thousands of acres)

	1954	1959	1964	Total losses (1954–64)	Percent lost (1954–64)
Maine	96.4	NA	96.4	<0.05	0.1
New Hampshire	9.9	NA	9.8	.1	1.4
Massachusetts	41.6	40.9	40.6	1.0	2.4
Connecticut	17.2	15.9	14.8	2.2	12.8
Rhode Island	2.3	2.2	2.2	.1	5.3
New York [1]	43.2	37.5	30.6	12.6	29.2
New Jersey	257.3	244.3	232.7	24.6	9.6
Delaware	120.1	116.9	115.5	4.6	3.8
Total	**588.0**	**NA**	**542.6**	**45.2**	**7.7**

[1] Long Island only.
Source: Inner City Fund. Based on U.S. Department of the Interior, Fish and Wildlife Service data.

planning to plan

The most imaginative and far-reaching proposal for the incorporation of the planning function into the structure of government is that of Tugwell in his draft of a new constitution. [Rexford Guy Tugwell, "Constitution for A United Republics of America—Version XXXVII," *The Center Magazine*, Vol. III, No. 5 (Sept., 1970)] He proposes that "planning" shall constitute one of six separate branches of government. In order to give some idea of what he suggests, a portion of Article III, The Planning Branch, from his latest draft Constitution follows. You will note that the technology assessment function is included here.

> ARTICLE III, THE PLANNING BRANCH Section 5. It shall be recognized that the six- and twelve-year development plans represent national intentions tempered by the appraisal of possibilities. The twelve-year plan shall be a general estimate of probable progress, both governmental and private; the six-year plan shall be more specific as to estimated income and expenditure.
>
> The purpose shall be to advance, through every agency of government, the excellence of national life; it shall be the further purpose to anticipate innovations, to estimate their impact, to assimilate them into existing institutions, or to moderate deleterious effects on the environment and on society.

An important part of the National Environmental Protection Act of 1969 is the requirement that an agency think before it acts: alternatives must be considered and secondary effects evaluated. Thus NEPA attempts to incorporate environmental values in the decision-making that takes place as part of all government planning.

The difficulty is that to allocate limited resources relatively properly requires a judgment process in which social, ethical, economic, and other values are evaluated together. Is wilderness more important than saw timber? Are beautiful views more important than the ore extracted from surface mines? Is the soil more valuable than the coal? And in this evaluative process, who will represent future generations?

Merely stating the problems makes clear that no man has the ability to make such decisions with unerring correctness. Nevertheless, two grievous faults in current practice are obvious.

Economic considerations, particularly short-term benefits, receive disproportionate consideration. Second, the decisions usually are made by small numbers of administrative agency heads whose chief qualification frequently is either long-term loyalty to a political party or long-term participation in the industry they regulate. And so a number of salient policy considerations are generally ignored.

The United States has sufficient economic capability to provide for the future without serious limitations on present well-being. We do, however, have a problem in the increasing number of persons who cannot happily do without work in this society and who seem to have little possibility of being absorbed into the private sector work force even in periods of high employment. Environmental protection and the work of undoing the destruction of the past could provide worthwhile employment. The Civilian Conservation Corps of the 1930's was an unqualified success. Yet, except for some recent activity in California to use conservation work as an alternative to the draft, and a limited Job Corps program, we have made little effort to make conservation work a source of employment. Even these programs, usually paramilitary in nature, seem strangely un-American. Would we expect municipal water treatment facility employees to be limited to single males, who live in barrack communes?

It is clear that employment possibilities exist, and that they exist both in rural America and the core central cities, the two areas of America that are subject to declining population and depressed economies.

Rural conservation projects can help stop the population shift that each year compacts more of our population onto less land. Urban conservation can help heal the wounds that have made cities ugly, unsafe, and unhuman. Having tried to pave over the central cities only to find a thousand failures, perhaps we should reverse the process and plant flower gardens. A political candidate might go far today on a pledge that if elected, he would let grass grow in the streets.

The task then, is two-fold. We must determine the real costs, social and economic, of our present way of life so that it is possible to have sufficient facts to reverse the "liquidation basis" upon which it is being run. Second, we must openly admit we have a planned economy, and force the planners to operate openly, allowing the allocation decisions to be made on the basis of a more wide-spread participation.

This radical concept is called democracy.

Selected Bibliography: Planning

CLAWSON, Marion & Held, Burnell & Stoddard, Charles, *Land for the Future,* Baltimore, Johns Hopkins Press, 1960

COOLEY, Richard A., and Wandesforde-Smith, Geoffrey, eds., *Congress and the Environment,* Seattle & London, Univ. of Washington Press, 1970

DANSEREAU, Pierre and Weadcock, Virginia A., eds., *Challenge for Survival—* Land, air, and water for man in megalopolis, New York, Columbia Univ. Press, 1970

DAVIES, J. Clarence, III, *The Politics of Pollution,* New York, Pegasus 1970 paper

EWALD, William R., Jr., ed., *Environment and Change: The Next Fifty Years,* Bloomington, Indiana Univ. Press, 1968 paper

FIFE, *Killing the Goose,* 13 Environment No. 3, April 1971 at 20

HANSE, *Creating New Institutional Arrangements for Environmental Quality Control,* 3 Natural Resource Law 739 Nov. 1970

HARRIS, Joseph, *Congressional Control of Administration,* Garden City, N.Y., Doubleday & Co., Inc., 1964 paper

HUTCHISON, *Bringing Conservation into the Main Stream of American Thought,* 9 Natural Resources Journal 518 1969

LANDSBERG, Hans H., *Natural Resources for U. S. Growth, Baltimore, Johns Hopkins Press, 1964* paper

MURPHY, *A Law for Life, 1969,* Wisconsin Law Review 733

REICH, *The Law of the Planned Society,* 75 *Yale Law Journal* 1227 1966

RESOURCES FOR THE FUTURE; *Science and Resources: Prospects and Implications of Technological Advance,* Essays by G. W. Beadle & Others, ed. by Henry Jarrett, Blatimore, Johns Hopkins Press, 1969

SAX, *Defending the Environment, A Strategy for Citizen Action,* Alfred A. Knopf, New York, 1971

SCIENTIFIC AMERICA, *Technology and Economic Development,* September, 1963

Evaluation

In the late 1930's our technology produced a mechanical cotton picker at the price within reach of agricultural users. The machine eliminated millions of hours of human drudgery. Yet it had side effects that were probably unforeseen and, at any rate, far from uniformly beneficial even for those who were saved from drudgery. The introduction of the mechanical cotton picker eventually forced millions of southern farm tenants, sharecroppers, and roving cotton pickers to move North and West. Now many of them and their children and grandchildren reside in the core of our large cities, many still unable to compete in an industrialized society. There they have an important role in our society, as statistics on poverty and crime express the secondary effects of technological development.

If we begin to speculate on the possibility of such developments, we must take note of the high capital cost of modern agriculture that makes small family farms obsolete, and is moving the total control of agriculture to large agricorporations and banks. Even more dangerous vertical integration monopolization is occurring, with economic control from field to market in a few hands.

The move toward "efficient" highly capital-intense agriculture further increases the political pressure for large-scale irrigated agriculture subsidized by the public. It also implies dependence on a single crop (monoculture), with its ever increasing needs for pesticides to control a biologically unstable environment. The varieties of food that can be obtained is reduced as plants are bred to be easily handled by machines. Travelers marvel at the huge variety of locally grown produce available in rural Mexico. In the United States, an agricultural area of the same size may be devoted to one or two crops, and only one type of apple may now be available where formerly a dozen types were grown. Thus the inexpensive food found in supermarkets carries with it additional costs both economic and environmental, paid for by the tax-payer and the consumer.

benefit-cost analysis

To control the governmental support for programs that seem beneficial requires more than superficial analysis. Evaluation goes by various names: systems analysis, technological assessment, benefit-cost studies. The governmental agencies oriented toward science and technology have the better systems, despite all their blunders, which says much about the quality of the social programs. Nevertheless, some kinds of assessment have been used for years in the natural resource area—particularly in the resource development programs.

The goal of benefit-cost analysis is to require an objective evaluation of the merits of each proposed government project, and thereby encourage an improved allocation of public funds. With the new emphasis on Federal public works during the 1930's, benefit-cost analysis developed as a tool for project evaluation. In the Flood Control Act of 1936, Congress enunciated a benefit-cost requirement which over the years has been broadened to other purposes. The Act requires ". . . that the Federal Government should improve or participate in the improvement of navigable waters or their tributaries, including watersheds thereof, for flood control purposes if the benefits to whomsoever they may accrue are in excess of the estimated costs, and if the lives and social security of people are otherwise adversely affected."[1]

The present system of benefit-cost analysis is determined by laws, regulations and policy discussions. Senate document 97[2] has helped coordinate and standardize Federal benefit-cost analysis and serves as the basis for present studies. Senate Document 97 supports the use of the benefit-cost system to evaluate tangible and intangible benefits and costs to

1. 49 Stat. 1570.

2. The President's Water Resources Council, *Policies, Standards, and Procedures in the Formulation, Evaluation and Review of Plans for Use and Development of Water and Related Land Resources,* 87th Cong., 2d Sess., Sen. Doc. 97 (1962).

the fullest extent possible and defines how Federal agencies should evaluate items in the analysis.

The result of a benefit-cost analysis is expressed as a ratio, with benefits in the numerator and costs in the denominator. A project is considered to be justified if this ratio exceeds one. The analysis requires conversion of all values into monetary terms. Thus, the validity of a benefit-cost analysis depends on the success of evaluating intangibles and benefits and costs with no established market value.

Tangible benefits are divided into primary and secondary benefits. Primary benefits denote the value obtained from project-produced goods and services. Secondary benefits are the value added to activities influenced by the project. Other tangible benefits include the employment of unemployed resources, economic stabilization, income redistribution, and regional development. Benefits such as outdoor recreation have no established market value, and are difficult to evaluate. General outdoor recreation is assigned a value between $0.50 and $1.50 per man-day, and specialized outdoor recreation is valued between $2.00 and $6.00 per man-day.[3] The quantification of intangible benefits such as environmental protection is even more difficult.

Costs include all construction and operating expenses. Any environmental impact created by the project should be included in the cost analysis, although these costs are often ignored. The evaluation of intangible benefits and environmental costs remains a persistent problem throughout the analysis.

Technological evaluation

A more fundamental problem is that most major technological developments require an almost endless number of effects and relationships to be considered. If these considerations are made, the number of subjective value judgments that must be made result in an almost useless assessment. If an all-encompassing study is not made so as to increase the validity of the assessment there is no assurance that the decision-maker (a politician or administrator) will not be swayed by considerations that were not part of the technological assessment. Nevertheless, the attempt to perfect an evaluation system continues. For example, the National Academy of Engineering has been given responsibility for making studies and recommendations on this. [A Study of Technology Assessment, Report of the Committee on Public Engineering Policy, National Academy of Engineering for the Committee on Science and Astronautics, July 1969].

Many government projects require large initial capital expenditures to achieve benefits over the life of the project. Costs and benefits involve comparisons of different time streams. The time streams are equated by using the discount rate. The discount rate is the cost of capital in investing funds and waiting for their yield, and is analogous to the interest rate used by the private sector.

Since many Federal undertakings will yield benefits for a substantial period of time (the estimated useful life of projects is often fifty years), changes in the discount rate will produce significant differences in the benefit-cost ratio. Thus, the higher the discount rate, the fewer the projects which will show a favorable benefit-cost ratio.

In the past, the discount rate was analogized to the average rate of interest payable by the Treasury on interest-bearing marketable securities of the United States. This was substantially lower than the interest rate used by the private sector, and did not reflect the social opportunity cost[4] of the funds. The discount rate remained between 2⅝% and 3¼% from 1960 to 1968. Recently, the discount rate was increased to 7%. It is expected that the new discount rate will produce more realistic benefit-cost ratios.

3. Ad Hoc Water Resources Council, *Evaluation Standards for Primary Outdoor Recreation Benefits* at 4-5 (1964).

4. Opportunity cost represents the return from the best alternative use of the funds or, in other words, the cost of an investment foregone.

The effect of the discount rate used in benefit-cost analysis is illustrated by the following hypothetical multiple purpose water resources project evaluated at a 3% and a 7% discount rate.

Project life: 50 years

Benefits

irrigation	$ 500,000/yr.
hydroelectric power	400,000/yr.
flood control	200,000/yr.
recreation	200,000/yr.
water supply	100,000/yr.
fish & wildlife enhancement	100,000/yr.
TOTAL	$1,500,000/yr.

Costs[1]

construction	$20,000,000
annual maintenance	$ 250,000/yr.

Applying a 3% discount rate (discount rates of about 3% were used from 1961–1968):

Present worth of benefits = $1,500,000 (P/A, 3%, 50)[2] = $1,500,000 (23.11)* = $34,665,000
Present worth of costs = $20,000,000 + $250,00 (23.11) = $25,777,500

Benefits/Costs = $34,665,000/$25,777,500 = 1.3 **At the 3% discount rate, the benefit-cost ratio is favorable.**

Applying a 7% discount rate (proposed for current water resources programs) to the same hypothetical:

Present worth of benefits = $1,500,000 (P/A, 7%, 50) = $1,500,000 (13.8)* = 20,700,000
Present worth of costs = $20,000,000 + $250,000 (13.8) = $23,450,000
Benefits/Costs = $20,700,000/$23,450,000 less than 1. **At the 7% discount rate, the benefit-cost ratio is unfavorable.**

*Conversion factors are tabulated in the appendix to James and Lee, Economics of Water Resources Planning (1971).

1. Flood control costs are non-reimbursable and are often not included by state and local governments in calculating the cost component.

2. (P/A, 3%, 50) indicates the conversion factor for calculating the present worth of a time stream at a 3% discount rate for a 50-year period.

evaluating environmental values

The Water Resources Council has formulated a revised procedure for Federal benefit-cost analysis.[5] The system attempts to remedy the overemphasis on monetary values inherent in the methods discussed by providing information on tradeoffs between monetary and nonmonetary values.

The Water Resources Council procedure requires planning to be carried out in the context of four broad objectives relating to national economic development, environmental quality, quality of life, and regional development. Listed as benefits to the national economic development are all increases in national output. Beneficial and adverse effects under the environmental quality objective are expressed in various quantitative units or in qualitative terms. Benefits and costs under the quality of life objective pertain to the beneficial and adverse effects of a plan on people. The regional development objective includes the effects of a plan on the region under consideration—i.e. regional income, employment, economic stability, or some environmental feature. This procedure is expected to facilitate recognition of tradeoffs inadequately represented in the present system and when adopted will supercede Senate Document 97.

The Department of Interior has published *A Procedure for Evaluating Environmental Impact*.[6] The primary purpose of the procedure is to provide a system for the analysis and numerical weighting of probable impacts. The analysis does not produce an overall quantitative rating, but reveals many value judgments. The system uses a matrix which has actions which cause environmental impact on one axis and existing environmental conditions that might be affected on the other.

5. Water Resources Council, *Principles and Standards for Planning Water and Land Resources.*

6. Geological Survey Circular 645.

The matrix consists of 100 possible actions and 88 environmental characteristics resulting in a total of 8,800 possible interactions. Interactions denoting the environmental impacts of a particular project are marked with a slash drawn from the upper right-hand corner to the lower left-hand corner of the box. The relative magnitude of the impact is indicated in the upper left-hand portion of the square and the relative importance of the action is shown in the lower right-hand portion. Magnitude and importance are evaluated on a scale from 1 to 10, with 10 being the greatest. The magnitude of the impact should be based on factual information, while the importance of the impact will be more subjective. This system should assist the reviewer in separating fact from preference.

While the present system of benefit-cost analysis, the proposed Principles and Standards for Planning Water and Land Resources, and the Procedure for Evaluating Environmental Impact, aid in the recognition and consideration of environmental values in government decision-making, no system has been developed that provides for the quantification of intangible benefits and costs. Until such a system is created, the consideration of environmental values will remain considerably subjective. The fact that a quantification procedure is unobtainable should not discourage efforts to refine existing methods of analysis.

Selected Bibliography: Evaluation

BROWN, George E. Jr., *The Problems of Implementing Technology Assessments: The Congressional Context,* Technology Assessment Seminar Series Program of Policy Studies in Science and Technology, The George Washington University, Dec. 3, 1970

HAMMOND, *Convention and Limitation in Benefit-Cost Analysis,* 6 Natural Resources Journal 1966

HAVEMAN, *Water Resource Investment and the Public Interest-An Analysis of Federal Expenditures in Ten Southern States* 1965

CONSERVATION FOUNDATION LETTER, Jan. 1971, Developing the Nation's Water Resources—A Study of Dubious Planning Techniques

KOHN, *Leaf Burning—An Economic Case Study,* Scientist and Citizen April 1967

WEISBROD, *Concepts of Benefits and Costs,* in Samuel B. Chase, Jr., ed. *Problems in Public Expenditure Analysis* 261 1968

KNETSCH, *Federal Natural Resource Developments, Basic Issues in Benefit and Cost Measurement* 1969

NEUZIL, *Uses and Abuses of Highway Benefit-Cost Analysis,* Sierra Club Bulletin, Jan. 1968 at 16

WHITE, Gilbert, *Strategies of American Water Management* 1969

HIBGEE, *Farms and Farmers in an Urban Age,* The Twentieth Century Fund, New York 1963

PORTNOY, *The Role of the Courts in Technology Assessment,* 55 Cornell L. Rev. 861 (1970)

KATZ, *The Funcion of Tort Liability in Technology Assessment,* 38 Univ. of Cincinnati L. Rev. 587 1969

KATZ, *The Role of the Legal System in Society's Implementation of Technology Assessment,* paper given at the Technology Assessment Implementation Project, The George Washington University, May 6, 1971

BARNES, *The Vanishing Small Farmer,* The New Republic, June 12, 1971 at 21

YEAGER, *Technology vs. Liberty,* 54 American Bar Assn. Journal 759 (1968)

CARPENTER, Richard A., *Technology Assessment and the Congress,* Science Policy Research Division, Legislative Reference Service, Library of Congress Feb. 19, 1969

KEIFER, David M., *Technology Assessment,* Chemical and Engineering News, Oct. 5, 1970 , pp. 42–54

U.S. CONGRESS, House Committee on Science and Astronautics, *Technology Assessment,* 90th Cong., 1st Sess., Aug. 1968

U.S. CONGRESS, House Committee on Science and Astronautics, H. Rept. 91-1437, 91st Cong., 2nd Sess., Sept. 9, 1970

e. Economic impact of pollution control

The costs of pollution control are unknown, despite several serious attempts and many flimsily founded estimates at determining those costs. Regardless of the totals, however, all seem to agree that the damage done by pollution is far greater than the costs of eliminating it. Aspects of this are discussed in the several chapters of this book dealing with various classes of pollutants.

But it may be worthwhile here to forestall a few tall tales that are beginning to obtain wide circulation. One is that industry is already well on its way to abating its pollution. Although expenditures in this field are vast, they remain but a tiny fraction of all new capital expenditures. And it should be remembered that through tax write-offs (to be discussed later) other tax payers pay for much of this, and that the expenses for pollution control equipment should be compared with all capital, not merely with new capital investments.

Various industry representatives have been quoted in the press as saying that industry will spend various huge sums for pollution control this year. These figures vary widely, but for the most part are apparently without foundation—no survey was made, no calculations are presented. The largest figures based on any sort of reasonable survey are those of McGraw-Hill. But even this survey has been criticized (by the Council on Environmental Quality, in their report for 1971 at 114) as possibly being on the high side: "industries with high costs are more often inclined to respond to a questionnaire."

The McGraw-Hill figures for 1972 indicate that nearly $5 billion would be spent during the year on industrial pollution control, and that this is about 5 percent of new capital investment. The highest percentage was in the paper industry (nearly 30 percent), while other high figures were 21.7 percent for nonferrous metals, 14 percent for stone, clay and glass; 13 percent for iron and steel, and 12 percent for machinery manufacturers. The highest dollar amount was for electric utilities ($1 billion), which was about 7 percent of new investment.

If these figures are correct, then industry is not making sufficient investment to meet even the current Federal standards. (*See* the CEQ report mentioned above.) The petroleum industry, for instance, needed an estimated $2.7 billion worth of equipment to meet current standards, while their investment was listed at about one-half billion dollars. Thus, in general, industry is installing pollution control equipment at a rate designed to bring industrial pollution down to current legal limits within four to five years. Yet new laws hopefully will set far stricter standards long before five years have passed. (*See* "Industry Reported Fighting Pollution More than Ever," *The Washington Post,* May 25, 1972 at H1.)

Two additional points on this: frequently the best methods of pollution control involve more than merely filtering emisions — a process or materials change is often superior. Also, it is quite possible that some of these changes, which often aid productivity, are being classified as changes for pollution control. There will be more about this sort of thing in several technical discussions later in this book.

plant closings

More than 10,000 businesses in the United States shut down each year; in fewer than a score of closings in the past few years has the need for pollution control played a major part in causing the shutdown. Yet in scores more, industry chiefs have told workers and the public that pollution control expenses forced the closings. I. W. Abel, president of the United Steelworkers, made this comment: "Many obsolete plants use environmental control as a convenient public relations tool to justify a production decision to terminate operations and rationalize past failures to modernize facilities."

An excellent study of this was by Gladwin Hill, "Costs of Cleanup, or, A Myth of Factory Closings Is Exploded," *The New York Times,* June 4, 1972, Sec. 3, page 1. Governmental Studies include *The Economic Impact of Pollution Control,* and "A Summary of Recent Studies," which is based on the former book (Prepared by the Council on Environmental Quality, the Department of Commerce, and the Environmental Protection Agency, GPO

1972). See also, *Economic Dislocation Resulting from Environmental Controls,* Hearings before the Subcommittee on Air and Water Pollution, Committee on Public Works, United States Senate, 92d. Cong., 1st. Sess., May 17 18, and June 28, 1971. The annual reports of the Council on Environmental Quality also treat the economic aspects of pollution control.

Some factories, certainly, have been forced to close due to their inability to meet pollution control standards. Federal figures show that about 1,500 persons already have lost their jobs in this way, and thousands more are threatened (*See The New York Times* article mentioned above). Yet some jobs have opened up in the plants that took over the business of those which closed, and many thousands more have found work designing, building, installing, and operating pollution control equipment. It is entirely likely that overall, more jobs will be created controlling pollution than will be lost in the closing of polluting facilities.

Two descriptions of the hardships that result from plant closings due in part to pollution control expenses can be found in *Newsweek,* June 12, 1972 at 47 (a pulp and paper mill), and in *The Wall Street Journal,* May 18, 1972 at 40 (a copper smelter).

See also the discussions of the economic impact of solid wastes, pp. Two-3 to Two-6; of air pollution, pp. Three-4 and Three-5, and of water pollution, pp. Four-19 through Four-25. Merely as samples, rather than as any attempt to survey the field, the following studies are republished photographically from *The Economic Impact of Pollution Control: A Summary of Recent Studies,* GPO, March 1972:

petroleum refineries

From 1972 through 1976, it was estimated that the petroleum refining industry would be required to make capital expenditures of $634 million to $1155 million to meet the air and water pollution abatement requirements that apply to the refining of petroleum. Annual costs of $2 million in 1972 rising to $21 million in 1976 would also be required. In addition, the cost of using low sulfur fuels in refinery operations was estimated to be $108 million annually by 1976. The average pollution abatement costs per barrel in 1976 were estimated to be $0.06, thus increasing the total cost per barrel by approximately 1.4%.

Because capital expenditures for pollution control equipment would equal only 5% of the $21.4 billion capital expenditures otherwise projected for the industry in the next ten years, it was considered that these expenditures would be manageable. A price increase of $0.08 per barrel was expected to help defray the added costs. In addition to the annual costs mentioned above, this $0.08 figure included an 8% return judged to be necessary to attract the capital required to install control equipment in new facilities. This price increase was assumed to be possible because imports are restricted by law and the demand for petroleum is not elastic.

Given this $0.08/bbl. price increase, it was estimated that most small producers will be able to sustain added pollution control costs. A few, perhaps 12, might be forced to close.

If a dozen small refineries do close, approximately 1,000 workers would become unemployed. These small refineries would probably be located near smaller communities, and thus would have a noticeable local impact. Otherwise, industry employment is expected to increase at about the rate projected without pollution control costs.

It was estimated that the total investment required to meet air and thermal pollution control requirements associated with the generation of electricity from 1972 to 1976 will be $10.7 billion. Of this, $7.5 billion would be required for air pollution control, and $3.2 billion for thermal pollution control. It has been suggested that the cost of installing pollution control equipment on existing plants might be twice those included in these estimates. If so, the total investment required through 1976 would reach $17.8 billion. Annual costs associated with pollution controls were estimated to rise from $338 million in 1972 to $2.5 billion in 1976. Costs per kilowatt hour in 1976 would range from 0.22 mills to 1.52 mills depending upon the region of the country. These costs did not include additional costs that might be required for the control of nitrogen oxides and radiation.

The impact of pollution control costs will vary from region to region across the U.S. depending upon the source of energy employed. In the West South Central, for example, almost all generators are gas-fueled, and will require almost no air pollution control facilities. Consequently, pollution control costs in this region in 1976 were estimated to total only 2.8% of 1970 average revenues. In the Tennessee Valley Authority region, on the other hand, approximately 80% of the generating facilities are coal-fired. These will be faced with the full cost of air and thermal pollution controls. This, combined with a low revenue level, was estimated to lead to pollution control costs in 1976 totaling 10.65% of average 1970 revenues. The average of all regions' air and thermal pollution control costs in 1976 was estimated to be 7% of 1970 average revenues.

In the philosophy of utility regulation, justified cost increases are passed on to the consumer. Thus, it can be assumed the above costs will ultimately be passed on completely to the electric ratepayers through higher electricity rates. Past experience, however, indicates that the passing on may not be complete and in any event will occur with some delay. Furthermore, given the complexity and variety of rate structures, it was not possible to determine how these price increases might be distributed among the various categories of consumers.

No adequate information was available on the demand responsiveness of the users of electricity to changes in electricity's price. The total demand for electricity was judged to be extremely unresponsive to price.

Six industries were identified for which electric power costs amounted to 5% or more of the total value of shipments. These are Atomic Energy Commission plants, primary aluminum, electrometallurgical products, alkalies and chlorine, industrial gases, and hydraulic cement. The anticipated increase in the price of electricity was expected to have little impact, even upon these industries.

cement production

Capital expenditures required from 1972 through 1976 to meet air and water pollution control requirements associated with the manufacturing of cement in kilns and clinker coolers were estimated to total $122 million. Annual costs were estimated to increase from $3.0 million in 1972 to $43 million in 1976. These costs average out to $0.08 to $0.10 per barrel of cement.

Projections of cash flow and capital needs including pollution abatement expenditures for the cement industry through 1980 indicated that the industry will be able to meet its cash needs. Given the most severe set of assumptions, however, many changes in the industry's financial policies would be required. These would include a reduction in the divident payout ratio from 59% to 49%, and an increase in the debt/equity ratio from 0.39:1 to 0.6:1. Both of these were considered manageable. Alternatively, a 4%-5% real price increase would be employed to provide most of the required funds.

Pollution control costs in the cement industry were expected to accelerate the current trend in the industry toward the closing of small, old plants and the construction of large, modern facilities. This, in turn, would increase the capital pressure upon the industry. The combined effect has been estimated to result in the closing of approximately 25 cement plants in the 1972-1976 period. The additional impact upon cement industry employment was expected to be minimal. Only one possible community impact has been identified.

The increase of prices because of pollution controls was expected to accelerate the current increase in cement imports. No estimate of the magnitude of this impact has been made, however.

steel making

Capital expenditures required by air and water pollution abatement regulations were estimated to total $2.4 billion to $3.5 billion for the period 1972 through 1976. Annual operating and maintenance costs were estimated to be $45 million to $70 million in 1972, increasing to $760 million to $1,100 million in 1976. Per net ton of steel shipped, these costs would average from $0.47 to $0.73 in 1972 and $6.60 to $9.60 in 1976.

Price increases to cover pollution abatement costs would be necessary to generate the cash required to meet projected expenditures. The estimated 0.7% to 1.5% annual increases were considered moderate, however, in relation to historical price increases.

It was expected that most facilities would be able to install pollution abatement equipment and continue operation. This conclusion was strengthened by the fact that the demand may exceed the capacity of the industry to supply steel so that the industry would need all of its current capacity.

fruit & vegetable canning and freezing

Water pollution abatement regulations were estimated to require the investment of approximately $120 million by the fruit and vegetable canning and freezing industry through 1976. Annual costs of pollution control equipment were estimated at $4.3 million in 1972 increasing to $21.3 million in 1976.

In the fruit and vegetable canning and freezing industry, the largest third of the plants produce about 80% of total industry volume. These plants enjoy a considerable cost advantage over the remaining plants, and are consequently much more profitable. This advantage has created a trend over the past 10-15 years toward fewer and larger processing plants. Census figures indicate that from 1958 to 1967 the total number of fruit and vegetable canning plants declined 25%. The number of fruit and vegetable freezing plants more than doubled from 1958 to 1964, but then decreased 6.6% through 1967. Both of these trends were expected to continue through 1980 with a 25% decrease projected from 1971 through 1980.

It was expected that the larger canning and freezing plants will also enjoy a cost advantage in installing and operating pollution control equipment. For those plants which must install their own facilities, for example, the price increase that would be required to offset abatement costs would be 5.5% for large plants, but 9.6% for small plants.

Given estimates that half of the plants will be able to find lower cost abatement solutions, and that 58% of the projected abatement technology is already installed, actual price increases were not expected to be as high as above. Prices were expected to rise 1.4% to 2.3%. Such an increase would cover the average costs of the larger producers, but not of the smaller plants.

The increased prices were expected to lead to a 0.5% to 1.0% decrease in consumption. Such a decrease would be less than the total annual increase expected in consumption because of population expansion and increases in per capita consumption.

The increased costs of pollution control were expected to further reduce the profits of the already marginally profitable small plants. Many of these plants will be able to tie into municipal systems or to find other low cost pollution abatement techniques that will enable them to stay in business. Experience in some states indicates that half of the small plants might be unable to find such alternatives. In this case, up to half of the small plants in the industry, or one-third of all plants, were expected to be forced to close. Of the 1,200 plants included in the industry directory, therefore, 400 might be forced to close because of pollution abatement costs. As noted above, 25% of the plants, or 300 of the 1,200, would be expected to close by 1980 in any event. Thus, the addition of pollution control costs was expected to lead to the additional closing of 100 plants, or 8.3% of the total. In addition, closing of the other plants was expected to occur some years earlier than otherwise.

It was estimated that the closing of 400 plants would result in the loss of jobs by approximately 28,000 employees. The disemployment created by the 100 plants that were estimated to close because of pollution controls would be one-fourth of that number or 7,000. Many of these would be in small towns and rural areas where reemployment would not be readily available. Up to 90% of the jobs lost would be part-time positions.

Because many of the plant closings would be in small towns or rural areas, the community impact of these closings could be significant. This would be further complicated if the farmers in the surrounding areas are unable to find alternate markets for their products. This possibility was suggested, but no careful analysis has been made of the experience in such cases or of the technical factors involved. Accordingly, no estimate is available for the magnitude of this impact.

The impact of increased prices in the industry upon the U.S. balance of payments was expected to be small.

pulp & paper mills

Approximately $3.3 billion was estimated to be required in capital expenditures by the paper industry for the period 1972-1976 to meet air and water pollution abatement requirements. Annual costs per ton of product were estimated to range from $5.50 to $12.50 depending upon product sector.

Because of an anticipated tightening of supply/demand balances, price increases were expected in the paper industry. These increases were likely to reflect the above-mentioned annual costs of pollution controls. Increases of this magnitude would represent a 3.5% to 10% increase over current prices depending upon product sector.

Given these increases it was anticipated that most mills will be able to manage pollution control expenditures. However, of the 752 pulp and paper mills in the U.S., 329 accounting for 15% of U.S. production have been identified as marginal. These mills currently have profit margins much below industry averages (-7.7% to 4.8% vs 6.6%) and may experience pollution control costs approximately twice as large as industry avarages. Price increases were not expected to cover their increased costs. This will reduce already low profit margins and create some difficulty in raising the capital required for pollution control equipment.

Even in the absence of pollution control requirements, 30-35 of these marginal mills were expected to close in the 1972-76 period. It was estimated that an additional 60-65 mills would be forced to close with the imposition of abatement regulations. These additional closings were expected to result in the loss of 16,000 jobs by 1976. A larger number of jobs will be made available in plants which are expected to expand, but these of course may not be in the same community. Many of the shut downs are likely to be in rural areas where they would have significant community impact.

smelting and refining of copper

The capital investment required in the copper industry, because of air and water pollution controls from 1972 through 1976, was estimated to total $300 million to $690 million, with a most likely estimate of $341 million. Annual costs were expected to increase from $6 million in 1972 to $95 million in 1976. Per pound of refined copper, these costs average $0.001 in 1972 and $0.025 in 1976, with a possible high estimate of $0.05 in 1976.

It is expected that the industry can finance the required capital expenditures.

The effect of cost increases has been analysed considering a basic projection for the copper industry without pollution control costs; and two alternative assumptions: (a) that foreign competition will not compete in the U.S. market, so that U.S. producers are able to raise prices, and (b) that foreign competition will prevent any price increase in the U.S. market as a result of pollution control costs. It was assumed that the actual impact of pollution control costs will lie somewhere between these two extremes.

If the average pollution control costs are considered, (a) U.S. production of copper in 1980 was expected to be approximately 7% less than the base projections of 4,169,000 short tons if foreign competition prevents price increases while prices and consumption would not change; (b) U.S. production would be 3.5% lower than base projections; U.S. consumption 4.6% lower; and U.S. prices 4% higher; if foreign competition is not a factor.

Thus depending upon costs and foreign competition,it was estimated that U.S. supply be reduced 3.5% to 14% and U.S. consumption 0% to 9%;and U.S. prices may increase 0% to 8% because of pollution controls.

It was estimated that most existing U.S. smelters will continue to operate under pollution control requirements. Two smelters were identified, however, as being forced to close. No estimate was made of additional smelters which might close.

With the imposition of pollution controls, employment in the copper industry was not expected to decline, but would grow more slowly than the base projections. Without pollution control costs, employment was expected to grow from 54,000 in 1970 to 76,900 in 1980. Pollution control costs were expected to reduce the 1980 employment by 2,800 to 10,900 or 3.6% to 14% depending upon the cost and foreign competition assumptions discussed above. Where individual smelters close, of course, all workers would become unemployed. The two smelters identified as closing currently employ 1,150 employees. No estimate was made of the associated mining employment. In both instances, a significant community impact was expected.

f. The role of taxes

The following article, by the author of this book and Glenn L. Reitze, who edited this book, was published initially in the February, 1971, issue of the American Bar Association Journal.

the stick is mightier than the carrot

THE STICK is more effective than the carrot: No man will spend $10 to bring himself a benefit simply because the government promises to return $5. Tax incentives are fiscal carrots. They are extremely expensive, but soft on pollution.

Until now the state and federal pollution control programs have been a disappointment to those who seek some improvement in our air and water.[1] Nevertheless, several thousand bills pertaining to pollution control have been introduced in Congress and state legislatures during the past several years.[2] Many of them offer little to control pollution; rather they extend tax incentives as rewards to polluters.[3]

In theory, these rewards eliminate pollution. In practice, they are ineffective and in many cases even discourage pollution control by promoting expenditures for the wrong things at a substantial cost to the public. In addition, government agencies that should be enforcing current pollution control regulations must devote their energies to processing increasing quantities of tax incentive applications.[4]

The federal law containing the major specific tax incentive for pollution control was passed in 1969, when the Tax Reform Act added Section 169 to the Internal Revenue Code. That section permits rapid (sixty-month) depreciation allowances for pollution-control hardware.

The bill's predecessor, no longer in effect for new investments, was Section 38 of the Internal Revenue Code, added in 1962. This section permitted a deduction directly from a firm's taxes of 7 per cent of the expenditure for pollution-control equipment, subject to certain varying restrictions.[5]

According to one authority, by March, 1970, at least thirty-one states had placed antipollution incentive provisions in one or more of their principal revenue-producing laws.[6]

All these incentive provisions, state and federal, provide rapid depreciation or forgiveness from property, income, sales and use, or franchise taxes. Their one key effect is to shift the cost of compliance with government pollution limitations from individual polluters to the taxpayer.

In addition, there apparently is widespread misuse (permitted by lax or overworked government officials) of tax incentive laws to purchase equipment that does not serve to improve the environment. A substantial part of the pollution control equipment being sold today and receiving tax credit reportedly is used to clean water coming into

1. The federal air pollution program has been criticized in Reitze, *The Role of the Region in Air Pollution Control*, 20 CASE W. RES. L. REV. 809 (1969), and the federal water pollution program in *Wastes, Water, and Wishful Thinking: The Battle of Lake Erie*, 20 CASE W. RES. L. REV. 5 (1968) See also, Reitze, *Environmental Pollution Control, Why Has It Failed?* 55 A.B.A.J. 923 (1969).

2. Thirty-nine bills directly related to the environment were introduced in the House during the period January 23-30, 1969. Fifteen months later, during "Earth Week", forty-two bills were introduced between April 23 and 30, 1970.

3. Bills have been proposed and many have become law to give relief from sales and use taxes, property taxes (real and tangible personal), fuel taxes, franchise taxes and income taxes. Benefits include fast write-offs, tax credits, and exemption from taxation.

4. In Ohio, a typical industrial state, the number and monetary value of pollution control exemptions granted have been increasing substantially each year. In the three years between January, 1966, and the end of 1969, Ohio received 148 exemption applications for purchases listed at $64.7 million. In the first half of 1970, there were thirty-eight applications for purchases totalling $31.98 million.

5. This section was temporarily suspended from October 10, 1966, to March 9, 1967. Certain water and air pollution facilities were exempted. INT. REV. CODE OF 1954, § 48(h) (12).

6. McNulty, *State Tax Incentives To Fight Pollution*, 56 A.B.A.J. 747, 748 (1970).

a plant for use in manufacturing rather than for controlling waste discharges.[7]

Tax incentives of this sort—which reward rather than punish those receiving the incentive (the latter may be referred to as negative tax incentives or tax penalties)—obviously cut government revenue. The key to determining the value of positive tax incentives, therefore, lies in evaluating the benefits to be gained by the government (public) in return for revenue lost.

tax benefits

Benefits that would be gained regardless of the tax incentive clearly must be excluded from the list of benefits gained in exchange for the loss. Thus, pollution expenditures made to comply with federal, state and local health or pollution laws cannot be considered public benefits gained by granting tax incentives, although businesses received that aid. This clarification will permit many a tax incentive to be seen for what it is—a subsidy rather than an exchange of tax forgiveness for desired behavior.[8]

The potential cost of even the present federal tax incentive programs for pollution control, if maintained, is immense, but it is virtually impossible to estimate with precision. Government officials predict expenditures by industry in the next five years of $3.3 billion for water pollution control, another $2 billion for thermal pollution prevention and $2.6 billion for control of four major air pollutants in one hundred metropolitan areas.[9] Additional solid waste disposal expenditures can bring the total to $10 billion.

These estimates are comparatively conservative. Yet, even without additional federal tax incentive legislation of this sort, the Federal Government's revenue loss with those expenditures could be a billion dollars per year.[10] The loss to state governments, with their many similar laws, is not included. For example, the loss of revenue to Ohio from air pollution exemptions alone in 1970 is estimated to be $6.3 million, according to the Research and Statistics Section of the Ohio Department of Taxation.

Other estimates of industry expenditures for pollution control equipment during the next five years center around $32 billion.[11] Bank of America Senior Vice President Alan K. Brown recently put the figure at $80 billion to $95 billion.[12]

The public sector loss, even under the low ($1 billion annual) federal tax loss estimate, is about eleven times what the Department of Health, Education and Welfare spends on all its air pollution control programs ($94.2 million).[13]

Even if we accept the projected federal revenue loss of $115 million in 1974, as estimated by the Senate Finance Committee in its report to accompany the Tax Reform Act of 1969, we still have a considerable loss when compared with federal antipollution expenditures.[14] But this estimate is based on a level of expenditure that would never control pollution.

Despite their cost, tax incentives fail to control pollution. The most basic reasons are five:

1. **Unprofitability.** They fail to give an incentive to invest in nonproductive facilities regardless of the lessened cost of those facilities.

2. **Badly Aimed.** As used today, they give credit for physical devices that often are only a small part of pollution control (switching fuel can often be far more significant) and give credit for facilities regardless of their effectiveness in controlling pollution.

7. BUSINESS WEEK, October 4, 1969, at 118.

8. For a criticism of tax exemptions in general, see Reitze, *Real Property Tax Exemptions in Ohio—Fiscal Absurdity*, 18 W. RES. L. REV. 64 (1966).

9. ENVIRONMENTAL QUALITY, FIRST ANNUAL REPORT OF THE COUNCIL ON ENVIRONMENTAL QUALITY 43, 72 (1970).

10. By contrast, the estimated federal funding for pollution control and abatement was $1,290,900,000 in fiscal year 1970 obligations. *Id.* at 320.

11. The Wall Street Journal, August 10, 1970, page 1.

12. B.N.A. Env. RPTR., August 28, 1970, at 467.

13. *Supra* note 9, at 320.

14. S. REP. No. 91-552, to accompany H.R. 13270, 91st Cong., 1st Sess. 646 (1969). Naturally those in favor of tax incentive legislation give lower estimates of tax losses. Section 169 has been estimated to have a maximum annual cost of only $120 million, an amount which could be reached by expenditures of one tenth of the amount needed for pollution control. See remarks of Senator Russell B. Long, 115 CONG. REC. S16206 (December 9, 1970).

3. **No Public Gain.** They pay for pollution control facilities required by other laws, bringing no gain to the public in exchange for the tax loss and lessening funds for governmental pollution control, among other things.

4. **Reverse Robin Hood.** They increase general taxes through tax burden distribution and provide substantial tax write-offs to wealthy corporations having the least need of public assistance to eliminate their pollution. Yet they fail to aid small and medium-sized companies unable to purchase required pollution control equipment.

5. **Pricing Quackery.** Because pollutions costs are shifted to the general public, sales prices do not reflect a product's true cost to society. The sales price does not reflect the propensity for environmental harm during a product's manufacture, use or disposal. The true costs to society are masked.

The categories, of course, overlap considerably.

The existence of the philosophy of pollution control through rewards to polluters, moreover, gives rise to a convenient analogy, which may or may not be a key factor, for making additional rewards. An example is the charge in John Esposito's study on air pollution that, when Los Angeles sought more low-sulphur fuel oil, the political price was a change in federal oil import regulations to allow refiners who produce low-sulphur residual fuel oil to import an additional barrel of foreign crude oil for each barrel of low-sulphur residual oil produced. To the oil firms, this reportedly is worth about 90¢ a barrel, and the companies involved thereby gain between $20,000 and $50,000 a day in return for producing the low-sulphur residual fuel for the West Coast states. Slightly less than half this sum, the report added, goes to Union Oil of California and to Atlantic-Richfield for doing precisely what they had been doing all along.[15]

Unprofitability of Pollution Control Affects Incentives

It is the inherent unprofitability of most pollution control that makes tax incentives meaningless as a method of stimulating investments in it. Labor relations, government regulatory actions, marketing considerations, antitrust problems and a host of other variables play their parts in investment decisions. But these variables should not obscure the fact that tax incentives give no incentive to invest in nonproductive facilities or operations.

For an investment with a productive potential, a tax incentive could reduce the cost so that the potential profit is realized. But very few pollution control investments have any profit potential, and therefore that possibility is remote.

The few profitable pollution control investments have received much publicity. Yet even this category of pollution-control investment often fails to be made. Company managers by and large seek the highest return on investment, and profitable pollution control investments are rarely the most profitable investment a firm can make.

tax benefits

While few pollution abatement controls will produce any profitable commodity, most tax incentive plans are drafted so that profitable abatement techniques will not qualify. For example, Section 169 (e) states that the federal certifying authority shall not certify any property under Section 169 (d) (1) (B) to the extent it appears that by reason of profits derived through recovery of wastes or otherwise in the operation of the property, its costs will be recovered over its actual useful life. In most states the statutory guideline for a tax benefit requires that the facility meet the test that its primary purpose be for pollution control or that it is used exclusively for pollution control purposes.

These tests have virtually nothing to do with developing a good pollution abatement program, for a good program is normally so closely related to the production process that very few expenditures will meet either the primary purpose or the exclusive use test.

It has been pointed out, moreover, that some of the largest companies—especially those in automobiles and oil—behave at times like independent political states rather than simple profit makers. Hence, there is all the more reason to attempt control through re-

15. Esposito, Vanishing Air 248 (1970).

gulating behavior rather than by appeals to a profit-making sense through tax burden redistribution.[16]

Devices to protect the health and safety of workers also are usually unprofitable, but government, union and insurance company regulations force their purchase and use, to the general benefit. Devices for the health and safety of the public may be considered in the same category and be imposed by regulation.

The furor over mine safety demonstrates again that some businessmen will not protect their workers' safety and health voluntarily and adequately. Yet few governmental rewards are given for corporate health and safety expenditures. We recognize that inherently unprofitable investments will not be made merely because the government absorbs part of the cost.

tax benefits

If the desire is to encourage industry to use a specific abatement technique or produce some other beneficial response in pollution control, we should utilize a more forthright approach—direct subsidies. We could, at least, more easily review whether the social benefit achieved is worth the public cost.

Businessmen in general respond to this approach less enthusiastically, for the grants must appear in budgets and the cost to the public is made obvious. And happily for some businessmen, tax incentives tend to continue long after the reason for the program has disappeared.[17]

The imprecision of tax incentives makes their use for any purpose of doubtful value; in the environmental area, their value appears to be nil. While they do not bring about pollution abatement, they do act to limit and hinder proper control programs for they encourage improper technical responses to pollution problems.

Pollution problems are usually an integral part of the production process. Their control requires a plan carefully integrated into the entire operation of the business. Nearly all industrial pollution can be controlled, and effective control is best managed if the production process is designed to minimize waste.

Some methods of control are to substitute fuels or power sources; substitute raw materials; use different production processes; change the design of the product; capture pollutants before they leave the plant; change disposal practices so as to encourage reclamation of waste products; and recycle either waste products or resources used in the productive process.[18]

The most drastic remedy for pollution would be to end production—a remedy that if applied to all pollution sources would have disastrous social and economic repercussions. However, a few products, when balanced against their capacity for environmental destruction, are so marginally useful to society that if they were priced to reflect these necessary pollution abatement costs, they would be priced out of the market. The use of products causing the release of heavy metals such as mercury might be limited by this approach.

Tax Incentives Have a Faulty Focus

The tax incentive program is harmful in its focus on capital costs of pollution control rather than the total cost, which includes, in many cases, substantial operating costs.

16. For a study of the oil industry as a political state, see TUGENDHAT, OIL: THE BIGGEST BUSINESS (1969). Professor Kenneth Galbraith in *The New Industrial State* points to evidence that for the mature corporation, the profit motive is subordinate to the desire for reasonable growth and stability. Hence, it may be difficult to get even profit-making pollution abatement equipment installed.

17. Sometimes budgets become sacroscant without a reason relating to public benefit. The federal gasoline tax enacted in 1932 was allocated to the highway trust fund in 1956 for highway construction. Now, with public mass transportation woefully underfinanced and highways proliferating everywhere, the highway lobby has convinced most legislators and much of the public that the gasoline tax is a sacred fund.

18. See NATIONAL RESEARCH COUNCIL COMMITTEE, NATIONAL ACADEMY OF SCIENCES, WASTE MANAGEMENT AND CONTROL, No. 1400 (1966). Techniques and costs of air pollution equipment are discussed in 3 STERN, AIR POLLUTION (2d ed. 1969). Water pollution costs can be found in THE COST OF CLEAN WATER, a Federal Water Quality Administration publication which comes in multiple volumes, each devoted to a different industry.

For example, an electric utility could substitute a cleaner-burning fuel at considerable expense and get no tax benefit except perhaps some small consideration for the costs of converting furnaces to burn a different fuel. However, a company that purchases a precipitator that has marginal total pollution control effectiveness can receive substantial tax benefits. To obtain a tax benefit, there is no legal requirement that an investment reduce pollution; the only requirement is that an investment be made.

Some common control equipment, such as electrostatic precipitators, are extraordinarily expensive. They can cost a million dollars, yet their operating costs are so high that many businesses would resist using them or turn them off in order to save on operating costs even if the Government paid the entire purchase price. This results in a situation in which companies that have spent the money for equipment required by law bypass the equipment at night, on holidays or between inspections in order to save on operating costs. In addition, a failure to make rapid repairs after a breakdown may result in an investment being inoperative much of the time.

The operating costs are such an important component of pollution control that any system of tax incentives must consider the total cost of abatement. By 1975, it is estimated, air pollution costs for operation, maintenance, depreciation and interest will run $1.9 billion.[19] These operating costs have always been tax deductible, yet this does not seem to have aided pollution control efforts.

A tax program that favors "hardware" expenditures encourages poor abatement responses from industry. By holding most of their expenditures not to be qualified for tax benefits, the program unfairly treats those industries that make a serious attempt at pollution control. In addition, there is the problem previously mentioned of possible widespread misuse of equipment purchased under tax exemptions to aid manufacturing, not to abate pollution.

The intimate relation of pollution control to the entire production process means that true pollution control cannot be separated from the total business operation. Here again the analogy to safety programs applies. Employee training, work layout, lighting, etc., is as important to safety as adding protective equipment to a machine.

Robin Hood Reversed; Rob the Poor To Help the Rich

The real financial problem in private sector pollution control is the inability of small or inefficient operations to obtain capital to pay for control. Tax incentives do not solve this problem; they benefit only those with capital to invest and income to be sheltered. The companies that can afford pollution controls will benefit.

For example, a $1 million expenditure for an electrostatic precipitator, even if subject to depreciation in sixty months, benefits fully only those businesses with $200,000 of spare income to shelter from taxes. Marginal enterprises get little benefit.

tax benefits

Thus, tax benefits aid the owners of large, successful businesses disproportionately, and their result will be to promote the elimination of small businesses as the cost of required pollution controls rise. A further obvious effect is the promotion of yet more control of our system by those who control the largest industries.

It is questionable whether large polluters need public financial assistance to meet their legal obligations to refrain from imposing pollution on others. But it is clear that the large polluters alone do account for a very large share of total pollution.

The Council on Environmental Quality reported this year:

> The more than 300,000 water-using factories in the United States discharge three to four times as much oxygen-demanding wastes as the sewered population of the United States. Moreover, many of the wastes discharged by industry are toxic.
>
> The output of industrial waste is growing several times faster than the volume of sanitary sewage. Although there is as yet no detailed inventory of industrial wastes, indications are that over half the volume discharged to water comes from four major industry groups—paper, organic chemicals, petroleum, and steel.[20]

19. *Supra* note 9, at 72.

20. *Supra* note 9, at 32.

tax benefits

In spite of the flood of publicity, little is spent by industry for pollution control when considered as a function of gross sales or profit.

Esposito, in *Vanishing Air,* explains:

> A February 1970 report by the National Industrial Conference Board indicates that the industry's 1969 capital appropriations for air and water pollution control dropped 56.9 percent below the 1968 appropriation. This reduction from 38 million in 1969, represents a drop in pollution control investments from less than four-tenths of 1 percent of 1968 gross revenues to something less than two-tenths of 1 percent for 1969.[21]

Republic Steel Corporation, the second largest industrial polluter of Lake Erie, according to the Federal Water Quality Administration,[22] in 1969 invested $28 million in pollution control from sales income of more than $1.5 billion created by property, plant and equipment valued at more than $2.25 billion.[23]

General Motors Corporation omitted its research budget for pollution control from its 1969 annual report, but the Esposito book on air pollution relates that G.M.'s official figure is $40 million annually since 1967, or about .17 of 1 per cent of gross sales. This figure is one sixth of G.M.'s annual advertising budget. It is just $13 million more than the $27 million G.M. is spending each year in a ten-year program to change signs at company dealerships.[24]

The justice of rewarding these large firms through tax incentives is at least questionable; nevertheless, it is of only peripheral interest. Rather than argue which tax benefit is "just" or proper, which is an approach that encourages the outpourings of public relations releases from corporations and trade associations, we should focus on the question of whether tax incentives create behavior that results in a reduction in pollution at a cost to the public that has a favorable cost to benefit ratio, judging, as William James taught, not by "first things, principles" but by the "last things, fruits, consequences, facts".[25]

Pricing Quackery Shifts Financial Burden to the Public

A basic reason for continued pollution is that the polluter shifts to the public, in terms of environmental destruction, the basic production costs that he avoids by not preventing pollution. Tax incentives augment that shift by placing the pollution control burden of business on the general public through tax burden redistribution.

To allow the general public (rather than the individual purchaser of a high pollution propensity product) to absorb pollution control costs is to thwart the function of the marketplace as a place of value exchange. To the extent a polluter can shift costs of control equipment to the general public, his products continue to avoid having their price reflect their pollution effect. Environmentally destructive products are enabled to compete with less harmful products without the market price reflecting their social costs. Because no incentive is provided in the marketplace to minimize pollution at the lowest cost per unit sold, the natural market competitiveness is not utilized to reward the producer who shifts the fewest negative social costs to the public.

Tax incentives such as those discussed also have the capacity to destroy state and local abatement programs. Most states require that the state pollution control board or its tax commission or revenue department, acting on the recommendation of the pollution control board, approve or certify the pollution control facility so as to qualify for the tax benefit,[26] as does the Federal Government.[27]

State agencies have been burdened with the obligation to process not only thousands of applications for exemptions to a variety of state taxes, but also by law they must provide businessmen with certification to meet exemption allowance requirements of Section 169 of the Internal Revenue

21. *Supra* note 5, at 84.
22. Lake Erie Report, August, 1968, at 7.
23. 1969 Annual Report, at 3, 10, 12 and 28.
24. *Supra* note 17, at 29.
25. *What Pragmation Means*, in Essays in Pragmatism 148 (1948).

26. The tax practitioner must not only be familiar with tax law but also must search pollution law for applicable tax authority. For an illustration see, Ohio Rev. Code §§ 6111.31 and 6111.03(M).
27. Int. Rev. Code of 1954, § 169 (D).

Code. This results in either a reduction of the agency's other enforcement, monitoring and planning efforts or in cursory examinations of the exemption applications. Abuses of the exemption allowances, therefore, are no surprise. And the failure of state inspection programs allows federal as well as state benefits to flow to the businessman because of the Section 169 requirements.

Only a few cities in the United States have meaningful air pollution programs with adequate staff. Most state programs are smaller than that of their larger cities.[28] Fifty per cent of the state agencies have fewer than ten positions budgeted.[29] With an estimated 8,000 additional personnel needed to implement the Clean Air Act properly, one wonders whether industry is unaware that enforcement can be effectively prevented by imposing onerous time-consuming responsibilities for processing tax exemptions on the pollution planning and enforcement agencies. While the cost of tax incentive legislation can be calculated in terms of revenue losses to the public treasury, it is much more difficult to evaluate the financial and social costs of having state pollution control agencies bogged down in the relentless pushing of paper to get industry their tax benefits.

The point about all of these laws, and the many similar bills proposed, is that they reward a limited number of taxpayers for "pollution control" expenditures. Not, we must note, pollution control effectiveness or the simple elimination of pollution.

28. O'Fallon, *Deficiencies in the Air Quality Act of 1967*, 33 LAW & CONTEMP. PROB. 275, 293, (1963).
29. *Supra* note 9, at 85.

POSTNOTE

After the preceding article was published originally, changes were made in the regulations governing the applicability of Sec. 169. However, these changes were insufficient to affect the validity of the basic criticisms expressed above. On May 17, 1971 the Treasury Department's final regulations on Sec. 169 were published in the Federal Register. These provide generally that a taxpayer may amortize over a 60-month period the cost of any pollution control facility that has been certified by the appropriate state agencies and the Environmental Protection Agency.

The EPA published its final regulations in the Federal Register May 26, 1971. They provide guidelines as to which facilities may be eligible for certification. Forms for the certification are available through EPA regional offices, where the eligibility determinations are to be made. The regulations were officially summarized as follows:

> "Under the new regulations, certification may be made for a treatment facility installed after December 31, 1968, when it is used in connection with a plant or other property that was in operation before January 1, 1969. A treatment facility is one that abates or controls air or water pollution by removing, altering, disposing of, or storing a pollutant, contaminant, waste, or heat.
>
> "A facility which is not a building may qualify for the tax deduction even though it performs functions in addition to the abatement of pollution. In such a case, EPA will determine the percentage of the cost of the facility which is allocable to its abatement function.
>
> "A building must be exclusively devoted to pollution control in order to qualify for the rapid write-off. The Treasury's regulations contain a detailed definition of a "building".
>
> "A facility used in connection with both pre-1969 and newer plants may also qualify for the fast tax write-off, with EPA determining the percentage of the cost of the facility that is allocable to the pre-1969 plant.
>
> "Section 169 does not apply to facilities whose costs will be recovered by profits they generate. Certification, therefore, will be denied for pollution-control facilities that are used to abate pollution generated by others than their owners, when fees are charged by the owners for the use of such facilities."

The Environmental Protection Agency's regulations concerning certification of pollution control facilities for accelerated amortization for federal tax purposes are published in this volume at page Appendix One-14.

Pollution Abatement Incentives For Industry

A Directory of Federal and State Laws

Republished below is the full text of a pamphlet from the National Association of Manufacturers, whom we thank for making our research so much easier.

This booklet was prepared by the Environmental Quality Subcommittee of the Area Industrial Problems Committee of the National Association of Manufacturers. It is designed to acquaint manufacturing companies and other interested persons with provisions of state laws relating to tax relief for nonproductive pollution abatement expenditures.

In the Tax Reform Act of 1969, provision was made for a 5-year write-off of pollution control equipment installed in industrial plants which were in operation on Dec. 31, 1968. NAM advocates accelerated amortization up to and including the immediate write-off of the facility, at the option of the taxpayer and tax credits to industrial companies. Numerous bills have been introduced in this and previous Congresses calling for a 1 to 5 year write-off and a 20 percent tax credit for *land, buildings and equipment* used for pollution control purposes.

Some of the states which have the strongest legislation and standards and the most effective enforcement provide tax relief for industrial companies. States like New York, New Jersey, California and Illinois have recognized the need and desirability of some form of mechanism to help companies absorb the heavy initial costs of abatement.

This relief is generally in three forms: first, allowing the purchaser to accelerate the depreciation write-off value over a period of from one to five years for income tax and/or franchise tax purposes; second, exempting the purchase of pollution abatement equipment from sales and use taxes; third, exempting pollution abatement installations from property taxes.

Federal Tax Credits

Under the new Tax Reform Act of 1969, an individual or corporation taxpayer is allowed to amortize the cost of a certified pollution control facility over a 60-month period. This facility must be certified by both state and federal agencies.

The amortization deduction is limited to pollution control facilities added to plants which were in operation on Dec. 31, 1968 and includes pollution control facilities placed in service up to Jan. 1, 1975.

The deduction is limited to the proportion of the cost of the property attributable to the first 15 years of its normal useful life. Where property has a normal useful life of more than 15 years, one portion of the facility is to be amortized over the 5-year period and the remaining portion is to receive regular depreciation based upon the entire normal useful life of the property.

The new law is applicable to the taxable years ending after Dec. 31, 1968.

ALABAMA

Property Tax—Air and water pollution devices are exempted under Act. 1137.

Sales & Use Tax—Air and water facilities are exempt from sales taxes under Act 1139 and Use Taxes under Act 1141.

Income or Franchise Taxes—Air and water pollution abatement facilities are exempted from income taxes under Act 1136 and franchise tax under Act 1138.

ALASKA

There are no state tax incentive laws for installation of pollution abatement equipment.

ARIZONA

Income or Franchise Taxes—A deduction for income and franchise taxes is granted with respect to the amortization of the adjusted basis of air and water facilities may be claimed, based upon a 60-month period. (Section 43-123.02).

ARKANSAS

Sales & Use Tax—Exemption granted under normal machinery and equipment exemption (Title 84-1904).

CALIFORNIA

Income or Franchise Taxes—For purposes of personal income tax, air and water facilities may be amortized either over a 60-month period (Sec 17226) or over a one-year period in the full amount of the expenditure (Sec 17226.5). Identical provisions exist for corporation income tax purposes (Sec 24372 and Sec 24372.5)

COLORADO

There are no state tax incentive laws for installation of pollution abatement equipment.

CONNECTICUT

Property Tax—Water (Sec 12-82.98) and air (Sec 12-82.102) facilities are exempt.

Sales & Use Tax—Water (Sec 12-412.95) and air (Sec 12-412.96) facilities are exempt.

Income or Franchise Tax—Corporations are allowed a tax credit equal to five percent of the amount expended on air and water pollution control after Jan. 1, 1967. Four year carryover allowed. (G.S. 12-217b; 12-217c; P.A. (1969) No. 291.)

DELAWARE

There are no state tax incentive laws for installation of pollution abatement equipment.

FLORIDA

Property Tax—Air and water equipment is assessed at no more than salvage value for property tax purposes. Replacing old equipment with new does not increase tax valuation (Sec 403. 241).

Sales & Use Tax—Legislature has repealed previous exemption from sales, use and privilege taxes under Sec 403.241.

GEORGIA

Property Tax—Air and water facilities are exempt (Ga. Code Ann Sec 92-201.1).

Sales & Use Tax—Approved air and water facilities are exempt (Ga. Code Ann 92-3403a C (2) (t.1)).

HAWAII

Property Tax—The state legislature passed S. B. 1007 before this booklet went to press and the governor was expected to sign the bill which excludes air pollution facilities from real property assessment.

Sales Tax—S. B. 1007 (See Property Tax) excludes air pollution control faciliites from 4% excise tax.

Income or Franchise Tax—The state legislature passed S. B. 986 before this booklet went to press and the governor was expected to sign the bill which allows five year amortization of air and water pollution control facilities.

IDAHO

Property Tax—Air and water facilities are exempt (Sec 63-105T).

ILLINOIS

Property Tax—For purposes of property taxation, air and water facilities are valued according to the fair cash value of their economic productivity, including resale value (Ch. 120, Sec 500.21a-1).

Sales & Use Tax—Air and water facilities are exempt from retailers' occupation (sales) tax (Ch.120, Sec 440a), service occupation tax (Ch. 120, Sec 439.120a), use tax (Ch.120, Sec 439.2a), and service occupation tax (Ch.120, Sec 439.32a).

INDIANA

Property Tax—Air (L. 1965, C 119, Sec 1) and water (Act 1967, S. 111, Sec 2) facilities are exempt.

Sales & Use Tax—Air and water facilities are exempt, unless they are constructed so as to be a part of realty.

IOWA

There are no state tax incentive laws for installation of pollution abatement equipment.

KANSAS

There are no state tax incentive laws for installation of pollution abatement equipment.

KENTUCKY

Sales & Use Tax—Exemption granted under normal machinery and equipment exemption (Reg 6-1).

LOUISIANA

Property Tax—Pollution abatement equipment is granted exemption (Art 10, Sec 4, Para 10) for ten years from state or local property taxes (Ten Year Tax Exemption Law).

MAINE

Property Tax—Exemption for all disposal systems that produce no salable product (RS 1963, c 414, Sec 103).

Sales & Use Tax—Amendment to Title 36 Sec 1760 provides that delineated water (sub sec 29) and air (sub sec 30) pollution control facilities are exempt from sales and use tax.

MARYLAND

Sales & Use Tax—Partial exemption granted under normal machinery and equipment exemption (Art 81, Ch 325).

MASSACHUSETTS

Property Tax—Air (Ch 59, Sec 5, Part 39) and water (Ch 59, Sec 5, Part 44) facilities are exempt.

Sales & Use Tax—Exemption granted under normal machinery and equipment (Ch. 64H, Sec 6).

Income or Franchise Tax—The cost of water pollution control equipment may be deducted in the year acquired for excise tax purposes (Ch 63, Sec 38D).

MICHIGAN

Property Tax—Air (Sec 336.4) and water (P.A. 1966, Act 222, Sec 4) facilities are exempt.

Sales & Use Tax—Air (Sec 336.4) and water (P.A. 1966, Act 222, Sec 4) facilities are exempt from sales and use taxes.

MINNESOTA

Property Tax—Real and personal property used primarily for the abatement and control of air and water pollution to the extent it is so used (Sec 272.02 (15)).

Income or Franchise Tax—A credit of 5% up to $50,000 in any taxable year for the cost of equipment installed and operated solely and exclusively to prevent air and water pollution may be deducted from the income and water pollution may be deducted from the income. Three year carryback and seven year carryover allowed. (Sec 290.06 (9)).

MISSISSIPPI

There are no state tax incentive laws for installation of pollution abatement equipment.

MISSOURI

Sales & Use Tax—Air (Sec 144.030.80) and water (Sec 144.030.85) facilities are exempt (must be certified).

MONTANA

Property Tax—Facilities, machinery and equipment, attached or unattached to real property, for air pollution control are exempted (Section 84-301, R.C.M. 1947, Class 7, Sec. b.)

NEBRASKA

There are no state tax incentive laws for installation of pollution abatement equipment.

NEVADA

There are no state tax incentive laws for installation of pollution abatement equipment.

NEW HAMPSHIRE

Property Tax—Pollution control property is exempt for 25 years for the percentage of the property so used (L. 1955, C 196).

NEW JERSEY

Property Tax—Air and water facilities are exempt (L. 1966, C 127, Sec 1).

Sales & Use Tax—Machinery and equipment used in sewerage systems are exempt (L. 1966, C 30, Sec 8.36).

NEW MEXICO

There are no state tax incentive laws for installation of pollution abatement equipment.

NEW YORK

Property Tax—Air (Real Property Tax Law, Sec 481) and water (Real Property Tax Law, Sec 477) facilities are exempt.

Sales & Use Tax—Water facilities are exempt from statewide and local upstate sales taxes, but not from New York City sales tax (Tax Law, Art 28, Sec 1115.61).

Income or Franchise Tax—A deduction is allowed for air and water expenditures (Tax Law, Sec 208.50).

NORTH CAROLINA

Property Tax—New air and water equipment shall not increase real estate tax valuation (Sec 105-294). Land (Sec 105-296) and equipment (Sec 105-297) used primarily for air and water pollution control are exempt from real estate tax.

Income or Franchise Tax—Persons (Sec 105-47) and corporations (Sec 105-130.10) may claim state income tax deductions for amortization of air and water facilities over a 60-month period.

NORTH DAKOTA

There are no state tax incentive laws for installation of pollution abatement equipment.

OHIO

Property Tax—Water (Sec 6111.31) and air (Sec 5709.25) facilities are exempt from personal property taxes. Must apply for certificate (SB174).

Sales & Use Tax—Water (Sec 6111.31) and air (Sec 5709.25) facilities are exempt from sales use tax. Must apply for certificate (SB 174).

Income or Franchise Tax—Water (Sec 6111.31) and air (Sec 5709.25) facilities are exempt from franchise taxes. Must apply for certificate (SB-174).

OKLAHOMA

Sales & Use Tax—Exemption granted under normal machinery and equipment exemption (Title 68, Art 31, Sec 1305).

Income or Franchise Tax—Income tax credit not more than 20 percent of net investment is allowed each year until entire net investment is recovered—for both water (L. 1967, S. 314, Sec 2) and air (L. 1969, S. 129, Sec 2) facilities.

OREGON

Taxpayer may elect either property tax exemption or income tax credit (Sec 449.635).

Property Tax—Air and water pollution facilities are exempt from property taxes for 20 years if built before 1970; for less time, if built after 1970. Only businesses conducted in Oregon before 1967 are eligible for exemption if pollution control facilities are built after 1970 (Sec 307.405).

Income or Franchise Tax—Credit against corporation (Sec 317.072) and individual (Sec 316.097) income taxes is a maximum 5% of the cost of the facility per year, up to a maximum 50% of the investment. Credit ends Dec. 31, 1978.

PENNSYLVANIA

Sales & Use Tax—Air and water pollution control facilities are exempt from both sales and use tax for manufacturers and processors, Reg 225 (a) (2) (f); for public utilities, Reg 227 (a) (2) (d); and for persons engaged in mining, Reg 228 (a) (2) (f).

RHODE ISLAND

Property Tax—Air and water facilities are exempt from property tax (Sec 44-3.45).

Sales & Use Tax—Air and water facilities are exempt from sales use tax (Sec 44-18-30.75).

Income or Franchise Tax—A deduction with respect to the amortization of the adjusted basis of air and water facilities may be claimed, based on a 60-month period (Sec 44-11-11-A).

SOUTH CAROLINA

Property Tax—Air and water facilities are exempt (Sec 65-1522.51-A).

Sales & Use Tax—Exemption granted under normal machinery and equipment exemption (Title 65, Ch 17, Art 3, Sec 65-1404).

SOUTH DAKOTA

There are no state tax incentive laws for installation of pollution abatement equipment.

TENNESSEE

Property Tax—All air and water pollution control equipment is exempted from property taxation under TCA 67-512.

Sales & Use Tax—Air and water pollution control equipment is classified as "industrial machinery" (TCA 67-3002) and is taxed at rate of 1% (TCA 67-3003).

TEXAS

There are no state tax incentive laws for installation of pollution abatement equipment.

UTAH

There are no state tax incentive laws for installation of pollution abatement equipment.

VERMONT
Property Tax—Water (Sec 3802.60) and air (L. 1967, No. 310, Sec 19) facilities are exempt.

VIRGINIA

Income Tax—An income tax deduction with respect to the amortization of the adjusted basis of air and water facilities may be claimed, based on a 60-month period in lieu of deduction for depreciation. (Sec 58-81.1).

WASHINGTON
Income or Franchise Tax—There are two options for newly constructed air and water facilities: (1) exemption from sales-use tax may be claimed, or (2) a credit may be taken against sales-use tax, business and occupation taxes, and public utilities taxes in the same amount as provided in (1) (L. 1967, C. 139, Sec 5 and Sec 5.5). After operation begins, an annual credit may be claimed against business and occupation taxes, sales-use tax, and public utilities taxes in the amount of 2 percent of the cost of the facility (L. 1967, C. 139, Sec 6.5).

WEST VIRGINIA
Sales & Use Tax—Exemption granted under normal machinery and equipment exemption (Ch 11, Act 15-A-3).

Income or Franchise Tax—The cost of air and water facilities may be deducted from federal taxable income in the year of installation (L. 1967, S 209, Sec 11-24-5.65).

WISCONSIN
Property Tax—Air and water facilities are exempt (Sec 70.11 (21) (a)).

Income or Franchise Tax—The cost of air and water facilities may be deducted from the taxable income base in the year paid, or may be depreciated or amortized over five year period. (Sec 71.04 (2b)).

WYOMING
Property Tax—Air pollution control facilities are exempt (Sec 35-501).

End, text of NAM pamphlet.

---

more gifts proposed

Although accelerated amortization for industrial air pollution abatement facilities was provided in the Tax Reform Act of 1969 (Public Law 91-172), bills continued to be introduced to enable industry to make the necessary investments for construction, operation, and maintenance of such facilities. Examples include the following:

Amend the Small Business Act to encourage the development and utilization of new and improved methods of waste disposal and pollution control; assist small business concerns to effect conversions to meet pollution control standards by insuring loans at rates below commercial rates;

Amend the Internal Revenue Code of 1954 to allow an incentive tax credit for a part of the cost of constructing or providing facilities for air or water pollution control, and permit the amortization of such cost within a period of from 1 to 5 years;

Amend the Internal Revenue Code of 1954 to provide for an income tax deduction for additions to reserves for estimated air and water pollution control expenses;

Amend the Internal Revenue Code of 1954 to encourage the abatement of pollution by allowing an individual taxpayer to deduct from gross income the cost of eligible pollution control equipment;

Amend the Small Business Act to provide "disaster loan assistance to any small business required to install antipollution equipment to meet national, state or local environmental quality standards" below rates available from commercial institutions.

tax penalties and other user charges

Most tax laws passed to achieve environmental improvement have been positive tax incentives. They provide a reward for those who do what the government desires. In the past year considerable interest has developed concerning the use of negative incentives. [Conservation Foundation, CF Letter, June 1971]. Such laws would use the tax system to penalize pollutors. Such a system is not new. It is the basic regulatory device of the German Ruhr District Authority that has been in existence since 1904. The German approach has been to tax the effluent discharged by pollutors based on a formula that considered both the quality and the quantity of the material discharged.* [Fair, Pollution Abatement in the Ruhr District, in Comparisons In Resource Management 143, Jarrett, ed., 1961].

The advantages of such a system are substantial. A given level of environmental quality could be achieved at a lower cost than if a common standard were imposed. The system is very flexible and gives all pollutors, even those who can meet a common standard, an incentive to reduce pollution. There is no incentive to delay abating pollution. At the same time each pollutor can reduce his discharge any way he desires and is encouraged to use new methods. A secondary benefit is that they generate revenue which forces commodity prices to reflect the true social cost of production.

The disadvantage is the danger that the assimilative capacities of air or water environments will be set too high, thus making the tax system a license to pollute. Political pressure to keep charges low will be exerted by industry, with the resulting low charges likely to discourage innovation in pollution technology. Another disadvantage is the difficulty of setting appropriate charges and administering them for the wide range of pollutants discharged into the environment.

Water pollution charges could be based on units of pollution discharged. Such a charge is relatively easy to make for organics, as it can be based on the *biochemical oxygen demand* (BOD) of the wastes. As more complex wastes are controlled, the charge system becomes more complex and equity can only be approximated. Such a system, however, requires a degree of monitoring that we do not have and administrative agencies of a size and competence not generally found. Such a system as part of a comprehensive program could, of course, be instituted in steps.

The following is excerpted from *Environmental Quality, The Second Annual Report of the Council on Environmental Quality,* August 1971:

effluent fees

> The "effluent fee" or pollution charge has been a key innovation in financing pollution control at the State level. However, its implementation so far has been limited. Vermont passed a law in 1969 levying a charge on dischargers not in compliance with State water quality standards.[46] The Vermont law provides that after July 1, 1971, a "temporary pollution permit" may be issued to a discharger ineligible for a "discharge permit." A discharge permit is issued only for discharges that will not reduce the quality of receiving waters below applicable standards. To receive a temporary permit and avoid legal action by the Water Resources Board, the discharger must show that he is making a bona fide effort to install or develop control facilities or systems, has no reasonable alternatives, and would suffer hardship if the permit were denied. He must also demonstrate that some public benefit will result from issuance of the permit and that the discharge will not unreasonably degrade water quality.
>
> Any temporary permit issued must contain various conditions specified by statute. One of these is periodic payment of a pollution charge, established by the Board "to approximate in economic terms the damage done to other [public and private] users of the waters." This is designed to give permit holders "the economic incentive . . . to reduce the volume and degrading quality

*This system is not a true effluent tax, but rather a program to distribute total treatment costs.

46. Vt. Sta. Ann. tit. 10, §912a.

of their discharges" during the limited period of time the permit allows to complete remedial action.

The Vermont effluent fee system deviates most sharply from the basic effluent fee concept, as advocated by welfare economists, in this way: The Vermont charge applies only to dischargers determined to be out of compliance with water quality standards. The basic effluent fee concept generally calls for charges to be levied against all dischargers. The July 1, 1971, deadline for implementing the effluent fee law recently was extended for 1 year by the Vermont Legislature to give firms more time to comply with water quality standards. However, firms not complying by July 1, 1972, will be assessed fees retroactive to July 1, 1971.

new types of taxes

Michigan recently enacted legislation establishing an effluent and water quality monitoring fee system. That law requires all manufacturing and other commercial dischargers to pay a fee "for the cost of surveillance of industrial and commercial discharges and receiving waters." [47] The fee, assessed annually by the Water Resources Commission and based on the volume and strength of discharge, may range from a $50 minimum administrative fee to $9,000 per location for discharges in conformance with the Commission's effluent restrictions. The law specifies no maximum fee for unlawful discharges. Thus, it apparently could be applied similarly to the Vermont law.

The new waste treatment and disposal program in Maryland, discussed earlier in this chapter, may also be used to impose an effluent fee. Maryland's new Environmental Service is authorized to charge for its services. The Environmental Service Act would permit MES to structure its charges to reflect the costs of environmental damage caused by pollution.

End, excerpt from CEQ report.

The legal problems involved in developing such taxes are considerable, but do not seem to be prohibitive. For instance, New York City ran into difficulties in court after trying to tax plastic containers so as to discourage their use, and so reduce waste disposal costs. (See pp. Two-65 to Two-76). Other municipalities and states have attempted related techniques of controlling solid waste (See Two-57 and Appendix Two-8, 9).

Another tax in this vein frequently suggested is a ban of phosphates in detergents (treated in Chapter Four).

Resource user taxes, such as a tax based on an automobile's horsepower, could discourage fuel consumption. A tax on the number of passengers in a vehicle using a bridge or tunnel, especially during rush hours, could discourage inefficient and socially costly transportation practices. The rates would be set in reverse ratio to the number of persons using the vehicle so as to encourage greater utilization of fewer vehicles.

To control air pollution, taxes on both lead and sulfur have been suggested by President Nixon. A sulfur tax was promised in "The President's 1971 Environmental Program" compiled by the Council on Environmental Quality, and some further information on such a proposal was made available for the President's 1972 Environmental Message in February. The tax as outlined in the latter message would vary between 10 and 15 cents a pound for the sulfur content of the fuel used, with rebates for successful control. It would go into effect in 1976. (*See* "Sulfur Tax: a Break for the Smelters," *The Wall Street Journal,* Feb. 17, 1972 at 8.

proposal for tax on sulfur

However, several months later, the Administration bill had not yet been introduced in Congress. Instead, a tougher bill proposed by some environmental groups under the label The Coalition to Tax Pollution (620 C Street S.E., Washington, D.C. 20003) found two Congressional sponsors, Sen, William Proxmire and Rep. Les Aspin, both of Wisconsin. The identical bills were S. 3057 and H.R. 10890.

Finally, when no Republican could be found to introduce the Administration's sulfur tax proposal, several Democrats introduced it,

47. Mich. Stat. Ann. §3.533.

possibly to embarrass the Administration. *See* "Sulfur Tax Lacks GOP Sponsors," *The Washington Post,* July 6, 1972 at G3. Since the Administration bill so far lacks real support except possibly as a means to weaken the other bill, it is the Proxmire-Aspin bill that we will discuss here. That bill has five key points:

proposal for tax on sulfur

1. That the charge on sulfur emitted to the environment be set at 20¢/lb. and that this level be achieved by 1975. The rate could be set at 5¢ in 1972, and increased by 5¢ every year until 1975. (A 20¢ tax on sulfur is equivalent to a 10¢ tax on sulfur dioxide.)
2. That the charge be applied uniformly throughout the nation in order to avoid creating havens for pollution and to keep the tax administratively simple.
3. That Congress rather than an agency set the level of the tax so that the debate is out in the open.
4. That the revenue not be ear-marked so that no one program funding is dependent on a lack of pollution control.
5. That no subsidies be given to industries, but that workers laid off as a result of plant closure receive assistance in the form of retraining, relocation, and unemployment compensation.

Reprinted below are portions of a flyer supporting the Proxmire-Aspin bill that was issued by the bill's unofficial sponsor, The Coalition to Tax Pollution. Comments by the author follow.

POLLUTION TAXES

- **What is a pollution tax system?**

The purpose of pollution taxes is to make pollution abatement in the self-interest of the polluter, by creating a strong economic incentive for industry to stop polluting. A pollution tax system places financial responsibility directly on the polluter according to the amount of pollution emitted. For the tax to be effective, it must cost the polluter more than the expense of abatement.

- **Why do we need pollution taxes?**

Despite all the public effort and concern, pollution is getting worse. We need to try a tactic that will really work. As things stand now, pollution control agencies have the overwhelming responsibility of policing all violations, yet with their usually inadequate staffs, they are unable to prosecute all violators. The result is selective enforcement, and the big polluters are usually overlooked because of their political pull. Even if enforcement agencies could prosecute all violators, there are so many opportunities for industry to delay compliance with standards that pollution can get much worse in the meantime.

Taxes and standards can and should be used together to control pollution, but taxes have four significant advantages:

1. The administration of pollution taxes is much simpler: the burden of proof is on the polluter rather than on the enforcement agency. Individual legal proceedings do not have to be brought against polluters; all companies simply pay the tax on all their pollution. Enforcement centers on spot-checking, rather than on proof of guilt.
2. The creative energies of industry are turned inward to determine how to stop pollution, rather than outward to argue with the standard-setters and obtain delays. Industry itself takes the initiative in finding the most economical and efficient way to abate pollution.
3. The incentive to reduce pollution continues even after standards are met, because the last pound of pollutant is taxed just as much as the first pound. This encourages continuous research and development of pollution-abatement technology, to eliminate more and more of the pollution.
4. Under the present mechanisms of pollution control, delay is always to the advantage of the polluters, because in the meantime they can continue to pollute as heavily as before. Litigation is less costly for them than abatement, so they have a strong incentive to go through every legal channel, even if they expect to lose the case eventually. With pollution taxes, there is a strong incentive to avoid delay of any kind, because the taxes keep mounting up as long as the pollution continues.

Tax breaks and subsidies have also been tried, but they bias industries to make large capital expenditures on pollution control equipment, often on treatment measures, do not encourage research into more effective technologies to prevent pollution, and do not insure that the equipment will continue to function. Pollution taxes, on the contrary, are "technologically neutral"; they encourage technological progress at all levels, progress measured in terms of how much pollution is reduced rather than on how much money is spent on equipment. A charge based strictly on the quantity of pollution emitted makes industry seek the best long-term means of pollution control.

"LICENSE TO POLLUTE"?

- **Won't pollution taxes just give industry a "license to pollute"? Couldn't industry simply pay the tax, pass the cost on to the consumer, and accomplish no pollution control?**

Many people, including some who are genuinely concerned about the quality of the environment, have been worried that a tax on pollution might constitute a "license to pollute," in other words, that pollution would be allowed upon payment of a fee. Environmentalists have taken a new look at pollution taxes, however, and have seen that if a tax per pound of pollutant is set at a high enough level (where pollution is more expensive than abatement), the economics of the situation will force polluters to choose pollution control. There are several factors which prevent this tax from being a "license to pollute."

COMPETITION: With a tax set at a high enough level, competitive factors will force polluters to control their pollution, thereby preventing them from simply passing the tax on to the consumer. Since polluting will be more expensive than abatement, any firm which chooses to reduce its pollution will have a competitive advantage over any firm which hasn't chosen this least-cost alternative. Out of economic self-preservation, firms will not be able to pay and pollute.

Some have suggested that in the case of the power industry, competitive factors do not apply. However, large power users always have the alternative of generating their own power if they think they can do it more cheaply. Electricity is generally very cheap for bulk users, but if power companies started adding on the full cost of the tax rather than controlling their pollution, they would lose their best customers, who would all have the option of choosing for themselves the least-cost alternative—pollution abatement.

ELASTICITY OF DEMAND: Another reason why industries are drawn toward least-cost alternatives is that consumers of many products would buy less if the price went up significantly. Consumption patterns very definitely correspond to the prices of products. For example, in the case of copper, many users have shifted over to aluminum, which is lighter and cheaper. Even in the case of electricity use, elasticity of demand is an important factor, because of alternative sources of energy (gas instead of electric stoves, steam or gas instead of electric heat, hand-powered instead of electric can-openers, to name a few), and many opportunities to conserve power use. Companies are anxious to keep consumption of their products at a maximum, and are therefore going to avoid a rise in prices which does not contribute to their profits. Adding on the full burden of the tax to the price of the product, rather than accomplishing pollution control, would be very much to the disadvantage of the firm: it would get no benefit from the higher prices that consumers were paying (since the tax money would all go to the government, and consumers would buy less of the product besides.

- **But isn't part of the purpose of a pollution tax to collect revenue?**

No. This tax is not a revenue measure. Although the concept of pollution taxes grew out of the conviction that the air and water should not be free dumping grounds, the goal of the tax is to make pollution control in the economic self-interest of the polluters, not to collect revenue. The revenue will decrease as environmental quality improves: after the initial adjustment period, there should be very little revenue and very little pollution. (To minimize revenue in the adjustment period, our proposal states that the tax should be phased in over four years.)

CONSUMERS

- **But won't the consumer have to pay more for goods, even if industry chooses to stop polluting?**

If industries choose to stop polluting instead of paying the tax, they will still have to pay for abatement, although this expense will be much less. This cost will be reflected in consumer prices. At the present time, goods that are produced in polluting processes are artificially cheap; part of their true cost is expressed in the form of environmental deterioration. Pollution taxes, by locating the cost of pollution and pollution abatement exactly at the source, cause goods to reflect more accurately the total costs that go into their production. But *any* effective pollution control will cause increased cost to the consumer, either in the form of higher prices (as in this case) or higher taxes (as in government-subsidized pollution control). Pollution taxes, in that they encourage the most economical means of pollution control, will cause the least rise in consumer costs consistent with pollution control.

WHICH POLLUTANTS?

- **Which pollutants should be taxed?**

Pollution taxes can be used on many pollutants, but they will prove particularly useful in cases where abatement will require a significant amount of technological research and development, and where the cost of abatement will be quite high. These are the situations in which, under the existing pollution control regulations, industry has a strong economic incentive to seek delay. These are also the situations in which industry needs the most incentive to carry out the needed research.

Sulfur oxides, one of the most serious and abundant air pollutants, fulfill these criteria. We propose a sulfur tax as a first objective. Other pollutants for which pollution taxes would be particularly appropriate are BOD (biological oxygen demand—a measure of water pollution) and nitrogen oxides (another serious air pollutant). The tax approach has also been suggested for non-returnable containers, for phosphate content of cleaning agents, and for solid wastes.

A SULFUR TAX

- **Why is sulfur a good pollutant to tax?**

Sulfur oxides are a very serious pollutant, causing severe damage to health and property. There is a well-documented case relating sulfur pollution to respiratory disease. The incidence of emphysema, bronchitis, and lung cancer—and death from these diseases—has been correlated with surfur in the air. Respiratory disease patients are even required to stay indoors on days when the sulfur level is especially high. It was recently reported in Houston, Texas that between April and July, 1971, 150 people have actually fallen sick in the street from breathing air polluted by sulfur from sulfuric acid plants. This is an example of a serious short-term effect; most of us suffer and will suffer from less obvious long-term effects. Although we may not fall in the street, our sickness and death rates will be higher. In addition to these health effects, sulfur pollution is responsible for damage to property. Houses have to be painted more often, clothes deteriorate faster, and in areas of especially high pollution, property values decline. A conservative estimate of the monetary costs of this damage was made by the Environmental Protection Agency. They estimated that society at large pays about 25 cents per pound of sulfur emitted to the air. This money is not paid by the polluters. It is paid by all of us.

Sulfur abatement technology needs much more research and development, and abatement costs will be high, so industry has little incentive to try to stop sulfur pollution. A tax would provide the needed incentive. In addition, sulfur is emitted from remarkably few sources; nearly all of it comes from less than 1000 fossil-fueled power plants, 262 oil refineries, 64 smelters, and 212 sulfuric acid plants.

There are several methods to abate sulfur pollution, but the technology is not yet adequate to solve every case. Refinement and construction of abatement equipment is going to be expensive, so a strong economic incentive is particularly needed.

LOW-SULFUR FUEL: The easiest short-term means of sulfur abatement is to switch to low-sulfur fuel, but for several reasons this is not an efficient or desirable long-term method. Because of present shortages, buying low-sulfur fuel is more expensive than the anticipated costs of stack gas removal, and the burgeoning exploitation of low-sulfur coal by strip-mining imposes severe environmental costs as well. In addition, even with low-sulfur fuel there is a significant amount of sulfur pollution, and stack gas removal might eventually have to be built anyway.

FUEL DESULFURIZATION: Another method is fuel desulfurization, but this will probably be in the most expensive range of costs for sulfur abatement. Taking the sulfur out of the stack gases will probably be a better approach, except in the case of household furnace oil users. Clearly it would be more efficient to have centralized desulfurization in this case. Since the tax on sulfur would make high-sulfur fuel more expensive than low-sulfur fuel, householders would be encouraged to buy desulfurized fuel, and users with abatement equipment would buy the high-sulfur fuel, take out the sulfur, and collect a rebate on the tax.

STACK GAS REMOVAL: Stack gas desulfurization is the approach with the most promising potential for controlling sulfur pollution. Various techniques for removal of sulfur gases from the smokestack are currently being tested in large experimental units. A tax would speed up the refinement of these methods, and their implementation on a large scale.

FOR SULFURIC ACID PLANTS: In the case of sulfur pollution from sulfuric acid plants, abatement consists of making the process more efficient. Abatement therefore results in more usable product.

FOR SMELTERS: Sulfur pollution from smelters results

om sulfur in the ore itself. Many smelters have sulfuric acid ants attached; sulfur is recovered and made into sulfuric acid. his technique is already well-developed, but not widely used in oper smelters, because it is not profitable. The tax would make profitable.

A tax on sulfur pollution will provide the needed incentive for dustry to perfect and use sulfur abatement technology. Gaps in ur present-day capabilities will be rapidly filled when the onomic incentive to do so is created.

How much should sulfur be taxed?

A tax of 20 cents per pound of sulfur would provide an verwhelming incentive to abate. (This amount is calculated per ound of sulfur rather than of SO_2 and other sulfur oxides. ince SO_2 weighs twice as much as sulfur, an equivalent tax on O_2 would be 10 cents per pound.) Estimates of the average ost of sulfur pollution abatement range between 5 and 15 cents er pound, depending on the specific fuel and process. Another uideline for setting the level of the tax is the Environmental rotection Agency's estimate that society pays about 25 cents er pound on the measurable health and property costs caused y sulfur oxides pollution. According to this estimate, stopping ollution is much cheaper than paying for its damage. The 0-cent tax level could be achieved in several increments, with 975 as a target for the full level.

Where should a tax on sulfur be applied?

It is possible to apply a pollution tax anywhere in the chain of upply of the polluting substance and still provide the same egree of incentive to stop pollution. In the case of sulfur ollution that comes from the combustion of fossil fuels, there re two efficient possibilities:

1. The tax could be assessed at the source of supply of the fuel, and a rebate could be given to any later owner of the fuel for the amount of sulfur removed. The overall result is the same as if the tax were assessed on the polluter, but it is easier to account for all the sulfur by assessing the tax before the fuel is distributed. In the case of residential fuel oil, a tax applied at the refinery would give the refiner an incentive to take the sulfur out before he sold the fuel to the dealer. Industrial purchasers will be willing to buy fuel that has the tax cost built in, if they have the means to remove the sulfur and get the rebate later on. Other purchasers will buy low-sulfur fuel, since they won't be able to remove sulfur themselves.
2. An alternative to having the fuel supplier actually pay the tax would be to measure the amount of sulfur in the fuel, figure the amount of tax due on the fuel, and issue a certificate of tax liability. This certificate would be passed on at the sale of the fuel. When sulfur is removed the amount of tax shown on the certificate is reduced accordingly.

Under both of these systems, sulfur removal must be neasured and proven by the company in question. Under the irst system, the rebate is given only if sulfur removal is proven; nder the second, the tax must be paid on the assessed amount f sulfur, minus the amount removed.

Taxing sulfur at the beginning of the chain of supply has two dvantages over applying the tax only at the point of actual ollution, although the end result (cutting pollution) is the same:

1. All sulfur is accounted for, including that in the fuel burned in residential furnaces.
2. The incentive to remove sulfur exists at all points.

Cases of sulfur pollution which do not fall in the above ategory (such as pollution from sulfuric acid plants) will have to e taxed directly at the point of pollution.

- **Who makes the decision on sulfur tax legislation?**

The sulfur tax measure will be discussed in the Finance Committee of the Senate and the Ways and Means Committee of the House.

SETTING POLLUTION TAXES

- **Who should set pollution taxes?**

The level of the tax is crucial. The decision on the rate of the charge is the equivalent of a decision on an acceptable level of environmental quality. The debate over the level of pollution charges should be as visible as possible; many values, some not measurable, must be taken into account. Industrial and regional self-interest should have to face squarely society's demand for effective pollution control. Agencies in the Executive branch are much more susceptible than Congress to arm-twisting, since their debates take place behind closed doors by people who are not directly accountable to the public. Therefore, Congress should be responsible for setting the level of pollution taxes.

- **Where should the revenue from pollution taxes go?**

Since the object of pollution taxes is to stop pollution rather than to collect revenue, any program which depended on the tax revenue for its funding would be dependent on a lack of pollution control. The more successful the tax is, the less revenue there will be. If we totally succeed in stopping pollution, no revenue will be collected. Therefore, what revenue there is should not be earmaked.

- **Should pollution taxes be applied uniformly throughout the nation, or should there be regional variations, according to pollution levels and/or economic difficulties?**

A variable tax would give industries an incentive to move to the areas where the tax was lowest. Even if they did not actually move, the opportunity to do so would give them leverage in their attempts to lower the tax in their areas. The notion of lower taxes in areas where there is less pollution implies that we are willing to tolerate more pollution in the areas that are clean now.

QUESTIONS FROM POLLUTERS

- **Isn't it too much to ask industry to pay the tax at the same time it is trying to make abatement expenditures?**

Pollution taxes give industry the choice of paying the tax or controlling their pollution, and weights the choice in favor of controlling pollution. We propose a period of grace during which the tax is low, but we believe there should be an incentive to stop pollution right at the beginning, because without the tax, it is always more profitable to delay.

- **If our goods cost more, won't the United States lose out in international competition?**

It is true that some products will cost more when we have effective pollution control; one of the effects of the pollution tax is to locate this added cost so that prices of goods reflect the environmental costs that go into their production. This will make some goods more expensive than those of countries which do not control their pollution. However, compared with other factors in the American economy which have made our products more expensive—minimum wage laws, high wage levels, social security, child labor laws, occupational safety regulations—pollution control costs will have a relatively minor effect. It has been suggested by some that the United States place special import taxes on goods from countries which do not control their pollution.

End, excerpts from a pro-sulfur tax flyer of The Coalition to Tax Pollution. Some comments by the author are on the following page.

tax proposal criticized

COMMENTARY

The proposed tax program described above has gathered quite considerable support, but not very much critical examination. Therefore the following criticisms are listed, that they might be kept in mind before a perhaps mistaken commitment is made to a method of control that can have immensely complicated effects.

• Although a tax on sulfur would encourage alternate fuel uses, those uses might not be less environmentally harmful. The increased use of nuclear power is an example. Also, demand for natural gas would increase; yet, as presently organized, that industry cannot meet present demand (but see section on Federal Power Commission later in this chapter).

• The tax, as conceived above, would go into effect virtually immediately, although the installation of equipment to control the emissions (and avoid the tax) could not be achieved for several years. Hence there would be considerable economic effect without environmental benefit. This would amount to yet another surcharge on the American public, since the tax cost would be passed to consumers, further promoting inflation. The amount of that tax would be about $1.75 billion in 1972.

• The cost of preventing sulfur emissions is calculated at about 7 cents per pound of sulfur removed, based on less than complete removal at newly constructed plants. Costs to older plants would in general be considerably higher. Tax rates set below the removal cost would be merely inflationary, while those above the removal cost would have profound effects on the industrial base of the nation, favoring industries that do not pollute (the goal) or which have other pollutants—a seldom-mentioned by-product of the proposed tax.

The singling out of sulfur oxides for this treatment makes some industries such as copper smelting subject to very severe sanctions while industries such as automobile manufacturers, cement producers, much of the chemical industry, and many others have no similar sanction. A competitive advantage for some industries such as aluminum over steel may be a side effect. Economic punishments (including possible plant closings) therefore could be inflicted without any improvement in the environment.

• The price of sulfur by-products, depended upon to hold down the cost of sulfur removal, would likely drop as more sulfur is made available.

• The uniformity of the regulations has obvious advantages, but some economic disadvantages. The copper industry may serve as an example. Although electric utilities can pass on additional costs to consumers, the copper industry in the United States cannot do so without extreme difficulty. Theirs is a world market; they either keep their prices close to the world market figures, or go out of business. From a strictly economic standpoint, a tax on sulfur emissions—especially one that cannot be avoided even with the best emissions controls—is a real danger to domestic copper production. From an environmental viewpoint, there is something to be said for the argument that much stricter standards are required in urban areas than in the rural areas where most of the copper smelters are located.

• To remove SO_2 from stack gases, they may be passed through a scrubbing tower's countercurrent to limewater, converting the sulfur dioxide to calcium sulfite. Producing the limewater requires lime, which is the heating of limestone (calcium carbonate) to a high temperature. Air generally is polluted in this way, and of course energy is consumed.

The objections above—some quite serious, others possibly frivolous—are offered as an example of one man's fairly brief consideration of possible problems.

g. Congress and the environment

The working unit of Congress is the standing committee. These are twenty-one standing committees in the House, and sixteen in the Senate. The Committee chairmen are the majority party's member with the longest service on the committee. These chairmen have a great deal of control over what legislation is passed.

Environmental bills in the Senate are usually within the jurisdiction of committees on: Agriculture and Forestry; Commerce; Government Operations; Interior and Insular Affairs; or Public Works. Atomic Energy matters are handled by the Joint [House and Senate] Committee on Atomic Energy. In addition, any money required for environmental activities requires legislation which must pass through the Appropriations Committee: this committee has subcommittees such as Agriculture and Forestry, Interior and Related Agencies, and Public Works.

Environmental bills in the House are usually handled by the committees on: Agriculture; Government Operations; Interior and Insular Affairs; Merchant Marine and Fisheries; or Public Works. Three other committees are important. The Ways and Means Committee considers legislation concerning revenue and taxation. The Committee on Rules supervises the way pending bills come to the floor for debate and this power can be used to block or slow legislation. The Committee on Appropriations writes the measures which provide the funds for government operations. This committee has many subcommittees paralleling the other standing committees. The result in that most government programs require two bills to pass each house; an authorizing bill creating a program, and an appropriation bill providing the funds to carry out the program.

There are 535 members of Congress (both houses), and, as of June 1, 1972, there were 334 regular committees and subcommittees, plus several study commissions and special committees. The number of committees has been growing rapidly in recent years. The working members of these staffs do much of the work attributed to Congress, although it must also be pointed out that a quite considerable number of these positions are not actually for committee work, and some are for virtually no work at all. Some even serve as chauffeurs for Congressmen and their families. There are staff professionals who undoubtedly deserve their $30,000 salaries, and there are receptionists in the private offices of Congressmen (paid for from committee funds, not the $150,000 individual Congressman's allowance for clerk hire, as they officially should be) gaining $30,800 annually. 14-year-old pageboys are paid $7,660 for running errands. Oddly, the size of a committee's staff does not reflect its responsibilities: for instance, the House Armed Services Committee, charged with overseeing the Federal government's biggest operations, employs 33 persons, while the House Internal Security Committee, with extremely little to do, employs 51. (*See, The Wall Street Journal,* June 1, 1972 at 1.)

The members of the committees and subcommittees can be found in the Environment Reporter (B.N.A.) §61:800- and in the CCH Congressional Index. Other books with this information are the Congressional Directory, Government Printing Office, Washington, D.C. 20402, $3.00 *paper* [available in most public libraries], and the Congressional Staff Directory, 300 New Jersey Ave., S.E., Washington, D.C. 20003, $12.50.

The League of Conservation Voters, c/o Friends of the Earth, 917 Fifteenth Street, N.W., Washington, D.C. 20005, is a conservation organization specifically set up to follow the actions of Congress.

Also very useful is the free weekly newsletter *Conservation Report,* published by the National Wildlife Federation. All federal environmental bills are listed, and key ones discussed. Their address is 1412 16th St., N.W., Washington, D.C. 20036.

THE CONGRESS OF THE UNITED STATES

(Committees considering natural resource legislation)

The following list is republished from the Conservation Directory 1972, which is available from the National Wildlife Federation, 1412 16th Street, N.W., Washington, D.C. 20036 ($2.00, paper).

UNITED STATES SENATE

COMMITTEE ON AGRICULTURE AND FORESTRY, Rm. 324, Old Senate Office Bldg., Washington, DC 20510 (202, 225-2035)

Consists of 14 Senators: agriculture generally; inspection of livestock and meat products; animal industry and diseases of animals; adulteration of seeds, insect pests, and protection of birds and animals in forest reserves; agricultural colleges and experiment stations; forestry in general and forest reserves other than those created from the public domain; agricultural economics and research; agricultural and industrial chemistry; dairy industry; entomology and plant quarantine; human nutrition and home economics; plant industry, soils, and agricultural engineering; agricultural educational extension services; extension of farm credit and farm security; rural electrification; agricultural production and marketing and stabilization of prices of agricultural products; crop insurance and soil conservation.

Subcommittees:
Agricultural Credit and Rural Electrification; Committee on Agricultural Exports; Agricultural Production, Marketing, and Stabilization of Prices; Agricultural Research and General Legislation; Environment, Soil, Conservation and Forestry; Rural Development

COMMITTEE ON APPROPRIATIONS, Rm. 1235, New Senate Office Bldg., Washington, DC 20510 (202, 225-3471)

Consists of 24 Senators: all proposed legislation, messages, petitions, memorials, and other matters relating to appropriation of the revenue for the support of the Government.

Subcommittees:
Agriculture, Environmental and Consumer Protection; Defense; District of Columbia; Foreign Operations; Housing and Urban Development, Space, and Science; Interior; Labor and Health, Education and Welfare; Legislative; Military Construction; Public Works; State, Justice, Commerce, the Judiciary; Transportation; Treasury, Post Office, General Government

COMMITTEE ON COMMERCE, Rm. 5202, New Senate Office Bldg., Washington, DC 20510 (202, 225-5115)

Consists of 10 Senators: interstate and foreign commerce generally; merchant marine generally; registering and and licensing of vessels and small boats; navigation and the laws relating thereto, including pilotage; rules and international arrangements to prevent collisions at sea; inland waterways; fisheries and wildlife, including research, restoration, refuges, and conservation.

Subcommittees:
Aviation; Communications; (The) Consumer; Environment; Foreign Commerce and Tourism; Merchant Marine; Oceans and Atmosphere; Surface Transportation

COMMITTEE ON INTERIOR AND INSULAR AFFAIRS, Rm. 3106, New Senate Office Bldg., Washington, DC 20510 (202, 225-4971)

Consists of 16 Senators: public lands generally, including entry, easements, and grazing thereon; mineral resources of the public lands; forfeiture of land grants and alien ownership, including alien ownership of mineral lands; forest reserves and national parks created from the public domain; military parks and battlefields, and national cemeteries; preservation of prehistoric ruins and objects of interest on the public domain; measures relating generally to the insular possessions of the U.S., except those affecting their revenue and appropriations; irrigation and reclamation, including water supply for reclamation projects, and easements of public lands for irrigation projects; interstate compacts relating to apportionment of waters for irrigation purposes; mining interests generally; mineral land laws and claims and entries thereunder; geological survey; mining schools and experimental stations; petroleum conservation and conservation of the radium supply in the U.S.; relations of the U.S. with the Indians and Indian tribes; measures relating to the care, education, and management of Indians, including the care and allotment of Indian lands and general and special measures relating to claims which are paid out of Indian funds.

Subcommittees:
Indian Affairs; Minerals, Materials and Fuels; Parks and Recreation; Public Lands; Territories and Insular Affairs; Water and Power Resources; Legislative Oversight

COMMITTEE ON PUBLIC WORKS, Rm. 4204, New Senate Office Bldg., Washington, DC 20510 (202, 225-6176)

Consists of 16 Senators: flood control and improvement of rivers and harbors; public works for the benefit of navigation and bridges and dams (other than international bridges and dams); water power; oil and other pollution of navigable waters; public buildings and occupied or improved grounds of the United States generally; measures relating to the purchase of sites and construction of post offices, customhouses, Federal courthouses, and Government buildings within the District of Columbia; measures relating to the Capitol building and the Senate and House Office Buildings; measures relating to the construction or reconstruction, maintenance, and care of the buildings, and grounds of the Botanic Gardens, the Library of Congress, and the Smithsonian Institution; public reservations and parks within the District of Columbia including Rock Creek Park and the Zoological Park; measures relating to the construction or maintenance of roads and post roads; air pollution control measures; disaster relief; economic development; environmental pollution control measures.

Subcommittees:
Air and Water Pollution; Economic Development; Environmental Science and Technology; Flood Controls, Rivers and Harbors; Public Buildings and Grounds; Roads

HOUSE OF REPRESENTATIVES

COMMITTEE ON AGRICULTURE, Rm. 1301, Longworth House Office Bldg., Washington, DC 20515 (202, 225-2171)

Consists of 36 Members: adulteration of seeds, insect pests, and protection of birds and animals in forest reserves; agriculture generally; agricultural and industrial chemistry; agricultural colleges and experiment stations; agricultural economics and research; agricultural education extension services; agricultural production and marketing and stabilization of prices of agricultural products; animal industry and diseases of animals; crop insurance and soil conservation; dairy industry; entomology and plant quarantine; extension of farm credit and farm security; forestry in general, and forest reserves other than those created from the public domain; human nutrition and home economics; inspection of livestock and meat products; plant industry, soils, and agricultural engineering; rural electrification.

Subcommittees:
Cotton; Dairy and Poultry; Forests; Livestock and Grains; Oilseeds and Rice; Tobacco; Conservation and Credit; Domestic Marketing and Consumer Relations; Departmental Operations; Family Farms and Rural Development

COMMITTEE ON APPROPRIATIONS, Rm. H-218, Capitol Bldg., Washington, DC 20515 (202, 225-2771)

Consists of 55 Members: appropriation of the revenue for the support of the Government.

Subcommittees:

Agriculture, Environmental and Consumer Protection; Defense; District of Columbia; Foreign Operations; Housing and Urban Development, Space, and Science; Interior and Related Agencies; Labor, Health, Education and Welfare; Legislative; Military Construction; Public Works; State, Justice, Commerce, and the Judiciary; Transportation; Treasury, Post Office, and General Government

COMMITTEE ON INTERIOR AND INSULAR AFFAIRS, Rm. 1324, Longworth House Office Bldg., Washington, DC 20515 (202, 225-2761)

Consists of 39 Members: forest reserves and national parks created from the public domain; forfeiture of land grants and alien ownership, including alien ownership of mineral lands; geological survey; interstate compacts relating to apportionment of waters for irrigation purposes; irrigation and reclamation, including water supply for reclamation projects, and easements of public lands for irrigation projects, and acquisition of private lands when necessary to complete irrigation projects; measures relating to the care, education, and management of Indians, including the care and allotment of Indian lands and general and special measures relating to claims which are paid out of Indian funds; measures relating to insular possessions of the U.S., except matters affecting their revenue and appropriations; military parks and battlefields, and national cemeteries; mineral land laws and claims and entries thereunder; mineral resources of the public lands; mining interests generally; mining schools and experimental stations; petroleum conservation on the public lands and conservation of the radium supply in the U.S.; preservation of prehistoric ruins and objects of interest on the public domain; public lands generally, including entry, easements, and grazing thereon; relations of the U.S. with the Indians and the Indian tribes.

Subcommittees:

Environment; Indian Affairs; Irrigation and Reclamation; Mines and Mining; National Parks and Recreation; Public Lands; Territorial and Insular Affairs

COMMITTEE ON INTERSTATE AND FOREIGN COMMERCE, Rm. 2125, Rayburn House Office Bldg., Washington, DC 20515 (202, 225-2927)

Consists of 43 Members: interstate and foreign communications; Weather Bureau; petroleum and natural gas, (including interstate oil compacts), interstate electric power; interstate and foreign transportation; inland waterways; motor vehicle safety; newsprint, pulp and paper, and brand names; public health and quarantine; food and drugs; air pollution.

Subcommittees:

Commerce and Finance; Communications and Power; Public Health and Environment; Transportation and Aeronautics; Investigations

COMMITTEE ON MERCHANT MARINE AND FISHERIES, Rm. 1334, Longworth House Office Bldg., Washington, DC 20515 (202, 225-4047)

Consists of 37 Members: merchant marine generally; registering and licensing of vessels and small boats; coast and geodetic surveys; fisheries and wildlife, including research, restoration, refuges and conservation.

Subcommittees:

Coast Guard, Coast and Geodetic Survey and Navigation; Fisheries and Wildlife Conservation; Merchant Marine; Oceanography; Panama Canal; Maritime Education and Training

COMMITTEE ON PUBLIC WORKS, Rm. 2167, Rayburn House Office Bldg., Washington, DC 20515 (202, 225-4472)

Consists of 37 Members: flood control and improvement of rivers and harbors; public works for the benefit of navigation, including bridges and dams (other than international bridges and dams); water power; oil and other pollution of navigable waters; public reservations and parks within the District of Columbia, including Rock Creek Park and the Zoological Park; measures relating to the construction or maintenance of roads and post roads, other than appropriations therefor.

Subcommittees:

Flood Control and Internal Development; Investigations and Oversight; Public Buildings and Grounds; Rivers and Harbors; Roads; Watershed Development; Economic Development Programs

h. The Federal budget and the environment

The job of building a better environment is not one for government alone.

—Richard Nixon, August 1970

"I couldn't afford to learn it," said the Mock Turtle with a sigh. "I only took the regular course."

"What was that?" inquired Alice.

"Reeling and Writhing . . . and then the different branches of Arithmetic— Ambition, Distraction, Uglification, and Derision."

—Lewis Carroll in *Alice in Wonderland*

Most of what is written about the Federal budget is absurd. Some of it, mostly that distributed by the government, is probably intentionally absurd (either that or the writers are quite insane), while some of it, including that in many highly respected newspapers, probably gets its absurdity simply from trying to make clear statements from figures that are often mis-labeled, frequently contradictory, and possibly even suffering from an occasional purely random number (there really isn't any way to tell). One gets the feeling that, among mathematicians, Einstein would have been incensed, while Lewis Carroll would have felt quite at home.

The process of obtaining money from the Federal government requires five or more steps. An understanding of these steps is necessary to avoid being misled by government releases. The process begins with an *authorization.* This normally is found in the statute creating the program. A program for solid waste, for example, might authorize $10 million a year for five years. The authorization provides an upper figure for funding, but authorization of large sums need not result in one cent actually being provided. The next step is a *budget request.* Congress need not follow the budget request, but in practice rarely deviates substantially from these requests except to cut them. Each year there may be a few items over which Congress refuses to follow the President's requests, and these often become newsworthy political fights. Most items are not controversial.

no budget from Congress

Congress does not prepare a national budget or a coordinated economic plan of any sort, although it has the Constitutional responsibility for raising revenues and appropriating monies. Its handling of the nation's finances over the past several years has been increasingly chaotic.

The budgetary process acts as a deterrent to major shifts in priorities. It is a true product of bureaucracy, with each agency almost always starting with the existing budget and attempting to expand. The public has virtually no input into the budget process. Rarely can an interest not already identified with a government agency successfully lobby for major sums.

The *budget request* in turn leads to legislation to appropriate money. These *appropriations* are the result of decisions made behind closed doors. Regardless of which Congressional committee authorized expenditures, it is the House Appropriations Committee that determines whether any money actually will be appropriated. The House committee is divided into subcommittees which deal with the various subjects that come before them. Perhaps of most importance to environmentalists is the Subcommittee on Agriculture and Environmental and Consumer Protection. Appropriations for both the Environmental Protection Agency and the Council of Environmental Quality are passed on by this committee. It is headed by Congressman Jamie Whitten of Mississippi. Congressman Whitten has not yet had the opportunity to build a favorable reputation from his Committee work concerning the environment. His best known effort in this area is his book "That We May Live," a pro-pesticide book written in an attempt to refute Rachel Carson's "Silent Spring." In 1970 he voted against increased funding for water pollution control, but in favor of the SST.

If money is appropriated it must be *obligated* by the various agencies. By not doing this, or by moving slowly, or through pressure from the President's Office of the Management and Budget, funds provided by Congress are not used.

After money is obligated, the goods or services are supplied to the government and as it pays the bills the money is *spent.*

Because of the many steps involved, political leaders can take advantage of voter innocence by pledging large authorizations for projects. The money, of course, may never be forthcoming. The spread between authorizations and appropriations is often great and this gap is particularly pronounced in the environmental area where rhetoric is more important than action.

An example of how the authorization to expenditure process works can be seen in the 1970 waste treatment plant construction program.

	IN MILLIONS
Authorized	$1,000
Requested in Budget	214
Appropriated	800
Obligated	425
Spent	176

It should be emphasized that this is the best funded environmental program and one of the few that has resulted in Congressional expenditures going well above budget requests. Its popularity may be in part due to the nature of the program, which provides Federal money to cities for clean-up efforts. The cities in turn spend these funds on new equipment and construction, funneling profits to equipment supply and construction businesses. The program is non-regulatory, with no compulsion to force political blocs to do anything.

The great publicity given environmental problems has not produced substantial change in budgeting. The cost overrun on one new military weapon amounts to more than the fiscal 1973 spending for elementary and secondary education and water pollution control. The spending in fiscal 1973 of $171.5 million for air pollution control is a little over 1 percent of what the Federal government estimates air pollution costs the American people each year.

Those who agree with present budgeting often defend spending priorities by comparing total government spending (federal, state, and local). As state and local government programs are not engaged in national defense, the percentage of spending for social welfare and other domestic programs increases.

Nevertheless, all sanitation programs, health programs, hospital support, and natural resource programs at all levels of government combined account for less than 10 percent of the government's spending, or less than a third of the defense and international spending.

As the interest in environmental protection has grown, the necessity for funds has resulted in a great deal of attention being given to the budget. Not surprisingly, these budget figures are interpreted in a variety of ways, muddied by the complexity of federal reporting such as whether trust funds and insurance programs are included. Nevertheless, sums spent for environmental protection by the federal government are increasing, though total expenditures for natural resource programs as a percentage of the total budget have remained low.

Natural resource expenditures, however, can be misleading, for about two-thirds of the natural resource budget is for water resource and power development projects. A high percentage are environmentally destructive, and many of the most publicized conservation battles have involved attempts by citizens to prevent ecological destruction financed by the federal treasury.

obtaining information on the budget

The United States Government publishes three book-size official documents concerning the President's proposed Federal Budget. These are:

1) *The Budget of the United States Government* (plus fiscal year number). This book, of 570 pages in Fiscal 1973, gives an account of how the tax pie is divided among agencies, excepting such secret operations as those of the Central Intelligence Agency. It is frequently too general to be of much analytical use; the summary tables in back, however, are useful in obtaining an overall picture of general priorities. The self-congratulatory text often contains conclusions that are arguable. Details of program expenditures are scarce. GPO, $2.50 (*paper*). (A summary pamphlet, *The Budget in Brief*, gives a still-more general treatment. GPO $0.60.)

2) *The Budget of the United States—Appendix*. This giant tome, 1,102 large pages in Fiscal 1973, contains less text and more tables than the *Budget* itself, but in general is usable without the *Budget* volume. The emphasis is on the expenditures of the individual agencies, for which tables of job slots and pay level summaries are supplied in a separate section.

The Appendix is filled with interesting bits of information—for instance, that for Fiscal 1973 the Indian Health Services section of HEW will have $367,000 for Printing and Reproduction, and the Army Corps of Engineers $1.5 million for the same purpose (a fact that fascinates our publisher, who says that a large pile of fat books could be printed for either figure), and that the Department of Defense-Civil will have $7,109,000 for gravestone procurement.

But sometimes the labeling of expenditures is less useful than it could be. For instance, although 11½ pages of small type are devoted to the Department of Agriculture's Soil Conservation Service, nowhere will the reader find mention of the now-infamous stream channelization program which has destroyed tens of thousands of miles of streams, turning them into ditches. The program is still in the Budget for vast sums, but it is difficult if not impossible to learn that from the information given.

Unfortunately, it is rare even in the Appendix to find a financial picture of any specific program, since the outlays are for the most part grouped only by agency. Thus it is possible to obtain a great deal more information, proportionally, about the programs of a very small agency than about most larger ones. An example may be useful.

On page 383 of the *Appendix*, we find one of the smallest agencies listed; this is "Wildlife Conservation" under the general heading, "Department of Defense-Civil." For the *Appendix*, Wildlife Conservation apparently was considered as an agency, rather than a mere program of some agency, or it would have been lumped with other expenditures, as are most programs. The portrait we find of this program, which is to support hunting and fishing preserves for military use, is informative. We find that there are four employees, whose salaries average $6,892, and that these salaries have changed only slightly from the preceding two years. But Supplies and Materials will cost $353,000, up from $199,000 in 1971; Other Services will cost $244,000, up from $82,000 in 1971, and Printing and Reproduction will cost $7,000, up from $4,000 in 1971. Total outlays are to be $641,000, up from $293,000 in 1971.

The above is an example of the *Appendix* at its most detailed and useful. The same categories of expenditures applied to the vastly larger and more complex Environmental Protection Agency, for instance, are of far less utility. GPO $8.50 (*paper*)

3) *Special Analyses—Budget of the United States Government*. Perhaps symbolically, this document bears one title on the spine and a different related one on the front cover. The figures inside bear the same relationship to those of the *Budget*: related, but not the same. An example will be given shortly. The authors of the *Analyses* take the same agency figures as did the authors of the *Budget*, and rearrange them in patterns to display other virtues of governmental operations. GPO $2.50 (*paper*)

Reitze

an overview of the budget

The U.S. Budget is calculated by fiscal years which run from July 1 to June 30, and are named for the year in which they end. Thus, Fiscal Year 1973 began on July 1, 1972.

A very general examination of the budget as a whole will help to give some perspective to the portion devoted to environmental protection. Revenues for the 1973 Fiscal Year were estimated at $220 billion, although that figure depended on a far rosier picture of the economy than was held likely by most economists; it assumed a sharp upward turn in economic activity that as of the late spring of 1972 had not yet occurred. Expenditures were estimated at $246 billion, thus assuming a deficit for the year of about $26 billion, or more than 10 per cent. The budget pie was to be sliced as follows:

SUMMARY OF BUDGET OUTLAYS

[In millions of dollars]

Function	Outlays				Recommended budget authority for 1973 [1]
	1969 actual	1971 actual	1972 estimate	1973 estimate	
National defense [2]	81,232	77,661	78,030	78,310	85,363
International affairs and finance	3,785	3,095	3,960	3,844	5,188
Space research and technology	4,247	3,381	3,180	3,191	3,378
Agriculture and rural development	6,218	5,096	7,345	6,891	7,746
Natural resources and environment	2,169	2,716	4,376	2,450	2,944
Commerce and transportation	7,921	11,310	11,872	11,550	12,654
Community development and housing	1,961	3,357	4,039	4,844	5,648
Education and manpower	6,525	8,654	10,140	11,281	12,416
Health	11,611	14,463	17,024	18,117	23,681
Income security	37,699	55,712	65,225	69,658	74,320
Veterans benefits and services	7,640	9,776	11,127	11,745	12,441
Interest	15,791	19,609	20,067	21,161	21,161
General government	2,866	3,970	5,302	5,531	5,747
General Revenue Sharing	-------	-------	2,250	5,000	5,300
Allowances:					
Pay raises (excluding Department of Defense)	-------	-------	250	775	800
Contingencies	-------	-------	300	500	700
Undistributed intragovernmental transactions:					
Employer share, employee retirement	−2,018	−2,611	−2,687	−2,893	−2,893
Interest received by trust funds	−3,099	−4,765	−5,190	−5,697	−5,697
Total	**184,548**	**211,425**	**236,610**	**246,257**	**270,898**
Expenditure account	183,072	210,308	235,597	246,463	269,407
Loan account	1,476	1,117	1,013	−206	1,490

[1] Compares with budget authority for 1969, 1971, and 1972, as follows:
1969: Total, $196,167 million (NOA, $194,652 million; LA, $1,515 million).
1971: Total, $236,406 million (NOA, $234,869 million; LA, $1,536 million).
1972: Total, $249,777 million (NOA, $247,684 million; LA, $2,093 million).

[2] Includes allowances for military retirement systems reform and civilian and military pay raises for Department of Defense.

It should be noticed in the table above that additional billions of dollars not listed under "national defense" are also basically military expenses. These include "veterans benefits and services" and "interest" on the national debt. Some juggling has also taken place to limit the apparent military budget in favor of other portions of the pie, but the extent of this can not be detailed from the information supplied in the budget publications. However, a few examples nevertheless are evident, and will be noted later. Another factor of relevance is that although the budget listed no substantial increase in military expenditures, in summing up the military program (*The Budget*, p. 77), the Government makes no mention of this, but stresses that *budget authority* would be increased by $6.3 billion, leading several publications to declare flatly that the military budget was to be augmented. In view of the greatly raised expenditures already evident by the spring of 1972 due to increased activity in the Vietnam War, such a "mistake" in interpretation may be no mistake at all.

The budget is important, for although money may not make the world go around, it is what makes governments function; without an adequate supply, key parts may wither away, or never see the light of day. Examples are easy to find. The Council on Environmental Quality, charged with (among other things) development of general U.S. environmental policy as well as the examination of hundreds of complex environmental impact statements submitted each month under the National Environmental Policy Act, has 65 jobs for Fiscal 1973. That compares with 70 for the government's Inter-American Social Development Institute; 143 for the government's Overseas Private Investment Corporation; 392 for the American Battle Monuments Commission; 721 for the Office of Civil Defense, and 351,925 (not counting military personnel or those supported by military research grants) for the Department of Defense.

The above figures are rough indications of what is held to be valuable or useful by those placed at the top of our political structure. Yet, ironically, ineptitude is shown even here. The country may well be less safe with its literally tens of thousands of atomic weapons than it might have been with a tenth that many; the environment clearly would have been better served if at least half the funds allocated to natural resources programs—particularly those of the Army Corps of Engineers, the Soil Conservation Service's stream channelization program, and various pesticide programs—had never been spent. Funding alone guarantees nothing.

'Natural Resources & the Environment'

For Fiscal Year 1973, the Federal Budget which the Executive Branch proposed was for a total of about $246 billion, a little less than 1 percent of which ($2.45 billion) was officially earmarked for "Natural Resources and Environment" programs. These programs include pollution control, the national parks system, the operations of the Tennessee Valley Authority, and many other activities. An additional $4.133 billion is to be used for these activities, but this was not included in most official calculations because these monies come from sale of mineral rights, etc. The receipts for 1973 are unusually high, and in recent years have averaged less than half that amount. Part of the increase is due to about a billion dollars in older receipts being released for Federal use after a long-time court embargo concerning a dispute with the states over offshore oil rights.

The 1973 Natural Resources and Environment category of the Federal Budget provides for expenditures of about $446 million more than in Fiscal 1972 ($6.585 billion to $6.139 billion). Roughly, then, expenditures were intended to just about keep pace with the nation's rate of inflation. But as the money provided by taxes for these programs was to be greatly reduced —from $4.376 billion to $2.450 billion—many newspaper and magazine writers stated without qualification that the proposed budget would reduce expenditures on environmental programs by almost half.

Pollution Control and Abatement expenditures will be treated at some length in this section because basically this is the subject of Volume One. The other elements of the Natural Resources and Environment category of the Federal Budget will be treated here only briefly, but will be examined in greater detail in Volume Two, where the subject matter corresponds to these expenditures.

Not all the above natural resources and environment expenditures go toward protection of the environment; many are actually quite environmentally destructive, but are billed, for public relations purposes, as expenditures for protection. A good deal of care must be exercised in examining the more detailed breakdown of these accounts.

The accompanying table is from the *Budget* at 529.

BUDGET OUTLAYS BY FUNCTION AND AGENCY
(in millions of dollars)

Function and department or other unit	EXPENDITURES 1971 actual	EXPENDITURES 1972 estimate	EXPENDITURES 1973 estimate	NET LENDING 1971 actual	NET LENDING 1972 estimate	NET LENDING 1973 estimate
400 NATURAL RESOURCES AND ENVIRONMENT						
401 Water resources and power:						
Department of Agriculture [1]	118	136	148	*	1	------
Department of Defense—Civil [1]	1,365	1,631	1,810	------	------	------
Department of the Interior [1]	501	598	672	5	14	15
Department of State	7	10	21	------	------	------
Other independent agencies:						
Federal Power Commission	20	22	23	------	------	------
Intergovernmental agencies	*	*	*	------	------	------
Temporary study commission	2	2	1	------	------	------
Tennessee Valley Authority	367	582	507	------	------	------
Water Resources Council [1]	6	9	10	------	------	------
Total 401	2,384	2,990	3,192	5	15	15
402 Land management:						
Department of Agriculture [1]	649	726	701	------	------	------
Department of the Interior [1]	188	208	217	------	------	------
Temporary study commission	------	------	------	1	*	------
Total 402	837	935	918	------	------	------
403 Mineral resources:						
Department of the Interior [1]	130	121	103	------	------	------
404 Pollution control and abatement:						
Environmental Protection Agency [1,3]	701	1,287	1,541	------	------	------
405 Recreational resources:						
Department of the Interior [1]	479	642	640	------	------	------
409 Other natural resources programs:						
Department of Defense—Civil	*	*	1	------	------	------
Department of the Interior	133	146	172	------	------	------
Department of State	3	3	3	------	------	------
Total 409	136	149	176	------	------	------
Deductions for offsetting receipts: [6]						
Interfund and intragovernmental transaction	−1	−2	−2	------	------	------
Proprietary receipts from the public	−1,956	−1,761	−4,133	------	------	------
Total natural resources and evironment	2,711	4,361	2,435	5	15	15

*Less than $500 thousand.
[1] Includes both Federal and trust funds.
[6] Excludes offsetting receipts which have been distributed by subfunction above: 1971, $0; 1972, $0; 1973, $3 million.

parks

One phase of the expenditures for Natural Resources and Environment which is particularly emphasized by the President is full funding of the Land and Water Conservation Fund, administered by the Bureau of Outdoor Recreation in the Department of the Interior. This means that of the $300 million receipts, all will be distributed. $197 million will go to State and local governments, $76.6 million to the National Park Service, $11 million for the Forest Service, $8.5 million for the Bureau of Sport Fisheries and Wildlife, and $1.8 million to the Bureau of Land Management.

Again, as in 1972, the major expenditure from the fund goes toward local recreational development in the urban areas, as represented by the large portion of the Fund directed to State and local governments. For the most part the facilities that will benefit from these funds are already in government ownership. The money for the purchase of lands for National Parks already approved by Congress is not being appropriated. While the need for urban and local parks and development is obvious, it is being satisfied by shifting money intended for national park and recreation areas in the Land and Water Conservation Fund to a new purpose. Those wild and scenic lands suitable for parks, if not purchased in the very near future, will largely be devoured by developers. The few pieces of land that are purchased to be reclaimed have been inflated in value in anticipation of Federal purchase, so that the Federal dollar has much smaller impact. The political advantage of the "parks for the people" program is obvious. Swimming pools in urban areas paid for by the Federal government are very popular. Land acquisition for Federal parks is usually opposed by the mining and timber industries, both having substantial influence through lobbying activities. It is truly unfortunate that our nation cannot afford both types of parks.

parks

Although this scheme of utilization of the Land and Water Conservation Fund is not as advantageous environmentally as it could be, still it does provide recreational resources to urban dwellers. Other expenditures under the heading of Natural Resources and Environment cannot be even slightly justified environmentally. Some of the more obviously destructive activities which will be funded include:

- Stream channelization and river flow control by the Soil Conservation Service and the Army Corps of Engineers. $121 million for "flood prevention" goes to the Soil Conservation Service to continue the construction of small watershed projects and begin 75 new dams. $1.708 billion will go to the Corps of Engineers for the same activities connected with large projects. This is an increase of nearly $208 million for the Corps.
- Research and development expenditures of $45 million by the Bureau of Mines, Office of Coal Research to find more efficient ways of mining and using coal. There could be more direct subsidy payments to the coal industry, but this certainly isn't terribly indirect.
- Acceleration of the program to lease the rights to the Outer Continental Shelf (a portion of the $92 million to the Bureau of Land Management). Under this program the oil industry, although not having proved that it can protect the environment from destructive oil pollution of the sea, will acquire the rights to begin exploration and exploitation of whatever natural resources can be found on earth's last frontier.

In reference to the above two items, the following official word on the subject is quoted from page 112 of the *Budget*:

mineral resources

> Mineral programs include research and resource development for coal, petroleum, oil shale, and other minerals, mining research, metallurgy research, and mineral investigations.
>
> Outlays for these programs in 1973 will be $103 million. Program increases for 1973 are aimed at environmental problems. Increased outlays of $11 million will permit pilot plant work on alternative processes for changing coal into fuel gas, in order to meet growing energy demands and reduce pollution. Research will also be conducted on the economic feasibility of removing sulfur dioxide from metal smelter gases. An increase of $7 million is provided for the proposed mined land regulation program, which will reduce the adverse environmental effects of mining operations. Legislation is also proposed to repeal the Mining Law of 1872, the Minerals Leasing Act of 1920, and related acts, and to substitute laws which will require increased use of competitive sales for minerals disposals, will improve land managers' control of minerals activities, and will require that minerals exploration and production on the public domain and acquired lands meet strengthened requirements for environmental safeguards.
>
> ***Other natural resources programs.***—These programs include topographic surveys and mapping, geological and mineral resource surveys and mapping, and water resources investigations. Outlays for these programs in 1973 will increase by $26 million to $176 million.
>
> Increased funds are provided for research on earthquake prediction and control, for processing of data from the experimental earth

resources technology satellite to be launched in 1972, and to investigate and evaluate geothermal resources, a potential source of power that is now largely unused. Funds are also provided to accelerate Outer Continental Shelf oil and gas leasing, and improve environmental safeguards for such leases.

---

pesticides

Pesticides are a particularly difficult subject to analyze from a budgetary point of view. The official view, like that on radioactive fallout, has changed so that practices once advocated without restraint are now carried out more circumspectly (at least as far as the accompanying rhetoric is concerned). But there is no doubt that the governmental subsidies to the big chemical firms, in the form of pesticides research and promotion, are scores of times greater than any recently-born attempt to limit use of these poisons.

The problem of interpretation is simple: the answer is difficult. Programs that for years have promoted pesticide use are re-labeled "activities to reduce or avoid the use of pesticides." Thus, the *Special Analyses'* authors (p. 300) find a total of $107 million devoted to this purpose ($51 million in a graph, $66 million additional mentioned in text), while the authors of the *Budget in Brief* pp. 52–53, apparently failed completely to notice that any money was being spent for such environmentally protective purposes.

The indices to the *Budget* and *Appendix* are remarkably uninformative on this subject.

Astonishingly enough, the same indices are even more silent concerning pesticide development or pest control, although the Federal government continues to spend 9-figure sums annually in this field. This paradox will be discussed further in the section of this work devoted to pesticides. (*See* Vol. 2.)

Some of the pesticides research will be to find poisons which are less harmful to the environment as a whole. But separating this research from that which is relatively unmindful of environmental damage is extremely difficult. It would be a serious mistake to consider any agency so vast as the Department of Agriculture—or the Environmental Protection Agency, for that matter—to be monolithic. Obviously almost any pesticide research could have either environmentally beneficial or harmful effects, depending upon the use to which it is put.

But what is clearly lacking in the Federal government is sufficient commitment to a search for alternate crop-protection methods. So much is said about pesticides that few persons are even aware that certain plants, in proximity to other plants, will protect them (through their smells) from harmful insects. Yet plant odors are still ignored: the commercial potential has not been seen. More work, but still too little, has been done on breeding defective insects (to block effective mating) and insects which protect plants by eating other insects or their eggs.

According to an analysis in the February 2, 1972 issue of the Conservation Foundation's *CF Newsletter,* the total Environmental Protection Agency's pesticide budget would be $23.1 million in Fiscal 1973, compared with $22.3 million the year before. Other studies of pesticides are made by the Food and Drug and Administration, the National Science Foundation, and several agencies of the Department of Agriculture, though all of these programs are not aimed at limiting the use of pesticides.

An "integrated pest-management research and development program" has been ordered formed by the agencies mentioned above, with total funding (including part of the mentioned EPA funds) of $11.7 million. This is a small amount compared with the sums to be spent on other pesticide research and promotion, but at least in theory is a hopeful sign. The Agriculture Department also pays large sums—$10,711,000 budgeted for Fiscal 1973 (*Budget* at 235) to compensate dairymen and beekeepers for the contamination of their products or death of their bees due to use of approved pesticides.

transportation

Highways continue to receive the most transportation money—$4.4 billion in Fiscal 1973—but this heavy emphasis has finally begun to subside slightly. The 1973 highway figure is down 11.6 percent from 1972, while urban mass transit expenditures are increased to $1 billion—up from $334 million in 1971 and $606 million in 1972. Of this $1 billion, $841 million is for buses and rail passenger cars. In addition, research on transportation —mostly "personal rapid transit"—would increase to $115 million from $62 million in 1972. The tax money subsidies to the present aircraft companies (which were formed almost exclusively with government-supplied funds) are, though often indirectly, much greater. (The airline industry which purchases their wares is also subsidized.) The Federal government recently guaranteed a loan of $250 million to the Lockhead Corp.

energy resources

Large increases were proposed in funding for the dangerous Liquid Metal Fast Breeder Reactor ($158 million in 1972 to $182 million in 1973) despite the fact that the Atomic Energy Commission still hasn't found any even slightly reasonable solution as to what to do with its immense amounts of wastes which are lethal for thousands of years. (The AEC's latest idea is to store these wastes, with half-lives of 24,000 years, in tank farms. See most any newspaper for May 19, 1972, including the *Wall Street Journal* at 18.) Such wastes are produced by all present atomic reactors, but the problem grows with each plant, making it steadily more possible to contaminate the entire planet.

Other than nuclear power, the only really substantial sums are for the gasification of coal ($39 million), which would almost certainly entail increased strip-mining, and for an acceleration of the leasing of offshore gas and oil ($18 million).

Solar power, which has far greater potential than most people realize, is again virtually ignored, although the funds have at least been raised from zero a few years ago to $4 million, all to the National Science Foundation. Adequate use of solar energy would destroy the present fuel companies, which control not only petroleum, but a great deal of the coal and nuclear fuel industries as well. (*See* Volume Two.)

reporting

Reporting on the Environment

The *Special Analyses* of the Budget contains a section on "Understnding, Describing, and Predicting the Environment." This is a catch-all category for various research and reporting activities concerned with the natural world, including the weather. Few of these activities are concerned with protecting the environment (even indirectly, as through research) in the sense used throughout this treatise. Indeed, the results of a considerable portion of the study done here may prove to be environmentally destructive. Note that such activities as the predicting of weather conditions (by the military's own weather service) for the dropping of bombs or pesticides in Vietnam are included. Various government expenditures to assist the natural resource exploitative industries also are included.

UNDERSTANDING, DESCRIBING, AND PREDICTING THE ENVIRONMENT[1,2]

Federal agencies conduct a wide variety of activities to understand, describe, and predict environmental conditions. Objectives range from the provision of routine weather forecasts to the scientific understanding of complex ecological systems. Funding for these activities will increase in 1973.

[In millions of dollars]

	1970 actual	*1971 actual*	*1972 estimate*	*1973 estimate*
Budget authority	719	914	1,031	1,101
Obligations	710	914	1,050	1,117
Outlays	702	856	951	1,051

[1] This section excludes activities reported under pollution control and abatement.
[2] Funding data are not available for 1969 on a basis comparable to 1970–73.

"Pollution Control & Abatement"

A foolish consistency is the hobgoblin of little minds.
—Emerson (*Self-Reliance*)

four views

The term "Pollution Control and Abatement" is used in the text or tables of both the Fiscal 1973 Federal *Budget* and its companion volume, the *Special Analyses.* It also serves as a caption to a graph on page 28 of the *Budget.* A similar term, "Abatement and Control," in reference to activities of the Environmental Protection Agency, is used in the separately published *Appendix* to the Budget. In each of the four cases, the figure cited for expenditures in the category mentioned is considerably different. This fact, though perhaps annoying to non-masochists, at least saved scores of journalists from writing tritely similar reports. The lack of uniformity alone was no lack of virtue: none of the figures (as labeled) could reasonably be regarded as "correct."

The key to the variety seems to have been semantic, rather than mathematical. With more accurate identification, each of the figures used in the text, tables or graphs may be useful. This assumes, of course, that there were no similar mistakes in gathering the preliminary figures not available for examination.

First View

On page 107 of the *Budget,* the figure $1.541 billion is calculable for Pollution Control and Abatement outlays from this listing of component expenditures:

[In millions of dollars]

Program or agency	Outlays 1971 actual	Outlays 1972 estimate	Outlays 1973 estimate	Recommended budget authority for 1973[1]
Pollution control and abatement:				
Sewage plant construction grants	478	908	1,100	2,000
Other present programs[3]	223	379	419	443
Proposed legislation	-------	-------	22	35

On page 108 of the *Budget,* we find that the figure calculated from the above is identical to that of the total Environmental Protection Agency expenditures, including $1.1 billion in grants to state and local governments for construction of municipal sewage treatment facilities:

Pollution control and abatement.—Environmental Protection Agency programs deal with problems of air, water, and noise pollution, solid waste management, use of pesticides, and radiation. Outlays for these programs will increase by $254 million in 1973 to $1,541 million.

The principal increase will occur in Federal grants to municipalities for the construction of sewage treatment plants. Outlays for this program will rise from $908 million in 1972 to $1,100 million in 1973. This continues the Administration's commitment to finance the full Federal share of the backlog of municipal sewage treatment plant construction.

Outlays for existing programs other than construction grants will increase by $40 million in 1973, to $419 million. Additional outlays of $22 million are also provided for proposed legislation relating to the regulation of ocean dumping, toxic substances, pesticides, and noise.

End quote.

Second View

The authors of the *Appendix* chose to look at EPA's expenditures differently, making the following breakdown, which excludes the sewage treatment grants mentioned above:

ENVIRONMENTAL PROTECTION AGENCY

Program and Financing (in thousands of dollars)

Identification code 20-00-0100-0-1-404	1971 actual	1972 est.	1973 est.
Program by activities:			
1. Research and development	134,013	167,966	178,601
2. Abatement and control	116,303	191,792	205,473
3. Enforcement	8,205	20,783	28,979
4. Facilities	1,087	2,812	36,094
5. Program direction and support	23,782	34,411	40,881
Total programs costs—obligations	283,390	417,764	490,028

EPA: view from the *Appendix* to the Budget

1. *Research and development.*—Activities deal with causes, sources, transport, fate, and effects of pollutants in ecological systems; and development of monitoring technology and pollution control criteria used in establishing standards and regulations. Several new efforts will be undertaken to define pollution control objectives and cost-effective solutions. Research will be expanded in health effects of air pollution and urban-regional scale modeling of relationships among air pollution emissions, atmospheric conditions, and ambient air quality. Funds will also support cost-sharing arrangements with industry to develop sulfur oxide control technology. Solid waste activities are being reoriented to focus upon economic and institutional constraints. A new strategy will be developed to encourage greater private sector involvement in the development and application of pollution control technology. Activities are conducted under grants, contracts, and other agreements involving universities, industry, nonprofit organizations, State and local governments, other Federal agencies, and through activities at EPA's laboratories and field locations.

2. *Abatement and control.*—Planning grants and control agency support grants are awarded to State, regional, and local agencies for planning, establishing, and improving environmental quality programs. Monitoring and surveillance are performed to determine baseline quality conditions, to measure pollutants, and to evaluate the performance of control devices. Pollution prevention, control, and abatement standards are generally established in cooperation with State and local agencies. Technical assistance is provided to Federal agencies, States, interstate regions, local communities, and industry. Environmental impact statements by Federal agencies are reviewed and evaluated. Education and training are supported through grants and other forms of assistance and in-house training programs are conducted for personnel of Federal, State, and local governments, industry, and educational institutions. Costs for services performed in the form of direct training activities and pesticides registration will be offset by charges.

3. *Enforcement.*—This activity includes the certification and permit programs; the enforcement of environmental pollution standards, including the gathering and preparation of evidential data and the conduct of enforcement proceedings; and legal services for the agency.

4. *Facilities.*—This activity provides for construction of laboratory facilities and alterations, repairs, and improvements to existing facilities.

5. *Program direction and support.*—This activity includes executive direction and leadership for all programs and support in such areas as public, legislative, and international affairs, equal employment opportunity, coordination of environmental impact statements and Federal agency pollution control activities, program planning, review and evaluation, economic analysis, budgeting, accounting, auditing, personnel management, organizational analysis, ADP operations, grants and contracting policy, facilities management, and other housekeeping activities. Activities involving analysis of economic input of pollution control activity are being greatly expanded. This activity also includes direction and leadership for all programs under the management of 10 regional administrators, and provision of administrative support services.

COMMENT

Thus, one official view is that the EPA budget is the total of Federal pollution abatement expenditures, while a second official view holds that only a small portion of the EPA budget is for that purpose. Two additional official government views are treated at page Introduction-74.

Neither of the above views, of course, is necessarily correct or incorrect: clearly most of what the Environmental Protection Agency does is somehow related to pollution control, and most Federal activity in this field is handled by EPA. Hence, there is some justification, if only that of simplicity, in regarding the EPA budget as synonymous with pollution control. The authors of the *Budget* seem to take this view throughout; the $1.541 billion figure is used for Pollution Control and Abatement in the general Budget breakdowns, and in *The Budget in Brief* (pp. 52-53).

EPA & the Budget

Since the Environmental Protection Agency's expenditures are being classified, at least by some members of the government, as synonymous with Federal pollution control and abatement outlays, a closer look at EPA's budget is in order.

In the 570-page *Budget,* the Environmental Protection Agency is mentioned six times, according to the index. On the first reference, we find only that EPA was established in 1970; on the second, there is no reference; on the third we find the total EPA expenditures, including the grants program; on the fourth, that the National Bureau of Standards will work with EPA in developing measuring devices; on the fifth, there again is no mention, and on the sixth, we get a chart of six items, three of which contain no entries for the past two years, plus summaries of the above. This chart is just slightly larger than that of the Battle Monuments Commission, and about 60 percent as large as the Smithsonian Institution's.

The *Appendix* tells us more about the Environmental Protection Agency, but still refrains from boring us with such details as a breakdown by program. Instead, we learn that about $11 million in general funds and $377,000 in intragovernmental exchanges are alloted for EPA travel and transportation of persons, but we learn nothing of what various programs, with two exceptions, are costing us. The exceptions are the sewage treatment grants program, and the pesticide certification program. In addition to a one-page list of higher-level job slots and summary of pay levels, 3½ of the 1,102 pages of the *Appendix* are devoted to the Environmental Protection Agency. Among the comparatively useful facts we can learn by shuffling between the several tables available is that there are funds for about 8,500 permanent employees and the equivalent of 811 other full-time jobs after adding up the hours of part-timers or temporary workers. All but about 300 of these positions come under the Government Service (GS) pay categories, and the average pay for these jobs was $13,562. There were seven positions higher than the GS levels, these paying $38,000 to $42,500.

By comparison, the Department of Commerce's Economic Development Administration, with expenditures of $161 million, has 7¼ pages in the main section of the *Appendix*, plus the job slot summary elsewhere. Less surprisingly, the Social and Economic Statistics Administration, with total outlays of $35 million, has eight full pages. Bulk alone, of course, means little; but so do statistics that are overly conglomerated.

The *Special Analyses* adds nothing.

Because of the paucity of information in the expected sources, the researcher is left with the task of assembling the EPA Humpty Dumpty from the shards of newspaper clippings, whose writers were supplied with press releases. From these we gather that:

- *Relative emphasis:* Without allowance for a special funding of $22 million to be specified later by the Administration, EPA's expenditures, excluding the sewage treatment grants program, could be divided as follows: air, 43.8 percent; water, 41.5 percent; solid wastes, 5.9 percent; pesticides, 5.9 percent; radiation, 2.6 percent, and noise, 0.3 percent. The additional $22 million was to be divided among water, pesticides, toxic substances, ocean dumping, and noise. The above figures are based on the entire EPA operations budget, not merely those in the pollution control and abatement category.

- *Air pollution:* expenditures would be raised from $145.7 million in 1972 to $168.2 million in 1973, but this newer figure is still only a fraction of the $490 million authorized for 1973. There has been some comment that this sum will not permit full enforcement of the 1970 Clean Air Act.

• *Water Pollution:* although the program to fund local sewage treatment plants construction would be greater by $190 million than in 1972 (for a total of $1.1 billion), the total is still far less than Congress has requested be spent. There is considerable bitterness that in past years, the Executive branch has withheld a large part of the money Congress directed be spent. It was expected that this item might be one Congress might choose to dispute with the President, although he holds the reins through ability to again refuse to spend the funds. In this, however, it was felt that similar actions were unlikely in an election year.

In addition to the grants for the construction of municipal sewage treatment plants, the EPA water pollution operations budget includes total expenditures of $154.6 million, including $20.6 million in grants to state agencies, $25.3 million for the development of waste water treatment and control technology, $6.2 million for eutrophication and lake studies, and $10.3 million for enforcement.

• *Solid Wastes:* No other environmental program has had a difference of such a high percentage between the authorization and the proposed outlays. In Fiscal 1973, the authorization is $216 million, but the proposed spending is $23.1 million or $20.5 million, depending on which source you trust. This is a reduction of either $12 or $15 million from 1972, and effectively prevents any serious Federal effort in this field.

Third View

The figure labeled Pollution Control and Abatement in the graph on page 28 of the *Budget* (about $1.9 billion) probably stems from the addition of the entire Environmental Protection Agency budget (including the $1.1 billion sewage treatment grants program) and the $272 million scheduled for pollution abatement at Federal facilities. However, no explanation is supplied.

Fourth View

The writers of the *Special Analyses,* use the term Pollution Control and Abatement (pp. 296–300) to represent some quite different activities from those found by the writers of the *Budget.* The phrase here encompasses the entire budget of the Environmental Protection Agency (including the sewage treatment grants program) and $3 million deducted in other mentions of the EPA budget because of offsetting receipts. It also includes $272 million for abatement of pollution at Federal facilities, and $624 million in assorted programs proportedly related to pollution control or abatement, including research. These are the figures they arrive at:

POLLUTION CONTROL AND ABATEMENT ACTIVITIES

(in millions of dollars)

Type of activity	Budget authority			Outlays		
	1971 actual	1972 estimate	1973 estimate	1971 actual	1972 estimate	1973 estimate
Financial aid to State and local governments	1,082	2,121	2,123	554	1,014	1,250
Research and development	442	516	599	366	474	561
Federal abatement and control operations	136	198	219	92	189	206
Manpower development	19	18	15	17	18	14
Reduce pollution from Federal facilities	116	280	315	74	186	272
Other pollution control and abatement activities	49	124	113	45	94	115
Separate transmittal [1]	--------	--------	35	--------	--------	22
Total	**1,823**	**3,258**	**3,419**	**1,149**	**1,975**	**2,440**

[1] Not reflected in preceding activity lines are proposals that will be transmitted subsequently for an estimated $35 million in budget authority and $22 million in outlays in 1973 for EPA for implementing legislation proposed by the administration.

The justification, or lack of it, for including the entire EPA budget in the tables labeled Pollution Control and Abatement has already been discussed. What about the rest? The $272 million for abatement activities at Federal facilities is perhaps the most directly efficient Federal clean-up money spent. Still, unless it is made clear that this is a component of a general abatement expenditures figure, it could be misleading.

There is some evidence that the Federal government is seriously attempting to abate pollution from Federal facilities. This is one of the few areas of environmental concern in which appropriations exceed actual expenditures (and the Office of Management and Budget is not restricting expenditures). Appropriations for Fiscal Year 1971 were $116 million; for FY 1972, $280 million; for FY 1973, they will probably be $315 million, though with expenditures of only $272 million. The actual expenditures for those years were $532 million. The money that was spent in FY 1971 and FY 1972 exceeded the original projected total costs of clean-up of $359 million.

Despite these expenditures, many Federal facilities are working toward clean-up deadlines as far ahead as 1977, while some projects may not be completed until several years beyond that date.

See Hill, Gladwin, "Officials Say Goal Is In Sight In Drive To Stop Pollution By Government Facilities," *The New York Times,* May 15, 1972 at C40.

The question of the remaining $624 million cannot be resolved simply by appending a footnote or inserting a very brief explanation. The *Special Analyses* does attempt an explanation through the brief prose passages which follow. But these are not adequate. An attempt to locate the corresponding figures in the agency breakdowns in the *Appendix* was far less fruitful than one might have hoped, since the categories were not the same, and nothing identified as pollution control programs could be found. This is not to say that the programs selected could not justifiably be termed abatement programs under another system of classification. But the overall accuracy of these *Special Analyses* figures cannot be checked.

Nevertheless, some extremely doubtful programs are identifiably included by the *Special Analyses* under Pollution Control and Abatement. Note that for the Department of Defense "reduction of smoke levels in propellants" is included, as is a program (incompletely identified) for the development of an all-terrain vehicle, now classified as "low pollution" engine development. Though this name change may be no lie, it is nevertheless deceptive, since the research and development would have been funded regardless of any chance environmental benefits.

The Department of Transportation's noise program may be regarded as a subsidy to airlines. Only a tiny fraction of total Federal noise pollution research is related to anything but jet aircraft. The Department of Agriculture's pesticide programs included here have traditionally been to encourage the use of pesticides. In addition, some of the agencies, such as the Atomic Energy Commission, are adding undisposable lethal substances to the world at such a rate that no amount of pollution control or abatement can ever result in a net gain.

We quote from the Special Analyses at 298-299; the figures placed alongside are from an accompanying table and explain the agencies' purported expeditures for pollution control and abatement:

For example, the *Department of Defense* will continue to expand its R. & D. and action programs to reduce pollution from its industrial production facilities, military bases, naval vessels, aircraft, and jet engine test facilities. Accomplishments include development of a new process for disposal of deteriorated explosives, development of biodegradable metal cleaners, reduction of smoke levels in propellants, and the development of a low pollution engine that is now being tested for use in automobiles. — $235 million

The *Atomic Energy Commission* will continue its major program of research, development, and monitoring relating to effects of ionizing radiation. Increases in 1973 are largely for research on the effects of — $154 million thermal alteration of lakes, streams, and estuaries and to provide information on the amount and nature of radioactivity and other potential pollutants released to the environment.

$139 million The *Department of Agriculture* makes grants and loans for waste treatment facilities in smaller localities and conducts research on agriculturally related pollution such as pesticides, animal and crop processing wastes and fertilizer and plant nutrients. Progress has been made in reducing pollution from facilities in National forests by a minimization of stream pollution and sediment, and prevention of logging residue disposition in stream channels.

$82 million The *Department of the Interior* will continue research relating to pollution sources and effects, will expand activities to reduce pollution from facilities in the national parks, and will increase research under pilot plant programs to develop methods of converting coal to fuel gas with less pollution.

$56 million The *Corps of Engineers* will continue construction of dikes for the containment of polluted material dredged from Great Lakes harbors.

$79 million The *Department of Transportation* will increase funding for work on reducing aircraft engine noise, studying environmental effects of aircraft, and reducing pollution from Coast Guard facilities.

$30 million The *Department of Commerce* provides grants for waste treatment facilities from the Economic Development Administration. The National Oceanic and Atmospheric Administration conducts environmental monitoring and prediction activities related to air and water pollution. The National Bureau of Standards defines and tests environmental standards and measurements.

$5 million The *General Services Administration* will continue work on pollution reduction at Federal installations using funds appropriated in previous years.

$29 million The *National Aeronautics and Space Administration* activities consist primarily of research and development on reduction of aircraft noise.

End quote.

Since the Government's analysts obviously came to different conclusions regarding how much of our Federal tax money is spent for pollution control and abatement, it may be a useful exercise for the reader to try a hand at coming up with yet another figure.

If, simply by definition, we exclude abatement activities at Federal facilities and research, we are left with, above all (financially) the $1.1 billion sewage treatment grants (though remembering that the Executive branch for several years has actually been very slow in spending the funds allocated for this program). We might add to that the part of the Environmental Protection Agency's expenditures that were classified as abatement and control activities in the *Appendix*—$205.5 million—or attempt to guess just how much real abatement activity occurs there.

There would be some logic in adding also a portion of the budget of the Department of Justice's Lands and Natural Resources Division ($5,334,000, which includes all civil suits relating to land matters, Indian Affairs, and other resources matters as well as pollution abatement). But that division also spends much of its energies defending environmentally destructive governmental activities, making much more detailed information necessary if it is to have any meaning in this context.

Programs which surprisingly seem to be on no one's list of Federal governmental pollution control activities are those for assistance in constructing sewer and water systems. The reason for this exclusion is well stated below in an excerpt from the *Special Analyses* (pp. 307-8). But the coincidental environmental benefits should not be ignored by those seeking a real understanding of the effects of the Federal government on pollution control.

Sewer and Water Programs

Assistance for the construction of sewer and water systems is provided through Federal grants, direct loans and insured loans. The primary objective of Federal sewer and water programs is not pollution control, but rather urban or rural development. To the extent assisted sewer projects provide environmental benefits, they do so as a result of their association with waste treatment and other abatement programs.

[In millions of dollars]

	1969 est.	1970 actual	1971 actual	1972 est.	1973 est.
Budget authority	295	252	573	765	150
Obligations	420	409	546	622	610
Outlays	300	364	331	465	550

Grants to finance water system and sewerline construction are made by five Federal agencies. The *Department of Housing and Urban Development* provides assistance for basic sewer and water facilities as part of its community development efforts. Approximately 400 grant reservations will be made in both 1972 and 1973. In addition, some public facility loans will be made to finance sewer and water facilities construction in each of these years. Outlays will increase in 1973 by 15%, from $155 million to $177 million. Grant reservations under HUD's water and sewer program will continue at the $200 million level in 1973. Unused balances are sufficient to fund the program in 1973, so no additional appropriation is necessary. Increases in this program have been limited, as Federal funds have been considered more important to expand the waste treatment construction program.

The *Department of Agriculture* provides grants and loans for basic water and waste facilities in rural communities with population not in excess of 5,500 people. The total program level—grants and loans—increased from $306 million in 1971 to $342 million in 1972 and 1973. Loans total $300 million in 1973. The number of rural families benefiting from the program increases from 266 thousand in 1970 to 500 thousand in 1973. Outlays (after deducting the repayment of prior year loans) will increase by 24% in 1973, from $231 million to $287 million.

The *Department of Commerce* provides assistance to municipalities as a part of its economic development efforts. Outlays will increase by 9% from $66 million in 1972 to $72 million in 1973. Other agencies providing sewer and water system grants are the Appalachian Regional Commission and the Department of the Interior (for the trust territory).

End quote.

Since coincidental effects on pollution control are being discussed, it should also not be overlooked that many Federal programs have a partial or total negative effect. Examples include not only the military's pesticide and other plant- and land-destruction programs in Vietnam, but also the Federal highway construction grants, scheduled to amount to $4.22 billion in Fiscal 1973.

On the environmentally beneficial side, there are several relatively small pollution control programs in agencies other than the Environmental Protection Agency. One of these is the Coast Guard's oil-spills search program. Patrols for this purpose are scheduled to rise from 3,000 in Fiscal 1972 to 6,000 in Fiscal 1973 (*Appendix* p. 689). A small program run by the Department of Commerce's Economic Development Administration gives grants, for, among other things, water pollution control facilities for the treatment of industrial wastes. But the specific expenditures involved in such programs are very rarely made clear in the *Budget,* the *Appendix,* or the *Special Analyses.* A guess is that all of these mini-programs devoted truly to pollution abatement total less than $40 million, though this clearly conflicts with the under-explained claims of the *Special Analyses* in the materials republished above.

budgeting summation

What this really shows is that the determination of what is a pollution-controlling activity is not simple. The locating of housing and stores to encourage people to walk rather than to ride their cars would be an example of a real pollution-controlling activity, yet would not likely be listed under Pollution Control and Abatement. In short, pollution control is dependent on life style, and many decisions besides those to build a sewage treatment plant or purchase smokeless propellants affect such control. The Federal Budget reflects literally hundreds of thousands of such life-style decisions.

i. Federal Government agencies dealing with the environment

The key Federal effort to protect the environment is centered in the **Environmental Protection Agency** (EPA), which has already been discussed in connection with the Federal Budget on pages Introduction 72-74. Additional information is furnished below. Another Federal agency with important environmental protection activities is the **Council on Environmental Quality** which is discussed on page One-48, 49 in connection with its mandate under the National Environmental Protection Act of 1969 and the Environmental Quality Act of 1970.

The **National Oceanic and Atmospheric Administration** is the key agency in regard to protecting the Oceans. It is discussed below within the Section on the Department of Commerce.

The **Department of the Interior**, once the focus for nearly all Federal environment protection operations, still carries on several important such activities, as well as supervising use of public lands.

The **Army Corps of Engineers** and the **Department of Agriculture** both preserve and destroy resources with different hands, and their operations should not be overlocked.

Except for EPA, treated first because of its preeminence, the agencies are listed alphabetically in four groups: *Agencies of the Executive Office of the President; Departments under the Executive Branch; Independent Agencies,* and *Selected Boards and Commissions.*

It should be remembered that no such list can be complete, since, under the National Environmental Policy Act (See Chapter One), all Federal agencies must weigh the environmental impact of their operations. Thus even regulatory agencies such as the Interstate Commerce Commission and Federal Communications Commission may engage in environmental protection.

Standard references are the materials mentioned in the Section on the Federal Budget (See Introduction-64) and the United States Government Organization Manual (GPO, $3.00 *paper*) from which most of the following has been taken. See also the listings on pp. Appendix One-8-12 concerning Federal Government agencies having expertise under the National Environmental Policy Act.

Environmental Protection Agency Regions

Regional Offices	Phone	States covered
Boston, Massachusetts 02203	617–223–7210	Connecticut, Maine, Massachusetts, New Hampshire, Rhode Island, Vermont
New York, New York 10007	212–264–2525	New Jersey, New York, Puerto Rico, Virgin Islands
Philadelphia, Pa. 19106	215–597–9151	Delaware, Maryland, Pennsylvania, Virginia, West Virginia, D.C.
Atlanta, Georgia 30309	404–526–5727	Alabama, Florida, Georgia, Kentucky, Mississippi, North Carolina, South Carolina, Tennessee
Chicago, Illinois 60606	312–353–5250	Illinois, Indiana, Michigan, Minnesota, Ohio, Wisconsin
Dallas, Texas 75202	214–749–2827	Arkansas, Louisiana, New Mexico, Oklahoma, Texas
Kansas City, Missouri 64106	816–374–5493	Iowa, Kansas, Missouri, Nebraska
Denver, Colorado 80203	303–837–3895	Colorado, Montana, North Dakota, South Dakota, Utah, Wyoming
San Francisco, Calif. 94102	415–556–4303	Arizona, California, Hawaii, Nevada, American Samoa, Guam, Trust Territories of Pacific Islands, Wake Island
Seattle, Washington 98101	206–442–1200	Alaska, Idaho, Oregon, Washington

Environmental Protection Agency

The description of the Environmental Protection Agency which follows is from an EPA booklet, "Toward a New Environmental Ethic," GPO, September, 1971:

The United States Environmental Protection Agency was established December 2, 1970, bringing together for the first time in a single agency the major environmental control programs of the Federal government. EPA is charged with mounting an integrated, coordinated attack on the environmental problems of air and water pollution, solid wastes management, pesticides, radiation, and noise.

Regional Offices are staffed by specialists in each program area and headed by a Regional Administrator possessing broad authority to act for EPA in matters within his jurisdiction.

EPA's creation marked the end of the piecemeal approach to our nation's environmental problems which has, so often in the past, inhibited progress—or merely substituted one form of pollution for another.

standards-setting and enforcement

The United States Environmental Protection Agency is, first and foremost, a regulatory agency, with responsibilities for establishing and enforcing environmental standards, within the limits of its various statutory authorities.

Establishment of standards is central to the whole pollution control effort, for it is in this way that we define what each of us may and may not do to the environment on which we all depend.

The standards set by EPA (in some cases, in cooperation with the States) have the force of law. They define the kinds of levels of pollutants which must be prevented from entering our air and water, and establish time-tables for achieving the prescribed quality. They set limits on radiation emissions and pesticide residues. Enforcement of environmental standards is, under certain laws, shared with the States, the Federal government acting only when the State fails to do so; in other instances, the Federal government has primary enforcement authority.

research and monitoring

EPA is also a research body, monitoring and analyzing the environment and conducting scientific studies into the causes and effects of pollution, the techniques of pollution control, and the environmental consequences of man's actions.

Effective action, particularly in standards-setting and enforcement, requires that EPA have sound data on what is being introduced into the environment, its impact on ecological stability, on human health, and on other factors important to human life. By close coordination of its various research programs, EPA strives to develop a synthesis of knowledge from the biological, physical and social sciences which can be interpreted in terms of total human and environmental needs.

Major aims of the Agency's research efforts at this time include:

- Expansion and improvement of environmental monitoring and surveillance to provide baselines of environmental quality.
- Advancement of understanding of long-term exposures to contaminants, of sub-acute or delayed effects on human and other organisms, of the combined and synergistic actions of chemical, biological, and physical stresses.
- Acceleration of progress in applied research into the control of pollutants, the recycling of so-called "wastes," and the development of sophisticated, non-polluting production processes.
- Improved assessment of trends of technical and social change and potential effects—first, second, and even third-order effects—on environmental quality.

review of federal activities

To ensure full consideration of environmental factors in Federal decision-making, each Federal agency is required to submit to the President's Council on Environmental Quality an *environmental impact statement* on any proposal for legislation or other major action significantly affecting the quality of the human environment. This must include:

- the environmental impact of the proposed action,
- any adverse environmental effects which cannot be avoided should the proposal be implemented,
- alternatives to the proposed action,
- the relationship between local short-term uses of man's environment and the maintenance and enhancement of long-term productivity, and
- any irreversible and irretrievable commitments of resources which would be involved in the proposed action should it be implemented.

Before filing with the Council, the statement must be circulated in draft to EPA and other appropriate federal, state, and local environmental agencies for their comments. These must accompany the final statement.

The final environmental impact statement, together with all comments, must be made available to the Congress and the public by the originating agency. Federal agencies must insure the fullest practicable provision of timely public information and understanding of the environmental impact of federal plans and programs including, whenever appropriate, public hearings.

EPA is specifically charged with making public its written comments on environmental impact statements and with publishing its determinations when these hold that a proposal is unsatisfactory from the standpoint of public health or welfare or environmental quality.

The Council on Environmental Quality considers all the evidence and advises the President as to the best course of action.

- Improved understanding of the transport of materials through the environment; their passage through the media of air, water, and land; their ability to cross the various interfaces; and their various changes of state that can make them innocuous at one point and hazardous at another.

In addition to performing research in its own laboratories in various locations throughout the country, EPA, through grants and contracts, supports the studies of scientists in universities and other research institutions. The Agency also consolidates and evaluates information as it is developed throughout the scientific community to develop the best possible scientific *base* for environmental action.

technical and financial assistance

EPA serves also as a catalyst for environmental protection efforts at all levels of government by providing technical and financial assistance to state, regional, and local jurisdictions.

EPA publishes and gives wide distribution to its technical and scientific findings in all program areas, to advance the total body of scientific knowledge and hasten the application of new, proven pollution-control techniques.

Its "Technology Transfer" program is specifically designed to bridge the gap between the development and application of new techniques to control pollution. Workshops and seminars are held for state and local officials, design engineers, industrial representatives, and the public to introduce them to new, practicable control technology; technical bulletins and design manuals are widely disseminated.

Through EPA's ten Regional Offices, prompt assistance is given to State and local authorities, industries, and citizens in the solution of technical problems.

In several program areas, Federal funds are made available for the construction and operation of facilities to reduce pollution and to demonstrate new technology. Financial assistance is also provided for state and local governments to aid their environmental control programs.

manpower development

EPA provides training both in its own extensive training facilities and in universities and other educational institutions, to help develop the highly skilled manpower the Nation needs to combat environmental problems. Technical training in control techniques and program management is given to employees of state and local governments, industry, and other organizations. Support is given to universities for environmental courses. Fellowships are available to qualified students for advanced training.

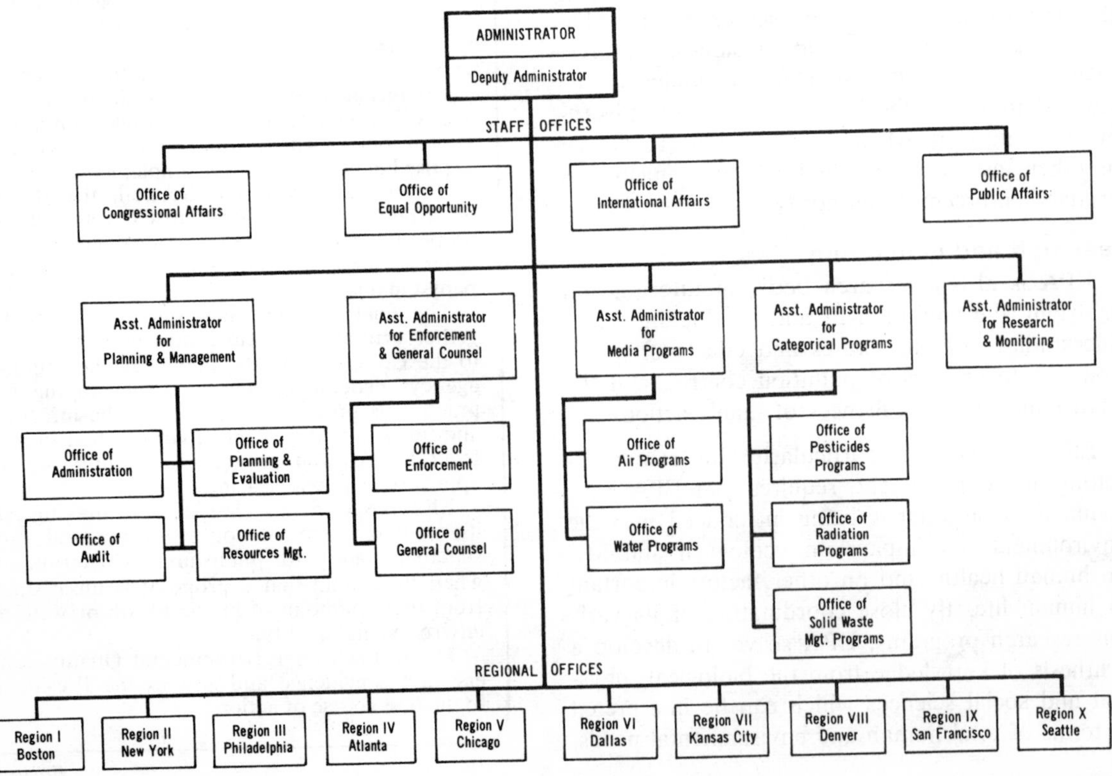

permanent Federal agencies, Executive Office of the President

Council on Environmental Quality

722 Jackson Place NW., Washington, D.C. 20006. Phone, 202—382-1415

Chairman	Russell E. Train.
Member	Robert Cahn.
Member	Dr. Gordon J. F. MacDonald.
Secretary	Boyd H. Gibbons III.

CREATION AND PURPOSE.—The Council on Environmental Quality was established by the National Environmental Policy Act of 1969 (83 Stat. 852; 42 U.S.C. 4321 et seq.), to formulate and recommend national policies to promote the improvement of the quality of the environment. The Office of Environmental Quality, which provides staff for the Council, was subsequently established by title II of the Environmental Quality Improvement Act of 1970 (84 Stat. 114; 42 U.S.C. 4372).

ORGANIZATION.—The Council consists of three members appointed by the President by and with the advice and consent of the Senate. One of the members is designated by the President as Chairman. The Council is located within the Executive Office of the President.

ACTIVITIES.—The Council develops and recommends to the President national policies which promote environmental quality, performs a continuing analysis of changes or trends in the national environment, and assists the President in the preparation of the annual environmental quality report to the Congress.

For further information, contact the Information Office, Council on Environmental Quality, Executive Office Building, Washington, D.C. 20506. Phone, 202—395-3266.

See also discussion on pages One-48 & 49.

Office of Management and Budget

Executive Office Building, Washington, D.C. 20503. Phone, 202—395-3000

The Office's functions include the following:

1. To aid the President to bring about more efficient and economical conduct of Government service.
2. To assist in developing efficient coordinating mechanisms to implement Government activities and to expand interagency cooperation.
3. To assist the President in the preparation of the budget and the formulation of the fiscal program of the Government.
4. To supervise and control the administration of the budget.
5. To conduct research and promote the development of improved plans of administrative management, and to advise the executive departments and agencies of the Government with respect to improved administrative organization and practice.
6. To assist the President by clearing and coordinating departmental advice on proposed legislation and by making recommendations as to Presidential action on legislative enactments, in accordance with past practice.
7. To assist in the consideration and clearance and, where necessary, in the preparation of proposed Executive orders and proclamations.
8. To plan and promote the improvement, development, and coordination of Federal and other statistical services.
9. To plan and develop information systems to provide the President with program performance data.
10. To plan, conduct, and promote evaluation efforts to assist the President in the assessment of program objectives, performance, and efficiency.
11. To plan and develop programs to recruit, train, motivate, deploy, and evaluate career personnel.
12. To keep the President informed of the progress of activities by agencies of the Government with respect to work proposed, work actually initiated, and work completed, together with the relative timing of work between the several agencies of the Government.

For further information, contact the Assistant to the Director for Adminstration, Office of Management and Budget, Executive Office Building, Washington, D.C. 20503. Phone, 202—395-4790.

See also discussions at page One-29 and at Introduction-63.

Office of Science and Technology

Executive Office Building, Washington, D.C. 20506. Phone, 202—395-3000

PURPOSE.—The Director of the Office of Science and Technology provides advice and assistance to the President with respect to developing policies and evaluating and coordinating programs to assure that science and technology are used most effectively in the interests of national security and general welfare.

ACTIVITIES.—Functions of the Office include:

1. Evaluation of major policies, plans, and programs of science and technology of the various agencies of the Federal Government, giving appropriate emphasis to the relationship of science and technology to national security and foreign policy, and measures for furthering science and technology in the Nation;

2. Assessment of selected scientific and technical developments and programs in relation to their impact on national policies;

3. Review, integration, and coordination of major Federal activities in science and technology giving due consideration to the effects of such activities as non-Federal resources and institutions.

For further information, contact the Executive Officer, Office of Science and Technology, Executive Office Building, Washington, D.C. 20506. Phone, 202—395-3577.

Federal Council for Science and Technology

216 Executive Office Building, Washington, D.C. 20506. Phone, 202—395-3534.

Executive Secretary.—Lawrence A. Goldmuntz.

The Council was established by Executive Order 10807 of March 13, 1959, amended by Executive Order 11381 of November 8, 1967, to promote closer cooperation among Federal agencies, to facilitate resolution of common problems and to improve planning and management in science and technology, and to advise and assist the President regarding Federal programs affecting more than one agency. Council membership includes the Chairman, designated by the President, and officers of policy rank from eleven departments and agencies. Designated representatives of seven other departments and agencies attend meetings as observers. Selected activities involving a number of agencies are coordinated through Council committees on Atmospheric Sciences, Materials Research and Development, High Energy Physics, Water Resources Research, Behavioral Sciences, Patent Policy, Long Range Planning, International Programs, Science Information, Academic Science and Engineering, Federal Laboratories, Environmental Quality, and Solid Earth Sciences. The Council Secretariat is provided by the Office of Science and Technology.

Federal Government agencies — Executive Departments

DEPARTMENT OF AGRICULTURE

Fourteenth Street and Independence Avenue SW., Washington, D.C. 20250. Phone, 202—737-4142

Farmers Home Administration

INDIVIDUAL SOIL AND WATER CONSERVATION LOANS.—Loans are made to owners or operators of farms and ranches including partnerships and domestic corporations to assist them in developing, conserving, and making proper use of their land and resources.

RECREATION LOANS.—Recreation loans enable farmers and ranchers to convert all or a portion of the farms or ranches owned or leased by them to outdoor income-producing recreational enterprises.

LOANS AND GRANTS TO ASSOCIATIONS.—Loans and grants for the construction of rural community water and waste disposal systems are made to public bodies and to nonprofit organizations.

WATERSHED PROTECTION AND FLOOD PREVENTION LOANS.—These loans enable local organizations to help finance projects that protect and develop land and water resources in small watersheds.

Dept. of Agriculture

RESOURCE CONSERVATION AND DEVELOPMENT LOANS.—Loans are available for natural resource conservation and development in designated areas. Such loans may be made for periods up to 30 years with repayment of principal and interest deferred up to 5 years, if necessary. The interest rate for loans made in fiscal 1971 is 3.463 percent.

APPALACHIA LOANS.—In certain areas in Appalachia loans may be made to finance all or a portion of the landowner's contribution to land conservation, stabilization, and erosion control measures called for in ASCS cost-sharing contracts. These loans bear 5 percent interest and are repayable over periods up to 40 years.

For further information, contact the Information Staff, Farmers Home Administration, Department of Agriculture, Washington, D.C. 20250. Phone, 202—388—4323.

Forest Service

NATIONAL FOREST SYSTEM.—The Forest Service manages 154 national forests and 19 national grasslands comprising 187 million acres in 41 States and Puerto Rico, under the principles of multiple use and sustained yield.

These lands are protected as much as possible from wildfire, epidemics of disease and insect pests, erosion, floods, and water and air pollution. Burned areas get emergency seeding treatment to prevent massive erosion and stream siltation. Roads and trails are built where needed to allow for closely regulated timber harvesting and to give the public access to outdoor recreation areas and provide scenic drives and hikes. Picnic, camping, water-sport, skiing, and other areas are provided with facilities for public convenience and enjoyment. Timber harvesting methods are used which will protect the land and streams, assure rapid renewal of the forest, provide food and cover for wildlife and fish, and have minimum impact on scenic and recreation values. Local communities benefit from the logging and milling activities. Rangelands are improved for millions of livestock and game animals. The national forests provide a refuge for many species of endangered birds, animals, and fish. Some 14.5 million acres are set aside for wilderness and primitive areas where timber will not be harvested.

The Forest Service operates 17 youth conservation centers on national forest land throughout the country to provide vocational training for underprivileged young people, and provides special manpower training for disadvantaged older rural people.

COOPERATION WITH THE STATES.—The Forest Service cooperates with State and local governments, agencies and organizations, forest industries, and private landowners, in the protection, reforestation, management, and utilization of 511 million acres of forested lands and associated lands vital for watershed protection.

All 50 States have cooperative agreements for participation in the Cooperative Forest Fire Control Program.

Technical Federal and State assistance is provided for private forest landowners and for operators and processors of primary forest products in the management of their operations for maximum efficiency consistent with wise conservation.

Problems of forests are dealt with in Vol. Two of this work.

FOREST RESEARCH.—The Forest Service carries on basic research throughout the country, often in cooperation with State agricultural colleges, under the authority of the McSweeney-McNary act of May 22, 1928 (45 Stat. 699; 16 U.S.C. 581–581i), as amended and supplemented. Research is carried on in all the fields previously mentioned in addition to many others including genetics, nutrition, improved methods of harvesting, prevention, detection, and mapping of lightning fires, better processing methods for forest products, environmental improvement, etc.

FIELD OFFICES—FOREST SERVICE

National Forest System Regions—Regional Forester

Region	Address
1. Northern	Federal Bldg., Missoula, Mont. 59801.
2. Rocky Mountain	Federal Center, Bldg. 85, Denver, Colo. 80225.
3. Southwestern	517 Gold Ave. SW., Albuquerque, N. Mex. 87101.
4. Intermountain	324 25th St., Ogden, Utah 84401.
5. California	630 Sansome St., San Francisco, Calif. 94111.
6. Pacific Northwest.	319 SW Pine St. (P.O. Box 3623), Portland, Oreg. 97208.
8. Southern	1720 Peachtree Rd. NW., Atlanta, Ga. 30309.
9. Eastern	633 W. Wisconsin Ave., Milwaukee, Wis. 53203.
10. Alaska	Federal Office Bldg. (P.O. Box 1628), Juneau, Alaska 99801.

For further information, contact the Division of Information and Education, Forest Service, Department of Agriculture, Washington, D.C. 20250. Phone, 202—388—3760.

Soil Conservation Service

Dept. of Agriculture

CONSERVATION OPERATIONS.—Assistance to individual district cooperators includes: (1) giving the cooperator a soil and land-capability map of his land; (2) giving him information about practical alternatives for treating and using the land within its capabilities as indicated on the map; (3) helping him develop an orderly plan for installing the treatment measures and making the land use changes needed; and (4) helping him apply parts of the plan that require special skills or knowledge.

SOIL SURVEYS.—One important basis for conservation planning is the National Cooperative Soil Survey for which the SCS is responsible. The work is carried out in cooperation with State agricultural experiment stations and other State and Federal agencies. The soil surveys provide information about soils that is needed for land-use planning on both agricultural and nonagricultural land. Users of the published surveys include farmers and ranchers, engineers, highway departments, planning and zoning bodies, builders, realtors, and others.

See also indices in Volume Two.

WATERSHEDS.—SCS has the responsibility for the watershed activities and river basin surveys and investigations of the Department of Agriculture. Under the Watershed Protection and Flood Prevention Act (68 Stat. 666, 16 U.S.C. 1001–1009), local sponsoring organizations are given technical and financial help for land treatment and structural measures for flood prevention, fish and wildlife development, recreation, and agricultural and municipal water supply in watersheds up to 250,000 acres in size.

Under authority of the Flood Control Act of 1944, SCS assists sponsors to plan and apply flood prevention measures and practices in 11 major watersheds comprising approximately 30 million acres. Detailed plans are prepared and applied to tributary watersheds.

River basin surveys are undertaken at the request of cooperating State or Federal agencies. These surveys provide a basis for coordinated resource development of river basin areas.

GREAT PLAINS.—SCS has administrative leadership of the Great Plains Conservation program under the act of August 7, 1956 (70 Stat. 1115, 16 U.S.C. 590p), as amended. This program is designed to promote greater agricultural stability in the critical Great Plains area. SCS helps landowners and operators develop plans for installing permanent soil and water conservation practices over a 3- to 10-year period.

RECREATION.—SCS has departmental leadership for establishing public recreation areas in watershed projects and for assistance to landowners and operators in developing recreation areas and facilities on private land. These areas help provide much-needed outdoor recreation space for America's growing population, and provide added income for America's rural landowners. Many landowners are shifting to recreation as their primary source of income.

RESOURCE CONSERVATION AND DEVELOPMENT.—Under the Food and Agriculture Act of 1962 (76 Stat. 608; 16 U.S.C. 1001 et seq.), SCS assists local sponsoring groups accelerate planning and development of land and water resources in multiple county areas. Projects may include such measures as flood prevention; developing water resources for recreation, wildlife, agricultural, municipal, or industrial use; conservation planning and establishment on individual land units; improving recreation facilities, including historical and scenic attractions; encouraging new industries to locate in the area and to process products of the area; improving markets for crop and livestock products; upgrading and protecting the quality of the environment; and long-range planning to coordinate public efforts in the area. Technical and financial assistance is available for planning and carrying out project measures.

OTHER PROGRAMS.—SCS gives technical help to landowners and operators who participate in the Rural Environmental Assistance Program, cropland conversion, and cropland adjustment programs of the Department of Agriculture and certifies to the adequacy of practices installed. SCS also gives technical help to the Farmers Home Administration in making soil and water conservation loans to landowners and operators.

The work of SCS is directed by the Administrator and his staff in Washington, D.C. State offices and a Caribbean office give technical and administrative supervision to about 2,800 local work units where conservation technicians work directly with landowners and operators, other users and developers, and community planning agencies.

For further information, contact the Information Division, Soil Conservation Service, Department of Agriculture, Washington, D.C. 20250. Phone, 202—388–4543.

Economic Research Service

The Economic Research Service conducts programs of research in agricultural economics and marketing, both domestic and in foreign commerce. The results of these studies are widely disseminated.

NATURAL RESOURCE ECONOMICS RESEARCH.—Land and water research involves studies of economic utilization of land and water resources, the impact of urban and industrial expansion, land tenure problems, legal-economic aspects of land and water use, and the relationship of resource use and tenure to income and values. River basin and watershed investigations are conducted relating to the formulation of comprehensive river basin plans and programs, watershed planning, development and management programs, and resource conservation projects.

ECONOMIC DEVELOPMENT RESEARCH.—This research is concerned with analyses of the characteristics, income, and employment opportunities of low-income rural people and of chronic depressed rural areas, as well as problems and programs of rural renewal and economic development and growth. It includes statistical and economic analysis of farm population, migration, manpower, and rural levels of living. Studies are made of problems of rural local government.

For further information, contact the Division of Information, Office of Management Services, Department of Agriculture, Washington, D.C. 20250. Phone, 202—388–7133.

Agricultural Research Service

RESEARCH PROGRAMS.—The Plant Science and Entomology program involves research to: improve the quality and yield of field and horticultural crops and related production technology; protect crops against diseases, pests, and pollutants; and control destructive insects and promote use of beneficial insects in relation to the production of crops, animals, and well-being of man, with consideration for non-pesticidal methods to avoid residues and pollution of the environment.

The Soils, Water, and Engineering program involves research to: mechanize crop and livestock production, harvest and process farm crops, improve farm structures, and develop new, safe, and effective farm uses for electrical energy; and effectively utilize the productive capacity of soil and water resources with concern for problems of pollution and preservation of these resources.

The Livestock program involves research to: develop superior strains of livestock, poultry, and domestic fur animals; improve feeding and management practices that provide efficient production while avoiding or minimizing pollution due to animal wastes; and determine causes and control of diseases and parasites affecting livestock, poultry, and domestic fur-bearing animals.

For further information, contact the Information Division, Agricultural Research Service, Department of Agriculture, Washington, D.C. 20250. Phone, 202—388–4433.

Agricultural Stabilization and Conservation Service

RURAL ENVIRONMENTAL ASSISTANCE PROGRAM.—The Rural Environmental Assistance Program (REAP), successor to the Agricultural Conservation Program (ACP), provides cost-sharing (generally on a 50–50 basis) with farmers to carry out needed conservation and environmental measures.

Program emphasis is on meeting some of the more pressing farm-related conservation and environmental problems in rural areas, on practices for long-range preservation of the environment, and on practices that will provide substantial benefits to the public at the least possible public cost.

For further information, contact the Information Division, Agricultural Stabilization and Conservation Service, Department of Agriculture, Washington, D.C. 20250. Phone, 202—388–5237.

DEPARTMENT OF COMMERCE

Fourteenth Street bet. Constitution Avenue and E Street NW., Washington, D.C. 20230. Phone, 202—783-9200

National Oceanic and Atmospheric Administration

(6010 Executive Boulevard, Rockville, Md. 20852. Phone, 301—656-4060)

CREATION AND AUTHORITY.—The National Oceanic and Atmospheric Administration (NOAA) was formed on October 3, 1970, by Reorganization Plan 4 of 1970. Its principal functions are authorized by title 15, chapter 9, U.S. Code (National Weather Service), title 33, chapter 17, U.S. Code (National Ocean Survey), title 16, chapter 9, U.S. Code (National Marine Fisheries Service).

PURPOSE.—The mission of NOAA is to explore, map, and chart the global oceans and translate new physical and biological knowledge into systems capable of assessing the sea's potential yield which the Nation and its industries can employ. To manage, use, and conserve these animal and mineral resources; monitor and predict the characteristics of the physical environment and the changes of the atmosphere, ocean, sun and solid earth, gravity and geomagnetism, and warn against impending environmental hazards, and ease the human burden of hurricanes, tornadoes, floods, tsunamis, and other destructive natural events.

ORGANIZATION.—NOAA consists of staff offices, six major components, and the field organization. The major components are: the National Marine Fisheries Service, the Environmental Data Service, the National Weather Service, the Environmental Research Laboratories, the National Ocean Survey, and the National Environmental Satellite Service.

FUNCTIONS AND ACTIVITIES.—Among its principal functions and activities, NOAA reports the weather of the United States and its possessions and provides weather forecasts to the general public; issues warnings against tornadoes, hurricanes, tsunamis, and floods; and provides special services to aeronautical, maritime, agricultural, and other weather-sensitive activities.

NOAA also prepares and issues nautical and aeronautical charts; conducts geodetic, oceanographic, and marine geophysical surveys; predicts tides, currents, and the state of the oceans; conducts biological research on the living resources of the sea; analyzes economic aspects of fisheries operations and seeks means of bringing more of the world's aquatic resources into economic and commercial production consistent with sound conservation principles.

FIELD ORGANIZATION—NATIONAL OCEANIC AND ATMOSPHERIC ADMINISTRATION

Field Organization	Address
1. National Weather Service Regions:	
EASTERN—Connecticut, Delaware, Maine, Maryland, Massachusetts, New Hampshire, New Jersey, New York, North Carolina, Ohio, Pennsylvania, Rhode Island, South Carolina, Vermont, Virginia, West Virginia.	585 Stewart Ave., Garden City, Long Island, N.Y. 11530.
CENTRAL—Colorado, Illinois, Indiana, Iowa, Kansas, Kentucky, Michigan, Minnesota, Missouri, Nebraska, North Dakota, South Dakota, Wisconsin, Wyoming.	601 E. 12th St., Kansas City, Mo. 64106.
SOUTHERN—Alabama, Arkansas, Florida, Georgia, Louisiana, Mississippi, New Mexico, Oklahoma, Tennessee, Texas, Puerto Rico.	819 Taylor St., Fort Worth, Tex. 76102.
WESTERN—Arizona, California, Idaho, Montana, Oregon, Nevada, Utah, Washington.	125 S. State St., Salt Lake City, Utah 84111.
ALASKA	632 6th Ave., Anchorage, Alaska 99501.
PACIFIC	1149 Bethel St., Honolulu, Hawaii 96813.
2. National Ocean Survey Field Director:	
MID-CONTINENT	601 E. 12th St., Kansas City, Mo. 64106.
3. National Ocean Survey Marine Centers:	
ATLANTIC	439 W. York St., Norfolk, Va. 23510.
PACIFIC	1801 Fairview Ave., East, Seattle, Wash. 98102.
4. National Ocean Survey Lake Survey Center:	Federal Building and U.S. Courthouse, Detroit, Mich. 38226.
5. National Marine Fisheries Service Regions:	
NORTHEAST—Connecticut, Delaware, Illinois, Indiana, Maine, Maryland, Massachusetts, Minnesota, New Hampshire, New Jersey, New York, Ohio, Pennsylvania, Rhode Island, Virginia, Vermont, West Virginia, Wisconsin.	14 Elm St., Gloucester, Mass. 01930.
SOUTHEAST—Alabama, Arkansas, Florida, Georgia, Iowa, Kansas, Kentucky, Louisiana, Mississippi, Missouri, Nebraska, North Carolina, Oklahoma, South Carolina, Tennessee, Texas, Puerto Rico, Virgin Islands.	144 First Ave., South, St. Petersburg, Fla. 33701.
NORTHWEST—Idaho, Montana, North Dakota, Oregon, South Dakota, Washington, Wyoming.	1319 Second Ave., Seattle, Wash. 98101.
SOUTHWEST—Arizona, California, Colorado, Nevada, New Mexico, Utah, Hawaii, Samoa, Guam, Trust Territories.	300 S. Ferry St., Terminal Island, Calif. 90731.
ALASKA	P.O. Box 1668, Juneau, Alaska 99801.

In addition, NOAA provides satellite observations of the environment by establishing and operating a national environmental satellite system; and conducts an integrated program of research and services relating to the oceans and inland waters, the lower and upper atmosphere, space environment and the earth to increase understanding of man's geophysical environment. NOAA acquires, stores, and disseminates worldwide environmental data through a system of meteorological, oceanographic, geodetic, and seismological data centers.

NOAA also administers and directs the National Sea Grant Program by providing grants to institutions for aquatic research, education, and advisory services; develops a national system of data buoys for automatically obtaining and disseminating marine environmental data; and tests and evaluates oceanographic instruments and maintains a national reference center for oceanographic instruments specifications and characteristics.

For further information, contact the Office of Public Affairs, National Oceanic and Atmospheric Administration, Rockville, Md. 20852. Phone, 301—496–8234.

DEPARTMENT OF DEFENSE

DEPARTMENT OF THE ARMY

Office of Civil Functions

The Office of Civil Functions is responsible for the civil functions of the Department of the Army, including the Civil Works Program of the Corps of Engineers, the National Cemetery Program, and miscellaneous civil functions as assigned.

CHIEF OF ENGINEERS.—The Chief of Engineers, as principal adviser to the Chief of Staff for all Army engineering matters, has Army staff responsibility for engineer functions throughout the Army and is commander of the Corps of Engineers.

Under the direction and supervision of the Secretary of the Army, he has responsibility for planning, programing, budgeting and engineering, construction, operation and maintenance, and real estate necessary for the improvement of rivers, harbors, and waterways for navigation, flood control, and related purposes; administration of laws for the protection and preservation of navigable waters; and administration of the purchase and sale of utilities services as the DA Power Procurement Officer. He also provides general and specialized engineering, construction, and real estate services for the Air Force and other governmental agencies as requested.

U.S. ARMY CORPS OF ENGINEERS, Office of the Chief of Engineers, Forrestal Bldg., Washington, DC 20314

Civil Works:

Director of Civil Works: MAJ. GEN. FRANK P. KOISCH (693-7154)

Chief, Recreation and Environmental Branch: DR. C. GRANT ASH (693-7290)

Chief, Fish and Wildlife Section: BERTON M. MacLEAN (693-7290)

DEPARTMENT OF HEALTH, EDUCATION, AND WELFARE

330 Independence Avenue SW., Washington, D.C. 20201. Phone, 202—962–2246

Public Health Service

Food and Drug Administration

BUREAU OF FOODS.—The Bureau conducts research and develops standards and policy on the composition, quality, nutrition, and safety of foods, food additives, colors, and cosmetics; conducts research designed to improve the detection, prevention, and control of contamination that may be responsible for illness or injury conveyed by foods, colors, and cosmetics; plans, coordinates, and evaluates FDA's surveillance and compliance programs relating to foods, colors, and cosmetics; reviews industry petitions and recommends the promulgation of regulations for food standards and to permit the safe use of color additives and food additives; and collects and interprets data on nutrition, food additives, and environmental factors affecting the total chemical insult posed by food additives.

Office of Education

ENVIRONMENT.—For programs with environmental education content, write to Environmental Education, Office of Education, Department of Health, Education, and Welfare, Washington, D.C. 20202.

DEPARTMENT OF HOUSING AND URBAN DEVELOPMENT

451 Seventh Street SW., Washington, D.C. 20410. Phone, 202—655-4000

OPEN SPACE LAND AND RELATED PROGRAMS.—These programs include grant programs for the acquisition and development of open space land, urban beautification and improvement, and historic preservation.

OFFICE OF COMMUNITY GOALS AND STANDARDS.—The Office is responsible for the workable program for community improvement; planning requirements for HUD and other specified Federal programs; environmental, transportation, and water resources planning; and relocation assistance policy and requirements.

COMMUNITY FACILITIES.—Community facilities provides grants for basic water and sewer facilities, neighborhood facilities grants, and public facilities loans.

OFFICE OF INTERSTATE LAND SALES REGISTRATION.—The Office carries out the Department's interstate land sales registration program.

The Interstate Land Sales Full Disclosure Act, authorized by title XIV of the 1968 Housing Act, requires statements of record from land developers offering to sell or lease, by the use of the mail or by any means in interstate commerce, any lot in any subdivision with 50 or more lots.

DEPARTMENT OF JUSTICE

Constitution Avenue and Tenth Street NW., Washington, D.C. 20530.
Phone, 202—737-8200

Land and Natural Resources Division

The Assistant Attorney General in charge of the Land and Natural Resources Division supervises all suits and matters of a civil nature in the Federal district courts, in the State courts, and in the Court of Claims relating to real property, including not only lands but water and other related natural resources and the Outer Continental Shelf and marine resources and to the protection of the environment. This encompasses condemnation proceedings for the acquisition of property, actions to remove clouds and to quiet title, to recover possession, to recover damages, to determine boundaries, to cancel patents, to set aside *ad valorem* taxes and tax sales, to establish rights in minerals, including mineral leases, in oil reserves, and in other natural resources, to establish water rights and protect water resources, to abate water and air pollution, to defend actions for compensation for the claimed taking by the United States of real property or any interest therein, and to defend actions seeking to establish an interest in real property adverse to the United States.

The Division is also responsible for criminal prosecutions for air and water pollution.

The Division is also charged with representing the interests of the United States in all civil litigation pertaining to Indians and Indian affairs, including the defense of Indian claims against the United States, whether in the Court of Claims or before the Indian Claims Commission. It defends officers of the United States, handles injunction and mandamus proceedings and litigation arising from contracts whenever those matters affect the rights of the United States in the use or title of its real property.

Except as delegated to the other departments and agencies, the Division passes upon the title to all real property and interests in real property acquired by the United States by direct purchase.

Among other functions of the Division are the review of legislative proposals affecting matters within the scope of its litigation responsibilities and the rendition of legal advice to Federal representatives to interstate water resource compacts.

DEPARTMENT OF THE INTERIOR

C Street between Eighteenth and Nineteenth Streets NW., Washington, D.C. 20240.
Phone, 202—343–1100

RESPONSIBILITY.—The jurisdiction of the Department includes the administration of over 533 million acres of Federal land, and trust responsibilities for approximately 50 million acres of land, mostly Indian reservations; the conservation and development of mineral and water resources; the promotion of mine safety and efficiency; the conservation, development, and utilization of fish and wildlife resources; the coordination of Federal and State recreation programs; the administration of the Nation's scenic and historic areas; the operation of Job Corps Conservation Centers and other manpower and youth training programs; the reclamation of arid lands in the West through irrigation; and the management of hydroelectric power systems. The Department of the Interior is also concerned with the social and economic development of the territories of the United States and in the Trust Territory of the Pacific Islands; and administers programs providing services to Indians and Alaska Native people.

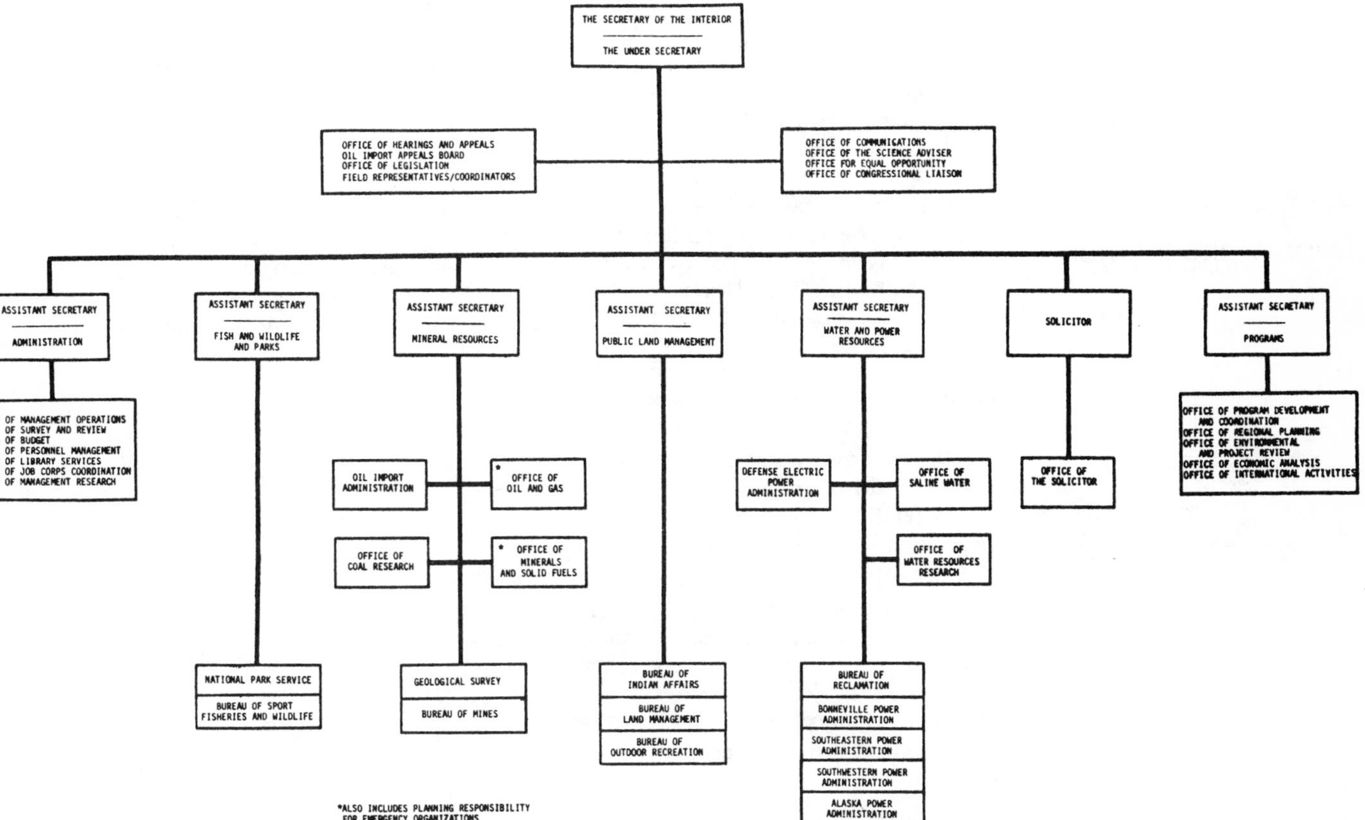

FIELD COMMITTEES—DEPARTMENT OF THE INTERIOR

Region	Title of Chairman	Address
NORTHEAST.—Connecticut, Delaware, Maine, Maryland, Massachusetts, New Hampshire, New Jersey, New York, Pennsylvania, Rhode Island, Vermont, and Virginia.	Regional Coordinator	John F. Kennedy Federal Bldg., Boston, Mass. 02203.
NORTH CENTRAL.—Illinois, Indiana, Iowa, Kentucky, Michigan, Minnesota, Ohio, West Virginia, and Wisconsin.	Field Representative	2510 Dempster St., Des Plaines, Ill. 60016.
SOUTHEAST.—Alabama, Florida, Georgia, Mississippi, North Carolina, South Carolina, Tennessee, and the Virgin Islands.	Field Representative	148 Cain St. NE., Atlanta, Ga. 30303.
MISSOURI BASIN.—Colorado, Kansas, Missouri, Montana, Nebraska, North Dakota, South Dakota, and Wyoming.	Regional Coordinator	Federal Office Bldg., P.O. Box 2530, Billings, Mont. 59103.
SOUTHWEST.—Arkansas, Louisiana, New Mexico, Oklahoma, and Texas.	Field Representative	Federal Bldg., Albuquerque, N. Mex. 87101.
PACIFIC NORTHWEST.—Idaho, Oregon, and Washington.	Field Representative	Federal Bldg., P.O. Box 3621, Portland, Oreg. 97208.
PACIFIC SOUTHWEST.—Arizona, California, Hawaii, Nevada, and Utah.	Field Representative	450 Golden Gate Ave., P.O. Box 36098, San Francisco, Calif. 94102.
ALASKA	Field Representative	338 Denali St., Anchorage, Alaska 99501.

Office of the Solicitor

The Office of the Solicitor performs all legal work for the entire Department with the exception of that performed by the Office of Hearings and Appeals, and specified territorial matters.

REGIONAL OFFICES—OFFICE OF THE SOLICITOR

Anchorage, Alaska, 99501	Federal Bldg.
Denver, Colo., 80225	Denver Federal Center.
Los Angeles, Calif., 90012	Federal Bldg.
Philadelphia, Pa., 19106	Second Bank Bldg.
Portland, Oreg., 97208	Federal Bldg.
Sacramento, Calif., 95825	Federal Bldg.
Salt Lake City, Utah, 84111	Federal Bldg.
Tulsa, Okla., 74103	Post Office and Federal Bldg.

United States Fish and Wildlife Service

Dept. of the Interior

Bureau of Sport Fisheries and Wildlife

ORGANIZATION.—The Bureau of Sport Fisheries and Wildlife consists of a headquarters office at Washington, D.C., five regional offices, wildlife refuges, fish hatcheries, research laboratories, and other offices located in the 50 States.

FISHERY PROGRAMS.—The Bureau has programs for research, development, and management of fish resources, Federal aid to State fish and wildlife agencies, and technical assistance in preserving and enhancing water and related resources for sport fishing. A system of nearly 100 fish hatcheries is operated for the propagation and distribution of various species of sport fishes, including trout, salmon, bass, and catfish. The stocking of public waters and farm fish ponds is carried out in cooperation with State fish and game departments.

WILDLIFE PROGRAMS.—

The approximately 30 million acre National Wildlife Refuge System includes 330 refuges and game ranges managed for migratory birds, protection of endangered species, public enjoyment of natural resources, and economic benefits from sales of land products and concessions.

INTERAGENCY PROGRAM. — Funds are received from other agencies to assist in Bureau programs such as land acquisition for recreation areas and for endangered species under the Land and Water Conservation Act; participation in planning and constructing fish and wildlife facilities on other agency water projects; operation of two Job Corps centers; and insect and disease control in cooperation with USDA.

TRAINING PROGRAMS.—Bureau, State, and private employees; students; and representatives of foreign governments secure training in fish and wildlife research and management programs at Bureau training centers, or in Cooperative Units functioning under agreements with universities and the fish and game department of the State where the unit is located. Under the Youth Conservation Corps Program the Bureau operates ten camps in the summer months.

FINANCIAL ASSISTANCE PROGRAMS.—Funds are allotted annually to State fish and wildlife departments for use in fish and game management programs; the conservation and development of anadromous fish occur through a State-Federal cooperative program.

ENVIRONMENTAL COORDINATION AND RIVER BASIN STUDIES.—The Bureau studies environmental impact statements and water use projects proposed by Federal or private agencies for the probable effects of such projects on fish and wildlife resources and recommends measures for their conservation and development.

REGIONAL OFFICES—BUREAU OF SPORT FISHERIES AND WILDLIFE

Region	Headquarters
1. Pacific*	730 NE. Pacific St., Portland, Oreg., 97208.
2. Southwest	Federal Bldg., Albuquerque, N. Mex., 87103.
3. North Central	Federal Bldg., Fort Snelling, Twin Cities, Minn., 55111.
4. Southeast	809 Peachtree-Seventh Bldg., Atlanta, Ga., 30323.
5. Northeast	U.S. Post Office and Courthouse, Boston, Mass., 02109.
*Alaska Area Office	6917 Seward Highway, Anchorage, Alaska, 99502.

Job Corps

Overall direction and all other Job Corps programs are handled by the Dept. of Labor.

Job Corps is a nationwide youth training program, offering comprehensive development for disadvantaged youth through centers with residential facilities for all or most of enrollees.

The Civilian Conservation Centers accommodating from 100 to 250 Corpsmen, are located on public lands and are operated by the conservation agencies of the Departments of Agriculture and the Interior and the Commonwealth of Puerto Rico. The education program in these centers as well as in the urban centers is designed to serve nonreaders as well as enable attainment of the high school equivalency General Educational Development Test (GED).

The work programs at these Conservation Centers have been redirected to be fully supportive of the vocational training programs.

Job Corps recruiting is accomplished primarily through the State Employment Services.

Corpsmembers are paid a basic living allowance of $30 per month, and increases may be earned depending on length of enrollment and satisfactory performance to a maximum of $50 per month. Corpsmembers who remain in the program for longer than 6 months receive, upon termination, and additional readjustment allowance of $50 for each month of satisfactory service in the Job Corps,

National Park Service

ORGANIZATION.—The National Park Service has 283 field areas which include national parks, monuments, recreation areas, and many types of historic areas. It has six regional offices; the Office of National Capital Parks; three service centers; and a headquarters staff in Washington, D.C.

ACTIVITIES.—National Park Service programs help the public learn, through direct observation, about the Nation's natural and historic heritage and how it may be enjoyed, enhanced, and protected. Service programs develop the recreational potential of the parks while protecting their environment. Educational programs for schoolchildren and adults are conducted in the areas of conservation and environmental awareness. Research is conducted in many areas of resource protection and management.

THE ENVIRONMENT.—The National Park Service, in cooperation with the National Education Association, has developed the National Environmental Education Development (NEED) program, a primary and secondary school curriculum integrating environmental concepts into school classwork. Field work under the NEED program takes place in Park Service National Environmental Study Areas (NESA) located in the parks.

REGIONAL OFFICES—NATIONAL PARK SERVICE

Northeast	143 S. 3d St., Philadelphia, Pa., 19106.
Southeast	Federal Bldg., Richmond, Va., 23240.
Midwest	1709 Jackson St., Omaha, Nebr., 68102.
Southwest	Box 728, Santa Fe, N. Mex., 87501.
Western	450 Golden Gate Ave., San Francisco, Calif., 94102.
Pacific Northwest	Fourth and Pike Bldg., Seattle, Wash. 98101.

Geological Survey

(General Services Building, Eighteenth and F Streets NW., Washington, D.C. 20242)

Dept. of the Interior

CONSERVATION.—Classify Federal lands as to their value for leasable minerals or for reservoir and waterpower sites; supervise the operations of private industry on mining and oil and gas leases on public domain, acquired, Indian, Outer Continental Shelf, and certain Naval Petroleum Reserve lands to ensure maximum utilization and prevent waste of the mineral resources, to limit damage or pollution to the total environment, and to secure the safety and promote the welfare of workmen; maintain production accounts and collect royalties; prepare and publish maps and reports of mineral and water resources investigations on Federal lands; and provide the Bureau of Land Management and other Federal agencies geologic and engineering advice, evaluations, and inspection services for the management and disposition of the public domain.

EROS PROGRAM.—The Earth Resources Observation Systems is a departmental program for acquiring, processing, distributing, and applying remote sensor data collected from aircraft and spacecraft toward the solution of resources and environmental problems.

Sources of Information

Inquiries on the following subjects should be directed to the specified office, Geological Survey, Department of the Interior, Washington, D.C. 20242.

THE ENVIRONMENT.—The Survey reviews environmental impact statements which are generated by action agencies and develops guidelines for effective impact reporting. Write the Assistant Director for Engineering, Room 5236, GSA Building.

Bureau of Mines

MINERAL RESOURCES AND ENVIRONMENTAL DEVELOPMENT.—Functions include surveillance and evaluations of the industrial and commercial outlook for minerals and fuel deposits; studies to determine the relationship of mineral supply, demand and technology to the national and world economy; studies and projects concerning the relationship of the mineral industries to environmental problems; collection, evaluation, and publication of mineral industry statistics; and conducting engineering studies regarding effective mining practices. Also included are research programs concerning extraction, processing, use, and disposal of minerals, mineral fuels, and helium production.

Bureau of Land Management

The Bureau is responsible for the management of 60 percent of the Nation's Federal lands and administers the Federal laws pertaining to these lands. This responsibility covers 20 percent of the Nation's total land base. Lands under its jurisdiction are located primarily in 10 States in the far West and in Alaska. However, scattered parcels of public land are located in an additional 14 States.

Public land resources managed by the Bureau include timber, minerals, wildlife habitat, livestock forage, public recreation values, and open space. Bureau programs provide for the protection, orderly development, and use of all these resources under principles of multiple use and sustained yield, and for a quality environment. It manages watersheds to protect soil and enhance water quality, develops recreation opportunity on public land, and makes public land available through sale or lease to individuals, organizations, local governments, and other Federal agencies when such transfer is in the public interest.

The Bureau is responsible for the survey of Federal lands and maintains public land records. It is responsible for mineral leasing on much of the public land held by other Federal agencies and for leasing the mineral deposits of the Outer Continental Shelf.

Sources of Information

THE ENVIRONMENT.—The Bureau administers the Department of the Interior's Johnny Horizon Environmental Program. A complete "how to" booklet is available from local Interior offices or by writing Johnny Horizon, Department of the Interior, Washington, D.C. 20240.

Bureau of Outdoor Recreation

ACTIVITIES.—Under the Land and Water Conservation Act of 1965, the Bureau administers a program of financial assistance grants to States for facilitating outdoor recreation planning, acquisition, and developmental activities. The Fund also helps finance the acquisition of Federal lands and water areas for recreational purposes and the Bureau participates directly in the planning, coordination, and establishment of uniform policies relating to recreation and fish and wildlife benefits and costs of Federal multipurpose water resource projects.

REGIONAL OFFICES—BUREAU OF OUTDOOR RECREATION

Region	Headquarters
Northeast	1421 Cherry St., Philadelphia, Pa., 19102.
Southeast	810 New Walton Bldg., Atlanta, Ga., 30303.
Lake Central	3853 Research Park Dr., Ann Arbor, Mich., 48104.
Mid-Continent	Denver Federal Center, Bldg. 41, Denver, Colo., 80225.
Pacific Northwest.	1000 2d Ave., Seattle, Wash., 98104.
Pacific Southwest.	450 Golden Gate Ave., San Francisco, Calif., 94102.

Bureau of Reclamation

ACTIVITIES.—Major functions include: investigation and development of plans for the regulation, conservation, and utilization of water and related land resources including basinwide water studies; administration of water research programs to develop maximum use of resources including by the Congress; operation and maintenance of projects and facilities constructed by the Bureau, and review of the operation and maintenance of Bureau-built projects and facilities which are operated and maintained by water users; settlement of public or acquired lands on Bureau projects; administration of the Small Reclamation Projects Act of 1956; and negotiation, execution, and administration of repayment contracts, water-user operation and maintenance contracts, and contracts required by statutes relating to the irrigation of excess lands.

The Bureau has responsibility for the sale, interchange, purchase, or transmission of electric power and energy generated at: (1) powerplants constructed and operated by the Bureau, except surplus electric power from nine hydroelectric plants operated by the Bureau in the Pacific Northwest; and (2) six powerplants on the Missouri River and one on the Rio Grande that were constructed by other Federal agencies.

The Bureau administers youth conservation programs, as assigned. It renders technical assistance to foreign countries in water resource development and utilization.

Other Departmental Offices

Office of Water Resources Research

The Office of Water Resources Research (OWRR) administers the program of water resources research and training authorized by the Water Resources Research Act of 1964, as amended (78 Stat. 329, 80 Stat. 129; 42 U.S.C. 1961). Major program purposes are to: develop through research new technology and more efficient methods for resolving local, State, and nationwide water resource problems; train water scientists and engineers through their on-the-job participation in research work; and facilitate water research coordination and the application of research results by furnishing information about ongoing and completed research. OWRR does not maintain its own laboratories or perform "in-house" research.

Under title I of the act, OWRR provides annual fund allotments to support one State university water resources research and training institute in each State and in Puerto Rico; additional funds are provided to these institutes for additional specific research project work on a dollar-for-dollar matching-fund basis. Other universities and colleges may participate in the title I program work of the designated State institutes. Under title II of the act, grants and contracts are made with academic, private, public, or other organizations and individuals having water research competence for support of urgently needed water resources research work.

OWRR also operates a water resources scientific information center to furnish information to the Nation's water resource community, in project abstract and other summary formats, regarding ongoing water research projects and the results obtained from completed water resources studies and investigations.

Information available to the public regarding OWRR activities is contained in the *OWRR Annual Report,* which can be obtained from the Office of Water Resources Research, Department of the Interior, Washington, D.C. 20240.

Office of Saline Water

The Office of Saline Water performs functions vested in the Secretary of the Interior by the act of July 3, 1952 (42 U.S.C. 1951 et seq.). This act authorizes the Secretary of the Interior to conduct research and development of practical means for the economical production, from sea or other saline water, of water suitable for agricultural, industrial, municipal, and other beneficial uses and for related studies and research.

Office of Coal Research

The Office of Coal Research was established pursuant to the Coal Research Act of July 7, 1960 (74 Stat. 336; 30 U.S.C. 661). The Office seeks to develop new and more efficient methods of mining, preparing, and utilizing coal to insure abundant supplies of clean energy.

All research is performed by contracts with public and private organizations. The Office of Coal Research (OCR) does not issue grants, maintain its own laboratories, or perform "in-house" research.

Office of Minerals and Solid Fuels

The Office provides advice and staff assistance to the Secretariat and initiates specialized studies and evaluations regarding departmental policy decisions affecting metals, minerals, and solid fuels.

The Office is responsible for planning and programing to provide for a supply of metals, minerals, and solid fuels adequate for essential civilian and military requirements under partial and full mobilization. It also assists the States in planning for the emergency management of solid fuels in coordination with efforts at the national level.

Office of Oil and Gas

The Office of Oil and Gas serves as a focal point for leadership and information on petroleum matters in the Federal Government, and the principal channel of communication between the Federal Government, the petroleum industry, and the oil producing States. It also maintains the capability to respond effectively to emergencies affecting the Nation's supply of oil and gas.

DEPARTMENT OF STATE

2201 C Street NW., Washington, D.C. 20520. Phone, 202—655-4000

Special Assistant for Fisheries and Wildlife: DONALD L. McKERNAN (Ext. 22335) Deputy Special Assistant for Fisheries and Wildlife: BURDICK H. BRITTIN (Ext. 20853)
Special Assistant for Environmental Affairs and Director, Office of Environmental Affairs: CHRISTIAN A. HERTER, JR. (Ext. 27964)

INTERNATIONAL SCIENTIFIC AND TECHNOLGICAL AFFAIRS.—The Bureau of International Scientific and Technological Affairs develops and directs the carrying out of policy recommendations relative to peaceful uses of atomic energy including participation in the International Atomic Energy Agency; international cooperation and relationships in space, atmospheric, and environmental sciences; and U.S. international science policy and cooperative programs in science and technology.

Agency for International Development

FOOD FOR PEACE.—Highest priority is given to improving the quality of life in less developed nations. Emphasis is placed on transforming traditional agricultural methods into more productive systems through the introduction of modern techniques, research, and changes in national policy. Malnutrition is dealt with through child-feeding programs, professional training, and nutritional research and development. Assistance is provided at the request of individual countries in population and family planning programs including provision for medical supplies and equipment.

DEPARTMENT OF TRANSPORTATION

400 Seventh Street SW., Washington, D.C. 20590. Phone, 202—426-4000

Assistant Secretary for Environment and Urban Systems

The Assistant Secretary for Environment and Urban Systems is responsible for environmental and overall urban transportation needs, goals, and policies; and innovative approaches to urban transportation and environmental enhancement programs. He serves as catalyst for the translation of these programs into balanced and responsive transportation systems.

Assistant Secretary for Systems Development and Technology

The Assistant Secretary for Systems Development and Technology is responsible for scientific and technological research and development advancing transportation capability as to its safety, effectiveness, economy, and viability; technological input to development of transportation policy; abatement of noise generated by transportation equipment; telecommunications; regulation of the transportation of hazardous materials; and regulation of the transportation of natural and other toxic gas by pipeline.

United States Coast Guard

(400 Seventh Street SW., Washington, D.C. 20591. Phone, 202—426-2158)

The Coast Guard cooperates with other agencies in their law enforcement responsibilities and enforces conservation laws and the Oil Pollution Act of 1961.

Federal Highway Administration

(400 Seventh Street SW., Washington, D.C. 20591. Phone, 202—426-0539)

administers the highway beautification program, the highway construction phase of the Appalachian regional development program, and is responsible for the survey and construction of forest highway system roads, defense highway and access roads, roads in national parks, and other highway related programs, as authorized.

Federal Railroad Administration

(400 Seventh Street SW., Washington, D.C. 20590. Phone, 202—426-4000)

Office of High Speed Ground Transportation

The Office administers a high speed ground transportation research and development program to advance intercity transportation systems, and conducts demonstrations with accompanying data collection and analyses to contribute to the improvement of the national transportation system.

Urban Mass Transportation Administration

(400 Seventh Street SW., Washington, D.C. 20590. Phone, 202—426-4011)

RESEARCH, DEVELOPMENT, AND DEMONSTRATION.—The Administration undertakes research, development, and demonstration projects in all phases of urban mass transportation for the purpose of assisting in the reduction of urban transportation needs, the improvement of mass transportation service, or meeting total urban transportation needs at minimum cost. Such projects may be undertaken directly, by grant or by contracting out and may be made with public bodies, universities, nonprofit and other organizations, and individuals in urban transportation research.

Grants may also be made to public and private nonprofit institutions of higher education for the support of multi-disciplinary programs combining comprehensive research in the problems of urban transportation and the training of persons in urban transportation research and related skills.

Federal Government — Independent agencies

APPALACHIAN REGIONAL COMMISSION

1666 Connecticut Avenue NW., Washington, D.C. 20235.
Phone, 202—967-3167

These programs include: construction of a development highway system, construction of access roads, construction and operation of multicounty health projects, construction of vocational education facilities, technical assistance and planning loans for low and moderate income housing construction, application of land treatment and erosion control measures, reclamation of land damaged by past mining practices, support of timber development organizations, research grants, operation of a comprehensive water resources survey, construction of sewage treatment facilities, and the supplementation of a number of existing grant-in-aid programs providing for the acquisition of land and the construction and equipment of public facilities.

PUBLICATIONS.—Copies of the *Annual Report of Fiscal Year 1970* and *Appalachia:* A Journal of the Appalachian Regional Commission are available upon request.

ATOMIC ENERGY COMMISSION

Washington, D.C. 20545. Phone, 301—973-1000

REGULATORY FUNCTIONS.—The Director of Regulation carries out the following AEC functions: licensing and regulation of the civilian use of nuclear materials and the construction and operation of nuclear reactors and other nuclear facilities.

ENVIRONMENT.—Environmental protection is a basic consideration in the development and conduct of AEC programs and in the granting of licenses to the public for possessing nuclear material and for building and operating nuclear reactors. Information about these programs is available from the Director, Office of Environmental Affairs, AEC Headquarters, or for programs affecting activities that are licensed or proposed for licensing, the Director of Regulation, AEC Headquarters.

PUBLIC DOCUMENT ROOM.—AEC has a public document room located at 1717 H Street NW., Washington, D.C.

DELAWARE RIVER BASIN COMMISSION

Office of the U.S. Commissioner: Room 5625, Department of the Interior Building, Washington, D.C. 20240. Phone, 202—343-5761

Office of the Executive Director: 25 State Police Drive (P.O. Box 360), Trenton, N.J. 08603. Phone, 609—883-9500

Under the terms of the Compact, the Delaware River Basin Commission is responsible for the development and maintenance of a comprehensive plan and for programing, scheduling, and controlling projects and activities within the Delaware River Basin, which will provide regulation and development of ground and surface water supplies for municipal, industrial, and agricultural uses; abatement of stream pollution; flood damage reduction; promotion of forestry, soil conservation, and watershed projects; propagation of fish and wildlife; development of water-related recreational facilities; and development of hydroelectric power potentialities.

FEDERAL MARITIME COMMISSION

1405 I Street NW., Washington, D.C. 20573. Phone, 202—393-3111

OIL POLLUTION.—The Commission administers section 11(p)(1) of the Water Quality Improvement Act of 1970 (84 Stat. 91; 33 U.S.C. 1101 note) with respect to evidence of financial responsibility by owners and operators of vessels which may be subjected to liability to the United States for the cost of removal of oil from the navigable waters of the United States, adjoining shorelines, or waters of the contiguous zone.

independent agencies

FEDERAL POWER COMMISSION

General Accounting Office Building, 441 G Street NW., Washington, D.C. 20426. Phone, 202—386-4506

FUNCTIONS AND ACTIVITIES.—The Federal Power Commission issues permits and licenses for non-Federal hydroelectric power projects; regulates the rates and other aspects of interstate wholesale transactions in electric power and natural gas; and issues certificates for interstate gas sales and construction and operation of interstate pipeline facilities; and requires maximum feasible protection of our natural environment in the construction of new hydroelectric projects and natural gas transmission lines consistent with the Nation's needs for adequate and reliable electric power and natural gas services. It also requires development of recreational facilities for the general public at hydroelectric projects.

The FPC is responsible for allocating the costs of certain Federal projects, and participates in the allocation of costs of other projects and determines headwater benefit charges against owners of non-Federal water power projects benefited by upstream improvements built by the U.S. or other licensees.

Sources of Information

THE ENVIRONMENT.—Contact the Office of the Advisor on Environmental Quality on programs of environmental matters.

GENERAL SERVICES ADMINISTRATION

General Services Building, Eighteenth and F Streets NW., Washington, D.C. 20405. Phone, 202—343-1100

ENVIRONMENT.—Information on the dual-fuel project, a method of powering vehicles on either gasoline or compressed natural gas, thereby reducing pollutants by 90 percent, may be obtained from the Deputy Commissioner (Transportation), Transportation and Communications Service, General Services Administration, Washington, D.C. 20405. Phone, 202—254-5374.

NATIONAL SCIENCE FOUNDATION

1800 G Street NW., Washington, D.C. 20550. Phone, 202—655-4000

ACTIVITIES.—Among the activities of the Foundation are:

1. Directing targeted research efforts designed and managed to respond to specific environmental, societal, and technological problems of national concern, and to assess new problem areas and the impact of technology on society and the environment.

SMITHSONIAN INSTITUTION

1000 Jefferson Drive SW., Washington, D.C. 20560. Phone, 202—628-4422

ENVIRONMENT.—The Chesapeake Bay Center for Environmental Studies promotes a program of research and education designed to develop ecological knowledge with emphasis on populations, communities and ecosystems.

NATIONAL MUSEUM OF NATURAL HISTORY.—This museum serves as a national and international center for the natural sciences. It maintains the largest reference collections in the Nation and conducts a broad program of basic research on man, plants, animals, fossil organisms, rocks, minerals, and materials from outer space: their classification, distribution, analysis, and environmental and ecological relationships. Its fundamental studies in systematics and biology are providing new information required for the solution of major national problems of conservation and pollution, food production, improvement of medical knowledge; for planning national and international programs leading to predictive ecology and environmental management; and for furnishing basic information to the scientific community and researchers engaged in environmental studies.

TENNESSEE VALLEY AUTHORITY

New Sprankle Building, Knoxville, Tenn. 37902; Woodward Building, Fifteenth and H Streets NW., Washington, D.C. 20444.
Washington Phone, 202—343-4537

ENVIRONMENTAL PROTECTION.—Division of Environmental Research and Development, TVA, 713 Edney Building, Chattanooga, Tenn. 37401. Also Division of Forestry, Fisheries, and Wildlife Development, TVA, Norris, Tenn. 37828.

independent agencies

SELECTED BOARDS, COMMITTEES, AND COMMISSIONS

Advisory Board on National Parks, Historic Sites, Buildings, and Monuments

National Park Service, Interior Building, Washington, D.C. 20240. Phone, 202—343-2012.

Executive Secretary.—Mrs. Helen C. Saults.

The Board was established by act of August 21, 1935 (49 Stat. 667; 16 U.S.C. 463), to advise on matters relating to national parks and other items covered by the act upon request of the Secretary of the Interior. It may also recommend policies pertaining to national parks and to restoration, reconstruction, conservation, and general administration of archaeologic sites and historic sites, buildings, and properties.

Advisory Council on Historic Preservation

Interior Building, Washington, D.C. 20240. Phone, 202—343-8607.

Executive Director.—George B. Hartzog, Jr.

The Council has the responsibility (1) for commenting on Federal, federally-assisted, and federally-licensed undertakings having an effect upon properties listed in the National Register of Historic Places; (2) for initiating studies of special preservation problems; (3) for recommending changes in existing laws and procedures pertaining to historic properties; (4) for recommending new regulations and legislation concerning historic preservation; (5) for coordinating the efforts of Federal, State, and local agencies; and (6) for generally advising the President and the Congress in historic preservation matters.

Citizens' Advisory Committee on Environmental Quality

1700 Pennsylvania Avenue NW., Washington, D.C. 20006. Phone, 202—223-3040.

Chairman.—Laurance S. Rockefeller.

The 15-member Committee was established by Executive Order 11472 of May 29, 1969, to advise the President and the Council on Environmental Quality on matters affecting environmental quality, including (1) the correlation of environmental quality considerations with other factors in Federal policies and programs, (2) stimulation of public and private participation in programs to protect against pollution of the Nation's air, water, land, and living resources, (3) cooperation between the Federal Government, State and local governments, and private organizations in environmental programs, (4) the effects of new and changing technologies on the environment, and (5) outdoor recreation and the beautification of our Nation's cities and countryside.

independent agencies

Federal Council for Science and Technology

216 Executive Office Building, Washington, D.C. 20506. Phone, 202—395-3534.

Executive Secretary.—Lawrence A. Goldmuntz.

The Council was established by Executive Order 10807 of March 13, 1959, amended by Executive Order 11381 of November 8, 1967, to promote closer cooperation among Federal agencies. Selected activities involving a number of agencies are coordinated through Council committees on Atmospheric Sciences, Materials Research and Development, High Energy Physics, Water Resources Research, Behavioral Sciences, Patent Policy, Long Range Planning, International Programs, Science Information, Academic Science and Engineering, Federal Laboratories, Environmental Quality, and Solid Earth Sciences. The Council Secretariat is provided by the Office of Science and Technology.

Migratory Bird Conservation Commission

Department of the Interior Building, Washington, D.C. 20240. Phone, 202—343-4676.

Secretary.—Walter R. McAllester.

The Commission was created by the Migratory Bird Conservation Act of February 18, 1929 (45 Stat. 1222; 16 U.S.C. 715–715r), to consider and pass upon any area of land and/or water that may be recommended by the Secretary of the Interior for purchase or rental for migratory bird refuges, and to fix a price at which such area may be purchased or rented.

National Forest Reservation Commission

1621 Kent Street, Arlington, Va. 22209. Phone, 703—557-9170.

Secretary.—Russell P. McRorey.

The Commission was established by the act of March 1, 1911 (36 Stat. 962; 16 U.S.C. 513), to consider and pass upon lands recommended by the Secretary of Agriculture for acquisition as national forests by purchase or exchange under the act, and to fix the consideration to be paid.

National Park Foundation

Department of the Interior Building, Washington, D.C. 20240. Phone, 202—343-8607.

Assistant Secretary.—Robert R. Garvey, Jr.

The Foundation, a non-profit, tax exempt corporation, was established by act of December 18, 1967 (81 Stat. 656; 16 U.S.C. 19e–19n), to accept and administer gifts of any nature for the benefit of or in connection with the National Park Service.

National Water Commission

800 North Quincy Street, Arlington, Va. 22203. Phone, 703—557-1960.

Executive Director.—Theodore M. Schad.

The Commission was established by act of September 26, 1968 (82 Stat. 868, 42 U.S.C. 1962a note), to consider ways of meeting U.S. water requirements in the future, and to sub-
more efficient use of water, reduction
mit reports on its studies to the President and the Congress.

The seven man commission is to terminate not later than September 26, 1973.

Water Resources Council

2120 L Street NW., Washington, D.C. 20037. Phone, 202—254-6303.

Director.—W. Don Maughan.

The Council was established by the Water Resources Planning Act of 1965 (79 Stat. 244; 42 U.S.C. 1962a), to maintain a continuing study of the adequacy of supplies of water necessary to meet the requirements in each water resource region in the United States, of the relation of regional or river basin plans and programs to the requirements of larger regions of the Nation, and of the adequacy of administrative and statutory means for the coordination of the water and related land resources policies and programs of the several Federal agencies. The Council also reviews the plans of the river basin commissions and transmits these plans with its recommendations to the President for his review and transmittal by him to Congress. It administers a program of Federal financial grants to States to aid them in comprehensive water and related land resource planning.

j. State Government agencies dealing with the environment

The following list of key state agencies concerned with protecting the environment is culled from the much more detailed listings in the Conservation Directory for 1972, which is published by the National Wildlife Federation, 1412 16th Street, N.W., Washington, D.C., and sold for $2.00. This directory is the most complete of its type in the field. State extension services are listed because in general they do much of the local environmental research, and are often good sources of information on ecological problems.

ALABAMA

DEPARTMENT OF CONSERVATION AND NATURAL RESOURCES, 64 N. Union St., Montgomery 36104 (205, 269-7221)

STATE EXTENSION SERVICES
Director of Extension Service: RALPH R. JONES, Auburn University, Auburn 36830 (205, 263-7521)

ALASKA

DEPARTMENT OF ENVIRONMENTAL CONSERVATION, Pouch 0, 419 Sixth St., Juneau 99801 (907, 586-5371)

DEPARTMENT OF NATURAL RESOURCES, Pouch M, Goldstein Bldg., Juneau 99801 (907, 586-6352)

STATE EXTENSION SERVICES
Director of Extension Service (and Sea Grant): DR. JAMES W. MATTHEWS, University of Alaska, College 99701 (202, 963-1110)

ARIZONA

STATE DIVISION OF SOIL CONSERVATION AND WATERSHED MANAGEMENT, 400 State Office Bldg., Phoenix 85007 (602, 271-4625)

STATE EXTENSION SERVICES
Director of Extension Service (and Sea Grant): DR. GEORGE E. HULL, University of Arizona, Tucson 85721 (602, 792-6011)

ARKANSAS

DEPARTMENT OF POLLUTION CONTROL AND ECOLOGY 1100 Harrington Ave., Little Rock 72202

STATE EXTENSION SERVICES
Director of Extension Service: C. A. VINES, P.O. Box 391, Little Rock 72203 (501, 372-4361)

CALIFORNIA

RESOURCES AGENCY, THE, 1416 Ninth St., Sacramento 95814 (916, 445-5656)

STATE EXTENSION SERVICES
Director of Extension Service: DR. GEORGE B. ALCORN, University of California, 2200 University Ave., Berkeley 94720 (415, 7252)

COLORADO

DEPARTMENT OF NATURAL RESOURCES, 1845 Sherman, Denver 80203 (303, 892-3311)

STATE EXTENSION SERVICES
Director of Extension Service: LOWELL H. WATTS, Colorado State University, Fort Collins 80521 (303, 297-0111)

CONNECTICUT

DEPARTMENT OF ENVIRONMENTAL PROTECTION, 539 State Office Building, Hartford 06115

STATE EXTENSION SERVICES
Director of Extension Services: DR. EDWIN J. KERSTING, University of Connecticut, Storrs, 06268 (203, 244-2000)

DELAWARE

DEPARTMENT OF NATURAL RESOURCES AND ENVIRONMENTAL CONTROL,
The Edward Tathall Bldg., Legislative Ave. and D St., Dover 19901

STATE EXTENSION SERVICES
Director of Extension Service: DR. SAMUEL M. GWINN, University of Delaware, Newark 19711 (302, 654-6131)

DISTRICT OF COLUMBIA

DEPARTMENT OF ENVIRONMENTAL SERVICES 1875 Connecticut Ave. N.W., Washington, DC 20009

STATE EXTENSION SERVICES
Director of Extension Service (and Sea Grant): DR. JOSEPH C. PAIGE, Federal City College, 1424 K. St., N.W., Washington, DC 20005 (202, 967-1221)

FLORIDA

DEPARTMENT OF NATURAL RESOURCES, Larson Bldg., Gaines St. at Monroe, Tallahassee 32304 (904, 224-7141)

STATE EXTENSION SERVICES
Director of Extension Service (and Sea Grant): DR. JOE N. BUSBY, University of Florida, Gainesville 32601 (904, 376-1681)

State agencies

GEORGIA

NATURAL AREAS COUNCIL, 544 Agriculture Bldg., 7 Hunter St., S.W., Atlanta 30303 (404, 656-3222)

STATE EXTENSION SERVICES
Director of Extension Service: DR. CHARLES P. ELLINGTON, University of Georgia, Athens 30601 (404, 548-5641)

HAWAII

DEPARTMENT OF AGRICULTURE, Agana 96910 (772-6866)
Director: JOSE T. BARCINAS
Assistant Director: GERALD S. A. PEREZ

GUAM

DEPARTMENT OF LAND AND NATURAL RESOURCES, Box 621, Honolulu 96809 (548-6550)

STATE EXTENSION SERVICES
Director of Extension Service: DR. C. PEAIRS WILSON, University of Hawaii, Honolulu 96822 (808, 944-8234)

IDAHO

DEPARTMENT OF AGRICULTURE, Suite 162, 1365 N. Orchard, P.O. Box 790, Boise 83701 (208, 384-3242)

DEPARTMENT OF HEALTH, Statehouse Boise 83707

STATE EXTENSION SERVICES
Director of Extension Service: DR. JAMES E. KRAUS, University of Idaho, Moscow 83843 (208, 342-2711)

ILLINOIS

DEPARTMENT OF CONSERVATION, 102 State Office Bldg., Springfield 62706 (217, 525-6302)

ENVIRONMENTAL PROTECTION AGENCY, 535 W. Jefferson St., Springfield 62704 (217, 525-3397)

STATE EXTENSION SERVICES
Director of Extension Service: DR. J. B. CLAAR, University of Illinois, Urbana 61801 (217, 525-4011)

INDIANA

DEPARTMENT OF NATURAL RESOURCES, 608 State Office Bldg., Indianapolis 46204

STATE EXTENSION SERVICES
Director of Extension Service: DR. HOWARD G. DIESSLIN, Purdue University, Lafayette 47907 (317, 633-7000)

IOWA

NATURAL RESOURCES COUNCIL, Grimes State Office Bldg., Des Moines 50319 (515, 281-5914)

STATE CONSERVATION COMMISSION, State Office Bldg., 300 4th St., Des Moines 50319 (515, 281-5145)

STATE EXTENSION SERVICES
Director of Extension Service (and Sea Grant): DR. MARVIN A. ANDERSON, Iowa State University, Ames 50010 (515, 294-4576)

KANSAS

STATE PARK AND RESOURCES AUTHORITY, 801 Harrison, Topeka 66612 (913, 296-2281)

STATE EXTENSION SERVICES:
Director of Extension Service (and Sea Grant): ROBERT A. BOHANNON, Ph.D., Kansas State University, Manhattan 66502 (913, 532-5820)

KENTUCKY

DEPARTMENT OF NATURAL RESOURCES, Executive Bldg., 209 St. Clair St., Frankfort 40601 (502, 564-3350)

STATE EXTENSION SERVICES:
Director of Extension Service: DR. CHARLES E. BARNHART, University of Kentucky, Lexington 40506 (606, 252-2775)

LOUISIANA

STATE DEPARTMENT OF CONSERVATION, P.O. Box 44275, Capitol Sta., Baton Rouge 70804 (504, 389-5161)

STATE EXTENSION SERVICES:
Director of Extension Service: JOHN A. COX, Louisiana State University, Baton Rouge 70803 (504, 388-2386)

MAINE

DEPARTMENT OF NATURAL RESOURCES, State Office Bldg., Augusta 04330 (207, 289-3821)

STATE EXTENSION SERVICES:
Director of Extension Service (and Sea Grant): EDWIN H. BATES, University of Maine, Orono 04473 (207, 942-8271)

MARYLAND

DEPARTMENT OF NATURAL RESOURCES, State Office Bldg., Annapolis 21401 (301, 267 plus extension)

STATE EXTENSION SERVICES:
Director of Extension Service (and Sea Grant): DR. ROBERT E. WAGNER, University of Maryland, College Park 20742 (301, 752-8460)

MASSACHUSETTS

DEPARTMENT OF NATURAL RESOURCES, Leverett Saltonstall Bldg., 100 Cambridge St., Boston 02202 (617, 727-3163)

STATE EXTENSION SERVICES:
Director of Extension Service: DR. ARLISS A. SPIELMAN, University of Massachusetts, Amherst 01002 (617, 223-2100)

MICHIGAN

DEPARTMENT OF NATURAL RESOURCES, Mason Bldg., Lansing 48926 (517, 373-1220)

STATE EXTENSION SERVICES:
Director of Extension Service: GEORGE S. McINTYRE, Michigan State University, East Lansing 48823 (517, 337-4283)

State agencies

MINNESOTA

DEPARTMENT OF NATURAL RESOURCES, 301 Centennial Bldg., 658 Cedar St., St. Paul 55101 (612, 221 plus extension)

POLLUTION CONTROL AGENCY, 717 Delaware St., S.E., Minneapolis 55440 (612, 378-1320)

STATE EXTENSION SERVICES
Director of Extension Service (and Sea Grant): DR. ROLAND H. ABRAHAM, University of Minnesota, St. Paul 55101 (612, 373-1223)

MISSISSIPPI

AIR AND WATER POLLUTION CONTROL COMMISSION, P.O. Box 827, Jackson 39205 (601, 354-6783)

STATE EXTENSION SERVICES
Director of Extension Service: DR. W. M. BOST, Mississippi State University, State College 39762 (601, 325-4436)

MISSOURI

DEPARTMENT OF CONSERVATION, P.O. Box 180, Jefferson City 65101 (314, 893-2626) (Organized: 1937)

STATE EXTENSION SERVICES
Acting Director of Extension Service (and Sea Grant): DR. CARL N. SCHENEMAN, University of Missouri, 309 University Hall, Columbia 65201 (314, 449-8186)

MONTANA

STATE DEPARTMENT OF HEALTH, Helena 59601 (406, 449-2544)

STATE SOIL CONSERVATION COMMITTEE, 422 Mitchell Bldg., Helena 59601 (406, 449-2608)

STATE EXTENSION SERVICES
Director of Extension Service: TORLIEF S. AASHEIM, Montana State University, Bozeman 59715 (406, 587-3121 Ext. 271)

NEBRASKA

DEPARTMENT OF ENVIRONMENTAL CONTROL, State House Sta., Box 94653, Lincoln 68509

STATE EXTENSION SERVICES
Director of Extension Service (and Sea Grant): DR. JOHN L. ADAMS, University of Nebraska, Lincoln 68503 (402, 472-7211

NEVADA

DEPARTMENT OF CONSERVATION AND NATURAL RESOURCES, Nye Bldg., Carson City 89701 (702, 882-7482)

ENVIRONMENTAL PROTECTION COMMISSION, State Health Div., 201 S. Fall St., Carson City 89701 (702, 882-7458)

STATE EXTENSION SERVICE
Director of Extension Service: DR. DALE W. BOHMONT, University of Nevada, Reno 89507 (702, 784-6611)

NEW HAMPSHIRE

COUNCIL OF RESOURCES AND DEVELOPMENT, State House Annex, Concord 03301 (603, 271-2155)

STATE EXTENSION SERVICES
Director of Extension Service (and Sea Grant): DR. MAYNARD C. HECKEL, University of New Hampshire, Taylor Hall, Durham 03824 (603, 868-7732)

NEW JERSEY

DEPARTMENT OF ENVIRONMENTAL PROTECTION, Labor and Industry Bldg., Box 1390, Trenton 08625 (609, 292-2886)
Commissioner: RICHARD J. SULLIVAN

STATE EXTENSION SERVICES
Director of Extension Services: DR. JOHN L. GERWIG, Rutgers - The State University, New Brunswick 08903 (201, 247-1766)

NEW MEXICO

ENVIRONMENTAL IMPROVEMENT AGENCY, P.O. Box 2348, Santa Fe 87501

STATE EXTENSION SERVICES
Director of Extension Service: DR. P. J. LEYENDECKER, New Mexico State University, Las Cruces, 88001 (505, 247-0311)

NEW YORK

BUREAU OF ENVIRONMENTAL PROTECTION, Dept. of Law, State of New York, 80 Center St., New York 10013

DEPARTMENT OF ENVIRONMENTAL CONSERVATION, 50 Wolf Rd., Albany 12201

STATE EXTENSION SERVICES
Director of Extension Service: DR. EDWARD H. SMITH, New York State College of Agriculture, Ithaca 14850 (607, 772-1050)

NORTH CAROLINA

DEPARTMENT OF CONSERVATION AND DEVELOPMENT, P.O. Box 27687, Raleigh 27611 (919, 829-4177)

STATE EXTENSION SERVICES
Director of Extension Service: DR. GEORGE HYATT, JR., North Carolina State University, Raleigh 27607 (919, 828-9031)

NORTH DAKOTA

DEPARTMENT OF HEALTH, Bismarck 58501

STATE PARK SERVICE, Rt. 2, Box 139, Mandan 58554 (701, 663-9571)

STATE EXTENSION SERVICES
Director of Extension Service (and Sea Grant): ARTHUR H. SCHULZ, North Dakota State University, Fargo 58102 (701, 237-5248)

State agencies

OHIO

DEPARTMENT OF NATURAL RESOURCES, 907 Ohio Departments Bldg., Columbus 43215 (614, 469-3770)

STATE EXTENSION SERVICES
Director of Extension Service (and Sea Grant): DR. ROY M. KOTTMAN, Ohio State University, 2120 Fyffe Ct., Columbus 43210 (614, 422-6891)

OKLAHOMA

DEPARTMENT OF WILDLIFE CONSERVATION, 1801 N. Lincoln, P.O. Box 53465, Oklahoma City 73105 (405, 521-3851)

STATE DEPARTMENT OF HEALTH, 3400 N. Eastern, Oklahoma City 73105 (405, 427-6561)

STATE EXTENSION SERVICES
Director of Extension Service (and Sea Grant): DR. JEAN C. EVANS, Oklahoma State University, Stillwater 74074 (405, 236-2517)

OREGON

DEPARTMENT OF ENVIRONMENTAL QUALITY, 1234 S.W. Morrison, Portland 97205

STATE EXTENSION SERVICES
Director of Extension Service: DR. LEE R. KOLMER, Oregon State University, Corvallis 97331 (503, 754-2713)

PENNSYLVANIA

DEPARTMENT OF ENVIRONMENTAL RESOURCES, Public Relations, Rm. 522, South Office Bldg., Harrisburg 17120

STATE EXTENSION SERVICES
Director of Extension Service: DR. RUSSELL E. LARSON, The Pennsylvania State University, University Park 16802 (814, 865-2541)

PUERTO RICO

DEPARTMENT OF HEALTH, P.O. Box 9342, Santurce 00908 (722-2050)

STATE EXTENSION SERVICES
Director of Extension Service (and Sea Grant): ENRIQUE R. ORTIZ, University of Puerto Rico, Rio Piedras 00928 (809, 765-8000)

RHODE ISLAND

DEPARTMENT OF NATURAL RESOURCES, 83 Park St., Providence 02903 (401, 277 plus extension)

STATE EXTENSION SERVICES
Director of Extension Service: DR. JAMES W. COBBLE, University of Rhode Island, Kingston 02881 (401, 528-1000)

SOUTH CAROLINA

POLLUTION CONTROL AUTHORITY, Box 11628, 1321 Lady St., Columbia 29211
Executive Director: H. J. WEBB (803, 758-2915)

STATE SOIL AND WATER CONSERVATION COMMISSION, 2414 Bull St., Columbia 29201 (803, 758-2824)

STATE EXTENSION SERVICES
Director of Extension Service (and Sea Grant): DR. WAYNE T. O'DELL, Clemson University, Clemson 29631 (803, 253-8371)

SOUTH DAKOTA

COMMITTEE ON WATER POLLUTION, State Department of Health, Pierre 57501

CONSERVATION COMMISSION, State Capitol, Pierre 57501 (605, 224-3258)

STATE EXTENSION SERVICES
Director of Extension Service: DR. JOHN T. STONE, South Dakota University, Brookings 57006 (605, 225-0250)
Extension Forester: LAWRENCE L. HELWIG, South Dakota University,

TENNESSEE

DEPARTMENT OF CONSERVATION, 2611 W. End Ave., Nashville 37203 (615, 741-2301)

STATE EXTENSION SERVICES
Director of Extension Service (and Sea Grant): DR. VERNON W. DARTER, University of Tennessee, P.O. Box 1071, Knoxville 37901 (615 524-4257)

TEXAS

STATE SOIL AND WATER CONSERVATION BOARD, 1018 First National Bldg., Temple 76501 (817, 773-2250)

WATER RIGHTS COMMISSION, P.O. Box 13207, Capitol Sta., Austin 78711 (512, 475-4514)

STATE EXTENSION SERVICES
Director of Extension Service: DR. JOHN E. HUTCHISON, Texas A & M University, College Station 77843 (713, 846-8821)

UTAH

STATE DEPARTMENT OF NATURAL RESOURCES, 225 State Capitol, Salt Lake City 84114

STATE EXTENSION SERVICES
Director Extension Service (and Sea Grant): DR. CLARK BALLARD, Utah State University, Logan 84321 (801, 753-7268)

VERMONT

AGENCY OF ENVIRONMENTAL CONSERVATION, Montpelier 05602 (802, 223-2311, Ext. 656)

STATE EXTENSION SERVICES
Director of Extension Service (and Sea Grant): R. P. DAVISON, University of Vermont, Burlington 05401 (802, 862-6501)

U.S. VIRGIN ISLANDS

STATE EXTENSION SERVICES
Acting Director of Extension Service (and Sea Grant): MORRIS HENDERSON, P.O. Box 166, Kingshill, St. Croix 00850 (809, 773-0246)

VIRGINIA

DEPARTMENT OF CONSERVATION AND ECONOMIC DEVELOPMENT, 911 E. Broad St., Richmond 23219 (703, 770-2121)

STATE EXTENSION SERVICES
Director of Extension Service: DR. W. E. SKELTON, Virginia Polytechnic Institute, Blacksburg 24061 (703, 649-3611)

WASHINGTON

DEPARTMENT OF ECOLOGY, Box 829, Olympia 98504 (206, 753-2800)

DEPARTMENT OF NATURAL RESOURCES, Box 168, Public Lands-Social Security Bldg., Olympia 98503 (206, 753-5327)

STATE EXTENSION SERVICES
Director of Extension Service: JOHN P. MILLER, Washington State University, Pullman 99163 (509, 838-4611)

WEST VIRGINIA

DEPARTMENT OF NATURAL RESOURCES, 1800 Washington St., East, Charleston 25305 (304, 348-2754)

STATE EXTENSION SERVICES
Director of Extension Service: DR. B. L. COFFINDAFFER, West Virginia University, 294 Coliseum, Morgantown 26505 (304, 296-3441)

WISCONSIN

DEPARTMENT OF NATURAL RESOURCES, Box 450, Madison 53701 (608, 266-2121)

STATE EXTENSION SERVICES
Director of Extension Service: DR. GALE L. VANDEBERG, University of Wisconsin, 432 North Lake St., Madison 53706 (608, 256-4441)

WYOMING

DEPARTMENT OF AGRICULTURE, 313 Capitol Bldg., Cheyenne 82001 (307, 777-7321)

State Conservation Commission:
Executive Secretary: MARVIN H. CRONBERG

DEPARTMENT OF HEALTH AND SOCIAL SERVICES, Div. of Health and Medical Services, State Office Bldg., Cheyenne 82001 (307, 777-7275)

STATE EXTENSION SERVICES
Director of Extension Service: DR. NEAL W. HILSTON, University of Wyoming, Box 3354, University Station, Laramie 82070 (307, 778-2220)

---

k. International organizations & agreements

SELECTED INTERNATIONAL ORGANIZATIONS in Which the United States Participates

International Boundary and Water Commission, United States and Mexico

United States Section: 818 Southwest Center, 300 Main Drive, El Paso, Tex. 79901.

ACTIVITIES.—Principal activities of the Commission have related to the construction, operation, and maintenance of diversion dams and flood control works, including the Rio Grande Rectification and Canalization Projects and the Lower Rio Grande Flood Control Project; construction and operation of international storage dams and powerplants on the Rio Grande; implementation of arrangements, including an international stream gaging program, for equitable distribution between the two countries of Rio Grande and Colorado River waters; carrying out . . . the construction and operation supervision of international sewage disposal plants serving specified border communities.

International Joint Commission—United States and Canada

United States Section: 1717 H Street NW., Washington, D.C. 20440. Phones, 202—296–2142 or 202—632–9456.

Chairman.—Christian A. Herter, Jr.
Secretary.—William A. Bullard.

ACTIVITIES.—The Commission has jurisdiction over all cases involving use, obstruction, or diversion of boundary waters between the United States and Canada; waters flowing from boundary waters; and waters at a lower level than the boundary in rivers flowing across the boundary.

Except in cases of special agreement, the approval of the Commission is required for the construction and maintenance of any works that would raise the natural level of boundary waters and for works that would back water above the natural level at the boundary in waters crossing the boundary. The Commission acts also to prevent pollution of boundary waters and waters crossing the boundary.

World Health Organization

Headquarters: Avenue Appia, Geneva, Switzerland.

Regional Office for the Americas: Pan American Sanitary Bureau, Twenty-third Street and Virginia Avenue NW., Washington, D.C. 20037. Phone, 202—223–4700.

Director General.—Dr. Marcolino G. Candau.

ACTIVITIES.—WHO assists countries in strengthening public health services, including such activities as communicable disease control, maternal and child health (including the health aspects of population dynamics), environmental health, and the education and training of both professional and paramedical personnel.

Pan American Health Organization

Executive Organ: Pan American Sanitary Bureau, 525 Twenty-third Street NW., Washington, D.C. 20037. Phone, 202—223–4700.
Director.—Dr. Abraham Horwitz.

By agreement between the World Health Organization and the Pan American Health Organization, effective July 1, 1949, the Bureau serves as Regional Office of WHO for the Americas.

World Meteorological Organization

Secretariat: 41 Avenue Giuseppe Motta, Geneva, Switzerland.

Secretary General.—David Arthur Davies.

This organization has no office in Washington, D.C. Information may be obtained from the Office of International Economic and Social Affairs, Department of State 20520, and the National Oceanic and Atmospheric Administration, Department of Commerce, Rockville, Md. 20852.

PURPOSE.—The purposes of the WMO are (1) to facilitate worldwide cooperation in the establishment of networks of stations for making meteorological observations or other geophysical observations,

references

BLEICHER, "An Overview of International Environmental Regulation," 2 *Ecology Law Quarterly* 1, 1972

STEIN. Robert, *The Potential of Regional Organizations in Managing the Human Environment,* Woodrow Wilson International Center for Scholars, May 1972

MCLAIN, Jon, "Stepping Across Boundaries," 14 *Environment,* No. 4, May 1972 at 16

U.N. Conference on the Human Environment

The United Nations Conference on the Human Environment was held in Stockholm in June of 1972. The conference's first major agreement was to recommend a 10-year ban on whaling (*Washington Post,* June 10, 1972 at A7), but the International Whaling Commission, which had power to implement that recommendation, ignored it (*Washington Post,* June 30, 1972 at 26).

The major achievement, besides the publicity given environmental problems, was creation of a new U.N. environmental agency that will have a ceiling budget of $20 million annually for the first five years. This compares with budgets of $250 million for the U.N.'s other specialized agencies. However, 10 of the 20 millions are to go towards a global monitoring and assessment program called Earthwatch, most of which has been in operation for 10 years under the name World Weather Watch. Since the World Meteorological Organization has in the past been unable to obtain the promised voluntary contributions for this program, it is hoped that the new name and somewhat expanded role will permit more ready funding.

The remaining $10 million authorized will be insufficient for the many surveys and research activities approved by the conference, though many such activities are already being conducted by the U.N., and must now be incorporated within the new agency.

The U.S. contribution to the new agency will be $8 million a year, but as the U.S. share of all U.N. expenses is to drop from 31 to 25 percent, net U.S. payments to the U.N. will drop by about $28 million a year.

See, Sterling, Clair, "Stockholm: A Summing Up", *The Washington Post,* June 25, 1972 at B6.

international agreements

Formal public agreements between the United States and other national political units are listed below. But a warning may be warranted for some readers. The political units (nations) which made these agreements are not always dominant in controlling the man-made forces which pass among their territories. At least since the Dutch East India Company, corporations and political states have vied for such control—sometimes in concert, sometimes in competition. Although corporate actions are generally quieter than in the heyday of the "banana republics," United Fruit still "loans" the U.S. Government an official to fill the top Latin American post in the State Department (undersecretary of state), and oil firms are considered to have better "political" sections in the Mideast than does the U.S. Government.The mistake would be to think of the corporations as controlling governmental policy, as though a shark needed pilot fish to determine where it would go. Rather, it must be realized that the corporations themselves are frequently by far the stronger entities, and that their own agreements, usually private, may be of far greater significance than those between or among governments. "At least eighty-five" multinational businesses reportedly have assets greater than those of 50 countries which are members of the United Nations (*Saturday Review*, May 20, 1972 at 65). Like any such figures, these are open to greatly varying interpretations, but there is little real doubt that Standard Oil of New Jersey is a great deal more powerful internationally than, say, Chad or Nicaragua. Unfortunately, we have no list available of key private agreements. Effects of these corporations within the United States will be alluded to briefly several times in this work, but a significant treatment is obviously beyond the scope of this work.

See generally: KEOHANE, Robert O., and NYE, Joseph S. Jr., eds., *Transnational Relations and World Politics,* Harvard University Press, Cambridge, Mass., 1972 (*paper*).

TREATIES AND OTHER INTERNATIONAL AGREEMENTS CONTAINING ANTI-POLLUTION PROVISIONS

Multilateral

Antarctica

The Antarctic Treaty, done at Washington December 1, 1959.
12 UST 794; TIAS 4780.

(Art. V prohibits nuclear explosions in Antarctica and the disposal there of radioactive waste material).

Interim guidelines for conservation of fauna and flora, adopted as Recommendation III-IX under the Antarctic Treaty at Brussels June 2-13, p964.
17 UST 991; TIAS 6058.

(Provides that each participating Government shall, to the extent feasible, take all reasonable measures towards the alleviation of pollution of the waters adjacent to the coast and ice shelves).

Aviation

Convention on International Civil Aviation, done at Chicago December 7, 1944.
61 Stat. 1180; TIAS 1591.

(Art. 12 requires contracting States to adopt measures to insure that every aircraft carrying its nationality mark shall comply with rules of the air in force wherever it is. It requires each State to keep its own regulations uniform, to the greatest possible extent, with those established under the Convention, and declares that over the high seas, the rules in force are those established under the Convention. Annex 2 (Rules of the Air) established under the Convention provides in Chapter 3, paragraph 3.1.4 that "Nothing shall be dropped or sprayed from an aircraft in flight except under conditions prescribed by the appropriate authority.")

Health

International sanitary regulations, adopted at Geneva May 25, 1951.
7 UST 2255; TIAS 3625.

(Article 14 provides that every airport shall also be provided with an effective system for the removal and safe disposal of excrement, refuse, waste water, condemned food, and other matter dangerous to health.)

(Article 29 provides that a health authority may take all practicable measures to control the discharge from any ship of sewage and refuse which might contaminate the waters of a port, river, or canal.)

(Article 31 provides that no matter capable of causing any epidemic disease shall be thrown or allowed to fall from an aircraft when it is in flight.)

(Article 63 provides that human dejecta, waste water including bilge-water, waste matter, and any matter which is considered to be contaminated shall not be discharged or unloaded without previous disinfection. Their safe disposal shall be the responsibility of the health authority.)

International health regulations, adopted at Boston July 25, 1969. Enters into force January 1, 1971 and will replace, as between the States bound by these regulations, the 1951 international sanitary regulations cited above.)

(Articles 14, 30, 32, and 65 contain provisions similar to those cited above.)

international agreements

Maritime matters

International convention for the prevention of pollution of the sea by oil, done at London May 12, 1954, as amended April 11, 1962.
12 UST 2989; TIAS 4900.
17 UST 1523; TIAS 6109 (amendments).

(Convention sets up prohibited zones around the coasts of all countries into which ships of Governments parties to the convention are prohibited from discharging oil or oily wastes.)

Convention on the high seas, done at Geneva April 29, 1958.
13 UST 2312; TIAS 5200.

(Art. 24 requires States parties to draw up regulations to prevent pollution of the seas by discharge of oil from ships or pipelines or resulting from exploitation and exploration of seabed and its subsoil. Art. 25 requires parties to prevent pollution of seas from dumping of radio-active waste and to co-operate with international organizations in measures for preventing pollution of seas or airspace above, resulting from activities with radio-active or other harmful agents.)

Convention on the continental shelf, done at Geneva April 29, 1958.
15 UST 471; TIAS 5578.

(Art. 5, para. 7, requires a coastal State party to undertake, in the safety zones around installations and devices for exploiting and exploring natural resources on its continental shelf, all appropriate measures for the protection of the living resources of the sea from harmful agents.)

International convention relating to intervention on the high seas in cases of oil pollution casualties, done at Brussels November 29, 1969. (The convention has been signed by the United States and submitted to the Senate for advice and consent to ratification but is not yet in force.)
Senate Executive G, 91st Congress, 2nd Session.

(Article 1 provides that parties to the present convention may take such measures on the high seas as may be necessary to prevent, mitigate or eliminate grave and imminent danger to their coastline or related interests from pollution or threat of pollution of the sea by oil, following upon a maritime casualty or acts related to such a casualty, which may reasonably be expected to result in major harmful consequences.

International convention on civil liability for oil pollution damage, done at Brussels November 29, 1969. (The convention has been signed by the United States and submitted to the Senate for advice and consent to ratification but is not yet in force.)
Senate Executive G. 91st Congress, 2nd Session. (The convention establishes rules relating to the liability of the owner of an oil-carrying vessel to governments and private parties for the damages caused by oil pollution.)

Nuclear (General)

The treaty banning nuclear weapon tests in the atmosphere, in outer space and under water, done at Moscow August 5, 1963.
14 UST 1313; TIAS 5433.

(Art. I prohibits any nuclear explosion in the atmosphere, outer space or under water and in any other environment if it causes radioactive debris outside the territorial limits of the State where the explosion is conducted.)

Outer Space

Treaty on principles governing the activities of states in the exploration and use of outer space, including the moon and other bodies, done at Washington, London and Moscow January 27, 1967.
18 UST 2410; TIAS 6347.

(Art. IX requires States parties to avoid harmfully contaminating Outer Space and adversely changing the environment of the earth by introducing extraterrestrial matter.)

Bilateral

Canada

Treaty relating to boundary waters and questions arising along the boundary between the U.S. and Canada, signed at Washington January 11, 1909.
36 Stat. 2448; TS 548; III Redmond 2607.

(Art. IV provides that the boundary waters and waters flowing across the boundary shall not be polluted on either side of the injury of health or property on the other. The International Joint Commission has made a number of recommendations to carry out the provisions of Art. IV of the Boundary Waters Treaty that have been approved by the U.S. and Canada. See "Documents On the Use and Control of the Waters of Interstate and International Streams," H. Doc. 319, 90th Cong., 2nd Sess., pp. 391-393.)

Convention between the U.S. and Canada concerning operation of smelter at Trail, British Columbia, signed at Ottawa April 15, 1935.
49 Stat. 3245; TS 893; IV Trenwith 4009.

(Provided for payment by Canada to U.S. of $350,000 in damages caused prior to 1932 byfumesdischarged from the smelter of the Consolidated Mining and Smelting Co. at Trail, British Columbia, to property in the State of Washington, in accordance with finding of International Joint Commission pursuant to Art. IX of 1909 Boundary Waters Treaty; submitted to arbitration the U.S. claim of damages after January 1, 1932.)

Agreement Between Canada and the United States of America on Great Lakes Water Quality, April 15, 1972.

Mexico

Convention between the U.S. and Mexico to facilitate the carrying out of the principles contained in the treaty of November 12, 1884, and to avoid the difficulties occasioned by changes which take place in the beds of the Rio Grande and Colorado River, signed at Washington March 1, 1889.
26 Stat. 1512; TS 232; I Malloy 1167.

(Establishes the International Boundary Commission to decide all questions and differences growing out of changes in the rivers, works constructed therein, or any other cause affecting the boundary.)

Treaty between the U.S. and Mexico relating to the utilization of waters of the Colorado and Tijuana Rivers and of the Rio Grande, signed at Washington February 3, 1944.
59 Stat. 1219; TS 994; 3 UNTS 313.

(Renames the Commission as the International Boundary and Water Commission, with a U.S. Section and Mexican Section, and with additional powers and duties. Art. 3 provides that in making provision for joint use of international waters, the Commission shall be guided by the following order of preferences: 1. domestic and municipal uses; 2. agriculture and stock-raising;

3. electric power; 4. industrial uses; 5. navigation; 6. fishing and hunting; 7. any other beneficial uses. All of the foregoing uses "shall be subject to any sanitary measures or works which may be mutually agreed upon by the two Governments, which hereby agree to give preferential attention to the solution of all border sanitation problems.")

Recommendations of the International Boundary and Water Commission to improve the quality of water reaching Morelos Dam in Mexico from the U.S., approved by the Presidents of the U.S. and Mexico on March 22, 1965.
52 Dept. of State Bulletin 556 (1965).

(Construction of a drain to permit control of the salinity of water impounded by and diverted from Morelos Dam for irrigation purposes.)

Panama

Isthmian canal convention between the U.S. and Panama, signed at Washington November 18, 1903:
33 Stat. 2234; TS 431; II Malloy 1349.

(Under Art. IV Panama grants to the U.S. in perpetuity the right to use the rivers, streams and other water for navigation, water supply, and for maintenance, operation, sanitation and protection of the Canal.)

General treaty of friendship and cooperation between the U.S. and Panama, signed at Washington March 2, 1936.
53 Stat. 1807; TS 945.

(Art. I declares that the 1903 Convention contemplates use, occupation and control by the U.S. of the Canal Zone and additional lands and waters under U.S. jurisdiction for the purposes of "efficient maintenance, operation, sanitation and protection of the Canal and its auxiliary works.")

international agreements

Agreement for enlargement and use by Canal Zone of sewerage facilities in Colon Free Zone Area, concluded by exchange of notes at Panama March 8 and 25, 1954.
5 UST 782; TIAS 2966.

(Facilities to be constructed at U.S. expense; to be owned by Panama, subject to continuous use by U.S.)

Spain

Agreement of cooperation and friendship, signed at Washington August 6, 1970. Enters into force September 26, 1970.

(Article 16 provides that cooperation will be developed between the parties to the fight against pollution in all its forms, especially in the atmosphere, in waters and in the soil.)

Union of Soviet Socialist Republics

Agreement on Certain fishery problems in the northeastern part of the Pacific Ocean off the coast of the United States, signed at Washington February 13, 1967, as amended and extended January 31, 1969.
18 UST 190; 20 UST 340; TIAS 6218, 6636.

(Paragraph 7 provides that both Governments will take appropriate measures to ensure that, to the extent practicable, waste materials are discharged at sea only in waters deeper than 1000 meters.)

Agreement on Cooperation in the Field of Environmental Protection between the U.S. and the U.S.S.R., signed May 23, 1972 in Moscow.

Article 5 provides for the establishment of a joint U.S.-U.S.S.R. committee to meet annually to approve concrete measures for cooperation. The treaty suggests that these measures may take the form of exchange of scientists, experts, and research scholars, the organization of meetings, the exchange of information, and "other forms of cooperation," but no specific project or exchange is mentioned in the treaty. In a press conference on the day of the signing, CEQ Chairman Russell E. Train indicated that nothing definite had yet been planned. This agreement had been signed by the President but not yet ratified by the Senate when this book went to press.

NOTE

Most of the above was compiled by the Treaty Affairs Section, Office of the Legal Adviser, Department of State, August 7, 1970; additions have been made by the author through the spring of 1972, but these additions may be incomplete.

CHAPTER ONE: Environmental Policy

the legal right to a clean environment

In rhetoric, at least, the United States government is formally committed to encouraging "productive and enjoyable harmony between man and his environment." This promise is made in the National Environmental Policy Act of 1969.[1] The importance of this Act is the principal topic of this chapter. We will also discuss the possibilities for a Constitutional right to a healthful environment, and, finally, the clear enunciation of such a right in recent amendments to some state constitutions.

The reader considering involvement in attempts to enforce the National Environmental Policy Act is referred also to the extensive materials in this chapter's index.

In brief, passage of the National Environmental Policy Act of 1969 (popularly known as NEPA—pronounced nee-pa) was an attempt to create a new frame of reference for the consideration of all major activities by the Federal government: a frame of reference that would include consideration of effects on the environment. Its means of doing this is to attempt to internalize within each agency processes which should require real thought concerning environmental impact.

origin of NEPA

NEPA was the culmination of a decade of previously unsuccessful Congressional attempts to define and put into practice a national environmental policy. The Resources and Conservation Act,[2] proposed in 1959, called on the Executive branch to coordinate its scattered conservation efforts. The Ecological Resources and Surveys Bill,[3] introduced several years later, contained provisions designed to remedy the inadequate use of environmental data by federal agencies. A bill very similar to the version of NEPA as introduced in the Senate was introduced without success in 1967.[4]

The original 1969 version of the bill which was to become NEPA, Senate Bill 1075, was introduced by Senator Henry Jackson of Washington. It had a three-fold purpose: to establish a national environmental policy; to authorize research concerning natural resources, and to establish a council of environmental advisors.

As introduced, Senator Jackson's bill did not contain any operational procedure to assure implementation of a national environmental policy. Although the language called for "a national strategy for management of the human environment," it did not provide any specific procedures for review, coordination or control of continuing activities or decision-making.[5] It was after the single-day hearing on S. 1075 before the Senate Interior and Insular Affairs Committee that the provision for an "action-forcing" or operational measure was added to the bill.[6] This added section was number 102(2)(C), which requires Federal agencies to prepare an "environmental impact" statement if any of their proposed actions might significantly affect the environment.

1. 42 U.S.C. § 4321 *et. seq.*

2. S. 2549, 86th Cong., 2d Sess. (1960).

3. S. 2282, 89th Cong., 2d Sess. (1966).

4. S. 2805, 90th Cong., 2d Sess. (1968).

5. Hearings on S. 1075 before the Senate Committee on Interior and Insular Affairs, Ninety-first Congress, 1st Session (1969).

6. *Ibid.*

NEPA, as enacted, represents a synthesis by a House-Senate conference committee of S. 1075 and its House counterpart, H. R. 6750, sponsored by Representative John S. Dingall of Michigan. Sections 101, 102, 103, 104 and 105 are based on S. 1075, while the remaining sections are based primarily on the House bill.

One purpose in enacting NEPA was to fulfill the need for an interdisciplinary approach to environmental management and decision-making in all branches and levels of the Federal government. Previously, President Nixon had attempted to improve the executive organization through his executive order of May 29, 1969, which created an interdepartmental, Cabinet-level Environmental Quality Council and a Citizen's Advisory Committee of Environmental Quality.[7]

NEPA in brief

NEPA provides four new approaches for dealing with environmental problems on a preventive and anticipatory basis, and represents a break from the previous practices of dealing only with environmental crises and attempting to reclaim resources from past abuse.

Section 101 provides a statement of national environmental policy and a declaration of national goals. Senator Jackson assessed the philosophy of the section in the following remarks:

> A statement of environmental policy is more than a statement of what we believe as a people and as a nation. It establishes priorities and gives expression to our national goals and aspirations. It provides a statutory foundation to which administrators may refer to for guidance in making decisions which find environmental values in conflict with other values.
>
> What is involved is a congressional declaration that we do not intend, as a a government or as a people, to initiate actions which endanger the continued existence or the health of mankind: That we will not intentionally initiate actions which will do irreparable damage to the air, land, and water which support life on earth.[8]

Section 102 provides the "action-forcing" procedures of the Act. All federal agencies are required to determine the environmental impact of their actions in decision-making. Section 102 requires agencies which propose actions to consult with federal and state agencies having jurisdiction or expertise in environmental matters and prepare an environmental impact statement in accordance with the specific provisions of the Section. Thus, Section 102 forces federal agencies to internalize the consideration of the environmental repercussions of their activities.

Title II of the Act establishes a Council on Environmental Quality in the Executive Office of the President. The Council is designed to provide the President with objective advice and maintain a continuing supervision of federal activities which affect the environment. The Council is required to establish a system for monitoring environmental indicators, maintain records on the status of the environment, and ensure that there will be complete data available for the anticipation of emerging environmental problems and trends. The Office of Environmental Quality, which comprises the staff for the Council, was created by the Environmental Quality Improvement Act of 1970,[9] the text of which is printed in the materials which follow.

NEPA did not create the kind of organization that was envisioned originally by its Congressional midwives. The concept of the Council on Environmental Quality as an independent group of environmental wisemen, charged with viewing the national situation broadly and setting goals accordingly, has largely disappeared. The Council as created by the Act is an arm of

7. Executive Order 11472, May 29, 1969.

8. 115 Cong. Rec. 40416 (1969) (remarks of Sen. Jackson).

9. P. L. 91-224, April 3, 1970.

the Office of the President, and as such speaks for the President. Its position as an independent voice is thus compromised by its relationship with the President: while the Council influences policy, policy influences the Council. Yet it is clearly undesirable to present to the public political decisions adorned with the oil-spotted halo of disinterested wisdom.

We have made great strides in our efforts to present to the President on a systematic basis essential environmental information. But a government-sponsored independent environmental watchdog has yet to be unleashed.

Section 201 of NEPA requires the President to submit an annual Environmental Quality Report to Congress. This report is similar to the annual Economic Report of the President, required by the Full Employment Act of 1946.

A reading of the National Environmental Policy Act, plus the related Environmental Quality Improvement Act and Executive Order 11514 (the texts of which follow) is recommended to all serious students. The text of Executive Order 11602, which offers further support for the NEPA philosophy, is printed in the appendix to Chapter Three, since it is concerned primarily with air pollution. Discussions of various aspects of NEPA follow the texts of the above-mentioned documents.

The National Environmental Policy Act of 1969

42 U.S.C. § 4321 *et seq.*

Public Law 91-190, January 1, 1970

AN ACT To establish a national policy for the environment, to provide for the establishment of a Council on Environmental Quality, and for other purposes

Be it enacted by the Senate and House of Representatives of the United States of America in Congress assembled, That this Act may be cited as the "National Environmental Policy Act of 1969".

PURPOSE

SEC. 2. The purposes of this Act are: To declare a national policy which will encourage productive and enjoyable harmony between man and his environment; to promote efforts which will prevent or eliminate damage to the environment and biosphere and stimulate the health and welfare of man; to enrich the understanding of the ecological systems and natural resources important to the Nation; and to establish a Council on Environmental Quality.

TITLE I

DECLARATION OF NATIONAL ENVIRONMENTAL POLICY

SEC. 101. (a) The Congress, recognizing the profound impact of man's activity on the interrelations of all components of the natural environment, particularly the profound influences of population growth, high-density urbanization, industrial expansion, resource exploitation, and new and expanding technological advances and recognizing further the critical importance of restoring and maintaining environmental quality to the overall welfare and development of man, declares that it is the continuing policy of the Federal Government, in cooperation with State and local governments, and other concerned public and private organizations, to use all practicable means and measures, including financial and technical assistance, in a manner calculated to foster and promote the general welfare, to create and maintain conditions under which man and nature can exist in productive harmony, and fulfill the social, economic, and other requirements of present and future generations of Americans.

(b) In order to carry out the policy set forth in this Act, it is the continuing responsibility of the Federal Government to use all practicable means, consistent with other essential considerations of national policy, to improve and coordinate Federal plans, functions, programs, and resources to the end that the Nation may—

(1) fulfill the responsibilities of each generation as trustee of the environment for succeeding generations;

(2) assure for all Americans safe, healthful, productive, and esthetically and culturally pleasing surroundings;

(3) attain the widest range of beneficial uses of the environment without degradation, risk to health or safety, or other undesirable and unintended consequences;

(4) preserve important historic, cultural, and natural aspects of our national heritage, and maintain, wherever possible, an environment which supports diversity, and variety of individual choice;

National Environmental Policy Act of 1969

(5) achieve a balance between population and resource use which will permit high standards of living and a wide sharing of life's amenities; and

(6) enhance the quality of renewable resources and approach the maximum attainable recycling of depletable resources.

(c) The Congress recognizes that each person should enjoy a healthful environment and that each person has a responsibility to contribute to the preservation and enhancement of the environment.

Sec. 102. The Congress authorizes and directs that, to the fullest extent possible: (1) the policies, regulations, and public laws of the United States shall be interpreted and administered in accordance with the policies set forth in this Act, and (2) all agencies of the Federal Government shall—

(A) utilize a systematic, interdisciplinary approach which will insure the integrated use of the natural and social sciences and the environmental design arts in planning and in decisionmaking which may have an impact on man's environment;

(B) identify and develop methods and procedures, in consultation with the Council on Environmental Quality established by title II of this Act, which will insure that presently unquantified environmental amenities and values may be given appropriate consideration in decisionmaking along with economic and technical considerations;

(C) include in every recommendation or report on proposals for legislation and other major Federal actions significantly affecting the quality of the human environment, a detailed statement by the responsible official on—

(i) the environmental impact of the proposed action,

(ii) any adverse environmental effects which cannot be avoided should the proposal be implemented,

(iii) alternatives to the proposed action,

(iv) the relationship between local short-term uses of man's environment and the maintenance and enhancement of long-term productivity, and

(v) any irreversible and irretrievable commitments of resources which would be involved in the proposed action should it be implemented.

Prior to making any detailed statement, the responsible Federal official shall consult with and obtain the comments of any Federal agency which has jurisdiction by law or special expertise with respect to any environmental impact involved. Copies of such statement and the comments and views of the appropriate Federal, State, and local agencies, which are authorized to develop and enforce environmental standards, shall be made available to the President, the Council on Environmental Quality and to the public as provided by section 552 of title 5, United States Code, and shall accompany the proposal through the existing agency review processes;

(D) study, develop, and describe appropriate alternatives to recommended courses of action in any proposal which involves unresolved conflicts concerning alternative uses of available resources;

(E) recognize the worldwide and long-range character of environmental problems and, where consistent with the foreign policy of the United States, lend appropriate support to initiatives, resolutions, and programs designed to maximize international cooperation in anticipating and preventing a decline in the quality of mankind's world environment;

(F) make available to States, counties, municipalities, institutions, and individuals, advice and information useful in restoring, maintaining, and enhancing the quality of the environment;

(G) initiate and utilize ecological information in the planning and development of resource-oriented projects; and

(H) assist the Council on Environmental Quality established by title II of this Act.

SEC. 103. All agencies of the Federal Government shall review their present statutory authority, administrative regulations, and current policies and procedures for the purpose of determining whether there are any deficiencies or inconsistencies therein which prohibit full compliance with the purposes and provisions of this Act and shall propose to the President not later than July 1, 1971, such measures as may be necessary to bring their authority and policies into conformity with the intent, purposes, and procedures set forth in this Act.

SEC. 104. Nothing in section 102 or 103 shall in any way affect the specific statutory obligations of any Federal agency (1) to comply with criteria or standards of environmental quality, (2) to coordinate or consult with any other Federal or State agency, or (3) to act, or refrain from acting contingent upon the recommendations or certification of any other Federal or State agency.

SEC. 105. The policies and goals set forth in this Act are supplementary to those set forth in existing authorizations of Federal agencies.

TITLE II

COUNCIL ON ENVIRONMENTAL QUALITY

SEC. 201. The President shall transmit to the Congress annually beginning July 1, 1970, an Environmental Quality Report (hereinafter referred to as the "report") which shall set forth (1) the status and condition of the major natural, manmade, or altered environmental classes of the Nation, including, but not limited to, the air, the aquatic, including marine, estuarine, and fresh water, and the terrestrial environment, including, but not limited to, the forest, dryland, wetland, range, urban, suburban, and rural environment; (2) current and foreseeable trends in the quality, management and utilization of such environments and the effects of those trends on the social, economic, and other requirements of the Nation; (3) the adequacy of available natural resources for fulfilling human and economic requirements of the Nation in the light of expected population pressures; (4) a review of the programs and activities (including regulatory activities) of the Federal Government, the State and local governments, and nongovernmental entities or individuals, with particular reference to their effect on the environment and on the conservation, development and utilization of natural resources; and (5) a program for remedying the deficiencies of existing programs and activities, together with recommendations for legislation.

SEC. 202. There is created in the Executive Office of the President a Council on Environmental Quality (hereinafter referred to as the "Council"). The Council shall be composed of three members who shall be appointed by the President to serve at his pleasure, by and with the advice and consent of the Senate. The President shall designate one of the members of the Council to serve as Chairman. Each member shall be a person who, as a result of his training, experience, and attainments, is exceptionally well qualified to analyze and interpret environmental trends and information of all kinds; to appraise programs and activities of the Federal Government in the light of the policy set forth in title I of this Act; to be conscious of and responsive to the scientific, economic, social, esthetic, and cultural needs and interests of the Nation; and to formulate and recommend national policies to promote the improvement of the quality of the environment.

SEC. 203. The Council may employ such officers and employees as may be necessary to carry out its functions under this Act. In addition, the Council may employ and fix the compensation of such experts and consultants as may be necessary for the carrying out of its functions under this Act, in accordance with section 3109 of title 5, United States Code (but without regard to the last sentence thereof).

SEC. 204. It shall be the duty and function of the Council—

(1) to assist and advise the President in the preparation of the Environmental Quality Report required by section 201;

(2) to gather timely and authoritative information concerning the conditions and trends in the quality of the environment both current and prospective, to analyze and interpret such information for the purpose of determining whether such conditions and trends are interfering, or are likely to interfere, with the achievement of the policy set forth in title I of this Act, and to compile and submit to the President studies relating to such conditions and trends;

(3) to review and appraise the various programs and activities of the Federal Government in the light of the policy set forth in title I of this Act for the purpose of determining the extent to which such programs and activities are contributing to the achievement of such policy, and to make recommendations to the President with respect thereto;

(4) to develop and recommend to the President national policies to foster and promote the improvement of environmental quality to meet the conservation, social, economic, health, and other requirements and goals of the Nation;

(5) to conduct investigations, studies, surveys, research, and analyses relating to ecological systems and environmental quality;

(6) to document and define changes in the natural environment, including the plant and animal systems, and to accumulate necessary data and other information for a con-

tinuing analysis of these changes or trends and an interpretation of their underlying causes;

(7) to report at least once each year to the President on the state and condition of the environment; and

(8) to make and furnish such studies, reports thereon, and recommendations with respect to matters of policy and legislation as the President may request.

SEC. 205. In exercising its powers, functions, and duties under this Act, the Council shall—

(1) consult with the Citizens' Advisory Committee on Environmental Quality established by Executive Order numbered 11472, dated May 29, 1969, and with such representatives of science, industry, agriculture, labor, conservation organizations, State and local governments and other groups, as it deems advisable; and

(2) utilize, to the fullest extent possible, the services, facilities and information (including statistical information) of public and private agencies and organizations, and individuals, in order that duplication of effort and expense may be avoided, thus assuring that the Council's activities will not unnecessarily overlap or conflict with similar activities authorized by law and performed by established agencies.

SEC. 206. Members of the Council shall serve full time and the Chairman of the Council shall be compensated at the rate provided for Level II of the Executive Schedule Pay Rates (5 U.S.C. 5313). The other members of the Council shall be compensated at the rate provided for Level IV of the Executive Schedule Pay Rates (5 U.S.C. 5315).

SEC. 207. There are authorized to be appropriated to carry out the provisions of this Act not to exceed $300,000 for fiscal year 1970, $700,000 for fiscal year 1971, and $1,000,000 for each fiscal year thereafter.

Approved January 1, 1970.

The Environmental Quality Improvement Act of 1970

Public Law 91-224, April 3, 1970

42 U.S.C. §§ 4371-4374

TITLE II—ENVIRONMENTAL QUALITY
(OF THE WATER QUALITY IMPROVEMENT ACT OF 1970)

SHORT TITLE

SEC. 201. This title may be cited as the "Environmental Quality Improvement Act of 1970."

FINDINGS, DECLARATIONS, AND PURPOSES

SEC. 202. (a) The Congress finds—

(1) that man has caused changes in the environment;

(2) that many of these changes may affect the relationship between man and his environment; and

(3) that population increases and urban concentration contribute directly to pollution and the degradation of our environment.

(b)(1) The Congress declares that there is a national policy for the environment which provides for the enhancement of environmental quality. This policy is evidenced by statutes heretofore enacted relating to the prevention, abatement, and control of environmental pollution, water and land resources, transportation, and economic and regional development.

(2) The primary responsibility for implementing this policy rests with State and local governments.

(3) The Federal Government encourages and supports implementation of this policy through appropriate regional organizations established under existing law.

(c) The purposes of this title are—

(1) to assure that each Federal department and agency conducting or supporting public works activities which affect the environment shall implement the policies established under existing law; and

(2) to authorize an Office of Environmental Quality, which, notwithstanding any other provision of law, shall provide the professional and administrative staff for the Council on Environmental Quality established by Public Law 91–190.

OFFICE OF ENVIRONMENTAL QUALITY

SEC. 203. (a) There is established in the Executive Office of the President an office to be known as the Office of Environmental Quality (hereafter in this title referred to as the "Office"). The Chairman of the Council on Environmental Quality established by Public Law 91–190 shall be the Director of the Office. There shall be in the Office a Deputy Director who shall be appointed by the President, by and with the advice and consent of the Senate.

(b) The compensation of the Deputy Director shall be fixed by the President at a rate not in excess of the annual rate of compensation payable to the Deputy Director of the Bureau of the Budget.

(c) The Director is authorized to employ such officers and employees (including experts and consultants) as may be necessary to enable the Office to carry out its functions under this title and Public Law 91–190, except that he may employ no more than ten specialists and other experts without regard to the provisions of title 5, United States Code, governing appointments in the competitive service, and pay such specialists and experts without regard to the provisions of chapter 51 and subchapter 111 of chapter 53 of such title relating to classification and General Schedule pay rates, but no such specialist or expert shall be paid at a rate in excess of the maximum rate for GS–18 of the General Schedule under section 5330 of title 5.

(d) In carrying out his functions the Director shall assist and advise the President on policies and programs of the Federal Government affecting environmental quality by—

(1) providing the professional and administrative staff and support for the Council on Environmental Quality established by Public Law 91–190;

(2) assisting the Federal agencies and departments in appraising the effectiveness of existing and proposed facilities, programs, policies, and activities of the Federal Government, and those specific major projects designated by the President which do not require individual project authorization by Congress, which affect environmental quality;

(3) reviewing the adequacy of existing systems for monitoring and predicting environmental changes in order to achieve effective coverage and efficient use of research facilities and other resources;

(4) promoting the advancement of scientific knowledge of the effects of actions and technology on the environment and encourage the development of the means to prevent or reduce adverse effects that endanger the health and wellbeing of man;

(5) assisting in coordinating among the Federal departments and agencies those programs and activities which affect, protect, and improve environmental quality;

(6) assisting the Federal departments and agencies in the development and interrelationship of environmental quality criteria and standards established through the Federal Government;

(7) collecting, collating, analyzing, and interpreting data and information on environmental quality, ecological research, and evaluation.

(e) The Director is authorized to contract with public or private agencies, institutions, and organizations and with individuals without regard to sections 3618 and 3709 of the Revised Statutes (31 U.S.C. 529; 41 U.S.C. 5) in carrying out his functions.

REPORT

SEC. 204. Each Environmental Quality Report required by Public Law 91–190 shall, upon transmittal to Congress, be referred to each standing committee having jurisdiction over any part of the subject matter of the Report.

AUTHORIZATION

SEC. 205. There are hereby authorized to be appropriated not to exceed $500,000 for the fiscal year ending June 30, 1970, not to exceed $750,000 for the fiscal year ending June 30, 1971, not to exceed $1,250,000 for the fiscal year ending June 30, 1972, and not to exceed $1,500,000 for the fiscal year ending June 30, 1973. These authorizations are in addition to those contained in Public Law 91–190.

Approved April 3, 1970.

Executive Order 11514, Protection and Enhancement of Environmental Quality, March 5, 1970

By virtue of the authority vested in me as President of the United States and in furtherance of the purpose and policy of the National Environmental Policy Act of 1969 (Public Law No. 91–190, approved January 1, 1970), it is ordered as follows:

SECTION 1. *Policy.* The Federal Government shall provide leadership in protecting and enhancing the quality of the Nation's environment to sustain and enrich human life. Federal agencies shall initiate measures needed to direct their policies, plans and programs so as to meet national environmental goals. The Council on Environmental Quality, through the Chairman, shall advise and assist the President in leading this national effort.

SEC. 2. *Responsibilities of Federal agencies.* Consonant with Title I of the National Environmental Policy Act of 1969, hereinafter referred to as the "Act", the heads of Federal agencies shall:

(a) Monitor, evaluate, and control on a continuing basis their agencies' activities so as to protect and enhance the quality of the environment. Such activities shall include those directed to controlling pollution and enhancing the environment and those designed to accomplish other program objectives which may affect the quality of the environment. Agencies shall develop

Executive Order 11514

programs and measures to protect and enhance environmental quality and shall assess progress in meeting the specific objectives of such activities. Heads of agencies shall consult with appropriate Federal, State and local agencies in carrying out their activities as they affect the quality of the environment.

(b) Develop procedures to ensure the fullest practicable provision of timely public information and understanding of Federal plans and programs with environmental impact in order to obtain the views of interested parties. These procedures shall include, whenever appropriate, provision for public hearings, and shall provide the public with relevant information, including information on alternative courses of action. Federal agencies shall also encourage State and local agencies to adopt similar procedures for informing the public concerning their activities affecting the quality of the environment.

(c) Insure that information regarding existing or potential environment problems and control methods developed as part of research, development, demonstration, test, or evaluation activities is made available to Federal agencies, States, counties, municipalities, institutions, and other entities, as appropriate.

(d) Review their agencies' statutory authority, administrative regulations, policies, and procedures, including those relating to loans, grants, contracts, leases, licenses, or permits, in order to identify any deficiencies or inconsistencies therein which prohibit or limit full compliance with the purposes and provisions of the Act. A report on this review and the corrective actions taken or planned, including such measures to be proposed to the President as may be necessary to bring their authority and policies into conformance with the intent, purposes, and procedures of the Act, shall be provided to the Council on Environmental Quality not later than September 1, 1970.

(e) Engage in exchange of data and research results, and cooperate with agencies of other governments to foster the purposes of the Act.

(f) Proceed, in coordination with other agencies, with actions required by section 102 of the Act.

SEC. 3. *Responsibilities of Council on Environmental Quality.* The Council on Environmental Quality shall:

(a) Evaluate existing and proposed policies and activities of the Federal Government directed to the control of pollution and the enhancement of the environment and to the accomplishment of other objectives which affect the quality of the environment. This shall include continuing review of procedures employed in the development and enforcement of Federal standards affecting environmental quality. Based upon such evaluations the Council shall, where appropriate, recommend to the President policies of environmental quality and shall, where appropriate, seek resolution of significant environmental issues.

(b) Recommend to the President and to the agencies priorities among programs designed for the control of pollution and for enhancement of the environment.

(c) Determine the need for new policies and programs for dealing with environmental problems not being adequately addressed.

(d) Conduct, as it determines to be appropriate, public hearings or conferences on issues of environmental significance.

(e) Promote the development and use of indices and monitoring systems (1) to assess environmental conditions and trends, (2) to predict the environmental impact of proposed public and private actions, and (3) to determine the effectiveness of programs of protecting and enhancing environmental quality.

(f) Coordinate Federal programs related to environmental quality.

(g) Advise and assist the President and the agencies in achieving international cooperation for dealing with environmental problems, under the foreign policy guidance of the Secretary of State.

(h) Issue guidelines to Federal agencies for the preparation of detailed statements on proposals for legislation and other Federal actions affecting the environment, as required by section 102(2)(C) of the Act.

(i) Issue such other instructions to agencies, and request such reports and other information from them, as may be required to carry out the Council's responsibilities under the Act.

(j) Assist the President in preparing the annual Environmental Quality Report provided for in section 201 of the Act.

(k) Foster investigations, studies, surveys, research, and analyses relating to (i) ecological systems and environmental quality, (ii) the impact of new and changing technologies thereon, and (iii) means of preventing or reducing adverse effects from such technologies.

SEC. 4. *Amendments of E. O. 11472.* Executive Order No. 11472 of May 29, 1969, including the heading thereof, is hereby amended:

(1) By substituting for the term "the Environmental Quality Council", wherever it occurs, the following: "the Cabinet Committee on the Environment".

(2) By substituting for the term "the Council", wherever it occurs, the following: "the Cabinet Committee".

(3) By inserting in subsection (f) of section 101, after "Budget,", the following: "the Director of the Office of Science and Technology,".

(4) By substituting for subsection (g) of section 101 the following:

"(g) The Chairman of the Council on Environmental Quality (established by Public Law 91–190) shall assist the President in directing the affairs of the Cabinet Committee."

(5) By deleting subsection (c) of section 102.

(6) By substituting for "the Office of Science and Technology", in section 104, the following: "the Council on Environmental Quality (established by Public Law 91–190)".

(7) By substituting for "(hereinafter referred to as the 'Committee')", in section 201, the following: "hereinafter referred to as the 'Citizens' Committee')".

(8) By substituting for the term "the Committee", wherever it occurs, the following: "the Citizens' Committee".

RICHARD NIXON.

THE WHITE HOUSE.

NEPA SUMMARIZED

The most important development in national policy has been the passage of the National Environmental Policy Act of 1969. This act attempts to create a new frame of reference for the consideration of environmental problems by all government agencies. Each agency whose actions have environmental side effects must consider these effects in addition to carrying out their primary mission. The aim is to internalize within each agency a procedure for assuring environmental protection.

Constitutional rights and NEPA

Life is not merely being alive, but being well.
—Martial, *Epigrams*

A question of considerable importance in interpreting the National Environmental Policy Act of 1969 is whether it creates an enforceable right to a healthful—and possibly aesthetically pleasing—environment. Section 101(b) of NEPA provides that:

ethos of NEPA: §101 (b)

> (b) In order to carry out the policy set forth in this Act, it is the continuing responsibility of the Federal Government to use all practicable means, consistent with other essential considerations of national policy, to improve and coordinate Federal plans, functions, programs, and resources to the end that the Nation may—
>
> (1) fulfill the responsibilities of each generation as trustee of the environment for succeeding generations;
>
> (2) assure for all Americans safe, healthful, productive, and esthetically and culturally pleasing surroundings;
>
> (3) attain the widest range of beneficial uses of the environment without degradation, risk to health or safety, or other undesirable and unintended consequences;
>
> (4) preserve important historic, cultural, and natural aspects of our national heritage, and maintain, wherever possible, an environment which supports diversity, and variety of individual choice;
>
> (5) achieve a balance between population and resource use which will permit high standards of living and a wide sharing of life's amenities; and
>
> (6) enhance the quality of renewable resources and approach the maximum attainable recycling of depletable resources.

The import of this section is to place the responsibility for environmental protection squarely on the shoulders of the Federal government. The Federal government is assigned the roles of trustee and protector of the environment. An essential determination in assessing the impact of Section 101(b) is the extent to which the Section creates third party rights which would enable citizens to compel the government as trustee and protector of the environment to comply with the provisions of the Section.

The existence of third party rights would allow citizens to redress environmental abuses by requiring the government to enforce the individual's right to a healthful environment. Presumably, this action would take the form of a mandamus against the Federal official charged with protecting the specific area of the environment in question. A third party right under Section 101(b) would also permit citizen suits to enjoin Federal activity that violated the government's duties as protector and trustee of the environment.

The extent to which Section 101(b) provides enforceable third party rights has not been determined. Since the language of the Section does not explicitly enunciate such a right, courts might be reluctant to interpret one. Certainly, the recognition of a Constitutional right to a decent environment (discussed below) would help bolster the judicial recognition of third party rights under Section 101(b). (This issue is also discussed in Chapter Five.)

Courts have been unreceptive to the assertion of a right to a decent environment under Section 101(b). In *Environmental Defense Fund v. Corps of Engineers,*[10] the plaintiffs contended that NEPA created substantive rights in addition to its procedural requirements on the basis of Section 101(b). The court held that the Act did not create such substantive rights and did not purport to vest in the plaintiffs or anyone else a "right to the type of environment envisioned therein."[11]

While a broad interpretation of Section 101(b) would enable citizens to compel the government to protect the environment, a liberal construction of Section 101(c) would allow an individual to litigate directly to stop an environmentally destructive activity. Section 101(c) states:

> The Congress recognizes that each person should enjoy a healthful environment and that each person has a responsibility to contribute to the preservation and enhancement of the environment.[12]

This language neither explicitly recognizes a Constitutional right to a clean environment nor clearly creates a statutory right. The Senate had previously passed a bill containing language that emphatically articulated a right to a decent environment:

> The Congress recognizes that each person has a fundamental and inalienable right to a healthful environment. . . .[13]

In light of the conference committee's change in the wording of this Section, it is difficult to assert an enforceable right under NEPA to a clean environment. Without a supporting Constitutional right, the enacted language of Section 101(c) would appear to be more the stating of a goal than provision for an enforceable right.

Constitutional possibilities

However, specific reference in the Constitution is not a prerequisite to a Constitutionally recognized right to environmental protection. The Ninth Amendment to the Constitution, which states that "the enumeration in the Constitution, of certain rights, shall not be construed to deny or disparage others retained by the people," may provide a basis for an unenumerated right to a clean environment.

Additional Constitutional underpinnings for a right to a decent environment may be provided by the due process clause of the Fifth Amendment:(". . . nor shall any person . . . be deprived of life, liberty or property, without due process of law"), as well as by the due process, equal protection, and privileges and immunities clauses of the Fourteenth Amendment:

> No State shall make or enforce any law which shall abridge the privileges or immunities of citizens of the United States; nor shall any State deprive any person of life, liberty or property without due process of law; nor deny to any person within its jurisdiction the equal protection of the laws

The Fourteenth Amendment would make applicable to the states an environmental right recognized as implicit in the Ninth Amendment.

10. 325 F.Supp. 749 (E.D. Ark. 1971). The case concerned an attempt by EDF to enjoin construction of the proposed Gillham Dam.

11. *Id.* at 755. The court in *Calvert Cliffs Coordinating Committee, Inc. v. U.S. Atomic Energy Commission,* ___F.2d___, 2 ERC 1779 (D.C. Cir. 1971), held the general substantive policy of Section 101(b) to be flexible and found that "[i]t leaves room for a responsible exercise of discretion and may not require particular substantive results in particular problematic instances." *Id.* at 1780. The court reiterated this interpretation of Section 101 stating:

> The reviewing court probably cannot reverse a substantive decision on its merits, under Section 101, unless it be shown that the actual balance of costs and benefits that was struck was arbitrary or clearly gave insufficient weight to environmental values. *Id.* at 1783.

12. 42 U.S.C. §4331 (C).

13. S.1075, 91st Cong., 2d Sess. §101(b) (1970).

The Supreme Court's decision in *Griswald v. Connecticut,*[14] illustrates how a court can find a Constitutional basis for an unenumerated right. The Court held that a Connecticut statute which prohibited the dissemination of birth control information to married couples was invalid because it intruded upon the marital relationship which was within the zone of privacy created by the First, Third, Fourth, Fifth and Ninth Amendments. Mr. Justice Douglas based his decision on the theory that the specific guarantees of the Bill of Rights are not complete in themselves, but include "peripheral rights" without which "the specific rights would be less secure."[15]

the halo around the first 10 Amendments

> [S]pecific guarantees in the Bill of Rights have penumbras, formed by emanations from those guarantees that help give them life and substance.[16]

Mr. Justice Goldberg based his concurring opinion on the Ninth Amendment, which he contended was drafted to protect fundamental rights that are not expressly enumerated in the first eight amendments.[17] In determining which rights are fundamental, judges must look to "the traditions and collective conscience of our people to determine whether a principle is so rooted as to be ranked as fundamental."[18] Surely, the right to a healthful environment should be considered a fundamental right. Mr. Justice Harlan used a substantive due process approach in concurring in *Griswald* to find a constitutional source for an unenumerated right.[19]

A judicially recognized constitutional right to a decent environment would have to develop on a case-by-case basis. The right would protect the public from unreasonable environmental degradation. The scope of reasonableness would evolve from a case-by-case adjudication. The judicial process could accommodate necessary concessions to individual liberty and societal progress.[20]

A Pyrrhic victory for those advocating that a right to a decent environment is embodied in the U.S. Constitution as it stands occurred in *Environmental Defense Fund v. Hoerner Waldorf Corp.,* ___F.Supp.___, 1 ERC 1640 (D.Mont.1970) when that suit was dismissed for lack of standing. The plaintiff organization maintained that the people have a fundamental right to be secure from environmental degradation (under the Ninth Amendment), and that the defendant was preventing the exercise of that right, and also that the public's property was being taken (used) without the due process of law, in violation of the 14th Amendment, in that a National Forest was being damaged. They based their right to represent the public in this latter point on *Parker v. U.S.,* 309 F.Supp. 593 (D. Colo. 1970) and *Illinois Central Railroad v. Illinois,* 146 U.S. 387 (1892).

The due process argument was dismissed on the grounds that the Constitution's Fifth and 14th Amendments prohibit only the taking without due process of private property for public use, not the taking of public property for private use.

The fundamental right to a decent environment under the Ninth Amendment was dismissed with the following sugar-coated "no":

14. 381 U.S. 479 (1965).

15. *Id.* at 483.

16. *Id.* at 484.

17. *Id.* at 492.

18. *Id.* at 493.

19. *Id.* at 499-502.

20. *See* Toward a Constitutionally Protected Environment, 56 Va. L. Rev. 458 (1970), *See also,* Roberts, The Right to a Decent Environment; E=MC²; Environment Equals Man Times Courts Redoubling Their Efforts, 55 Cornell L. Rev. 691 (1970). [Additional material is found in Chapter 5 of this text]

> The Court has no difficulty in finding that the right to life and liberty and property are constitutionally protected . . . and surely a person's health is what, in a most significant degree, sustains life. So it seems to me that each of us is constitutionally protected in our natural and personal state of life and health. But the constitutional protection is against governmental action either federal or state.

And the court found no Federal or state activity involved, suggesting that the plaintiff may have done better by bringing the suit as a simple nuisance action. (These are dealt with in Chapter Five of this book.)

Hence, *EDF v. Hoerner Waldorf* seemed to find some sort of NEPA rights already in the Constitution, but that those rights apply only to governmental actions.

faint praise
in the courts

In general, however, the courts have been more reluctant to recognize any such constitutionally protected right to a decent environment. The plaintiffs in *Environmental Defense Fund v. Corps of Engineers*[21] claimed that the right to live in an environment that preserves the unquantified amenities of life was part of the liberty protected by the Fifth and Fourteenth Amendments, and was one of the unenumerated rights retained by the people under the Ninth Amendment.[22] The court expressed its conviction in the sincerity and possible validity of plaintiffs' claim.

> Those who would attempt to protect the environment through the courts are striving mightily to carve out a constitutional mandate from the existing provisions of the constitution. Such claims even under our present Constitution are not fanciful and may indeed someday, in one way or another, obtain judicial recognition.[23]

The court went on to predict that the Ninth Amendment may prove to be as important in the development of Constitutional law during the remainder of this century as the Fourteenth Amendment had been since the beginning of this century.[24] But the district judge declined the opportunity to break new Constitutional ground quoting from Judge Leonard Hand in *Spector Motor Service, Inc. v. Walsh*:[25]

> Nor is it desirable for a lower court to embrace the exhilarating possibilities of anticipating a doctrine which may be in the womb of time, but whose birth is distant.[26]

The favorable reception accorded plaintiff's constitutional argument is encouraging. Possibly, if an alternative legal basis for enjoining the defendant's activities had not been available, the court would have overcome its reticence to ruling on plaintiff's Constitutional claim. In *EDF*, NEPA provided plaintiffs with an adequate remedy. The *Griswald* court did not have the luxury of an alternative legal theory to support their holding and were forced to make a Constitutional decision. Judicial economy would appear to militate against a judicially declared Constitutional right to a clean environment. Since necessity appears to be the mother of judicial innovation, the assertion of a Constitutional environmental right must await a *Griswald*-like predicament.[27]

21. 325 F.Supp. 728 (E.D. Ark. 1971).

22. *Id.* at 739.

23. *Id.* at 739.

24. *Id.* at 739.

25. 139 F.2d 809 (2d Cir. 1944).

26. *Id.* at 823.

27. Similar constitutional claims were presented in *Ely v. Velde*, __F.2d__, 3 ERC 1280 (4th Cir. 1971), but the Fourth Circuit declined to consider the constitutional concerns of the appellant. The court found an adequate remedy in NEPA. The court found no state action in the case.

the scope of NEPA

The list of "environmental considerations" in NEPA must not be regarded as exhaustive. In a decision in the U.S. Court of Appeals for the Second Circuit (*Hanly v. Mitchell,* May 17, 1972, 4 ERC 1152), it was declared that NEPA "must be construed to include protection of the quality of life for city residents. Noise, traffic, overburdened mass transportation systems, crime, congestion, and even availability of drugs all effect the urban 'environment'. . . ." See also the discussion on pages One-50-51.

NEPA, as presently interpreted, neither provides a right to a decent environment nor reflects an announced Constitutional right to a healthful environment. While the language of Sections 101(b) and (c) are not likely to be interpreted as creating an enforceable environmental right, the penumbras of the Bill of Rights would appear to encompass a Constitutional right. A Constitutional amendment would provide a direct solution to the problem of creating an environmental right.

The theory that a Constitutional amendment is an appropriate vehicle for protecting such a right is based on the parallelism between today's environmental anxieties and the fears of political repression that motivated the drafters of the original Bill of Rights.[28] The Bill of Rights was addressed to the major social apprehensions of the time. Since the framers were unable to respond to an issue which had not yet arisen, the enactment of a constitutional amendment would be in keeping with the philosophy that inspired the Bill of Rights.[29] A Constitutional amendment should be self-executing to provide an enforceable right to a decent environment.

amending the Constitution

Former Rep. Richard L. Ottinger of New York introduced the following environmental amendment in 1968:

> Section 1. The right of the people to clean air, pure water, freedom from excessive and unnecessary noise, and the natural scenic, historic and esthetic qualities of their environment shall not be abridged.
>
> Section 2. The Congress shall within three years after the enactment of this article, and within every subsequent term of ten years or lesser term as the Congress may determine, and in such manner as they shall by law direct, cause to be made an inventory of the natural, scenic, esthetic and historic resources of the United States with their state of preservation and provide for protection as a matter of national purpose.
>
> Section 3. No Federal or State agency, body, or authority shall be authorized to exercise public work, issue any permit, license or concession, make any rule, execute any management policy, or other official act which adversely affects the people's heritage of lands and waters now or hereafter placed in public ownership without first giving reasonable notice to the public and holding a public hearing thereon.[30]

This amendment could be improved by substituting the word "infringe" for "abridge" in Section 1. Abridge connotes government action, whereas infringe would include the impact of private conduct. The inventory required by Section 2 would be of immense magnitude and, in view of its extent and complexity, it would be of dubious value. Section 3 provides for environmental due process and incorporates the notion that procedural safeguards are required to ensure adequate environmental protection. The deletion of the word "adversely" would strengthen this Section.[31] The Ottinger Amendment died in committee.

28. *See* Platt, Toward Constitutional Recognition of the Environment, 56 A.B.A.J. 1061, 1062 (1970).

29. *See* Platt, *supra* note 28 at 1062.

30. H.R.J.Res. 1321, 90th Cong. 2d Sess. (1968).

31. *See* Platt, *supra* note 28 at 1062.

Rep. John B. Dingell of Michigan and four colleagues have introduced an amendment that would restore the original declaration of S.1075 Section 101(c) that "every person has a fundamental right to a healthful environment." Additionally, the amendment would provide that any person who is engaged in interstate commerce and

> . . . who is responsible for any pollution of air or water or for the creation of any unreasonable noise shall be subject to liability in monetary damages, injunction, declaratory judgment, or other appropriate relief in a class action brought by any person representing the interest of a group or class of persons whose lives, safety, health, property or welfare has been endangered or adversely affected in any way by such pollution or noise.[32]

This amendment would provide a private right of action to redress environmental harm. The use of private lawsuits and class actions offers a promising means of abating environmental degradation.[33]

Senator Nelson of Wisconsin has proposed an amendment that:

> Every person has the inalienable right to a decent environment. The United States and every State shall guarantee this right.[34]

The National Environmental Policy Act in use

standing and sovereign immunity with NEPA

This subsection and the following one—on Federal Jurisdiction under NEPA—presuppose that the reader is already somewhat acquainted with the basics of litigation, and therefore can appreciate fairly readily some of the special aspects of that art as applied to the National Environmental Policy Act. The complete beginner might do well to read first some of Chapter Five, which gives a review of private environmental litigation in general, before attempting these subsections. There is some intentional overlapping of material between these chapters.

To be permitted to carry on a law suit—that is, to maintain standing—a plaintiff must satisfy the court that he has met two requirements:

> 1) the plaintiff must have alleged that he has suffered or will suffer injury (economic or otherwise), and
> 2) the interest that the plaintiff seeks to protect must be within the zone of interests regulated or protected by the statute or section of the Constitution which the plaintiff invokes.[35]

The Supreme Court, in articulating these tests for standing, stated explicitly that the interest sought to be protected may at times reflect "aesthetic, conservation and recreational" values.[36] Economic values traditionally have been protected.

NEPA expands the scope of statutory interest in the environment, enabling plaintiffs to allege more convincingly the injury required for a law suit to be accepted by the courts.

32. H.R. 15578, 91st Cong. 2d Sess. (1970).

33. *See generally,* Sax, Defending the Environment, A Strategy for Citizen Action (1971).

34. S.J.Res. 169, 91st Cong., 2d Sess. (1970).

35. *See Association of Data Processing Service Organizations, Inc. v. Camp,* 397 U.S. 151 (1970).

36. *Id.* at 154, citing *Scenic Hudson Preservation Conference v. FPC,* 354 F.2d 608 (2d Cir. 1965).

> We mention these noneconomic values to emphasize that standing may stem from them as well as from the economic injury on which plaintiffs rely here. *Data Processing* at 154.

In recent years, the courts generally have been receptive to granting standing to conservation organizations seeking to maintain actions to protect environmental and conservation interests.[37] The Ninth Circuit sought to enunciate an exception to this trend in *Sierra Club v. Hickel*.[38] In determining that the Sierra Club was not within the required zone of interest to maintain standing, the court stated:

> We do not believe such club without a showing of more direct interest can constitute standing in the legal sense sufficient to challenge the exercise of responsibilities on behalf of all the citizens by two cabinet level officials of the government acting under Congressional and Constitutional authority.[39]

The Supreme Court, in upholding this decision,[40] gave only a tiny setback for the conservation movement because the Court stressed that there was a way that standing could be maintained through the inclusion, as plaintiffs, of individuals whose pleasure would be reduced. The text of this judicial impediment to the conservationist movement is in Chapter Five of this work. (Restyled *v. Morton; See* p. Five-8).

Even before the Supreme Court made its decision, the Ninth Circuit view was skirted by several courts, carefully distinguishing the cases before them from that rejected by the Ninth Circuit. In *West Virginia Highway Conservancy v. Island Creek Coal Co.*,[41] for example, the Fourth Circuit found that plaintiffs alleged injury in terms of aesthetic, conservational and recreational values which were sufficient to confer standing. Additionally, the court found that the plaintiffs sought to protect the same conservation interests with which NEPA and the Wilderness Act are concerned. Thus, NEPA was used to expand the zone of interest to encompass the plaintiffs.[42] The court was careful to distinguish *Sierra Club v. Hickel* by showing that plaintiff was a conservation organization composed of local residents and users of the area affected by administrative action.

rights for foreign interests

The question whether a foreign national or a foreign country on behalf of its citizens can come within the zone of interests protected by NEPA still awaits clarification by the courts. The possibility that an injured foreigner might meet the standing tests as enumerated in the *Data Processing* case mentioned above is suggested by §102(2) (E) of NEPA, which "recognizes the worldwide . . . character of environmental problems."

An attempt to test this idea[43] occurred when Canadian interests, arguing that more than a billion dollars of Canadian interests were affected, sought standing in litigation testing whether the U.S. Secretary of the Interior had complied with NEPA prior to issuing a permit for the transAlaska pipeline.[44] Standing was granted, but on the basis of Rule 24 (a) of the Federal Rules of Civil Procedure, which allows intervention where applicants have an interest "that may be antagonistic" to the interests of plaintiffs "which would make their [applicant's] representation by plaintiff's

37. *See e.g., Environmental Defense Fund v. Corps of Engineers,* 325 F.Supp. 728 (E.D.Ark. 1971); *Pennsylvania Environmental Council v. Bartlett,* 315 F.Supp. 238 (M.D. Pa. 1970).

38. 433 F.2d 24 (9th Cir. 1970) *certiorari granted* 401 U.S. 907 (1971).

39. *Id.* at 30. The court also noted that the Sierra Club could not bolster its argument for standing by the fact that no one else was willing to maintain the suit.

> Nor does the fact that no one else appears on the scene who is in fact aggrieved and is willing or desirous of taking up the cudgels create a right in appellee. The right to sue does not inure to one who does not possess it, simply because there is no one else willing and able to assert it. *Id.* at 32.

40. The court cited *Citizens Committee for the Hudson Valley v. Volpe,* 425 F.2d 197 (2d Cir. 1970) and *Parker v. U.S.,* 307 F.Supp. 685 (D.Colo. 1969).

41. 441 F.2d 232 (4th Cir. 1971).

42. *Id.* at 234.

43. Copyrights and patents offer partial precedents to the legislative granting of legal rights within the United States to foreign citizens residing within their own countries.

44. *Wilderness Society v. Morton,* ____ F.2d ____, 4 ERC 1101 (D.C. Cir., May 11, 1972).

counsel inadequate. . . ." No mention was made in the opinion of NEPA §102(2)(E).

standing for U.S. actions abroad[45]

Another standing problem may arise if environmentalists attempt to bring actions against Federal agencies engaged in international activities. Agencies whose programs have extraterritorial environmental impacts have been reluctant to comply with NEPA.[45] Even if national environmental groups are able to overcome the zone of interest requirements, an attempt to obtain judicial review of activities related to foreign policy may encounter opposition. The foreign relations area is regarded traditionally as reserved for the Executive branch, and courts have been reluctant to interfere. The present standing requirements would have to be liberally interpreted to permit American organizations to maintain actions to redress foreign or worldwide environmental problems. The fact that the environmental degradation is being perpetrated by the U.S. government with American tax revenues would appear to strengthen an organization's case for standing.[46] (See also the subsection later in this chapter on the application of NEPA to U.S. activities abroad.)

Standing of Americans to redress U.S. international activities which affect the worldwide environment, has not been determined. Since environmental problems are not confined by political boundries, the concepts of standing must be reexamined and expanded to accommodate the realities of the problems involved.

The Supreme Court has emasculated the doctrine of sovereign immunity with its finding that "only upon a showing of clear and convincing evidence of a contrary legislative intent" can courts deny judicial review of agency actions.[47] Sovereign immunity does survive in other actions against the United States and its officers, and can be grounds for dismissal unless exceptions are pleaded. These exceptions are:

(1) action by officers beyond their statutory powers and

(2) action, even though within the scope of the official's authority, when the powers themselves or the manner in which they are exercised are constitutionally void.[48]

An allegation that a Federal official exceeded the requirements of NEPA would be sufficient to overcome the defense of sovereign immunity. In *Environmental Defense Fund v. Corps of Engineers,*[49] the court found that defendants were proceeding with the Gillham Dam project without complying with the provisions of NEPA, and held that defendants may be acting in excess of their statutory authority and, therefore, the suit was not barred by the doctrine of sovereign immunity.[50] Plaintiffs should anticipate the defense of sovereign immunity in drafting their complaints and allege *ultra vires* official activity in violation of NEPA or other statutory constraints on Federal action to avoid the defense.

Federal Jurisdiction in NEPA Cases

Federal jurisdiction in NEPA cases

(For selection of a court in general, see Chapter Five.) NEPA enables plaintiffs to invoke "Federal question" jurisdiction under 28 U.S.C. §1331. In 28 U.S.C. §1331, the requirement that the matter in controversy exceed the value of $10,000 is imposed. A series of particular statutes grant jurisdiction, without regard to the amount in controversy, in almost all areas that would otherwise fall under the general Federal question statute.[51] NEPA does not contain such a grant of federal jurisdiction regardless of

45. *See* the discussion of the Application of NEPA Abroad

46. *See e.g., Flast v. Cohen,* 392 U.S. 83 (1968).

47. *See Abbott Laboratories v. Gardiner,* 387 U.S. 136 (1967). *See also,* Chapter 5 of this text.

48. *See Larson v. Domestic & Foreign Commerce Corp.,* 337 U.S. 682 (1949), *see also Dugan v. Rank,* 372 U.S. 609 (1962).

49. 325 F.Supp. 728 (E.D. Ark. 1970).

50. *Id.* at 733.

51. *See* Wright, Federal Courts at 108-10.

Federal jurisdiction in NEPA cases

jurisdictional amount, and unless an alternative jurisdiction statute waiving the $10,000 minimum is applicable, the $10,000 requirement of 28 U.S.C. §1331 must be satisfied. Almost always the problem of jurisdictional amount has been resolved by one or more of three factors:

1) if plaintiff claims damage in excess of $10,000 in good faith, the court will not dismiss unless it appears to a legal certainty that the claim is really for less than the jurisdictional amount;[52]

2) lack of judicial concern for jurisdictional amount;[53] and

3) a tolerant attitude in allowing rights not inherently measurable in monetary terms to be appraised as having a high money value.[54]

This last theory would be most valuable in environmental suits where aesthetic, conservation and recreational interests are involved.

A district court has suggested that a refusal to decide Constitutional issues for lack of jurisdictional amount might be deemed a denial of due process.[55] This theory would enable litigants to allege Constitutional environmental issues and obtain a Federal forum for the entire case under pendent jurisdiction.[56] This would provide for a judicial determination of a constitutional right to a decent environment and establish federal jurisdiction.

Under Section 702 of the Administrative Procedure Act, "a person suffering legal wrong because of agency action . . . is entitled to judicial review thereof."[57] Although the section does not confer a specific grant of Federal jurisdiction, the Supreme Court, in the opinion of at least one commentator, has assumed that "one who is entitled to review under the APA cannot be denied review on the ground that a district court lacks jurisdiction to provide it."[58] Thus, 5 U.S.C. §702 provides Federal jurisdiction for persons aggrieved by agency actions with no $10,000 limitation. Since many environmental plaintiffs are pleading the APA, the question of standing and jurisdiction becomes very complex. It would seem that some attorneys seek standing under NEPA but get jurisdiction under the APA. The shotgun approach of using a variety of jurisdictional statutes provides in tangible results what it lacks in intellectual precision: courts find that they have jurisdiction over cases in which NEPA is pleaded.

See Chapter Five for a more general discussion of the selection of a forum.

52. *See Saint Paul Mercury Idem. Co. v. Red Cab Co.,* 303 U.S. 283 (1938).

53. *See e.g., Flast v. Cohen,* 392 U.S. 83 (1968); *Leedom v. Kyne,* 358 U.S. 184 (1958).

54. *See* Davis, Administrative Law Treatise at 789-94 (1970 supplement).

55. *See Murry v. Vaughn,* 300 F.Supp. 688 (D.R.I. 1969).

56. *See United Mine Workers of America v. Gibbs,* 383 U.S. 715 (1966).

57. 5 U.S.C. §702.

58. Davis, *supra* note 55 at 789 *discussing Rusk v. Cort,* 369 U.S. 367 (1962).

Sec. 102 of NEPA

Section 102 is the heart of NEPA. The Section requires all federal agencies to consider the environmental effects of *major Federal actions* and proposals for legislation. The provisions of Section 102 are to force the agencies to internalize environmental considerations and provide for full disclosure of the environmental impact of proposed actions. The intention is for decisions to be made "in the light of public scrutiny."[59]

The environmental statement is to be prepared by a "responsible official," and, be a full analysis of the environmental impact; it should not be an attempt to justify a particular decision.[60]

The requirements of Section 102 have been brought to their present state by a myriad of Council on Environmental Quality guidelines, agency regulations and judicial decisions. The following discussion attempts to assess these Section 102 requirements to date.

The CEQ guidelines require all federal agencies to submit an environmental impact statement for the following: [61]

1) recommendations (or favorable reports) relating to legislation, including appropriations;

2) projects and continuing activities directly undertaken by federal agencies (including those supported through federal grants, contract subsidies, loans), and activities involving a federal lease, permit, license or certificate, and

3) policy, regulations and procedure-making.

identifying actions covered by NEPA

According to the CEQ guidelines, the statutory clause "major federal actions significantly affecting the quality of the human environment" is interpreted as requiring compliance with Section 102 as follows:

> Such actions may be localized in their impact, but if there is potential that the environment may be significantly affected, the statement is to be prepared. Proposed actions, the environmental impact of which is likely to be highly controversial, should be covered in all cases. In considering what constitutes a major action significantly affecting the environment, agencies should bear in mind that the effect of many Federal decisions about a project or complex of projects can be individually limited but cumulatively considerable. This can occur when one or more agencies over a period of years puts into a project individually minor but collectively major resources, when one decision involving a limited amount of money is a precedent for action in much larger cases or represents a decision in principle about a future major course of action, or when several Government agencies individually make decisions about partial aspects of a major action.[62]

The court in *Scherr v. Volpe*[63] held that a federal agency did not have discretion to determine whether a project is a major action. The court found that Section 102 provided a command to the agency to make a detailed statement required by NEPA to the fullest extent possible.[64]

59. *See* 115 Cong. Rec. 40416 (1969) (remarks of Senator Jackson).

60. But the statement need not be "perfect" See *Environmental Defense Fund v. Army Corps of Engineers*, reprinted *infra* at Appendix One-33.

61. 36 Fed. Reg. 7724 (1971).

62. *Id.* at 7724.

63. 3 ERC 1588 (W.D. Wis. 1971).

64. *Id.* Judge Wright discussed this point in *Calvert Cliffs Coordinating Committee v. U.S. Atomic Energy Commission*, __F.2d__, 2 ERC 1779 (D.C. Cir. 1971) stating:

> Of course, all of these Section 102 duties are qualified by the phrase "to the fullest extent possible." We must stress as forcefully as possible that this language does not provide an escape hatch for footdragging agencies; it does not make NEPA's procedural requirements somehow "discretionary." Congress did not intend the Act to be such a paper tiger. Indeed, the requirement of environmental consideration "to the fullest extent possible" sets a high standard for the agencies, a standard which must be rigorously enforced by the reviewing courts.

In *Natural Resources Defense Council v. Grant*[65], the court defined a major federal action as "a federal action that requires substantial planning, time, resources or expenditure."[66] The term "significantly affecting the quality of the human environment" was construed to mean a project "having an important or meaningful effect, direct or indirect, upon a broad range of aspects of the human environment."[67] The cumulative impact of other projects is to be considered in determining whether a specific action meets the standard.

identifying actions covered by NEPA

The requirements of a major federal action have been broadly interpreted to include most Federal activities. The award of a Law Enforcement Assistance Administration grant to build a state correctional facility was considered a major federal action requiring the preparation of an environmental statement despite the routine nature of the grant program.[68] Cancellation of helium purchase contracts by the Department of Interior was held to require compliance with Section 102(2)(C).[69] The termination of an unprofitable railroad operation required the ICC to consider the environmental consequences of its action.[70]

The court in *Cohen v. Price Commission*[71] determined that NEPA was not applicable to the Price Commission—a temporary agency, and one required to act upon matters within its authority with dispatch. The court based its holding on the fact that Congress intended no hindrance to expeditious action as evidenced by the fact that it exempted the Commission from the normal requirements of the Administrative Procedure Act.[72] The substantial time period required for compliance with NEPA would defeat the Commission's ability to act rapidly on implementing an emergency program. Obviously, for greater clarity, Congress would have done well to incorporate this exemption from NEPA in the Economic Stabilization Act (the enabling legislation for the Price Commission) if that had been desired.

A four-day cold-weather training exercise which entailed a 900-Marine bivouac in Reid State Park, Maine, was determined not to be a major federal action requiring the preparation of an environmental impact statement.[73] The district judge, apparently impressed with the Navy's precautions to protect the ecosystem of the park, found that the requirements of NEPA had been satisfied. Although in this case the environmental impact had been minimized (and such consideration was consistent with NEPA), excusing compliance with Section 102(2)(C) on the basis that the operation did not constitute a major Federal action sets a very unfortunate precedent.

When two or more federal agencies are involved in a project, the agency which has primary authority for committing the government to a course of action with significant environmental effects (the "lead agency") should prepare the Section 102 statement.[74] This principle was applied in

65. __F.Supp.__, 3 ERC 1883 (E.D.N.C. 1972).

66. *Id.* at 1890. The court held that the Chicod Creek Watershed Project, which called for sixty-six miles of stream channelization and the expenditure of $1,503,831 ($706,684 of which was to be federally funded), was a major federal action. In addition, the court noted that the project had been in the planning and preparation stages for several years, and that construction would entail a substantial amount of time and labor. *Id.* at 1890.

67. *Id.* at 1890.

68. *See Ely v. Velde,* __F.2d__, 3 ERC 1280 (4th Cir. 1971).

69. *See National Helium Corp. v. Morton,* __F.2d__, 3 ERC 1129 (10th Cir. 1971).

70. *See City of New York v. U.S.*, 3 ERC 1571 (E.D.N.Y. 1972).

71. __F.Supp.__, 3 ERC 1548 (S.D.N.Y. 1972).

72. *Id.* at 1552.

73. *Citizens for Reid State Park v. Laird,* 336 F.Supp. 783 (D. Me. 1972).

74. 36 Fed. Reg. 7724, 7725 (1971).

Upper Pecos Assn. v. Stans.[75] The plaintiff contended that the Department of Commerce did not comply with NEPA because it failed to consider the environmental impact of a road to be built with a Department of Commerce agency grant in the area of the Santa Fe National Forest. The court found that, despite the Department of Commerce's financial assistance, the Forest Service was the lead agency, since it had to grant the right of way and permit the use of Forest Service lands for the highway. The court determined that the Department of Commerce was excused from preparing an environmental impact statement.

Adverse significant effects include actions that "degrade the quality of the environment, curtail the range of beneficial uses of environment, and serve short-term (to the disadvantage of long-term) environmental goals."[76] Actions which have both beneficial and detrimental effects, require a Section 102 statement even if, after balancing the effects, the agency believes that the net effect will be beneficial.[77]

application to agencies

The legislative history of NEPA tends to suggest that the Act was to be applicable to "the environmental impact agencies"rather than the environmental enhancement agencies, such as the Federal Water Pollution Control Administration or National Air Pollution Control Administration.[78] In a poorly articulated opinion, the court in *Gibson v. Ruckelshaus*[79] granted an injunction against condemnation proceedings or federal financing for a sewage treatment facility on the ground that the Environmental Protection Agency had failed to comply with NEPA. In light of *Gibson* and differing interpretations of the legislative history, the exclusion of environmental enhancement agencies from the requirements of NEPA is in doubt. Nothing in the Act would appear to exempt environmental protection agencies. The unqualified language of Section 102(2) making the provisions applicable to "all agencies of the federal government" can only be interpreted as including environmental enhancement agencies.

However, most people, including those setting EPA policy, feel that Section 102(2)(C) is not applicable to their activities. This view takes on increased significance as a pending water pollution bill[80] would move the existing program from the Army Corps of Engineers where 102 statements are required, to EPA where such a requirement might not be required.

The Section 102(2)(C) process is initiated with the compilation of a draft statement. The agency must circulate the draft to Federal agencies with jurisdiction by law or special expertise with respect to any environmental impact involved. The CEQ requests that ten copies of the draft statement, comments and final statement be supplied to the Council. Agencies must delay preparation of a final impact statement until 90 days after the draft has been circulated for comment. Administrative action should not be taken until 30 days after the final statement is made available to the Council and the public. Agencies unable to comply with the minimum periods specified in the guidelines should consult the Council concerning appropriate modification.

See the list of agencies with expertise under §102 of NEPA at Appendix One-7, and the list of offices for the coordination of statements at Appendix-13. Availability to the public is discussed *infra* at One-46.

75. 328 F.Supp. 332 (D.N. Mex. 1971).

76. 36 Fed. Reg. 7724, 7725 (1971).

77. *Id.* at 7725.

78. *See* 115 Cong. Rec. 40425 (1969). Both the programs mentioned are now part of the Environmental Protection Agency.

79. __F.Supp.__, 3 ERC 1028 (E.D. Tex. 1971).

80. See pp. Four 36-37 of this text.

content of impact statements

The Council on Environmental Quality requires the following points to be covered in an environmental impact statement:

1) a description of the proposed action including information and technical data adequate to permit an assessment of the environmental impact by commenting agencies,

2) the probable impact of the proposed action on the environment,

3) adverse environmental effects which cannot be avoided,

4) alternatives to the proposed action,

5) the relationship between local short-term uses of the environment and the maintenance of long-term productivity,

6) any irreversible and irretrievable commitments of resources which would be involved in the proposed action, and

7) a discussion of any problems and objections raised by federal, state or local agencies and by private organizations and individuals in the review process and the disposition of the issues involved.[81]

Natural Resources Defense Council, Inc. v. Morton[82] (see text in this book) raised a question as to the scope of the requirement that environmental impact statements contain a discussion of alternatives. The case concerned the Department of Interior's proposed sale of oil and gas leases for submerged lands on the continental shelf off eastern Louisiana. This policy was responsive to the directive in President Nixon's Message on Supply of Energy and Clean Air.[83]

The Department of Interior prepared an environmental impact statement which adequately disclosed the environmental problems of the proposed action, but which NRDC contended did not sufficiently discuss alternatives to the proposed sale. The court ruled that the Department of Interior's impact statement did not adequately evaluate alternatives.[84] The D.C. Circuit viewed the impact statement as providing a basis for the evaluation of benefits of a proposed project in light of its environmental risks and the comparison of the net balance for the proposed project with the environmental risks of alternative courses of action.[85] The court attempted to establish a standard of reasonableness for agency consideration of alternatives.

> . . . the discussion of environmental effects of alternatives need not be exhaustive. What is required is information sufficient to permit a reasoned choice of alternatives so far as environmental aspects are concerned. As to alternatives not within the scope of authority of the responsible official, reference may of course be made to studies of other agencies—including other impact statements. Nor is it appropriate . . . to disregard alternatives merely because they do not offer a complete solution to the problem.[86]

See also CEQ regulations in the Appendix to this chapter.

In *Conservation Council v. Froehlke,* ___ F.2d ___, (4th Cir., May 2, 1972) 4 ERC 1044, the court ruled that the Army Corps of Engineers' environmental impact statement for a North Carolina dam that included full disclosure of all possible environmental effects and that fully discussed alternatives to dam complied with the National Environmental Policy Act, even though costs of the project exceed benefits, and even though strong evidence was presented that casts doubt on the advisibility of continuing with the project.

81. 36 Fed. Reg. 7724, 7725 (1970).

82. ___F.2d___, 3 ERC 1558 (D.C. Cir. 1972).

83. The text of the message appears at 112 Cong. Rec. S.8313-17 (6/4/71).

84. ___F.2d___, 3 ERC 1558 (D.C. Cir. 1972).

85. *Id.* at 1561. The court felt that the Department of Interior should have investigated reducing the oil import quota.

86. *Id.* at 1763.

circulation of impact statements

A federal agency considering an action requiring an environmental statement must consult with and obtain comment on the impact of the action from other agencies with jurisdiction by law or special expertise with respect to environmental impacts involved.[87] Agencies are required to circulate draft environmental statements and allow 30 days for reply. After 30 days, it may be presumed (unless the agency consulted requests a specific extension of time) that the agency consulted has no comment to make. Agencies are requested to comply with time extensions up to 15 days.[88]

Neither NEPA nor the CEQ guidelines require agencies to comment on environmental statements. Thus, agencies have no affirmative duty to participate in the circulation process, and, without guidance from the CEQ, participation will remain voluntary. This voluntary participation could result in commenting agencies' tacit approval of draft environmental statements in an attempt to promote comity with other agencies and maintain an administrative status quo, or to protect agency jurisdiction. The role of the commenting agencies requires greater definition to insure meaningful inputs into the circulation process, and to realize the coordination of government activities as envisioned in Section 102(A).

agency internalization of statement preparation

The "action forcing" provisions of Section 102 were intended to compel agencies to internalize environmental considerations.[89] It is, therefore, not surprising that the delegation of the preparation of environmental impact statements to the applicant for a federal license has encountered judicial opposition. The Federal Power Commission in *Greene County Planning Board v. F.P.C.*[90] contended that the applicant's draft statement,[91] reviewed as to form and circulated by the Commission, sufficed for the purposes of Section 102(2)(C) and that the Commission was not required to make its own statement until it filed its final decision. Petitioners argued that the Commission must issue its own statement prior to any formal hearings. The court agreed with petitioners and held that the F.P.C. had "abdicated a significant part of its responsibility" by substituting the applicant's statement for its own.[92] The court went on to state that:

> The danger of this procedure, and one obvious shortcoming, is the potential, if not the likelihood, that the applicant's statement will be based upon self-serving assumptions.[93]

The Second Circuit in articulating its decision aptly employed the often quoted principle it expounded in *Scenic Hudson Preservation Conference v. F.P.C.*[94] that the Commission's role as representative of the public interest "does not permit it to act as an umpire blandly calling balls and strikes for adversaries appearing before it; the right of the public must re-

87. 36 Fed. Reg. 7724, 7725 (1971).

88. *Id.* at 7725. (5-20)

89. To insure that the policies and goals defined in this act are infused into the ongoing programs and actions of the Federal Government, the act also established some important 'action forcing' procedures. 115 Cong. Rec. at 40416 (1969) (remarks of Senator Jackson).

90. __F.2d__, 3 ERC 1595 (2d Cir. 1972). 1-25 Text is printed *infra* at Appendix One-37.

91. The applicant, Power Authority of the State of New York, needed FPC authorization to construct a high-voltage transmission line.

92. Green County, *supra* note 90 at 1599.

93. *Id.* at 1599-1600.

94. 354 F.2d 608 (2d Cir. 1965) *cert. denied sub. nom. Consolidated Edison Co. of New York v. Scenic Hudson Preservation Conference,* 384 U.S. 941 (1966).

ceive active and affirmative protection at the hands of the Commission."[95] Thus, environmental impact statements must be completed by the agency at all stages of the proceedings.[96]

While the licensing agency is charged with drafting the statement required by Section 102(2)(C), studies and investigations compiled by the applicant may be used in some limited situations. The court in *Sierra Club v. Hardin*[97] found that investigations conducted by the applicant, U.S. Plywood, were sufficient for the Forest Service to use in environmental studies. U.S. Plywood had spent substantial sums to insure that the impact of the proposed mill would be minimized through comprehensive site planning and the most advanced technology available. Mill site selection had been supervised by a panel of experts from American and Canadian universities and a field study by the applicant had produced a 70-page report.[98] The court, apparently impressed by the applicant's diligence, stated:

> It seems unlikely that an investigation by federal experts would have been more comprehensive or unbiased.[99]

While the court may have been correct in its assessment of the sincerity of the applicant's investigations, allowing the Forest Service to substitute the applicant's studies for its own determination establishes a dangerous precedent. University professors in the employ of large corporations seeking valuable permits are not necessarily unbiased, and detailed reports are not always impartial. Independent agency studies are necessary to fulfill the mandate of NEPA.

The court in *Sierra Club v. Hardin* did attempt to circumscribe its ruling by stating:

> Considering the impressive credentials of the U.S.P. panel of environmental experts assigned to the project, the high quality of its research project, the advanced stage of planning as of January 1, 1970, and the exhorbitant cost of any further delay, the Forest Service was justified in its reliance upon U.S.P.'s environmental studies. Nothing in this opinion should be construed as implying that the procedures followed by the Forest Service in its efforts to comply with NEPA in this case will be found acceptable in the future under circumstances where it is fair to impute notice of the Act's provisions to all parties at or before the time a major federal project is conceived.[100]

In light of the above disclaimer and the holding of *Greene County* (see above) a licensing agency would be advised to draft its own environmental impact statements based on independent research.

In *Environmental Defense Fund v. Corp of Engineers,* (E.D. Ark. May 5, 1972) 4 ERC 1097, the court concluded that the "objectivity" requirements of NEPA are met if, (1) "At a minimum, the involved federal agency must make a good faith effort to comply with the provisions of NEPA," and, (2) the environmental impact statement is not "consciously slanted or biased." It added that, "The judiciary can delay the construction of the dam pending compliance by the defendants with . . . NEPA but, ultimately, plaintiffs' only chance to stop the dam . . . lies in their ability . . . to convince the decision-makers of the wisdom and correctness of their views on the merits." This decision is printed at Appendix One-33.

95. *Greene County, supra* note 90 at 1599.

96. The FPC has filed a petition for rehearing in the Second Circuit and suggested *en banc* reconsideration of the decision. The Commission has announced that it will seek review by the United States Supreme Court, if necessary.

97. 325 F.Supp. 99 (D. Alas. 1971). Action to enjoin a timber sale in a National Forest and prevent the issuance of a patent to use national forest land for processing timber.

98. *Id.* at 126.

99. *Id.* at 126.

100. *Id.* at 127.

applying NEPA to projects begun before January 1, 1970

One of the most difficult questions presented in early cases brought under NEPA concerned the effect of the Act on federal projects that were approved or under construction prior to January 1, 1970, the effective date of the Act. Specifically, the courts were required to determine:

1) at what point a project was sufficiently complete to make compliance with NEPA unnecessary, and

2) whether NEPA was retroactively applicable to on-going Federal undertakings regardless of their state of completion.

Pennsylvania Environmental Council v. Bartlett[101] provided an early test of NEPA's application prior to January 1, 1970. The case concerned an attempt to enjoin the construction of a Federally financed highway for failure to file an environmental impact statement as required by NEPA. All planning for the road had been done before NEPA was enacted and the construction contract had been awarded prior to the effective date of the Act. Only the actual construction remained after January 1, 1970. The court held that the project had been sufficiently completed to make the application of NEPA retroactive and refused to interpret the Act retroactively, citing *Union Pacific Railroad Co. v. Laramie Stock Yards:*[102]

> [T]he first rule of construction is that legislation must be considered as addressed to the future, not the past . . . [and] a retrospective operation will not be given to a statute which interferes with antecedent rights . . . unless such be the unequivocal and inflexible import of the terms, and the manifest intention of the legislature.[103]

The court construed the language of Section 102 requiring the Federal government to implement the requirements of the Section "to the fullest extent possible" as imposing a restraint on agency compliance. This interpretation would appear to be at odds with the legislative history of the Section which states:

> Thus, it is the intent of the conferees that the provision 'to the fullest extent possible' shall not be used by any Federal agency as a means of avoiding compliance with the directives set out in Section 102.[104]

The *Bartlett* court found no manifest congressional intuition or unequivocal or inflexible import in the language used to indicate that the Act should have been applied retroactively.[105]

The Council on Environmental Quality's Interim Guidelines announced on April 30, 1970,[106] the same day as the *Bartlett* decision was handed down, appear to resolve some of the questions relating to the application of Section 102(C) procedures to existing projects.

> To the fullest extent possible the Section 102(2)(C) procedure should be applied to further major Federal actions having a significant effect on the environment even though they arise from projects or programs initiated prior to enactment of Public Law 91-190 on January 1, 1970. Where it is not practicable to reassess the basic course of action, it is still important that further incremental major actions be shaped so as to minimize adverse environmental conse-

101. 315 F.Supp. 238 (M.D. Pa. 1970).

102. 231 U.S. 190 (1913).

103. *Id.* at 199. *See also Greene v. U.S.*, 376 U.S. 149, 160 (1964).

104. H.R. Rep. No. 91-762, 91st Cong. 1st Sess. at 9, 10 (1969).

105. Bartlett, *supra* note 101.

106. 35 Fed. Reg. 7390 (1969).

applying NEPA to projects begun before January 1, 1970

quences. It is also important in further action that account be taken of environmental consequences not fully evaluated at the outset of the project or program.[107]

These guidelines would appear to carry significant weight in relation to the *Bartlett* decision. Mr. Justice Cardozo indicated the importance of such an administrative interpretation in *Norwegian Nitrogen Products Co. v. U.S.*:

> [. . . an administrative interpretation] will not be overturned except for very cogent reasons . . . [Such an interpretation] has peculiar weight when it involves a contemporaneous construction of a statute by the men charged with the responsibility of setting its machinery in motion, of making the parts work efficiently and smoothly while they are yet untried and new.[108]

The application of NEPA to the Gillham Dam project authorized in 1958 and from a financial point of view 63 percent complete at the time the suit was filed was attempted in *Environmental Defense Fund v. Corps of Engineers.*[109] While no work had been done on the dam itself, $9,496,000 of the estimated $14,800,000 cost of the project had been expended. Plaintiffs sought to have the court apply NEPA to anticipated future actions on the project, while the defendants argued that NEPA permitted a "double standard" with respect to on-going projects which were underway at the time of the passage of the Act. The court stressed the language of Sections 101(a) and (b) concerning "the continuing responsibility of the Federal government" to protect the environment and to "improve and coordinate Federal plans, functions and resources to accomplish that objective." It held that the Act required defendants to improve existing plans and programs."[110]

> [A]s the court interprets NEPA, the Congress of the United States is intent upon requiring the agencies of the United States government . . . to objectively evaluate all of their projects regardless of how much money has already been spent thereon and regardless of the degree of completion of the work.[111]

The *EDF* decision appears to be in consonance with the legislative history of NEPA and the CEQ's Interim Guidelines, and would appear to be an intelligent solution to the problem of the application of NEPA to projects begun prior to its effective date.

Several recent decisions have resolved the retroactive application of NEPA along the lines taken in *EDF v. Corps of Engineers.*[112] In light of these decisions, *Bartlett* would now appear to be a minority viewpoint concerning the application of NEPA to on-going federal projects.

A limited exception to the retroactivity doctrine of *EDF v. Corps of Engineers* was enunciated in *Jicarilla Apache Tribe v. Morton.*[113] The court held that an environmental impact statement was not required for a major federal action that completes or contributes to the completion of a project initiated prior to the effective date of the Act where it is not practical to reassess the basic course of action.[114]

107. *Id.* at 7390.

108. 288 U.S. 294, 315 (1933).

109. 325 F.Supp. 728 (E.D. Ark. 1971).

110. *Id.* at 743.

111. *Id.* at 746.

112. *See Natural Resources Defense Council v. Grant,* __F.Supp., 3 ERC 1883 (E.D.N.C. 1972); *Environmental Defense Fund v. TVA,* __F.Supp.__, 3 ERC 1553 (E.D. Tenn. 1972); *Morningside Lenox Park Assn. v. Volpe,* __F.Supp.__, 3 ERC 1327 (N.D. Ga. 1971).

113. __F.Supp.__, (D.C. Cir. March 14, 1972), 3 ERC 1919.

114. 104. *Id.* at 1921.

coordination of impact statements

The Office of Management and Budget serves as the Federal Government's budget agency; it is charged with improving the management and organization within the Executive branch. OMB coordinates and examines legislative proposals from the President and has substantial control over which agency requests for money or programs are presented to Congress. The OMB's duties as coordinator of the activities of the Executive branch and as a legislative liaison enable it to play a key role in implementing the policies of NEPA.

Where an environmental impact statement is required in connection with the submission of a legislative proposal or report, it is sent to OMB for clearance pursuant to Circular No. A-19. The OMB is requested to have a statement prepared in time for informational copies of it to accompany the proposal or report.[115]

OMB has proposed consultation with CEQ in all cases where agencies submit or intend to submit 102 statements. In cases where the clearance process discloses the need for an environmental statement, and none is under preparation, the responsible agency will be requested to submit one.[116] Thus, the OMB does not propose to review the content of impact statement, but, merely, to check agency compliance with NEPA during the legislative clearing process.[117] The delegation of substantive review of environmental statements to the CEQ is consistent with OMB's management function and the procedural checks established by the regulations will help insure agency procedural compliance with Section 102.

The shortcomings of this procedure remain the shortcomings of both the OMB and the CEQ (see also the discussion on the latter agency). Both agencies are direct arms of the Executive branch; as they are not independent, there is a political cast to them that can never be erased. It is not wild supposition to imagine that on occasion the OMB might do more to the environmental reports it supervises than merely assure their existence. (Office of Management and Budget has been guilty of withholding from the public environmental reports.) There is, of course, the chance that such intervention might be on the side of the angels. But we are left to the graces of men not directly accountable (and generally quite unknowable) to the public, though in general quite well-known to Washington's higher-paid lobbyists.

OMB regulations require annual budget estimates to be accompanied by a summary list of those specific actions covered by the estimates which require an impact statement.[118] The list must include: 1) identification of the agency actions and individual projects and activities requiring preparation of a 102 statement, 2) the amount of funds involved in the budget year, 3) the status of the statement—the agency must indicate in each instance, if a draft statement has been completed, whether comments from interested parties have been received and whether final statements have been completed, and 4) a statement of any unusual aspects of the project including unresolved issues, potential controversy and unusual impact on the environment.[119] In addition to the summary list, agencies must notify the appro-

115. OMB Regulations *See* 36 Fed. Reg. 23710 (1971).

116. *Id.* at 23710.

117. The OMB regulations are careful to separate the substantive consideration of environmental factors from procedural compliance with the requirements of Section 102(2)(C), as follows:

> Compliance with the 102(2)(C) statement does not, of course, relieve any agency or Office of Management and Budget from responsibility for giving the fullest consideration to environmental factors in developing its views on legislative proposals or reports in accordance with Circular A-19. The responsible agency should transmit its 102(2)(C) statements on legislative proposals and reports to the appropriate Congressional committees in accordance with section 10(c) of the revised guidelines of the Council on Environmental Quality. *Id.* at 23711.

118. *Id.* at 23711.

119. *Id.* at 23711.

priate OMB budget examiner of any action expected to be included in the agency's budget estimate which will have a particularly significant impact on the environment or potentially controversial nature.[120] The regulations do not reveal OMB's motives for these requirements. The OMB may be interested in cataloging agency activities having environmental impacts. Such a procedure would provide an overview of which agencies are heavily engaged in environmentally destructive projects.

OMB Circular No. A-95 is designed to provide coordination of federally assisted projects with state and local governments. The procedures established by this Circular will permit state and local review of environmental impact statements.[121]

agency regulations

Federal agencies are required by Section 102(B) of NEPA to:

> . . . identify and develop methods and procedures . . . which will insure that presently unquantified environmental amenities and values may be given appropriate consideration in decisionmaking along with economic and technical considerations.[122]

Section 103 instructs all Federal agencies to

> . . . review their present statutory authority, administrative regulations, and current policies and procedures for the purpose of determining whether there are any deficiencies or inconsistencies therein which prohibit full compliance with the purposes and provisions of this Act and shall propose to the President not later than July 1, 1971, such measures as may be necessary to bring their authority and policies into conformity with the intent, purposes, and procedures set forth in this Act.[123]

Although agencies have often been less than enthusiastic about promulgating regulations to implement NEPA,[124] most agencies have finally done so.[125]

Agency regulations recently have come under judicial attack for failure to comply with the congressional policy of NEPA. [126] *Calvert Cliff's Coordinating Committee, Inc. v. U.S. Atomic Energy Commission*[127] was a landmark decision, firmly imposing the NEPA mandate on agency activities. Petitioners claimed that the AEC's rules governing the consideration of environmental matters failed to satisfy the standard imposed by NEPA. The Commission, on the other hand, argued that NEPA was vague, allowing room for discretion, and that the AEC's rules fell within the broad scope of the Act.[128]

120. *Id.* at 23711.

121. *See* 36 Fed. Reg. 7726, §9(a) (1971).

122. 42 U.S.C. §4332(B).

123. 42 U.S.C. §4333.

124. *See Calvert Cliff's Coordinating Committee v. U.S. Atomic Energy Commission,*___F.2d ___, 2 ERC 1779 (D.C. Cir. 1971). The A.E.C. issued its first, short policy statement on implementation of NEPA's procedural provisions on April 2, 1970. Two months later, the Commission published a notice of proposed rule-making in the Federal Register. (35 Fed. Reg. 8594, June 3, 1970). Finally on December 3, 1970, eleven months after the passage of NEPA, the A.E.C. issued a formal amendment to its governing regulations (35 Fed. Reg. 18469, December 4, 1970); *see also,* Note, *The National Environmental Policy Act: A Sheep in Wolf's Clothing?,* 35 Brooklyn L. Rev. 139, 148-9 (1970).

125. *See* 36 Fed. Reg. 23666 (1971).

126. *See* Calvert Cliff's, *supra,* note 124; *Kalur v. Resor,* 3 ERC 1458 (D.D.C. 1971).

127. ___F.2d___ 2 ERC 1779 (D.C. Cir. 1971).

128. *Id.* at 1780.

The AEC rules provided for the consideration of environmental issues outside the hearing process when such issues were not raised by a party to the proceedings.[129] Environmental data was only required to "accompany" an application through the review process, but would receive no consideration from the hearing board. Circuit Judge J. Skelly Wright had this to say:[130]

> *We believe that the [Atomic Energy] Commission's crabbed interpretation of NEPA makes a mockery of the Act. What possible purpose could there be in the Section 102(2)(C) requirement (that the 'detailed statement' accompany proposals through agency review processes) if 'accompany' means no more than physical proximity—mandating no more than the physical act of passing certain folders and papers? . . . NEPA was meant to do more than regulate the flow of papers in the federal bureaucracy.*

The court expressed disapproval of the substantial time lag between the passage of NEPA and the imposition of the Commission's rules on March 4, 1971.[131] The AEC sought to explain its apparent lack of diligence claiming the time lag was "intended to provide an orderly period of transition in the Commission's regulatory proceedings and to avoid unreasonable delay in the construction and operation of nuclear power plants urgently needed to meet national requirements for electric power."[132] The court was unimpressed with the Commission's arguments and termed the delay "shocking."[133]

The court went on to censure the AEC's abdication of responsibility by deferring to water quality standards devised and administered by the states and other federal agencies. *Calvert Cliffs* puts Federal agencies on notice that the courts will demand strict compliance with NEPA. As Judge Wright noted:

> Our duty, in short, is to see that important legislative purposes heralded in the halls of Congress are not lost or misdirected in the vast hallways of the federal bureaucracy.[134]

On August 25, 1971, this author visited the Calvert Cliffs construction site. The U.S. court of appeals decision had not slowed construction. Now the plant is about halfway into the six-year period scheduled for construction. Its cost will be over $300 million.

For the citizen who visits the construction site, the gas and electric company has a 16-page color comic book entitled: *The Atom, Electricity and You,* which explains:"... The electric companies are very conscious of the radiation problems—and have successfully **solved** them!"[emphasis in original] To which the comic book's "intelligent citizen" type replies:

> "Thanks for showing us the real facts about **nuclear generation!** One thing's sure—it's going to be a **great** thing for all of us!"

On March 25, 1972 the AEC gave notice that it is considering issuance of licenses to Baltimore Gas Electric Company to operate Units 1 and 2 of its Calvert Cliffs Nuclear Power Station.

129. The regulations provided:

> When no party to a proceeding***raises any [environmental] issue***such issues will not be considered by the atomic safety and licensing board. Under such circumstances, although the Applicant's Environmental Report, comments thereon, and the Detailed Statement will accompany the application through the Commission's review processes, they will not be received in evidence, and the Commission's responsibilities under the National Environmental Policy Act of 1969 will be carried out in toto outside the hearing process. 10 C.F.R. § App. D. at 249.

130. Calvert Cliff s *supra* note 124 at 1784-5.

131. *See* 10 C.F.R. §50, App. D at 249.

132. Calvert Cliff's *supra* note 124 at 1786, citing 35 Fed. Reg. 18470 (1970).

133. *Id.* at 1786.

134. *Id.* at 1780.

CALVERT CLIFFS' COORDINATING COMMITTEE, INC., v. U.S. ATOMIC ENERGY COMMISSION

___ F.2d ___ (D.C. Cir. 1971), 2 ERC 1779

Before WRIGHT, TAMM and ROBINSON, *Circuit Judges.*

WRIGHT, *Circuit Judge*: These cases are only the beginning of what promises to become a flood of new litigation—litigation seeking judicial assistance in protecting our natural environment. Several recently enacted statutes attest to the commitment of the Government to control, at long last, the destructive engine of material "progress."[1] But it remains to be seen whether the promise of this legislation will become a reality. Therein lies the judicial role. In these cases, we must for the first time interpret the broadest and perhaps most important of the recent statutes: the National Environmental Policy Act of 1969 (NEPA).[2] We must assess claims that one of the agencies charged with its administration has failed to live up to the congressional mandate. Our duty, in short, is to see that important legislative purposes, heralded in the halls of Congress, are not lost or misdirected in the vast hallways of the federal bureaucracy.

NEPA, like so much other reform legislation of the last 40 years, is cast in terms of a general mandate and broad delegation of authority to new and old administrative agencies. It takes the major step of requiring all federal agencies to consider values of environmental preservation in their spheres of activity, and it prescribes certain procedural measures to ensure that those values are in fact fully respected. Petitioners argue that rules recently adopted by the Atomic Energy Commission to govern consideration of environmental matters fail to satisfy the rigor demanded by NEPA. The Commission, on the other hand, contends that the vagueness of the NEPA mandate and delegation leaves much room for discretion and that the rules challenged by petitioners fall well within the broad scope of the Act. We find the policies embodied in NEPA to be a good deal clearer and more demanding than does the Commission. We conclude that the Commission's procedural rules do not comply with the congressional policy. Hence we remand these cases for further rule making.

I

We begin our analysis with an examination of NEPA's structure and approach and of the Atomic Energy Commission rules which are said to conflict with the requirements of the Act. The relevant portion of NEPA is Title I, consisting of five sections.[3] Section 101 sets forth the Act's basic substantive policy: that the federal government "use all practicable means and measures" to protect environmental values. Congress did not establish environmental protection as an exclusive goal; rather, it desired a reordering of priorities, so that environmental costs and benefits will assume their proper place along with other considerations. In Section 101(b), imposing an explicit duty on federal officials, the Act provides that "it is the continuing responsibility of the Federal Government to use all practicable means, consistent with other essential considerations of national policy," to avoid environmental degradation, preserve "historic, cultural, and natural" resources, and promote "the widest range of beneficial uses of the environment without * * * undesirable and unintended consequences."

Thus the general substantive policy of the Act is a flexible one. It leaves room for a responsible exercise of discretion and may not require particular substantive results in particular problematic instances. However, the Act also contains very important "procedural" provisions—provisions which are designed to see that all federal agencies do in fact exercise the substantive discretion given them. These provisions are not highly flexible. Indeed, they establish a strict standard of compliance.

NEPA, first of all, makes environmental protection a part of the mandate of every federal agency and department. The Atomic Energy Commission, for example, had continually asserted, prior to NEPA, that it had no statutory authority to concern itself with the adverse environmental effects of its actions.[4] Now, however, its hands are no longer tied. It is not only permitted, but compelled, to take environmental values into account. Perhaps the greatest importance of NEPA is to require the Atomic Energy Commission and other agencies to *consider* environmental issues just as they consider other matters within their mandates. This compulsion is most plainly stated in Section 102. There, "Congress authorizes and directs that, to the fullest extent possible: (1) the policies, regulations, and public laws of the United States shall be interpreted and administered in accordance with the policies set forth in this Act * * *." Congress also "authorizes and directs" that "(2) all agencies of the Federal Government shall" follow certain rigorous procedures in considering environmental values.[5] Senator Jackson,

---

[1] *See, e.g.,* Environmental Education Act, 20 U.S.C.A. § 1531 (1971 Pocket Part); Air Quality Act of 1967, 42 U.S.C. § 1857 (Supp. V 1965-1969); Environmental Quality Improvement Act of 1970, 42 U.S.C.A. §§ 4372-4374 (1971 Pocket Part); Water and Environmental Quality Improvement Act of 1970, Pub. L. 91-224, 91st Cong., 2d Sess. (1970).

[2] 42 U.S.C.A. § 4321 *et seq.* (1971 Pocket Part).

[3] The full text of Title I is printed as an appendix to this opinion.

[4] Before the enactment of NEPA, the Commission did recognize its separate statutory mandate to consider the specific radiological hazards caused by its actions; but it argued that it could not consider broader environmental impacts. Its position was upheld in *State of New Hampshire* v. *Atomic Energy Commission,* 1 Cir., 406 F.2d 170, *cert. denied,* 395 U.S. 962 (1969).

[5] Only once—in § 102(2)(B)—does the Act state, in terms, that federal agencies must give full "consideration" to environmental impact as part of their decision making processes. However, a requirement of consideration is clearly implicit in the substantive mandate of § 101, in the requirement of § 102(1) that all laws and regulations be "interpreted and administered" in accord with that mandate, and in the other specific procedural measures compelled by § 102(2). The only circuit to interpret NEPA to date has said that "[t]his Act essentially states that every federal agency shall consider ecological factors when dealing with activities which may have an impact on man's environment." *Zabel* v. *Tabb,* 5 Cir., 430 F.2d 199, 211 (1970). Thus a purely mechanical compliance with the particular measures required in § 102(2)(C) & (D) will not satisfy the Act if they do not amount to full good faith *consideration* of the environment. *See* text at pages 14-18 *infra.* The requirements of § 102(2) must not be read so narrowly as to erase the general import of §§ 101, 102(1) and 102(2)(A) & (B).

NEPA's principal sponsor, stated that "[n]o agency will [now] be able to maintain that it has no mandate or no requirement to consider the environmental consequences of its actions." [6] He characterized the requirements of Section 102 as "action-forcing" and stated that "[o]therwise, these lofty declarations [in Section 101] are nothing more than that." [7]

The sort of consideration of environmental values which NEPA compels is clarified in Section 102(2)(A) and (B). In general, all agencies must use a "systematic, interdisciplinary approach" to environmental planning and evaluation "in decisionmaking which may have an impact on man's environment." In order to include all possible environmental factors in the decisional equation, agencies must "identify and develop methods and procedures * * * which will insure that presently unquantified environmental amenities and values may be given appropriate consideration in decisionmaking along with economic and technical considerations." [8] "Environmental amenities" will often be in conflict with "economic and technical considerations." To "consider" the former "along with" the latter must involve a balancing process. In some instances environmental costs may outweigh economic and technical benefits and in other instances they may not. But NEPA mandates a rather finely tuned and "systematic" balancing analysis in each instance.[9]

To ensure that the balancing analysis is carried out and given full effect, Section 102(2)(C) requires that responsible officials of all agencies prepare a "detailed statement" covering the impact of particular actions on the environment, the environmental costs which might be avoided, and alternative measures which might alter the cost-benefit equation. The apparent purpose of the "detailed statement" is to aid in the agencies' own decision making process and to advise other interested agencies and the public of the environmental consequences of planned federal action. Beyond the "detailed statement," Section 102(2)(D) requires all agencies specifically to "study, develop, and describe appropriate alternatives to recommended courses of action in any proposal which involves unresolved conflicts concerning alternative uses of available resources." This requirement, like the "detailed statement" requirement, seeks to ensure that each agency decision maker has before him and takes into proper account all possible approaches to a particular project (including total abandonment of the project) which would alter the environmental impact and the cost-benefit balance. Only in that fashion is it likely that the most intelligent, optimally beneficial decision will ultimately be made. Moreover, by compelling a formal "detailed statement" and a description of alternatives, NEPA provides evidence that the mandated decision making process has in fact taken place and, most importantly, allows those removed from the initial process to evaluate and balance the factors on their own.

Of course, all of these Section 102 duties are qualified by the phrase "to the fullest extent possible." We must stress as forcefully as possible that this language does not provide an escape hatch for footdragging agencies; it does not make NEPA's procedural requirements somehow "discretionary." Congress did not intend the Act to be such a paper tiger. Indeed, the requirement of environmental consideration "to the fullest extent possible" sets a high standard for the agencies, a standard which must be rigorously enforced by the reviewing courts.

Unlike the substantive duties of Section 101(B), which require agencies to "use all practicable means consistent with other essential considerations," the procedural duties of Section 102 must be fulfilled to the "fullest extent possible." [10] This contrast, in itself, is revealing. But the dispositive factor in our interpretation is the expressed views of the Senate and House conferees who wrote the "fullest extent possible" language into NEPA. They stated [11]:

> "* * * The purpose of the new language is to make it clear that each agency of the Federal Government shall comply with the directives set out in * * * [Section 102(2)] unless the existing law applicable

---

On April 23, 1971, the Council on Environmental Quality—established by NEPA—issued guidelines for federal agencies on compliance with the Act. 36 FED. REG. 7723 (April 23, 1971). The Council stated that "[t]he objective of section 102(2) (C) of the Act and of these guidelines is to build into the agency decision making process an appropriate and careful consideration of the environmental aspects of proposed action * * *." *Id.* at 7724.

[6] *Hearings on S.1075, S. 237 and S. 1752 Before Senate Committee on Interior and Insular Affairs,* 91st Cong., 1st Sess. 206 (1969). Just before the Senate finally approved NEPA, Senator Jackson said on the floor that the Act "directs all agencies to assure consideration of the environmental impact of their actions in decisionmaking." 115 CONG. REC. (Part 30) 40416 (1969).

[7] *Hearings on S. 1075, supra* Note 6, at 116. Again, the Senator reemphasized his point on the floor of the Senate, saying: "To insure that the policies and goals defined in this act are infused into the ongoing programs and actions of the Federal Government, the act also established some important 'action-forcing' procedures." 115 CONG. REC. (Part 30) at 40416. The Senate Committee on Interior and Insular Affairs Committee Report on NEPA also stressed the importance of the "action-forcing" provisions which require full and rigorous consideration of environmental values as an integral part of agency decision making. S. Rep. No. 91-296, 91st Cong., 1st Sess. (1969).

[8] The word "appropriate" in § 102(2) (B) cannot be interpreted to blunt the thrust of the whole Act or to give agencies broad discretion to downplay environmental factors in their decision making processes. The Act requires consideration "appropriate" to the problem of protecting our threatened environment, not consideration "appropriate" to the whims, habits or other particular concerns of federal agencies. *See* Note 5 *supra.*

[9] Senator Jackson specifically recognized the requirement of a balancing judgment. He said on the floor of the Senate: "Subsection 102(b) requires the development of procedures designed to insure that all relevant environmental values and amenities are considered in the calculus of project development and decisionmaking. Subsection 102(c) establishes a procedure designed to insure that in instances where a proposed major Federal action would have a significant impact on the environment that the impact has in fact been considered, that any adverse affects which cannot be avoided are justified by some other stated consideration of national policy, that short-term uses are consistent with long-term productivity, and that any irreversible and irretrievable commitments of resources are warranted." 115 CONG. REC. (Part 21) 29055 (1969).

[10] The Commission, arguing before this court, has mistakenly confused the two standards, using the § 101(B) language to suggest that it has broad discretion in performance of § 102 procedural duties. We stress the necessity to separate the two, substantive and procedural, standards. *See* text at page 37 *infra.*

[11] The Senators' views are contained in "Major Changes in S. 1075 as Passed by the Senate," 115 CONG. REC. (Part 30) at 40417-40418. The Representatives' views are contained in a separate statement filed with the Conference Report, 115 CONG. REC. (Part 29) 39702-39703 (1969).

to such agency's operations expressly prohibits or makes full compliance with one of the directives impossible. * * * Thus, it is the intent of the conferees that the provision 'to the fullest extent possible' shall not be used by any Federal agency as a means of avoiding compliance with the directives set out in section 102. Rather, the language in section 102 is intended to assure that all agencies of the Federal Government shall comply with the directives set out in said section 'to the fullest extent possible' under their statutory authorizations and that no agency shall utilize an excessively narrow construction of its existing statutory authorizations to avoid compliance."

Thus the Section 102 duties are not inherently flexible. They must be complied with to the fullest extent, unless there is a clear conflict of *statutory* authority.[12] Considerations of administrative difficulty, delay or economic cost will not suffice to strip the section of its fundamental importance.

We conclude, then, that Section 102 of NEPA mandates a particular sort of careful and informed decisionmaking process and creates judicially enforceable duties. The reviewing courts probably cannot reverse a substantive decision on its merits, under Section 101, unless it be shown that the actual balance of costs and benefits that was struck was arbitrary or clearly gave insufficient weight to environmental values. But if the decision was reached procedurally without individualized consideration and balancing of environmental factors—conducted fully and in good faith—it is the responsibility of the courts to reverse. As one District Court has said of Section 102 requirements: "It is hard to imagine a clearer or stronger mandate to the Courts." [13]

In the cases before us now, we do not have to review a particular decision by the Atomic Energy Commission granting a construction permit or an operating license. Rather, we must review the Commission's recently promulgated rules which govern consideration of environmental values in all such individual decisions.[14] The rules were devised strictly in order to comply with the NEPA procedural requirements—but petitioners argue that they fall far short of the congressional mandate.

The period of the rules' gestation does not indicate overenthusiasm on the Commission's part. NEPA went into effect on January 1, 1970. On April 2, 1970—three months later—the Commission issued its first, short policy statement on implementation of the Act's procedural provisions.[15] After another span of two months, the Commission published a notice of proposed rule making in the Federal Register.[16] Petitioners submitted substantial comments critical of the proposed rules. Finally, on December 3, 1970, the Commission terminated its long rule making proceeding by issuing a formal amendment, labelled Appendix D, to its governing regulations.[17] Appendix D is a somewhat revised version of the earlier proposal and, at last, commits the Commission to consider environmental impact in its decision making process.

The procedure for environmental study and consideration set up by the Appendix D rules is as follows: Each applicant for an initial construction permit must submit to the Commission his own "environmental report," presenting his assessment of the environmental impact of the planned facility and possible alternatives which would alter the impact. When construction is completed and the applicant applies for a license to operate the new facility, he must again submit an "environmental report" noting any factors which have changed since the original report. At each stage, the Commission's regulatory staff must take the applicant's report and prepare its own "detailed state-

---

[12] § Section 104 of NEPA provides that the Act does not eliminate any duties already imposed by other "specific statutory obligations." Only when such specific obligations conflict with NEPA do agencies have a right under § 104 and the "fullest extent possible" language to dilute their compliance with the full letter and spirit of the Act. *See* text at pages 28-35 *infra*. Sections 103 and 105 also support the general interpretation that the "fullest extent possible" language exempts agencies from full compliance only when there is a conflict of statutory obligations. Section 103 provides for agency review of existing obligations in order to discover and, if possible, correct any conflicts. *See* text at pages 21-22 *infra*. And § 105 provides that "[t]he policies and goals set forth in this Act are supplementary to those set forth in existing authorizations of Federal agencies." The report of the House conferees states that § 105 "does not * * * obviate the requirement that the Federal agencies conduct their activities in accordance with the provisions of this bill unless to do so would clearly violate their existing statutory obligations." 115 CONG. REC. (Part 29) at 39703. The section-by-section analysis by the Senate conferees makes exactly the same point in slightly different language. 115 CONG. REC. (Part 30) at 40418. The guidelines published by the Council on Environmental Quality state that "[t]he phrase 'to the fullest extent possible' * * * is meant to make clear that each agency of the Federal Government shall comply with the requirement unless existing law applicable to the agency's operations expressly prohibits or makes compliance impossible." 36 FED. REG. at 7724.

[13] *Texas Committee on Natural Resources* v. *United States*, W.D. Tex., 1 Envir. Rpts—Cas. 1303, 1304 (1970). A few of the courts which have considered NEPA to date have made statements stressing the discretionary aspects of the Act. *See, e.g., Pennsylvania Environmental Council* v. *Bartlett*, M.D. Pa., 315 F.Supp. 238 (1970); *Bucklein* v. *Volpe*, N.D. Cal., 2 Envir. Rpts—Cas. 1082, 1083 (1970). The Commission and intervenors rely upon these statements quite heavily. However, their reliance is misplaced, since the courts in question were not referring to the *procedural* duties created by NEPA. Rather, they were concerned with the Act's substantive goals or with such peripheral matters as retroactive application of the Act.

The general interpretation of NEPA which we outline in text at pages 4-11 *supra* is fully supported by the scholarly commentary. *See, e.g.,* Donovan, *The Federal Government and Environmental Control: Administrative Reform on the Executive Level*, 12 B.C. IND. & COM. L. REV. 541 (1971); Hanks & Hanks, *An Environmental Bill of Rights: The Citizen Suit and the National Environmental Policy Act of 1969*, 24 RUTG. L. REV. 231 (1970); Sive, *Some Thoughts of an Environmental Lawyer in the Wilderness of Administrative Law*, 70 COLUM. L. REV. 612, 643-650 (1970); Peterson, *An Analysis of Title I of the National Environmental Policy Act of 1969*, 1 ENVIR. L. RPTR 50035 (1971); Yannacone, *National Environmental Policy Act of 1969*, 1 ENVIR. LAW 8 (1970); Note, *The National Environmental Policy Act: A Sheep in Wolf's Clothing?*, 37 BROOKLYN L. REV. 139 (1970).

[14] In Case No. 24,871, petitioners attack four aspects of the Commission's rules, which are outlined in text. In Case No. 24,839, they challenge a particular application of the rules in the granting of a particular construction permit—that for the Calvert Cliffs Nuclear Power Plant. However, their challenge consists largely of an attack on the substance of one aspect of the rules also attacked in Case No. 24,871. Thus we are able to resolve both cases together, and our remand to the Commission for further rule making includes a remand for further consideration relating to the Calvert Cliffs Plant in Case No. 24,839. *See* Part V of this opinion, *infra*.

[15] 35 FED. REG. 5463 (April 2, 1970).

[16] 35 FED. REG. 8594 (June 3, 1970).

[17] 35 FED. REG. 18469 (December 4, 1970). The version of the rules finally adopted is now printed in 10 C.F.R. § 50, App. D, pp. 246-250 (1971).

ment" of environmental costs, benefits and alternatives. The statement will then be circulated to other interested and responsible agencies and made available to the public. After comments are received from those sources, the staff must prepare a final "detailed statement" and make a final recommendation on the application for a construction permit or operating license.

Up to this point in the Appendix D rules petitioners have raised no challenge. However, they do attack four other, specific parts of the rules which, they say, violate the requirements of Section 102 of NEPA. Each of these parts in some way limits full consideration and individualized balancing of environmental values in the Commission's decision making process. (1) Although environmental factors must be considered by the agency's regulatory staff under the rules, such factors need not be considered by the hearing board conducting an independent review of staff recommendations, unless affirmatively raised by outside parties or staff members. (2) Another part of the procedural rules prohibits any such party from raising non-radiological environmental issues at any hearing if the notice for that hearing appeared in the Federal Register before March 4, 1971. (3) Moreover, the hearing board is prohibited from conducting an independent evaluation and balancing of certain environmental factors if other responsible agencies have already certified that their own environmental standards are satisfied by the proposed federal action. (4) Finally, the Commission's rules provide that when a construction permit for a facility has been issued before NEPA compliance was required and when an operating license has yet to be issued, the agency will not formally consider environmental factors or require modifications in the proposed facility until the time of the issuance of the operating license. Each of these parts of the Commission's rules will be described at greater length and evaluated under NEPA in the following sections of this opinion.

II

NEPA makes only one specific reference to consideration of environmental values in agency review processes. Section 102(2)(C) provides that copies of the staff's "detailed statement" and comments thereon "shall accompany the proposal through the existing agency review processes." The Atomic Energy Commission's rules may seem in technical compliance with the letter of that provision. They state:

> "12. If any party to a proceeding * * * raises any [environmental] issue * * * the Applicant's Environmental Report and the Detailed Statement will be offered in evidence. The atomic safety and licensing board will make findings of fact on, and resolve, the matters in controversy among the parties with regard to those issues. Depending on the resolution of those issues, the permit or license may be granted, denied, or appropriately conditioned to protect environmental values.
>
> "13. When no party to a proceeding * * * raises any [environmental] issue * * * such issues will not be considered by the atomic safety and licensing board. Under such circumstances, although the Applicant's Environmental Report, comments thereon, and the Detailed Statement will accompany the application through the Commission's review processes, they will not be received in evidence, and the Commission's responsibilities under the National Environmental Policy Act of 1969 will be carried out in toto outside the hearing process." [18]

The question here is whether the Commission is correct in thinking that its NEPA responsibilities may "be carried out in toto outside the hearing process"—whether it is enough that environmental data and evaluations merely "accompany" an application through the review process, but receive no consideration whatever from the hearing board.

We believe that the Commission's crabbed interpretation of NEPA makes a mockery of the Act. What possible purpose could there be in the Section 102(2)(C) requirement (that the "detailed statement" accompany proposals through agency review processes) if "accompany" means no more than physical proximity—mandating no more than the physical act of passing certain folders and papers, unopened, to reviewing officials along with other folders and papers? What possible purpose could there be in requiring the "detailed statement" to be before hearing boards, if the boards are free to ignore entirely the contents of the statement? NEPA was meant to do more than regulate the flow of papers in the federal bureaucracy. The word "accompany" in Section 102(2)(C) must not be read so narrowly as to make the Act ludicrous. It must, rather, be read to indicate a congressional intent that environmental factors, as compiled in the "detailed statement," be *considered* through agency review processes.[19]

Beyond Section 102(2)(C), NEPA requires that agencies consider the environmental impact of their actions "to the fullest extent possible." The Act is addressed to agencies as a whole, not only to their professional staffs. Compliance to the *"fullest"* possible extent would seem to demand that environmental issues be considered at every important stage in the decision making process concerning a particular action—at every stage where an overall balancing of environmental and nonenvironmental factors is appropriate and where alterations might be made in the proposed action to minimize environmental costs. Of course, consideration which is entirely duplicative is not necessarily required. But independent review of staff proposals by hearing boards is hardly a duplicative function. A truly independent review provides a crucial check on the staff's recommendations. The Commission's hearing boards automatically consider nonenvironmental factors, even though they have been previously studied by the staff. Clearly, the review process is an appropriate stage at which to balance conflicting factors against one another. And, just as clearly, it provides an important opportunity to reject or significantly modify the staff's recommended action. Environmental factors, therefore, should not be singled out and excluded, at this stage, from the proper balance of values envisioned by NEPA.

The Commission's regulations provide that in an uncontested proceeding the hearing board shall on its own "determine whether the application and the record of the proceeding contain sufficient information, and the review of the application by the Commission's regulatory staff has been adequate, to support affirmative findings on" various

[18] 10 C.F.R. § 50, App. D, at 249.

[19] The guidelines issued by the Council on Environmental Quality emphasize the importance of consideration of alternatives to staff recommendations during the agency review process: "A rigorous exploration and objective evaluation of alternative actions that might avoid some or all of the adverse environmental effects is essential. Sufficient analysis of such alternatives and their costs and impact on the environment should accompany the proposed action through the agency review process in order not to foreclose prematurely options which might have less detrimental effects." 36 FED. REG. at 7725. The Council also states that an objective of its guidelines is "to assist agencies in implementing not only the letter, but the spirit, of the Act." *Id.* at 7724.

nonenvironmental factors.[20] NEPA requires at least as much automatic consideration of environmental factors. In uncontested hearings, the board need not necessarily go over the same ground covered in the "detailed statement." But it must at least examine the statement carefully to determine whether "the review * * * by the Commission's regulatory staff has been adequate." And it must independently consider the final balance among conflicting factors that is struck in the staff's recommendation.

The rationale of the Commission's limitation of environmental issues to hearings in which parties affirmatively raise those issues may have been one of economy. It may have been supposed that, whenever there are serious environmental costs overlooked or uncorrected by the staff, some party will intervene to bring those costs to the hearing board's attention. Of course, independent review of the "detailed statement" and independent balancing of factors in an uncontested hearing will take some time. If it is done properly, it will take a significant amount of time. But all of the NEPA procedures take time. Such administrative costs are not enough to undercut the Act's requirement that environmental protection be considered "to the fullest extent possible," *see* text at pages 9-11 *supra.* It is, moreover, unrealistic to assume that there will always be an intervenor with the information, energy and money required to challenge a staff recommendation which ignores environmental costs. NEPA establishes environmental protection as an integral part of the Atomic Energy Commission's basic mandate. The primary responsibility for fulfilling that mandate lies with the Commission. Its responsibility is not simply to sit back, like an umpire, and resolve adversary contentions at the hearing stage. Rather, it must itself take the initiative of considering environmental values at every distinctive and comprehensive stage of the process beyond the staff's evaluation and recommendation.[21]

III

Congress passed the final version of NEPA in late 1969, and the Act went into full effect on January 1, 1970. Yet the Atomic Energy Commission's rules prohibit any consideration of environmental issues by its hearing boards at proceedings officially noticed before March 4, 1971.[22] This is 14 months after the effective date of NEPA. And the hearings affected may go on for as much as a year longer until final action is taken. The result is that major federal actions having a significant environmental impact may be taken by the Commission, without full NEPA compliance, more than two years after the Act's effective date. In view of the importance of environmental consideration during the agency review process, *see* Part II *supra,* such a time lag is shocking.

The Commission explained that its very long time lag was intended "to provide an orderly period of transition in the conduct of the Commission's regulatory proceedings and to avoid unreasonable delays in the construction and operation of nuclear power plants urgently needed to meet the national requirements for electric power." [23] Before this court, it has claimed authority for its action, arguing that "the statute did not lay down detailed guidelines and inflexible timetables for its implementation; and we find in it no bar to agency provisions which are designed to accommodate transitional implementation problems." [24]

Again, the Commission's approach to statutory interpretation is strange indeed—so strange that it seems to reveal a rather thoroughgoing reluctance to meet the NEPA procedural obligations in the agency review process, the stage at which deliberation is most open to public examination and subject to the participation of public intervenors. The Act, it is true, lacks an "inflexible timetable" for its implementation. But it does have a clear effective date, consistently enforced by reviewing courts up to now. Every federal court having faced the issues has held that the procedural requirements of NEPA must be met in order to uphold federal action taken after January 1, 1970.[25] The absence of a "timetable" for compliance has never been held sufficient, in itself, to put off the date on which a congressional mandate takes effect. The absence of a "timetable," rather, indicates that compliance is required forthwith.

The only part of the Act which even implies that implementation may be subject, in some cases, to some significant delay is Section 103. There, Congress provided that all agencies must review "their present statutory authority, administrative regulations, and current policies and procedures for the purpose of determining whether there are any deficiencies or inconsistencies therein which prohibit full compliance" with NEPA. Agencies finding some such insuperable difficulty are obliged to "propose to the President not later than July 1, 1971, such measures as may be necessary to bring their authority and policies

[20] 10 C.F.R. § 2.104(b) (2) (1971).

[21] In recent years, the courts have become increasingly strict in requiring that federal agencies live up to their mandates to consider the public interest. They have become increasingly impatient with agencies which attempt to avoid or dilute their statutorily imposed role as protectors of public interest values beyond the narrow concerns of industries being regulated. *See, e.g., Udall* v. *FPC,* 387 U.S. 428 (1967); *Environmental Defense Fund, Inc.* v. *Ruckelshaus,* —— U.S.App.D.C. ——, 439 F.2d 584 (1971); *Moss* v. *C.A.B.,* 139 U.S.App.D.C. 150, 430 F.2d 891 (1970); *Environmental Defense Fund, Inc.* v. *U.S. Dept. of H. E. & W.,* 138 U.S.App. D.C. 381, 428 F.2d 1083 (1970). In commenting on the Atomic Energy Commission's pre-NEPA duty to consider health and safety matters, the Supreme Court said "the responsibility for safeguarding that health and safety belongs under the statute to the Commission." *Power Reactor Development Co.* v. *I.U.E.R.M.W.,* 367 U.S. 396, 404 (1961). The Second Circuit has made the same point regarding the Federal Power Commission: "In this case, as in many others, the Commission has claimed to be the representative of the public interest. This role does not permit it to act as an umpire blandly calling balls and strikes for adversaries appearing before it; the right of the public must receive active and affirmative protection at the hands of the Commission." *Scenic Hudson Preservation Conference* v. *FPC,* 2 Cir., 354 F.2d 608, 620 (1965).

[22] 10 C.F.R. § 50, App. D, at 249.

[23] 35 FED. REG. 18470 (December 4, 1970).

[24] Brief for respondents in No. 24,871 at 49.

[25] In some cases, the courts have had a difficult time determining whether particular federal actions were "taken" before or after January 1, 1970. But they have all started from the basic rule that any action taken after that date must comply with NEPA's procedural requirements. *See* Note, *Retroactive Application of the National Environmental Policy Act of 1969,* 69 MICH. L. REV. 732 (1971), and cases cited therein. Clearly, any hearing held between January 1, 1970 and March 4, 1971 which culminates in the grant of a permit or license is a federal action taken after the Act's effective date.

into conformity with the intent, purposes, and procedures set forth in this Act."

The Commission, however, cannot justify its time lag under these Section 103 provisions. Indeed, it has not attempted to do so; only intervenors have raised the argument. Section 103 could support a substantial delay only by an agency which in fact discovered an insuperable barrier to compliance with the Act and required time to formulate and propose the needed reformative measures. The actual review of existing statutory authority and regulations cannot be a particularly lengthy process for experienced counsel of a federal agency. Of course, the Atomic Energy Commission discovered no obstacle to NEPA implementation. Although it did not report its conclusion to the President until October 2, 1970, that nine-month delay (January to October) cannot justify so long a period of noncompliance with the Act. It certainly cannot justify a further delay of compliance until March 4, 1971.

No doubt the process of formulating procedural rules to implement NEPA takes some time. Congress cannot have expected that federal agencies would immediately begin considering environmental issues on January 1, 1970. But the effective date of the Act does set a time for agencies to begin adopting rules and it demands that they strive, "to the fullest extent possible," to be prompt in the process. The Atomic Energy Commission has failed in this regard.[26] Consideration of environmental issues in the agency review process, for example, is quite clearly compelled by the Act.[27] The Commission cannot justify its 11-month delay in adopting rules on this point as part of a difficult, discretionary effort to decide whether or not its hearing boards should deal with environmental questions at all.

Even if the long delay had been necessary, however, the Commission would not be relieved of all NEPA responsibility to hold public hearings on the environmental consequences of actions taken between January 1, 1970 and final adoption of the rules. Although the Act's effective date may not require instant compliance, it must at least require that NEPA procedures, once established, be applied to consider prompt alterations in the plans or operations of facilities approved without compliance.[28] Yet the Commission's rules contain no such provision. Indeed, they do not even apply to the hearings still being conducted at the time of their adoption on December 3, 1970—or, for that matter, to hearings initiated in the following three months. The delayed compliance date of March 4, 1971, then, cannot be justified by the Commission's long drawn out rule making process.

Strangely, the Commission has principally relied on more pragmatic arguments. It seems an unfortunate affliction of large organizations to resist new procedures and to envision massive roadblocks to their adoption. Hence the Commission's talk of the need for an "orderly transition" to the NEPA procedures. It is difficult to credit the Commission's argument that several months were needed to work the consideration of environmental values into its review process. Before the enactment of NEPA, the Commission already had regulations requiring that hearings include health, safety and radiological matters.[29] The introduction of environmental matters cannot have presented a radically unsettling problem. And, in any event, the obvious sense of urgency on the part of Congress should make clear that a transition, however "orderly," must proceed at a pace faster than a funeral procession.

In the end, the Commission's long delay seems based upon what it believes to be a pressing national power crisis. Inclusion of environmental issues in pre-March 4, 1971 hearings might have held up the licensing of some power plants for a time. But the very purpose of NEPA was to tell federal agencies that environmental protection is as much a part of their responsibility as is protection and promotion of the industries they regulate. Whether or not the spectre of a national power crisis is as real as the Commission apparently believes, it must not be used

---

[26] *See* text at pages 12-13 *supra*.

[27] As early as March 5, 1970, President Nixon stated in an executive order that NEPA requires consideration of environmental factors at public hearings. Executive Order 11514, 35 FED. REG. 4247 (March 5, 1970). *See also* Part II of this opinion.

[28] In Part V of this opinion, we hold that the Commission must promptly consider the environmental impact of projects initially approved before January 1, 1970 but not yet granted an operating license. We hold that the Commission may not wait until construction is entirely completed and consider environmental factors only at the operating license hearings; rather, before environmental damage has been irreparably done by full construction of a facility, the Commission must consider alterations in the plans. Much the same principle—of making alterations while they still may be made at relatively small expense—applies to projects approved without NEPA compliance *after* the Act's effective date. A total reversal of the basic decision to construct a particular facility or take a particular action may then be difficult, since substantial resources may already have been committed to the project. Since NEPA must apply to the project in some fashion, however, it is essential that it apply as effectively as possible—requiring alterations in parts of the project to which resources have not yet been inalterably committed at great expense.

One District Court has dealt with the problem of instant compliance with NEPA. It suggested another measure which agencies should take while in the process of developing rules. It said: "The NEPA does not require the impossible. Nor would it require, in effect, a moratorium on all projects which had an environmental impact while awaiting compliance with § 102(2)(B). It would suffice if the statement pointed out this deficiency. The decisionmakers could then determine whether any purpose would be served in delaying the project while awaiting the development of such criteria." *Environmental Defense Fund, Inc.* v. *Corps of Engineers,* E.D. Ark., 325 F.Supp. 749, 758 (1971). Apparently, the Atomic Energy Commission did not even go this far toward *considering* the lack of a NEPA public hearing as a basis for delaying projects between the Act's effective date and adoption of the rules.

Of course, on the facts of these cases, we need not express any final view on the legal effect of the Commission's failure to comply with NEPA after the Act's effective date. Mere *post hoc* alterations in plans may not be enough, especially in view of the Commission's long delay in promulgating rules. Less than a year ago, this court was asked to review a refusal by the Atomic Energy Commission to consider environmental factors in granting a license. We held that the case was not yet ripe for review. But we stated: "If the Commission persists in excluding such evidence, it is courting the possibility that if error is found a court will reverse its final order, condemn its proceeding as so much waste motion, and order that the proceeding be conducted over again in a way that realistically permits de novo consideration of the tendered evidence." *Thermal Ecology Must be Preserved* v. *AEC,* 139 U.S.App.D.C. 366, 368, 433 F.2d 524, 526 (1970).

[29] *See* 10 C.F.R. § 20 (1971) for the standards which the Commission had developed to deal with radioactive emissions which might pose health or safety problems.

to create a blackout of environmental consideration in the agency review process. NEPA compels a case-by-case examination and balancing of discrete factors. Perhaps there may be cases in which the need for rapid licensing of a particular facility would justify a strict time limit on a hearing board's review of environmental issues; but a blanket banning of such issues until March 4, 1971 is impermissible under NEPA.

IV

The sweep of NEPA is extraordinarily broad, compelling consideration of any and all types of environmental impact of federal action. However, the Atomic Energy Commission's rules specifically exclude from full consideration a wide variety of environmental issues. First, they provide that no party may raise and the Commission may not independently examine any problem of water quality—perhaps the most significant impact of nuclear power plants. Rather, the Commission indicates that it will defer totally to water quality standards devised and administered by state agencies and approved by the federal government under the Federal Water Pollution Control Act.[30] Secondly, the rules provide for similar abdication of NEPA authority to the standards of other agencies:

> "With respect to those aspects of environmental quality for which environmental quality standards and requirements have been established by authorized Federal, State, and regional agencies, proof that the applicant is equipped to observe and agrees to observe such standards and requirements will be considered a satisfactory showing that there will not be a significant, adverse effect on the environment. Certification by the appropriate agency that there is reasonable assurance that the applicant for the permit or license will observe such standards and requirements will be considered dispositive for this purpose." [31]

The most the Commission will do is include a condition in all construction permits and operating licenses requiring compliance with the water quality or other standards set by such agencies.[32] The upshot is that the NEPA procedures, viewed by the Commission as superfluous, will wither away in disuse, applied only to those environmental issues wholly unregulated by any other federal, state or regional body.

We believe the Commission's rule is in fundamental conflict with the basic purpose of the Act. NEPA mandates a case-by-case balancing judgment on the part of federal agencies. In each individual case, the particular economic and technical benefits of planned action must be assessed and then weighed against the environmental costs; alternatives must be considered which would affect the balance of values. *See* text at pages 7-9 *supra.* The magnitude of possible benefits and possible costs may lie anywhere on a broad spectrum. Much will depend on the particular magnitudes involved in particular cases. In some cases, the benefits will be great enough to justify a certain quantum of environmental costs; in other cases, they will not be so great and the proposed action may have to be abandoned or significantly altered so as to bring the benefits and costs into a proper balance. The point of the individualized balancing analysis is to ensure that, with possible alterations, the optimally beneficial action is finally taken.

Certification by another agency that its own environmental standards are satisfied involves an entirely different kind of judgment. Such agencies, without overall responsibility for the particular federal action in question, attend only to one aspect of the problem: the magnitude of certain environmental costs. They simply determine whether those costs exceed an allowable amount. Their certification does not mean that they found no environmental damage whatever. In fact, there may be significant environmental damage (*e.g.,* water pollution), but not quite enough to violate applicable (*e.g.,* water quality) standards. Certifying agencies do not attempt to weigh that damage against the opposing benefits. Thus the balancing analysis remains to be done. It may be that the environmental costs, though passing prescribed standards, are nonetheless great enough to outweigh the particular economic and technical benefits involved in the planned action. The only agency in a position to make such a judgment is the agency with overall responsibility for the proposed federal action—the agency to which NEPA is specifically directed.

The Atomic Energy Commission, abdicating entirely to other agencies' certifications, neglects the mandated balancing analysis. Concerned members of the public are thereby precluded from raising a wide range of environmental issues in order to affect particular Commission decisions. And the special purpose of NEPA is subverted.

Arguing before this court, the Commission has made much of the special environmental expertise of the agencies which set environmental standards. NEPA did not overlook this consideration. Indeed, the Act is quite explicit in describing the attention which is to be given to the views and standards of other agencies. Section 102 (2)(C) provides:

> "Prior to making any detailed statement, the responsible Federal official shall consult with and obtain the comments of any Federal agency which has jurisdiction by law or special expertise with respect to any environmental impact involved. Copies of such statement and the comments and views of the appropriate Federal, State, and local agencies, which are authorized to develop and enforce environmental standards, shall be made available to the President, the Council on Environmental Quality and to the public * * *."

Thus the Congress was surely cognizant of federal, state and local agencies "authorized to develop and enforce environmental standards." But it provided, in Section 102 (2)(C), only for full consultation. It most certainly did not authorize a total abdication to those agencies. Nor did it grant a license to disregard the main body of NEPA obligations.

Of course, federal agencies such as the Atomic Energy Commission may have specific duties, under acts other than NEPA, to obey particular environmental standards. Section 104 of NEPA makes clear that such duties are not to be ignored:

[30] 10 C.F.R. § 50, App. D, at 249. Appendix D does require that applicants' environmental reports and the Commission's "detailed statements" include "a discussion of the water quality aspects of the proposed action." *Id.* at 248. But, as is stated in text, it bars independent consideration of those matters by the Commission's reviewing boards at public hearings. It also bars the Commission from requiring—or even considering—any water protection measures not already required by the approving state agencies. *See* Note 31 *infra.*

The section of the Federal Water Pollution Control Act establishing a system of state agency certification is § 21, as amended in the Water Quality Improvement Act of 1970. 33 U.S.C.A. § 1171 (1970). In text below, this section is discussed as part of the Water Quality Improvement Act.

[31] 10 C.F.R. § 50, App. D, at 249.

[32] *Ibid.*

"Nothing in Section 102 or 103 shall in any way affect the specific statutory obligations of any Federal agency (1) to comply with criteria or standards of environmental quality, (2) to coordinate or consult with any other Federal or State agency, or (3) to act, or refrain from acting contingent upon the recommendations or certification of any other Federal or State agency."

On its face, Section 104 seems quite unextraordinary, intended only to see that the general procedural reforms achieved in NEPA do not wipe out the more specific environmental controls imposed by other statutes. Ironically, however, the Commission argues that Section 104 in fact allows other statutes to wipe out NEPA.

Since the Commission places great reliance on Section 104 to support its abdication to standard setting agencies, we should first note the section's obvious limitation. It deals only with deference to such agencies which is compelled by "specific statutory obligations." The Commission has brought to our attention one "specific statutory obligation": the Water Quality Improvement Act of 1970 (WQIA).[33] That Act prohibits federal licensing bodies, such as the Atomic Energy Commission, from issuing licenses for facilities which pollute "the navigable waters of the United States" unless they receive a certification from the appropriate agency that compliance with applicable water quality standards is reasonably assured. Thus Section 104 applies in some fashion to consideration of water quality matters. But it definitely cannot support—indeed, it is not even relevant to—the Commission's wholesale abdication to the standards and certifications of any and all federal, state and local agencies dealing with matters other than water quality.

As to water quality, Section 104 and WQIA clearly require obedience to standards set by other agencies. But obedience does not imply total abdication. Certainly, the language of Section 104 does not authorize an abdication. It does not suggest that other "specific statutory obligations" will entirely replace NEPA. Rather, it ensures that three sorts of "obligations" will not be undermined by NEPA: (1) the obligation to "comply" with certain standards, (2) the obligation to "coordinate" or "consult" with certain agencies, and (3) the obligation to "act, or refrain from acting contingent upon" a certification from certain agencies. WQIA imposes the third sort of obligation. It makes the granting of a license by the Commission "contingent upon" a water quality certification. But it does not *require* the Commission to grant a license once a certification has been issued. It does not preclude the Commission from demanding water pollution controls from its licensees which are *more strict* than those demanded by the applicable water quality standards of the certifying agency.[34] It is very important to understand these facts about WQIA. For all that Section 104 of NEPA does is to reaffirm other "specific statutory obligations." Unless those obligations are plainly mutually exclusive with the requirements of NEPA, the specific mandate of NEPA must remain in force. In other words, Section 104 can operate to relieve an agency of its NEPA duties only if other "specific statutory obligations" clearly preclude performance of those duties.

Obedience to water quality certifications under WQIA is not mutually exclusive with the NEPA procedures. It does not preclude performance of the NEPA duties. Water quality certifications essentially establish a *minimum condition* for the granting of a license. But they need not end the matter. The Commission can then go on to perform the very different operation of balancing the overall benefits and costs of a particular proposed project, and consider alterations (above and beyond the applicable water quality standards) which would further reduce environmental damage. Because the Commission *can* still conduct the NEPA balancing analysis, consistent with WQIA, Section 104 does not exempt it from doing so. And it, therefore, *must* conduct the obligatory analysis under the prescribed procedures.

We believe the above result follows from the plain language of Section 104 of NEPA and WQIA. However, the Commission argues that we should delve beneath the plain language and adopt a significantly different interpretation. It relies entirely upon certain statements made by Senator Jackson and Senator Muskie, the sponsors of NEPA and WQIA respectively.[35] Those statements indicate that Section 104 was the product of a compromise intended to eliminate any conflict between the two bills then in the Senate. The overriding purpose was to prevent NEPA from eclipsing obedience to more specific standards under WQIA. Senator Muskie, distrustful of "self-policing by Federal agencies which pollute or license pollution," was particularly concerned that NEPA not undercut the independent role of standard setting agencies.[36] Most of his and Senator Jackson's comments stop short of suggesting that NEPA would have *no* application in water quality matters; their goal was to protect WQIA, not to undercut NEPA. Our interpretation of Section 104 is perfectly consistent with that purpose.

Yet the statements of the two Senators occasionally indicate they were willing to go farther, to permit agencies such as the Atomic Energy Commission to forego at least some NEPA procedures in consideration of water quality. Senator Jackson, for example, said, "The compromise worked out between the bills provides that the licensing agency will not have to make a detailed statement on water quality if the State or other appropriate agency has

---

[33] The relevant portion is 33 U.S.C.A. § 1171. *See* Note 30 *supra.*

[34] The relevant language in WQIA seems carefully to avoid any such restrictive implication. It provides that "[e]ach Federal agency * * * shall * * * insure compliance with applicable water quality standards * * *." 33 U.S.C.A. § 1171 (a). It also provides that "[n]o license or permit shall be granted until the certification required by this section has been obtained or has been waived * * *. No license or permit shall be granted if certification has been denied * * *." 33 U.S.C.A. § 1171(b)(1). Nowhere does it indicate that certification must be the final and only protection against unjustified water pollution—a fully sufficient as well as a necessary condition for issuance of a federal license or permit.

We also take note of § 21(c) of WQIA, which states: "Nothing in this section shall be construed to limit the authority of any department or agency pursuant to any other provision of law to require compliance with applicable water quality standards. * * *" 33 U.S.C.A. § 1171(c).

[35] The statements by Senators Jackson and Muskie were made, first, at the time the Senate originally considered WQIA. 115 CONG. REC. (Part 21) at 29052-29056. Another relevant colloquy between the two Senators occurred when the Senate considered the Conference Report on NEPA. 115 CONG. REC. (Part 30) at 40415-40425. Senator Muskie made a further statement at the time of final Senate approval of the Conference Report on WQIA. 116 CONG. REC. (daily ed.) S4401 (March 24, 1970).

[36] 115 CONG. REC. (Part 21) at 29053.

made a certification pursuant to [WQIA]." [37] Perhaps Senator Jackson would have required some consideration and balancing of environmental costs—despite the lack of a formal detailed statement—but he did not spell out his views. No Senator, other than Senators Jackson and Muskie, addressed himself specifically to the problem during floor discussion. Nor did any member of the House of Representatives.[38] The section-by-section analysis of NEPA submitted to the Senate clearly stated the overriding purpose of Section 104: that "no agency may substitute the procedures outlined in this Act for more restrictive and specific procedures established by law governing its activities." [39] The report does not suggest there that NEPA procedures should be entirely abandoned, but rather that they should not be "substituted" for more specific standards. In one rather cryptic sentence, the analysis does muddy the waters somewhat, stating that "[i]t is the intention that where there is no more effective procedure already established, the procedure of this act will be followed." [40] Notably, however, the sentence does not state that in the presence of "more effective procedures" the NEPA procedure will be abandoned entirely. It seems purposefully vague, quite possibly meaning that obedience to the certifications of standard setting agencies must alter, by supplementing, the *normal* "procedure of this act."

This rather meager legislative history, in our view, cannot radically transform the purport of the plain words of Section 104. Had the Senate sponsors fully intended to allow a total abdication of NEPA responsibilities in water quality matters—rather than a supplementing of them by strict obedience to the specific standards of WQIA—the language of Section 104 could easily have been changed. As the Supreme Court often has said, the legislative history of a statute (particularly such relatively meager and vague history as we have here) cannot radically affect its interpretation if the language of the statute is clear. *See, e.g., Packard Motor Car Co.* v. *NLRB,* 330 U.S. 485 (1947); *Kuehner* v. *Irving Trust Co.,* 299 U.S. 445 (1937); *Fairport, Painesville & Eastern R. Co.* v. *Meredith,* 292 U.S. 589 (1934); *Wilbur* v. *United States ex rel. Vindicator Consolidated Gold Mining Co.,* 284 U.S. 231 (1931). In a recent case interpreting a veterans' act, the Court set down the principle which must govern our approach to the case before us:

> "Having concluded that the provisions of § 1 are clear and unequivocal on their face, we find no need to resort to the legislative history of the Act. Since the State has placed such heavy reliance upon that history, however, we do deem it appropriate to point out that this history is at best inconclusive. It is true, as the State points out, that Representative Rankin, as Chairman of the Committee handling the bill on the floor of the House, expressed his view during the course of discussion of the bill on the floor that the 1941 Act would not apply to [the sort of case in question] * * *. But such statements, even when they stand alone, have never been regarded as sufficiently compelling to justify deviation from the plain language of a statute. * * *"

United States v. *Oregon,* 366 U.S. 643, 648 (1961). (Footnotes omitted.) It is, after all, the plain language of the statute which *all* the members of both houses of Congress must approve or disapprove. The courts should not allow that language to be significantly undercut. In cases such as this one, the most we should do to interpret clear statutory wording is to see that the *overriding purpose* behind the wording supports its plain meaning. We have done that here. And we conclude that Section 104 of NEPA does not permit the sort of total abdication of responsibility practiced by the Atomic Energy Commission.

V

Petitioners' final attack is on the Commission's rules governing a particular set of nuclear facilities: those for which construction permits were granted without consideration of environmental issues, but for which operating licenses have yet to be issued. These facilities, still in varying stages of construction, include the one of most immediate concern to one of the petitioners: the Calvert Cliffs nuclear power plant on Chesapeake Bay in Maryland.

The Commission's rules recognize that the granting of a construction permit before NEPA's effective date does not justify bland inattention to environmental consequences until the operating license proceedings, perhaps far in the future. The rules require that measures be taken *now* for environmental protection. Specifically, the Commission has provided for three such measures during the pre-operating license stage. First, it has required that a condition be added to all construction permits, "whenever issued," which would oblige the holders of the permits to observe all applicable environmental standards imposed by federal or state law. Second, it has required permit holders to submit their own environmental report on the facility under construction. And third, it has initiated procedures for the drafting of its staff's "detailed environmental statement" in advance of operating license proceedings.[41]

The one thing the Commission has refused to do is take any independent action based upon the material in the environmental reports and "detailed statements." Whatever environmental damage the reports and statements may reveal, the Commission will allow construction to proceed on the original plans. It will not even consider requiring alterations in those plans (beyond compliance with external standards which would be binding in any event), though the "detailed statements" must contain an analysis of possible alternatives and may suggest relatively inexpensive but highly beneficial changes. Moreover, the

[37] *Ibid. See also id.* at 29056. Senator Jackson appears not to have ascribed major importance to the compromise. He said, "It is my understanding that there was never any conflict between this section [of WQIA] and the provisions of [NEPA]. If both bills were enacted in their present form, there would be a requirement for State certification, as well as a requirement that the licensing agency make environmental findings." *Id.* at 29053. He added, "The agreed-upon changes mentioned previously would change the language of some of these requirements, but their substance would remain relatively unchanged." *Id.* at 29055. Senator Muskie seemed to give greater emphasis to the supposed conflict between the two bills. *See id.* at 29053; 115 CONG. REC. (Part 30) at 40425; 116 CONG. REC. (daily ed.) at S4401.

[38] The Commission has called to our attention remarks made by Congressman Harsha. The Congressman did refer to a statement by Senator Muskie regarding NEPA, but it was a statement regarding application of the Act to established environmental control agencies, not regarding the relationship between NEPA and WQIA. 115 CONG. REC. (Part 30) at 40927-40928.

[39] *Id.* at 40420.

[40] *Ibid.*

[41] 10 C.F.R. § 50, App. D, ¶ ¶ 1, 14.

Commission has, as a blanket policy, refused to consider the possibility of temporarily halting construction in particular cases pending a full study of a facility's environmental impact. It has also refused to weigh the pros and cons of "backfitting" for particular facilities (alteration of already constructed portions of the facilities in order to incorporate new technological developments designed to protect the environment). Thus reports and statements will be produced, but nothing will be done with them. Once again, the Commission seems to believe that the mere drafting and filing of papers is enough to satisfy NEPA.

The Commission appears to recognize the severe limitation which its rules impose on environmental protection. Yet it argues that full NEPA consideration of alternatives and independent action would cause too much delay at the pre-operating license stage. It justifies its rules as the most that is "practicable, in the light of environmental needs and 'other essential considerations of national policy'."[42] It cites, in particular, the "national power crisis" as a consideration of national policy militating against delay in construction of nuclear power facilities.

The Commission relies upon the flexible NEPA mandate to "use all practicable means consistent with other essential considerations of national policy." As we have previously pointed out, however, that mandate applies only to the substantive guidelines set forth in Section 101 of the Act. *See* pages 9-10 *supra.* The procedural duties, the duties to give full *consideration* to environmental protection, are subject to a much more strict standard of compliance. By now, the applicable principle should be absolutely clear. NEPA requires that an agency must—to the *fullest* extent possible under its other statutory obligations—consider alternatives to its actions which would reduce environmental damage. That principle establishes that consideration of environmental matters must be more than a *pro forma* ritual. Clearly, it is pointless to "consider" environmental costs without also seriously considering action to avoid them. Such a full exercise of substantive discretion is required at every important, appropriate and nonduplicative stage of an agency's proceedings. *See* text at pages 16-17 *supra.*

The special importance of the pre-operating license stage is not difficult to fathom. In cases where environmental costs were not considered in granting a construction permit, it is very likely that the planned facility will include some features which do significant damage to the environment and which could not have survived a rigorous balancing of costs and benefits. At the later operating license proceedings, this environmental damage will have to be fully considered. But by that time the situation will have changed radically. Once a facility has been completely constructed, the economic cost of any alteration may be very great. In the language of NEPA, there is likely to be an "irreversible and irretrievable commitment of resources," which will inevitably restrict the Commission's options. Either the licensee will have to undergo a major expense in making alterations in a completed facility or the environmental harm will have to be tolerated. It is all too probable that the latter result would come to pass.

By refusing to consider requirement of alterations until construction is completed, the Commission may effectively foreclose the environmental protection desired by Congress. It may also foreclose rigorous consideration of environmental factors at the eventual operating license proceedings. If "irreversible and irretrievable commitment[s] of resources" have already been made, the license hearing (and any public intervention therein) may become a hollow exercise. This hardly amounts to consideration of environmental values "to the fullest extent possible."

A full NEPA consideration of alterations in the original plans of a facility, then, is both important and appropriate well before the operating license proceedings. It is not duplicative if environmental issues were not considered in granting the construction permit. And it need not be duplicated, absent new information or new developments, at the operating license stage. In order that the pre-operating license review be as effective as possible, the Commission should consider very seriously the requirement of a temporary halt in construction pending its review and the "backfitting" of technological innovations. For no action which might minimize environmental damage may be dismissed out of hand. Of course, final operation of the facility may be delayed thereby. But some delay is inherent whenever the NEPA consideration is conducted—whether before or at the license proceedings. It is far more consistent with the purposes of the Act to delay operation at a stage where real environmental protection may come about than at a stage where corrective action may be so costly as to be impossible.

Thus we conclude that the Commission must go farther than it has in its present rules. It must consider action, as well as file reports and papers, at the pre-operating license stage. As the Commission candidly admits, such consideration does not amount to a retroactive application of NEPA. Although the projects in question may have been commenced and initially approved before January 1, 1970, the Act clearly applies to them since they must still pass muster before going into full operation.[43] All we demand is that the environmental review be as full and fruitful as possible.

VI

We hold that, in the four respects detailed above, the Commission must revise its rules governing consideration of environmental issues. We do not impose a harsh burden on the Commission. For we require only an exercise of substantive discretion which will protect the environment "to the fullest extent possible." No less is required if the grand congressional purposes underlying NEPA are to become a reality.

Remanded for proceedings consistent with this opinion.

[42] Brief for respondents in No. 24,871 at 59.

[43] The courts which have held NEPA to be nonretroactive have not faced situations like the one before us here—situations where there are two, distinct stages of federal approval, one occurring before the Act's effective date and one after that date. *See* Note, *supra* Note 25.

The guidelines issued by the Council on Environmental Quality urge agencies to employ NEPA procedures to minimize environmental damage, even when approval of particular projects was given before January 1, 1970: "To the maximum extent practicable the section 102(2)(C) procedure should be applied to further major Federal actions having a significant effect on the environment even though they arise from projects or programs initiated prior to enactment of [NEPA] on January 1, 1970. Where it is not practicable to reassess the basic course of action, it is still important that further incremental major actions be shaped so as to mimimize adverse environmental consequences. It is also important in further action that account be taken of environmental consequences not fully evaluated at the outset of the project or program." 36 FED. REG. at 7727.

postscript to *Calvert Cliffs*

NOTE: Considerable additional materials related to this section are published in the appendix to this chapter. Substantive aspects of energy production, plus more on the specific effects of NEPA in this field, are in Vol. Two.

As a result of the Calvert Cliffs decision, the Atomic Energy Commission on Aug. 27, 1971 released proposed rules intended to impose environmentally protective restrictions on all nuclear power plants except seven which entered operation prior to the signing of NEPA on Jan. 1, 1971. Such rules were adopted on Sept. 3, 1971, and were expected to delay construction of 81 nuclear plants, and affect the operations of 15 others. The costs to utility companies for these changes and delays were estimated at $25 million. Five nuclear plants in operation were given 40 days to show why their licenses should not be suspended. Harold L. Price, AEC Director of Regulations, was quoted as saying: "We now have to go back and study things like water quality where we didn't even think we had jurisdiction." (Washington Post, Sept. 4, 1971, at 1)

access to information under NEPA

In legal theory, a citizen has access to a great deal more information concerning the formation of decisions by the Federal government than is the case in practice. The theoretical access is provided by the Freedom of Information Act (5 U.S.C. §552), which is discussed in Chapter Five.

However, difficulties in obtaining information still exist, and so lawyers seeking to protect the environment recently have turned to seeking information under the ageis of NEPA's §102 or under a combination of both the Freedom of Information Act and NEPA.

The several lawsuits filed by environmentalists prior to the underground nuclear tests at Amchitka Island, Alaska, in October, 1971, were, from a legal point of view, more attempts to obtain information than actually to stop the test. The case brought under the Freedom of Information Act is treated in Chapter Five. In the one brought under NEPA, environmentalists at least pierced momentarily the Atomic Energy Commission's hegemonic veil by convincing the court to review the AEC's test plans.[134a] Chief Justice Bazelon relied on Calvert Cliffs Coordinating Committee v. AEC[134b] in ruling that:

NOTE: See also pp. Five 50-55.

> "the court has a responsibility to determine whether the agencies involved have fully and in good faith followed the procedure contemplated by Congress [in the National Environmental Policy Act]: that is, setting forth the environmental factors involved in order that those entrusted with ultimate determination whether to authorize, abandon, or modify the project, shall be clearly advised of the environmental factors which they must take into account."

The court then held that:

> ". . . [T]he officials making the ultimate decision, whether within or outside the agency, must be informed of the full range of responsible opinion on the environmental effects in order to make an informed choice."
>
> * * *
>
> ". . . [The court's] *function is only to assure that the [environmental impact] statement sets forth the opposing scientific views,* and does not take the arbitrary and impermissible approach of completely omitting from the statement, and hence from the focus that the statement was

134 a. *Committee for Nuclear Responsibility v. Seaborg,* ___ F.2d ___, No. 71-1732 (D.C. Cir., October 5, 1971), reversing an earlier district court order dismissing plaintiffs' suit to enjoin the test. The lower court had predicated its judgment on the government's contention that Congress' passage of authorization and appropriation bills for the test had conclusively established the sufficiency of the AEC's environmental impact statement. Mimeograph opinion at 2, 3.

134 b. ___ F.2d ___, No. 24,839 (D.C. Cir., July 23, 1971).

intended to provide for the deciding officials, any reference whatever to the existence of responsible scientific opinions concerning possible adverse environmental effects." (emphasis supplied)

The full text of this and related cases are published in the appendix to this chapter.

NEPA & the SEC

The Securities and Exchange Commission has proposed revisions to its corporate disclosure regulations to comply with NEPA. Under the proposed rules, corporations will be required to report all governmental proceedings involving environmental matters, regardless of the amount of damages involved, and all civil claims involving the environment where damages exceed 10 percent of the company's current assets.[135] The 10 percent of assets limitation would appear to frustrate the efficacy of the new regulations, since large corporations could escape disclosure of many significant private claims. While initially the disclosure requirements were intended to provide information to investors concerning the financial affairs of the issuer, NEPA requires the consideration of more than economic issues, and a revised disclosure formula would further the implementation of the policies of the Act. One possibility would be to require disclosure of all private civil actions in federal courts and all state court actions involving a specified amount (e.g. $10,000).

The Natural Resources Defense Council and the Project on Corporate Responsibility have filed a rule-making petition with the SEC asking the SEC for stronger regulations to implement NEPA. The NRDC-PCR proposed regulations would require corporations to disclose the adverse environmental effects of their activities and to discuss their efforts to remedy pollution problems. The petition requested that the SEC require any registered corporation whose product, services or operations cause "material environmental pollution" or "material injury to valuable natural areas or resources" to include in its registration statement and periodic reports to the Commission a description of the following:

1) the nature and extent of the pollution or injury,
2) the feasibility of curbing the pollution under existing technology,
3) plans and prospects for improving that technology,
4) existing and projected expenditures for curbing the pollution,
5) applicable legal environmental compliance with environmental protection standards.[136]

The NRDC-PCR petition is based on sections 102(1) and 103 of NEPA and Executive Order 11514. Section 103 has the potential for enabling private parties to petition federal agencies to review their present policies and statutory authority to determine compliance with NEPA.

application of NEPA abroad

Section 102(E) would appear to require the application of NEPA to extraterritorial governmental activities. The section recognizes that environmental problems are not confined by political boundaries and authorizes and directs all agencies of the Federal government that have international responsibilities to anticipate and prevent a decline in the quality of the worldwide environment.[137] In assessing the environmental impact of over-

135. *See* statement of William J. Casey, Chairman of the Securities and Exchange Commission, Before the Subcommittee on Fisheries and Wildlife Conservation of the House of Representatives Committee on Merchant Marine and Fisheries.

136. Memorandum on the Natural Resources Defense Council-Project on Corporate Responsibility NEPA Petition to SEC (Feb. 11, 1972).

137. 115 Cong. Rec. 40420 (12/20/69).

seas activities, agencies are constrained to act in a manner consistent with the foreign policy of the United States.[138] While this constraint may limit the scope of an impact statement or impose restrictions on public review in some cases, it does not relieve agencies with international responsibilities from complying with the mandate of Section 102(E) of NEPA.

But agencies engaged in international activities with environmental ramifications showed great reluctance to obey the law. The Agency for International Development (AID), under the jurisdiction of the State Department, until recently asserted that it is exempt from compliance with Section 102. AID spends two billion dollars annually to provide economic and technical assistance to developing countries and finances many projects which have an environmental impact on the host country, as well as the world environment.[139] Very recently, AID finally has attempted to comply with NEPA's procedural requirements by implementing a new procedure for environmental review of capital projects.[140] This procedure integrates the environmental considerations established by Section 102 into project feasibility studies. Copies of these environmental studies will be transmitted to the CEQ. The CEQ has indicated that the new procedures are responsive to NEPA.[141]

According to AID's new procedures, environmental reports will become available "at the time when a capital project is authorized by A.I.D. and when the borrower/grantee is notified of the authorizing action . . ."[142]

application of NEPA abroad

Although the new procedure enables AID to internalize environmental considerations, the provisions for public disclosure and the opportunity for public participation in the decisionmaking process are inadequate. The public is presented with a fait accompli. NEPA requires the opportunity for public participation at all stages of the decision-making process.[143]

If AID is required to integrate the procedural provisions of NEPA into its decisionmaking, it must achieve the same standard of compliance that is imposed on other agencies.[144] Certainly, the agency's previous intransigent attitude towards implementing the provisions of NEPA should not enable AID to escape full compliance with the Act. While foreign policy considerations may require a relaxation of the requirements in certain cases, the present agency guidelines would appear to be inadequate.[146]

The Department of Defense (DOD) regulations require the preparation of an environmental statement for actions conducted anywhere in the world, except when conducted in, or partly in, areas which are in or under the jurisdiction of another country.[147] In those cases, the DOD Component responsible for the action must provide full particulars, a recommendation as to whether or not a statement should be prepared, reasons for the recommendation and an assessment of the effects of a statement on

138. *Id.* at 40420.

139. AID finances various projects including the construction of bridges, dams, airports, power plants, irrigation facilities, steel mills, waste disposal facilities, thermal power plants, fertilizer plants, sewage facilities and roads. *Environmental Activities Report of the Agency for International Development,* July, 1971.

140. *See* Strausberg, *The National Environmental Policy Act and the Agency for International Development,* January 1972 (unpublished paper of the Environmental Law Program of the George Washington University).

141. *Id.*

142. Manual Circular 1214.1.

143. *See* discussion of the availability of impact statements and public participation *infra.*

144. *See Green County Planning Board v. F.P.C., supra* note 83.

145. *See Calvert Cliffs Coordinating Committee, Inc. v. U.S. Atomic Energy Commission, supra* note 109; *Kalur v. Resor,* __F.Supp.__, 3 ERC 1458 (D.D.C. 1971).

146. 36 Fed. Reg. 15750-15754. (1971)

147. *Id.* at 15750-1.

U.S. foreign relations to the Assistant Secretary of Defense who will advise the DOD Component.[148] This procedure in effect excuses compliance with NEPA for most of DOD's overseas activities. The regulations do provide that:

> The DOD Component shall comply with applicable environmental laws and policies, even though an environmental statement is not required. In countries or areas not under U.S. control or administration, projects or activities are subject to the environmental laws, regulations, and stipulations of the foreign government concerned.[149]

But the DOD exemption for the procedural requirements of NEPA for actions that do not involve foreign policy problems is unjustifiable. As Senator Jackson testified ". . . the problems of the environment do not, for the most part, raise questions related to ideology, national security or the balance of world power."[150] Furthermore NEPA only requires an agency to think.

Environmental statements are not required for multi-national activities, such as NATO, when the DOD component involved does not have primary decision-making responsibility. Combat or combat-related activities in a combat zone, riot control activities and other emergency actions do not require impact statements.[151]

application of NEPA abroad

An interesting problem concerns the compliance with NEPA by international negotiators.[152] The preparation and release of an impact statement might prematurely disclose a negotiating position, while noncompliance would result in a disregard of environmental factors. A possible solution would be to prepare a 102 statement to be reviewed only by the CEQ. This would force the negotiating agency to consider the environmental effects of their positions, but prevent any detrimental disclosure. Although this procedure would foreclose any citizen participation, the realities of international negotiation and the foreign policy interests of the United States would have to take precedence. This would be consistent with the constraint of Section 102(E) that agencies act in a manner consistent with the foreign policy of the United States.

The CEQ would have to exercise considerable diligence in reviewing these statements to compensate for the lack of public disclosure. Under such a procedure, the environmental impact statement would be prepared before the negotiating session. Ideally, environmental considerations would be incorporated into all stages of the pre-negotiation planning, and an impact statement covering foreseeable bargaining positions and the anticipated agreement should be submitted for review before an agreement is negotiated. This procedure would be analogous to the Section 102(2)(C) requirements for legislative proposals.

A detailed environmental statement should be prepared and released for all negotiated agreements that require Senate ratification.

See also the section on international agreements at Introduction-105, and the discussion of standing for affected foreign citizens under NEPA at One-19.

148. *Id.* at 15751.

149. *Id.* at 15751.

150. 115 Cong. Rec. S. 17451-17454 (daily ed. Dec. 20, 1969).

151. 36 Fed. Reg. 15751 (1971).

152. *See The Washington Post*, Feb. 1, 1972 at A3, col. 1.

availability of
impact statements

Availability of Impact Statements and Public Participation

"The National Environmental Policy Act, for example, requires all federal agencies to provide the public with "environmental impact statements," which outline the expected effects on the environment of proposed projects. But an enterprising Federal Aviation Administration official, Robert F. Bacon, has found an effective means of limiting the circulation of these statements. He simply charges an exorbitant price for them. Citizens seeking an environmental impact statement on the proposed Palmdale Intercontinental Airport outside Los Angeles were told the standard fee is 50 cents a page. For the 115-page statement, this comes to $57.50—plus a stiff extra charge if the citizen also wants the accompanying maps." The Washington Post, Thursday, July 8, 1971, at G7

NEPA embraces the concept that agency decisions should be made "in the light of public scrutiny."[153] According to Section 101(C), every person has "a responsibility to contribute to the preservation and enhancement of the environment." Environmental statements are intended to disclose the environmental impact of Federal activities, and allow meaningful public participation in the decision-making process. As one court aptly stated, "[A]t the very least NEPA is an environmental full disclosure law . . . intended to make [agency] decision-making more responsive and responsible."[154]

In order to understand the procedure involved in the preparation and distribution of 102 statements, it may be helpful to use an example of a Federal project which requires a 102 statement; for instance, the plans for a new airport. The 102 statement process would begin when a sponsor, usually a local or state airport authority, contacts the area or district Federal Aviation Administration (FAA) office and asks for instructions about how to proceed with his applications for FAA approval. The district FAA office will furnish the sponsor with a copy of the FAA guidelines for implementing Section 102(2)(C) which explains the procedure and requirements for filing and submitting a 102 environmental impact statement.*

See also CEQ Guidelines at Appendix One-1

The sponsor then has the responsibility for preparing the initial version of the draft 102 statement while consulting with other state and local agencies to determine the environmental impact in the area of the new airport. After the statement is prepared, the sponsor sends it back to the district FAA office which performs the first environmental review. If the district office finds that the statement is adequate and that it should be further processed, it is sent to the Regional FAA office.

The Regional office receives the draft statement and reproduces it for distribution for comments from those Federal agencies which have "jurisdiction by law or expertise" and to the FAA Airport Services office in Washington. In turn, the Airport Services office makes copies of the draft statement and sends them to both the Council on Environmental Quality and to the Assistant Secretary's Office on Environment and Urban Systems in the Department of Transportation (hereafter TEU). All of these

153. 115 Cong. Rec. 40416 (1969) (remarks of Senator Jackson).

154. *EDF v. Corps of Engineers,* 325 F.Supp. 749, 759 (E.D. Ark. 1971).

* A sponsor must prepare a draft 102(2) (C) environmental statement in accordance with instructions and guidance of the order for all major Federal airport development actions without exception. If the action is not a major Federal airport development, as defined in paragraph 9(g) of the order, the sponsor may submit a *negative declaration* if within the applicant's studied judgment the project WILL NOT PRODUCE OR RESULT in a significant effect upon the environment when assessed against the criteria contained in para. 9(f).

The Negative Declaration must contain the following points:

(1) A description of the proposed action and its purpose.

(2) A discussion of the proposed method of accomplishment including construction techniques and safeguards, etc., to be utilized to abrogate possible short-term adverse effects upon the environment.

(3) A positive statement that the end product development will in no way alter the airport's impact upon its surrounding environment beyond the existing level.

consultants have thirty days in which to comment to the Regional FAA office on the draft statement. After thirty days, the Regional office prepares a final statement considering all the comments which have been made, and distributes this final statement to the FAA Airport Services office, which sends copies to the Council and TEU. If after fourteen days no response has been received, the FAA Airport Services office gives the Regional office clearance to allow final approval of the proposed airport project. However, if at any point in the process, the Regional office, the Airport Services office, or TEU express dissatisfaction with the statement, the sponsor may be asked to furnish further information or proof of his allegations in the statement.

The process places primary responsibility on the sponsor for developing the basic environmental information. The FAA Airport Services office hopes eventually to be able to eliminate the first draft circulation process when the other agencies and FAA offices become accustomed to the environmental statement process.

It would be nearly impossible for a Federal agency in Washington to submit the first draft of a detailed environmental statement on an airport project in Mississippi, for example, and include the necessary "detailed" information.

See also 'expertise' at Appendix One-9, and 'coordination' at Appendix One-13

In most cases, the Federal agencies have designated field offices to receive copies of the draft statements for review. Where no field office exists, the draft statement must be sent to the next higher level to be reviewed.

As the process grows, questions undoubtably will be raised as to the competence and ability of the field offices to handle the number of 102 statements that will be submitted within each jurisdiction. Most Federal agency field offices are not equipped with the expert personnel or financial resources to study and effectively evaluate the environmental impact of local or state projects, and possibly, many local and state agencies required to comment on these draft statements will consider the entire process simply more bothersome red tape.

availability of impact statements

The CEQ guidelines require agencies to develop procedures to insure the provision of timely public information of federal plans and programs with environmental impact in order to obtain the views of interested parties.[155] The procedures are to include, whenever appropriate, provision for public hearings and provide the public with relevant information including alternative courses of action.[156] Draft environmental statements are to be made public at least fifteen days prior to the hearings.[157] The agency which prepares the Section 102 statement is responsible for making the statement, with comments, available to the public, pursuant to the provisions of the Freedom of Information Act.[158] Agencies are required to implement public information procedures.[159] (See also pp. Five 50-52.)

The National Wildlife Federation's comments on the CEQ guidelines are especially critical of the public information and participation provisions. National Wildlife contends that the guidelines do not provide for sufficient public notice of proposed actions, nor for adequate public access to the information which relates to proposed actions affecting the environment.

The CEQ guidelines make no provision for early public notice of proposed actions. The first official notification usually occurs when a draft statement is circulated for comment. Even then, the public is not directly

155. 36 Fed. Reg. 7724, 7726 (1971).

156. *Id.* at 7726.

157. *Id.* at 7726.

158. *Id. at 7726. "[E]xcept where the agency prepares the draft statement on the basis of a hearing subject to the Administrative Procedure Act and preceded by adequate public notice and information to identify the issues. . ." Id.* at 7726.

159. *Id.* at 7726-7. Interagency memoranda commenting on the impact statement must be included.

notified of the draft, but may get a copy on request. Draft statements often contain conclusions as to environmental impact without revealing the background data. The guidelines allow departments to alter the comments of Federal agencies on environmental impact before they are made public. It would be better if agency comments were disclosed without departmental consolidation.

Agencies should be required to submit a draft statement which would include detailed information concerning the sources and references used to compile the environmental statement. All background data should be made available to the public on request. The failure to provide complete technical information would preclude intelligent citizen participation in the review process. The draft statements should be public information, and should be circulated to other agencies for comment. All comments should be available to the public. A period of at least 30 days for public scrutiny following the agency comment period is necessary to allow for meaningful public review. Public hearings should be mandatory in all controversial cases. After the public hearing is held, or following the period for public comments, the agency should prepare a final draft.

Greene County Planning Board v. FPC appears at App. One-37.

The court in *Greene County Planning Board v. FPC* specified procedures for allowing the necessary public participation. The Commission's staff must prepare a detailed statement before the Presiding Examiner makes his initial decision.[160] Intervenors must have a reasonable opportunity to comment on the statement. The court goes on to state:

> But, since the statement may well go to waste unless it is subject to the full scrutiny of the hearing process, we also believe that the intervenors must be given the opportunity to cross-examine both PASNY [the applicant] and Commission witnesses in light of the statement.[161]

Environmental statements are catalogued monthly in the *102 Monitor* published by the Council on Environmental Quality, and available on a subscription basis at $6.50 a year from the Council at 722 Jackson Place, N.W. Washington, D.C.

Council on Environmental Quality

The Council on Environmental Quality (CEQ) was created by Title II of NEPA. The Council is composed of three members appointed by the President with the advice and consent of the Senate, who serve at the pleasure of the President. The members of the Council are to be persons of broad experience and training with the competence to analyze and interpret environmental trends and developing problems.[162] The President selects one member of the Council as Chairman.

The duties of the CEQ include: assisting the President in the preparation of the annual environmental quality report required by Section 201; carrying on studies related to the status of the environment; reviewing Federal programs which affect the quality of the environment; assisting in the formulation of national priorities to foster and improve the quality of the environment; and conducting other studies that the President may request. The staff for the CEQ was provided by the Environmental Quality Improvement Act of 1970[163] (the text of which is reprinted in this book.)

160. Greene County, *supra.* note 83 at 1600-1.

161. *Id.* at 1601. The court quoting from the CEQ Report, 1 ELR 50059 added:

> Often individuals and groups can contribute data and insights beyond the expertise of the agency involved. *Id.* at 1412.

162. 115 Cong. Rec. 40421 (1969)

> The members of the Council, therefore, should not necessarily be selected for depth of training or expertise in any specific discipline, but rather for the ability to grasp broad national issues, to render public service in the national interest, and to appreciate the significance of choosing among present alternatives in shaping the country's future environment. *Id.* at 40421.

163. P.L. 91-224, April 3, 1970.

The Council functions primarily as a Presidential advisor on environmental matters, rather than as an environmental ombudsman. The CEQ was designed to give the President impartial and objective advice, and to provide insight into the long-range needs and priorities of the country.[164] The Council by virtue of its position in the Executive Office of the President owes its primary allegiance to the President.

The CEQ reviews all environmental impact statements, but the extent of its powers and responsibilities remains undefined. While NEPA requires that Section 102 statements be made available to the Council, the Act does not require agency action to await any responsive comments from the CEQ. The main function of the Council in its review of Federal programs appears to be keeping the President informed on the extent to which these activities may effect the policies set forth in the Act. The conference committee's report on the duties of the CEQ states:

> It is not the committee's intent that the Council be involved in the day-to-day decision-making processes of the Federal Government or that it be involved in the resolution of particular conflicts between agencies and departments.[165]

Thus, the Council has no police powers over Federal agencies, and can only evaluate their activities. The Council has attempted to resolve problems resulting from inadequate compliance with Section 102 through the use of informal conferences. As one court defined the CEQ's role:

> Thus, the Council's function is in no way regulatory. Its purpose is to take information and to coordinate the reporting of governmental activities so as to aid the policy makers.[166]

So far, the Council has not had to deal with the problem publicly. The Council has continued to use the conference method of informally resolving their problems with the agencies. The draft statement procedure has also helped to limit possible conflict. At present, the Council has been more successful in playing the role of "counselor" than "monitor."

The President did, however, give the Council the power to "issue such other instructions to agencies and request such reports and other information from them as may be required to carry out the Council's responsibilities under the Act."* The Council could interpret this as providing the necessary authority to require an agency to resubmit a more adequate statement. Aside from rejecting a statement and requiring an agency to resubmit a more adequate one, the Council has no other sanction which they can impose to require an agency to respond or comply.

The CEQ is required to comment on draft impact statements. Usually these comments accompany the draft statement and the final statement and are available to the public. However, the Council has taken an exception to this rule, and considers its comments unavailable to the public. The CEQ does not consider itself a commenting agency by "law or expertise," and does not regard its comments as subject to the Freedom of Information Act. This policy is also based on the Council's role as a Presidential advisor, which confers a traditional right to privileged communications with the President. The Council's role as a presidential advisor and its position in the Executive Office of the President precludes any impartial review of the environmental impacts of proposed Federal actions.

164. *See* 115 Cong. Rec. 40421.

165. *Id.* at 40421.

166. *See National Helium Corp. v. Morton*, ___F.2d___, 3 ERC 1129, 1133 (10th Cir. 1971).

* Executive Order 11514, Subsection 3(i), dated March 5, 1970 (35 Federal Register 4247).

some thoughts on future developments

NEPA has provided the statutory basis for encouraging environmental protection, and has enabled environmentalists to enjoin some ecologically destructive activities. NEPA has developed into a successful tool for compelling Federal agencies to consider the environmental impact of their activities. Future development and application of the substantive rights and requirements imposed by the Act may be expected.

The development of a judicially recognized right to a healthful environment may emerge. This right could be recognized as either a Constitutional right, third-party rights under Section 101(b), or a substantive right to a decent environment under Section 102(1). Section 102(1) incorporates the policies of Section 101 of NEPA into the statutory authorizations which govern the actions of all Federal agencies. Given the proper judicial construction, Section 102(1) may be used to force agencies to further the goals of Section 101.[167] Section 103 can be expected to be tested as public interest groups attempt to force agencies to comply with the spirit and the letter of NEPA.

Greater public participation in agency decision-making is desirable to make Federal programs more responsive and environmentally responsible. Increased access to environmental data and a Federal commitment to encouraging public participation is needed.

Until now, most NEPA cases have been concerned with the procedural requirements of Section 102(2)(C). These cases have largely resolved the problems of retroactive application of the Act, the preparation of impact statements by the applicant, and the activities requiring compliance with NEPA. We are about to embark on the second generation of NEPA suits where the substantive requirements of Section 102(2)(C) will be exposed to judicial scrutiny. *Natural Resources Defense Council v. Morton,* which is published in this text, is indicative of the type of decision that will determine the substantive requirements of environmental statements.

For an excellent discussion of the cases decided under the National Environmental Policy Act up to April 1, 1972, *see* GREEN, Harold, *The National Environmental Policy Act in the Courts,* The Conservation Foundation (1972).

Procedural inadequacies remain, and should be clarified either administratively or judicially. Specifically, the requirements for circulation and agency comments on draft impact statements should be defined more explicitly. The requirements for public hearings need additional clarification.

The responsibilities of the Council on Environmental Quality should be examined and also made more explicit. The CEQ should be given the power to compel agency compliance. This could be accomplished by a formal procedure whereby the CEQ could require the Office of Management and Budget to withhold funding for any Federal program not in compliance with NEPA.

The evolution of NEPA and its implementation will continue. The CEQ is presently considering a revision of its guidelines. Agency regulations implementing the Act were opened to public comment, and changes may be expected in the coming year. Recent judicial interpretation of the Act has shaped agency response, giving promise for a higher standard of administrative compliance in the future.

NEPA is amenable to flexible judicial construction. As the agencies become aware of the Act and its implications, a certain amount of administrative chagrin can be expected. The consideration of the environmental ramifications of agency actions is not simple, but this review is necessary if the narrow pursuit of agency goals at the expense of environmental values is to be avoided.

The successful implementation of NEPA will require additional manpower and money to make the necessary environmental studies. In the long run, these expenditures may prove to be a financial as well as an environ-

167. *See* Cohen & Warren, Developing Judicial Recognition of the Substantive Requirements of the National Environmental Policy Act of 1969, January 1972 —13 *Bos. Col. Ind. & Comm. L. Rev.* 685 (March 1972)

mental bargain. Ecologically undesirable projects may be avoided, alternatives adopted, and environmental protection incorporated early in the planning, when the cost of implementation is lower.

NEPA represents a change in government policy. Until the passage of the Act, economic studies had been the primary basis for evaluating actions. NEPA adds a new parameter to the calculus of government planning. NEPA mandates a consideration of the future implications of Federal actions. While economic considerations will continue to be important, NEPA recognizes the environmental values necessary for successful, long-run government planning.

Recently courts have affirmed the inclusion under NEPA of protection of *quality of life* (see page One-16). Other suits on which judgment had yet to be passed have tried to utilize this concept so broadly that NEPA seems to be viewed as a considerable extension, if not replacement, for the Bill of Rights. *Time* magazine of May 29, 1972 at page 12 reports that a group of 19 community organizations in Chicago have filed suit to block a low-income housing project from "polluting" their neighborhood with persons of different social characteristics. It remains to be seen if this will be taken seriously. See also pp. One-12-15.

The relative success of NEPA has won it many enemies on Capitol Hill, because its application has delayed pork-barrel projects. The opposition is open in some cases, and more subtile in others: Congressmen who in private curse the Act and the "environmental extremists" who use it to block construction projects, in public praise NEPA lightly, and introduce bills supposedly "to correct problems" created by the Act and its judicial interpretation. (According to the CEQ, about 15 percent of the cases filed under NEPA during 1971 resulted in project delays.)

Many bills to weaken NEPA were introduced during 1972. One of these, Public Law 92-307 (June 2, 1972) Permitted the Atomic Energy Commission to issue temporary operating permits for atomic reactors without following the procedures of NEPA. (See, *Federal Register,* Vol. 37, No. 116, June 15, 1972 at 11871.) The following are a few of the other such bills that have been introduced. The passage of even a few would effectively destroy NEPA.

> H.R. 14137: Amends NEPA to allow the President at his discretion to declare an emergency, suspending compliance with the provisions of NEPA for a particular project for a 180-day period. No hearings need be held to examine whether an emergency really exists. A similar bill is being proposed in the Senate.
>
> H.R. 5277: Power Plant Siting Bill: Sets up a procedure for the long range planning and state certification of bulk power generating facilities while specifically eliminating the need to file environmental impact statements as required by NEPA.
>
> S. 3381: Would set up regional commissions for administering public works development projects. Authorized projects would not need environmental impact statements as required by NEPA.
>
> Federal-Aid Highway Act for 1972: Amendments are being drafted to the Highway Transportation Act which would relieve the Department of Transportation of responsibility for filing Environmental Impact Statements for highway projects, as now required by NEPA.

REFERENCES

VOIGHT, Harry H., *The National Environmental Policy Act and The Independent Regulatory Agency: Some Unresolved Conflicts,* 5 Natural Resources Lawyer 13, January 1972.

HANKS & HANKS, *An Environmental Bill of Rights: The Citizen Suit and the NEPA of 1969,* 24 Rutgers Law Review 230 (1970).

COLEMAN, Virginia, *Possible Repercussions of the National Environmental Policy Act of 1969 on the Private Law Governing Pollution Abatement Suits,* 3 Nat. Res. Lawyer 647 (November 1970).

Rights to clean environment: the States

In Illinois, there is now a constitutional right to a healthful environment.

Constitution of the State of Illinois (1970)

Article XI
Environment

Section 1. PUBLIC POLICY—LEGISLATIVE RESPONSIBILITY

The public policy of the State and the duty of each person is to provide and maintain a healthful environment for the benefit of this and future generations. The General Assembly shall provide by law for the implementation and enforcement of this public policy.

Section 2. RIGHTS OF INDIVIDUALS

Each person has the right to a healthful environment. Each person may enforce this right against any party, governmental or private, through appropriate legal proceedings subject to reasonable limitation and regulation as the General Assembly may provide by law.

New or added attention to conservation and environmental quality is found in either the constitution or its amendments in the following states:

Florida .... Const., Art. II, §7, effective Nov. 5, 1968;
Michigan .... Const., Art. 4, §52, effective Jan. 1, 1964;
New York........... Const., Art. XIV, §4, amendment effective Jan. 1, 1970;
Pennsylvania .... Const., Art. I, §28, amendment effective 1971;
Rhode Island......... Const., Art. I, §17, amendment adopted Nov. 3, 1970;
Virginia .... Const., Art. XIV, §2, effective July, 1971.

Other state constitutions provide for the rights of fishery, free access to the shore, rights to use navigable waters, special status for oyster beds and limitations on the disposition of public trust properties. For an excellent discussion of this subject, *See,* Howard, A.E. Dick, "State Constitutions and the Environment," 58 Virginia L. Rev. 193 (Feb. 1972).

There have been some efforts to create such a policy by statute as well, notably in the Illinois Environmental Protection Act of 1970, H.B. 3788, BNA Environment Reporter, State Water Pollution Laws, 766:0101, which set up a pollution control board with the authority to determine and implement environmental control standards for the state in regard to the requirements of Federal law.

The citizen has standing to affect the Board's actions in three ways; first, one may file a proposal to adopt, amend, or repeal any Board procedural regulation under the Act; second, one may file a complaint against anyone for violation of an air or water quality standard or other regulations promulgated under the Act; and finally, one may formally object to the grant of a variance putting the burden of proof upon the party seeking the variance.

Any party to a Board hearing, any person filing a complaint which was denied by the Board, any person who has been denied a permit or variance and any person adversely affected by a final order or determination of the Board may obtain judicial review from the Appellate Court for the District in which the cause of action arose.

Michigan was the first state to provide a statutory right by citizens to sue to protect the environment for the general good. The text of the act, drafted by Professor Joseph L. Sax, follows. Such legislation has been most forcefully advocated by Professor Sax, particularly in his excellent book, *Defending the Environment* (Alfred A. Knopf, New York, 1971).

The Michigan Environmental Protection Act of 1970

Act 127 P.A. 1970, Mich. Comp. Laws, Ann. §§691-1201-1207 (West's 3 Mich. Leg. Serv. 1970)

AN ACT to provide for actions for declaratory and equitable relief for protection of the air, water and other natural resources and the public trust therein; to prescribe the rights, duties and functions of the attorney general, any political subdivision of the state, any instrumentality or agency of the state or of a political subdivision thereof, any person, partnership, corporation, association, organization or other legal entity; and to provide for judicial proceedings relative thereto.

The People of the State of Michigan enact:

Sec. 1. This act, shall be known and may be cited as the "Thomas J. Anderson, Gordon Rockwell environmental protection act of 1970".

Sec. 2. (1) The attorney general, any political subdivision of the state, any instrumentality or agency of the state or of a political subdivision thereof, any person, partnership, corporation, association, organization or other legal entity may maintain an action in the circuit court having jurisdiction where the alleged violation occurred or is likely to occur for declaratory and equitable relief against the state, any political subdivision thereof, any instrumentality or agency of the state or of a political subdivision thereof, any person, partnership, corporation, association, organization or other legal entity for the protection of the air, water and other natural resources and the public trust therein from pollution, impairment or destruction.

(2) In granting relief provided by subsection (1) where there is involved a standard for pollution or for an anti-pollution device or procedure, fixed by rule or otherwise, by an instrumentality or agency of the state or a political subdivision thereof, the court may:

(a) Determine the validity, applicability and reasonableness of the standard.

(b) When a court finds a standard to be deficient, direct the adoption of a standard approved and specified by the court.

Sec. 2a. If the court has reasonable ground to doubt the solvency of the plaintiff or the plaintiff's ability to pay any cost or judgment which might be rendered against him in an action brought under this act the court may order the plaintiff to post a surety bond or cash not to exceed $500.00.

Sec. 3. (1) When the plaintiff in the action has made a prima facie showing that the conduct of the defendant has, or is likely to pollute, impair or destroy the air, water or other natural resources or the public trust therein, the defendant may rebut the prima facie showing by the submission of evidence to the contrary. The defendant may also show, by way of an affirmative defense, that there is no feasible and prudent alternative to defendant's conduct and that such conduct is consistent with the promotion of the public health, safety and welfare in light of the state's paramount concern for the protection of its natural resources from pollution, impairment or destruction. Except as to the affirmative defense, the principles of burden of proof and weight of the evidence generally applicable in civil actions in the circuit courts shall apply to actions brought under this act.

(2) The court may appoint a master or referee, who shall be a disinterested person and technically qualified, to take testimony and make a record and a report of his findings to the court in the action.

(3) Costs may be apportioned to the parties if the interests of justice require.

Sec. 4. (1) The court may grant temporary and permanent equitable relief, or may impose conditions on the defendant that are required to protect the air, water and other natural resources or the public trust therein from pollution, impairment or destruction.

(2) If administrative, licensing or other proceedings are required or available to determine the legality of the defendant's conduct, the court may remit the parties to such proceedings, which proceedings shall be conducted in accordance with and subject to the provisions of Act No. 306 of the Public Acts of 1969, being sections 24.201 to 24.313 of the Compiled Laws of 1948. In so remitting the court may grant temporary equitable relief where necessary for the protection of the air, water and other natural resources or the public trust therein from pollution, impairment or destruction. In so remitting the court shall retain jurisdiction of the action pending completion thereof for the purpose of determining whether adequate protection from pollution, impairment or destruction has been afforded.

(3) Upon completion of such proceedings, the court shall adjudicate the impact of the defendant's conduct on the air, water or other natural resources and on the public trust therein in accordance with this act. In such adjudication the court may order that additional evidence be taken to the extent necessary to protect the rights recognized in this act.

(4) Where, as to any administrative, licensing or other proceeding, judicial review thereof is available, notwithstanding the provisions to the contrary of Act No. 306

of the Public Acts of 1969, pertaining to judicial review, the court originally taking jurisdiction shall maintain jurisdiction for purposes of judicial review.

Sec. 5. (1) Whenever administrative, licensing or other proceedings, and judicial review thereof are available by law, the agency or the court may permit the attorney general, any political subdivision of the state, any instrumentality or agency of the state or of a political subdivision thereof, any person, partnership, corporation, association, organization or other legal entity to intervene as a party on the filing of a pleading asserting that the proceeding or action for judicial review involves conduct which has, or which is likely to have, the effect of polluting, impairing or destroying the air, water or other natural resources or the public trust therein.

(2) In any such administrative, licensing or other proceedings, and in any judicial review thereof, any alleged pollution, impairment or destruction of the air, water or other natural resources or the public trust therein, shall be determined, and no conduct shall be authorized or approved which does, or is likely to have such effect so long as there is a feasible and prudent alternative consistent with the reasonable requirements of the public health, safety and welfare.

(3) The doctrines of collateral estoppel and res judicata may be applied by the court to prevent multiplicity of suits.

Sec. 6. This act shall be supplementary to existing administrative and regulatory procedures provided by law.

Sec. 7. This act shall take effect October 1, 1970.

This act is ordered to take immediate effect.

Michigan Act in the courts

The first case brought under the Michigan Environmental Protection Act, *Roberts v. Michigan*[1] was a taxpayer's suit against the Secretary of State and the state highway director seeking an injunction against the issuance of motor vehicle licenses or permission to use automobiles on state roads until new emission standards were imposed by or at the direction of the court. The complaint was based on Section 2(2) (b) of the Act. The Michigan Circuit Court for Ingham County held that the Section was an illegal delegation of legislative authority, asking the courts to engage in law making, but upheld the rest of the Act.

The Michigan Circuit Court for Livingston County in *Lakeland Property Owners v. Township of Northfield*[2] took issue with the *Roberts* decision, stating:

> This Court does not believe Act 127, 1970 [The Michigan Environmental Protection Act] is unconstitutional by virtue of it having contained therein a prohibited delegation of powers. Said Act simply states that when a Court finds a standard to be unreasonable or deficient the Court may set an acceptable standard which the Court may enforce directly or order the agency involved to enforce such standard.[3]

The Court stated that it was not controlled by the *Roberts* decision and found that any dispute between the circuits must be resolved by a higher tribunal. On the basis of Section 2(2) (b) of the Michigan Environmental Protection Act, the court directed the State Water Resources Commission to adopt a different pollution standard.

As of June 1971, nine months after the Michigan Environmental Protection Act took effect, 13 lawsuits had been brought under the Act, six of which were brought by units of the state or county governments. This is certainly not the flood of litigation which the opponents of the Act predicted.

1. 2 E.R.C. 1612.
2. 3 E.R.C. 1893.
3. *Id.* at 1901.

Michigan

A second action brought after *Roberts v. Michigan* was decided in May 1971. In that case, *Muskegon County v. Environmental Protection Organization,* citizens opposed a county planned sewage treatment project which involved tertiary treatment by spray irrigation. The citizens claimed that the water table was only a few feet below the surface and that liquid wastes would percolate through the soil too quickly contaminating ground water. The county instituted an action for a declaratory judgment against the Environmental Protection Organization requesting that the project be declared not to constitute a nuisance. The citizens counter-claimed under the Environmental Protection Act. The court found that the proposal was not a nuisance and did not violate the Environmental Protection Act. The court reserved the power to reevaluate the plant after it is in operation if there is evidence that pollution is occurring.

In the most publicized case to date, a Wayne County circuit jury found the Chrysler corporation liable for damage to homes, cars, and personal health that occurred because of emissions from their foundry. As some 300 homes were involved, the damages may exceed $1 million. *See,* Newsweek, July 10, 1972 at 70.

other states

The Florida Environmental Protection Act of 1971[1] and the Minnesota Environmental Rights Act[2] also provide citizens with the right to sue to remedy environmental abuses. The Washington Environmental Quality Reorganization Act of 1970 establishes a right to a healthful environment; this may serve as a basis for the assertion of citizen rights. California, Nebraska, New York, and Pennsylvania have recently enacted legislation reorganizing state administration of environmental protection.

Similar legislative proposals have been introduced in other states (New York, Massachusetts, Colorado, Tennessee and Pennsylvania—see also Chapter 5). They are usually primarily concerned with giving the citizen standing to sue in court to protect the environment, and the change in policy is a secondary benefit.

federal level

On the Federal level, Senators Philip Hart and George McGovern were sponsoring legislation similar to the Michigan Act that would allow citizen suits for environmental protection. A key difference would be that only injunctions and other equitable remedies would be permitted — no monetary damages would be allowed.

TEXT OF MICHIGAN CITIZEN SUIT CASE,

ROBERTS V. MICHIGAN, IS ON NEXT PAGE

1. Florida Statutes Annotated, Ch. 71-343 (1971).

2. Minnesota Statutes Annotated, Ch. 952 (1971).

ROBERTS v. MICHIGAN
Civ. Action No. 12428-C (Mich. Cir. Ct. Ingham City, May 4, 1971)

Warren, C.J.:

Plaintiff Charles G. Roberts brings this action under the provisions of the Thomas J. Anderson, Gordon Rockwell Environmental Protection Act of 1970 (1948 CL 691.1201 *et seq.;* MSA 14.528(201) *et seq.;* 1970 PA 127) which act provides in part as follows:

> (1) . . . any person...may maintain an action in the circuit court ...for declaratory and equitable relief against the state, any political subdivision thereof, any instrumentality or agency of the state ...for the protection of the air, water and other natural resources and the public trust therein from pollution, impairment or destruction.

After alleging that the operation of motor vehicles is a major cause of pollution, Plaintiff asks injunctive relief against the Secretary of State, the Director of State Department of Highways, and the State of Michigan to prevent the further issuance of licenses to operators of motor vehicles, to prevent the use of streets and highways, and to prevent the use of tax monies for the construction of highways etc. until sufficient safeguards, standards, rules, and regulations are adopted and enforced. At paragraph 16 of Plaintiff's First Amended Complaint he alleges that:

> This Court has the power and the authority, and is hereby requested, under the aforesaid Act 127, PA 1970, (Enrolled House Bill No. 3055) to order, impose or establish rules and regulations governing the replacement, repair and protection of the natural resources and the water of the State of Michigan and regulating the use of streets and highways therein to prevent or restrict pollution of the air, and to enjoin the Defendants... (etc.)
>
> (A similar statement and request is set forth in paragraph 11.)

The Attorney General has moved for Summary Judgment and Accelerated Judgment as to all Defendants alleging that as to the Secretary of State and the Director, State Department of Highways neither of these persons have the authority to adopt standards, rules, regulations, and safeguards in relation to pollution arising out of the operation of motor vehicles. The Court, after hearing arguments and reviewing the pleadings concurs in this conclusion, i.e. that the case should be dismissed as to the Secretary of State and Director, State Department of Highways so far as Plaintiff claims these persons have authority to adopt rules, regulations, standards, and safeguards *for vehicles other than as Plaintiff describes in paragraph 17 of his Complaint.* ("First Amended Complaint"). The want of authority to adopt rules, regulations, standards and safeguards as to vehicles owned or operated by these two Defendants in their respective departments has not been demonstrated, and for this reason they should remain as defendants. (This conclusion however bows to the conclusions hereinafter stated in relation to the validity of the Act. It is stated only to avoid duplication of consideration in the event that the conclusions of the Court hereinafter stated are not adopted by a higher court on appeal.)

DETERMINATION

At least as applied to the matter of alleged pollution arising from the operation of motor vehicles, this court concludes that the Act is unconstitutional for the reason that it purports to delegate legislative authority and responsibility to the courts.

BASIS FOR DETERMINATION

Sub-paragraph 2 of Section 2 of the Act reads as follows:

> (2) In granting relief provided by subsection (1) where there is involved a standard for pollution or for an anti-pollution device or procedure, fixed by rule or otherwise, by an instrumentality or agency of the state or a political subdivision thereof, the court may:
>
> (a) Determine the validity, applicability and reasonableness of the standard.
>
> (b) When a court finds a standard to be deficient, direct the adoption of a standard approved and specified by the court.

Historically the matter of prescribing rules and regulations for the operation of motor vehicles has been within the province of the legislature. The legislature, for example, caused to be drafted and adopted Act 300 of the Public Acts of 1949—the Michigan Vehicle Code (MCLA 257.1 et seq.; MSA 9.1801 et seq.). This Act repealed other and earlier acts passed by the legislature relating to the operation of motor vehicles.

The legislature did adopt a standard for pollution or for an anti-pollution device or procedure in the Vehicle Code. Section 707 (MCLA 257.707; MSA 9.2407) provides:

> (a) Every motor vehicle shall at all times be equipped with a muffler in good working order and in constant operation to prevent excessive or unusual noise and *annoying smoke....* (emphasis added)
>
> (b) The engine and power mechanism of every motor vehicle shall be so equipped and adjusted to prevent the escape of *excessive fumes or smoke.* (emphasis added)

Quite clearly the legislature did adopt standards, and quite clearly those standards are deficient.

This gives rise to the first question which is this: "Just who is it that this Court will 'direct' to adopt adequate standards?" Could it be any body other than the legislature? (The Court recognizes that the statute uses the word "may" in relation to the Court directing the adoption of approved and specified standards. However, to treat this provision as meaning anything other than "shall direct," after having determined that the standards are deficient, would render the legislation meaningless.) This Court is disinclined to attempt to "direct" the legislative branch of government. Courts should resist the temptation to legislate and to substitute themselves and their judgment for that of the duly elected representatives of the general public. *Knibbe v City of Warren,* 363 Mich 283 (1961).

The second question presented is this: "What real tools does this Court have to determine what adequate standards are?"

The third question is this: "Wouldn't the public be better served with an enactment of the legislature which would be uniform throughout the State?"

Fourthly, in a time when the public is crying for attention to, and disposition of, the backlog of untried cases in our trial courts, common sense would seem to dictate that the legislature, not the courts, establish the standards involved in the operation of motor vehicles.

Turning, however, to the more legalistic approach, Article 4, Section 1 of the Constitution of 1963 provides:

> The legislative power of the State of Michigan is vested in a senate and a house of representatives.

"Legislative power" is authority to make, alter, amend, and repeal laws. *Harsha v City of Detroit,* 261 Mich 586 (1933). The legislature is the repository of all legislative power subject only to restrictions imposed by state or federal constitutions. *Oakland County Taxpayers' League v Board of Supervisors of Oakland County,* 355 Mich 305 (1959).

Legislative power may not be delegated. 1 Cooley, *Constitutional Limitations* (6th Ed.) p. 137; *King v Concordia Fire Insurance Co.,* 140 Mich 258; *Chemical Bank & Trust Co. v County of Oakland,* 264 Mich 684 (1933); *O'Brien v State Highway Commissioner,* 375 Mich 545 (1965). While certain delegations of power to be exercised in accordance with guidelines established by the legislature have been upheld, and while certain delegations of power as to the execution of the law have been upheld, these are to be distinguished from an attempted delegation of the power to make the law. This Court concludes that it is being called upon to make law when, after determining the standards to be deficient (in relation to pollution arising from the use of motor vehicles) it is then to "direct the adoption of a standard approved and specified by the court."

For the foregoing reasons the Court concludes that this Act, so far as it pertains to pollution arising from the operation of motor vehicles is unconstitutional. An order may enter accordingly.

APPENDIX—Chapter One

CEQ guidelines on NEPA § 102 environmental statements*

1. *Purpose.* This memorandum provides guidelines to Federal departments, agencies, and establishments for preparing detailed environmental statements on proposals for legislation and other major Federal actions significantly affecting the quality of the human environment as required by section 102(2)(C) of the National Environmental Policy Act (Public Law 91–190) (hereafter "the Act"). Underlying the preparation of such environmental statements is the mandate of both the Act and Executive Order 11514 (35 F.R. 4247) of March 4, 1970, that all Federal agencies, to the fullest extent possible, direct their policies, plans and programs so as to meet national environmental goals. The objective of section 102(2)(C) of the Act and of these guidelines is to build into the agency decision making process an appropriate and careful consideration of the environmental aspects of proposed action and to assist agencies in implementing not only the letter, but the spirit, of the Act. This memorandum also provides guidance on implementation of section 309 of the Clean Air Act, as amended (42 U.S.C. 1857 et seq.).

2. *Policy.* As early as possible and in all cases prior to agency decision concerning major action or recommendation or a favorable report on legislation that significantly affects the environment, Federal agencies will, in consultation with other appropriate Federal, State, and local agencies, assess in detail the potential environmental impact in order that adverse effects are avoided, and environmental quality is restored or enhanced, to the fullest extent practicable. In particular, alternative actions that will minimize adverse impact should be explored and both the long- and short-range implications to man, his physical and social surroundings, and to nature, should be evaluated in order to avoid to the fullest extent practicable undesirable consequences for the environment.

3. *Agency and OMB procedures.* (a) Pursuant to section 2(f) of Executive Order 11514, the heads of Federal agencies have been directed to proceed with measures required by section 102(2)(C) of the Act. Consequently, each agency will establish, in consultation with the Council on Environmental Quality, not later than June 1, 1970 (and, by July 1, 1971, with respect to requirements imposed by revisions in these guidelines, which will apply to draft environmental statements circulated after June 30, 1971), its own formal procedures for (1) identifying those agency actions requiring environmental statements, the appropriate time prior to decision for the consultations required by section 102(2)(C), and the agency review process for which environmental statements are to be available, (2) obtaining information required in their preparation, (3) designating the officials who are to be responsible for the statements, (4) consulting with and taking account of the comments of appropriate Federal, State, and local agencies, including obtaining the comment of the Administrator of the Environmental Protection Agency, whether or not an environmental statement is prepared, when required under section 309 of the Clean Air Act, as amended, and section 8 of these guidelines, and (5) meeting the requirements of section 2(b) of Executive Order 11514 for providing timely public information on Federal plans and programs with environmental impact including procedures responsive to section 10 of these guidelines. These procedures should be consonant with the guidelines contained herein. Each agency should file seven (7) copies of all such procedures with the Council on Environmental Quality, which will provide advice to agencies in the preparation of their procedures and guidance on the application and interpretation of the Council's guidelines. The Environmental Protection Agency will

* 36 Fed. Register, 7724–7729, Apr. 23, 1971.

assist in resolving any question relating to section 309 of the Clean Air Act, as amended.

(b) Each Federal agency should consult, with the assistance of the Council on Environmental Quality and the Office of Management and Budget if desired, with other appropriate Federal agencies in the development of the above procedures so as to achieve consistency in dealing with similar activities and to assure effective coordination among agencies in their review of proposed activities.

(c) State and local review of agency procedures, regulations, and policies for the administration of Federal programs of assistance to State and local governments will be conducted pursuant to procedures established by the Office of Management and Budget Circular No. A–85. For agency procedures subject to OMB Circular No. A–85 a 30-day extension in the July 1, 1971, deadline set in section 3(a) is granted.

(d) It is imperative that existing mechanisms for obtaining the views of Federal, State, and local agencies on proposed Federal actions be utilized to the extent practicable in dealing with environmental matters. The Office of Management and Budget will issue instructions, as necessary, to take full advantage of existing mechanisms (relating to procedures for handling legislation, preparation of budgetary materials, new procedures, water resource and other projects, etc.).

CEQ guidelines on impact statements

4. *Federal agencies included.* Section 102(2)(C) applies to all agencies of the Federal Government with respect to recommendations or favorable reports on proposals for (i) legislation and (ii) other major Federal actions significantly affecting the quality of the human environment. The phrase "to the fullest extent possible" in section 102(2)(C) is meant to make clear that each agency of the Federal Government shall comply with the requirement unless existing law applicable to the agency's operations expressly prohibits or make compliance impossible. (Section 105 of the Act provides that "The policies and goals set forth in this Act are supplementary to those set forth in existing authorizations of Federal agencies.")

5. *Actions included.* The following criteria will be employed by agencies in deciding whether a proposed action requires the preparation of an environmental statement:

(a) "Actions" include but are not limited to:

(i) Recommendations or favorable reports relating to legislation including that for appropriations. The requirement for following the section 102(2)(C) procedure as elaborated in these guidelines applies to both (i) agency recommendations on their own proposals for legislation and (ii) agency reports on legislation initiated elsewhere. (In the latter case only the agency which has primary responsibility for the subject matter involved will prepare an environmental statement.) The Office of Management and Budget will supplement these general guidelines with specific instructions relating to the way in which the section 102 (2)(C) procedure fits into its legislative clearance process;

(ii) Projects and continuing activities: directly undertaken by Federal agencies; supported in whole or in part through Federal contracts, grants, subsidies, loans, or other forms of funding assistance; involving a Federal lease, permit, license, certificate or other entitlement for use;

(iii) Policy, regulations, and procedure-making.

(b) The statutory clause "major Federal actions significantly affecting the quality of the human environment" is to be construed by agencies with a view to the overall, cumulative impact of the action proposed (and of further actions contemplated). Such actions may be localized in their impact, but if there is potential that the environment may be significantly affected, the statement is to be prepared. Proposed actions, the environmental impact of which is likely to be highly controversial, should be covered in all cases. In considering what constitutes major action significantly affecting the environment, agencies should bear in mind that the effect of many Federal decisions about a project or complex of projects can be individually limited but cumulatively considerable. This can occur when one or more agencies over a period of years puts into a project individually minor but collectively major resources, when one decision involving a limited amount of money is a precedent for action in much larger cases or represents a decision in principle about a future major course of action, or when several Government agencies individually make decisions about partial aspects of a major action. The lead agency should prepare an environmental statement if it is reasonable to anticipate a cumulatively significant impact on the environment from Federal action. "Lead agency" refers to the Federal agency which has primary authority for committing the Federal Government to a course of action with significant environmental impact. As necessary, the Council on Environmental Quality will assist in resolving questions of lead agency determination.

(c) Section 101(b) of the Act indicates the broad range of aspects of the environment to be surveyed in any assessment of significant effect. The Act also indicates that adverse significant effects include those that degrade the quality of the environment, curtail the range of beneficial uses of the environment, and serve short-term, to the disadvantage of long-term, environmental goals. Significant effects can also include actions which may have both beneficial and detrimental effects, even if, on balance, the agency believes that the effect will be beneficial. Significant adverse effects on the quality of the human environment include both those that directly affect human beings and those that indirectly affect human beings through adverse effects on the environment.

CEQ guidelines on impact statements

(d) Because of the Act's legislative history, environmental protective regulatory activities concurred in or taken by the Environmental Protection Agency are not deemed actions which require the preparation of environmental statements under section 102(2)(C) of the Act.

6. *Content of environmental statement.* (a) The following points are to be covered:

(i) A description of the proposed action including information and technical data adequate to permit a careful assessment of environmental impact by commenting agencies. Where relevant, maps should be provided.

(ii) The probable impact of the proposed action on the environment, including impact on ecological systems such as wildlife, fish, and marine life. Both primary and secondary significant consequences for the environment should be included in the analysis. For example, the implications, if any, of the action for population distribution or concentration should be estimated and an assessment made of the effect of any possible change in population patterns upon the resource base, including land use, water, and public services, of the area in question.

(iii) Any probable adverse environmental effects which cannot be avoided (such as water or air pollution, undesirable land use patterns, damage to life systems, urban congestion, threats to health or other consequences adverse to the environmental goals set out in section 101(b) or the Act).

(iv) Alternatives to the proposed action (section 102(2)(D) of the Act requires the responsible agency to "study, develop, and describe appropriate alternatives to recommended courses of action in any proposal which involves unresolved conflicts concerning alternative uses of available resources"). A rigorous exploration and objective evaluation of alternative actions that might avoid some or all of the adverse environmental effects is essential. Sufficient analysis of such alternatives and their costs and impact on the environment should accompany the proposed action through the agency review process in order not to foreclose prematurely options which might have less detrimental effects.

(v) The relationship between local short-term uses of man's environment and the maintenance and enhancement of long-term productivity. This in essence requires the agency to assess the action for cumulative and long-term effects from the perspective that each generation is trustee of the environment for succeeding generations.

(vi) Any irreversible and irretrievable commitments of resources which would be involved in the proposed action should it be implemented. This requires the agency to identify the extent to which the action curtails the range of beneficial uses of the environment.

(vii) Where appropriate, a discussion of problems and objections raised by other Federal, State, and local agencies and by private organizations and individuals in the review process and the disposition of the issues involved. (This section may be added at the end of the review process in the final text of the environmental statement.)

CEQ guidelines on impact statements

(b) With respect to water quality aspects of the proposed action which have been previously certified by the appropriate State or interstate organization as being in substantial compliance with applicable water quality standards, the comment of the Environmental Protection Agency should also be requested.

(c) Each environmental statement should be prepared in accordance with the precept in section 102(2)(A) of the Act that all agencies of the Federal Government "utilize a systematic, interdisciplinary approach which will insure the integrated use of the natural and social sciences and the environmental design arts in planning and decisionmaking which may have an impact on man's environment."

(d) Where an agency follows a practice of declining to favor an alternative until public hearings have been held on a proposed action, a draft environmental statement may be prepared and circulated indicating that two or more alternatives are under consideration.

(e) Appendix 1 prescribes the form of the summary sheet which should accompany each draft and final environmental statement.

7. *Federal agencies to be consulted in connection with preparation of environmental statement.* A Federal agency considering an action requiring an environmental statement, on the basis of (i) a draft environmental statement for which it takes responsibility or (ii) comparable information followed by a hearing subject to the provisions of the Administrative Procedure Act, should consult with, and obtain the comment on the environmental impact of the action of, Federal agencies with jurisdiction by law or special expertise with respect to any environmental impact involved. These Federal agencies include components of (depending on the aspect or aspects of the environment):

Advisory Council on Historic Preservation.
Department of Agriculture.
Department of Commerce.
Department of Defense.
Department of Health, Education, and Welfare.
Department of Housing and Urban Development.
Department of the Interior.
Department of State.
Department of Transportation.
Atomic Energy Commission.
Federal Power Commission
Environmental Protection Agency.
Office of Economic Opportunity.

For actions specifically affecting the environment of their geographic jurisdictions, the following Federal and Federal-State agencies are also to be consulted:

Tennessee Valley Authority.
Appalachian Regional Commission.
National Capital Planning Commission.
Delaware River Basin Commission.
Susquehanna River Basin Commission.

Agencies seeking comment should determine which one or more of the above listed agencies are appropriate to consult on the basis of the areas of expertise identified in Appendix 2 to these guidelines. It is recommended (i) that the above listed departments and agencies establish contact points, which often are most appropriately regional offices, for providing comments on the environmental statements and (ii) that departments from which comment is solicited coordinate and consolidate the comments of their component entities. The requirement in section 102(2)(C) to obtain comment from Federal agencies having jurisdiction or special expertise is in addition to any specific statutory obligation of any Federal agency to coordinate or consult with any other Federal or State agency. Agencies seeking comment may establish time limits of not less than thirty (30) days for reply, after which it may be presumed, unless the agency consulted requests a specified extension of time, that the agency consulted has no comment to make. Agencies seeking comment should endeavor to comply with requests for extensions of time of up to fifteen (15) days.

CEQ guidelines on impact statements

8. *Interim EPA procedures for implementation of section 309 of the Clean Air Act, as amended.* (a) Section 309 of the Clean Air Act, as amended, provides:

SEC. 309. (a) The Administrator shall review and comment in writing on the environmental impact of any matter relating to duties and responsibilities granted pursuant to this Act or other provisions of the authority of the Administrator, contained in any (1) legislation proposed by any Federal department or agency, (2) newly authorized Federal projects for construction and any major Federal agency action (other than a project for construction) to which section 102(2)(C) of Public Law 91–190 applies, and (3) proposed regulations published by any department or agency of the Federal Government. Such written comment shall be made public at the conclusion of any such review.

(b) In the event the Administrator determines that any such legislation, action, or regulation is unsatisfactory from the standpoint of public health or welfare or environmental quality, he shall publish his determination and the matter shall be referred to the Council on Environmental Quality.

(b) Accordingly, wherever an agency action related to air or water quality, noise abatement and control, pesticide regulation, solid waste disposal, radiation criteria and standards, or other provisions of the authority of the Administrator if the Environmental Protection Agency is involved, including his enforcement authority, Federal agencies are required to submit for review and comment by the Administrator in writing: (i) proposals for new Federal construction projects and other major Federal agency actions to which section 102(2)(C) of the National Environmental Policy Act applies and (ii) proposed legislation and regulations, whether or not section 102(2)(C) of the National Environmental Policy Act applies. (Actions requiring review by the Administrator do not include litigation or enforcement proceedings.) The Administrator's comments shall constitute his comments for the purposes of both section 309 of the Clean Air Act and section 102(2)(C) of the National Environmental Policy Act. A period of 45 days shall be allowed for such review. The Administrator's written comment shall be furnished to the responsible Federal department or agency, to the Council on Environmental Quality and summarized in a notice published in the FEDERAL REGISTER. The public may obtain copies of such comment on request from the Environmental Protection Agency.

CEQ guidelines on impact statements

9. *State and local review.* Where no public hearing has been held on the proposed action at which the appropriate State and local review has been invited, and where review of the environmental impact of the proposed action by State and local agencies authorized to develop and enforce environmental standards is relevant, such State and local review shall be provided as follows:

(a) For direct Federal development projects and projects assisted under programs listed in Attachment D of the Office of Management and Budget Circular No. A-95, review of draft environmental statements by State and local governments will be through procedures set forth under Part 1 of Circular No. A-95.

(b) Where these procedures are not appropriate and where a proposed action affects matters within their jurisdiction, review of the draft environmental statement on a proposed action by State and local agencies authorized to develop and enforce environmental standards and their comments on the environmental impact of the proposed action may be obtained directly or by distributing the draft environmental statement to the appropriate State, regional and metropolitan clearinghouses unless the Governor of the State involved has designated some other point for obtaining this review.

10. *Use of statements in agency review processes; distribution to Council on Environmental Quality; availability to public.* (a) Agencies will need to identify at what stage or stages of a series of actions relating to a particular matter the environmental statement procedures of this directive will be applied. It will often be necessary to use the procedures both in the development of a national program and in the review of proposed projects within the national program. However, where a grant-in-aid program does not entail prior approval by Federal agencies of specific projects the view of Federal, State, and local agencies in the legislative process may have to suffice. The principle to be applied is to obtain views of other agencies at the earliest feasible time in the development of program and project proposals. Care should be exercised so as to not to duplicate the clearance process, but when actions being considered differ significantly from those that have already been reviewed pursuant to section 102(2)(C) of the Act an environmental statement should be provided.

(b) Ten (10) copies of draft environmental statements (when prepared), ten (10) copies of all comments made thereon (to be forwarded to the Council by the entity making comment at the time comment is forwarded to the responsible agency), and ten (10) copies of the final text of environmental statements (together with all comments received thereon by the responsible agency from Federal, State, and local agencies and from private organizations and individuals) shall be supplied to the Council on Environmental Quality in the Executive Office of the President (this will serve as making environmental statements available to the President). It is important that draft environmental statements be prepared and circulated for comment and furnished to the Council early enough in the agency review process before an action is taken in order to permit meaningful consideration of the environmental issues involved. To the maximum extent practicable no administrative action (i.e., any proposed action to be taken by the agency other than agency proposals for legislation to Congress or agency reports on legislation) subject to section 102(2)(C) is to be taken sooner than ninety (90) days after a draft environmental statement has been circulated for comment, furnished to the Council and, except where advance public disclosure will result in significantly increased costs of procurement to the Government, made available to the public pursuant to these guidelines; neither should such administrative action be taken sooner than thirty (30) days after the final text of an environmental statement (together with comments) has been made available to the Council and the public. If the final text of an environmental statement is filed within ninety (90) days after a draft statement has been circulated for comment, furnished to the Council and made public pursuant to this section of these guidelines, the thirty (30) day period and ninety (90) day period may run concurrently to the extent that they overlap.

(c) With respect to recommendations or reports on proposals for legislation to which section 102(2)(C) applies, the final text of the environmental statement and comments thereon should be available to the Congress and to the public in support of the proposed legislation or report. In cases where the scheduling of congressional hearings on recommendations or reports on proposals for legislation which the Federal agency has forwarded to the Congress does not allow adequate time for the completion of a final text of an environmental statement (together with comments), a draft environmental statement may be furnished to the Congress and made available to the public pending transmittal of the comments as received and the final text.

(d) Where emergency circumstances make it necessary to take an action with significant environmental impact without observing the provisions of these guidelines concerning minimum periods for agency review and advance availability of environmental statements, the Federal agency proposing to take the action should consult with the Council on Environmental Quality about alternative arrangements. Similarly, where there are overriding considerations of expense to the Government or impaired program effectiveness, the responsible agency should consult the Council concerning appropriate modifications of the minimum periods.

CEQ guidelines on impact statements

(e) In accord with the policy of the National Environmental Policy Act and Executive Order 11514 agencies have a responsibility to develop procedures to insure the fullest practicable provision of timely public information and understanding of Federal plans and programs with environmental impact in order to obtain the views of interested parties. These procedures shall include, whenever appropriate, provision for public hearings, and shall provide the public with relevant information, including information on alternative courses of action. Agencies which hold hearings on proposed administrative actions or legislation should make the draft environmental statement available to the public at least fifteen (15) days prior to the time of the relevant hearings except where the agency prepares the draft statement on the basis of a hearing subject to the Administrative Procedure Act and preceded by adequate public notice and information to identify the issues and obtain the comments provided for in sections 6–9 of these guidelines.

(f) The agency which prepared the environmental statement is responsible for making the statement and the comments received available to the public pursuant to the provisions of the Freedom of Information Act (5 U.S.C., sec. 552), without regard to the exclusion of interagency memoranda when such memoranda transmit comments of Federal agencies listed in section 7 of these guidelines upon the environmental impact of proposed actions subject to section 102(2)(C).

(g) Agency procedures prepared pursuant to section 3 of these guidelines shall implement these public information requirements and shall include arrangements for availability of environmental statements and comments at the head and appropriate regional offices of the responsible agency and at appropriate State, regional, and metropolitan clearinghouses unless the Governor of the State involved designates some other point for receipt of this information.

11. *Application of section 102(2)(C) procedure to existing projects and programs.* To the maximum extent practicable the sec-

CEQ guidelines on impact statements

tion 102(2)(C) procedure should be applied to further major Federal actions having a significant effect on the environment even though they arise from projects or programs initiated prior to enactment of the Act on January 1, 1970. Where it is not practicable to reassess the basic course of action, it is still important that further incremental major actions be shaped so as to minimize adverse environmental consequences. It is also important in further action that account be taken of environmental consequences not fully evaluated at the outset of the project or program.

12. *Supplemetary guidelines, evaluation of procedures.* (a) The Council on Environmental Quality after examining environmental statements and agency procedures with respect to such statements will issue such supplements to these guidelines as are necessary.

(b) Agencies will continue to assess their experience in the implementation of the section 102(2)(C) provisions of the Act and in conforming with these guidelines and report thereon to the Council on Environmental Quality by December 1, 1971. Such reports should include an identification of the problem areas and suggestions for revision or clarification of these guidelines to achieve effective coordination of views on environmental aspects (and alternatives, where appropriate) of proposed actions without imposing unproductive administrative procedures.

RUSSELL E. TRAIN,
Chairman.

appendix

A summary sheet should accompany each environmental statement submitted, consisting of no more than one page, and covering the following items:

(Check one) ( ) Draft. ( ) Final Environmental Statement.

Name of Responsible Federal Agency (with name of operating division where appropriate).

1. Name of Action. (Check one) ( ) Administrative Action. ( ) Legislative Action.
2. Brief description of action indicating what States (and counties) particularly affected.
3. Summary of environmental impact and adverse environmental effects.
4. List alternatives considered.
5. a. (For draft statements) List all Federal, State, and local agencies from which comments have been requested.

b. (For final statements) List all Federal, State, and local agencies and other sources from which written comments have been received.

6. Dates draft statement and final statement made available to Council on Environmental Quality and public.

Expertise under § 102 of NEPA

According to Section 102(2)(C) of the NEPA which requires environmental impact statements to be filed, the responsible Federal Official shall consult with and obtain the comments of any Federal agency which has jurisdiction by law or special expertise with respect to any environmental impact involved. What is expertise? This is the government's answer (reprinted from "Environmental Quality, the Second Annual Report of the Council on Environmental Quality", August, 1971):

air

air quality and air pollution control—Department of Agriculture: Forest Service (effects on vegetation).

Department of Health, Education, and Welfare (health aspects).
Environmental Protection Agency: Air Pollution Control Office.

Department of the Interior:
Bureau of Mines (fossil and gaseous fuel combustion).
Bureau of Sport Fisheries and Wildlife (wildlife).
Department of Transportation:
Assistant Secretary for Systems Development and Technology (auto emissions).
Coast Guard (vessel emissions).
Federal Aviation Administration (aircraft emissions).

weather modification—Department of Commerce: National Oceanic and Atmospheric Administration.
Department of Defense: Department of the Air Force.
Department of the Interior: Bureau of Reclamation.

energy

environmental aspects of electric energy generation and transmission—Atomic Energy Commission (nuclear power).
Environmental Protection Agency:
Water Quality Office.
Air Pollution Control Office.
Department of Agriculture: Rural Electrification Administration (rural areas).
Department of Defense: Army Corps of Engineers (hydro-facilities).
Federal Power Commission (hydro-facilities and transmission lines).
Department of Housing and Urban Development (urban areas).
Department of the Interior—(facilities on Government lands).

natural gas energy development, transmission and generation—Federal Power Commission (natural gas production, transmission and supply).
Department of the Interior:
Geological Survey.
Bureau of Mines.

hazardous substances

Expertise under §102 of NEPA

toxic materials—Department of Commerce: National Oceanic and Atmospheric Administration.
Department of Health, Education and Welfare (health aspects).
Environmental Protection Agency.
Department of Agriculture:
Agricultural Research Service.
Consumer and Marketing Service.
Department of Defense.
Department of the Interior: Bureau of Sport Fisheries and Wildlife.

pesticides—Department of Agriculture:
Agricultural Research Service (biological controls, food and fiber production).
Consumer and Marketing Service.
Forest Service.
Department of Commerce:
National Marine Fisheries Service.
National Oceanic and Atmospheric Administration.
Environmental Protection Agency: Office of Pesticides.
Department of the Interior:
Bureau of Sport Fisheries and Wildlife (effects on fish and wildlife).
Bureau of Land Management.
Department of Health, Education, and Welfare (health aspects).

herbicides—Department of Agriculture:
Agricultural Research Service.
Forest Service.

Environmental Protection Agency: Office of Pesticides.
Department of Health, Education, and Welfare (Health aspects).
Department of the Interior:
Bureau of Sport Fisheries and Wildlife.
Bureau of Land Management.
Bureau of Reclamation.

transportation and handling of hazardous materials—Department of Commerce:
Maritime Administration.
National Marine Fisheries Service.
National Oceanic and Atmospheric Administration (impact on marine life).
Department of Defense:
Armed Services Explosive Safety Board.
Army Corps of Engineers (navigable waterways).
Department of Health, Education, and Welfare: Office of the Surgeon General (health aspects).
Department of Transportation:
Federal Highway Administration Bureau of Motor Carrier Safety.

Coast Guard.
Federation Railroad Administration.
Federal Aviation Administration.
Assistant Secretary for Systems Development and Technology.
Office of Hazardous Materials.
Office of Pipeline Safety.
Environmental Protection Agency (hazardous substances).
Atomic Energy Commission (radioactive substances).

land use and management

coastal areas: wetlands, estuaries, waterfowl refuges, and beaches—Department of Agriculture: Forest Service.
Department of Commerce:
National Marine Fisheries Service (impact on marine life).
National Oceanic and Atmospheric Administration (impact on marine life).
Department of Transportation: Coast Guard (bridges, navigation).
Department of Defense: Army Corps of Engineers (beaches, dredge and fill permits, Refuse Act permits).
Department of the Interior:
Bureau of Sport Fisheries and Wildlife.
National Park Service.
U.S. Geological Survey (coastal geology).
Bureau of Outdoor Recreation (beaches) .
Department of Agriculture: Soil Conservation Service (soil stability, hydrology).
Environmental Protection Agency: Water Quality Office.

historic and archeological sites—Department of the Interior: National Park Service.
Advisory Council on Historic Preservation.
Department of Housing and Urban Development (urban areas).

Expertise under
§ 102 of NEPA

flood plains and watersheds—Department of Agriculture:
Agricultural Stabilization and Research Service.
Soil Conservation Service.
Forest Service.
Department of the Interior:
Bureau of Outdoor Recreation.
Bureau of Reclamation.
Bureau of Sport Fisheries and Wildlife.
Bureau of Land Measurement.
U.S. Geological Survey.
Department of Housing and Urban Development (urban areas).
Department of Defense: Army Corps of Engineers.

mineral land reclamation—Appalachian Regional Commission.
Department of Agriculture: Forest Service.
Department of the Interior:
Bureau of Mines.
Bureau of Outdoor Recreation.
Bureau of Sport Fisheries and Wildlife.
Bureau of Land Management.
U.S. Geological Survey.
Tennessee Valley Authority.

parks, forests, and outdoor recreation—Department of Agriculture:
Forest Service.
Soil Conservation Service.
Department of the Interior:
Bureau of Land Management.
National Park Service.
Bureau of Outdoor Recreation.
Bureau of Sport Fisheries and Wildlife.
Department of Defense: Army Corps of Engineers.
Department of Housing and Urban Development (urban areas).

soil and plant life, sedimentation, erosion and hydrologic conditions—Department of Agriculture:
Soil Conservation Service.
Agricultural Research Service.
Forest Service.
Department of Defense: Army Corps of Engineers (dredging, aquatic plants).
Department of Commerce: National Oceanic and Atmospheric Administration.
Department of the Interior:
Bureau of Land Management.
Bureau of Sport Fisheries and Wildlife.
Geological Survey.
Bureau of Reclamation.

noise

noise control and abatement—Department of Health, Education, and Welfare (health aspects).

Department of Commerce: National Bureau of Standards.

Department of Transportation:

Assistant Secretary for Systems Development and Technology.

Federal AviationAdministration (Office of Noise Abatement).

Environmental Protection Agency (Office of Noise).

Department of Housing and Urban Development (urban land use aspects, building materials standards).

physiological health and human well being

chemical contamination of food products—Department of Agriculture: Consumer and Marketing Service.

Department of Health, Education, and Welfare (health aspects).

Environmental Protection Agency: Office of Pesticides (economic poisons).

food additives and food sanitation—Department of Health, Education, and Welfare (health aspects).

Environmental Protection Agency: Office of Pesticides (economic poisons, e.g., pesticide residues).

Department of Agriculture: Consumer Marketing Service (meat and poultry products).

microbiological contamination—Department of Health, Education, and Welfare (health aspects).

radiation and radiological health—Department of Commerce: National Bureau of Standards.

Atomic Energy Commission.

Environmental Protection Agency: Office of Radiation.

Department of the Interior: Bureau of Mines (uranium mines).

sanitation and waste systems—Department of Health, Education, and Welfare (health aspects).

Department of Defense: Army Corps of Engineers.

Environmental Protection Agency:

Solid Waste Office.

Water Quality Office.

Department of Transportation: U.S. Coast Guard (ship sanitation).

Department of the Interior:

Bureau of Mines (mineral waste and recycling, mine acid wastes, urban solid wastes).

Bureau of Land Management (solid wastes on public lands).

Office of Saline Water (demineralization of liquid wastes).

shellfish sanitation—Department of Commerce:

National Marine Fisheries Service.

National Oceanic and Atmospheric Administration

Department of Health, Education, and Welfare (health aspects).

Environmental Protection Agency: Office of Water Quality.

transportation

air quality—Environmental Protection Agency: Air Pollution Control Office.

Department of Transportation: Federal Aviation Administration.

Department of the Interior:

Bureau of Outdoor Recreation.

Bureau of Sport Fisheries and Wildlife.

Department of Commerce: National Oceanic and Atmospheric Administration (meteorological conditions).

water quality—Environmental Protection Agency: Office of Water Quality.

Department of the Interior: Bureau of Sport Fisheries and Wildlife.

Department of Commerce: National Oceanic and Atmospheric Administration (impact on marine life and ocean monitoring).

Department of Defense: Army Corps of Engineers.

Department of Transportation: Coast Guard.

urban

congestion in urban areas, housing and building displacement—Department of Transportation: Federal Highway Administration.

Office of Economic Opportunity.

Department of Housing and Urban Development.

Department of the Interior: Bureau of Outdoor Recreation.

environmental effects with special impact in low-income neighborhoods—Department of the Interior: National Park Service.

Office of Economic Opportunity.

Department of Housing and Urban Development (urban areas).

Department of Commerce (economic development areas).

Economic Development Administration.

Department of Transportation: Urban Mass Transportation Administration.

rodent control—Department of Health, Education, and Welfare (health aspects).
Department of Housing and Urban Development (urban areas).

urban planning—Department of Transportation: Federal Highway Administration.
Department of Housing and Urban Development.
Environmental Protection Agency.
Department of the Interior:
Geological Survey.
Bureau of Outdoor Recreation.
Department of Commerce: Economic Development Administration.

Expertise under § 102 of NEPA

water

water quality and water pollution control—Department of Agriculture:
Soil Conservation Service.
Forest Service.
Department of the Interior:
Bureau of Reclamation.
Bureau of Land Management.
Bureau of Sports Fisheries and Wildlife.
Bureau of Outdoor Recreation.
Geological Survey.
Office of Saline Water.
Environmental Protection Agency: Water Quality Office.
Department of Health, Education, and Welfare (health aspects).
Department of Defense:
Army Corps of Engineers.
Department of the Navy (ship pollution control).
Department of Transportation: Coast Guard (oil spills, ship sanitation).
Department of Commerce: National Oceanic and Atmospheric Administration.

marine pollution—Department of Commerce: National Oceanic and Atmospheric Administration.
Department of Transportation: Coast Guard.
Department of Defense:
Army Corps of Engineers.
Office of Oceanographer of the Navy.

river and canal regulation and stream channelization—Department of Agriculture: Soil Conservation Service.
Department of Defense: Army Corps of Engineers.
Department of the Interior:
Bureau of Reclamation.
Geological Survey.
Bureau of Sport Fisheries and Wildlife.
Department of Transportation: Coast Guard.

wildlife

Environmental Protection Agency.
Department of Agriculture:
Forest Service.
Soil Conservation Service.
Department of the Interior:
Bureau of Sport Fisheries and Wildlife.
Bureau of Land Management.
Bureau of Outdoor Recreation.

Coordination of § 102 statements

federal agency offices for receiving and coordinating comments upon environmental impact statements

advisory council on historic preservation

Robert Garvey, Executive Director, Suite 618, 801 19th Street NW., Washington, DC 20006, 343–8607.

department of agriculture

Dr. T. C. Byerly, Office of the Secretary, Washington, D.C., 20250, 388–7803.

appalachian regional commission

Orville H. Lerch, Alternate Federal Co-Chairman, 1666 Connecticut Avenue NW., Washington, DC 20235, 967–4103.

department of the army (corps of engineers)

Col. J. B. Newman, Executive Director of Civil Works, Office of the Chief of Engineers, Washington, D.C. 20314, 693–7168.

atomic energy commission

For nonregulatory matters: Joseph J. DiNunno, Director, Office of Environmental Affairs, Washington, D.C. 20545, 973–5391.

For regulatory matters: Christopher L. Henderson, Assistant Director for Regulation, Washington, D.C. 20545, 973–7531.

department of commerce

Dr. Sydney R. Galler, Deputy Assistant Secretary for Environmental Affairs, Washington, D.C. 20230, 967–4335.

department of defense

Dr. Louis M. Rousselot, Assistant Secretary for Defense (Health and Environment), Room 3E172, The Pentagon, Washington, DC 20301, 697–2111.

delaware river basin commission

W. Brinton Whitall, Secretary, Post Office Box 360, Trenton, NJ 08603, 609–883–9500.

environmental protection agency

Charles Fabrikant, Director of Impact Statements Office, 1626 K Street NW., Washington, DC 20460, 632–7719.

federal power commission

Frederick H. Warren, Commission's Advisor on Environmental Quality, 441 G Street NW., Washington, DC 20426, 386–6084.

general services administration

Rod Kreger, Deputy Administrator, General Services Administration–AD, Washington, D.C. 20405, 343–6077.

Alternate contact: Aaron Woloshin, Director, Office of Environmental Affairs, General Services Administration–ADF, 343–4161.

department of health, education, and welfare

Coordination of §102 statements

Roger O. Egeberg, Assistant Secretary for Health and Science Affairs, HEW North Building, Washington, D.C. 20202, 963–4254.

department of housing and urban development [1]

Charles Orlebeke, Deputy Under Secretary, 451 Seventh Street SW., Washington, DC 20410, 755–6960.

Alternate contact: George Wright, Office of the Deputy Under Secretary, 755–8192.

department of the interior

Jack O. Horton, Deputy Assistant Secretary for Programs, Washington, D.C. 20240, 343–6181.

national capital planning commission

Charles H. Conrad, Executive Director, Washington, D.C. 20576, 382–1163.

office of economic opportunity

Frank Carlucci, Director, 1200 19th Street, NW., Washington, DC 20506, 254–6000.

department of state

Christian Herter, Jr., Special Assistant to the Secretary for Environmental Affairs, Washington, D.C. 20520, 632–7964.

---

[1] Contact the Deputy Under Secretary with regard to environmental impacts of legislation, policy statements, program regulations and procedures, and precedent-making project decisions. For all other HUD consultation, contact the HUD Regional Administrator in whose jurisdiction the project lies, as follows:

James J. Barry, Regional Administrator I, Attention: Environmental Clearance Officer, Room 405, John F. Kennedy Federal Building, Boston, MA 02203, 617–223–4066.

S. William Green, Regional Administrator II, Attention: Environmental Clearance Officer, 26 Federal Plaza, New York, NY 10007, 212–264–8068.

Warren P. Phelan, Regional Administrator III, Attention: Environmental Clearance Officer, Curtis Building, Sixth and Walnut Street, Philadelphia, PA 19106, 215–597–2560.

Edward H. Baxter, Regional Administrator IV, Attention: Environmental Clearance Officer, Peachtree-Seventh Building, Atlanta, GA 30323, 404–526–5585.

George Vavoulis, Regional Administrator V, Attention: Environmental Clearance Officer, 360 North Michigan Avenue, Chicago, IL 60601, 312–353–5680.

Richard L. Morgan, Regional Administrator VI, Attention: Environmental Clearance Officer, Federal Office Building, 819 Taylor Street, Fort Worth, TX 76102, 817–334–2867.

Harry T. Morley, Jr., Regional Administrator VII, Attention: Environmental Clearance Officer, 911 Walnut Street, Kansas City, MO 64106, 816–374–2661.

Robert C. Rosenheim, Regional Administrator VIII, Attention: Environmental Clearance Officer, Samsonite Building, 1051 South Broadway, Denver, CO 80209, 303–837–4061.

Robert H. Baida, Regional Administrator IX, Attention: Environmental Clearance Officer, 450 Golden Gate Avenue, Post Office Box 36003, San Francisco, CA 94102, 415–556–4752.

Oscar P. Pederson, Regional Administrator X, Attention: Environmental Clearance Officer, Room 226, Arcade Plaza Building, Seattle, WA 98101, 206–583–5415.

susquehanna river basin commission

Alan J. Summerville, Water Resources Coordinator, Department of Environmental Resources, 105 South Office Building, Harrisburg, PA. 17120, 717-787-2315.

tennessee valley authority

Dr. Francis Gartrell, Director of Environmental Research and Development, 720 Edney Building, Chattanooga, TN 37401, 615-755-2002.

department of transportation

Herbert F. DeSimone, Assistant Secretary for Environment and Urban Systems, Washington, D.C. 20590, 426-4563.

department of treasury

Richard E. Slitor, Assistant Director, Office of Tax Analysis, Washington, D.C. 20220, 964-2797.

EPA Regulations Concerning Certification of Pollution Control Facilities

for accelerated amortization under Sec. 704, Tax Reform Act of 1969, P.L. 91-172

FEDERAL REGISTER, VOL. 36, NO. 102- MAY 26, 1971

Part 602 to Title 18, Chapter V, as set forth below is hereby adopted.

Effective date. This revision shall become effective on the date of its publication in the FEDERAL REGISTER.

Dated: May 21, 1971.

WILLIAM D. RUCKELSHAUS,
Administrator.

AUTHORITY: The provisions of this Part 602 issued pursuant to section 301, 80 Stat. 378, 5 U.S.C. 301, and sec. 704 of the Tax Reform Act of 1969, 83 Stat. 667.

§ 602.1 Applicability.

The regulations of this part apply to certifications by the Administrator of water or air pollution control facilities for purposes of section 169 of the Internal Revenue Code of 1954, as amended, 26 U.S.C. 169. Applicable regulations of the Department of the Treasury are set forth at 26 CFR 1.169 et seq.

§ 602.2 Definitions.

As used in this part, the following terms shall have the meaning indicated below:

(a) "Act" means, when used in connection with water pollution control facilities, the Federal Water Pollution Control Act, as amended (33 U.S.C. 1151 et seq.) or, when used in connection with air pollution control facilities, the Clean Air Act, as amended (42 U.S.C. 1857 et seq.).

(b) "State certifying authority" means:

(1) For water pollution control facilities, the State health authority, except that, in the case of any State in which there is a single State agency, other than the State health authority, charged with responsibility for enforcing State laws relating to the abatement of water pollution, it means such other State agency; or

(2) For air pollution control facilities, the air pollution control agency designated pursuant to section 302(b)(1) of the Act; or

(3) For both air and water pollution control facilities, any interstate agency authorized to act in place of the certifying agency of a State.

(c) "Applicant" means any person who files an application with the Administrator for certification that a facility is in compliance with the applicable regulations of Federal agencies and in furtherance of the general policies of the United States for cooperation with the States in the prevention and abatement of water or air pollution under the Act.

(d) "Administrator" means the Administrator, Environmental Protection Agency.

(e) "Regional Administrator" means the Regional designee appointed by the Administrator to certify facilities under this part.

(f) "Facility" means property comprising any new identifiable treatment facility which removes, alters, disposes of or stores pollutants, contaminants, wastes, or heat.

(g) "State" means the States, the District of Columbia, the Commonwealth of Puerto Rico, the Canal Zone, Guam, American Samoa, the Virgin Islands, and the Trust Territory of the Pacific Islands.

§ 602.3 General provisions.

(a) An applicant shall file an application in accordance with this part for each separate facility for which certification is sought: *Provided,* That one application shall suffice in the case of substantially identical facilities which the applicant has installed or plans to install in connection with substantially identical properties; *Provided further,* That an application may incorporate by reference material contained in an application previously submitted by the applicant under this part and pertaining to substantially identical facilities.

(b) The applicant shall, at the time of application to the State certifying authority, submit an application in the form prescribed by the Administrator to the Regional Administrator for the region in which the facility is located.

(c) Applications will be considered complete and will be processed when the Regional Administrator receives the completed State certification.

(d) Applications may be filed prior or subsequent to the commencement of construction, acquisition, installation, or operation of the facility.

(e) An amendment to an application shall be submitted in the same manner as the original application and shall be considered a part of the original application.

(f) If the facility is certified by the Regional Administrator, notice of certification will be issued to the Secretary of the Treasury or his delegate, and a copy of the notice shall be forwarded to the applicant and to the State certifying authority. If the facility is denied certification, the Regional Administrator will advise the applicant and State certifying authority in writing of the reasons therefor.

(g) No certification will be made by the Regional Administrator for any facility prior to the time it is placed in operation and the application, or amended application, in connection with such facility so states.

(h) An applicant may appeal any decision of the Regional Administrator which:

(1) Denies certification;

(2) Disapproves the applicant's suggested method of allocating costs pursuant to § 602.8(e); or

(3) Revokes a certification pursuant to § 602.10.

Any such appeal may be taken by filing with the Administrator within 30 days from the date of the decision of the Regional Administrator a written statement of objections to the decision appealed from. Within 60 days, the Administrator shall affirm, modify, or revoke the decision of the Regional Administrator, stating in writing his reasons therefor.

§ 602.4 Notice of intent to certify.

(a) On the basis of applications submitted prior to the construction, reconstruction, erection, acquisition, or operation of a facility, the Regional Administrator may notify applicants that such facility will be certified if:

(1) The Regional Administrator determines that such facility, if constructed, reconstructed, erected, acquired, installed, and operated in accordance with such application will be in compliance with requirements identified in § 602.8; and if

(2) The application is accompanied by a statement from the State certifying authority that such facility, if constructed, reconstructed, acquired, erected, installed, and operated in accordance with such application, will be in conformity with the State program or requirements for abatement or control of water or air pollution.

(b) Notice of actions taken under this section will be given to the appropriate State certifying authority.

§ 602.5 Applications.

Applications for certification under this part shall be submitted in such manner as the Administrator may prescribe, shall be signed by the applicant or agent thereof, and shall include the following information:

(a) Name, address, and Internal Revenue Service identifying number of the applicant;

(b) Type and narrative description of the new identifiable facility for which certification is (or will be) sought, including a copy of schematic or engineering drawings, and a description of the function and operation of such facility;

(c) Address (or proposed address) of facility location;

(d) A general description of the operation in connection with which such facility is (or will be) used and a description of the specific process or processes resulting in discharges or emissions which are (or will be) controlled by the facility;

(e) If the facility is (or will be) used in connection with more than one plant or other property, one or more of which were not in operation prior to January 1, 1969, a description of the operations of the facility in respect to each plant or other property, including a reasonable allocation of the costs of the facility among the plants being serviced, and a description of the reasoning and accounting method or methods used to arrive at such allocation;

(f) Description of the effect of such facility in terms of type and quantity of pollutants, contaminants, wastes or heat, removed, altered, stored, or disposed of by such facility;

(g) If the facilty performs a function other than removal, alteration, storage, or disposal of pollutants, contaminants, wastes or heat, a description of all functions performed by the facility, including a reasonable identification of the costs of the facility allocable to removal, alteration, storage, or disposal of pollutants, contaminants, wastes or heat, and a description of the reasoning and the accounting method or methods used to arrive at such allocation;

(h) Date when such construction, reconstruction, or erection will be completed or when such facility was (or will be) acquired;

(i) Date when such facility is placed (or is intended to be placed) in operation;

(j) Identification of the applicable State and local water or air pollution control requirements and standards, if any;

(k) Expected useful life of facility;

(l) Cost of construction, acquisition, installation, operation, and maintenance of the facility;

(m) Estimated profits reasonably expected to be derived through the recovery of wastes or otherwise in the operation of the facility over the period referred to in paragraph (a)(6) of 26 CFR 1.169-2;

(n) Such other information as the Administrator deems necessary for certification.

§ 602.6 State certification.

The State certification shall be by the State certifying authority having jurisdiction with respect to the facility in accordance with 26 U.S.C. 169 (d)(1)(A) and (d)(2). The certification shall state that the facility described in the application has been constructed, reconstructed, erected, or acquired in con-

EPA regulations on facilities

EPA regulations on facilities

ormity with the State program or requirements for abatement or control of water or air pollution. It shall be executed by an agent or officer authorized to act on behalf of the State certifying authority.

§ 602.7 General policies.

(a) The general policies of the United States for cooperation with the States in the prevention and abatement of water pollution are: To enhance the quality and value of our water resources; to eliminate or reduce the pollution of the nation's waters and tributaries thereof; to improve the sanitary condition of surface and underground waters; and to conserve such waters for public water supplies, propagation of fish and aquatic life and wildlife, recreational purposes, and agricultural, industrial, and other legitimate uses.

(b) The general policy of the United States for cooperation with the States in the prevention and abatement of air pollution is to cooperate with and to assist the States and local governments in protecting and enhancing the quality of the Nation's air resources by the prevention and abatement of conditions which cause or contribute to air pollution which endangers the public health or welfare.

§ 602.8 Requirements for certification.

(a) Subject to § 602.9, the Regional Administrator will certify a facility if he makes the following determinations:

(1) It has been certified by the State certifying authority.

(2) It removes, alters, disposes of, or stores pollutants, contaminants, wastes or heat, which, but for the facility, would be released into the environment.

(3) The applicant is in compliance with all regulations of Federal agencies applicable to use of the facility, including conditions specified in any permit issued to the applicant under section 13 of the Rivers and Harbors Act of 1899, as amended.

(4) The facility furthers the general policies of the United States and the States in the prevention and abatement of pollution.

(5) The applicant has complied with all the other requirements of this part and has submitted all requested information.

(b) In determining whether use of a facility furthers the general policies of the United States and the States in the prevention and abatement of water pollution, the Regional Administrator shall consider whether such facility is consistent with the following, insofar as they are applicable to the waters which will be affected by the facility:

(1) All applicable water quality standards, including water quality criteria and plans of implementation and enforcement established pursuant to section 10 (c) of the Act or State laws or regulations;

(2) Recommendations issued pursuant to section 10 (e) and (f) of the Act;

(3) Water pollution control programs established pursuant to section 3 or 7 of the Act.

(c) In determining whether use of a facility furthers the general policies of the United States and the States in the prevention and abatement of air pollution, the Regional Administrator shall consider whether such facility is consistent with and meets the following requirements, insofar as they are applicable to the air which will be affected by the facility;

(1) Plans for the implementation, maintenance, and enforcement of ambient air quality standards adopted or promulgated pursuant to section 110 of the Act;

(2) Recommendations issued pursuant to sections 103(e) and 115 of the Act which are applicable to facilities of the same type and located in the area to which the recommendations are directed;

(3) Local government requirements for control of air pollution, including emission standards;

(4) Standards promulgated by the Administrator pursuant to the Act.

(d) A facility which removes elements or compounds from fuels which would be released as pollutants when such fuels are burned may not be certified whether or not such facility is used in connection with the applicant's plant or property where such fuels are burned.

(e) Where a facility is used in connection with more than one plant or other property, one or more of which were not in operation prior to January 1, 1969, or where a facility will perform a function other than the removal, alteration, storage or disposal of pollutants, contaminants, wastes, or heat, the Regional Administrator will so indicate on the notice of certification and will approve or disapprove the applicant's suggested method of allocation of costs. If the Regional Administrator disapproves the applicant's suggested method, he shall identify the proportion of costs allocable to each such plant, or to the removal, alteration, storage or disposal of pollutants, contaminants, wastes, or heat.

§ 602.9 Cost recovery.

Where it appears that, by reason of estimated profits to be derived through the recovery of wastes, through separate charges for use of the facility in question, or otherwise in the operation of such facility, all or a portion of its costs may be recovered over the period referred to in paragraph (a)(6) of 26 CFR 1.169–2, the Regional Administrator shall so signify in the notice of certification. Determinations as to the meaning of the term "estimated profits" and as to the percentage of the cost of a certified facility which will be recovered over such period shall be made by the Secretary of the Treasury, or his delegate: *Provided,* That in no event shall estimated profits be deemed to arise from the use or reuse by the applicant of recovered waste.

§ 602.10 Revocation.

Certification hereunder may be revoked by the Regional Administrator on 30 days written notice to the applicant, served by certified mail, whenever the Regional Administrator shall determine that the facility in question is no longer being operated consistent with the § 602.8 (b) and (c) criteria in effect at the time the facility was placed in service. Within such 30-day period, the applicant may submit to the Regional Administrator such evidence, data or other written materials as the applicant may deem appropriate to show why the certification hereunder should not be revoked. Notification of a revocation under this section shall be given to the Secretary of the Treasury or his delegate. See 26 CFR 1.169–4(b)(1).

COUNCIL ON ENVIRONMENTAL QUALITY

IMPLEMENTATION OF NATIONAL ENVIRONMENTAL POLICY ACT

Notice of Opportunity for Public Comment on Procedures

DECEMBER 3, 1971.

Following its annual practice, the Council on Environmental Quality invites comment and suggestions from interested parties with respect to possible revisions of the Council's Guidelines on the preparation of environmental impact statements pursuant to section 102 (2)(C) of the National Environmental Policy Act (NEPA) (42 U.S.C. sec. 4332 (2)(C)). These Guidelines, dated April 23, 1971, are available from the Council and appear at 36 F.R. 7724–7729.

The Council also invites similar comment and suggestions with respect to the procedures adopted by agencies to implement NEPA and the Council's Guidelines. These procedures, to the extent they have been adopted, are available as follows:

DEPARTMENT OF AGRICULTURE

Departmental procedures dated November 12, 1971 (text follows this notice).
Agricultural Stabilization and Conservation Service (no separate procedures).
Animal Plant and Health Service (no separate procedures).
Cooperative State Research Service (no separate procedures).
Economic Research Service (no separate procedures).
Extension Service (no separate procedures).
Farmers Home Administration (no separate procedures).
Forest Service
Procedures dated July 31, 1971 (text follows this notice).
Rural Electrification Administration, Procedures dated June 17, 1971 (text follows this notice).
Soil Conservation Service, Procedures dated November 15, 1971 (text follows this notice).

APPALACHIAN REGIONAL COMMISSION

Procedures dated June 7, 1971 (text follows this notice).

ATOMIC ENERGY COMMISSION

Regulatory activities—procedures dated September 9, 1971; 36 F.R. 18071–18076; Supplement, 36 F.R. 22851–22854.
Nonregulatory activities—procedures dated July 16, 1971; 36 F.R. 13233–13235.

CANAL ZONE GOVERNMENT

Procedures dated July 1, 1971 (text follows this notice).

CIVIL AERONAUTICS BOARD

Procedures dated July 1, 1971; 36 F.R. 12513–12515.

DELAWARE RIVER BASIN COMMISSION

Procedures dated October 21, 1971; 36 F.R. 20381–20382.

DEPARTMENT OF COMMERCE

Departmental procedures dated November 6, 1971; 36 F.R. 21368–21370.
Economic Development Administration, Procedures dated November 16, 1971.
Maritime Administration (no separate procedures).
National Bureau of Standards (no separate procedures).
National Oceanographic and Atmospheric Administration (no separate procedures).

DEPARTMENT OF DEFENSE

Departmental procedures dated August 18, 1971; 36 F.R. 15750–15754.
Army Corps of Engineers, procedures dated June 11, 1971; 36 F.R. 11309–11318.

DEPARTMENT OF HEALTH, EDUCATION, AND WELFARE

Departmental procedures dated November 23, 1971 (text follows this notice).
Facilities Engineering and Construction Agency (no separate procedures).
Food and Drug Administration (no separate procedures).
Health Service and Mental Health Administration (no separate procedures).
National Institute of Health (no separate procedures).

DEPARTMENT OF HOUSING AND URBAN DEVELOPMENT

Departmental procedures dated November 19, 1971.
Federal Housing Authority (no separate procedures).
Urban Renewal Program (no separate procedures).
Water and Sewer Grants (no separate procedures).
Model Cities Program (no separate procedures).
Open Space and Public Facilities Assistance (no separate procedures).
Mortgage Insurance Programs (no separate procedures).

DEPARTMENT OF THE INTERIOR

Departmental procedures dated October 2, 1971; 36 F.R. 19343–19347.
Bonneville Power Administration (no separate procedures received).
Bureau of Indian Affairs (no separate procedures received).
Bureau of Land Management (no separate procedures received).
Bureau of Mines (no separate procedures received).
Bureau of Outdoor Recreation (no separate procedures received).
Bureau of Reclamation (no separate procedures received).
Bureau of Sport Fisheries and Wildlife (no separate procedures received).
National Park Service (no separate procedures received).
Office of Coal Research (no separate procedures received).
Office of Saline Water (no separate procedures received).
U.S. Geological Survey (no separate procedures received).

DEPARTMENT OF JUSTICE

Law Enforcement Assistance Administration, Procedures dated October 27, 1971; 36 F.R. 20613–20617.

DEPARTMENT OF STATE

Departmental procedures dated December 1, 1971.
Agency for International Development, Special procedures for Capital Projects dated September 1, 1971.
International Boundary Water Commission (United States-Mexico), Procedures dated August 21, 1971.

DEPARTMENT OF TRANSPORTATION

Departmental procedures dated October 4, 1971 (text follows this notice).
Coast Guard, Procedures dated October 13, 1971 (text follows this notice).
Federal Aviation Administration, Airport Development Aid Program Procedures dated December 7, 1970, amended June 25, 1971 (text follows this notice).
Federal Highway Administration, Procedures dated August 24, 1971 (text follows the notice).
St. Lawrence Seaway Administration (no separate procedures received).
Urban Mass Transportation Administration (no separate procedures received).

ENVIRONMENTAL PROTECTION AGENCY

Procedures dated December 1, 1971 (text to be published separately).

FEDERAL COMMUNICATIONS COMMISSION

(No procedures received.)

FEDERAL MARITIME COMMISSION

(No procedures received.)

FEDERAL POWER COMMISSION

Procedures dated December 15, 1970; 35 F.R. 18958–18960.
Amendments dated April 16, 1971; 36 F.R. 7232–7233; November 30, 1971; 36 F.R. 22738–22741.

FEDERAL TRADE COMMISSION

Procedures dated December 1, 1971; 36 F.R. 22814–22815.

GENERAL SERVICES ADMINISTRATION

Federal Supply Service, Procedures dated September 15, 1971 (text follows this notice).
Property Management and Disposal Service, Procedures dated September 15, 1971 (text follows this notice).
Public Buildings Service, Procedures dated September 15, 1971; 36 F.R. 23336–23338, 23652–23654.
Transportation and Communications Service, Procedures dated June 30, 1971; 36 F.R. 23274–23275.

INTERSTATE COMMERCE COMMISSION

Procedures dated May 26, 1971; 36 F.R. 10807–10810.

NATIONAL AERONAUTICS AND SPACE ADMINISTRATION

Procedures dated October 31, 1971; 36 F.R. 21753–21755 (Published in the FEDERAL REGISTER under Title 14, Chapter V, Subpart 1204.11).

NATIONAL CAPITAL PLANNING COMMISSION

Procedures dated August 9, 1971 (text follows this notice).

NATIONAL SCIENCE FOUNDATION

Procedures dated November 15, 1971 (text follows this notice).

OFFICE OF ECONOMIC OPPORTUNITY

Procedures dated July 1, 1971.

OFFICE OF MANAGEMENT AND BUDGET

Procedures dated September 14, 1971 (text follows this notice).

SMALL BUSINESS ADMINISTRATION

(No procedures received.)

TENNESSEE VALLEY AUTHORITY

Procedures dated November 2, 1971; 36 F.R. 21010–21014.

DEPARTMENT OF THE TREASURY

Departmental procedures dated July 31, 1971; 36 F.R. 14221–14222.
Internal Revenue Service, Procedures dated August 12, 1971; 36 F.R. 15061–15062.

UNITED STATES POSTAL SERVICE

(No procedures received.)

Summary of NEPA environmental impact statements filed with the CEQ through January 31, 1972 (by agency)

Agency	Draft 102's for actions on which no final 102's have yet been received	Final 102's on legislation and actions	Total actions on which final or draft 102 statements for federal actions have been received.
Agriculture, Department of	51	97	148
Appalachian Regional Commission	1	0	1
Atomic Energy Commission	36	28	64
Commerce, Department of	1	7	8
Defense, Department of	3	2	5
Air Force	2	3	5
Army	6	7	13
Army Corps of Engineers	182	273	455
Navy	7	4	11
Delaware River Basin Commission	3	0	3
Environmental Protection Agency	10	9	19
Federal Power Commission	18	5	23
General Services Administration	15	24	39
HEW, Department of	0	1	1
HUD, Department of	13	15	28
Interior, Department of	59	36	95
International Boundary and Water Commission--U.S. & Mexico	1	4	5
National Aeronautics and Space Admin.	14	8	22
National Science Foundation	1	1	2
Office of Science and Technology	0	1	1
Tennessee Valley Authority	10	4	14
Transportation, Department of	846	570	1416
Treasury, Department of	1	3	4
U.S. Water Resources Council	5	0	5
Veterans Administration	1	0	1
	1286	1102	2388

Summary of NEPA environmental impact statements filed with the CEQ through January 31, 1972 (By project type)

	Draft statements for actions on which no final statements have yet been filed	Final statements on legislation and actions	Total actions on which final or draft statements for federal actions have been taken
AEC nuclear development	9	11	20
Aircraft, ships and vehicles	0	5	5
Airports	34	133	167
Buildings	1	5	6
Bridge permits	10	8	18
Defense systems	2	2	4
Forestry	2	4	6
Housing, urban problems, new communities	8	10	18
International boundary	4	2	6
Land acquisition, disposal	13	29	42
Mass transit	2	2	4
Mining	4	2	6
Military installations	14	4	18
Natural gas & oil			
Drilling and exploration	3	5	8
Transportation, pipeline	5	3	8
Parks, wildlife refuges, recreation facilities	20	16	36
Pesticides, herbicides	10	11	21
Power			
Hydroelectric	19	5	24
Nuclear	26	16	42
Other	16	1	17
Transmission	7	7	14
Railroads	0	1	1
Roads	665	397	1062
Plus roads through parks	126	27	153
Space programs	4	4	8
Waste disposal			
Detoxification of toxic substances	6	2	8
Munition disposal	2	3	5
Radioactive waste disposal	5	1	6
Sewage facilities	9	5	14
Solid wastes	1	0	1
Water			
Beach erosion, hurricane protection	5	20	25
Irrigation	17	9	26
Navigation	53	97	150
Municipal & Industrial supply	7	1	8
Permit (Refuse Act, dredge and fill)	9	1	10
Watershed protection & flood control	128	229	357
Weather Modification	7	4	11
Research & Development	14	6	20
Miscellaneous	19	14	33
	1286	1102	2388

Background and sources of NEPA

Excerpted from <u>Selected Materials on the Calvert Cliffs Decision, Its Origin and Aftermath,</u> Joint Committee on Atomic Energy, Congress of the United States, 68-699 GPO, 1972 at 14 & 32.

NOTE: This discussion of the background of the National Environmental Policy Act of 1969 was not available when the main body of this chapter was prepared. It is added here to give the reader an alternate view to that given in the opening pages of this chapter.

I. General Background and Brief Legislative History

S. 1075 was introduced on February 18, 1969, by Senator Jackson D-Wash., and referred to the Senate Committee on Interior and Insular Affairs.[1] The bill as introduced was substantially different from the bill as reported by the Committee and passed by the Senate. Hearings on S. 1075 and two related bills introduced by Senators Nelson, D-Wisc., (S. 1752), and McGovern, D-S.D., (S. 237), were held on April 16, 1969, before the full Committee on Interior and Insular Affairs.[2] At the hearings, spokesmen for the Administration indicated opposition to the measure on the ground that the role of the Council on Environmental Quality which would be established by the bill in the Executive Office of the President [3] would duplicate the role of an "Environmental Quality Council" which the President was planning to establish.[4] However, these same spokesmen indicated general support for a declaration of a national environmental policy.[5] On May 29, 1969, Senator Jackson introduced an amendment to S. 1075 which incorporated into Title I of the bill an elaborate declaration of national environmental policy.[6] On June 18, 1969, the measure was considered by the Committee in executive session and ordered reported ot the Senate. However, at the request of the Director of the Office of Science and Technology and representatives of the BOB, the Committee voted on July 8, 1969, to reconsider the measure for the purpose of considering additional amendments. These amendments were proposed by the BOB in a July 7, 1969, letter to Senator Jackson, the Committee Chairman. The BOB proposed amendments to Titles I and II of S. 1075 were adopted while the BOB proposed amendments to Title III were adopted in part and rejected in part. Following the adoption of other amendments suggested by members of the Committee, the measure was again ordered reported to the Senate on July 8, 1969.[7] The Report was filed in the Senate on July 9, 1969,[8] and, upon the grant of a unanimous consent request that it be considered, the bill was passed by the Senate the next day.[9]

The House version of the measure was H.R. 12549, a bill introduced by Congressman Dingell, D-Mich., on July 1, 1969, and referred to the House Committee on Merchant Marine and Fisheries. H.R. 12549 contained nothing similar to the declaration of policy in Title I of S. 1075 in the form in which S. 1075 passed the Senate. Numerous other bills substantially identical to H.R. 12549 were also introduced and referred to Merchant Marine and Fisheries.[10] In addition, bills with an elabo-

[1] 115 Cong. Rec. S1780 (daily ed., February 18, 1969).

[2] *National Environmental Policy, Hearings Before the Committee on Interior and Insular Affairs, United States Senate, on S. 1075, S. 237, and S. 1752,* 91st Cong., 1st Sess. (1969) [hereinafter cited as "Hearings"]. See also *Joint House-Senate Colloquim to Discuss a National Policy for the Environment, Hearings Before the Committee on Interior and Insular Affairs, United States Senate, and the Committee on Science and Astronautics, U.S. House of Representatives,* 90th Cong., 2d Sess. (1968).

[3] The "Council on Environmental Quality" was changed to the "Board of Environmental Quality Advisers" in S. 1075 as reported and passed by the Senate. The conferees changed the name back to "Council on Environmental Quality."

[4] An "Environmental Quality Council" and a "Citizens' Advisory Committee on Environmental Quality" were both established by Executive Order 11472 on May 29, 1969.

[5] Hearings at 3, 6, 7. 73, 84, 90, 95.

[6] 115 Cong. Rec. S5995 (daily ed., June 5, 1969); 115 Cong. Rec. S5819 (daily ed., May 29, 1969).

[7] The information as to Committee reconsideration of the measure was obtained from the Senate Report and from an exhibit inserted into the Congressional Record by Senator Jackson in connection with instructions to the conferees on S. 1075 and debate on S. 7. 115 Cong. Rec. S12124 (daily ed., October 8, 1969). The BOB letter of July 7, 1969, is printed in S. Rep. No. 91-296, 91st Cong., 1st Sess. (1969).

[8] S. Rep. No. 91-296, 91st Cong., 1st Sess. (1969); 115 Cong. Rec. S7726 (daily ed., July 9, 1969).

[9] 115 Cong. Rec. S7813 (daily ed., July 10, 1969).

[10] These included H.R. 13042, H.R. 12603, H.R. 12932, H.R. 12928, H.R. 12877, H.R. 12573, H.R. 12527, H.R. 12525, H.R. 12511, H.R. 12507, H.R. 12506, H.R. 12503, H.R. 12228, H.R. 12209. H.R. 12207, H.R. 12180, H.R. 12077, H.R. 11942, and H.R. 11886.

rate declaration of national environmental policy substantially identical to that in S. 1075 as passed by the Senate were introduced and referred variously to the House Committees on Science and Astronautics,[11] Merchant Marine and Fisheries,[12] Interior and Insular Affairs,[13] and Government Operations.[14] Because of a question over which committee or committees had legislative jurisdiction over the subject matter of the bill, S. 1075 as passed by the Senate was not referred to any House committee, but rather held on the Speaker's table.[15] H.R. 12549 was reported to the House on July 11, 1969,[16] and passed by the House, with amendments, on September 23, 1969. Passage of H.R. 12549 was then vacated, S. 1075 taken from the Speaker's table, amended by substituting the text of the House-passed bill H.R. 12549, and passed by the House as so amended. The House then insisted upon its amendments to the Senate-passed S. 1075, requested a conference with the Senate, and appointed conferees.[17]

Because of the possible overlap between the Board of Environmental Quality Advisors which would have been established by Title III of the Senate-passed S. 1075,[18] and the Office of Environmental Quality which would have been established by Title II of S. 7,[19] the provisions of S. 1075 came up for discussion on the Senate floor during Senate consideration of S. 7. During consideration of S. 7, an amended version of Title II of S. 7 was agreed upon, the Senate formally disagreed to the House amendments to S. 1075, agreed to the House request for a conference on the measure, appointed Senate conferees, and then instructed these conferees to insist upon an amended version of S. 1075 (different from the Senate or House-passed versions) in the conference.[20]

A Conference Report and accompanying Statement by the House conferees were filed in the House on December 17, 1969.[21] The version of the bill recommended by the conferees generally followed the lines of the Senate-passed version but differed in several specifics both from the Senate-passed version and from the version the Senate conferees had been instructed to insist upon. The Conference Report was filed in and agreed to by the Senate on December 20, 1969,[22] and the Report was agreed to by the House on December 22, 1969.[23]

The President approved the measure on January 1, 1970.

S. 1075 as passed by the Senate July 10, 1969

SHORT TITLE

SECTION 1. That this Act may be cited as the "National Environmental Policy Act of 1969".

PURPOSE

SEC. 2. The purposes of this Act are: To declare a national policy which will encourage productive and enjoyable harmony between man and his environment; to promote efforts which will prevent or eliminate damage to the environment and biosphere and stimulate the health and welfare of man; to enrich the understanding of the ecological systems and natural resources important to the Nation; and to establish a Board of Environmental Quality Advisers.

TITLE I

DECLARATION OF NATIONAL ENVIRONMENTAL POLICY

SEC. 101. (a) The Congress, recognizing that man depends on his biological and physical surroundings for food, shelter, and other needs, and for cultural enrichment as well; and recognizing further the profound influences of population growth, high-density urbanization, industrial expansion, resource exploita-

[11] H.R. 13272 (Daddario, D–Conn.).
[12] H.R. 12143 (Nedzi, D–Mich.).
[13] H.R. 12900 (Saylor, R–Pa.) and H.R. 11937 (Foley, D–Wash.).
[14] H.R. 11952 (Reuss, D–Wisc.). Hearings on H.R. 11952 were held on July 9, 1969, before the Committee.
[15] This was apparently done upon a determination that S. 1075, as passed by the Senate, was "substantially the same as" H.R. 12549 as reported. *See* House of Representatives Rule XXIV, cl. 2.
[16] H.R. Rep. No. 91–378, 91st Cong., 1st Sess. (1969).
[17] 115 Cong. Rec. H8263 (daily ed., Sept. 23, 1969).
[18] See note 3, *supra*.
[19] S. 7 was introduced by Senator Muskie, D–Maine, on January 15, 1969. The provisions of S. 7 establishing an Office of Environmental Quality in the Executive Office of the President first appeared in the bill as reported by the Senate Public Works Committee on August 7, 1969. S. Rep. No. 91–351, 91st Cong., 1st Sess. (1969).
[20] S. 1075 was discussed in 115 Cong. Rec. S12108–S12147 (daily ed., October 8, 1969). The amended version of S. 1075 is printed in 115 Cong. Rec. S12109 (daily ed., October 8, 1969).
[21] 115 Cong. Rec. H12633 (daily ed., December 17, 1969), H.R. Rep. No. 91–765, 91st Cong., 1st Sess. (1969).
[22] 115 Cong. Rec. S17462 (daily ed., December 20, 1969).
[23] 115 Cong. Rec. H13096 (daily ed., December 23, 1969).

tion, and new and expanding technological advances on our physical and biological surroundings and on the quality of life available to the American people; hereby declares that it is the continuing policy and responsibility of the Federal Government to use all practicable means, consistent with other essential considerations of national policy, to improve and coordinate Federal plans, functions, programs, and resources to the end that the Nation may—

(1) fulfill the responsibilities of each generation as trustee of the environment for succeeding generations;

(2) assure for all Americans safe, healthful, productive, and esthetically and culturally pleasing surroundings;

(3) attain the widest range of beneficial uses of the environment without degradation, risk to health or safety, or other undesirable and unintended consequences;

(4) preserve important historic, cultural, and natural aspects of our national heritage, and maintain, wherever possible, an environment which supports diversity and variety of individual choice;

(5) achieve a balance between population and resource use which will permit high standards of living and a wide sharing of life's amenities; and

(6) enhance the quality of renewable resources and approach the maximum attainable recycling of depletable resources.

(b) The Congress recognizes that each person has a fundamental and inalienable right to a healthful environment and that each person has a responsibility to contribute to the preservation and enhancement of the environment.

Sec. 102. The Congress authorizes and directs that the policies, regulations, and public laws of the United States to the fullest extent possible, be interpreted and administered in accordance with the policies set forth in this Act, and that all agencies of the Federal Government—

(a) utilize to the fullest possible a systematic, interdisciplinary approach which will insure the integrated use of the natural and social sciences and the environmental design arts in planning and in decisionmaking which may have an impact on man's environment;

(b) identify and develop methods and procedures which will insure that presently unquantified environmental amenities and values may be given appropriate consideration in decisionmaking along with economic and technical considerations;

(c) include in every recommendation or report on proposals for legislation and other major Federal actions significantly affecting the quality of the human environment, a finding by the responsible official that—

(i) the environmental impact of the proposed action has been studied and considered;

(ii) any adverse environmental effects which cannot be avoided by following reasonable alternatives are justified by other stated considerations of national policy;

(iii) local short-term uses of man's environment are consistent with maintaining and enhancing long-term productivity; and that

(iv) any irreversible and irretrievable commitments of resources are warranted.

(d) study, develop, and describe appropriate alternatives to recommended courses of action in any proposal which involves unresolved conflicts concerning alternative uses of land, water, or air;

(e) recognize the worldwide and long-range character of environmental problems and lend appropriate support to initiatives, resolutions, and programs designed to maximize international cooperation in anticipating and preventing a decline in the quality of mankind's world environment; and

(f) review present statutory authority, administrative regulations, and current policies and procedures for conformity to the purposes and provisions of this Act and propose to the President and to the Congress such measures as may be necessary to make their authority consistent with this Act.

Sec. 103. The policies and goals set forth in this Act are supplementary to, but shall not be considered to repeal the existing mandates and authorizations of Federal agencies.

TITLE II

Sec. 201. To carry out the purposes of this Act, all agencies of the Federal Government in conjunction with their existing programs and authorities, are hereby authorized—

(a) to conduct investigations ,studies, surveys, research, and analyses relating to ecological systems and environmental quality;

(b) to document and define changes in the natural environment, including the plant and animal systems, and to accumulate necessary data and other information for a continuing analysis of these changes or trends and an interpretation of their underlying causes;

(c) to evaluate and disseminate information of an ecological nature to public and private agencies or organizations, or individuals in the form of reports, publications, atlases, and maps;

(d) to make available to States, counties, municipalities, institutions, and individuals, advice and information useful in restoring, maintaining, and enhancing the quality of the environment;

(e) to initiate and utilize ecological information in the planning and development of resource-oriented projects;

(f) to conduct research and studies within natural areas under Federal ownership which are under the jurisdiction of the Federal agencies; and

(g) to assist the Board of Environmental Quality Advisers established under title III of this Act and any council or committee established by the President to deal with environmental problems.

Sec. 202. (a) In carrying out the provisions of this title, the President is authorized to designate an agency or agencies to—

(1) make grants, including training grants, and enter into contracts or cooperative agreements with public or private agencies or organizations, or

individuals, and to accept and use donations of funds, property, personal services, or facilities to carry out the purposes of this Act;

(2) develop and maintain an inventory of existing and future natural resource development projects, engineering works, and other major projects and programs contemplated or planned by public or private agencies or organizations which make significant modifications in the natural environment;

(3) establish a system of collecting and receiving information and data on ecological research and evaluations which are in progress or are planned by other public or private agencies or organizations, or individuals; and

(4) assist and advise State and local government, and private enterprise in bringing their activities into conformity with the purposes of this Act and other Acts designed to enhance the quality of the environment.

(b) There are hereby authorized to be appropriated $500,000 annually for fiscal years 1971 and 1972, and $1,000,000 for each fiscal year thereafter.

SEC. 203. In recognition of the additional duties which the President may assign to the Office of Science and Technology to support any council or committee established by the President to deal with environmental problems and in furtherance of the policies established by this Act, there is hereby established in the Office of Science and Technology an additional office with the title "Deputy Director of the Office of Science and Technology." The Deputy Director shall be appointed by the President by and with the advice and consent of the Senate, shall perform such duties as the Director of the Office of Science and Technology shall from time to time direct, and shall be compensated at the rate provided for Level IV of the Executive Schedule Pay Rates (5 U.S.C. 5315).

TITLE III

SEC. 301. (a) There is created in the Executive Office of the President a Board of Environmental Quality Advisers (hereinafter referred to as the "Board"). The Board shall be composed of three members who shall be appointed by the President to serve at his pleasure, by and with the advice and consent of the Senate. Each member shall, as a result of training, experience, or attainments, be professionally qualified to analyze and interpret environmental trends of all kinds and descriptions and shall be conscious of and responsive to the scientific, economic, social, esthetic, and cultural needs and interest of this Nation. The President shall designate the Chairman and Vice Chairman of the Board from such members.

(b) Members of the Board shall serve full time and the Chairman of the Board shall be compensated at the rate provided for Level II of the Executive Schedule Pay Rates (5 U.S.C. 5313). The other members of the Board shall be compensated at the rate provided for Level IV of the Executive Schedule Pay Rates (5 U.S.C. 5315).

SEC. 302. (a) The primary function of the Board shall be to study and analyze environmental trends and the factors that effect these trends relating each area of study and analysis to the conservation, social, economic, and health goals of this Nation. In carrying out this function, the Board shall—

(1) report at least once each year to the President on the state and condition of the environment;

(2) provide advice, assistance, and staff support to the President on the formulation of national policies to foster and promote the improvement of environmental quality; and

(3) obtain information using existing sources, to the greatest extent practicable, concerning the quality of the environmental and make such information available to the public.

(b) The Board shall periodically review and appraise Federal programs, projects, activities, and policies which affect the quality of the environment and make recommendations thereon to the President.

(c) It shall be the duty and function of the Board to assist and advise the President in the preparation of the annual environmental quality report required under section 303.

(d) The Board and the Office of Science and Technology shall carry out their duties under the provisions of this Act at the direction of the President and shall perform whatever additional duties he may from time to time direct.

SEC. 303. The President shall transmit to the Congress, beginning June 30, 1970, an annual environmental quality report which shall set forth: (a) the status and condition of the major natural, manmade, or altered environmental classes of the Nation: and (b) current and foreseeable trends in quality, management, and utilization of such environments and the effects of those trends on the social, economic, and other requirements of the Nation.

SEC. 304. The Board may employ such officers and employees as may be necessary to carry out its functions under this Act. In addition, the Board may employ and fix the compensation of such experts and consultants as may be necessary for the carrying out of its functions under this Act, in accordance with section 3109 of title 5, United States Code (but without regard to the last sentence thereof).

SEC. 305. There are hereby authorized to be appropriated $1,000,000 annually to carry out the purposes of this title.

Amend the title so as to read: "A bill to establish a national policy for the environment; to authorize studies, surveys, and research relating to ecological systems, natural resources, and the quality of the human environment; and to establish a Board of Environmental Quality Advisers."

S. 1075 as passed by the House September 23, 1969

Motion offered by Mr. DINGELL: Strike out all after the enacting clause of S. 1075 and insert in lieu thereof the provisions of H.R. 12549, as passed, as follows:

"That the Congress, recognizing the profound impact of man's activity on the interrelations of all components of the natural environment, both living and nonliving, and the critical importance of restoring and maintaining environmental quality to the overall welfare and development of man, declares that it is the continuing policy of the Federal Government, in cooperation with State and local governments, urban and rural planners, industry, labor, agriculture, science, and conservation organizations, to use all practicable means and measures, including financial and technical assistance, in a manner calculated to foster and promote the general welfare, to create and maintain conditions under which man and nature can exist in productive harmony, and fulfill the social, economic and other requirements of present and future generations of Americans.

"SEC. 2. The President shall transmit to the Congress annually beginning June 30, 1970, an Environmental Quality Report (hereinafter referred to as the 'report') which shall set forth (1) the status and condition of the major natural, manmade, or altered environmental classes of the Nation, including, but not limited to, the air, the aquatic, including marine, estuarine, and fresh water, and the terrestrial environment, including, but not limited to, the forest, dryland, wetland, range, urban, suburban, and rural environment; (2) current and foreseeable trends in management and utilization of such environments and the effects of those trends on the social, economic, and other requirements of the Nation; (3) the adquacy of available natural resources for fulfilling human and economic requirements of the Nation in the light of expected population pressures; (4) a review of the programs and activities (including regulatory activities) of the Federal Government, the State and local governments, and nongovernmental entities or individuals, with particular reference to their effect on the environment and on the conservation, development, and utilization of natural resources; and (5) a program for remedying the deficiencies of existing programs and activities, together with recommendations for legislation.

"SEC. 3. There is created in the Executive Office of the President a Council on Environmental Quality (hereafter referred to as the "Council"). The Council shall be composed of five members who shall be appointed by the President, one of whom the President shall designate as chairman, and each of whom shall be a person who, as a result of his training, experience, and attainments, is exceptionally qualified to analyze and interpret environmental information of all kinds, to appraise programs and activities of the Government in the light of the policy set forth in subsection (a) of this section, and to formulate and recommend national policy to promote the improvement of our environmental quality.

"SEC. 4. The Council may employ such officers and employees as may be necessary to carry out its functions under this Act. In addition, the Council may employ and fix the compensation of such experts and consultants as may be necessary for the carrying out of its functions under this section, in accordance with section 3109 of title 5, United States Code (but without regard to the last sentence thereof).

"SEC. 5. It shall be the duty and function of the Council—

"(a) to assist and advise the President in the preparation of the Environmental Quality Report;

"(b) to gather timely and authoritative information concerning the conditions and trends in environmental quality both current and prospective, to analyze and interpret such information for the purpose of determining whether such conditions and trends are interfering, or are likely to interfere, with the achievement of the policy set forth in subsection (a) of this section, and to compile and submit to the President studies relating to such conditions and trends;

"(c) to appraise the various programs and activities of the Federal Government in the light of the policy set forth in subsection (a) of this section for the purpose of determining the extent to which such programs and activities are contributing to the achievement of such policy, and to make recommendations to the President with respect thereto;

"(d) to develop and recommend to the President national policies to foster and promote the improvement of environmental quality to meet social, economic, and other requirements of the Nation; and

"(e) to make and furnish such studies, reports thereon, and recommendations with respect to matters of policy and legislation as the President may request.

"SEC. 6. The Council shall make an annual report to the President in May of each year.

"SEC. 7. In exercising its powers, functions, and duties under this section—

"(a) the Council shall consult with such representatives of science, industry, agriculture, labor, conservation, organizations, State and local governments, and other groups, as it deems advisable; and

"(b) the Council shall, to the fullest extent possible, utilize the services, facilities, and information (including statistical information) of public and private agencies and organizations, and individuals, in order that duplication of effort and expense may be avoided.

"SEC. 8. (a) Section 5313 of title 5, United States Code, is amended by adding at the end thereof the following:

"(20) Chairman, Council on Environmental Quality."

"(b) Section 5315 of title 5, United States Code, is amended by adding, at the end thereof, the following:

"(92) Members, Council on Environmental Quality."

"SEC. 9. Nothing in this Act shall increase, decrease, or change any responsibility or authority of any Federal official or agency created by other provision of law.

"SEC. 10. There are authorized to be appropriated to carry out the provisions of this Act not to exceed $300,000 for fiscal year 1970, $500,000 for fiscal year 1971, and $1,000,000 for each fiscal year thereafter.

"Amend the title so as to read: 'An Act to provide for the establishment of a Council on Environmental Quality, and for other purposes.' "

Court decisions under NEPA

CUMULATIVE LIST OF REPORTED JUDICIAL DECISIONS INVOLVING THE NATIONAL ENVIRONMENTAL POLICY ACT OF 1969 THROUGH DECEMBER 31, 1971

UNITED STATES SUPREME COURT

Supreme Court

Committee for Nuclear Responsibility v. Seaborg, ___U.S.___, 3 ERC 1276 (Douglas, Brennan, and Marshall, JJ., dissenting). The court denied an injunction, pending action on a petition for certiorari, against the underground nuclear test Cannikin. Justice Douglas' dissent discusses possible defects in the AEC's 102 statement.

San Antonio Conservation Society v. Texas Highway Dept., 2 ERC 1083, 1 ELR 20069 (12/21/70) (Black, Douglas, Brennan, JJ., dissenting from denial of cert.). The dissenting Justices stated that NEPA does apply to Federally funded State highway projects, and that the Supreme Court should have taken for review, prior to decision in Court of Appeals, this dispute concerning a highway project for which an environmental statement under section 102(2)(C) was not prepared. There has been a further decision in the 5th Circuit referred to below.

2606.84 Acres v. United States, 2 ERC 1623, 1 ELR 20155 (4/19/71) (Douglas, Black, JJ., dissenting from denial of cert.). A landowner challenged the taking of his land for a Corps of Engineers project on the ground that the project had been expanded so radically since its authorization by Congress that a new authorization was required. The Fifth Circuit rejected this claim, and the Supreme Court denied certiorari. The dissenting Justices argued that the case warranted review partially to determine whether the Corps had complied with NEPA with respect to future work on the project.

UNITED STATES COURTS OF APPEALS

U.S. Courts of Appeals

Calvert Cliffs' Coordinating Comm. v. AEC, 2 ERC 1779, 1 ELR 20346 (D.C. Cir. 7/23/71). The court found the AEC's rules for implementing NEPA in licensing nuclear power plants invalid in four respects: (1) the rules failed to require hearing boards to consider environmental factors unless raised by the regulatory staff or outside persons; (2) they excluded nonradiological environmental issues in all cases where the notice of hearing was published before 3/4//71; (3) they prohibited reconsideration of water quality impacts where a certification of compliance with State standards had been obtained; and (4) they failed to provide for environmental review of cases in which a construction permit had been granted prior to NEPA's effective date but the time was not yet ripe for granting an operating license.

Committee for Nuclear Responsibility v. Seaborg, 3 ERC 1126, 1210, 1256 (D.C. Cir. 10/5/71, 10/28/71, 11/3/71). The court reversed a summary judgment for defendants, holding that plaintiffs had alleged a legally sufficient claim that the AEC's 102 statement on the underground nuclear test Cannikin was deficient under NEPA. The court later upheld the district judge's order requiring release of Government documents, which were not part of the 102 statement, discussing environmental aspects of the proposed test. However, the court refused to stay the test *pendente lite.* Finally, after release of the documents, the court refused on national security grounds to delay the test—without deciding whether NEPA had been satisfied. (The Supreme Court later upheld this refusal.)

Ely v. Velde, 3 ERC 1280 (4th Cir. 11/8/71). The court, in reversing a district court decision, held that the Law Enforcement Assistance Administration must prepare a 102 statement on the portion of a block grant to the State of Virginia that will be used to construct a prison facility in a historic area.

Lathan v. Volpe, 3 ERC 1362 (9th Cir. 11/15/71). The court held that citizens were entitled to a preliminary injunction against further acquisition of property by the State of Washington for Interstate 90 in Seattle until Federal officials prepared a 102 statement.

National Helium Corp. v. Morton, 3 ERC 1129, 1 ELR 20478 (10th Cir. 10/4/71). The court upheld a preliminary injunction against the Interior Department's cancellation of contracts to buy helium, on the basis of noncompliance with NEPA.

Pennsylvania Environmental Council v. Bartlett, 3 ERC 1421 (3d Cir. 12/1/71). The court upheld a district court ruling that a 102 statement was not required for a Federal-aid highway project for which all Federal approvals were given and all contracts awarded prior to enactment of NEPA.

San Antonio Conservation Society v. Texas Highway Department, 2 ERC 1872, 1 ELR 20379 (5th Cir. 8/5/71). The court stayed construction of a highway through a park in San Antonio, on the basis of noncompliance with NEPA and other laws. The court held that the "segments" of the highway adjacent to the park must be considered together with the park "segment" in the application of these laws. It further held that, since the highway had been approved for Federal funding, the State could not defeat the application of the Federal laws by proceeding without Federal funds.

Scenic Hudson Preservation Conf. v. FPC, 3 ERC 1232 (2d Cir. 10/22/71). The court upheld the FPC's grant of a license for the Storm King pumped storage power plant. The court found that the FPC had considered all relevant factors as required by NEPA, and that its findings were supported by substantial evidence.

Thermal Ecology Must Be Preserved v. AEC, 2 ERC 1379, 1 ELR 20078 (D.C. Cir. 7/20/70). The court refused to grant an order restraining AEC hearings on a permit application for a nuclear power plant near South Haven, Michigan. Citizen groups claimed the hearings were illegal under NEPA because the AEC was refusing to consider the dangers of thermal pollution or of cumulative radiation. However, the court said that this question could be raised only on review of a final AEC order.

Thermal Ecology Must Be Preserved v. AEC, 2 ERC 1405 (7th Cir. 8/24/70). The court refused to grant an order restraining AEC hearings on a permit application for a nuclear power plant near South Haven, Michigan. The court relied on the D.C. Circuit ruling of the same name.

Upper Pecos Assn. v. Stans, 2 ERC 1418 (10th Cir. 12/7/71). The court affirmed a district court ruling that the Economic Development Administration did not have to prepare a 102 statement on a grant for road construction, since the Forest Service was the lead agency in developing the road and had prepared a statement on it. Although the Forest Service's 102 statement was not prepared until after the EDA had made an offer of funds, the court held that this timing satisfied NEPA because the Forest Service still had full authority to grant or deny a right-of-way, and the application for EDA funds was made prior to enactment of NEPA.

West Virginia Highlands Conservancy v. Island Creek Coal Co., 2 ERC 1422, 1 ELR 20160 (4th Cir. 4/6/71). The court upheld the standing of a citizen group under NEPA and the Wilderness Act to challenge the Forest Service's permission of private timber cutting and road construction in Monongahela National Forest. The citizen group charged that a 102 statement should have been prepared, and that the area was protected by the Wilderness Act until studied for wilderness character. Without deciding these claims, the court found them sufficiently strong to justify a preliminary injunction pending further proceedings in the district court.

Zabel v. Tabb, 1 ERC 1449, 1 ERC 20023 (5th Cir. 7/16/70), *cert. denied,* 39 U.S.L.W. 3360 (2/22/71). The court held that the Army Corps of Engineers has authority to deny a dredge and fill permit under 33 U.S.C. 403 on ecological grounds, basing its holdings in part on NEPA.

U.S. District Courts

UNITED STATES DISTRICT COURTS

Arlington Coalition on Transportation v. Volpe, 3 ERC 1138 (E.D. Va. 10/8/71). The court dismissed a suit to enjoin construction of Interstate 66 through Arlington. It held that NEPA was inapplicable to portions of the highway approved before January 1, 1970, and found that a 102 statement would be prepared before approval of additional work. The decision was reversed by the 4th Circuit, in an unreported opinion.

Berkson v. Morton, 3 ERC 1121 (D. Md. 10/1/71. The court issued a 10-day temporary restraining order against construction in the C&O Canal National Historic Park without compliance with NEPA and other Federal statutes. This order has subsequently been extended.

Brooks v. Volpe, 2 ERC 1004, 1571, 1 ELR 20045, 20286 (W.D. Wash. 9/25/70, 4/6/71). The court held that a 102 statement was not required for an Interstate highway segment whose location had been approved in 1967. The court upheld the standing of the individual plaintiffs to bring the suit, but denied the standing of the environmental groups.

Bucklein v. Volpe, 2 ERC 1082, 1 ELR 20043 (N.D. Cal. 10/29/70). The court refused an injunction against disbursement of Federal emergency funds for a road relocation project. The plaintiff challenged the location of the road as an abuse of discretion, arguing that an alternative location was environmentally preferable. The court found that there had been "ample consideration" of environmental factors, and stated that it is unlikely that the policy declaration in Section 101 of NEPA was intended to create "court enforcible duties."

Businessmen for the Public Interest v. Resor, 3 ERC 1216 (N.D. Ill. 10/14/71). The court ruled that citizens could not sue to challenge the application of the Refuse Act permit program to Lake Michigan until the Corps of Engineers proposed to issue a permit under the program. However, the court went on to uphold the regulations implementing the program, relying in part on NEPA.

Citizens to Preserve Foster Park v. Volpe, 3 ERC 1031, 1 ELR 20389 (N.D. Ind. 8/18/71). The court denied a preliminary injunction against further work on a federally assisted highway. The court found that a 102 statement prepared in June 1970 complied with NEPA "to the extent possible" even though it did not comply with guidelines and procedures issued before that date. The court stressed that the park affected by the highway was already as "torn up" as it would be from further construction.

Coastal Petroleum Co. v. Secretary of the Army, 1 ERC 1475 (S.D. Fla. 7/1/70). The court held, on the basis of the District Court ruling (later reversed) in *Zabel v. Tabb,* that the Corps of Engineers has no authority to deny a permit under 33 U.S.C. 403 on other than navigational grounds. However, the court refused to order the Corps to grant a permit for limestone mining in Lake Okeechobee because of environmental danger and because other remedies were available to protect the applicant's financial interests. NEPA was discussed in supplemental briefs after the trial, but the court found it "not to be applicable." The court later reversed itself, without opinion, on the basis of the 5th Circuit's decision in *Zabel.*

NEPA decisions: U.S. District Courts

Daly v. Volpe, 2 ERC 1506, 1 ELR 20242 (E.D. Wash. 4/9/71). Local residents sought an injunction against construction of an interstate highway segment near North Bend, Washington, asserting that the Department of Transportation had not complied with the requirements of NEPA. The segment, on which planning and hearings had begun before enactment of NEPA, was approved on November 30, 1970. At that time a draft environmental statement had been prepared, but agency comments were not received or a final statement prepared until after the approval. The court held that the Department of Transportation had substantially complied with NEPA in approving the segment, since the plans had been coordinated with many groups before approval, and agency procedures for formal circulation of draft environmental statements were still being developed.

Delaware v. Pennsylvania New York Central Transp. Co., 2 ERC 1355, 1 ELR 20106 (D. Del. 2/24/71). The court granted standing to a State and private persons to challenge the Corps of Engineers' issuance of permits to Penn Central for a dike and fill operation along the foreshore of the Delaware River. Plaintiffs allege, *inter alia,* that the Corps violated NEPA by giving inadequate consideration to the environmental effects of the operation. However, consideration of plaintiffs' claims will be delayed pending Penn Central's bankruptcy proceedings in another Federal court.

Dorothy Thomas Foundation v. Hardin, 1 ERC 1679 (W.D.N.C. 8/31/70). The court denied a preliminary injunction against timber cutting in a National Forest, finding that plaintiffs had not proven that the Federal defendants had failed to consider the factors required by NEPA and the Multiple Use and Sustained Yield Act.

Echo Park Residents Comm. v. Romney, 3 ERC 1255 (C.D. Cal. 5/11/71). The court upheld the finding by HUD that Federal assistance for a 66-unit apartment project would not significantly affect the environment and did not need a 102 statement.

Elliot v. Volpe, 2 ERC 1498, 1 ELR 20243 (D. Mass. 4/20/71). Plaintiffs sued to halt construction of interstate highway segments through Somerville, Massachusetts, asserting that the Department of Transportation had not complied with the requirements of NEPA. The court denied an injunction, on the ground that the planning and location of the segments had been completed and approved in 1966, and substantial construction had taken place before the enactment of NEPA. The court concluded that it would be an unwarranted "retroactive" application of NEPA to require a total halt in construction while the NEPA procedures were followed for the remaining action on the segments.

Ely v. Velde, 2 ERC 1185, 1 ELR 20082 (E.D. Va. 1/22/71). In a suit by neighboring property owners to contest a Federal grant to a State for construction of a prison facility, the court held that NEPA did not require the Federal granting agency to consider the environmental impact of the facility. The court stated that the Safe Streets Act of 1968 imposed a mandatory duty to award the funds, which was not modified by enactment of the "discretionary" provisions of NEPA in 1970. The decision was later reversed by the 4th Circuit.

Environmental Defense Fund, Inc. v. Corps of Engineers, 1 ELR 20130, 2 ERC 1260 (E.D. Ark. 2/19/71). Plaintiff environmental groups sued to enjoin further construction of The Gillham Dam, on which the Corps has prepared an environmental statement under section 102(2)(C). The court upheld plaintiffs' standing and held that NEPA was applicable even though the project was partially constructed prior to January 1, 1970. On the merits, the court rejected plaintiffs' argument that section 101 creates an enforceable duty not to undertake environmentally damaging projects. However, it found the environmental statement legally inadequate and enjoined further construction until the Corps has complied with sections 102(2)(A) (B), (C), (D) of NEPA.

Environmental Defense Fund, Inc. v. Corps of Engineers, 2 ERC 1173, 1797, 1 ELR 20079, 20366 (D. D.C. 1/27/71, 7/27/71). The court granted a preliminary injunction against further construction of the Cross-Florida Barge Canal. The court held that a 102 statement was required for further actions even though the project was begun before January 1, 1970. The case was later consolidated with others involving the canal and transferred to M.D. Fla. for pretrial proceedings.

NEPA decisions: U.S. District Courts

Environmental Defense Fund, Inc. v. Corps of Engineers, 3 ERC 1085, 1 ELR 20466 (D. D.C. 9/21/71). The court granted a preliminary injunction against construction of the Tennessee-Tombigbee Waterway. It ruled that the plaintiffs had made a sufficient showing of noncompliance with NEPA to warrant an injunction pending trial.

Environmental Defense Fund, Inc. v. Hardin, 2 ERC 1424, 1 ELR 20207 (D. D.C. 4/14/71). The court ruled that the Department of Agriculture's fire ant control program, involving dissemination of the pesticide Mirex, was a major action requiring an environmental statement under Section 102(2)(C) of NEPA. However, it refused a preliminary injunction against the program, on the ground that the Department had performed adequate studies of the program's environmental effects and had prepared an environmental statement discussing those effects in sufficient detail to satisfy all procedural requirements of Section 102(2)(C).

Gibson v. Ruckelshaus, 3 ERC 1028, 1 ELR 20337 (E.D. Tex. 3/1/71). The court granted an injunction against condemnation proceedings or Federal financing for a sewage treatment facility, on the ground that the Environmental Protection Agency had failed to comply with NEPA and the Federal Water Pollution Control Act. The 5th Cir. later reversed and remanded the case on the basis of the plaintiff's refusal to cooperate with the court (8/9/71, 3 ERC 1370.)

Goose Hollow Foothills League v. Romney, 3 ERC 1087 (D. Ore. 9/9/71). The court enjoined construction of a Federally assisted college high-rise housing project for failure to prepare a 102 statement. However, the court stayed its injunction for 90 days to permit the filing of the statement. The injunction was made effective on 12/8/71, 3 ERC 1457.

Harrisburg Coalition Against Ruining the Environment v. Volpe, 2 ERC 1671, 1 ELR 20237 (M.D. Pa. 5/12/71). In a suit to enjoin construction of Interstate 81 through a park, the court found that the Secretary of Transportation had not made the findings required by Section 4(f) of the DOT Act. The case was remanded for new findings by the Secretary and for preparation of a 102 statement in accordance with the CEQ guidelines.

Investment Syndicates, Inc. v. Richmond, 1 ERC 1713, 1 ELR 20044 (D. Ore. 10/27/70). A landowner sued to enjoin construction of a power line across his land on the basis of the failure of Bonneville Power Administration to prepare an environmental statement under section 102(2)(C). The court held that a statement was not required, noting that the project had been approved and funded and nearly half of the necessary easements purchased before January 1, 1970, and that evidence of the proposed right of way was visible on plaintiff's land when he purchased it.

Izaak Walton League v. Macchia, 2 ERC 1661 (D. N.J. 6/16/71). The court upheld the plaintiff's standing to sue private developers and the Corps of Engineers to stop the developers from dredging in navigable waters under a Corps permit. The court also rejected the defenses of sovereign immunity and laches, and continued the case for trial. The suit challenges the validity of the permit under NEPA and other Federal laws.

Izaak Walton League v. Schlesinger, 3 ERC 1453 (D. D.C. 12/13/71). The court granted a preliminary injunction against the AEC's issuance of a partial operating license for the Quad Cities nuclear reactor pending completion of the NEPA review of the application for a full operating license. The court held that the partial license was itself a major action requiring a 102 statement.

Izaak Walton League v. St. Clair, 1 ERC 1401 (D. Minn. 6/1/70). The court denied the Government's motion to dismiss a suit brought to invalidate private mineral claims in the Boundary Waters Canoe Area (a Wilderness Area). The court upheld the plaintiff's standing to sue and ruled that the suit was not barred by sovereign immunity.

Kalur v. Resor, 3 ERC 1485 (D. D.C. 12/21/71). In an action to review the Corps of Engineers' regulations governing the Refuse Act permit program, the court found the regulations invalid in two respects: (1) the regulations permitted the issuance of permits for discharges into nonnavigable tributaries of navigable waters; and (2) they failed to require 102 statements for the issuance of permits. The court enjoined further issuance of permits under the program.

LaRaza Unida v. Volpe, 3 ERC 1306 (N.D. Cal. 11/8/71). The court granted a preliminary injunction against construction or property acquisition for a Federally assisted highway in Alameda County. The court based its order on violations of other Federal statutes, leaving a claimed violation of NEPA for consideration at trial.

Lever Bros. Co. v. FTC, 2 ERC 1648, 1 ELR 20185 (D. Me. 4/19/71). Detergent manufacturers sought an injunction forbidding the FTC to hold hearings on a proposed rule to require special labeling of detergents, including a pollution warning on detergents containing phosphorus. The manufacturers claimed that the hearings were illegal because the FTC had not prepared an environmental impact statement under NEPA on the proposed rule. The district court denied an injunction on the ground that the legality of the FTC's procedures could be reviewed only on review of the final adoption of a rule. The manufacturers then moved in the First Circuit Court of Appeals for an injunction pending appeal, which was denied by a single judge on the ground that as long as an environmental statement will be released prior to adoption of a rule, the manufacturers will not suffer sufficient hardship to justify court review prior to such adoption. (4/20/71, 2 ERC 1651, 1 ELR 20328.) The appeal was apparently dropped before hearing in the full court of appeals.

NEPA decisions:
U.S. District Courts

Lloyd Harbor Study Group, Inc. v. Seaborg, 2 ERC 1380, 1 ELR 20188 (E.D. N.Y. 4/2/71). A citizen group sought a court order under NEPA requiring the AEC to consider nonradiological environmental effects in its hearings on a permit application for a nuclear power plant in Shoreham, Long Island. The AEC had refused to receive evidence of such effects. The court dismissed the suit on the ground that this refusal could be reviewed only by a Court of Appeals after entry of a final AEC order.

McQueary v. Laird, 3 ERC 1185 (D. Colo. 10/2/71). A citizen group sought a court order under NEPA requiring the AEC to consider nonradiological environmental effects in its hearings on a permit application for a nuclear power plant in Shoreham, Long Island. The AEC had refused to receive evidence of such effects. The court dismissed the suit on the ground that this refusal could be reviewed only by a Court of Appeals after entry of a final AEC order.

McQueary v. Laird, 3 ERC 1185 (D. Colo. 10/2/71). In a suit to enjoin the Defense Department from storing chemical and biological warfare agents at Rocky Mountain Arsenal, the court held that NEPA did not create a substantive right to prevent the storage. The court held that the decision to store the agents was within the Department's discretion.

Monroe County Conservation Assn. v. Hansen, 1 ELR 20362, 3 ERC 1208 (W.D. N.Y. 6/6/71). The court denied a preliminary injunction against Corps of Engineers dumping of dredge spoil into Lake Ontario, saying that under the circumstances no law, including NEPA, required an immediate halt to the dumping.

Morningside-Lenox Park Assn. v. Volpe, 3 ERC 1327 (N.D. Ga. 11/22/71). The court preliminarily enjoined further work on Interstate 485 in Atlanta, holding that a 102 statement was required for further actions even though location approval was given before January 1, 1970.

National Helium Corp. v. Morton, 2 ERC 1372, 1 ELR 20157 (D. Kan. 3/27/71). The court held that the Secretary of the Interior's cancellation of contracts for Federal purchase of helium constituted a "major action" requiring an environmental impact statement under Section 102(2)(C) of NEPA, and that the contractor had standing to seek compliance with this requirement. The court issued a preliminary injunction against termination of the contracts until the Secretary complied with NEPA. The injunction was subsequently affirmed by the 10th circuit.

Nolop v. Volpe, 3 ERC 1338 (D. S.D. 11/11/71). The court upheld the standing of minor students at U.S.D. to sue as a class (through a guardian ad litem) to prevent construction through the campus of a Federally funded highway. It granted a preliminary injunction against further construction until a 102 statement is prepared.

Northwest Area Welfare Rights Orgn. v. Volpe, 2 ERC 1704, 1 ELR 20186 (E.D. Wash. 12/3/70). The court denied a preliminary injunction against further development of a highway project in Spokane. The court held that a claim of violation of NEPA was premature, since the only Federal participation was funding of an area transportation study.

NRDC v. Morton, 3 ERC 1473 (D. D.C. 12/16/71). The court preliminarily enjoined a proposed sale of leases for oil and gas extraction on the Outer Continental Shelf off eastern Louisiana. The court held that a substantial question had been raised about the legal sufficiency of Interior's 102 statement, particularly in the scope of alternative actions discussed.

NRDC v. TVA, 3 ERC 1468 (S.D. N.Y. 12/8/71). The court denied the defendants' motion to dismiss, which was premised on these grounds: (1) improper service of process; (2) improper venue; (3) lack of jurisdiction; and (4) failure to join indispensable parties. It granted the motion of the Audubon Society to intervene as a plaintiff.

Pennsylvania Environmental Council v. Bartlett, 1 ERC 1271 (M.D. Pa. 4/30/70). The court held that a conservation group had standing to challenge the Secretary of Transportation's approval of a State secondary highway relocation project, but that NEPA did not apply to a project for which planning and the award of a contract preceded January 1, 1970. In dictum, the court also expressed doubt that NEPA requires the Secretary to study the environmental impact of State secondary highway projects before approving them. The decision was later affirmed by the 3d Circuit.

NEPA decisions: U.S. District Courts

Petterson v. Resor, 3 ERC 1170 (D. Ore. 10/4/71). The court upheld citizens' standing to challenge a Corps of Engineers dredge-and-fill permit for the expansion of the Portland airport. However, it ruled that the permit was not one for which congressional approval was required under 33 U.S.C. 401. A NEPA violation was claimed, but the court only mentioned it without dealing with it.

Sierra Club v. Hardin, 2 ERC 1385, 1 ELR 20161 (D. Alaska 3/25/71). The court upheld the standing of conservation groups to challenge the Forest Service's sale of timber in Tongass National Forest as violative of NEPA and other statutes. However, the court found that the Forest Service's reliance on the report of a panel of conservationists complied with NEPA "to the fullest extent possible" in view of the advanced stage of the transaction at the time of NEPA's passage. It found the claims under other statutes to be barred by laches. The decision has been appealed.

Sierra Club v. Laird, 1 ELR 20085 (D. Ariz. 6/23/70). Plaintiff conservation groups sued to enjoin the Corps of Engineers from proceeding with a channel-clearing project on the Gila River, which had been authorized prior to January 1, 1970. The court granted a preliminary injunction on the basis of the Corps' failure to comply with section 102(2)(C), Executive Order 11514, and paragraph 11 of CEQ's Interim Guidelines.

State Committee to Stop Sanguine v. Laird, 317 F. Supp. 665 (W.D. Wis. 1970). In a suit by conservationists to enjoin the operation of a signal-system test facility for noncompliance with section 102(2)(E) (requiring *inter alia* that Federal agencies support international environmental initiatives), the court refused an injunction because of plaintiffs' failure to make specific allegations of noncompliance.

Texas Committee v. Resor, 1 ELR 20466 (E.D. Tex. 6/29/71). The court granted a preliminary injunction against work on the Cooper Dam project until the Corps of Engineers prepares a 102 statement.

Texas Committee v. United States, 1 ERC 1303 (W.D. Tex. 2/5/70), *dismissed as moot* (5th Cir. 8/25/70). The court granted a preliminary injunction to prevent Farmers Home Administration from financing a golf-course project that allegedly threatened important wildlife habitat. The project had been approved, but not commenced, before January 1, 1970. The basis for the injunction was that FHA had not considered the environmental impact as required by NEPA. The case was dismissed as moot when the golf course was located elsewhere.

United States v. Brookhaven, 2 ERC 1761, 1 ELR 20377 (E.D. N.Y. 7/2/71). The court granted a preliminary injunction against dredging by a municipality in navigable waters without a Corps of Engineers permit. It held that the Corps, which had issued a permit in 1967, was not required to grant a subsequent permit, since the law had changed with the passage of NEPA.

United States v. Joseph G. Moretti, Inc., 1 ELR 20443, 3 ERC 1052 (S.D. Fla. 9/2/71). The court issued an injunction against further private dredging in Florida Bay without a Corps of Engineers permit. The injunction also required restoration of the defendant's past damage to the bay. The court relied on NEPA to justify considering ecological damage.

United States v. 247.37 Acres, 3 ERC 1099 (S.D. Ohio 9/9/71). In a suit to condemn land for the Corps of Engineers' East Fork Reservoir project, the court refused to grant summary judgment for the Government. The court held that failure to comply with NEPA was a valid defense to the condemnation suit.

Upper Pecos Assn. v. Stans, 2 ERC 1614, 1 ELR 20228 (D. N.M. 6/1/71). The court upheld the plaintiff's standing to challenge an Economic Development Administration grant for construction of a road. However, the court held that a 102 statement was not required on the grant because the Forest Service, which was the lead agency in developing the road, had prepared a 102 statement on it. The decision was affirmed on appeal.

Wilderness Society v. Morton, 1 ERC 1335, 1 ELR 20042 (D. D.C. 4/23/70). In a suit by conservation groups, the court enjoined the issuance by the Secretary of the Interior of a permit for a road across Federal lands on the basis, among others, of the Secretary's failure to prepare a statement under section 102(2)(C) discussing the environmental impact of both the road and the related Trans-Alaska Pipeline.

PREFATORY NOTE

The great Alaskan oil strike—the largest ever in the Western Hemisphere—occurred in June of 1968. Had it occurred even a year earlier, there is little doubt that the oil companies would have rolled without a squeak over whatever feeble opposition that might have developed to its swift exploitation.

But by early 1970, with the Santa Barbara (Calif.) oil spill a recent memory, and, more importantly, the National Environmental Policy Act of 1969 now the law of the land, a double handful of conservationists halted the project, and forced the first serious examination—public or private of the potential effects of man's massive entry into the cold land north of Fairbanks.

WILDERNESS SOCIETY v. HICKEL

__F.Supp.__(D. D.C. April 23, 1970)

Hart, J. This matter having come on for hearing on plaintiffs' Motion for a Preliminary Injunction and after consideration of the Motion, the opposition thereto, the pleadings, exhibits, and argument of counsel, and it appearing to the Court that the defendant is about to issue a permit to the Trans-Alaska Pipeline System or its constituent companies to build a haul road across public lands in Alaska from Prudhoe Bay to the Yukon River and to use gravel from the public lands therefor, all in connection with the proposed Trans-Alaska pipeline;

It further appearing that the defendant, by the issuance of any permit to Trans-Alaska Pipeline System for pipeline purposes, would thereby violate the National Environmental Policy Act of 1969, 83 Stat. 852, and the Mineral Leasing Act of 1920, 30 U.S.C. § 185, and that unless a preliminary injunction should issue the plaintiffs would suffer irreparable injury, it is by the Court this 23rd day of April, 1970,

Ordered, that defendant, his agents, officers, servants, employees, attorneys, and any persons in active concert or participation with them, be and they are hereby enjoined until the final determination of plaintiffs' application for an injunction and other relief from issuing a permit in connection with the Trans-Alaska Pipeline System to any person or corporation to (1) construct a haul road over public lands of the United States from Prudhoe Bay to the Yukon River or any part of such road or (2) to the use of gravel from the public lands of the United States for such a road.

It is further ordered, that defendant, his agents, officers, servants, employees and attorneys, and any persons in active concert or participation with them, be and they are hereby enjoined until the final determination of plaintiffs' application for an injunction and other relief from, directly or indirectly, issuing a permit to any person or corporation for construction of any other section or component of the Trans-Alaska Pipeline System unless plaintiffs are given fourteen (14) days' notice prior to the planned issuance thereof and plaintiffs are given an opportunity to challenge the legality of said permit;

It is further ordered, that plaintiffs file a bond for the payment of such costs and damages as may be suffered by any party who is found to have been wrongfully or unlawfully restrained herein, in the amount of One Hundred Dollars ($100.00); and

It is further ordered, that the United States Marshal shall serve a copy of this Order forthwith upon the defendant.

I. FINDINGS OF FACT

1. Amerada Hess Corporation; Atlantic Pipe Line Company, a subsidiary of Atlantic Richfield Company; B.P. Pipe Line Company, a subsidiary of B.P. Alaska, Inc.; Home Pipe Line Company, a subsidiary of Home Oil Company of Canada; Humble Pipe Line Company, a subsidiary of Humble Oil and Refining Co.; Mobil Pipe Line Company, a subsidiary of Mobil Oil Co.; Phillips Petroleum Co.; and Union Oil Company of California; (also collectively known as the Trans Alaska Pipe Line System (TAPS) and referred to thereinafter as "the Companies") have applied to Defendant for certain permits involving public lands of the United States under the jurisdiction of Defendant.

2. The Companies have applied for the following permits:

a. An oil pipe line right-of-way 54 feet in width extending from Valdez on the Pacific South Coast of Alaska to Prudhoe Bay on the Arctic North Coast, a distance of approximately 800 miles;

b. A special land-use permit for an additional access and construction space extending 11 feet on one side and 35 feet on the opposite side of said oil pipe line right-of-way;

c. A special land-use permit for an area 200 feet in width extending from the Yukon River to Prudhoe Bay for a construction surface and haul road.

3. For the purpose of constructing the pipe line and the haul road, in excess of 12 million cubic yards of gravel will be needed from the public lands administered by Defendant from various sites near the route.

4. Defendant is ready to issue a permit for the construction surface and haul road referred to in paragraph 2(c) hereof and to authorize the sale of gravel from the public lands for the construction thereof.

5. Plaintiffs are three conservation organizations. Plaintiff, The Wilderness Society, a nonprofit corporation incorporated under the laws of the District of Columbia, was organized in 1935 and claims a membership of approximately 60,000 persons. Plaintiff Friends of the Earth is a nonprofit corporation organized under the laws of the State of New York. Plaintiff Environmental Defense Fund, Inc. is a nonprofit corporation organized under the laws of the State of New York.

6. Plaintiffs have submitted affidavits to the Court in support of their motion for a preliminary injunction, and Defendant has submitted affidavits in opposition thereto.

7. Attorneys for Plaintiffs and Defendant presented argument on Plaintiffs' motion for preliminary injunction on April 13, 1970.

8. Defendant has at all times treated the application of the Companies for the construction surface and haul road as separate and distinct from the other applications. Defendant has not yet met all of the procedural requirements of the National Environmental Policy Act with respect to the application for the oil pipe line right-of-way or the application for adjacent temporary access space.

II. CONCLUSIONS OF LAW

1. The Court has jurisdiction over the subject matter of the complaint and the parties hereto.

2. Plaintiffs have standing to maintain this action.

3. For the purpose of this preliminary injunction, it appears that the three aforementioned applications are, in effect, a single application for a pipe line right-of-way.

4. It appears that Defendant has not fully complied with the requirements of the National Environmental Policy Act of 1969 with respect to said application, when considered together.

5. It appears that said applications, when considered together, request a pipe line right-of-way in excess of the width permissible under Section 28 of the Mineral Leasing Act of 1920, 30 U.S.C. § 185.

6. If a preliminary injunction does not issue, it would appear that Plaintiffs will suffer irreparable injury.

7. Based upon the foregoing, a preliminary injunction against Defendant should issue.

ENVIRONMENTAL DEFENSE FUND v. ARMY CORPS OF ENGINEERS
___F.Supp.___(E.D. Ark. May 5, 1972), 4 ERC 1097

MEMORANDUM OPINION NUMBER SIX

EISELE, D.J.:

If this Court is correct in its interpretation of the NEPA, the plaintiffs here cannot look to the judiciary to reverse or modify any decision with respect to the building of the embankment across the Cossatot. If that decision is to be changed or modified, it must be through the actions of the appropriate decision-makers in the executive or legislative branches of our government. The judiciary can delay the construction of the dam pending compliance by the defendants with the congressionally mandated provisions of the NEPA but, ultimately, plaintiffs' only chance to stop the dam, or to alter same, lies in their ability—perhaps with the aid of others—to convince the decisionmakers of the wisdom and correctness of their views on the merits.

The NEPA sets up certain requirements which, if followed, will insure that the decision-maker is fully aware of all the pertinent facts, problems and opinions with respect to the environmental impact of the proposed project. But the plaintiffs are not relegated solely to the provisions of the NEPA in contacting, and attempting to influence, those decision-makers. In addition, there are formal and informal, direct and indirect, means which the plaintiffs, and other citizens, may use in their attempt to reach and influence those decision-makers. The Court mentions this because it is obvious that the Congress must have been aware of such alternative methods of communication when it enacted the NEPA. The environmental impact statement is not to be equated to a trial court record which is examined on appeal by a higher court. Although the impact statement should, within reason, be as complete as possible, there is nothing to prevent either the agency involved, or the parties opposing proposed agency action, from bringing new or additional information, opinions and arguments to the attention of the "upstream" decision-makers even after the final EIS has been forwarded to CEQ. So it is not necessary to dot all the I's and cross all the T's in an impact statement.

Congress, we must assume, intended and expected the courts to interpret the NEPA in a reasonable manner in order to effectuate its obvious purposes and objectives. It is doubtful that any agency, however objective, however sincere, however well-staffed, and however well-financed, could come up with a perfect environmental impact statement in connection with any major project. Further studies, evaluations and analyses by experts are almost certain to reveal inadequacies or deficiencies. But even such deficiencies and inadequacies, discovered after the fact, can be brought to the attention of the decision-makers, including, ultimately, the President and the Congress itself. All of the usual methods of communication, political and otherwise, are still available for this purpose.

The Court does not believe that the Congress intended that the NEPA be used as a vehicle for the continual delay and postponement of legislative and executive decisions. From the very beginning of this case the Court has emphasized the freedom of the defendants to comply with the provisions of the NEPA and thereby to avoid the injunctive power of the courts. In the months between the filing of this action and the hearing upon the merits, the defendants could have complied with the Act and thereby have avoided the injunction. They chose, however, to stand upon a 12-page environmental impact statement, which, admittedly, was a mere recast of information already in defendants' files. Now, after having been enjoined, pending compliance with the NEPA, they have filed a voluminous report which, the Court is advised, cost the taxpayers approximately a quarter of a million dollars.The Court cannot say that either the costs or the delays were necessary or justified in this case. In any event, those costs and delays were occasioned by the defendants' failure to comply with the law.

The Court is satisfied that the new EIS, although obviously not as fair and impartial and objective as if it had been compiled by a disinterested third person, meets the full disclosure requirements of the NEPA and is a record upon which a decision-maker could arrive at an informed decision. It may be that that decision-maker, in order to fully comprehend the objections and arguments advanced by the plaintiffs and others who oppose the project, will have to look carefully into the "back pages" and the appendices of the EIS. But there is no way that he can fail to note the facts and understand the very serious arguments advanced by the plaintiffs if he carefully reviews the entire environmental impact statement. Whether that decision-maker is influenced by such facts, opinions and arguments, or whether such facts, opinions and arguments cause that decision-maker to call for further studies and investigations, is another matter—not one over which this, or any other court, has any control.

The Court reaffirms the conclusions of law set forth in its prior decisions in this case. 325 F.Supp. 728 and 325 F.Supp. 749, [2 ERC 1260] (1971).

The defendants, having now complied with the law, are no longer acting *ultra vires*. The basis of the Court's jurisdiction has therefore been removed. The injunction will be vacated and the case dismissed.

Dated this 5th day of May, 1972.

KALUR v. RESOR

___F.Supp.___(D.C.D. Dec. 16, 1971), 3 ERC 1456

[Other portions of this case relating principally to water pollution laws are printed at p. Four-120, with a discussion following the case there.]

The National Environmental Policy Act (NEPA) takes the major step of requiring al federal agencies to consider values of environmental preservation in their spheres of activity, prescribing certain procedural measures to ensure that those values are in fact fully respected. Plaintiffs argue that regulations recently adopted by the Corps of Engineers to govern consideration of environmental matters fail to satisfy the rigor demanded by the NEPA. The defendants contend that since the Corps of Engineers is an agency dedicated to guarding the environment, that the provisions and purposes of NEPA do not rationally apply to it. This Court finds the policies and added in that to be clear. The regulations issued by the Corps of Engineers and acquiesced in by the other defendants do not comply with the congressional policy required detailed statements. Hence, further rulemaking is ordered.

The National Environmental Policy Act reads in part:

(All agencies of the Federal Government shall

* * * * * * *

(C) include in every recommendation or report on proposals for legislation and other major Federal actions significantly affecting the quality of the human environment, a detailed statement by the responsible official on

1. the environmental impact of the proposed action,
2. any adverse environmental effects which cannot be avoided should the proposal be implemented,
3. alternatives to the proposed action,

4. the relationship between local short-term uses of man's environment and the maintenance and enhancement of long-term productivity, and,

5. any irreversible and irretrievable commitments of resourcess which would be involved in the proposed action should it be implemented.

The Corps of Engineers and the other defendants in this case rely upon the remarks of several Senators on the floor of the Senate in positing the argument that they are not bound by NEPA's requirement that "all agencies" of the government must file a detailed statement as outlined above. They argue this position in support of the following regulation:

> (2) Section 102(2)(C) statements will not be required in permit cases where it is likely that the proposed discharge will not have any significant impact on the human environment. Moreover, the Council on Environmental Quality has advised that such statements will not be required where the only impact of proposed discharge or deposit will be on water quality and related water quality considerations because these matters are specifically addressed under subsections 21(b) and (c), the Federal Water Pollution Control Act, as amended.

It must be noted here, that if no detailed statement is required when the only impact of the proposed discharge will be on water quality and related considerations, the Corps of Engineers has successfully eliminated from its purview most of the times when reports would otherwise be required. As the permits are issued to allow refuse to be dumped into navigable waters it would appear that water quality considerations should be foremost in that agencies decision making process.

The recent case of *Calvert Cliffs'* v. *Atomic Energy Commission* is dispositive of this question. There, the Circuit Court for the District of Columbia scrutinized NEPA, its policies, and the total picture of the Act's legislative history in deciding that the Atomic Energy Commission violated NEPA in providing that no party may raise, and the Commission may not independently examine any problem of water quality. There the Commission indicated that it would defer totally to water quality standards administered by state agencies and approved by the federal government under the Federal Water Pollution Control Act. This is a similar regulation to the one presently before this Court. Here too the agency involved has rejected the requirement of filing a detailed statement when concerned with water quality, in deference to the Federal Water Pollution Control Act.

Here also, the agency has abdicated much of its decision making responsibility on water quality. Recognizing the expertise of the Environmental Protection Agency (EPA), the Corps will accept the findings, determinations and interpretations, as the Regional Representative of the EPA decides, concerning the applicability of water quality considerations upon requests for permits to dump refuse into navigable waters. Even if disagreement should arise between the Regional Director of the EPA and the Corps District Engineer, the Secretary of the Army, after due consultation, shall accept the findings, determinations, and interpretations of the Administrator of EPA as to water quality standards and related water quality considerations. This is analogous to the Atomic Energy Commission stating that it would not independently examine any problem of water quality. These cases having distinctions without meaning it is held that the *Calvert Cliffs'* reasoning applies here with equal force.

The Court found in *Calvert Cliffs'* that the Commission's rule was in fundamental conflict with the basic purpose of the Act. NEPA mandates a case by case balancing judgment on the part of federal agencies. In each individual case, the particular economic and technical benefits of planned action must be assessed and then weighed against the environmental costs; alternatives must be considered that would effect the balance of values. The point of the individualized balancing analysis is to ensure that, with possible alterations, the optimally beneficial action is finally taken.

Furthermore, certification by another agency (here the Federal Water Pollution Control Agency) that its own environmental standards are satisfied involves an entirely different kind of judgment.

> Such agencies, without overall responsibility for the particular federal action in question, attend only to one aspect of the problem:

> the magnitude of certain environmental costs. They simply determine whether those costs exceed an allowable amount. Their certification does not mean that they found no environmental damage (*e.g.*, water pollution), but not quite enough to violate applicable (*e.g.*, water quality) standards. Certifying agencies do not attempt to weigh that damage against the opposing benefits. Thus, the balancing analysis remains to be done. It may be that the environmental costs, though passing prescribed standards, are nonetheless great enough to outweigh the particular economic and technical benefits involved in the planned action. *The only agency in a position to make such a judgment is the agency with overall responsibility for the proposed federal action—the agency to which NEPA is specifically directed.*

The procedural requirement of the detailed statements is to ensure that this process occurs. Without it the Corps accepts by rote the determinations of other agencies. The Circuit Court succinctly stated:

> NEPA established environmental protection as an integral part of the Atomic Energy Commission's basic mandate. The primary responsibility for fulfilling that mandate lies with the Commission. Its responsibility is not simply to sit back, like an umpire, and resolve adversary contentions at the hearing stage. Rather, it must itself take the initiative of considering environmental values at every distinctive and comprehensive stage of the process beyond the staff's evaluation and recommendation.

Kalur v. Resor

Congress has provided that the Corps of Engineers may consult with other agencies and states before deciding, but it provided, in Section 102(2)(C) only for full consultation, not an abdication to those other agencies or states. It certainly did not grant a license to disregard the main body of the NEPA obligations. There are no specific statutory obligations that the Corps of Engineers has that prevents it from complying with the letter of the NEPA. Certainly, standards set by other agencies, in this case the Federal Water Pollution Control Agency, are to be recognized.

Abdication to them, however, is not authorized. Obedience to water quality certifications under the Water Quality Improvement Act is not mutually exclusive with the NEPA procedures. It does not preclude performance of the NEPA duties. Water quality certifications essentially establish a minimum condition for the granting of a license. But they need not end the matter. The Corps of Engineers can then go on to perform the very different operation of balancing the over-all benefits and costs of a particular proposed project, and consider alterations above and beyond the applicable water quality standards that would further reduce environmental damage. The Corps of Engineers may still conduct the NEPA balancing analysis consistent with the Water Quality Improvement Act and Section 104 of NEPA does not exempt it from doing so. Therefore, the Corps must conduct the obligatory analysis under the prescribed procedures of NEPA.

The Court in *Calvert Cliffs'* reviewed the section by section analysis of NEPA submitted to the Senate.[53] The Court concluded that this analysis clearly stated the overriding purpose of Section 104: that no agency may substitute the procedures outlined in the Act for more restrictive and specific procedures established by law governing its activities. Morever, this rather meager legislative history could not radically transform the purport of the plain words of Section 104.

> Had the Senate sponsors fully intended to allow total abdication of NEPA responsibilities in water quality matters—rather than a supplementing of them by strict obedience to the specific standards of the Water Quality Improvement Act—the language of Section 104 could easily have been changed. It is, after all, the plain language of the statute which all the members of both houses of Congress must approve or disapprove. The courts should not allow the language to be significantly undercut.

Courts should interpret clear statutory wording to see that the overriding purpose behind the wording supports its plain meaning. NEPA did not permit the sort of total abdication of responsibility practiced by the Atomic Energy Commission in *Calvert Cliffs'*—it does not permit it here with the Corps of Engineers.

The Circuit Court for the District of Columbia held that NEPA contains very important procedural provisions. These provisions were designed to see that all Federal agencies do in fact exercise the substantive discretion given them. "*These provisions are not highly flex-*

ible. Indeed, they establish a strict standard of compliance." (Emphasis added.) The regulations before the Court today clearly fly in the face of NEPA's mandate that all agencies of the Federal Government shall make such reports and include detailed statements as described. There is no exception, as defendants have argued, carved out for those agencies that may be viewed as environmental improvement agencies.

Plaintiff's motion for summary judgment is granted.

AUBREY E. ROBINSON, JR.,
U.S. District Judge.

DECEMBER 16, 1971.

GREENE COUNTY PLANNING BOARD v. FEDERAL POWER COMMISSION

___ F.2d. ___ (2d Cir. Jan. 17, 1972, Nos. 434, 435)

KAUFMAN, *Circuit Judge:*

We are called upon to assess the licensing procedures of the Federal Power Commission in a proceeding upon the application [1] of the Power Authority of the State of New York (PASNY) for authorization to construct a high-voltage transmission line. Although the petitioners—Greene County Planning Board, the Town of Durham, New York, and the Association for the Preservation of Durham Valley—raise several interesting arguments, the dispute centers on compliance with the procedural mandates of Section 102(2)(C) of the National Environmental Policy Act of 1969 (NEPA), 42 U.S.C.A. § 4332(2)(C), which requires all federal agencies to issue a "detailed statement" on the environmental impact of all "major Federal actions significantly affecting the quality of the human environment...." This section is an essential "action forcing" provision [2] in legislation designed "[t]o declare a national policy which will encourage productive harmony between man and his environment; to promote efforts which will prevent or eliminate damage to the environment and biosphere and stimulate the health and welfare of man; to enrich the understanding of the ecological systems and natural resources important to the Nation; and to establish a Council on Environmental Quality." [3] NEPA § 2, 42 U.S.C.A. § 4321. In addition, petitioners ask us to decide that the Commission has discretion in the public interest, to pay the attorneys' fees and other expenses of the intervenors in the proceedings. We find that the Commission has not complied with NEPA and remand for further proceedings, but under the circumstances presented to us, we refuse to order the Commission or PASNY to pay the expenses and counsel fees of the private intervenors.

A brief statement of the proceedings thus far will aid in comprehending the arguments advanced. On August 15, 1968, PASNY filed an application to construct, operate and maintain a 1,000,000 kilowatt pumped storage power project [4] along the middle reaches of Schoharie

---

[1] Application was made pursuant to Section 4(e) of the Federal Power Act, 16 U.S.C. § 797(e), which provides in pertinent part:

The Commission is hereby authorized and empowered—

* * *

(e) To issue licenses to citizens of the United States, or to any association of such citizens, or to any corporation organized under the laws of the United States or any State thereof, or to any State or municipality for the purpose of constructing, operating, and maintaining dams, water conduits, reservoirs, power houses, transmission lines, or other project works necessary or convenient for the development and improvement of navigation and for the development, tranmission, and utilization of power across, along, from or in any of the streams or other bodies of water over which Congress has jurisdiction under its authority to regulate commerce with foreign nations and among the several States, or upon any part of the public lands and reservations of the United States (including the Territories), or for the purpose of utilizing the surplus water or water power from any Government dam. . . .

[2] *See* S. Rep. No. 91–296, 91st Cong., 1st Sess. 20 (1969); *Environmental Quality, the Second Annual Report of the Council on Environmental Quality* ch. 5 (Aug. 1971), reprinted in 1 Environmental L. Rep. 50057, 50064 [hereinafter cited as *CEQ Report*].

[3] *See generally* Hanks & Hanks, *An Environmental Bill of Rights: The Citizen Suit and the National Environmental Policy Act of 1969,* 24 Rutgers L. Rev. 230 (1970); Peterson, *An Analysis of Title I of the National Environmental Policy Act of 1969,* 1 Environmental L. Rep. 50035.

[4] A pumped storage power facility is designed to provide energy during the hours of peak kilowatt demand. The functioning of such a facility is explained in our decision in *Scenic Hudson Preservation Conference* v. *Federal Power Commission,* 354 F.2d 608, 612 (2d Cir. 1965), *cert. denied sub nom. Consolidated Edison Co. of New York* v. *Scenic Hudson Preservation Conference,* 384 U.S. 941 (1966). *See also* Loving, *A Vast New Warehouse for Electricity,* Fortune 88 (Dec. 1971).

Creek in the towns of Blenheim and Gilboa, New York, some forty miles southwest of Albany. The project as proposed, *inter alia*, consisted of: (1) an upper reservoir; (2) a lower reservoir (including a dam across Schoharie Creek); (3) an outdoor power house and (4) three 345 kilovolt transmission lines—one from the switchyard adjacent to the powerhouse to a substation at New Scotland, one to a substation at Fraser and at the last to a substation at Leeds.[5] After consulting with several federal agencies, the Commission granted the license. Power Authority of the State of New York, Project No. 2685, 41 F.P.C. (June 6, 1969). Article 34 of the license, however, specifically prohibited construction of the transmission lines until further Commission approval was given to "plans for preservation and enhancement of the environment as it may be affected by the transmission lines design and location."[6] *Id.* at 718. In preparing the plans, PASNY was required to "give appropriate consideration to recognized guidelines for protecting the environment and to beneficial uses, including wildlife, of the transmission lines right-of-way." *Ibid.*

PASNY applied for construction authorization of the three lines on November 24, 1969. When no protests or petitions were filed with respect to the Gilboa-New Scotland and Gilboa-Fraser lines, the Commission approved construction of these two lines without holding a hearing. Power Authority of the State of New York, Project No. 2685, 43 F.P.C. 521 (April 10, 1970). Nevertheless, the Commission, after conducting a full inspection and conferring with PASNY's staff and consultants, "concluded that from an aesthetic and environmental values point of view, the selected locations of the two lines involved herein are preferable to all of the alternative routings that were considered." *Id.* at 522–23.

The Commission, however, received several protests with respect to the Gilboa-Leeds line which was to run from the project in Schoharie County, through the Durham Valley, past the town of Durham (in Green County) to the Leeds Substation less than two miles from the Hudson River near Catskill. Motions to intervene were filed by the Greene County Planning Board, the Town of Durham, the Association for the Preservation of the Durham Valley,[7] the Sierra Club and several individuals.[8] Intervention was granted on May 19, 1970, but participation was limited to the issues raised in the petitions to intervene—namely, the impact of the line on the Durham Valley in particular and Greene County in general.

NEPA became effective on January 1, 1970, after PASNY applied for the transmission line permits, but before the permits were issued for the Gilboa-New Scotland and Gilboa-Fraser lines. It was not until almost a year later, on December 2, 1970, that the Commission issued Order No. 415 to implement procedures in accord with NEPA. 18 C.F.R. §§ 2.80–.82 (January 1, 1971). Section 2.81(b) of the regulations required each applicant for a license for a "major project" to file its own detailed statement of environmental impact, developing fully the five factors listed in section 102(2)(C) of NEPA.[9] Although the regulations required the Commission staff to prepare a detailed statement in the case of all uncontested applications, no such statement was required where applications were contested.[10] *See* 18 C.F.R. §§ 2.81(e)-(f) (January 1, 1971.)

In accordance with Commission regulations, PASNY filed its impact statement on March 21, 1971, covering the proposed Gilboa-Leeds line and two alternative routings. The Commission reviewed the state-

[5] Exhibit R to PASNY's application proposed a recreational use plan including overlook areas and a State Park.

[6] Other restrictions on the license included provisions for flood control, additional studies with respect to fish and wildlife resources, protection for the covered Blenheim Bridge and development of a plan to blend the project works with the natural view.

[7] The Association is a voluntary, unincorporated, nonprofit association organized in 1960 to protect and preserve the scenic, historical and ecological values of the Durham Valley area. In January, 1970, the Association had over 100 members who in the aggregate owned more than 5,000 acres of land in Durham Valley and its immediate vicinity.

[8] The individual intervenors own land in the Durham Valley.

[9] The five factors are:

(i) the environmental impact of the proposed action.

(ii) any adverse environmental effects which cannot be avoided should the proposal be implemented.

(iii) alternatives to the proposed action.

(iv) the relationship between local short-term uses of man's environment and the maintenance and enhancement of long-term productivity, and

(v) any irreversible and irretrievable commitments of resources which would be involved in the proposed action should it be implemented.

[10] Under Section 2.81(e)(1), the Commission staff was expected to "specifically analyze and evaluate the evidence in the light of the environmental criteria. . . ."

The Commission revised its rules by Order No. 415–B, issued November 19, 1971. 36 Fed. Reg. 22738 (Nov. 30, 1971). Section 2.81 no longer requires the Commission to prepare its own statement in uncontested proceedings.

ment as to sufficiency of form, *see* 18 C.F.R. § 2.81(b) (January 1, 1971), and then circulated it for comment to agencies with "special expertise with respect to any environmental impact involved."[11] *See* NEPA § 102(2)(C) 42 U.S.C.A. § 4332(2)(C).

Finally, by order issued May 4, 1971, the Commission ordered a hearing on PASNY's proposals and set a prehearing conference for June 22, 1971. At this conference, Durham and Green County moved that PASNY, or alternatively the Commission, pay the expenses and fees, including attorneys' fees, incurred by the intervenors in the proceeding. Greene County also requested the Presiding Examiner to set a date for the Commission to file its own impact statement pursuant to NEPA. Then, by motions filed July 6 and July 12, 1971, the intervenors moved for an order vacating, rescinding or suspending the June 6, 1969, license of the entire project and enjoining further construction, alleging that the Commission did not comply with the notice requirements of the Federal Power Act and the mandates of NEPA.[12]

The Presiding Examiner denied each of the motions, and the movants filed timely notices of appeal to the Commission. *See* 18 C.F.R. § 1.28 (January 1, 1971). Although each appeal was denied *sub silentio* by operation of law,[13] the Commission granted rehearings and by orders dated October 28 and 29, 1971, it formally denied the appeals. Petitioners ask us to review those orders. *See* Federal Power Act § 313, 16 U.S.C. § *825l*.

Before passing to the merits of petitioners' contentions, we note that the latest round of hearings commenced on November 9, 1971. Petitioners moved for a stay of these hearings in this Court, but the motion was denied on November 1. To date, the hearings have been concerned with cross-examination of PASNY and Commission witnesses. They are expected to continue for several months. In addition, the entire project, exclusive of the Gilboa-Leeds transmission line, is now more than 80% complete.[14]

Greene County Planning Board v. F.P.C.

I. Compliance With NEPA

A. Gilboa-Leeds Transmission Line

Section 102(2)(C) of NEPA, as we stated at the outset, requires every federal agency to "include in every recommendation or report on proposals for . . . major Federal actions significantly affecting the quality of the human environment" a detailed environmental impact statement. Prior to making the statement, the agency must "consult with and obtain the comments of any Federal agency which has jurisdiction by law or special expertise with respect to any environmental impact involved." The detailed statement, however, "*must accompany the proposal through the existing agency review processes. . . .*"[15] (Emphasis added.)

It is conceded that authorization of the Gilboa-Leeds line, an integral part of the Blenheim-Gilboa Project, would constitute a major federal action. The parties, however, are in vigorous disagreement

[11] The statement was circulated to the Hudson River Valley Commission, the Secretary of the Interior, the Secretary of Agriculture, the Army Corps of Engineers, the New York Department of Environmental Conservation and the Environmental Protection Agency.

[12] Intervenors made several motions, either orally or in writing, which are not recounted here, since they were mainly variations of the theme we already have presented.

Intervenors, however, unsuccessfully moved that they be provided copies of the transcript without charge, that their non-expert witnesses be allowed to testify orally without first filing written testimony, and that the hearings be held in Greene County. The Commission denied appeals from the Presiding Examiner's decisions, noting that it is within his discretion to determine procedural matters relating to the hearings. Although petitioners preserved their objections to the Presiding Examiner's decisions by petitioning for review of the Commission's orders, they have not raised these issues on appeal. Nevertheless, we are constrained to note that the Commision at nearly every turn had made it difficult procedurally for the intervenors. For example, intervenors were forced to go to court to compel disclosures under the Freedom of Information Act. *See Town of Durham* v. *Federal Power Commission,* 71 Civ. 3993 (S.D.N.Y. Oct. 26, 1971). We suggest that the Federal Power Commission, as well as other Federal Agencies, must review their rules and rethink encrusted, entrenched positions in light of the provision in NEPA that, "to the fullest extent possible," all regulations of the agencies must be interpreted and administered in accordance with the policies of the Act. NEPA § 102(1), 42 U.S.C.A. § 4332(1). We fully agree with the Council on Environmental Quality that compliance is required not only with the letter, but the spirit of the Act. Council on Environmental Quality. Guidelines § 1, 36 Fed. Reg. 7724 (April 23, 1971).

[13] Section 1.28(c) of the Commission's rules provides in part:

> (c) *Commission action.* Unless the Comm acts upon questions referred by presiding officers to the Commission for determination or upon appeals taken to the Commission from rulings of presiding officers within thirty days after referral or filing of the appeal, whichever is later, such referrals or appeals shall be deemed to have been denied.

[14] We are told that more than 75% of the estimated $160,000,000 total cost has been spent or committed.

[15] Section 102(2)(C) provides in full:

> Sec. 102. The Congress authorizes and directs that, to the fullest extent possible: . . . (2) all agencies of the Federal Government shall—
> (C) include in every recommendation or report on proposals for legislation and other

over when the Commission must make its impact statement. The Commission argues that PASNY's statement, reviewed as to form by the Commission and circulated by it, suffices for the purposes of Section 102(2)(C) and that the Commission is not required to make its *own* statement until it files its final decision. Petitioners argue that the Commission must issue its statement prior to any formal hearings. PASNY, perhaps recognizing that the Commission's position is untenable, but nevertheless anxious to expedite the proceedings, proposes a third course of action. It urges that the Commission can draft its statement on the basis of the hearings, but to be circulated by it for comment before its final decision. It is clear to us that petitioners offer the correct interpretation.

Section 101(a) of NEPA, 42 U.S.C.A. §4331(a), declares that "it is the continuing policy of the Federal Government . . . to use all practicable means and measures . . . in a manner calculated to foster and promote the general welfare, to create and maintain conditions under which man and nature can exist in productive harmony, and fulfill the social, economic, and other requirements of present and future generations of Americans." To this end the government must "coordinate Federal plans, functions, programs, and resources. . . ." NEPA §101(b), 42 U.S.C.A. §4331(b). As long as six years ago, this Court remanded a case to the Commission because, in granting a license for the construction of a similar pumped storage power project at Storm King Mountain on the Hudson River it had failed to weigh the factors of "the conservation of natural resources, the maintenance of natural beauty, and the preservation of historic sites." [16] *Scenic Hudson Preservation Conference* v. *Federal Power Commission* [*Scenic Hudson I*], 354 F.2d 608, 614 (1965), *cert. denied sub nom. Consolidated Edison Co. of New York* v. *Scenic Hudson Preservation Conference*, 384 U.S. 941 (1966). We commented there: "In this case, as in many others, the Commission has claimed to be the representative of the public interest. This role does not permit it to act as an umpire blandly calling balls and strikes for adversaries appearing before it; the right of the public must receive active and affirmative protection at the hands of the Commission." *Id.* at 620. But NEPA, which was a response to the urgent need for a similar approach in all federal agencies,[17] went far beyond the requirement that the agency merely consider enviroinmental factors and include those factors in the record subject to review by the courts.

In addition to the environmental impact statement, Section 102(2) requires the agency, *inter alia*, to:

> (A) utilize a systematic, interdisciplinary approach which will insure the integrated use of the natural and social sciences and the environmental design arts in planning and in decisionmaking which may have an impact on man's environment;
>
> * * *
>
> (D) study, develop, and describe appropriate alternatives to recommended courses of action in any proposal which involves unresolved conflicts concerning alternative uses of available resources;
>
> * * *

major Federal actions significantly affecting the quality of the human environment a detailed statement by the responsible official on—

(i) the environmental impact of the proposed action.

(ii) any adverse environmental effects which cannot be avoided should the proposal be implemented,

(iii) alternatives to the proposed action,

(iv) the relationship between local short-term uses of man's environment and the maintenance and enhancement of long-term productivity, and

(v) any irreversible and irretrievable commitments of resources which would be involved in the proposed action should it be implemented.

Prior to making any detailed statement, the responsible Federal official shall consult with and obtain the comments of any Federal agency which has jurisdiction by law or special expertise with respect to any environmental impact involved. Copies of such statement and the comments and views of the appropriate Federal, State, and local agencies, which are authorized to develop and enforce environmental standards, shall be made available to the President, the Council on Environmental Quality and to the public as provided by section 552 of title 5, United States Code, and shall accompany the proposal through the existing agency review processes;

[16] The decision was based upon Section 10(a) of the Federal Power Act, 16 U.S.C. § 803, which provides:

> All licenses issued under this Part shall be on the following conditions:
>
> (a) That the project adopted, including the maps, plans, and specifications, shall be such as in the judgment of the Commission will be best adapted to a comprehensive plan for improving or developing a waterway or waterways for the use or benefit of interstate or foreign commerce, for the improvement and utilization of waterpower development, and for other beneficial public uses, including recreational purposes; and if necessary in order to secure such plan the Commission shall have authority to require the modification of any project and of the plans and specifications of the project works before approval.

See also Udall v. *Federal Power Commission*, 387 U.S. 428 (1967).

[17] *See* Hanks & Hanks, *supra* note 3, at 265–69.

> (E) recognize the worldwide and long-range character of environmental problems . . .

We view this section as did the District of Columbia Circuit. It is a mandate to consider environmental values "at every distinctive and comprehensive stage of the [agency's] process." The primary and non-delegable responsibility for fulfilling that function lies with the Commission. *Calvert Cliff's Coordinating Committee, Inc.* v. *Atomic Energy Commission*, 449 F. 2d 1109, 1119 (D.C. Cir. 1971) (holding that rules of the AEC which did not require a detailed statement in an uncontested licensing proceeding did not comply with Section 102(2)(C)).

The Federal Power Commission has abdicated a significant part of its responsibility by substituting the statement of PASNY for its own. The Commission appears to be content to collate the comments of other federal agencies, its own staff and the intervenors and once again to act as an umpire.[18] The danger of this procedure, and one obvious shortcoming, is the potential, if not likelihood, that the applicant's statement will be based upon self-serving, assumptions.[19] In fact, PASNY's statement begins: "Neither the construction nor the operation of the Gilboa-Leeds transmission line will have any significant adverse impact on the environment." But, the Gilboa-Leeds line, if constructed as proposed, will cut a swath approximately 35 miles long and 150 feet wide across the face of Greene and Schoharie Counties. It is small consolation that the line will not scar either existing historical sites or designated park land.

Moreover, although decision like *Scenic Hudson I* have greatly expanded the concept of standing to challenge administrative action,[20] intervenors generally have limited resources, both in terms of money and technical expertise, and thus may not be able to provide an effective analysis of environmental factors.[21] It was in part for this reason that Congress has compelled agencies to seek the aid of all available expertise and formulate their own position early in the review process. The Commission argues, however, that written testimony of its staff demonstrates that the Commission has not left the applicant and the intervenors to develop the record. It insists that its staff has undertaken field research in an effort to investigate alternatives proposed by PASNY and also any additional feasible alternatives. It is clear to us that this testimony cannot replace a single coherent and comprehensive environmental analysis, which is itself subject to scrutiny during the agency review processes. If this course of action we approve were not followed, alternatives might be lost as the applicant's statement tended to produce a *status quo* syndrome.

The danger that the review process will bog down once an initial decision has been rendered is fully recognized by the Council on Environmental Quality[22] in Section 10(b) of its Guidelines suggesting procedures for compliance with NEPA, 36 Fed. Reg. 7724 (April 23, 1971):

> It is important that draft environmental statements be prepared and circulated for comment and furnished to the Council early enough in the agency review process before an action is taken in order to permit meaningful consideration of the environmental issues involved. To the maximum extent practicable no administrative action . . . is to be taken sooner than ninety (90) days

Greene County Planning Board v. F.P.C.

---

[18] The Commission did not face squarely the issue of compliance with NEPA in its orders. In upholding the Presiding Examiner's refusal to delay the hearings until the Commission had prepared its statement, the Commission said:

> . . . they [Durham and Greene County] simply ask the Commission to reconsider that which the Presiding Examiner found to be not in the public interest. For the reasons given in connection with the preceding appeal [the Presiding Examiner has broad discretion over hearing procedures], reconsideration of such procedural matter will be denied. . . .

[19] *Cf. Scenic Hudson I,* 354 F.2d at 619: "self-serving general statements by officials of Consolidated Edison. . . ."

[20] *See, e.g., Association of Data Processing Service Organizations* v. *Camp,* 397 U.S. 150, 153 (1970); *Citizens Committee for the Hudson Valley* v. *Volpe,* 425 F.2d 97 (2d Cir.), *cert. denied,* 400 U.S. 949 (1970). *See generally* Hanks & Hanks, *supra* note 3, at 231–44; Peterson, *supra* note 3, at 50047–48.

[21] *See Calvert Cliffs',* 449 F.2d at 1118–19 ("It is, moreover, unrealistic to assume that there will always be an intervenor with the information, energy and money required to challenge a staff recommendation which ignores environmental costs."); Gellhorn, *Public Participation in Administrative Hearings,* Report Prepared for the Committee on Agency Organization and Procedure of the Administrative Conference of the United States 29–37 (October 29, 1971).

[22] The Council was established pursuant to Subchapter II of NEPA, 42 U.S.C. §§ 4341 *et seq.* Its duties include assisting the President in the preparation of the annual Environmental Quality Report to be transmitted to Congress and conducting investigations and developing programs concerning environmental quality.

> after a draft envronmental statement has been circulated for comment, furnished to the Council and . . . made available to the public . . .

It is interesting that the Commission relies on these Guidelines to sustain its position. Initially, it directs us to Section 7 which would allow an agency, when it seeks the advice of other agencies pursuant to Section 102(2)(C), to circulate "(i) a draft environmental statement for which it takes responsibility or (ii) comparable information . . ." And, Section 2.81(b) of the Commission's latest rules (issued after the Guidelines) provides that the applicant's draft statement "shall be deemed to be information comparable to an agency draft statement pursuant to Section 7 of the Guidelines of the Council on Environmental Quality." The Commission then calls our attention to Section 10(e) of the Guidelines, which provides:

> Agencies which hold hearings on proposed administrative actions or legislation should make the draft environmental statement available to the public at least fifteen (15) days prior to the time of the relevant hearings except where the agency prepares the draft statement on the basis of a hearing subject to the Administrative Procedure Act and preceded by adequate public notice and information to dentify the issues and obtain the comments provided for in sections 6-9 of these guidelines.

Greene County Planning Board v. F.P.C.

The Commission argues that the proviso relieves it of its obligation to prepare an environmental statement prior to the licensing hearings and that the applicant's statement, "information comparable" to a statement of its own, sufficiently identifies the issues. Although the Guidelines are merely advisory and the Council on Enviornmental Quality has no authority to prescribe regulations governing compliance with NEPA, we would not lightly suggest that the Council, entrusted with the responsibility of developing and recommending national policies "to foster and promote the improvement of the environmental quality," NEPA § 204, 42 U.S.C.A. § 4344, has misconstrued NEPA. Although the Commission's interpretation of Section 10(e) of the Guidelines is superficially appealing, it flies in the face of Section 102(2)(C) of NEPA which explicitly requires the agency's *own* detailed statement to "accompany the proposal through the existing agency review processes."[23] There can be no question that the hearings on PASNY's application, ordered pursuant to Section 308 of the Federal Power Act, 16 U.S.C. § 825g, and Section 1.20 of the Commission's rules, 18 C.F.R. § 1.20 (January 1, 1971), constitute an existing agency review process.

Though we conclude that the Commission was in violation of NEPA by conducting hearings prior to the preparation by *its staff* of its own impact statement,[24] we are of the view that it did not seek improperly the advice of other agencies on the basis of PASNY's application. Section 102(2)(C) compels the agency to seek this advice before preparing its statement. Section 102(1), however, directs that "to the fullest extent possible" regulations should be interpreted and administered in accordance with the policies of NEPA. In this record, it would be insructive for the Commission to consult the rules of the Atomic Energy Commission, 36 Fed. Reg. 18071 (Sept. 9, 1971), promulgated after the decision in *Calvert Cliff's* charged the AEC with a "crabbed interpretation of NEPA [which made] a mockery of the Act." 449 F.2d at 117. The Atomic Energy Commission, although it still requires an

[23] An alternative interpretation, and one we would deem acceptable under the Act, is that the agency may hold two hearings—one solely to gather information to aid the Commission in formulating its statements, the second to consider the merits of the license application.

It is interesting to note that the Council on Environmental Quality assumed that when the Commission circulated the PASNY report, it subsequently would circulate its own report. In its June 1971 official monthly bulletin the Council published the following notice of the PASNY report:

> Applicant's drafts. (These are not official FPC drafts. They will be followed by staff-prepared draft statements.) . . .

[24] In its brief to this Court, the Commission argued that it would be in contravention of Section 8(a) of the Administrative Procedure Act, 5 U.S.C. § 557, which prohibits Commission participation in the decisionmaking process until the record is completely developed, if it were required to adopt a position in an environmental impact statement. Certainly no one has suggested that the detailed statement prepared before the hearings must be prepared by Commission members. It is sufficient for the purpose of EPA if the statement is prepared by the Commission's staff on the basis of the staff's investigations. Counsel for the Commission conceded at oral argument that this procedure would not violate the APA. *See also* Section 6(d) of the Guidelines of the Council on Environmental Quality:

> Where an agency follows a practice of declining to favor an alternative until public hearings have been held on a proposed action, a draft environmental statement may be prepared and circulated indicating that two or more alternatives are under consideration.

applicant to submit its environmental report, prepares a draft report of its own in advance of seeking the advice of other federal agencies. Then, on the basis of comments received from these agencies and all interested parties, it prepares its final detailed statement, which is offered in evidence at a contested hearing.

In light of our foregoing discussion, we must consider the most efficient procedure for ensuring that the policies of NEPA are implemented in Commission proceedings on the Gilboa-Leeds line. For the reasons we have set forth, we deem it essential that the Commission's staff should prepare a detailed statement before the Presiding Examiner issues his initial decision. Moreover, the intervenors must have a reasonable opportunity to comment on the statement. But, since the statement may well go to waste unless it is subject to the full scrutiny of the hearing process, we also believe that the intervenors must be given the opportunity to cross-examine both PASNY and Commission witnesses in light of the statement. "Often individuals and groups can contribute data and insights beyond the expertise of the agency involved."*CEQ Report*, 1 Environmental L. Rep. at 50059. We leave to the Commission to determine the most efficient procedure for meeting this mandate.

Fully recognizing that delay unfortunately is incident to our mandate and PASNY's claim that the Blenheim-Gilboa project is a vitally needed power facility, we can only add our voice to that of the District of Columbia Circuit in *Calvert Cliffs'* : Delay is a concomitant of the implementation of the procedures prescribed by NEPA, and the spectre of a power crisis "must not be used to create a blackout of environmental consideration in the agency review process." 449 F.2d at 1122. "It is far more consistent with the purposes of the Act to delay operation at a stage where real environmental protection may come about than at a stage where corrective action may be so costly as to be impossible." *Id.* at 1128.

Greene County Planning Board v. F.P.C.

The petitioners inform us also that the Commission has violated its comprehensive planning duties by not requiring PASNY to divulge in its environmental statement any plans it may have with respect to future power projects and transmission lines. PASNY has admitted that the Gilboa-Leeds line is part of a plan which may include three massive pumped storage hydroelectric projects, six 345 kilovolt transmission lines and three 765 kilovolt transmission lines. The Commission responds that its planning responsibility under Section 10(a) of the Federal Power Act, 16 U.S.C. § 803(a),[25] does not require analysis of future projects which are not presented in license applications. PASNY adopts the benign position that it has disclosed the feasibility studies presently in progress [26] and that the Commission should take them into account in considering the Gilboa-Leeds line.

We cannot agree with petitioners that the Commission erred when it did not require PASNY to supplement its impact statement. NEPA places the onus of formulating the statement solely on the Commission, and, unless there is any indication that the Commission's procedures will not allow it to comply with its statutory duty this Court should defer to the Commission's discretion as to the proper information gathering techniques.

In an effort to avoid any confusion or misunderstanding on remand, we are constrained to comment on the Commission's planning responsibility. Under Section 10(a) of the Federal Power Act, the Commission cannot issue a license unless the project is "best adapted to a comprehensive plan . . . for the improvement and utilization of waterpower development and for other beneficial public uses, including recreational purposes; . . . " In *Scenic Hudson I* we commented that the Commission's failure to inform itself of Consolidated Edison's future interconnection plans "cannot be reconciled with its planning responsibility under the Federal Power Act." 345 F.2d at 622. And, less than two years later, Justice Douglas writing for the Supreme Court in *Udall* v. *Federal Power Commission*, 387 U.S. 428 (1967), made it clear that the Federal Power Act does not command the immediate construction of as many projects as possible and that the determination whether to license any one project "can be made only after an exploration of all issues relevant to the 'public interest,' including future power demand and supply, alternate sources of power, [and]

[25] *See* note 16 *supra*.
[26] PASNY is making a study to determine the physical, environmental and economic feasibility of constructing additional pumped storage facilities downstream from the Blenheim-Gilboa project.

the public interest in preserving reaches of wild rivers and wilderness areas. . . ." *Id.* at 450. Although these decisions may not have established long-range planning requirements,[27] they evidence a clear intent that the Commission at least should consider all available and relevant information in performing its functions.

The Commission's "hands-off" attitude is even more startling in view of the explicit requirement in NEPA that the Commission "recognize the worldwide and long-range character of environmental problems" and interpret its mandate under the Federal Power Act in accordance with the policies set forth in NEPA. NEPA §§ 102(1), (2)(E), 42 U.S.C.A. §§ 4332(1), (2)(E). Any doubt about the intent of these provisions is obviated by the following statement in the Senate Report accompanying the Act:

> "Environmental problems are only dealt with when they reach crisis proportions. Public desires and aspirations are seldom consulted. Important decisions concerning the use and the shape of man's future environment continue to be made in small but steady increments which perpetuate rather than avoid the recognized mistakes of previous decades." S. Rep. No. 91–296, 91st Cong., 1st Sess. 5 (1969).

The Commission has indicated that the June 6, 1969, license of the Blenheim-Gilboa Project did not commit it to authorize construction of the Gilboa-Leeds line. But we fail to see how the Commission, if it is to fulfill the demanding standard of "careful and informed decisionmaking," *Calvert Cliffs'*, 449 F.2d at 1115, can disregard impending plans for further power development. For example, it may be that it would be proper to defer decision on the Gilboa-Leeds line until these plans were crystallized, particularly if there is a likelihood that future development might affect the optimum location of the line or even make the line unnecessary. Although the basic defect of current planning and licensing processes is "the inevitably narrow scope of the decision the agency [has] to make: whether or not to license a single and specific [project]," [28] we cannot tolerate the Commission cutting back on its expanded responsibility by blinding itself to potential developments notwithstanding its lack of authority to compel future, alternate construction.

Greene County Planning Board v. F.P.C.

B. Blenheim-Gilboa Project and Approved Transmission Lines

Petitioners ask us to stay construction of the pumped storage facility and the two approved transmission lines, now 80% complete, pending compliance with NEPA.[29] Although there can be no question that the Act applies to all major federal actions taken after January 1, 1970, despite the fact that construction of the project under consideration may have commenced prior to that date, *see, e.g., Calvert Cliffs'*, 449 F.2d at 1127–29 (construction permit for nuclear facility granted prior to effective date, but operating license not yet issued); *Environmental Defense Fund, Inc.* v. *Corps of Engineers*, 325 F. Supp. 728, 743–49 (E.D. Ark. 1971) (Gillham Dam to be built as part of on-going Millwood Reservoir project), we see no basis for applyingN EPA retroactively [30] to the licensing of the basic project which became final nearly six months prior to the effective date of the Act. *See Pennsylvania Environmental Council* v. *Bartlett*, 315 F. Supp. 238 (M.D. Pa. 1970).

With respect to the Gilboa-New Scotland and Gilboa-Fraser lines, however, there can be no question that the Commission failed to comply with NEPA. The lines were approved on April 10, 1970, but the Commission failed to issue the requisite detailed environmental statement. Nevertheless, we find no compelling basis for halting construction of the lines so far advanced and decline to reopen the authorization proceedings. It is of no small consequence that petitioners, having made timely motions to intervene, offered no objections to the construction of the two lines and did not petition this Court or the District of

[27] The author of this opinion has suggested that:

> . . . a major share of the blame for the unnecessary delays and ineffectual public planning in the United States may be laid at the doorstep of fragmented government regulation of power development. We sorely lack a federal agency—with sufficient authority, power and purse to choose among the infinite patterns of potential development—responsible for planning and controlling the growth and dispersal of electric generating capacity over a realistically extensive span of space and time.

Kaufman, *Power for the People—and by the People: Utilities, the Environment and the Public Interest*, 46 N.Y.U.L. Rev. 867, 872–73 (1971).

[28] *Id.* at 872.

[29] Petitioners before the Commission also challenged the license and the approval of the Gilboa-New Scotland and Gilboa-Fraser lines on the ground that the Commission did not comply with the notice provisions of the Federal Power Act, and the lengthy order of October 28, 1971, deals solely with that point. Petitioners have not raised the objection here.

[30] *See generally* Note, *Retroactive Application of the National Environmental Policy Act of 1969*, 69 Mich. L. Rev. 732 (1971).

Columbia Circuit for review within 60 days as provided by Section 313(b) of the Federal Power Act, 16 U.S.C. § 825*l*(b). Thus, construction of the lines began pursuant to a *final* order of the Commission. Although we might arrive at a different conclusion if there were significant potential for subversion of the substantive policies expressed in NEPA, *cf. Calvert Cliffs'*, 449 F.2d at 1121 n. 28, the Commission did require PASNY in submitting its plans to "give appropriate consideration to recognize guidelines for protecting the environment" [31] and also conducted its own independent investigation of alternative routings. Moreover, it would be unreasonable to expect instant compliance with all of the Act's procedural requirements, *see id.* at 1121, and there is no indication (as there is with respect to the Gilboa-Leeds line) of obstinate refusal to comply with NEPA. *Compare Scenic Hudson Preservation Conference* v. *Federal Power Commission [Scenic Hudson II]*, 1970 Slip Op. 5279, 5314–16 (2d Cir. Oct. 22, 1971).

II. Expenses and fees

The petitioners' final request is for an order requiring PASNY, or in the alternative the Commission, to pay the expenses and fees incurred by petitioners. Recognizing as they do that a rule requiring reimbursement of all intervenors would be subject to abuse, they limit their request to reasonable out-of-pocket expenses, including fees for experts as they are incurred, and reasonable attorneys' fees at the conclusion of the proceedings before the Commission in the event that their participation is determined to have been in the public interest.

As we read the Commission's order of October 29, 1971, the Commission denied petitioner's motion for payment of fees on the ground that it had no authority to grant them. But, in an effort to buttress its argument that the petitions for review are in this regard untimely, the Commission now argues that it has foreclosed only the present award of fees and has left open the question of whether ultimately to award them when the proceedings have come to an end. Whether or not the Commission will entertain renewed motions at the close of its proceedings, we find that the petitions are timely and that his Court has jurisdiction to review the Commission's order.

Section 313(b) of the Federal Power Act, 16 U.S.C. § 8251(b), provides that "[a]ny party to a proceeding under [the Act] aggrieved by an order issued by the Commission in such proceedings may obtain a review of such order. . . ." This language, unlike those provisions limiting review to "final orders," *see, e.g.*, Section 10(f) of the National Labor Relations Act, 29 U.S.C. § 160(f), seemingly would allow review of all Commission orders. But the courts, sensitive to the policies underlying the requirement of exhaustion of administrative remedies, have declined jurisdiction where the issues raised could be disposed of in review of a final Commission order without serious detriment to the rights of the parties. *See, e.g., Federal Power Commission* v. *Metropolitan Edison Co.*, 304 U.S. 375, 383–84 (1938); *Mid-American Pipeline Co.* v. *Federal Power Commission*, 299 F.2d 126 (D.C. Cir. 1962). Review is available, however, where an interlocutory order has "an impact upon rights and [is] of such a nature as will cause irreparable injury if not challenged." *Amerada Petroleum Corp.* v. *Federal Power Commission*, 285 F.2d 737, 739 (10th Cir. 1960) (interpreting the review provision of the Natural Gas Act, identical to Section 313 (b) of the Federal Power Act). In *Environmental Defense Fund, Inc.* v. *Ruckelshaus*, 439 F.2d 584 (D.C. Cir. 1971), the District of Columbia Circuit, considering the Federal Insecticide, Fungicide, and Rodenticide Act, which provides for judicial review "[i]n a case of actual controversy as to the validity of any order" of the Secretary of Agriculture, stated that the applicable test is not whether there are further administrative proceedings available, but "whether the impact of the order is sufficiently 'final' to warrant review in the context of the particular case." *Id.* at 591. *See also Environmental Defense Fund, Inc.* v. *Hardin*, 428 F.2d 1093, 1098–99 (D.C. Cir. 1970). In light of the new congressional mandates in NEPA, this test is particularly appropriate when agency action affects the environment.

Greene County Planning Board v. F.P.C.

In accordance with these precepts we find that the petitions are reviewable. Despite the Commission's argument that petitioners have made an inadequate showing of financial hardship, it is clear to us that a refusal to award petitioners expenses as they are incurred, particularly expenses related to production of expert witnesses, may significantly hamper a petitioner's efforts to represent the public interest before the Commission.[32] And, a retroactive award of experts' fees would be small consolation to a petitioner if the hearings are finished, the record is complete and these experts were not called because of inadequate funds.

Having determined that the petition for review is timely, we find

[31] *See, e.g.*, Guidelines for the Protection of Natural, Historic, Scenic, and Recreational Values in the Design and Location of Right-of-Way and Transmission Facilities, Report of the Working Committee on Utilities of the President's Council on Recreation and Natural Beauty (Dec. 27, 1968), reprinted in Commissioner Bagge's concurrence in the June 6, 1969, license. 41 F.P.C. at 725.

[32] *See* page 1408 and note 21 *supra*.

Greene County Planning Board v. F.P.C.

ourselves in agreement with the Commission's position that at this posture of the proceedings and under current circumstances, without a clearer congressional mandate we should not order the Commission or PASNY to pay the expenses and fees of petitioners, either as they are incurred or at the close of the proceedings.

Petitioners rely on two provisions of the Federal Power Act—Sections 309 and 314(c), 16 U.S.C. §§ 825h, 825m(c)—and buttress their interpretations of those sections with the mandate in Section 102(1) of NEPA that all public laws, "to the fullest extent possible," should be interpreted in accordance with national environmental policies. Section 309 empowers the Commission "to perform any and all acts, and to prescribe, issue, make, amend, and rescind such orders, rules, and regulations as it may find necessary or appropriate to carry out the provisions of [the Federal Power Act]." Although this section, which carries the title "Administrative powers of Commission; rules, regulations, and orders," is not restricted to "procedural minutiae," *Niagara Mohawk Power Corporation* v. *Federal Power Commission*, 379 F.2d 153, 158 (D.C. Cir. 1967) (FPC empowered to backdate a license), we perceive no basis in the terms of the provision to extend the Commission's power to include paying or awarding the expenses or fees of intervenors. We would need a far clearer congressional mandate to afford the relief requested, especially in dealing with counsel fees, when Congress has not hesitated in other circumstances explicitly to provide for them when to do so was in the public interest. See Clayton Act, 15 U.S.C. § 15; Communications Act of 1934, 47 U.S.C. § 206; Interstate Commerce Act, 49 U.S.C. § 16(2).

Nor is there any basis for reaching a different conclusion with respect to counsel fees under Section 314(c) of the Federal Power Act. It provides that "[t]he Commission may employ such attorneys as it finds necessary for proper legal aid and service of the Commission...." The legislative history bears out the only reasonable interpretation so clear on the face of the statute: "Subsection (c) authorizes the Commission to employ such attorneys as it needs for *its* legal work." H.R. Rep. No. 1318, 74th Cong., 1st Sess. 34 (emphasis added).

Finally, petitioners rely on the Supreme Court's decision in *Mills* v. *Electric Auto-Lite Co.*, 396 U.S. 375 (1970), which held that plaintiffs who successfully brought a derivative action under Section 14(a) of the Securities Exchange Act of 1934 were entitled to an award of costs, including counsel fees, against the corporation, even if the corporation recovered no money as a result of the action. Noting that the Securities Exchange Act did not provide for counsel fees, the Court based its decision on its equitable power to enforce the policies of the Act and to prevent unjust enrichment: "The dissemination of misleading proxy solicitations was a 'deceit practiced on the stockholders as a group,' *J. I. Case Co.* v. *Borak*, 377 U.S., at 432, and the expenses of petitioners' lawsuit have been incurred for the benefit of the corporation and the other shareholders." 396 U.S. at 392. Whether or not *Mills* could support such an award as petitioners seek without a more specific congressional mandate,[33] we do not find compelling need for it at this point, in view of our direction as to the role required of the Commission here.

Fully mindful that petitioners invoke our equitable powers, we cannot ignore parallel developments in this rapidly changing area of administrative law. As recently as December 7, 1971, the Administrative Conference of the United States refused to adopt a recommendation which would have endorsed the principle of reimbursing the legal expenses incurred by intervenors in administrative proceedings. The Conference, however, did adopt a recommendation which would oblige agencies to minimize filing and distribution requirements, to minimize the costs of obtaining transcripts, to make available the agency's technical files and to experiment with allowing access to their staff as advisers and witnesses. Recommendation 28, Public Participation in Administrative Hearings §D, adopted December 7, 1971. Without a showing of compelling need, it would be premature for us to inject the federal courts into this area of administrative discretion, perhaps foreclosing more flexible approaches through agency action or rules.

The petitions for review are granted in part and denied in part, and the case is remanded for further proceedings in accordance with this opinion.

[33] *See* Note, *The Allocation of Attorneys Fees after Mills* v. *Electric Auto-Lite*, 38 U. Chi. L. Rev. 316, 329–30 (1971).

COMMITTEE FOR NUCLEAR RESPONSIBILITY, INC., v. SEABORG

___F.2d___(D.C. Cir. Oct. 5, 1971)

Before BAZELON, *Chief Judge,* and LEVENTHAL and ROBINSON, *Circuit Judges.*

PER CURIAM: Plaintiffs seek to enjoin an underground nuclear test, code-named Cannikin, to be conducted by the defendant Atomic Energy Commission (A.E.C.). The district court granted summary judgment for defendants, and plaintiffs appealed.[1] The case came on for consideration of plaintiffs' motion for a stay pending appeal and expedited consideration of the appeal. The parties stipulated at the time of oral argument that since briefs on the merits had already been submitted by both parties, the case should be heard on the merits. Accordingly, we consider in this opinion the substantive questions presented. We reverse, and remand the case to the district court for continued proceedings consistent with this opinion.

I.

The A.E.C. is completing plans for an underground test of a nuclear warhead on Amchitka Island, Alaska.[2] As required by the National Environmental Policy Act (NEPA), 42 U.S.C. 4331 *et seq.* (1970), the Commission issued an impact statement evaluating the environmental effects of the test. Plaintiffs, seven conservation groups, seek to enjoin the test primarily on the grounds that the impact statement did not satisfy NEPA's requirements.[3]

Plaintiffs commenced discovery proceedings in an effort to establish the deficiency of the impact statement's treatment of potential dangers of the test. Defendants moved for dismissal of the complaint or in the alternative for summary judgment, and all discovery was stayed pending the outcome of the motion to dismiss. Immediately at the conclusion of the argument on the motion, the district court denied the motion to dismiss but granted summary judgment for defendants. This appeal followed.

II

The district court specifically upheld the sufficiency of the motion to dismiss. The court did not articulate its reasons for granting summary judgment, but from the record in the case, including the expedition with which the motion for summary judgment was granted, we conclude that the district court accepted the validity of the contention that was most strongly pressed by the Government: that Congress's passage of authorization and appropriations bills for the test represented a conclusive determination of the sufficiency of the impact statement. This contention was, in our view, erroneous, and in order to avoid the continuance of an order that was predicated on an impermissible basis, the judgment of the District Court must be reversed. See *The Delaware and Hudson Ry. Co.* v. *United Transportation Union,* No. 71-1183, March 31, 1971.

Congress could, of course, withdraw the question of the statement's compliance from the courts by repealing NEPA as it applied to the Cannikin test. But it is well settled that repeal by implication is disfavored, and the doctrine applies with full vigor when, as here, the subsequent legislation is an appropriations measure,[4] and when the prior Act is to continue in its general applicability, as construed by the courts, but the claim is made that it is to be subject to a particularized legislative exception.[5] Congress must be free to provide authorizations and appropriations for projects proposed by the executive even though claims of illegality on grounds of noncompliance with NEPA are pending in the courts. There is, of course, nothing inconsistent with adoption of appropriations and authorizations measures on the *pro tanto* assumption of validity, while leaving any claim of invalidity to be determined by the courts.[6] That is the effect of the authorization and appropriations measures relating to the Cannikin test. This conclusion is established by the general principles just discussed. Nothing in the legislative history leads to a different result. On the contrary, there is an affirmative indication that at least some of the Congressmen voting for the authorization and appropriations measures specifically contemplated that the claim of illegality remained for resolution by the courts.[7] The legislative history indicates that while the impact statement was used as reference material by both proponents and opponents of the test, Congress did not purport to make a binding determination on the issue whether the statement was in compliance with NEPA.

Thus, plaintiffs clearly presented a cognizable claim under NEPA,[8] and summary judgment would be appropriate only if they failed to provide any factual underpinning for their claim.[9]

[1] For purposes of this opinion we refer to appellants in this court as "plaintiffs" and appellees as "defendants."

[2] The precise yield of the nuclear test has not been released although it is in the range of five megatons. The test was originally scheduled for October, 1971, but Congress has provided that it may not take place sooner than May, 1972, unless the President gives his direct approval for an earlier date.

[3] Appellants also rested their claim for injunctive relief on three other grounds, asserted violations of:
(1) The Nuclear Test Ban Treaty,
(2) Various statutes designed to protect wildlife, and
(3) The rights under the Fifth and Ninth Amendments of citizens endangered by Cannikin.

[4] *See, e.g., United States* v. *Langston,* 118 U.S. 389 (1886).

[5] *Cf., District of Columbia Civic Assn.* v. *Volpe,* —— U.S. App. D.C. ——, 434 F.2d 436, 444-47 (1970).

[6] That was precisely the conclusion as to the intent of Congress reached in another NEPA case by the court in *Environmental Defense Fund, Inc.* v. *Corps of Engineers,* 325 F.Supp. 749, 762-63 (E.D. Ark. 1971).

[7] Thus, Representative Price, in voting for the project, stated concerning the issue of whether the impact statement complied with NEPA: "This matter is before the court. I submit that if there has been any violation of the law, the court will supply the appropriate remedy." 112 CONG. REC. 6785, July 15, 1971.

[8] In view of our disposition of the case, it is not necessary to rule on whether any of plaintiffs' other three grounds for relief state a claim on which relief can be granted. Our order does not foreclose the district court, on remand, from striking any or all of those grounds for failure to state a claim.

[9] Rule 56, Fed.R.Civ.Pro., permits summary judgment only when no material issue of fact is in dispute and the moving party is by law entitled to judgment. *See Sartor* v. *Arkansas Gas Corp.,* 321 U.S. 620, 627 (1944).

III

Section 102 of NEPA requires, *inter alia,* that an impact statement assess adverse environmental effects and discuss alternatives to the proposed action.[10] On the ultimate issue whether a project should be undertaken or not, a matter involving the assessment and weighing of various factors, the court's function is limited. However, the court has a responsibility to determine whether the agencies involved have fully and in good faith followed the procedure contemplated by Congress: that is, setting forth the environmental factors involved in order that those entrusted with ultimate determination whether to authorize, abandon or modify the project, shall be clearly advised of the environmental factors which they must take into account. See *Calvert Cliffs' Coordinating Committee* v. *Atomic Energy Commission,* No. 24,839, slip opinion at 11.

The statement has importance in focusing the environmental factors involved even when the officials ultimately responsible are in, or more likely the head of, the office or agency that prepared the report. The ultimate decision must of course take into account matters other than environmental factors, but insofar as staff has prepared the environmental statement for transmission and consideration throughout the entire executive process, the officials making the ultimate decision, whether within or outside the agency, must be informed of the full range of responsible opinion on the environmental effects in order to make an informed choice. Moreover, the statement has significance in focusing environmental factors for informed appraisal by the President, who has broad concern even when not directly involved in the decisional process, and in any event by Congress and the public.

When, as here, the issue of procedure relates to the sufficiency of the presentation in the statement, the court is not to rule on the relative merits of competing scientific opinion. Its function is only to assure that the statement sets forth the opposing scientific views, and does not take the arbitrary and impermissible approach of completely omitting from the statement, and hence from the focus that the statement was intended to provide for the deciding officials, any reference whatever to the existence of responsible scientific opinions concerning possible adverse environmental effects.[11] Only *responsible* opposing views need be included and hence there is room for discretion on the part of the officials preparing the statement; but there is no room for an assumption that their determination is conclusive. The agency need not set forth at full length views with which it disagrees, all that is required is a meaningful reference that identifies the problem at hand for the responsible official. The agency, of course, is not foreclosed from noting in the statement that it accepts certain contentions or rejects others.[12]

By means of discovery and the introduction of the affidavit of a scientific expert, plaintiffs attempted to prove that the requirement of the law was not met "fully and in good faith" by the A.E.C. The district court's grant of summary judgment erroneously foreclosed this line of inquiry to plaintiffs.

Summary judgment is only appropriate when there is no bona fide material issue, and Rule 56 clearly contemplates that the parties shall have opportunity for deposition in order to establish the existence of a material issue.[13] Here, plaintiffs sought to establish that there was responsible scientific opinion as to possible adverse environmental consequences, a fact that would be material in support of their legal claim that omission of all reference to such scientific opinion was contrary to the process prescribed by NEPA.[14]

Plaintiffs also alleged the existence of reports by federal agencies recommending against Cannikin specifically because of potential harm to the environment. NEPA clearly indicates that the agency responsible for a project should obtain and release such adverse reports.[15] If these reports exist, and they are not subject to some statutory exemp-

[10] NEPA, section 102, 42 U.S.C. 4332 (1970):

> The Congress authorizes and directs that, to the fullest extent possible: (1) the policies, regulations, and public laws of the United States shall be interpreted and administered in accordance with the policies set forth in this chapter, and (2) all agencies of the Federal Government shall—
>
> (A) utilize a systematic, interdisciplinary approach which will insure the integrated use of the natural and social sciences and the environmental design arts in planning and in decisionmaking which may have an impact on man's environment;
>
> (B) identify and develop methods and procedures, in consultation with the Council on Environmental Quality established by subchapter II of this chapter, which will insure that presently unquantified environmental amenities and values may be given appropriate consideration in decisionmaking along with economic and technical considerations;
>
> (C) include in every recommendation or report on proposals for legislation and other major Federal actions significantly affecting the quality of the human environment, a detailed statement by the responsible official on—
>
> (i) the environmental impact of the proposed action,
>
> (ii) any adverse environmental effects which cannot be avoided should the proposal be implemented,
>
> (iii) alternatives to the proposed action,
>
> (iv) the relationship between local short-term uses of man's environment and the maintenance and enhancement of long-term productivity, and
>
> (v) any irreversible and irretrievable commitments of resources which would be involved in the proposed action should it be implemented.
>
> Prior to making any detailed statement, the responsible Federal official shall consult with and obtain the comments of any Federal agency which has jurisdiction by law or special expertise with respect to any environmental impact involved. Copies of such statement and the comments and views of the appropriate Federal, State, and local agencies, which are authorized to develop and enforce environmental standards, shall be made available to the President, the Council on Environmental Quality and to the public as provided by section 552 of Title 5, and shall accompany the proposal through the existing agency review processes; . . .

[11] *Compare Environmental Defense Fund, Inc.* v. *Corps of Engineers,* 325 F.Supp. 749, 759 (E.D.Ark. 1971).

[12] *Compare Environmental Defense Fund, Inc.* v. *Corps of Engineers,* 325 F.Supp. 749, 759 (E.D.Ark. 1971).

[13] *Cf.,* Rule 56(f), Fed.R.Civ.Pro., *Berne Street Enterprises, Inc.* v. *American Export Isbrandtsen Co., Inc.,* 298 F.Supp. 195 (S.D.N.Y. 1968), 6 Moore's *Federal Practice,* § 56.24.

[14] We do not here decide that the statement is inadequate, but only that the district court is not to foreclose an opportunity to plaintiffs to make their submission on this point.

[15] 42 U.S.C. 4332 (1970).

tion, plaintiffs must prevail on this contention as well.[16] Plaintiffs attempted, through deposition of the A.E.C. and through attempted deposition of the agencies whom they believed to have such reports, to uncover facts supporting their claim. The grant of summary judgment prematurely terminated the discovery process and foreclosed plaintiffs' opportunity to substantiate their allegations.

Since unresolved questions of fact existed as to both of plaintiffs' arguments under NEPA, summary judgment was plainly inappropriate. On remand, plaintiffs' discovery—subject of course to the possible interposition of valid claims of privilege—should be allowed to continue.[17]

Reversed and remanded.

[16] We do not consider whether the court may decline to order the release of agency comments on the ground that they are not so related to the impact statement as to require their inclusion therein, or on the ground that they are exempt from public disclosure by virtue of exemptions set forth in the Freedom of Information Act, 5 U.S.C. 552 (1970), which should be transported into NEPA. No such grounds were presented to us at this time, and accordingly we express no opinion thereon.

[17] Since defendants stated that the test would not take place without ample notice to the plaintiffs, we see no need to consider whether or not to issue a stay *pendente lite*. If the need arises, the question of a stay may, of course, be addressed to the district court.

COMMITTEE FOR NUCLEAR RESPONSIBILITY, INC., v. SEABORG

___ F.2d ___ (D.C. Cir. Oct. 28, 1971)

Per Curiam: This appeal presents a new chapter in the litigation concerning the proposed underground nuclear test, code-named Cannikin, on Amchitka Island, Alaska. In *Committee for Nuclear Responsibility, Inc. v. Seaborg*, No. 71-1732, October 5, 1971, we held that plaintiffs—conservation groups—had presented a cognizable claim, which the courts were obligated to determine, that the Atomic Energy Commission had failed to carry out the mandate of Congress in the National Environmental Policy Act (NEPA), 42 U.S.C. §§ 4331 *et seq.* (1970), to set forth all pertinent environmental effects of the project, and thus to provide the disclosure which is indispensable to informed appraisal of the project by the Executive, Congress, and, the public. We remanded the case to the District Court so that plaintiffs might present evidence in support of their allegations, and continue the pretrial discovery that had been untimely curtailed by the government's motion to dismiss the lawsuit.

On remand plaintiffs sought to have the government produce documents in its possession allegedly containing information needed by plaintiffs for substantiation of their claim. The government resisted and raised a claim of executive privilege. To resolve the question of privilege, the District Court ordered the government to submit the documents at issue for personal *in camera* inspection by the District Court after excising any and all materials reflecting military and diplomatic secrets as distinguished from possible environmental hazards of the test. The order included a certification under 28 U.S.C. § 1292(b) of the controlling importance of the questions presented.[1] The government filed an application for allowance of an immediate appeal, challenging the District Court's order on the grounds that executive privilege precludes even *in camera* screening by the District Court. We grant the appeal and affirm the order of the District Court. Respondents in this proceeding, plaintiffs below, request a stay of the blast *pendente lite*. For the reasons set forth below, we deny the stay.

I.

Disposition of the matters before us has been expedited in view of the announcement, made to the Court at oral argument yesterday afternoon, that less than two hours earlier the Atomic Energy Commission had issued a press release stating as follows:

STATEMENT BY AEC CHAIRMAN
JAMES R. SCHLESINGER

> The Atomic Energy Commission is now planning to proceed with the Cannikin test. We have now received the requisite authority to go ahead including detonation. Stemming operations at the test site, which make it impractical to recover the device, will begin today. We expect to be in a readiness state to detonate within a week.
>
> The primary purposes of Cannikin are to proof test the Spartan warhead and to obtain measurements on yield and on x-ray flux and spectrum. Testing is regarded as a desirable and prudent step before large investment of funds is made on that component of the Safeguard system. From the national security standpoint no serious objection has been raised against conducting the test. On that score the case is straightforward.
>
> Some objections have been raised on environmental grounds. In the careful examination of these issues within the Executive Branch environmental damage has been exhaustively considered and overriding requirements of national security have, of necessity, taken precedence.

The government suggests that the developments recounted in the statement may render the case moot. That suggestion is not sound. As our opinion of October 5 made clear, the recent action of Congress[2] requiring the President personally to approve the test before it can go forward does not negate the AEC's obligation to comply with NEPA. Approval by the President and compliance with NEPA are two separate statutory requirements which

[1] A copy of the District Court's order is appended to this opinion. The District Court had previously filed with this Court, on October 20, 1971, a *Request for Further Guidance on the Perimeters of Discovery* contemplated by our first opinion in this case, No. 71-1732. In a Memorandum Order, filed the following day, we indicated our appreciation of the District Court's initiative shown in the request, but declined to give further guidance because at that juncture, the Court had:

> not been apprised of the particular objections made by the Government to plaintiffs' applications for discovery. Our Memorandum Order of October 19, 1971, requested that the Government advise us of those objections, but a statement of objections was not supplied because the proceedings before us were mooted by the Government's disclosure that detonation would not in any event take place prior to October 27, 1971.

We left open, however, the possibility of a future interlocutory appeal pursuant to 28 U.S.C. 1292(b). The District Court, in following that procedure here, has now focused the issues involved for our decision.

[2] Pub. L. No. 92-134, 85 Stat. 365 (1971).

must be satisfied if the test is to be lawfully carried out. The President's decision satisfies one requirement. This Court, as to the second requirement of law, is left with the responsibility to determine whether the AEC disregarded the will of Congress in preparing the environmental impact statement required by NEPA.

II.

Documents such as those encompassed in the District Court's order would normally remain part of the internal files of the agencies involved in the absence of an appropriate demand. When such demand is made in conjunction with discovery sought in the courts, the settled rule is that the court must balance the moving party's need for the documents in the litigation against the reasons which are asserted in defending their confidentiality.[3]

The government's interest in confidentiality is plain where the documents make reference to military or diplomatic secrets. But plaintiffs indicated clearly that they seek no such secrets, and the District Court's order explicitly provides that the government is not required to produce any documents or parts of documents which contain such secret material.

The government may still have an interest, however, in avoiding disclosure of documents which reflect intra-executive advisory opinions and recommendations whose confidentiality contributes substantially to the effectiveness of government decision-making processes.[4] *In camera* inspection of allegedly privileged documents—as ordered here by the District Court—is a procedure approved by the courts at least where, as here, military and diplomatic secrets are not at issue.[5] Of course, the party seeking discovery must make a preliminary showing of necessity to warrant even *in camera* disclosure,[6] but there is no claim on this appeal that plaintiffs have not made such a showing or that the District Court's order is erroneous for lack of such a showing.

The purpose of *in camera* inspection by the District Court is to permit the District Judge to examine the documents and determine which documents, or which portions of documents, may properly be disclosed to the other party, and which should continue to be held in a confidential status. This determination may come to require e.g., separation of those documents or portions of documents that set forth facts from those that present comments that must be held confidential in order to maintain the integrity of the executive decision-making process.

However, the government seeks to distinguish all those cases [7] where it was required to produce documents for *in camera* inspection on the ground that in those cases the government gave reasons to the court for withholding disclosure. In this case, says the government, it is invoking "true" executive privilege—and is not offering any reasons to the court. The claim of privilege consists of the filing of affidavits from the five officials heading the agencies where the documents are located. Each of those officials avers that he has determined that the documents in his official custody may not be produced for the personal *in camera* inspection of the judge, on the ground that such disclosure even to the judge would be contrary to the public interest. The government's position—sharpened at oral argument yesterday—is that this determination by the executive official is conclusive upon the court, and the court has no judicial authority to require the production of the documents in the possession of an executive department, once the head of that department has filed this formal claim of privilege. Government counsel further asserts that this executive determination is conclusive even where the document only relates to certain factual material that is essential for disposition of the lawsuit, and even where the document is such that the court may readily separate factual material to be disclosed to the other party from the kind of recommendations and discussion that would be an integral part of the decision-making process.

In our view, this claim of absolute immunity for documents in possession of an executive department or agency, upon the bald assertion of its head, is not sound law.

There are some cases that hold that the court may not require production from a subordinate official when his departmental regulation requires that the decision on production should be first presented to the head of the department. *Boske v. Comingore* 177 U.S. 459 (1900); *U.S. Ex rel Touhy v. Ragen* 340 U.S. 462 (1951). But as Justice Reed pointed out in the latter case, these decisions went to the point of "centralizing determination as to whether subpoenas *duces tecum* will be willingly obeyed or challenged," 340 U.S. at 468. When it is the *head* of the executive department who presents a challenge to an order requiring the production of documents, the claim of privilege is one for consideration by the court, which could give attention to the reasons presented by the head of the agency for failing to produce the information.

These early cases were based on a "housekeeping" provision, now codified as 5 U.S.C. § 301 (1970), which authorized each department to issue regulations with respect to custody of its papers. This statute does permit centralization of responsibility in a department whether to claim a privilege. But as the Fifth Circuit has held, it does not confer a privilege, and this view of its intendment is fortified by the 1958 amendment which added the following language: "This section does not authorize withholding information from the public or limiting the availability of records to the public." [8] Such statutes must be read in

[3] *See, e.g.,* United States v. Reynolds, 345 U.S. 1, 11 (1953), Carl Zeiss Stiftung v. V.E.B., Carl Zeiss, Jena, 40 F.R.D. 318, 327, (1966) (hereinafter *Zeiss*) *aff'd on the basis of the opinion of the District Court* in 128 U.S. App. D.C. 10, 384 F.2d 979, *cert. den'd* 389 U.S. 952 (1967).

[4] *Zeiss* at 324.

[5] *See, e.g.,* Freeman v. Seligson, 132 U.S. App. D.C. 56, 69 n.65, 405 F.2d 1326, 1339 n.65 (1968), Boeing Airplane Co. v. Coggeshall, 108 U.S. App. D.C. 106, 114, 280 F.2d 654, 662 (1960).

[6] *See, e.g.,* United States v. Reynolds, 345 U.S. 1, 11 (1953), *Zeiss* at 327.

[7] *E.g.,* Machin v. Zuckert, 114 U.S. App. D.C. 335, 316 F.2d 336 (1963), *cert. denied* 327 U.S. 896 (1963).

[8] *See,* N.L.R.B. v. Capitol Fish Co., 294 F.2d 868, 875 (5th Cir., 1961):

> 5 U.S.C.A. § 22 [now § 301] cannot be construed to establish authority in the executive departments to determine whether certain papers and records are privileged. Its function is to furnish the departments with housekeeping authority. It cannot bar a judicial determination of the question of privilege or a demand for the production of evidence found not privileged. Had there been any doubt of this before, the doubt was removed by the amendment of 5 U.S.C.A. § 22 [now § 301] in 1958 making explicit the fact that the section does not of itself create a privilege. This amendment added the

light of the importance of the rule of law, and the fair administration of justice, of permitting limited disclosures in judicial proceedings, with judicious use of protective orders. *See Freeman v. Seligson,* 132 U.S. App. D.C. 56, 78, 405 F.2d 1326, 1348 (1968).

The last claim of the government is an appeal to the doctrine of Separation of Powers. It is argued that the inherent constitutional powers of the executive branch give it the legal authority to determine what documents in its possession will be produced in court.

There is no direct Supreme Court precedent. The question was noted, but not decided, in *United States v. Reynolds,* 345 U.S. 1, 16 (1952). The view of this Court is determined by fundamental legal principles, and principally the root conception of the rule of law in our democratic society. An essential ingredient of our rule of law is the authority of the courts to determine whether an executive official or agency has complied with the Constitution and with the mandates of Congress which define and limit the authority of the executive. Any claim to executive absolutism cannot override the duty of the court to assure that an official has not exceeded his charter or flouted the legislative will.

Of course the court exercises its authority with due deference to the position of the executive. It will take into account all proper considerations, including the importance of maintaining the integrity of executive decision-making processes. But no executive official or agency can be given absolute authority to determine what documents in his possession may be considered by the court in its task. Otherwise the head of an executive department would have the power on his own say so to cover up all evidence of fraud and corruption when a federal court or grand jury was investigating malfeasance in office, and this is not the law.

With the power of the District Court to determine the question of privilege thus firmly established in the context of the controversy as it has been presented to us, we think it is plain that the judgment of the District Court must be affirmed. We are issuing our order so that the executive officials may proceed at once to carry out the order of the District Court. When the documents are produced before the District Judge for his personal *in camera* inspection, he will consider whether the plaintiffs' need for access to the documents, or any part of the documents, for purposes of this litigation must be overridden by some higher requirement of confidentiality.

Normally this balancing process will require an excision, from the factual data in the documents, of material which consists purely of advice, deliberations and recommendations.[9] Certain of the documents, though, may constitute agency comments whose existence prior to the issuance of the impact statement in final form required their inclusion in the statement by virtue of section 102 of NEPA, 42 U.S.C. 4332(C) (1970).

sentence, "This section does not authorize withholding information from the public or limiting the availability of records to the public." 72 Stat. 547 (1958). As a matter of comity, courts frequently do not require disclosure of the evidence when the circumstances indicate that the records should be confidential; if the court wishes to scrutinize it to make sure, the evidence may be examined in camera. But the ultimate determination of the privilege remains with the courts. (Citations omitted)

[9] *See Zeiss* at 324.

The Atomic Energy Commission, which prepared the environmental impact statement, was "responsible for making the statement and the comments received available to the public pursuant to the provisions of the Freedom of Information Act." *See* 36 Fed. Reg. 7724, 7726-27, § 10(f) (1971). These regulations, promulgated by the Council on Environmental Quality to implement NEPA, specify that the exemption for inter-agency memoranda is not applicable concerning the comments of federal agencies to be consulted in connection with the preparation of an environmental statement. And section 7 of those regulations specifically states that the project agency "should consult with and obtain the comment on the environmental impact of the action of federal agencies with jurisdiction by law or special expertise with respect to any environmental impact involved." [10] The Environmental Protection Agency—one of the agencies from whom a document was requested by the District Court—is specifically identified in this regulation as one of the agencies within the contemplation of section 7. The answer to the question of whether the statement by the Environmental Protection Agency mentioned in the District Court's order is required by NEPA to be included in the impact statement can only be determined after an *in camera* view.[11]

As to the documents not related to the NEPA process, the District Court's responsibility requires that it balance the need of the plaintiffs in the litigation brought to assure conformance to legislative will, against the necessity for confidentiality, as detailed above.[12]

We are not now addressing ourselves to the question of the obligation of the Atomic Energy Commission to include in the environmental statement other information that came into its possession prior to the issuance of that document. That is the ultimate issue for the District Court to determine in this litigation. Nor are we required to determine which official reports should be disclosed to the plaintiffs, or what portions of those reports should be disclosed. The only question which we decide now is that the District Court was correct in requiring an *in camera* investigation as a first step in ruling on the plaintiffs' request for disclosure and the proper extent of any government privilege.

[10] 36 Fed. Reg. 7724, 7725, § 7 (1971).

[11] Our opinion of October 5, 1971, indicated that an agency responsible for a project should obtain and release reports of federal agencies on the environmental effect of a project, but specifically reserved, at page 9, note 16, the question of disclosure of agency comments that are not so related to the impact statement as to require their inclusion therein, or are included within the exemptions of the Freedom of Information Act.

[12] In this process, the District Court must make, e.g., the judgments required to separate fact from opinion. And, as already noted in our opinion of October 5, the facts in this litigation include whether there is a body of opinion that was not fairly reflected in the AEC environment statement; either opinion of government officials or agencies, or a body of other responsible scientific opinion. The District Court may be able to determine the existence of such responsible opinion, without undertaking to pass on its ultimate scientific validity.

When analyzing the technical data *in camera,* the District Court judge may find it helpful, in order to enhance his comprehension of the documents lodged with him, to consider requesting a consultation with an expert provided by the government. This consultation should be undertaken with the corollary procedure of transcription of the comments in chambers, as reported by someone acceptable to the government, with the transcript to be kept under seal.

Plaintiffs' application for a stay *pendente lite* confronts the Court with an inherent limitation on its scope and information. The AEC release yesterday, reflecting the President's approval of the test, states that the Executive Branch has considered problems of environmental damage and has given precedence to "overriding requirements of national security." The Court is concerned solely with the question of legality of the AEC action under NEPA and its obligation to determine that question. It is in no position to consider or appraise the national security aspects of the test underlying the President's determination. It is the responsibility of the Executive to take into account both the considerations of national security and the serious issues of legality, identified by the opinions of this Court, relating to the claim that the AEC has failed to comply with NEPA and thus to permit the informed appraisal, by the Executive, Congress and the public, contemplated by that statute. The Court limits its actions in this litigation to matters within the judicial province; it is in no position at this juncture to enter a stay order that would interject the Court into national security matters that lie outside its province.

The mandate will issue at 4 p.m. this afternoon, but will be stayed for an additional 24 hours if the Court is advised that the government wishes to present an application to the Supreme Court for review and stay.

APPENDIX

ORDER OF THE DISTRICT COURT

IT IS HEREBY ORDERED that the defendants furnish to this Court the documents hereafter listed (with respect to which defendants have formally invoked executive privilege) for in camera inspection to determine whether they contain a presentation or discussion of an environmental hazard of substance not alluded to in the environmental statement relating to the Cannikin test. All matters relating to the environment in these documents shall be included, but no matter that is involved directly in national security, as differentiated from the environment, or as involves foreign relations, as differentiated from the environment, shall be included in the material produced for the Court's inspection.

The documents referred to are as follows:

1. With reference to Annex B to the Larson affidavit (Exhibit 18) and item except Ia 1(a) item 1-A.

2. With reference to the Irwin affidavit (Exhibit 13) item 5-C.

3. With reference to the David affidavit (Exhibit 12) item 3.

4. With reference to the Ruckelshaus affidavit (Exhibit 14) item 5.

5. With reference to the Train affidavit (Exhibit 11), items 3(a), 3(b) and 3(c).

Pursuant to the provisions of 28 U.S.C. 1292(b) it is the opinion of the Court that the foregoing order involves a controlling question of law as to which there is substantial ground for difference of opinion and that an immediate appeal from the order may materially advance the ultimate termination of this litigation.

IT IS FURTHER ORDERED that the execution of this order is stayed pending review by the Court of Appeals pursuant to the provisions of 28 U.S.C. 1292(b).

COMMITTEE FOR NUCLEAR RESPONSIBILITY, INC., v. SEABORG

__F.2d__(D.C. Cir. Nov. 3, 1971)

Before Bazelon, *Chief Judge*, and Leventhal and Robinson, *Circuit Judges*.

Per Curiam: Plaintiffs, conservation groups seeking to enjoin an underground nuclear explosion (code-named Cannikan) on Amchitka Island, Alaska, appeal from the District Court's denial of a preliminary injunction, and seek leave to appeal under 28 U.S.C. § 1292(b) from the District Court's order resolving certain questions of discovery. Plaintiffs have pressed their case with increasing urgency in court as the proposed detonation becomes ever more imminent. On October 28, 1971, we denied plaintiff's motion to stay the test, but affirmed the District Court's order requiring the Government to produce for *in camera* inspection certain documents which plaintiffs had been attempting to discover for months. Following *in camera* inspection on October 30, the District Court entered an order on November 1, which directed that some of these documents be released to plaintiffs (per Schedule A), but upheld the Government's objection to the release of other documents (in Schedule B). The Government does not seek to appeal, under § 1292(b), the rulings requiring disclosure.

Plaintiffs immediately appealed from the denial of a preliminary injunction. They move for summary reversal and stay. We deny that motion.

With regard to the discovery order, we have concluded that it would be inappropriate to entertain an appeal on this interlocutory matter at this time. The application for leave to appeal is denied.

I

The denial of a preliminary injunction was accompanied by findings of fact and conclusions of law in which the District Court indicated, *inter alia,* (1) that the Impact Statement issued by the Atomic Energy Commission (AEC) satisfied all of the requirements of the National Environmental Policy Act (NEPA), 42 U.S.C. §§ 4331 *et seq.* (1970); (2) that none of the documents examined *in camera* by the District Court contained discussion of environmental hazards of substance not "alluded to" in the AEC's Impact Statement; (3) that defendants have complied with NEPA and all applicable law and are not threatening to engage in illegal action; and (4) that the courts lack jurisdiction to enjoin this "presidential decision."

While we do not modify the order of the District Court, we do not accept the propositions upon which it relied. In our view the case does present a substantial question as to the legality of the proposed test. But it does not necessarily follow that plaintiffs are entitled to an injunction against the test.

It is distressing that the case has come to require even limited judicial consideration at a moment when the time available for that consideration is even more limited. Although the action was begun four months ago, and plaintiffs moved promptly for discovery, this discovery was ordered discontinued. It is only within the past few days that important documents were produced by the Government. We are not to be taken as saying this in a spirit of assessment of blame. The Government's counsel were entitled to press its contentions—which we subsequently rejected—first that NEPA had been suspended, and second that the Executive had an absolute constitutional privilege to withhold from the courts such documents as the Executive determined to withhold, even though the courts specifically excluded any call on documents in the area of military or diplomatic secrecy.

The fact remains, however, that judicial consideration at this time has been drastically foreshortened. We have examined *in camera* the papers presented to the District Court, including the papers which the District Court did not disclose. We are left with difficult questions about the validity of the AEC's environmental statement. But a hurried review of several hundred pages of technical documents cannot provide a satisfactory basis for resolving this litigation.

Our failure to enjoin the test is not predicated on a conviction that the AEC has compiled with NEPA in setting forth the dangers of environmental harm. The NEPA process—which is designed to minimize the likelihood of harm—has not run its course in the courts. We are in no position to calculate the dangers from the Cannikin test.

As to the harms which will accrue if the test is enjoined, they were presented to us by the Government in a paper filed October 26, 1971. The Government indicated that the process of stemming the test hole was scheduled to begin that day, and it did apparently begin on schedule. The Government's paper stated:

> Stemming involves putting gravel and other materials down the test hole on top of the nuclear device. This prevents release of radioactive materials into the atmosphere. Stemming makes it impractical to recover the test device. If the device were not detonated at full yield, it would probably be destroyed with a non-nuclear charge.
>
> If we were to start stemming and then discover we could not conduct the full-yield test, we would be prevented from another test for at least a year since there is not another device or test hole readily available. Such a delay would prevent the deployment of the Spartan interceptor in the Safeguard system by at least a year or force us to enter into production of the Spartan warhead when it has not been fully tested. Moreover, the cost of preparation for this test, which are not recoverable if the test does not proceed, would be at least 118 million dollars. Moreover, an additional 70 to 120 million dollars would be required to prepare again for another test.
>
> The risks increase substantially each day because the weather deteriorates in the Amchitka area from this time on; reasonably good weather is necessary for proper observation of the test by ground stations and for other supporting operations. Also, the device is already at the bottom of the test hole and any delay increases the risk of mechanical problems. For instance, the device is protected from the environment at 6,000 feet depth by a life-support system which has a limited life. In short, a period of bad weather combined with technical problems, both of which are unpredictable, could prevent the test. Each day of delay substantially increases these risks.

The Government also indicated that an injunction, and the resulting disruption of the Safeguard-ABM missile system, could well jeopardize the Strategic Arms Limitation Talks.

While the Government's assertion of monetary damage from an injunction is not minimal, it does not weigh as heavily with us as its assertions of potential harm to national security and foreign policy—assertions which we obviously can not appraise—and given the meager state of the record before us, we are constrained to refuse an injunction. *Cf.* Reynolds v. Sims, 377 U.S. 533, 585 (1964); Note, *Developments in the Law—Injunctions,* 78 Harv.L. Rev. 994, 1005-08 (1965). While we deny preventive relief, it should be clear that plaintiffs may yet prevail in their claim that the AEC failed to comply with NEPA in approving the Cannikin test.

II

Plaintiffs have also filed a motion for leave to appeal under 28 U.S.C. § 1292(b) from the District Court's order withholding certain documents from discovery. The order was predicated on a finding, made after an *in camera* investigation, that the documents in question consisted of intra-executive recommendations and deliberations whose confidentiality was required in order to maintain the integrity of the Executive's decision-making process.

Section 1292(b) permits an appellate court to grant an interlocutory appeal when resolution of the questions presented would materially advance the ultimate termination of the litigation. The transcript reveals the District Court's effort to apply our ruling of October 28. What is now involved on review is not so much a matter of stating controlling principles as reviewing their application. We cannot resolve this issue in the short span of time before the detonation of the blast. Whatever the consequences of the detonation, its mere occurence will not moot the issue of the Government's compliance with laws designed to insure that environmental factors involved in a decision of this magnitude are considered and set forth fully and candidly, pursuant to the Congressional mandate, for the information of the executive and legislative branches and the public. Review of the District Court's order withholding certain documents will await review of its final disposition of the case.

The plaintiffs' motion for summary reversal of the order of the District Court denying the motion for a preliminary injunction is denied. We also deny plaintiffs' application for leave to appeal the order of the District Court withholding certain documents from plaintiffs on the grounds of privilege.

So ordered.

See also the materials on
the Freedom of Information Act
at Five-51

ELY v. VELDE

___F.2d___(4th Cir. Nov. 8, 1971), 3 ERC 1280

SOBELOFF, J.:

This appeal calls upon us to consider an alleged conflict between several recently formulated federal policies. On the one hand, there is a congressional commitment against federal interference with a state's use of federal funds allocated to it for law enforcement; and, on the other, there are congressional mandates to all federal agencies to act so as to preserve and protect the natural environment and the historic and cultural foundations of the nation.

Appellants, who are residents of the Green Springs area of Louisa County, Virginia, brought an action to halt the proposed funding and construction in their neighborhood of a Medical and Reception Center ("Center") for Virginia prisoners. To this end, they sought to enjoin appellees Richard W. Velde and Clarence M. Coster, Associate Administrators of the Law Enforcement Assistance Administration ("LEAA"), from allocating to Virginia $775,000 of federal funds for the construction of the center. The complaining residents prayed, in addition, for an injunction against Otis L. Brown, Director of the Virginia Department of Welfare and Institutions, to prevent him from locating the contemplated institution in Green Springs.

[The court then discussed NEPA and the National Historic Preservation Act (NHPA), and determined that the LEAA had failed to comply with the mandatory procedural requirements of both statutes.]

An ancillary argument of the complaining parties, not vigorously pressed, is that apart from NHPA and NEPA, the federal Constitution was violated by Brown's "unreasonable and arbitrary action" in placing the proposed Center in Green Springs. We decline the invitation to elevate to a constitutional level the concerns voiced by the appellants. While a growing number of commentators argue in support of a constitutional protection for the environment[1], this newly-advanced constitutional doctrine has not yet been accorded judicial sanction; and appellants do not present a convincing case for doing so.

Appellants baldly attempt to stretch rights, protected by law against infringement by federal agencies only, to cover the states and their officers in disregard of the plainly limited character of the legislation. They make their assertion without citation of a single relevant authority and with no attempt to develop supporting reasons. The general concept of conservation and protection of the environment has, in the recent past, made vast advances, prompting the adoption of NHPA, NEPA and other legislation. But without any showing whatever, we are not free to lay upon the State of Virginia new obligations on constitutional grounds.

Neither the statutes nor the Constitution confers rights on the appellants which are enforceable vis-a-vis the State of Virginia under 28 U.S.C. Sec. 1983.

To summarize, we hold that the LEAA is duty-bound, in approving the grant at issue here, to comply with the procedural requirements of NHPA and NEPA. We reverse the judgment as to appellees Velde and Coster and we remand for the entry of an appropriate order in accord with this opinion.

However, for the reasons stated above, the denial of an injunction against appellee Brown is afirmed.

Affirmed in part, reversed in part, and remanded.

1/ E.G., Sive, Some Thoughts of an Environmental Lawyer in the Wilderness of Administrative Law, 70 Colum. L. Rev. 612, 642-43 (1970); Roberts, The Right to a Decent Environment, 55 Cornell L. Rev. 674, 688-92 (1970); Note, Toward a Constitutionally Protected Environment, 46 Va. L. Rev. 458 (1970).

CHAPTER TWO: Solid Wastes & Recycling

a. Solid wastes: an overview

Solid waste is the first class of pollutants to be treated extensively in this book, but it cannot be treated in isolation, for all pollution, indeed all ecological problems, are interconnected in an infinite number of ways.

Solid waste is the trash discarded by the apartment dweller; it is the corn stalks left to rot in a farmer's field; it is the ore tailings sent streaming into Lake Superior; it is the automobile sold to the scrap dealer, and the one abandoned along a country road; it is what is left when man has touched nature and moved on.

The interconnections are complex, sometimes circular, and never so simple that any single "solution" to a disposal problem does not then create some other problem. Matter is neither created nor destroyed: merely turned into waste, useful products, or relatively neutral substances.

Our own survival is based on the waste cycle: not only do we feast on bread and wine and cheese, but the plentitude of our soil and our seas is based on the waste cycle.

By bulk and weight, agricultural waste is the biggest element in U.S. solid waste. Mineral waste is second in terms of the tons of waste produced. But it is the industrial, commercial, institutional, and residential waste that is the major environmental problem. The effect of this environmental assault is most pronounced in the poverty areas of urban America. When added to the host of other problems of our inner cities the filth overwhelms the body, mind, and spirit. This condition is one more example of our institutional failures. Cities have other priorities, and the Federal government has minimal interest in this subject. Federal money might provide funds for cleaning our urban areas. But unless any Federal money granted is available only for this purpose, city governments will allocate it for some other purpose.

It is ironic that while unemployment in inner city areas is a national disgrace, there is no money available to clean the streets let alone provide the parks and gardens that make many foreign cities so attractive. To paraphrase what has been said before—we need to use our entrenching tools for gardening implements.

If we were serious about cleaning our urban environments, money is necessary and just as important as new laws. Money could be given for local programs such as "clean sweep" and "stay clean" programs. The Public Health Service, HEW, should expand its rodent control program. HUD has programs such as Model Cities that could give more priority to solid waste problems.

Other programs of technical assistance and occasional financial assistance include those of: Development of Housing and Urban Development under the 701 Planning Assistance Program and 704 Advance Acquisitions of Land Program (HUD); Farmers Home Administration (Department of Agriculture); Economic Development Administration (Department of Commerce); Bureau of Outdoor Recreation, Geological Survey, and Bureau of Mines (Department of the Interior); and Soil Conservation Service (Department of Agriculture).

Despite the need, there is little money available. The Federal solid waste program of Fiscal Year 1972 was funded at about $61 million. In FY

1973 the expenditures for this program were listed at $64 million, though these expenditures were too small to be detailed in the Federal Budget publications. (Figures used are from the *Special Analysis,* 1973, p. 300. The government gives lower figures elsewhere, but lack of further information makes analysis impossible.)

The following is excerpted from the *Environmental Quality, the First Annual Report of the Council on Environmental Quality,* August, 1970:

Solid wastes: an overview

The total solid wastes produced in the United States in 1969 reached 4.3 billion tons as shown in the following table:

	Million tons
Residential, Commercial and Institutional wastes	250
Collected	(190)
Uncollected	(60)
Industrial wastes	110
Mineral wastes	1, 700
Agricultural wastes	2, 280
Total	4, 340

Sources: Bureau of Solid Waste Management, Department of Health, Education, and Welfare; Division of Solid Wastes, Bureau of Mines, Department of the Interior.

Most of it originated from agriculture and livestock. Other large amounts arose from mining and industrial processes. A little under 6 percent, or 250 million tons, was classified as residential, commercial, and institutional solid wastes. And only three-fourths of this was collected.

Although wastes from homes, businesses, and institutions make up a small part of the total load of solid waste produced, they are the most offensive and the most dangerous to health when they accumulate near where people live. Agricultural and mineral wastes, although much greater in volume, are generally spread more widely over the land. They are more isolated from population concentrations and may not require special collection and disposal. Nevertheless, as more is learned about the effects of agricultural and mineral wastes on the quality of air, water, and esthetics, steps to curb their production and facilitate disposal seem likely.

agricultural wastes

The largest single source of solid wastes in this country is agriculture. It accounts for over half the total. The more than 2 billion tons of *agricultural wastes* produced each year includes animal and slaughterhouse wastes, useless residues from crop harvesting, vineyard and orchard prunings, and greenhouse wastes.

Herds of cattle and other animals, once left to graze over large open meadows, are now often confined to feedlots where they fatten more rapidly for market. On these feedlots, they generate enormous and concentrated quantities of manure that cannot readily and safely be assimilated by the soil. Manure permeates the earth and invades waterbodies, contributing to fish kills, eutrophied lakes, off-flavored drinking waters, and contaminated aquifers. Feedlots intensify odors, dusts, and the wholesale production of flies and other noxious insects. Animal waste disposal is a growing problem because the demand for animal manure as a soil conditioner is declining. Easier handling, among other advantages, favors chemical fertilizers.

About 110 million tons of *industrial solid wastes* (excluding mineral solid wastes) are generated every year. More than 15 million tons of it are scrap metal, and 30 million tons are paper and paper product wastes; a miscellaneous bag of slags, waste plastics, bales of rags, and drums of assorted products discarded for various reasons make up the rest. The electric utility industry produced over 30 million tons of fly ash in 1969 from burning bituminous coal and lignite. By 1980, the figure could rise to 40 million tons. Currently, only about 20 percent of ash material finds any use.

mineral wastes

In the past year, 1,700 million tons of *mineral solid wastes*, comprising 39 percent of total solid wastes, were generated in the United States—most of it from the mineral and fossil fuel mining, milling, and processing industries. Slag heaps, culm piles, and mill tailings accumulate near extraction or processing operations. Eighty mineral industries generate solid waste, but only eight of them are responsible for 80 percent of the total. Copper contributes the largest waste tonnage, followed by iron and steel, bituminous coal, phosphate rock, lead, zinc, alumina, and anthracite. By 1980, the Nation's mineral industries will be generating at least 2 billion tons of waste every year.

In 1969, Americans threw away more than 250 million tons of *residential, commercial, and institutional solid wastes*. Approximately 190 million tons were collected by public agencies and private refuse firms. The remainder was abandoned, dumped, disposed of at the point of origin, or hauled away by the producer to a disposal site. About $3.5 billion was spent last year handling the 190 million tons of collected solid wastes—an average of $18 per ton. Collection accounts for 80 percent of the cost ($14 per ton), disposal for the rest. A considerably higher rate of spending would be needed to upgrade existing systems to acceptable levels of operation.

household wastes

The solid waste collected annually includes 30 million tons of paper and paper products; 4 million tons of plastics; 100 million tires; 30 billion bottles; 60 billion cans; millions of tons of demolition debris, grass and tree trimmings, food wastes, and sewage sludge; and millions of discarded automobiles and major appliances.

In 1969, 43.8 billion *beverage containers* for beer and soft drinks were made in the United States. If the trend to throw-away containers continues, by 1980, 100 billion of these bottles and cans will be produced and discarded every year. Beverage containers already comprise 3.9 percent of all collected refuse, and the number is growing at a rate of nearly 7.5 percent per year—compared to 4 percent for all refuse. Bottles and cans constitute a major part of what is left in incinerators after burning. They must be hauled to land disposal sites. Each year an estimated 1 to 2 billion glass and metal beverage containers end up as litter on highways, beaches, parks, and other public areas. Severe penalties for littering have not worked in the face of the rising sales of the throw-away bottle and can, and strict enforcement of these laws has been difficult.

Paper constitutes almost 60 percent of roadside litter and is difficult to collect. Last year, 58.3 million tons of paper were consumed in the United States. Nineteen percent of this was recycled. Fifteen percent was temporarily retained or lost its identity in manufacturing processes. The remaining two-thirds—or 40 million tons—was discarded as residential, commercial, institutional, and industrial solid wastes. Typically, paper comprising 40 to 50 percent of mixed refuse is disposed of at an annual cost of over $900 million. Paper production is a multiple polluter. It crops up as a factor in timber wastes, in air and water pollution, and in the removal of organic materials from soils in managed forests. Much of the discarded paper consists of technically reusable fiber. Although the United States recycles only 19 percent of its paper, Japan reclaims and reprocesses nearly half of the paper its people use.

Plastics comprise an increasingly worrisome element in solid wastes. They are virtually indestructible, do not degrade naturally, and resist the compression plates of compactor trucks. In incinerators most plastics tend to melt rather than burn and to foul the grates. One range of plastics, polyvinyl chloride (PVC), is a new arrival in the packaging market. When burned, it produces hydrochloric acid. Although not yet widely used in the United States, in Germany it has already been blamed for increased air pollution, damage to incinerator stacks, and—in rare cases—destruction of nearby flora.

Another potential problem arises from disposing of *pesticides*. As stronger legislation and regulation of these agents take effect, the proper disposal of undesirable or condemned commodities becomes important. Even the containers used to market pesticides may retain considerable toxicity after discard. Although there have as yet been no serious cases, concentration of these agents in sanitary landfills and open dumps could contaminate ground water and imperil public health.

End, excerpt from the 1970 Council on Environmental Quality report. The following two paragraphs are from the very brief treatment given solid wastes in the 1971 report:

> Strewn garbage, besides being unattractive and odorous, also invites rodents. Rats feed on easily accessible garbage and present a health problem to inner city residents. Greater than the danger of the diseases they carry is the insecurity and fear they inspire, especially in parents with small children.
>
> An estimated 60 to 90 percent of rat bites occurs in inner city neighborhoods. Eighty percent occurs after midnight when most victims are asleep. The problem is intensified by large-scale building demolition in old, inner city areas, where rats are dislodged and then flee to other parts of the city. The presence of rats in an apartment often has nothing to do with the particular building's cleanliness. Substandard housing often is replete with holes in basement walls or around windows and pipes, giving rats entry points from which they fan out through a building.

End, *Environmental Quality* excerpt.

b. Collecting urban solid wastes

Before wastes are recycled or disposed of, they must be collected. New York City, for instance, has about 15,000 persons in its sanitation department, two-thirds of these working directly on the streets as garbagemen or street cleaners. Their pay at the time this book went to press averaged about $9,419 annually, but is scheduled to go to nearly $13,000 when the wage freeze ends. Still, the streets of New York are filthy—and much more so where four-fifths of all New York City residents live: in the boroughs other than Manhattan. Almost one-third of the city's sanitation effort is on Manhattan, particularly in the areas where tourists and commuters are plentiful.

New York faces many of the same problems as do other cities. Dogs (about 482,000 of them) leave a great deal behind: the estimates on droppings range from 10 million to 40 million pounds a year. Their urine sprayed in public places is estimated at 600,000 to 1 million gallons per year. Sunday newspapers alone in New York contribute 17 million pounds of solid waste per week. The streets total approximately 6,000 miles, all to be swept. Total collected non-industrial solid waste in New York City is almost 9 billion pounds a year. (See "Filth City: New York Wallows," *Washington Post,* Sept. 6, 1971, page 1)

The collection aspect of solid waste disposal accounts for 80 percent of the total cost of handling waste.

In 56 percent of the U.S. cities, public agencies handle waste collection. In 32 percent of the cities private collectors are used. Sometimes these are contract arrangements with the cities and sometimes the collector deals directly with the customer. In 12 percent of the cities the individual must haul away his own refuse. Private collectors haul away the greater portion of commercial (62 percent), industrial (57 percent), and agricultural wastes. Whether public or private systems are used, political interference is very common. This in turn often means poor administration, resulting in high costs and poor service.

About 337,000 men are employed in the United States as refuse collectors or drivers. Labor costs comprise 60 to 80 percent of the total costs of collection. Turnover is extremely high and the injury rate nearly nine times that of the average of U.S. industry is exceeded only by logging activities.

inner city problems

The following is excerpted from

Our Urban Environment and Our Most Endangered People

[Draft version], A Report to the Administrator of Environmental Protection Agency by The Task Force on Environmental Problems of the Inner City, September 1971:

The inner city is in greatest need of assistance in solid waste management. Oftentimes, projects that aid the typical city resident only scratch the surface of the inner city resident's problems. The solid waste problems of the inner city can not be treated in the same fashion as those of the rest of the city or the suburbs.

Inner city people must contend with over-flowing garbage cans that line their sidewalks or alleys; rodents and insects which thrive in this refuse; and housing that offers little protection from the rats generated by solid waste.

Their solid waste problem can be categorized as follows:

1. Rodents and insects
2. Litter (paper, bottles and cans, car parts and furniture)
3. Abandoned automobiles
4. Garbage

Rats and Garbage—Rats and household insects are a constant threat to the inner city.

Diseases—Such diseases as rat bite fever, leptospirosis,

salmonallosis, and murine typhus fever are spread by rats and insects which breed in solid wastes. The young, the sick and the old are vulnerable, and especially so after midnight when rats are most active and dangerous

Play time, as well as sleep time, holds dangers for children of the inner city. Bacteria in garbage and litter can infect those playing in the mounds of solid wastes. The very handling of this rubble can spread disease. (And the children must play on the streets for lack of recreational areas. Here again, garbage litter and abandoned automobiles contend with the children for space.)

Economic Loss Due to Rats—The direct economic loss to the nation due to rats is estimated between $500,000,000 and $1,000,000,000 annually. The estimate of loss is based on a rat population in the United States of one rat for every person. Even if recent improvements in environmental sanitation and rodent control have cut the rat population in half, the United States still has some 100,000,000 rats, each of which damages between $1 and $10 worth of food and other materials per year by gnawing and feeding, and contaminates 5 to 10 times more.

Litter and Abandoned Automobiles—The problems of litter and strewn garbage, plus abandoned automobiles, are distressing both to the residents of the inner city and to visitors.

inner city problems

Industrial Pollution—In addition to poor quality housing, neighborhoods in the inner city may be further degraded by their location to marginal industries. G.L. Morris, Acting Director of Categorical Programs in the Dallas Regional Office, reports, "Many of these industrial installations are negligent in the handling and disposal of solid wastes. Frequent violations of good practice include substandard storage at the plant, hauling in open vehicles, open dumping on company property near residential areas and improper operation of poorly designed incinerators which discharge noxious smoke, mist and fumes."

Bitterness—Solid wastes cause disease and economic loss, but there's an additional factor. They cause bitterness among the inner city residents. Feelings of depression, discouragement and despair result from lack of progress in environmental improvement.

* * *

The task force finds that inner city residents consider solid waste and the associated rat problem their Number 1 environmental problem. The task force finds that improved collection of solid waste, rather than transfer or disposal, the most pressing aspect of their problem. Moreover, the task force finds that the job of achieving, in the inner city, a level of cleanliness comparable to middle class areas is enormous. Such an undertaking in all our major cities would undoubtedly be a multi-billion dollar program.

End, excerpt from *Our Urban Environment and Our Most Endangered People.*

Again we quote from the 1971 report of the Council on Envitonmental Quality:

> Junk and litter accumulated in streets, on sidewalks, and in vacant lots and doorways are a familiar sight in poverty areas and cannot help having a psychological effect on those who live there. The resident often despairs of keeping his small living space clean when all around him are litter and garbage. He may conclude that since refuse collection is a public service, the abundance of uncollected litter indicates that his neighborhood is being discriminated against. Residents in 9 of 20 cities surveyed by the National Advisory Commission on Civil Disorders listed inadequate sanitation and garbage removal as significant grievances. Many cities able to set their own priorities with Federal funds have placed emphasis on sanitation services such as collecting garbage, buying trash and

garbage containers for the city poor, removing abandoned automobiles, cleaning up littered vacant lots, and increasing the number of sanitation workers.

Solving the problem involves more than merely upgrading municipal services. Some New York City poverty areas have garbage pickups six times a week, compared to three times a week elsewhere in the city. In Chicago, inner city poor are served by three collections a week, compared to one collection in the rest of the city. Yet inner city littering and unsanitary conditions continue, and there is widespread disenchantment at the failure of cleanup campaigns to have any lasting effect.

inner city problems

The reasons for this failure to maintain sanitary conditions in the inner city are complex and interrelated. Frustration over limited opportunities for housing, employment, and education can lead residents of the inner city to withdraw from active efforts to improve conditions around them. This psychological impact is worsened by physical conditions which work against sanitation. Buildings designed in earlier days have been subdivided into numerous crowded living units, with little provision for storage areas, common spaces, or refuse collection systems. Receptacles are often nonexistent, makeshift, or in poor condition—all leading to a situation in which wind, animals, and vandals spread litter throughout houses and neighborhoods. The abundance of vacant lots and abandoned structures, already strewn with refuse, encourage further junk, garbage, and other debris. Together these forces work to frustrate even the most willing city sanitation department in working with residents toward a cleaner neighborhood. Also, sanitation collection services have been criticized as perfunctory in some poverty areas. Often such services are confined to curbside collection of packaged refuse, ignoring litter in lots, sidewalks, and gutters.

End, excerpt from CEQ report.

The following three paragraphs are again from *Environmental Quality*, 1970:

collection methods

Refuse collection methods in most of the United States do not differ substantially from what they were when workers picked up the trash in horse-drawn wagons before the turn of the century. This lack of technological advance is particularly burdensome because up to 80 percent of the funds spent on solid waste management goes into collecting the waste and hauling it to a processing plant or a dump.

The one significant advance has been the compactor truck. These closed-body vehicles now make up a large part of the 150,000 refuse collection trucks in the United States. With hydraulic presses, they compress waste, usually at a 3-to-1 ratio, thus saving vehicle space and cutting the number of trips necessary to cover collection routes. However, the compactor has disadvantages. Because refuse of different types is mixed and crushed, recyclables are lost or contaminated by unusable waste. It is also hazardous to operators.

Efforts are underway to modernize trash collection. Under one Federal grant, researchers at The Johns Hopkins University are studying the practicability of transfer points in waste collection systems serving large cities. Under another, the University of Pennsylvania is studying the possibility of pipelines for collecting and removing domestic solid wastes. The pipeline method may be technologically feasible and economically attractive. But these are just beginnings. More research is mandatory.

End quote.

collection by pipeline

And more research has been done, although much more had already been done than was implied in this government report. By 1970, the Swedish suburban city of Sundeberg had for eight years been successfully using a pneumatic tube system to collect the refuse from nearly 5,000 apartments, some as far as 1.7 miles from the collection center. Although even a car battery reportedly was sent through the system, the tubes had never been clogged. (New York City's first subway, a six-foot in diameter bullet-shaped projectile in a pneumatic tube two-blocks' long, was a demonstration built in hope of receiving a contract to build a full system. After much ado and charges that considerable bribes had been passed, the Tammany Hall leaders opted for the elevated railroad. The subway, however, kept open as a novelty for about two years, reportedly worked quite well.) The refuse in Sundeberg feeds an incinerator, which makes steam, sent back to heat some of the area's buildings.

A pneumatic tube system of solid waste collection is in operation at the Disney amusement park near Orlando, Florida. *See,* Blake, Peter, "Walt Disney World," *The Architectural Forum.* Vol. 136, No. 5, June, 1972 at 32.

As mentioned briefly in the quoted CEQ report, a team headed by Dr. Iraj Zandi of the University of Pennsylvania's Towne School of Civil and Mechanical Engineering has made extensive studies of pneumatic and slurry (solids mixed in water) pipeline systems, concluding that a combination slurry and pneumatic network in central Philadelphia was technologically practical and economically worthwhile. No consideration, however, was given to possible economic advantages to be gained by making the receiving center a recycling plant; the stress was laid on moving the refuse away from the city. Such systems obviously would be more economical if they could be installed at the same time as sewage lines. One account of Professor Zandi's findings appears in *Environmental Science and Technology,* Vol. 3 No. 9, Sept. 1969.

See also, Johansson, "Whisking the Garbage," *Saturday Review,* July 3, 1971 at 40.

NATIONAL UTILIZATION OF MANPOWER IN SOLID WASTE COLLECTION (1968)

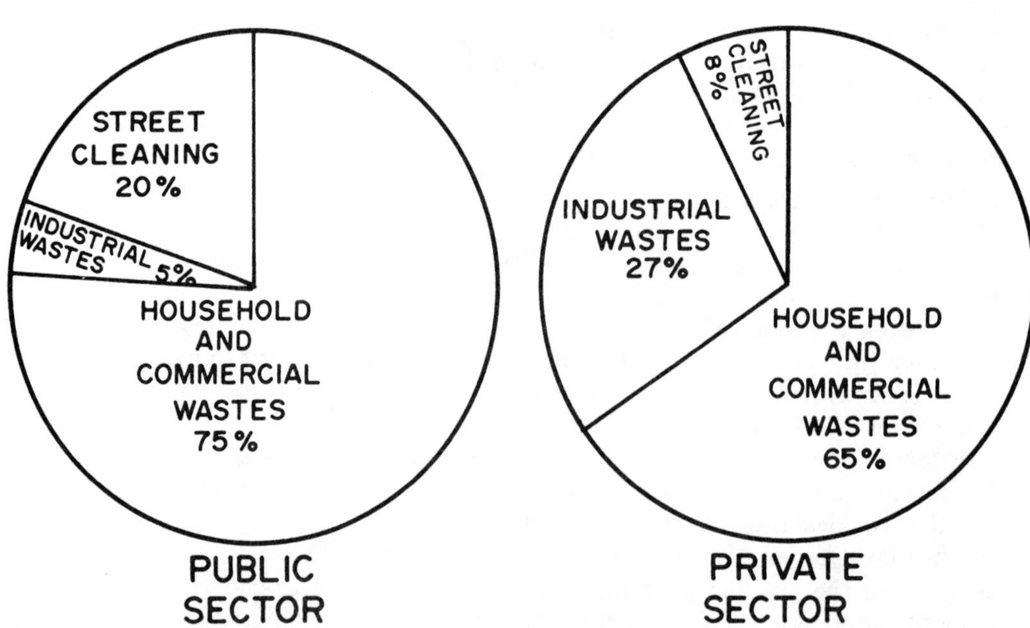

TOTAL: 337,000 workers, with 53 percent in the public sector, and 47 percent in the private sector.
SOURCE: *The National Solid Waste Survey,* an interim report, Bureau of Solid Waste Management, October, 1968.

average of solid wastes collected

(Pounds per person per day)

Solid wastes	Urban	Rural	National
Household	1.26	0.72	1.14
Commercial	0.46	0.11	0.38
Combined	2.63	2.60	2.63
Industrial	0.65	0.37	0.59
Demolition, construction	0.23	0.02	0.18
Street and alley	0.11	0.03	0.09
Miscellaneous	0.38	0.08	0.31
TOTALS	5.72	3.93	5.32

NOTE: Figures include only material known or estimated to be collected; they do not include household, commercial, industrial, demolition, agricultural, and other wastes transported, disposed of, or left by the individual generators. SOURCE: *The National Solid Wastes Survey,* An Interim Report, Bureau of Solid Waste Management, October, 1968 at 13.

c. Disposal systems

What the United States now uses for waste disposal would make a 200 B.C. rat feel quite at home. This is good for rats, bad for people.

The essence of the solution to this problem is extremely simple: we must not waste. And though it may surprise most of us, the technology to come very close to achieving that goal is available, and there are several thousand engineers, some of them unemployed, who have the know-how to help us save ourselves.

But it should be kept in mind that for some, waste—left as waste—means money. For example, bottle makers can sell 18 to 20 nonreturnable bottles for each returnable bottle they might otherwise have made, since the returnable bottles on the average are refilled that often before breakage.

Again we quote, for the following five paragraphs, from the 1970 Council on Environmental Quality report, before giving our own account:

mostly dumps

The final disposal point for an estimated 77 percent of all collected solid wastes is 14,000 open dumps in the country. Thirteen percent is deposited into properly operated sanitary landfills, where wastes are adequately covered each day with earth of the proper type. Nearly all of the remaining 10 percent is burned. Incinerators are used primarily in large cities, where the volume of refuse and the high cost of land make incineration an attractive disposal method. Small quantities of solid wastes are turned into nutrient-rich soil conditioners by composting operations. And a small but troublesome percentage is dumped at sea.

Land disposal of solid wastes can range from the most offensive fly- and rat-infested open dump to technically advanced practices that end in the creation of parklands, golf courses, outdoor theaters, and other public facilities. Disposal sites in or near urban areas can be reclaimed for use as attractive open space if proper sanitary landfill practices are employed.

Imaginative thinking in land disposal practices is not widespread. Collected refuse is dumped in whatever area is available, with little or no provision for soil cover. Often city fathers blame spontaneous com-

Disposal

bustion for fires at these dumps. But in at least some cases, local sanitation officials set fire to wastes to reduce their volume because dumps are overloaded. Burning at open dumps remains a major cause of air pollution in some cities. Improper landfill techniques can spawn large quantities of methane gas and breed armies of rats, flies, and other pests. Disposal sites often mar wetlands and scenic areas. Some are uneconomical because of their distance from the city. In California, filling canyons and other natural areas has been censored by conservation groups.

Improved equipment for landfilling is being developed. For example, with a grant from the Bureau of Solid Waste Management, King County (Seattle), Wash., is constructing a machine called the "Mole," which will compact refuse at high pressure and dispose of it below ground level. Under another grant, a landfill operation near Virginia Beach, Va., will be turned into a huge manmade hill for an amphitheater. A similar site near Chicago will be developed for tobogganing and skiing.

The city of Madison, Wis., has a grant to build and operate a hammer reduction mill to test the economic feasibility of salvaging paper and metals. Preliminary investigations of salvage possibilities are inconclusive, but disposal aspects of the mill look promising. It may be possible, for example, that milled refuse may safely be deposited in a landfill without earth cover.

Nearly 10 percent of domestic solid wastes is processed through *incineration*; 300 municipal incinerators account for about half the tonnage burned; the rest is consumed in thousands of small, privately owned trash burners. After incineration, about 25 percent of the waste by weight remains—as ashes, glass, metals, and unburned combustibles. These then must be removed and recycled, or disposed of in some way.

Since municipal incineration is often cited as a polluter of air, research is underway to improve incinerator technology. A German process involves a mechanically stoked rotary drum incinerator designed for small communities. West Virginia University is studying a fluidized-bed incinerator fueled by mixtures of domestic and industrial solid wastes.

End quote from *CEQ* report.

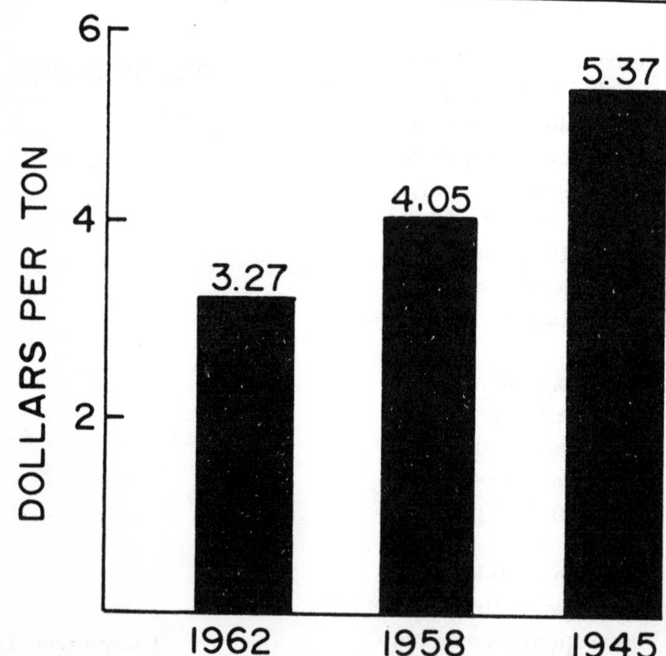

INCINERATOR OPERATING COSTS COMPARED BY AVERAGE AGES

Costs and weight and volume of residues all go down substantially on the newer incinerators. The size of these newer plants, however, is much greater. In 1968, when this graph was made, incinerators were used to dispose of an estimated 8 percent of the collected solid wastes in the United States, while hogs on feeding lots consumed about 4 percent. SOURCE: The National Solid Wastes Survey, an interim report, Bureau of Solid Waste Management, October, 1968.

Disposal

Members of few communities would tolerate an open dump if they had to live near it. But most U.S. dumps are in the least-populated sections of urban counties, or in some other political jurisdiction. A problem is that rural areas close to populated areas are becoming less common, and those who live there don't like being dumped on.

Every day local governments must deal with an estimated 5.3 pounds of solid waste for each person in the nation. That is more than a billion pounds per day.

The problem continues to get worse. Population keeps increasing. The weight of waste per person continues to rise. By 1980 it is expected to be 8 pounds per person each day. And the volume of wastes increases more rapidly than the weight. This fact increases collection and disposal costs.

What can we do about solving the problem? In the long run, we must reclaim these wastes and recycle them to produce new products. In one year, Americans junk most of 48 billion cans, 26 million jars and bottles, and 65 billion metal and plastic container caps.

Manufacturers are not much better than consumers at reusing production. Only about 10 per cent of the 8 billion pounds of plastic, and about 15 per cent of the 3.5 billion pounds of rubber products are reclaimed.

incinerators

Dumps encourage propagation of rodents and insects which carry diseases, and they present safety problems. One hundred and fifty persons burned to death last year at dumps: many of these were children. Dumps are aesthetic nuisances and present odor problems. They burn frequently and are sources of air pollution.

Incinerators can be a partial answer, and some ideas now under study are particularly attractive. But with present practices, a dump or a landfill is still needed to take care of non-burnable refuse and incinerator residue, which currently is 20 to 25 per cent by weight of the waste placed within them for burning.

Most incinerators are nuisances. They burn incompletely and distribute the community's wastes as air pollution. Water used to quench the ashes becomes a water pollution problem.

An incinerator theoretically can be designed so as not to be an air and water pollution problem, but the number in this country that are not nuisances could be counted on your fingers.

General Electric Co., with a $50,000 grant from the U.S. Department of Health, Education and Welfare, is studying possible construction of an incinerator at Lynn, Mass., that would use garbage to generate electricity for the huge GE plant there.

Normal municipal solid waste has a rather high energy value, producing as much heat when burned as low-grade coal. It is estimated that burning municipal wastes could provide 10 per cent of a community's electric power needs.

Solid wastes remaining after burning could be used for building materials. This aspect of waste reuse is further advanced in an incinerator type proposed by the Illinois Institute of Technology Research Institute. Using an especially high temperature—2,800 degrees Fahrenheit in place of the usual incinerator's 2,000 degrees—glass and metal would be separated for use in a variety of products.

sanitary landfills

However, there is still something to be said for the fabled "sanitary" landfill. Done properly, it can be an acceptable short-term solution to waste disposal. But it rarely is done properly, and dumps are still dumps.

Federal officials say that 94 percent of all "landfills" are mere dumps, and that such dumps receive 90 percent of all collected urban solid waste.

Sanitary landfills vary quite broadly in design, but their essential characteristics are simple. A pit, natural or excavated, is required. Waste is dumped and then compacted with tractors designed for this work.

Each day a layer of earth covers the accumulation. Eventually the trench or pit is filled with many cells and layers of waste, each covered with earth. A final layer of earth is applied, and the landfill is ready to be used as a park or parking lot or for some other use which does not require heavy foundation support.

A location chosen properly from a geological point of view, plus proper design for drainage, prevents most water pollution. Daily covering eliminates rodent and insect problems. Fire and consequential air pollution is minimized.

A major problem to be considered when selecting a waste disposal site on land is the possible impairment of the quality of the surrounding ground and surface waters. A booklet which addresses this question and outlines procedures to minimize the possibility of water contamination from "sanitary landfills" is Cummins, "Effects of Land Disposal of Solid Wastes on Water Quality", U.S. Dept. of Health, Education and Welfare (Public Health Service). Bureau of Solid Waste Management (Cincinnati: 1969).

With intelligent planning and management, a landfill can be an asset. That potential benefit, however, is generally in areas that have land already destroyed by man—for instance, by surface mining. An excellent presentation of the virtues of sanitary landfills under such conditions appears in "An Abandoned Strip Mine is to Fill," *Environmental Science And Technology,* Vol. 2, No. 6, June 1968, and, as updated, in the Vol. 6, No. 5, May 1972, issue of the same magazine. The latter issue also contains a fine survey of the entire field of waste disposal in an article by Alex Hershaft, "Solid Waste Treatment Technology." Names of firms engaging in various aspects of solid waste disposal are listed there; their addresses may be found in the annual September directory issue of that magazine. See also generally the Bibliography to this chapter.

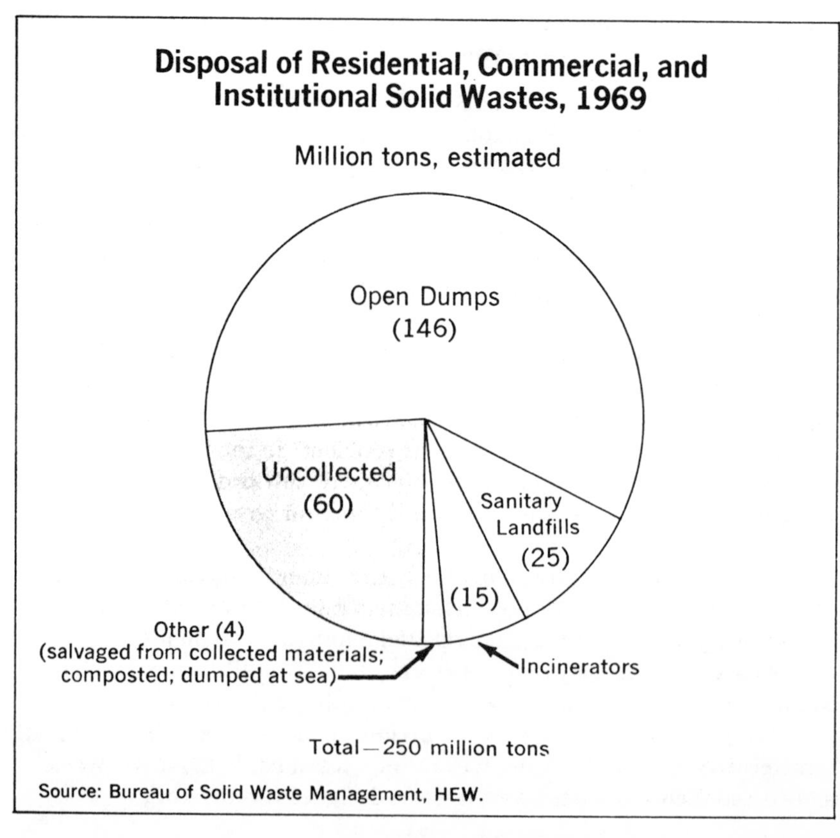

SANITARY LANDFILLS

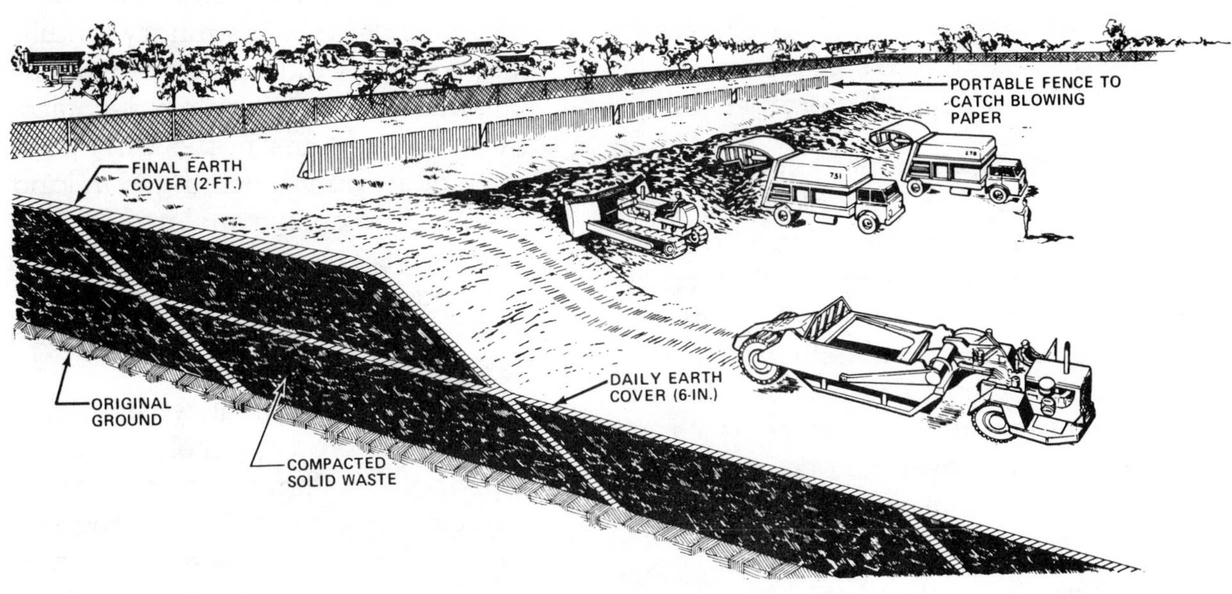

FIGURE 1. AREA METHOD. The bulldozer spreads and compacts solid wastes. The scraper (foreground) is used to haul the cover material at the end of the day's operations. Note the portable fence that catches any blowing debris. This is used with any landfill method.

FIGURE 2. TRENCH METHOD. The waste collection truck deposits its load into the trench where the bulldozer spreads and compacts it. At the end of the day the dragline excavates soil from the future trench; this soil is used as the daily cover material. Trenches can also be excavated with a front-end loader, bulldozer, or scraper.

SOURCE: Sanitary Landfill Facts, Bureau of Solid Waste Management, GPO, 1970

OPERATING A SANITARY LANDFILL

Wet Weather Operation. Wet weather can seriously hamper the operations of a sanitary landfill by making the soil too soft, mucky, or slippery for equipment operation.

Winter Operations. Experience has shown that with good planning and proper operating techniques, a sanitary landfill can be operated even in the severe winters of the northern states. If the trench method is used, the trenches should be excavated before the cold weather. It may be necessary to stockpile cover material and cover it with straw, leaves, or other material to prevent freezing.

Dust. In dry weather, dust may constitute a nuisance at a sanitary landfill operation. Dust at the unloading area can be controlled by sprinkling the unloading area and the deposited refuse with water.

Blowing Paper. In a 1959 survey of sanitary landfill operations by the American Society of Civil Engineers, the operating problem most frequently reported was blowing paper. The common method of controlling blowing paper is with a combination of permanent and portable fences.

Drainage. Ponding on the landfill surface will result in excessive seepage into the landfill and must be prevented. Precautions must be taken to prevent runoff water from eroding the cover material and exposing the wastes.

Water Pollution. Under certain geological conditions, the burial of solid wastes is a real potential for chemical and bacteriological pollution of ground and surface waters.

Air Pollution. Air pollution caused by smoke should not occur. Burning is not permitted at a properly operated sanitary landfill. If an accidental fire does occur, it should be extinguished immediately.

COMPLETED SANITARY LANDFILL

Decomposition. Little information is available on the decomposition of buried material in a sanitary landfill. It is extremely difficult to predict the time required for complete decomposition. Many items, particularly paper, have been found unchanged in landfills that had been completed for 15 to 25 years. The rate of decomposition is primarily dependent upon the moisture content and generally takes place at a very slow rate.

Decomposition of the wastes will result in the production of gases, principally methane, carbon dioxide, nitrogen, hydrogen, and hydrogen sulfide. The rate of gas production will usually reach a peak within the first 2 years and then slowly taper off.

Methane gas causes the most concern because of its explosive character. Precautions should be taken that will prevent the gas from concentrating in sewers or other structures located on or near the landfill.

Settlement. Settlement of the landfill is dependent on the depth of the fill, composition, compaction of the material, moisture content, and other factors. Studies have indicated that approximately 90 percent of the ultimate settlement will occur in the first 5 years.

Underground Fires. Although underground fires rarely occur in a completed landfill, the possibility does exist. All underground fires should be dug up and extinguished. The cell construction of a sanitary landfill helps to confine and restrict the spread of the fire should one occur.

Maintenance. Completed landfills generally require maintenance because of differential settlement. Maintenance consists primarily of resloping the surface to maintain good drainage and filling in small depressions that result from uneven settlement.

d. Composting

Composting, a solid waste disposal process utilizing bacteria, is in a way a return to agricultural technology, rather than that of industry. It facilitates the transformation of organic matter into soil and soil additives. Although suffering throughout its modern history from a pejorative view by the general public that its adherents were "organic food nuts," we have much to learn from this science. The opposition has often been mindless. Nevertheless, there is still no fully successful large-scale, long-term composting operation based on urban solid waste that can be held up to confound its critics.

Mark Twain joked of how the German farmers' wealth was calculated by the size of their compost heaps (which include manure). The science of composting has come a long way since then, and unpleasant (and unhealthy) odors are no longer part and parcel of the bacterial action.

Scientific composting of urban solid waste in the United States goes back about to 1951, when a plant was constructed in Altoona, Pennsylvania. Since that time others have been built in several states, including in recent years at Houston, Texas; Gainesville, Fla.; St. Petersburg, Fla.; Boulder, Colo.; Mobile, Ala., and Johnson City, Tenn. The last-named was constructed by the U.S. Public Health Service, the Tennessee Valley Authority, and Johnson City, to test composting of both urban refuse and sewage sludge.

But the path for composters has been filled with severe trials, most based simply on the fact that they couldn't find a market sufficient for their product: humus earth as a soil conditioner. Chemicals are cheaper, and weigh less.

As of the end of 1971, only two U.S. composting plants reportedly were operating—Altoona Farm, Inc., in Altoona, Pa., and Ecology, Inc., in Brooklyn, N.Y. Four other plants (at Boulder, Houston, Mobile and St. Petersburg) were operating on a demand basis in response to compost sales.

The Council on Economic Quality summed up composting in this paragraph (1970):

> An insignificant amount of collected solid wastes in the United States is *composted*. Metals, glass, and similar inorganics are sorted from mixed refuse, and the remainder is converted to a peat-like organic fertilizer and soil conditioner. This process is widely used in Europe. Madrid composts 200 tons daily and Moscow is opening a new 600-ton-per-day facility. Composting has never been popular in the United States for several reasons. Compared to many Western European nations, land available for disposal sites in the United States is inexpensive. The compost product has not always been of uniform quality here; nor has it competed with commercial soil conditioners. Also, the composition of refuse in the United States makes it more difficult to compost, since its organic content is low. Finally, composting was first sold to American cities as a profitmaking venture. When it did not pay off, many cities considered the enterprise a failure. The Bureau of Solid Waste Management, jointly with the Tennessee Valley Authority, is operating an experimental composting plant in Johnson City, Tenn. But the results have not been encouraging. In recent years almost all composting plants in this country have shut down.

End quote from CEQ report.

If organically grown foods, however, become a permanent, even if quite minor, part of the U.S. economic scene, perhaps a place can be found for composting within our industrialized society.

For the proponent's point of view, see the works published by Rodale Press, 33 E. Minor St., Emmaus, Pa. 18049.

the process of composting

In composting, organic material is attacked by a variety of microorganisms. Some of the material is used by the organisms, some components pass into the air, and some of the material is converted into a dark-colored mass called humus, which is familiar to most of us as produced naturally. Composting produces humus more rapidly than is normal in nature because the bacteria are given ideal conditions. Humus contributes to soil fertility by:

1. adding nutrients such as nitrogen and phosphorus;
2. holding soil moisture, and
3. permitting air circulation.

Composting can utilize a variety of wastes as raw materials. In the United States, these suitable wastes could include:

1. half of the more than 260 million tons of municipal wastes;
2. nearly all of the 550 million tons of inedible portions of crops and forestry waste;
3. the 1,560 million tons of animal and poultry manure and processing wastes, and
4. vegetable and fruit processing wastes.

But there are many difficulties, the most serious of which are economic, to the commercial production of compost. Some of these difficulties are:

1. the lack of steady markets;
2. high initial investment and operating costs;
3. the required handling of noncompostable wastes;
4. chemical nutrients must often be added to make compost effective as a fertilizer;
5. heavy metals can contaminate plants fertilized with compost made from wastes containing such metals, particularly in acidic soil.

Composting nevertheless has many benefits:

1. the soil-conditioning capabilities of compost are usually superior to those of chemical fertilizers;
2. compost does not cause a deterioration of soil structure as often occurs with the use of chemical fertilizers; and
3. the production of compost does not require the large amounts of electrical power needed to produce nitrogen fertilizers.

To be considered successful, a composing plant must not simply produce humus, it must also avoid being a health hazard. These are the basic potential problems:

1. odors;
2. disease-causing bacteria;
3. flies.

Composting can take place with or without oxygen. The aerobic (with oxygen) process destroys bacteria and produces no offensive odors, and is therefore the preferred method.

In addition, a plant may be unsightly, and if it does not process the wastes sufficiently rapidly, it will have the full range of problems associated with the storage of wastes. But all of these potential problems have been successfully avoided through correct composting practices. Health problems were associated primarily with the early, primitive composting operations; there is now an extensive body of literature and experience concerning the avoidance of these problems.

Commercial operations have found it necessary to remove salvageable and noncompostable meterials prior to composting. Since a product of uniform and generally pleasing appearance is usually required for sale, shredding is carried out. Objects that cannot be shredded must also be removed. Shredding also aids in achieving uniform decomposition.

Care must be taken to keep the carbon-to-nitrogen ratio between 4-to-1 and 2-to-1, and the moisture content sufficient to assure aerobic conditions, but high enough to permit the process to proceed.

Composting can take place in windrows: such piles can be of any length, but are generally four or five feet high, and eight to 12 feet wide at the bottom. However, more modern plants often use mechanized and enclosed digesters to speed-up composting and better control the end product.

The cost of composting plants can vary widely. Capital costs can run from $0.55 to $1.91 per ton for windrow plants, and $1.18 to $3.98 for digester plants. Operating expenses can run from $1.51 to $2.76 per ton. Revenue from the compost, together with the revenue from salvage, is usually insufficient to make a profit. In part, this is due to the fact that the environmentally destructive results of the run-off of organic fertilizers into our waters, and the pollution created by the production of electricity used in the manufacture of inorganic fertilizers, is not reflected in the marketplace. Environmentally irresponsible solid waste disposal is simpler, and may be cheaper, if social values are not accounted for. The result is that composting is seldom used, despite its environmental benefits.

See: MEYER, Judith, "Renewing the Soil," 14 *Environment* 2, March 1972 at 22, and "Solid Waste Management of Composting–European Activity and American Potential," Report SW-2c to the Solid Wastes Program, GPO 1968. The entire report is recommended. See also "Municipal Composting Research at Johnson City, Tennessee," in *Compost Science,* Vol. 9, No. 4, winter, 1969 at 4, and Kupchick, G.J., "Economics of Composting Municipal Refuse in Europe and Israel with special reference to possibilities in the U.S.A.," *Bulletin of the World Health Organization,* May 1966 at 798, and "Composting," 6 *Environmental Science & Technology* 5, May, 1972 at 417.

composting plants: two examples from Europe

Schweinfurt, Germany

Population served, 85,000

Type of plant, Caspari-Brikollare

A new process, the "Brikollare Verfahren," or briquette process, is used to make compost at a plant erected in Schweinfurt in 1965. Previously, all municipal solid wastes, including industrial waste from two large ball-bearing manufacturers and one heavy-machinery fabricator, were buried in a landfill. That was changed with the construction of a $1,000,000 composting plant for domestic and commercial waste and a $1,250,000 incinerator for industrial waste.

The incoming domestic and commercial refuse is elevated from the receiving bunker by a belt conveyor. One man inspects the refuse as it is conveyed and removes materials that might damage the mechanisms, but he does not really salvage any material. Iron is removed by a magnetic separator, and then the refuse falls into Dorr-Oliver raspers for shredding. The shredded refuse is then run through a ballistic separator, where gravel, broken glass, and similar hard, heavy material is removed. The ground compostable refuse is then elevated to a surge tank.

Meanwhile, digested sewage sludge from the city's treatment plant is vacuum filtered to increase the solids content from 12 to 30 percent (nearly three-quarters of the water in the sludge is removed). The dewatered sludge is mixed with the ground refuse in an auger conveyor and conveyed to the briquetting machine. Here, an elaborate machine produces briquettes, approximately 15 inches by 9 inches by 6 inches in size, that have a "tunnel" on the underside. These are placed automatically on pallets that are moved to a "curing shed," where the actual composting takes place. The briquettes quickly heat to 130° to 140° F (55° to 60° C), a surface fungal growth develops, and the briquettes both dry out and compost. The salient feature of the process is this concurrent biological-physical change. The metabolic heat of composting promotes surface drying, while the compacted nature of the refuse caused by the pressing of the briquettes allows capillary transfer of moisture from the center to the surface. Concurrently, as moisture is removed, air enters the capillaries of the briquette and sustains the aerobic fungal and bacterial organisms that attack the refuse and convert it to compost. The close stacking of the individual briquettes, along with their tunnel form, gives adequate opportunity for air transfer while still conserving the heat of composting. Even the outside-corner briquettes attain a temperature of 120° to 130° F (50° to 55° C). In the curing process the moisture content drops from about 65 to about 13 percent (wet weight basis).

The cured briquettes are stacked outside in a yard like normal building bricks. In the fall of the year, when compost can be marketed to nearby grape farmers, the briquettes are run through a simple hammermill, and the finished compost is sold.

Versailles, France

Population served, 82,000 Type of plant, silo

Incoming domestic refuse amounts to some 150 metric tons (165 short tons) per day. The metal is removed with a magnetic separator, and the refuse is then ground with a heavy-duty Hazemag hammermill. The ground refuse is rough screened (scalpings go to an incinerator) and then put into the four silos, each with a capacity of 320 metric tons—about 700 cubic meters (350 English tons—915 cubic yards).

Air is blown through the silo for aeration, and each silo is equipped with a bottom unloading device. The removed compost is sieved a second time and then piled outside for curing and to await sale.

sewage sludge

Besides compost, another product of waste treatment technology that can be used to improve the fertility of soil is sewage sludge. This is discussed here because of its similarity in potential use to compost, and also because sewage sludge can be utilized, as in the Schweinfurt plant described above, in the composting process. An additional discussion of sewage sludge occurs in Chapter Three: Water Pollution.

Sewage sludge is what is removed from ordinary residential sewage in the most common sewage treatment plants. It is mainly a somewhat purified human excrement with a black color, gooey consistency, and tar-like smell. It is not especially odorous.

Researchers have known for years that sewage sludge is an excellent soil additive, but only recently has any major city succeeded in making large-scale use of this product. The reason for this has simply been the existence of a taboo system in the United States against utilization of a product that has passed in another state through the human digestive system.

Sludge can be burned to produce heat or produce methane gas (for both, see Chapter Three), but a better use is to improve soil, particularly acidic land that has been ruined by surface mining (*See* Volume Two).

The Chicago Sanitary District now disposes of its sludge in Fulton County, Illinois, tremendously improving the land for crops (*Time* Sept. 27, 1971 at 93). The sanitary district expects to purchase about 50,000 acres to restore in this manner. The Chicago sludge is moved by barge via canals. Sludge can be piped directly to the farm fields (See Sheaffer, John R., "Reviving the Great Lakes," *Saturday Review* Nov. 7, 1970 at 62).

The literature on sewage sludge disposal is quite considerable. The EPA's Office of Solid Waste Management, 5555 Ridge Ave., Cincinnati, Ohio 45213, has sponsored a score or more of research projects in this area, and has several publications on its projects. The Federal Water Pollution Control Administration of the Department of the Interior (transferred to EPA) in January, 1968 published "Agricultural Utilization of Sewage Sludge Effluent and Sludge, An Annotated Bibliography," 89 pp., GPO.

e. Recycling

The techniques for handling solid waste have changed little since primitive times. Most cities are running out of reasonably accessible land for landfills. Moreover, few communities welcome the exported wastes of other areas. Ocean dumping must be banned. Incinerators, even when equipped with pollution controls, are still intolerable sources of air pollution. As we move to more strict air and water pollution limitations, the material that is captured by the control devices is added to the quantity of solid waste requiring disposal.

For these reasons, as well as the incredible waste of natural resources engendered by present practices, new solutions must be found. Such solutions will not only alleviate this pollution problem but could have major beneficial secondary effects. By recycling our waste we can reduce the drain on our natural resources and thus decrease the environmental destruction caused by the energy industry as well as strip mining, oil transportation and a host of other environmental problems.

bulk reduction

The problem of disposing of solid wastes has engendered some bizarre "solutions," many of which are promoted by American industry in typical huckster fashion. One outstanding example is the Trash Masher, a home appliance smaller than a dishwasher which crams barrels of trash into a 16 inch-tall paper bag, and is a bargain at just $249.95. Not only does this item do no more than convert one pound of solid waste into one pound of solid waste, it increases the home electric power demand, and makes the separation required for recycling extremely difficult. For a report on the biggest Trash Masher of them all, *see* "The Tezuka Refuse Compression System," U.S. Dept. of HEW (Public Health Service), Bureau of Solid Waste Management (Cincinnati: 1969). Actually, this large-scale municipal solid waste refuse compacter, which compresses solid waste into large bales, could significantly reduce the cost of transporting solid wastes, the most expensive aspect of current disposal operations. But the initial cost of the Tezuka system is impressively high (a 250 ton/day capacity installation would cost $2.125 million installed, *id.* at 38), and the end product is *non*-recyclable, and can only be disposed of through sanitary landfilling or environmentally-harmful ocean dumping.

industrial waste

The disposal of solid wastes generated by industry is normally a responsibility of the industry's management, subject to appropriate state laws and/or municipal ordinances. The 1971 *Industrial Pollution Control Handbook,* edited by Herbert F. Lund (New York, McGraw-Hill), appears to be the most comprehensive publication in this field, discussing the evolution of industrial pollution control, giving industry-by-industry problem analysis, and explaining pollution control equipment and operations.

resources in urban wastes

The ores from which we extract metals for our industrial society rarely contain more than a few percent of the target metal, and this waste (tailings)mountsup at an incredible rate: more than 1 billion tons a year in the United States alone. Copper, for instance, is standardly mined in the American West from ore containing only one to two percent of the metal. A famous exception to such low percentages is the great iron ore deposit of northern Minnesota, the exhaustion of which is already foreseeable.Those deposits contain about 30 percent iron.

The residue from incinerated U.S. municipal waste is about 30 percent iron. There is also, by weight, about 50 percent glass, which makes such residues compare favorably with the foam building material which can be (but isn't) made from Minnesota iron ore tailings.

The burning of municipal wastes can provide about one-third the heating power per ton as does a goodgrade of coal. That heat can(and does in many parts of Europe) generate electricity.

Investments in coal companies by power companies are not unusual. Because the demand for coal is growing, hundreds of thousands of acres in the majority of our states have been denuded, their soil destroyed, and hundreds of thousands more are already targets for plunderers.

ESTIMATED VALUE OF SCRAP IN NEW YORK CITY MUNICIPAL WASTE FLOW (PER YEAR)

scrap value of wastes

	Approximate number of tons	Current dealer's scrap value per ton [1]	Total estimated scrap value
Aluminum cans	12,000	$200	$2,400,000
Steel (from tin-free cans [2])	23,000	10	230,000
Steel (from detinning and remaining bimetal containers)	169,000	3	507,000
Glass containers	348,000	17	5,920,000
Newspapers	500,000	17	8,500,000
Paper corrugated and folding container of all types	1,480,000	10	14,800,000
Subtotal	2,532,000		32,357,000
Abandoned cars [3]	100,000	15–20	1.5–2,000,000
Total	2,632,000		[4] 34,000,000

[1] Average current market price when dealers sell to reprocessing plants. Includes dealer's costs and markup. Prices vary widely depending on density of collection input and grade of scrap material. These figures therefore represent only rough approximations.
[2] Approximately 12 percent of total steel containers of 192,000.
[3] 75,000 cars at 1 to 1.5 ton per car. Most abandoned cars are now recycled.
[4] Approximate.

SOURCE: New York City Environmental Protection Administration

In the long-run, the prospects for recycling are enhanced by the shortage of landfill sites. It is ironic that the waste of resources does not affect us as a society with as much concern as does the lack of disposal sites. Of major U.S. cities, 25 have sufficient landfill space for less than five years.

Reclamation of many resources in solid wastes is now practical under several systems and combinations of present systems. Some approach total use of the waste, either as raw material or fuel.

"total use" recycling plants

The Black Clawson Co., 605 Clark St., Middletown, Ohio 45042, recently turned its papermaking technology into the design of a joint solid waste disposal and sewage treatment plant. The plants reenforce each other through the sewage treatment plant's cleaning of water used in the solid waste plant, while the solid waste plant incinerates the sewage sludge as well as parts of the collected solid waste. No mention is made of heat utilization from the incinerator, but this latter is a successful feature of many plants in Europe and a handful in North America. (e.g. Montreal's Des Carrieres plant and Chicago's Northwest incinerator; see *Environmental Science and Technology,* Vol. 5, No. 3, March, 1971).

See also pp. Two 60-61

The Black Clawson plant is in successful use at Franklin, Ohio, operated by the Miami [River Valley] Conservancy District of Dayton, Ohio. Construction of the plant was sponsored by Bureau of Solid Waste Management, the U.S. Department of Housing and Urban Development, and the City of Franklin. An article describing the plant in a fairly detailed manner appears in *Public Works* magazine, June, 1971.

The Aluminum Association manufactured quite a bit of publicity late in 1970 by putting together, on paper, a solid waste reclamation system suitable for handling all municipal trash.

The technology of the suggested plant was borrowed: key elements were the blown-air classifier developed at Stanford Research Institute, and the post-incineration refuse separator developed by the Bureau of Mines at College Park, Maryland. But the idea itself basically seems sound, and it is to be regretted that no funding was provided, especially since the sponsors maintained it could make money. The following is a summary description of the proposed plant culled from the Aluminum Association's own description:

The plant is a full-size unit capable of handling refuse from a typical city of 175,000 to 225,000 population. Its main processing line includes incinerators to burn all combustible materials that are not reclaimed. Excess steam will be available for sale to potential users depending upon the site location. This revenue would offset part of the cost of operating the plant.

The residue from the incinerators is processed by a material recycling system that separates glass, ferrous metals and non-ferrous metals for reuse by industry. These revenues will also be applied against operating costs.

The plant has been designed as an aesthetically attractive unit with prime consideration for the control of odor, atmospheric emissions and wastewater discharge. It is as self-sustaining and reliable as human ingenuity and scientific technology can make it. It can be operated independently or be installed in conjunction with an existing wastewater treatment plant to become an integrated solid-liquid waste disposal facility.

The receiving and shredding area is designed to process 500 tons per day of solid municipal waste (refuse) as received in 20-cubic-yard packer trucks. Since a loaded truck will deliver about six tons of raw refuse each trip, approximately 85 truck loads will be received each day to reach the 500-tons-per-day rate, an average of 11 truck loads each hour. The receiving station normally operates 8 hours a day, 5 days a week; however, it is designed to handle incoming refuse in 7 hours, for an average of 12 truck loads each hour (71.5 tons of refuse per hour). There are two unloading stations. Each station can handle six trucks an hour, allowing ten minutes for each truck to enter the plant, dump its load, and leave.

Two incinerator units, each sized to burn 200 tons per day of shredded municipal waste, are provided. These units include a water-cooled furnace and a waste-heat boiler section. Steam is generated at 400 pounds per square inch (psi), 700° F, for in-plant drive turbine use and for potential sale to a user.

Air condensers are provided to condense the steam when its use is not required. The units will be fired 24 hours a day, seven days a week. Residue from the units is quenched and stored for labor processing in a material recycling system. Flue gases are cleaned by passing through electrostatic precipitator units and a wet scrubber. Feedwater treatment equipment is supplied to support the boiler requirements.

"total use" recycling plant

Steam is used for turbine drive units as needed throughout the refuse demonstration plant. The balance of steam is available for sale to an outside user. It is estimated that a maximum of 85,000 pounds per hour of steam will be generated with two incinerators in service and that approximately 35,000 pounds per hour will be required for in-house use in turbine drives, feedwater de-aeration and heating.

The pyrolysis unit is designed to handle a feed of 1250 tons of shredded refuse a week. It operates 90 per cent of the time. The feed rate is 8.5 tons per hour, assuming 151 operating hours in a seven-day week (90 per cent of the time). The pyrolysis unit consists of a surge bin, a feeder, and a kiln with the proper auxiliary units for gas scrubbing and quenching the residue.

The purpose of the incinerator residue recovery system (Bureau of Mines Unit) is to process the residue of the incinerator and pyrolysis unit for reusable materials. The recovered materials are classified generally as ferrous metals, non-ferrous metals, non-magnetic (colorless) glass, magnetic (colored) glass, and sand. The materials are separated and stored for shipment to users.

The system is sized to process 180 tons per day of wet residue (126 tons dry) from incinerator storage, 5 days a week, 8 hours a day. The system, with some modification, is based upon the pilot plant system of the U.S. Bureau of Mines unit at College Park, Maryland.

Two electromagnetic separators are installed, one for the output of each shredder. Each separator removes up to 3 tons per hour of magnetic materials (depending upon the consistency of incoming refuse). The separators are suspended over the belt conveyor carrying refuse from the shredder. Magnets are located within the belt loop of a short conveyor placed above and at right angles to the refuse conveyor. Magnetic materials are drawn up out of the shredded refuse, cling to the underside of the short belt conveyor, and are carried away from the main refuse conveyor. The materials removed from the refuse drop into a chute and are collected in a bin.

The screening area consists of a covered doubledeck vibrating screen designed to separate ten tons per hour of shredded refuse into three fractions. The top screen (or perforated plate) has 3/4-inch openings and the bottom screen has 3/16-inch openings.

"total use" recycling plant

The screen processes shredded refuse produced by the shredders described in the receiving and shredding area. The input refuse can be magnetically separated or not as desired.

The air classification system is designed to process 30 tons of shredded material per hour; it consists of three pairs of centrifugal separators arranged in series, six large diameter mechanical cyclones, and six exhaust fans. A cyclone and an exhauster are connected to each separator. By rotating the separators at a high rpm and by exhausting air upward through them, materials of different specific gravities and sizes are separated.

The fiber reclaiming area is a wet process which receives 224 tons per 8-hour day of shredded or unshredded waste from the receiving and shredding area. The waste is estimated to contain 75 per cent solids and 25 per cent moisture. A conveying system will also be provided for processing reclaimed raw paper from the air classifier units and paper wastes directly from a separate unloading station. These alternate feed arrangements allow evaluation and study of the hydropulper in the fiber recovery system.

Mixed paper consisting of newsprint, machine boards, bags, and other paper fibers are processed and reclaimed from solid municipal waste. The mixed fiber pulp consists of kraft sulfate and sulfite fibers, groundwood from newsprint, semi-chemical fibers from corrugating medium, and products from other pulping processes. The metals, glass, dirt, sand, plastics, and other materials are separated from the paper fibers and processed in other areas.

See also:

Bureau of Mines Research Programs on Recycling and Disposal of Mineral-Metal-, and Energy-Based Solid Wastes, United States Department of the Interior, Bureau of Mines Information Circular/1971, IC 8529.

An extensive bibliography can be found in *A Systems Approach to the Problems of Solid Waste and Litter,* Management and Behavioral Science Center, University of Pennsylvania, 1971 at 170.

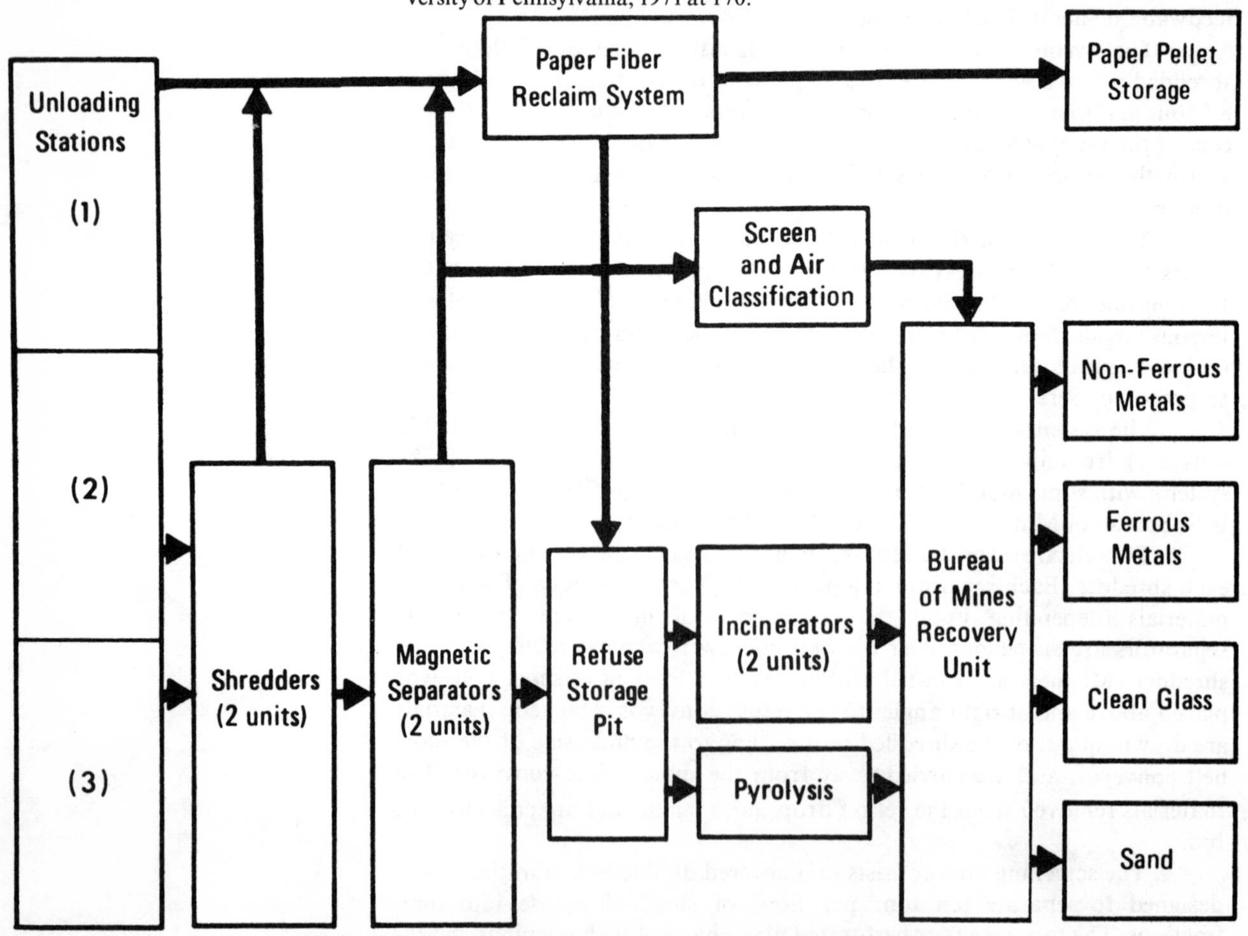

RECYCLING PLANT FLOWCHART

Selected resources for secondary use

Paper

About 30 million tons of paper found its way into the nation's dumps in 1971. Surveys show that 40 to 45 percent of municipal solid wastes are paper and paper products. Surely there is some relation between this and the oft-mentioned fact that the average solid waste per person in urban collections has risen from three pounds a day in 1920 to six pounds per day in 1970—and it was still rising sharply.

A low percentage of all U.S. paper waste is recycled, and a very low percentage indeed is recycled that reaches the individual, noncorporate, customer. The figure generally given for the percentage of U.S. paper that is recycled is 20 percent. But this can be misleading, due to conflicting definitions of what is recycled, and at any rate applies principally (70 percent) to cardboard production.

Paper, textiles, aluminum and zinc have very low recycling rates, but the paper industry is experiencing a rapid decline in the use of recycled material. According to the National Association of Secondary Materials Industries, we have declined from a 35% recycling rate in the mid-1940's to almost half that rate in the late 1960's. Paper constitutes nearly one-half this country's municipal solid waste. We are using 58 million tons of paper a year but only recycling 11 million tons. The largest user of waste paper is the paperboard industry, yet its use of recycled material went from 42% to 28% in just 10 years.

Why isn't most paper recycled? Why do we use wood at all with so much paper going to rot after only brief use?

materials for paper

The waste in paper making and use applies not only to the failure to recycle paper, but also to the choice of materials and methods of manufacture. Beginning centuries ago, a wide variety of fibrous plants were used for papermaking. The Egyptians, as every schoolboy ought to know, used the marsh plant papyrus. The Chinese used silk and various plant fibers. The Japanese used three plants—the *kooso, gampi,* and *mitsumata*—, while the Indians of central Mexico used the bark of the wild fig tree, and Europeans used rags of various fibers. Sugar cane waste (bagasse) is currently used to manufacture a large part of Mexico's paper, and the same material is used by the small Valentine Paper Co. plant in Lockport, Louisiana. Bagasse is the crushed, juiceless, fibrous residue of sugar cane stalks after the mills have finished extracting the sugar. If not recycled, this waste is usually burned, creating air pollution. By recycling, you eliminate a solid waste disposal problem and avoid using trees. The Wells Fargo Bank of San Francisco is using this material for checks and estimates the 200 million checks made of 80 percent bagasse each year saves 8,000 trees. Wood, indeed, has been a late-comer to papermaking, and some still unused materials such as various members of the century plant family (grown in immense numbers in Yucatan and central Mexico) have been shown to be quite usable for papermaking.

Wood pulp now comprises about 98 percent of all U.S. papers, with cotton making up most of the remainder.

The first commercial process for the use of wood in papermaking was invented in 1840. In this, the wood was simply ground. This process results in paper of almost as great weight as the wood that went into its making (minus the bark), and is relatively pollution free—especially if adequate filtration is used. This method, although still in use for rougher papers, is disliked because of the greater time consumed in its manufacture, and because occasional wood chips can be seen on the paper's surface, marring it for print, and because paper from pure groundwood pulp gives some difficulty in use on very high-speed presses.

The more common processes today use various chemicals to break down the wood fibers, destroying more than half the wood. But since trees are relatively cheap, this is the preferred method today.

In the process of manufacture, considerable ripping and other damage occurs. This waste paper is known as "mill broke" or simply "broke." This unsoiled paper has always been tossed back into the papermaking process. Prior to 1971, all paper companies insisted that "broke" was virgin material. Like just about everyone else, they tended to de-emphasize recycled materials; the government prohibits "excess" use of reused materials, and kid sisters resented hand-me-downs.

Then came the great awakening—or yawning, perhaps. With more mature tastes, what for years of hard use was known as virgin was now termed "recycled". This is obviously silly, but the government has a way of turning bad jokes into nightmares.

After strong urgings by several Congressmen, President Nixon in February of 1971 asked the General Services Administration (the Federal Government's purchasing agency) to examine their purchasing specifications and revise them to encourage the use of recycled materials. During the summer the GSA announced in reference to its forthcoming paper specifications that they would "have the effect of excluding from the definition of recycled fiber content some mill wastes known as mill broke which are normally recycled as virgin materials." So far, so good: logical and truthful.

A forceful industry lobbying movement was then set underway, led by the American Paper Institute, an industry association.

effect of lobbying

The result was that when the specifications came out in August of 1971, the definition of recycled fiber managed, in an involved, technical manner, to permit virtually all mill broke to qualify as recycled fiber. Not only that, but the specifications required recycled fibers in only 14 of the 122 paper purchasing categories, and the percentages were ridiculously low, including requiring 50 percent recycled materials in items such as paper towels and corrugated boxes that had been generally 100 percent recycled.

The redefinition of recycled paper to include mill broke was hailed as a triumph in industry magazines, but their victory was only almost complete. A counter effort by a score of Congressmen and lobbyists from a recycling industry association managed to settle the issue over the heads of GSA, and the traditional definition of mill broke as virgin fiber was restored. But the low specifications for recycled paper stayed, and the government's $140,000,000 purchases of about 400,000 tons of paper continue to encourage cutting rather than recycling.

Thereafter, GSA moved extremely slowly to increase the amount of recycled content in the paper products it purchases. But by June of 1972, they still required a recycled content in only 33 of their paper categories, and in only 10 of these categories did the recycled material have to come from post-consumer uses. (*I.e.*—Nearly all of these modest recycled content requirements could be met with clean scrap generated at paper wholesalers, binders and printers prior to use.)

(Though it has nothing to do with paper, it might be added here in defense of GSA, that another department of that agency not under the control of the same man as is paper buying, has done admirably in raising the requirements for use of retreaded tires from 3.5 percent to 50 percent of the 120,000 tires the Government replaces each year.)

Under the GSA requirements, only two of the categories (cardboard backing for memo pads, and chipboard) required 50 percent post-consumer waste; of the remaining eight categories, one required 20 percent (looseleaf binder covers), seven required 10 percent (four types of boxes and three types of computing and shorthand machine papers), and one (triple-wall fiberboard boxes) required 5 percent.

See also "Use of Recycled Paper by Congress," Hearings before the Committee on Rules and Administration, United States Senate, 92d Congress, 1st Session, August 3, 1971.

But a bigger question emerges: Why is the paper industry generally so opposed to recycling?

The most common answers, which are those promulgated by the paper industry itself and a major element, owners of American newspapers and magazines, are that recycled paper is, 1) inferior, 2) more expensive. Let us look.

question of quality

There is a small amount of truth in the charge that recycled papers are inferior in that the average length of fibers in recycled wood pulp papers is reduced, making it slightly weaker than paper made from 100 percent virgin wood fiber. But this weakness is not so marked as to rule out the use of recycled pulps in most paper uses. Folded maps which are likely to face heavy use are an exemplary case of a type of paper use in which virgin fibers are to be preferred. Another case is grocery bags, where recent experiments have still not been successful in making a cheap, recycled bag that is as strong as a virgin fiber one after it has been wetted. While dry, there is no problem. But even here, some recycled paper can be used without important loss of strength.

de-inking

Besides strength, recycled papers that have been printed upon must be de-inked if they are to be indistinguishable from standard bleached papers made from virgin fibers. The de-inking, however, although practical, is not even a necessity for many uses. Bergstrom Paper Co. of Neenah, Wisconsin, ignores de-inking, taking ordinary trash paper of all sorts and producing a line of printing and bond papers that have been used commercially with considerable success. The July, 1971, issue of *Chem 26 Paper Processing,* a 120-page trade journal, was the first commercial magazine printed on such paper. The difference from paper made from bleached virgin fibers is obvious, but the recycled paper is not unattractive. The paper is speckled with tiny spots of various colors, somewhat like the paper of a dollar bill. (Dollar bills, however, are made from pure cotton, which is much stronger than wood pulp.) Bleaching weakens paper fibers.

Recycling paper without de-inking leaves about 3 per cent solid waste, compared with 30 percent solid waste from the de-inked recycled papers Bergstrom also produces. The various processes for making recycled, de-inked papers produce even more pollutants than the production of similar qualities of paper from virgin pulp, but these pollutants can be controlled through adequate closed-system water filtration systems. The magazine mentioned above, *Chem 26 Paper Processing,* is recommended as a source for additional technical information.

Two other recycling methods are worthy of mention in this brief discussion. One is the technique used by the Riverside Paper Corp. at their mill in Appleton, Wisconsin. Riverside takes the mill broke from a nearby manufacturer of milk cartons, paper cups, etc., and turns these containers coated with wax and polyethylene into a variety of writing and printing papers. Using a technique developed at the company and licensed for manufacture to the Black Clawson Co., super-heated tricholoethylene in a closed system is sprayed onto the waste cartons. The resultant sludge is then removed from the tanks with common fuel oil, and this mixture is used to fuel the boilers that cook the mixture. The excellent paper produced can, of course, be recycled an indefinite number of times. The yield by weight in new paper is about 87 percent that of the waste paper used as material, and most of the remaining material is used as fuel. Indeed, the use of mill waste as fuel seems to have considerable commercial possibilities, while the use of mill waste as a food for Torula yeast is well underway. Boise Cascade Corp. has a $2.5 million plant under construction that will have an initial capacity of 12 million pounds of the protein additive, according to *Chem 26 Paper Processing.* The plant will use waste liquids from the pulping mill at Salem, Oregon.

purchasing paper

The current GSA definitions of two categories of recycled fiber for paper making are useful (the original definition was not). Part I is post-

defining recycled paper

consumer waste; Part II other materials, the use of which is also environmentally useful:

GSA DEFINITION

The paper stock shall contain not less than 35 percent by weight of reclaimed fibers as listed in Part I and Part II, but not less than 10 percent by weight as listed in Part I. A certificate shall be submitted with each bid indicating compliance with these requirements. The certificate should identify the types of reclaimed fiber to be used in the material listed in the invitation.

Part I

A. Paper, paperboard and fibrous wastes from factories, retail stores, office buildings, homes, etc., after they have passed their end-usage as a consumer item including:

1. Used corrugated boxes;
2. Old newspapers;
3. Old magazines;
4. Mixed waste paper;
5. Tabulating cards; and
6. Used cordage.

B. All paper, paperboard and fibrous wastes that enter and are collected from municipal solid waste.

Part II

A. Dry paper and paperboard waste generated after completion of the papermaking process [1] including:

1. Envelope cuttings, bindery trimmings and other paper and paperboard waste, resulting from printing, cutting, forming and other converting operations;
2. Bag, box and carton manufacturing wastes; and
3. Butt rolls, mill wrappers and rejected unused stock.

B. Finished paper and paperboard from obsolete inventories of paper and paperboard manufacturers, merchants, wholesalers, dealers, printers, converters or others.

C. Fibrous by-products of harvesting, manufacturing, extractive or woodcutting processes, flax straw, linters, bagasse, slash and other forest residues.

D. Wastes generated by the conversion of goods made from fibrous materials; i.e., waste rope from cordage manufacture, textile mill waste and cuttings.

E. Fibers recovered from waste water which otherwise would enter the waste stream.

---

[1] The papermaking process is defined as those manufacturing operations up to and including the cutting and trimming of the paper machine reel into smaller rolls or rough sheets.

The following is from a prepared statement by Jeffrey S. Padnos of the New York City Environmental Protection Agency at Hearings before the Subcommittee on Fiscal Policy of the Joint Economic Committee, Congress of the United States, November 9, 1971, (70-4220, GPO, 1972 at 116):

Buying environmentally beneficial products, particularly products made from secondary materials, is one of the most significant actions an individual, corporation, or government agency can take to encourage expanded recycling.

As described in the separate testimony I mentioned earlier, New York City has begun its environmental purchasing program with recycled paper. Our objective in the work we have done to date has been to write specifications which will encourage the use of "post-consumer waste," waste from products which have served their use in society and which enter our solid waste stream if not reclaimed. We want to encourage expanded utilization of those secondary fibres, which, under existing economic incentives, are not being reclaimed.

Our most recently developed definition of "recycled paper" is as follows:

> (Napkins, towels, etc.) shall contain a minimum of (25%) recycled fibres by weight. For the purposes of this requirement, recycled fibres are fibres reclaimed from post-consumer waste, including de-inked fibres, as well as fibres from old corrugated, newspapers, magazines, waste from office buildings or banks (shredded or unshredded), mixed papers, or other paper or paperboard products which have been used for the purpose originally intended, and returned to a paper mill for reuse. Post-consumer waste does not include waste generated in manufacuring, concerting, or printing processes, such as mill broke, roll trim, shavings, or kraft, corrugated, or envelope cuttings.

This definition is still under review, and has not yet been adopted. It does indicate, however, what we are trying to accomplish. New York City recently used a similar definition in a competitively bid contract for the purchase of corrugated boxes. The contract was recently awarded to a company which is supplying City with boxes which meet all of our technical standards at a price lower than the lowest bid submitted a year ago.

Unfortunately, a good deal of controversy and confusion still surrounds the question of defining recycled paper. Strong leadership from the Federal General Services Administration could settle this matter, but that leadership has not yet been forthcoming. The original standards proposed by the GSA were so lax that most paper mills could meet them simply by changing the name of their existing practices, so that use of production wastes would qualify as recycling. Subsequent specifications have shown some improvement, but they still seem to indicate a greater commitment to preserving existing practices than to providing new incentives for solid waste utilization.

overspecification

A second major area for standards investigation is overspecification. In many instances today, we are buying more product capability than we actually require for a given job. Overspecification places a needless added strain upon the environment, both in raw material consumption and in waste generation. It can also limit the applicability of secondary materials, particularly paper. A prime example of this is the brightness specification in many grades of paper. Over the years, paper companies have sought to compete with one another by increasing the brightness of their products. The results in some cases have actually been disfunctional—some printing papers are so bright that they are uncomfortable to read.

This is not simply harmless folly. Research performed by Resources for the Future, Inc., indicates that the higher the brightness requirement for either virgin or recycled paper, the greater the amount of solid, liquid, and gaseous wastes generated in the manufacturing process.

Another example is corrugated boxes. Some manufacturers have reported to us that at a given thickness, using secondary fibres means a slight sacrifice in the strength of the box. But how strong must our boxes be? On what are our present standards based? American manufacturers generally sneer at "flimsy" Japanese boxes. But those flimsy boxes are apparently capable of protecting delicate electronic equipment through ship, air, truck and rail transport from manufacturing centers in Japan to retail outlets in this country.

Earlier testimony by another member of the New York City Environmental Protection Agency, Marvin Gerstein, furnished information concerning the price, availability, and quality of the recycled paper obtained under the above definition (*ibid.* at 95):

Motivation

New York City's solid waste burden is growing rapidly. The Department of Sanitation currently disposes of over 24,000 tons of refuse every day—almost 15 billion pounds last year. Between 1960 and 1970, the City's population remained essentially constant, yet the solid waste load increased 40%.

A final solution to the City's solid waste problem is still being sought. It is hoped that recycling will become a major, if not total, part of that solution.

Our research indicates that existing economic incentives are such that almost all manufacturing and converting waste—including wood residuals such as sawdust and chips, "mill broke", and "cuttings" or "clippings" from envelopes or cartons—are already being reclaimed. For this reason, we decided to focus our efforts upon the post-consumer wastes, including newspapers, containers, and mixed papers (such as office building waste), which constitutes the bulk of the nearly 40 million tons of paper products entering our nation's solid waste stream every year.

Availability and price

availability

On February 2, 1971, Mayor Lindsay announced the beginning of New York City's environmental purchasing program. A few weeks later, the Purchase Department solicited bids for office bond paper, with the recycling requirement included. On March 19, 1971, we received bids from paper distributors representing five paper manufacturers. (Two other bids were received, but the manufacturers did not meet the recycling requirement.)

In order to gain perspective on the price of recycled paper, the Purchase Department requested bids for bond paper with no recycling requirement. On April 5, 1971, we received bids from distributors representing six paper manufacturers. We found the prices to be comparable. The lowest recycled paper bid of $354,177 for 365,000 reams was lower than five of the six virgin paper bids. Among those five was the brand of paper the City had bought in 1970. The lowest virgin paper bid was approximately $30,000 or 8.4% below the lowest recycled paper bid.

Shortly thereafter, the Mayor announced the award of the contract to the lowest recycled paper bidder.

Quality

To date the City has taken delivery on over 50,000 reams, approximately 250,000 pounds, of the recycled paper, and we have encountered no problems in use.

Response

The response to the City's actions has been tremendous. We have answered hundreds of requests for information regarding recycled paper, including more than sixty from other government agencies.

The City of Buffalo recently solicited two bids for paper, one using their old specification, the other including the recycling requirement for bond paper quoted above. Buffalo's Purchase Department has reported that the lowest of all bids received was for recycled paper, and a contract has been awarded.

The paper industry is also responding to the environmental concern being voiced around the country. Several new lines of recycled paper have come onto the market in recent months. One paper manufacturer reported that it is reactivating a waste paper deinking system which has been in mothballs for 10 years.

In conclusion, we can say that on the basis of our experience to date, the City is working to expand its program to other products, including corrugated containers mentioned previously. We feel that a strong Federal commitment to purchase environmentally beneficial products such as recycled paper is necessary, if recycling is to expand to levels that will have significant impact on municipal solid waste problems.

In the same hearings (*ibid.* at 140-141 and 145), Blair T. Bower, an economist for Resources for the Future, Inc., had this to say in response to questions concerning basic comparative costs of recycled and virgin papers:

comparative costs: recycled and virgin papers

What should be compared are the costs of preparing the raw material as an input to the paper machine in both cases. From the paper machine on, the costs are essentially the same. There is some controversy, I will admit, about that. But the technical people with whom we are working say that essentially one can assume that if the pulp that goes to the head box of the paper machine meets certain specifications, it does not matter what the source is. So we can start and look at the costs preceding the paper machine.

Chairman GRIFFITHS. Yes, look at the costs preceding.

Mr. BOWER. There are two kinds of costs involved, direct costs and indirect costs. The direct costs are those in the case of virgin roundwood of getting the raw material from the forest and producing the pulp.

The costs in the case of the paper residual are those of obtaining the paper residual from, say, the metropolitan area, and the costs of processing. The latter costs together are roughly 50 to 75 percent of the former.

If, in addition, one takes into account—which should be done—the residuals management costs associated with both of those operations, you probably would get an additional differential, but, as I said in my prepared statement, this is not necessarily clear, depending on whether it is more costly to handle the additional amount of suspended solids generated in processing the paper residual as against the gaseous residuals generated in the pulping operation.

Furthermore, we have not included, unquestionably, I think, the extra costs associated with some of our logging operations. These stem both from such forest management activities as the use of herbicides, but more importantly, probably, from the sediment generated in logging operations, and the esthetic impact of some of those activities on the landscape, which can be measured in terms of economic costs, as is being shown by the current controversy over the U.S. Forest Service management practices.

In summary, I would suggest, but only as an order of magnitude based on preliminary estimates—but the costs of processing paper residuals are clear, and those of pulping are available—that there is probably a differential of somewhere between 50 and 75 percent. That is, to use paper residuals to produce a given product costs 50 to 75 percent of using the virgin roundwood.

One other caveat: That differential assumes something about the location of the processing activity. Obviously if you have to ship the paper residual all the way to Seattle from St. Louis, you are incurring substantial transport costs.

In terms of the technical production processes involved in using paper residuals, in contrast to the production processes for pulping round wood or chips from round wood, there is no question but that the basic costs are less for using paper residuals. You are already starting with a material that has been pulped, and you do not have to go through the basic operation of separating the lignin from the cellulose which is all that the pulping operation does. Processing paper residuals is not a very capital-intensive kind of operation, relatively. So that one of the things which is clear, which has happened in the last couple of years, with the interest in so-called recycled products, is that firms which have been using converting residuals since time immemorial, but not saying anything about it, have climbed on the bandwagon and advertised them as 100 percent recycled. In some cases they have increased the price and gotten it, because people think they are doing something great by buying these products, whereas they actually aren't changing anything at all.

In practice, by mid-1972 the demand was so great for recycled papers that the prices asked and received by the better-known recycling mills were often markedly higher than for comparable virgin papers. But there seems to be general agreement with Mr. Bower concerning the theoretical price possibilities.

But Mr. Bower seemed to be the only one to believe that use of recycled fiber would little affect use of pulpwood (*ibid.* at 139):

Chairman GRIFFITHS.

I would like to ask you, Mr. Bower, if we pass laws that require that all bottles be green and all paper towels and toilet tissue and face tissue be brown, what would the estimated saving be?

Mr. BOWER. I wish I could give you an explicit answer to that, Madam Chairman. I would say that in another 6 months I could give you that answer. But the saving unquestionably would be substantial. By that I mean millions of dollars, if for no other reason than the decrease in cost of bleaching chemicals and the residuals management costs stemming from the use of those bleaching chemicals.

costs of bleaching

Chairman GRIFFITHS. What would the savings be in resources? Would there be savings in resources?

Mr. BOWER. On that I would suggest that the savings would be minimal, for the reason that this oft-quoted number of 17 trees for every ton of paper residual used is not a valid number. It is not valid for several reasons. One of the main reasons is the one I indicated in my prepared statement; namely, that the bulk of the raw material inputs into paper production, at least in the Northwest, comes from wood products residue. Consequently, substituting paper residuals would save only a very small number of trees. The resource costs saved relate not so much to the forests as to the cost of chemicals, the cost of energy for processing—and bleaching is an energy intensive process—the cost of water, and the residual management cost associated with those processes.

Chairman GRIFFITHS. But anyhow, it would be really worth doing, would it not?

Mr. BOWER. I would say very definitely.

Do you not think so, Mr. Padnos?

Mr. PADNOS. Yes.

The facts that Mr. Bower utilizes below in his prepared statement (*ibid.* at 131) invalidate his claim that there are only "a very small number of trees" to be saved by recycling waste paper. Note that the high percentages of wood residuals going into papermaking are confined largely to the Northwest, and yet the entire western half of the United States only produces about one-eighth of the paper produced in the nation (exhibit of the American Paper Institute, *ibid* at 73).

use of wood residues

An example—paper residuals and the production of paper products

There are three types of possible raw materials for production of paper products: (1) virgin roundwood or chips from such roundwood, the latter in situations where the chipping is done in the woods; (2) residues from wood products operations, such as saw mills; and (3) paper residuals. In turn, the last is comprised basically of two subcategories, converting residuals and user residuals (See Figure 1). Neglecting any imperfections in the market, the relative quantities of the three types of raw materials utilized for production of paper products is a function of their relative costs to the manufacturer. Even before the advent of air pollution controls in recent years, and before the current agitation for increased "recycling", wood products residues were comprising an increasing proportion of the raw material input for paper production. This stemmed from the fact that the cost of this input has been becoming less than the cost of the alternative source of raw material, virgin round wood. In northern California, Oregon, and Washington, by the end of the sixties, 60%–70% of the input into paper manufacture was wood products residues. Even in the southeast, the area of fast growing pine, the proportion rose in the decade of the sixties from 10% to 20%.

Virgin pulpwood costs are tending to increase for various reasons, perhaps not the least of these is the increasing competition for alternative outputs from the forest land—recreation in particular. Labor costs have continued to rise and although productivity has increased, the net result has been, and is likely to remain, a trend toward increased cost of virgin round wood. Note that these trends in costs and use would take place in the absence of any pollution controls or any pressure for recycling. Consequently, basic use of wood products residues does not meet the first assumption noted above, namely, that recycle means making use of something which previously had not been utilized. It *is* valid to say that in the last few years *increased* use of wood products residues has been stimulated by air pollution controls, at least in the Northwest where air quality standards could not be met with use of the traditional teepee burner. But the incremental addition to total use because of this factor appears relatively small.

Turning to the third category of raw material, paper residuals—specifically converting residuals, the percentage of residuals generated in converting operations varies from two to three percent in printing newspapers to about 20% in making folding cartons. Converting residuals have desirable characteristics as raw materials—large quantities in a single location, high degree of homogeneity or little contamination, and if contamination exists it is of a known, specific nature. Consequently the large bulk of converting residuals has been used for many years. In 1969, about five million tons of converting residuals were generated, of which about four million tons were used. This use has occurred by virtue of the fact that the raw material cost represented by converting residuals was less than that of the alternative raw material of virgin round wood. Thus, the bulk of converting residuals has been and is being used, in the absence of pollution controls or "recycling" pressure.

pollution from recycling

The significance in relation to the second assumption noted originally is obvious, both with respect to wood products residues and with respect to converting residuals. That is, there would be little decrease in the solid wastes management problem because the bulk of converting residuals and much of wood products residues are being used. What it means is that in cases where costs for pollution and residuals disposal are imposed directly on converting and wood products operations, these costs will stimulate some further use of residuals.

The third assumption may or may not be valid. That is, in order to utilize paper residuals—or any other type of residuals—as raw material, processing of the residual is required, just as the raw iron ore must be processed. The processing operation itself requires inputs, such as energy, and results in the generation of residuals. Whether or not these residuals are less environmentally damaging than those generated in the use of virgin raw material depends on the quantities and characteristics of the residuals generated and on the costs of reducing or modifying the residuals before discharge into the environment. For example, if 100% waste paper is used to make a paper product in contrast to softwood using the kraft pulping process, the former results in the generation of no gaseous residuals, but substantially more dissolved and suspended solids than the kraft process. Whether or not the gaseous residuals generated in the kraft process are more damaging and/or more costly to modify, depends on the particular situation.

One other point merits mention in the context of comparing the economics of using residuals with using virgin raw materials, namely, the importance of product specifications. Depending on those specifications, greater or lesser amounts of paper residuals can be used, and greater or lesser amounts of residuals are generated because the degree of processing required is directly related to the product specifications. For example, if a brown paper towel is acceptable rather than a white paper towel, no bleaching is necessary either for the paper residuals as raw material or for virgin round wood. Because bleaching is a major generator of residuals, this takes on added significance. But it should be emphasized that different paper products require different component inputs, computer punch cards in contrast to newsprint, for example. Many paper residuals simply cannot physically be used for certain products.

Paper & Paperboard Production and Waste Paper Consumption - 1970

(In Thousand Tons)

	1970 Production	1970 WASTE PAPER CONSUMPTION					
			Bulk Grades			High Grades	
		Total	Mixed Papers	Old Corrugated Boxes & Clippings	Newspapers	Pulp Substitutes	De-ink
PAPER							
Newsprint	3,309	400			400		
Printing, writing & related	10,845	695				465	230
Unbleached Kraft Packaging, Industrial Converting, Special Industrial and Other	5,318	179	5	52	25	77	20
Tissue	3,671	690		30	40	340	280
Paper Sub-Total	23,143	1,964	5	82	465	882	530
PAPERBOARD							
Woodpulp paperboard (unbleached kraft, solid bleached and semi-chemical)	18,511	810		792		18	
Combination Paperboard	6,982	7,856	1,840	3,282	1,629	884	221
Paperboard Sub-Total	25,493	8,666	1,840	4,074	1,629	902	221
CONSTRUCTION PAPER AND BOARD, WET MACHINE AND MOLDED PRODUCTS	3,960	1,370	761	202	298	91	18
GRAND TOTAL	52,596	12,000	2,606	4,358	2,392	1,875	769

American Paper Institute - July 20, 1971 JRE:mrb

We continue to quote from the same source:

STATEMENT OF JAMES R. TURNBULL, EXECUTIVE VICE PRESIDENT, NATIONAL FOREST PRODUCTS ASSOCIATION

Madam Chairman and members of the committee: My name is James R. Turnbull. I am Executive Vice President of the National Forest Products Association which is a federation of 21 regional, species and products organizations representing manufacturers of lumber, plywood and other wood products throughout the United States.

Some observers might wonder why manufacturers of lumber, plywood and other solid wood products seek to be heard at hearings related to the recycling of paper. Their answer lies in the excellent definition for recycled materials for paper-making which was released August 2 by Robert L. Kunzig, Administrator of the General Services Administration.

supporting the *status quo*

I ask, Madam Chairman, that Mr. Kunzig's statement to the press on this subject and the GSA definition be placed in the hearing record at this point.

GSA TAKES NEW STEPS TO SPUR PAPER RECYCLING

The Federal Government is taking still another step in its drive to encourage the use of recycled waste paper, the General Services Administration announced today.

Administrator Robert L. Kunzig of GSA which does most of the Government's buying, said that effective immediately his agency will require the inclusion of '"post-consumer" wastes in the corrugated fiberboard it buys to line package cartons.

The specification change will require at least 35 percent waste fibers. Of this at least 10 percent must be post-consumer wastes. Post-consumer wastes include materials which have passed through their intended use and have been collected from homes, offices, factories, or municipal solid waste. The remainder will be of manufacturing wastes, forest residues and other wastes.

The GSA definition of recyclable materials properly takes into account the wastes from sawmills and plywood plants as well as the substantial quantities of wood fiber which are increasingly recovered from branches, limbs, stumps, bark and even needles which were previously left on the ground after harvest.

Any legislation or other action which would oblige papermakers to depend heavily upon waste paper as the basis for their production would simply be transferring pollution problems from the wastebaskets of the nation to the yards of sawmill and plywood manufacturers.

It must be recognized as well that burning of these wastes, which was until recently an accepted practice in most areas of the country where volumes were excess to potential consumption, has now been severely restricted by Federal, state or local air pollution regulations.

Residuals from sawmill and plywood operations have, moreover, become a substantial source of revenues for individual companies and for the nation as a whole. In 1953 the State of Oregon was able to use only about six percent of sawmill residues for paper and composition boards; by 1967 that percentage had risen to 60 percent and the total volume for domestic and export use rose to six million tons. Two years later the volume was eight million tons. These residues have become a cash crop from wood manufacturing operations.

The direct cash benefit to the nation as a whole must not be overlooked. The export of wood residues in the form of chips have become a significant factor in the U.S. balance of trade picture. In 1969 about 1.7 million tons of wood chips were exported to Japan from Oregon alone and helped substantially to alleviate the American deficit trade position.

Consumption of Fibrous Materials to Produce 52.4 Million Tons of Paper and Paperboard in 1970

	Thousand Tons	% of Total
Waste Paper	12,000	22.0
Other Fibrous Materials	900	1.6
Wood Residues	11,700	21.4
Sub-Total	24,600	45.0
Woodpulp from Roundwood	30,000	55.0
Total	54,600	100.0

Source: American Pulpwood Association and American Paper Institute

July 20, 1971

An undisguised industry viewpoint is given below in the testimony of John F. Darrow, Vice President of the American Paper Institute, an industry association. Of particular interest are the figures given for total use of waste paper, wood products waste, and other waste fibers. According to the testimony as published, this total apparently is about 64 percent, with wood cut specifically from papermaking supplying the remainder. In fact, the 20 percent figure for other waste materials is contradicted by the American Paper Institute's own studies (as entered into the hearing record) in addition to the oral testimony (*ibid.* at 81—see graph on preceding page). Perhaps "two percent" was the intended figure.

The paper industry has been recyclers of paper for many years. At the present time about 22 percent of our fibers that we use are actually waste paper. Wood residues, sawdust, chips and slabs are other very important waste products that we use. They constitute about another 22 percent of our fiber. About another 20 percent is also waste material such as rags, cotton, linters, flax, and bagasse. So, the paper industry is very concerned with and deeply involved in the consumption of waste products.

As a generalization, the lower quality waste paper cannot be used to make a higher quality of paper. For example, the newsprint cannot be recycled and then made into a higher quality of paper, into very fine stationery, because the fibers themselves which have been used in making newsprint to begin with are lower quality of fiber. You can't upgrade the use of the fiber; you can downgrade but you cannot upgrade.

cardboard

To give you some idea as to the complexity of this problem, last year in the United States we used 12 million tons of waste paper. That was about 22 percent of our total raw material. Now, it is true, as was mentioned earlier this morning that the ratio has dropped from about 35 percent consumption during World War II down to about 22 percent at the present time. Quite obviously during World War II when conditions were different and there wasn't the demand for the high quality of paper, much more waste paper proportionately could be used.

On the other hand, the 12 million tons of paper that we are now consuming is a record level. In terms of tons we are at the high point. In terms of the proportion of the total, we dropped down from 35 percent to about 22 percent.

In terms of tons, I mentioned earlier that we consumed 12 million tons of waste paper. In the manufacture of newsprint it is less than 400,000 tons. In white paper, such as that is used for business and stationery purpoes, about 700,000 tons of waste paper is used, of which only 300,000 tons are deinked—in other words, the stock has to be deinked.

In the tissue area, the manufacturing of tissue paper, less than 1 million tons of waste paper are used. The largest area where waste papers are used today is in what we call combination boxboard. This is the board that is used for the boxes that you are familiar with in which you get your haberdashery; in which you get your laundry, et cetera. Here the consumption of waste paper is about 6 and a half million tons, with another almost two million tons consumed in other types of paperboard.

So, it is in the paperboard area where the largest consumption of waste paper is today, and where, in my opinion, concentration must be placed for increased use in the future.

At the present time in the United States there is a total capacity—let me put the frame of reference in this way: we produce at the present time about 54 million tons of paper and board each year. Against that the capacity to deink paper is approximately 1,200,000 tons. Projecting increases in capacity in the deinking of wastepaper for 1973, there is only a very modest increase in the wastepaper which will be deinked for use in paper manufacturing.

And I believe primarily the low rate at which the deinking capacity is projected to increase is a matter of economics.

The following is from Mr. Darrow's prepared statement (*ibid.* at 64):

I would like to make one general comment with respect to an Associated Press dispatch on November 8 with respect to the hearings before the Fiscal Policy Subcommittee which quoted one of the witnesses, Mr. M. G. Mighdoll, as stating, "The paper industry would soon increase its utilization of recycled paper stock from the present 20 per cent to at least 50 per cent of their raw material and would thus increase the annual conservation of trees from 200 million to 500 million." For the record, I would like to comment that whatever incentives the Congress might offer, it would not be possible for the paper industry to "soon increase" its utilization of recycled paper stock from 20 to at least 50 per cent as Mr. Mighdoll is quoted as saying. In my judgment, it is highly unlikely that a 50 per cent figure ever could be obtained under the most favorable circumstances. During World War II 35 per cent was the highest ever attained under maximum conditions.

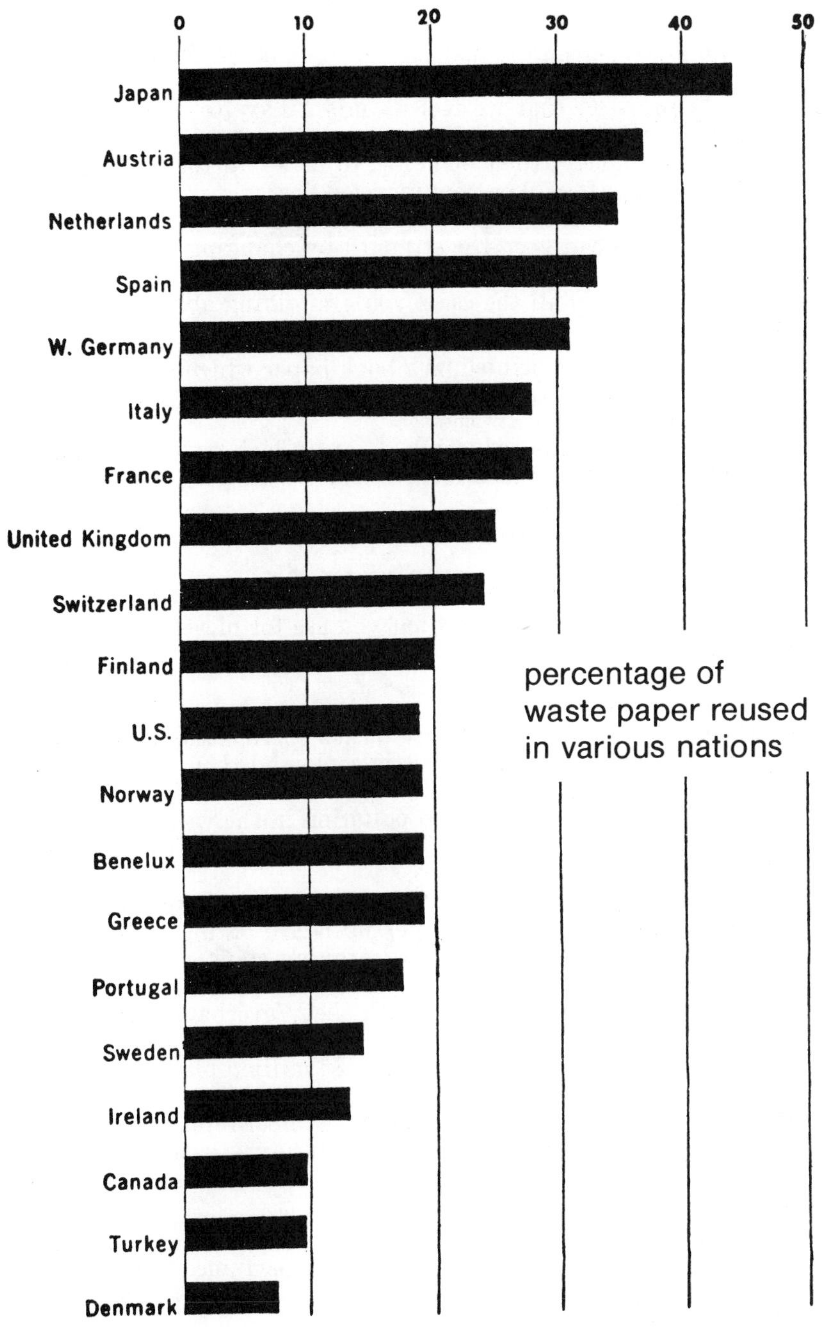

Percentage of wastepaper reused in various countries, cerca 1970. Source: Hearings before the Committee on Rules and Administration, United States Senate, Aug. 3, 1971, GPO, at page 28.

the paper in this book

The paper used for this book contains about 50 percent recycled paper, and was made by the Fitchburg Paper Company. A sister firm of the Fitchburg Company the Valentine Paper Company makes paper from bagasse (sugarcane waste). This latter paper may be used for supplements or future additions of this work. Excerpts from the testimony of a member of the Fitchburg firm follows (*Use of Recycled Paper by Congress Hearings before the Committee on Rules and Administration, United State Senate,* August 3, 1971, 66-182 GPO at 46):

Mr. GRADO. The products I will show here are No. 5 bond, offset printing papers, tablet papers, greeting card papers, technical papers such as those used for blueprints, that type of thing. My purpose is to show that with a broad range of papers recycled fibers can be used without sacrifice of quality or appearance.

We have been told, by our technical people, that they feel they can go as high as 70 percent by making certain changes in other parts of the formulation.

The only property that we feel we might have to change by using recycled fiber, when we get to 70 percent, is that we must put in something like a chemical called blancfor, to make up for the brightness that might be lost after 70 percent recycled fiber.

The CHAIRMAN. The strength would be all right?

Mr. GRADO. We can keep the strength by changing the other parts of our formulation.

The CHAIRMAN. In all the cases you are talking about wood fibers.

Mr. GRADO. Yes, so far.

This paper, which is printed, is a book paper which is made by our Fitchburg mill and contains 50 percent recycled fiber.

The CHAIRMAN. What are they?

Mr. GRADO. Deinked board, deinked papers back from carton plants. All deinked stock coming back from outside of our company, furnished to us by wastepaper dealers.

The CHAIRMAN. That would be a waste from printing plants, is that right?

Mr. GRADO. Printing plants, box board plants, that type of thing.

The CHAIRMAN. Do you know what you use for bleaching?

Mr. GRADO. We cook it in caustic to remove the ink. I am talking now about deinked.

The CHAIRMAN. I understand.

Mr. GRADO. In Louisiana, when we bleach corrugated, it would be a soda process, which would be a caustic cook, and then bleach it with chlorine and chlorine dioxide.

The CHAIRMAN. Do you run into pollution in the wash water?

Mr. GRADO. There is pollution. That is one remark I think should be elaborated on a little bit.

The CHAIRMAN. Caustic is a very big offender going into streams.

Mr. GRADO. Yes, sir; but the paper mills are taking care of their pollution. Both our plants are already taking steps. Our Louisiana mill has no pollution. It has already taken care of it. Our Fitchburg mill just signed a joint agreement with the Weyerhauser Paper Co. and with the city of Fitchburg, Mass., to put in a pollution control plant which will take care of that. It is a $5 million plant. That is all part of the cost of doing business.

I think we have to look at what this deinked fiber replaces, because it is replacing pulp. Making pulp is also a polluting situation. I daresay that deinking is no more—and may not even be as much—a pollutant as making raw pulp from wood.

The CHAIRMAN. I went to a papermill facility not long ago. You know, it has a little odor. They said, "It is perfume. We like that odor."

I know that is also a problem.

Mr. GRADO. Yes, sir.

Now this is a technical paper which you may have seen in blueprints. These have been coated and printed. This is called direct process paper. There are not many mills in the country that make it. It is a fairly technical grade, a fairly hard grade to make. We are the only papermill making this paper that does not make pulp. We are selling this in competition with virgin mills, meeting the quality specifications, and meeting the price. We are a major factor in this market, and this paper contains 30 percent recycled fiber.

The CHAIRMAN. Do you use any newsprint at all?

Mr. GRADO. No, sir; because in our type of mill we could not use ground wood. Newsprint is made from ground wood. For these types of papers, we cannot use ground wood. It has to be a cooked pulp.

Now these are papers that are made from agricultural waste at our mill in Louisiana. That is the waste after sugarcane has been used to make sugar. Currently that waste is being burned. It is causing fly ash pollution problems, air pollution problems in Louisiana and Florida. All those sugar mills are under great pressure right now to desist from burning bagasse. We are the only papermill that is making paper from it. It is made in all parts of the world, and in many countries it is the only source of paper, but in the United States there is only one mill using it, and that is ours. We are probably using 10 percent of the available bagasse fiber right now to make paper. This is clearly a postconsumer fiber. It has been used once to make sugar and the alternative to what we are doing with is to burn it and produce air pollution.

The following is excerpted from a publication of the American Forest Institute, Washington, D.C., a forest industry trade association. Other ramifications of the topics discussed here will be dealt with in the second volume of this work.

other uses for wood pulp

Present per capita paper consumption in the United States is between 560 and 575 pounds. By the year 2000 the estimated need will be 1,000 pounds per person. In 1900, the average American used only 50 pounds of paper.

Pulp and its chemical derivatives are used in many products that bear little resemblance to wood, including extenders for ice cream, photographic film, food flavoring and explosives.

Another important source of raw material for papermaking is the residue from the manufacture of other wood products such as lumber and plywood. In 1970, this amounted to over 19 million cords, more than one-quarter of all the wood used to manufacture pulp. This compares with a total of 15 million cords of wood from all sources used to make paper in 1945.

In Washington State alone, use of sawmill and plywood production residue recovers fiber equivalent to the annual growth on 3 million acres of forest.

Reclaimed wastepaper provides 20 percent of the raw material now used to make new paper, and another 25 percent is provided by lumber and plywood residues. One percent is fiber reclaimed from mill waste water. So, 46 percent of all raw material for paper comes from what once was considered waste.

But recycling creates some additional problems. One is that current waste pickup systems aren't geared to separate paper that can be reused from paper that cannot. Ways must be found to dispose of old ink and coatings from the paper that is to be reused. And the recycling process can be more expensive than using new fiber. Finally, wood fibers lose strength each time they are reused. Therefore, recycled fiber must usually be bolstered by unused fiber.

effects of repeated recycling

Although the statements above are made by an industry group with strong economic incentives to discourage recycling of paper, their objections can not be dismissed on grounds of prejudice alone. Their last point is one to which apparently little attention has been devoted, but which is critical to the eventual development of any relatively closed system of paper recycling. Nevertheless, even for those actively engaged in the recycling of paper, this point so far has been of surprising little importance. Mr. William E. Hancock of the Garden State Paper Company, newsprint recyclers, testified before the Senate Committee on Rules and Administration, August 3, 1971, that so little paper was presently recycled that the gradual shortening of fibers in the recycling process was not a factor of any noticeable importance.

The firm's technical director, Frank W. Lorey, added that they had determined there would be no problems if a fourth of the waste paper they used had previously been recycled, and that he believed "upwards of 50 percent" could be used without problems.

A separate factor was that "in laboratory conditions" Garden State's "best. . . newest mill" incurs approximately a 12 percent shrinkage. "If you were to put a pound of recycled newsprint into a vacuum situation, you would lose 12 percent just in moisture, the loss of the weight of the ink and of the small fibers which are washed away" (*ibid.* at 59). Although useful, that explanation does not confine itself to fiber loss alone. [For recycling losses by other processes, See page Two-25.] What is clear is that under current technology, the recycling of printed papers can not be done indefinitely without additional inputs of new fibers, although those other fibers might themselves be wastes of one sort or another. But because the fibers—especially the shortest, weakest ones—gradually are eliminated by the recycling process, the problem of significant weakening due to repeated recycling may well cure itself, since only a very small proportion of fibers would survive more than a limited number of recyclings. For example, in the case of newsprint being recycled 10 times with a 22 percent input of virgin fiber from other wastes—including 12 percent to make up for that lost in the reprocessing—there is little chance statistically of any significant amount of the original fiber still being in the paper. (It should be pointed out that the fiber and ink residues from recycling can be used as fuel; see page Two-25.) Assuming that both virgin and recycled fibers are replaced proportionally, a paper that was recycled once with the addition of 22 percent virgin fiber (the present average utilization in paper and cardboard combined of wastes from timber processing), the percentage of original fiber that would remain would be 78 percent. After a second recycling, the percentage would be 61; after a third, 48; fourth, 40; fifth; 31, sixth, 24; seventh, 19; eighth, 8; ninth, 6; 10th, 5; 11th, 4; 12th, 3, etc.

effects of repeated recycling

If only 50 percent of the material used was waste paper, the percentage of the original fiber remaining in a series of recyclings such as the above would be reduced much more rapidly. After the first recycling, with the same assumption of proportional replacement of new and used fiber, the percentage of original fiber would be 50; after two, 25 percent; three, 13.5 percent, four, 6.25 percent, 5th, 3.1 percent, etc.

Actually, the replacement of original fiber should be more rapid than in the above simple mathematical formulas, since the very smallest fibers fall through the screens on which paper is made, and are discarded in waste water unless stringent pollution controls are exercised. The effect of the smallest fibers that remain is mimimal: they add little to the strength of the paper, but otherwise do it no harm.

Hence, some virgin material is required if paper recycling is to be done for an indefinite number of times, but that virgin material may be

Waste Paper Utilization in Paper and Paperboard Manufacture

Estimated Future Consumption THOUSANDS OF TONS

END PRODUCT	1971	1972	1973
TOTAL ALL GRADES AND MOLDED PULP	12,345	12,686	13,071
TOTAL PAPER	2,381	2,455	2,600
NEWSPRINT	392	403	474
PRINTING, WRITING and RELATED	812	861	879
UNBL. KRAFT PKG., IND. CONV., SPECIAL IND. and OTHER	156	148	148
TISSUE	1,021	1,043	1,099
TOTAL PAPERBOARD	8,483	8,717	8,942
UNBLEACHED KRAFT and SOLID BLEACHED	296	289	331
SEMI-CHEMICAL	843	930	995
COMBINATION	7,344	7,498	7,616
CONSTRUCTION PAPER AND BOARD, MOLDED PULP AND OTHER	1,481	1,514	1,529

PAPER STOCK GRADES

Mixed Papers: Number 1 & 2 mixed papers, super mixed papers, boxboard cuttings, mill wrappers.

Newspapers: Number 1 news, over-issue news, super news. Any grade to be used as a news substitute.

Corrugated: Old containers both corrugated and solid fiber, container plant cuttings.

Pulp Substitutes & High Grade De-Inking: Ledger, tabulating cards, bleached sulphate shavings (unless used as a news substitute). Envelope and bleached sulphite and sulphate cuttings, book and magazine stock, news and publication blanks, kraft paper and bags, and all other grades not classified above.

(Source: American Paper Institute)

waste—sawdust, as in the Northwest, straw as in Spain, or perhaps even corn stalks.

But would sufficient long fibers remain in recycled materials after several recyclings to be useful in regard to strength? The experience of the Garden State firm in newspaper recycling, in which slightly stronger papers were obtained after recycling, would tend to indicate that the shortening of fibers would not occur so rapidly as to eliminate their utility.

newsprint recycling capacity

According to records of a recycling briefing given in June of 1971 in St. Petersburg, Florida, there are only three newsprint de-inking plants in the United States: the one in New Jersey, and ones in Illinois and California. Their total capacity was listed at 400,000 tons of newsprint annually, which is less than the newsprint consumption of Florida alone. An additional plant in the Ohio Valley is being considered by the Louisville newspapers. A pilot operation in Madison, Wisconsin, collected 2,400 tons of newspapers in its second year of operation. Of the 7,000 tons of newsprint used in a year in that city, 500 tons had been recycled.

The three newsprint recycling plants mentioned above are all part of Garden State Paper Company, which has been recycling 100 percent newsprint for more than a dozen years. Among those buying at least part of their paper from Garden State are *The Washington Post,* the *New York Post,* the *Chicago Sun-Times-Daily News, Newsday,* and several other large and medium-size newspapers. The recycled newsprint, in 1971, was selling at about $7.50 less per ton than virgin paper. The following is excerpted from the testimony of William E. Hancock of Garden State (*ibid.* at 57).

The chairman interviewing Mr. Hancock in the following is Sen. B. Everett Jordan of North Carolina.

> The Garden State process was developed in the late 1950's by Richard B. Scudder, publisher of the Evening News of Newark, N.J. Our first mill was built in Garfield, N.J., in 1960, and we produced our first roll of saleable newsprint in the fall of 1961. We added a second paper machine in Garfield in 1966, and constructed our Pomona, Calif., mill in 1967. In 1968, we entered into a joint venture with Field Enterprises in Chicago, and built the FSC Paper Corp., which Garden State operates, using our process.
>
> The Garden State process utilizes 100 percent old newspaper as its sole raw material furnish, and we currently consume nearly 400,000 tons of old newspaper annually. This makes Garden State the largest single consumer of old newspaper in the world.
>
> The availability of recycled newsprint today is in direct proportion to the availability of raw material and the availability of customers in a given area. A one-machine newsprint mill must have 300 tons of old newspaper daily in order to produce a minimum of 80,000 tons of newsprint annually or the operation is not economical. In addition, besides this, a capital expenditure of approximately $25 million is required, in addition to roughly 30 acres of land and adequate sewage treatment facilities and water supplies.
>
> After 3 years of investigation and study, we are convinced that an adequate supply of old newspapers currently exists in the country to support our mills and that this raw material supply is sufficiently abundant to support considerable expansion of our existing operation.
>
> I should like to note here that our Pomona mill was operating just 12 months after groundbreaking and that the Chicago facility took 14 months to build despite the inclement weather of the Midwest.
>
> The CHAIRMAN. You have mills in California, Chicago, and New York?
>
> Mr. HANCOCK. That's right. I have been remiss in mentioning here that the Chicago mill is the FSC Paper Corp. and is identified as such in some of our charts. We are located close to our source of raw material and close to our customers.
>
> At all three mills, waste water goes to municipal sewage treatment systems, and Garden State pays its fair share of the treatment costs. No waste process water is discharged directly into a river. The requirements for quality and quantity of waste water differs in all three mills. Pomona has a quantity restriction which was met by installing clari-

and 3 million gallons of effluent go into the municipal sewer, but as I mentioned earlier, the effluent is nontoxic and treatable, and is a small part of the 500 million daily gallons processed by the treatment plant.

Garden State burns low sulphur fuel at all three locations—gas at Pomona and Alsip, and oil at Garfield. The Garfield powerhouse was a coal-burning facility that was formerly owned by a textile mill, and conversion to oil was made to significantly reduce air pollution, although with coal an effective scrubbing system was used to minimize fly ash emission.

Other than water vapor, there is no gas emission of any kind from the papermaking process.

The paper mills are not noisy operations, and in general render sounds no worse than the hum of motors and the sound of turning rolls. The worse noise situation is the sound of escaping steam which happens only on upset conditions, and silencers have been installed on all steam vent lines. The three mills have proved to be good neighbors, and in Garfield where all stacks are equipped with silencers, a row of new houses were built directly adjacent to the mill property after the mill started operation.

recycling operation

This is an area I trust will be of some enlightened value. The quality of newsprint, recycled newsprint.

The characteristics of newsprint made from 100 percent deinked newspaper differ somewhat from those of virgin newsprint, but most of the differences are a plus factor to the consumer. In the end result, the key characteristic is pressroom runability which the newspapers report as breaks per 100 rolls or rolls per break. Recycled newsprint manufactured by our process ranks very well with virgin newsprint as Mr. Lorey will explain by use of the attached reports.

We won't go through all of them. No newsprint manufacturer has a perfect runability record in any pressroom and naturally Garden State has a problem similar to those confronting other newsprint fication equipment in the mill and reusing 60 percent of the water. Alsip, being on inland waterways, has a very strict quality restriction as well as a quantity limitation, and much money was spent in water treatment equipment to successfully meet the standards. The mill effluents contain no toxic substance, and are easily treated when mixed with domestic sewage.

The function of municipal sewage treatment systems is to collectively treat domestic and industrial effluents. Each day, Garden State's Pomona mill for instance, uses 3 million gallons of fresh water manufacturers. But you will see from Mr. Lorey's figures and from the reports supplied by the American Newspaper Publisher's Association itself, that recycled newsprint ranks well above the national and regional averages in printability, opacity and tearing strength, the latter being recognized by the industry as the most critical strength property.

Additional light was thrown on Garden States operations by the following statement, which appeared in *The Economics of Recycling Waste Materials,* Hearings of the Subcommittee on Fiscal Policy in the United States, 70-4220, G.P.O., 1972 at 56:

PREPARED STATEMENT OF RICHARD SCUDDER

Madam Chairman, my name is Richard B. Scudder, and I am Chairman of the Board of Garden State Paper Company with headquarters in Newark, New Jersey.

Garden State Paper Company began ten years ago to make newsprint out of waste paper and this is our only business. Our approximately 350 employees operate mills in New Jersey, Illinois, California and divert from solid waste and recycle over a thousand tons a day of old newspapers.

To support one of our mills, an annual supply of 120,000 tons of old newspapers is necessary. In most parts of the country, collection of such large amounts means long supply lines. To build a mill in Texas, for example, would require tapping the waste market along the Mississippi Valley, and even the West Coast. Freight rates on waste paper have been a major hindrance to a successful economic venture in Texas.

Normally, our mills pay from $26 to $28 a ton for waste paper. Our New Jersey mill, which is suffering a shortage of raw material at the moment, is forced to import from Montreal, Cleveland, and Detroit, at freight rates of $27.40 per ton from Montreal, $16.00 per ton from Cleveland and $16.60 per ton from Detroit. Normally, it costs us $3 or $4 a ton to bring paper from New York or Newark, each ten miles away, and considerably more from Philadelphia and Boston.

While there are huge amounts of waste paper in the New York metropolitan area, and while the city of New York describes itself as "suffocating in waste paper", we have not been able to achieve any economic means of separating it from the waste stream in adequate quantities given the overbearing freight rates which we must pay.

It is also difficult to sell large additional amounts of newsprint in today's market when most large newspapers are able to buy from Canadian firms at very large discounts.

Finally, Garden State has a tissue and toweling mill at Lititz, Pennsylvania, known as Morgan Mills, which has been losing money during the last two years because of inability to sell its product, although we believe the product to be competitive in quality and price. Government incentives are greatly needed to stimulate the sale of products made from waste.

freight rates & paper recycling

The National Association of Secondary Materials Industries, Inc., based in New York City, is an organization primarily of scrap dealers that supports a lobbying effort in Washington by the Smathers & Merrigan law firm. The association (NASMI) and their lobbyists have assembled considerable material to justify a claim that both freight rates (set by the Interstate Commerce Commission) and elements of the tax structure are unfair to the recycling industry. Although the evidence gathered by them is generally sound, it of course must be realized that the source is not unbiased, and it is possible that such aspects as the relationship of bulk, ease of handling, and mass quantity factors may not have entered adequately into the analysis of the figures from NASMI given below. But although independent study is needed, the lack of such study should not be used as an excuse to continue indefinitely practices that are, at least environmentally (if not economically) unsound. Additional mention of apparently unfair rates for scrap materials is made in the discussion of metals later in this chapter.

It should be remembered, however, that ICC's rate structure is not set up on some simple table of weight (or bulk) times distance, but rather is an incredible assemblage of pricing based in part on the value of the goods moved. *Time* magazine (May 8, 1972 at 82) reported that "The ICC maintains an unindexed file of 43 trillion different rates on varying weights of varying commodities moving varying distances" over the nation's railways.

The two graphs below were submitted with testimony reprinted on page Two-43, but they are included here because they are of greater relevance to the principal topic being considered on this and the following page.

OCEAN FREIGHT RATES FOR PULP AND WASTE PAPER

Origin	Destination	Pulp: Dollar per ton	Pulp: Selling price [1]	Pulp: Percent transportation to selling price (percent)	Waste paper: Dollar per ton	Waste paper: Selling price [2]	Waste paper: Percent transportation to selling price (percent)
Pacific west coast	Korea (Inchon)	$30.00	$100.00	30	$40.20	$24.00	165
Do	Thailand	35.50	100.00	35	41.50	24.00	170
Do	South Vietnam	43.00	100.00	43	44.65	24.00	185
Do	Australia	34.00	100.00	34	46.50	24.00	190
Do	Colombia	36.00	100.00	36	79.00	24.00	310
East Coast and gulf	Japan—main ports	35.25	100.00	35	48.00	24.00	200
Do	Formosa	36.25	100.00	36	54.25	24.00	226
East coast (North Atlantic)	Spain	29.25	100.00	29	34.00	24.00	142
Do	United Kingdom	30.00	100.00	30	37.75	24.00	157

[1] Unbleached kraft.
[2] Corrugated containers.

RATES, RAIL/100,000-LB. CARS, PULP AND WASTE PAPER

Origin	Destination	Woodpulp: Cost per ton	Woodpulp: Selling price [1]	Woodpulp: Percent transportation to selling price	Waste paper: Cost per ton	Waste paper: Selling price [2]	Waste paper: Percent transportation to selling price
Portland	Ft. Howard, Wis	$29.80	$150	20	$30.00	$19	157
Los Angeles	East coast	31.60	150	21	42.20	19	222
Phoenix	Denver, Colo	23.20	150	15	30.00	19	157
San Antonio	Santa Clara, Calif	27.80	150	18	30.80	19	162

[1] Unbleached Kraft.
[2] Corrugated containers.

Below is an excerpt from the statement of M. J. Mighdoll, executive vice-president of the National Association of Secondary Materials Industries, Inc., before the Subcommittee on Fiscal Policy of the Joint Economic Committee, U.S. Congress, Nov. 8, 1971, 70-4220, G.P.O., 1972 at 15:

freight rates

A significant cost factor in the recovery and utilization of recycled materials is that related to transporting the material to its natural and most economical market. Through past years, the transportation rates established by the Nation's railroads and steamship companies have discriminated against recycled materials as compared to their virgin counterparts, in spite of urgent appeals by the Council on Environmental Quality, the Environmental Protection Agency, and the Department of Commerce, who have asked the ICC to eliminate such discrimination.

There are numerous examples to illustrate the inequitable rate structure that exists between a virgin commodity and the same or comparable commodity in a solid waste or recycled form. Exhibit D attached to our prepared statement gives ample illustration of this discriminatory policy that has been applied by railroad and steamship conference ratemaking in recent years.

EXHIBIT D

RAIL FREIGHT RATE COMPARISON, PULPWOOD VERSUS PAPER WASTE

[Rate: In cents per hundred pounds]

Territory	Miles	Pulpwood: Rate, M/W 23 cords or 103,500	Pulpwood: Revenue per car	Paper waste: Rate, M/W 80,000	Paper waste: Revenue per car
Eastern	95	14	$144.38	28	$224
	225	20¼	209.99	40	320
	298	24½	254.84	43	344
		M/W 21 cords or 105,000 [1]		M/W 80,000	
Southern	100	9.8	$102.90	18	$144
	168	12.0	126.00	22	176
	205	13.9	145.95	27	216
		M/W 55,000		M/W 50,000	
Western	150	16.8	$100.80	37	$185
	300	24.5	142.00	50	250
	500	31.3	172.15	63	315

Source: Item 6287-2, Supp. 262, Tarriff T/C 754; item 75660, Tarriff TL-TCRTB-E-2009-H; item 75660, Tarriff SFTB No. S-2011L; Item 3920, Tarriff W-2000J; Item 2005 SFA 777; WTL pulpwood scale.

[1] Cars move in multiples of 10.

OCEAN FREIGHT RATE COMPARISON, WOODPULP VERSUS PAPER WASTE

[Rates expressed in dollars per long ton]

	Paper waste	Woodpulp
TO JAPANESE PORTS		
From:		
Pacific Coast:		
Under 50′ S/T	32.00	[1] 19.00
75′ to 90′ S/T	37.75	23.00
Atlantic Coast:		
Under 60 cft	44.85	[1] 25.25
Over 75 cft	53.75	
TO NORTHERN EUROPEAN PORTS		
From: Atlantic Coast:		
Up to 50 cft	40.43	31.90
TO AUSTRALIAN AND NEW ZEALAND PORTS		
From: Pacific Coast:		
Prior to June 1, 1971	[2] 52.00	[3] 38.00
After June 1, 1971	(4)	(5)

[1] Open rate—rate negotiated with individual line.
[2] Per long ton; with excess cube penalty.
[3] No excess penalty.
[4] Penalty cube excess increased.
[5] No increase.

Source: Pacific Westbound Conference Tariff circular No. 75, Item 2188, Item 2230 and 2231. Far East Conference Tariff No. 25, FMC No. 5, North Atlantic Continental Freight Conference No. 28 FMC-3, PCAT B, Tariff No. 15 FMC No. 4.

Since the transportation cost element is a significant proportion of the total costs involved in marketing materials or products, any inequitable or discriminatory rate must have an immediate and direct effect on the consumption of those materials and products. So it has been in the case of many recycled materials, which as has been illustrated previously, must compete directly with virgin commodities. Many freight rates are as much as 50 percent higher for the recycled material that can be used by a manufacturer instead of, or in addition to, comparable virgin materials.

Many virgin commodities enjoy point-to-point rate bases, calculated on a mileage scale. Most recycled materials must move on a commodity scale of rates. The net result is a distinct ton-per-mile advantage for virgin commodities. Furthermore, most recycled materials move longer distances to their points of consumption. For instance, in the eastern part of the United States, pulp wood is transported from forest to mill on the average of 136 miles, whereas wastepaper averages a distance of 434 miles from recovery point to consumption point.

The incidence of inequities is astounding, and it is reflected in ocean freight rates as well as in domestic rail rates. Many recycled materials represent surpluses to our domestic needs, but they are commercially prohibited from being exported to potential consumers abroad by steamship lines which impose excessive rates and unrealistic shipping conditions.

End, testimony of the recycling industry official.

ownership of forests

The economies of paper recycling can be deceptive, and there are powerful interests intent on continuing that deception. The basis for big profits in the paper-using world is the vertical trust, from forest to urban monopoly on printed advertising. In the United States, tree cutters in 1971 received a potential tremendous gift from the President when by executive order he vastly increased the amount of national forest that could be logged, including by clear-cutting, which permits far greater erosion than does selective cutting. That expansion had been specifically voted down the year before when it was presented to Congress. [This is covered in greater detail in Volume II]

Forest industry companies own about 65 million acres in the United States, plus huge holdings in Canada and Finland. The U.S. holdings are mostly in the East, particularly in the Southeast, and these holdings are equal in area to approximately all of New England plus New Jersey. In the West, forest industry companies largely rely on use of public lands.

Few of the firms which make pulp for paper are not also engaged in some type of wood product manufacture—often plywood. Hence, determining the amount of land owned by paper companies as such is difficult. However, industry sources seem to agree that the total forest land owned by the forest industry which is intended for pulpwood production is about 50 million acres.

In Maine, where about 80 percent of the land is forested, paper companies control about 36.2% of the total land, according to statistics compiled by the American Forest Institute. International Paper Company is the largest private landowner in the United States, third in total land ownership only to the U.S. government and possibly the government of the State of Minnesota.

In addition, the paper firms lease several million acres.

Despite this huge land and forest ownership, the American Paper Institute reports in *The Paper Industry's Part in Protecting the Environment* that "two thirds of the industry's wood requirements are currently being met from lands of farmers, other private owners, and state and federal agencies."

NOTE: Studies by University of Maine Prof. Harold E. Young indicate that a third of total woody fiber content (useful for pulp) is wasted in standard wood harvesting. *See:* "Puckerbrush Forestry", *American Forests*; Vol. 78, No. 3, March 1972 at 36.

A ton of paper recycled can take the place of about 1.6 tons of pulpwood, which is equal to about the annual growth of one-half to one-and-one-half acres of woodland. Put another way, that's about 15 to 20 trees.

Other aspects of forest resources are discussed in Volume Two of this work. Mention should be made, however, that advanced forestry practices could reduce waste considerably.

Senator B. Everett Jordon of North Carolina, while conducting hearings August 3, 1971 before the Senate Committee on Rules and Administration (66-182 G.P.O., 1971 at 39) had this to say about the forest industry:

growing pulp wood

> You know the tremendous amount of cuttage in the pulpwood areas—principally, the South. Of course, there is a great deal of replanting going on, but at the same time I think it is true they are still cutting down trees faster than they are able to grow. Ten to 12 years in good land is about the proper length of time for pine to grow. It has to be good land. Trees are just like any other crop. They are planted and cared for just like any other crop.
>
> We are increasing our consumption, as you pointed out, very rapidly. North Carolina is the principal producer of wooden furniture in the world. We furnish a great many things, but that is just one of them. It has been just a few years since all furniture went out crated in wooden crates. Today none of it goes out in wooden crates. It is packaged in corrugated cases of marvelous strength. You can get most any strength cardboard you want for packing cases.
>
> The same thing exists with the handling of a great many other products. It is all paper today. There is a big demand, and it is increasing all the time. Consequently, there is a resulting increased need to conserve our forests.
>
> I happen to be a member of the Committee on Agriculture and Forestry, as you know. One of that committee's major responsibilities is the conservation of our forests. We have to look after them and take care of them, or else we will run out.
>
> Some of the big pulpmills and papermills own tremendous acreages of forest for their own protection. They usually retain some of the larger trees and cut out the smaller timber for pulp. They also buy from the farmers in the area a great percentage of their pulpwood in order to help the local economy, but they always keep their own forest as a safety valve for their own consumption in case the production of wood pulp on the outside is not sufficient to run their mills. It is a big industry and a big business.

End quote.

more reasons why paper recycling is opposed

It is clear that the ownership of vast forests is a factor in the paper industry's resistance to recycling. Also of importance is the web of tax and tariff laws in the United States and Canada and the availability of low-cost timber on public lands.

The federal internal revenue code provides a number of tax benefits to the timber owner. Most important is section 631 with its provisions that, along with those of section 1231, allow disposal of timber at capital gains rates. Other provisions allow expenditures that provide benefits over a substantial period to be expensed out or capitalized, depending upon the desire of the taxpayer.

Below is an excerpt from the prepared statement of Thomas A. Davis of Smathers & Merrigan, lobbyists for much of the recycling industry (*Hearings Before the Subcommittee on Fiscal Policy of the Joint Economic Committee, Congress of the United States,* Nov. 8, 1971, 70-422 G.P.O., 1972 at 41):

effect of taxes

CAPITAL GAIN TREATMENT FOR TIMBER

The Internal Revenue Code provides that the owner of standing timber can elect to treat the difference between the cost of the trees and their fair market value at the beginning of the year such trees are cut.[1] Under this provision, a paper company which cuts its own timber for use in the production of paper can elect capital gain treatment on the appreciated value of those trees which are cut. The owner of timber who sells such timber under a contract in which he retains an economic interest, such as a so-called pay-as-cut contract, can also elect capital gain treatment.[2]

For example, a paper corporation which purchases a tract of timber for $1,000 and several years later cuts the trees then valued at $2,000 for pulp can treat the $1,000 increase in value of the trees as a capital gain subject to the 30 percent tax rate.

[1] Internal Revenue Code § 631(a).
[2] Internal Revenue Code § 631(b).

As a result of this capital gain treatment, paper companies using trees as a source of raw material have an overall effective tax rate that is less than a company which utilizes recycled material. Based on information contained in the Treasury Department Studies and Proposal of 1969, paper companies paid an effective tax rate of about 5 percent less than other types of manufacturing industries.[3] Looking at more current information contained in the 1968 Corporation Statistics of Income compiled by the Internal Revenue Service, it appears that the differential continues to be at least as great even after applying the new 30 percent capital gain rate provided under the 1969 Tax Reform Act. A company which produces or utilizes only recycled material would fall into the category of other manufacturing and thus has the higher effective tax rate.

The lower effective tax rate resulting from the use of trees obviously results in higher after-tax profits. Management necessarily must turn to the utilization of trees rather than purchasing recycled materials.

By bringing this capital gain provision to your attention, we do not mean to imply that such tax treatment should be changed. The provision was enacted in the Revenue Act of 1943 as an incentive device for conservation, reforestation and good forest management. It was discussed in the hearings during the enactment of the 1969 Tax Reform Act. These hearings indicate that capital gain treatment for timber has been effective toward the intended purpose.[4] There is and will be a continuing need to conserve and manage our forest lands. Recycled material can obviously not substitute for timber.

NOTE: Taxing timber sales as capital gains rather than as ordinary income costs the U.S. Treasury $130 million per year, according to a study published by the Joint Economic Committee of Congress on July 15, 1972. More than half these savings went to five corporations. See, The Washington Post, July 16, 1972 at A16.

End quote.

Further testimony from a similar viewpoint is excerpted in the following. Exhibits A and B mentioned are not reproduced in this book; Exhibits C and D are on page Two-39. This testimony and the preceeding is all part of a well coordinated lobbying effort, and reflects a uniformity of belief that it is easier to obtain more tax exemptions from Congress than it would be to eliminate the exemptions already granted to users of virgin materials. The relative scarcity of opposing testimony at these two hearings undoubtedly stems partly from an allegiance to the "lobbyists' ethic" (plenty-of-plums-for-all-of-us), and partly because of the relative economic insignificance of the recycling industry. In this case the full statement is printed here (*ibid* at 44):

lobbyists' ethic

Madam Chairman, I am very pleased to have this opportunity to appear before the distinguished members of the Fiscal Policy Subcommittee. My name is Haskell Stovroff—I am Chairman of the Board of Directors and Chief Executive Officer of Consolidated Fibers—one of the oldest and the largest independently owned domestic and export marketers of secondary fibers in the United States.

Our company, with 247 employees, operates ten waste paper processing plants within New York, California, Arizona, and Oregon. We collect secondary fibers from paper converters, industrial producers, and others in order to divert these raw materials from becoming solid waste. We then sort, process and bale these secondary fibers to transform them into valuable raw material for manufacturers of such paper products as printing papers, tissue, toweling, combination boxboard (used in production of folding cartons), liner board and corrugated medium for production of shipping cases, building board, roofing and insulation, as well as many other paper specialty products. Several of these plants divert from solid waste and recover over 5,000 tons of secondary fiber per month.

There are a number of inequities present today in Federal tax regulations, purchasing specifications and freight rates which are serious impediments to reducing the 38 to 40 million tons of paper and paperboard that were disposed of by being buried or incinerated in this country last year. If our projections are accurate, this amount will double in less than fifteen years unless the Congress provides increased economic incentives for the collection, processing and recycling of our nation's solid waste.

The Internal Revenue Code of 1954 allows a deduction in computing taxable income for depletion of timber. This tax provision gives an unmistakable competitive advantage to producers of paper and paperboard who have "integrated" woodland operations within their corporate tax structure or who buy pulpwood to manufacture pulp. This depletion provision has also impeded the increased use of waste paper as a raw material for the manufacture of paper and paperboard at a time when the virgin paper industry has undergone spectacular growth.

Manufacturers of paper and paperboard who produce their produces from reclaimed waste fibers do not enjoy such tax allowances and Exhibit A dramatically illustrates the decline in the share of the market for these mills.

Likewise there is a sharp drop in the number of paper machines in operation to produce paper and paperboard which generally use waste paper as their raw material furnish. These are called cylinder machines. Exhibit B is an illustration of this decline.

Please do not misinterpret my position. I do not prescribe a repeal of the timber depletion allowance. In order, however, to increase the reutilization of

[3] Tax Reform Studies and Proposals, U.S. Treasury Department, Part 3, p. 434 (Feb. 5, 1969).

[4] Hearings before the Committee on Ways and Means, House of Representatives, 91st Cong., first sess., on the subject of Tax Reform, 1969; Part 8, beginning on p. 2823.

waste materials, we mush give equal tax treatment to paper manufacturers who harvest our landfills and incinerators instead of, or in addition to, our shrinking timber supply.

This equal tax treatment is not only a matter of fundamental fairness, it is the most practical way to eliminate our nation's solid waste problem. Perhaps you have heard that one ton of reused waste paper saves so many trees. There is, I feel, a better comparison to be made. Experts have said that municipal refuse is disposed of today at an average cost of $25 to $30 per ton. These estimates would lead one to conclude that the secondary fibers industry therefore saved our taxpayers upwards of $250 million.

To collect, sort and process the 40 million tons of scrap paper we can recover in the future will require enormous capital investments. It is for these reasons that we need economic incentives to recycle solid waste.

Finally, there are gross inequities between government regulated freight rates for waste paper and "virgin" pulp. Exhibit C vividly points out these discrepancies in domestic shipments.

What is inequitable is not only the 20 cents per ton difference, but the fact that the product we are shipping has a selling price of about $40 per ton. That makes the cost of transportation 75% of the cost of the material. Pulp, on the other hand, travelling at 20 cents per ton less has an announced selling price of around $175 per ton. These freight costs are only 17% of the cost of the product. This incredible situation is truly unfair.

My last exhibit, Exhibit D, reflects the similar inequities in ocean freight rates between "virgin" pulp and waste paper. Inasmuch as these rates are subject to government regulation as well, I believe Congress can and should take immediate action to remedy these discriminations.

End quote.

state & local property taxes

State and local governments often allow timber lands to escape property taxes by using a more favorable tax at the time of cutting. Other states assess property taxes on timber lands at a very low assessed value. Whether such a tax system is justified because of the many years of investment before timber can be marketed is beyond the scope of the present chapter, But *see:*

BRIGGS, Charles, "Capital Gain and Loss Treatment for Timber," and UTZ, Keith, "Effect of Ad Valorem Taxes on a Tree Farm Investment," *Forest Farmer,* Manual Edition, March 1972 at 50. 58.

BREEDING & BURTON, *Income Taxation of Natural Resources,* Prentice Hall, Englewood Cliffs, N.J., 1971

See also: U.S. Dept. of Agriculture. Forest Service, *Forest Taxation and the Preservation of Rural Values in New York,* Agricultural Economic Report 160, April 1969.

U.S. Dept. of Agriculture, Forest Service, *The Timber Owner and His Federal Income Tax, Agriculture Handbook No. 274,* December 1964.

Condrell, *Effect of Tax Reform Act of 1969 on Taxpayers in the Timber Industry,* 3 Nat. Res. Lawyer 637 (November 1970).

postscript on cardboard

The recycling of paper for the manufacture of corrugated cardboard is a thriving business despite the government's tax incentives to the environmentally destructive. Cardboard manufacturers use about 7 million of the 10 million tons of paper products recycled annually in the United States. The cost for building a plant for cardboard production from trash paper would be about 20 percent less than the cost of one to work from virgin materials, according to *Chem 26, Paper Processing.* Bjorn O. Lehto, a specialist in this field for Chas. T. Main, Inc., adds that "If we add the cost of the woodland to the cost of this (virgin materials) mill, it has to generate three times as much profit per ton in order to produce a return on investment equal to that produced by the mill based on reclaimed fibers."

economics of cardboard

But these economics don't always operate even in this corner of the paper field, for the forest-owning plant gets the tax breaks, and so not even all corrugated cardboard is made from reclaimed fibers.

The same lessons apply to recycled pulp used for other papers. Industry estimates put the prices for recycled pulps of similar grades to virgin pulps at about $130 per ton to $165 to $170 per ton respectively. ("The Economics of Recycling," *Chem 26 Paper Processing,* July, 1971 at 61.)

Metals

The following seven paragraphs on the problem of auto disposal are from the *Annual Report of the Council on Environmental Quality,* August, 1970:

automobiles

A number of specific components in solid wastes present particular problems and require special mention. Abandoned autos are one of the most conspicuous solid waste disposal problems. On the average, 9 million autos are retired from service every year. Although statistics on the annual number of abandoned vehicles are subject to dispute, it is thought that approximately 15 percent are abandoned on city streets, in back alleys, along rural roads, and in vacant lots throughout the Nation. Most autos are abandoned because they are no longer serviceable and have little or no parts value to auto wreckers. The total number of abandoned cars in the country is even harder to ascertain, but has been estimated between 2.5 and 4.5 million.

The 85 percent of autos that are properly turned in by their owners enter a complex recycling system, usually beginning with the auto wrecker, whose chief business is selling the parts that can be removed. Some wreckers claim to obtain 97 percent of their sales revenues from parts. The high value of junk cars for parts and their often negligible value for scrap means that wreckers have little incentive to move their inventories to scrap processors. Except when there is demand for scrap, the junk cars just pile up.

Auto wreckers eventually, however, have to move the hulks to scrap processors. Most processors, using powerful hydraulic presses, reduce the cars to small bales containing high percentages of nonferrous materials—copper, upholstery, chrome, plastic, and glass. The bales are then sold to steel mills, which turn them into products which do not require high quality steel, or pass them on to mills which have sufficient capacity to dilute their contaminants. A growing number of processors produce a higher priced scrap through mechanical shredding and electromagnetic separation. Costs for shredding equipment, however, have limited the widespread use of this process, particularly by small scrap processors.

use as scrap

Steel mills and foundries are major users of ferrous scrap. In 1969, 50 percent of the material used for the production of all steel products was scrap. Six percent of that scrap was from junk autos. But changes in steel production techniques make it difficult to predict future scrap needs. Basic oxygen furnaces and electrical induction furnaces are partially replacing the open hearth furnace. The first requires less scrap, but the second uses more. It is even more difficult to predict export scrap demand and the effects of new fabricating and casting processes on the scrap market.

In his February 10 Message on the Environment, the President asked the Council on Environmental Quality to take the lead in recommending a bounty payment or some other system to promote the prompt scrapping of all junk automobiles. The Council has reviewed the range of alternatives leading to a Federal or State bounty system and concluded that under present conditions it is not practicable.

Most of the systems considered by the Council would be funded by a tax on the sale of all automobiles sold in the future or the collection of a fee from all present owners and future buyers. The bounty payment would be made to the scrap processor, the auto wrecker, or the owner of the car being junked. All of these proposals would put an unfair burden on the owners of the 85 percent of autos that are properly turned over to auto wreckers, in order to take care of the remainder which are not. Furthermore, the Council is not persuaded that the demand for auto scrap would be improved by such a system, nor that it would in fact influence the economics affecting abandonment. The resulting fund of payments would divert billions of dollars from other investments in the private economy. Administration and enforcement of the system would require excessive increases in government personnel and expenditures. The Council also determined that firm penalties against abandonment and improvement of State title and transfer laws alone, particularly for cars of low value, might substantially reduce abandonment and put abandoned vehicles more promptly into the scrapping cycle. Such laws should be strengthened.

Any attempt to solve the problem of abandoned cars, however, must consider the problems of fluctuating scrap demand, steel production technology, transportation rates for scrap, export scrap markets, availability of shredding equipment, and characteristics of the auto parts market.

End, excerpt from the CEQ report.

steel: problem of contamination

It should be added that a key problem is contamination of the steel by copper, which, even in small quantities, is a serious worry. The problem is caused by the fact that the average complete automobile, weighing about 1,200 pounds, has about four pounds of copper wiring, much of it in inaccessable locations. The shredding equipment mentioned above, which in conjunction with electro magnets make obtaining relatively pure ferrous scrap easier, cost from $500,000 to $3 million.

Metal scrap shredders that can consume as many as 1,000 cars a day are being used to reduce vast scrap heaps of discarded automobiles. In 1971, about 2.6 million cars were recycled with shredders, 700,000 more than in 1970. Since 1968, the number of shredders has increased from 67 to 108. The current going rate for a car at the shredder is from $15 to $20. After shredding, steel salvagers sell the pulverized car to steel mills for about 434.

There are an estimated 14 million to 20 million cars rusting in American junkyards or along the nation's highways. Every year, six million to seven million additional cars are discarded. The California legislature has passed a law which will require all car owners in the state to pay an extra $1 registration fee to finance a $14.4 million one-time clean-up of abandoned cars for disposal in shredding machines. *See* "Shredders Slowly Reducing Heaps of Junked Cars." *The New York Times,* March 26, 1972 at 60.

The auto scrap reclaiming industry employs about 100,000 workers in about 15,000 companies, half of which have five or fewer workers; 17 percent are one-man operations. California alone has about 2,000 firms. According to an auto scrap industry survey, the average junked car brought in about $500, nearly all for parts. The "No. 2 bundles" into which individual cars (complete with engine) are crushed for sale to steel mills, brought in only about $20 each. (Source: National Auto and Truck Wreckers Assn., San Mateo, Calif.)

The following is from the testimony of Jeffrey S. Padnos of the New York City Environmental Protection Agency before the Subcommittee on Fiscal Policy of the Joint Economic Committee, Congress of the United States (70-4220, G.P.O., 1972 at 111):

New York City has a very effective program for removing the cars from our streets, but it costs us money. The cars are spotted and tagged by sanitation personnel, and removed by private contractors. The contractor either pays the city or is paid, depending on the location of the car.

In Manhattan, the city pays $10 for each car removed; in the other boroughs, the city receives a small amount, but not enough to cover administrative expenses. Since contracts are let on a competitive basis, the amount the city receives is related to the value of scrap steel. Discriminatory freight rates reduce the value of the scrap in abandoned autos and thus increase the city's costs for handling them.

End quote

costs of scrap transportation

Transportation costs obviously are a factor in determining the extent to which any material is recycled. However, reliable information in this field seems exceptionally difficult to obtain.

In regard to steel scrap, a research report by the Battelle Laboratories* has concluded that, on the average, the Interstate Commerce Commission's railroad freight rate structure was prejudicial against the movement of iron and steel scrap, in comparison with iron ore, by about $1.49 per ton.

Since there seems to be no convincing logic behind the ICC's rate-making methods, trying to determine what is fair or unfair within the system may be as useless as trying to calculate the number of angels that can dance on the head of a pin.

For the moment it must be concluded that, although rate disparities between recycled and new materials might be demonstrable, those between ores and scrap are still possibly doubtful unless economic values are assigned aspects traditionally ignored, such as disposal problems and conservation of irreplaceable resources.

The next quotation is excerpted from a conversation among Albert J. Wein, of Steelmet, Inc., Mr. M. D. Schwartz of Pacific Smelting Co., (whose prepared statements are reprinted below), and Congresswoman Martha W. Griffith of Michigan (*ibid.* at 58, 59):

Mr. Wein. The scrap car itself is usually shipped, I would say, within a radius of 40, 50, maybe up to 100 miles. The economics would prevent the shipping of it any further. But once the scrap is processed it may then be shipped all the way around the world. As a matter of fact, I would say—I don't know the percentage, but a large percentage of the scrap reclaimed from secondary metals, reclaimed from the scrap cars is shipped to Japan, Europe, and parts of South America.

Mr. Schwartz. It has been estimated that there are between 17 and 20 million abandoned automobiles in the United States. I am in the same business, and this represents 500,000 tons of raw material. And at that same time this material is unobtainable because of freight.

In our particular industry we are running at two-thirds capacity because of the lack of means of bringing this material to market. It is bulky and it has high freight costs. And in the West they will bring automobiles in on a break-even basis maybe 200 miles. Our roads are probably better and travel can be much faster out there but it is unfortunate that this material is lying above ground. We have the facilities and consumers who will buy it; it is a question of freight and economics strictly.

Chairman Griffiths. Now, how could we go about correcting the freight rate as to make it feasible? Do you have a distinction between the freight rates on that or are those cars shipped at the same price than an automobile is shipped today out of Detroit?

Mr. Schwartz. No; a new one is shipped at a different rate; however, if you consider an automobile as a very bulk object, and when it is wrecked you take out the cast aluminum parts, the motor, differential and so forth, you only have about one ton of weight. If cars are pressed as they are, it still is a bulky item, and you can't get very much weight on a truck or a freight car. So, you can't ship it very far.

End quote.

*BARNES, T. M., *The Impact of Railroad Freight Rates on the Recycling of Ferrous Scrap*, Battelle Memorial Institute, Columbus, Ohio, Jan. 14, 1972. Barnes concludes that his calculated $1.49 per ton freight rate bias in favor of ore raises the price of steel (which costs about $69 to $74 a ton) by $4.21 a ton. Though the author of this book has made a considerable effort to make some sense of this—including asking for and receiving a detailed explanation from the author of the report—he remains unconvinced. Scrap, incidentally, consists of only 40% or less of the raw material, though in the less-used electric furnace process, it can completely take the place of ore.

The following passage is from testimony by Blair T. Bower of Resources for the Future, Inc. (*ibid.* at 129):

> As the high quality iron ore deposits of the Mesabi range neared exhaustion, costs for processing iron ore increased, thereby making scrap more attractive as a raw material, given the predominance of the open hearth method for producing steel. The next event was the development of pelletizing, which enabled economic upgrading of low grade iron ores, 35–40%, to high grade ores, 66–67%.[3] This shifted the balance back toward iron ore as the raw material.
>
> Traditionally the technology for processing junked vehicles involved compressing a stripped and burned out hulk into a chunk of impure "No. 2" scrap. As long as the open hearth was the predominant method of producing steel, this raw material had utility, for about 70% of the charge to the open hearth could be relatively impure scrap.[4] With the advent and growing use of the basic oxygen furnace (BOF) for producing steel—a less expensive production process than the open hearth—the bottom dropped out of the scrap steel market, because the maximum charge to the BOF is about 40%, the limiting factor being the impurities in the scrap raw material.[5] By 1970 BOF steel production exceeded open hearth steel production in the U.S.[6]
>
> Around 1960 a technological development on the residual side was introduced, the automobile shredder. This process takes whole automobile hulks and grinds them into small pieces, enabling better extraction of impurities and producing a raw material of far better quality than the old No. 2 bundle. A shift in relative prices in favor of the residual tended to result.
>
> The shredding plants installed in the decade of the 1960's have typically been highly capital intensive, large-volume operations, i.e., plant costs—$3 million; plant capacity—one car per minute.[7] This means that almost all such plants have been located in major metropolitan areas, leaving significant numbers of abandoned vehicles still resting in the environment.
>
> Even so, the growth in the use of the BOF process and the increasing number of available abandoned cars, stemming from the continued increase in the U.S. car population, tended to keep scrap prices low. This availability of low cost scrap in turn stimulated the initiation of a number of small steel mills around the country based on the electric furnace, with annual capacities of 50 to 500 thousand tons of steel. By 1969 about forty of these mills existed, producing about 2.3 million tons of raw steel.[8] Essentially 100% of the charge to an electric furnace can be scrap. This evolution, and the development in the last few years of the mobile automobile crusher and the mini automobile-shredder[9] suggest a likely increase in the use of the abandoned vehicle residual.
>
> Technological developments can affect not only the type of residuals which can be used in a production process but also the quantity of residuals generated in that process. Continuous casting, a recent development in the steel industry, reduces scrap generated internally in a steel mill. Such scrap is generated, in conventional steel production, in ingot and slab trimming and in rolling operations, in an amount up to 30% of the steel poured. Continuous casting cuts these losses to 10% or less.[10] Because the BOF operates on a low scrap charge, minimizing internal scrap generation is desirable. Thus the BOF and continuous casting go well together, further tending to shift the relative prices of virgin ore and scrap as raw materials and inducing more electric furnace capacity, which will tend to counteract that shift.
>
> At the same time as these various technological developments have taken place, there has been a change in the product output specifications for automobiles, in terms of the component materials. As indicated above, the value of a residual is a function of the quality of the material which can be produced from it, and of course of the cost of processing. But the quality depends in turn on the original quality of the residual. The more impurities in scrap steel, the lower its value. With respect to automobiles, the trend has been ever upward in the amount of non-ferrous materials utilized. The average 1970 model car contained about 100 pounds of zinc, 75 pounds of aluminum, 38 pounds of copper, and about 100 pounds of plastics. The last was about five times the amount used in 1960.[11] Increased impurities in the residual increase the cost of processing and/or decrease the quality and hence the value.

use of scrap in steel processing

End quote. *See also*:

Committee on Public Works, U.S. Senate. *Disposal of Junked and Abandoned Motor Vehicles.* Hearings before the Subcommittee on Air and Water Pollution on S.4197 and S.4204, 91st Cong., 2d Sess., 1970.

Below, Mr. M. J. Mighdoll of the National Association of Secondary Industries gives a general portrait of the metals recycling industry (*ibid.* at 21):

> The recycling activities of these companies are in no sense new. Many of the members of our industry date back to the last century, and in war and other national emergencies, they have contributed an essential service, to wit, the supply of recycled materials whose virgin counterparts had become critically scarce. From the standpoint of size, our industry members are a heterogeneous mix.

---

[3] For example see Anon., 1969, Savage River Mines, *Civil Engineering*, 39, 1, p. 62.

[4] Reinfeld, W., 1968. An economic analysis of recent technological trends in the U.S steel industry, Ph. D. Thesis, p. 93.

[5] Reinfeld, op. cit.

[6] Neely, H. C., 1970, The steel industry, *Chemical and Engineering News*, 48, 12, p. 48.

[7] Haltenhoff, C. E., 1971, Mini automobile-shredding plant for wastern Michigan, *Civil Engineering*, 41, 4, p. 55.

[8] Neely, op. cit., p. 56.

[9] Haltenhoff, op. cit.

[10] Neely, op. cit., p. 55.

[11] Anon., 1970, Detroit's minis grab new-car spotlight, *Chemical and Engineering News*, 48, 40, pp. 18, 19 and Anon., 1970, Aluminum use in autos climbs, *Chemical and Engineering News*, 49, 4, p. 23.

They range from small, individual-type businesses to large corporations employing hundreds of workers in multi-plant operations. However, the foundation of our recycling industry is the small, local business concerns which take the first crucial recycling steps—the collection and processing of various solid wastes so that these discarded commodities may be converted into new raw materials for use in the manufactured products of the American economy. In this connection, I direct the Committee's attention to Exhibit A to my statement which contains a *Profile of Companies in the Recycling Industry.* It shows (a) that the average plant and equipment investment for companies in our industry is presently approximately $1,500,000, (b) that the average company employs 71 employees, and (c) that the average company had gross sales in 1969 of only about $7.5 million.

STATE OF THE INDUSTRY'S RECYCLING ART

As an industry, however, recycling concerns presently process over 3,000,000 tons of non-ferrous scrap metals each year, including 1,500,000 tons of copper and brass scrap, 700,000 tons of lead scrap, 700,000 tons of aluminum scrap, 225,000 tons of zinc scrap, and 25,000 tons of nickel base scrap, not to mention large quantities of ferrous metals (iron and steel). In addition, scrap dealers and brokers handle substantial scrap metal which enters our international export trade. The export of non-ferrous scrap metal alone in 1964 amounted to about 225,000 tons with a dollar value of approximately $100,000,000.

For example—

(1) approximately 45% of our country's total available copper is now recovered from scrap produced by the recycling industry;

(2) about 30% of all aluminum, 18% of of all zinc, and more than 50% of the total domestic lead supplies are derived from scrap.

proportion of metals recovered

EXHIBIT C

PROPORTION OF RECOVERABLE MATERIAL RESOURCES CURRENTLY BEING RECYCLED [1]

Material	Short tons available for recycling	Short tons recycled	Percent recycled
Aluminum	2,215,000	1,056,000	48
Copper	2,456,000	1,489,000	61
Lead	1,406,000	585,000	42
Zinc	1,271,000	182,000	14
Nickel	106,000	42,100	40
Steel	141,000,000	36,700,000	26
Stainless steel	429,000	378,000	88
Precious metals (troy ounces)	105,000,000	79,000,000	75
Paper	46,800,000	11,400,000	19
Textiles	4,700,000	800,000	17

[1] Based on statistics and estimates provided to NASMI by Battelle Memorial Institute for Environmental Protection Agency Study.

End quote.

The following paragraphs are excerpted from testimony given by various other recycling industry executives, *ibid.* at 50-55:

PREPARED STATEMENT OF ALBERT J. WEIN

My name is Albert J. Wein, and I am the Executive Vice President of Steelmet, Inc. I wish to thank the Committee for the privilege of appearing here today on this subject of such importance to my company.

Steelmet is a major recycler of stainless steel, and both ferrous and non-ferrous scrap. Steelmet's operations begin when we collect scrap metal from various industries, from automobile wreckers, and from scrap metal dealers. This scrap is then sorted, by our company, processed, and recycled into new raw material which is sold to manufacturers of metal products.

Our plants are located in Pennsylvania, Florida, Kentucky, Rhode Island, and Massachusetts, and our approximately 425 employees are engaged in the business of annually recovering and recycling hundreds of thousands of tons of metal scrap, including some 400,000 to 500,000 tons of ferrous scrap, into new raw materials.

In our industry, I am deeply concerned with two basic problems, inequitable freight rates and unequal tax treatment.

Freight rates for secondary metals do not reflect the value of the commodities shipped. During the past several years, for example, freight rates have steadily increased while the value of the metal shipped has steadily decreased. This disasterous trend along with all of the increased costs of collecting and processing scrap has worked to prevent the recycling of more cans, automobiles and other scrap metal products which clutter our countryside.

Besides the discrimination in freight rates between recycled commodities and their virgin counterparts, I am deeply concerned about the unfair discrimination in freight rates between domestic and foreign rates. For example, the freight rates on metal scrap shipped from New England to such domestic consumption points as Pittsburgh and Cleveland range from $11.00 to $17.00 per gross ton. On the other hand, ocean freight rates from the same points to foreign consumers range between $3.50 to $7.00 per gross ton. Because the commodity which we ship is very low in value (approximately $20 to $30 per ton), we have no choice but to ship to foreign markets. Then, when foreign markets dry up because of changing price considerations, these discriminatory freight rates prevent domestic recycling of metal scrap such as that in automobiles and tin cans.

If there were equal freight rates for domestic and ocean shipments, we could ship our products to more domestic consumers and thus collect and process more scrap metal. Furthermore, our customers would have a continuous source of supply at stable prices and some of the wide price fluctuations which exist in the metal markets would be eliminated.

Madam Chairman, my second major concern is the unequal tax treatment for recycled metals compared to virgin metals. Those who mine primary metals receive a substantial depletion allowance which, of course, has no counterpart in the secondary metals industry. Equal tax treatment would enable our industry to more rapidly beautify the scrap processing facilities which we operate, and, of course, allow us to collect, sort, and process more scrap metal which would enable us to reduce solid waste which is otherwise uneconomical to process.

Prepared Statement of M. D. Schwartz

zinc

Madam Chairman, my name is M. D. Schwartz, and I am the President of the Pacific Smelting Company of Torrance, California. Our company, with approximately 150 employees, is the largest independent secondary zinc smelter in the world. We buy zinc scrap from metal dealers, industries, and others and smelt this scrap into ingots which provide a new raw material for producing a full line of zinc products. Our current capacity is over one million pounds of zinc per week but due to several very important economic impediments to recycling which I wish to briefly discuss, we are presently operating at only ⅔ capacity.

The scrap metal which we consume is generally in the lowest value nonferrous metal handled by the recycling industry. Even so, our buying area consists of the entire Western half of the United States and we have spent in excess of two million dollars in the past five years to improve and expand our facilities.

Currently, our company could increase its recycling of scrap zinc by ⅓ to ½ if the freight rates for scrap zinc were not almost unbearably prohibitive. Where would this additional scrap come from? There are today between seventeen and twenty million abandoned automobiles in the United States that have not been brought to market. Most of this scrap is uneconomical to ship because of freight costs. The zinc-base metals in these automobiles alone represent approximately 500,000 tons of raw material which could be recycled except for prohibitive freight rates. Recently, scrap zinc worth approximately $130 per ton net, had a freight rate of approximately $25 per ton. Now this rate has skyrocketed to nearly $50 per ton. This problem has become so severe that it is not unusual for freight charges to constitute one half of the cost of this scrap metal when it arrives at our secondary smelting plant. In addition to the obvious impediment to recycling which these ever-rising freight rates provide, there is also severe discrimination in rates between the scrap or recycled form of zinc and zinc in its virgin form.

Furthermore, the processing of scrap metal is further hampered compared to primary metals because scrap is a heterogeneous commodity which requires special furnaces and other very high cost equipment for processing. This is particularly burdensome because most secondary plants are in urban areas which require more extensive pollution abatement equipment. We certainly support the necessity for pollution abatement, but zinc recyclers, because of their urban location, bear a far heavier burden in this regard than virgin producers. Finally, only the virgin producers of zinc have had the important economic advantage of the depletion allowance—even though their capital expenditures are used to procure the less expensive homogeneous feed equipment.

aluminum

Prepared Statement of Edward Bergman

My name is Edward Bergman and I am the Chief Executive Officer of the U.S. Reduction Co., a leading secondary aluminum smelter. I am also President of the Aluminum Smelting & Recycling Institute, a trade association for the secondary aluminum industry.

Our company buys scrap aluminum, refines it into ingots and sells this recovered raw material to others for making aluminum castings and deoxidizing steel. Our company has over 1,000 employees, and we have offices and plants in Indiana, Illinois, Ohio, Alabama, and California. Last year we shipped over 220 million pounds of recycled aluminum.

While a few aluminum smelters are divisions of large corporations and a few are publicly owned corporations, for the most part the 50 or so aluminum smelters are small independently owned businesses. Secondary aluminum smelters have existed for almost 70 years, and the industry is now producing in excess of a billion pounds per year, or approximately 15 to 20% of the primary aluminum production.

The aluminum smelting industry produces secondary aluminum, aluminum produced from scrap, as opposed to primary aluminum which is made from ore which must be mined, usually in some distant country, refined into alumina and then elecrolytically reduced to aluminum. This then must be alloyed with other metals such as copper, silicon manganese, magnesium, chrome, titanium and zinc to produce a useable product. Secondary aluminum is used mainly in casting alloys and for the deoxidation of steel. The alloying ingredients for the most part are already in the aluminum scrap so recycling not only uses aluminum which has already been mined, shipped, refined and alloyed, but it also reuses the other metals which are present as alloying ingredients. We are producing a product in which the natural resources of labor, electrical energy and raw materials have already been expended, and in using this raw material we are helping to remove the waste which threatens to engulf our country.

Aluminum scrap consists of new scrap, the result of manufacturing processes (which is historically about 20% of primary aluminum production) and old scrap which is the obsolete product of our everyday living. In the past years the industry anticipated that 75 to 80% of the scrap would be new and 20 to 25% of the scrap would be old. Strangely enough this balance has not been maintained; for during the past 10 years, primary aluminum production has doubled from 4 billion pounds per year to 8 billion pounds per year. The amount of new scrap recovered has risen from 1 billion pounds per year to 2 billion pounds per year. But—the amount of old scrap moving to market has remained almost consistent at about 350 million pounds per year, in spite of the fact that more and more aluminum has gone into products which have a rapid obsolescence rate and should rapidly reappear as scrap.

Examples of these items are the automobile, which is using an average of about 70 pounds per car, and the all aluminum can, which is using about 500 million pounds of aluminum per year as against only 62 million pounds in 1965. This is despite the fact that aluminum is a high-priced commodity and aluminum scrap commands prices many times that of scrap steel, plastics and many non-ferrous materials.

These figures, I believe, point out problems of our industry that Government must help us to solve. The major problem is that economic incentives are urgently needed to bring the 300 to 400 million pounds per year of aluminum scrap now going to dumps and becoming litter back into the economic stream.

While others have followed Reynolds Metals' lead in attempting to collect aluminum cans for reuse, this plan is uneconomical for nation-wide coverage in its present form. An already existing network of dealers and smelters is available, but there must be an incentive in some form to make it economical to collect, sort, recycle and ship the huge quantity of aluminum going into food and beverage packaging. The tremendous scrap mine above ground must be worked on a daily basis in order to keep our communities clean. This scrap must be shipped when it's ready and sometimes will have to be shipped to locations far distant from where the scrap originates. This means that the very heavy shipping rates and demurrage charges have perhaps the decisive influence on the ability of the aluminum smelters to handle and remelt recycled aluminum.

Prepared Statement of Bert Romberg

copper & other metal

My name is Bert Romberg. I am Vice President in charge of Non-Ferrous Marketing for Commercial Metals Company. Please let me take this opportunity to thank you, Senator Proxmire and Congresswoman Griffiths for this opportunity to appear before your committee in connection with your review of the economics of recycling. Our Company, with headquarters in Dallas, Texas, is one of the largest in the recycling of scrap metal. Each year we supply over 1 million tons of raw material to major metal consuming industries in this country and throughout the world. Our 1,600 employees serve in operating twenty (20) scrap processing plants geographically spread from Florida to California. We also maintain five (5) domestic and nine (9) foreign offices which serve administrative and trading functions in support of our plant operations. In addition, we own an electric furnace steel mill manufacturing reinforcing bars and small shapes, and a copper tube mill which both consume secondary metals as their major source of raw materials. Traditionally, our business orientation has been approximately 60% toward the domestic market and 40% overseas, although this ratio is subject to wide variations depending on economic conditions around the world.

Our major business is to collect society's waste materials and turn them into useable raw materials. We have been ecologists all our industrial lives. To date we have done this without any governmental help, in fact, unfortunately, our operations have often suffered distinct governmental hindrances at all levels—Municipal, County, State and Federal. Therefore, we very much appreciate this opportunity to discuss with you some obvious economic hurdles with which our industry has had to struggle, so that your Committee can act effectively before it is too late, to stimulate the recycling of our dwindling natural resources.

Our company is vitally concerned with two economic problems which have severely limited our ability to recycle the vast quantity of scrap metal in this country. First, the inequitable freight rates which have discriminated against recycled materials, and second, the need for economic incentives to encourage investment in the very expensive, and short-lived equipment required for the processing of scrap metals.

In the non-ferrous metals field, we are faced with steadily rising freight rates for scrap, in many cases far higher than competing virgin metals are charged. Parenthetically, we should add that each time the railroads have succeeded in getting freight rate increases, their service to the shipper has become proportionately worse.

From the South, Southeast and Southwest to major consuming areas such as Midwest and Northeast points, freight rates for non-ferrous scrap are now between 1¢ and 1½¢ per pound. This means, in copper scrap, 2% to 5% of the delivered value; in aluminum scrap, 8% to 15%; in stainless steel scrap, 10% to 20%. Furthermore, the disparity between rates for virgin material compared to scrap gets continually larger. Some examples of these differences are:

	Per hundred weight
Refined copper:	
Hurley, N. Mex., to Detroit	$1.49
El Paso to New York	1.70
Copper scrap or copper-containing scrap:	
Dallas to Detroit	1.50
Dallas to New York	1.72

Please note that we pay equivalent or higher rates for hauls that are *600 miles shorter.*

freight rates &
non-ferreous metals

Aluminum ingots:	*Per hundred weight*
Los Angeles to Cableton, Mich	$1.75
Los Angeles to Cleveland, Ohio	2.18
Aluminum scrap:	
Los Angeles to Cableton, Mich	2.29
Los Angeles to Cleveland, Ohio	2.42

Similar disparities exist in export rates. On a shipment of primary metal versus scrap metals from Atlantic and Gulf ports to Japan, the following rate relationship exists:

Prime copper per 2,000 pounds	$31.25	Scrap copper per 2,000 pounds	$44.00
Prime aluminum per 2,000 pounds	28.00	Scrap aluminum per 2,000 pounds	45.25
Prime lead per 2,240 pounds	31.50	Scrap lead per 2,000 pounds	46.00
Prime zinc per 2,250 pounds	31.50	Scrap zinc per 2,000 pounds	44.00

The preparation of secondary materials for recycling is becoming a more sophisticated and investment-oriented business (in terms of money invested in machinery). Some of this machinery runs into the hundreds of thousands of dollars and in many cases a completely equipped processing center can run into the millions of dollars.

The cost of a complete plant for fragmentizing old automobile hulks can easily run into millions of dollars. In times of good business, net returns after taxes in our industry are in the range of 1% to 2% on sales volume. In times of poor business as we presently have, margins, for all practical purposes, disappear. We therefore feel that incentives are vitally necessary to encourage the business man to make such investments which even in good times are extremely marginal.

Finally, consideration must be given to the unusually rapid rate of attrition involved in the operation of equipment required in recycling; particularly machines such as automobile shredders which, by their very nature rapidly destroy themselves in use and simply do not last as long as the machinery used in the production of virgin metals.

End quote.

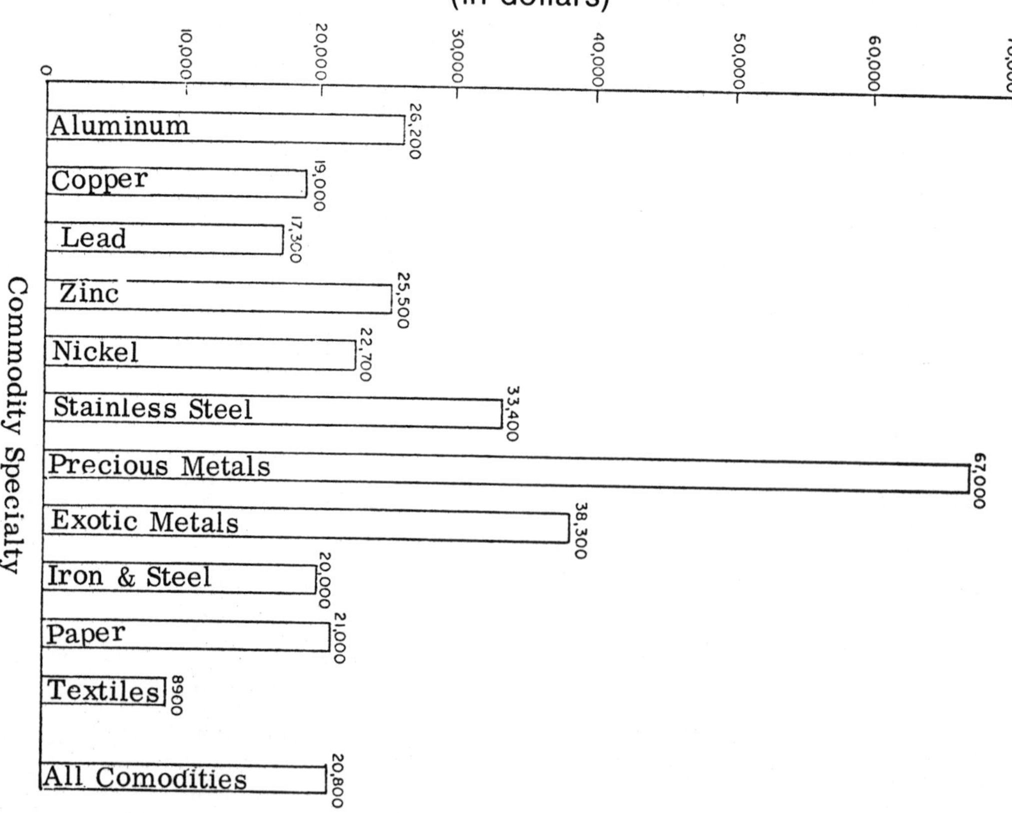

AVERAGE INVESTMENT PER EMPLOYEE BY RECYCLING COMPANIES
source: National Association of Seconary Material Industries, Inc.

information problems on freight rates

It should be stressed that the frequent use of the expression "discriminatory freight rates" in this chapter is a means of expressing an opinion, not a simple statement of fact. To make any simple statement about U.S. freight rates, other than perhaps that "they are a mess," is to leave the realm of provable assertion and enter the unreal world of the ICC's incredible bureaucracy. (See the *Time* quote on page Two-39.) What is seldom considered by the pro-recyclers is the economics of scale and to a lessor extent the problems of comparable bulk. That the selling price of the commodity moved should enter into the calculation of its freight rate is a patent absurdity. But this alone does not make their assertions of injustices incorrect. The obvious course of remedying such injustices is simply to let the nation's transportation systems utilize the free market of capitalism—a stage it has never really experienced, since from the days of the colonies the government has supported, subsidized and/or ruined every widely used form of transportation in existence. This includes even walking when account is taken of the difficulties given to this ecologically sound mode of transportation by government support of the automobile-roadbuilding-petroleum industry complex. This will be discussed at much greater length in Volume Two.

The Minerals Depletion Allowance gives producers of metals and petroleum from virgin sources a subsidy on the use of these materials, making it easier for virgin materials to sell for less than recycled ones. The obvious and best solution, ecologically, is to eliminate this subsidy, though political realities point up the fact that many Congressmen are reluctant to bite the hand that feeds them campaign money.

Therefore, the secondary industry (recycling) lobbyists have chosen to seek similar tax benefits for themselves. This is at least fairer than what we have, but it is not best. It does, however, have a certain sense of historic logic to it: over the years as efforts were made to eliminate this tax subsidy to oil millionaires, the result was that it was spread to virtually all mineral extractors. Thus the recycling lobbyists may be logically mad but politically clever. Proposals by the recycling lobbyists concerning other aspects of taxes—tax credits, for instance—have shown a similar pattern.

taxes: present & proposed

The following is from testimony of Jeffrey S. Padnos of the New York City Environmental Protection Agency before the Subcommittee on Fiscal Policy of the Joint Economic Committee, Congress of the United States, Nov. 9, 1971 (70-4220 GPO, 1972 at 111):

> The second tax I would like to suggest is a Reclamation Allowance. A manufacturer or material's processor could be paid a fixed sum for each ton of secondary raw material reclaimed from the solid waste stream. Another alternative would be to follow normal percentage depletion procedures and allow a reclaimer of secondary materials to deduct a percentage of his gross sales from his pre-tax earnings.
>
> Congress could find justification for a reclamation allowance in two basic ways. First, if an allowance could stimulate significantly higher levels of recycling, lower tax revenues would be offset by lower government expenditures for solid waste handling.
>
> But for those who may not be satisfied by seeing lower federal revenues offset by lower municipal expenditures, there is another basis for a reclamation allowance: equity. The record of federal material policy in this century is one of continuous incentive and subsidy to the extractive industries. This assistance has at time worked unwittingly to the detriment of the recycling industries as well as the environment.
>
> According to the United States Treasury Department (the figures that follow are based upon testimony by former Treasury Secretary Joseph W. Barr before the Joint Economic Committee in January, 1969), the total subsidy to all extractive industries is roughly $4 billion annually. More than $1.7 billion of this total results from tax provisions including expensing of exploration and development costs, allowing percentage instead of cost depletion, and granting capital gains treatment for certain profits from timber, coal, and iron ore.
>
> Another $2 billion subsidy comes in the form of direct budget outlays for such agencies as the Forest Service, the Bureau of Mines, the Geological Survey, or the Office of Coal Research.
>
> My purpose here is not to debate the merits of these expenditures, although some of them are certainly debatable. What I do want to emphasize is the unbalanced effect these policies have had upon the way in which our economy has grown. By subsidizing the cost of virgin raw materials, our country's natural resource policy has encouraged the substitution of virgin materials for both labor and secondary materals. This may have been the country's best path toward economic maturity. Today, however, as our nation suffers from both a glut of wasted resources in our disposal facilities, as well as a scarcity of jobs in the

labor market, it is time to re-examine a policy which can only aggrevate these conditions.

A reclamation allowance could mitigate or even remove the existing federal policy bias against recycling, even if subsidies to virgin-materials industries are left untouched.

Price Support System for Materials Reclaimed from Solid Waste

A related proposal, which could have much the same effect as a reclamation allowance, is a price support system for materials reclaimed from the solid waste stream. It might even be possible to administer this program through existing government agencies.

End quote.

Administration speaks of taxes

On June 2, 1972 *The Wall Street Journal* reported (p. 28) that the Nixon Administration was giving active consideration to tax allowance for the use of recycled materials. Beneficiaries would get a reduction in their income taxes in relation to the amount of glass, metal, paper or energy recovered from "municipal solid waste." Recovery from industrial sources would not be included. "But for those companies found eligible," the report continued, "one administration source says, the break would be 'at least comparable' to present depletion allowances, which range up to 22.5% for petroleum."

However, immediate action on this proposal was not considered likely.

Positive governmental actions to encourage recycling or research in this field are treated in the end of this chapter.

Fly ash

Fly ash—the type of ash that will go up the chimney if you don't stop it—is the major by-product of electricity produced by the burning of coal. And coal remains the fuel most-used for this purpose in this nation.

Fly ash accumulates in vast amounts, at some plants at several thousand tons a day. The overall U.S. production of fly ash by electric utilities alone is estimated at 40 million tons a year. With air pollution laws actually being enforced in some parts of the U.S., more of it is being trapped in filtering systems, rather than being set free to cover the country and cityside. Traditionally its disposal has been a problem, today costing about an average of $2 a ton for carting and dumping. In Europe relatively high percentages (40 to 70 percent) are being constructively utilized. In the United States, the percentage of utilization was listed in 1970 at about 17.4 percent, but with signs of greater use noted.

The current use is primarily in building materials, although out-moded building codes in some areas have seriously limited that use. The Tennessee Valley Authority(which pays for much of the strip mining of coal that destroys West Virginia to subsidize electricity for industry in other states) uses fly ash in its newest projects. The Corps of Engineers uses fly ash in more than 5 million cubic yards of concrete annually.

Sintered (heat-fused) fly ash forms a lightweight aggregate for large building blocks and things that most people, except owners of clay-brick factories, would call bricks. Up to 35 percent fly ash can be used in some applications, and the quality is superior to concretes made with other aggregates.

But other major possibilities for fly ash are still in the experimental-only stage. The possibilities are there because of the high aluminum oxide content, and small but valuable amounts of titanium oxide, sodium, potassium oxide, gallium and germanian. Enercon, Ltd., of Hamilton, Ont., is the first to withdraw these materials in commercial quantities, using 450 tons of ash daily from the Ontario Hydro Company's Lakeview plant.

A smaller but significant use of fly ash was developed at Uniroyal, Inc., in Mishawaka, Indiana, as an aid to the incineration of industrial sludge—effectively saving two dirty birds with one stone. See "Fly Ash Aids in Sludge Disposal," by Fred W. Moehle, *Environmental Science and Technology,* Vol. 1, No. 5, May, 1967, and "How to Resurrect Bricks From Ashes," *Business Week,* Aug. 1, 1970 at 48.

BOTTLES, CANS, AND OTHER CONTAINERS

Containers and other packaging are major contributors to the Nation's solid waste problem. In 1966, 52 million tons of packaging materials were produced, but only 10 percent of this amount was reused or recycled back into industrial raw material. The 90 percent which became solid waste accounted for over 13 percent of the Nation's total volume of solid waste from residential, commercial, and industrial sources. This packaging cost the American Consumers $25 billion in 1966, and today the cost and the problem is greater.[1] This expenditure provides the convenience associated with the disposable life style, but results in litter, other solid waste problems, higher prices to consumers, and a drain on resources. Containers for beverages make up about one-half of all food and beverage containers sold in the United States.

In 1970, an estimated 47.4 billion fillings of soft drinks and 35.6 billion containers of beer were sold in the United States. All of these did not become waste, for some beverage containers are still reused.[2]

In 1970 glass containers shipped domestically included:

SHARE OF SOFT DRINK AND BEER MARKETS USING CANS AND USING BOTTLES[3]

		Soft drinks	Beer
Bottles	(*returnables*)	54.9%	27.0%
	(*nonreturnables*)	17.5%	20.2%
	total bottles	72.4% of market	47.2%
Cans		27.6% of market	52.8%

Domestic shipment of glass bottles for all uses in 1970 reached 38,086,000,000, or 185 per capita.[4]

Thus, though some recycling exists, the beverage market uses 53.4 percent of the new manufactured glass containers.[5]

The beverage industry also uses metal cans. In 1970 there were over 64 million cans used in this country. There were 13,098,500 used for beer. Thus beverage cans accounted for nearly half of all cans used. Nonfood uses accounted for about one-sixth of the cans.[6]

USE OF BOTTLES BY BEVERAGE TYPE

Wine & Liquor			20,638 thousand gross
Beer	(*in returnables*)	2,347	
	(*nonreturnables*)	50,279	
	total for beer		52,626
Soft drinks	(*in returnables*)	11,317	
	(*nonreturnables*)	59,937	
	total soft drinks		69,254

1. Darnay, Arsen and Franklin, William, "The Role of Packaging in Solid Waste Management 1966," U.S. Dept. of H.E.W. Public Health Service Pub. No. 1855, 1969.

2. Folk, Hugh, "Employment Effects of the Mandatory Deposit Regulation," Center for Advanced Computation, Univ. of Illinois, 1972.

3. *Ibid.*

4. *Glass Containers,* 1971 edition, Glass Containers Manufacturers Institute, Inc., at 28.

5. *Supra* note 4 at 25.

6. "A Recycling Incentive Tax," Bureau of the Budget City of New York, November 1971 at C-15.

the rise of the returnable bottle

Between 1958 and 1970, beverage consumption rose 1.6 times, but container consumption rose 4.2 times.

Returnable Bottle Market

SHARE (PERCENTAGE) OF SOFT DRINKS, BEER PACKAGED IN RETURNABLE BOTTLES

	1958	1966	1976
Soft drinks	98% in returnables	80%	32% (projection)
Beer	58% in returnables	35%	20% (projection)

Today, returnable bottles are being returned less frequently. From a high of 40 return trips per soft drink container, the national average has declined to about 15 trips.[7] Thus, while our population is increasing at about 1 percent a year, collected refuse is increasing at 4% a year, but waste beverage containers are increasing at 7.5 percent a year.[8]

The public now must deal with a problem created by decisions made by private industry that have resulted in millions of bottles and cans being added to the already overwhelming quantity of solid waste. New York City, for example, expects its current refuse collection to almost double by 1985. This increase in less than 15 years is expected in a city whose population is not increasing.[9]

In the late 1940's and early 1950's, the steel industry began to produce one-way beverage containers. In the mid 1950's, the aluminum companies introduced the all-aluminum beer can. Subsequently the bi-metal steel can with aluminum tops appeared. The new can was popular among inner city consumers, where shopping on foot is common. However, the retailer quickly developed a resistance to returnables because of their need for handling and storage. In 1960, 40 percent of the supermarket space was devoted to nonselling storage. In 1970 only 10 percent of the space was used for storage. But due to the diversity of beverage containers, the bottler's storage space had increased significantly.[10]

The impact of metal cans on the beverage container market resulted in the glass bottle industry also producing throw-away containers.

The throw-away container has also aided the centralizing tendency of the industry. In 1950 there were 6,662 soft drink plants in the United States, but in 1970 the number had dropped to 3,054. (At the same time, annual per capita consumption of soft drink beverages went from 1,260 ounces to 2,750 ounces.[11])

Opposing this trend toward fewer bottling plants is the franchising system used by the major beverage makers. But the large food chains have countered with development of "private-label" nonreturnable soft drinks produced in large centralized plants. The result of this economic interplay is the continuing movement toward nonreturnables which cost the consumer an estimated $1.4 billion per year and has increased the solid waste and perhaps the litter problem.[12]

7. Hannon, Bruce, "Bottles, Cans, Energy," *Environment*, Vol. 14, No. 2, March 1972 at 11.

8. *Environmental Quality*, Council on Environmental Quality, (GPO) 1970 at 117.

9. "Use of Recycled Paper by Congress," Hearing before the Committee on Rules and Administration, U.S. Senate, 92 Cong., 1st Sess., S.2266 and S.2267, August 3, 1971 at 40.

10. *Supra*, note 7.

11. National Soft Drink Association, Soft Drink Industry, 1970-71 Annual Manual at 1-363.

12. *Supra*, note 7.

Vermont tax on containers

In April, 1972, Vermont enacted a bill imposing a .4 cent tax on beverage containers sold or distributed in the state if made of glass, metal, paper, plastic or any combination of those materials. Biodegradable containers, however, are exempt.

The tax will be used to provide revenue for landfills and state solid waste recycling centers. The state's 246 towns would get $1 million or 50 percent in the first year. The state would use whatever additional revenue was generated for environmental purposes. The deposit, which would become mandatory at the end of the one-year tax provision, would be refundable through retail stores if the wholesaler paid for the additional costs involved in handling. If the retailers refused to collect the beverage containers, the wholesalers and distributors would be responsible for providing at least one collection center in each town.

This is just one example of a recent nationwide state and local effort to reduce the solid waste problem caused by beverage containers. A summary of such legislation and ordinances appears in the appendix to this chapter.

As of September 10, 1971 there were 36 bills in Congress for proposed packaging legislation. There were 235 bills on this topic before the legislatures of 45 states. *See* also page Two-65.

energy requirements

Only very recently has there been any considerable amount of interest in the attempts by physicists to determine the relative efficiency of complex activities by measuring energy used in reference to the amount of fuel consumed for the power used. The goal, as it was for the first stop-watch-equipped "efficiency experts," is the conservation of energy.

Dr. Bruce Hannon of the Center for Advanced Computation at the University of Illinois, Urbana, recently published a study called "System Energy and Recycling: A Study of the Beverage Industry" that is of considerable interest to us here. Dr. Hannon compared the energy used to supply a customer with a beverage in 16-ounce bottles. To furnish one gallon, 58,100 British thermal units (BTU) were used when the bottles were throw-aways, and not recycled. Somewhat more energy was used if the throw-away bottles were recycled (crushed and new bottles made): 62,035 BTUs. If the bottle were filled eight times and returned, the energy used was 19,970 BTUs. The per-trip energy use was reduced for each trip the bottle made.

The national average in 1972 for the reuse of returnable bottles was calculated at 15 trips (refillings), which is down considerably from the 40-trip average in the 1950's. Dr. Hannon concluded that less energy was used to supply a given quantity of a beverage to the customer if returnable bottles were used, providing they were used about five times. At the eight fillings mentioned above, the energy used to furnish the beverage in throw-away bottles which are not recycled was about three times as great as the energy used to furnish the beverage in returnable bottles. If the bottles are filled 15 times (the national average), the energy used for the throw-aways is 4.4 times as great. Studies of sizes other than 16-ounce containers showed similar patterns.

The cost to bottlers, according to Dr. Hannon, for 12-ounce refillable bottles, throw-away bottles, and cans is respectively about nine, four, and five cents.

Soft drink cans required 11 percent less energy than throw-away glass bottles of the same size, but in this case the comparative scarcity of metals to glass sands must be remembered. Still, returnable glass bottles were immensely more efficient. Beer packaged in 12-ounce throw-away bottles and cans respectively required 4.2 and 3.4 times as much energy as bottles filled eight times.

Half-gallon paper containers for milk were shown to require 1.8 times as much energy use as their glass (reusable) counterparts.

If the beverage industry were converted entirely to returnable containers, the container energy system, which accounts for 0.34 percent of the total U.S. demand, would be reduced by 55 percent, according to Dr. Hannon's calculations.

The above few paragraphs do not, of course, give the full supporting detail of the original study, a version of which is reprinted in *Environment* magazine, Vol. 14, No. 2, March 1972 at 11.

Further findings of the above study are that the energy required to retrieve scrap glass from waste is far higher than the energy cost of mining raw material. When crushed glass is used as a substitute for crushed stone in road-paving, 60 times as much energy is used as for obtaining crushed stone.

recycling *vs.* refilling

Total waste recycling is advantageous from many points of view, but it is not advantageous from the point of view of energy use compared with producing glass from raw materials. This is especially true under present recycling systems, in which only 30 percent of the glass entering the system is reused as bottle glass. Some of the problems are that color sorting is considered necessary (though it has been pointed out that considerable savings could result if bottle color was regarded as unimportant), and bottles that leave metal rings attached after opening (such as those used by 7-Up) would create bottles with metal spots if they were recycled (which they presently are not).

Since the raw materials for glass are very common, the container industry's support of recycling efforts is primarily for public relations purposes: it makes no direct economic sense for them. Nevertheless, they realize that it is of great economic use to them if in this manner they can stall-off efforts to force the reuse of bottles, since their profits from making many recycled bottles are far higher than making the comparably fewer returnable bottles, despite the greater individual cost of the returnable bottles.

As an example of the industry point of view we reprint the following excerpted testimony from the "Hearings Before the Subcommittee on Fiscal Policy of the Joint Economic Committee, Congress of the United States," Nov. 9, 1971 (70-4220 GPO 1972 at 157):

STATEMENT OF J. J. WUERTHNER, JR., VICE PRESIDENT-PUBLIC AFFAIRS, GLASS CONTAINER MANUFACTURERS INSTITUTE, INC.

My name is J. J. Wuerthner, Jr. and I am Vice President-Public Affairs, of the Glass Container Manufacturers Institute, an association representing more than 90% of this country's glass container and closure manufacturing capacity.

We applaud the intent of this Subcommittee in exploring the means of reclaiming valuable materials from solid waste and conserving this country's natural resources. We in the glass container industry are convinced that the only viable long-range solution to the solid waste management problem is separation, salvage, and recycling. It is in this connection that I should like briefly to examine with you the work of the glass container industry and GCMI looking to the recovery and recycling of our products.

Some 20 months ago, in the spring of 1970, GCMI started a test pilot bottle reclamation and recycling program in the greater Los Angeles area. We offered to pay a half-cent a bottle or a penny a pound, which is $20 a ton for all used glass containers brought to reclamation centers at the plants of the 8 glass companies operating in the Los Angeles region by citizens and public service organizations. In the first week some 30,000 containers were reclaimed. The volume was soon up to one million a week and is now averaging about two million a week at the eight Los Angeles plants.

The success of the test program was so immediate that two months later in June of 1970 we extended the program to virtually every bottle-making plant in America. Today, reclamation centers are operating at more than 90 glass bottle factories in 25 states. Approximately 565 million bottles and jars have been recovered and recycled. Glass container manufacturers have paid almost $3 million for this glass.

While the reclaimed bottles represent only a small percentage of the industry's annual production. I want to emphasize that this is no one-shot public relations stunt. The bottle reclamation program is a serious first step effort looking to the day when it will be possible to mechanically separate all re-usable components of solid waste at municipal or regional collection centers for recycling into primary and secondary products.

Our bottle reclamation program has several fundamental objectives:

1. To accumulate meaningful volumes of waste glass to develope techniques for recycling large volumes of used containers back into the bottle-making process.

2. To provide a source of waste container glass for secondary products re-use exploration, such as road-building and home construction materials.

3. To help educate the public on the need for and feasibility of recycling waste glass and the other components of solid waste.

4. Finally, to make an immediate—even if a small dent—in the nation's solid waste and litter accumulations.

I am pleased to report that we have made real progress toward these objectives. The glass container industry traditionally has used small amounts of crushed glass, called cullet in the trade, in its furnaces. The cullet facilitates the melting of the virgin raw materials—sand, limestone and soda ash. We have now demonstrated, however, that salvaged glass, properly cleaned and processed, can provide from one-third to one-half of the raw material mix. This opens a potential market for some 5 million or more tons of reclaimed container glass a year at current production rates.

Such large-scale re-use of container glass would result in meaningful conservation of natural resources, despite the fact that glass is made of the most abundant raw materials on earth.

The chief drawbacks on the use of reclaimed glass as cullet are: that it must be free of foreign matter; it must be sorted by color; and it cannot be economically transported for great distances from its source to glass container plants. For these reasons, the glass container industry is sponsoring a major research effort toward developing secondary products made from salvaged glass in areas remote from glass plants, as well as uses for sub-standard cullet which cannot go back into the bottle-making process.

We have worked closely, for example, with the U.S. Bureau of Mines on the development of bricks and building blocks made with glass salvaged from incinerator residue. We have contracted with Tekology, Inc., in New Jersey, to make bricks—know as Tekbricks—with salvaged glass and resins. Through another GCMI-financed contract, the Colorado School of Mines Research Institute is developing construction panels using very high percentages of salvaged container glass. We are supporting a test project at the University of California, Los Angeles, to make various building materials from salvaged glass and cow manure.

Indeed, building materials promise a very large outlet for reclaimed glass. The products that now seem feasible in addition to those just named, include glass wool insulation, terrazzo flooring, shingles, siding and land tile.

reusing glass

Another large potential use for salvaged container glass is in new road building material known as glasphalt. This is asphalt in which crushed glass serves as aggregate instead of crushed stone. Glasphalt was developed at the University of Missouri at Rolla, with the aid of a federal grant. GCMI has more recently funded further research to determine what amount of impurities can be tolerated in the crushed glass aggregate without impairing the durability of the glasphalt.

A dozen or more experimental strips, streets and roads of glasphalt have been laid in public and private areas in the U.S. and Canada. Reports indicate that the new paving is performing well through all kinds of weather and traffic loads.

Glasphalt alone offers a potential market for salvaged glass far exceeding the availability of low-cost waste glass from solid waste and litter now or in the foreseeable future.

I might add in this connection that we also are seeking the approval of the Interstate Commerce Commission, through an action known as Ex Parte MC–85, to establish the authority to transport waste glass and other materials by truck in interstate commerce at reasonable rates.

The development of potential primary and secondary markets for salvaged container glass at this time has outstripped the availability of the material. The full realization of these markets, indeed, awaits the development of the mechanical means of economically separating the components of solid waste in large volume. Consistent with our conviction that the solution of the solid waste problem lies in large volume mechanical separation together with development of markets for the salvaged materials, we are working extensively with other companies and groups on the development of various technologies for separating glass from the refuse stream and then processing it for recycling into primary and secondary products.

We do not believe that the answer to this challenge lies in any one system. Local circumstances call for specialized solutions. For this reason, we are working in several directions. For example, we have conducted research with Stanford Research Institute of California on an air classification system of solid waste separation. Members of our industry are working on a so-called dense media system in which the components of waste are separated in a liquid media on the basis of their specific gravity.

Nor have we discarded the concept of home separation of certain elements of waste, such as paper, glass and metal. Separation of solid waste at the source is practiced in some communities today. Others are looking in that direction. It may provide a useful interim solution leading to the development of more sophisticated separation and recycling concepts.

Finally, we are seeking to perfect the techniques for sorting salvaged glass by color so it can be recycled back into glass furnaces. To this end, we are working with the U.S. Bureau of Mines on a high intensity magnetic system and with the Sortex Corporation of America, in Michigan on an optical sorting system. Both show real promise.

Indeed, all these separation systems are producing highly promising results in the laboratory and we are now moving on to the field testing stage.

You will be interested to know that some 10 tons of amber glass separated by magnetic techniques at the U.S. Bureau of Mines laboratory in Maryland is about to be shipped for a trial run in a glass container furnace.

These and similar programs are described in more detail in the attached reprint of a paper, "SEPARATION OF GLASS FROM MUNICIPAL REFUSE."

given at the Solid Waste Resource Conference, Battelle Memorial Institute, May 13, 1971, by Dr. Robert J. Ryder of Brockway Glass Company, Inc. and John H. Abrahams, Jr., of GCMI. We are also attaching a policy statement of the glass container industry in the solid waste management and litter control fields.

reusing glass

SEPARATION OF GLASS FROM MUNICIPAL REFUSE (EDITED)

by
Robert J. Ryder
Brockway Glass Company, Inc., Brockway, Pennsylvania
and
John H. Abrahams, Jr.
Glass Container Manufacturers Institute, Inc., Washington, D. C.

The nation's glass container manufacturers are convinced that the long-range solution to the presence of glass in solid waste can be found in the separation systems and markets for waste glass which are currently being developed. These systems are designed to separate the various salvageable components of refuse, and glass is but one of these. The enriched, mixed colored glass is a by-product left after other materials are separated, and thus it starts with a zero value, or even a negative value since disposal in a landfill could cost several dollars a ton.

As we have seen, two potential markets are developing for this glass mixture. One is the use of waste glass as cullet in the bottle-making process; the other is its use in various secondary products. By using materials handling methods, glass fragments 1/4 to 3/4 inches across can be freed of contaminants and color sorted for remelting and reforming into containers. Less refined or smaller sized fragments are usable in secondary products also. As indicated earlier, the U. S. Bureau of Mines is developing a system using commercial equipment which is capable of separating sand-sized particles by color.

Today there are perhaps three major approaches to separation. These are wet separation, dry separation, and separation after incineration or pyrolysis. The glass container industry is working closely in the development of several of these systems in order to evaluate the quality of waste container glass produced and the potential markets. Systems using one or more of these basic systems are nearing the stage of practical demonstration.

One of the best known systems is the Hydrasposal method developed by the Black Clawson Company of Middletown, Ohio. A prototype of this wet separation system is being constructed at Franklin, Ohio. When fully installed, this plant will be one of the most complete systems in the country for processing the waste products of our society. The Hydrasposal and Fiberclaim systems, manufactured by Black Clawson, are designed to handle nearly all normal municipal residue except bulky items. Coordinated with this is a modern sewage disposal plant to be built soon by the Miami (Ohio) Conservancy District which will serve Franklin and the surrounding area as well and will process contaminated waste water from the solid waste plant.

The Black Clawson demonstration plant is being designed to handle 50 tons of refuse in an 8-hour day, with a salvage potential over 50 per cent of the total tonnage (see Flow Diagram). The process will first crush the refuse into a liquid slurry small enough to pass a 3/4 or 1 inch diameter opening. Heavy materials settle out, and ferrous metals are removed magnetically. Inorganic materials are then removed in a liquid cyclone, which leaves a residue of heavy materials consisting of 80 per cent glass and nonferrous metals. The light organic portion is reduced into discreet fibers with contaminants screened out.

The glass container industry is interested in the heavy portion containing the 80 per cent glass and has designed a system to refine the glass fraction into a material usable in glass manufacturing furnaces. As such, the glass must be clean, uncontaminated, free of metals, and sorted by color.

POSTSCRIPT: As of mid-June, 1972, the recycling complex at Franklin was in partial operation—that is, the initial stages of separation were being accomplished, and magnetic metals and paper were being sold. The Sortex glass separator was to be installed near the end of the year. Hence, the agglutinated mass of glass and non-magnetic metals was still being buried in a landfill. There were no immediate plans at EPA for use of the non-magnetic metals.

See also pp. Two-20-22

Essential Details and Flow Diagram of the Proposed Subsystem for the Municipal Separation Plant at Franklin, Ohio.

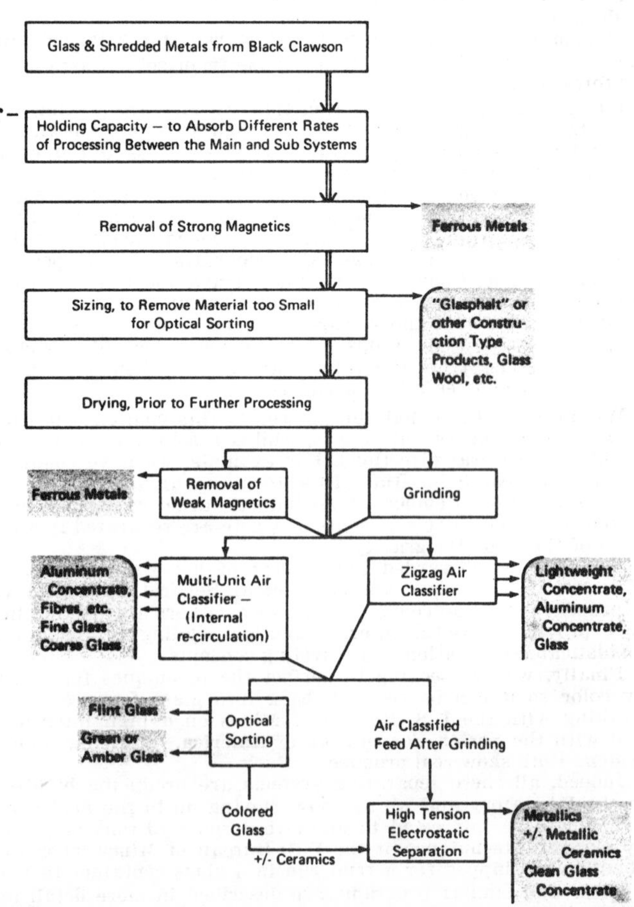

In preparation for the Sortex separator, the large fragments (1/4 inch to 3/4 inch) will be subjected to a cyclone air classifier and a zig-zag classifier. These two separation systems will be in service for this experimental subsystem, but the most efficient of the two systems probably would be used in a second generation subsystem. The Sortex optical sorter scans each fragment as it passes through a filtered beam of light and sorts the clear glass from colored glass and contaminants. A second pass of the rejects would then sort the greens from the remaining mixture, until all economically salvageable glass fragments are removed.

Hopefully, future generations will see a nation-wide network of refuse processing stations, perhaps designed along the order of the Franklin, Ohio, pilot project, where municipalities, or even utilities, will separate wastes mechanically and automatically and subsequently sell the recyclable materials to manufacturers or refiners. Such systems, we believe, will result in the much needed conservation of our natural resources and reduce pollution from solid waste.

End quote.

economic impact of change to reusable bottles

A study of the employment effects of the mandatory deposit regulation for Illinois indicates that a net employment gain would result from the imposition of a five-cent deposit on all beverage containers. Assuming a complete shift to returnable containers, a net increase of 6,500 jobs is anticipated. The transition to returnable containers would result in a reduction of employment in glass and metal container manufacturing and waste disposal, but would increase employment in other areas. Much of this shift in employment would be ameliorated by (voluntary) attrition in the glass bottle and metal can industries. The voluntary job-leaving rate in the glass bottle industry is close to 2 percent per month; this would produce the necessary 5 percent reduction in three months. The attrition rate in the metal can industry is about 1 percent a month, and so the reduction of 17 percent would impose a greater adjustment problem. The following chart illustrates the extent of the reductions and increases, and reveals a net increase in employment of about 1,500 jobs.

Employment Effects

Reductions in employment	
Metal cans	1,605
Glass containers	554
Litter collection and waste disposal	550
Indirect employment effects from metal cans	2,988
Indirect employment effects from glass containers	204
Total reductions	5903
Increases in employment	
Retail trade	6,750
Soft-drink bottlers	120
Brewers and beer distributers	627
Total increases	7,397
Net increase in employment	1,494

In addition to those effects, about $71.4 million of consumer expenditures will be diverted to other consumer goods from beverages. This represents about .007 percent of GNP. This expenditure would create about 5,000 additional jobs. Thus the total employment effects of the mandatory deposit regulation and a complete shift to returnables should be about 6,500 jobs.

See FOLK, *Employment Effects of the Mandatory Deposit Regulation,* Center for Advanced Computation, University of Illinois, Urbana, January, 1972.

Other techniques for control of beverage containers can be the banning of all nonreturnable bottles or the placing of a high tax on nonreturnables. Such an approach shifts the costs of collection and storage back to the retailers and wholesalers. It is unlikely to reduce litter greatly. It also places a burden on the beer and carbonated beverage industry that is not shared by the producers of the wine, hard liquor, fruit juice and other beverages.

Returnable glass bottles can also be standardized within the beverage industry, with labels to identify the brand. Such an approach simplifies collecting and reusing bottles, and has been successfully used in Denmark.

The tax approach to encouraging recycling is discussed toward the end of this chapter. The case *Society of Plastics Industry v. New York,* reprinted there, is a key part of that discussion. See also p. Two-57 and the list of laws and ordinances pertaining to containers in the Appendix to this chapter.

container reclamation programs

Voluntary reclamation programs are inefficient and produce only a minor reduction in solid waste and litter. However, specific programs can be relatively successful. But for large cities, the logistics of such operations are prohibitive.

The following is from a letter from Mrs. Nancy Bollows of the *Recycle Groups, Boston Environment, Inc.,* submitted for the Hearings before the Subcommittee on Fiscal Policy of the Joint Economic Committee, U.S. Congress, November 8-9, 1971 at 151:

> As for cans, we have calculated that Wellesley has recycled an average of 13.6% of its cans, Concord 11.1%, Needham 7.0% and Lexington 6.7% during the months of June, July and August 1971. These figures are based on weighing data from American Can, the rate of can consumption and the weight of an average can.
>
> With data from Glass Container Corporation, we have determined that the weight of glass brought to this plant (located in Dayville, Conn.) from Massachusetts from August 1970 to August 1971 is equivalent to one entire year's glass container consumption for 14,000 people.
>
> These figures show that even with the economics of recycling as they are now, some towns find it profitable or at least break-even to incorporate recycling into their solid waste system. I am certain that more towns would be able to follow this lead if there existed a stronger market for all secondary materials and thus further alleviating our solid waste burden.
>
> A different aspect of recycling involves the mills and salvage dealers themselves. Our experience has been that many greater Boston salvage dealers are threatened with extinction because of their 'undesirable' nature. In fact, the city of Chelsea, the location of many large and small dealers, will be 'urban renewed', forcing the dealers to relocate or go out of business entirely. Apparently one of the stipulations for the Federal renewal funds is that no salvage dealers remain in the area.

End quote.

Aluminum reclamation programs have been most successful because the metal has a reasonable salvage value. However, the most successful program, run by Adolph Coors Co., has had only a 25% return rate. But aluminum accounts for only about 0.3 percent of solid waste by weight and only 0.1 percent is aluminum beverage containers (though this figure could increase to 1 percent if the "all aluminum" can is widely adopted). The use of bi-metal containers, usually steel and aluminum, complicates recycling.

mandatory deposits

Mandatory deposit programs can encourage recycling, but many of the costs would be imposed on retailers and consumers. A substantial amount of money may be tied up in deposits to the benefit of someone, probably the retailer, but the interest value of these deposits can balance some of his additional collection costs. Senators William Proxmire and Gaylord Nelson have proposed a federally administered revolving fund for the upgrading of municipal waste facilities, to be financed by a 1 cent-per-pound tax on all products entering the solid waste stream within ten years. However, the tax is not related either to disposal costs or the expenditures for any specific program. There is no allowance or incentive for recycling.

See Management and Behavioral Science Center, *A Systems Approach to the Problems of Solid Waste and Litter,* Wharton School of Finance and Commerce, University of Pennsylvania, Philadelphia, September 1971.

Plastics emerged as a major container material during the 1960's. With an average annual growth rate of 12 percent a year since 1966, they are by far the fastest growing container material. Plastics are generally nondegradable and hard to compact, and some give off harmful by-products such as hydrochloric acid when incinerated. Once used and mixed with other plastics, recycling is virtually impossible. However, plastics are sufficiently new that research may obviate some or all of these difficulties. A food chain of 250 outlets, Der Wienerschnitzel, has scheduled use of biodegradable plastic lids for paper cups. *See,* "A Vanishing Coffee Cup," *Newsweek,* July 10, 1972 at 99.

plastic containers

Plastics have the highest per-unit solid waste management cost of any material, and there is little hope of limiting the costs they now impose once they are marketed, because they are virtually unrecyclable, and almost never reused. They also pose a severe rural litter problem because of the nondegradability of the types now in general use.

As of 1972, most beverages (both alcoholic and non-alcoholic) are retailed in glass or metals containers. However, it seems likely that plastics may take over a large part of this market, and possibly much of the food packaging as well. Research in this field has been going on for several years, and some test marketing has been conducted by at least two major soft drink manufacturers. *See* plastics trade journals in general, as well as the pamphlet, "Plastic Wastes in the Coming Decade," GPO 1970.

Indeed, it may well be that current recycling efforts aimed at municipal wastes that are high in glass and metals and relatively low on plastics, are like soldiers in the oft-told story, "training to fight the last war."

Special mention must be made of the polyvinyl chloride class of polymer plastics. These are widely used in clothing and beverage containers, and release hydrochloric acid when burned, creating both air pollution and incinerator maintenance problems. But these plastics can be, and to some extent already have been, replaced by less-harmful ones.

Despite the environmental dangers inherent in the use of polyvinyl chloride bottles, the Internal Revenue Service (Alcohol and Firearms Division) is moving to allow the use of such bottles as liquor containers. The IRS's dismally poor draft NEPA 102 statement was filed on February 14, 1972. *See:* Publication PB 206 561-D, Jan. 28, 1972, National Technical Information Service, Springfield, Virginia.

polyethylenes

The following is edited from a book length technical study, *Disposal of Polyethylene Plastic Waste,* Report SW-14c, of the EPA Solid Waste Management Program, 1971:

Although the home market for plastic products is small in proportion to the total volume of synthetics manufactured in this country, this market deserves consideration in municipal waste disposal problems, because consumer goods are increasingly reaching their final destination in public disposal sites.

The production of polyolefins, which include polyethylene as a major constituent, has steadily increased during the past decade and is expected to reach a volume of 6 billion lb by 1969. Polyethylene is therefore entering communal and industrial wastes in substantial amounts. About 40 percent of polyethylene waste derived from commercial sources is burned in incinerators. Disposing of polyethylene by burning it in combustion units is not entirely satisfactory, because polymers, such as polyethylene, block the air supply by depositing on the grate in a molten mass. The high calorific value of plastics is also responsible for the excessive heat generated during their combustion and the damage incurred by the gratings.

Although incineration of plastic waste, as found in municipal refuse, does not present unusual difficulties at the present level of synthetics in waste (1-2%), engineers in sanitation departments of large cities, such as Chicago, are concerned with the growing amount of plastic materials in garbage, because it is believed that a 3- to 4-percent waste content causes problems in city incinerators. This level may soon be reached because of the increasing use of disposable plastic products and packaging materials.

The potential problems of plastic waste incineration in heterogeneous municipal refuse are closely related to the large differences in the combustion properties of plastic and other waste constituents and to the pollution danger associated with the discharge of hydrocarbon combustion products. The excess oxygen required for adequate combustion of organic polymers is substantially greater than that needed for low-calorific refuse. Consequently, the thermal output (20,000 Btu) exceeds the combustion ratings of municipal refuse (5,000 Btu) by a factor of 3. It is therefore not surprising to find unsatisfactory performance of refuse incinerators in those applications in which a substantial amount of polymers is present in the waste. The manufacturers of incinerators generally claim that the difficulties encountered could be alleviated by redesigning conventional combustion furnaces. They believe that changes in the construction of the furnace, proper stack design, and maintenance of optimum gas-pressure relationships in the incinerator will improve the combustibility of plastics.

Disposal of communal and industrial wastes in landfills has been attempted in this country with some success. The practice of burying decomposable waste (garbage, cellulosic refuse, and metals) has an advantage in that the disposal site can be reused after the materials completely decompose or corrode. However, synthetic plastics, with very few exceptions, do not undergo significant decomposition when deposited in landfills. These materials survive intact for many years, and thus delay reuse of the site. There are no known microorganisms that attack polyolefins at a rate sufficiently rapid to promote effective disposal.

The application of composting techniques to plastics, particularly polyolefins, is rather ineffective because of the pronounced biological inertness of these synthetic materials. However, the possibility of subjecting chemically treated polymers to microorganisms that could utilize the modified material makes the composting approach for the disposal of plastics theoretically feasible.

The chemical and biological inertness of polyethylene, which is primarily due to its hydrocarbon nature and its ordered structure, makes the disposal of polyolefin waste by chemical and biological methods difficult. However, despite this difficulty the experimental studies conducted in the course of this program have shown that chemical treatment of plastic can modify the mechanical, thermal, and biochemical properties of the material in such a way as to facilitate the ultimate disposal of plastic. The approach that has appeared particularly attractive involves the oxidative degradation and concomitant nitration of polyethylene by exposure to RFNA, or binary systems including HNO_3, as a constituent. Considerations for this approach follow.

- Thermal treatment of polyethylene, following exposure to HNO_3, resulted in pronounced embrittlement of this inherently flexible plastic to the extent that it could be shattered by impact force. This behavior is important in the disposal of polyethylene, because effective compaction reduces the volume of solid waste and minimizes space requirements in landfill and incineration processes.
- Thermal response of acid-treated polyethylene changed noticeably in comparison with untreated material, as indicated by DTA and calorimetric measurements. A 30-percent reduction in the heat of combustion was observed for the oxidized polymer.
- Although polyethylene resists attack by fungal and bacterial microorganisms, nitration modified the polyhydrocarbon to an extent that its utilization by bacteria (Pseudomonas) became apparent after a 72-hr exposure.

Attention should be given to the degradation of the polymer in multicomponent oxidizing systems, the effects of the latter on biodegradability, and the use of selected catalysts. Following sanitary landfilling, special studies should be made to determine if there could be groundwater pollution due to leaching of the treated polyethylene.

End, excerpt.

New York City's government has as a primary goal the reduction of the solid waste generated in the city. This might best be accomplished by reducing volume through recycling. It is estimated that if scrap dealers handled an additional 5,400 tons a day, the city could reduce its present solid waste load by 25 percent. The city would save $46 million a year in collection costs, $22 million a year in operating costs, and the $200 million capital investment for a 6,000 ton-a-day incinerator that is being considered to meet the growing solid waste problem.

Most municipal waste technically could be recycled by sorting, composting, or pyrolysis followed by resale. However, two barriers exist.

1) It is very difficult to sort out the components of highly heterogenous municipal wastes. The existing secondary materials industries collect their wastes from more homogeneous sources. However, these problems are being overcome. The U.S. Bureau of Mines is funding a number of pilot projects dealing with sorting.

2) The lack of markets for recycled products is considered a still more difficult problem. The gap between salvage supply and market demand can be closed by lowering the costs of salvaging while increasing the demand for salvaged materials. An incentive tax could achieve this goal by counterbalancing the existing disincentives. Taxes could also be used to discourage waste and encourage reuse, particularly with packaging.

tax approach to container control

A tax could take several forms. It could be a recycling incentive tax, a simple differential user charge, a waste collection fee, or a mandatory deposit/bounty tax. New York City engaged the McKinsey & Company to study this subject, and their report recommends the use of a recycling incentive tax. This tax would tax each product in proportion to the costs it typically imposes on the city's solid waste process, with offsetting credits to induce greater use of recycled material in the product's manufacture and encourage reuse of the product. The tax also would encourage manufacturers to make products recyclable by varying the tax rate according to the relative recyclability and disposability of the products. By taxing different size containers at the same rate, the use of large containers can be encouraged. *See,* McKinsey & Company, Inc., *A Recycling Incentive Tax,* Bureau of the Budget, City of New York, November 1971.

The disadvantage of such a tax approach is that it deals with only a small part of the domestic solid waste load. Beverage containers constitute only about 3.5% of domestic solid waste. Furthermore, even a high tax would not prevent many containers from breaking or otherwise becoming solid waste. At best, litter could be reduced 20 percent through a packaging control; actual reduction could be expected to be substantially less. This means that beverage controls cannot solve the solid waste problem. However, the number of discarded beverage containers is so large and the rate of growth is so rapid that legislation directed at containers would seem to be worthwhile. In addition, it should be remembered that the components of municipal waste can vary. While beverage containers may make up a small part of the total national solid waste load, they may be a much larger part of any specific municipality's wastes.

Jeffrey S. Padnos of the New York City Environmental Protection Agency gave this description on August 9, 1971 of an ordinance which was tested in court and found wanting. The text of the relevant case begins on the following page.

> The proposed tax—the New York State Legislature has given the city authorization to enact the tax in full. To date, however, the New York City Council has implemented only the plastics portion—is a 1-to-3-cent levy at the wholesale level on rigid and semirigid paper, glass, metal, and plastic containers for all nonfood items sold at retail. Any container made of a prescribed percentage of recycled material is allowed a 1-cent credit against the tax. Wholesalers purchasing products from manufacturers reusing old containers would receive an additional 1-cent credit per container. As a result of the combinations of credits, all taxes are avoidable on paper, glass, aluminium, and tin-free steel cans. Thus, the more successful the tax, the less revenue it actually generates.

SOCIETY OF PLASTICS INDUSTRY v. NEW YORK CITY

326 N.Y. Supp. 2d 788 (1971)

Saul S. Streit, Justice:

Plaintiffs seek a declaratory judgment determining that Local Law No. 43 (1971) of the City of New York is unconstitutional and invalid. They also ask for permanent injunctive relief against its enforcement by defendants.

It is plaintiffs' contentions herein that Local Law No. 43, as enacted by the City Council of the City of New York (1) fails to comply with the provisions of the State's "enabling legislation" (Art. 29, Sec. 1201 [f], Tax Law, as amended by chapter 399, Laws of 1971; (2) unconstitutionally discriminates against them because it imposes a tax *only* upon plastic containers and not upon other similar items specifically enumerated in the enabling act; (3) deprives them of property without due process of law (allegedly forcing some of the plaintiffs out of business) and (4) imposes an undue burden on interstate commerce in violation of Article 1, Section 8 of the Constitution of the United States.

Plaintiffs' initial contention is that Local Law No. 43 was not authorized by the State Legislature and thus violates the provisions of Article III, Section 1 and Article XVI, Section 1 of the New York State Constitution.

It is well settled that these constitutional provisions grant all taxing power in New York State to the State Legislature and provide that such power may be delegated to municipalities only through laws which specifically designate the tax that can be imposed (See, *Genet v. City of Brooklyn,* 99 N.W. 296, 1 N.E. 777). A municipal corporation does not possess the inherent power to assess and levy taxes. Its power to tax is derived solely from state legislative enactment (see *County Securities, Inc. v. Seacord,* 278 N.Y. 34, 37, 15 N.E.2d 179, 180; Rhyne, "Municipal Law", Sec. 28-1). Thus, the Court of Appeals in *United States Steel Corp. v. Gerosa,* 7 N.Y.2d 454, 459, 199 N.Y.S.2d 475, 478, 166 N.E.2d 489, 491, stated that the State Legislature has the exclusive power to tax, "* * * including the power to determine the class of persons to be taxed * * *, which it may delegate to its municipal subdivisions, including the City of New York". The Court cautioned, however, that "* * * any taxes imposed by the [City of New York] must be within the expressed limitations * * * and unless authorized, a tax so levied is constitutionally invalid (*Long Island R. Co. v. Hylan,* 240 N.Y. 199, 148 N.E. 189)".

It is also well settled that statutes authorizing the levey of taxes are to be strictly construed (see, 16 McQuillen, *Municipal Corporations* §44-13, 3d Ed., 1963). City tax ordinances must strictly conform to the provisions of their enabling acts. If the authority of the City to tax is doubtful, the doubt must always be resolved *against* the tax.

The Enabling Act authorizing the city to impose the subject tax (L.1971, c. 399) added a new subdivision (f) to Section 1201 of Article 29 of the Tax Law. Tax Law Article 29 is an omnibus enabling statute authorizing various localities of the State to impose a variety of taxes. Section 1201, dealing with taxes administered by cities of one million or more in population, authorizes such cities to adopt and amend local laws imposing "any or all of the types of taxes set forth in the following subdivisions of this section * * *". Subdivision (f) of this section is entitled,

> An act to amend the tax law, by adding thereto provisions enabling any city with a population of one million or more to impose taxes to promote the recycling of containers and reduce the cost of solid waste disposal to such city.

This subdivision authorized New York City to impose,

> Taxes on the sale of containers made in whole or in part of rigid or semi-rigid paper board, fibre, glass, metal, plastic or any combination of such materials * * * intended for use in packing or packaging any product intended for sale.

The Enabling Act set the maximum rates of taxes on the different kinds of materials at three cents for each plastic bottle, two cents for each other plastic container, two cents for each glass container, and two cents for each metal container, except one cent for each metal container made of only one metal. Where a container is made of a combination of two or more of these materials, it is taxable as if it were made of the component material having the highest rate on the following table: fiber and paperboard—one cent; metal—two cents; glass—two cents; plastic—three cents. (Presumably, the tax on containers made solely of fiber or paperboard was intended to be one cent each, although the Enabling Act fails to list a maximum rate for containers made solely of said materials.)

The Enabling Act requires that the local law imposing the taxes allow specific credits against the taxes on the basis of the percentage of "recycled material" of which the container is made, the required percentages being 80% for paper and fiberboard; 30%—40% for metal; 20%—30% for glass and 30% for plastic.

In June, 1971, allegedly pursuant to this Enabling Act, the City Council of the City of New York passed, and the Mayor signed, Local Law No. 43 of 1971, which added a new Title F to Chapter 46 of the Administrative Code of the City of New York.

The stated purposes of the Local Law are, *"raising revenue by imposing taxes on plastic containers and to promote the recycling of such containers and reduce the cost of solid waste disposal of the city."*

This Local Law provided, inter alia, for a tax of two cents on the sale of every "rigid or semi-rigid" plastic container by a seller or supplier to a retailer on or after July 1, 1971 and for the allowance of one cent for each taxable container that is manufactured with a minimum of 30% recycled material.

Plaintiffs contend that this local enactment, exempting from taxation all containers made of metal, glass, fibre and paperboard, is invalid because it fatally deviates from and exceeds the delegation of taxing power granted by the Enabling Act. Plaintiffs argue that the Enabling Act fixed the "taxable class" as "containers made in whole or part of rigid or semi-rigid paperboard, fibre, glass, metal, plastic or any combination of such materials", and that if the City chose to act pursuant to the taxing authority delegated to it, the City must impose a tax on the entire taxable class.

Defendants contend, however, that the blanket authorization contained in Section 1201 of the Tax Law to impose "any or all of the types of taxes set forth" therein, empowers the City to pick and choose from the types of materials enumerated in the container tax enabling act. Analogizing to the broad scope of authority granted under "Local Home Rule", defendants urge a liberal construction of the Enabling Act. In their trial memorandum, defendants argue that,

> Considering the purpose sought to be achieved by the Enabling Act, it is inconceivable to believe that it was intended that the City should not have the same right to exercise its judgment and make distinctions between the different containers therein mentioned, similar to those the State Legislature could make, on the basis of their qualities and characteristics in relation to waste disposal problems. Obviously the intent was to enable the City to try out the possibility of reducing the difficulties and cost of waste disposal created by containers, by imposition of taxes on those categories of containers which presented the greatest waste disposal burdens for the City * * *. The use of taxes for waste disposal control purposes is a novel device not before used. * * * It would

> be unreasonable to believe that in embarking upon this experiment the City would not have the right first to try out this method with respect to one of the authorized types of containers which presents the greatest problem, before applying it to the others.

At the outset, the parties all agreed that this challenge to the validity of the local law raised only a question of law. While it so appeared to the court as well, decision on this issue was withheld until the presentation of all evidence, to determine if there was any validity to defendant's argument that the uniqueness of this ecologically-inspired tax took it out of the general rules for construction of municipal implementation of delegated taxing authority.

All the evidence having been presented, I find no merit in defendants' contentions. Home Rule principles are simply inapplicable in the determination of the scope of delegated local tax powers (see, *Weber v. City of New York,* 18 Misc.2d 543, 195 N.Y.S.2d 269; see also County Securities, Inc. v. Seacord, supra). The blanket authorization of Tax Law §1201 does permit New York City to impose "any or all of the types of taxes" set forth in its various subdivisions. However, the *type* of tax set forth in subdivision (f) was a tax on rigid and semi-rigid containers made of five specified types of materials. The contention that each type of container material may thus be the subject of a separate tax strains the plain meaning of the law and contravenes the tenet of strict construction of tax statutes. Moreover, I find the decision in *Glen Cove Theatres, Inc. v. City of Glen Cove,* 36 Misc.2d 772, 233 N.Y.S.2d 972, to be most persuasive authority for the position urged by plaintiffs. The court in *Glen Cove* rejected an argument similar to that urged by defendants herein, with respect to the blanket authorization contained in Tax Law §1201, on the basis of internal evidence in the statute itself.

The type of tax authorized by subdivision (c) of Section 1201 is a "privilege tax" on coin-operated amusement devices. That subdivision, however, specifically authorizes municipalities, when exercising its taxing authority, to pick and choose from among the various types or classes of such devices. The Court in *Glen Cove,* in rejecting a selective "amusement tax" imposed upon only a portion of the class enumerated in the enabling act (then subdivision [f] of Section 1201), noted that the specific grant of discretion contained in the coin-operated amusement device subdivision negated any implied or inherent right of discretion with respect to any other subdivision. "There would be no need for such language except on the assumption that without it, there existed no right to pick and choose." (36 Misc.2d at 778, 233 N.Y.S.2d at 978.)

It would appear that the *Glen Cove* decision is but a judicial confirmation of a long-standing administrative interpretation given the Tax Law by the State Tax Commission. A subsequent law review commentary, co-authored by the then Commissioner of the N. Y. State Department of Taxation and Finance, notes that,

> It has long been the position of the Tax Commission as advisor to municipalities on questions arising under the act enabling them to impose nonproperty taxes of various kinds, that the municipality *must take certain categories of taxes as a package, not exempting items or activities to be taxed which were not exempted by the terms of the enabling act.* * * * Glen Cove Theater, Inc. v. City of Glen Cove provides us with the first judicial affirmation of this position within New York." [emphasis added] (J. Murphy and E. Rook, "State and Local Taxation," 15 Syracuse L.Rev. 227.)

Finally, the legislative history of the Enabling Act itself supports the conclusion that the State Legislature intended to impose a tax on all the enumerated container materials. Indeed, the entire scheme of the tax authorized by the State Legislature (characterized by its proponents as a "Recycling Incentive Tax") is premised upon the taxation of all such containers. Quite apart from the claimed right of a municipality to pick and choose from among the component members of a taxable class, as an abstract legal proposition, such discrimination *in the instant case* would necessarily defeat the purpose and intent of the Enabling Act.

Unless the tax were imposed upon all the enumerated types of container materials there could be no "incentive" to recycle containers nor to reduce significantly the amount of solid waste or the cost of its disposal. The only "incentive" created by a tax on one, rather than all types of containers, would be the incentive to switch from the taxed type to the exempted types, with no reduction in the volume of containers used and no recycling.

When the City chose to tax only plastic containers, it did not, as it contends, simply enact a "lesser" included tax. Rather, it legislated an entirely different tax; one whose true purpose and effect was, as conceded by defense counsel, "to curtail the amount of plastics, and to eliminate as many plastics as possible." (Trial Minutes, p. 607). Nothing in the Enabling Act or its legislative history supports the contention that the Legislature contemplated or authorized the resulting destruction of the plastic container industry, for the ultimate benefit of the paper, glass and metal industries in New York City.

I conclude that Local Law No. 43 exceeds the authorization granted by the State Legislature, is thus violative of the provisions of Article III, Section 1, and Article XVI, Section 1 of the State Constitution, and is, therefore, invalid.

Plaintiffs also contend that the challenged tax violates the Equal Protection Clauses of the Fourteenth Amendment and Article 1, Section 11 of the N. Y. State Constitution in that it imposes unreasonable and arbitrary classifications unrelated to the object of the legislation. They further argue the imposition of the tax will destroy their businesses and that this constitutes a deprivation of property without due process of law in contravention of the Federal and State Constitutions.

At the outset, defendants challenge the basic premise that a court may inquire as to whether the tax imposed bears a reasonable relation to the object of the enabling legislation. They contend that any imaginable state of facts which could justify a separate treatment of plastics would enable the City to impose a tax on it under the Equal Protection Clause. Abandoning their initial contentions and concessions with respect to the primary objects of this law, defendants now assert that this is merely a revenue-raising statute and any effect it may also have on reducing solid wastes, and promoting recycling is "purely incidental and tangential." We are told to ignore the title and stated purposes of the Enabling Act and Local Law and are directed to cases espousing the familiar rule of statutory construction that the title of a statute does not conclusively establish its objects and purposes.

I find no merit in the position here taken by defendants. The presumption of constitutionality which attaches to legislative action is a presumption of fact, of the existence of factual conditions supporting the legislation. As such, it is a rebuttable rather than a conclusive presumption. There is no rule of law which makes legislative edict invulnerable to constitutional assault. Nor is such an immunity achieved by treating any fanciful conjuncture as sufficient to repel attack (see, *Borden's Co. v. Baldwin,* 293 U.S. 194, 209, 55 S.Ct. 187, 79 L.Ed. 281 and cases cited therein). In a recent decision involving an equal protection challenge to a state law, the Supreme Court stated the present day view that,

> In determining whether or not a state law violated the Equal Protection Clause, we must consider the facts and circumstances behind the law, the interests which the State claims to be protecting and the interests of those who are disadvantaged by the classification. (*Williams v. Rhodes,* 393 U.S. 23, 30, 89 S.Ct. 5, 10, 21 L.Ed. 2d 24.)

Likewise with respect to the related due process argument, a recent commentary observes that,

> Substantive due process litigation illustrates, as well as any area does, the importance of facts in constitutional adjudication and the function of the courts in regard to such facts. It can be stated very broadly that virtually all of the facts persuasive to a legislator in voting for or against legislation are within the judicial scrutiny in passing upon the constitutionality of laws attacked as violative of due process. (2 C. J. Antieu, "Modern Constitutional Law" §15:37 at 703.)

Indeed, an examination of the authorities cited by defendants themselves supports this position. Defendants place great reliance upon *Magnana Co. v. Hamilton,* 292 U.S. 40, 54 S.Ct. 599, 78 L.Ed. 1109, 1934, which they assert is "dispositive of and indistinguishable from the equal protection question raised here." In that case, the U.S. Supreme Court sustained a tax on oleomargarine which was so high as to place it at an economic disadvantage with its principal competitor, butter. The Court dismissed an equal protection clause argument with the terse comment that ". . . it is obvious that the differences between butter and oleomargarine are sufficient to justify their separate classification for purposes of taxation . . .," and declined to make judicial inquiry into the collateral purposes and motives behind an otherwise lawful tax levy. Defendants assert that the differences between plastic containers and all the other types is also so obvious as to justify their separate classification for tax purposes. What defendants overlook is that *Magnano* was preceded by a line of oleomargarine tax cases (see, e.g., *Hammond Packing Co. v. Montana,* 233 U.S. 331, 34 S.Ct. 596, 58 L.Ed. 985; *McCray v. United States,* 195 U.S. 27, 24 S.Ct. 769, 49 L.Ed. 78; *Capital City Dairy Co. v. Ohio,* 183 U.S. 238, 22 S.Ct. 120, 46 L.Ed. 171; *In re Kollock,* 165 U.S. 526, 17 S.Ct. 444, 41 L.Ed. 813), wherein the factual basis underlying the distinction between the two products was judicially examined in extensive detail before any conclusion on the equal protection or due process assertions was reached. Not only was there careful consideration of such things as the ingredient composition of the two products and the danger of consumer fraud and deception (passing off colored margarine as pure butter), but also consideration of the legitimate State interest in protecting the dairy farming industry (which formed the principal tax base in states adopting such legislation) from the destructive onslaught of cheaply produced butter substitutes.

This court perceives no *obvious* distinction between plastic containers and all other types and, in line with impressive precedents, has put the parties to their proof on this question.

Defendants' contention that the mere titles of the challenged law and Enabling Act are not to be deemed controlling on the issue of the purpose and objectives of the legislation is not questioned. However, a problem only arises with the title of a statute when it is sought to be used to improperly extend, restrict or alter the unambiguous text of the statute (see, McKinney's Consol. Laws, Statutes §123, subd. a [Vol. 1] at pp. 246-247; *Squadrito v. Griebsch,* 1 N.Y.2d 471, 475, 154 N.Y.S.2d 37, 40, 136 N.E. 2d 504, 506). There can be no dispute that the object of a statute is to be determined by its provisions, and not merely by its title (see, *People v. O'Brien,* 111 N.Y. 1, 59, 18 N.E. 692, 707). Nevertheless, this fact adds nothing to defendants' case. An examination of the provisions of the Enabling Act, including its mandatory tax credit provisions for use of recycled materials, its requirement that implementing regulations promulgated by the Finance Administrator be based upon the recommendation, *inter alia,* of the department or agency charged with the duty of waste collection and disposal, its provisions that the granting of tax exemptions, credits and surcharges be based upon considerations of difficulty of recycling, re-use and relative cost of disposal of containers, and a host of other provisions, establish beyond question that the title of the Enabling Act accurately and unambiguously reflects the purpose and objectives of the tax. *These are:* to promote the recycling of containers and reduce the cost of solid waste disposal to the City. Moreover, any doubts as to the legislative intent are dispelled by the legislative history. This legislation is the brainchild of the City's Environmental Protection Administration, which conducted investigations and hearings, drafted the proposed Enabling Act, and, together with the City's Legislative Representative, lobbied for its passage. A review of the correspondence supporting this so-called "New York City Recycling Incentive Tax," sent to members of the legislature by Jerome Kretchmer, the City's EPA Administrator and Richard Brown, the Mayor's Legislative Representative, demonstrates that the purpose and objectives of this legislation were, from its inception, exactly as stated in the title of the Act.

An examination of the text of Local Law No. 43, with its critical provision for a tax credit for the use of recycled material and its express statement that it is to be construed and enforced in conformity with the Enabling Act (Chap. 399 of Laws of 1971) "pursuant to which it is enacted," leads to the conclusion that the Local Law was ostensibly enacted for the very same objectives and purposes. An interesting footnote to the legislative history of Local Law No. 43 is that the original bill introduced in the City Council was in exact conformity with the Enabling Act, imposing a tax upon containers made of glass, metal, paperboard and fibre, as well as plastic. The legislative process and reasoning, whereby the final product which emerged from the City Council so varied with the original, is concededly a mystery to both sides in this case. From the evidence presented to this Court, the enactment of a tax only on plastic containers, allegedly in conformity with the Enabling Act, does not appear to be the result of any rational or reasonable legislative process.

Society of Plastics Industry v. New York City

Plaintiffs' assertion that the discrimination against plastic containers was an arbitrary one appears valid. Plaintiffs' further assertion that this discrimination was not grounded on any difference having a fair and substantial relation to the object of the legislation was established by an overwhelming preponderance of the credible evidence presented.

I find the expert testimony established that it costs no more, and probably less, to collect plastic containers than to collect paper, metal or glass containers. The significant cost factor in the municipal collection of solid waste is the weight of the refuse load. Plaintiffs' expert witness conclusively demonstrated that plastics, being lighter than the other materials, was easier to lift and carry, thus increasing the productivity of sanitationmen. It follows that if the enforcement of this law resulted in the substitution of paper, glass or metal containers for plastic containers, the costs of solid waste collection would increase rather than decrease.

Once collected, the City's solid wastes are disposed of by two methods—incineration and sanitary landfill. Expert testimony established that plastic containers are cheaper to dispose of by incineration than glass or metal containers. These latter types do not burn and some thirty percent of the cost of incineration is removal of the residue left after incineration. Defendants' experts attempted to show that plastic containers increase the cost of incineration because (1) excessive heat generated by burning plastic damages vital parts of the incinerator; (2) combustion of plastics require more air than presently equipped incinerators can feed to insure clean (i.e., pollution free) burning and modification of existing incinerators would be very costly; (3) melting plastics damage and impair the operation of the incinerators; and (4) one type of commonly used plastic polyvinylchloride, when burned, emits chlorine gas which, combining with water vapor, forms an acid (HCL) which damages vital parts of the incinerator. However, these contentions were based upon the presence in the waste load to be incinerated of a percentage of plastic far in excess of that shown to presently exist or projected in the foreseeable future. Defense experts conceded that plastic content not in excess of 10% of the total of an incineration load was within the capabilities of the City's present incinerators and does not produce the dire results enumerated. Plaintiffs challenged this 10% percent figure as too low but established in any event, that plastic containers constitute no more than 1.5% of the City's solid waste load. (Surprisingly, defendants could point to no current survey conducted by the City which established the actual composition of the City's solid waste.) Polyvinylchloride, the only type of plastic packaging which produces HCL, comprises at most only 10% of the 1.5% of plastic containers, an insignificant portion of the total solid waste loads. There was no credible evidence that this minute amount causes any acid damage to the City's incinerators. Moreover, it was conceded that other waste materials produce HCL upon incineration, including paper, grass cuttings and common table salt, but no percentages, proportions or amounts of HCL thus produced were presented by defendants. In sum, defendants failed to establish that plastic containers cause any damage or increase in repair costs to the City's incinerators.

Expert testimony also established that plastic containers occupy no more space in the City's collection trucks or in the City's sanitary landfills than an equal number of glass, metal or paper containers and may well occupy less space therein. It is condeded by plaintiffs that plastics are not biodegradable. While defendants laid stress on the desirability of biodegradable waste for sanitary landfills, plaintiffs' expert refuted this contention, noting that biodegradable waste may cause leaching, with resultant pollution of ground water, settling of the landfill (making it unsuitable for many uses), and the production of noxious hydrogen sulfide gas and explosive methane gas. Thus, the desirability of biodegradable waste for landfill is at best arguable. In any event, it was established that neither glass nor metal are biodegradable. Consequently, whatever its merits, this property of waste materials forms no basis for distinguishing between plastic, glass and metal.

Accordingly, plaintiffs have demonstrated by convincing proof that the discrimination against plastic containers does not rest upon any ground of difference having any relation to the objective of the legislation to reduce the City's cost of solid waste disposal.

With respect to the objective of recycling containers, it has already been noted that the Local Law not only fails to induce or require recycling of present containers made of glass, metal, paperboard and fibre, but logically will lead to an increase of such containers in use, defeating both objectives of the Enabling Act. It remains to be considered whether Local Law No. 43, directed only to plastic containers, will lead, or can lead, to recycling of that one type of container.

The Local Law defines "recycled material" as "component materials which have been derived from previously used material or from new or old scrap material." Plaintiffs' witnesses established that "new scrap" is generated in the very process of molding plastic containers and that such scrap is immediately recovered and returned to the process for re-use. As a consequence, the bulk of plastic containers now contain "recycled" materials as defined by the Local Law. The same witnesses asserted, without contradiction, that aside from special orders (e.g., certain government contracts) the percentage of recycled materials (i.e., new scrap) in plastic containers presently manufactured is at least 30%. Since this is the percentage required for the tax credit incentive to be operative, the Local Law can hardly be deemed to promote that which is already being done. To the extent that recycling is sought from materials contained in the City's solid waste, expert evidence established that there is no economically feasible way to reclaim any of the types of containers enumerated in the Enabling Act from the solid mass of waste collected by the City. Indeed, whether the assumption be valid or not, it appears that the City proceeded on the assumption that plastic containers *cannot be recycled,* in the sence of being reclaimed after consumer disposal and ground up for use in a new product. Defendants' expert witness indicated that he was unaware of any plastic container recycling. Significantly, the aforementioned letter from Jerome Kretchmer, Administrator of the City's Environmental Protection Administration, addressed to all members of the State Legislature and City Council urging enactment of the tax, asserts that plastic containers are "generally unrecyclable." If the Local Law was grounded upon this assumption then it is to be doubly damned, for there was not one shred of evidence presented herein which demonstrates that any form of container, glass, metal or paperboard, is any more recyclable than plastic containers; secondly, if the claimed objective of recycling plastic was preordained by its authors as impossible, then the statute is a fraud.

It thus appears that the discrimination against plastic containers does not rest on any reasonable basis in relation to the objective of promoting the recycling of containers, plastic or otherwise.

During the trial, defendants attempted to show that one of the prime differences between plastic and the other container materials was plastic's alleged adverse contribution to air pollution upon incineration and that the City sought this tax as an air pollution control measure. Defendants' proof that plastic containers are significant air pollutants was weak and inconclusive. Defendants' proof that the Enabling Act was sought as an air pollution control measure was non-existent. Aside from a passing reference to air pollution resulting from incineration of total solid wastes contained in the letter from the Mayor's State Legislative Representative to members of the Legislature, no proof was offered that any responsible City official advised the Legislature that the City sought the power to destroy the plastic container industry to aid in the fight against air pollution.

Society of Plastics Industry v. New York City

In sum, I find from the evidence adduced that the discriminatory classification established by the Local Law is unreasonable and arbitrary and does not rest on any ground of difference having any relation to the object of the Legislation (see, *Royster Guano Co. v. Virginia,* 253 U.S. 412, 415, 40 S.Ct. 560, 64 L.Ed. 989; *Louisville Gas & Electric Co. v. Coleman,* 277 U.S. 32, 48 S.Ct. 423, 72 L.Ed. 770; *Quaker City Cab Co. v. Pennsylvania,* 277 U.S. 389, 48 S.Ct. 553, 72 L.Ed. 927; *Merchants Refrigerating Co. v. Taylor,* 275 N.Y. 113, 9 N.E.2d 799),whether in terms of the City's cost of collection and disposal of solid wastes or promotion of recycling of containers or, indeed, the raising of revenues.

I conclude that plaintiffs have established by a preponderance of the credible evidence that Local Law No. 43 is violative of the Equal Protection clauses of the Federal and State Constitutions.

Referring again to plaintiffs' contention that the Local Law also violates the constitutional protection of Due Process, the essential proof here offered by plaintiffs was that they have already suffered severe financial losses and face certain destruction of their businesses. Having already demonstrated that the Local Law was arbitrary in its inception, incapable of accomplishing its avowed objectives in its execution, and lacks any other legitimate legislative purpose, plaintiffs assert that the loss and destruction of their businesses constitutes a deprivation of property without due process of law in contravention of the Fourteenth Amendment and Article 1, Section 6 of the State Constitution.

A statute which interferes with or takes away a person's property must be reasonably calculated to accomplish some proper public purpose (see, e.g., *Fisher Co. v. Woods,* 187 N.Y. 90, 79 N.E. 836). The mere fact that this is a tax statute will not save it from invalidation for constitutional infirmity *(Grosjean v. American Press Co.,* 297 U.S. 233, 56 S.Ct. 444, 80 L.Ed. 660). Indeed, the contention that Local Law No. 43 is purely a revenue-producing measure and that all other consequences of its enforcement are incidental is, in light of the evidence adduced, sham. The avowed primary purpose of the law is clearly to promote the recycling of plastic containers and to reduce the cost of solid waste disposal. The actual result of the law, as plaintiffs' evidence establishes, is the destruction of an industry to the benefit of its competitors without proof of any legitimate public reason therefor.

Defendants have not seriously attempted to refute plaintiffs' proof of present damage and certain future destruction of their businesses, as a result of this Local Law. Uncontradicted testimony of witness after witness, bolstered by documentary proof, has established that the mere passage of this tax has already cost individual plaintiffs hundreds of thousands of dollars in business (i.e., cancelled orders) and that implementation of the tax will result in the total destruction of the business of many plaintiffs. One of the most significant reasons for such dire consequences is that in a great many cases the tax imposed by the law equals or exceeds the price of the article taxed, and in almost all instances, it greatly exceeds the profit margin available to the manufacturer or seller. A further reason is that the tax attaches to each and every plastic container, so that the currently popular use of multiple containers within a single packaged product gives rise to a multiple tax, with the potential for increasing by up to 50% the retail price of products ranging from cigars to sanitary napkins.

Equally important is the complex record keeping requirement of the law. Quite logically, retailers have concluded that they can avoid the burden and expense of any possible record keeping by the simple expedient of switching to one of the untaxed type of containers for their products.

Ironically, several plaintiffs testified that they were encouraged into developing their plastic container businesses by various governmental agencies, including in one case, defendant Finance Administrator, and to employ and train disadvantaged and unskilled workers. In this respect, the passage of Local Law No. 43 has already required the lay off of many hundreds of such workers and its enforcement would result in returning all to the unemployment rolls.

(Further irony is found in the fact that contemporaneously with the development of this tax, the City has been encouraging and requiring the use of plastic bags for garbage, because plastics are light, durable and cut collection costs. Not surprisingly, defendants' experts perceived no problems connected with the collection or incineration of this particular type of plastic container.)

I find from the credible evidence presented that Local Law No. 43 will operate arbitrarily to damage or destroy plaintiffs' businesses without serving any permissible public objective and thus deprives plaintiffs of property without due process of law in violation of the Federal and State Constitutions and is, therefore, invalid (*Fisher v. Woods, supra; Grosjean v. American Press Co., supra*).

Plaintiffs assert a further basis for their claim of denial of due process, namely that the statute is unduly vague. Although the Local Law imposes a tax which must be paid under threat of criminal prosecution, it gives no standards by which the terms "rigid or semi-rigid plastic" can be defined. The Enabling Act is of no assistance here, since it also fails to define these terms. The City Finance Administrator's "Information Bulletin" CT-1 gives illustrations of what that office views as "rigid and semi-rigid" plastic, but some of its illustrations are so at variance with common sense that even defense counsel was compelled to concede their error. The only reference cited to the Court by defense counsel was "any dictionary". Indeed, one of defendants' experts confessed that he did not know what was intended by these terms and sought a definition from the Court.

As the Supreme Court stated in *Connally v. General Construction Co.*, 269 U.S. 385, 391, 46 S.Ct. 126, 127, 70 L.Ed. 322:

> [A] statute which either forbids or requires the doing of an act in terms so vague that men of common intelligence must necessarily guess at its meaning and differ as to its application violates the first essential of due process of law.

For the additional reason of vagueness, then, I find that Local Law No. 43 is violative of the Due Process Clauses of the Federal and State Constitutions.

Plaintiffs' final contention is that Local Law No. 43 imposes an undue burden on interstate commerce in violation of Article 1, Section 8, of the U.S. Constitution. Plaintiffs base this contention on three grounds: (1) that the law favors New York City wholesalers of plastic containers over out-of-state wholesalers; (2) products packaged in plastic containers are distributed on a national basis and the possibility of inconsistent legislation passed by various localities will impose an undue burden on interstate commerce; and (3) the excessive record keeping requirements of the Local Law discourages interstate traffic in plastic containers.

Under Local Law No. 43 the taxable event is the sale of a plastic container by a wholesaler or supplier to a retailer for use in connection with or as part of a sale to the consumer. The tax is imposed upon the wholesaler or seller, but if he fails to pay, the retailer must do so. Out-of-state wholesalers, however, are exempt from the tax, so that their local retailers bear the primary burden of paying the tax. Plaintiffs argue that there is an improper discrimination against out-of-state wholesalers since retailers who continue using plastic containers despite enactment of Local Law No. 43 will undoubtedly favor local suppliers in order to avoid having to pay the tax personally and to avoid the onerous record keeping requirements of the law. I do not find merit in this contention. The scheme of taxation is not novel in this particular feature and it would seem permissible to hold a local vendee liable for the tax even though the goods are shipped interstate, without doing violence to the Commerce Clause (see, *McGoldrick v. Berwind White Coal Mining Co.,* 309 U.S. 33, 60 S.Ct. 388, 84 L.Ed. 565; cf. *Henneford v. Silas Mason Co.,* 300 U.S. 577, 57 S.Ct. 524, 81 L.Ed. 814 [compensating use tax]; see also, *National Bellas Hess, Inc. v. Dept of Revenue,* 386 U.S. 753, 87 S.Ct. 1389, 18 L.Ed.2d 505).

Society of Plastics Industry v. New York City

With respect to the burden of record keeping incidental to liability for the tax, I do not believe that this feature of the tax standing alone is sufficient to condemn the law as a burden on interstate commerce.

Plaintiffs have called the Court's attention to the recent enactment by Congress of the "Solid Waste Disposal Act" (42 U.S.C. §3251 et seq.) wherein Congress announces a finding that the problem of solid waste is a matter "national in scope", and directed the Secretary of Health, Education and Welfare to conduct an investigation to determine, inter alia,

> the necessity and method of imposing disposal or other charges on packaging, containers * * * which charges would reflect the cost of final disposal, the value of recoverable components of the item, and any social costs associated with nonrecycling or uncontrolled disposal of such items. (42 U.S.C. §3253a [a] [7]).

Plaintiffs contend that in the face of this declaration by Congress, individual communities should not be permitted to begin enacting locally-conceived, locally-oriented legislation because of the danger of creating a welter of conflicting and inconsistent regulations (see, *National Bellas Hess, Inc. v. Dept. of Revenue, supra,* at pp. 759-760, 87 S.Ct. 1389). While this raises an interesting question, plaintiffs did not, upon the trial, sufficiently pursue the matter so as to permit a finding that the problem of solid waste disposal control has been federally preempted. I find, therefore, that plaintiffs failed to sustain the burden of proof on this last contention.

In recapitulation, I find that (1) the Local Law was not authorized by the State Legislature and thus violates the provisions of Article III, Section 1, of the new York State Constitution; (2) the imposition of the tax only on plastic containers, exempting glass, metal, paperboard and fibre containers, is an arbitrary classification bearing no reasonable relation to the objectives of the legislation and thus violates the Equal Protection clauses of the Fourteenth Amendment of the U.S. Constitution and Article 1, Section 11, of the New York State Constitution; and (3) the Local Law will operate arbitrarily to damage or destroy plaintiffs' businesses without thereby serving any legitimate public purpose and said law is so vague in its essential terms that it constitutes a deprivation of property without due process of law and contravenes the Fourteenth Amendment of the U.S. Constitution and Article 1, Section 6, of the New York State Constitution.

I therefore declare that Local Law No. 43 of 1971 is unconstitutional, invalid and void. Defendants, their agents, attorneys, servants and employees are permanently enjoined from enforcing, carrying out, implementing or otherwise giving effect to the provisions of said Local Law.

---

litigation

Few cases have been litigated to date on the question of controlling solid waste disposal, largely because the only federal law in the area, The Solid Waste Disposal Act of 1965, as amended, is relatively new, and has generally dealt only with State financial assistance and the promotion of research and occupational development and training grants to the states.

The preceding case, *Society of Plastics Industry v. City of New York,* therefore is a rarity. Other cases dealing with solid waste have dealt with the substantial issues of solid waste only peripherally, the decisions being made on common law grounds (See Chapter Five). Excellent examples of this sort of suit dealing with solid waste problems are *City of Miami v. City of Coral Gables,* 233 So. 2d 7, District Ct. of Appeals of Florida, 3rd District, March 10, 1970 (nuisance); and *Zengerle v. Board of County Commissioners,* 2 ERC 1512, Md. __A.2d __, Maryland Ct. of Appeals No. 256, May 6, 1971; *Garren v. City of Winston-Salem*, U.S. Ct. of Appeals, 4th Circuit, March 2, 1971; and *Appelbaum v. St. Louis County* 451 S.W. 2d 107, Supreme Ct. of Missouri, Feb. 9, 1970 (all three concerning zoning regulations).

See cases in Appendix to Chapter Five

Rubber tires

Approximately 100 million worn-out tires are discarded annually in the United States. About 25 percent of once-used tires are recapped for a second use, but this figure is small compared with that of some other nations, where about 80 percent of all worn-out tires are recapped.

A relatively small amount of scrap rubber—about 250,000 pounds, mostly from tires—is reclaimed annually in the U.S. This is less than 10 percent of new rubber production. As a result of such low demand, the market price for scrap tires at collection points reportedly is only about 10 cents—about ½ cent a pound. In 1945, the share of production for reclaimed rubber was about 30 percent, although even that was far less than was possible. Growing up in Jersey City, for ten years after the war the stench of burning tires—in lots filled with hundreds of thousands—was a weekly nuisance.

Tires present some unique disposal problems. They are difficult to destroy except by burning, yet this creates a host of air pollution problems because of the many chemicals released. When buried, tires tend to rise to the surface, due to pressures within the soil, although the trip may take several years.

New disposal methods are sorely needed, and several are being investigated. Tires are being used to construct artificial reefs to improve sport fishing along the coasts. Their great durability and ability to collect barnacles and seaweed make them excellent for this purpose. The reefs are constructed by bailing tires, weighing them down with concrete, and dumping them in appropriate locations. Estimates are that such reefs might utilize 1.6 billion tires at a disposal cost of 20 to 40 cents per tire.

Tire cremation plants are another possible solution, although recycling is still the obvious and best answer. Goodyear is installing a $550,000 smokeless furnace at their plant in Jackson, Michigan, that will burn tires as fuel. The heat will be used to generate steam for curing new tires and other industrial purposes. The heat energy in tires is easily understood when it is remembered that they are comprised principally of petroleum products.

Scrap tires have value as fuel, higher than that of most coals, but the sulfur content makes them smell like rotten eggs. Hence excellent emission control devices would be needed, were they to be used as fuel. Tires are not burned in most municipal incinerators because their residues tend to gum up the works. Still, the English have shown quite a bit of interest.

About the best possibilities seem to be in the Firestone—U.S. Government experiments. At the Coal Carbonization Center of the EPA's Solid Wastes Management Office, it has been shown that a ton of scrap tires yield 40 to 60 percent of its weight in liquid oils, plus gas equivalent in heating value to natural gas. The yield for one ton of tires is as much as 140 gallons of liquid oils (similar to those of most coal chemicals) and 1500 cubic feet of heating gas, plus a high-carbon residue.

Other proposed uses for old tires include the construction of highway crash barriers, inclusion as a component of asphalt road surfaces, distillation to recapture gases, oils and other ingredients, and burning them in special vessels to render carbon black.

See: "The Tire Makers Try All Sorts of Methods to Destroy Old Tires but Not Environment," *The Wall Street Journal,* April 27, 1972 at 38.

tires

Below are two excerpts from testimony concerning recycling in the textile industry. (*Hearings Before the Subcommittee on Fiscal Policy of the Joint Economic Committee, Congress of the United States,* 70-4220 GPO 1972 at 28 and 49). The fact that this testimony is with no more comment than this should not be interpreted as meaning that the opinions voiced are not debatable. On the contrary, both statements are part of a single, very much self-interested lobbying effort. But space limitations will permit only one more lengthy discussion of a resource for recycling. Hence, for this one and many never mentioned the reader is on his own.

The following is quoted from the statement of the National Association of Secondary Materials Industry in the Hearings Before the Subcommittee on Fiscal Policy of the Joint Economic Committee, Congress of the United States, August 9, 1971, at 28:

Textiles

Prepared Statement of Richard H. Frankel

Madam Chairman, my name is Richard H. Frankel, and I am the Vice President of Frankel Bros. & Co., Inc. of Rochester, New York.

I am a recycler of secondary textiles. That is, my company buys textile waste of all varieties including cutting room scrap from all over the country. We then sort, grade, and bale this waste product which would otherwise have to be buried or burned, in order to create a new raw material for paper mills, roofing mills, floor covering industries, woolen mills and other consumers.

As a direct result of various governmental impediments and policies, my company, which approximately 5 years ago processed some 30 million pounds of textile waste per year, is now processing only 15 million pounds per year. I now have only half as many employees as I had 5 years ago.

Why is this so? First, the textile industry finds itself with many complex factors to cope with in the development of a more expansive recycling program. There are economic, technological, psychological and legal restraints which keep the recycling of textiles from similar growth patterns as those experienced by other industries. At the present time, greater and greater tonnages of textiles are finding their way to the solid waste pile, so hampered is the reprocessing of these materials. It seems that it is only in various local areas where textile wastes are generated, that the public becomes aware of the problem of disposing of this material. Some 10 million pounds of discarded textile wastes are sorted in this nation every week. About 40% of this tonnage is collected, processed, and reused as wiping rags by industry. Some of the balance finds its way into other uses. But this is only a small percentage of the nation's generation of textile wastes—some 1.2 million tons are in the solid waste stream each year—potential recycled fibers and material for new uses and product applications.

The greatest single setback the textile recycling industry has experienced was as a result of the labeling restrictions imposed through the Wool Products Labeling Act and the Textile Fiber Identification Act. The rules and regulations imposed by this legislation have led to the consumer's fear of reused and reprocessed products; it gave birth to and promoted consumer attitudes that precluded the acceptance of products containing recycled fibers. "Virgin" products were supposed to be better products under the labeling umbrella promoted by the wool growing interests. In actuality, products made with recycled materials were of the finest quality and gave American consumers fine products at lower costs. In the last thirty years this country has seen the collapse of the New England economic community with the closing of almost all the mills that bought woolens, cleansed, garnetted, respun, and rewove them for use into new clothing and other textile products. We all know that employees were hurt, considerable money was lost, and communities disappeared. We do not want that to happen again and economic incentives and changes in legislation regulating the labeling of textiles are essential to our survival.

Furthermore, freight charges average 20% to 30% of the total sales price of textile products. In simplest terms, as these ever-increasing freight rates have risen we have been forced to recycle less. In some instances, particularly the lower valued grades which are the high volume items, freight is as high as 60% to 70% of the sale price. For example, the freight rates for shipping Mixed Synthetics to Arrowhead, New York, are as follows:

	Per hundredweight delivered
Sale price	2.30
Average freight to my plant	.78
Average freight to a customer in Arrowhead, N.Y.	.33
Total	1.11

Freight equals 48% of sale.

Sweepings to Toronto sell for $1.75 cwt. delivered:

Average freight to my plant	$0.78
Average freight to a customer in Toronto	.59
Total	1.37

Freight equals 78% of sale price.

In addition, there is a very serious discrimination between domestic freight rates and export rates. As in other recycled commodities, domestic rates for recycled textiles are much higher than export rates. This means that when foreign buyers can purchase textile waste abroad at a lower cost than buying from us we must rely on sales to domestic markets. Because, however, the domestic freight rates are so much higher, we cannot sell our textile wastes at a price which is sufficient to cover what it costs to collect, process and ship this textile waste.

Finally, incentives are particularly necessary for research and development in the textile segment of the recycling industry because of the advent of an increased use of synthetics which cannot be used for the same purposes as 100% Cotton (Cellulose fiber). The value of the 100% Cotton after sorting simply is not high enough to pay for the cost of sorting out the synthetic blends. With economic incentives to encourage further research and technological development we are convinced that more and more of these blends and synthetic wastes can be recycled.

Therefore, we urge this Committee and the Congress to support the NASMI proposals for tax and other incentives to recycle textile wastes. If such a package of incentives were adopted my company could surely recycle 100% more textile wastes.

Prepared Statement of M. J. Mighdoll

My name is M. J. Mighdoll and I am Executive Vice President of the National Association of Secondary Material Industries (NASMI) which has its main offices in New York City.

Many mills are recycling only half as many textile products as they were just 5 years ago. Although some 5,000 tons of discarded textile wastes are recycled each week, some 1.2 million tons are generated as solid waste each year—a virtually hopeless battle.

We, therefore, urge the Congress to immediately study this matter. We realize that it is important to adequately inform and protect the textile consumer. But we believe that labeling of textile products must be carried out without unfairly stigmatizing the recycling industry.

One of the last surviving segments of the textile recycling industry is the wiping cloth industry. This small, but vitally important segment of the recycling industry collects and purchases some four million pounds of discarded textiles each week. These textiles are then washed, sterilized, stripped of buttons and other abrasives and cut into wiping cloths of various sizes and shapes.

Then, these cloths are packaged in cartons ranging in weight from approximately 5 pounds to 50 pounds, or in bales varying from approximately 25 to as high as 1,000 or more pounds. Historically, for more than 70 years, the industry's sale of wiping cloths has been on a gross weight basis, with a certain stated maximum percentage of tare. Now, a bureau of the Commerce Department unilaterally seeks to destroy this totally accepted industrial practice by forcing the industry to adopt a net weight system.

The penalty of adopting such a system would surely be the ultimate demise of one of the last remaining segments of the textile recycling industry. Even now, textile recyclers are going out of business because of prohibitive costs and dwindling markets. The exorbitant expense of restructuring the processing and weighing of recycled textiles and additional labor and equipment required, would simply destroy this industry.

We urge the Congress to eliminate such unnecessary regulations which benefit no one and threaten to destroy recycling.

Unfortunately, the many foreign aid and grant programs which the Federal Government has established have often had an adverse effect on stimulating domestic recycling. First, these aid programs have built up the underdeveloped world to such a point that many foreign markets which have historically purchased recycled raw materials have been virtually eliminated. Second, with the increased emphasis on multilateral aid rather than unilateral assistance, United States dollars are not being used to purchase United States products.

Lubricating oil

by Jeffrey E. Howard and Dennis P. Koehler, J.D.'s, June, 1972, The National Law Center, The George Washington University

In the United States, approximately two and one-half billion gallons of lubricating oils are sold annually for industrial and automotive uses. One-half of this oil is consumed during use, and the remaining 1.25 billion gallons are drained periodically to be replaced with new oil.[1] The following chart, appearing in the Bureau of the Census' Industrial Reports, Sales of Lubricating Oils and Greases, January 1971, provides the most recent information available in mid-1972 on trends in domestic lubricating oil demand.

TYPES OF OILS (add 000 gallons)

Year	*Total*	*Automotive*	*Aviation*	*Industry Lubricating*	*Other*
1969	2,184,031	1,050,935	9,894	781,206	341,996
1967	2,058,953	1,031,784	13,064	699,120	314,985
1965	2,028,963	1,015,809	15,363	659,966	337,825
1962	1,766,094	945,493	22,357	510,823	287,621

Drained oil which has become physically and chemically contaminated during use is termed "waste" or "used" oil. In spite of the fact that used oil can relatively easily be recycled (see discussion below), as much as 75% of all such oil available for recycling may be disposed of in some environmentally harmful fashion.[2] The following table, prepared by the American Petroleum Institute (API), offers a somewhat more conservative estimate of the fate of the nation's used oils.[3]

AMERICAN PETROLEUM INSTITUTE'S ESTIMATE OF FATE OF OILS

Use		*Volume-Gal/Year*
Reprocessed [recycled] for reuse	37–40%	500 million
Road oil use	12%	150 million
Farm use	3%	40 million
Dumped on ground	23–25%	300 million
Dumped into sewers	1%	12 million
Fate unknown	18–20%	250 million

It should be noted that the API's estimate for the amount of used oil recyled each year is five times the Environmental Protection Agency's (EPA) estimates of the recycled oil industry's capacity — "about 100 million gallons per year in 1971."[4] Even if the API's estimates are regarded as accurate, they reveal that at least 750 million of the 1.25 billion gallons of used oil drained each year are harmfully added to the environment of the United States, ruining soil and causing water pollution.

water pollutant

Because lubricating oils will not break down under the extreme temperatures and pressures for which they are designed, so will they not break down when discarded into the environment. With the exception of

1. Appearing in Bernard, "Embroiled in Oil," reprinted in the Proceedings of the Joint Conference on Prevention and Control of Oil Spills, Washington, D.C. (June 15-17, 1971) 91 at 92.

2. Statement of the Association of Petroleum Re-Refiners, appearing in "The Economics of Recycling Waste Materials," Hearings before the Subcommittee on Fiscal Policy of the Joint Economic Committee of the United States (November 8-9, 1971) at 179.

3. "Embroiled in Oil," *supra* note 1, at 92.

4. *Ibid.*

recycling, virtually all "uses" found for waste or used oils are ecologically harmful. Oil dumped on the surface of the ground penetrates that ground; once this oil reaches the ground water table the water can no longer serve as a source of potable water supply. For example, in chalky rock or limestone areas, where ground water runs through fractures in the rock formation, there have been numerous cases where minute quantities of oil have irretrievably rendered wells unfit for human water use. Even if diluted to a ratio of one part of oil to a million parts of water, the taste of groundwater is affected by oil.

water pollutant

The API "use" chart indicated that 150 million gallons of used oil are spread on roads annually. Recent tests conducted by EPA, however, have indicated that used oil does not perform such dust suppression functions very well. It emulsifies quickly during rainstorms and washes off the road or penetrates into the ground.[5] It appears that slightly larger initial expenditures to purchase an oil or other product designed specifically for road use would result in a substantial long-term saving and serve to reduce the environmental damage caused by such use.

Used oils which find their way into sanitary sewer systems inhibit useful bacterial growth at sewage treatment plants, and thereby decrease the efficiency of the plants. Oils entering receiving streams as effluents from sewage treatment plants, or directly from storm drainage systems tend to adhere to floating particulates in the stream and sink to the bottom. The resulting bottom pollution destroys bottom-dwelling plants and lowers marine life often irretrievably.

In addition, some waste oil reportedly is sold to fuel oil distributors who blend it with heating oil and sell it to unsuspecting customers. The danger is that such waste oil may contain additives such as lead, iron, zinc, barium, and phosphrous. When the oil is burned, these additives are released to the atmosphere. See *Environment,* Vol. 14, No. 1, Jan./Feb. 1972 at 27, and Vol. 14, No. 3, April 1972 at 55.

The following is quoted from the Statement of the Association of Petroleum Re-refiners at the "Hearings Before the Subcommittee on Fiscal Policy of the Joint Economic Committee, Congress of the United States," November 8 and 9, 1971, GPO.

U.S. Oil Week on January 25, 1971 quotes Harold Bernard, of the Federal Water Quality Administration as saying on page 4, "We polled (FWOA's) regional directors. Six of the nine indicated that used oil, dumped into sewers, is a serious problem in the sewerage treatment plants and has caused fires in these plants, as well as caused treatment upheaval".

A UPI report from New York, dated December 26, 1970, tells this story: "The city environment protection administration says that city gasoline service stations are creating a serious pollution problem by illegally dumping waste oil into sewer systems to avoid paying a fee for removing it to re-refiners . . . Another agency spokesman (the UPI report continues) said there are only three re-refiners left in the area now because recycling has become too expensive to be profitable. A major factor, the spokesman said, was additives the oil companies have added that makes it more expensive to clean the oil . . ."

In an address to the National Petroleum Council a year ago last January Walter J. Hickel spoke about the missing millions of gallons, and said: "The hero of this action used to be the re-refiners, who would collect the waste oil and make something saleable and useful out of it. But the re-refiner is decreasing in numbers, and the sanitary sewer system is taking his place as the collector of waste oils in all too many cases."

A telegram from Hans G. Tanzler, Mayor of Jacksonville, Florida, was received on February 19, 1970. It read, in part: ". . . we were faced with an insurmountable problem of the disposal of waste oil from service stations, garages, and so on, in that no one would pick the oil up, and waste oils would be disposed of through our sewer systems, both storm and sanitary, creating fire hazards and pollution problems in the St. Johns River and its tributaries. The disposal of waste oil in any sizeable urban area is a vital point in environmental control that must not be overlooked."

The events leading up to this telegram were typical—a re-refiner closing down in a large urban area, leaving a potentially virulent pollution problem. What was NOT typical was the quick and intelligent action taken by the Mayor in appealing for help to have some other re-refiners take over in Jacksonville, in this case Seaboard Industries, Inc., from neighboring Doraville, Georgia.

One immediate solution is to burn used oils instead of recycling it. This would reduce or eliminate water pollution caused by dumping such oils—but there is a hitch.

5. *id.* at 93.

Perhaps the single most significant development in the growing concern about disposition of used oil without pollution has been the recent work of the task force on used oil disposal set up by the American Petroleum Institute, the organ of the new oil major refining industry. The final report of the task force published last fall favored burning over the recycling of waste oils. But, they admit in the Report's foreword that "the amount of used lubricating oil in the fuel blend should not exceed 25%," and in the next sentence, they argue that this blend policy will "obviate any health problems which might otherwise result from air contaminants". But there's a hitch in this happy solution . . . several hitches, in fact.

1. Walter C. McCrone Associates, Inc., of Chicago was asked to analyze the combustion products present in waste oils before they are re-refined . . . There are the oils recommended for burning by API. As the attached summary shows, more than 1,000 *pounds of metal oxides* are released when 10,000 gallons of waste motor oils are burned. Consider this alongside estimates of waste oil collectors that 260 million gallons last year were indeed burned. (This total related only to waste oil picked up by truck; the remaining non-recycled oil cannot be traced.) Simple arithmetic leads to the conclusion that at least 26 million pounds of metallic oxides would have been released into the environment just last year by burning!

2. The January 1971 issue of *Fortune* included an article . . . Metallic Menaces in the Environment . . . which quotes Dr. Henry A. Schroeder of Dartmouth Medical School as pointing out:

> "Pollution by toxic metals is a much more serious and much more insidious problem than is pollution by organic substances such as pesticides, weed killers, sulphur dioxide, oxides of nitrogen, carbon monoxide and other gross contaminants of air and water. Most organic substances are degradable by natural processes; *no metal is degradable*.
>
> "Little wonder that we are now witnessing the beginning of restrictions on metallic pollutants. Federal authorities will suggest criteria this year for permissable amounts of lead in the ambient air. (If you'll check the McCrone figures you'll see that in all areas sampled, lead amounts to at least half the oxides released by burning oil.) Guidelines for beryllium will follow next year. Later on cadmium, copper, manganese, nickel, vanadium, zinc, chromium and air-borne mercury will come under control. Similar restrictions on the disposal of these substances in water are either already in effect or soon will be."

POUNDS OF COMBUSTION PRODUCTS PER 10,000 GALLONS OF DRAININGS[1]

	Jackson, Miss.	Oklahoma City, Okla.	Washington, D.C.	Doraville, Ga.	San Carlos, Calif.	Dearborn, Mich.	St. Louis, Mo.	Houston, Tex.	Lyons, Ill.
Zinc	36.0	46.0	58.0	33.0	54.0	45.0	32.0	32.0	44.0
Copper	1.1	.9	1.4	1.2	1.6	1.4	1.2	1.3	1.5
Aluminum	4.6	5.1	2.6	5.1	4.4	4.8	4.5	4.4	6.3
Barium	43.0	25.0	57.0	20.0	31.0	9.3	33.0	45.0	38.0
Calcium	136.0	220.0	162.0	131.0	220.0	147.0	120.0	162.0	168.0
Nickel	.2	.3	.3	2.4	.5	.6	.3	.9	.7
Chromium	2.6	2.9	4.8	1.5	3.8	2.6	2.2	2.9	1.2
Iron	34.0	32.0	17.0	30.0	28.0	36.0	32.0	30.0	42.0
Silicon	29.0	22.0	13.0	24.0	24.0	27.0	64.0	19.0	24.0
Lead	650.0	650.0	400.0	570.0	480.0	720.0	650.0	570.0	650.0
Tin	.6	.6	.6	1.0	.9	1.0	.9	1.3	.9
Phosphorus	225.0	225.0	255.0	211.0	173.0	264.0	189.0	189.0	173.0
Boron	3.6	3.6	2.8	4.3	3.6	5.9	3.6	3.8	5.9
Magnesium	23.0	10.0	23.0	36.0	19.0	31.0	25.0	61.0	25.0
Total	1,188.7	1,243.4	997.5	1,070.5	1,043.8	1,295.6	1,157.7	1,122.6	1,180.5

[1] Calculated as oxides.

3. Apart from the above there is a serious problem of physically burning the oil—whether or not it can be burned effectively and safely. Mr. Harold Bernard of FWOA is again quoted by *U.S. Oil Week* as saying: "How can one be assured that the oil will be used in the prescribed ratio of 1 to 3? How can such a system be enforced without bringing public agencies into the picture?" He took out a plastic tube filled with pieces of oil burner deposit. "Here is an example of the results of using crankcase oil as a fuel without proper safeguards. They were rodded out of fire tubes . . . after only a few days of operation. Even with proper safeguards, the long term effects are unknown. Many metals are added during use. What happens to them in the burner?"

4. Quoting from the A.P.I. task force itself, they quote major oil companies: Humble says, "Nozzles seemed to plug up in burner barrels and wasn't easy to remove". American says, "Heavy deposits in tubes (averaging 1/16 in. and ½ in. at openings) were enough to shut down boiler once every two weeks for a day, a situation that could impose problems, particularly in the winter". Gulf's tests, "In burning 25% waste oil and 75% distillate at 3 gph up to 28% of the lead in the blend was found in fuel gas emission." Shell—"Using waste oil in a 3 to 1 ratio to normal refinery fuel, found burners were plugged four times during month long test; normal plugging rate is once in two months. Burner tips were clogged with small bits of rubber and metal shavings".

A gallon of oil saved by recycling is worth MORE than the original gallon because it is prevented from polluting the environment and causing extensive damage.

Last year, despite unwarranted or unjustified obstacles planted in their way, the petroleum re-refiners recycled 120 million gallons. We can lick the *billion* gallon problem if permitted adequate profit incentives.

End, excerpt from "Statement of the Association of Petroleum Re-refiners."

effect of retailing

The problem of waste oil disposal is further exacerbated by what has literally been a revolution in automotive oil sales — the shift from the service station to the mass marketer. Service stations, which in 1961 accounted for 70% of total automotive motor oil sales, saw their share of the market slashed to roughtly 45% by 1971[6] The majority of the decrease has been taken up by the large drug chains and discount houses, which usually sell name brand lubricating oils direct to consumers at savings of 65-75%. Bradlees, for example, a large South Plainfield, New Jersey discount house, sells four quarts of Quaker State for $1, while the suggested retail price is 85 cents per quart.[7]

The real environmental question posed by this change in motor oil sales patterns is: What are the people who buy their oil from these sources doing with their drained waste oils? Positive incentives must be developed to ensure that they are not merely dumped onto the ground or into sewers, or incinerated before dangerous contaminants are removed.

oil recycling industry

The "oil re-refiners" industry in the United States is small and getting smaller. These re-refiners, operating their own collection facilities or contracting with independent used oil collectors, acquire used lubricating oils from varied automotive and industrial sources. They re-refine the used oil by subjecting it to physical and chemical processes similar in type but not in range to those used in refining the crude oil. The re-refined or recycled lubricating oils, after the addition of appropriate oil additives and, in some cases, after blending with refined virgin oils to meet user viscosity requirements, are substantially identical to new oils and are sold for the same uses as new oils of comparable quality. To meet prejudices against used products, however, these recycled oils generally are sold for less than virgin oils. In some instances, the recycled oil may possibly even be superior for its intended use to many virgin oil products. *Aero* magazine reported in its May/June 1970 issue at page 39:

> Private pilots, flying school operators, distributors, dealers, and mechanics who use re-refined engine lubricating oil prefer it to "new," "fresh," "virgin" oil. Why so? They claim it gives longer engine life . . . at considerable savings.

problems of oil recycling

Even though it is clear that waste oils can be recycled into usable oil products, the American Petroleum Institute's study of the "fate" of the nation's used oils (referred to above) conservatively estimates that 750 million gallons of used oils are not recycled each year. In 1965 there were approximately 150 used oil re-refiners; today there are approximately 50 remaining.[8] The capacity of the re-refining industry was about 300 million gallons.[9] A few years ago it was generally profitable for re-refiners and independent used-oil collectors to pay several cents per gallon for used oil; today those seeking to dispose of used oil often must pay several cents per gallon to have it hauled away. What has caused this decline in the oil recycling industry at a period when concern for the nation's environment has grown tremendously? The answer seems to include adverse Federal government actions and technological problems.

(1) *Government action.* In 1965 the Excise Tax Reduction Act leveled a double-barreled blast at the re-refiners. Before that time there had been a 6-cents-per-gallon tax levied on the manufacturer of lubricating oil which was paid by the first user of this oil. Since re-refiners were exempt from paying this tax—the tax on the original oil had already been paid—the

6. Special Report, "Motor-Oil Sales Flow From Stations to Mass Merchandisers," *National Petroleum News* (August 1971) at 52.

7. *id.* at 53.

8. "The Economics of Recycling Waste Materials," *supra* note 2, at 182.

9. *Environmental Science & Technology, supra* note 7, at 25.

net result was a 6 cent per gallon competitive edge. The Internal Revenue Service changed all that in 1965, when it ruled that since these funds were to go into the Highway Trust Fund, off-highway users, notably railroads, could be refunded their full tax payments at the end of the tax year when they purchased 100 percent new lubricating oil. The IRS also refused to allow tax refunds on any new oils that were used in blending re-refined oil. Thus the re-refiners lost their 6 cents per gallon margin in competing for the off-highway user market, and were required in addition to pay the 6 cents per gallon excise tax on all new oils purchased.

prejudicial labels

Also in 1965, the Federal Trade Commission ruled that all containers of re-refined oil produced for sale to the public had to be prominently labeled "previously used." While a true description, the obvious connotation of inferiority quickly plummeted retail sales of re-refined oil to half the previous level, and the industry never recovered its share of this massive consumer market.

Even today, in fact, recycled automotive oil can be produced and sold at prices substantially lower than those of new automotive oils. But most consumers will not buy it. Potential users of this recycled oil must be convinced that it is as good as new oil. Changing the label from "previously used" to "recycled" might help.

The effect of the FTC ruling was exacerbated by the lack of any objective methods for comparing recycled oil with new oil. Neither the Federal government nor private oil interests have ever developed general performance specifications or economically feasible testing procedures for new oils, a failure which has largely frustrated the oil recyclers' efforts to convince the public of their products' comparative worth.

A provision for a law in this field might enable purchasers of automotive oils to return their used oil in leakproof containers on which a deposit has been placed. It also would be relatively easy, because of present tax record laws, to require adequate record-keeping concerning the disposition of such oils, makiing checking for massive dumpings easier.

Maryland, in July of 1971, was advised that it should set up a waste oil recycling plant. The proposal was put forth by Wilfred H. Shields, Jr., chief of solid waste services for the Maryland Environmental Service, and Walter A. Miles, head of monitoring-surveillance for the State Department of Health and Mental Hygiene. They pointed out that 13.5 million gallons of waste oil are produced annually in the state, and that there are no technological barriers whatever to its being recycled to a "lubricating oil . . . identical in every respect . . . to the original product." They added that contaminants are removed from crude oil, just as they would be from the waste oil.

Nevertheless, current Federal procurement policy is that all government-purchased oil must be new and may not be used or reconditioned. Yet the reduced drain on the nation's oil reserves which could result from across-the-board recycled oil procurement by the Federal government would be in the national interest.

Obviously Federal purchases of virgin materials rather than recycled ones significantly affect the quality of our environment. Therefore such actions require the filing of section 102 environmental impact statements under the National Environmental Policy Act of 1969. And certain of these actions must be illegal under terms of the same Act. The Solid Waste Disposal Act, as an example of specific Congressional intent in this area, sections 202(a)(5) and 202(b)(1), might also be of some assistance here. Yet such thinking has not yet entered widespread cognizance among conservationists, much less within the Federal bureaucracy.

The full text of the Solid Waste Disposal Act as amended by the Resource Recovery Act of 1970 appears in the appendix to this chapter.

For an examination of new methods in oil re-refining and the pollution problems of re-refiners, *See:* "Waste lube oils pose disposal dilemma," *Environmental Science & Technology,* Vol. 6, No. 1, January 1972 at 25.

(2) *Additives.* The tremendous increase in the use of oil additives in recent years presents additional problems to the oil recycling industry. These additives, of course, have clearly beneficial performance functions, most notably an increase in the life of certain types of oils. Automotive lubricating oil, for example, is now advertised as lasting for 4,000 miles, where several years ago oil changes were recommended every 1,000 miles. The longer useful "oil life" results in a relative decrease in consumption.

These same additives, however, must be removed in the early stages of the used oil recycling process. The very nature of the additive design—ability to withstand high temperatures, great pressures, and complex chemical reactions—makes them extremely difficult and costly to remove from used oil. Adding to this problem is the constant development of new additives; as soon as the oil recyclers succeed in removing one complex new additive from used oil, another, more complex oil additive appears on the market. There is no easy way out of this dilema, except perhaps to discourage the use of new additives unless their total benefits clearly outweigh the total costs, including those to be incurred by the oil recycling industry.

Different technologies apply in recycling automotive and industrial lubricating oils. Used automotive oils are surprisingly uniform across the country, once the relatively small quantities taken from individual service stations and other collection points are mixed together by the used oil re-refiner. The re-refiner thus can use the same recycling process for all used oils collected, minimizing research and development expenses. The introduction of new oil additives can temporarily disrupt existing recycling techniques, but once a method of removing these new additives is found, the entire oil recycling industry benefits. In any event, a significant portion of the total cost of recycling used automotive oil is due to the high cost of its collection.

Used industrial oil, on the other hand, is anything but uniform. Some of these used oils are generated in tremendous quantities by single industrial plants, so that recycling is most economical when performed on the premises of such a plant. Different contaminants found in differing sources sources of used industrial oils may make uniform recycling processes impossible. Recycling costs thus may be related directly to the used industrial oil source, often requiring significantly larger outlays for recycling research and development. In fact, some of these used industrial oils may present insurmountable technical recycling problems.

(3) *Sludge.* The final reason for the decrease in the amount of used oil actually recycled is environmental. Conventional re-refining technology yields a high percentage of acid/sludge residue and other solid waste by-products—as much as 30% of the total used oil processed.[10] The recycling industry is finding that these unrefinable sludges pose serious waste disposal problems, and cannot be disposed of without some type of further treatment if Federal and state pollution laws are to be complied with. Because the oil recycling industry's profit margins are generally low, the added costs of such treatment may prove to be prohibitive, forcing even more oil recyclers out of business.

Fortunately, new used-oil re-refining technologies may alleviate this problem. Preliminary results from an EPA grant-funded research effort to develop such new recycling techniques indicate that the percentage of acid/sludge residue can be reduced to as little at 5% of the volume of used oil processed, and can be of a type which satisfied sanitary landfill requirements.[11] EPA believes that this new technology will prove to be more attractive economically than conventional used oil recycling processes.

4. *Monopoly* The businesses engaged in the extraction of petroleum from the earth have tremendous economic powers which they can and do exert on both the very governments that granted them that economic power

10. "Embroiled in Oil," *supra* note 1, at 92.

11. Interview with Harold Bernard, Agricultural and Marine Pollution Control Branch, Division of Applied Science and Technology, Environmental Protection Agency (April 28, 1972).

and on individuals as powerless as the operator of a service station. A very important provision for any remedial legislation in this field would be to make illegal the practice by oil companies of prohibiting service stations or other lubricating oil retailers from stocking recycled oil products or selling the used oil they collect. A more general law to make such practices illegal in all industries would be logical and overall environmentally useful, though its special application clearly would be in those industries exploiting irreplaceable resources.

Although lubricating oil is only a small part of all petroleum consumption, the politically powerful oil bloc in the Federal and many state governments might find such recycling unacceptable. Looming as an unpleasant specter would be lost mineral depletion allowance benefits and unused domestic and foreign oil rights. A situation similar to that for paper recycling occurs, as indeed it does for so many of our natural resources.

Selected Bibliography: Solid Wastes & Recycling

National Research Council Committee on Pollution, *Waste Management and Control,* Washington, National Academy of Sciences—National Research Council 1966

Hanks, Thrift G., M.D., *Solid Waste Disease Relationships,* A Literature Survey, U.S. Department of Health, Education & Welfare Public Health Service, Cincinnati, 1967

Cleaning Our Environment The Chemical Basis for Action, American Chemical Society, 1969 paper

Legal Framework of Solid Waste Disposal, 3 *Indiana Legal Forum* 415 (Sept. 1970).

Solid Waste Management: A List of Available Literature, U.S. Department of Health, Education, and Welfare, Public Health Service, Environmental Health Service, June 1970

Policies for Solid Waste Management, (1970) 64 p. from U.S.D. HEW, Public Health Service, Bureau of Solid Waste Management, Wash., D.C. 20201

Systems Analysis of Regional Solid Waste Handling (1970) 210 p. technical methodology and computer programs. Bureau of Solid Waste Management, Wash., D.C. 20201

Special Studies for Incinerators, U.S. Department of Health, Education, and Welfare, Public Health Service, 1968

Solid Waste Processing, A state-of-the-art report on unit operations and processes, U.S. Department of Health, Education, and Welfare, Public Health Service, 1969

Solid Waste Management: Abstracts and Excerpts from the Literature, Vol. 1 & 2, U.S. Department of Health, Education, and Welfare, Public Health Service, 1970

Comprehensive Studies of Solid Waste Management, U.S. Department of Health, Education, and Welfare, Public Health Service, 1970

Effective Technology for Recycling Metal, National Assn. of Secondary Materials Industries, New York, 1971

Articles which discuss recycling include:

(a) Gumpert, "Reclaiming Refuse," The Wall Street Journal, June 23, 1970, p. 1.

(b) "Recycling: Ultimate answer to problem of Solid Wastes?," Product Engineering, September 28, 1970, p. 32.

(c) "Recycling Resources for Environmental Management," National Assoc. of Secondary Material Industries, Inc. (mimeograph), 1971.

(d) Special Report, "Turning Junk and Trash into a Resource," Business Week, October 10, 1970, p. 66.

(e) Grinstead, The New Resource, 12 Environment 10, December 1970 at 2.

An article, however, which points out industry's tendency to capitalize on the public relations value of recycling while doing little to actually recycle their products appears in Taylor, "Debunking Madison Avenue," Environmental Action, April 17, 1971, p. 8.

See also the books and articles mentioned on pages Two-8, 12, 15, 17, 18, 20, 22, 24, 25, 32, 44, 46, 48, 54, 55, 56, 63, 65, 77, 79 and 82.

Federal legislation

The Bureau of Mines of the Department of the Interior has been studying the reclaiming and recycling of minerals and metals for more than 30 years. Such authority is inherent in the Organic Act of May 16, 1910, as amended in 1913, which established the Bureau of Mines. This authority was continued when Congress enacted the Solid Waste Disposal Act, P.L. 89-272, October 20, 1965 though major responsibility for solid waste programs was placed in the Environmental Protection Agency. [For a description of the Bureau of Mines programs *see* Kenahan, "Solid Waste: Resources Out of Place," 5 *Env. Sci. & Tech.* No. 7, July 1971 at 594].

Congress enacted the Solid Waste Disposal Act. P.L. 89-272, Oct. 20, 1965. Although this Act was designed "to develop efficient means of disposing of the millions of tons of solid wastes that clog the nation's cities and countryside," it was limited to providing the States with technical and financial assistance and establishing a national research and development program. In 1968, the Senate Public Works Committee published a report (Senate Report No. 1447, July 22, 1968) calling for new legislation "next year" to "provide new direction to this important program to preserve and enhance environmental quality and protect the health of the American people." Sen. Rpt. No. 1447, at 9. (The bill which this report accompanied merely extended the life of the Act—its appropriations—by one year; no other substantive changes in the federal approach were enacted).

The new directions actually came about in 1970 when the Solid Waste Disposal Act was amended by the Resource Recovery Act, P.L. 91-512, Oct. 26, 1970. Once again, the Federal government continued its policy of recognizing solid waste disposal as primarily a state or local problem, as it expanded the Act considerably in the areas of research grants, funding and training programs, and resource recovery system demonstrations for the States. Perhaps the most significant of the Act's new provisions are those requiring a report to Congress on National Disposal Sites, including a list of materials subject to disposal therein (Act as amended, Sec. 212), requiring the Director of EPA to promulgate guidelines and model statutes for solid waste recovery, collection, separation, and disposal systems (*id.* Sec. 209); and Title II of the Act, which established a National Materials Policy, recognizing the fact that U.S. resources were not unlimited and requiring their efficient utilization in anticipation of both future U.S. and world needs (*id.,* Title II, Sec. 202).

The National Association of Secondary Materials Industries, Inc. has made this criticism:

> Under the Resource Recovery Act of 1970, appropriations ranging from $35 million in 1971 to $75 million in 1974 were authorized for research and development in recycling. Some of these funds went to on-going research programs in the Environmental Protection Agency while the remainder went to States, local agencies, and others.
>
> The Senate Report on this legislation, however, stresses that the private sector has its research problems as well:
>
> "Solutions to the solid wastes problems facing this Nation require application of the knowledge and expertise of people from both the public and private sector. *The Committee does not believe that capabilities of the private sector have been adequately utilized.*
>
> Because the Resource Recovery Act specifically provides in Section 205 that no grants may be made to "profit making organizations" private industry research and development on the important question of recycling receives no assistance at all from the Federal Government. While we certainly appreciate some of the reasons behind this policy, we feel that the private sector, which has had years of technological expertise in recycling, and which must ultimately carry the burden of recycling, should receive some attention to its research needs.

End quote

As evidenced by a report accompanying one of the bills, S.2005 (later amended and passed as H.R. 11833), the new emphasis was on recoverable resources, "those which maintain useful physical or chemical properties throughout their process of use and therefore can be continuously recycled in the production-consumption process" (remarks of Sen. Muskie, Sen. Rpt. No. 91-1034, July 23, at 2, 1970), and the bill's intent was "to stimulate the development of resource recovery methods which will provide for more economic use of wastes." *id.*

The Environmental Protection Agency was scheduled to issue proposed guidelines for municipal incinerators in mid-July of 1972. The guidelines are required under the Solid Waste Disposal Act Amendments of 1970. Final municipal incinerator guidelines were scheduled for August. Guidelines for sanitary landfills also were reportedly under development.

It should be noted, however, that federal financial assistance to communities for the construction of new or improved resource recovery systems or solid waste treatment facilities—literally the "meat" of this new legislation—is virtually non-obtainable at this time. The current Federal regulations which control the grants for these projects (42 C.F.R. §458.1, et. seq.) include a whole host of "special requirements" which few if any interested communities can hope to meet (*id.*, §§ 458.8, 458.9). Disgust with this type of federal non-action has been voiced. A recent note in 5 Suffolk Univ. L. R. 962 (Spring 1971), "Control of Redeemable Solid Waste: A Proposed National Bill" finds that "[because] the [redeemable solid waste] problem is of a sufficient national magnitude that the individual states cannot adequately deal with the problem, [o]nly a uniform national system will be the answer." *id.* at 964. The author finds a basis for such federal action both in the Constitution's Commerce Clause and in the Solid Waste Disposal Act, and includes as an appendix his own national bill.

EPA guidelines grants

The Environmental Protection Agency's General Grant Regulations and Procedures, State and Local Assistance [Interim Regulations] may be found in the *Federal Register,* Vol. 37, No. 112, June 19, 1972 at 11649. These grants concern state and local water quality, solid waste, and air pollution programs.

However, some progress is being made. An EPA news release of April 1972 reports "Eight open burning dumps have been closed down in Des Moines, Iowa, with the ninth and last scheduled to close later in the spring. The city's success — cited as an "example of what can be done by communities throughout the country", was accomplished by a new regional solid waste disposal agency which in just 15 months closed the dumps and improved collection service.

EPA supported the project with $209,874 in grants from its Office of Solid Waste Management Programs; Des Moines' contribution was $120,-000.

EPA initiated a citizen solid waste management campaign in 1971 to encourage communities to close open dumps. The goal is 5,000. To date more than 1,600 dumps have closed — largely through state and community action.

state-Federal relationships

The Solid Waste Disposal Act [42 U.S.C. 3251] demands that State solid waste management plans funded under the Act include an inventory of waste disposal facilities and a survey of problems and practices. The 1970 Act [42 U.S.C.A. 325(a) (2)] requires that provisions for recycling or recovery of materials from waste must be included where possible. A chart on page 48 of the second annual report of the Council on Environmental Quality (August 1971) shows that status of these programs. Ten states are in the inventory stage. Twenty-five states have plans at the draft stage. Seventeen states have completed solid waste management plans. However, state laws dealing with solid waste are rudimentary at best. A few states are attempting to ban or tax beverage containers. *See also* page Two-57, and the Appendix to this chapter.

The following is excerpted from *Environmental Quality: The Second Annual Report of the Council on Environmental Quality,* Washington, 1971:

> Regulation of solid waste management practices, other than for public health protection, is in a rudimentary state. However, statewide and regional solid waste planning is on the rise. And it is leading to increased regulatory activity—such as prohibitions against open dumps and controls over landfill practices.
>
> In New Jersey, the Department of Environmental Protection

was empowered to register all solid waste disposal operations, to formulate a statewide waste management plan, and to encourage regional action. It was also empowered to build disposal facilities on an experimental basis.[20] The State plan, recently issued by the Department, recommends incineration and landfill districts.

A new Kansas law calls for limited State regulation of solid waste management.[21] It creates a Solid Waste Advisory Council to recommend ways to finance solid waste systems and standards to govern the operation of disposal facilities. North Carolina has armed its State Board of Health with new solid wastes research, standard-setting, and inspection responsibilities.[22]

The Solid Waste Disposal Act[23] demands that State solid waste management plans funded under the Act include an inventory of waste disposal facilities and a survey of problems and practices. Under the 1970 Amendments, provision for recycling or recovery of materials from waste must be included whenever possible.[24]

End quote.

State & Local laws & planning

In many cases the State's legislative authority is not clearly defined or lacks adequate power. The authority in this field within some states often is based on general health or nuisance laws or for the control of dumping refuse on public and private property without permission. This last group could be considered anti-litter laws. Only a few of the States have specific legislation giving authority to the State health department for the control of the storage, collection, and disposal of solid wastes.

State leadership is essential to successfully attack solid waste problems in metropolitan areas. Two recent studies have concluded that State legislation must complement local governmental action in order to make it possible to provide adequate refuse disposal services for metropolitan areas. These studies were made in the Northeastern Illinois and the Hartford, Connecticut, metropolitan areas. Both reports point out the need for area-wide refuse disposal agencies. Unfortunately, few states have delegated the authority necessary to establish area-wide refuse collection and/or disposal systems. The *Census of Governments: 1962,* for example, reports that only nine states—California, Connecticut, Kentucky, Michigan, New Jersey, Ohio, South Carolina, Tennessee, and Washington—have provisions for the formation of districts or authorities to organize and operate such area-wide systems.

Several States have, however, made important contributions toward the solution of solid waste problems. New York and New Jersey, for example, have recently revised their State sanitary codes to control the use of open dumps for refuse disposal. Extensive studies of ground water pollution by refuse fills have been sponsored by the State of California.

Local governmental officials have used a variety of legal provisions and technical approaches to solve solid waste problems in some metropolitan areas. The Los Angeles County Sanitation Districts, for example, made a detailed study and report, which led to the establishment of a system of transfer stations and sanitary landfills, which now serve more than fifty cities and a large unincorporated area in the county. In neighboring Orange County, the Highway Department prepared a *Master Plan of Refuse Disposal,* which anticipated the county's disposal needs up to the year 2000. The county-wide system of transfer stations and sanitary landfills was subsequently established with the support of all the cities and other local governmental units.

20. N.J. Stat. Ann. §13:1D–1 *et seq.*
21. Ch. 264, [1970] Kansas Laws.
22. N. C. Gen. Stat. §130–166.18.
23. 42 U.S.C. §3251.
24. 42 U.S.C.A. §325(a)(2).

Criticism of local laws as well as local practices in this field is not unusual. The following two paragraphs are again from comments made by the National Association of Secondary Materials Industry, Inc.:

Often when municipal and state governments seek to cope with their solid waste problems, they foster discriminatory policies and take regulatory actions which impede recycling. Many municipal and state governments still enforce antiquated licensing, zoning, record-keeping and other discriminatory policies which adversely affect the recycling industry. Some companies processing or utilizing recycled material do not enjoy the same zoning privileges as do other industrial companies. Many cities and states license and tax recycling companies on a different basis than other raw material and manufacturing companies. One state during this past year sought to bring the recycling industry under the domination of public utility laws as it sought to "do something" about the solid waste problem.

These discriminatory policies directly affect recycling. They add additional cost burdens to many companies and, in other cases, actually bring about the dislocation of entire business activities. A study our Association recently conducted vividly indicated that recycling plants had been forced out of the very municipalities that were seeking to encourage recycling.

We clearly need constructive Federal policies in this area to provide reasonable and uniform standards to municipalities and states so that they may truly encourage, not discourage recycling.

End quote.

planning

A recent survey by the Housing and Home Finance Agency reports that twenty-four planning agencies have completed seventeen solid waste disposal studies, fourteen others are underway, and six more are anticipated. The planning agencies doing these studies are evenly divided between three types—multijurisdictional, city-county, and county.

Comprehensive planning is an essential step in the design of efficient area-wide refuse collection and disposal services. Local conditions must be evaluated, the possible solutions investigated, and the best methods of providing service determined. Such engineering studies can be made by either local public works agencies or consulting engineering firms.

An attorney can often be of the greatest benefit to the community considering the implementation of a solid waste disposal program at that program's inception. EPA's Bureau of Solid Waste Management will provide information outlining model programs in sanitary landfills or incinerator operations to interested state or local government units. *See Elements of Solid Waste Management,* Training Course Manual prepared by the BSWM Training Institute (Cincinnati: January 1970) which includes detailed rating methods for landfill and incinerator operations and checklist evaluations, and *Developing a State Solid Waste Management Plan,* U.S. Dept. of HEW Environmental Health Service (BSWM) publication SW-42ts (1970). A recent study of the special water pollution problems created by municipal handling of sludge (the solid substance remaining from water and wastewater treatment) is found in *A Study of Sludge Handling and Disposal,* U.S. Dept. of the Interior, FWPCA Pub. No. WP-20-4 (May 1968). For a report of recent observations of solid waste processing operations in Europe, *See* Jensen, OBSERVATIONS OF CONTINENTAL EUROPEAN SOLID WASTE MANAGEMENT PRACTICES, HEW's BSWM, Public Health Service Pub. No. 1880 (Washington, D.C. 1969).

The following is excerpted from *Solid Waste Handling in Metropolitan Areas,* February 1964, U.S. Department of Health, Education, and Welfare:

Although municipalities generally have ample legal authority to regulate solid waste handling within their corporate limits, few States have enacted laws which enable local governmental units in metropolitan areas to deal effectively with solid wastes. While municipalities can exercise the power of eminent domain within their corporate limits, the land available for refuse disposal is frequently insufficient to meet their needs. Even when a city finds land to purchase in a neighboring community or an unincorporated area, political boundaries are formidable obstacles which may prevent the site from being used for refuse disposal facilities.

local powers

Few state laws provide any protection for city residents from the effects of nuisances that are maintained in neighboring communities. Illinois is one exception. The Criminal Code of Illinois authorizes municipalities to prohibit any offensive or unwholesome business or establishment located within one mile of their corporate limits (Illinois Revised Statutes (1961) ch. 24, Sect. 11-42-9, ch. 100-1/2, Sect. 27). In the recent case of the *City of Chicago v. Fritz,* 184 N.E. 2d. 713 (1962), the City sought to enjoin Fritz from operating a dump within one mile of the corporate limits of Chicago. The dump, where garbage was burned, was found to be both a statutory public nuisance violation of the Criminal Code and a common law public nuisance. Therefore, the operation was abated by court injunction.

State legal authority to provide refuse services on an area-wide basis is urgently needed in metropolitan areas. A few cities are currently sharing disposal facilities on a fee or prorated cost basis, and some counties have county-wide refuse disposal systems, but State statutes often do not provide the legal authority for establishing and financing refuse disposal services on an area-wide basis. Although communities naturally wish to retain their rights of home rule, and therefore are often reluctant to give up their jurisdiction over such matters, scarcity of disposal sites and the economic advantages of using area-wide refuse disposal systems are forcing more metropolitan areas to consider this approach.

The question which so frequently confronts communities that are considering metropolitan-wide refuse services is, "What level of the local government should provide refuse collection and disposal services?" One of the biggest obstacles to organizing efficient refuse collection and disposal systems in metropolitan areas is the multitude of local governmental units. In Allegheny County, Pennsylvania, for example, there are 129 local political subdivisions. These local political subdivisions may be separated by natural boundaries, such as rivers or mountains, or by the political bounaries of satellite communities that surround a central city. The provision of economical service under such conditions is complicated and may be further hampered by State or international boundaries.

Traditionally, small and large cities have provided their own "total" service. During the last few years, however, there is a trend in metropolitan areas toward each community continuing to provide collection service, with disposal service provided on an area-wide basis. The increasing population and higher population density has resulted in a shortage of land for disposal sites, an increase in the quantities of refuse that must be collected, and longer hauling distances to disposal sites that may even be located beyond the limits of the urbanized area.

Area-wide refuse disposal service is being provided in a few metropolitan areas by special purpose districts, by counties, or by cooperative agreements between cities and other local political subdivisions. Unfortunately, many States do not have enabling legislation, which permits special purpose districts to be formed or counties to provide these services, with the result that investments are needlessly duplicated and some areas are not provided adequate service. The scarcity of disposal sites and the economic advantages gained by using transfer stations with fewer and larger scale disposal facilities are forcing more metropolitan areas to consider the establishment of some type of metropolitan-wide refuse disposal service.

End quote from HEW publication.

See also in Chapter Five the discussion and cases involving nuisance and zoning.

Litter

Litter creates aesthetic problems. In certain circumstances, health problems are created, and the public must pay. A little is known about the motivation of those who are slobs, but virtually nothing is known about the effectiveness of anti-litter campaigns. Keep American Beautiful, Inc., (KAB) is a non-profit organization sponsored by industry that studies the problem and leads the fight against litter. Studies show paper items to compose more than half of the litter, with beverage containers accounting for about 20 percent. But most research data is of marginal utility.

These are some sample annual state expenditures for litter control, along with a per capita cost calculation: Oregon, $600,000 ($0.30); Missouri, $484,000 ($0.11); Massachusetts, $750,000 ($0.14); Texas, $1,900,000 ($0.20); Maine, $220,000 ($0.23); Florida, $850,000 ($0.14). These are some sample per capita municipal expenditures for litter control: New York City, $1.12; Washington, D.C., $2.00; Lincoln, Neb., $1.30; Tucson, $0.56; Atlanta, $1.00, and Philadelphia, $1.00.

Although the above sample is far too small to obtain any reliable figure for a nationwide average, it would come to $280 million dollars ($1.35 per person, combining state and municipal expenses). What is not included is the aesthetic cost, nor the loss of resources, since the level of expenditures clearly is far less than is needed to keep our city streets and countryside clean.

See, Management and Behavioral Science Center, *A Systems Approach to the Problems of Solid Waste and Litter,* Wharton School of Finance and Commerce, University of Pennsylvania, September 1971.

How to Control Litter

1. Anti-litter campaigns may reduce somewhat the amount of litter, but our knowledge is limited. What kinds of campaigns work best would be a useful field of research. Education to increase peer group pressure against littering may be a prerequisite to any meaningful improvement.
2. A tax on all items that become litter would provide funds for control, while giving industry an incentive to produce packaging that minimizes litter.
3. More effective trash containers such as bags, tied at the top, would limit trash spillage.
4. More litter containers at convenient locations would make it easier for people to discard material properly.
5. Anti-litter laws with low fines similar to parking fines but regularly enforced could help, though the danger of selective enforcement against unpopular groups remains.
6. Litter that does collect should be collected regularly.

Following are two cases dealing with (1) an anti-littering ordinance, and (2) an ordinance to restrain dogs.

VAN NUYS PUBLISHING CO. INC., v. CITY OF THOUSAND OAKS

489 P.2d 809 (Calif. Supreme Ct. 1971)

[Edited]

TOBRINER, Associate Justice.

Plaintiff Van Nuys Publishing Company instituted this action to enjoin defendant City of Thousand Oaks from enforcing a newly enacted "anti-littering" ordinance on the ground that the provision on its face and as applied, constituted an unconstitutional abridgement of First Amendment rights.

[W]e have concluded that the city's present, broadly phrased, anti-littering ordinance cannot be squared with established First Amendment precepts.

[T]he City of Thousand Oaks has, by the instant enactment, undertaken an extensive interference with the distribution and circulation of all types of written material; as such, the challenged provision unquestionably exhibits the familiar unconstitutional vice of "overbreadth," proscribing constitutionally protected activity along with "littering."

Section 4 of city ordinance No. 98, provides in full: "No person may throw, cast, distribute, scatter, deposit, pass out, give away, circulate or deliver any handbill, dodger, circular, newspapers, paper, booklet, poster, other printed matter or advertising literature of any kind in the yard or grounds of any house, building structure, on any porch, doorstep vestibule, in any public hallway, or upon any vacant lot or other private property without having first obtained permission of the owner or of an adult resident or occupant thereof," Violators of this ordinance are guilty of a misdemeanor.

The problem of accumulating litter constitutes a major concern for many modern municipalities, and the City of Thousand Oaks' avowed goal in enacting the present legislation—the reduction of litter throughout the community—is, of course, a legitimate and, indeed an increasingly urgent, government objective. In attempting to achieve this unquestionably valid goal through a broad proscription of the dis emination of written literature, however, the instant ordinance collides with the constitutionally enshrined rights of freedom of speech and press.

[T]he present section adopts a "broad brush" solution to litter control and thereby discloses its complete insensitivity to the constitutional freedoms it endangers.

Over 30 years ago in *Schneider v. State* (1939) 308 U.S. 147, 60 S.Ct. 146, 84 L.Ed. 155, the United States Supreme Court rejected as incompatible with the First Amendment a claim that a municipality could broadly curtail the dissemination of written literature in order to control litter, essentially the same proposition now unearthed by the City of Thousand Oaks.

[T]he public convenience in respect of cleanliness of the streets does not justify an exertion of the police power which invades the free communication of information and opinion secured by the Constitution." (308 U.S. at pp. 162-163, 60 S.Ct. at 151.)

A city cannot preserve "privacy" (or attack "litter") by prohibiting all distribution without "prior consent," as the City of Thousand Oaks has attempted to do here. The potentially devasting effect on First Amendment rights of such a provision necessitates that the city adopt a less restrictive alternative method to achieve its legitimate goals.

In sum, though attempting to meet the very real problem of accumulation of litter, the present penal enactment goes substantially beyond what is necessary to achieve the city's anti-littering objective and, in so doing, treads directly on First Amendment rights.

The gravity of the dangers inherent in the instant ordinance is perhaps best appreciated through a brief glance back to our country's revolutionary beginnings. If the present law had been in force in eighteenth century America, the colonies may well have preserved the cleanliness of their streets only at the price of stilling the dissident voices of such pamphleteers as Thomas Paine, Andrew Eliot and John Carmichael. Without the unique contribution of the political pamphlet; our country's founders might have been deprived of Common Sense's vigorous call to "[S]tand forth! Every spot of the old work is overrun with oppression. Freedom hath been hunted round the Globe. Asia and Africa have long expelled her. Europe regards her like a stranger, and England hath given her warning to depart. O! receive the fugitive, and prepare in time an asylum for mankind."[10]

10. Thomas Paine, Common Sense (Philadelphia 1776) in The Writings of Thomas Paine 100-101 (Conway ed. 1894—1896).

TOWN OF NUTLEY (N.J.) v. FORNEY
283 A.2d 142 (1972)

[Edited]

KAPP, J. C. C.

James Forney was tried and convicted in the Nutley Municipal Court on March 24, 1971 for violating section 7-C of an ordinance entitled, "An Ordinance [No. 961] to Regulate the Licensing of Dogs, to Regulate and Prevent the Running at Large of Dogs, and to Authorize the Destruction of Dogs Running at Large," and the amendments and supplements thereto, which, in pertinent part, provide that:

> No person owning, harboring, keeping, or in charge of any dog shall cause, suffer, or allow such dog to soil, defile, defecate on nor commit any nuisance on any common thoroughfare, sidewalk, passageway, bypath, play area, park, or any place where people congregate or walk, or upon any public property whatsoever, or upon any private property without the permission of the owner of said property. The restriction in this section shall not apply to that portion of the street lying between the curb lines, which shall be used to curb such dog under the following conditions:
>
> (1) The person who so curbs such dog shall immediately remove all feces deposited by such dog by any sanitary method approved by the local Health Authority.
>
> (2) The feces removed from the aforementioned designated area shall be disposed of by the person owning, harboring, keeping, or in charge of any dog curbed in accordance with the provisions of this Ordinance, in a sanitary manner approved by the local Health Authority.

He was sentenced to pay a fine of $10, and now appeals pursuant to R. 3:23.

The facts are these: Frank Plinio, a citizen who resides at 204 Walnut Street, Nutley, complained that on March 19, 1971 at 6:35 P.M. he saw Forney in front of 203 Walnut Street with a large Great Dane dog. He observed the dog squat and defecate in the street, about one foot from the curb. When Forney failed to pick up the excrement he called out to defendant that he was in violation of the ordinance, whereupon defendant remarked, "What are you worried about, I'm not doing it on your lawn." Defendant then left the area with the dog without removing the dung, which an officer, who responded to the scene, described as "a large deposit" and who opined that it was the dropping of a large dog.

Defendant here contends that section 7-C, *supra,* offends the equal protection clauses of our Federal and State Constitutions since it contains an unreasonable classification in singling out dogs for this type of regulation, and that it is unrelated in any substantial degree to the health, safety and welfare of the community and its inhabitants. Defendant further alleges that the ordinance fails to provide an adequate standard for the enabling means of disposition of the excrement.

A dog is not a nuisance *per se. Smith v. Costello,* 77 Idaho 205, 290 P.2d 742 (Supp.Ct. 1955), citing 39 Am.Jur. 347 §65; 66 C.J.S. Nuisances §32, at 785. But it has also been of the essence of civilized society, where many individuals live as neighbors, for each to exercise his rights with due regard to the rights of all—*sic utere tuo ut alienum non laedas.* Under such circumstances, this limitation of one's rights, if necessary to protect the rights of all, is not to be adjudged a taking of property without due process of law but, on the contrary, if properly carried out, it is but the use of due process of law for the protection of the rights of all *Mansfield & Swett, Inc.*

v. West Orange, 120 N.J.L. 145, 198 A. 225 (Supp.Ct. 1938); *Annett v. Salsberg,* 135 N.J.L. 122, 50 A.2d 841 (Sup.Ct. 1947); *Mugler v. Kansas,* 123 U.S. 623, 8 S.Ct. 273, 31 L.Ed. 205 (Sup.Ct. 1887); *Hudson County Water Co. v. McCarter,* 209 U.S. 349, 28 S.Ct. 529, 52 L.Ed. 828 (Sup.Ct. 1908).

So it is held, in 62 C.J.S. Municipal Corporations §218, at 402, that

> The right to the possession of dogs in a municipal corporation is subject to the limitation that such possession must not interfere with the health, security, and comfort of the other inhabitants of the corporation. It has generally been held that such possession may be subject to regulation by municipal corporations. The keeping of dogs is subject not only to many general ordinances against animals, but has also been made the subject of many special regulations.

Is this ordinance within the competency of the municipality to enact?

There was a time when dog owners loved their animals as pets, but today we find that such large dogs are being employed extensively for security purposes as well, because of the alarming increase in crimes of violence. The tons of solid waste and urine that are daily deposited by dogs have undeniably fouled our streets, our walks and parks to the extent that it has become well-nigh intolerable, threatening the health and safety of our citizens. The admixture of excrement with other litter, in and about our public walks and highways, has desecrated the landscape. Dog droppings have become a scourge, a form of environmental pollution, no less dangerous and degrading than the poisons that we exude and dump into our air and water. Persons stepping into dog feces on sidewalks or in streets while crossing, or when entering or alighting from automobiles, can easily carry it on their shoes, and thence into their homes. Infants crawling about a rug or floor upon which such animal feces have been deposited may ingest them, since young children, especially babies, are known to be constantly placing their fingers into their mouths. Following a heavy rainfall, dog feces are known to find their way into sewers, along with other litter and debris. In the Town of Nutley the sewers have a direct connection to the streams and estuaries of the Passaic River, a river which has been designated by environmentalists as one of the ten most polluted rivers in the country.

There is abundant medical authority to the effect that when the eggs or larva of the Toxocara Canis worm, which is found in the dog feces, infects a human it courses through the body and may well result in an attack upon a vital organism, such as the brain, lungs, liver or eyes.

Adverting now to the appellant's assault upon the ordinance, we find that it is bottomed upon the authority conferred by N.J.S.A. 40:48-2, which provides that

> Any municipality may make, amend, repeal and enforce such other ordinances, regulations, rules and by-laws not contrary to the laws of this state or of the United States, as it may deem necessary and proper for the good government, order and protection of persons and property, and for the preservation of the public health, safety and welfare of the municipality and its inhabitants, and as may be necessary to carry into effect the powers and duties conferred and imposed by this subtitle, or by any law.

In considering such municipal measures as are designed to deal with problems of public health, regard must be had for the presumptive validity of an ordinance. *Zampieri v. River Vale Tp.,* 29 N.J. 599, 152 A.2d 28 (1959); *Mullin v. Ringle,* 27 N.J. 250, 142 A.2d 216 (1958). With respect to the validity of such regulations concerning dogs, all presumptions are likewise in favor of validity. 62 C.J.S., Municipal Corporations §218, at 403, citing *State v. Mueller,* 220 Wis. 435, 265 N.W. 103 (Supp.Ct.

1936); Regard must also be had for the doctrine that the governing body is entitled to wide latitude in its efforts at necessary municipal regulation and that the enactment that finally issues forth should not be disturbed unless it is palpably unreasonable or in conflict with some superior statutory or constitutional limitation. Nor may we lose sight of the mandate in N.J. Constitution (1947), Art. IV, §VII, par. 11, to liberally construe legislation concerning municipal power. *Marangi Bros. v. Board of Comm'rs, Ridgewood,* 33 N.J.Super. 294, 110 A.2d 131 (App.Div. 1954).

In the case of *Jones v. Haridor Realty Co.,* 37 N.J. 384, 181 A.2d 481 (1962) Justice Francis said:

> One of the basic functions of government is to safeguard the health, safety and welfare of its people. Upon the appearance of conditions detrimental to their welfare, it has the duty to apply remedial measures. The courts in turn are required to respect and sustain such efforts as an exercise of the legislative police power so long as they are not clearly arbitrary and are reasonably related to the objective sought to be attained. [at 393, 181 A.2d at 485.]

While such a regulation, albeit lawful, may be considered by some to be drastic in its operation, yet the court is not at liberty to substitute its judgment for that of the municipality. *Peoples Rapid Transit v. Atlantic City,* 105 N.J.L. 286, 144 A. 630 (Sup.Ct. 1929), aff'd, *Parlor Car DeLuxe Coach Co. v. Atlantic City,* 106 N.J.L. 587, 149 A. 893 (E. & A. 1930); *Newark v. Charlton Holding Co.,* 9 N.J. Super. 433, 74 A.2d 641 (Cty.Ct. 1950). All such questions of policy, wisdom and expediency are for the legislative and not the judicial branch of the government. *Jones v. Haridor Realty Corp., supra.*;"The wisdom of legislative action is reviewable only at the polls. The judicial role is tightly circumscribed." *Kozesnik v. Montgomery Tp.,* 24 N.J. 154, 167, 131 A.2d 1, 8 (1957). Furthermore, merely because an ordinance is burdensome or distasteful to some individuals will not render it arbitrary or unreasonable *per se.*

Town of Nutley v. Forney

In the means employed to advance the public health and safety, the legislative authority has broad discretion. *Amodio v. Board of Comm'rs, West New York,* 133 N.J.L. 220, 43 A.2d 889 (Sup.Ct. 1945). A state may grant to cities and towns the right to exercise such parts of the police power as to dogs as it may deem proper. 4 Am.Jur.2d, Animals, §23, at 269. It is apparent therefore that the ordinance itself bears a substantial relation to the security of the public health.

Defendant next claims that the ordinance is invalid in that it contains an unreasonable classification in singling out dogs for this type of regulation. Not so. The governing body is endowed with a high degree of discretion where, as here, the legislation is inspired by considerations of public health. Dogs are generally made the subject matter of "special and peculiar regulations." 4 Am.Jur.2d, Animals, §3, at 252. And this "without depriving their owners of any constitutional right." Id. §6, at 254; §23, at 269, citing *Nicchia v. New York,* 254 U.S. 228, 41 S.Ct. 103, 65 L.Ed. 235, 13 A.L.R. 826 (1920); *Sentell v. New Orleans & C. R. Co.,* 166 U.S. 698, 17 S.Ct. 693, 41 L.Ed. 1169 (1897); *Simpson v. Los Angeles,* 40 Cal.2d 271, 253 P.2d 464, app. dism. 346 U.S. 802, 74 S.Ct. 37, 98 L.Ed. 333, reh. den. 346 U.S. 880), 74 S.Ct. 118, 98 L.Ed. 387 (Sup.Ct. 1953); *McPhail v. Denver,* 59 Colo. 248, 149 P. 257 (Sup.Ct. 1915); *Shadoan v. Barnett,* 217 Ky. 205, 289 S.W. 204, 49 A.L.R. 843 (Ct.App. 1926); *Blair v. Forehand,* 100 Mass. 136 (Sup.Ct. 1868); *Van Horn v. People,* 46 Mich. 183, 9 N.W. 246 (Sup.Ct. 1881); *Julienne v. Jackson,* 69 Miss. 34, 10 So. 43 (Sup.Ct. 1891); *Carthage v. Rhodes,* 101 Mo. 175, 14 S.W. 181 (Sup.Ct. 1890); *State v. Harrell,* 203 N.C. 210, 165 S.E. 551 (Sup.Ct. 1932); *Dickinson v. Thress,* 69 N.D. 748, 290 N.W. 653 (Sup.Ct. 1940); *Commonwealth v. Haldeman,* 288 Pa. 81, 135 A. 651 (Sup.Ct. 1927); *State v. Anderson,* 144 Tenn. 546, 234 S.W. 768, 19 A.L.R. 180 (Sup.Ct. 1920). Annotation: 49 A.L.R. 847.

The defendant further claims that the ordinance is deficient because it fails to set forth a definitive standard for the disposition and removal of the dog feces, except to declare that it shall be "in a sanitary manner approved by the local Health Authority." This contention is untenable. It does not require any degree of ingenuity to understand that the measure mandates the owner to remove the droppings of his dog from the prohibited area, and to dispose of them. It is fair to assume that a master who truly values his pet will not find it to be unduly oppressive or demeaning to remove the excrement, encase it in a wrapper or a container and dispose of it in a garbage receptacle or in some other suitable manner. See *Brandon v. Montclair,* 124 N.J.L. 135, 11 A.2d 304 (Sup.Ct. 1940); aff'd 125 N.J.L. 367, 15 A.2d 598 (E. & A. 1940), where Justice Heher rightly noted that

> A statute often speaks as plainly by inference, and by means of the purpose which underlies it, as in any other manner. That which is clearly implied is as much a part of the law as that which is expressed. [at 143, 11 A.2d at 309.]

See also *West Jersey and Seashore R. R. Co. v. Board of Public Utility Comm'rs,* 87 N.J.L. 170, 94 A. 57 (E. & A. 1915).

In *Annett v. Salsberg, supra,* Justice Wachenfeld declared that

> The prohibition contained in the instant law [R.S. 26:3B-7, L. 1945, c. 192] is palpably in the interest of public health. The statute bears a direct and substantial relation to it and is obviously a regulation designed to protect the community from the ravages of disease and contagion. It is reasonable, advisable and necessary and therefore, we think, unassailable.
>
> The statute is not so vague as to make it unconstitutional. Its mandates so clearly express the acts condemned that the ordinary person could intelligently and easily conclude what is prohibited. Reasonable certainty fulfills the constitutional requirement and liberal effect is always given to the legislative intent, where possible.

The principle is also aptly expressed by Justice Heher in *Mansfield & Swett, Inc., v. West Orange, supra:*

> The state possesses the inherent authority—it antedates the Constitution—to resort, in the building and expansion of its community life, to such measures as may be necessary to secure the essential common material and moral needs. The public welfare is of prime importance; and the correlative restrictions upon individual rights—either of person or of property—are incidents of the social order, considered a negligible loss compared with the resultant advantages to the community as a whole. Planning confined to the common need is inherent in the authority to create the municipality itself. It is as old as government itself; it is of the very essence of civilized society.

Now, with respect to the claim of unreasonableness of that part of the ordinance which mandates that the owner shall curb his dog in the street between the curb lines: in *McGonnell v. Comm'rs of Orange,* 98 N.J.L. 642, 121 A. 135 (Supp.Ct. 1923), the court declared:

> The power of a city council or other body to pass ordinances relating to the various matters entrusted by the legislature to its jurisdiction, carries with it the implication (expressed in many cases) that such ordinances must be reasonable. Every intendment is made in favor of their reasonable character, and to support them a construction will be placed on them which will make them reasonable rather than unreasonable; but the question of their reasonable character is for the court, which will not hesitate to declare them void if plainly unreasonable. This is familiar law, acted on in a multitude of cases, in many of which the court confined its action to the particular part of the ordinance shown to be unreasonable, leaving the rest to stand. Some of the cases fol-

low: *Long v. Jersey City,* 37 N.J.L. 348, 351; *Pennsylvania Railroad Co. v. Jersey City,* 47 N.J.L. 286, 288, in the Court of Errors and Appeals , where Chief Justice Beasley said in the opinion: "If this bylaw [ordinance] be subject to this imputation [that it is unreasonable] there can be no doubt that it would be the duty of this court to pronounce it a nullity."

Again in *Wagman v. Trenton,* 102 N.J.L. 492, 134 A. 115 (Sup.Ct. 1926), we find:

> Where, as here, the subject-matter of the ordinance is within the police power of the city and the ordinance is adopted by the proper legislative body of the city, the presumption is (until the contrary be shown) that the ordinance is reasonable. The question of reasonableness is a question of fact, and the burden of proof is upon the prosecutor who attacks the ordinance to show its unreasonableness. The court should not interfere unless it is shown that the ordinance, either upon the fact of its provisions or by reason of its operation in the circumstances under which it is to take effect, is unreasonable or oppressive. *Falco v. Atlantic City,* 99 N.J.L. 19, 122 A. 610; *North Jersey Street Railway Co. v. Jersey City,* 75 N.J.L. 349, 67 A. 1072.

Town of Nutley v. Forney

In the leading case on the exercise and the limitations of police power, Justice Heher in *New Jersey Good Humor, Inc. v. Bradley Beach,* 124 N.J.L. 162, 11 A.2d 113 (E. & A. 1940), stated:

> The restraints and regulations imposed for the general good and welfare must needs have the virtue of reasonableness. There cannot be, in the name of police regulation, an unreasonable and oppressive curtailment of personal or property rights. [at 168, 11 A.2d at 117.]

The public right of reasonable regulation for the common good and welfare is denominated as the police power. The exertion of this sovereign authority is controlled by constitutional and statutory delineation. The restraint thus laid upon individual rights—either of person or of property—may not go beyond the public need; and the means employed must be both reasonable and appropriate to that end.

If a person is required to exercise or walk his dog only in the street, it exposes him and his dog heedlessly and unnecessarily to the dangers of vehicular traffic and therefore runs counter to the public safety. This is particularly true where the owner resides in a congested area on a main thoroughfare where the flow of traffic may be unusually heavy and the likelihood of injury readily foreseeable. So long as the owner of the dog is required to remove its feces, it is of no consequence that they may be dropped between the curb lines or elsewhere.

That part of the measure which mandates that the owner shall curb his dog in the street between the curb lines is unreasonable, arbitrary and dangerous to life and limb and therefore invalid.

However, since such invalidity of a portion of an ordinance does not render another part invalid, where the two parts are separable and are not dependent on each other, *State v. Western Union Telegraph Co.,* 13 N.J. Super. 172, 80 A.2d 342 (Cty.Ct. 1951); *Affiliated Distillers Brands Corp., v. Sills,* 56 N.J. 251, 265 A.2d 809 (1970); 62 C.J.S., Municipal Corporations §218, at 403, we have determined that the underlying purpose of the ordinance, *i.e.,* to remove the excrement and to dispose of it in a sanitary manner is a valid exercise of the municipal power inasmuch as it is designed to safeguard the health and wellbeing of the populace.

Affirmed.

National Commission on Materials Policy

The National Commission on Materials Policy is made up of seven members appointed by the President, with the advice and consent of the Senate. The Commission is to submit a report by June 30, 1973 and terminate within 90 days after the report is submitted.

To date, the commission has identified the segments of American society with an interest in the development of a comprehensive National Materials Policy and is participating with the Executive Branch, industry, the academic and scientific communities, and environmental and consumer groups in discussions on what is needed.

The commission formed the NCMP Inter-Agency Steering Committee which includes one member from the eight Government agencies with a direct interest. The agencies are the Atomic Energy Commission; Departments of Agriculture, Commerce, Interior, and State; the Environmental Protection Agency; the Office of Emergency Preparedness, and the Council on International Economic Policy.

The Commission has asked the federal agencies to supply basic data on the supply and demands for natural resources as far ahead as 2000.

NCMP is working with over 200 trade associations such as the American Mining Congress, Automobile Manufacturers Association, Institute of Scrap Iron and Steel, National Association of Secondary Material Industries, American Ceramics Institute, American Forestry Association, American Paper Institute, American Chemical Society, American Petroleum Institute, and the National Solid Waste Management Association. Thus industry has the opportunity to shape policy.

The commission plans to sponsor eight forums in cooperation with the academic community in an effort to obtain "realistic input." The forums to be held in the spring of 1972 at the University of California, Los Angeles; Pennsylvania State University; Massachusetts Institute of Technology; Stanford University; the Colorado University School of Mines; University of Texas, Austin; University of Michigan, and Georgia Institute of Technology. Each of the schools will hold a three to four-day session and bring together between 50 and 100 academic experts to discuss topics assigned by the commission and to attempt to develop realistic solutions. The universities will be instructed that the forums must be interdisciplinary and include engineering scientists, economists, political scientists, social scientists, lawyers, and medical men.

Although the academic community and the scientific communities overlap, the NCMP is working with the scientific community through the National Academy of Sciences and the National Academy of Engineering because this will assure that nonacademic scientists will be included, the commission said. The scientific community program is not final.

NCMP also is working on a program with labor, particularly the AFL-CIO, under the guidance of Commissioner Lee Minten, President emeritus of the Glass Bottle Blowers Association. Additional programs with environmental and consumer groups are being worked out to insure their input will be included in the discussions. *See also,* BNA *Environment Reporter* 51:5601.

APPENDIX — Chapter Two

The Solid Waste Disposal Act as amended

Title II of Public Law 89-272, Oct. 20. 1965
and Public Law 95-512, Oct. 26, 1970

AN ACT To authorize a research and development program with respect to solid-waste disposal, and for other purposes.

* * * * *

TITLE II—SOLID WASTE DISPOSAL [1]

SHORT TITLE

SEC. 201. This title (hereinafter referred to as "this Act") may be cited as the "Solid Waste Disposal Act".

FINDINGS AND PURPOSES

SEC. 202. (a) The Congress finds—

(1) that the continuing technological progress and improvement in methods of manufacture, packaging, and marketing of consumer products has resulted in an ever-mounting increase, and in a change in the characteristics, of the mass of material discarded by the purchaser of such products;

(2) that the economic and population growth of our Nation, and the improvements in the standard of living enjoyed by our population, have required increased industrial production to meet our needs, and have made necessary the demolition of old buildings, the construction of new buildings, and the provision of highways and other avenues of transportation, which, together with related industrial, commercial, and agricultural operations, have resulted in a rising tide of scrap, discarded, and waste materials;

(3) that the continuing concentration of our population in expanding metropolitan and other urban areas has presented these communities with serious financial, management, intergovernmental, and technical problems in the disposal of solid wastes resulting from the industrial, commercial, domestic, and other activities carried on in such areas;

(4) that inefficient and improper methods of disposal of solid wastes result in scenic blights, create serious hazards to the public health, including pollution of air and water resources, accident hazards, and increase in rodent and insect vectors of disease, have an adverse effect on land values, create public nuisances, otherwise interfere with community life and development;

(5) that the failure or inability to salvage and reuse such materials economically results in the unnecessary waste and depletion of our natural resources; and

(6) that while the collection and disposal of solid wastes should continue to be primarily the function of State, regional, and local agencies, the problems of waste disposal as set forth above have become a matter national in scope and in concern and necessitate Federal action through financial and technical assistance and leadership in the development, demonstration, and application of new and improved methods and processes to reduce the amount of waste and unsalvageable materials and to provide for proper and economical solid-waste disposal practices.

(b) [2] The purposes of this Act therefore are—

(1) to promote the demonstration, construction, and application of solid waste management and resource recovery systems which preserve and enhance the quality or air, water, and land resources;

(2) to provide technical and financial assistance to States and local governments and interstate agencies in the planning and development of resource recovery and solid waste disposal programs;

(3) to promote a national research and development program for improved management techniques, more effective organizational arrangements, and new and improved methods of collection, separation, recovery, and recycling of solid wastes, and the environmentally safe disposal of nonrecoverable residues;

(4) to provide for the promulgation of guidelines for solid waste collection, transport, separation, recovery, and disposal systems; and

(5) to provide for training grants in occupations involving the design, operation, and maintenance of solid waste disposal systems.

DEFINITIONS

SEC. 203.[3] When used in this Act:

(1) [3a] The term "Secretary" means the Secretary of Health, Education, and Welfare; except that such term means the Secretary of the Interior with respect to problems of solid waste resulting from the extraction, processing, or utilization of minerals or fossil fuels where the generation, production, or reuse of such waste is or may be controlled within the extraction, processing, or utilization facility or facilities and where such control is a feature of the technology or economy of the operation of such facility or facilities.

(2) The term "State" means a State, the District of Columbia, the Commonwealth of Puerto Rico, the Virgin Islands, Guam, and American Samoa.

(3) The term "interstate agency" means an agency of two or more municipalities in different States, or an agency established by two or more States, with authority to provide for the disposal of solid wastes and serving two or more municipalities located in different States.

[1] Title I of P.L. 89–272 amended the Clean Air Act (P.L. 88–206).

[2] Sec. 202(b) amended by sec. 101, P.L. 91–512.
[3] Sec. 203 amended by sec. 102, P.L. 91–512.
[3a] Reorganization Plan Number 3 of 1970 transferred authority to the Administrator, Environmental Protection Agency.

(4) The term "solid waste" means garbage, refuse, and other discarded solid materials, including solid-waste materials resulting from industrial, commercial, and agricultural operations, and from community activities, but does not include solids or dissolved material in domestic sewage or other significant pollutants in water resources, such as silt, dissolved or suspended solids in industrial waste water effluents, dissolved materials in irrigation return flows or other common water pollutants.

(5) The term "solid-waste disposal" means the collection, storage, treatment, utilization, processing, or final disposal of solid waste.

(6) The term "construction," with respect to any project of construction under this act, means (A) the erection or building of new structures and acquisition of lands or interests therein, or the acquisition, replacement, expansion, remodeling, alteration, modernization, or extension of existing structures, and (B) the acquisition and installation of initial equipment of, or required in connection with, new or newly acquired structures or the expanded, remodeled, altered, modernized or extended part of existing structures (including trucks and other motor vehicles, and tractors, cranes, and other machinery) necessary for the proper utilization and operation of the facility after completion of the project; and includes preliminary planning to determine the economic and engineering feasibility and the public health and safety aspects of the project, the engineering, architectural, legal, fiscal, and economic investigations and studies, and any surveys, designs, plans, working drawings, specifications, and other action necessary for the carrying out of the project, and (C) the inspection and supervision of the process of carrying out the project to completion.

(7) the term "municipality" means a city, town, borough, county, parish, district, or other public body created by or pursuant to State law with responsibility for the planning or administration of solid waste disposal, or an Indian tribe.

(8) The term "intermunicipal agency" means an agency established by two or more municipalities with responsibility for planning or administration of solid waste disposal.

(9) The term "recovered resources" means materials or energy recovered from solid wastes.

(10) The term "resource recovery system" means a solid waste management system which provides for collection, separation, recycling, and recovery of solid wastes, including disposal of nonrecoverable waste residues.

RESEARCH, DEMONSTRATIONS, TRAINING, AND OTHER ACTIVITIES

SEC. 204.[4] (a) The Secretary shall conduct, and encourage, cooperate with, and render financial and other assistance to appropriate public (whether Federal, State, interstate, or local) authorities, agencies, and institutions, private agencies and institutions, and individuals in the conduct of, and promote the coordination of, research, investigations, experiments, training, demonstrations, surveys, and studies relating to—

(1) any adverse health and welfare effects of the release into the environment of material present in solid waste, and methods to eliminate such effects;

(2) the operation and financing of solid waste disposal programs;

(3) the reduction of the amount of such waste and unsalvageable waste materials;

(4) the development and application of new and improved methods of collecting and disposing of solid waste and processing and recovering materials and energy from solid wastes; and

(5) the identification of solid waste components and potential materials and energy recoverable from such waste components.

(b) In carrying out the provisions of the preceding subsection, the Secretary is authorized to—

(1) collect and make available, through publications and other appropriate means, the results of and other information pertaining to, such research and other activities, including appropriate recommendations in connection therewith;

(2) cooperate with public and private agencies, institutions, and organizations, and with any industries involved, in the preparation and the conduct of such research and other activities; and

(3) make grants-in-aid to public or private agencies and institutions and to individuals for research, training projects, surveys, and demonstrations (including construction of facilities), and provide for the conduct of research, training, surveys, and demonstrations by contract with public or private agencies and institutions and with individuals; and such contracts for research or demonstrations or both (including contracts for construction) may be made in accordance with and subject to the limitations provided with respect to research contracts of the military departments in title 10, United States Code, section 2353, except that the determination, approval, and certification required thereby shall be made by the Secretary.

(c) Any grant, agreement, or contract made or entered into under this section shall contain provisions effective to insure that all information, uses, processes, patents and other developments resulting from any activity undertaken pursuant to such grant, agreement, or contract will be made readily available on fair and equitable terms to industries utilizing methods of solid-waste disposal and industries engaging in furnishing devices, facilities, equipment, and supplies to be used in connection with solid-waste disposal. In carrying out the provisions of this section, the Secretary and each department, agency, and officer of the Federal Government having functions or duties under this Act shall make use of and adhere to the Statement of Government Patent Policy which was promulgated by the President in his memorandum of October 10, 1963. (3 CFR, 1963 Supp., p. 238.)

SPECIAL STUDY AND DEMONSTRATION PROJECTS ON RECOVERY OF USEFUL ENERGY AND MATERIALS

SEC. 205.[5] (a) The Secretary shall carry out an investigation and study to determine—

(1) means of recovering materials and energy from solid waste, recommended uses of such materials and energy for national or international welfare, including identification of potential markets for such recovered resources, and the impact of distribution of such resources on existing markets;

(2) changes in current product characteristics and production and packaging practices which would reduce the amount of solid waste;

[4] Sec. 204(a) amended by Sec. 103, P.L. 91–512.

[5] Sec. 205 added by sec. 104(a) of P.L. 91–512.

(3) methods of collection, separation, and containerization which will encourage efficient utilization of facilities and contribute to more effective programs of reduction, reuse, or disposal of wastes;

(4) the use of Federal procurement to develop market demand for recovered resources;

(5) recommended incentives (including Federal grants, loans, and other assistance) and disincentives to accelerate the reclamation or recycling of materials from solid wastes, with special emphasis on motor vehicle hulks;

(6) the effect of existing public policies, including subsidies and economic incentives and disincentives, percentage depletion allowances, capital gains treatment and other tax incentives and disincentives, upon the recycling and reuse of materials, and the likely effect of the modification or elimination of such incentives and disincentives upon the reuse, recycling and conservation of such materials; and

(7) the necessity and method of imposing disposal or other charges on packaging, containers, vehicles, and other manufactured goods, which charges would reflect the cost of final disposal, the value of recoverable components of the item, and any social costs associated with nonrecycling or uncontrolled disposal of such items.

The Secretary shall from time to time, but not less frequently than annually, report the results of such investigation and study to the President and the Congress.

(b) The Secretary is also authorized to carry out demonstration projects to test and demonstrate methods and techniques developed pursuant to subsection (a).

(c) Section 204 (b) and (c) shall be applicable to investigations, studies, and projects carried out under this section.

INTERSTATE AND INTERLOCAL COOPERATION

SEC. 206.[6] The Secretary shall encourage cooperative activities by the States and local governments in connection with solid-waste disposal programs; encourage where practicable, interstate, interlocal, and regional planning for, and the conduct of, interstate, interlocal, and regional solid-waste disposal programs; and encourage the enactment of improved and, so far as practicable, uniform State and local laws governing solid-waste disposal.

GRANTS FOR STATE, INTERSTATE, AND LOCAL PLANNING

SEC. 207.[7] (a) The Secretary may from time to time, upon such terms and conditions consistent with this section as he finds appropriate to carry out the purposes of this Act, make grants to State, interstate, municipal, and intermunicipal agencies, and organizations composed of public officials which are eligible for assistance under section 701(g) of the Housing Act of 1954, of not to exceed 66⅔ per centum of the cost in the case of an application with respect to an area including only one municipality, and not to exceed 75 per centum of the cost in any other case, of—

(1) making surveys of solid waste disposal practices and problems within the jurisdictional areas of such agencies and

(2) developing and revising solid waste disposal plans as part of regional environmental protection systems for such areas, providing for recycling or recovery of materials from wastes whenever possible and including planning for the reuse of solid waste disposal areas and studies of the effect and relationship of solid waste disposal practices on areas adjacent to waste disposal sites,

(3) developing proposals for projects to be carried out pursuant to section 208 of this Act, or

(4) planning programs for the removal and processing of abandoned motor vehicle hulks.

(b) Grants pursuant to this section may be made upon application therefor which—

(1) designates or establishes a single agency (which may be an interdepartmental agency) as the sole agency for carrying out the purposes of this section for the area involved;

(2) indicates the manner in which provision will be made to assure full consideration of all aspects of planning essential to areawide planning for proper and effective solid waste disposal consistent with the protection of the public health and welfare, including such factors as population growth, urban and metropolitan development, land use planning, water pollution control, air pollution control, and the feasibility of regional disposal and resource recovery programs;

(3) sets forth plans for expenditure of such grant, which plans provide reasonable assurance of carrying out the purposes of this section;

(4) provides for submission of such reports of the activities of the agency in carrying out the purposes of this section, in such form and containing such information, as the Secretary may from time to time find necessary for carrying out the purposes of this section and for keeping such records and affording such access thereto as he may find necessary; and

(5) provides for such fiscal-control and fund-accounting procedures as may be necessary to assure proper disbursement of and accounting for funds paid to the agency under this section.

(c) The Secretary shall make a grant under this section only if he finds that there is satisfactory assurance that the planning of solid waste disposal will be coordinated, so far as practicable, with and not duplicate other related State, interstate, regional, and local planning activities, including those financed in part with funds pursuant to section 701 of the Housing Act of 1954.

GRANTS FOR RESOURCE RECOVERY SYSTEMS AND IMPROVED SOLID WASTE DISPOSAL FACILITIES

SEC. 208.[8] (a) The Secretary is authorized to make grants pursuant to this section to any State, municipal, or interstate or intermunicipal agency for the demonstration of resource recovery systems or for the construction of new or improved solid waste disposal facilities.

(b)(1) Any grant under this section for the demonstration of a resource recovery system may be made only if it (A) is consistent with any plans which meet the requirements of section 207(b)(2) of this Act; (B) is consistent with the guidelines recommended pursuant to section 209 of this Act; (C) is designed to provide areawide resource recovery systems consistent with the purposes of this Act, as determined by the Secretary, pursuant to regulations promulgated under subsection (d) of this section; and (D) provides an equitable system for distributing the costs associated with construc-

[6] Previous sec. 205 redesignated as sec. 206 by sec. 104(a) of P.L. 91–512.

[7] Sec. 207 added by sec. 104(b) of P.L. 91–512.

[8] Sec. 208 added by sec. 104(b) P.L. 91–512.

tion, operation, and maintenance of any resource recovery system among the users of such system.

(2) The Federal share for any project to which paragraph (1) applies shall not be more than 75 percent.

(c) (1) A grant under this section for the construction of a new or improved solid waste disposal facility may be made only if—

(A) a State or interstate plan for solid waste disposal has been adopted which applies to the area involved, and the facility to be constructed (i) is consistent with such plan, (ii) is included in a comprehensive plan for the area involved which is satisfactory to the Secretary for the purposes of this Act, and (iii) is consistent with the guidelines recommended under section 209, and

(B) the project advances the state of the art by applying new and improved techniques in reducing the environmental impact of solid waste disposal, in achieving recovery of energy or resources, or in recycling useful materials.

(2) The Federal share for any project to which paragraph (1) applies shall be not more than 50 percent in the case of a project serving an area which includes only one municipality, and not more than 75 percent in any other case.

(d) (1) The Secretary, within ninety days after the date of enactment of the Resource Recovery Act of 1970, shall promulgate regulations establishing a procedure for awarding grants under this section which—

(A) provides that projects will be carried out in communities of varying sizes, under such conditions as will assist in solving the community waste problems of urban-industrial centers, metropolitan regions, and rural areas, under representative geographic and environmental conditions; and

(B) provides deadlines for submission of, and action on, grant requests.

(2) In taking action on applications for grants under this section, consideration shall be given by the Secretary (A) to the public benefits to be derived by the construction and the propriety of Federal aid in making such grant; (B) to the extent applicable, to the economic and commercial viability of the project (including contractual arrangements with the private sector to market any resources recovered); (C) to the potential of such project for general application to community solid waste disposal problems; and (D) to the use by the applicant of comprehensive regional or metropolitan area planning.

(e) A grant under this section—

(1) may be made only in the amount of the Federal share of (A) the estimated total design and construction costs, plus (B) in the case of a grant to which subsection (b) (1) applies, the first-year operation and maintenance costs;

(2) may not be provided for land acquisition or (except as otherwise provided in paragraph (1) (B)) for operating or maintenance costs;

(3) may not be made until the applicant has made provision satisfactory to the Secretary for proper and efficient operation and maintenance of the project (subject to paragraph (1) (B)); and

(4) may be made subject to such conditions and requirements, in addition to those provided in this section, as the Secretary may require to properly carry out his functions pursuant to this Act.

For purposes of paragraph (1), the non-Federal share may be in any form, including, but not limited to, lands or interests therein needed for the project or personal property or services, the value of which shall be determined by the Secretary.

(f) (1) Not more than 15 percent of the total of funds authorized to be appropriated under section 216(a) (3) for any fiscal year to carry out this section shall be granted under this section for projects in any one State.

(2) The Secretary shall prescribe by regulation the manner in which this subsection shall apply to a grant under this section for a project in an area which includes all or part of more than one State.

RECOMMENDED GUIDELINES

SEC. 209.[9] (a) The Secretary shall, in cooperation with appropriate State, Federal, interstate, regional, and local agencies, allowing for public comment by other interested parties, as soon as practicable after the enactment of the Resource Recovery Act of 1970, recommend to appropriate agencies and publish in the Federal Register guidelines for solid waste recovery, collection, separation, and disposal systems (including systems for private use), which shall be consistent with public health and welfare, and air and water quality standards and adaptable to appropriate land-use plans. Such guidelines shall apply to such systems whether on land or water and shall be revised from time to time.

(b) (1) The Secretary shall, as soon as practicable, recommend model codes, ordinances, and statutes which are designed to implement this section and the purposes of this Act.

(2) The Secretary shall issue to appropriate Federal, interstate, regional, and local agencies information on technically feasible solid waste collection, separation, disposal, recycling, and recovery methods, including data on the cost of construction, operation, and maintenance of such methods.

GRANTS OR CONTRACTS FOR TRAINING PROJECTS.

SEC. 210.[10] (a) The Secretary is authorized to make grants to, and contracts with, any eligible organization. For purposes of this section the term "eligible organization" means a State or interstate agency, a municipality, educational institution, and any other organization which is capable of effectively carrying out a project which may be funded by grant under subsection (b) of this section.

(b) (1) Subject to the provisions of paragraph (2), grants or contracts may be made to pay all or a part of the costs, as may be determined by the Secretary, of any project operated or to be operated by an eligible organization, which is designed—

(A) to develop, expand, or carry out a program (which may combine training, education, and employment) for training persons for occupations involving the management, supervision, design, operation, or maintenance of solid waste disposal and resources recovery equipment and facilities; or

(B) to train instructors and supervisory personnel to train or supervise persons in occupations involving the design, operation, and maintenance of solid waste disposal and resource recovery equipment and facilities.

(2) A grant or contract authorized by paragraph (1) of this subsection may be made only upon application to the Secretary at such time or times and containing such information as he may prescribe, except that no such application shall be approved unless it provides for the same procedures and reports (and access to such re-

[9] Sec. 209 added by sec. 104(b) P.L. 91–512.
[10] Sec. 210 added by sec. 104(b) P.L. 91–512.

ports and to other records) as is required by section 207(b) (4) and (5) with respect to applications made under such section.

(c) The Secretary shall make a complete investigation and study to determine—

(1) the need for additional trained State and local personnel to carry out plans assisted under this Act and other solid waste and resource recovery programs;

(2) means of using existing training programs to train such personnel; and

(3) the extent and nature of obstacles to employment and occupational advancement in the solid waste disposal and resource recovery field which may limit either available manpower or the advancement of personnel in such field.

He shall report the results of such investigation and study, including his recommendations to the President and the Congress not later than one year after enactment of this Act.

APPLICABILITY OF SOLID WASTE DISPOSAL GUIDELINES TO EXECUTIVE AGENCIES

SEC. 211.[11] (a)(1) If—

(A) an Executive agency (as defined in section 105 of title 5, United States Code) has jurisdiction over any real property or facility the operation or administration of which involves such agency in solid waste disposal activities, or

(B) such an agency enters into a contract with any person for the operation by such person of any Federal property or facility, and the performance of such contract involves such person in solid waste disposal activities,

then such agency shall insure compliance with the guidelines recommended under section 209 and the purposes of this Act in the operation or administration of such property or facility, or the performance of such contract, as the case may be.

(2) Each Executive agency which conducts any activity—

(A) which generates solid waste, and

(B) which, if conducted by a person other than such agency, would require a permit or license from such agency in order to dispose of such solid waste,

shall insure compliance with such guidelines and the purposes of this Act in conducting such activity.

(3) Each Executive agency which permits the use of Federal property for purposes of disposal of solid waste shall insure compliance with such guidelines and the purposes of this Act in the disposal of such waste.

(4) The President shall prescribe regulations to carry out this subsection.

(b) Each Executive agency which issues any license or permit for disposal of solid waste shall, prior to the issuance of such license or permit, consult with the Secretary to insure compliance with guidelines recommended under section 209 and the purposes of this Act.

NATIONAL DISPOSAL SITES STUDY

SEC. 212.[12] The Secretary shall submit to the Congress no later than two years after the date of enactment of the Resource Recovery Act of 1970, a comprehensive report and plan for the creation of a system of national disposal sites for the storage and disposal of hazardous wastes, including radioactive, toxic chemical, biological, and other wastes which may endanger public health or welfare. Such report shall include: (1) a list of materials which should be subject to disposal in any such site; (2) current methods of disposal of such materials; (3) recommended methods of reduction, neutralization, recovery, or disposal of such materials; (4) an inventory of possible sites including existing land or water disposal sites operated or licensed by Federal agencies; (5) an estimate of the cost of developing and maintaining sites including consideration of means for distributing the short- and long-term costs of operating such sites among the users thereof; and (6) such other information as may be appropriate.

LABOR STANDARDS

SEC. 213.[13] No grant for a project of construction under this Act shall be made unless the Secretary finds that the application contains or is supported by reasonable assurance that all laborers and mechanics employed by contractors or subcontractors on projects of the type covered by the Davis-Bacon Act, as amended (40 U.S.C. 276a—276a–5), will be paid wages at rates not less than those prevailing on similar work in the locality as determined by the Secretary of Labor in accordance with that Act; and the Secretary of Labor shall have with respect to the labor standards specified in this section the authority and functions set forth in Reorganization Plan Numbered 14 of 1950 (15 F.R. 3176; 5 U.S.C. 133z–15) and section 2 of the Act of June 13, 1934, as amended (40 U.S.C. 276c).

OTHER AUTHORITY NOT AFFECTED

SEC. 214. This Act shall not be construed as superseding or limiting the authorities and responsibilities, under any other provisions of law, of the Secretary of Health, Education, and Welfare, the Secretary of the Interior, or any other Federal officer, department, or agency.

GENERAL PROVISIONS

SEC. 215.[14] (a) Payments of grants under this Act may be made (after necessary adjustment on account of previously made underpayments or overpayments) in advance or by way of reimbursement, and in such installments and on such conditions as the Secretary may determine.

(b) No grant may be made under this Act to any private profitmaking organization.

SEC. 216.[15] (a)(1) There are authorized to be appropriated to the Secretary of Health, Education, and Welfare for carrying out the provisions of this Act (including, but not limited to, section 208), not to exceed $41,500,000 for the fiscal year ending June 30, 1971.

(2) There are authorized to be appropriated to the Secretary of Health, Education, and Welfare to carry out the provisions of this Act, other than section 208, not to exceed $72,000,000 for the fiscal year ending June 30, 1972, and not to exceed $76,000,000 for the fiscal year ending June 30, 1973.

(3) There are authorized to be appropriated to the Secretary of Health, Education, and Welfare to carry out

[11] Sec. 211 added by sec. 104(b) P.L. 91–512.

[12] Sec. 212 added by sec. 104(b) of P.L. 91–512.

[13] Former secs. 207 through 210 redesignated as secs. 213 through 216 by sec. 104(b) of P.L. 91–512.

[14] Sec. 215 as redesignated by sec. 104(b) of P.L. 91–512 further amended by sec. 104(c) of that Act.

[15] Sec. 216 as redesignated by sec. 104(b) of P.L. 91–512 further amended by sec. 105 of that Act.

section 208 of this Act not to exceed $80,000,000 for the fiscal year ending June 30, 1972, and not to exceed $140,-000,000 for the fiscal year ending June 30, 1973.

(b) There are authorized to be appropriated to the Secretary of the Interior to carry out this Act not to exceed $8,750,000 for the fiscal year ending June 30, 1971, not to exceed $20,000,000 for the fiscal year ending June 30, 1972, and not to exceed $22,500,000 for the fiscal year ending June 30, 1973. Prior to expending any funds authorized to be appropriated by this subsection, the Secretary of the Interior shall consult with the Secretary of Health, Education, and Welfare to assure that the expenditure of such funds will be consistent with the purposes of this Act.

(c) Such portion as the Secretary may determine, but not more than 1 per centum, of any appropriation for grants, contracts, or other payments under any provision of this Act for any fiscal year beginning after June 30, 1970, shall be available for evaluation (directly, or by grants or contracts) of any program authorized by this Act.

(d) Sums appropriated under this section shall remain available until expended.

NOTE: The Environmental Protection Agency's Regulations on Solid Waste Disposal and Resource Recovery Grants can be found in the Federal Register, Volume 36, Number 181, of September 17, 1971.

National Materials Policy Act of 1970

Public Law 91-512; Title II of H.R. 11833

Sec. 201. This title may be cited as the "National Materials Policy Act of 1970".

Sec. 202. It is the purpose of this title to enhance environmental quality and conserve materials by developing a national materials policy to utilize present resources and technology more efficiently, to anticipate the future materials requirements of the Nation and the world, and to make recommendations on the supply, use, recovery, and disposal of materials.

Sec. 203. (a) There is hereby created the National Commission on Materials Policy (hereafter referred to as the "Commission") which shall be composed of seven members chosen from Government service and the private sector for their outstanding qualifications and demonstrated competence with regard to matters related to materials policy, to be appointed by the President with the advice and consent of the Senate, one of whom he shall designate as Chairman.

(b) The members of the Commission shall serve without compensation, but shall be reimbursed for travel, subsistence, and other necessary expenses incurred by them in carrying out the duties of the Commission.

Sec. 204. The Commission shall make a full and complete investigation and study for the purpose of developing a national materials policy which shall include, without being limited to, a determination of–

(1) national and international materials requirements, priorities, and objectives, both current and future, including economic projections;

(2) the relationship of materials policy to (A) national and international population size and (B) the enhancement of environmental quality;

(3) recommended means for the extraction, development, and use of materials which are susceptible to recycling, reuse, or self-destruction, in order to enhance environmental quality and conserve materials;

(4) means of exploiting existing scientific knowledge in the supply, use, recovery, and disposal of materials and encouraging further research and education in this field;

(5) means to enhance coordination and cooperation among Federal departments and agencies in materials usage so that such usage might best serve the national materials policy;

(6) the feasibility and desirability of establishing computer inventories of national and international materials requirements, supplies, and alternatives; and

(7) which Federal agency or agencies shall be assigned continuing responsibility for the implementation of the national materials policy.

(b) In order to carry out the purposes of this title, the Commission is authorized–

(1) to request the cooperation and assistance of such other Federal departments and agencies as may be appropriate;

(2) to appoint and fix the compensation of such staff personnel as may be necessary, without regard to the provisions of title 5, United States Code, governing appointments in the competitive service, and without regard to the provisions of chapter 51 and subchapter III of such title relating to classification and General Schedule pay rates; and

(3) to obtain the services of experts and consultants, in accordance with the provisions of section 3109 of title 5, United States Code, at rates for individuals not to exceed $100 per diem.

(c) The Commission shall submit to the President and to the Congress a report with respect to its findings and recommendations no later than June 30, 1973, and shall terminate not later than ninety days after submission of such report.

(d) Upon request by the Commission, each Federal department and agency is authorized and directed to furnish, to the greatest extent practicable, such information and assistance as the Commission may request.

Sec. 205. When used in this title, the term "materials" means natural resources intended to be utilized by industry for the production of goods, with the exclusion of food.

Sec. 206. There is hereby authorized to be appropriated the sum of $2,000,000 to carry out the provisions of this title.

Legal restrictions on retailed beverage containers (as of December, 1971)

STATE	place	effective date	action taken	postscript
CALIFORNIA				
	Davis	1/31/72	bans all nonreturnables	
	South San Francisco	7/1/71	bans all nonreturnables	city council rescinds 8/2/71
MARYLAND				
	Bowie	4/1/71	5-cent deposit required	a previous ban ordinance had been rescinded in passing this one, which was under court challenge. It was not being enforced.
	Howard County	7/1/71	bans all nonreturnables and requires 5-cent deposit	being challenged, and not being enforced.
	Rockville	2/1/72	bans all nonreturnables	rescinded by city council 11/23/71.
MASSACHUSETTS				
	Bedford	6/1/72	bans all nonreturnables	state attorney general declares unconstitutional 7/8/71.
	Marlboro	6/1/72	bans all nonreturnables	vetoed by mayor.
MICHIGAN				
	Davidson	1/1/72	bans all nonreturnables	city council rescinds
	Garden City	1/1/72	bans all glass nonreturnables	
	Lake County	1/1/72	bans all nonreturnables	county prosecutor declares he he will not enforce w/o state act.
	Livonia (res.)	1/1/72	recommendation that nonreturnables not be used	not legally binding.
	Northville	1/1/72	bans all glass nonreturnables	
	Plymouth	1/1/73	bans all glass nonreturnables	
	Sterling Hgts.	1/1/72	bans all nonreturnables	
	Troy	1/1/72	bans all nonreturnables	
	Wayne	1/1/72	bans all glass nonreturnables	
MINNESOTA				
	Deephaven	1/1/72	bans beer, soft drink nonreturnables	being reconsidered
	East Bethel (res.)	1/1/72	recommends ban on beer, soft drink non-returnables	not legally binding
	New Hope	not set	bans nonreturnables	to go into effect only if all 30 municipalities in county also pass ban.
	Princeton	1/1/72	bans all nonreturnables	
	St. Louis Park	9/1/72	bans all nonreturnables	city council announces that enforcement is intended only if other nearby communities also pass similar ban.
NEW JERSEY				
	Edgewater	1969	bans all nonreturnables for soft drinks when sold in less than six-pack	

State	Locality	Date	Provision	Status
NEW YORK				
	New York City	7/1/71	taxed all plastic containers 2 cents	declared invalid; see Two-66 - 76.
NEVADA				
	Clark County	8/2/71	requires 4-cent minimum deposit for beer, soft drinks, bans detachable tops, and places 1-cent tax.	to be made effective only if four cities in county adopt.
OHIO				
	Barberton	4/1/72	bans all nonreturnables	
	Oberlin	1/1/72	bans all nonreturnables, and makes possession of them a criminal offense	legal opposition intend
OREGON		10/1/72	requires deposit of 2 cents on containers certified for use by more than one bottler, 5 cents on other containers (beer and soft drinks; also bans detachable opener sections on cans.	legal opposition intended.
PENNSYLVANIA				
	Colwyn	spring, 1971	bans nonreturnable soft drink bottles when less than 6-pack sold	
VERMONT				
	Northfield	7/1/71	bans all nonreturnables	attorney general rules unconstitutional
VIRGINIA	Loudoun County	1/1/72	deposit required in 6-16 ounce sizes	legal challenge underway.
WISCONSIN				
	Madison	7/1/71	forbits sale of beer and soft drinks in nonreturnable containers unless such products are also offered in returnable containers.	

NOTE

During 1971 and the early months of 1972, activities by councils and legislative bodies related to the regulation of beverage containers were so common as to require almost fulltime work just to keep relatively fully informed. In a survey taken September 10, 1971, there were 36 such bills before the U.S. Congress, and 235 before the legislatures of 45 states. The number of cities and towns considering such ordinances was considered beyond reasonable computation. Lawsuits could be assumed for virtually any of the proposals that became law. Despite the great lack of success such measures were meeting, the basic idea of attempting to control production or sales of items destined by their natures to enter the solid waste burden of communities is too logical to be discarded without further consideration. It may well be that the failures here will lay the groundwork for more effective measures.

Inner city recommendations

The following are edited recommendations concerning solid waste from *Our Urban Environment and Our Most Endangered People* [draft version], a Report to the U.S. Environmental Protection Agency by the Task Force on Environmental Problems of the Inner City, September, 1971. Though these recommendations are far from being innovative or definitive, they offer a starting point for those having to consider these problems. Certainly more thought is needed to this subject. See also the report's findings on page Two-5 and Two-6.

1. *Supplemental Trash Containers—Plastic Bags*

The task force finds that the use of plastic bags can be a highly cost-effective method of immediately improving the inner city solid waste problem. Plastic bags have several important advantages, they:

1. accelerate the trash collection process (The sanitation worker does not have to return an empty trash can to the curb.)
2. provide an odor barrier and thus are not an open invitation to rats and insects as are conventional trash cans.
3. are available in unlimited supply while inner city people have limited and usually inadequate number of metal containers. Thus, all trash can be packaged, and overflows can be drastically reduced.
4. are quieter than metal containers.

The task force recommends grants to inner city areas for the purchase and distribution of plastic trash bags. (See National Clean Sweep Recommendation for Budget.) These bags might have suitable civic pride inscriptions on them, for example, "Help Keep Your Street Clean," or "Help Protect Your Environment."

The task force recognizes that plastic bags have at least two environmental disadvantages:

1. They are not biodegradable in sanitary landfills.
2. They create noxious fumes when incinerated.

The task force feels, however, that the pressing solid waste problems of inner cities dictate, in the short run, the use of plastic bags. For the long run, however, the task force feels EPA should accelerate research to develop plastic bags which are both biodegradable and free of toxic fumes when incinerated.

The task force suggests that the Administrator set forth a challenge to the membership of the American Chemical Society to develop such a plastic by June 1973, with a progress report to be made to the Administrator by June 1972. An enormous market could be mandated for such a product, and this market would be sufficient incentive for chemists everywhere to join the quest.

2. *Demonstration City Pilot Recycling Plant*

The task force recommends the establishment of a pilot recylcing plant in Demonstration City (Washington, D.C.). This recycling center could be run by a black-owned and operated corporation or community action group. Possibly this center could be built at the site of D.C.'s incinerator #5.

In general recycling would pose an alternative to other forms of solid waste disposal, such as incineration, which adds to the air pollution problem. EPA would thus be putting into action its desire to recycle some of this nation's natural resources, as well as providing employment and capitalization to minority groups.

Initially, this recycling center would serve only a segment of the city. A long range goal would be to expand this operation to the entire city.

In such a system, the city government's sanitation department could handle the collection services for this recycling center. All garbage from the service community would be brought to the center. The garbage would be sorted by recycling center personnel. Solid waste which can't be recycled would be shipped to some sort of disposal facility, preferably a sanitary landfill.

This demonstration would be in keeping with one of the goals of the Solid Waste Program, i.e., to recycle solid waste. Also, this would be a unique demonstration project since we are dealing with inner city residents, as opposed to the middle class residents who benefit from the recycling effort in Berkeley, California, which is a Solid Waste Program Demonstration Grant project.

The facility will need bins for the sorted solid waste, a glass crusher, a distribution mechanism (trucks, rail, etc.), and work stations for the recycling center personnel. However, the most important need is the technical expertise of Solid Waste Program personnel.

This recycling center would not alleviate the solid waste problem by itself. It must be accompanied by an imaginative solid waste collection scheme. However, this recycling center will provide financial help for the inner city community and be a beginning step in completing the cycle of conservation. Jobs will be created by the center's operation, and some of the money would be funneled back into the inner city community.

3. *Inner City Coordinator*

The task force recommends the establishment of a liaison position within the Solid Waste Program which is the focal point for solid waste problems of the inner city. One of the reasons the Task Force on the Environmental Problems of the Inner City was established was that we had no one in EPA assessing the effort of our Agency relative to the urban poor. If the Office of Solid Waste Management Programs (and other EPA Program areas) had an "urban specialist" who kept abreast of problems in the urban environment, coordinated program resources in researching solutions, and was receptive to requests for assistance to the urban poor, then we would have come a long way in showing that we are truly trying to relate to the urban poor.

4. *Public Education*

A. *The task force recommends the making of urban solid waste films that enable the viewer to see corrective actions applied to problems.* Most of the present films make one aware of how severely solid waste can damage the environment, both physically and aesthetically. This is good in that the problem is being emphasized, and this helps create a concerned work force and public. However, we should also emphasize solutions to these solid waste problems.

The proposed film could be used by community action groups to emphasize to residents that there *are* solutions to their waste problems. Also, it may serve as an inspiration to the community to clean up its neighborhoods.

B. *The task force recommends establishment of curriculum in public school systems, colleges, and universities relating urban solid waste problems and possible solutions to students.* We do not propose solely the creation of "urban specialists" by this recommendation, but the encouragement of students to take courses dealing with urban environmental issues. These courses will help sustain an environmentally aware nation. Also, these young people will bring fresh thinking to our urban poor's problems, and help provide workable solutions.

5. *Demonstration Grants*

The task force recommends the demonstration and evaluation of equipment and methods for improving solid waste storage in densely populated, low-income, inner-city residential areas for the benefit of the users, and the collection agency. This is in line with a currently proposed Solid Waste Demonstration Grant entitled "Inner City Storage Demonstration and Evaluation."

It will provide alternative solutions for the many problems of solid waste storage for inner city areas. Various solid waste storage rechniques will be utilized, such as refuse bags, metal, plastic, or rubber containers, special compactors, bulk containers. New and improved storage techniques which show promise for the inner city is especially encouraged.

One possible solution might be the placing of bins at strategic locations within the inner city community. One problem frequently encountered is that there are not enough storage containers in the inner city for garbage disposal. Thus, garbage becomes piled on the ground next to those insufficient numbers of trash containers residents can afford. Sometimes collection crews are very careless about picking up this "additional" trash, and it doesn't get picked up. This syndrome possibly can be avoided if there are adequate numbers of containers in the first place. Additional data would have to be gathered, however, and a cost analysis performed before such a plan could be implemented.

6. *Monitoring*

The task force recommends the establishment of a monitoring program for the inner city solid waste problem.. This could either be run by the Solid Waste Program, or the city government with technical assistance from the Solid Waste Program. This monitoring program will be needed in order that any concerted solid waste project in the inner city might have lasting effectiveness.

We would make an inspection of the garbage and litter before our efforts and afterwards to attain some measure of effectiveness. Then we make periodic inspections afterwards to make sure the level of clearance was maintained. We would also take note of the types and frequencies of complaints by the residents. This would be accompanied by a survey of community reaction to the project or campaign.

In this manner, the Solid Waste Program can assure that its efforts to aid the urban poor are more than one-shot affairs. By our monitoring program, we can assure that problems that arise can be remedied, and that our efforts won't have been in vain.

CHAPTER THREE: Air Pollution

a. History and effects of air pollution

Natural air pollution such as from volcanic eruptions or dust storms has occurred for millions of years. The letters of Pliny the Younger to Tacitus, the Roman historian, tell of the death of Pliny's uncle, presumably from sulfurous gases, following the eruption of Mount Vesuvius in 79 A.D.

Primitive man polluted the air with his cooking and warming fires. But it was not until the introduction of "seacoal" in 13th century England that air pollution was serious enough to be subject to government regulation. The industrial revolution late in the 18th century led to serious pollution problems, and during the 19th century London was subject to periods of severe air pollution that resulted in loss of life.

In the 20th century the problem continued to increase in severity. Population growth combined with urbanization intensified the problem. An increased standard of living required more manufactured goods, and this required energy, the release of which causes pollution. The introduction of petroleum as a major source of energy brought additional pollutants. By the 1940's Los Angeles was suffering the smog caused by oxidants, peroxides, ozonides and various other hydrocarbon reactions. In recent years new processes in the steel, petroleum, and chemical industries have intensified industrially caused pollution.

By the early 20th century, the English physician, Dr. Des Voeux, coined the word "smog" to describe the air pollution he blamed for respiratory diseases. Later, air pollution episodes resulted in acute illness and sudden death: in December of 1930, in the Meuse River Valley in Belgium, thousands of people fell ill, and 60 died. In October of 1948, in Donora, Pennsylvania, out of a population of 14,000, nearly 6,000 fell ill, and 18 died. In December, 1952, in London, England, the worst air pollution disaster occurred, killing 4,000 people. In 1962 another period of severe air pollution took 750 lives. In London, six incidents previous to these two going back to 1873 had taken more than 2,500 lives.

In New York City periods of severe air pollution occurred in 1953, 1962, 1963, and 1966. The last two attacks brought 405 and 168 deaths respectively, though the causes of such fatalities can be demonstrated only by careful statistical analysis of mortality figures.

meteorological factors

The above occurrences were during *inversions.* Normally warm air rises and mixes with cooler air. When the rising air is cooled and meets air its equal in temperature, the vertical movements stop. The distance to the ground is known as the mixing depth. Seasons change the mixing depth. During the summer daylight hours it is usually at several thousand feet, but in the winter it may be only a few hundred feet from the ground. When a layer of warm air moves over a layer of cooler air, the cooler bottom level of air is trapped, and as it fills with the pollutants of the community, it becomes injurious.

There are two common types of inversions. A *subsidence inversion* occurs when a layer of air in a high-pressure air mass sinks down upon an area. Such inversions occur some 340 days of the year on the western coast of the United States. A *radiation inversion* is a normal nighttime formation. The ground, cooling rapidly, makes a layer of air cooler than the upper layers. The layer breaks up as the morning sun heats the ground, but in valleys surrounded by steep mountains, such inversions can last throughout the day. Valleys can also act to inhibit horizontal movement of contaminants by the wind currents.

If fog is present, it can intensify an inversion, and air pollutants can also create the nuclei to create fog. Fog can turn harmful gases into acids and help carry the poisonous material deep into the lungs.

Another phenomenon that encourages the entrapment of pollutants is the *heat island* effect created by a city being warmer than the countryside. This creates air circulation patterns that intensify the entrapment of air pollution. Thus acute episodes of air pollution are the result of nature's inability to disperse the pollutants. Given time, most pollutants wash out in rain or snow, causing water and soil pollution. Some pollutants such as pesticides and radiation are removed from the air by entering the life chain. Thus, if we don't breathe air pollutants, we may drink them or eat them.

The major air pollution disasters attract a great deal of attention, but since the 1950's not much research has been done into the problems created by the daily exposure to levels of pollution substantially below those found in the major disasters. It has become evident that air pollution is a major health problem, but specific proof of cause and effect is difficult to achieve.

effects on health

Epidemiological studies can show statistically the effects of exposure on populations, but cannot show that any specific individual case is due to air pollution. With daily exposures to a multitude of pollutants, identifying the causative agent is difficult. Cigarette smoking can further conceal the effects of air pollution.

Clinical studies and laboratory experiments are important, but usually cannot duplicate the wide variety of harmful exposures that the individual is subjected to because they cannot control all the variables. This problem of pollutants creating different effects in combination than alone makes study of these effects more difficult. For example, small particulate matter, by reducing the body's defense mechanisms, can make the effect of sulfur dioxide much more harmful. When we attempt to deal with the synergisms of air and water pollution, food additives, excessive noise and radiation on the human body, we encounter a possible nightmare.

Nevertheless, we have now amassed sufficient data to conclude that air pollution can produce chronic airway resistance; bronchial asthma can be triggered by air pollution, and, though physicians differ on the proper terminology, asthmatic bronchitis or Tokyo-Yokohama asthma is developed from exposure to air pollution, though it is often also related to smoking.

Asthma outbreaks and air pollution levels are clearly linked.

Chronic bronchitis has been the subject of numerous British studies that show it statistically related to air pollution. Cigarette smoking is so overwhelmingly significant that identifying the role of air pollution is complicated. The increase in chronic bronchitis, however, is frightening. In the 10 years ending with 1961, the death rate from chronic bronchitis increased 50 percent and the same-sized increase occurred in the following five years. These figures are probably low, for the disease is often listed as a contributing rather than the primary cause of death.

Pulmonary emphysema is the fastest-growing cause of death in the United States. Between 1950 and 1966 deaths due to this disease increased 17 fold. No single cause for the disease has yet been found, but the disease is aggravated by air pollution, and the close relationship between community air pollution levels and this disease is well established. The economic costs of this disease is high: over six percent of those receiving Social Security disability payments are disabled by this disease.

Lung cancer deaths in the largest metropolitan areas are twice that of rural areas. The rate is generally proportional to the size of the city, as is, generally the air pollution level. Even adjusting the figures for smoking habits still results in lung cancer rates being one-third higher in cities.

Other ailments for which air pollution is implicated include heart disease and eye irritation. Preliminary investigations show a relationship to fertility, newborn survival, premature aging, and psychological damage.

The following, concerning research activities by the Air Pollution Control Office (then HEW; transferred to EPA), is excerpted from *Progress in the Prevention of Air Pollution* [92nd Cong. Doc. 92-11]. This was the required annual report (calendar year 1970) on implementation of the Clean Air Act. Submitted March 5, it was ordered printed May 3, 1971:

One epidemiological study conducted by APCO in the Chattanooga region has provided, for the first time, evidence that ambient air levels of nitrogen dioxide are associated with adverse health effects (beyond the effects resulting from the involvement of nitrogen oxides in formation of photochemical smog). Within the Chattanooga region, the occurrence of respiratory illness was studied in areas of differing nitrogen dioxide levels. In the area with higher nitrogen dioxide levels, there was a higher rate of respiratory illness during an A2/Hong Kong influenza epidemic and during the period between the A2 epidemic and a subsequent influenza B epidemic. The rate was higher among second grade schoolchildren included in the study, their brothers and sisters and their parents. The rate was nearly 19 percent higher in the area of higher nitrogen dioxide levels. In that area, the second grade schoolchildren also produced significantly poor results on test of ventilatory performance.

In another area, an APCO study showed a consistent relationship between sulfur dioxide levels and the rate of asthma attacks among members of the group studied.

A laboratory study demonstrated that animals repeatedly exposed to ozone and nitrogen dioxide develop some degree to tolerance to these pollutants but that the tolerance is limited. It was found that while direct injury to lung tissue becomes less acute after repeated exposure, the occurrence of subtle alterations in cellular chemistry and morphology, which are associated with exposure to nitrogen dioxide, does not subside.

See also the section on effects of air pollution on residents of the inner city: Appendix Three-4.

End quote

The following is from *Environmental Quality: The First Annual Report of the Council on Environmental Quality,* August, 1970.

effects on plants

Air pollution inflicts widespread and costly damage on plant life and buildings and materials. Some experiences of the past warned of the effects of air pollution on plant life. Sulfur dioxide fumes from a large copper smelting plant set up after the Civil War in Copper Basin, Tenn., damaged 30,000 acres of timberland. Much of this originally forested mountain land is still barren. Today, the damage to plant life is less dramatic than in the days of unrestricted smelter operations. But the slower, chronic injury inflicted on agricultural, forest, and ornamental vegetation by increasing quantities and varieties of air pollutants has now spread to all parts of the country.

Smog in the Los Angeles basin contributes to the slow decline of citrus groves south of the city and damages trees in the San Bernardino National Forest 50 miles away. Fluoride and sulfur oxides, released into the air by phosphate fertilizer processing in Florida, have blighted large numbers of pines and citrus orchards. Livestock grazing on fluoride-tainted vegetation develop a crippling condition known as fluorosis. In New Jersey, pollution injury to vegetation has been observed in every county and damage reported to at least 36 commercial crops.

At sulfur oxide levels routinely observed in some of our cities, many plants suffer a chronic injury described as "early aging." Nitrogen dioxide produces similar injury symptoms and seems to restrict the growth of plants even when symptoms of injury are not visible. Ozone, a major photochemical oxidant, is a significant threat to leafy vegetables, field and forage crops, shrubs, and fruit and forest trees—particularly conifers. The damage from ozone in minute quantities can be great. Extended ozone exposure to 0.05 parts per million can reduce a radish yield 50 percent. Tobacco is sensitive to ozone at a level of 0.03 parts per million.

effects on materials

Air pollutants also damage a wide variety of materials. Sulfur oxides will destroy even the most durable products. Steel corrodes two to four times faster in urban industrial areas than it does in rural areas where much less sulfur-bearing coal and oil are burned. When particulate matter is also present in the air, the corrosion rates multiply. One-third of the replacement cost of steel rails in England is estimated to be caused by sulfur pollution. The rise of sulfur oxides levels in the air is accelerating the erosion of statuary and buildings throughout the world, and in some cities, works of art made of stone, bronze, and steel must be moved indoors to preserve them from deterioration. Particulate matter in the air not only speeds the corrosive action of other pollutants but by itself is responsible for costly damage and soiling. Clothes and cars must be washed, houses painted, and buildings cleaned more often because of the particulates in the air. Ozone damages textiles, discolors dyes, and greatly accelerates the cracking of rubber.

effects on materials

Air pollution dims visibility, obscures city skylines and scenic beauty, interferes with the safe operation of aircraft and automobiles, and disrupts transportation schedules. In one recent year, low visibility from smoke, haze, and dust was the suspected cause of 15 to 20 plane crashes. In Los Angeles, visibility in the smog frequently lowers to less than 3 miles. During the air pollution alert in the eastern States during July 1970, visibility was almost totally obscured in some areas. The Federal Aviation Administration's visibility safety factor for airplane operation without instruments is 5 miles. Nitrogen dioxide, which reaches peak levels during morning rush-hour traffic, is responsible for the whiskey-brown haze that stains the sky over many cities. Particulates, however, are the major villain in reducing visibility. Particles (ash, carbon, dust, and liquid particles) discharged directly to the air scatter and absorb light, reducing the contrast between objects and their backgrounds. Particles are also formed in the atmosphere by photochemical reactions and by the conversion of sulfur dioxide to sulfuric acid mist. Wherever sulfur pollution is significant—which is wherever large amounts of coal and oil are burned—visibility diminishes as relative humidity rises.

costs of pollution

The total costs of air pollution in the United States cannot be precisely calculated, but they amount to many billions of dollars a year. Economic studies are beginning to identify some of the more obvious costs. To paint steel structures damaged by air pollution runs an estimated $100 million a year. Commercial laundering, cleaning, and dyeing of fabrics soiled by air pollution costs about $800 million. Washing cars dirtied by air pollution costs about $240 million. Damage to agricultural crops and livestock is put at $500 million a year or more. Adverse effects of air pollution on air travel cost from $40 to $80 million a year. Even more difficult to tie down are the costs of replacing and protecting precision instruments or maintaining cleanliness in the production of foods, beverages, and other consumables. It is equally difficult to assess damage, soiling, and added maintenance to homes and furnishings or how air pollution acts on property values. The cost of fuels wasted in incomplete combustion and of valuable and potentially recoverable resources such as sulfur wasted into the air is also hard to count. It is still more difficult to determine the dollar value of medical costs and time lost from work because of air pollution—or to calculate the resulting fall in productivity of business and industry.

The total investment necessary through 1975 to control the major industrial and municipal sources of particulate matter, sulfur oxides, hydrocarbons, and carbon monoxide in 100 metropolitan areas of the United States has been estimated at $2.6 billion. This includes costs for controlling both existing and new sources. By 1975, it will cost another $1.9 billion for operation, maintenance, depreciation, and interest.

These estimated costs are based on assumed future control requirements. Still, the yearly cost to control the industrial sources of these four major pollutants is relatively low, less than 1 percent of the value of the annual output of the industries involved, although the costs to some industries is much greater.

End, selection from *Environmental Quality,* 1970. The following is from the *CEQ's Environmental Quality,* 1971:

> The damage estimates due to the major pollutants are admittedly crude and at this stage, can only approximate the real costs of air pollution.
>
> Scientific evidence on what air pollution does to human health is far from complete. Serious air pollution episodes have demonstrated how air pollution can severely impair health. Further research is spawning a growing body of evidence which indicates that even the long-term effects of exposure to low concentrations of pollutants can damage health and cause chronic disease and premature death, especially for the most vulnerable—the aged and those already suffering from respiratory diseases. Major illnesses linked to air pollution include emphysema, bronchitis, asthma, and lung cancer.
>
> Data from 1963 suggest that a 50 percent reduction in air pollution existing in major urban areas at that time would lower the costs of damage to health by $2.08 billion in a single year.
>
> The Environmental Protection Agency (EPA) estimates that the economic cost of human mortality and morbidity from all air pollution is in the neighborhood of $6 billion annually. However, these estimated health costs relate only to medical care and work loss. If the costs of discomfort, frustration, and anxiety were included, these estimates would be greatly increased.
>
> Vegetation and materials damage have also been assessed. Air pollution corrodes and damages materials and stunts and kills trees, plants, and crops. The direct costs of air pollution on both materials and vegetation are estimated at $4.9 billion annually.
>
> A study of property values suggests that prices are sensitive to pollution levels. Averaging the effect of increased pollution on property values in a number of cities, EPA estimates lowered nationwide values of property from air pollution at $5.2 billion annually.
>
> The annual toll of air pollution on health, vegetation, materials, and property values has been estimated by EPA at more than $16 billion annually—over $80 for each person in the United States. In all probability, the estimates of cost will be even higher when the impact on esthetic and other values are calculated, when the cost of discomfort from illness is considered, and when damage can be more precisely traced to pollutants. Also, the estimates may increase as more is known about the damages of long-term exposure to very low levels of any one pollutant or many in combination. It must be emphasized, however, that these cost estimates only crudely approximate the damages from air pollution.

* * *

trends in air pollution

The greatest single source of air pollution, when measured by pollutant weight, is the automobile. Transportation contributed more pollution than all other sources together, and carbon monoxide alone, primarily from automobiles, outweighed the other four major pollutants combined. However, it is significant that the contribution of transportation sources declined slightly in

1969. We have apparently reached the peak level of automobile pollution, and as older cars are replaced by newer ones with pollution devices, which were first installed in the 1967 models in California and in the 1968 models nationwide, we can expect automobile-related pollution to decline. The 1975 and 1976 emission standards will quicken this decline. But in the long run, if the number of cars on the road continues to increase at the present rate, even the effect of these controls eventually could be negated—unless something else is done.

There are no firm data on the reasons for the slight decline in solid waste emissions. However, it is probably due to a reduction in open burning at municipal dumps.

It is somewhat misleading to consider air pollutants in terms of their aggregate weight. We worry about pollutants because of their effects, and, other things being equal, a pound of sulfur oxides is a far more serious threat to health and welfare than a pound of carbon monoxide.

measuring pollutants

Measuring pollutants by tons emitted also ignores their geographical distribution. We are generally concerned with the concentration of pollutants in a particular place, but measuring total weight of emissions tells us nothing about their concentration. One might expect that the increase in total emissions over the past several years would cause corresponding increases in ambient concentration levels (often referred to as air quality). But, in fact, this has not been the case, as Figure 1 shows. Ambient levels of sulfur dioxide and carbon monoxide have decreased. Levels of particulate matter (TSP—total suspended particulates) have stayed about the same.

The disparity between weight of emissions and ambient levels is due partly to the application of controls in the larger cities where ambient levels are measured. New York City, the State of New Jersey, and other locations have succeeded in lowering emissions of sulfur oxides and particulates through stringent enforcement of standards. Thus the air quality in the urban areas has improved, but total weight of emissions has continued to increase outside these areas.

The disparity is also due partly to the method by which ambient levels are measured. The trends in Figure 1 are based on only one sampling station in each city. Thus it is uncertain how well the figures for each city actually represent the air quality in the entire community. The movement of heavy industry to loca-

Figure 1

Trends in Ambient Levels of Selected Air Pollutants

TSP is total suspended particles

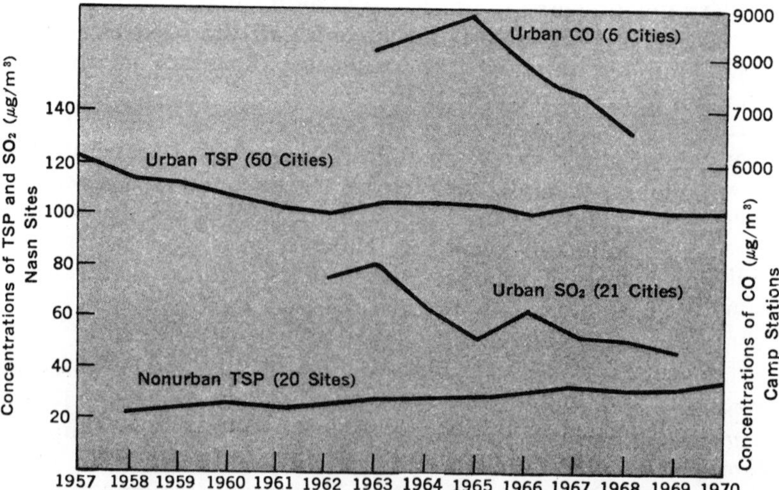

Source: The Mitre Corp. MTR–6013. Based on Environmental Protection Agency data.

tions outside the central city improves air quality in the city but does not reduce the total amount of pollutants emitted. On the other hand, the figures for total weight of pollutants emitted are based on extrapolations from a variety of data sources and not on actual measurements. Therefore their validity is also uncertain.

The importance of where the monitoring site is located within a particular community cannot be overemphasized. Wide variations in recorded ambient air levels can occur from site to site within the same city, depending on the location of the sites. For example, although EPA's National Air Sampling Network (NASN) sites are generally located in the central city, State and local sites may be closer to major pollutant sources, because such stations are often sited for possible enforcement actions. Thus the NASN data often show much cleaner air conditions than the State and local data.

effects on climate

The dispersion of pollutants may create other problems, such as changes in global climate or atmospheric conditions. It has been hypothesized, for example, that an increase in carbon dioxide levels could raise the global temperature enough to raise the level of the ocean because of melting of the polar icecaps. Measurements at the National Oceanographic and Atmospheric Agency's Mauna Loa Observatory indicate that compared with 1958 through 1968, the rate of increase of atmospheric carbon dioxide nearly doubled during 1969 and 1970. The earlier data point to an average annual increase of 0.7 parts per million. But the recent measurements show that the carbon dioxide content at Mauna Loa has climbed 1.35 parts per million during each of the last 2 years. Scientists now are investigating the reasons for this accelerated rate of change. The complete carbon dioxide cycle must be studied intensely and mathematical models must be developed to simulate the effects of changes in the atmospheric content upon climate.

Figure 1 shows that levels of total suspended particulates are much higher in urban than in nonurban areas. However, the differences seem to be diminishing, perhaps because of greater dispersion of industrial plants and the movement of population out of central cities. Figure 2 shows that the ambient levels of

Figure 2

Relationship of Air Pollution and Population, Second Half 1969—First Half 1970

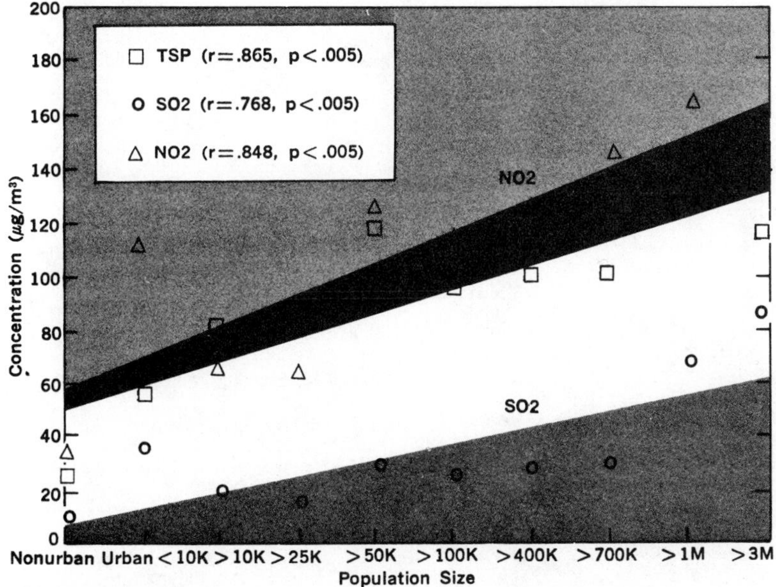

Source: The Mitre Corp. MTR–6013. Based on Environmental Protection Agency data.

particulates, sulfur dioxide, and nitrogen oxides correlate with population size: the larger the population of the community, the higher the levels of pollution.

Figures 1 and 2 both give values which are aggregated for many communities. However, there are wide variations in levels of air pollution from city to city. The variation can be seen from Table 2, which shows the levels of major air pollutants in six large cities. There are also regional variations in pollution levels because of the type of fuels used and the patterns of population distribution.

variations in exposure

Another indicator of variations in pollution levels from city to city and of the problems with using *average* air quality figures are so-called "episodes." These are periods when the air pollution in a particular community reaches dangerously high levels. A good example of such an episode occurred in Birmingham, Ala., this year. In previous years, levels of particulate matter, measured in micrograms per cubic meter of air, had averaged 155 during April in Birmingham. From April 15 to 21, 1971, they soared to an average of 372, reaching a peak of 607 during April 19–20. Families living in high exposure areas suffered from increased respiratory irritation symptoms, including cough, burning of throat or chest, and shortness of breath. Calls or visits to physicians were more frequent, and more persons reported restricted activity. Most pollution episodes are due to a combination of high continuous levels of pollution output aggravated by meteorological conditions, particularly inversions, which prevent the pollutants from dispersing.

The data in this section do not provide any easy answer to the question of whether air pollution in the United States is getting better or worse. Overall emissions, measured by weight, are still

Table 2

Annual Average Levels of Selected Air Pollutants in Selected Cities[1]

Location and pollutant (mg/m^3)	1962	1963	1964	1965	1966	1967	1968
Chicago:							
SO_2	282	393	458	341	215	327	307
NO_2	81	77	87	81	105	94	90
CO	[2]NA	9,430	13,915	19,665	14,375	10,120	7,130
Cincinnati:							
SO_2	92	68	100	79	81	55	44
NO_2	56	56	60	66	68	53	60
CO	NA	8,050	7,015	4,600	5,635	6,440	6,440
Denver:							
SO_2	NA	NA	NA	55	29	13	34
NO_2	NA	NA	NA	68	64	70	68
CO	NA	NA	NA	8,280	9,085	8,740	6,210
Philadelphia:							
SO_2	231	181	215	223	238	257	212
NO_2	73	71	71	68	73	81	73
CO	NA	NA	8,165	9,315	7,820	7,245	9,890
St. Louis:							
SO_2	NA	NA	155	123	113	76	73
NO_2	NA	NA	62	64	64	45	43
CO	NA	NA	7,245	7,475	6,670	6,440	5,270
Washington, D.C.:							
SO_2	144	131	126	121	115	126	97
NO_2	56	66	68	66	66	81	88
CO	6,095	7,705	6,555	4,255	3,795	5,635	3,910

[1] Data for 1969 and 1970 not available until December 1971 because of change in computer processing methods.

[2] NA—not available.

Source: The Mitre Corp. MTR-6013. Based on Environmental Protection Agency data.

increasing along with increases in population and production, although the expected reduction in automobile emissions probably will begin to reverse this trend. Ambient air quality levels seem to be generally improving, at least in the places where the sampling stations are located. Most large cities still must make a major effort to reach newly set national air quality standards.

inner city studies

The special environmental problems of the inhabitants of the inner city are dealt with in chapter 6, p. 189, of the Second Annual Report of the Council on Environmental Quality (August 1971). The exposure to air pollutants, it is shown, varies inversely with income.

An article by Virginia Brodine, entitled A Special Burden [13 Environment #2, March 1971 at 22] shows that the health problems created by air pollution fall most heavily on the poor, the old, and the infirm.

See, in the appendix to this chapter, the excerpts from Our Urban Environment and Our Most Endangered People.

b. Types and sources of air pollution

Air pollution is found in a variety of forms which affect both its capacity for harm and the efforts necessary for control. The following general categories are usually recognized:

definitions

An **aerosol** is a solid or liquid of microscopic size in a gas (including air).

Dust is solid particles temporarily suspended in the air.

Droplets are small liquid particles that fall in still air but may be suspended in turbulent conditions.

Fly Ash is fine particles of ash found in the gas arising from combustion.

Fume is technically the solid particles formed by condensation from a gaseous state but can mean almost any kind of contamination.

Gas is matter having no independent shape, a volume which tends to expand indefinitely within the gravitation field in which it is held.

Mist is liquid particles of large size.

Particles are a small mass of solid or liquid.

Smoke is finely divided aerosol particles from incomplete combustion.

Soot is particles of carbon impregnated with tar.

Vapor is the gaseous phase of material that is liquid or solid at normal temperature and pressure.

CLASSIFICATION OF POLLUTANTS *

Major classes	*Sub-classes*	*Typical members of sub-classes*
ORGANIC GASES	Hydrocarbons	Methane, butane, octane, benzene, acetylene, ethylene, butadiene
	Aldehydes & Ketones	Formaldehyde, acetone
	Other organics	Chlorinated hydrocarbons, benzopyrene, alcohols, organic acid
INORGANIC GASES	Oxides of nitrogen	Nitrogen dioxide, nitric oxide, nitrous oxide
	Oxides of sulfur	Sulfur dioxide, sulfur trioxide
	Oxides of carbon	Carbon monoxide, carbon dioxide
	Other inorganics	Hydrogen sulfide, hydrogen fluoride, ammonia, chlorine
PARTICULATES	Solid particulates	Dust, smoke
	Liquid particulates	Mist, spray

* Modified from a table in *Elements of Air Quality Management*, U.S. Department of Health, Education and Welfare, August 1967.

The Federal government has made studies of Air Quality Criteria for several individual pollutants. These studies are available from the National Technical Information Service, U.S. Department of Commerce, 5285 Port Royal Road, Springfield, Va., 22151.

See also the selected bibliography on page Three-25.

sources of air pollution

Air pollution can come from natural or man-made sources. The former are rarely of concern to lawyers. Man-made sources frequently are divided between stationary and mobile sources. From an administrative and control point of view, such a division is useful, as mobile sources can quickly change legal jurisdictions, are very numerous, and therefore difficult to control.

From an engineering point of view, mobile sources, particularly the internal combustion engine, present difficult technical problems. The pollution abatement equipment must be limited in size, weight, and cost, and must function with little maintenance effort if it is to serve its intended purpose.

Mobile sources are the major source of air pollution, and the automobile accounts for most of the problem. These air pollutants eventually poison our waters as well. According to Dr. John Middleton, Acting Commissioner, Air Pollution Control Office of EPA:

> "The automobile is the source of around 60 percent of all man-made air pollution in 57 urban areas containing about 60 percent of the nation's population. In these areas, the contribution of emissions from the automobile to the total pollution of the air ranges from 17.2 percent in industrialized Steubenville, Ohio, to 91.7 percent in urbanized Los Angeles. The automobile is the source of two-thirds of the carbon monoxide that is discharged into the air of the United States each year. It is the chief source of lead and, in some cities, it is a significant source of undifferentiated particulate matter."

Other writers would add asbestos from brakes and rubber from tires to the list of specific pollutants from automobiles.

The smog problem which found fame originally in Los Angeles is created by nitrogen dioxide and hydrocarbons and sunlight combining to create ozone, which recombines with nitrogen dioxide to create chemicals usually labeled photochemical smog. One common chemical which forms is peroxyacetyl nitrate (PAN), others are the aldehydes including formaldehyde.

Pollution from stationary sources is much more diverse. Milling of grain, demolition, crushing and grinding operations produce dust or particulates. Home heating, incineration, refuse burning and fossil fuel power plants produce the byproducts of incomplete combustion. These byproducts include sulfur oxides, nitrogen oxides, carbon monoxide, smoke, flyash, vapors, and odors.

Manufacturing processes produce a wide variety of pollutants. Metallurgical plants, chemical plants, petroleum refineries, and paper and pulp mills are among the worst air (as well as water) pollutors. Manufacturing plants produce all of the pollutants of incomplete combustion as well as hundreds of other toxic substances. Very little is known of their combined effects. Agricultural activities produce some particulate pollution, but the main problem is the wide dissemination of pesticides. The nuclear energy industry in its ore preparation, fuel fabrication, nuclear fission, spent fuel reprocessing, and nuclear testing, creates radioactive air pollutants. These problems are discussed in Volume Two of this work.

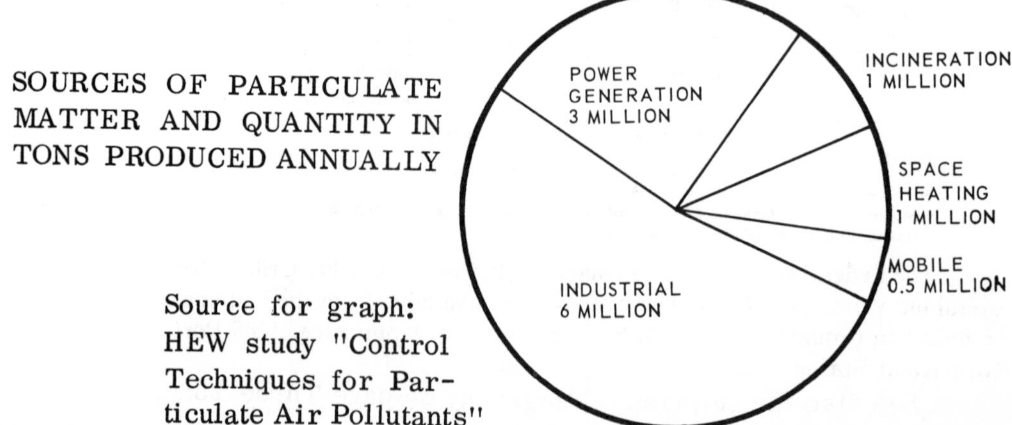

SOURCES OF PARTICULATE MATTER AND QUANTITY IN TONS PRODUCED ANNUALLY

Source for graph: HEW study "Control Techniques for Particulate Air Pollutants"

asbestos

Asbestos has long been known as a serious health problem. For a depressing introduction to the field, the various studies of the fate of asbestos workers are recommended. One, condensed in the *Washington Post* of October 21, 1971 from an article appearing that same week in the *New Yorker* magazine, explains that of a statistical 285 deaths otherwise to be expected among persons who worked during World War II in an asbestos factory, 425 were dead by 1970. Forty-seven had died of asbestosis (a lung disease), while 161 had died of cancer. Surprisingly, the cancer was often in the stomach or colon, rather than in the lungs. The study indicated that persons who worked for as little as a year in an asbestos factory had a cancer death rate five times the U.S. average.

The study and others mentioned in the article showed that a supposedly "safe" type of asbestos—the amosite variety—was as dangerous as the more common type—the chrysotile variety.

Regulation of this contaminant in the outdoor atmosphere is needed because of the large amounts released from automobile brake linings and from the use of asbestos as a fireproofing material in construction. Asbestos used for the latter purpose is also released during demolition.

On October 8, 1971, the National Academy of Sciences warned that the major sources of man-made asbestos emission, industrial processing and the use of products containing asbestos, must be defined and controlled, or asbestos ambient air concentrations in some localities would approach those encountered by workers in the asbestos industry. See "Asbestos: The Need for and Feasibility of Air Pollution Controls," NAS Printing and Publishing Office, Washington, D.C.

REFERENCE

See, SAX, Dangerous Properties of Industrial Materials, 1968.

Industrial process and control summary

Industry or process	Source of emissions	Particulate matter	Method of control
Iron and steel mills	Blast furnaces, steel making furnaces, sintering machines.	Iron oxide, dust, smoke	Cyclones, baghouses, electrostatic precipitators, wet collectors.
Gray iron foundries	Cupolas, shake out systems, core making.	Iron oxide, dust, smoke, oil, grease, metal fumes.	Scrubbers, dry centrifugal collectors.
Metallurgical (non-ferrous)	Smelters and furnaces	Smoke, metal fumes, oil, grease.	Electrostatic precipitators, fabric filters.
Petroleum refineries	Catalyst regenerators, sludge incinerators.	Catalyst dust, ash from sludge.	High-efficiency cyclones, electrostatic precipitators, scrubbing towers, baghouses.
Portland cement	Kilns, dryers, material handling systems.	Alkali and process dusts	Fabric filters, electrostatic precipitator, mechanical collectors.
Kraft paper mills	Chemical recovery furnaces, smelt tanks, lime kilns.	Chemical dusts	Electrostatic precipitators, venturi scrubbers.
Acid manufacture-phosphoric, sulfuric.	Thermal processes, phosphate rock acidulating, grinding and handling systems.	Acid mist, dust	Electrostatic precipitators, mesh mist eliminators.

SOURCE: "Control Techniques for Particulates," HEW publication, 1969.

Emissions of Air Pollutants from Stationary Sources in 298 Metropolitan Areas and in Total United States

(Tons in thousands)

Pollutant	Emissions in 298 areas (tons)	Total U.S. emissions (tons)	Percent covered in 298 areas	Percent reduction expected in 1976
Process Sources				
Particulates	4,601	6,915	67	93
Sulfur oxides	5,156	6,695	77	72
Carbon monoxide	7,520	9,400	80	95
Hydrocarbons	1,412	2,034	69	51
Fluorides	53	72	74	88
Lead	21	22	95	67
Combustion Sources				
Particulates	3,247	8,937	36	76
Sulfur oxides	11,416	22,130	52	67

Source: Environmental Protection Agency.

SOURCE for the table above: "Environmental Quality," the second annual report of the Council on Environmental Quality, August, 1971.

SOURCE for the two tables below: "Control Techniques for Particulates," HEW publication, 1969.

Examples of particulate emission factors

Source	Specific process	Particulate emission rate, uncontrolled
Aircraft	Four engine fan jet	7.4 lb/flight.
Solid waste disposal	Open burning dump	16 lb/ton of refuse.
Phosphoric acid manufacturing.	Thermal process	0.2–10.8 lb/ton of phosphorus burned.
Sulfuric acid manufacturing.	Contact process	0.3–7.5 lb/ton of acid produced.
Food and agricultural	Coffee roasting, direct fired	7.6 lb/ton of green beans.
	Cotton ginning and incineration of trash	11.7 lb/bale of cotton.
Feed and grain mills	General operation	6 lb/ton of product.
Primary metal industry	Iron and steel manufacturing furnace, open hearth (oxygen lance).	22 lb/ton of steel.
Secondary metal industry	Aluminum smelting, chlorination-lancing	1000 lb/ton of chlorine.
	Brass and bronze smelting reverberatory furnace.	26.3 lb/ton of metal charged.
	Gray iron foundry cupola	17.4 lb/ton of metal charged.

Installed costs of control equipment

Collector type	Approximate installed cost, in thousands of dollars — Gas flow rates (1000 actual cubic feet per minute)						
	2	5	10	15	100	300	500
Gravity	0.5	1.2	2.6	15	28	------	------
Mechanical	------	------	4	13	23	80	------
Wet	------	7.5	10	30	55	150	------
High-voltage electrostatic precipitator	------	------	------	85	120	265	415
Low-voltage electrostatic precipitator	------	13	24	105	200	------	------
Fabric filter:							
High temperature (550° F.)	------	------	30	88	155	430	720
Medium temperature (250° F.)	------	------	15	45	82	225	375
Afterburner, direct flame catalytic	8.2	12	18	------	------	------	------
	16	20	29	------	------	------	------

Reitze

Six main classes of air pollutants are found in the air over the United States. These are particulates, sulfur oxides, hydrocarbons, carbon monoxide, nitrogen oxides, and photochemical oxidants. Each of these have been studied by the federal government and are found in documents required by law and designated as Air Quality Criteria. A Summary and Conclusion pamphlet of about 13 pages is available for each of these pollutants.

c. Control devices for stationary sources

The reduction of air pollution can be achieved by process modification (using a higher-temperature incinerator); material substitution (gas for high-sulfur coal); or by cleaning the gases that result from combustion or manufacturing processes. It is this third technique that this subsection will discuss.

The amount of reduction in the emission of air pollutants is determined by the efficiency of the removal equipment. One hundred percent efficiency is a goal that is difficult to achieve, and as such efficiency of reduction is approached, costs of abatement increase rapidly. Often the combination of equipment used will be based on the need to meet an emission standard. For example, particulate concentration of .02 grains per standard cubic foot (gr/SCF) in stack gases will satisfy most air pollution standards of performance. The equipment is then selected with sufficient reduction efficiency to reach such emission standards.

Once such equipment is installed, it becomes progressively more difficult to meet lower emission standards. In industrial areas for example, even the .02 grain emission might be found too high to meet atmospheric quality goals. Under federal, state, and some local laws, air pollution control is based on the reduction of emissions to reach a predetermined atmospheric quality. Such an approach can require an emission source to increase continuously the reduction efficiency as emission limitations are made more restrictive.

The cleaning of emissions can be divided into gas cleaning processes and the removal of particulates. Odors and some of the pollutants, especially from the chemical industry, can present special problems.

There are three categories of methods for removing pollutants from gases: (1) absorption into a liquid, (2) withdrawal onto a solid, and, (3) chemical change. Examples of these three categories are, respectively: spray towers, bag systems, and burning.

wet collectors

Wet collectors usually use water. Their advantages include the ability to handle high humidity gases, minimal space requirements, gas and particulate collection is simultaneous, and high temperature gas is cooled. Their disadvantages include stream plume problems and the disposal of the liquid and/or removal of the pollutants. Thus, air pollution control can increase water pollution.

There are many kinds of wet collectors, including spray chambers, cyclone scrubbers, induced draft scrubbers, packed beds, venturi scrubbers, foam scrubbers and wetted filter scrubbers. All seek to clean air by dirtying a liquid, usually water.

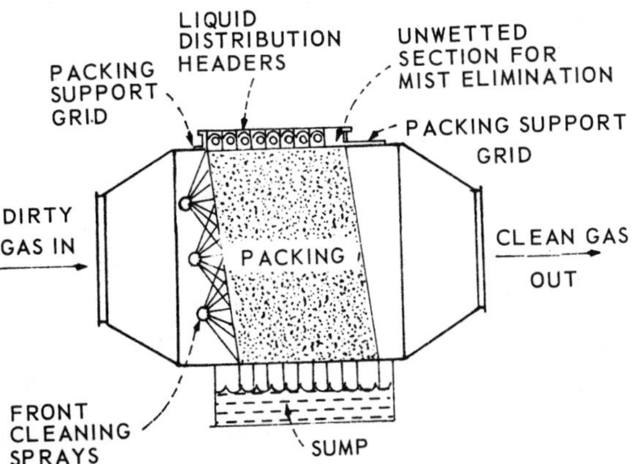

PACKED-BED SCRUBBER OF CROSS-FLOW TYPE

wet collectors

For washing pollutants from gases, absorption equipment may form a packed, plate, or tray tower. In these systems a liquid enters one end of the system (a vertical or horizontal cylinder) and the gases enter the opposite end. In traveling through the system the gases are absorbed.

In a spray tower the principle is the same, though there are engineering advantages and disadvantages. There is much less gas-liquid interfacial area, but at the same time the gases entering the system have a much smaller pressure drop. In a Venturi scrubber, both liquid and gas enter near the throat and flow with the gas, moving into an entrainment separator. This is a less satisfactory gas removal process because of the large pressure drops incurred. Floating bed scrubbers use a floating bed-sieve tray arrangement. Its use is most advantageous when gas streams contain particulates.

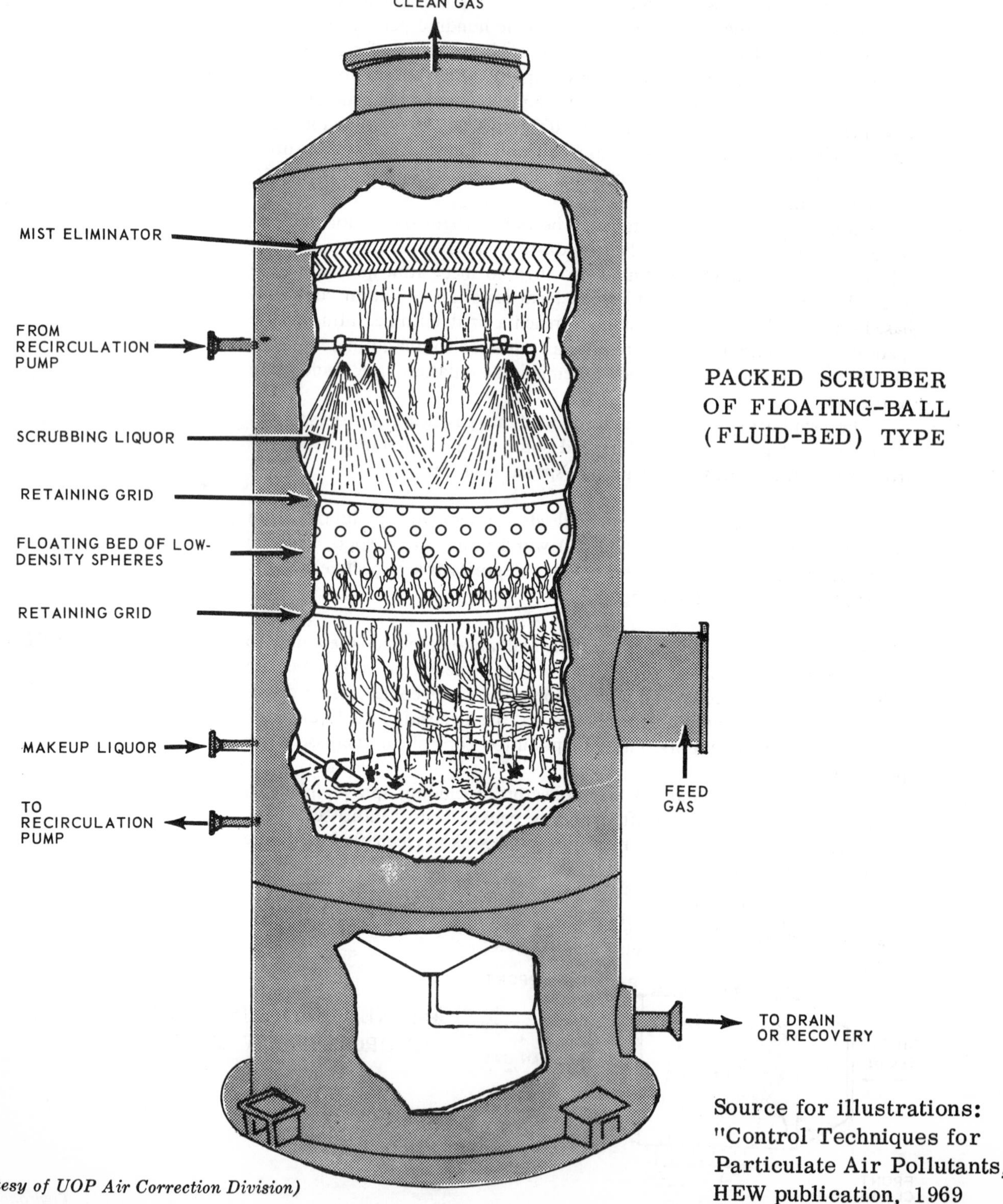

PACKED SCRUBBER OF FLOATING-BALL (FLUID-BED) TYPE

(Courtesy of UOP Air Correction Division)

Source for illustrations: "Control Techniques for Particulate Air Pollutants," HEW publication, 1969

a.

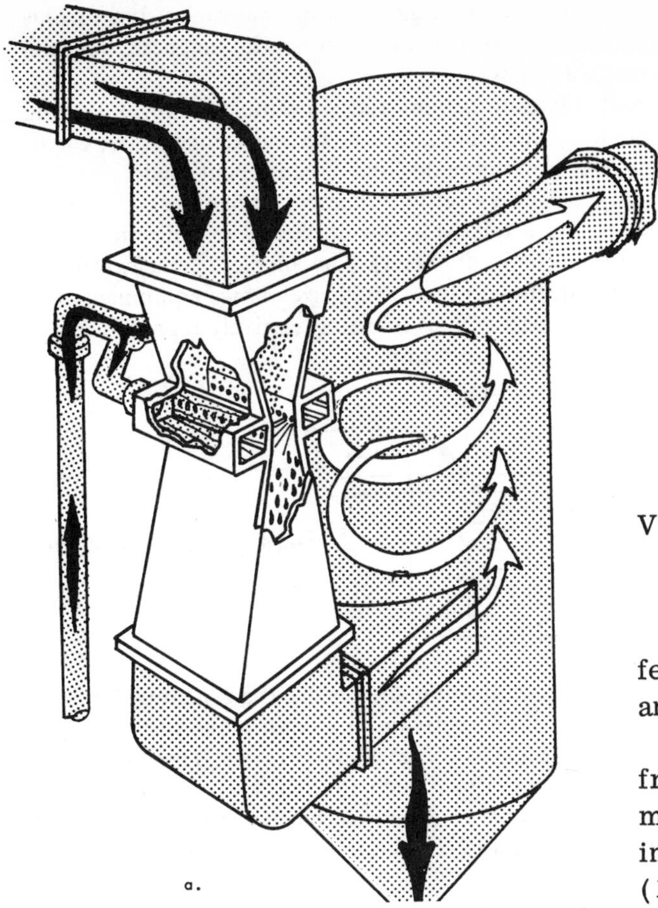

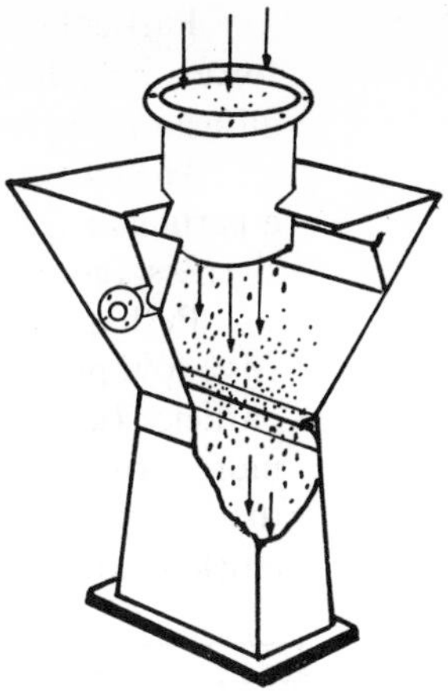

b.

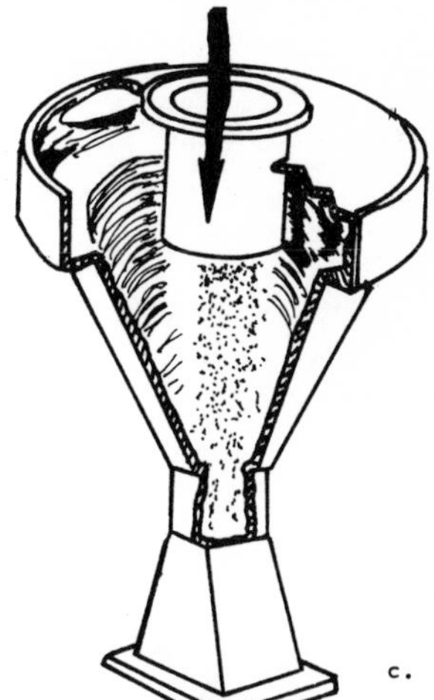

c.

VENTURI SCRUBBERS OF THREE TYPES

In figure (a), the scrubbing liquid is fed via jets; in (b) it goes over a weir, and in (c) it is sent swirling over a shelf.

Venturi scrubbers derive their name from their similarity to the device for measuring the flow of a fluid which was invented by Italian physicist G. B. Venturi (1746 - 1822).

BELOW, OTHER TYPES OF WET COLLECTORS FOR GASES

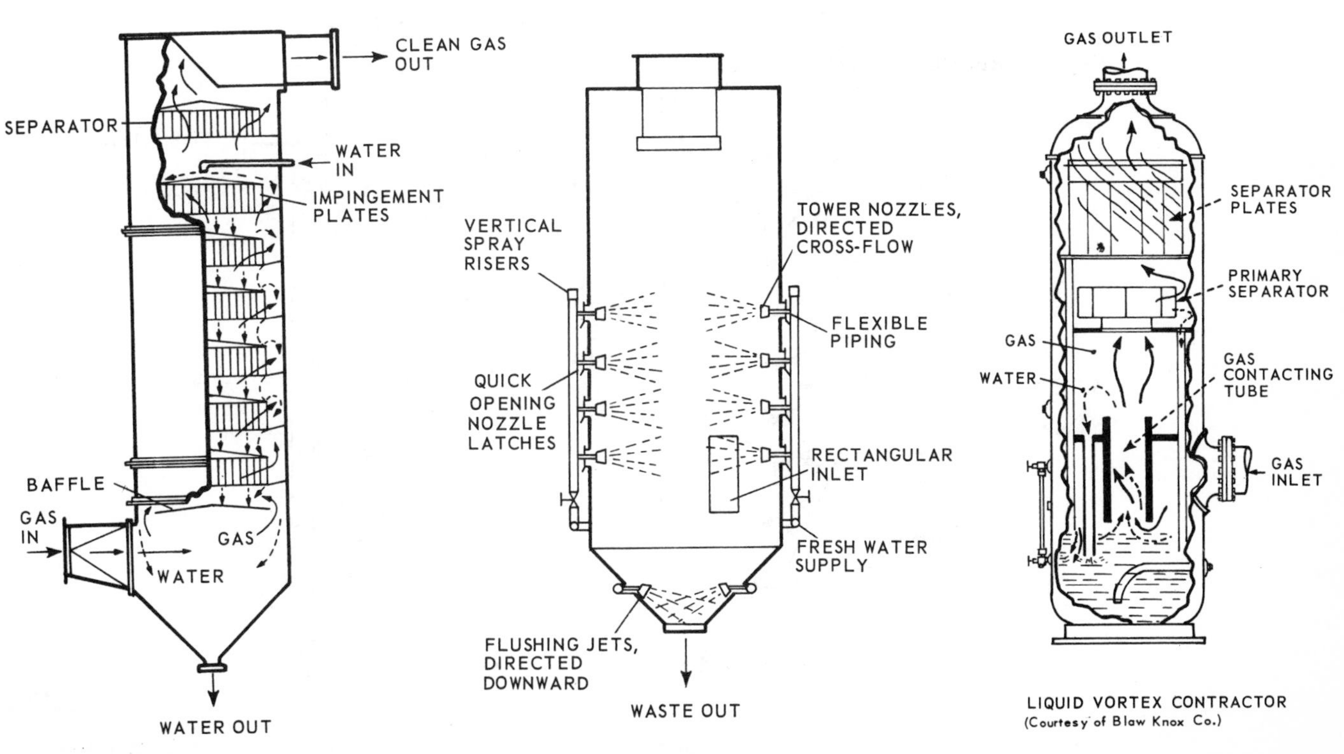

MULTI-WASH SCRUBBER.
(Courtesy of Claude B. Schneible Company)

CYCLONIC SPRAY SCRUBBER.
(Courtesy of Buffalo Forge Company)

LIQUID VORTEX CONTRACTOR
(Courtesy of Blaw Knox Co.)

withdrawing onto a solid

Particulates can be removed from gases by mechanisms using various forces, including gravitational, centrifugal, electrostatic, magnetic, thermal diffusion, and Brownian diffusion.

The size of the particulates to be removed is a critical factor in utilizing a particular technique, but other characteristics such as temperature, corrosiveness, flammability, etc., determine the kind of equipment used.

Perhaps the simplest device is a settling chamber. It has low construction cost, low pressure drop, but a relatively low efficiency in collecting small particles (less than 50 microns in diameter). The smaller particles are the more serious health hazard, though their small size allows equipment with the ability to trap only large particulates to claim relatively high percentage efficiencies in reducing particulate pollution.

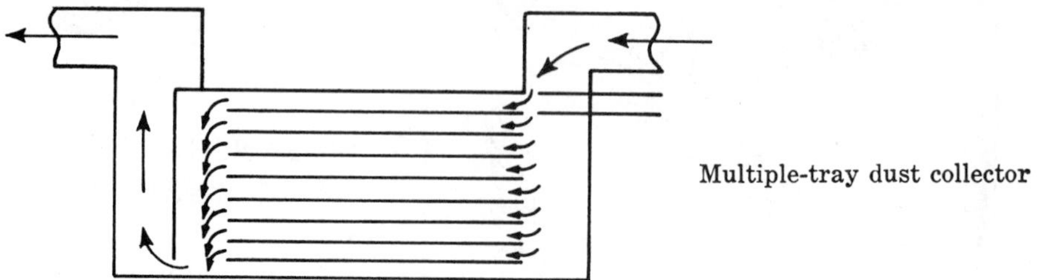

Multiple-tray dust collector

The most commonly used collection devices are the **centrifugal collectors** or **cyclones.** These move the gas stream in a continuous spiral, simply letting the large particles fall aside as the gas (smoke) rises. These are often cleaned simply by beating them, after which the particles become a solid waste disposal problem. It is simple to construct, has no moving parts, and can be designed in a variety of ways, though the tangential inlet cyclone is the most common.

The collection efficiency is dependent upon a number of factors. Large particles are collected more efficiently; the physical design is important (narrow diameter with high inlet gas velocity increases efficiency). However, pressure in the particulate collection hopper caused by an improperly maintained system or one with air leaks can reduce efficiency.

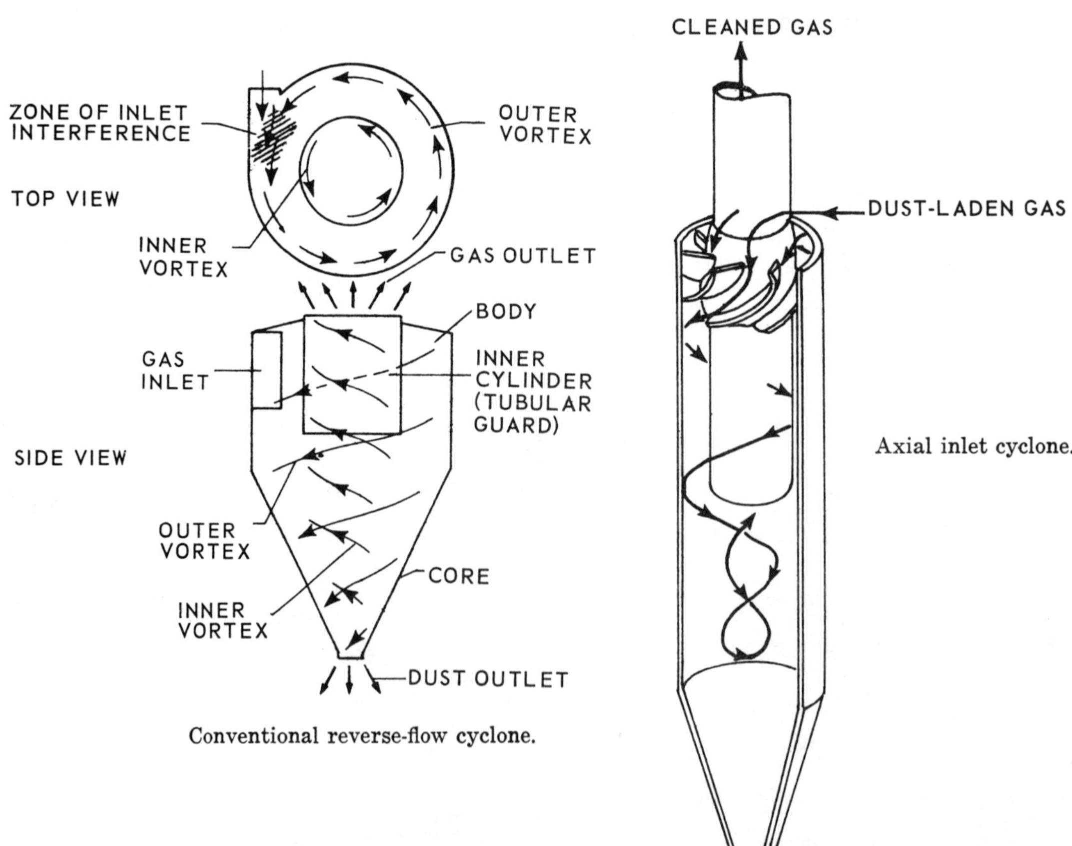

Conventional reverse-flow cyclone.

Axial inlet cyclone.

Filter collectors (bag systems) are porous structures which remove particulate matter passing through them. Two types are common, fibrous or deep-bed, and cloth or paper filters, the latter having a high efficiency.

Fibrous filters are common in air conditioners. In industrial air pollution control systems, cloth or fabric filters are arranged as bags. They are cleaned by shaking, or with air jets or reverse air flow. Cotton, wool, asbestos, glass and synthetics can be used, for the choice of filters depends upon the characteristics of the gas and its pollutants.

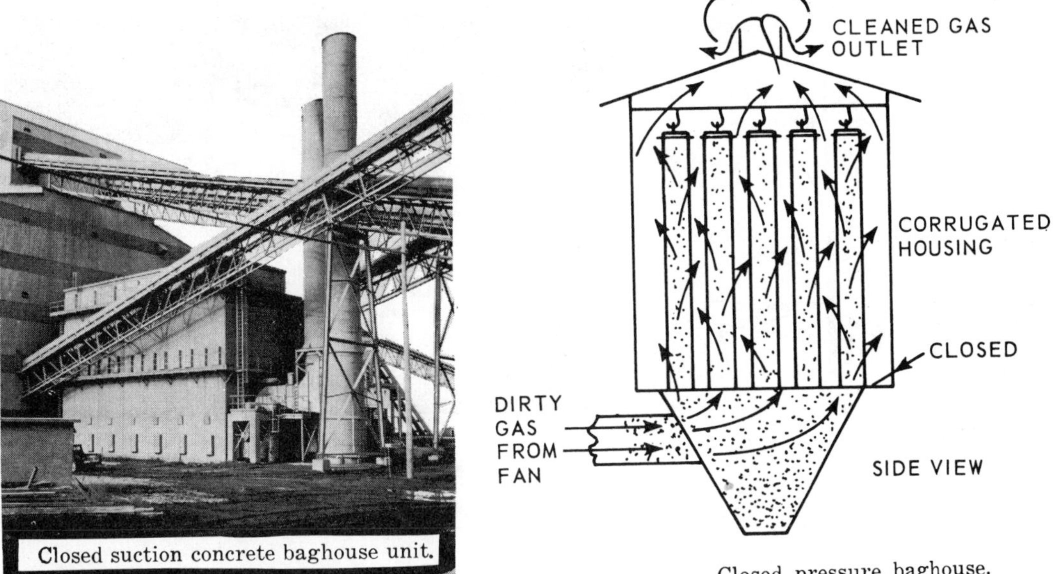

Closed suction concrete baghouse unit.
(Courtesy of the Wheelabrator Corporation)

Closed pressure baghouse.

Electrostatic precipitators use an electric field to charge particles which are attracted to a plate or tube (the positive electrode). The particles are removed by rapping, scraping, brushing, or washing. Their disposal can be a water purity or solid waste problem. The precipitators can be two-stage-low-voltage or single-stage-high-voltage types. Efficiencies can be high if designed properly, but both capital and operating costs are high.

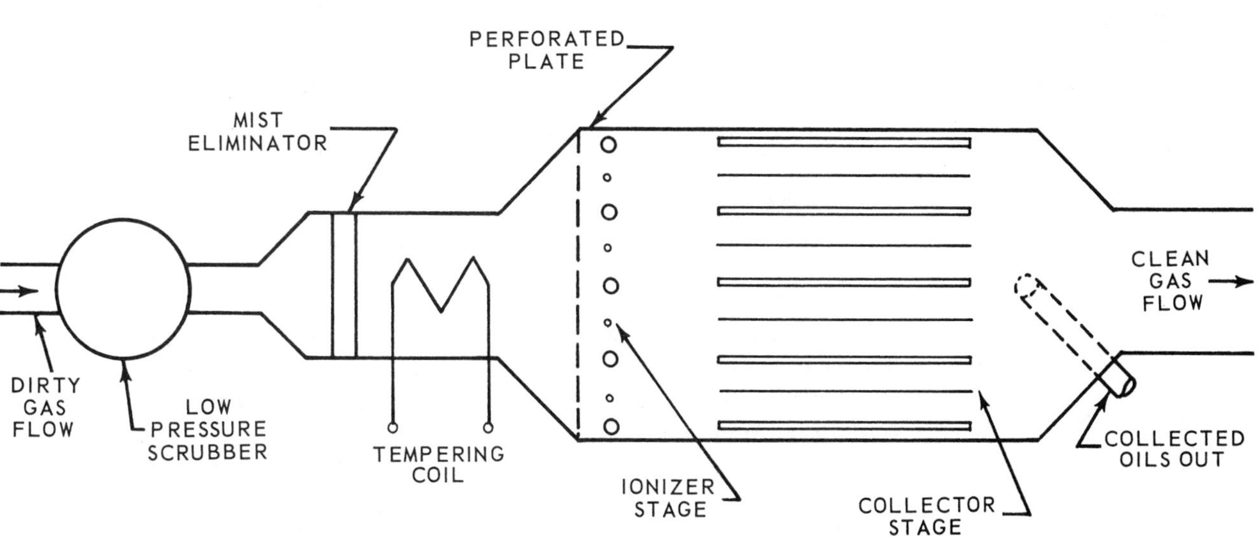

Two-stage electrostatic precipitator with auxiliary scrubber, mist eliminator, tempering coil, and gas distribution plate (top view).

chemical change

Combustion processes depend upon a proper temperature, combustion time, and fuel-oxygen mixing to convert gaseous pollutants into carbon dioxide and water. Two common types of these devices are flame combustion and catalytic combustion.

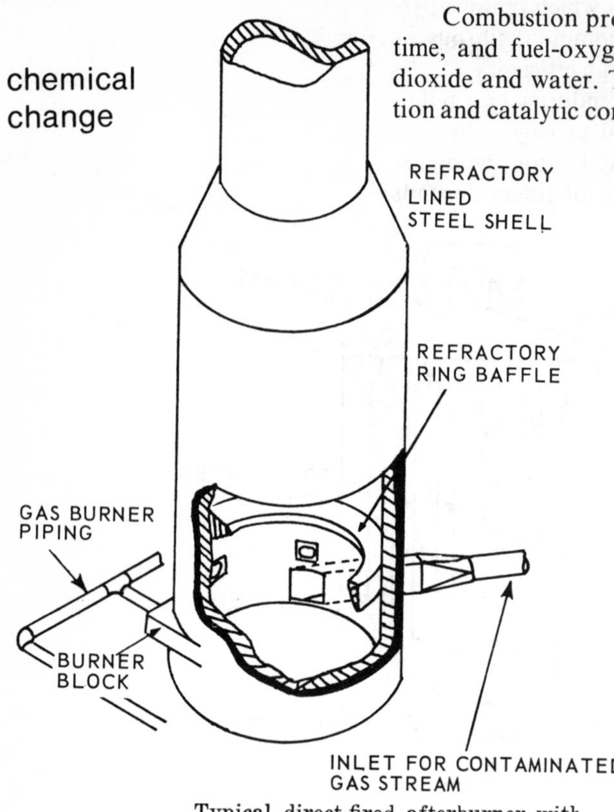

Typical direct-fired afterburner with tangential entries for both fuel and contaminated gases.

Multiple-port high-intensity premix burner.
(Courtesy of Maxon Premix Burner Company)

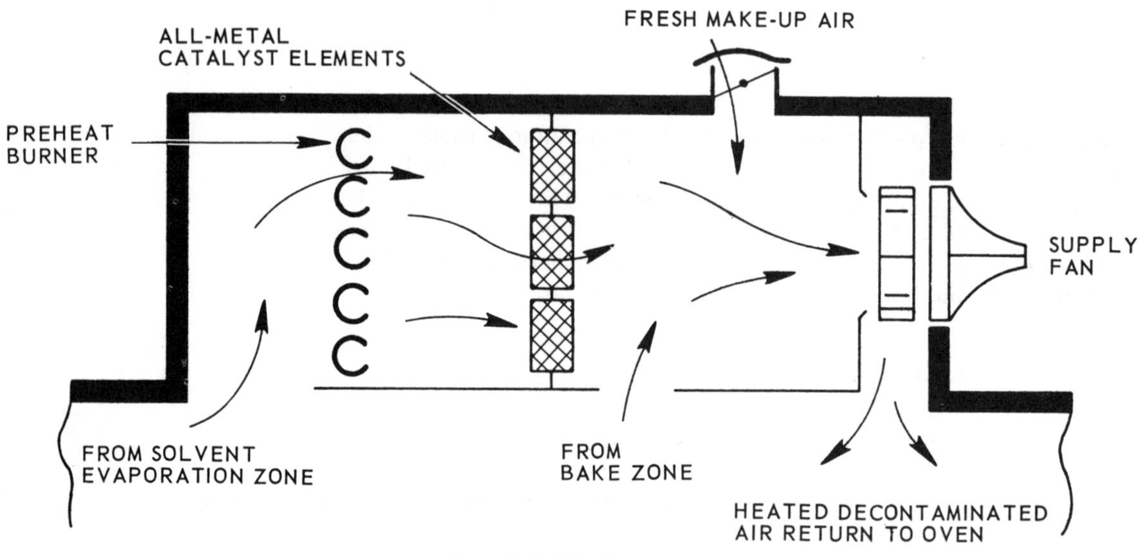

Direct recirculation of combustion gases to recover heat.

The removal of the wide variety of air pollutants from the various industrial processes requires solutions tailored to the industry. Both the combination of pollutants and the form in which they are produced must be considered. Many processes can be controlled only by expensive installations. Odors can be controlled by dispersal, combustion, or absorption. Much research needs to be done to perfect the air pollution abatement equipment to increase efficiency, decrease size, and reduce the costs involved in their use, but present technology can go immensely further toward eliminating present pollutants. The frequent contention by factory owners that the "state of the art" isn't sufficient to clean their emissions much more efficiently is nearly always bunk.

As one of the requirements of the 1967 Air Quality Act, the Federal government must release documents on control techniques for each of the air pollutants for which criteria are issued. Thus a book exists on control techniques for: Particulate Air Pollutants, Sulfur Oxide, Carbon Monoxide. Photochemical Oxidants, Hydrocarbons, Nitrogen Oxides

Short summaries of these control documents can be found in the Environment Reporter (BNA).

Advantages and disadvantages of various collection devices

Collector	Advantages	Disadvantages
Gravitational	Low pressure loss, simplicity of design and maintainance.	Much space required. Low collection efficiency.
Cyclone	Simplicity of design and maintainance	Much head room required.
	Little floor space required	Low collection efficiency of small particles.
	Dry continuous disposal of collected dusts	Sensitive to variable dust loadings and flow rates.
	Low to moderate pressure loss.	
	Handles large particles.	
	Handles high dust loadings.	
	Temperature independent.	
Wet collectors	Simultaneous gas absorption and particle removal.	Corrosion, erosion problems. Added cost of wastewater treatment and reclamation.
	Ability to cool and clean high-temperature, moisture-laden gases.	Low efficiency on submicron particles.
	Corrosive gases and mists can be recovered and neutralized.	Contamination of effluent stream by liquid entrainment.
	Reduced dust explosion risk	Freezing problems in cold weather.
	Efficiency can be varied	Reduction in buoyancy and plume rise. Water vapor contributes to visible plume under some atmospheric conditions.
Electrostatic precipitator.	99+ percent efficiency obtainable	Relatively high initial cost.
	Very small particles can be collected	Precipitators are sensitive to variable dust loadings or flow rates.
	Particles may be collected wet or dry	Resistivity causes some material to be economically uncollectable.
	Pressure drops and power requirements are small compared to other high-efficiency collectors.	Precautions are required to safeguard personnel from high voltage.
	Maintenance is nominal unless corrosive or adhesive materials are handled.	Collection efficiencies can deteriorate gradually and imperceptibly.
	Few moving parts	
	Can be operated at high temperatures (550° to 850° F.).	
Fabric filtration	Dry collection possible	Sensitivity to filtering velocity.
	Decrease of performance is noticeable	High-temperature gases must be cooled to 200° to 550° F.
	Collection of small particles possible	Affected by relative humidity (condensation).
	High efficiencies possible	Susceptibility of fabric to chemical attack.
Afterburner, direct flame.	High removal efficiency of submicron odor-causing particulate matter.	High operational cost. Fire hazard.
	Simultaneous disposal of combustible gaseous and particulate matter.	Removes only combustibles.
	Direct disposal of non-toxic gases and wastes to the atmosphere after combustion.	
	Possible heat recovery	
	Relatively small space requirement	
	Simple construction	
	Low maintenance	
Afterburner, catalytic.	Same as direct flame afterburner	High initial cost.
	Compared to direct flame: reduced fuel requirements, reduced temperature, insulation requirements, and fire hazard.	Catalysts subject to poisoning. Catalysts require reactivation.

SOURCE: "Control Techniques for Particulates," HEW publication, 1969.

Nationwide sources of sulfur dioxide emissions, 1966

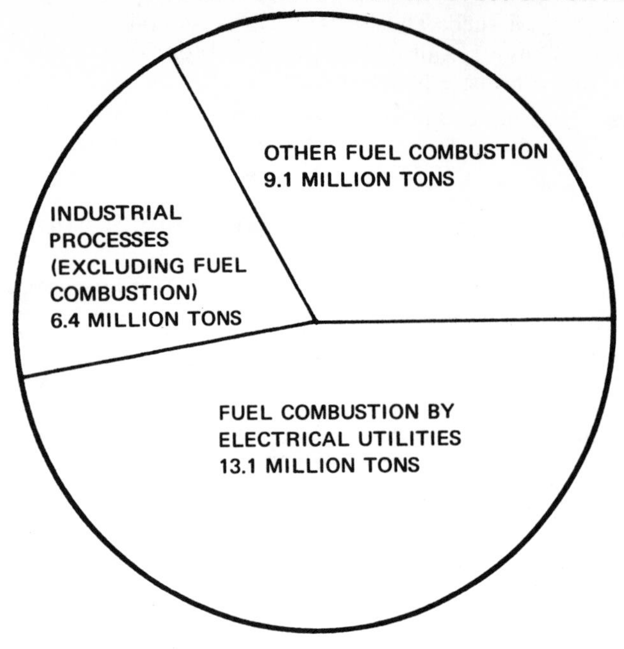

SOURCE for graph and both tables: "Control Techniques for Sulfur Oxide Air Pollutants," HEW, 1969

SO_2 emissions from fuel combustion, 1966

Source	SO_2 emissions, tons
Utility coal	11,925,000
Utility oil	1,218,000
Other coal	4,700,000
Other oil	4,386,000
Natural gas	3,500
Total	22,232,500

SO_2 emissions from industrial processes, 1966

	SO_2 emissions, tons
Ore smelting	3,500,000
Petroleum	1,583,000
Sulfuric acid manufacturing	550,000
Coke processing	500,000
Refuse burning	200,000
Miscellaneous[a]	75,000
Total industrial process	6,408,000

[a]Includes chemical manufacturing, and pulp and paper production.

sulfur oxides

An oxide of sulfur is any chemical combination of sulfur and oxygen. However, this section deals with only two such oxides, sulfur dioxide (SO_2) and sulfur trioxide (SO_3), which are the most common sulfur oxide pollutants. Sulfur dioxide is an invisible, nonflammable, acidic gas that oxidizes to sulfur trioxide in the atmosphere at varying rates depending on temperature and other substances. Sulfur trioxide combines readily with water to form sulfuric acid mist (H_2SO_4) or combines with other materials in the atmosphere to form sulfate compounds.

The 3 paragraphs which follow form a summary of the control techniques for emissions of sulfur oxides. It is reprinted from *Environmental Quality: The First Annual Report of the Council on Environmental Quality,* August, 1970:

At present about 65 percent of the energy for generating electricity stems from coal; gas, oil, and hydroelectric sources account for about 34 percent; and nuclear energy the remaining 1 percent. By 1980, 22 percent of the total installed electric power capacity is expected to be nuclear. By 1990, it will be 40 percent. However, by far the greatest source of energy is now, and will continue to be for the rest of this century, the burning of coal and oil. The amount of coal used for power by the year 2000 will be four times greater than it is today.

A number of alternatives are available to control sulfur oxide pollution over the next decade. Switching fuels is possible, but only when an alternative, low-sulfur fuel is available. Most coal near the Nation's centers of population and power demand is high in sulfur. Low-sulfur coal not only is far away but also commands a higher price for use as coke by domestic and foreign steelmakers. North Africa and other areas are rich in low sulfur oil but are limited by low production and refinery capabilities. Oil import quotas bar it from certain areas of the Midwest and the West Coast, although the oil may be imported to other areas of the United States. The United States will probably continue to rely primarily on residual oil from the Western Hemisphere. And that oil will have to be desulfurized before it is used. Natural gas carries an insignificant sulfur content, but it is the scarcest of fossil fuels, and most of it is being conserved for nonpower purposes.

Sulfur can be separated from coal and oil, but the processes are costly, and some are not fully developed technically. Methods to remove sulfur from the stack gases after the fuel is burned are under development. However, none of these processes is yet in large-scale use and the costs are not yet known. Some of the stack control processes recover sulfur or a sulfur byproduct, which can be sold to help offset costs. Some are also being evaluated for their potential in reducing pollution from nitrogen oxides.

End, excerpt from *Environmental Quality,* 1970.

The French have come up with what may be the most unusual method yet of ridding a city of the sulphuric acid mist that the sulfur oxides produce. Rather than place control on the sources of the emissions, they have erected in Paris a pair of test "pollution traps" which suck in air, remove the pollutants, and eject the clean air. The traps are 16½-foot-tall, five-foot-wide towers with fans capable of processing 557,000 cubic feet of air daily. They were commissioned by the nation's electricity monopoly, Electricite de France (New York Times News Service story with United Press International photo in the Washington *Evening Star,* Oct. 21, 1971 at A-12).

The following four paragraphs sum up the Federal government's research efforts in this field. They are from *Progress in the Prevention and Control of Air*

sulfur control research

Pollution, the annual report on implementation of the Clean Air Act, May 3, 1971:

Two of the projects involve demonstrations of privately developed flue gas desulfurization processes, both of which result in recovery of sulfuric acid. The magnesium oxide wet scrubbing process, developed by the Chemico Corp., is to be demonstrated at an oil-fired electric generating plant operated by the Boston Edison Co., testing is expected to begin late in 1971. The catalytic oxidation process, developed by the Monsanto Co., is to be demonstrated at a coal-fired electric generating plant operated by the Illinois Power Co.; testing is expected to begin mid-1972. These two processes are known to be technically feasible; the projects now underway will demonstrate the reliability economics of the processes on a large scale.

Another sulfur oxides control process, one developed by APCO and the Tennessee Valley Authority, is already undergoing large-scale demonstration testing at a TVA electric generating plant; this process is known as dry limestone injection. Following completion of the dry limestone project, demonstration of a second process, the limestone injection and wet scrubbing process, will be undertaken at the same plant. Though these processes do not yield a byproduct now considered usable, they are relatively close to commercial applicability. It is anticipated that limestone injection and wet scrubbing will be capable of achieving better than 90 percent removal of sulfur oxides, that it will also remove particulate matter, and that its costs will be reasonable.

Through a demonstration grant to the city of Key West, Fla., APCO is supporting another demonstration of limestone injection and wet scrubbing at an electric generating facility. Because of the availability of a local supply of limestone (derived from coral), an ample low-cost water supply, and inexpensive waste treatment in a diked lagoon, the Key West facility provides a unique opportunity to demonstrate the economic and technical feasibility of the wet limestone process.

Among the processes described above, it is anticipated that one or more will go into commercial use within the next few years, particularly at electric generating plants, which are major sources of sulfur oxides pollution. But it is not expected that these processes will provide a full solution to the sulfur oxides problem. Accordingly APCO is supporting pilot-scale investigations of several other processes; the purpose is to identify processes that may have a higher sulfur oxides control efficiency, have more favorable economics, produce elemental sulfur rather than sulfuric acid as a byproduct, and simultaneously remove more than one pollutant. Four such processes currently are under investigation: the Westvaco regenerable char process, which produces elemental sulfur (easier and cheaper to store and ship than is sulfuric acid); the Tyco modified chamber process to remove sulfur oxides, nitrogen oxides, and particulate matter with production of sulfuric and nitric acids as byproducts; Atomics International's molten carbonate process, which produces elemental sulfur; and the ammonia scrubbing process, which can be made to produce sulfuric acid.

End quote.

On June 4, 1971, President Nixon's Energy Message contained a request for an increase of $15 million for FY 72 making a total of $26 million available to develop and demonstrate, in partnership with industry, the technology for removing sulfur from the stack gases of power plants and industrial plants burning coal and oil.

See also the section beginning on page Introduction-38 in which a proposed tax on sulfur emissions is discussed.

The following brief glossary, borrowed from one in A Citizen's Guide to Clean Air (available free from the Conservation Foundation, 1717 Massachusetts Ave., N.W., Washington, D.C. 20036), is intended both as a quick review for the student, and as an aid to understanding the remaining sections of this chapter. The glossary is not intended to be complete, as the terms used in this field fill fair-sized technical dictionaries.

GLOSSARY

Air quality criteria—the levels of pollution and lengths of exposure at which, based on currently available scientific information, specific adverse effects on health and welfare are known to occur. These are delineated by EPA in "criteria documents."

Ambient air—the unconfined space occupied by the atmosphere; i.e., outdoor air. See: troposphere.

Ambient air quality standard—a limit on the amount of a given pollutant which will be permitted in the ambient air:

—long-term standard—typically a limit for one year for a given pollutant. It is usually expressed as an annual geometric mean or arithmetic mean.

—short-term standard—a limit for a short period of time for a given pollutant, such as one day, three hours, and so on.

—primary standard—a limit for a given pollutant that, according to the Act, is to be set by EPA at a level stringent enough to protect the public health.

—secondary standard—a limit for a given pollutant that, according to the Act, is to be set by EPA at a level stringent enough to protect the public welfare.

Anti-degradation clause—a provision in air quality standards that prohibits deterioration of air quality in areas where the pollution levels are presently below those allowed by the standards.

Area source—small, diffused individual pollutant sources such as automobiles, home or commercial heating units, small home incinerators.

Arithmetic mean—the sum of a given number of factors divided by the number of factors, e.g., $3+4+5+6 = 18 \div 4 = 4.5$. Arithmetic means tend to be higher than geometric means.

Background level—amounts of pollutants present in the ambient air due to natural sources. Examples: marsh gases, pollen.

BTU (British Thermal Unit)—the amount of heat needed to raise the temperature of one pound of water one degree Fahrenheit.

Carbon monoxide (CO)—a colorless, odorless, very toxic gas produced by any process that involves the incomplete combustion of carbon-containing substances such as coal, oil, gasoline and natural gas.

Carcinogenic—cancer-producing.

Chilling effect—phenomenon in which the increase in atmospheric particulates inhibits penetration of the sun's energy, thus gradually lowering the temperature of the earth.

Coh—abbreviation for "coefficient of haze," a unit for the measurement of visibility interference.

Compliance schedule—a legally enforceable detailed timetable of actions to be taken by a pollution source to bring it into accord with implementation plans or other regulations.

Control strategy—the combination of measures (such as emission limitations, land-use plans, emission taxes) designed to reduce levels of a specific pollutant in the ambient air.

Control techniques—methods, equipment and devices applicable to the prevention and control of air pollutants at their sources, such as process changes, flue gas stack devices, stack height requirements, fuel use limitations, plant location rules, and so on. They are described in EPA's control-techniques documents.

Effluent—an outflow; a discharge or emission of a liquid or gas.

Electrostatic precipitator—a device that uses electrical (rather than mechanical or chemical) attraction to collect particulates for measurement, analysis or control.

Geometric mean—the Nth root of the product of N factors (N = number of factors), e.g., $3 \times 4 \times 5 \times 6 = \sqrt[4]{360} = 4.35+$. Geometric means are often lower than arithmetic means.

Greenhouse effect—the phenomenon in which the sun's energy, in the form of light waves, passes through the atmosphere and is absorbed by the earth, which then radiates the energy as heat waves that the air is able to absorb. The air thus behaves like glass in a greenhouse, allowing the passage of light while trapping heat.

Hazardous air pollutant—defined by the Act as a pollutant which, in EPA's judgment, "may cause, or contribute to, an increase in mortality or in serious irreversible, or incapacitating reversible, illness." These pollutants include asbestos, beryllium, cadmium, and mercury.

Hydrocarbons—any of a vast family of compounds originating in materials containing carbon and hydrogen in various combinations. Some may be carcinogenic; other are active participants in photochemical processes in combination with oxides of nitrogen.

Implementation plan—a state blueprint of the steps that will be taken to ensure attainment of an air quality standard within a specified time period.

Inversion—the phenomenon in which a layer of cool air is trapped by a layer of warmer air above it so that the botton layer cannot rise.

Margin of safety—the difference between an allowable level for a given pollutant and a criteria level at which adverse effects have been noted, assuming that the allowable level is numerically lower. Significance is normally expressed in units of 5, e.g., 75 $\mu g/m^3$, 80 $\mu g/m^3$, 85, etc., rather than in units of 1 or 2 $\mu g/m^3$.

Mean—see: arithmetic mean, geometric mean.

Micrograms per cubic meter ($\mu g/m^3$)—a weight per unit volume measurement. Micro is a prefix meaning 1/1,000,000.

Monitoring—sampling by local, state, and regional agencies as part of a surveillance system for measuring pollutants present in the atmosphere or pollutants emitted from an individual point source, e.g., a factory stack.

Oxide—a compound of two elements, one of which is oxygen.

Ozone (O_3)—a pungent, colorless, toxic gas; one component of photochemical smog.

Parts per million (ppm)—a volume unit of measurement; the number of parts of a given substance in a million parts of air.

Photochemical process—the chemical changes and interactions brought about by the radiant energy of the sun acting upon foreign substances in the air. Results in smog.

Point source—a stationary source that emits a given pollutant in amounts above specified levels (such as 25 tons per year).

Ringelmann charts—a series of charts, scaled from 0 to 5, for measuring the density of black smoke rising from stacks and other sources (5 is the most dense, 0 the least). These charts are often used in setting emission standards and checking on compliance.

Scrubber—a device that uses a spray to remove aerosol and gaseous pollutants from an air stream; used for both measurement and control of pollution.

Smog—the irritating haze resulting from the sun's effect on certain pollutants in the air, notably those from automobile exhaust. (Also a mixture of smoke and chemical "fog.")

Source—see: point source, area source.

Standard of performance—an emission limitation imposed on a particular category of pollution sources, either by EPA or by a state. Limitations may take the form of emission standards or of requirements for specific operating procedures.

Sulfur dioxide (SO_2)—a heavy, pungent, colorless gas formed primarily by combustion of coal, oil, and other sulfur-bearing compounds, but also produced in chemical plants and by processing metals and burning trash.

Surveillance system—a required part of implementation plans, established to monitor all aspects of progress toward attainment of air quality standards and to identify potential episodes of high pollutant concentrations in time to take preventive action. Also, the ambient monitoring network.

Synergism—the cooperative action of separate substances in such a way that the total effect is greater than the sum of the effects of the substances acting independently.

Troposphere—the innermost part of the 12-mile layer of air encircling the earth; it extends outward about 5 miles at the poles and 10 at the equator.

Variance—sanction granted by a governing body for delay or exception in the application of a given law, ordinance, or regulation.

West-Gaeke method (modified)—a colorimetric technique for measurement of sulfur dioxide and sulfite salts which can be modified to compensate for interferences produced by the presence of nitrogen oxides, ozone, or heavy metal salts in the sample. (EPA prefers the modified method.)

Selected Bibliography

EDELMAN, *The Law of Air Pollution Control,* 1970

KEENER, Kenneth, "A Current Survey of Federal Air Quality Control Legislation and Regulations," 5 *Nat. Res. L.* No. 1, January 1972 at 42.

Air Pollution Control, Symposium, 33 Law and Contemporary Problems #2, Spring 1968

MIDDLETON, Air Pollution Control: New Goals in the Law, 59 Kentucky L.J. 644 1971

ROSSANO, ed., *Air Pollution Control, Guidebook for Management,* 1969

WARD, ed., *Man and His Environment,* 1970

National Tuberculosis and Respiratory Disease Association, *Air Pollution Primer,* 1969

DAVIES III, *The Politics of Pollution,* 1970

BRODIE, Episode 104, 13 Environment #1, Jan-Feb 1971 at 2

"Air Pollution Control: A Symposium," 33 *Law & Contemporary Problems,* 195 Sept. 1968

"Air Pollution Symposium 1968," *Wash. U.L.Q.* 205, Sept. 1968

"Air Pollution Symposium," 10 *Airz. L. Rev.* 1, summer 1968

AYRES, R. U., "Air Pollution in Cities," 9 *Nat. Res. L.* 1, June 1969

CORCHET, T. D., "Some Economies of Air Pollution Control," 8 *Nat. Res. J.* 236, April 1968

DELOGEE, O.E., "Legal Aspects of Air Pollution Control and Proposed State Legislation for Such Control," 1969 *Wisc. L. Rev.* 884, 1969

ESPOSITO, J. C., "Air & Water Pollution: What to do While Waiting for Washington," 5 *Harv. Civil Rights, Civil Liberties Law Rev.* 32, June 1970

WOLOZIN, Harold, ed. *The Economics of Air Pollution; Papers,* 1st ed. New York, W.W. Norton 1966

STERN, Arthur Cecil, *Air Pollution,* 2 ed., 3 Vol. New York, Academic Press 1968 NL S839a

LEWIS, Howard R. *With Every Breath You Take,* New York, Crown Publishers, Inc. 1965

CLARK, G. Havighurst, *Air Pollution Control,* Dobbs Ferry, N.Y., Oceana Publications 1969

ZIMMERMAN, I. F., "Political Boundaries & Air Pollution Control," 46 *J. Uuban L.* 173, 1968

MOODY, J. E., "Air Quality Improvements—A Look Ahead," 2 *Nat. Res. Law. June 1969*

Biological Effects of Atmospheric Pollutants, Fluorides, National Academy of Sciences (1971).

For more information on control techniques for air pollutants:

TITLE	GPO NO.	GPO PRICE	NTIS NO.
Control Techniques for Particulate Air Pollutants	FS2.300: AP-51	$1.75	PB 190253
Control Techniques for Sulfur Oxide Air Pollutants	FS2.300: AP-52	$1.25	PB 190254
Control Techniques for Carbon Monoxide Emissions from Stationary Sources	FS2.300: AP-65	$0.70	PB 190263
Control Techniques for Co, NOx, and Hydrocarbon Emissions from Mobile Sources	FS2.300: AP-66	$1.25	PB 190264
Control Techniques for Nitrogen Oxide Emissions from Stationary Sources	FS2.300: AP-67	$1.00	PB 190265
Control Techniques for Hydrocarbon and Organic Solvent Emissions from Stationary Sources	FS2.300: AP-68	$1.00	PB 190266

Obtaining information from the Environmental Protection Agency

The following information sheet from the Environmental Protection Agency is a photographic reproduction of the original, to convey the precise policy information from EPA in regard to obtaining information concerning air pollution problems and control methods:

ENVIRONMENTAL PROTECTION AGENCY (EPA)
OFFICE OF AIR PROGRAMS
OFFICE OF TECHNICAL INFORMATION AND PUBLICATIONS
* * *
AIR POLLUTION TECHNICAL INFORMATION CENTER
Research Triangle Park, N. C. 27711

The Office of Technical Information and Publications (OTIP) provides a complete system of technical information and communication activities. The principal element of OTIP charged with the responsibility of technical literature communication is the Air Pollution Technical Information Center (APTIC). APTIC is responsible for the collection and dissemination of all domestic and foreign technical literature related to air pollution. Toward this end, APTIC performs six basic services:

1. Preparation of a monthly bulletin containing informative abstracts of approximately 1000 technical articles. Air Pollution Abstracts has a world-wide distribution of 10,000, with coverage including 1100 domestic and foreign serial publications, patents, government reports, preprints, technical society papers, and proceedings.

2. Provision of literature searches on an individual basis. More than 30,000 technical documents are accessible through APTIC's computer-based information retrieval system.

   > Individual literature searches are conducted without charge. In order to receive a highly relevant bibliography one should describe both his area of interest and specific items of concern. A knowledge of one's overall objectives is also valuable. Requests should be directed to the above address, or by telephone to (919) 549-8411 Ext. 2135, or from Government FTS telephones, to (919) 549-2135.

3. Response to inquiries concerning the secondary distribution of federally-produced air pollution-related documents.

4. Preparation for publication of comprehensive bibliographies and state-of-the-art summaries of major air pollution topics.

5. Translation of certain foreign journals cover-to-cover (e.g. the German Staub and the Russian Hygiene and Sanitation) and of selected Russian literature, and individual translation of numerous foreign articles. The former are published through the National Technical Information Service, Springfield, Virginia 22151; the latter, initially for EPA use, are available to the public through the National Translations Center, 35 West 33rd Street, Chicago, Illinois 60616 or through interlibrary loan.

6. Provision of complete conventional library services, primarily for EPA use.

d. Creating the Federal air pollution program

Between 1950 and 1954 a number of unsuccessful resolutions and bills were introduced in Congress. The Donora incident of 1948 and the efforts of Los Angeles to control smog were the factors that led to this interest—albeit unsuccessful. The first bill to pass was signed by President Eisenhower in 1955 (P.L. 84-159); it authorized $5 million each year for five years for research and control efforts, and for grants to states and educational institutions for training personnel. But President Eisenhower and the Budget Bureau opposed Federal enforcement authority, and so meaningful legislation could not be passed. In 1959 the 1955 act was extended for four more years.

In 1961 President Kennedy began to press for effective legislation. In 1960 and 1961 bills had passed the Senate. In 1962 the President tried to get the House to pass the bill that had been passed by the Senate. The bill that President Kennedy wanted was finally signed into law by President Johnson on December 17, 1963, as the Clean Air Act (P.L. 88-206).

Under this Act, for pollution within a state, at state request, the Department of Health, Education and Welfare could hold public hearings, then a conference, and finally, if necessary, request Federal court action. If pollution in one state affected persons in another, HEW could act without state permission. This act will be further discussed later in this chapter.

The 1963 Clean Air Act provided for abatement conferences. With the passage of the 1967 Act the emphasis shifted to the developing and enforcing of standards, but the conference provision remained in the law, though essentially ignored. The Clean Air Amendments of 1970 did not abolish the conference procedure, and it remains as Sec. 115 of the Clean Air Act.

Since the passage of the 1963 Act, ten enforcement conferences have been held. Four have dealt with single sources of pollution; six have considered all sources of pollution within major metropolitan areas, including the metropolitan areas of New York, New Jersey, Kansas City, and Washington, D.C.

The conference system is cumbersome and time consuming. However, its failure to be used to achieve air quality improvement is due at least as much to the failure of the federal government seriously to attempt to stop pollution as to the weaknesses of the Act. **Only one case has ever been taken to the courts.** That case, *U.S. v. Bishop Processing Company,* follows. The time sequence is interesting, for it shows the ability of a government agency to solve pollution problems. This case must be used for illustration purposes, as it is the only suit ever brought. Under the 1967 Act, to be discussed in the following subsection, not a single case has ever been brought. If the federal government sues a second pollutor, they can report a 100 percent increase in enforcement efforts.

For a discussion of the conference technique see: "Air Pollution in the Marietta-Parkersburg Area—A Case History," 32 Ohio S.L.J. 58 (1971)

Back to Bishop:

1956 order to stop emitting odors by Worcester County Circuit Court;
1959 to 1965 both Delaware and Maryland attempt to abate Bishop's pollution.
1965 Conference held;
1967 Public hearing held;
1968 Suit begun in Federal District Court;
1968 Nov. Consent decree entered;
1969 Hearings on motions, decree to stop operations;
1970 March U.S. Ct. of Appeals upholds decision;
1970 order stayed for appeal to U.S. Sup. Ct. [Cert. denied]
June 4, 1970 the plant was ordered to cease all operations forever—but see also the note following the case.

UNITED STATES v. BISHOP PROCESSING CO., 423 F.2d 469 4th Cir., decided March 3, 1970

Certiorari Denied May 18, 1970.
See 90 S. Ct. 1695

[Footnotes omitted]

Before Sobeloff, Boreman and Bryan, Circuit Judges.

Sobeloff, Circuit Judge:

This appeal is the most recent chapter in a long series of proceedings, in and out of court, stretching over more than a decade. The states of Delaware and Maryland, later joined by the federal government, have been endeavoring to bring relief to affected communities from alleged air pollution stemming from the appellant's rendering plant.

From approximately 1959 to 1965 the two states engaged in futile efforts to induce Bishop Processing Company, operator of the rendering and animal reduction plant located near Bishop, Maryland, to abate the malodorous air pollution which allegedly moves across the state line to pollute the air of nearby Selbyville, Delaware. Finally in 1965, the United States Secretary of Health, Education and Welfare received a request from the Delaware authorities to "take the necessary action under P. L. 88-206, section 5 (the Clean Air Act, 42 U.S.C. section 1857 et seq.), to secure the abatement of the air pollution problem." In response to this request the Secretary initiated hearing procedures provided in the Act.

As recited in the District Judge's opinion, the initial step was a conference held in Selbyville on November 9 and 10,1965. The parties attending the conference represented, as specified in the Act, the air pollution control agencies of the states and municipalities concerned. The Secretary forwarded to the participants a summary of the conference discussions and recommendations, which called upon Maryland to require Bishop to take certain remedial action by September 1, 1966

Since the recommended remedial action was not taken, the Secretary instituted the next step envisioned in the Act, by calling a public hearing which was held on May 17 and 18, 1967. At this hearing Bishop was represented by counsel who extensively cross-examined witnesses and otherwise fully participated. The hearing board forwarded its findings and recommendations to the Secretary, who in turn transmitted them to Bishop with the instruction to abate the pollution not later than December 1, 1967 by installing adequate and effective pollution control system.

This step also proving fruitless, the Secretary, in the exercise of the authority granted him in section 1857 d, filed a complaint on March 7, 1968 in the United States District Court for Maryland seeking to enjoin Bishop from discharging malodorous air pollutants. There followed discussions between the parties and on October 4, 1968, the action then pending was disposed of by settlement. A consent decree was entered in which Bishop agreed, in the precise terms it had suggested, to "cease all manufacturing and processing" upon the "filing of an affidavit by the Director, Air Pollution Control Division, State of Delaware Water and Air Resources Commission, stating that the defendant is discharging malodorous air pollution reaching the State of Delaware * * *."

The Director accordingly instituted a surveillance program to determine to what extent, if any, the obnoxious odors persisted and reached Delaware. Odor logs were kept at the instance of the Director and he made personal observations. On this basis the Director found that Bishop had been recurringly discharging malodorous air pollutants which reached the State of Delaware since November 1, 1968. These findings and conclusions the Director embodied in an affidavit.

Based upon this affidavit and pursuant to the consent decree, the United States moved for an order directing the defendant to cease operations. A hearing on this motion was held on March 3 and 4, 1969, in which the District Judge declared that the "Court would prefer to have more evidence" that Bishop is engaging in air pollution, and announced his interpretation of the consent decree "for the guidance of * * * members of the staff who may be participating in any further investigations." In this way the judge indicated to the parties the type of evidence he would consider requisite for a showing of air pollution upon which an order could be based.

On September 12, 1969, the United States filed a second motion accompanied by affidavits in compliance with the consent decree and the court prescribed evidentiary requirements. After a further hearing, the court found the evidence substantial and entered the order to cease operations. The appeal is from this order.

The appellant presses the contention that the District Court erred in ruling that the Director performed his duties in accordance with the consent decree. Bishop argues that the decree was entered into with various "understandings" which contemplated certain procedures to be followed by the Director in his investigation. Specifically, Bishop asserts its "understandings" that (1) the Director was not to rely on citizen complaints or on testimony of representatives of the federal government in determining whether it committed air pollution and (2) that the Director's finding was to be based upon "generally accepted sampling techniques."

Whatever merit this argument might have in other circumstances, it must fail here. The consent decree is plain in its terms. Nowhere and at no time was it intimated that any finding of air pollution was to be based upon unexpressed "understandings" with respect to the investigative procedures. Neither before the entry of the consent decree, nor when the judge held a hearing and announced his interpretation of the decree for the guidance of the parties did Bishop disclose the existence of any "understandings" or reservations on its part.

Bishop had ample opportunity to propose incorporation in the decree of any protection it may have felt necessary, and to object to procedures it deemed contrary to its understanding of the decree's terms. It cannot now ask the court to revise the decree by inserting language or to interpret it to embrace matters which, if present at all, were lurking in the recesses of Bishop's corporate mind.

Apparently as an afterthought, appellant now complains that the government witnesses lacked objectivity. It is contended that information supplied by employees of the United States should not have been considered, for the federal government is an adversary in this proceeding. It was argued to us that appellant had faith in the Delaware Director but not in the federal officials and that appellant's expectation was that the Delaware official would not rely upon federal representations made to him. There are many examples of administrative agencies that act upon the testimony of their investigators. It does not derogate from the investigators' objectivity that the agency by whom they are employed has the regulatory function. Of course the fact finder must consider every witness' relationship to the parties and to the subject matter, but a government employee is not disqualified as a witness by reason of his employment.

But the issue is a false one here, for the Director, whom the appellant chose to determine the facts, did not exceed the terms of his authority in the consent decree. Like considerations apply to appellant's belated challenge to citizens' complaints.

Bishop's further contentions, variously repeated, are in substance an attack on the sufficiency of the evidence upon which the finding of air pollution was based. As above stated, at the first hearing the District Judge explained, with no caveat whatever from Bishop, the type and quantum of evidence he felt was necessary. After a second hearing he found that the Government had complied with his directions and adduced sufficient evidence to show that Bishop continues to pollute the air. Certainly the factual finding, so carefully arrived at, cannot be deemed clearly erroneous.

Pollution is a severe and increasing problem of which the courts and other branches of government have become acutely conscious. The residents of the area in the neighborhood of Bishop's plant have the right to demand that the air they breathe shall not be defiled by what witnesses described as a "horrible" and "nauseating" stench. The afflicted neighbors have striven long and in vain to vindicate that right. Relief is due them now.

The appellant cannot complain that the decree came suddenly, unexpectedly, or without awareness of the complaints, nor that it was denied full opportunity to meet them. In light of the entire history we perceive no inequity.

This court is not unmindful of the serious consequences to appellant's business from the District Court's order. It is, however, precisely the remedy which Bishop suggested and agreed to in order to avoid a trial, and seems inescapable since it has over a long period failed to take effective measures to solve the problem.

The order of the District Court is affirmed.

It is further ordered that if appellant applies to the Supreme Court for certiorari within 15 days from the filing of this opinion, the injunctive order of the District Court will be further stayed until final disposition of the case in the Supreme Court; otherwise the District Court's injunction shall become operative.

Affirmed.

POSTNOTE

According to the *Washington Post* of July 29, 1971, at B1, the Bishop plant is still in operation. Private information confirms this, but corrects the article concerning what the plant is currently doing. It has stopped rendering chickens, but continues to blend fats.

Judge Thomsen of the United States District Court in Baltimore on July 14, 1971, held the company in contempt of court for failure to close down on June 4, 1970. No penalty was imposed for the contempt finding. The Judge ruled the plant could remain open if they followed a specific timetable in installing air pollution control equipment, and if they cleaned the plant weekly. According to the *Post* article, the Justice Department's attorney said there was no odor now from the plant, and that the department was suing to force the company to install equipment to abate it. [Sic] To this incredible exercise in the bureaucratic mentality this author can only add the famous French proverb: *Plus ca change, plus c'est la meme chose.* Marcus Aurelius, never at a loss for words, put it another way: "All things are now as they were in the day of those whom we have buried!"

history of various Federal bills

The next major federal act was the 1965 Motor Vehicle Air Pollution Control Act (P.L. 89-272). Motor vehicle research was first authorized in a 1960 act (P.L. 86-493) that directed the Surgeon General to study public health effects of motor vehicle exhaust fumes.

Little happened during the 1960 to 1965 period. In January of 1965, Senator Edmund Muskie of Maine introduced a bill to regulate automobile emissions. President Johnson opposed the bill, preferring a voluntary program by the industry. Political pressure caused a reversal of the President's position, and the bill was passed and signed on October 20, 1965. Industry made little objection, as the bill prevented state control of new automobiles. The Act gave HEW authority to establish permissible emission levels from new motor vehicles. The act also included a provision allowing HEW to call a conference to focus on potential sources of air pollution.

Between 1963 and 1966 public interest in air pollution grew. The existing legislation was clearly inadequate. In January of 1967, President Johnson called for new legislation that would include national emission standards for major industrial sources and have regional commissions to enforce control measures. Between February and May, Senator Muskie held hearings on the administration bill. Industry opposed the bill, while HEW, by calling for stringent sulfur emissions standards, threatened the coal industry.

Senator Muskie's committee was a subcommittee of the Public Works Committee chaired by Senator Jennings Randolph of West Virginia. Thus, Senator Randolph could influence the bill to protect the coal industry. This and other pressure resulted in a substantially weakened bill being reported out of committee and passing the Senate by a unanimous vote.

The House reduced the appropriation authorizations and made several minor changes. The conference committee quickly reconciled the versions, and on November 21, 1967, President Johnson signed the Air Quality Act (P.L. 90-148) into law. This Act also is discussed in the material which follows. The weakness of the 1967 act led to the Clean Air Amendments of 1970 (P.L. 91-604). All legislation passed after 1963 form amendments to the Clean Air Act of 1963, so that the existing statute, 42 U.S.C. 1857 et seq. is known as The Clean Air Act.

e. The Air Quality Act of 1967

AUTHOR'S NOTE OF CAUTION: The 1967 Act discussed here has been amended virtually out-of-existence. However, an understanding ot it will greatly aid in understanding the 1970 law currently in force.

The Air Quality Act of 1967 provided for an intergovernmental system for the prevention and control of air pollution on a regional basis. To put this system into operation, the Department of Health, Education, and Welfare (EPA now) was required to designate air quality control regions and issue air quality criteria and reports on control techniques. State governments were then expected to establish air quality standards for the air quality control regions and to adopt plans for implementation of the standards. The air quality standards and implementation plans were then to be submitted to the Department for review.

These regions are designated on the basis of meteorological and topographical factors, urban-industrial concentrations, jurisdictional boundaries, and other factors relevant to effective implementation of air quality standards. Air quality control regions may lie entirely within a single State or include portions of two or more States.

The Department of Health, Education, and Welfare was responsible for developing and issuing air quality criteria reflecting available scientific knowledge of the adverse effects of air pollutants on public health and welfare. Air quality criteria documents summarize available information on the relationship between exposures to air pollutants and their effects on man and his environment, including injury to health, damage to materials and vegetation, reduction of visibility, economic losses, and so on.

For those types of air pollutants for which air quality criteria are issued, the Department of Health, Education, and Welfare must also develop and issue reports on control techniques. These reports provide information on the availability and applicability of techniques for the prevention and control of air pollutants at their sources and on the cost and effectiveness of such techniques.

The Department of Health, Education, and Welfare has issued air quality criteria and reports on control techniques for sulfur oxides and particulate matter, as well as carbon monoxide, photochemical oxidents, hydrocarbons, and nitrogen oxides.

1967 act analyzed

The Act calls on state governments to adopt—for application in air quality control regions—air quality standards for those types of pollutants for which air quality criteria and reports on control techniques are issued. Public hearings must be held as part of the standard-setting process. States are also called upon to adopt plans for implementation of the air quality standards.

States must take these steps in accordance with the following timetable:

> 1. No later than 90 days after the issuance of air quality criteria and a report on control techniques for a given type of air pollutant, the Governor of any State in which an air quality control region has been designated must notify the Secretary in writing of the State's intent to adopt air quality standards applicable to that pollutant in that air quality control region.
>
> 2. No later than 180 days after the end of the above 90-day period, the State must adopt such air quality standards, after holding public hearings, and must submit the standards to the Department of Health, Education, and Welfare for review.
>
> 3. No later than 180 days after the end of the above 180-day period, the State must adopt a plan for implementation of the air quality standards and must submit the plan to the Department for review.

In setting an air quality standard for a given type of air pollutant, a State is defining an air quality goal in terms of a desired limit on levels of that pollutant in the air. The need for protection of public health is the most important consideration involved in establishing such goals. In its report on the Air Quality Act, the Committee on Public Works stated:

> The committee feels that under any circumstances protection of health should be considered a minimum requirement, and wherever possible standards should be established which enhance the quality of the environment.

An implementation plan is a blueprint of the steps that will be taken to insure attainment of an air quality standard within a reasonable time. It includes all the steps to be taken to abate and control pollutant emissions from existing sources in an air quality control region and to prevent urban and economic growth from adding to a region's air pollution problems.

An implementation plan for an air quality standard must be designed to bring about the attainment of that standard within a reasonable time. Every implementation plan must include a timetable for obtaining compliance with the projected requirements for the prevention, abatement, and control of air pollution.

The various requirements included in an implementation plan must be enforceable by State action. This did not mean that States must assume exclusive responsibility for enforcement. They might rely on the capabilities of local and regional agencies; however, to comply with the Air Quality Act,

States were required to have the legal authority necessary to conduct enforcement activities.

A surveillance system was necessary to monitor all aspects of progress toward attainment of air quality standards and to identify potential episodes of high pollutant concentrations in time to take preventive action. These provisions could include arrangements for surveillance activities and the monitoring of emissions to be conducted by local and regional agencies.

Air quality standards and implementation plans were required to be submitted to the Department of Health, Education, and Welfare for review. If they were approved, they became the Federal standards and plans for the air quality control region involved.

The Air Quality Act authorized the Department of Health, Education and Welfare to take steps to insure adoption of appropriate air quality standards in the event that a State failed to establish such standards for an air quality control region or if the standards established by a State cannot be approved. The Act also authorized the Department to take appropriate enforcement action if a State failed to take reasonable action to insure the attainment and maintenance of an approved air quality standard.

summation

The 1967 Act was nearly unworkable. The processes required were cumbersome and extremely time consuming. By tying any regulation of what came out of smokestacks to atmospheric monitoring and the development of air quality goals the effort to develop programs that could abate air pollution moved at a snail's pace. The main effect of the 1967 Act was to delay any serious attempt to improve the air.

If proper leadership had existed, it is probable that a control program based on emission standards could have been begun in the mid or late 1960's. At the same time, information could have been gathered that might have permitted later a more sophisticated management program incorporating air quality standards. But the cart was put before the horse, and the horse wasn't even untied.

The following is excerpted from an article by the author of this book which criticized the Federal air pollution program that existed prior to passage of the 1970 amendments. Although specifically of historic interest now, this excerpt is included because it contains a detailed damnation of a type of legal program that is still being proposed in many parts of the nation.

Air Quality Act of 1967 Analyzed

AUTHOR'S NOTE OF CAUTION: The 1967 Act discussed here has been amended virtually out-of-existence. However, an understanding of it will aid greatly in understanding the 1970 law currently in force.

When in recent years it became generally recognized that our uncoordinated and desultory governmental regulation process, largely based on local ordinances, was unable to provide the broad range of institutional responses necessary to solve our air pollution problems, Congress responded with a series of acts which eventually led to the important Air Quality Act of 1967.[1] This act provided for the involvement of the federal, state, and local governments in a cooperative program to achieve improved air quality. The approach chosen was similar to that used in the Water Quality Act of 1965[2] but with some significant differences. Under the 1967 Act the federal government through the Secretary of the Department of Health, Education and Welfare (HEW) provides technical and financial assistance to state and local governments to assist them in develop-

[1] 42 U.S.C. 1857b-1 (Supp. III, 1967) [hereinafter cited by section number without reference to the *United States Code*].

[2] 33 U.S.C. 466 (Supp. III, 1967).

ing air pollution prevention and control programs. But, the Secretary also issues criteria of air quality necessary for the protection of the public health and welfare. Thus, the federal government can determine what is acceptable air quality — a power they do not have in the field of water quality regulation. The Secretary must also provide information concerning the control techniques which can be utilized to achieve the air quality goals set forth in the federal criteria.

The states also have an important role in pollution abatement. After the Secretary of HEW issues air quality criteria, recommends control techniques, and designates a specific control region, the governor of a target state must, within 90 days, file a letter of intent indicating that his state will comply with the Air Quality Act. The Act then requires that within 180 days after filing the letter of intent the governor will hold public hearings and adopt quality standards applicable to the control region or regions. Within an additional 180 days, the state must adopt a plan for the implementation, maintenance, and enforcement of the air quality standards.

1967 act analyzed

The purpose of joint federal and state activity is to develop a *regional* air pollution program.[9] Air pollution can only be abated when specific steps are taken to reduce the harmful emissions of specific pollutors. While coordination to provide a uniform response is useful, only a local program designed to meet local needs can effectively achieve a reduction in the degree of air pollution.[10] The success or failure of the federal program will depend upon the "front line" action which takes place within the control regions. These regions are designated on the basis of political boundaries, the degree of urbanization, and atmospheric conditions. In June 1968, the National Air Pollution Control Administration of HEW named 32 of the largest and most severely polluted urban communities in the country as the initial air quality control regions. Ohio, which prides itself in its national leadership, continued to maintain this position of eminence by having five of its cities (Cincinnati, Cleveland, Dayton, Toledo, and Steubenville) within the first 32 control regions. By 1970 an additional 25 control regions will be formally designated. The control regions will then include 70 percent of our urban population.

Under the federal law the regions must have uniform standards within the region and an overall long-range abatement plan. Thus, existing county and municipal public health and air pollution control organizations will still be required. Many of these existing organizations can best function by being incorporated into the regional organization. Thus, implementation of the regional plan may be accomplished by the existing county and municipal organizations, while direction and control will be exercised by the regional authorities. The framework for an air pollution control program is being provided by the federal government. Local action will determine whether such control ever achieves the desired emission reductions so as to provide results that can be verified by objective measurement.

It would appear that the intended function of this present legislation is to bide time until the public realizes the impact of air pollution, and then demands meaningful legislation — in other words, don't rock the boat until the public makes waves.

The federal government will also obstruct the programs of the regions by limiting the pollution sources that can be regulated. The most serious source of pollution is the automobile, as its emissions account for about 60 percent by weight of all atmospheric pollutants. However, the federal government has seen fit to prohibit the states or any political subdivision thereof from requiring pollutant control devices on new motor vehicles.

The federal government has provided a series of sanctions in the event the states do not cooperate in developing an air pollution abatement program.[33] These sanctions are similar to those used in the water pollution control legislation. They can be characterized by saying that they probably will not work, since if used, they would delay the development of a program for many years. We cannot afford to wait — our health is at stake. Recently the State of Iowa told the federal government, in so many words, that it is not going to follow federal prescriptions in dealing with their waters.[34]

1967 act analyzed

Citizen involvement is critically needed to develop a proper legislative framework for an air pollution program, because of the unusual democratic process provided in the Air Pollution Act. The federal government by establishing criteria will inform the citizenry that a specific concentration of a given pollutant is harmful. They will also provide information concerning the available control techniques. Each region will then hold hearings and in a very democratic manner decide whether that region will adopt the federal criteria. This may be the rebirth of the democratic process involved in the New England town meeting as compared to representative democracy or government by a technocratic bureaucracy. We have never been allowed to decide how many cases of small pox we are willing to have in our communities, and the federal government keeps trying to stamp out tuberculosis without having "grassroot" hearings.

The air pollution program will either maintain or effectively stifle citizen interest by having many hearings. Since there are five regions in Ohio there will be five hearings for sulfur oxides. When the hearings on sulfur oxides are completed we should be ready for hearings on nitrogen oxides, and still later we can debate the merits of carbon monoxide poisoning. For many years we will be able to have hearings. Some communities may opt for clean air and some others may decide cancer is more desirable. By the time standards are set for the dozens of different pollutants new updated criteria should be available for the oxides of sulfur and we can start over again.

As analytical statistical information becomes more sophisticated, each community will be able to choose the level of deaths from respiratory diseases that it finds desirable. These hearings then may be used to build community cohesiveness since hundreds of people with little knowledge of the subject will be involved in intimate deliberation for many years in deciding whether the federal scientists' conclusion that air pollution is harmful to your health should be accepted. The Air Pollution Act of 1967 may not improve the atmosphere but it should provide for additional employment.

---

[32] *See* note 24 *supra.* COMMITTEE ON PUBLIC WORKS, AIR QUALITY ACT OF 1967, S. REP. NO. 780, 90th Cong., 1st Sess. 10 (1967).

[33] § 1857d.

[34] N.Y. Times, Apr. 21, 1969, at 22.

Assuming that the hearings result in a setting of a standard which is similar to the federal criteria, the atmosphere will not improve until an implementation plan is developed which will require specific emission sources to reduce their discharge of pollutants. It is interesting to note that the 1967 Act provides for minimal federal responses if the state does not set standards that meet federal approval. After a long administrative procedure the federal government can set standards. If one state is involved, action can be taken only if the governor of that state requests such action. After all administrative actions are complete the standards are still subject to a trial de novo which could probably include a review of the HEW criteria and recommended control techniques.[35]

1967 act analyzed

II. The State Government and the Region

The state government is given substantial responsibility under the federal act. The state government's general disinterest in the subject and their lack of concern for urban problems make this level of government the natural choice for having primary responsibility for the air pollution abatement program. The governor, as we have seen, is required to hold hearings, set standards, and develop a plan to achieve the desired standards. Considerable flexibility is given to the states since the 1967 Act does not specify what type of governmental organizations, if any, will be created to achieve the Act's goals.

AUTHOR'S NOTE OF CAUTION: The 1967 Act discussed here has been amended virtually out-of-existence. However, an understanding of it will aid greatly in understanding the 1970 law currently in force.

III. Local Government and the Region

The role of the local government in the federal air pollution control program is not yet clear. The state-oriented federal program leaves implementation to the discretion of the states. The state may or may not choose to use existing local government organizations or to allow new local government organizations to develop.

Municipal governments have traditionally possessed air pollution ordinances. These ordinances are generally patterned as nuisance abatement acts and have little relevance to the problems of our sophisticated technology.

What is disquieting is that the states, which have such a poor record concerning environmental protection activities, have been given so much control in effectuating the federal program.

A plan to create regional authorities subject to federal control, but without state involvement would have made sense from an environmental science, if not a political, point of view. Few people desire an expanded central government, but the states have generally shown themselves incapable of providing for the needs of their citizens. This vacuum is generally filled by federal programs.

End, selection from article by the author of this book analyzing the 1967 Federal air pollution control legislation, which, as modified, forms part of the current law.

---

[35] § 1857d(c).

f. The Clean Air Act amendments of 1970

Public Law 91-604

The Clean Air Amendments of 1970, enacted in December 31, 1970, remedied most of the defects of the previous legislation. With the passage of that Act, air pollution became the only environmental problem to have a statutory base sufficient for meaningful Federal action. The solid waste, noise pollution, and pesticide legislation as of the fall of 1971, can barely be considered to be the basis for programs. The water pollution act is nearly hopelessly deficient but that is the subject of chapter four.

Major changes in Air Pollution Law Created by the 1970 Amendments

[Sections are to the Clean Air Act as Amended]

Clean Air Act amendments summarized

Section 107 gave the administrator of EPA 90 days to designate any air quality regions he deemed necessary or appropriate. Any portion of a state not in a control region was a control region subject to further subdivision by the State with EPA approval. The result is that the country has been divided into about 250 regions. These regions are based on considerations of climate, meteorology, topography, urbanization, and politics.

Section 108 requires the Administrator to provide criteria documents and control information. The criteria documents give the levels at which pollutants, by themselves and in combination, have adverse effects. The control technique documents include information on the technology, the costs, and the economic feasibility of alternative control methods.

Section 109 provided for the Administrator to establish national primary and secondary air quality standards. Primary air quality standards to be those necessary to protect the public health, allowing an adequate margin of safety. Secondary standards are those which in the judgment of the Administrator protect the public from adverse effects associated with air pollution. But the Federal government, not the states, will set standards, and these will be uniform except that Section 116 allows states to set more stringent standards.

Section 110 requires states to develop implementation plans. However, unlike the 1967 Act, the Administrator has virtually complete control over the development of the plan. Primary standards must be achieved within three years, while secondary standards must be achieved in a reasonable time. If the plan is considered inadequate by the Administrator he can essentially take over the state's program. The implementation plan can be used to prevent new construction or modification of air pollution sources if it will prevent the attainment or maintenance of a primary or secondary standard.

The U.S. District Court for the District of Columbia has held that the Administrator of the Environmental Protection Agency has authority under the Clean Air Act to require state air pollution control plans submitted to EPA pursuant to Section 110 to provide against deterioration of existing air quality. *Sierra Club v. Ruckelshaus,* ___ F.Supp. ___ (D.C.D. June 2, 1972), 4 ERC 1205 being,appealed. See text of case at Appendix three-17.

For a case interpreting Section 110(a)(1) and 307, *see Getty Oil v. Ruckelshaus,* ___ F.Supp. ___ (D. Del. May 10, 1972), 4 ERC 1141. The case is being appealed.

Section 111 requires new stationary sources to install the best system of emission reduction which the Administrator determines has been adequately demonstrated. Modification of an existing source can bring it within the provisions of this section. The Administrator shall also establish performance standards for new stationary sources in categories that he determines may contribute significantly to the endangerment of public health or welfare. The states subject to the Administrator's approval can take the responsibilities of implementation and enforcement. The states are required to set state performance standards, under EPA prescribed procedures, for all existing unmodified sources in the categories covered by emission limits on new facilities.

Section 112 requires the administrator to set emission standards for hazardous air pollutants. Such pollutants are defined to exclude those to which air quality standards are applicable, but virtually any other substance could be included, though the legislative history makes clear the more toxic materials such as beryllium were intended to be controlled. Both new and existing stationary sources are covered although existing sources may get waivers of up to two years from the Administrator if health is protected. The President may exempt sources of pollution for two-year periods if control techniques available will not permit the pollutor to meet the standards.

Clean Air Act amendments summarized

Section 113 provides for Federal enforcement. If a person violates an implementation plan the violator and the State are to be notified by the Administrator. After 30 days the Administrator may issue a compliance order or bring a civil action. If the violations *appear* to result from a failure of state enforcement, after 30 days notice, the Administrator may enforce the plan. The Administrator may start a civil action for an injunction or other appropriate relief whenever any person—

(1) violates or fails to comply with an order; or

(2) violates an implementation plan during Federal enforcement and after 30 days notice; or

(3) violates emission limits under sections 111 or 112; or

(4) fails to comply with the inspection, monitoring, and entry provisions of section 114.

Penalties for violation of these provisions can be no more than $25,000 per day and/or one year in prison. After a first conviction, the possible penalties double. A knowingly false statement or record required under the Act or tampering with a monitoring device can bring a fine of up to $10,000 and/or six months imprisonment.

Section 114 gives the Administrator the power to require the operator of any emission source to keep such records and do such monitoring or sampling as he may require. A right of entry and a right to inspect emission records and data is provided. Records and information are to be public information unless the Administrator determines they would divulge trade secrets. Emission data are specifically exempted from such protection.

Section 115 saved but substantially limited the possible use of the conference procedure of the 1963 Act.

Section 116 gives the States the right to promulgate or enforce stricter controls except to the extent the Federal government has preempted control of new motor vehicles.

Section 117 made some changes in the section requiring consultation with the President's Air Quality Advisory Board and Advisory Committee.

Section 118 makes Federal facilities subject to Federal, State, interstate and local air pollution law. There are limited exemptions that can be granted by the President.

Section 303 gives the Administrator the right to seek a restraining order in Federal District Court when pollution presents an imminent and substantial endangerment to health, and state or local authorities have not acted.

Section 304 allows citizen suits against any person including the U.S. and other governmental units except to the extent protected by the 11th amendment, for violating an emission standard or an order of the Administrator. The Administrator can be sued only for violating a nondiscretionary duty. Federal district courts have jurisdiction without regard to amount in controversy or citizenship of parties. Sixty days notice must be given before action can be commenced in some circumstances. If the Administrator or State is diligently pursuing a civil action, then citizen suits are barred but they can intervene as a matter of right.

The Environmental Protection Agency has issued rules concerning such suits, including those against the EPA Administrator. These rules are printed in the appendix to this chapter.

The court can award costs including attorney fees and expert witness fees to *any* party. Bond may be required.

Section 305 allows EPA attorneys to represent the Administrator in civil actions if after request the Attorney General does not represent him.

Section 306 forbids a Federal agency from contracting for the procurement of goods or services at a facility convicted under section 113(c)(1). The President can make exemptions.

Clean Air Act amendments summarized

Section 307 gives the Administrator subpoena power. Emission data cannot be made confidential though other information may be. Challenges to the Administrator's general actions must be filed in the U.S. Court of Appeals for the District of Columbia; other reviews are directed to U.S. Courts of Appeal for the appropriate circuit. There is some modification of the Administrative Procedure Act and specific court review limitations that are applicable to the Administrator.

Section 308 can make licensing mandatory for patents relating to pollution.

Section 309 makes the Administrator review and comment on the environmental impact of projects or matters that would not be otherwise covered by the National Environmental Policy Act.

The provisions of the Clean Air Act dealing with motor vehicles were changed substantially but these will be dealt with in subsequent sections of this material.

CLEAN AIR ACT

The following statutory and regulatory material comprises the basic body of law applicable to emissions from stationary sources. (Motor vehicle programs will be found in a subsequent section). This program builds on the 1967 Act by giving the Federal Government power and responsibilities formerly handled by the states. The 1970 amendments, however, still anticipate that the states and regions will be the primary groups developing and enforcing implementation plans. The basic change is that the Administrator has almost unlimited discretion in telling the States and Regions how to do the job.

TITLE II of the Clean Air Act 1963, as amended by the Motor Vehicle Air Pollution Control Act 1965 (Public Law 89-272) is published at Three-61; a brief analysis of the section proceeds it at Three-59, and discussion of air pollution from mobile sources follows at Three-67.

Titles I and III of the Clean Air Act of 1963 (Public Law 88-206) as amended by Clean Air Act Amendments of 1966 (Public Law 89-675), the Air Quality Act of 1967 (Public Law 90-148) and the Clean Air Amendments of 1970 (Public Law 91-604).

THE CLEAN AIR ACT as amended Title I and III

"TITLE I—AIR POLLUTION PREVENTION AND CONTROL

"FINDINGS AND PURPOSES

"SEC. 101. (a) The Congress finds—

"(1) that the predominant part of the Nation's population is located in its rapidly expanding metropolitan and other urban areas, which generally cross the boundary lines of local jurisdictions and often extend into two or more States;

"(2) that the growth in the amount and complexity of air pollution brought about by urbanization, industrial development, and the increasing use of motor vehicles, has resulted in mounting dangers to the public health and welfare, including injury to agricultural crops and livestock, damage to and the deterioration of property, and hazards to air and ground transportation;

"(3) that the prevention and control of air pollution at its source is the primary responsibility of States and local governments; and

"(4) that Federal financial assistance and leadership is essential for the development of cooperative Federal, State, regional, and local programs to prevent and control air pollution.

"(b) The purposes of this title are—

"(1) to protect and enhance the quality of the Nation's air resources so as to promote the public health and welfare and the productive capacity of its population;

"(2) to initiate and accelerate a national research and development program to achieve the prevention and control of air pollution;

"(3) to provide technical and financial assistance to State and local governments in connection with the development and execution of their air pollution prevention and control programs; and

"(4) to encourage and assist the development and operation of regional air pollution control programs.

"COOPERATIVE ACTIVITIES AND UNIFORM LAWS

"SEC. 102. (a) The Administrator shall encourage cooperative ·tivities by the States and local governments for the prevention nd control of air pollution; encourage the enactment of improved nd, so far as practicable in the light of varying conditions and eeds, uniform State and local laws relating to the prevention and ontrol of air pollution; and encourage the making of agreements nd compacts between States for the prevention and control of air ollution.

"(b) The Administrator shall cooperate with and encourage ooperative activities by all Federal departments and agencies aving functions relating to the prevention and control of air ollution, so as to assure the utilization in the Federal air pollu-on control program of all appropriate and available facilities nd resources within the Federal Government.

"(c) The consent of the Congress is hereby given to two or ore States to negotiate and enter into agreements or compacts, ot in conflict with any law or treaty of the United States, for (1) ooperative effort and mutual assistance for the prevention and ontrol of air pollution and the enforcement of their respective ws relating thereto, and (2) the establishment of such agencies, oint or otherwise, as they may deem desirable for making effec-ve such agreements or compacts. No such agreement or compact hall be binding or obligatory upon any State a party thereto nless and until it has been approved by Congress. It is the intent f Congress that no agreement or compact entered into between tates after the date of enactment of the Air Quality Act of 1967, hich relates to the control and abatement of air pollution in an ir quality control region, shall provide for participation by a tate which is not included (in whole or in part) in such air uality control region.

"RESEARCH, INVESTIGATION, TRAINING, AND OTHER ACTIVITIES

"SEC. 103. (a) The Administrator shall establish a national re-earch and development program for the prevention and control f air pollution and as part of such program shall—

"(1) conduct, and promote the coordination and acceleration of, research, investigations, experiments, training, demonstrations, surveys, and studies relating to the causes, effects, extent, prevention, and control of air pollution;

"(2) encourage, cooperate with, and render technical services and provide financial assistance to air pollution control agencies and other appropriate public or private agencies, institutions, and organizations, and individuals in the conduct of such activities;

"(3) conduct investigations and research and make surveys concerning any specific problem of air pollution in cooperation with any air pollution control agency with a view to recommending a solution of such problem, if he is requested to do so by such agency or if, in his judgment, such problem may affect any community or communities in a State other than that in which the source of the matter causing or contributing to the pollution is located;

"(4) establish technical advisory committees composed of recognized experts in various aspects of air pollution to assist in the examination and evaluation of research progress and proposals and to avoid duplication of research.

"(b) In carrying out the provisions of the preceding subsection the Administrator is authorized to—

"(1) collect and make available, through publications and other appropriate means, the results of and other information, including appropriate recommendations by him in connection therewith, pertaining to such research and other activities;

"(2) cooperate with other Federal departments and agencies, with air pollution control agencies, with other public and private agencies, institutions, and organizations, and with any industries involved, in the preparation and conduct of such research and other activities;

"(3) make grants to air pollution control agencies, to other public or nonprofit private agencies, institutions, and organizations, and to individuals, for purposes stated in subsection (a)(1) of this section;

"(4) contract with public or private agencies, institutions, and organizations, and with individuals, without regard to sections 3648 and 3709 of the Revised Statutes (31 U.S.C. 529; 41 U.S.C. 5);

"(5) provide training for, and make training grants to, personnel of air pollution control agencies and other persons with suitable qualifications;

"(6) establish and maintain research fellowships, in the Environmental Protection Agency and at public or nonprofit private educational institutions or research organizations;

"(7) collect and disseminate, in cooperation with other Federal departments and agencies, and with other public or private agencies, institutions, and organizations having related responsibilities, basic data on chemical, physical, and biological effects of varying air quality and other information pertaining to air pollution and the prevention and control thereof; and

"(8) develop effective and practical processes, methods, and prototype devices for the prevention or control of air pollution.

"(c) In carrying out the provisions of subsection (a) of this section the Administrator shall conduct research on, and survey the results of other scientific studies on, the harmful effects on the health or welfare of persons by the various known air pollutants.

"(d) The Administrator is authorized to construct such facilities and staff and equip them as he determines to be necessary to carry out his functions under this Act.

"(e) If, in the judgment of the Administrator, an air pollution problem of substantial significance may result from discharge or discharges into the atmosphere, he may call a conference concerning this potential air pollution problem to be held in or near one or more of the places where such discharge or discharges are occurring or will occur. All interested persons shall be given an opportunity to be heard at such conference, either orally or in writing, and shall be permitted to appear in person or by representative in accordance with porcedures prescribed by the Administrator. If . . . the Administrator finds, on the basis of evidence presented at such conference, that the discharge or discharges if permitted to take place or continue are likely to cause or contribute to air pollution subject to abatement under section 115, he shall send such findings, together with recommendations concerning the measures which he finds reasonable and suitable to prevent such pollution, to the person or persons whose actions will result in the discharge or discharges involved; to air pollution agencies of the State or States and of the municipality or municipalities where such discharge or discharges will originate; and to the interstate air pollution control agency, if any, in the jurisdictional area of which any such municipality is located. Such findings and recommendations shall be advisory only, but shall be admitted together with the record of the conference, as part of the proceedings under subsections (b), (c), (d), (e), and (f) of section 115.

"(f) (1) In carrying out research pursuant to this Act, the Administrator shall give special emphasis to research on the short- and long-term effects of air pollutants on public health and welfare. In the furtherance of such research, he shall conduct an accelerated research program—

"(A) to improve knowledge of the contribution of air pollutants to the occurrence of adverse effects on health, including, but not limited to, behavioral, physiological, toxicological, and biochemical effects; and

"(B) to improve knowledge of the short- and long-term effects of air pollutants on welfare.

"(2) In carrying out the provisions of this subsection the Administrator may—

"(A) conduct epidemiological studies of the effects of air pollutants on mortality and morbidity;

"(B) conduct clinical and laboratory studies on the immunologic, biochemical, physiological, and the toxicological effects including carcinogenic, teratogenic, and mutagenic effects of air pollutants;

"(C) utilize, on a reimbursable basis, the facilities of existing Federal scientific laboratories and research centers;

"(D) utilize the authority contained in paragraphs (1) through (4) of subsection (b); and

"(E) consult with other appropriate Federal agencies to assure that research or studies conducted pursuant to this subsection will be coordinated with research and studies of such other Federal agencies.

"(3) In entering into contracts under this subsection, the Administrator is authorized to contract for a term not to exceed 10 years in duration. For the purposes of this paragraph, there are authorized to be appropriated $15,000,000. Such amounts as are appropriated shall remain available until expended and shall be in addition to any other appropriations under this Act."

"GRANTS FOR SUPPORT OF AIR POLLUTION PLANNING AND CONTROL PROGRAMS

"SEC. 105. (a) (1) (A) The Administrator may make grants to air pollution control agencies in an amount up to two-thirds of the cost of planning, developing, establishing, or improving, and up to one-half of the cost of maintaining, programs for the prevention and control of air pollution or implementation of national primary and secondary ambient air quality standards.

"(B) Subject to subparagraph (C), the Administrator may make grants to air pollution control agencies within the meaning of paragraph (1), (2), or (4) of section 302(b) in an amount up to three-fourths of the cost of planning, developing, establishing, or improving, and up to three-fifths of the cost of maintaining, any program for the prevention and control of air pollution or implementation of national primary and secondary ambient air quality standards in an area that includes two or more municipalities, whether in the same or different States.

"(C) With respect to any air quality control region or portion thereof for which there is an applicable implementation plan under section 110, grants under subparagraph (B) may be made only to air pollution control agencies which have substantial responsibilities for carrying out such applicable implementation plan."

"(2) Before approving any grant under this subsection to any air pollution control agency within the meaning of sections 302 (b)(2) and 302(b)(4) the Administrator shall receive assurances that such agency provides for adequate representation of appropriate State, interstate, local, and (when appropriate) international, interests in the air quality control region.

"(3) Before approving any planning grant under this subsection to any air pollutant control agency within the meaning of sections 302(b)(2) and 302(b)(4), the Administrator shall receive assurances that such agency has the capability of developing a comprehensive air quality plan for the air quality control region, which plan shall include (when appropriate) a recommended system of alerts to avert and reduce the risk of situations in which there may be imminent and serious danger to the public health or welfare from air pollutants and the various aspects relevant to the establishment of air quality standards for such air quality control region, including the concentration of industries, other commercial establishments, population and naturally occurring factors which shall affect such standards.

"(b) from the sums available for the purposes of subsection (a) of this section for any fiscal year, the Administrator shall from time to time make grants to air pollution control agencies upon such terms and conditions as the Administrator may fi necessary to carry out the purpose of this section. In establishi regulations for the granting of such funds the Administrat shall, so far as practicable, give due consideration to (1) t population, (2) the extent of the actual or potential air polluti problem, and (3) the financial need of the respective agenci No agency shall receive any grant under this section during a fiscal year when its expenditures of non-Federal funds for oth than nonrecurrent expenditures for air pollution control prograr will be less than its expenditures were for such programs duri the preceding fiscal year; and no agency shall receive any gra under this section with respect to the maintenance of a progra for the prevention and control of air pollution unless the Admi istrator is satisfied that such grant will be so used as to suppl ment and, to the extent practicable, increase the level of Stat local, or other non-Federal funds that would in the absence such grant be made available for the maintenance of such pr gram, and will in no event supplant such State, local, or oth non-Federal funds. No grant shall be made under this section unt the Administrator has consulted with the appropriate official designated by the Governor or Governors of the State or Stat affected.

"(c) Not more than 10 per centum of the total of funds appr priated or allocated for the purposes of subsection (a) of th section shall be granted for air pollution control programs in a one State. In the case of a grant for a program in an area cros ing State boundaries, the Administrator shall determine the pc tion of such grant that is chargeable to the percentage limitati under this subsection for each State into which such area extenc

"(d) The Administrator, with the concurrence of any recipie of a grant under this section, may reduce the payments to su recipient by the amount of the pay, allowances, traveling e penses, and any other costs in connection with the detail of a officer or employee to the recipient under section 301 of this Ac when such detail is for the convenience of, and at the request c such recipient and for the purpose of carrying out the provisio of this Act. The amount by which such payments have been r duced shall be available for payment of such costs by the Admi istrator, but shall, for the purpose of determining the amount any grant to a recipient under subsection (a) of this section, deemed to have been paid to such agency.

"INTERSTATE AIR QUALITY AGENCIES OR COMMISSIONS

"SEC. 106. For the purpose of developing implementation pla for any interstate air quality control region designated pursua to section 107, the Administrator is authorized to pay, for tv years, up to 100 per centum of the air quality planning progra costs of any agency designated by the Governors of the affect States, which agency shall be capable of recommending to t Governors plans for implementation of national primary and se ondary ambient air quality standards and shall include represe tation from the States and appropriate political subdivisio within the air quality control region. After the initial two-ye period the Administrator is authorized to make grants to suc agency in an amount up to three-fourths of the air quality pla ning program costs of such agency.

"AIR QUALITY CONTROL REGIONS

"SEC. 107. (a) Each State shall have the primary responsibili for assuring air quality within the entire geographic area con prising such State by submitting an implementation plan for suc State which will specify the manner in which national prima and secondary ambient air quality standards will be achieved ar maintained within each air quality control region in such Stat

"(b) For purposes of developing and carrying out implement tion plans under section 110—

"(1) an air quality control region designated under th section before the date of enactment of the Clean Air Amen ments of 1970, or a region designated after such date und subsection (c), shall be an air quality control region; and

"(2) the portion of such State which is not part of any suc designated region shall be an air quality control region, b such portion may be subdivided by the State into two or mo air quality control regions with the approval of the Admini trator.

"(c) The Administrator shall, within 90 days after the da of enactment of the Clean Air Amendments of 1970, after co sultation with appropriate State and local authorities, designa as an air quality control region any interstate area or major intr state area which he deems necessary or appropriate for the attai ment and maintenance of ambient air quality standards. The A ministrator shall immediately notify the governors of the affecte States of any designation made under this subsection.

AIR QUALITY CRITERIA AND CONTROL TECHNIQUES

"SEC. 108. (a) (1) For the purpose of establishing national primary and secondary ambient air quality standards, the Administrator shall within 30 days after the rate of enactment of the Clean Air Amendments of 1970 publish, and shall from time to time thereafter revise, a list which includes each air pollutant—

"(A) which in his judgment has an adverse effect on public health and welfare;

"(B) the presence of which in the ambient air results from numerous or diverse mobile or stationary sources; and

"(C) for which air quality criteria had not been issued before the date of enactment of the Clean Air Amendments of 1970, but for which he plans to issue air quality criteria under this section.

"(2) The Administrator shall issue air quality criteria for an air pollutant within 12 months after he has included such pollutant in a list under paragraph (1). Air quality criteria for an air pollutant shall accurately reflect the latest scientific knowledge useful in indicating the kind and extent of all identifiable effects on public health or welfare which may be expected from the presence of such pollutant in the ambient air, in varying quantities. The criteria for an air pollutant, to the extent practicable, shall include information on—

"(A) those variable factors (including atmospheric conditions) which of themselves or in combination with other factors may alter the effects on public health or welfare of such air pollutant;

"(B) the types of air pollutants which, when present in the atmosphere, may interact with such pollutant to produce an adverse effect on public health or welfare; and

"(C) any known or anticipated adverse effects on welfare.

"(b) (1) Simultaneously with the issuance of criteria under subsection (a), the Administrator shall, after consultation with appropriate advisory committees and Federal departments and agencies, issue to the States and appropriate air pollution control agencies information on air pollution control techniques, which information shall include data relating to the technology and costs of emission control. Such information shall include such data as are available on available technology and alternative methods of prevention and control of air pollution. Such information shall also include data on alternative fuels, processes, and operating methods which will result in elimination of significant reduction of emissions.

"(2) In order to assist in the development of information on pollution control techniques, the Administrator may establish a standing consulting committee for each air pollutant included in a list published pursuant to subsection (a) (1), which shall be comprised of technically qualified individuals representative of State and local governments, industry, and the academic community. Each such committee shall submit as appropriate, to the Administrator information related to that required by in paragraph (1).

"(c) The Administrator shall from time to time review, and, as appropriate, modify, and reissue any criteria or information on control techniques issued pursuant to this section.

"(d) The issuance of air quality criteria and information on air pollution control techniques shall be announced in the Federal Register and copies shall be made available to the general public.

"NATIONAL AMBIENT AIR QUALITY STANDARDS

"SEC. 109. (a) (1) The Administrator—

"(A) within 30 days after the date of enactment of the Clean Air Amendments of 1970, shall publish proposed regulations prescribing a national primary ambient air quality standard and a national secondary ambient air quality standard for each air pollutant for which air quality criteria have been issued prior to such date of enactment; and

"(B) after a reasonable time for interested persons to submit written comments thereon (but no later than 90 days after the initial publication of such proposed standards) shall by regulation promulgate such proposed national primary and secondary ambient air quality standards with such modifications as he deems appropriate.

"(2) With respect to any air pollutant for which air quality criteria are issued after the date of enactment of the Clean Air Amendments of 1970, the Administrator shall publish, simultaneously with the issuance of such criteria and information, proposed national primary and secondary ambient air quality standards for any such pollutant. The procedure provided for in paragraph (1) (B) of this subsection shall apply to the promulgation of such standards.

"(b) (1) National primary ambient air quality standards, prescribed, under subsection (a) shall be ambient air quality standards the attainment and maintenance of which in the judgment of the Administrator, based on such criteria and allowing an adequate margin of safety, are requisite to protect the public health. Such primary standards may be revised in the same manner as promulgated.

"(2) Any national secondary ambient air quality standard prescribed under subsection (a) shall specify a level of air quality the attainment and maintenance of which in the judgment of the Administrator, based on such criteria, is requisite to protect the public welfare from any known or anticipated adverse effects associated with the presence of such air pollutant in the ambient air. Such secondary standards may be revised in the same manner as promulgated.

"IMPLEMENTATION PLANS

"SEC. 110. (a) (1) Each State shall, after reasonable notice and public hearings, adopt and submit to the Administrator, within nine months after the promulgation of a national primary ambient air quality standard (or any revision thereof) under section 109 for any air pollutant, a plan which provides for implementation, maintenance, and enforcement of such primary standard in each air quality control region (or portion thereof) within such State. In addition, such State shall adopt and submit to the Administrator (either as a part of a plan submitted under the preceding sentence or separately) within nine months after the promulgation of a national ambient air quality secondary standard (or revision thereof), a plan which provides for implementation, maintenance, and enforcement of such secondary standard in each air quality control region (or portion thereof) within such State. Unless a separate public hearing is provided, each State shall consider its plan implementing such secondary standard at the hearing required by the first sentence of this paragraph.

"(2) The Administrator shall, within four months after the date required for submission of a plan under paragraph (1), approve or disapprove such plan for each portion thereof. The Administrator shall approve such plan, or any portion thereof, if he determines that it was adopted after reasonable notice and hearing and that—

"(A) (i) in the case of a plan implementing a national primary ambient air quality standard, it provides for the attainment of such primary standard as expeditiously as practicable but (subject to subsection (e)) in no case later than three years from the date of approval of such plan (or any revision thereof to take account of a revised primary standard); and (ii) in the case of a plan implementing a national secondary ambient air quality standard, it specifies a reasonable time at which such secondary standard will be attained;

"(B) it includes emission limitations, schedules, and timetables for compliance with such limitations, and such other measures as may be necessary to insure attainment and maintenance of such primary or secondary standard, including, but not limited to, land-use and transportation controls;

"(C) it includes provision for establishment and operation of appropriate devices, methods, systems, and procedures necessary to (i) monitor, compile, and analyze data on ambient air quality and, (ii) upon request, make such data available to the Administrator;

"(D) it includes a procedure, meeting the requirements of paragraph (4), for review (prior to construction or modification) of the location of new sources to which a standard of performance will apply;

"(E) it contains adequate provisions for intergovernmental cooperation, including measures necessary to insure that emissions of air pollutants from sources located in any air quality control region will not interfere with the attainment or maintenance of such primary or secondary standard in any portion of such region outside of such State or in any other air quality control region;

"(F) it provides (i) necessary assurances that the State will have adequate personnel, funding, and authority to carry out such implementation plan, (ii) requirements for installation of equipment by owners or operators of stationary sources to monitor emissions from such sources, (iii) for periodic reports on the nature and amounts of such emissions; (iv) that such reports shall be correlated by the State agency with any emission limitations or standards established pursuant to this Act, which reports shall be available at reasonable times for public inspection; and (v) for authority comparable to that in section 303, and adequate contingency plans to implement such authority;

"(G) it provides, to the extent necessary and practicable, for periodic inspection and testing of motor vehicles to enforce compliance with applicable emission standards; and

"(H) it provides for revision, after public hearings, of such plan (i) from time to time as may be necessary to take account of revisions of such national primary or secondary ambient air quality standard or the availability of improved or more expeditious methods of achieving such primary or secondary standard; or (ii) whenever the Administrator finds on the basis of information available to him that the plan is substantially inadequate to achieve the national ambient air quality primary or secondary standard which it implements.

"(3) The Administrator shall approve any revision of an implementation plan applicable to an air quality control region if he determines that it meets the requirements of paragraph (2) and has been adopted by the State after reasonable notice and public hearings.

"(4) The procedure referred to in paragraph (2) (D) for review, prior to construction or modification, of the location of new sources shall (A) provide for adequate authority to prevent the construction or modification of any new source to which a standard of performance under section 111 will apply at any location which the State determines will prevent the attainment or maintenance within any air quality control region (or portion thereof) within such State of a national ambient air quality primary or secondary standard, and (B) require that prior to commencing construction or modification of any such source, the owner or operator thereof shall submit to such State such information as may be necessary to permit the State to make a determination under clause (A).

"(b) The Administrator may, wherever he determines necessary, extend the period for submission of any plan or portion thereof which implements a national secondary ambient air quality standard for a period not to exceed eighteen months from the date otherwise required for submission of such plan.

"(c) The Administrator shall, after consideration of any State hearing record, promptly prepare and publish proposed regulations setting forth an implementation plan, or portion thereof, for a State if—

"(1) The State fails to submit an implementation plan for any national ambient air quality primary or secondary standard within the time prescribed,

"(2) the plan, or any portion thereof, submitted for such State is determined by the Administrator not to be in accordance with the requirements of this section, or

"(3) the State fails, within 60 days after notification by the Administrator or such longer period as he may prescribe, to revise an implementation plan as required pursuant to a provision of its plan referred to in subsection (a) (2) (H).

If such State held no public hearing associated with respect to such plan (or revision thereof), the Administrator shall provide opportunity for such hearing within such State on any proposed regulation. The Administrator shall, within six months after the date required for submission of such plan (or revision thereof), promulgate any such regulations unless, prior to such promulgation, such State has adopted and submitted a plan (or revision) which the Administrator determines to be in accordance with the requirements of this section.

"(d) For purposes of this Act, an applicable implementation plan is the implementation plan, or most recent revision thereof, which has been approved under subsection (a) or promulgated under subsection (c) and which implements a national primary or secondary ambient air quality standard in a State.

"(e) (1) Upon application of a Governor of a State at the time of submission of any plan implementing a national ambient air quality primary standard, the Administrator may (subject to paragraph (2)) extend the three-year period referred to in subsection (a) (2) (A) (i) for not more than two years for an air quality control region if after review of such plan the Administrator determines that—

"(A) one or more emission sources (or classes of moving sources) are unable to comply with the requirements of such plan which implement such primary standard because the necessary technology or other alternatives are not available or will not be available soon enough to permit compliance within such three-year period, and

"(B) the State has considered and applied as a part of its plan reasonably available alternative means of attaining such primary standard and has justifiably concluded that attainment of such primary standard within the three years cannot be achieved.

"(2) The Administrator may grant an extension under paragraph (1) only if he determines that the State plan provides for—

"(A) application of the requirements of the plan which implement such primary standard to all emission sources in such region other than the sources (or classes) described in paragraph (1) (A) within the three-year period, and

"(B) such interim measures of control of the sources (or classes) described in paragraph (1) (A) as the Administrator determines to be reasonable under the circumstances.

"(f) (1) Prior to the date on which any stationary source or class of moving sources is required to comply with any requirement of an applicable implementation plan the Governor of the State to which such plan applies may apply to the Administrator to postpone the applicability of such requirement to such source (or class) for not more than one year. If the Administrator determines that—

"(A) good faith efforts have been made to comply with such requirement before such date,

"(B) such source (or class) is unable to comply with such requirement because the necessary technology or other alternative methods of control are not available or have not been available for a sufficient period of time,

"(C) any available alternative operating procedures and interim control measures have reduced or will reduce the impact of such source on public health, and

"(D) the continued operation of such source is essential to national security or to the public health or welfare,

then the Administrator shall grant a postponement of such requirement.

"(2) (A) Any determination under paragraph (1) shall (i) be made on the record after notice to interested persons and opportunity for hearing, (ii) be based upon a fair evaluation of the entire record at such hearing, and (iii) include a statement setting forth in detail the findings and conclusions upon which the determination is based.

"(B) Any determination made pursuant to this paragraph shall be subject to judicial review by the United States court of appeals for the circuit which includes such State upon the filing in such court within 30 days from the date of such decision of a petition by any interested person praying that the decision be modified or set aside in whole or in part. A copy of the petition shall forthwith be sent by registered or certified mail to the Administrator and thereupon the Administrator shall certify and file in such court the record upon which the final decision complained of was issued, as provided in section 2112 of title 28, United States Code. Upon the filing of such petition the court shall have jurisdiction to affirm or set aside the determination complained of in whole or in part. The findings of the Administrator with respect to questions of fact (including each determination made under subparagraphs (A), (B), (C), and (D) of paragraph (1)) shall be sustained if based upon a fair evaluation of the entire record at such hearing.

"(C) Proceedings before the court under this paragraph shall take precedence over all the other causes of action on the docket and shall be assigned for hearing and decision at the earliest practicable date and expedited in every way.

"(D) Section 307 (a) (relating to subpenas) shall be applicable to any proceeding under this subsection.

"STANDARDS OF PERFORMANCE FOR NEW STATIONARY SOURCES

"SEC. 111. (a) For purposes of this section:

"(1) The term 'standard of performance' means a standard for emissions of air pollutants which reflects the degree of emission limitation achievable through the application of the best system of emission reduction which (taking into account the cost of achieving such reduction) the Administrator determines has been adequately demonstrated.

"(2) The term 'new source' means any stationary source, the construction or modification of which is commenced after the publication of regulations (or, if earlier, proposed regulations) prescribing a standard of performance under this section which will be applicable to such source.

"(3) The term 'stationary source' means any building, structure, facility, or installation which emits or may emit any air pollutant.

"(4) The term 'modification' means any physical change in, or change in the method of operation of, a stationary source which increases the amount of any air pollutant emitted by such source or which results in the emission of any air pollutant not previously emitted.

"(5) The term 'owner or operator' means any person who owns, leases, operates, controls, or supervises a stationary source.

"(6) The term 'existing source' means any stationary source other than a new source.

"(b) (1) (A) The Administrator shall, within 90 days after the date of enactment of the Clean Air Amendments of 1970, publish (and from time to time thereafter shall revise) a list of categories of stationary sources. He shall include a category of sources in such list if he determines it may contribute significantly to air pollution which causes or contributes to the endangerment of public health or welfare.

"(B) Within 120 days after the inclusion of a category of stationary sources in a list under subparagraph (A), the Administrator shall propose regulations, establishing Federal standards of performance for new sources within such category. The Administrator shall afford interested persons an opportunity for written comment on such proposed regulations. After considering such comments, he shall promulgate, within 90 days after such publication, such standards with such modifications as he deems appropriate. The Administrator may, from time to time, revise such standards following the procedure required by this subsection for promulgation of such standards. Standards of performance or revisions thereof shall become effective upon promulgation.

"(2) The Administrator may distinguish among classes, types, and sizes within categories of new sources for the purpose of establishing such standards.

"(3) The Administrator shall, from time to time, issue information on pollution control techniques for categories of new sources and air pollutants subject to the provisions of this section.

"(4) The provisions of this section shall apply to any new source owned or operated by the United States.

"(c) (1) Each State may develop and submit to the Administrator a procedure for implementing and enforcing standards of performance for new sources located in such State. If the Administrator finds the State procedure is adequate, he shall delegate to such State any authority he has under this Act to implement and enforce such standards (except with respect to new sources owned or operated by the United States).

"(2) Nothing in this subsection shall prohibit the Administrator from enforcing any applicable standard of performance under this section.

"(d) (1) The Administrator shall prescribe regulations which shall establish a procedure similar to that provided by section 110 under which each State shall submit to the Administrator a plan which (A) establishes emission standards for any existing source for any air pollutant (i) for which air quality criteria have not been issued or which is not included on a list published under section 108(a) or 112(b) (1) (A) but (ii) to which a standard of performance under subsection (b) would apply if such existing source were a new source, and (B) provides for the implementation and enforcement of such emission standards.

"(2) The Administrator shall have the same authority—

"(A) to prescribe a plan for a State in cases where the State fails to submit a satisfactory plan as he would have under section 110(c) in the case of failure to submit an implementation plan, and

"(B) to enforce the provisions of such plan in cases where the State fails to enforce them as he would have under sections 113 and 114 with respect to an implementation plan.

"(e) After the effective date of standards of performance promulgated under this section, it shall be unlawful for any owner or operator of any new source to operate such source in violation of any standard of performance applicable to such source.

"NATIONAL EMISSION STANDARDS FOR HAZARDOUS AIR POLLUTANTS

"SEC. 112. (a) For purposes of this section—

"(1) The term 'hazardous air pollutant' means an air pollutant to which no ambient air quality standard is applicable and which in the judgment of the Administrator may cause, or contribute to, an increase in mortality or an increase in serious irreversible, or incapacitating reversible, illness.

"(2) The term 'new source' means a stationary source the construction or modification of which is commenced after the Administrator proposes regulations under this section establishing an emission standard which will be applicable to such source.

"(3) The terms 'stationary source,' 'modification,' 'owner or operator' and 'existing source' shall have the same meaning as such terms have under section 111(a).

"(b) (1) (A) The Administrator shall, within 90 days after the date of enactment of the Clean Air Amendments of 1970, publish (and shall from time to time thereafter revise) a list which includes each hazardous air pollutant for which he intends to establish an emission standard under this section.

"(B) Within 180 days after the inclusion of any air pollutant in such list, the Administrator shall publish proposed regulations establishing emission standards for such pollutant together with a notice of a public hearing within thirty days. Not later than 180 days after such publication, the Administrator shall prescribe an emission standard for such pollutant, unless he finds, on the basis of information presented at such hearings, that such pollutant clearly is not a hazardous air pollutant. The Administrator shall establish any such standard at the level which in his judgment provides an ample margin of safety to protect the public health from such hazardous air pollutant.

"(C) Any emission standard established pursuant to this section shall become effective upon promulgation.

"(2) The Administrator shall, from time to time, issue information on pollution control techniques for air pollutants subject to the provisions of this section.

"(c) (1) After the effective date of any emission standard under this section—

"(A) no person may construct any new source or modify any existing source which, in the Administrator's judgment, will emit an air pollutant to which such standard applies unless the Administrator finds that such source if properly operated will not cause emissions in violation of such standard, and

"(B) no air pollutant to which such standard applies may be emitted from any stationary source in violation of such standard, except that in the case of an existing source—

"(i) such standard shall not apply until 90 days after its effective date, and

"(ii) the Administrator may grant a waiver permitting such source a period of up to two years after the effective date of a standard to comply with the standard, if he finds that such period is necessary for the installation of controls and that steps will be taken during the period of the waiver to assure that the health of persons will be protected from imminent endangerment.

"(2) The President may exempt any stationary source from compliance with paragraph (1) for a period of not more than two years if he finds that the technology to implement such standards is not available and the operation of such source is required for reasons of national security. An exemption under this paragraph may be extended for one or more additional periods, each period not to exceed two years. The President shall make a report to Congress with respect to each exemption (or extension thereof) made under this paragraph.

"(d) (1) Each State may develop and submit to the Administrator a procedure for implementing and enforcing *emission standards for hazardous air pollutants* for stationary sources located in such State. If the Administrator finds the State procedure is adequate, he shall delegate to such State any authority he has under this Act to implement and enforce such standards (except with respect to stationary sources owned or operated by the United States).

"(2) Nothing in this subsection shall prohibit the Administrator from enforcing any applicable *emission* standard under this section.

"FEDERAL ENFORCEMENT

"SEC. 113. (a) (1) Whenever, on the basis of any information available to him, the Administrator finds that any person is in violation of any requirement of an applicable implementation plan, the Administrator shall notify the person in violation of the plan and the State in which the plan applies of such finding. If such violation extends beyond the 30th day after the date of the Administrator's notification, the Administrator may issue an order requiring such person to comply with the requirements of such plan or he may bring a civil action in accordance with subsection (b).

"(2) Whenever, on the basis of information available to him, the Administrator finds that violations of an applicable implementation plan are so widespread that such violations appear to result from a failure of the State in which the plan applies to enforce the plan effectively, he shall so notify the State. If the Administrator finds such failure extends beyond the thirtieth day after such notice, he shall give public notice of such finding. During the period beginning with such public notice and ending when such State satisfies the Administrator that it will enforce such plan (hereafter referred to in this section as 'period of Federally assumed enforcement'), the Administrator may enforce any requirement of such plan with respect to any person—

"(A) by issuing an order to comply with such requirement, or

"(B) by bringing a civil action under subsection (b).

"(3) Whenever, on the basis of any information available to him, the Administrator finds that any person is in violation of section 111(e) (relating to new source performance standards) or 112(c) (relating to standards for hazardous emissions), or is in violation of any requirement of section 114 (relating to inspections, etc.), he may issue an order requiring such person to comply with such section or requirement, or he may bring a civil action in accordance with subsection (b).

"(4) An order issued under this subsection (other than an order relating to a violation of section 112) shall not take effect until the person to whom it is issued has had an opportunity to confer with the Administrator concerning the alleged violation. A copy of any order issued under this subsection shall be sent to the State air pollution control agency of any State in which the violation occurs. Any order issued under this subsection shall state with reasonable specificity the nature of the violation, specify a time for compliance which the Administrator determines is reasonable, taking into account the seriousness of the violation and any good faith efforts to comply with applicable requirements. In any case in which an order under this subsection (or notice to a violator under paragraph (1)) is issued to a corporation, a copy of such order (or notice) shall be issued to appropriate corporate officers.

"(b) The Administrator may commence a civil action for appropriate relief, including a permanent or temporary injunction, whenever any person—

"(1) violates or fails or refuses to comply with any order issued under subsection (a); or

"(2) violates any requirement of an applicable implementation plan during any period of Federally assumed enforcement more than 30 days after having been notified by the Administrator under subsection (a) (1) of a finding that such person is violating such requirement; or

"(3) violates section 111(e) or 112(c); or

"(4) fails or refuses to comply with any requirement of section 114.

Any action under this subsection may be brought in the district court of the United States for the district in which the defendant is located or resides or is doing business, and such court shall have jurisdiction to restrain such violation and to require compliance. Notice of the commencement of such action shall be given to the appropriate State air pollution control agency.

"(c) (1) Any person who knowingly—

"(A) violates any requirement of an applicable implementation plan during any period of Federally assumed enforcement more than 30 days after having been notified by the Administrator under subsection (a) (1) that such person is violating such requirement, or

"(B) violates or fails or refuses to comply with any order issued by the Administrator under subsection (a), or

"(C) violates section 111(e) or section 112(c)

shall be punished by a fine of not more than $25,000 per day of violation, or by imprisonment for not more than one year, or by both. If the conviction is for a violation committed after the first conviction of such person under this paragraph, punishment shall be by a fine of not more than $50,000 per day of violation, or by imprisonment for not more than two years, or by both.

"(2) Any person who knowingly makes any false statement, representation, or certification in any application, record, report, plan, or other document filed or required to be maintained under this Act or who falsifies, tampers with, or knowingly renders inaccurate any monitoring device or method required to be maintained under this Act, shall upon conviction, be punished by a fine of not more than $10,000, or by imprisonment for not more than six months, or by both.

"INSPECTIONS, MONITORING, AND ENTRY

"SEC. 114. (a) For the purpose (i) of developing or assisting in the development of any implementation plan under section 110 or 111(d), any standard of performance under section 111, or any emission standard under section 112(ii) of determining whether any person is in violation of any such standard or any requirement of such a plan, or (iii) carrying out section 303—

"(1) the Administrator may require the owner or operator of any emission source to (A) establish and maintain such records, (B) make such reports, (C) install, use, and maintain such monitoring equipment or methods, (D) sample such emissions (in accordance with such methods, at such locations, at such intervals, and in such manner as the Administrator shall prescribe), and (E) provide such other information, as he may reasonably require; and

"(2) the Administrator of his authorized representative, upon presentation of his credentials—

"(A) shall have a right of entry to, upon, or through any premises in which an emission source is located or in which any records required to be maintained under paragraph (1) of this section are located, and

"(B) may at reasonable times have access to and copy any records, inspect any monitoring equipment or method required under paragraph (1), and sample any emissions which the owner or operator of such source is required to sample under paragraph (1).

"(b) (1) Each State may develop and submit to the Administrator a procedure for carrying out this section in such State. If the Administrator finds the State procedure is adequate, he may delegate to such State any authority he has to carry out this section (except with respect to new sources owned or operated by the United States).

"(2) Nothing in this subsection shall prohibit the Administrator from carrying out this section in a State.

"(c) Any records, reports or information obtained under subsection (a) shall be available to the public, except that upon a showing satisfactory to the Administrator by any person that records, reports, or information, or particular part thereof, (other than emission data) to which the Administrator has access under this section if made public, would divulge methods or processes entitled to protection as trade secrets of such person, the Administrator shall consider such record, report, or information or particular portion thereof confidential in accrdance with the purposes of section 1905 of title 18 of the United States Code, except that such record, report, or information may be disclosed to other officers, employees, or authorized representatives of the United States concerned with carrying out this Act or when relevant in any proceeding under this Act.

"ABATEMENT BY MEANS OF CONFERENCE PROCEDURE IN CERTAIN CASES

"SEC. 115. (a) The pollution of the air in any State or States which endangers the health or welfare of any persons and which is covered by subsection (b) or (c) shall be subject to abatement as provided in this section.

"(b) (1) Whenever requested by the Governor of any State, State air pollution control agency, or (with the concurrence of t Governor and the State air pollution control agency for the Sta in which the municipality is situated) the governing body of a municipality, the Administrator shall, if such request refers air pollution which is alleged to endanger the health or welfare persons in a State other than that in which the discharge or di charges (causing or contributing to such pollution) originat give formal notification thereof to the air pollution control agen of the municipality where such discharge or discharges originat to the air pollution control agency of the State in which su municipality is located, and to the interstate air pollution contr agency, if any, in whose jurisdictional area such municipality located, and shall call promptly a conference of such agency agencies and of the air pollution control agencies of the munic palities which may be adversely affected by such pollution, a the air pollution control agency, if any, of each State, or for ea area, in which any such municipality is located.

"(2) Whenever requested by the Governor of any State, a Sta air pollution control agency, or (with the concurrence of the Go ernor and the State air pollution control agency for the State which the municipality is situated) the governing body of a municipality, the Administrator shall, if such request refers alleged air pollution which is endangering the health or welfa of persons only in the State in which the discharge or discharg (causing or contributing to such pollution) originate and if municipality affected by such air pollution, or the municipality which such pollution originates, has either made or concurred such request, give formal notification thereof to the State air po lution control agency, to the air pollution control agencies of t municipality where such discharge or discharges originate, and the municipality or municipalities alleged to be adversely affecte thereby, and to any interstate air pollution control agency, who jurisdictional area includes any such municipality and sha promptly call a conference of such agency or agencies, unless the judgment of the Administrator, the effect of such pollution not of such significance as to warrant exercise of Federal jurisdi tion under this section.

"(3) The Administrator may, after consultation with Sta officials of all affected States, also call such a conference wheneve on the basis of reports, surveys, or studies, he has reason to be lieve that any pollution referred to in subsection (a) is occurrin and is endangering the health and welfare of persons in a Stat other than that in which the discharge or discharges originat The Administrator shall invite the cooperation of any municipa State, or interstate air pollution control agencies having jurisdic tion in the affected area on any surveys or studies forming th basis of conference action.

"(4) A conference may not be called under this subsection wit respect to an air pollutant for which (at the time the conferenc is called) a national primary or secondary ambient air qualit standard is in effect under section 109.

"(c) Whenever the Administrator, upon receipt of reports, sur veys, or studies from any duly constituted international agency has reason to believe that any pollution referred to in subsectio (a) which endangers the health or welfare of persons in a foreig country is occurring, or whenever the Secretary of State request him to do so with respect to such pollution which the Secretary o State alleges is of such a nature, the Administrator shall giv formal notification thereof to the air pollution control agency o the municipality where such discharge or discharges originate, t the air pollution control agency of the State in which such munici pality is located, and to the interstate air pollution control agency if any, in the jurisdictional area of which such municipality i located, and shall call promptly a conference of such agency o agencies. The Administrator shall invite the foreign countr which may be adversely affected by the pollution to attend an participate in the conference, and the representative of such coun try shall, for the purpose of the conference and any further pro ceeding resulting from such conference, have all the rights of State air pollution control agency. This subsection shall apply onl to a foreign country which the Administrator determines ha given the United States essentially the same rights with respec to the prevention or control of air pollution occurring in tha country as is given that country by this subsection.

"(d) (1) The agencies called to attend any conference under thi section may bring such persons as they desire to the conference The Administrator shall deliver to such agencies and make avail able to other interested parties, at least thirty days prior to an such conference, a Federal report with respect to the matters be fore the conference, including data and conclusions or finding (if any); and shall give at least thirty days' prior notice of th conference date to any such agency, and to the public by publica tion on at least three different days in a newspaper or newspaper of general circulation in the area. The chairman of the conferenc shall give interested parties an opportunity to present their view to the conference with respect to such Federal report, conclusion or findings (if any), and other pertinent information. The Ad ministrator shall provide that a transcript be maintained of th oceedings of the conference and that a copy of such transcript made available on request of any participant in the conference the expense of such participant.

"(2) Following this conference, the Administrator shall prepare ıd forward to all air pollution control agencies attending the nference a summary of conference discussions including (A) currence of air pollution subject to abatement under this Act; 3) adequacy of measures taken toward abatement of the pollu- on; and (C) nature of delays, if any, being encountered in abat- g the pollution.

"(e) If the Administrator believes, upon the conclusion of the nference or thereafter, that effective progress toward abatement such pollution is not being made and that the health or welfare any persons is being endangered, he shall recommend to the ap- opriate State, interstate, or municipal air pollution control gency (or to all such agencies) that the necessary remedial ac- on be taken. The Administrator shall allow at least six months om the date he makes such recommendations for the taking of ıch recommended action.

"(f) (1) If, at the conclusion of the period so allowed, such re- edial action or other action which in the judgment of the Ad- inistrator is reasonably calculated to secure abatement of such ollution has not been taken, the Administrator shall call a public earing, to be held in or near one or more of the places where the scharge or discharges causing or contributing to such pollution iginated, before a hearing board of five or more persons ap- ointed by the Administrator. Each State in which any discharge ausing or contributing to such pollution originates and each State aiming to be adversely affected by such pollution shall be given n opportunity to select one member of such hearing board and ıch Federal department, agency, or instrumentality having a ıbstantial interest in the subject matter as determined by the dministrator shall be given an opportunity to select one member such hearing board, and one member shall be a representative the appropriate interstate air pollution agency if one exists, nd not less than a majority of such hearing board shall be per- ons other than officers or employees of the Environmental Pro- ection Agency. At least three weeks' prior notice of such hearing ıall be given to the State, interstate, and municipal air pollution ontrol agencies called to attend such hearing and to the alleged olluter or polluters. All interested parties shall be given a reason- ble opportunity to present evidence to such hearing board.

"(2) On the basis of evidence presented at such hearing, the earing board shall make findings as to whether pollution referred in subsection (a) is occurring and whether effective progress ward abatement thereof is being made. If the hearing board nds such pollution is occurring and effective progress toward batement thereof is not being made it shall make recommenda- ons to the Administrator concerning the measures, if any, which finds to be reasonable and suitable to secure abatement of such ollution.

"(3) The Administrator shall send such findings and recom- endations to the person or persons discharging any matter caus- ıg or contributing to such pollution; to air pollution control gencies of the State or States and of the municipality or munici- alities where such discharge or discharges originate; and to any terstate air pollution control agency whose jurisdictional area ıcludes any such municipality, together with a notice specifying reasonable time (not less than six months) to secure abatement f such pollution.

"(g) If action reasonably calculated to secure abatement of the ollution within the time specified in the notice following the ublic hearing is not taken the Administrator—

(1) in the case of pollution of air which is endangering the health or welfare of persons (A) in a State other than that in which the discharge or discharges (causing or contributing to such pollution) originate, or (B) in a foreign country which has participated in a conference called under subsec- tion (c) of this section and in all proceedings under this section resulting from such conference, may request the At- torney General to bring a suit on behalf of the United States in the appropriate United States district court to secure abatement of the pollution.

"(2) in the case of pollution of air which is endangering the health or welfare of persons only in the State in which the discharge or discharges (causing or contributing to such pollution) originate, at the request of the Governor of such State, shall provide such technical and other assistance as in his judgment is necessary to assist the State in judicial pro- ceedings to secure abatement of the pollution under State or local law or, at the request of the Governor of such State, shall request the Attorney General to bring suit on behalf of the United States in the appropriate United States district court to secure abatement of the pollution.

"(h) The court shall receive in evidence in any suit brought in United States court under subsection (g) of this section a tran- cript of the proceedings before the board and a copy of the oard's recommendations and shall receive such further evidence s the court in its discretion deems proper. The court, giving due consideration to the practicability of complying with such standards as may be applicable and to the physical and economic feasibility of securing abatement of any pollution proved, shall have jurisdiction to enter such judgment, and orders enforcing such judgment, as the public interest and the equities of the case may require.

"(i) Members of any hearing board appointed pursuant to subsection (f) who are not regular full-time officers or employees of the United States shall, while participating in the hearing conducted by such board or otherwise engaged on the work of such board, be entitled to receive compensation at a rate fixed by the Administration, but not exceeding $100 per diem, including traveltime, and while away from their homes or regular places of business they may be allowed travel expenses, including per diem in lieu of subsistence, as authorized by law (5 U.S.C. 73b–2) for persons in the Government service employed intermittently.

"(j) (1) In connection with any conference called under this section, the Administrator is authorized to require any person whose activities result in the emission of air pollutants causing or contributing to air pollution to file with him, in such form as he may prescribe, a report, based on existing data, furnishing to the Administrator such information as may reasonably be required as to thq character, kind, and quantity of pollutants discharged and the use of devices or other means to prevent or reduce the emission of pollutants by the person filing such a report. After a conference has been held with respect to any such pollution the Administrator shall require such reports from the person whose activities result in such pollution only to the extent recommended by such conference. Such report shall be made under oath or otherwise, as the Administrator may prescribe, and shall be filed with the Administrator within such reasonable period as the Administrator may prescribe, unless additional time be granted by the Administrator. No person shall be required in such report to divulge trade secrets or secret processes and all information reported shall be considered confidential for the purposes of section 1905 of title 18 of the United States Code.

"(2) If any person required to file any report under this subsection shall fail to do so within the time fixed by the Administrator for filing the same, and such failure shall continue for thirty days after notice of such default, such person shall forfeit to the United States the sum of $100 for each and every day of the continuance of such failure, which forfeiture shall be payable into the Treasury of the United States, and shall be recoverable in a civil suit in the name of the United States brought in the district where such person has his principal office or in any district in which he does business: *Provided,* That the Administrator may upon application therefor remit or mitigate any forfeiture provided for under this subsection and he shall have authority to determine the facts upon all such applications.

"(3) It shall be the duty of the various United States attorneys, under the direction of the Attorney General of the United States, to prosecute for the recovery of such forfeitures.

"(k) No order or judgment under this section, or settlement, compromise, or agreement respecting any action under this section (whether or not entered or made before the date of enactment of the Clean Air Amendments of 1970) shall relieve any person of any obligation to comply with any requirement of an applicable implementation plan, or with any standard prescribed under section 111 or 112.

"RETENTION OF STATE AUTHORITY

"SEC. 116. Except as otherwise provided in sections 209, 211(c)(4), and 233 (preempting certain State regulation of moving sources) nothing in this Act shall preclude or deny the right of any State or political subdivision thereof to adopt or enforce (1) any standard or limitation respecting emissions of air pollutants or (2) any requirement respecting control or abatement of air pollution; except that if an emission standard or limitation is in effect under an applicable implementation plan or under section 111 or 112, such State or political subdivision may not adopt or enforce any emission standard or limitation which is less stringent than the standard or limitation under such plan or section.

"PRESIDENT'S AIR QUALITY ADVISORY BOARD AND ADVISORY COMMITTEES

"SEC. 117. (a) (1) There is hereby established in the Environmental Protection Agency an Air Quality Advisory Board, composed of the Administrator or his designee, who shall be Chairman, and fifteen members appointed by the President, none of whom shall be Federal officers or employees. The appointed members, having due regard for the purposes of this Act, shall be selected from among representatives of various State, interstate, and local governmental agencies, of public or private interests contributing to, affected by, or concerned with air pollution, and of other public and private agencies, organizations, or groups demonstrating an active interest in the field of air pollution prevention and control, as well as other individuals who are expert in this field.

"(2) Each member appointed by the President shall hold office for a term of three years, except that (A) any member appointed to fill a vacany occurring prior to the expiration of the term for which his predecessor was appointed shall be appointed for the remainder of such term, and (B) the terms of office of the members first taking office pursuant to this subsection shall expire as follows: five at the end of one year after the date of appointment, five at the end of two years after such date, and five at the end of three years after such date, as designated by the President at the time of appointment, and (C) the term of any member under the preceding provisions shall be extended until the date on which his successor's appointment is effective. None of the members shall be eligible for reappointment within one year after the end of his preceding term, unless such term was for less than three years.

"(b) The Board shall advise and consult with the Administrator on matters of policy relating to the activities and functions of the Administrator under this Act and make such recommendations as it deems necessary to the President.

"(c) Such clerical and technical assistance as may be necessary to discharge the duties of the Board and such other advisory committees as hereinafter authorized shall be provided from the personnel of the Environmental Protection Agency.

"(d) In order to obtain assistance in the development and implementation of the purposes of this Act including air quality criteria, recommended control techniques, standards, research and development, and to encourage the continued efforts on the part of industry to improve air quality and to develop economically feasible methods for the control and abatement of air pollution, the Administrator shall from time to time establish advisory committees. Committee members shall include, but not be limited to, persons who are knowledgeable concerning air quality from the standpoint of health, welfare, economics, or technology.

"(e) The members of the Board and other advisory committees appointed pursuant to this Act who are not officers or employees of the United States while attending conferences or meetings of the Board or while otherwise serving at the request of the Administrator, shall be entitled to receive compensation at a rate to be fixed by the Administrator, but not exceeding $100 per diem, including traveltime, and while away from their homes or regular places of business they may be allowed travel expenses, including per diem in lieu of subsistence, as authorized by section 5703 of title 5 of the United States Code for persons in the Government service employed intermittently.

"(f) Prior to—

"(1) issuing criteria for an air pollutant under section 108(a)(2),

"(2) publishing any list under section 111(b)(1)(A) or 112(b)(1)(A),

"(3) publishing any standard under section 111(b)(1)(B) or section 112(b)(1)(B), or

"(4) publishing any regulation under section 202(a),

the Administrator shall, to the maximum extent practicable within the time provided, consult with appropriate advisory committees, independent experts, and Federal departments and agencies.

"CONTROL OF POLLUTION FROM FEDERAL FACILITIES

"SEC. 118. Each department, agency, and instrumentality of the executive, legislative, and judicial branches of the Federal Government (1) having jurisdiction over any property or facility, or (2) engaged in any activity resulting, or which may result, in the discharge of air pollutants, shall comply with Federal, State, interstate, and local requirements respecting control and abatement of air pollution to the same extent that any person is subject to such requirements. The President may exempt any emission source of any department, agency, or instrumentality in the executive branch from compliance with such a requirement if he determines it to be in the paramount interest of the United States to do so, except that no exemption may be granted from section 111, and an exemption from section 112 may be granted only in accordance with section 112(c). No such exemption shall be granted due to lack of appropriation unless the President shall have specifically requested such appropriation as a part of the budgetary process and the Congress shall have failed to make available such requested appropriation. Any exemption shall be for a period not in excess of one year, but additional exemptions may be granted for periods of not to exceed one year upon the President's making a new determination. The President shall report each January to the Congress all exemptions from the requirements of this section granted during the preceding calendar year, together with his reason for granting each such exemption.

"ADMINISTRATION

"SEC. 301. (a) The Administrator is authorized to prescrib such regulations as are necessary to carry out his functions unde this Act. The Administrator may delegate to any officer or em ployee of the Environmental Protection Agency such of his power and duties under this Act, except the making of regulations, as h may deem necessary or expedient.

"(b) Upon the request of an air pollution control agency, per sonnel of the Environmental Protection Agency may be detailed t such agency for the purpose of carrying out the provisions of th Act.

"(c) Payments under grants made under this Act may be mad in installments, and in advance or by way of reimbursement, a may be determined by the Administrator.

"DEFINITIONS

"SEC. 302. When used in this Act—

"(a) The term 'Administrator' means the Administrator of th Environmental Protection Agency.

"(b) The term 'air pollution control agency' means any of th following:

"(1) A single State agency designated by the Governor o that State as the official State air pollution control agency fo purposes of this Act;

"(2) An agency established by two or more States an having substantial powers or duties pertaining to the preven tion and control of air pollution;

"(3) A city, county, or other local government healt authority, or, in the case of any city, county, or other loca government in which there is an agency other than the healt authority charged with responsibility for enforcing ordir ances or laws relating to the prevention and control of ai pollution, such other agency; or

"(4) An agency of two or more municipalities located i the same State or in different States and having substantia powers or duties pertaining to the prevention and control o air pollution.

"(c) The term 'interstate air pollution control agency' means—

"(1) an air pollution control agency established by two o more States, or

"(2) an air pollution control agency of two or more muni cipalities located in different States.

"(d) The term 'State' means a State, the District of Columbia the Commonwealth of Puerto Rico, the Virgin Islands, Guam, an American Samoa.

"(e) The term 'person' includes an individual, corporation partnership, association, State, municipality, and political sub division of a State.

"(f) The term 'municipality' means a city, town, borough county, parish, district, or other public body created by or pur suant to State law.

"(g) The term 'air pollutant' means an air pollution agent o combination of such agents.

"(h) All language referring to effects on welfare includes, bu is not limited to, effects on soils, water, crops, vegetation, man made materials, animals, wildlife, weather, visibility, and climate damage to and deterioration of property, and hazards to transpor tation, as well as effects on economic values and on personal com fort and well-being.

"EMERGENCY POWERS

"SEC. 303. Notwithstanding any other provisions of this Act the Administrator upon receipt of evidence that a pollution sourc or combination of sources (including moving sources) is present ing an imminent and substantial endangerment to the health o persons, and that appropriate State or local authorities have no acted to abate such sources, may bring suit on behalf of the Unite States in the appropriate United States district court to immedi ately restrain any person causing or contributing to the allege pollution to stop the emission of air pollutants causing or contrib uting to such pollution or to take such other action as may b necessary.

"CITIZEN SUITS

"SEC. 304. (a) Except as provided in subsection (b), any persor may commence a civil action on his own behalf—

"(1) against any person (including (i) the United States and (ii) any other governmental instrumentality or agency to the extent permitted by the Eleventh Amendment to the

Constitution) who is alleged to be in violation of (A) an emission standard or limitation under this Act or (B) an order issued by the Administrator or a State with respect to such a standard or limitation, or

"(2) against the Administrator where there is alleged a failure of the Administrator to perform any act or duty under this Act which is not discretionary with the Administrator.

The district courts shall have jurisdiction, without regard to the amount in controversy or the citizenship of the parties, to enforce such an emission standard or limitation, or such an order, or to order the Administrator to perform such act or duty, as the case may be.

"(b) No action may be commenced—

"(1) under subsection (a) (1)—

"(A) prior to 60 days after the plaintiff has given notice of the violation (i) to the Administrator, (ii) to the State in which the violation occurs, and (iii) to any alleged violator of the standard, limitation, or order, or

"(B) if the Administrator or State has commenced and is diligently prosecuting a civil action in a court of the United States or a State to require compliance with the standard, limitation, or order, but in any such action in a court of the United States any person may intervene as a matter of right.

"(2) under subsection (a) (2) prior to 60 days after the plaintiff has given notice of such action to the Administrator, except that such action may be brought immediately after such notification in the case of an action under this section respecting a violation of section 112(c) (1) (B) or an order issued by the Administrator pursuant to section 113(a). Notice under this subsection shall be given in such manner as the Administrator shall prescribe by regulation.

"(c) (1) Any action respecting a violation by a stationary source of an emission standard or limitation or an order respecting such standard or limitation may be brought only in the judicial district in which such source is located.

"(2) In such action under this section, the Administrator, if not a party, may intervene as a matter of right.

"(d) The court, in issuing any final order in any action brought pursuant to subsection (a) of this section, may award costs of litigation (including reasonable attorney and expert witness fees) to any party, whenever the court determines such award is appropriate. The court may, if a temporary restraining order or preliminary injunction is sought, require the filing of a bond or equivalent security in accordance with the Federal Rules of Civil Procedure.

"(e) Nothing in this section shall restrict any right which any person (or class of persons) may have under any statute or common law to seek enforcement of any emission standard or limitation or to seek any other relief (including relief against the Administrator or a State agency).

"(f) For purposes of this section, the term 'emission standard or limitation under this Act' means—

"(1) a schedule or timetable of compliance, emission limitation, standard of performance or emission standard, or

"(2) a control or prohibition respecting a motor vehicle fuel or fuel additive,

which is in effect under this Act (including a requirement applicable by reason of section 118) or under an applicable implementation plan.

"APPEARANCE

"SEC. 305. The Administrator shall request the Attorney General to appear and represent him in any civil action instituted under this Act to which the Administrator is a party. Unless the Attorney General notifies the Administrator that he will appear in such action, within a reasonable time, attorneys appointed by the Administrator shall appear and represent him.

"FEDERAL PROCUREMENT

"SEC. 306. (a) No Federal agency may enter into any contract with any person who is convicted of any offense under section 113(c) (1) for the procurement of goods, materials, and services to perform such contract at any facility at which the violation which gave rise to such conviction occurred if such facility is owned, leased, or supervised by such person. The prohibition in the preceding sentence shall continue until the Administrator certifies that the condition giving rise to such a conviction has been corrected.

"(b) The Administrator shall establish procedures to provide all Federal agencies with the notification necessary for the purposes of subsection (a).

"(c) In order to implement the purposes and policy of this Act to protect and enhance the quality of the Nation's air, the President shall, not more than 180 days after enactment of the Clean Air Amendments of 1970 cause to be issued an order (1) requiring each Federal agency authorized to enter into contracts and each Federal agency which is empowered to extend Federal assistance by way of grant, loan, or contract to effectuate the purpose and policy of this Act in such contracting or assistance activities, and (2) setting forth procedures, sanctions, penalties, and such other provisions, as the President determines necessary to carry out such requirement.

"(d) The President may exempt any contract, loan, or grant from all or part of the provisions of this section where he determines such exemption is necessary in the paramount interest of the United States and he shall notify the Congress of such exemption.

"(e) The President shall annually report to the Congress on measures taken toward implementing the purpose and intent of this section, including but not limited to the progress and problems associated with implementation of this section.

"GENERAL PROVISION RELATING TO ADMINSITRATIVE PROCEEDINGS AND JUDICIAL REVIEW

"SEC. 307 (a) (1) In connection with any determination under section 110(f) or section 202(b) (5), or for purposes of obtaining information under section 202(b) (4) or 210(c) (4), the Administrator may issue subpenas for the attendance and testimony of witnesses and the production of relevant papers, books, and documents, and he may administer oaths. Except for emission data, upon a showing satisfactory to the Administrator by such owner or operator that such papers, books, documents, or information or particular part thereof, if made public, would divulge trade secrets or secret processes of such owner or operator, the Administrator shall consider such record, report, or information or particular portion thereof confidential in accordance with the purposes of section 1905 of title 18 of the United States Code, except that such paper, book, document, or information may be disclosed to other officers, emplyees, or authorized representatives of the United States concerned with carrying out this Act, to persons carrying out the National Academy of Sciences' study and investigation provided for in section 202(c), or when relevant in any proceeding under this Act. Witnesses summoned shall be paid the same fees and mileage that are paid witnesses in the courts of the United States. In cases of contumacy or refusal to obey a supena served upon any person under this subparagraph, the district court of the United States for any district in which such person is found or resides or transacts business, upon application by the United States and after notice to such person, shall have jurisdiction to issue an order requiring such person to appear and give testimony before the Administrator to appear and produce papers, books, and documents before the Administrator, or both, and any failure to obey such order of the court may be punished by such court as a contempt thereof.

"(b) (1) A petition for review of action of the Administrator in promulgating any national primary or secondary ambient air quality standard, any emission standard under section 112, any standard of performance under section 111 any standard under section 202 (other than a standard required to be prescribed under section 202(b) (1)), any determination under section 202(b) (5), any control or prohibition under section 211, or any standard under section 231 may be filed only in the United States Court of Appeals for the District of Columbia. A petition for review of the Administrator's action in approving or promulgating any implementation plan under section 110 or section 111(d) may be filed only in the United States Court of Appeals for the appropriate circuit. Any such petition shall be filed within 30 days from the date of such promulgation or approval, or after such date if such petition is based solely on grounds arising after such 30th day.

"(2) Action of the Administrator with respect to which review could have been obtained under paragraph (1) shall not be subject to judicial review in civil or criminal proceedings for enforcement.

"(c) In any judicial proceeding in which review is sought of a determination under this Act required to be made on the record after notice and opportunity for hearing, if any party applies to the court for leave to adduce additional evidence, and shows to the satisfaction of the court that such additional evidence is material and that there were reasonable grounds for the failure to adduce such evidence in the proceeding before the Administrator, the court may order such additional evidence (and evidence in rebuttal thereof) to be taken before the Administrator, in such manner and upon such terms and conditions as to the court may deem proper. The Administrator may modify his findings as to the facts, or make new findings, by reason of the additional evidence so taken and he shall file such modified or new findings, and his recommendation, if any, for the modification or setting aside of his original determination, with the return of such additional evidence.

"MANDATORY LICENSING

"SEC. 308. Whenever the Attorney General determines, upon application of the Administrator—

"(1) that—

"(A) in the implementation of the requirements of section 111, 112, or 202 of this Act, a right under any United States letters patent, which is being used or intended for public or commercial use and not otherwise reasonably available, is necessary to enable any person required to comply with such limitation to so comply, and

"(B) there are no reasonable alternative methods to accomplish such purpose, and

"(2) that the unavailability of such right may result in a substantial lessening of competition or tendency to create a monopoly in any line of commerce in any section of the country,

the Attorney General may so certify to a district court of the United States, which may issue an order requiring the person who owns such patent to license it on such reasonable terms and conditions as the court, after hearing, may determine. Such certification may be made to the district court for the district in which the person owning the patent resides, does business, or is found.

"POLICY REVIEW

"SEC. 309. (a) The Administrator shall review and comment in writing on the environmental impact of any matter relating to duties and responsibilities granted pursuant to this Act or other provisions of the authority of the Administrator, contained in any (1) legislation proposed by any Federal department or agency, (2) newly authorized Federal projects for construction and any major Federal agency action other than a project for construction to which section 102(2)(C) of Public Law 91–190 applies, and (3) proposed regulations published by any department or agency of the Federal Government. Such written comment shall be made public at the conclusion of any such review.

"(b) In the event the Administrator determines that any such legislation, action, or regulation is unsatisfactory from the standpoint of public health or welfare or environmental quality, he shall publish his determination and the matter shall be referred to the Council on Environmental Quality.

"OTHER AUTHORITY NOT AFFECTED

"SEC. 310. (a) Except as provided in subsection (b) of this section, this Act shall not be construed as superseding or limiting the authorities and responsibilities, under any other provision of law, of the Administrator or any other Federal officer, department, or agency.

"(b) No appropriation shall be authorized or made under section 301, 311, or 314 of the Public Health Service Act for any fiscal year after the fiscal year ending June 30, 1964, for any purpose for which appropriations may be made under authority of this Act.

"RECORDS AND AUDIT

"SEC. 311. (a) Each recipient of assistance under this Act shall keep such records as the Administrator shall prescribe, including records which fully disclose the amount and disposition by such recipient of the proceeds of such assistance, the total cost of the project or undertaking in connection with which such assistance is given or used, and the amount of that portion of the cost of the project or undertaking supplied by other sources, and such other records as will facilitate an effective audit.

"(b) The Administrator and the Comptroller General of the United States, or any of their duly authorized representatives, shall have access for the purpose of audit and examinations to any books, documents, papers, and records of the recipients that are pertinent to the grants received under this Act.

"COMPREHENSIVE ECONOMIC COST STUDIES

"SEC. 312. (a) In order to provide the basis for evaluating programs authorized by this Act and the development of new programs and to furnish the Congress with the information necessary for authorization of appropriations by fiscal years beginning after June 30, 1969, the Administrator, in cooperation with State, interstate, and local air pollution control agencies, shall make a detailed estimate of the cost of carrying out the provisions of this Act; a comprehensive study of the cost of program implementation by affected units of government; and a comprehensive study of the economic impact of air quality standards on the Nation's industries, communities, and other contributing sources of pollution, including an analysis of the national requirements for and the cost of controlling emissions to attain such standards of air quality as may be established pursuant to this Act or applicable State law. The Administrator shall submit such detailed estimate and the results of such comprehensive study of cost for the fiv year period beginning July 1, 1969, and the results of such oth studies, to the Congress not later than January 10, 1969, and sh submit a reevaluation of such estimate and studies annual thereafter.

"(b) The Administrator shall also make a complete investig tion and study to determine (1) the need for additional train State and local personnel to carry out programs assisted pursua to this Act and other programs for the same purpose as this Ac (2) means of using existing Federal training programs to tra such personnel; and (3) the need for additional trained personn to develop, operate and maintain those pollution control faciliti designed and installed to implement air quality standards. I shall report the results of such investigation and study to t President and the Congress not later than July 1, 1969.

"ADDITIONAL REPORTS TO CONGRESS

"SEC. 313. Not later than six months after the effective date this section and not later than January 10 of each calendar ye beginning after such date, the Administrator shall report to th Congress on measures taken toward implementing the purpo and intent of this Act including, but not limited to, (1) the pro ress and problems associated with control of automotive exhau emissions and the research efforts related thereto; (2) the d velopment of air quality criteria and recommended emission co trol requirements; (3) the status of enforcement actions take pursuant to this Act; (4) the status of State ambient air stan ards setting, including such plans for implementation and er forcement as have been developed; (5) the extent of developmer and expansion of air pollution monitoring systems; (6) progres and problems related to development of new and improved contr techniques; (7) the develpment of quantitative and qualitativ instrumentation to monitor emissions and air quality; (8) stanc ards set or under consideration pursuant to title II of this Act (9) the status of State, interstate, and local pollution control prc grams established pursuant to and assisted by this Act; and (10 the reports and recommendations made by the President's Ai Quality Advisory Board.

"LABOR STANDARDS

"SEC. 314. The Administrator shall take such action as may b necessary to insure that all laborers and mechanics employed b contractors or subcontractors on projects assisted under this Ac shall be paid wages at rates not less than those prevailing for th same type of work on similar construction in the locality as de termined by the Secretary of Labor, in accordance with the Act o March 3, 1931, as amended, known as the Davis-Bacon Act (4 Stat. 1494; 40 U.S.C. 276a—276a–5). The Secretary of Labo shall have, with respect to the labor standards specified in thi subsection, the authority and functions set forth in Reorganiza tion Plan Numbered 14 of 1950 (15 F.R. 3176; 64 Stat. 1267) an section 2 of the Act of June 13, 1934, as amended (48 Stat. 948 40 U.S.C. 276c).

"SEPARABILITY

"SEC. 315. If any provision of this Act, or the application o any provision of this Act to any person or circumstance, is helc invalid, the application of such provision to other persons or circumstances, and the remainder of this Act, shall not be affectec thereby.

"APPROPRIATIONS

"SEC. 316. There are authorized to be appropriated to carry out this Act, other than sections 103(f)(3) and (d), 104, 212, and 403, $125,000,000 for the fiscal year ending June 30, 1971, $225,000,000 for the fiscal year ending June 30, 1972, and $300,000,000 for the fiscal year ending June 30, 1973.

g. Implementation of Federal air legislation

The Air Pollution Amendments of 1970 created an entirely new program. In spite of the time that had elapsed since the passage of the 1967 Act, the states were far behind on the time schedules that would eventually produce an implementation plan to control emissions. For several years most state effort went into developing the air quality standards and emission inventories. Development of standards required public hearing for each region and in interstate regions there were multiple hearings. As new criteria and control technique documents were released by the Federal government, the states had to hold new hearings on those pollutants.

personnel shortage

The regions often required new state legislation or administrative agreements in order to function. States often contracted with local agencies to perform required functions. Both local and state agencies had to increase their staff to carry out the federal mandate. Qualified people are hard to find and training became and remains an important part of State and local efforts. The Federal government states that an increased need for State and local agency employment from 2,300 in 1969 to 8,000 in 1974 is projected. An increase in the positions in the National Air Pollution Control Administration from 1,000 to 2,900 is likewise projected. The amount of effort required by the private sector is forecast to increase from 20,000 to 40,000 man-years to meet the compliance requirements of State and local laws and regulations. A need for training 400,000 combustion equipment operators and 600,000 automobile mechanics is likewise identified. [Manpower and Training Needs for Air Pollution Control, Report of the Secretary of HEW, 91st Cong., 2d Sess., Senate Document No. 9198 (August 7, 1970)]

monitoring

Very few cities in the United States had any real idea of what their air quality was when the 1967 Act passed. For a control system to be based on the reaching of atmospheric goals, an accurate knowledge of the air quality was mandatory. Few cities had monitoring; those that did were of such poor quality that data was of marginal value. The number of pollutants tested was very limited, testing technique was not uniform, testing sites were located with little relationship to accurate measurement. The result was a nearly meaningless information base concerning atmospheric air quality. Since then the Federal government has spent much effort in developing this information, a job that is far from complete. A monitoring system known as the National Air Surveillance Network was created and is now under EPA administration. Federal and local monitoring stations contribute their data to the system. To date, however, the stations are too few, and too limited in their scope to provide for national surveillance. It is doubtful whether a surveillance system based on technology presently utilized could ever work. One study showed that four stations per square mile would be needed to monitor sulfur dioxide with 25 percent accuracy. Only one quarter the number would be needed to monitor particulates, but most of the more complex pollutants would require at least four per square mile. With automated monitoring stations costing upward of $10,000 and requiring costly maintenance, such monitoring would be prohibitively expensive. Even if these stations were provided, their accuracy is further limited by the inability to predict regional atmospheric conditions from the raw data provided by these fixed monitoring stations. Such predictability is dependent upon the quality of the mathematical model (also called dispersion model) that has been developed for the region which in turn is affected by a vast number of variables including the need for a sophisticated knowledge of meteorological conditions. The result of these problems is that pollution profiles to date are an educated guess concerning atmospheric quality. With the present state of the art to control emissions, a control program aimed at maintaining a given level of air quality is wishful thinking. There is, however, a possibility that such predictability will be developed in the near future.

One promising development is the correlation spectrometer that is based on dispersing sunlight (or artificial light) through a prism. If gases are present in the atmosphere their molecules absorb light in specific spectrum and thus produce lines in the rainbow of colors in the spectrum. The larger the amount of gas the greater the intensity of the lines. Each gas has its own characteristic lines and so the instrument can be equipped to measure any gas. At present masks have been designed to identify the optical footprints of sulfur dioxide, nitrogen dioxide, and iodine gas. Currently being designed are masks for carbon monoxide, some hydrocarbons, ozone and nitrogen oxide. This instrument is portable and gives a reading not of a point source but of a pollution concentration of a band of air whose length can be controlled to read either a line of sight distance, or from the ground to the inversion layer, or from an airplane to the ground. [See Coble, Langan, and McCaull, "New Eye on the Air," 13 *Environment* #4, May 1971 at 34]

emission inventories

Even if a Control Region had a clear picture of its air quality it could still not mount an effective control effort unless it had an accurate emission inventory of the location of all pollution sources, and the time and kind of pollutants that were being discharged. When the 1967 Act passed, except for Los Angeles and perhaps one or two other locations, such information was unavailable. Getting the information has not been easy. In many regions a dozen or two dozen inspectors would be responsible for thousands of emissions. Many companies had no idea of what they spewed into the atmosphere; few had much interest in finding out. Often stack measurement and/or continuous monitoring was needed, but in older plants it was often difficult to do this. Laws did not exist to require the pollutor to provide the needed information and cities had neither the money, manpower, or skill to do so. [See Cooper, and Rossano, Source Testing for Air Pollution Control, 1971] Meaningful inspection was also hampered by the economic, political, and psychological power of big pollutors. An air pollution inspector would be stopped at the plant gate by the plant security guard. The inspector could quote Supreme Court decisions but nonetheless he would be delayed until the proper company officials could meet him and accompany his inspection. If he raised objections to what he saw, the company's scientific and engineering experts could be used to overwhelm him. If this didn't work the following general argument in outline form would be used—it is not really pollution, it doesn't harm anyone, the equipment is unavailable for control but it has nonetheless been on order for months, it can't be operated without breakdown, and if forced to abate the company will reduce operations (close down, or not carry out a planned expansion).

The effect of these problems is that the various activities that were designed to take place under the 1967 Act fell far behind schedule. The pollution control effort that existed in 1967 was based on various attempts to control emissions—usually limited to industrial sources and perhaps incinerators. The 1967 Act called for a program based on atmospheric quality. As we have just seen, the information was not available and could not easily be made available. To set standards required much manpower. The emission inventory necessary to proceed required money, manpower, and often new legislation. The Regional control effort created legal, political, and financing difficulties.

Thus, when the 1970 amendments passed no implementation plans had been approved by the Federal government though many plans were in various stages of development and implementation. Proposed regulations for new implementation plans came out in April of 1971 but most Regions continued pretty much as they had been.

Twenty-one implementation plans were submitted in 1970 by 15 states for 13 air quality control regions, and were originally required to meet state air quality standards under the Clean Air Act before it was amended. However, under the 1970 amendments, state plans must satisfy a number of other new requirements.

On August 13, 1971, EPA announced it had approved portions of several regional air pollution control plans for sulfur oxide and particulate matter. The plans were prepared by state governments prior to the Clean Air Act Amendments of 1970. The action marked the first time that the EPA had approved such state plans.

The Environmental Protection Agency issued its final regulations concerning implementation of state programs under the 1970 Clean Air Act amendments on August 14, 1971.

The full text of these regulations appears in the Federal Register, Vol. 36, No. 158, August 14, 1971 at 15486.

regional plans

Under the 1970 amendments all of the nation will be in a region or the residual region provided for in section 107 of the Clean Air Act. By the end of 1970, there were 100 regions containing 140 million persons, about 70 percent of the nation. Many of these regions are interstate and thus create special administrative problems.

For the list of Air Quality Control Regions and their geographical coverage, see 42 C.F.R. Chapter IV, Subchapter C, Part 481, *Environment Reporter* 31:1201.

The Environmental Protection Agency, on May 31, 1972, approved 11 state implementation plans, but allowed 18 of the most densely populated states until mid-1977 to comply with the 1975 standards for control of emissions from vehicles. Parts of nearly all state implementation plans were approved. *See, The Wall Street Journal,* at 3, and *The New York Times* at 1, both June 1, 1972, and the *Federal Register,* Vol. 37, No. 105, May 31, 1972 at 10842. EPA later proposed substitute implementation plans for states that failed to present fully acceptable plans. *See, Federal Register,* Vol. 37, No. 115, June 14, 1972 at 11826, and proposed amendments to these plans at Vol. 37, No. 119, June 20, 1972 at 12155.

See the annual reports to Congress from EPA on Implementation of the Clean Air Act; the fourth was due in mid-1972.

See, "Air Pollution over the States," (a report on state implementation of the Federal laws) *Environmental Science & Technology,* Vol. 6, No. 2, February, 1972 at 111.

An air pollution program that would give informants one-half of the fine paid by a polluter has been given preliminary approval by the District of Columbia City Council, and was expected to receive final approval before this book returns from the bindery. The proposed regulations reportedly were the first in the country to provide a bounty on air polluters. The maximum fine was set at $300, with provision that no one person can collect more than $1,000 in a year.

The District of Columbia's program is in implementation of the Federal air laws, as the city in this case is treated as a state. See, *The Washington Post,* June 7, 1972 at B1.

Emergency Powers

Section 303 gives the Administrator the power to go to court to abate pollution creating an imminent and substantial danger to health when appropriate State and Local authorities have not acted. This provision has been used once to close down the steel and other industries of Birmingham, Alabama for 31 hours on November 18, 1971. For a discussion of this action *see* Sloyan, Patric, "The Day They Shut Down Birmingham," *The Washington Monthly,* May 1972 at 41.

progress?

The question then must be faced as to how well we are meeting our goals of cleaning up the air. It is difficult to say. The demands of the 1967 act could not be met without years of laying the foundation. Much of the groundwork has now been done but as the pressure increases to comply with the implementation plans a countervailing pressure can be expected as industry stalls or complies only after legal command. Every effort will be made to lower the requirements of the implementation plans and to "be reasonable". There will, of course, also be increased pressure to have the public pay the cost of pollution control. The method of emission or source control was replaced by the Federal government with the atmospheric air quality control concept. That didn't work and won't work, at least for the next several years, though we still pretend that implementation plans are really geared to atmospheric modeling concepts. In the 1970 amendments several provisions were made that are based on the philosophy of the pre-1967 efforts. Section 112 allows for emission control of hazardous pollutants. These are defined so that all but six categories of pollutants can be subject to Federal emission limits. Section 111 allows Federal emission limits on new stationary sources. The control efforts of these programs do not depend on meeting any atmospheric quality goals. However, the program carried on under the implementation plan (Sec. 110) is based on achieving primary and secondary standards of atmospheric quality. (These standards are reprinted in the appendix to this chapter.)

SOURCE OF TABLE: A Citizen's Guide to Clean Air, by the Conservation Foundation under contract to the Environmental Protection Agency, 1972. Additional materials from this publication concerning air polution control plans and the timetable for state plans are reprinted in the Appendix to this chapter.

NATIONAL AMBIENT AIR QUALITY STANDARDS

Pollutant	*Primary*	*Secondary*
Particulate Matter		
Annual geometric mean	75	60
Maximum 24-hour concentration*	260	150
Sulfur Oxides		
Annual arithmetic mean	80 (.03 ppm)	60 (.02 ppm)
Maximum 24-hour concentration*	365 (.14 ppm)	260 (.1 ppm)
Maximum 3-hour concentration*		1,300 (.5 ppm)
Carbon Monoxide		
Maximum 8-hour concentration*	10 (9 ppm)	
Maximum 1-hour concentration*	40 (35 ppm)	same as primary
Photochemical Oxidants		
Maximum 1-hour concentration*	160 (.08 ppm)	same as primary
Hydrocarbons		
Maximum 3-hour (6-9 am) concentration*	160 (.24 ppm)	same as primary
Nitrogen Oxides		
Annual arithmetic mean	100 (.05 ppm)	same as primary

(All measurements are expressed in micrograms per cubic meter ($\mu g/m^3$) except for those for carbon monoxide, which are expressed in milligrams per cubic meter (mg/m^3). Equivalent measurements in parts per million (ppm) are given for the gaseous pollutants.)

* Not to be exceeded more than once a year.

Standards for such other pollutants as fluorides, polycyclic organic matter, and odorous substances may be proposed in the future.

too many cookbooks

So we are pursuing two concepts of control simultaneously, putting those subject to these controls in a position of knowing that whatever efforts they make now will probably require expensive upward revision. We also penalize those who attempt to abate. The cost of control increases very rapidly after some base control efforts are made. If an implementation plan fails to lead to a desired level of atmospheric purity, then everyone must then reduce his emissions further, and those who have done most could be faced with the most expensive additional requirements. For this reason we are beginning to realize that if the program goal is really to reach a predefined atmospheric purity, the effort to force everyone to abate under an implementation plan will be much more costly than a system based on an economic model. Some industries can achieve major pollution reduction at a relatively low cost; others give society the benefits of a smaller reduction at a very high cost. The mechanics of administering a pollution control program aimed at achieving a result at the lowest possible cost can vary. An effluent or emission charge or tax is the most common proposal. Administered poorly, an effluent tax could result in the government's granting of licenses to kill (people and the environment). Administered properly, it could produce a desired result at a much lower total cost. The major technical weakness of such a proposal is that the system would depend upon an information base that is not available and may or may not be available in the near future. We do not really know what the effects of air pollution are; we do not know what is emitted into the atmosphere; we do not know what happens in the atmosphere. While these information gaps are serious limitations on the development of any program, they are much more serious if the control program becomes tied exclusively to atmospheric quality goals administered so as to allow some people to buy the right to pollute. Meanwhile our schizophrenic program continues. If in 1967 we had adopted serious emission limitations, even if limited only to major sources, we would have been years ahead in our program. Such an action would not have precluded atmospheric studies, emission inventories, and the development of better instrumentation.

The new amendment in 1970 put us, for the time being, back on the emission control track. The state implementation plan, section 111 (new stationary sources) and section 112 (hazardous emissions) will be the primary determinants of whether clean air is to be achieved. EPA is the power that determines whether such efforts will be sustained. At this time it is very difficult to analyze their efforts. The time for setting up a government program is past, yet the time for achieving demonstrable improvement under existing programs has not yet really arrived. The 1970 amendments required new activities to take place on a new time schedule and in August of 1971 many of the required actions have yet to take place. It will be several months before the implementation plans show how serious EPA is going to be. Continued expansion of budgets will also be necessary to achieve results. Vigorous enforcement (perhaps a second lawsuit) will be needed.

EPA regulations on new stationary sources

What very little evidence now exists indicates that the Environmental Protection Agency will keep up its pressure as long as the demand for improvement continues to be heard by the political leadership. If pressure slackens—so will efforts. On March 31, 1971 (36 F.R. 5931) EPA listed the sources to be subject to emission limits under section 111. They are:

1. Contact Sulfuric Acid Plants
2. Fossil Fuel-Fired Steam Generators of more than 250 million Btu/hr. heat input
3. Incinerators of more than 2000 lbs./hr. charging rate. (Municipal type refuse)
4. Nitric Acid Plants
5. Portland Cement Plants

It is interesting to note that the major air polluting industries—steel, aluminum, petroleum, pulp and paper, and organic chemicals—are not on the list. They are expected to be made subject to the regulations, however, in the summer of 1972.

On December 23, 1971, the Environmental Protection Agency promulgated regulations under section 111 for new or seriously modified stationary sources. [36 Fed. Reg. 24876] The regulations set emissions standards, test methods and procedures and provide for procedures by which owners could request EPA to review plans for the construction or important modification of their plants. A supplemental statement in connection with the final regulations was issued on March 21, 1972 [37 Fed. Reg. 5767].

On March 31, 1971, EPA released a list of substances to be subject to future control under section 112 (hazardous emissions). Asbestos, beryllium, and mercury were listed along with the statement that other substances may be designated later. On December 3, 1971, EPA issued proposed standards for the three materials just mentioned (36 Fed. Reg. 23239, Dec. 7. 1971), with the promise that final standards would follow within six months.

HEW has determined that ozone is a toxic gas capable of causing serious physical injury [e.g. pulmonary edema.] Accordingly, the department has proposed regulations for ozone generators and other devices emitting ozone. See *Federal Register,* Vol. 37, No. 124 at 12644.

Federal facilities

Performance standards for Federal Facilities are found in 42 C.F.R. part 76. Under section 118 of the 1970 amendments, Federal facilities must meet all Federal, State, interstate and local requirements. Refer to that section for the limited exceptions.

h. Natural gas and the role of the FPC

One of the most effective and easiest ways to meet air quality goals is to substitute a clean burning fuel for a dirty one. Natural gas is the best fuel, for both particulate and sulfur oxides, the two major contaminants from stationary combustion sources, are essentially absent. One of the major stationary pollutors is the electric generating industry. This industry has attempted to meet its air pollution emission requirement by using natural gas, low sulfur oil and coal, and gas turbines for peak power needs. Utilities however are limited in their discretion both because of the need to recover increased costs and because they are regulated by both State and Federal agencies. [See Luce, Utility Responsibility for Protection of the Environment, 10 Arizona L. Rev. 68 (1968) and Sillin, Environmental Considerations Facing the Public Utility Industry, 2 Nat. Res. Law. No. 1, Jan., 1969 at 20]

See also Committee on Public Works, United States Senate, Some Environmental Implications of National Fuels Policy, 91 Cong. 2d Sess., December 1970.

Environmental problems of power generation are discussed at much greater depth in Volume Two of this work. Alternate sources of energy, including atomic and solar, are also examined there.

If utilities desire to use natural gas they must obtain permission of the Federal Power Commission. The Commission has a duty to protect and conserve natural gas as the supply is limited. For these reasons they have taken the position that boiler fuel gas is of lowest priority in the possible uses for this fuel. This "end use" theory was upheld by the Supreme Court in *FPC v. Transcontinental Gas Pipe Line Corp.* [365 U.S. 1 (1961)].

See the FPC staff report, Air Pollution and the Regulated Electric Power and Natural Gas Industry (1968).

Subsequently the FPC decided in three cases that the reduction of air pollution under the circumstances before them did not justify the use of gas as a substitute for other fossil fuels for electric power production.

In the Transwestern Pipeline Case, known also as the Gulf Pacific case [36 F.P.C. 176 (1966)] the Commission refused to supply the gas to Los Angeles. In Florida Gas Transmission Co. [37 F.P.C. 466 (1967)] the Commission approved the sale but for economic reasons and considered the air pollution argument on balance to be essentially irrelevant. The strongest case for gas to reduce air pollution was Transcontinental Pipe Line Corporation [38 F.P. C. 906 (1967)] where such gas for New York City would have a substantial effect in reducing air pollution. The sale of gas was approved but again on the basis of economic arguments. Only one Commissioner felt such arguments gave much weight to his vote.

The Federal Power Commission's position on this subject seems not to have changed substantially since the boiler gas cases of 1967. The FPC's annual report for FY 1970 recognizes the shortage of natural gas, but devotes little more than one page to a discussion of fuels, and makes no mention at all of boiler gas.

The most recent FPC decision in this area is Chandeleur Pipe Line Company, __FPC__, Opinion No. 560-A, (December 31, 1970), appeal filed, Civ. No. 71-1197, 71-1198, 71-1289 (April 30, 1971, D.C.C.A.).

See also generally the *Oil & Gas Journal,* a weekly publication, and specifically the following articles from the issue of Oct. 25, 1971: "U.S. utilities flood over $1 billion into gas search"; "AGA told gas supply may never catch up," and "Study will answer Arctic gas-pipeline questions."

In order to obtain the information necessary to develop a more effective environmental program the Federal Power Commission developed a steam-electric plant and water quality control data program. It was designed to be coordinated with the National Air Pollution Control Administration and the Federal Water Quality Administration, now both part of EPA. Control data was required to be supplied to the FPC by electric utilities generating power from plants of 25 megawatts or more. 18 CFR 141.59 issued October 22, 1970.

The problem of supplying natural gas for electric utilities has become one part of the larger problem of obtaining sufficient natural gas to supply the existing and expanding demand. The reason such a shortage developed at this time is primarily due to the regulatory activities of the F.P.C., though what they have done wrong is somewhat dependent upon the interest represented by the critique. See MacAvoy, The Regulation-Induced Shortage of Natural Gas, 14 Job Law & Economics 167 (April 1971) for a study sponsored by the independent Brookings Institution. To blame the F.P.C., however, requires that one ignore the political aspect of appointments to the F.P.C. In recent months claims of F.P.C.-suppressed reports that are unfavorable to industry have been made.

According to columnist Jack Anderson [*Washington Post*, May 13, 1971 at G7], of the 41 members of the Presidentially appointed National Gas Survey Executive Advisory Committee, 32 are from gas companies, and of the remainder, only one could be considered a "real consumer member." The committee gives the Federal Power Commission advice on regulating the gas industry. Anderson listed some of these members as having contributed heavily to the Republican Party.

Of greater importance than these advisors are the members of the FPC and the role of its chairman, John Nassikas. However, the view of many is that here there is little difference in point of view between the advisors and the advised.

state role

State government regulating agencies can also affect the use of fuels, thus modifying the effect of FPC decisions. The following information on such a case in Illinois is from the CEQ annual report, 1971:

indirect pollution controls—In come cases, pollution control requirements may be imposed indirectly, rather than through standards. For example, the Illinois Public Utility Commission, at the urging of the State Attorney General, granted a rate increase to a large electric utility, Commonwealth Edison, on the condition that the utility take several specific pollution abatement actions. If Commonwealth Edison fails to take the actions within the allotted time, the State may reduce the rate increase 50 percent. This is believed to be the first rate regulation in the Nation to contain explicit and extensive environmental quality requirements. The requirements call for the utility to convert to cleaner fuels to protect air quality and to install cooling facilities to prevent thermal water pollution.

methane use

Natural gas is a mixture of low-molecular-weight hydrocarbons. Methane is almost always the major constituent. ("Control Techniques for Sulfur Oxide Air Pollutants," HEW, 1969 at 4-31.) Most of it is relatively free of sulfur, hence its usefulness as an alternate fuel to reduce pollution.

The natural gas deposits upon which we can draw were formed millions of years ago, and lie under vast sections of 23 of our 50 states. But gas continues to be formed—in bogs, streams, garbage dumps, and cesspools. Before do-it-yourself technology got out of style for governmental units, utilization of the methane formed at municipal secondary water treatment plants was not uncommon. A few of these still make use of the methane, but in many cases the bother isn't considered worthwhile. In Cleveland, for example, the sewage sludge is placed in a large steel digester, the methane is drawn off, and the gas used to power a generator for the sewage plant's electrical use. This system had been in operation for many years when the author visited it a couple of years ago, but there was sentiment there too for discontinuing the system.

Like most of the better solutions to pollution problems, the production of methane gas from organic wastes simultaneously affects several of the traditional pollution categories: solid waste, air pollution, water pollution, and, to a minor extent, noise pollution.

It has been mentioned earlier that natural methane production by decomposition of organic matter is a serious problem in landfills. Yet efficient recycling should use such potential energy sources. Since it is clearly possible to speed up greatly the production of methane from decomposing wastes, it seems possible that methane production may have a role in municipal waste utilization. The possible uses for methane are many, including heating, powering of vehicles, and production of electricity.

methane autos

An account of one inventor's success in building methane-powered vehicles appears in "The Marvelous Chicken-Powered Motorcar," in *The Mother Earth News* No. 10, July, 1971 at 14 (See also editorial note at 13.) The fanciful title stems from the fact that the organic material that British inventor Harold Bate uses to produce the methane used in his cars is 75 percent a 1-to-1 mixture of chicken and hog manure, plus 25 percent straw.

The excreta-straw mixture is sprinkled with water and stacked in a compost pile with some of the previous batch (to speed-up decomposition) and left for 24 hours. It is then shoveled into a heavy steel container, maintained at about 85 to 90 degrees F., and the gas is withdrawn periodically over several weeks with a high-pressure compressor.

A 300-pound batch of manure-straw reportedly yields about 1,500 cubic feet of methane gas, the equivalent of about 62 U.S. gallons of gasoline. Bate calculates his costs at about 3 cents per gasoline gallon equivalent, but the article was unclear as to whether this made allowance for raw materials' costs—which it may not have, since Bate has a chicken farm. From an air pollution viewpoint, this is relevant: combustion of methane in the vehicles using it was listed at 97 to 98 percent. From a water pollution viewpoint, the lack of lead (as in gasoline) eliminates the problem of air-borne lead entering water supplies following precipitation.

See also in *The Mother Earth News* No. 3 "Solution to Pollution, Electricity From Manure Gases," and "How to Generate Power From Garbage."

It should be obvious that chicken-manure-powered automobiles are hardly likely to be handcrafted by every commuter in the country. But the use of organic wastes for energy production is far too sensible a concept to be dismissed totally as a quaint curiosity.

Use of natural gas is not the only alternative to burning coal or oil. Obvious other possibilities are solar and atomic energy. These are discussed extensively in Volume Two of this work.

i. Mobile sources of air pollution

Transportation contributes by weight more air pollution than all other sources combined.

The greatest single source of air pollution is the automobile [see subsection on sources of pollution]. Futhermore, the demand for gasoline creates pollution problems from petroleum production (the Santa Barbara spill), its transportation (the Torrey Canyon wreck), and its refining (the Port Newark area, New Jersey). The need for new sources affects our foreign policy and creates environmental threats such as the Trans Alaska Pipeline (TAPS). These problems are in part due to the promotional and sales practices of the automobile industry which encourages the horsepower race, with the corresponding increase in the consumption of gasoline.

a kingdom for horsepower

But because pollution from automobiles is a complex problem, car size alone does not determine pollution rate. [See Craig, *Not A Question of Size,* 12 Environment #5, June 1970 at 2, and *EPA Auto, Truck Test Results,* Environmental News EPA, April 12, 1971]. But ever-increasing consumption of petroleum products is a major part of the air pollution problem.

Another aspect of the air pollution problem has been the evolvement of the automobile engine in the past twenty years. Between 1954 and 1959 average horsepower almost doubled. The climb slowed in the 1960's, but since then has continued up. This horsepower race is only one aspect of a change in design to emphasize performance characteristics better suited for racing than for transportation. Today's engines often obtain maximum torque at road speeds as high as 60 to 80 mph, and maximum horsepower at speeds in excess of 100 mph. To achieve this "performance" requires a series of trade-offs in engine design that lower fuel economy and increase the volume of exhaust gases; the increased compression ratios result in higher peak temperatures which increase the production of nitrogen oxides. Such engines also require increased use of lead-based additives. [See Macinko, *The Tailpipe Problem,* 12 Environment #5, June 1970 at 6].

emission controls for automobiles

The primary legal problems concerning automobile emissions are no longer over whether they should be controlled. Now the arguments will be over the regulations designed for control.

The legal issues can manifest themselves in arguments such as due process, administrative discretion, and general equity principles. Economic considerations will, or course, be important. However, the real issues, regardless of the legal label, will be whether it is possible to control the emissions with existing technology at an economic and social price Americans are willing to pay. In either case, the lawyer is a secondary participant with the engineers and scientists battling over how best to control the problem.

The major air pollutants from automobiles are hydrocarbons, carbon monoxide, nitrogen oxides, lead compounds, and a number of fuel additives. The amount produced depends upon the design and condition of the vehicle, how it is operated, and the composition of the fuel. If the car has no controls, about 65 percent of the hydrocarbons will come from the exhaust gas. The fuel tank and carburetor will account for about 15 percent, and the remainder, about 20 percent, will be blowby or crankcase emissions from around the piston rings. The other pollutants are emitted almost entirely in the exhaust gases.

Crankcase Emission of hydrocarbons from this source was largely eliminated by the PCV system (positive crankcase ventilation) installed since the 1963 model year. These systems recycle crankcase air and blowby gases back into the engine intake. Sludge may develop from the acidic blowby gases and plug the PCV value. Thus engine oils with polymeric dispersants and metallic detergents began to be used.

Evaporation Efforts to prevent evaporation of fuel from the carburetor and fuel system have resulted in the development of systems which either store fuel vapors in the crankcase or in charcoal canisters, which recycle hydrocarbons to the engine. The problem is to prevent the disruption of carburetion. Although fuel modification techniques which reduced fuel volatility would result in emission controls for all cars, not just new ones, industry continues to pursue the mechanical approach. It may be cheaper than changing the fuel but whether their efficiency remains high and maintenance free for the life of the engine is not yet fully confirmed. Such devices were first used on the 1960 model year sold in California.

Exhaust Two approaches have been used to control hydrocarbon and carbon monoxide. The first approach is to add air into the exhaust manifold where exhaust gas temperatures are highest and thus increase oxidation. The second approach is to design the cylinders and adjust the combustion process to get better combustion. Most 1968 models use the second method, though air injection is used on manual transmission vehicles. Meeting post-1970 standards requires more complex systems. The exhaust manifold thermal reactor and the catalytic converter are two such devices. The exhaust manifold increases the time exhaust gases are held at high temperature and thus allows more complete oxidation. It can be damaged by lead compounds. Catalytic converters would fit into the auto's exhaust system but the technical problems in their use are substantial because of the wide range of gas temperatures and flow rates. Several companies built systems certified by California in 1964. The automobile manufacturers instead made modifications in their vehicles that meant that these devices were never used. Now research efforts are progressing once again. Changing the composition of the fuel is also possible. California regulates the content of reactive hydrocarbons in gasoline.

Nitrogen Oxides Adjustments to automobiles to reduce carbon monoxide and hydrocarbon emissions by using a lean and hotter burning fuel can produce more nitric oxide. These tradeoffs complicate control of emissions with further tradeoffs against vehicle performance being necessary for emission control. It is very likely that much of the control effort to date has resulted in increasing the nitric oxide emissions. The material which follows discusses the direction of present research efforts.

References: *Cleaning Our Environment, The Chemical Basis for Action,* American Chemical Society 1969 at 47, and *Air Pollution Primer,* National Tuberculosis and Respiratory Disease Association 1969, at 23.

California's program

The seriousness of the air pollution problem was first recognized in California. There the intensity of use of the automobile coupled with the poor meteorological conditions created the infamous Los Angeles smog. In 1959 the California legislature provided for the first automobile emission control program. Additional legislation was passed on a regular basis, and when the first Federal standards were set under the 1965 Amendments to the Clean Air Act, the California program had become the model for the nation—a position it continues to maintain though the gap has narrowed. [See Kennedy and Weekes, *Control of Automobile Emissions—California's Experience and the Federal Legislation,* 33 Law & Contemporary Problems No. 2 Spring 1968, at 297].

The 1965 Federal Act required the installation of air pollution controls that would meet standards set by the Department of Health, Education, and Welfare. These standards required complete control of crankcase hydrocarbons and carbon monoxide and applied to the 1968 model year vehicles.

The Air Quality Act of 1967 settled the question of Congress' intent to preempt the regulation of new motor vehicles by specifically stating such an intention. [Now section 209 of the Clean Air Act] A grandfather clause allowed California to be more strict [209(b)].

By 1970 it was becoming clear that there were major deficiencies in the 1965 Amendments to the Clean Air Act. Under the Act, NAPCA tested only a small number of vehicles submitted by the manufacturer. If the test vehicle met the Federal standards, all similar models sold by the manufacturer were deemed to have met the standards. The result was that there was a major difference between the emission characteristics of those vehicles sold and those tested by NAPCA. Furthermore emission increased rapidly as the vehicle was used. [See Esposito, *Vanishing Air,* 1970].

In July of 1970, HEW proposed new test procedures. At the same time standards for 1975 models for hydrocarbons and carbon monoxide were confirmed. It was further stated that nitrogen oxide and particulate standards proposed in February of 1970 would be confirmed as soon as test procedures for these standards were developed.

In December of 1970 The Clean Air Amendments became law, vastly strengthening the Act.

CLEAN AIR ACT AMENDMENTS ANALYZED

Title II

Section 202 made several important policy changes. Standards, of course, are now the responsibility of the Administrator of EPA, not HEW. Standards are to be based on emission levels to protect the public health and welfare. Existing technology is not relevant, nor is the cost (except politically). Standards are applicable to vehicles and engines for their useful life. Useful life is defined in the regulations as 100,000 miles, with the emissions at 50,000 miles being considered the average emission level over its useful life. This regulation applies to both exhaust and fuel evaporative emission standards. 45 CFR 1201.92 Crankcase emission tests are based on 100,000 miles for vehicles or 3,000 hours for engines. 45 CFR 1201.12. Congress, however, gave little discretion to the Administrator, for 202(d) requires at least a 50,000 mile useful life.

202(b) (1) is the heart of the act. Carbon monoxide and hydrocarbons from model year 1975 must be reduced by 90 percent of the model year 1970 allowable emissions. Oxides of nitrogen must be reduced 90 percent by model year 1976 based on the actual average emission from model year 1971. Since the Administrator determines the basis for measurement, this is an area of controversy and political pressure between the industry and government.

202(b) (2) calls for needed emission standards and measurement techniques to be prescribed by regulation within 180 days.

202(b) (3) shows respect for the automobile industry lawyers by allowing the Administrator to define "model year".

202(b) (4) requires the Administrator to report to Congress each July 1st concerning his progress. It gives the administrator the power to hold hearings and issue subpoenas [section 307(a)].

202(b) (5) provides the possibility of a one-year suspension of any emission standard, but interim standards reflecting the greatest degree of control (considering applicable technology and the cost of applying such technology) are required in the time available to manufacturer.

202(b) (5) (D) limits the discretion of the Administrator and **(E)** emphasizes the extension cannot exceed one year.

202(c) authorizes the National Academy of Sciences to study the feasibility of meeting the emission standards.

202(d) provides for regulations concerning the useful life of vehicles [see 202(a)].

202(e) gives the Administrator the power to postpone certification of a new power source until he has prescribed standards for air pollution from such a vehicle.

Section 203(a) prohibits the introduction into commerce or importation of new vehicles or engines unless covered by a certificate of conformity. The section also prohibits a number of other actions that would thwart the purpose of making sure that vehicles sold have engines that meet emission standards.

Section 204 established injunction proceedings and provides inter-jurisdictional subpoenas for the acquisition of witnesses.

Section 205 provides civil penalties of up to $10,000 for violation of section 203(a), each vehicle or engine violation constituting a separate offense; this multiple penalty does not apply to persons making control devices inoperative.

Section 206 provides for the testing of new motor vehicles and new engines under procedures to be specified by regulation. If the vehicle or engine meets standards the Administrator will issue a verification of compliance. He is also required to make the results of such tests public. The Federal Certification Test Results for 1971 Model Year can be found in 36 Fed. Reg. 6934 (Sat., April 10, 1971).

The act also provides for the rejection of vehicles and engines that do not meet test requirements, with section 206(b) (2) (B) providing for court review by a U.S. court of appeals.

Clean Air Act, Title II, summarized

206(c) gives the government the right to enter the manufacturer's plants to test vehicles or engines, or to inspect records and facilities.

206(d) requires the Administrator to establish regulations concerning testing.

206(e) directs the Administrator to make available to the public, in a nontechnical manner, the test results comparing vehicle and engine performance.

Section 207 requires a warranty from the manufacturer to the ultimate purchaser that the vehicle or engine meets the requirements of section 202 and regulations thereunder. The cost of meeting the warranty of satisfactory performance for the useful life is to be borne by the manufacturer. If the Administrator determines that vehicles or engines are not meeting standards for their useful life, the manufacturer can be required to remedy the nonconformity including those already sold. If the manufacturer disagrees, a public hearing is held, followed by an order. Judicial review is covered by section 307(c).

207(e) places conditions on any advertising concerning the cost or value of emission control.

Section 208 requires that manufacturers maintain and make available to the public all records except those the Secretary deems entitled to protection as trade secrets.

Section 209 continues the federal preemption concerning the regulation of new vehicles or new engines, except for California.

209(b) Allows states to continue to regulate used vehicles, and section 210 provides for grants for state emission testing and control programs.

Section 211 (Regulation of Fuels), and **Section 212** (Development of Low-Emission Vehicles) are discussed subsequently. **Section 213** provides definitions. **Section 301** to **316** cover general administration. Statutory materials can be found in the section on air pollution from stationary sources.

THE CLEAN AIR ACT as amended Title II

Clean Air Act (42 U.S.C. 1857 et seq.) includes the Clean Air Act of 1963 (P.L. 88-206), and amendments made by the "Motor Vehicle Air Pollution Control Act"—P.L. 89-272 (October 20, 1965), the "Clean Air Act Amendments of 1966—P.L. 89-675 (October 15, 1966), the "Air Quality Act of 1967"—P.L. 90-148 (November 21, 1967), and the "Clean Air Amendments of 1970"—P.L. 91-604—(December 31, 1970).

TITLE II—EMISSION STANDARDS FOR MOVING SOURCES

"SHORT TITLE

SEC. 201. This title may be cited as the 'National Emission Standards Act.'

PART A—MOTOR VEHICLE EMISSION AND FUEL STANDARDS

ESTABLISHMENT OF STANDARDS

SEC. 202. (a) Except as otherwise provided in subsection (b)—

(1) The Administrator shall by regulation prescribe (and from time to time revise) in accordance with the provisions of this section, standards applicable to the emission of any air pollutant from any class or classes of new motor vehicles or new motor vehicle engines, which in his judgment causes or contributes to, or is likely to cause or to contribute to, air pollution which endangers the public health or welfare. Such standards shall be applicable to such vehicles and engines for their useful life (as determined under subsection (d)), whether such vehicles and engines are designed as complete systems or incorporate devices to prevent or control such pollution.

(2) Any regulation prescribed under this subsection (and any revision thereof) shall take effect after such period as the Administrator finds necessary to permit the development and application of the requisite technology, giving appropriate consideration to the cost of compliance within such period.

(b) (1) (A) The regulations under subsection (a) applicable to emissions of carbon monoxide and hydrocarbons from light duty vehicles and engines manufactured during or after model year 1975 shall contain standards which require a reduction of at least 90 per centum from emissions of carbon monoxide and hydrocarbons allowable under the standards under this section applicable to light duty vehicles and engines manufactured in model year 1970.

(B) The regulations under subsection (a) applicable to emissions of oxides of nitrogen from light duty vehicles and engines manufactured during or after model year 1976 shall contain standards which require a reduction of at least 90 per centum from the average of emissions of oxides of nitrogen actually measured from light duty vehicles manufactured during model year 1971 which are not subject to any Federal or State emission standard for oxides of nitrogen. Such average of emissions shall be determined by the Administrator on the basis of measurements made by him.

(2) Emission standards under paragraph (1), and measurement techniques on which such standards are based (if not promulgated prior to the date of enactment of the Clean Air Amendments of 1970), shall be prescribed by regulation within 180 days after such date.

(3) For purposes of this part—

(A) (i) The term 'model year' with reference to any specific calendar year means the manufacturer's annual production period (as determined by the Administrator) which includes January 1 of such calendar year. If the manufacturer has no annual production period, the term 'model year' shall mean the calendar year.

(ii) For the purpose of assuring that vehicles and engines manufactured before the beginning of a model year were not manufactured for purposes of circumventing the effective date of a standard required to be prescribed by subsection (b), the Administrator may prescribe regulations defining 'model year' otherwise than as provided in clause (i).

(B) The term 'light duty vehicles and engines' means new light duty motor vehicles and new light duty motor vehicle engines, as determined under regulations of the Administrator.

(4) On July 1 of 1971, and of each year thereafter, the Administrator shall report to the Congress with respect to the development of systems necessary to implement the emission standards established pursuant to this section. Such reports shall include information regarding the continuing effects of such air pollutants subject to standards under this section on the public health and welfare, the extent and progress of efforts being made to develop the necessary systems, the costs associated with development and application of such systems, and following such hearings as he may deem advisable, any recommendations for additional congressional action necessary to achieve the purposes of this Act. In gathering information for the purposes of this paragraph and in connection with any hearing, the provisions of section 307(a) (relating to subpenas) shall apply.

(5) (A) At any time after January 1, 1972, any manufacturer may file with the Administrator an application requesting the suspension for one year only of the effective date of any emission standard required by paragraph (1) (A) with respect to such manufacturer. The Administrator shall make his determination with respect to any such application within 60 days. If he determines, in accordance with the provisions of this subsection, that such suspension should be granted, he shall simultaneously with such determination prescribe by regulation interim emission standards which shall apply (in lieu of the standards required to be prescribed, by paragraph (1) (A)) to emissions of carbon monoxide or hydrocarbons (or both) from such vehicles and engines manufactured during model year 1975.

(B) At any time after January 1, 1973, any manufacturer may file with the Administrator an application requesting the suspension, for one year only of the effective date of any emission standard required by paragraph (1) (B) with respect to such manufacturer. The Administrator shall make his determination with respect to any such application within 60 days. If he determines, in accordance with the provisions of this subsection, that such suspension should be granted, he shall simultaneously with such determination prescribe by regulation interim emission standards which shall apply (in lieu of the standards required to be prescribed by paragraph (1) (B)) to emissions of oxides of nitrogen from such vehicles and engines manufactured during model year 1976.

(C) Any interim standards prescribed under this paragraph shall reflect the greatest degree of emission control which is achievable by application of technology which the Administrator determines is available, giving appropriate consideration to the cost of applying such technology within the period of time available to manufacturers.

(D) Within 60 days after receipt of the application for any such suspension, and after public hearing, the Administrator shall issue a decision granting or refusing such suspension. The Administrator shall grant such suspension only if he determines that (i) such suspension is essential to the public interest or the public health and welfare of the United States, (ii) all good faith efforts have been made to meet the standards established by this subsection, (iii) the applicant has established that effective control technology, processes, operating methods, or other alternatives are not available or have not been available for a sufficient period of time to achieve compliance prior to the effective date of such standards, and (iv) the study and investigation of the National Academy of Sciences conducted pursuant to subsection (c) and other information available to him has not indicated that technology, processes, or other alternatives are available to meet such standards.

(E) Nothing in this paragraph shall extend the effective date of any emission standard required to be prescribed under this subsection for more than one year.

(c) (1) The Administrator shall undertake to enter into appropriate arrangements with the National Academy of Sciences to conduct a comprehensive study and investigation of the technological feasibility of meeting the emissions standards required to be prescribed by the Administrator by subsection (b) of this section.

(2) Of the funds authorized to be appropriated to the Administrator by this Act, such amounts as are required shall be available to carry out the study and investigation authorized by paragraph (1) of this subsection.

(3) In entering into any arrangement with the National Academy of Sciences for conducting the study and investigation authorized by paragraph (1) of this subsection, the Administrator shall request the National Academy of Sciences to submit semiannual reports on the progress of its study and investigation to the Administrator and the Congress, beginning not later than July 1, 1971, and continuing until such study and investigation is completed.

(4) The Administrator shall furnish to such Academy at its request any information which the Academy deems necessary for the purpose of conducting the investigation and study authorized by paragraph (1) of this subsection. For the purpose of furnishing such information, the Administrator may use any authority he has under this Act (A) to obtain information from any person, and (B) to require such person to conduct such tests, keep such records, and make such reports respecting research or other activities conducted by such person as may be reasonably necessary to carry out this subsection:

(d) The Administrator shall prescribe regulations under which the useful life of vehicles and engines shall be determined for purposes of subsection (a) (1) of this section and section 207. Such regulations shall provide that useful life shall—

(1) in the case of light duty vehicles and light duty vehicle engines, be a period of use of five years or of fifty thousand miles (or the equivalent), whichever first occurs; and

(2) in the case of any other motor vehicle or motor vehicle engine, be a period of use set forth in paragraph (1) unless the Administrator determines that a period of use of greater duration or mileage is appropriate.

(e) In the event a new power source or propulsion system for new motor vehicles or new motor vehicle engines is submitted for certification pursuant to section 206(a), the Administrator may postpone certification until he has prescribed standards for any air pollutants emitted by such vehicle or engine which cause or contribute to, or are likely to cause or contribute to, air pollution which endangers the public health or welfare but for which standards have not been prescribed under subsection (a).

PROHIBITED ACTS

SEC. 203. (a) The following acts and the causing thereof are prohibited—

(1) in the case of a manufacturer of new motor vehicles or new motor vehicle engines for distribution in commerce, the sale, or the offering for sale, or the introduction, or delivery for introduction, into commerce, or (in the case of any person, except as provided by regulation of the Administrator), the importation into the United States, of any new motor vehicle or new motor vehicle engine, manufactured after the effective date of regulations under this part which are applicable to such vehicle or engine unless such vehicle or engine is covered by a certificate of conformity issued (and in effect) under regulations prescribed under this part (except as provided in subsection (b));

(2) for any person to fail or refuse to permit access to or copying of records or to fail to make reports or provide information, required under section 208;

(3) for any person to remove or render inoperative any device or element of design installed on or in a motor vehicle or motor vehicle engine in compliance with regulations under this title prior to its sale and delivery to the ultimate purchaser, or for any manufacturer or dealer knowingly to remove or render inoperative any such device or element of design after such sale and delivery to the ultimate purchaser; or

(4) for any manufacturer of a new motor vehicle or new motor vehicle engine subject to standards prescribed under section 202—

(A) to sell or lease any such vehicle or engine unless such manufacturer has complied with the requirements of section 207(a) and (b) with respect to such vehicle or engine, and unless a label or tag is affixed to such vehicle or engine in accordance with section 207(c) (3), or

(B) to fail or refuse to comply with the requirements of section 207(c) or (e).

(b) (1) The Administrator may exempt any new motor vehicle or new motor vehicle engine from subsection (a), upon such terms and conditions as he may find necessary for the purpose of research, investigations, studies, demonstrations, or training, or for reasons of national security.

(2) A new motor vehicle or new motor vehicle engine offered for importation or imported by any person in violation of subsection (a) shall be refused admission into the United States, but the Secretary of the Treasury and the Administrator may, by joint regulation, provide for deferring final determination as to admission and authorizing the delivery of such a motor vehicle or engine offered for import to the owner or consignee thereof upon such terms and conditions (including the furnishing of a bond) as may appear to them appropriate to insure that any such motor vehicle or engine will be brought into conformity with the standards, requirements, and limitations applicable to it under this part. The Secretary of the Treasury shall, if a motor vehicle or engine is finally refused admission under this paragraph, cause disposition thereof in accordance with the customs laws unless it is exported, under regulations prescribed by such Secretary, within ninety days of the date of notice of such refusal or such additional time as may be permitted pursuant to such regulations, except that disposition in accordance with the customs laws may not be made in such manner as may result, directly or indirectly, in the sale, to the ultimate consumer, of a new motor vehicle or new motor vehicle engine that fails to comply with applicable standards of the Administrator under this part.

(3) A new motor vehicle or new motor vehicle engine intended solely for export, and so labeled or tagged on the outside of the container and on the vehicle or engine itself, shall be subject to the provisions of subsection (a), except that if the country of export has emission standards which differ from the standards prescribed under subsection (a), then such vehicle or engine shall comply with the standards of such country of export.

(c) Upon application therefor, the Administrator may exempt from section 203(a) (3) any vehicles (or class thereof) manufactured before the 1974 model year from section 203(a) (3) for the purpose of permitting modifications to the emission control device or system of such vehicle in order to use fuels other than those specified in certification testing under section 206(a) (1), if the Administrator, on the basis of information submitted by the applicant, finds that such modification will not result in such vehicle or engine not complying with standards under section 202 applicable to such vehicle or engine. Any such exemption shall identify (1) the vehicle or vehicles so exempted, (2) the specific nature of the modification, and (3) the person or class of persons to whom the exemption shall apply.

INJUNCTION PROCEEDINGS

SEC. 204. (a) The district courts of the United States shall have jurisdiction to restrain violations of paragraph (1), (2), (3), or (4) of section 203(a).

(b) Actions to restrain such violations shall be brought by and in the name of the United States. In any such action, subpenas for witnesses who are required to attend a district court in any district may run into any other district.

"PENALTIES

SEC. 205. Any person who violates paragraph (1), (2), (3), or (4) of section 203(a) shall be subject to a civil penalty of not more than $10,000. Any such violation with respect to paragraph (1), (2), or (4) of section 203(a) shall constitute a separate offense with respect to each motor vehicle or motor vehicle engine.

MOTOR VEHICLE AND MOTOR VEHICLE ENGINE COMPLIANCE TESTING AND CERTIFICATION

SEC. 206. (a) (1) The Administrator shall test, or require to be tested in such manner as he deems appropriate, any new motor vehicle or new motor vehicle engine submitted by a manufacturer to determine whether such vehicle or engine conforms with the regulations prescribed under section 202 of this Act. If such vehicle or engine conforms to such regulations, the Administrator shall issue a certificate of conformity upon such terms, and for such period (not in excess of one year), as he may prescribe.

(2) The Administrator shall test any emission control system incorporated in a motor vehicle or motor vehicle engine submitted to him by any person, in order to determine whether such system enables such vehicle or engine to conform to the standards required to be prescribed under section 202(b) of this Act. If the Administrator finds on the basis of such tests that such vehicle or engine conforms to such standards, the Administrator shall issue a verification of compliance with emission standards for such system when incorporated in vehicles of a class of which the tested vehicle is representative. He shall inform manufacturers and the National Academy of Sciences, and make available to the public, the results of such tests. Tests under this paragraph shall be conducted under such terms and conditions (including requirements for preliminary testing by qualified independent laboratories) as the Administrator may prescribe by regulations.

(b) (1) In order to determine whether new motor vehicles or new motor vehicle engines being manufactured by a manufacturer do in fact conform with the regulations with respect to which the certificate of conformity was issued, the Administrator is authorized to test such vehicles or engines. Such tests may be conducted by the Administrator directly or, in accordance with conditions specified by the Administrator, by the manufacturer.

(2) (A) (i) If, based on tests conducted under paragraph (1) on a sample of new vehicles or engines covered by a certificate of conformity, the Administrator determines that all or part of the vehicles or engines so covered do not conform with the regulations with respect to which the certificate of conformity was issued, he may suspend or revoke such certificate in whole or in part, and shall so notify the manufacturer. Such suspension or revocation shall apply in the case of any new motor vehicles or new motor vehicle engines manufactured after the date of such notification (or manufactured before such date if still in the hands of the manufacturer), and shall apply until such time as the Administrator finds that vehicles and engines manufactured by the manufacturer do conform to such regulations. If, during any period of suspension or revocation, the Administrator finds that a vehicle or engine actually conforms to such regulations, he shall issue a certificate of conformity applicable to such vehicle or engine.

(ii) If, based on tests conducted under paragraph (1) on any new vehicle or engine, the Administrator determines that such vehicle or engine does not conform with such regulations, he may suspend or revoke such certificate insofar as it applies to such vehicle or engine until such time as he finds such vehicle or engine actually so conforms with such regulations, and he shall so notify the manufacturer.

(B) (i) At the request of any manufacturer the Administrator shall grant such manufacturer a hearing as to whether the tests have been properly conducted or any sampling methods have been properly applied, and make a determination on the record with respect to any suspension or revocation under subparagraph (A); but suspension or revocation under subparagraph (A) shall not be stayed by reason of such hearing.

(ii) In any case of actual controversy as to the validity of any determination under clause (i), the manufacturer may at any time prior to the 60th day after such determination is made file a petition with the United States court of appeals for the circuit wherein such manufacturer resides or has his principal place of business for a judicial review of such determination. A copy of the petition shall be forthwith transmitted by the clerk of the court to the Administrator or other officer designated by him for that purpose. The Administrator thereupon shall file in the court the record of the proceedings on which the Administrator based his determination, as provided in section 2112 of title 28 of the United States Code.

(iii) If the petitioner applies to the court for leave to adduce additional evidence, and shows to the satisfaction of the court that such additional evidence is material and that there were reasonable grounds for the failure to adduce such evidence in the proceeding before the Administrator, the court may order such additional evidence (and evidence in rebuttal thereof) to be taken before the Administrator, in such manner and upon such terms and conditions as the court may deem proper. The Administrator may modify his findings as to the facts, or make new findings, by reason of the additional evidence so taken and he shall file such modified or new findings, and his recommendation, if any, for the modification or setting aside of his original determination, with the return of such additional evidence.

(iv) Upon the filing of the petition referred to in clause (ii), the court shall have jurisdiction to review the order in accordance with chapter 7 of title 5, United States Code, and to grant appropriate relief as provided in such chapter.

(c) For purposes of enforcement of this section, officers or employees duly designated by the Administrator, upon presenting appropriate credentials to the manufacturer or person in charge, are authorized (1) to enter, at reasonable times, any plant or other establishment of such manufacturers, for the purpose of conducting tests of vehicles or engines in the hands of the manufacturer, or (2) to inspect at reasonable times, records, files, papers, processes, controls, and facilities used by such manufacturer in conducting tests under regulations of the Administrator. Each such inspection shall be commenced and completed with reasonable promptness.

(d) The Administrator shall by regulation establish methods and procedures for making tests under this section.

(e) The Administrator shall announce in the Federal Register and make available to the public the results of his tests of any motor vehicle or motor vehicle engine submitted by a manufacturer under subsection (a) as promptly as possible after the enactment of the Clean Air Amendments of 1970 and at the beginning of each model year which begins thereafter. Such results shall be described in such nontechnical manner as will reasonably disclose to prospective ultimate purchasers of new motor vehicles and new motor vehicle engines the comparative performance of the vehicles and engines tested in meeting the standards prescribed under section 202 of this Act.

COMPLIANCE BY VEHICLES AND ENGINES IN ACTUAL USE

SEC. 207. (a) Effective with respect to vehicles and engines manufactured in model years beginning more than 60 days after the date of the enactment of the Clean Air Amendments of 1970, the manufacturer of each new motor vehicle and new motor vehicle engine shall warrant to the ultimate purchaser and each subsequent purchaser that such vehicle or engine is (1) designed, built, and equipped so as to conform at the time of sale with applicable regulations under section 202, and (2) free from defects in materials and workmanship which cause such vehicle or engine to fail to conform with applicable regulations for its useful life (as determined under sec. 202(d)).

(b) If the Administrator determines that (i) there are available testing methods and procedures to ascertain whether, when in actual use throughout its useful life (as determined under section 202(d)), each vehicle and engine to which regulations under section 202 apply complies with the emission standards of such regulations, (ii) such methods and procedures are in accordance with good engineering practices, and (iii) such methods and procedures are reasonably capable of being correlated with tests conducted under section 206(a)(1), then—

(1) he shall establish such methods and procedures by regulation, and

(2) at such time as he determines that inspection facilities or equipment are available for purposes of carrying out testing methods and procedures established under paragraph (1), he shall prescribe regulations which shall require manufacturers to warrant the emission control device or system of each new motor vehicle or new motor vehicle engine to which a regulation under section 202 applies and which is manufactured in a model year beginning after the Administrator first prescribes warranty regulations under this paragraph (2). The warranty under such regulations shall run to the ultimate purchaser and each subsequent purchaser and shall provide that if—

(A) the vehicle or engine is maintained and operated in accordance with instructions under subsection (c)(3),

(B) it fails to conform at any time during its useful life (as determined under section 202(d)) to the regulations prescribed under section 202, and

(C) such nonconformity results in the ultimate purchaser (or any subsequent purchaser) of such vehicle or engine having to bear any penalty or other sanction (including the denial of the right to use such vehicle or engine) under State or Federal law,

then such manufacturer shall remedy such nonconformity under such warranty with the cost thereof to be borne by the manufacturer.

(c) Effective with respect to vehicles and engines manufactured during model years beginning more than 60 days after the date of enactment of the Clean Air Amendments of 1970—

(1) If the Administrator determines that a substantial number of any class or category of vehicles or engines, although properly maintained and used, do not conform to the regulations prescribed under section 202, when in actual use throughout their useful life (as determined under section 202(d)), he shall immediately notify the manufacturer thereof of such nonconformity, and he shall require the manufacturer to submit a plan for remedying the nonconformity of the vehicles or engines with respect to which such notification is given. The plan shall provide that the nonconformity of any such vehicles or engines which are properly used and maintained will be remedied at the expense of the manufacturer. If the manufacturer disagrees with such determination of nonconformity and so advises the Administrator, the Administrator shall afford the manufacturer and other interested persons an opportunity to present their views and evidence in support thereof at a public hearing. Unless, as a result of such hearing the Administrator withdraws such determination of nonconformity, he shall ,within 60 days after the completion of such hearing, order the manufacturer to provide prompt notification of such nonconformity in accordance with paragraph (2).

(2) Any notification required by paragraph (1) with respect to any class or category of vehicles or engines shall be given to dealers, ultimate purchasers, and subsequent purchasers (if known) in such manner and containing such information as the Administrator may by regulations require.

(3) The manufacturer shall furnish with each new motor vehicle or motor vehicle engine such written instructions for the maintenance and use of the vehicle or engine by the ultimate purchaser as may be reasonable and necessary to assure the proper functioning of emission control devices and systems. In addition, the manufacturer shall indicate by means of a label or tag permanently affixed to such vehicle or engine that such vehicle or engine is covered by a certificate of conformity issued for the purpose of assuring achievement of emissions standards prescribed under section 202. Such label or tag shall contain such other information relating to control of motor vehicle emissions as the Administrator shall prescribe by regulation.

(d) Any cost obligation of any dealer incurred as a result of any requirement imposed by subsection (a), (b), or (c) shall be borne by the manufacturer. The transfer of any such cost obligation from a manufacturer to any dealer through franchise or other agreement is prohibited.

(e) If a manufacturer includes in any advertisement a statement respecting the cost or value of emission control devices or systems, such manufacturer shall set forth in such statement the cost or value attributed to such devices or systems by the Secretary of Labor (through the Bureau of Labor Statistics). The Secretary of Labor, and his representatives, shall have the same access for this purpose to the books, documents, papers, and records of a manufacturer as the Comptroller General has to those of a recipient of assistance for purposes of section 311.

(f) Any inspection of a motor vehicle or a motor vehicle engine for purposes of subsection (c)(1), after its sale to the ultimate purchaser, shall be made only if the owner of such vehicle or engine voluntarily permits such inspection to be made, except as may be provided by any State or local inspection program.

(b) The amendments made by this section shall not apply to vehicles or engines imported into the United States before the sixtieth day after the date of enactment of this Act.

"RECORDS AND REPORTS

SEC. 208. (a) Every manufacturer shall establish and maintain such records, make such reports, and provide such information as the Administrator may reasonably require to enable him to determine whether such manufacturer has acted or is acting in compliance with this part and regulations thereunder and shall, upon request of an officer or employee duly designated by the Administrator, permit such officer or employee at reasonable times to have access to and copy such records.

(b) Any records, reports or information obtained under subsection (a) shall be available to the public, except that upon a showing satisfactory to the Administrator by any person that records, reports, or information, or particular part thereof (other than emission data), to which the Administrator has access under this section if made public, would divulge methods or processes entitled to protection as trade secrets of such person, the Administrator shall consider such record, report, or information or particular portion thereof confidential in accordance with the purposes of section 1905 of title 18 of the United States Code, except that such record, report, or information may be disclosed to other officers, employees, or authorized representatives of the United States concerned with carrying out this Act or when relevant in any proceeding under this Act. Nothing in this section shall authorize the withholding of information by the Administrator or any officer or employee under his control, from the duly authorized committees of the Congress.

STATE STANDARDS

SEC. 209. (a) No State or any political subdivision thereof shall adopt or attempt to enforce any standard relating to the control of emissions from new motor vehicles or new motor vehicle engines subject to this part. No State shall require certification, inspection, or any other approval relating to the control of emissions from any new motor vehicle or new motor vehicle engine as condition precedent to the initial retail sale, titling (if any), or registration of such motor vehicle, motor vehicle engine, or equipment.

(b) The Administrator shall, after notice and opportunity for public hearing, waive application of this section to any State which has adopted standards (other than crankcase emission standards) for the control of emissions from new motor vehicles or new motor vehicle engines prior to March 30, 1966, unless he finds that such State does not require standards more stringent than applicable Federal standards to meet compelling and extraordinary conditions or that such State standards and accompanying enforcement procedures are not consistent with section 202(a) of this part.

(c) Nothing in this part shall preclude or deny to any State or political subdivision thereof the right otherwise to control, regulate, or restrict the use, operation, or movement of registered or licensed motor vehicles.

STATE GRANTS

SEC. 210. The Administrator is authorized to make grants to appropriate State agencies in an amount up to two-thirds of the cost of developing and maintaining effective vehicle emission devices and systems inspection and emission testing and control programs, except that—

(1) no such grant shall be made for any part of any State vehicle inspection program which does not directly relate to the cost of the air pollution control aspects of such a program;

(2) no such grant shall be made unless the Secretary of Transportation has certified to the Administrator that such program is consistent with any highway safety program developed pursuant to section 402 of title 23 of the United States Code; and

(3) no such grant shall be made unless the program includes provisions designed to insure that emission control devices and systems on vehicles in actual use have not been discontinued or rendered inoperative.

REGULATION OF FUELS

SEC. 211. (a) The Administrator may by regulation designate any fuel or fuel additive and, after such date or dates as may be prescribed by him, no manufacturer or processor of any such fuel or additive may sell, offer for sale, or introduce into commerce such fuel or additive unless the Administrator has registered such fuel or additive in accordance with subsection (b) of this section.

(b) (1) For the purpose of registration of fuels and fuel additives, the Administrator shall require—

(A) the manufacturer of any fuel to notify him as to the commercial identifying name and manufacturer of any additive contained in such fuel; the range of concentration of any additive in the fuel; and the purpose-in-use of any such additive; and

(B) the manufacturer of any additive to notify him as to the chemical composition of such additive.

(2) For the purpose of registration of fuels and fuel additives, the Administrator may also require the manufacturer of any fuel or fuel additive—

(A) to conduct tests to determine potential public health effects of such fuel or additive (including, but not limited to, carcinogenic, teratogenic, or mutagenic effects), and

(B) to furnish the description of any analytical technique that can be used to detect and measure any additive in such fuel, the recommended range of concentration of such additive, and the recommended purpose-in-use of such additive, and such other information as is reasonable and necessary to determine the emissions resulting from the use of the fuel or additive contained in such fuel, the effect of such fuel or additive on the emission control performance of any vehicle or vehicle engine, or the extent to which such emissions affect the public health or welfare.

Tests under subparagraph (A) shall be conducted in conformity with test procedures and protocols established by the Administrator. The result of such tests shall not be considered confidential.

(3) Upon compliance with the provision of this subsection, including assurances that the Administrator will receive changes in the information required, the Administrator shall register such fuel or fuel additive.

(c) (1) The Administrator may, from time to time on the basis of information obtained under subsection (b) of this section or other information available to him, by regulation, control or prohibit the manufacture, introduction into commerce, offering for sale, or sale of any fuel or fuel additive for use in a motor vehicle or motor vehicle engine (A) if any emission products of such fuel or fuel additive will endanger the public health or welfare, or (B) if emission products of such fuel or fuel additive will impair to a significant degree the performance of any emission control device or system which is in general use, or which the Administrator finds has been developed to a point where in a reasonable time it would be in general use were such regulation to be promulgated.

(2) (A) No fuel, class of fuels, or fuel additive may be controlled or prohibited by the Administrator pursuant to clause (A) of paragraph (1) except after consideration of all relevant medical and scientific evidence available to him, including consideration of other technologically or economically feasible means of achieving emission standards under section 202.

(B) No fuel or fuel additive may be controlled or prohibited by the Administrator pursuant to clause (B) of paragraph (1) except after consideration of available scientific and economic data, including a cost benefit analysis comparing emission control devices or systems which are or will be in general use and require the proposed control or prohibition with emission control devices or systems which are or will be in general use and do not require the proposed control or prohibition. On request of a manufacturer of motor vehicles, motor vehicle engines, fuels, or fuel additives submitted within 10 days of notice of proposed rulemaking, the Administrator shall hold a public hearing and publish findings with respect to any matter he is required to consider under this subparagraph. Such findings shall be published at the time of promulgation of final regulations.

(C) No fuel or fuel additive may be prohibited by the Administrator under paragraph (1) unless he finds, and publishes such finding, that in his judgment such prohibition will not cause the use of any other fuel or fuel additive which will produce emissions which will endanger the public health or welfare to the same or greater degree than the use of the fuel or fuel additive proposed to be prohibited.

(3) (A) For the purpose of evidence and data to carry out paragraph (2), the Administrator may require the manufacturer of any motor vehicle or motor vehicle engine to furnish any information which has been developed concerning the emissions from motor vehicles resulting from the use of any fuel or fuel additive, or the effect of such use on the performance of any emission control device or system.

(B) In obtaining information under subparagraph (A), section 307(a) (relating to subpenas) shall be applicable.

(4) (A) Except as otherwise provided in subparagraph (B) or (C), no State (or political subdivision thereof) may prescribe or attempt to enforce, for purposes of motor vehicle emission control, any control or prohibition respecting use of a fuel or fuel additive in a motor vehicle or motor vehicle engine—

(i) if the Administrator has found that no control or prohibition under paragraph (1) is necessary and has published his finding in the Federal Register, or

(ii) if the Administrator has prescribed under paragraph (1) a control or prohibition applicable to such fuel or fuel additive, unless State prohibition or control is identical to the prohibition or control prescribed by the Administrator.

(B) Any State for which application of section 209(a) has at any time been waived under section 209(b) may at any time prescribe and enforce, for the purpose of motor vehicle emission control, a control or prohibition respecting any fuel or fuel additive.

(C) A State may prescribe and enforce, for purposes of motor vehicle emission control, a control or prohibition respecting the use of a fuel or fuel additive in a motor vehicle or motor vehicle engine if an applicable implementation plan for such State under section 110 so provides. The Administrator may approve such provision in an implementation plan, or promulgate an implementation plan containing such a provision, only if he finds that the State control or prohibition is necessary to achieve the national primary or secondary ambient air quality standard which the plan implements.

(d) Any person who violates subsection (a) or the regulations prescribed under subsection (c) or who fails to furnish any information required by the Administrator under subsection (c) shall forfeit and pay to the United States a civil penalty of $10,000 for each and every day of the continuance of such violation, which shall accrue to the United States and be recovered in a civil suit in the name of the United States, brought in the district where such person has his principal office or in any district in which he does business. The Administrator may, upon application therefor, remit or mitigate any forfeiture provided for in this subsection and he shall have authority to determine the facts upon all such applications.

DEVELOPMENT OF LOW-EMISSION VEHICLES

SEC. 212. (a) For the purpose of this section—

(1) The term 'Board' means the Low-Emission Vehicle Certification Board.

(2) The term 'Federal Government' includes the legislative, executive, and judicial branches of the Government of the United States, and the government of the District of Columbia.

(3) The term 'motor vehicle' means any self-propelled vehicle designed for use in the United States on the highways, other than a vehicle designed or used for military field training, combat, or tactical purposes.

(4) The term 'low-emission vehicle' means any motor vehicle which—

(A) emits any air pollutant in amounts significantly below new motor vehicle standards applicable under section 202 at the time of procurement to that type of vehicle; and

(B) with respect to all other air pollutants meets the new motor vehicle standards applicable under section 202 at the time of procurement to that type of vehicle.

(5) The term 'retail price' means (A) the maximum statutory price applicable to any class or model of motor vehicle; or (B) in any case where there is no applicable maximum statutory price, the most recent procurement price paid for any class or model of motor vehicle.

(b) (1) There is established a Low-Emission Vehicle Certification Board to be composed of the Administrator or his designee, the Secretary of Transportation or his designee, the Chairman of the Council on Environmental Quality or his designee, the Director of the National Highway Safety Bureau in the Department of Transportation, the Administrator of General Services, and two members appointed by the President. The President shall designate one member of the Board as Chairman.

(2) Any member of the Board not employed by the United States may receive compensation at the rate of $125 for each day such member is engaged upon work of the Board. Each member of the Board shall be reimbursed for travel expenses, including per diem in lieu of subsistence as authorized by section 5703 of title 5, United States Code, for persons in the Government service employed intermittently.

(3) (A) The Chairman, with the concurrence of the members of the Board, may employ and fix the compensation of such additional personnel as may be necessary to carry out the functions of the Board, but no individual so appointed shall receive compensation in excess of the rate authorized for GS–18 by section 5332 of title 5, United States Code.

(B) The Chairman may fix the time and place of such meetings as may be required, but a meeting of the Board shall be called whenever a majority of its members so request.

(C) The Board is granted all other powers necessary for meeting its responsibilities under this section.

(c) The Administrator shall determine which models or classes of motor vehicles qualify as low-emission vehicles in accordance with the provisions of this section.

(d) (1) The Board shall certify any class or model of motor vehicles—

(A) for which a certification application has been filed in accordance with paragraph (3) of this subsection;

(B) which is a low-emission vehicle as determined by the Administrator; and

(C) which it determines is suitable for use as a substitute for a class or model of vehicles at that time in use by agencies of the Federal Government.

The Board shall specify with particularity the class or model of vehicles for which the class or model of vehicles described in the application is a suitable substitute. In making the determination under this subsection the Board shall consider the following criteria:

(i) the safety of the vehicle;
(ii) its performance characteristics;
(iii) its reliability potential;
(iv) its serviceability;
(v) its fuel availability;
(vi) its noise level; and
(vii) its maintenance costs as compared with the class or model of motor vehicle for which it may be a suitable substitute.

(2) Certification under this section shall be effective for a period of one year from the date of issuance.

(3) (A) Any party seeking to have a class or model of vehicle certified under this section shall file a certification application in accordance with regulations prescribed by the Board.

(B) The Board shall publish a notice of each application received in the Federal Register.

(C) The Administrator and the Board shall make determinations for the purpose of this section in accordance with procedures prescribed by regulation by the Administrator and the Board, respectively.

(D) The Administrator and the Board shall conduct whatever investigation is necessary, including actual inspection of the vehicle at a place designated in regulations prescribed under subparagraph (A).

(E) The Board shall receive and evaluate written comments and documents from interested parties in support of, or in opposition to, certification of the class or model of vehicle under consideration.

(F) Within ninety days after the receipt of a properly filed certification application, the Administrator shall determine whether such class or model of vehicle is a low-emission vehicle, and within 180 days of such determination, the Board shall reach a decision by majority vote as to whether such class or model of vehicle, having been determined to be a low-emission vehicle, is a suitable substitute for any class or classes of vehicles presently being purchased by the Federal Government for use by its agencies.

(G) Immediately upon making any determination or decision under subparagraph (F), the Administrator and the Board shall each publish in the Federal Register notice of such determination or decision, including reasons therefor and in the case of the Board any dissenting views.

(e) (1) Certified low-emission vehicles shall be acquired by purchase or lease by the Federal Government for use by the Federal Government in lieu of other vehicles if the Administrator of General Services determines that such certified vehicles have procurement costs which are no more than 150 per centum of the retail price of the least expensive class or model of motor vehicle for which they are certified substitutes.

(2) In order to encourage development of inherently low-polluting propulsion technology, the Board may, at its discretion, raise the premium set forth in paragraph (1) of this subsection to 200 per centum of the retail price of any class or model of motor vehicle for which a certified low-emission vehicle is a certified substitute, if the Board determines that the certified low-emission vehicle is powered by an inherently low-polluting propulsion system.

(3) Data relied upon by the Board and the Administrator in determining that a vehicle is a certified low-emission vehicle shall be incorporated in any contract for the procurement of such vehicle.

(f) The procuring agency shall be required to purchase available certified low-emission vehicles which are eligible for purchase to the extent they are available before purchasing any other vehicles for which any low-emission vehicle is a certified substitute. In making purchasing selections between competing eligible certified low-emission vehicles, the procuring agency shall give priority to (1) any class or model which does not require extensive periodic maintenance to retain its low-polluting qualities or which does not require the use of fuels which are more expensive than those of the classes or models of vehicles for which it is a certified substitute; and (2) passenger vehicles other than buses.

(g) For the purpose of procuring certified low-emission vehicles any statutory price limitations shall be waived.

(h) The Administrator shall, from time to time as the Board deems appropriate, test the emissions from certified low-emission vehicles purchased by the Federal Government. If at any time he finds that the emission rates exceed the rates on which certification under this section was based, the Administrator shall notify the Board. Thereupon the Board shall give the supplier of such vehicles written notice of this finding, issue public notice of it, and give the supplier an opportunity to make necessary repairs, adjustments, or replacements. If no such repairs, adjustments, or replacements are made within a period to be set by the Board, the Board may order the supplier to show cause why the vehicle involved should be eligible for recertification.

(i) There are authorized to be appropriated for paying additional amounts for motor vehicles pursuant to, and for carrying out the provisions of, this section, $5,000,000 for the fiscal year ending June 30, 1971, and $25,000,000 for each of the two succeeding fiscal years.

(j) The Board shall promulgate the procedures required to implement this section within one hundred and eighty days after the date of enactment of the Clean Air Amendments of 1970.

"DEFINITIONS FOR PART A

SEC. 213. As used in this part—

(1) The term 'manufacturer' as used in sections 202, 203, 206, 207, and 208 means any person engaged in the manufacturing or assembling of new motor vehicles or new motor vehicle engines, or importing such vehicles or engines for resale, or who acts for and is under the control of any such person in connection with the distribution of new motor vehicles or new motor vehicle engines, but shall not include any dealer with respect to new motor vehicles or new motor vehicle engines received by him in commerce.

(2) The term 'motor vehicle' means any self-propelled vehicle designed for transporting persons or property on a street or highway.

(3) Except with respect to vehicles or engines imported or offered for importation, the term 'new motor vehicle' means a motor vehicle the equitable or legal title to which has never been transferred to an ultimate purchaser; and the term 'new motor vehicle engine' means an engine in a new motor vehicle or a motor vehicle engine the equitable or legal title to which has never been transferred to the ultimate purchaser; and with respect to imported vehicles or engines, such terms mean a motor vehicle and engine, respectively, manufactured after the effective date of a regulation issued under section 202 which is applicable to such vehicle or engine (or which would be applicable to such vehicle or engine had it been manufactured for importation into the United States).

(4) The term 'dealer' means any person who is engaged in the sale or the distribution of new motor vehicles or new motor vehicle engines to the ultimate purchaser.

(5) The term 'ultimate purchaser' means, with respect to any new motor vehicle or new motor vehicle engine, the first person who in good faith purchases such new motor vehicle or new engine for purposes other than resale.

(6) The term 'commerce' means (A) commerce between any place in any State and any place outside thereof; and (B) commerce wholly within the District of Columbia.

regulations on auto emissions

As this book went to press in July of 1972, the automobile manufacturers and the Environmental Protection Agency were engaged in a legal battle over whether the 1975 auto emissions control standards would be enforced. (*See,* "Auto 'Big 3' Suing to Review Deadline by EPA on Exhaust," *The Wall Street Journal,* June 9, 1972 at 3.)

In addition the Ford Motor Company was having problems obtaining certification for its 1973 models because its employees cheated on emissions' tests by performing 442 instances of unauthorized maintenance on 26 test vehicles. This figure of 442 did not become public until a study was made by the U.S. General Accounting Office, which found the test procedures in general to be extremely lax. *See* "GAO Says Ford Fixed Test Cars 442 Times without Telling EPA," *The Wall Street Journal,* June 13, 1972 at 17. *See also,* "Ford Imbroglio Shows Clean Air Enforcers How Weak they Are," *The Wall Street Journal,* June 6, 1972 at 1.

Because the situation was being altered daily, this book will make no attempt to establish the current status of these disputes. For general discussions of the the subject, *see,* "Is there a '73 Car in Ford's Future," *Newsweek,* June 5, 1972 at 75, and Malin, Mary and Lewicke, Carol, "Pollution-Free power for the automobile," *Environmental Science & Technology,* Vol. 6, No. 6, June, 1972 at 512. The latter article also gives an excellent summation of major new power sources under development.

The 1970 automobile emission requirements were the most controversial aspect of the amendments to the Clean Air Act. To force the most powerful corporations in the United States (automotive and petroleum) to change their ways and to develop a technology that is not fully available is a difficult task. History has shown the automobile companies have successfully resisted regulation while investing minimal money and manpower in safety and pollution emission improvements. The ability to quash the antitrust suits that sought to penalize them for delaying installation of air pollution devices is just one example of their power. [see the Nader-affiliated task force report by John Esposito, *Vanishing Air,*

regulations on auto emissions

1970] For this reason the passage of the 1970 Act did not end the political maneuvering to avoid its requirement. The issuance of regulations and their enforcement is an important part of the total program and in August of 1971 such regulations continue to be modified. It is not unusual to see high officials of EPA state that the most rigorous regulations must be met and a week later state that there is guarded optimism that they will be met.

For a case in which the Supreme Court directed eighteen states to seek relief in federal district court from an alleged conspiracy on the part of the nation's four leading automobile producers to restrain the development of emission control equipment, *see Washington v. General Motors Corp., ___ U.S. ___,* 40 U.S. L.W. 4437 (April 24, 1972), reprinted at the end of Chapter Five.

Since the efforts of the automobile companies will be in proportion to the intensity of governmental pressure, the informal agreements that are made become very important. Seemingly insignificant changes in regulations can mean substantial differences in industry costs and the amount of reduction of pollutants that is actually achieved. For example, EPA has proposed changing emission tests which now emphasize the cool portion of the cycle. New requirements would require four test bags with two hot and two cold starts. The Automobile Manufacturers Association opposed increasing the number of samples. So we have a proposal on July 27, 1971 to change regulations issued 25 days earlier. This kind of activity can be expected to continue.

The following is from *A Citizen's Guide to Clean Air,* published by the Conservation Foundation, Washington, D.C., 1972 :

> On June 30, 1971, EPA announced the numerical equivalents of the required reductions. The 1970 standards permitted emissions of 34 grams of carbon monoxide per vehicle mile (gm/mi). The 1975 standards will allow 3.4 gm/mi. Hydrocarbon limits were set at 4.1 gm/mi; the 1975 levels will be .41 gm/mi. There were no 1970 standards for nitrogen oxides; 1976 levels will be .4 gm/mi, down from 1970 average emissions of 4.0 gm/mi. (For nitrogen oxides, EPA has also set an interim standard of 3.0 gm/mi, effective with 1973 models.)

End, excerpt from *A Citizen's Guide to Clean Air.*

The basic regulatory effort is in Code of Federal Regulation, Title 45, Subtitle A, Part 1201. The control of Air Pollution From New Motor Vehicles and New Motor Vehicle Engines was the subject of regulations issued on January 15, 1972, 37 Fed. Reg. 669.

Continued changes in the regulations can be expected. The Act backed-up by public pressure, makes it clear that auto emission control is mandatory. However, the degree to which pollutants are controlled and the concomitant costs of control are closely related to how the progress is to be measured. Thus the regulations concerning testing procedures become very important to those being regulated. We can therefore expect bitter fights to take place away from public view. Technical questions arising out of subjects that are to be controlled by regulations that for nearly everyone are obscure points are the real determinants of what kind of results flow from the government's program.

Federal regulations are kept up to date in the *Environment Reporter* (B.N.A.) 31:1601 et. seq.

On July 14, 1971, the Environmental Protection Agency announced that controls to meet both 1975 and 1976 automobile emission standards have not yet been developed, but that the agency is "moderately optimistic that the 1975 standards can be attained."

The agency's comments came in its first annual report to the Congress on the development of systems to reduce auto exhaust emissions. The report is required by the Clean Air Act.

The Act requires that 1975-model cars achieve a 90 per cent

reduction in emissions of hydrocarbons and carbon monoxides from 1970 levels and that 1976-model cars achieve a 90 per cent reduction in emissions of oxides of nitrogen compared with uncontrolled 1971-model cars.

EPA said its hopes for meeting the 1975 standards hinged in part on the expectation that unleaded gasoline would be generally available by 1975. Unleaded gasoline is needed for the operation of some proposed devices to control emissions of hydrocarbons and carbon monoxide, the report said.

The agency said the achievement of the 1976 standard would require a technological breakthrough beyond the present state of the art. EPA said it is "hopeful" that such a breakthrough would occur.

On September 25, 1971, EPA Administrator William D. Ruckelshaus announced that an engine under development for several years previous to the announcement "represents a break-through in emissions control technology and means that the truly clean car is not as far away as many people thought." (Washington *Evening Star,* Sept. 25, 1971 at A3.)

The announcement explained that the engine mentioned uses a "stratified charge principle," mixing fuel with air inside the combustion cylinder instead of in a carburetor. Development costs of the car originally had been paid by the Army, to obtain an engine that could be run on a wide variety of fuels. Costs of development during two years prior to the Ruckelshaus announcement had been shifted to EPA, the Army, Ford, and Texaco, Inc.

EPA said the engine met the 1976 emissions tests for short periods. A spokesman for Ford said the engine ran well only for 5,000 to 6,000 miles, and that the company did not believe the engine could be perfected in time for production by the 1975 model year. (Tooling up begins two-to-three years before introduction of a model on the market.)

The EPA said that U.S. automakers are now spending more than $330 million a year for research and development on emission reduction, focused on the present internal combustion engine to meet mass production requirements of the industry within the tight time limits set by the Clean Air Act. The report says that the auto industry, other independent companies and inventors, and EPA-sponsored researchers also are at work on various alternative power systems which show varying degrees of promise. These include the turbine engine, the Rankine-cycle engine, a stratified charge system, electric power sources and others.

One of the major requirements of the report is to assess the projected costs of the control technologies. The agency said it is developing ways to assess the cost and effectiveness of various emission control strategies and their effect on ambient air quality. The report, however, cited industry projections showing that price increases of $80 to $600 per car would be needed to meet the 1975 standards. These estimates did not include costs resulting from warranties, maintenance, expected increases in fuel consumption or reduced operating performance.

costs

Estimated Investment and Operating Costs for Mobile Sources of Air Pollution, 1971–76

Year	Investment cost (per vehicle)		Additional operating costs (per year)		Total annual investment for mobile sources (millions)	Annual operating cost (millions)
	Autos and light trucks	Heavy-duty trucks	Autos and light trucks	Heavy-duty trucks		
1971	$ 17	$ 9	—$ 2.70	0	$ 131.1	—$175
1972	17	9	—2.70	0	136.6	—209
1973	42	21	7.90	$ 3.50	346.3	—154
1974	42	21	7.90	3.50	498.5	— 50
1975	240	46	20.70	13.50	2,068.7	744
1976	240	46	20.70	13.50	3,031.7	909

[1] Negative values indicate savings in operating costs.

Source: Environmental Protection Agency.

The following is the Council on Environmental Quality's explanation for the preceding graph, taken from "Environmental Quality," 1971:

The standards will result in increased costs for automobiles and in increased fuel consumption. But it may cost somewhat less to maintain a car using unleaded gasoline.

The estimated investment costs of implementing auto and truck standards for model years 1967 through 1976 are estimated at nearly $6.3 billion—$5.1 billion for 1975 and 1976 alone (see Table A–7). The operating costs for the 1967 to 1976 period would be $800 million. However, this low total is largely due to expected operating savings in the early years. For 1975 and 1976, the increased operating expenses are estimated at about $1.7 billion.

The projected per auto costs of meeting the 1975 auto standards are in dispute. The figures in Table A–7 are probably at the low range of estimates. The total costs of meeting the 1976 standards on nitrogen oxides are unknown, because no feasible control technology has yet been developed. Table A–7

The following is the Council on Environmental Quality's summation of the situation in regards to automobile emission controls ("Environmental Quality," August, 1971 at 41):

auto emissions—Under the Federal Clean Air Act, State and local governments retain authority to regulate pollution from automobiles in use. But authority to regulate emissions from new motor vehicles is reserved to the Federal Government. California is an exception. Under section 209(a) of the Federal Clean Air Act, California is eligible for a waiver from EPA permitting it to establish emission standards for new motor vehicles stiffer than Federal standards if needed to meet "compelling and extraordinary conditions" in that State. California, whose regulation of automotive emissions established the precedent for present Federal law, has obtained several waivers since the Federal law was enacted in 1965. In 1971, waivers were granted by EPA for emission standards and test procedures for various classes of vehicles in the 1972, 1973, and 1975 model years.

A number of State and local governments have "antismoke" laws, which prohibit annoying, visible exhaust from vehicles. Michigan's vehicle code is one example. Although many such laws are rarely enforced, some jurisdictions are moving to strengthen their implementation. For example, officials in Jacksonville and in Dade County, Fla., have announced that they are intensifying enforcement of their recently enacted antismoke laws. On a nationwide basis, however, much more needs to be done to enforce such laws.

Several States are studying the possibility of establishing emission testing and inspection programs. Section 210 of the Clean Air Act authorized Federal grants to assist such programs.

End, excerpt from "Environmental Quality."

The industry view is not monolithic, but is generally favorably inclined toward the feasibility of such auto emission testing. The sub-council Report of the National Industrial Pollution Control Council (March 1971), entitled *Maintaining Vehicular Emission Control System Integrity,* recommends state inspection of new cars, but only within high pollution areas. Used car testing should be expanded to provide more information on deterioration factors. Development of tests suitable for rapid state inspection, especially NO_X should be considered. However, manufacturers should be required to inspect only a sample of assembly-line cars to confirm compliance with prototype performance standards.

The Vehicle Emissions Inspection Panel of the Automobile Manufacturers Association, Inc. has recommended that engine maintenance inspections be required in order to minimize vehicle emissions.

An EPA report published on September 24, 1971, recommended no legislative changes to the Clean Air Act's auto emission standards provisions, citing costs of achieving the 1975-76 standards as prohibitive. The EPA report, "Development of Systems to Attain Established Motor Vehicle and Engine Emission Standards," also reflected the auto industry's consensus that the gasoline-fueled internal combustion engine is the only mass-producible prospect for 1975-76, and that current technology is unavailable to permit attainment of the emission standards.

In an apparent effort to demonstrate that it means business, EPA requested the Justice Department in October 1971 to bring suit against the Ford Motor Company for shipping 207,500 1972-model cars and trucks to its dealers on consignment before certificates of compliance with 1970 Clean Air Act emission standards were issued. Ford claimed that the shipments were initiated because EPA had been late in issuing emission standards for the 1972 models, and that compliance would have resulted in an assembly line shutdown, laying off 70,000 production workers.

EPA has proposed stricter national standards to control air pollution from new heavy duty gasoline and diesel engines. These standards, published in 36 Federal Register 193 (Oct. 5, 1971), would apply to 1973 and later model engines, American-made and imported.

For heavy duty gasoline engines, the 1973 standards would lower the current allowable exhaust emission levels of hydrocarbons by 40% (to 160 ppm); of carbon monoxide by 45% (to 0.8%); and would place new limits on nitrogen oxides (2000 ppm).

The new standards would also place limits on emissions from heavy duty diesel engines, to 3 grams per brake horsepower-hour (gm/bhp-hr) for hydrocarbons; to 7.5 gm/bhp-hr for carbon monoxide; and to 12.5 gm/bhp-hr for nitrogen oxides.

On August 15, 1971, the Environmental Protection Agency announced that, in cooperation with state and local air pollution control agencies, it had begun a three-month study in more than 30 urban air quality control regions to determine existing levels of automobile-related air pollutants.

The study is intended to provide base data for the design of state plans to achieve the national air quality standards for carbon monoxide, photochemical oxidant (ozone), and nitrogen dioxide, as required by the Clean Air Act.

The study, involving the use of more than $500,000 worth of new instruments operated by specially trained local technicians, began on July 1, 1971. Air quality data are transmitted daily to a centralized collection point where they are validated, computer-summarized, and returned to cooperating State agencies.

Regions in the study are urban areas where complete measurements are not routinely being made by the EPA, or state or local pollution control agencies.

REFERENCES AND SELECTED BIBLIOGRAPHY

CURRIE, *Motor Vehicle Air Pollution:* State Authority and Federal Pre-Emption.

For technical information see publications of the Society of Automotive Engineers, Inc., 2 Pennsylvania Plaza, New York, N.Y. 10001, and specifically DICKINSON, G. W.; ILDRAD, H. H. and BERGIN, R.J.; "Tune-up Inspection a Continuing Emission Control." SAE Paper 690141 Jan. 13-17, 1969.

See also,

ELSTON, John C.; ANDREATCH, A. J.; and MILASK, L. S.; *Reduction of Exhaust Pollutants through Automotive Inspection Requirements,* International Conference on Air Pollution, Washington, D.C., Feb. 1971.

Idle Emission Standards for Highway Light Duty Vehicle Inspection, State of California Air Resources Board, adopted March 17, 1971

ANDREATCH, ELSTON, and LAHEY, *The New Jersey Repair Project Tune-up at Idle,* paper presented at the 64th Annual Meeting of the Air Pollution Control Association June 27–July 2, 1971

New Jersey State Department of Environmental Protection, Air Pollution Control Code, Proposed Chapter 15 *Control and Prohibition of Air Pollution from Light-Duty Gasoline—Field Motor Vehicles* May 27, 1971

"Air Pollution: the Problem of Motor Vehicle Emissions," 3 *Conn. L. Rev.* summer 1970

"Air Quality Act of 1967," 54 *Iowa L. Rev.* 115, Aug. 1968

"Air Pollution—automobile smog: A Proposed Remedy," 14 *De Paul L. Rev., 436, 1965*

Vehicle Emission Inspection presented to AAMVA Committee on Engineering and Vehicle Inspection, August 19, 1970, by J.H. St. John, AMA Inspection Handbook Committee, Ford Motor Company.

INNES, W.B.; "Rapid Vehicle Exhaust Inspection by Selective Combusion Analysis," Air Pollution Control Association Meeting, New York City, June 1969.

Exhaust Emission Analyzer Test and Evaluation Report, Department of California Highway Patrol, March, 1970.

PATTISON, J. N.; "The New Federal Driving Cycle for Emissions Tests." APCA Meeting, Atlantic City, New Jersey, June 27 to July 1, 1971.

American Conference of Governmental Industrial Hygienists, Committee on Air Sampling Instruments, *Air Sampling for Evaluation of Atmospheric Contaminants,* 3rd. ed. Cincinnati 1966

American Public Health Association Program Area Committee on Air Pollution *Guide to the appraisal and control of air pollution,* 2d ed. New York, American Public Health Assn. 1969

BATTAN, Louis J., *The Unclean Sky,* Anchor Books, Doubleday & Co., Inc. Garden City, New York 1966

CARR, Donald Eaton, *The Breath of Life,* 1st ed., New York, Norton 1965

National Tuberculosis and Respiratory Disease Administration, *Air Pollution Primer,* New York, 1969 paper

American Chemical Society, *Cleaning Our Environment, The Chemical Basis for Action,* Washington, 1969 paper

Symposium: Air Pollution, 10 Arizona Law Review No. 1, Summer 1969

lead alkyls

Back in 1923 lead alkyls were added to gasoline to improve engine efficiency. High compression engines were designed to burn this fuel, and except for the premium gasoline marketed in Eastern areas by the American Oil Company, a division of Standard Oil Co. (Indiana), non-leaded gasoline was generally unavailable In early 1970, California Standard's Chevron subsidiary began marketing a lead-free gasoline.

Lead poisoning is as old as history. Lead was used for water pipes in ancient Rome and caused many cases of poisoning. Today it is an industrial hygiene problem—primarily for workers engaged in manufacturing lead batteries and paint and among tinsmiths and typographers. It is also a serious health problem among children—an estimated 112,000 to 225,000 children fall victim to this "silent epidemic" each year. Primarily poor children suffer, for the lead comes from paint. Local ordinances usually ban lead-based paint indoors, but old homes, painted with lead-based paints, have the plaster and paint peel off to be ingested by children.

Cores of polar ice dating to 800 B.C. formed from snow that fell during the infancy of Greek civilization, contain almost too little lead to measure, according to Dr. Tsaihwa Chow, a research chemist at Scripps Institution of Oceanography near San Diego.

After 1750, Dr. Chow has found, the lead content of polar ice was moderately increased by smelting operations and coal-burning during the Industrial Revolution. But snow that has fallen at the poles since 1940 contains up to 500 times more lead than the pristine snows of pre-Christian times.

Standard texts on industrial toxicology list lead compounds as severly toxic when absorbed into the body by inhalation, ingestion or through the skin. Lead poisoning can come about from air pollution or by eating and drinking lead contaminants. When lead is inhaled, absorption takes place more easily and symptoms develop more quickly. When lead is ingested much of it passes through the body unabsorbed. This means that larger amounts of lead and more time are needed to be lead poisoned by wa ter pollution. Lead is a cumulative poison, like pesticides and radioactivity. Eventually the body stores enough to produce symptoms and disability. Lead poisoning can kill, but for many, lead poisoning is such that the individual never realizes that he has the problem—or something else is blamed. Complaints include constipation and/or diarrhea, loss of appetite, metallic taste, nausea and vomiting, lassitude, insomnia, weakness, joint and muscle pains, irritability, headache and dizziness. A possibility is that broad dissemination of lead may cause some of these symptoms to appear in the entire population and to be accepted as normal. The result is a lower quality life for all those affected.

lead in air

For years then we have been pouring lead into our atmosphere from automobiles,knowing its insidious character. Storage battery manufacturing is the largest user of lead with gasoline antiknock additives the second largest user—together accounting for more than half the national lead consumption. Refineries consumed 237,589 metric tons of lead in the form of tetraethyl lead in 1968. Most of this lead becomes a pollution problem—that is if you admit it exists.

This lead is emitted into the atmosphere, but oddly enough most studies have not categorized it as a serious general air pollutant. This is probably due to the investigations, for they have not been conducted in locations of heavy automobile concentration or use. A Cincinnati study revealed that 1,700 pounds of lead were produced each day from the combustion of leaded gasolines. What happens is that lead falls out of the air to become a water and soil pollutant. As a result, general urban air pollution levels for lead range from about one to three micrograms per cubic meter of air (ug/m^3), while atmospheric measurements taken near automobile traffic can run as high as 40 ug/m^3. For those who breathe near automobile concentrations, lead poisoning from air pollution is indeed a health problem.

lead in water, soil, and plants

With 6 billion pounds of lead alkyls burned since 1923, the lead must be going somewhere. In 1926 a special advisory committee to the U.S. Surgeon General advised the U.S. Public Health Service to monitor lead levels in the environment and its effects on the public. This advice was generally ignored and the few studies made indicated that lead in air was not dangerous. The industry continues to use scientific studies to claim lead does not cause pollution of air. The key word, however, is air. In highly motorized areas lead in water, soil, and vegetables can be several times higher than normal background values. The U.S. Geological Survey found lead in amounts as high as 3,000 parts per million in the ash of grasses near Denver. A study of mosses along major roads in Sweden showed 300 to 500 parts per million (ppm) on the sides of selected roads. Beyond 100 meters from the road lead concentration was less than 100 ppm. Background would be 20 to 40 ppm. A Public Health Service study states 0.05 mg/liter as the limit for lead in drinking water, yet this was shown to be exceeded by stations along such rivers as the Maumee, Ohio, Wabash, Little Miami, and the Illinois. The result of this dissemination process is that most of us have .05 mg of lead per 100 grams of blood. Symptoms of lead poisoning have been found at .08 mg per 100 grams of blood. This difference is small, though still a significant margin, but it is indicative of a problem created by our industry.

More recently we have begun to appreciate the amount of lead in the air. In mid-Manhattan the average lead content is 7.5 micrograms per cubic meter of lead, nearly four times the 2 ug/m^3 limit the World Health Organization considers advisable for the general population. The freeways in Los Angeles sometimes have 72 ug/m^3. When it rains the lead spikes the drinking water.

Health is being exposed to a hazard and ecological consideration is pushed aside to provide a production benefit. Leaded gasoline provides better performance characteristics, this benefits us all.

However, it was the oil industry and the automotive industry that made the decision. Why? From their view leaded gasoline provides a higher average octane, a slightly higher percentage of premium gasoline on total gasoline and a higher percentage of gasoline from crude. Thus a side effect of lead additives is conservation of our petroleum resources but the reason for its adoption is that leaded gasoline is more efficient—if we ignore our environment.

It is this new concern for the environment that has brought pressure to abandon lead additives. They interfere with catalysts that are packed into devices for removing pollutants from auto exhausts. Lead itself is a pollutant which adds to the problem of meeting particulate limitations in the new federal standards. And we are also beginning to recognize the danger from this ancient poison.

Getting rid of lead is necessary, but gasoline is likely to be more expensive and perhaps of lower octane. Worse yet it may bring new pollution problems. The additional light volatile gasoline created by producing non-leaded gasolines could increase evaporation losses or hydrocarbon emissions. Like most modern pollution problems, answers are not easy to find.

Nevertheless, in late 1970 there were still no federal or state laws to control the lead content of fuels. However, from 1926 to 1958 industry practice set a 3 gram per gallon lead limit, based on limits recommended by the Surgeon General. In 1958 this was increased to 4 grams per gallon.

See also: "Octane Maneuvers Bleed Motorists" the Jack Anderson *Washington Merry-Go-Round* column in the *Washington Post*, Oct. 9, 1971 at D 15.

Once again we quote from the annual report for 1970 on implementation of the Clean Air Act:

Under the Clean Air Act, manufacturers of fuels and fuel additives may be required to register any additives used in a fuel sold in interstate commerce. Registration is solely for the purpose of gathering information; no regulatory activity is involved.

On June 13, 1970, motor gasoline, excluding aviation gasoline was designated as the first fuel to be covered. On the same day, regulations for registration of motor fuel additivies were published in the Federal Register. [42 CFR 79]

Producers of the designated fuel had 90 days to notify APCO of the names of additives used in the fuel, the purpose and range of concentration of each such additive, and the additive manufacturer's name and address. They also were expected to provide summaries of available information on the emission products resulting from the use of the additive and on the toxicity of such emission products.

Additive manufacturers then are required to furnish information on the recommended purposes and concentrations of all additives identified by fuel producers, and on the chemical composition and structure of the additives. They are required to furnish summaries of available information on emission products and their toxicity.

On December 15, 1970, 226 additives, including lead additives, were registered. Notifications of such registration were sent to the 35 companies which manufacture these additives and to the 98 fuel manufacturers which had reported use or anticipated use of them. After January 9, 1971, no fuel manufacturer or processor may use an additive in motor gasoline (with the exception of aviation gasoline) introduced into interstate commerce unless the additive is registered and the manufacturer has complied with registration requirements.

End, report on implementation of Clean Air Act.

availability of unleaded gasoline

On August 18, 1971, EPA announced that according to its own study, "Lead-free gasoline apparently could be made generally available by 1975 at an increase in cost to consumers ranging from two-tenths to nine-tenths of a cent per gallon." The variation in cost, EPA said, would depend upon how soon industry would have to provide the lead-free gasoline and whether it would have to be for all grades. However, it will be 1976 before all gasoline grades could be made lead-free, the study reported.

As part of its effort to develop information, the Agency commissioned a seven-month study of the economic and technical implications of various hypothetical schedules for the regulation of lead additives. The study was performed by Bonner & Moore Associates of Houston, Texas.

The Bonner & Moore study envisaged the availability of a lead-free grade of gasoline having a research octane rating of 93. Gasoline having a research octane rating of 93 is adequate for cars made in 1971 and later. The 93-octane gas would be an addition to the conventional regular and premium leaded gasolines.

Using this three-fuel approach, the study said, various regulatory strategies could be devised to remove the lead from gasoline at different rates of speed.

Copies of the full Bonner & Moore report may be obtained from the National Technical Information Service, U.S. Department of Commerce, 5285 Port Royal Road, Springfield, Va. 22151. The publication number is NTIS-PB-201033.

The Clean Air Act authorizes EPA to regulate the uses of fuel additives on the basis of their adverse effects on public health and welfare, or on the performance of motor vehicle emission control systems.

EPA regulations

EPA issued proposed regulations on the regulation of fuels and fuel additives in February, 1972 (37 Fed. Reg. 3882, Feb. 23, 1972). The regulations prescribe a decrease in the lead content of gasoline from 2.0 grams of lead per gallon in 1974 to 1.25 grams per gallon in 1977. The regulations also require that lead-free gasoline be generally available after July 1, 1974. Lead-free gasoline is defined as gasoline containing not more than 0.05 grams of lead per gallon. Since lead impairs the performance of emission control systems that include catalytic converters which motor vehicle manufacturers are developing to meet 1975-76 motor vehicle emissions standards, the availability of lead-free gasoline is required to maintain the efficacy of proposed emission control systems. Phosphorous, another fuel additive which effects the performance of catalytic converters, is restricted to 0.01 grams per gallon. The EPA additives document is also published in the *Environment Reporter* 31:2641. Because of some doubts concerning the information needed, EPA re-opened the period for commenting on June 14, 1972 for 30 days. EPA's reasons are explained in the *Federal Register* Vol. 37, No. 115, at 11787.

See also discussion of lead in the inner city at App. Three-7

A group of urban, labor and environmental organizations, the Urban Environment Coalition, has opposed the proposed EPA lead regulation. The coalition contends that the .05 gram per gallon standard is not stringent enough to prevent lead poisoning in ghetto children who are subject to a high automobile emissions exposure from auto-clogged, inner-city streets.

The following is from *The President's 1971 Environmental Program,* by the Council on Environmental Quality, GPO, March, 1971 at 30:

Lead in gasoline adds to the automotive air pollution problem in two ways. First, lead fouls some of the major emission control systems now being developed to meet the 1975 air quality standards.

Second, lead itself is a pollutant. Over 95 percent of the total lead emitted into the atmosphere derives from additives in gasoline. Lead particles can penetrate the lungs and can be retained and absorbed in the bloodstream. In urban areas, the margin of safety between blood levels of lead in humans and levels at which lead poisoning symptoms have been identified are growing smaller. While no clear case has been found of lead poisoning from automobile emissions, there is ample reason for concern.

The Clean Air Amendments of 1970 authorize control of lead levels in gasoline. However, a total ban is not feasible because over one-half of the vehicles now on the road require high octane gasoline which, in general, can only be achieved using lead additives. The Federal Government can and will require that unleaded gasoline be available, but it cannot assure that people will buy it. Since the cost of low-lead or nonleaded gasoline is higher, there is little incentive for car owners to purchase it. In fact, current low-lead or nonleaded gasoline is not selling well.

proposal for tax on lead

The President is again proposing a special tax on lead additives in gasoline. The tax would allow consumers to buy the low or unleaded fuels at no price disadvantage over leaded gasolines, and hence creates an economic incentive for refiners to produce more low or unleaded gasoline. This special charge would help to bring about, at reasonable costs, the gradual transition to use of unleaded gasoline, which is essential to reduce lead emissions and to meet the other emission control standards scheduled to come into effect for the 1975 automobiles.

End, excerpt from Presidential program.

other additives

Lead additives to improve "performance" have already been discussed. Many other additives are used. These additives have secondary effects. They often prevent an efficient combustion and thus increase air pollution. The additives can also undergo chemical changes and are emitted as additional air pollutants. Additives are added to: remove lead oxide from valves and spark plugs; alter the chemical composition of combustion chamber deposits; prevent fuel deterioration; prevent the catalytic action of trace copper; prevent rust; prevent icing; prevent carburetor deposits; and to lubricate cylinders to prevent valve and ring sticking.

See MACINKO, "The Tailpipe Problem," 12 *Environment* No. 5, June 1970 at 6.

REFERENCES AND SELECTED BIBLIOGRAPHY

SAX, *Dangerous Properties of Industrial Materials,* 1968

U.S. Dept. HEW, *Symposium on Environmental Lead Contamination,* Public Health Service Pub. No. 1440, March 1966

GILLETTE, "The Economics of Lead Poisoning," 55 *Sierra Club Bul.* #9, Sept. 1970

"Will the new gasolines lick auto pollution," 36 *Consumer Reports* #3, March 1971 at 156

MACINKO, "The Tailpipe Problem," 12 *Environment* #5, June 1971 at 14

For the petition and supporting memorandum by the Environmental Defense Fund (EDF) to the Department of H.E.W. on May 5, 1970 seeking to eliminate lead from automobile exhausts, see LANUAD and RHEINGOLD, *The Environmental Law Handbook*, 1971 at 306

The federal government's program to date has resulted in a decline in air pollution from automobiles from its high in 1969. Reductions could be more rapidly attained if the 1975-1976 standards are vigorously pursued. However, as long as the number of cars continues to increase, it is unlikely that pollution from this source will not start to rise again even with a vigorous program. Thus, some major shift in the means of transportation away from the internal combustion engine will be mandatory.

low-emission vehicles

Sec. 212 of the Clean Air Act provides for the development of a low emission vehicle. It also provides for the purchase of such vehicles at procurement costs of up to 150 percent of alternative substitutes. The purchase price can go up 200 percent if an inherently low polluting propulsion system is used.

For several years the Japanese firm Toyo Kogyo has manufactured the low-polluting Mazda automobile. Recently these have been imported to the U.S. West Coast (Seattle, Wash.) and to Texas and Florida (Jacksonville). Two models of the Mazda use the Wankel engine.

Wankel engines use a triangular rotor in a combustion chamber instead of a piston, have fewer parts, achieve better combustion, and hence

Wankel, Rankine & Lear

pollute less. Mercedes-Benz, Rolls-Royce, Alfa Romeo, and Citroen also have Wankel engines under development. General Motors paid $50 million for rights to the Wankel. A potential conflict of interest lies in the fact that U.S. auto firms make far higher profits on parts than on new cars, and so a simpler engine might well cut into their profits.

Burning hydrogen in a converted Wankel engine reportedly results in emissions that are cleaner than the air that enters the engine. Such a car was built by Roger E. Billings, who was then a senior in engineering at Brigham Young University, Provo, Utah, See *The New York Times,* June 8, 1972 at 53.

The possible propulsion systems that have the potential for replacing the internal combustion engine are quite varied. Liquid Natural Gas (LNG) and Compressed Natural Gas (CNG) are one possibility. LNG systems exist but the fuel supply limits the range of travel of the vehicle, and requires insulated tanks to maintain its low temperatures. CNG systems and propane (LPG) systems can be put into conventional automobiles for $300 to $400. However, the national supply of gas is so limited that it would be necessary to deal with complex politics of the regulated gas industry before creating a large new market for gas. Turbine engines produce fewer pollutants but their nitrogen oxide emissions are high. A wide variety of electric vehicles has been studied. Technology is inadequate, particularly involving fuel cells, one of the more promising innovations. The potential is high for the development of electric vehicles, especially small commuting vehicles. One disadvantage is that their recharging, unless fuel cells were used, would require increased electric generation and the pollution from that source would increase.

For regulations on certification of low-emission vehicles, see the Federal Register, Vol. 36, No. 125, of June 29, 1971

Late in October of 1971, a turbine car was tested by the Environmental Protection Agency's laboratory in Ann Arbor, Mich. The car passed the emission tests for 1975 model cars, and EPA scientists reportedly were enthusiastic about this automobile's possibilities. The car had been developed by a small firm called Williams Research Corp., of Walled Lake, Mich., under a $240,000 grant from New York City. General Motors and Volkswagen have both requested Williams to develop engines for them, and Chrysler was to have their turbine engine tested by EPA in December of 1971. Although the turbine engine is a workable reality, full production is not considered possible at least until 1979. (See *Time,* Nov. 8, 1971, at 101.)

Steam engines seem to be another satisfactory alternative to the internal combustion engine. One of these, the Rankine engine, has attracted Japanese industrial interest. The famous inventor William Lear has been working for several years on a steam car using a fluid called Learium.

The Ford Motor Company and Thermo-Electric Corp. of Waltham, Massachusetts are developing a Rankine-Cycle vapor engine, See, *The Wall Street Journal,* June 17, 1972 at 32.

The development of a steam bus has been proceeding under a grant from the Urban Mass Transportation Administration of the U.S. Department of Transportation to the California Assembly Rules Committee. The Assembly and the Southern California Rapid Transit District have in turn contracted with several firms to test different designs. All work on water in a closed cycle system.

REFERENCES

U.S. Department of Health, Education, and Welfare, Public Health Service, *Power Systems for Electric Vehicles,* Bureau of Disease Prevention and Environmental Control, National Center for Air Pollution Control, Cincinnati, Ohio 1967

2 *Steambus Newsletter* #2, October 28, 1970

HOHENEMSER and Mc CAULL, "The Windup Car," 12 *Environment* #5, June 1970 at 14 Environmental Action, *Earth Tool Kit,* New York, Balletine Books, 1971 at 114

For an examination of the state of the art of building low-polluting vehicles, *See:* MALIN, Marty and Lewicke, Carol, "Pollution-free power for the automobile," *Environmental Science 9 technology,* Vol. 6, No. 6, June 1972, at 513.

j. Pollution from aircraft

From 1967 to 1969 the National Air Pollution Control Administration of H.E.W. [now in EPA] tried to obtain a voluntary emission control program from the aircraft industry. In August 1969, NAPCA invited forty-three airlines to a meeting to sign a memorandum of agreement to limit pollution from airlines. Seventeen airlines did not accept the invitation, the other twenty-four were represented by one man, who refused to sign. The airlines had their own program but one which called for modifying the JT8D engine on a slower schedule than NAPCA's.

Meanwhile New Jersey filed suit against seven airlines. The airlines claimed only the Federal government could regulate them. The FAA acted to establish limits, whereupon Senator Muskie charged the FAA was attempting to protect the airlines from state law.

On January 30, 1970, the airlines signed an agreement with the Department of Transportation and H.E.W. to reduce sharply smoke emissions from jet engines by 1972. The terms were not satisfactory to the States and in January of 1970, New York sued eighteen airlines. In September, Massachusetts sued 10 airlines.

The emission of air pollutants from airplanes is a tiny portion (1%) of the total but still accounts for some 400 billion pounds annually. Since 80 percent of aircraft emission occur during takeoff and landing these pollutants are highly concentrated around the larger airports. Furthermore, aircraft pollution control devices designed to limit particulate emissions through higher combustion temperatures add to air pollution problems by increasing NO_X pollution.

REFERENCES

SCHAEFFER, "Smokeless jet engines really aren't," *Environmental Action,* October 31, 1970 at 5.

For the documents and agreement in the N.J. case see LANDAU & RHEINGOLD, *The Environmental Law Handbook,* 1971 at 276.

The following is from the official report on implementation of the Clean Air Act during the year 1970:

> Following a meeting in January 1970 with the Secretary of Health Education, and Welfare and the Secretary of Transportation, virtually all of the Nation's airlines agreed to initiate a program to reduce smoke emissions from about 3,300 jet aircraft engines. The program involves installation of new types of combustors in JT8D engines. New combustors are to be installed during routine overhauls of such engines; on the average, such engines undergo routine overhaul after every 5,000 hours of operation. As of November 15, 1970, the new cumbustors had been installed on nearly 10 percent of the engines, and production of additional new combustors was reported to be on schedule. The program is to be completed by December 31, 1972.
>
> In October 1970, after learning that jet aircraft ordinarily discharge into the air the fuel that seeps from engines during stops, APCO asked the airlines to take steps to curtail this practice. APCO estimated that such fuel dumping may result in release of about 110 tons of fuel per year in the vicinity of National Airport in Washington, D.C., and that nationally, the total may be in excess of 7,700 tons (2 million gallons) annually. The airlines indicated that they are interested in developing a long-range solution to this problem and that they would submit a proposal to APCO by February 1, 1971.

The following is from Nature and Control of Aircraft Engine Exhaust Emissions, Report 91-9 of the Secretary of HEW to Congress, December, 1968 at 3:

A. Impact of Aircraft Emissions

1. Exhaust emissions from piston and jet aircraft include the same pollutants emitted by highway vehicles, as well as certain other pollution sources, and, consequently, participate in the same air pollution problems.

2. The present contribution of aircraft emissions to the total atmospheric pollution burden of the community is considered small. The magnitude of this relative contribution is expected to grow, largely as a result of effective emission control legislation applicable to highway vehicles. By 1980, for example, carbon monoxide from aircraft is expected to account for 3 to 5 percent of the carbon monoxide emissions in Los Angeles County versus a present contribution of less than 1 percent.

3. Based on emission densities, the average level of atmospheric pollution at selected air terminals and their immediate vicinity is calculated to be of comparable magnitude to that in the communities in which the terminals are located.

4. Under conditions of heavy airport traffic, exposures to high concentrations of exhaust contaminants are likely to occur in aircraft loading areas and in the cabins of aircraft lined up awaiting takeoff.

5. The public's reaction to air pollution in the form of smoke and odor from jet aircraft is evident from complaints and newspaper accounts. Response, both in the form of legislative action and attempts by industry to find a solution to the visible emissions problem, has been notable.

B. Control of Aircraft Emissions

1. Principles of combustion and engine operating conditions similar to those which account for emissions from highway vehicles are responsible for emissions from aircraft engines. Subject to special safety considerations, aircraft engine emissions are generally amenable to the same principles as applied to motor vehicle emission control technology.

2. Turbine-engine combustor technology for effectively eliminating the visible plume seems assured for application in the very near future, both to new engines and to replacement combustor components for existing engines. When applied to existing aircraft, according to regular replacement schedules of such engines and combustor units, the cost is not expected to be a significant factor. Safety, in terms of engine relight characteristics, is not expected to be degraded thereby.

3. Total particulates, hydrocarbons and carbon monoxide emissions reduction from turbine engines may be realized as a consequence of improved combustion design for improved performance and for the control of visible emissions.

4. Aircraft engine emissions in the lower atmosphere are primarily the result of ground operations, and the approach and takeoff segments of an aircraft's flight pattern. Airport designs which minimize aircraft ground operations, plus the use of low-pollution aircraft-to-terminal transportation can produce meaningful results in all receptor areas.

5. Control measures applicable to aircraft piston engine emissions are dependent on developing definitive data on emission impact and the development of control technology.

6. The control of oxides of nitrogen from aircraft is not deemed to be feasible on the basis of current information.

7. Control of aircraft emissions by altering fuel composition is not indicated in the light of the control potential of other approaches considered.

C. Conclusions and Recommendation

1. Reduction of particulate emissions from jet aircraft is both desirable and feasible. Engine manufacturers and airlines have indicated that improvements in turbine engine combustor design can be built into new engines and retrofitted on engines already in use. Testing programs are already underway. Furthermore, they have indicated that application of this technology will be underway by the early 1970's. While there are no laws or regulations to compel the industry to follow through on this work, it appears that public pressures resulting primarily from the adverse effects of odors and visibility obscuration will lead industry to initiate the application of this technology as soon as possible and to complete it within the shortest possible time. Accordingly, it is the intention of this Department to encourage such action by engine manufacturers and airline operators and to keep close watch on their progress. If, at any time, it appears that progress is inadequate or that completion of the work will be unduly prolonged, or that the concern of the industry lags, the Department will recommend regulatory action to the Congress that statutory authority for such action be provided.

2. Further research is needed to define more precisely the present and probable future nature and magnitude of all other air pollution problems associated with aircraft activity in the United States and to identify needs for control measures. Emphasis must be placed particularly on assessment of air pollutant levels in the air terminal environment and their effects on health and safety and on evaluation of possible long-term effects of upper atmospheric pollution resulting from aircraft flight activity. The Department will undertake research appropriate to the solution of this problem.

3. As further research results in identification of needs for additional measures to control air pollution from any type of aircraft, and as measures to achieve such control become available through research and development, it is the Department's expectation that engine manufacturers, airline operators, and other segments of the aviation community will take the initiative in the development and application of such control measures. If the private sector fails to provide adequate controls, the Department will not hesitate to recommend to the Congress that Federal regulatory action be authorized.

4. In light of the relatively small contribution of aircraft to community air pollution in all places for which adequate data are available, and in view of the practical problems that would result from State and local regulatory action in this field, it is the Department's conclusion that adoption and enforcement of State or local emission control regulations pertaining to aircraft cannot be adequately justified at this time. The Department recommends that, if and when regulations become necessary, the rationale used to develop Federal rather than local emission standards for motor vehicles be applied to aircraft.

5. The Department recognizes that State and local agencies, in cooperation with the Federal Aviation Administration and other cognizant agencies, are the most appropriate groups to insure that control of airport pollution hazards will be given adequate consideration in the selection of airport sites, planning for expansion and reconstruction of airports, design of airports, and planning and conduct of ground operations.

6. The Department will include information on progress in the control of air pollution from aircraft in the annual report which must be submitted under section 306 of the Air Quality Act.

End, HEW report.

Federal pre-emption—Is it complete?

In the 1970 amendments, Section 233 preempts the control of emissions of any air pollutant from any aircraft or engine.

However, is *Huron Cement Company v. Detroit,* 362 U.S. 440 (1960) applicable? The United States Supreme Court, in *Huron Portland Cement Co. v. City of Detroit,* held that the smoke abatement code of the City of Detroit could be applied to ships docked at the Port of Detroit even though the ships were engaged in interstate commerce. The Court held that the federal inspection laws did not preempt local regulations to protect the health of the community. Perhaps this case can be used to challenge federal actions that attempt to control subjects that have significant impact on health, safety and welfare—matters traditionally of concern to state and local government. The fight over the attempt by Minnesota to set standards for discharges from nuclear power plants that are more restrictive than those of the Atomic Energy Commission is another example of this type of problem. (See the material on electric power generation in Volume Two).

In that case, the Supreme Court held that an atomic energy generating plant that had complied with all AEC regulations was not required to comply with stricter Minnesota pollution control regulations governing the discharge of radioactive wastes, because a 1959 amendment to the Atomic Energy Act preempted the field. *Minnesota v. Northern States Power Co.,* 40 U.S.L.W. 3479 (April 4, 1972).

Title II, Part B, Sec. 231 of the 1970 Clean Air Act, (42 U.S.C. 1857, et. seq.) requires EPA to complete a study of emissions of air pollutants from aircraft and publish a report of such study, accompanied by proposed aircraft emission standards, no later than September 27, 1971. In mid-April of 1972 the report was said to be completed and submitted, but could not be obtained from EPA.

THE CLEAN AIR ACT
Title II, Part B

42 U.S.C. 1857 *et seq*

PART B—AIRCRAFT EMISSION STANDARDS

ESTABLISHMENT OF STANDARDS

SEC. 231 (a) (1) Within 90 days after the date of enactment of the Clean Air Amendments of 1970, the Administrator shall commence a study and investigation of emissions of air pollutants from aircraft in order to determine—

(A) the extent to which such emissions affect air quality in air quality control regions throughout the United States, and

(B) the technological feasibility of controlling such emissions.

(2) Within 180 days after commencing such study and investigation, the Administrator shall publish a report of such study and investigation and shall issue proposed emission standards applicable to emissions of any air pollutant from any class or classes of aircraft or aircraft engines which in his judgment cause or contribute to or are likely to cause or contribute to air pollution which endangers the public health or welfare.

(3) The Administrator shall hold public hearings with respect to such proposer standards. Such hearings shall, to the extent practicable, be held in air quality control regions which are most seriously affected by aircraft emissions. Within 90 days after the issuance of such proposed regulations, he shall issue such regulation with such modifications as he deems appropriate. Such regulations may be revised from time to time.

(b) Any regulation prescribed under this section (and any revision thereof) shall take effect after such period as the Administrator finds necessary (after consultation with the Secretary of Transportation) to permit the development and application of the requisite technology, giving appropriate consideration to the cost of compliance within such period.

(c) Any regulations under this section, or amendments thereto, with respect to aircraft, shall be prescribed only after consultation with the Secretary of Transportation in order to assure appropriate consideration for aircraft safety.

ENFORCEMENT OF STANDARDS

SEC. 232 (a) The Secretary of Transportation, after consultation with the Administrator, shall prescribe regulations to insure compliance with all standards prescribed under section 231 by the Administrator. The regulations of the Secretary of Transportation shall include provisions making such standards applicable in the issuance, amendment, modification, suspension, or revocation of any certificate authorized by the Federal Aviation Act or the Department of Transportation Act. Such Secretary shall insure that all necessary inspections are accomplished, and, may execute any power or duty vested in him by any other provision of law in the execution of all powers and duties vested in him under this section.

(b) In any action to amend, modify, suspend, or revoke a certificate in which violation of an emission standard prescribed under section 231 or of a regulation prescribed under subsection (a) is at issue, the certificate holder shall have the same notice and appeal rights as are prescribed for such holders in the Federal Aviation Act of 1958 or the Department of Transportation Act, except that in any appeal to the National Transportation Safety Board, the Board may amend, modify, or revoke the order of the

Secretary of Transportation only if it finds no violation of such standard or regulation and that such amendment, modification, or revocation is consistent with safety in air transportation.

STATE STANDARDS AND CONTROLS

SEC. 233. No State or political subdivision thereof may adopt or attempt to enforce any standard respecting emissions of any air pollutant from any aircraft or engine thereof unless such standard is identical to a standard applicable to such aircraft under this part.

DEFINITIONS

SEC. 234. Terms used in this part (other than Administrator) shall have the same meaning as such terms have under section 101 of the Federal Aviation Act of 1958.

FEDERAL AVIATION ACT OF 1968

49 U.S.C. 1421

(1) Section 601 of the Federal Aviation Act of 1958 (49 U.S.C. 1421) is amended by adding at the end thereof the following new subsection:

AVIATION FUEL STANDARDS [1]

(d) The Administrator shall prescribe, and from time to time revise, regulations (1) establishing standards governing the composition or the chemical or physical properties of any aircraft fuel or fuel additive for the purpose of controlling or eliminating aircraft emissions which the Administrator of the Environmental Protection Agency (pursuant to section 231 of the Clean Air Act) determines endanger the public health or welfare, and (2) providing for the implementation and enforcement of such standards.

(2) Section 610(a) of such Act (49 U.S.C. 1430(a)) is amended by striking out "and" at the end of paragraph (7); by striking out the period at the end of paragraph (8) and inserting in lieu thereof "; and" and by adding after paragraph (8) the following new paragraph:

(9) For any person to manufacture, deliver, sell, or offer for sale, any aviation fuel or fuel additive in violation of any regulation prescribed under section 601(d).

(3) That portion of the table of contents contained in the first section of the Federal Aviation Act of 1958 which appears under the side heading

SEC. 601 General Safety Powers and Duties.

is amended by adding at the end thereof the following:

(d) Aviation fuel standards.

---

[1] These amendments to the Federal Aviation Act were made by the Clean Air Amendments of 1970 and are included herein because of their relationship to the Clean Air Act.

k. State and local regulation of air pollution

Smoke regulations in England go back to the 13th century, though enforcement seems sporadic at best and even limited success was not achieved until recent times. In the United States, smoke ordinances were adopted in 1881 by Chicago and Cincinnati. By 1900, similar ordinances were in effect in St. Louis, the City of Brooklyn, and New York City. These ordinances were generally enacted after the demonstrated futility of trying to control the emissions of an industrialized nation through the use of public nuisance actions on a case-by-case basis.

In the ensuing years many cities passed ordinances, but they were of limited value—usually based on some prohibition against smoke. Since many of the most harmful pollutants are invisible, this fact alone limits their utility.

Nevertheless, until the beginning of serious control efforts by the Federal government in 1967, cities were the main governmental units dealing with air pollution. Some of the cities, particularly the larger ones, had passed more sophisticated ordinances, and many programs had sizable budgets. At the state level, thirty-five states had programs by 1967. A common characteristic of these programs was that they were usually much smaller than the program of the largest city in the state.

1967 figures, for example, showed:

	1967 Budget	**Personnel Man Years**
California	$2,407,000	98
Los Angeles County	3,758,200	305
Massachusetts	10,500	.5
Boston Metro.	134,300	20
New York	2,371,280	50
N. Y. C.	1,509,900	120
Ohio	128,000	8
Cleveland	276,700	33

The result of these conditions is that when the 1967 act was passed, the trained manpower and experienced organizations were in the cities, yet the federal government dealt directly with the states. This has created numerous political and administrative problems, but progress, though limited, has occurred. Federal matching grants under the 1963 program resulted in increased expenditures. However, of the 55 State and territorial programs being financed, only six have reached an annual per capita expenditure of 25 cents, which is generally considered a minimum expenditure needed. [Note the estimated economic cost of air pollution is $65 per capita per year.] Only 23 (including the six) are spending ten cents per person per year. At the local level 64 of the 144 grantees are spending at least 40 cents per capita per year. Prior to the passage of the Clean Air Act of 1963, only nine states had adopted air pollution control regulations; by 1967, 30 had. Local agencies have proliferated from 85 in 1962 to more than 200 in 1970.

LOCAL CONTROL OF AIR POLLUTION

Prior to 1967 a local air pollution program could exist independently of state efforts. In many states there were no programs and where programs existed they were dominated by the activities of the larger cities. [See O'Fallon, *Deficiencies in the Air Quality Act of 1967,* 33 Law and Contemporary Problems 275, 293 (Spring 1968)] Since 1967 the states have been forced by Federal law to develop air pollution implementation plans. Because of these Federal laws every state now has some program. However, since the combined federal, state and local expenditures in F.Y. 1971 in South Dakota is twenty-one thousand dollars compared with California's expenditures of over twelve and one-half million dollars, there is considerable variation in state and local efforts. Nevertheless, the ability of a

funding of state and local air pollution agencies

Funding and Manpower for State and Local Air Pollution Control Agencies, 1970–71

(In thousands of dollars)

State	Fiscal year 1970 funding			Fiscal year 1971 budgeted [1]			Fiscal year	
	Federal	State and local [2]	Total	Federal	State and local [2]	Total	1970 man-years	1971 man-years
Alabama	15	156	171	15	169	184	10	12
Alaska	54	21	75	54	23	77	5	6
Arizona	314	243	557	314	382	696	48	47
Arkansas	49	44	93	60	49	109	4	10
California	2,069	7,665	9,734	2,463	10,114	12,577	614	635
Colorado	567	560	1,127	611	636	1,247	71	74
Connecticut	407	272	679	448	484	932	48	56
Delaware	249	148	397	197	172	369	26	31
District of Columbia	213	107	320	234	117	351	21	21
Florida	488	658	1,146	961	734	1,695	90	123
Georgia	316	192	508	358	344	702	35	65
Hawaii	0	73	73	0	205	205	7	14
Idaho	46	37	83	47	38	85	6	2
Illinois	1,391	3,477	4,868	1,255	2,831	4,086	212	291
Indiana	380	454	834	323	580	903	61	71
Iowa	87	86	173	92	180	272	9	29
Kansas	127	61	188	141	94	235	29	31
Kentucky	341	393	734	534	529	1,063	54	76
Louisiana	120	106	226	154	182	336	15	16
Maine	54	27	81	36	18	54	2	6
Maryland	1,307	899	2,206	1,426	910	2,336	124	173
Massachusetts	415	324	739	575	436	1,011	33	61
Michigan	1,336	662	1,998	1,331	956	2,287	59	116
Minnesota	346	231	577	350	369	719	42	46
Mississippi	44	23	67	46	24	70	3	6
Missouri	733	583	1,316	761	598	1,359	104	107
Montana	106	85	191	131	97	228	10	17
Nebraska	30	15	45	90	46	136	3	8
Nevada	148	130	278	159	136	295	22	26
New Hampshire	32	34	66	45	38	83	6	7
New Jersey	788	796	1,584	1,430	1,323	2,753	149	177
New Mexico	78	87	165	217	148	365	11	23
New York	2,332	7,876	10,208	2,629	8,784	11,413	628	720
North Carolina	454	246	700	578	396	974	55	81
North Dakota	15	13	28	15	12	27	3	4
Ohio	730	1,054	1,784	904	1,422	2,326	84	129
Oklahoma	90	84	174	105	114	219	13	21
Oregon	557	420	977	547	524	1,071	55	57
Pennsylvania	1,958	1,641	3,599	2,604	2,424	5,028	204	295
Rhode Island	114	66	180	83	42	125	8	12
South Carolina	224	166	390	295	359	654	23	44
South Dakota	0	0	0	14	7	21	0	3
Tennessee	503	259	762	788	416	1,204	58	100
Texas	1,139	693	1,832	1,475	960	2,435	155	182
Utah	123	80	203	99	122	221	12	17
Vermont	21	15	36	53	26	79	3	6
Virginia	231	146	377	320	306	626	34	42
Washington	1,222	981	2,203	1,212	1,246	2,458	93	85
West Virginia	138	110	248	221	226	447	14	27
Wisconsin	57	34	91	100	137	237	7	14
Wyoming	16	9	25	26	14	40	3	4
Guam	0	0	0	9	7	16	0	1
Puerto Rico	144	108	252	141	104	245	25	25
Virgin Islands	30	16	46	39	20	59	4	4
Total	**22,748**	**32,666**	**55,414**	**[3]27,115**	**[4]40,630**	**67,745**	**3,414**	**[5]4,256**

[1] Data represent activities of air quality agencies, not expenditures for pollution control facilities. Most States follow the Federal July–June fiscal year, although some use the calendar year or another 12-month period.

[2] Data for State and local agencies are substantially complete although they include only agencies receiving Federal financial assistance.

[3] 19.19 percent increase over 1970 level.

[4] 24.38 percent increase over 1970 level.

[5] 24.69 percent increase over 1970 level.

Source: Environmental Protection Agency, Office of Air Programs.

city to decide to either control or not control air pollution is no longer possible. Some programs governing the emission within a city are in existence or soon will be. Thus the local control of air pollution will have some kind of relationship to the federal-state effort. The following possible relationships can exist:

1. The local program can deal with emissions not covered by the federal state program or be more strict (when allowed by state law);

2. The local program can handle minor matters as a coordinated part of the federal-state programs. For example it might license and inspect apartment incinerators;

3. The local program can be one of several programs within a Federal Air Pollution Control Region in which the state's role is small and primarily tnat of a coordinator;

4. The local program can dominate the Federal Air Pollution Control Region and provide services to areas outside the local jurisdiction by contract;

5. The local government can have its power to control air pollution completely taken away and given to the Federal Air Pollution Control Region.

The local government that attempts to regulate air pollution can do so through a variety of programs ranging from the primitive to the multi million dollar program of Los Angeles County. The term ordinance will be used in the following discussion but in most cases what is said could apply to county, regional, or state codes or statutes. The simplest program requires no legislation but utilizes abatement actions based on public nuisance. [Chapter 5 deals with public nuisance in greater detail.] Local governments might sue under the general grant of police power to protect the health, safety, and morals of the community, a specific ordinance prohibiting some activity passed under the police power, or a general health ordinance.

The local government can pass an ordinance identifying some conduct as a public nuisance. Such conduct could be smoke, excessive smoke, pollution, unreasonable pollution, etc. A Ringelmann chart can be used as a basis for declaring a discharge to be a nuisance. Such a chart compares smoke to various degrees of darkness, one being white and five being black. This will be discussed in greater detail in the subsequent discussion of the Cleveland code.

The following cases are reprinted here:

- **Hadacheck v. Sebastian:** Concerns the right of a city to attempt to prevent air pollution through property use regulation that is not based on nuisance abatement or on health protection. For a more obvious legal point, the right of a city to pass an ordinance making the emission of dense smoke a nuisance, see the equally venerable case, *Northwestern Laundry v. City of Des Moines,* 239 U.S. 486 (1915).
- **Bortz Coal Co. v. Air Pollution Commission:** Right to control air pollution through comprehensive legislation utilizing an administrative agency.
- **New Jersey v. Mundet Cork Corp.** and **Board of Health v. New York Central Railroad:** Two cases concerning ordinances based on use of the Ringelmann Smoke Chart. Statutory interpretation problems are shown.
- **Oriental Boulevard Co. v. Heller:** A case concerning an ordinance controlling refuse incinerators. Note that the adequate banking of such incinerators in a large city would create massive problems of additional solid waste disposal. Disposal of waste from privately owned incinerators generally is a private sector expense, while municipal solid waste disposal usually is a public sector expense.
- **Department of Health v. Owens-Corning Fiberglas Corp.:** A principal case on odor control.

HADACHECK v. SEBASTIAN, Chief of Police of the City of Los Angeles, 239 U.S. 394 (1915)

Mr. Justice McKenna delivered the opinion of the court.

Habeas corpus prosecuted in the Supreme Court of the State of California for the discharge of plaintiff in error from the custody of defendant in error, Chief of Police of the City of Los Angeles.

Plaintiff in error, to whom we shall refer as petitioner, was convicted of a misdemeanor for the violation of an ordinance of the City of Los Angeles which makes it unlawful for any person to establish or operate a brick yard or brick kiln, or any establishment, factory or place for the manufacture or burning of brick within described limits in the city. Sentence was pronounced against him and he was committed to the custody of defendant in error as Chief of Police of the City of Los Angeles.

Being so in custody he filed a petition in the Supreme Court of the State for a writ of *habeas corpus.* The writ was issued. Subsequently defendant in error made a return thereto supported by affidavits, to which petitioner made sworn reply. The court rendered judgment discharging the writ and remanding petitioner to custody. The Chief Justice of the court then granted this writ of error.

The petition sets forth the reason for resorting to *habeas corpus* and that petitioner is the owner of a tract of land within the limits described in the ordinance upon which tract of land there is a very valuable bed of clay, of great value for the manufacture of brick of a fine quality, worth to him not less than $100,000 per acre or about $800,000 for the entire tract for brick-making purposes, and not exceeding $60,000 for residential purposes or for any purpose other than the manufacture of brick. That he has made excavations of considerable depth and covering a very large area of the property and that on account thereof the land cannot be utilized for residential purposes or any purpose other than that for which it is now used. That he purchased the land because of such bed of clay and for the purpose of manufacturing brick; that it was at the time of purchase outside of the limits of the city and distant from dwellings and other habitations and that he did not expect or believe, nor did other owners of property in the vicinity expect or believe, that the territory would be annexed to the city. That he has erected expensive machinery for the manufacture of bricks of fine quality which have been and are being used for building purposes in and about the city.

That if the ordinance be declared valid he will be compelled to entirely abandon his business and will be deprived of the use of his property.

That the manufacture of brick must necessarily be carried on where suitable clay is found and the clay cannot be transported to some other location, and, besides, the clay upon his property is particularly fine and clay of as good quality cannot be found in any other place within the city where the same can be utilized for the manufacture of brick. That within the prohibited district there is one other brick yard besides that of plaintiff in error.

That there is no reason for the prohibition of the business; that its maintenance cannot be and is not in the nature of a nuisance as defined in § 3479 of the Civil Code of the State, and cannot be dangerous or detrimental to health or the morals or safety or peace or welfare or convenience of the people of the district or city.

That the business is so conducted as not to be in any way or degree a nuisance; no noises arise therefrom, and no noxious odors, and that by the use of certain means (which are described) provided and the situation of the brick yard an extremely small amount of smoke is emitted from any kiln and what is emitted is so dissipated that it is not a nuisance nor in any manner detrimental to health or comfort. That during the seven years which the brick yard has been conducted no complaint has been made of it, and no attempt has ever been made to regulate it.

That the city embraces 107.62 square miles in area and 75% of it is devoted to residential purposes; that the district described in the ordinance includes only about three square miles, is sparsely settled and contains large tracts of unsubdivided and unoccupied land; and that the boundaries of the district were determined for the sole and specific purpose of prohibiting and suppressing the business of petitioner and that of the other brick yard.

That there are and were at the time of the adoption of the ordinance in other districts of the city thickly built up with residences brick yards maintained more detrimental to the inhabitants of the city. That a petition was filed, signed by several hundred persons, representing such brick yards to be a nuisance and no ordinance or regulation was passed in regard to such petition and the brick yards are operated without hindrance or molestation. That other brick yards are permitted to be maintained without prohibition or regulation.

That no ordinance or regulation of any kind has been passed at any time regulating or attempting to regulate brick yards or inquiry made whether they could be maintained without being a nuisance or detrimental to health.

That the ordinance does not state a public offense and is in violation of the constitution of the State and the Fourteenth Amendment to the Constitution of the United States.

That the business of petitioner is a lawful one, none of the materials used in it are combustible, the machinery is of the most approved pattern and its conduct will not create a nuisance.

There is an allegation that the ordinance if enforced fosters and will foster a monopoly and protects and will protect other persons engaged in the manufacture of brick in the city, and discriminates and will discriminate against petitioner in favor of such other persons who are his competitors, and will prevent him from entering into competition with them.

The petition, after almost every paragraph, charges a deprivation of property, the taking of property without compensation, and that the ordinance is in consequence invalid.

We have given this outline of the petition as it presents petitioner's contentions, with the circumstances (which we deem most material) that give color and emphasis to them.

But there are substantial traverses made by the return to the writ, among others, a denial of the charge that the ordinance was arbitrarily directed against the business of petitioner, and it is alleged that there is another district in which brick yards are prohibited.

There was a denial of the allegations that the brick yard was conducted or could be conducted sanitarily or was not offensive to health. And there were affidavits supporting the denials. In these it was alleged that the fumes, gases, smoke, soot, steam and dust arising from petitioner's brick-making plant have from time to time caused sickness and serious discomfort to those living in the vicinity.

There was no specific denial of the value of the property or that it contained deposits of clay or that the latter could not be removed and manufactured into brick elsewhere. There was, however, a general denial that the enforcement of the ordinance would "entirely deprive petitioner of his property and the use thereof."

How the Supreme Court dealt with the allegations, denials and affidavits we can gather from its opinion. The court said, through Mr. Justice Sloss, 165 California, p. 416: "The district to which the prohibition was applied contains about three square miles. The petitioner is the owner of a tract of land, containing eight acres, more or less, within the district described in the ordinance. He acquired his land in 1902, before the territory to which the ordinance was directed had been annexed to the city of Los Angeles. His land contains valuable deposits of clay suitable for the manufacture of brick, and he has, during the entire period of his ownership, used the land for brickmaking, and has erected thereon kilns, machinery and buildings necessary for such manufacture. The land, as he alleges, is far more valuable for brickmaking than for any other purpose."

The court considered the business one which could be regulated and that regulation was not precluded by the fact "that the value of investments made in the business prior to any legislative action will be greatly diminished," and that no complaint could be based upon the fact that petitioner had been carrying on the trade in that locality for a long period.

And, considering the allegations of the petition, the denials of the return and the evidence of the affidavits, the court said that the latter tended to show that the district created had become primarily a residential section and that the occupants of the neighboring dwellings are seriously incommoded by the operations of petitioner; and that such evidence, "when taken in connection with the presumptions in favor of the propriety of the legislative determination, overcame the contention that the prohibition of the ordinance was a mere arbitrary invasion of private right, not supported by any tenable belief that the continuance of the business was so detrimental to the interests of others as to require suppression."

The court, on the evidence, rejected the contention that the ordinance was not in good faith enacted as a police measure and that it was intended to discriminate against petitioner or that it was actuated by any motive of injuring him as an individual.

The charge of discrimination between localities was not sustained. The court expressed the view that the determination of prohibition was for the legislature and that the court, without regard to the fact shown in the return that there was another district in which brick-making was prohibited, could not sustain the claim that the ordinance was not enacted in good faith but was designed to discriminate against petitioner and the other brick yard within the district. "The facts before us," the court finally said, "would certainly not justify the conclusion that the ordinance here in question was designed, in either its adoption or its enforcement, to be anything but what it purported to be, viz., a legitimate regulation, operating alike upon all who came within its terms."

We think the conclusion of the court is justified by the evidence and makes it unnecessary to review the many cases cited by petitioner in which it is decided that the police power of a state cannot be arbitrarily exercised. The principle is familiar, but in any given case it must plainly appear to apply. It is to be remembered that we are dealing with one of the most essential powers of government, one that is the least limitable. It may, indeed, seem harsh in its exercise, usually is on some individual, but the imperative necessity for its existence precludes any limitation upon it when not exerted arbitrarily. A vested interest cannot be asserted against it because of conditions once obtaining. *Chicago & Alton R. R.* v. *Tranbarger*, 238 U. S. 67, 78. To so hold would preclude development and fix a city forever in its primitive conditions. There must be progress, and if in its march private interests are in the way they must yield to the good of the community. The logical result of petitioner's contention would seem to be that a city could not be formed or enlarged against the resistance of an occupant of the ground and that if it grows at all it can only grow as the environment of the occupations that are usually banished to the purlieus.

The police power and to what extent it may be exerted we have recently illustrated in *Reinman* v. *Little Rock*, 237 U. S. 171. The circumstances of the case were very much like those of the case at bar and give reply to the contentions of petitioner, especially that which asserts that a necessary and lawful occupation that is not a nuisance *per se* cannot be made so by legislative declaration. There was a like investment in property, encouraged by the then conditions; a like reduction of value and deprivation of property was asserted against the validity of the ordinance there considered; a like assertion of an arbitrary exercise of the power of prohibition. Against all of these contentions, and causing the rejection of them all, was adduced the police power. There was a prohibition of a business, lawful in itself, there as here. It was a livery stable there; a brick yard here. They differ in particulars, but they are alike in that which cause and justify prohibition in defined localities—that is, the effect upon the health and comfort of the community.

The ordinance passed upon prohibited the conduct of the business within a certain defined area in Little Rock, Arkansas. This court said of it: granting that the business was not a nuisance *per se*, it was clearly within the police power of the State to regulate it, "and to that end to declare that in particular circumstances and in particular localities a livery stable shall be deemed a nuisance in fact and in law." And the only limitation upon the power was stated to be that the power could not be exerted arbitrarily or with unjust discrimination. There was a citation of cases. We think the present case is within the ruling thus declared.

There is a distinction between *Reinman* v. *Little Rock* and the case at bar. There a particular business was prohibited which was not affixed to or dependent upon its locality; it could be conducted elsewhere. Here, it is contended, the latter condition does not exist, and it is alleged that the manufacture of brick must necessarily be carried on where suitable clay is found and that the clay on petitioner's property cannot be transported to some other locality. This is not urged as a physical impossibility but only, counsel say, that such transportation and the transportation of the bricks to places where they could be used in construction work would be prohibitive "from a financial standpoint." But upon the evidence the Supreme Court considered the case, as we understand its opinion, from the standpoint of the offensive effects of the operation of a brick yard and not from the deprivation of the deposits of clay, and distinguished *Ex parte Kelso*, 147 California, 609, wherein the court declared invalid an ordinance absolutely prohibiting the maintenance or operation of a rock or stone quarry within a certain portion of the city and county of San Francisco. The court there said that the effect of the ordinance was "to absolutely deprive the owners of real property within such limits of a valuable right incident to their ownership,—viz., the right to extract therefrom such rock and stone as they might find it to their advantage to dispose of." The court expressed the view that the removal could be regulated but that "an absolute prohibition of such removal under the circumstances," could not be upheld.

In the present case there is no prohibition of the removal of the brick clay; only a prohibition within the designated locality of its manufacture into bricks. And to this feature of the ordinance our opinion is addressed. Whether other questions would arise if the ordinance were broader, and opinion on such questions, we reserve.

Petitioner invokes the equal protection clause of the Constitution and charges that it is violated in that the ordinance (1) "prohibits him from manufacturing brick upon his property while his competitors are permitted, without regulation of any kind, to manufacture brick upon property situated in all respects similarly to that of plaintiff in error"; and (2) that it "prohibits the conduct of his business while it permits the maintenance within the same district of any other kind of business, no matter how objectionable the same may be, either in its nature or in the manner in which it is conducted."

If we should grant that the first specification shows a violation of classification, that is, a distinction between businesses which was not within the legislative power, petitioner's contention encounters the objection that it depends upon an inquiry of fact which the record does not enable us to determine. It is alleged in the return to the petition that brickmaking is prohibited in one other district and an ordinance is referred to regulating business in other districts. To this plaintiff in error replied that the ordinance attempts to prohibit the operation of certain businesses having mechanical power and does not prohibit the maintenance of any business or the operation of any machine that is operated by animal power. In other words, petitioner makes his contention depend upon disputable considerations of classification and upon a comparison of conditions of which there is no means of judicial determination and upon which nevertheless we are expected to reverse legislative action exercised upon matters of which the city has control.

To a certain extent the latter comment may be applied to other contentions, and, besides, there is no allegation or proof of other objectionable businesses being permitted within the district, and a speculation of their establishment or conduct at some future time is too remote.

In his petition and argument something is made of the ordinance as fostering a monopoly and suppressing his competition with other brickmakers. The charge and argument are too illusive. It is part of the charge that the ordinance was directed against him. The charge, we have seen, was rejected by the Supreme Court, and we find nothing to justify it.

It may be that brick yards in other localities within the city where the same conditions exist are not regulated or prohibited, but it does not follow that they will not be. That petitioner's business was first in time to be prohibited does not make its prohibition unlawful. And it may be, as said by the Supreme Court of the State, that the conditions justify a distinction. However, the inquiries thus suggested are outside of our province.

There are other and subsidiary contentions which, we think, do not require discussion. They are disposed of by what we have said. It may be that something else than prohibition would have satisfied the conditions. Of this, however, we have no means of determining, and besides we cannot declare invalid the exertion of a power which the city undoubtedly has because of a charge that it does not exactly accommodate the conditions or that some other exercise would have been better or less harsh. We must accord good faith to the city in the absence of a clear showing to the contrary and an honest exercise of judgment upon the circumstances which induced its action.

We do not notice the contention that the ordinance is not within the city's charter powers nor that it is in violation of the state constitution, such contentions raising only local questions which must be deemed to have been decided adversely to petitioner by the Supreme Court of the State.

Judgment affirmed.

BORTZ COAL v. AIR POLLUTION COMMISSION, 2 E.R.C. 1744, Commonwealth Court of Pennsylvania No. 297 C.D. 1970, decided July 9, 1971

[Edited]

This is an appeal by the Bortz Coal Company, appellant, (Bortz) from an adjudication (Abatement Order) of the Air Pollution Commission, appellee, (Commission) dated December 1, 1970, in which the Commission affirmed an air pollution abatement order (dated August 22, 1969) of the Department of Health under the Air Pollution Control Act, Act of January 8, 1960, P. L. 2119, 35 P. S. 4001, et seq.

The abatement order, in pertinent part, provides:

"(1) that the Bortz Coal Company shall on and after Jan. 1, 1970, operate the beehive coke ovens at its Smithfield coke plant located in George's Township, Fayette County, in such a manner that the emissions from these operations do not exceed the limits set forth in Section 13 of Air Pollution Commission

(2) That the Bortz Coal Company shall on and after January 1, 1970, operate the coke pressure, conveyor belts, screens, truck hauling and dumping and open storage piles at its Smithfield coke plant located in George's Township, Fayette County, in such a manner that the air contaminants from these operations are not detectable beyond the plant's property line.

(3) That the Bortz Coal Company shall on or before November 1, 1969, submit to the Department of Health a plan setting forth the procedures to be used to comply with paragraphs (1) and (2) of this Order. The plan is to contain a detailed description of the methods or devices to be used to control the air pollution."

The Commission in its adjudication of December 1, 1970, affirmed the abatement order of the Department quoted above in all particulars but extended the dates in paragraph (1) to January 1, 1971, and in paragraph (2) to June 1, 1971, and in paragraph (3) to February 1, 1971.

It is this latter adjudication from which Bortz appeals to this Court.

The record, including the transcript of the hearing before the Commission, reveals that Bortz has owned and operated 70 beehive coke ovens at its Smithfield coke plant for about 50 years. The ovens were built in 1898. Apparently the first discussions between the State air pollution authorities and Bortz concerning alleged air pollution violations by Bortz occurred in 1963. In 1965, Bortz was ordered to file a plan for the control of particulate matter emissions from its ovens. Bortz complied and filed such a plan. In 1969, the problem was again discussed with Bortz by the Region V Air Pollution Control Association*. Subsequent to the discussion with the Association the Health Department issued the aba ment order.

Bortz raises five issues which will be discussed a ruled upon in the enumerated paragraphs of this opini

Because of the fact that for all practical purposes this case represents the first venture of an appellate court of this Commonwealth into what in all probabili will become a major development in the law, known generally as environmental law, we believe it would be beneficial to the bar and to the public, to the regu agencies and to the courts, to make several preparat comments.

Although one would be led to believe from the avalanche of recent publications on the subject of air pollution that it is something new, created by scientist and crusaded by modern youth, it should be pointed ou that the law has been concerned with air pollution for centuries. As early as 1306, A. D., the use of "sea-co (as distinguished from charcoal) as fuel was forbidden on penalty of death. City of Portland v. Lloyd A. Fry Roofing Company, 472 P.2d 826 (1970) and Air Pollutio Its Control and Abatement, Kennedy and Porter; 8 Van L. Rev. 854 (1954-55). During her reign, Queen Eliza beth of England forbade the burning of coal in London during sessions of Parliament, and in 1661 A. D., ther was a plan to remove all industries in the city of Lond to its leeward side and to plant sweet-smelling flowers and trees on the windward side. See Fumifugium Natio al Smoke Abatement Society, Manchester, England (1953). Blackstone (Book III, Chapter 13, pages 167 a 217) describes the legal problems of a lead smelter, t fumes from whose plant were a nuisance, killing the neighboring farmer's corn. See 77 Eng. Rep. 816 and Appeal of Pennsylvania Coal Company, 96 Pa. 116 (1880). *

The point in citing these proofs of prior concern is merely to remind the reader that the law always provided for the protection against private nuisances. Th has been formed a new public policy in this State, as well as other States of this Nation, that there is need for protection of the public against public nuisances.

That new policy is found in Section 2 of the Air Pollution Control Act, January 8, 1960, P. L. 2119, as amended, by the Act of June 12, 1968, P. L.____, No. 92, 35 P. S. 4002, which reads as follows:

"It is hereby declared to be the policy of the Comm wealth of Pennsylvania to protect the air resources of the Commonwealth to the degree necessary for th (i) protection of public health, safety and well-being of its citizens, (ii) prevention of injury to plant and animal life and to property; (iii) protection of the comfort and convenience of the public and the protection of the recreational resources of the Commo

*The Association is specifically provided for in section 6 of the Act (35 P. S. 4006) and is composed of citizens from the air pollution region with certain enumerated powers and duties.

*Even William Shakespeare, over 300 years ago, placed the following words in the mouth of Hamlet, prince of Denmark: "This most excellent canopy, the air, look you, this grave o'erhanging firmament... appeareth no other thing to me than a foul and pestulae congregation of vapors."

wealth; and (iv) development, attraction and expansion of industry, commerce, and agriculture."

In carrying out this public policy, the Legislature created the Air Pollution Commission (35 P. S. 4005), under the Department of Health. * The Commission was directed by the Legislature to establish rules, regulations and standards for the enforcement of the Act. There can be no doubt from a reading of the Act that the legislative intent is to clean the air insofar as is reasonably possible under the policy powers granted to the Commonwealth in both the State and Federal Constitutions.

It is well recognized as a principle of American jurisprudence that the Legislature may utilize the establishment of administrative agencies as a part of the legislative process in our tripartite system of government to regulate and control that segment of our society which the Legislature in its wisdom deems necessary of control. See Metro. Edison Co. v. P. S. C., 127 Pa. Super. 11, 191 A. 678 (1937).

The Legislature may not delegate its legislative function but it may authorize an agency to carry out the legislative intent described in general terms through rules, regulations and standards established by the agency. See Belovsky v. Philadelphia, 357 Pa. 329, 54 A. 2d 277 (1947). There are certain constitutional tests to determine whether or not the Legislature has gone too far in its delegation. For example, see Cott Beverage Corp. v. Horst, 380 Pa. 113, 110 A. 2d 405 (1955), Commonwealth v. Zasloff, 338 Pa. 457, 13 A. 2d 67 (1940), and Harris v. State Board of Optometrical Examiners, 287 Pa. 531, 135 A. 2d 237 (1926). The rules, regulations and standards of the regulatory agency must be reasonable, understandable, available, and must not violate the constitutional rights of any citizen.

Because of the well recognized problems involved in combining, in administrative agencies all three functions of a tripartite form of government, viz., legislative , executive and judicial, the agencies and the courts must take care in carrying out their primary function of protecting the public, that they be vigilant to make certain that the individual citizen's rights in property and due process are not violated. Because it is common for the employees of the adjudicating regulatory agency to assume the role of prosecutor, witness and judge of the quasi-judicial functions of the agency, the courts must scrutinize the proceedings, the attitude and approach of the regulatory agency to assure that four centuries of well developed standards of fairness, procedure and substantive law are not washed away with the intense shower of exuberance and well meaning desires. Some environmental lawyers believe that right to a decent environment may be within the penumbra of the unenumerated natural rights guaranteed by the Ninth Amendment of the United States Constitution. See Griswold v. Connecticut, 381 U. S. 479 (1965). Some lawyers believe that the protection of the environment comes within the public trust doctrine. See 68 Michigan L. Rev. 471 (1970). Only time will tell how far environmental control of the air will be developed, but no matter how it is developed, it must be done within the framework of the law.

We turn now to the five issues raised in this case.

1. The Air Pollution Control Act, supra, does not constitute an unlawful delegation of legislative authority to the Air Pollution Commission and the Department of Health.

The Pennsylvania Supreme Court has set down many times the guidelines for reviewing courts of this State to follow in cases where parties attempt to have a statute declared unconstitutional. In Loomis v. Philadelphia School District Board of Education, 376 Pa. 428, 431, 103 A. 2d 769, 770 (1954) the Court said:

> "Nothing but a clear violation of the Constitution will justify the judiciary in nullifying a legislative enactment. Every presumption must be indulged in its favor, and one who claims an Act is unconstitutional has a very heavy burden of proof..."

In the case of City of Philadelphia v. Depuy, 431 Pa. 276, 279, 241 A. 2d 741, 743 (1968) the Court said.

> "We start with the well established proposition that one seeking to show a statute unconstitutional must carry a very heavy burden. This doctrine was most recently reiterated in Commonwealth v. Life Assurance Company of Pennsylvania, 419 Pa. 370, 214 A. 2d 209 (1965)... Moreover, the taxpayer's burden will be deemed met only if the challenged statute 'clearly, palpably, and plainly violates the Constitution.' Daly v. Hemphill, 411 Pa. 263, 271, 191 A. 2d 835, 840 (1963)."

The appellant in this case has not met this heavy burden on any of the constitutional questions involved in this case.

With regard to the specific issue of an unlawful delegation of legislative power, we are referred to the case of Dauphin Deposit Trust Company v. Myers, 388 Pa. 444, 449, 130 A. 2d 686, 688 (1957) where the court said: "Where the standard fixed by the Legislature is not arbitrary or unlimited, but is definite and reasonable, the delegation of power or discretion will be sustained as constitutional. In considering the standard, regard must be had to the purpose and scope of the act, the subject matters covered therein, the duties prescribed, and the broad or narrow powers granted, because those factors will often determine whether or not a sufficiently clear, definite and reasonable standard has been established."

In the Dauphin Deposit Trust Company case, the Court held that the agency had exceeded the powers granted and reversed the action of the agency.

We hold that a careful reading of the Air Pollution Control Act, supra, indicates a sufficiently clear, definite and reasonable delegation of the powers to the Commission.

* As of January 19, 1971, these public authorities were combined in the new Department of Environmental Resources, Act of December 3, 1970, P. L. Act No. 275.

The statute, as amended, at 35 P. S. 4003(5) defines air pollution as:

> "(5) 'air pollution.' The presence in the outdoor atmosphere of any form of contaminant including but not limited to the discharging from stacks, chimneys, openings, buildings, structures, open fires, vehicles, processes, or any other source of any smoke, soot, fly ash, dust, cinders, dirt, noxious or obnoxious acids, fumes, oxides, gases, vapors, odors, toxic or radioactive substances, waste, or any other matter in such place, manner, or concentration inimical or which may be inimical to the public health, safety, or welfare or which is, or may be injurious to human, plant or animal life, or to property, or which unreasonably interferes with the comfortable enjoyment of life or property."

After setting forth what it was that the Legislature desired to be controlled by the above-quoted definition, the Legislature thereafter in Sections 4 and 5 of the Act (35 P. S. 4004 and 4005) set forth the powers and procedures under which the Department of Health and the Air Pollution Commission would carry out the legislative intent, including the establishment of rules and regulations as set forth in 35 P. S. 4005 (d) (2) and (7). This approach to governmental regulation is indeed the accepted and proper method for delegating authority to an administrative agency One of the discretionary determinations to be made by the Commission is the scientific or technical rules and regulations which determine that amount of the air pollution which should be prohibited in carrying out the legislative intent. If the regulatory agency sets forth unreasonable standards or fails to establish any standards of air pollution , the citizens are protected through the appeal provisions of the Act. Certainly the possibility of such an unreasonable determination should not be the basis for a holding that there has been an unlawful delegation of power. As stated before, we hold that there is not an unlawful delegation of powers in the Air Pollution Control Act.

2. The enforcement of the rules and regulations of the Air Pollution Commission does not constitute a confiscation of property without due process of law in violation of the Constitution of Pennsylvania (Article I. Section 10), or the Constitution of the United States (Fourteenth Amendment).

There is no doubt in this writer's mind after a review of the record in this case that operation of beehive coke ovens cannot practically or feasibly meet the minimum air pollution standards set in the rules and regulations of the Commission insofar as air pollution is concerned. Unless some unforeseen method for controlling the emission of particulate matter from these coke ovens is invented or developed, the beehive coke oven industry in this State will be forced out of business. In spite of the fact that this writer may believe that the disappearance of a large recognized industry in this State will be a socio-economic tragedy for thousands of citizens of this Commonwealth, this Court cannot pass upon the advisability of such an economic occurrence. That determination has been made by the Legislature, and this Court can do nothing but follow the mandates of that body.

Strangely enough, one of the cases cited by the appellant sets the stage for a discussion of this problem In White's Appeal, 287 Pa. 259, 265, 134 A. 409, 411 (1926), Mr. Justice Kephart says:

> "The power of judicial investigation does not concern itself with the wisdom of the policy emanating from the legislative branch, or whether the best of all possible means of achieving the desired result has been selected. It is concerned only with the questions of whether the statute has a recognized police purpose and whether it has a reasonable relation to the object to be attained.
>
> Generally, the right concerns, as here, property and rights issuing out of it. No matter how seemingly complete our scheme of private ownership may be under our system of government, all property is held in subordination to the right of its reasonable regulation by the government clearly necessary to preserve the health, safety or morals of the people. Obedience to such regulation is not taking property without due process; that clause does not qualify the police power: C. B. and Q. Ry. Company v. Drainage Commissioners, 200 U. S. 561; Salem v. Maynese, 123 Mass. 372; In ré Cherry, 201 AppDiv N. Y. 856, 193 N. Y. S. 57, affirmed 234 N. Y. 607, 138 N. E. 465. Property is held under the implied obligation that the owner shall use it in such way as not to be injurious to the community: Windsor v. Whitney, 95 Conn. 357, 111 A. 354."

Justice Kephart, in this well reasoned opinion, goes on to state how firm the property rights of the individuals are under our form of government, but throughout this opinion, he consistently states that one may use his property in any way he sees fit so long as that use harms no one.

The basic premise, then, is that coke oven operators in this State may use their property so long as they do no injury to other citizens of the Commonwealth in violation of the law. It matters not under the law that these coke ovens in question have been in continuous use since 1898. There is no prescriptive right to cause injury to another, and this basic premise has existed every day of the operation of these coke ovens. They were always subject to the prohibition. In the Air Pollution Act, supra, the Legislature has established that certain air pollution is injurious to the public health, welfare and safety, and, now, it need only be determined whether or not those technical standards which were set by the Commission are reasonable, so as not to violate Bortz's constitutional rights.

Bortz nowhere in this case challenges the technical level of air pollution as established by the Commssion as being violative of Bortz's rights. It has offered no testimony, evidence or argument that the standards set by the Commission were unreasonable except that those standards could not be met by Bortz in the operation of its coke ovens. Standards set by the Commission are applicable not only to Bortz, but to all citizens in e Commonwealth; and they are equally applicable to ery coke oven operator in this state.

3. Exclusion of governmental bodies from the nalties section of the Air Pollution Act, supra, does t constitute an unlawful discrimination and violation the Pennsylvania Constitution (Article III, Section) or of the United States Constitution (Fourteenth nendment).

As we have already pointed out, Bortz carries a avy burden of proof to establish the unconstitutionality this statute. Bortz argues that it is discriminated ainst because of the elimination of governmental bodies om the penalty section of the Act (35 P. S. 4009). This gument has no merit, because the Legislature rtainly had the power to determine that it would make sense to penalize the government itself. This does t mean that a governmental body could not be ordered a court to cease and desist emitting air pollution as termined by the Commission. Clearly, governmental dies could be so restricted by a court; but to even tempt to hold some governmental body of this Common-ealth to a fine or imprisonment makes no sense. ontempt proceedings for the failure of a governmental dy to abide by an order of court is adequate enforce-ent. Exclusions of Section 9 (35 P. S. 4009) are proper, d do not constitute an unlawful discrimination. See ir Pollution Commission. Coated Materials Company, Dauphin 274 (1970).

4. The evidence presented by the Commission was t sufficient to establish a violation of the Air Pollution ontrol Act, supra, or the rules and regulations of the ommission.

Under Section 5 (35 P.S. 4005) the Commission is iven the power and duty to hold hearings as follows:

> "Hear and determine all appeals from orders issued by the department in accordance with the provisions of this act. Any and all action by the Commission taken with reference to any such appeal shall be in the form of an adjudication, and all such action shall be subject to the provisions of the Administrative Agency Law, the act of June 4, 1945, (P. L. 1388), as amended, insofar as the rights of any person aggrieved are concerned. Any party aggrieved as defined in the act of June 4, 1945 (P. L. 1388), as amended, known as the 'Administrative Agency Law', by any adjudication of the Commission shall have the right to appeal such adjudication in the manner provided by and subject to the 'Administrative Agency Law'."

The Administrative Agency Law (71 P. S. 1710 et seq.) provides the procedural due process guarantees under which the rights of citizens are protected.

In view of the fact that the Department of Health is the moving party seeking to abate the emission of particulate matter by Bortz, the Commonwealth had the burden of proving that acts of Bortz were in violation of the Air Pollution Act. In order to meet that burden, the Commission had to prove that under the statute and its rules, regulations and standards, Bortz had violated the law necessitating the abatement order.

We have already pointed out that the delegation of power to the Commission to establish rules and regulations in keeping with the legislative intent was proper. We now must determine whether or not the rules and regulations which establish the standards are enforceable. The abatement order refers to violations of Section 1.3 of the Air Pollution Commission regulation IV, which reads as follows:

> "Section 1.3 Limits for Particulate Matter Emissions
> In the absence of a determination by the Commission imposing more stringent or less stringent limits, as provided for in Section 1.4 of this regulation, a local air pollution problem shall be deemed to exist:
> (1) If any person causes, suffers, allows or permits smoke from any combustion unit, the shade or appearance of which is darker than No. 2 of the Ringelmann Smoke Chart, to be emitted into the outdoor atmosphere.
> Exception: Smoke emitted during the cleaning of a firebox or the building of a new fire may be darker than No. 2 of the Ringelmann Smoke Chart for a period or periods aggregating not more than 6 minutes in any 60 consecutive minutes.
> (2) If any person causes, suffers, allows or permits particulate matter (including smoke) to be emitted into the outdoor atmosphere from any air contamination source such that the actual or calculated emission rate of particulate matter from such source (as determined in accordance with Section 1.5) may be expected to cause a ground level concentration at any point outside the person's property in excess of either 150 micrograms of suspended particulate matter per cubic meter of air or 0.6 milligrams of particle fall per square centimeter per month at any time.
> Whenever particulate matter from one air contamination source is discharged through two or more flues, the quantity that may be discharged from all of the flues shall not exceed the emission that would be permitted by assuming that all of the particulate matter is being emitted from a single flue having an effective height calculated in the following manner:
>
> > Multiply the effective height of each flue by the percentage of the total air contaminant emission rate emitted through the flue, add the products and divide the sum by 100.
>
> Whenever particulate matter from more than one air contamination source is discharged through less flues than the number of air contamination sources, the quantity that may be discharged from each flue shall not exceed the emission permitted by this Section 1.3(2) for each flue except under unusual conditions (see Section 1.4).
> (3) If any person causes, suffers, allows or permits fugitive dust to be emitted into the outdoor atmosphere from any air contamination source or sources in such a manner that the ground level concentration of fugitive dust (as determined in accordance with Section 1.5) from the air contamination source or sources at any point outside the person's property exceeds a concentration of 2.0 miligrams per cubic meter of air above background concentration, for any 10 minute period.

Whenever a local air pollution problem is deemed to exist, the Department may, in accordance with the procedures provided in the Air Pollution Control Act, issue an order directing the person or persons charged with causing, suffering, allowing or permitting such air pollution problem to control, abate or prevent such air pollution problem."

Besides the test of whether or not the restrictions stated in the standards of Section 1.3 are reasonable (which issue has not been raised by Bortz), we must determine if Section 1.3 gives a reasonable notice to the citizens of the Commonwealth of what is expected of them insofar as meeting the minimum standards is concerned. We hold that the above quoted regulations of Section 1.3 are reasonably understandable and adequately specific and therefore legally sufficient.

We next turn to the record in this case to determine whether or not the Commission presented sufficient evidence to support the regulatory action it desired to take. In this regard, we refer to the Administrative Agency Law, supra, 71P. S. 1710. 44, which states:

"The court to which the appeal is taken shall hear the appeal without a jury on the record certified by the agency. After hearing, the court shall affirm the adjudication unless it shall find that the same is in violation of the constitutional rights of the appellant, or is not in accordance with law, or that the provisions of sections 31 to 35 inclusive of this act have been violated in the proceeding before the agency, or that any finding of fact made by the agency and necessary to support its adjudication is not supported by substantial evidence. If the adjudication is not affirmed, the court may set aside or modify it, in whole or in part, or may remand the proceeding to the agency for further disposition in accordance with the order of the court."

The pertinent portion of this section is whether or not the finding of fact by the Commission is supported by "substantial evidence". "Substantial evidence" is such relevant evidence as a reasonable mind might accept as adequate to support a conclusion, and more is required than a mere scintilla of evidence or suspicion of the existence of a fact to be established. See Pennsylvania State Board of Medical Examiners v. Schireson, 360 Pa. 129, 61 A. 2d 343 (1948); Erie Resistor Corporation v. Unemployment Compensation Board, 194 Pa. Super 278, 166 A. 2d 96 (1960).

In this case the Commonwealth presented the testimony of four witnesses. One was an official of the Commission who verified procedural records to the date of the hearing. Two housewives testified concerning dirt and soot in or about their homes caused by the coke ovens of Bortz. The fourth witness, who was the chief witness of the Commission, was an air pollution control engineer employed by the Department of Health in Region V where Bortz's coke ovens are situated. This engineering witness testified, in addition to his qualifications, to a visit to the scene of Bortz's coke ovens, to his taking photographs (which were not made part of the record) indicating smoke plumes and soot deposits and to his observations concerning the emission of smoke from the operation of Bortz's coke ovens. This witness described smoke blowing across the roadway towards some houses. He then testified that, based upon some literature, which was never identified, he was able to determine that 25 per cent of the coal charge to the beehive ovens was lost in the form of smoke and particulate, and that based upon the tons of coke pulled from the ovens four days a week, he was able to estimate that each coke oven in Bortz's operation emitted more than 45 pounds of particulate matter per hour for each oven. From his observations he testified that the smoke emissions were in excess of the permissible allowance of smoke as established by the Commission's regulation utilizing the Ringelmann Smoke Chart. He used none of the available instruments for testing smoke emissions or falling particulate matter.

The problem arises in that this witness, though admittedly an expert, for the purposes of this record, did not make any stack tests, nor did he utilize any of the available instrumentation to measure the amount of falling particulate, emitting particulate, or smoke density.

If we are to permit employees of the Commission to determine that smoke and particulate matter emissions are in violation of the Commission's regulations based solely upon visual observations, then there is really no need to have standards and regulations at all. The standard is not what this witness or any single employee of the regulatory agency might deem to be a violation of what the Legislature intended. What is relevant is proof that the standards set forth by the regulatory agency have been met or violated in accordance with those specific standards. Visual tests and observations are not adequate evidence of a violation where recognized scientific tests are available. As was pointed out in the oral argument of this case, this Commonwealth in a Motor Vehicle Code violation case would not permit a qualified expert state policeman with 25 years' experience observing speeding automobiles on the Turnpike to testify to the speed of an automobile without the use of available instruments, such as radar and a tested speedometer. This Court cannot close its eyes to the necessity of a regulatory agency proving its case. Somehow, regulatory agencies such as the Air Pollution Commission and its employees take the attitude that because they represent the government, there is no need for them to prove facts, except as established by the estimates and observations of their experts. Merely because the Commonwealth employs experts in the various fields of regulation does not necessarily mean that the Commonwealth need not prove its case. In the event it should occur in a case that there is no scientific measurement instrument, or no method for determining a violation, then, as in all adjudicated matters in this Commonwealth, violations will have to be determined upon the weight of the evidence produced. However, where there is an available, established method for determining violations, those methods must be used.

The Legislature certainly intended this approach to gulation. Why else would they provide for access to citizen's property and specifically authorize tests as t forth in the Act at 35 P. S. 4004?

The Commonwealth here, in effect, is ordering the utdown of Bortz's coke ovens. This is no small atter. To permit the Commission to order an abate-ent based solely upon the visual tests and observations one employee strikes at the heart of fairness envi-oned in every judicial process known to our system of risprudence.

If the engineering witness' testimony can be verified established tests, then there is no doubt that the ommission can accomplish its purpose in this matter. e will remand this case back to the Commission for e purpose of having the Commission properly estab-sh substantial evidence to prove the violation alleged this case. If the Commission cannot establish that ortz has violated the minimum standards set forth in ection 1.3 of its regulation IV through available tests, en it should establish other sufficient and credible vidence, or the abatement order must be dismissed. here is no way for this Court to determine from the resent state of this record whether or not the particu-ate matter was in excess of 150 micrograms of sus-ended particulate matter per cubic meter of air, or n excess of 0.6 milligrams of particle fall per square entimeter per month.

This Court is not unfamiliar with the Ringelmann Smoke Chart, and therefore the Court is puzzled why such an inexpensive method of testing was not used in his case. In the case of City of Portland v. Lloyd A. Fry Roofing Company, 472 P. 2d 826, 827 (1970), the ourt gave a description of a Ringelmann Chart as follows:

> "It is a plain white piece of paper divided into four sections, numbered from one to four, and each about five and three quarters x seven and three quarters inches in size. On each of these sections is printed a series of intersecting heavy black lines of uniform width for each section, with the lines growing progressively wider from section one to to section four, until on section four the black covers much more than half of the surface.
> This chart refers to Bureau of Mines Information Circular No. 6888, a copy of which is also in the record. From the chart and this circular, it appears that the chart is to be posted at a distance of 50 feet from the observer. When so posted the black lines and the white spaces merge into each other by a process of optical illusion, so as to present the appearance of a series of gray rectan - gles of different color densities, number 4 being the densest. Estimate of the density of smoke may be made by glancing from this chart so displayed to smoke, and picking out the section on the chart which most nearly resembles the smoke. This mode of measuring the density of smoke has been in use, it appears, for over fifty years. This affords a reason-ably certain mode of determining and stating the density and opacity of smoke, and we think that the statute adopting it is not lacking in certainty."

From this description, we are at a loss to understand why an engineer employed by this Commonwealth would not be equipped with a piece of paper such as described by the California Court. A citizen whose business is about to be destroyed by an abatement order is certain-ly entitled to that much consideration (the use of the test instrument) in the establishment of his alleged violation.

5. The refusal of the hearing examiner to permit testimony on the economic factors involved in this case was error.

As is clearly shown in the order of the Air Pollution Commission from which this appeal arose, there is power in the Commission to set time limits within which compliance with the Commission's orders may be set. It is conceivable that economic factors could very well persuade the Commission to set a deadline at some time different than it would otherwise set it without such information. In view of the fact that one of the declared policies of the Commonwealth, as noted above (35 P. S. 4002), is to protect the air resources of the Common-wealth to the degree necessary for the protection of the citizen's "well-being", "property" and the "expansion of industry", it is conceivable that economic factors could be very relevant to the Commission for it to properly carry out the Legislative intent. This is not to say that the Commission must give weight to the economic factor evidence. We do say, however, that without such evidence, if it has been offered, the Com-mission cannot fully carry out the legislative intent.

SUMMARY

As has already been pointed out, the Administrative Agency Law, supra, at Section 44, authorizes this Court within the scope of its jurisdiction to remand these proceedings back to the agency for further dispo-sition in accordance with this opinion. We therefore

ORDER

AND NOW, this 9th day of July, 1971, it is hereby ordered that this matter be remanded to the Air Pollu-tion Commission for the purpose of establishing sub-stantial evidence of the alleged air pollution violation of appellant and to receive evidence in accordance with this opinion.

Harry A. Kramer, Judge

Judge Manderino concurs in result only.

NEW JERSEY v. MUNDET CORK CORP., 8 N.J. 359, 86 A.2d 1 (1952)

[Edited]

BURLING, J.

This is an appeal by the Mundet Cork Corporation, a New Jersey corporation, defendant, from a judgment of conviction entered against it in the Union County Court upon a complaint charging it with violation of an air pollutant ordinance of the plaintiff, the Township of Hillside, a municipal corporation of this State. The appeal was addressed to the Superior Court, Appellate Division; prior to hearing there certification of the Appeal to this court was granted on our own motion.

The defendant processes raw cork in the manufacture of cork board insulation, cork gaskets and similar products, a business which it has been conducting at its plant in Hillside since 1918. About 60 per cent of the output of the plant consists of products made from cork board which is the end result of a steam baking process. This process is described as one wherein quantities of ground cork are placed in metal containers or moulds, baking chambers, then compressed and subjected to contact with superheated steam, which, as it passes through the cork, causes the particles to become fused or sealed together. The steam is then drawn off through a water wash and passed into the air outside the plant through a gooseneck stack.

On August 28, 1929, the township committee of the plaintiff passed an ordinance entitled "An Ordinance Regulating the Emission of Smoke from Chimneys of Buildings (Boilers, Engines, etc.) within the Township of Hillside," which prohibited "the emission of dense smoke from any smokestack or chimney connected with any stationary engine, steam boiler, locomotive * * * or other similar machine, or from any smokestack or chimney of any * * * establishment, or private residence using oil burners, or any building used as a factory, or for any purpose of trade, or from any tar kettle, or other machine, furnace or contrivance within the corporate limits of the Township of Hillside, which smoke contains soot or other substance in sufficient quantities to permit the deposit of such soot or other substance on any surface within the limits of said Township." An ordinance adopted on July 22, 1931, amended sections 1 and 2 of the ordinance. The pertinent section 1(b) of the amended ordinance contains the following language: "(b) the production or emission within the Township of Hillside of smoke, fly ash or fumes, the density or shade of which is equal to or greater than No. 2 of the Ringelmann Smoke Chart, as published by the United States Bureau of Mines, or which is so dense as to be dimly seen through at the point of emission into the external air from any stack or open fire, except that of a locomotive for a period or for periods aggregating twelve minutes or more in any period of one hour, * * * is hereby prohibited." (Emphasis supplied.)

Section 2 of the amended ordinance contains the following pertinent language: "* * * any owner of any locomotive engine, steam roller, steam derrick or tar kettle, or other machine, furnace or contrivance within the limits of the Township of Hillside who permits or allows to be emitted from any such chimney or smokestack, locomotive, engine, steam roller, steam derrick, tar kettle or other machine, furnace or contrivance, or private residence using oil burners, smoke, fly ash or fumes in violation of Section 1 of this ordinance shall, upon receipt of notice in writing duly served upon him or them by the Smoke Inspector, without delay, file a plan or statement of proposed alterations to remedy the cause of such violation, and shall, within thirty days after the receipt of such notice, entirely eliminate said smoke, fly ash or fumes, as violate this ordinance, and upon conviction thereof in a court of competent jurisdiction, be fined not more than One Hundred Dollars ($100.00) * * *."

The defendant was charged with a violation of section 1 (b) and non-compliance with section 2 of the foregoing ordinance (as amended) by complaint in writing dated August 31, 1950. Judgment of conviction was entered against it in the Municipal Court of the Township of Hillside on October 7, 1950. The defendant appealed to the Union County Court. The appeal resulted in a trial of novo to the Union County Court, Law Division, without a jury; the judgment of conviction of the defendant by the court was filed on June 14, 1951 and the defendant appealed.

The appeal presents several questions, including construction of the ordinance aforementioned, proof of violation thereof, and constitutional rights of the defendant.

We consider first the question of construction of the ordinance. The premise of the defendant is that the ordinance is ambiguous and must be construed to exclude the vaporous emanation, exhaust steam from the cork baking process, expelled into the atmosphere from defendant's stack. This question must be resolved against the defendant.

The emphasis in this type of ordinance for centuries has been placed on smoke regulation. (In response to a petition by the citizens of London, a royal proclamation was issued by Edward I of England in 1306 to prohibit artificers from using sea coal as distinguished from charcoal, in their furnaces, and making the use of sea coal a capital offense. See Prentice on Police Powers, p. 35 (1894).) In more recent generations other air pollutants have been subjected to control. See Regulation of Smoke and Air Pollution in Pennsylvania, 10 U. Pitt. L. Rev. 493 (1948-1949). Ordinances designed to regulate and control air pollution in the interest of the public health and welfare have been held valid and enforceable in this State. With this general background in mind we turn to examination of the meaning of the ordinance now before us. The defendant relies upon four rules of construction: that judicial construction of ordinances is governed by the same rules as judicial construction of statutes; that where an ordinance is ambiguous reference may be had to its title to determine the legislative intent of the enacting body; that penal ordinances are to be strictly construed; and that the doctrine of ejusdem generis is pertinent and if applied would confine the meaning of the terms used in the amended ordinance ("smoke, fly ash, or fumes") to emissions caused by combustion. We are of the opinion that the foregoing terms of the ordinance in question are not ambiguous and therefore the rules of construction adverted to by the defendant are not appropriate. A penal ordinance or statute is to be strictly construed and will not be held to create a liability when the words of the enactment are not clear in fixing it, but where there is no ambiguity it is settled that there is no need to resort to this rule of construction. The doctrine of ejusdem generis, that a word is known from its associates, is an aid to construction where the expression is of doubtful meaning. Likewise, generality of language, or the natural import of the words employed according to their common sense, clearly and unambiguously expressed in the enacting clause of a statute or ordinance will not be restrained or narrowed by a particular reference in the title or preamble.

Smoke was the subject regulated by the ordinance adopted in 1929, but air may be polluted by the presence of varied foreign matter such as fluorine, fly ash, sulphur dioxide, and fumes. Compare 10 U. Pitt. L Rev., supra, at p. 494. The word "fume" in common parlance is defined inter alia as a noun to be "a smoky or vaporous exhalation, usually odorous", and as a verb to mean "to throw off fumes, as in combustion or chemical action; to rise up, as vapor," and also "to pass or move in fumes or vapors" and "throw off in vapor, or as in the form of vapor." Webster's New International Dictionary (2nd ed. 1947) p.1018. Noxious fumes, gases or vapors have long been considered in the category of public nuisances. See Blackstone's Commentaries (Browne's ed. 1897), pp. 432, 641; 39 Am. Jur., Nuisances, secs. 58, 59, pp. 340, 341. If we were to deprive the word "fumes" as used in the amended ordinance of its natural import, we would render impotent the clearly and unambiguously expressed intention of the legislative body. Limitation of the meaning of "fumes" as used in the ordinance to products of combustion would render its inclusion meaningless for the word "smoke" includes visible products of combustion in the normally accepted sense. The references in the ordinance to sources of smoke, fly ash or fumes, including "engine, steam roller, steam derrick or tar kettle or other machine, furnace or contrivance," clearly are all inclusive and not restricted to apparatus used for combustion. We hold that a vaporous exhalation containing contaminants is a "fume" within the meaning of the word "fumes" as used in the ordinance in question.

It is next urged by the defendant that the judgment is against the weight of the evidence in that the proofs do not establish beyond a reasonable doubt a violation of the ordinance by the defendant. This contention is not supported by the record. One of the Township's witnesses testified that on the day when the alleged violation of the ordinance occurred they "observed heavy fumes, vapors fumes coming out of the gooseneck stack" of the defendant's plant "the full depth of the 18-inch stack for about 50 feet high spread over the neighborhood," so dense that "you could not see through it," and it continued for about 30 minutes. another of the township's witnesses, while corroborating the foregoing testimony, also testified that the emission was a "gaseous smoke substance" with an irritating, obnoxious odor, that it could be "barely seen through" for 30 to 50 feet from the point of emission from the stack, that it had a brownish cast the appearence of "adulterated steam." This witness also testified that the emission from the stack "has a residue that comes forth from the stack in the steam, and when the steam evaporates into the air, the residue which is heavier than air, settles to the ground and settles on the homes in the vicinity, and along with it is a pungent odor that is prevalent at that time when the plant is in operation" and is noticeable at a considerable distance from the defendant's plant. It was also testified that the defendant was notified of the alleged violation and that the defendant filed no plan or statement of proposed alterations to remedy the cause thereof, as required by the ordinance, and failed to comply with the requirement of the ordinance that the condition constituting the violation be eliminated within 30 days after notice.

The defendant's witnesses admitted that the exhaust steam or substance emanating from the gooseneck stack has a "characteristic" odor, which is rather strong and is such as made by burning leaves or wood but claimed it is not irritating. The defendant's witnesses also testified that the odor clings to the clothing; that it is detectable at times as one approaches the plant. They further testified that there are natural rosins in the cork and that the odor comes from those rosins; that the rosins leave the baking mould with the steam; that some of the rosins are solids but the solids are eliminated by a water wash; that the steam as it leaves the stack contains volatiles described as rosin contaminates or chemicals that are dropped out as it condenses and these volatiles may be acid distillates. It was also admitted that a gaseous substance is contained in the exhaust steam, and a gas can be a fume; that there is a percentage of both solid material and volatile substances discharged with the steam into the atmosphere.

The defendant's witnesses gave testimony that the exhaust has the appearance of pure white steam but is not pure steam. They testified that it contains contaminates resulting from the cork baking process. The defendant's plant manager testified that nothing had been done to change the conditions, although there was considerable testimony as to experimentation in that direction.

The township, on rebuttal, introduced the testimony of residents of the neighborhood of the defendant's plant, to the effect that the odor "smells like cork" and caused coughing; that the smoky emission from defendant's gooseneck stack could not be seen through; that it creates a "cloud bank" making driving difficult and that it is "stifling"; that the aroma clings to anything exposed to the substance.

To summarize, there is no support for the defendant's contention that the judgment was against the weight of the evidence. The proof are beyond a reasonable doubt that there was on the day in question emission from defendant's contrivance of fumes so dense as to be dimly seen through at the point of emission into the external air for periods aggregating 12 minutes or more in any period of one hour; that the defendant failed to file a statement or plan of proposed alterations to remedy the condition and failed to eliminate the condition within 30 days after notice as provided in the ordinance.

The defendant contends, however, that in order to support a conviction under an ordinance such as the one under consideration, the township must prove that the defendant's conduct constituted a common law nuisance, and that there exists in the record no proof that any person had been injuriously affected by the vaporous emanation from its plant. This appears to be an argument that regardless of density of the emission no conviction may be had unless injury is proved.

A statute or ordinance of this nature constitutes a legislative declaration that certain conditions or circumstances causing air pollution are deemed a public nuisance and are prohibited for the reason that they constitute a hazard to the public welfare. Enactment of a regulatory ordinance of this type is a function of the police power conferred on municipalities by R. S. 40: 48–2, N. J. S. A. (originally enacted in 1917) for the protection of the welfare of their residents. It is exercised for prevention of threatened injury and not solely for punishment of accomplished harm. The exercise of the legislative judgment is not subject to judicial superintendence unless it is plainly beyond the realm of the police power or palpably unreasonable. In determining the question of reasonableness cognizance must be taken of the problem to be solved by the municipality, for example the requirement necessary to minimize the offensive character of the conduct to be regulated. The testimony, which has been adverted to above, showed that persons had been stifled and annoyed by the fumes from the defendant's stack and that driving on the public streets was at times made dangerous thereby. These are elements of injury, and except for erroneous exclusion of proffered evidence at the trial it appears that other comparable evidence of injury would have been introduced. Further, actual injury to health or property is not necessary to the proof of conviction of violation of the ordinance, since whether persons or property are or may be injured by the continued exercise of the prohibited conduct or industrial operations is relative to the question of reasonableness of the ordinance and not to the question of fact as to what constitutes violation thereof. The burden of proof is upon those who attack the ordinance to show clearly that it is unreasonable.

The ordinance here in question is a reasonable exercise of legislative authority.

The final question to be disposed of is the asserted defense of the doctrine of "unavoidable necessity." The effect of such assertion runs to the reasonableness of the ordinance. Regardless of the philosophy of the doctrine, the facts do not support the application thereof.

The pertinent evidence is as follows: Bruns, vice-president and director of the defendant, testified that the defendant had been conducting experiments in the control of steam, including washing, ozonization, chlorination, electrical precipitation and secondary combustion, and that the defendant was working on and and installing a carbon eliminator, which it hoped would be successful, but which it had not disclosed in detail because the process was believed patentable. Magrum, a vice-president of defendant in charge of manufacturing and engineering at the Hillside plant, testified that additional equipment had been ordered by the defendant and the problem was well on the way to solution, although delivery of the equipment might suffer delay due to the national emergency. Magrum testified that it was possible through the use of a mere condensation device to eliminate the emission of steam into the atmosphere, that such a method had not been employed because "it becomes a mechanical problem" to take out the necessary amount of heat, that it is a matter of expense and space, but the matter of expense would not be insuperable. He testified that no mechanical process could be introduced to absorb the steam coming from a stack of the diameter used by the defendant. Magrum further testified that use of absorbent oils proved "quite promising" in experimental work but had not been used in actual operation although use of such oils might be a feasible solution to the condition. He admitted that it would be feasible to eliminate the fumes and that the conditions were susceptible to exclusion; that laboratory tests had the "appearance" of success. Simeral, who largely related his testimony to plants of other companies with different equipment and at different locations, was offered as an expert witness and testified that there is no way of eliminating all odors emanating from baking cork. He testified that at a Camden, N. J. plant there is no exhaust steam emitted into the atmosphere "because we condense the steam immediately after it leaves the moulds." However, he also testified that at the Camden plant an unlimited supply of Delaware River water was available for use in the condensation equipment. Schwartz, an expert not familiar with the details of operation of the defendant's plant testified that there is no "scientifically effective and economically feasible" method for "entirely eliminating all steam and odor bi-products of the cork baking process" (emphasis supplied), but we noted that entire elimination of all steam and odor is not required by the ordinance, which prohibits fumes of designated densities.

Analysis of the foregoing testimony, introduced by defendant to prove unavoidable necessity, shows that experimentation in various methods of elimination of the exhaust vapor condition at defendant's plant have been conducted; that some of these experiments show success but have not been applied; that a condensation device could be used but has not been used because "it is a mechanical problem," although the expense is not insuperable; and that a condensation method is in successful use elsewhere in a locality where river water is available for the type of condensation apparatus involved. There was no evidence introduced to show that compliance with the provisions of the ordinance by reduction of density of the emission, as opposed to complete elimination thereof, had been attempted or was not possible.

It is to be noted that the ordinance affords the defendant an opportunity to present a plan to remedy the cause of the violation, and contemplates the withholding of enforcement within a limited time pending the performance of a plan designed for compliance therewith.

The defendant finally contends that its motion to dismiss made at the close of the township's case should have been granted. The motion was addressed to the trial court on the sole ground that the ordinance applied only to smoke and there was no proof of emission of products of combustion. This motion was properly denied. We have discussed the construction of the ordinance ante, and our conclusions in that respect govern our determination as to the motion.

We find no merit in the remaining questions presented.

For the reasons stated, the judgment of the Union County Court is affirmed.

BOARD OF HEALTH OF WEEHAWKEN TOWNSHIP v. NEW YORK CENTRAL RAILROAD, and NEW YORK CENTRAL RAILROAD v. COONS, 72 A2d 511, No. A-95 Supreme Ct. of New Jersey, March 27, 1950.

Heher, J.:

The defendants New York Central Railroad Company and Coons appealed to the Appellate Division of the Superior Court from judgments of conviction entered in the Municipal Court of Weehawken upon complaints severally charging them with permitting or causing the emission of smoke from Central's power plant on Pershing Road, Weehawken, on October 8, 1949, between 8:30 p. m. and 9:30 p. m., "of a density greater than the density described as No. 2 on the Ringelmann Chart published by the United States Bureau of Mines," in contravention of an ordinance of the local Board of Health which embodied at length the standards of that bureau. Coons was Central's stationary engineer at the plant. The Appellate Division ordered the consolidation of the appeals for argument. Thereafter, we certified the appeals here on our own motion; and since there was uncertainty at the bar as to the right of appeal in cases of this class directly to the Appellate Division until the later determination of this Court in State v. Yaccarino, 3N. J. 291, 70 A. 2d 84 (1949), and the issues raised are of public concern, we granted defendants' motion on the oral argument for certification of the causes for appeal to the Municipal Court. Constitution of 1947, Article VI, section V, paragraph 1(d), N. J. S. A.; Rule 1:2-1 of this Court.

Section 2 of the ordinance denounces as a public nuisance the emission within the municipality of smoke of the proscribed density; and the insistence is that under Pennsylvania Railroad Co. v. Jersey City, 84 N. J. L. 761, 87 A. 467 (E. &A. 1913), such a direction against a railroad company is ultra vires and void. The ratio decidendi of these cases is that the non-negligent emission of smoke from the smokestacks of locomotives used in the operation of a railroad is an irremediable incident of the exercise of the legislative franchise, and not within local control except as expressly provided. But it is said that the principle is by analogy applicable to a railroad power plant as a necessary operating facility. We do not perceive the analogy.

Quite different considerations govern the use of locomotives in the operation of a railroad through the State and the management of a local power plant such as we have here. It is beyond the local province to proscribe smoke in the operation of locomotives under a railroad charter, unless its escape be attributable to negligence or want of care. There cannot be in the nature of things a delegation of regulative power which in its varying local applications would render function under the State's charter impracticable. State v. Erie Railroad Co., 84 N. J. L. 661, 87 A. 141, 46 L. R. A., N. S., 117 (E. &A. 1913). The principle has no bearing upon the functioning of terminal facilities and fixed installations, such as engine houses and repair shops. Beseman v. Pennsylvania Railroad Co., 50 N. J. L. 235, 13 A. 164 (Sup. Ct. 1888), affirmed 52 N. J. L. 221, 20 A. 169 (E. &A. 1889); Ridge v. Pennsylvania Railroad Co., 58 N. J. Eq. 172, 43 A. 275 (Ch. 1899); Baltimore & Potomac R. R. Co. v. Fifth Baptist Church, 108 U. S. 317, 2 S. Ct. 719, 27 L. Ed. 739 (1883).

The ordinance here does not offend against the cited principle. It is designed to "regulate and control air pollution," in the interest of "the public health and welfare," by barring the "excessive emission of dense smoke" within the confines of the Township. "Dense smoke," within the intendment of the regulation, is that which has "a density of No. 2 or greater as established by the Ringelmann Chart" therein incorporated. This proscription is indubitably within the competency of the local boards of health. The function of these agencies is to advance and secure the public health by means and measures reasonably appropriate to that end. The preservation of the public health is a vital element of the police power inherent in sovereignty.

The power thus exercised is within the grant contained in R. S. 26:3-64, N. J. S. A., and ch. 177 of the Session Laws of 1947, to be found also in N. J. S. A. 26:1A-9, N. J. S. A. The inherent general authority to conserve and protect the public health thereby conferred and recognized is not curtailed by the specific enumeration of R. S. 26:3-31, N. J. S. A. Atlantic City v. Abbott, 73 N. J. L. 281, 62 A. 999 (Sup. Ct. 1906); Schwarz Bros. Co. v. Board of Health, 83 N. J. L. 81, 83 A. 762 (Sup. Ct. 1912), affirmed on this point 84 N. J. L. 735, 87 A. 148 (E. &A. 1913); Fenton v. Atlantic City, 90 N. J. L. 403, 103 A. 695 (Sup. Ct. 1917); Kurinsky v. Board of Health of Lakewood Township, 128 N. J. L. 185, 24 A. 2d 803 (Sup. Ct. 1942); Potter v. Weleck, 131 N. J. L. 155, 35 A. 2d 627 (Sup. Ct. 1944). The cited act of 1947 is affirmative legislative acquiescence in the judicial finding of the general power in the preexisting statutes.

And there can be no doubt that the regulation under review has a substantial relation to the public health. Dense smoke, a carrier as it is of dust, soot and cinders, contaminates and pollutes the atmosphere and deteriorates its normal healthful attributes and qualities, and therefore cannot but be harmful to the public health, especially in populous areas. This is a matter of common experience, so much so that it is properly a subject of judicial notice. City of Rochester v. Macauley-Fien Milling Co., 199 N. Y. 207, 92N. E. 641, 32 L. R. A., N. S. 554 (1910); Bowers v. City of Indianapolis, 169 Ind. 105, 81 N. E. 1097, 13 Ann. Cas. 1198 (1907). In Garrett v. State, 49 N. J. L. 94, 693, 7 A. 29, 33, 60 Am. Rep. 592 (Sup. Ct. 1886), it was indicated that the corruption of the air by noisome odors and smells, to the annoyance and inconvenience of the public, would constitute a public nuisance suppressible by the local board of health. It was said that the local boards of health were created "to prevent nuisances in conservation of the public health", and "to prevent disease and discomfort, such as might arise from contamination of air, water, or food." See also, Nicoulin v. Lowery, 49 N. J. L. 391, 8 A. 513 (Sup. Ct. 1887). At common law, an action of nuisance will lie for substantial discomfort or inconvenience. But the inconvenience must be more than fanciful; it is not actionable unless it is one "materially interfering with the ordinary comfort physically of human existence, not merely according to elegant or dainty modes and habits of living, but according to plain and sober and simple notions among the English People." Walter v. Selfe, (1851) 4 DeG. &Sm. 322. The common law judges by no Spartan standards. The loss of even one night's sleep is not deemed a trivial matter. Andreae v. Selfridge (1937) 3 A. E. R. 261; Salmond on the law of Torts (10th Ed. 1945) 224. Of course, the standard of convenience and comfort varies according to local conditions and needs. It suffices to say as to this that the conditions constituting a nuisance at a given time and place may not be a nuisance at another time and place. And it may be added that the complexities of our modern society due in large part to congestion of population and concentration of industry and business impose an ever increasing demand for individual consessions to the common good. There are no constitutional restraints upon state action against the emission of dense smoke injurious to the common welfare; the only requirement is that the regulation be free from arbitrariness. Northwestern Laundry v. DeMoines, 239 U. S. 486, 36 S. Ct. 206 L. Ed. 396 (1916).

It is also urged that if R. S. 26:3-64, N. J. S. A., be deemed a grant of the power here exercised, it is violative of article IV, section I, paragraph 1 of the State Constitution of 1947, for failure to prescribe "standards to guide the administrative agencies in the exercise of the powers delegated" –citing State by Van Riper v. traffic Telephone Workers' Federation of N. J., 2 N. J. 335, 353, 66 A. 2d 616 (1949).

The local boards of health in the exertion of the authority thus conferred exercise, not an administrative function, but rather a portion of the police power to serve the public health. They are "governmental agencies by which the police law of the state is locally exerted." Fredericks v. Board of Health, 82 N. J. L. 200, 82 A. 528, 529 (Sup. Ct. 1912). See, also, Bradshaw v. City Council of Camden, 39 N. J. L. 416 (Sup. Ct. 1877); State Board of Health of Jersey City v. Schwarz Bros. Co., 84 N. J. L. 500, 87 A. 147 (Sup. Ct. 1913), affirmed sub-nom. Schwarz Bros. Co. v. State Board of Health, Id., 735, 87 A. 463 (E. &A. 1913). There is a delegation to these agencies of the "lawmaking function * * * as an admitted exception to the general doctrine of constitu-

al legislation". Bohan v. Weehawken, 65 N. J. L. 490, A. 446, 447 (Sup. Ct. 1900). See also, Fenton v. Atlan- City, supra, 90 N. J. L. 403, 103 A. 695. Borden's ndensed Milk Co. v. Board of Health, 81 N. J. L. 218, 30 (Sup. Ct. 1911); Courter v. Newark, 54 N. J. L. 325, A. 949 (Sup. Ct. 1892); Earruso v. Board of Health, N. J. L. 463, 200 A. 755 (Sup. Ct. 1938).

d, by the same reasoning it would seem that in this gard there is no merit in the contention that R. S. 26: 5, N. J. S. A., contravenes Article III of the Consti- ion of 1947, providing for a division of the powers of vernment. It is said that the power to declare and ine nuisances is in essence judicial, and that such laration as to the "emission of dense smoke, even ten seconds, in anticipation of the event," constitutes invasion of the judicial province. But there is no need consider the section in its entirety. It suffices to y that the authority exercised here is legislative in ality. As to this, see State, Marshall, Pros. v. eet Commissioners of Trenton, 36 N. J. L. 283 ıp. Ct. 1873).

he reasonableness of the regulation is not open to estion. It does not proscribe all smoke, no matter at the conditions, but merely smoke of a density and deleterious to the public health. Indeed, it is ged that the enforcement of the regulation against fendants was arbitrary and unreasonable because e smoke was the result of the temporary use of gh volatile coal made unavoidable by a miners' strike work stoppage at the time which "prevented shipment freshly mined, medium volatile coal to Weehawken." ıt unavoidable necessity was not established by the oofs.

t is said, also that the exemption of one- and two-fam- y residences from the mandate of the ordinance is rbitrary and the regulation constitutes a denial of the qual protection of the laws within the meaning of the ourteenth Amendment of the Federal Constitution.

There are manifest differences of circumstance and egree between power plants such as Central's and rivate residences in relation to the prevention and orrection of the injurious consequences of dense smoke the public health. The exigency and the remedy were eculiarly within the judgment of the local legislative ody; and unless there be an utter lack of basis for the lassification, the action taken is not discriminatory in ne constitutional sense. Ring v. North Arlington, 136 J. J. L. 494, 56 A. 2d 744 (Sup. Ct. 1948), affirmed 1 J. J. 24, 61 A. 2d. 508 (1948); Amodio v. West New York, 133 N. J. L. 220, 43 A. 2d 889 (Sup. Ct. 1945). The Legislature may make distinctions of degree having a rational basis; and they will be presumed to rest on hat basis if there be any conceivable state of facts which would afford reasonable ground for its action. Washington National Insurance Co. v. Board of Review of U. C. C., N. J. 545, 64 A. 2d 443 (1948). The legislative author- ity "is not bound to extend its regulation to all cases which it might possibly reach. The Legislature 'is free to recognize degrees of harm and it may confine its restrictions to those classes of cases where the need is deemed to be clearest.' If 'the law presumably hits the evil where it is most felt, it is not to be overthrown because there are other instances to which it might have been applied.'" West Coast Hotel Co. v. Parrish, 300 U. S. 379, 57 S. Ct. 578, 585, 81 L. Ed. 703, 108 A. L. R. 1330 (1937).

And the proofs support the convictions. There was evidence of the emission during the period specified in the complaints of smoke of a density greater than that permitted by the ordinance, according to the standard of the Ringelmann Chart; and it stood uncontradicted. One witness characterized it as "dense black smoke;" another as "heavy black smoke." There was no attempt at refutation. As we have seen, the defense really was that the medium volatile coal ordinarily used was not obtainable; but it was not sustained.

We find no prejudicial error in the rulings on evidence. The judgments are affirmed.

For affirmance: Chief Justice **VANDERBILT**, and justices **CASE**, **HEHER**, **OLIPHANT**, **WACHENFELD** and **BURLING**—6

For reversal: None.

ORIENTAL BOULEVARD CO. v. HELLER, 27 N.Y. 2d 212, 265 NE 2d 72, Ct. of Appeals of New York, decided Nov. 12, 1970

BREITEL, Judge.

Plaintiffs question the power of the City of New York to regulate by a particular local ordinance the use of fuel burners and refuse incinerators to control the emission of aerial pollutants. The original plaintiffs and several hundred intervenors, all apartment house owners, sought a declaratory judgment to annul and enjoin enforcement of the ordinance on the ground of its unconstitutionality. Special Term granted summary judgment in part in favor of defendant municipal officials, holding that there was power to enact the ordinance and that it was constitutional in design and application. A trial, however, was ordered on the limited issue of whether the time schedule for compliance by owners was unconstitutionally too short (58 Misc. 2d 920, 297 N. Y. S. 2d 431). The Appellate Division unanimously modified by eliminating the trial as to the time compliance schedule (34 A. D. 2d 811, 311 N. Y. S. 2d 635).

The principal contentions are: the State has preempted the regulation of air pollution; the local ordinance is impossible of compliance within the time schedule provided; the upgrading of equipment is disproportionately costly; the daily accumulative penalties are confiscatory and would discourage justifiable resistance to the ordinance; and the provisions for summary sealing of incinerators and fuel burners are violative of constitutional limitations. Plaintiffs particularly urge that the effect of the ordinance in reducing air pollution would be either nonexistent or so minimal as not to justify the extraordinary expense imposed on property owners.

Other arguments are made but do not require present discussion. They have been adequately treated at Special Term or have insufficient substance.

The amended ordinance is a detailed statute aimed at multiple dwelling uses of fuel and refuse burners (Administrative Code of City of New York, Secs. 892-1.0 to 897-2.0, as amd. by Local Laws, 1966, No. 14, and Local Laws, 1968, No. 14 of City of New York). It requires the commissioner of air pollution control to issue operating certificates for fuel burners and incinerators (Secs. 892-4.2, 892-4.3, subd. b). Owners must conduct such tests as the commissioner deems necessary to determine the compliance of equipment with the new standards (Sec. 892-4.1, subd. c). The law sets new standards for lower sulphur content of fuel. It requires the owners to install sulphur emission monitoring and recording devices, and to forward the records to the commissioner (Sec. 893-1.0, subd. b, par. 1). Installation of apparatus in the fuel burners, entailing substantial outlays, was required within two years (Sec. 892-4.2, subd. b). Varying with the number of apartments dependent upon an incinerator, owners are required to install additional apparatus within staggered periods up to two years (Sec. 892-4.3, subd. b, pars. 1, 2, 2 as amd.). After compliance dates have passed, the commissioner is empowered to seal any equipment for which permits have not been obtained as explicitly required by the ordinance, and, in addition, but only after notice and hearing, to seal any other equipment which is emitting harmful substances (Secs. 892-6.0; 892-4.3, subd. e). A fine from $25 to $200 a day and imprisonment up to 60 days may be imposed for each day of improper operation of an incinerator (Sec. 892-4.3, subd. f).

The ponderous argument made that pollution caused by incinerators and oil burning equipment is of trivial effect in the overall solution of a massive problem is fallacious. Accepting the contention that there is only a 2 percent daily contribution of pollutants by private apartment houses, this contribution still aggregates over 186 tons per day. Moreover, government is and must be entitled to attack massive problems piecemeal, and to select those most susceptible areas which permit of the least destructive effect on the economy (see 2 Cooley, Constitutional Limitations [8th ed.] p. 1231; United States v. Carolene Prods. Co., 304 U.S. 144, 151, 58 S.Ct. 778, 82 L.Ed. 1234). Thus, while, by common belief, the automobile is the grossest offender in air pollution, the only immediate corrective, evidently, would be its banishment, a socially and economically intolerable solution worse than the condition to be cured.

This is not to say that there are not serious questions raised as to the wisdom and the practicality of th undoubtedly rigorous measures required by the ordinance. But the ultimate conclusion must be that these a questions within the domain of legislative and executive discretion because they involve among alternative reasonable courses of action based on the presently limited knowledge of the extent of the pollution evil and methods of cure. So long as there is reasonable basis in available information, and rationality in chosen courses of conduct to alleviate an accepted evil, there is no constitutional infirmity (United States v. Carolene Prods. Co., supra, at pp. 151-154, 58 S. Ct. 778; Borden's Farm Products Co. v. Baldwin, 293 U.S. 19 209-210, 55 S. Ct. 187, 79 L. Ed. 281; Lindsley v. Natural Carbonic Gas Co., 220 U.S.61, esp. pp. 80-81, 31 S. Ct. 337, 55 L. Ed. 369; People v. Charles Schweinle Press, 214 N.Y.395, 406-408, 108 N. E. 639, 641-643). It is in this context that some may accord respect to arguments made by appellants to the effect that the city in a panic has adopted measures which will not achieve what is hoped or, if so, at a greater cost than necessary. Yet, the rebuttal is that such arguments, however cogent they may appear to be, do not affect the constitutionalit of the ordiannce. Efforts at solution of serious problem will not wait on perfect knowledge or the application of optimal methods of alleviation to the exclusion of trial and error experimentation. * Unfortunately, the extent of the pollution problem, its life-threatening acceleration, and the high economic and social costs of control are exceeded in gravity by only one or two other domestic or even international issues.

With respect to the effect of cumulative penalties, were this a novel proposition, plaintiffs perhaps might have a substantial contention. However, the courts hav long sustained a pyramiding of penalties as valid means of control (People v. Spencer, 201 N.Y. 105, 111, 94 N.E. 614, 616; Suydam v. Smith, 52 N.Y. 383, 388-389 But on the other hand, if the requirements of the statute were impossible to satisfy, cumulative penalties would be confiscatory, as any penalty would be invalid becaus irrational (see City of Buffalo v. New York Cent. R. R. Co., 125 Misc. 801, 212 N.Y.S. 1, affd. 218 app Div. 810, 218 N.Y.S. 713, affd. 271 N.Y. 658, 3 N.E. 2d 471). Thus, barring a showing of impossibility of compliance, this argument lacks weight. Moreover, as a practical matter, the property owners are not so vulnerable to oppressive action, and the authorities have indicated that there is no likelihood that cumulative penalties would be invoked to obstruct landlords who wish to litigate the issue or who establish that, for one reason or another, they are unable to comply within the statutory time schedules.

On another somewhat similar issue plaintiffs urge that the regional shortage of pollution control engineers and related service firms would have prevented many multiple dwelling owners from complying with the ordinance had all sought at one time to comply with the ordinance within its time limits. Because plaintiffs do not ntend that they, rather than all owners, found timely rformance impossible, they fail to show that they are grieved. Statutes will not be struck down unless the aintiffs are actually aggrieved (Headley v. City of ochester, 272 N. Y. 197, 205-206, 5 N. E. 2d 198, 201-2; see, also, People v. Merolla, 9 N. Y. 2d 62, 68-69, 1 N. Y. S. 2d 155, 159-160, 172 N. E. 2d 541, 545).

It is not without practical significance, if not theo-etical relevance, that more than two and four years ave passed since the respective local laws were enacted, which time much, if not all, of the change-overs equired could have been accomplished. In the meantime, aintiffs have made no effort to comply. Hence, it is ot persuasive, on the limited issue affecting the com-iance time schedule, that, as plaintiffs argue, per-rmance is not possible because all could not have per-ormed within the original time schedules in the amended rdiance. Plaintiffs may have been reasonable in esisting enforcement of the ordinance for other easons, but not because all members of the class ould not have complied.

While it is true that compliance in particular uildings will involve the outlay of varying substantial ums in the range of $3,500 to $14,000, or even $19,000, o upgrade fuel burners and incinerators, the amounts nly seem enormous when totaled as a whole for the ity. Related to the particular properties, considering he serious health hazard represented by aerial pollution, here is no showing that the amounts are disproportion-te to the capital investment or the benefits to be obtain-d. Equally significant outlays have been required in he past from owners of multiple dwellings and sustained s constitutional (see, e. g., Tenement House Dept. of City of New York v. Moeschen, 179 N. Y. 325, 330, 72 N. E. 231, 232; Health Dept. of City of New York v. Rector of Trinity Church, 145 N. Y. 32, 40-43, 39 N. E. 833, 835, 837). At a time when weather agencies in the city report almost daily that the air is unsatisfactory or unhealthy, it is hardly permissible to allow aerial pollution to continue untrammeled because the necessary outlays to avoid the condition would cut into profit mar-gins or require "hardship" adjustments in controlled rents. In any event, there is no patent unconstitutional-ity involved and the balance to be struck is a legislative and not a judicial obligation.

Also unsound is plaintiffs' argument of State pre-emption. The Environmental Conservation Law, Consol. Laws, c. 43-B, was recently enacted, effective July 1, 1970 (L. 1970, ch. 140). Section 10 provides that: "It shall further be the policy of the state to improve and coordinate the environmental plans, functions, powers and programs of the state, in cooperation with the fed-eral government, regions, local governments".

Paragraph 21 of section 14 empowers the newly created department to: "Encourage activities consis-tent with the purposes of this chapter by advising and assisting local governments, institutions, industries and individuals." These provisions explicitly recognize that local units of government are intended to function in the air pollution area.

Lastly, the argument that the summary sealing of equipment, without notice and hearing, is unconstitu-tional is lacking in substance. The ordinance authorizes summary sealing only in the case of specified classes of fuel burners and incinerators for which permits have not been obtained and whose operation has thus become unlawful (§§ 892-6.0; 892-4.3, subd. e). Moreover, a hearing for the affected owner, even after the summary sealing obtainable by judicial proceedings of a summary or plenary character, is sufficient to insure constitution-ality so long as the health hazard to be controlled is sufficiently widespread and grave, and immediate action is desirable (Ewing v. Mytinger & Casselberry, 339 U. S. 594, 599, 70 S. Ct. 870, 94 L. Ed. 1088; North Amer. Cold Stor. Co. v. Chicago, 211 U. S. 306, 315, 317, 320-321, 29 S. Ct. 101, 53 L. Ed. 195; Phillips v. Commissioner, 283 U. S. 589, 596-597, 51 S. Ct. 608, 75 L. Ed. 1289; City of Newburgh v. Park Filling Sta., 273 App. Div. 24, 27, 75 N. Y. S. 2d 439, 441, affd. 298 N. Y. 649, 82 N. E. 2d 39; 1 Davis, Administrative Law Treatise, § 7.08; see, also, relevant to the need of notice to one who has knowledge of a nuisance by reason of operation or control, Matter of 300 West 154th St. Realty Co. v. Department of Bldgs. of City of N. Y., 26 N. Y. 2d 538, at p. 543, 311 N. Y. S. 2d 899, at p. 902, 260 N. E. 2d 543, at p. 536).

As to other equipment of classes not specified in the ordinance, there must be notice and hearing before the offending equipment may be sealed on the ground that it is emitting noxious substances. Also, if it had been true, as it is not, that the ordinance failed to provide for adequate notice and hearing, the requirement would be implied (Matter of Buttonow, 23 N. Y. 2d 385, 393, 297 N. Y. S. 2d 97, 103, 244 N. E. 2d 677, 681; Matter of Hecht v. Monaghan, 307 N. Y. 461, 468-469, 121 N. E. 2d 421, 424-425).

Accordingly, the order of the Appellate Division should be affirmed, with costs.

FULD, C. J., and BURKE, SCILEPPI, BERGAN, JASEN and GIBSON, JJ., concur.

Order affirmed.

*That the effort has not been unrewarding in stimu-lating inventive and strenuous schemes to control pollution is demostrated by an article which ap-peared in a trade journal. The Real Estate News, for September, 1970, at p. 12 et seq.

DEPT. OF HEALTH, State of New Jersey v. OWENS-CORNING FIBERGLAS CORP., 100 N.J. Super. 366, 242 A.2d 21 (1968); affirmed *per curiam,* 53 N.J. 248, 250 A.2d 11 (1969), decided April 17, 1968

[Edited]

GOLDMANN, S. J. A. D.

Defendant Owens-Corning Fiberglas Corporation (Owens-Corning) appeals from an order and amended order of the State Department of Health (Department) directing that it cease violation of chapter VI, section 2.1 of the New Jersey Air Pollution Control Code (Code) and forthwith take certain specified interim measures to minimize air pollution caused by its plant operations.

I

The proceedings before the Department were instituted by a complaint, dated September 28, 1966, alleging that on ten specified dates during July and August of 1966 Owens-Corning

"did cause, suffer, allow or permit air pollution by emitting substances into the outdoor atmosphere from [its premises in Barrington, Camden County] in such quantities as to be injurious to human or plant life, or property, or to unreasonably interfere with the comfortable enjoyment of life and property in violation of Chapter VI, Section 2.1 of the New Jersey Air Pollution Control Code, a copy of which is annexed hereto and made a part hereof."

Chapter VI, section 2.1 of the Code provides:

"No person shall cause, suffer, allow or permit to be emitted into the outdoor atmosphere substances in quantities which shall result in air pollution."

"Air pollution," as used in chapter VI, is defined in chapter I, section 1.10 of the Code in the same language as appears in the Air Pollution Control Act (1954), N. J. S. A. 26: 2C-2:

"'Air pollution' * * * shall mean the presence in the outdoor atmosphere of substances in quantities which are injurious to human, plant or animal life or to property or unreasonably interfere with the comfortable enjoyment of life and property throughout the State and in such territories of the State as s shall be affected thereby and excludes all aspects of the employer-employee relationship as to health and safety hazards."[1]

Accompanying the Department's complaint was a notice directed to Owens-Corning of the hearing on October 25, 1966. The hearing began as scheduled and continued over series of dates until early 1967. The hearing officer throughout all phases of this matter was E. Powers Mincher of the Department. Since chapter VI of the Code does not provide measurable standards in the form of specific limits for emissions to the atmosphere, this first or preliminary hearing was a procedural prerequisite to the issuance of any order, by reason of N. J. S. A. 26: 2C-14, third paragraph, which reads:

"In any case where no code, rule or regulation has been promulgated which sets specific limits for emissions to the atmosphere of the type discovered and alleged, no order to cease such emissions shall be issued until the holding of a preliminary hearing thereon which shall be held upon not less than 15 days' notice by the department [State Department of Health] to all interested persons."

On March 9, 1967 State Commissioner of Health Kandle issued the first of the two orders under appeal. It recited that he had given due consideration to the transcript of hearing, the findings and recommendations of the hearing officer, and the brief submitted by counsel for Owens-Corning. He found that the company had violated chapter VI, section 2.1 of the Code and directed that it cease such violation on or before January 1, 1968 and forthwith take interim measures (set out at length) to minimize the effects resulting from its plant operations.

II

Owens-Corning owns and operates a plant in Barrington, Camden County, where it manufactures various fiberglas products. It uses four production lines, known as U–1, U–2, T and P–20, in its operation. The basic process on all four lines is this: Raw materials are conveyed from a storage area and fed into a glass melting furnace. The material is then passed through a spinning operation which converts the molten glass into fiberglas, at which time a phenol formaldehyde resin is injected for binding purposes. The material is then cooled and conveyed into a curing oven after passing through several conveyors which control the thickness of the material. From the curing oven the material enters the fabricating stage where it is cut to size and packaged. The completed product is then sent to the warehousing area for shipment.

The issue to be determined at the first (preliminary) hearing was whether Owens-Corning had violated chapter VI, section 2.1 of the Code on the dates specified. The Department presented its case in two separate but related main phases. The first consisted of the testimony of 11 witnesses who lived close to or within a reasonable distance of the plant. They testified to the fumes, smoke and blue haze coming from the plant and to the effects they had suffered therefrom, demostra-

; how, in various ways, their daily lives and proper- ıad been interfered with. Their complaints included ›aring and burning of the eyes, "runny" noses, a and "funny " taste in the mouth, nausea and cough- . The odor and smoke are unbearable. Almost all tified that they had to close their windows and stay oors because of the conditions experienced.

The second phase of the Department's presentation olved technical evidence given by Joseph A. Rziga- ski, enforcement supervisor for the Department's sanitation (pollution control) program. His qualifi- ions as an air pollution expert were not challenged. had visited the plant on a number of occasions and scribed the manufacturing process on the four pro- tion lines. Rzigalinski explained that two areas in ticular generated gaseous emissions—the forming a and the curing area. He was present at the plant February 17, 1966 at defendant's invitation, the pur- se being to observe an odor tracer survey of the issions from the dehumidification tower stack. Dr. ıos Turk conducted the survey on behalf of Owens- rning, and this was done when only the U-1 line and odor abatement equipment were in operation, all ıer production lines being shut down. Dr. Turk's st was solely for the detection of phenol odors. Des- te all precautions taken by the plant, he found low vel peaks of phenol odors during the test.

Rzigalinski visited the plant on May 19, 1966, again defendant's invitation, to observe tests of phenol lor emissions from the dehumidification tower stack the U-1 line. The test, conducted for defendant by illiam R. Bradley Associates, indicated that 0.22 rts of phenol per million parts of air were being nitted from the stack. According to Rzigalinski, 0.22 m. is below the so-called "odor threshold level" for enol of 0.29 ppm. None of the other production lines ere tested for its emissions, nor was the test concer- ed with odors other than phenol. On this visit Rziga- nski detected strong formaldehyde odors coming from of ventilators above the curing oven and from open- gs on the roof above the melting and spinning opera- ons.

Although Rzigalinski's visits and the two surveys all redated the July and August 1966 complaint dates bout which the Department's 11 witnesses testified, ere is a definite correlation between the two eviden- al patterns. Samuel Thomas, Owens-Corning's Direc- r of Environmental Control, admitted that the air pol- ıtion control equipment or devices at the plant were the ame at the time he testified on January 9, 1967 as they ad been for well over a year, except for a modification n the P-20 line in the fall of 1966. Moreover, there ad been no substantial changes in the production pro- ess in that time except for some changes in chemicals r chemicals processes in 1966. From this it may easonably be said that conditions at the plant had not varied in any substantial degree as regards odor or smoke emissions between the dates of Rzigalinski's inspections and the two surveys, and the dates set out in the complaint.

The record reveals that the Department had as early as May 1961, if not before, discussed with representa- tives of Owens-Corning the necessity of controlling emissions from its plant into the atmosphere. The com- pany recognized the existence of the condition and was apparently trying to correct it. Numerous conferences and exchanges of correspondence followed over the next five years, all dealing with the air pollution problem. Although Owens-Corning repeatedly assured the Depart- ment that it was taking definite steps to eliminate the condition, it failed to comply with its own timetables as well as the Department's repeated requests that it control the emissions.

The Department's long and patient wait for Owens-Corning to solve the air pollution problem came to an end when it received a letter from company vice-pre- sident Briley on June 21, 1966. He wrote that the com- pany was dissatisfied with the dehumidification tower on the U-1 line and accordingly did not intend to install similar equipment on the other three lines. Instead, Owens-Corning had directed its research center in Ohio to undertake a "crash" program at the Barrington plant. There would be a complete evaluation of these changes within the next six months, at which time the company would be in a position to know whether they were feasi- ble. A timetable would then be developed to make the necessary process modifications as rapidly as posible. The Department filed its complaint soon after receipt of the Briley letter.

We take note of the reservation contained in Owens-corning's brief that all that had taken place before be- tween the company and the Department was not to be considered as any admission of violation on its part. This flies directly in the face of the company's very clear knowledge that emissions from its plant had for years been polluting the air in Barrington and neighbor- ing communities. This was made manifest in its confer- ences with Department representatives, in the letters it had written to the Department, and in its continued and protracted efforts to correct the situation.

Owens-Corning presented seven lay witnesses at the preliminary hearing. They denied they had ever experi- enced any of the complaints testified to by the 11 Depart- ment witnesses, or that the plant operations had ever interfered with their enjoyment of life and property. In evaluating the testimony of these witnesses it is to be observed that one lived next door to the company's pur- chasing agent Maguire; another admitted that her son dated his daughter; a third testified that the company had always been very cooperative in donating door prizes for local sports events of which he was chairman; a fourth lived around the corner from Maguire, and yet another witness was a friend of his.

Owens-Corning produced three expert witnesses, the testimony of only one of whom Thomas, concerns us here. He said that environmental control in the type of plant defendant operates is an entirely new field. He gave a history of the various tests that had been made and the equipment that had been installed in order to alleviate the complained-of condition. The company had spent over $3,289,000 on this program.

III

During the pendency of the appeal Owens-Corning filed two motions. The first sought leave to present additional evidence dealing with the population (1960 census figures) of the three municipalities from which the Department drew its witnesses. In its brief opposing the motion the Department included the 1966 population estimates of the State Department of Conservation and Economic Development. We received both sets of figures without prejudice as to their materiality or relevance.

The second motion was addressed to the record filed by the Department with this court on August 14, 1967. The record included the report, findings and recommendations made by the hearing officer after the preliminary hearing as well as those made after the grievance hearing. Owens-Corning contended that it had never been given an opportunity to review the reports, findings and recommendations, and to respond to, explain or controvert them. It moved that the proceedings be remanded to the Department for a de novo hearing or, in the alternative, for an opportunity to appear before the commissioner to counter the hearing officer's reports. We denied the motion.

IV

Defendant contends that the Air Pollution Control Act, N. J. S. A. 26:2C–1 et seq., is unconstitutional because it delegates legislative power to an administrative agency, the Air Pollution Control Commission, without setting up a standard or standards to guide it in the exercise of that power.

The Air Pollution Control Act of 1954 does not offend the requirement that there be sufficient standards for the guidance of the administrative agency. In this definitive sense, "air pollution" is in itself a standard, albeit a broad one. That aside, an entirely adequate standard appears in the very definition of "air pollution" contained in N. J. S. A. 26:2C–2. By force of that definition, contamination of the air may be prohibited or controlled only under specifically defined circumstances, namely, where there is proof of injury to health or unreasonable interference with the comfortable enjoyment of life and property.

Our Supreme Court's description of the contents of the act in N. J. Dept. of Health v. Roselle, 34 N. J. 331, 169 A. 2d 153 (1961), would militate against defendant's present contention:

"* * * The Commission and the Department are given wide powers to meet the pressing dangers of air pollution. The Commission is authorized to adopt a code or rules and regulations 'controlling and prohibiting air pollution,' N. J. S. A. 26:2C–8. The Department is directed to 'control air pollution in accordance with any code, rule or regulation promulgated by the commission,' with power to '(e) Receive or initiate complaints * * * and institute legal proceedings for the prevention of air pollution and for the recovery of penalties in accordance with this act.' N. J. S. A. 26:2C-9

The statute lays down the steps for enforcement of the code. * * * Thus the statute directs the Department to determine in plain terms what shall be done. * * *" (at pages 347-348, 169 A. 2d at page 161.)

Considering the nature and purpose of the Air Pollution Control Act, its need for flexibility, its standards when compared to those of other statutes that have been held valid, and its plainly sufficient procedural safeguards (e. g., N. J. S. A. 26:2C–8, 14, 14.1, 19 and 20), we conclude that the act does not lack adequate standards and that defendant has failed to sustain its burden in challenging the statute's constitutionality.

IX

We have also considered defendant's argument that the orders were improper in that they attempted to regulate odors, since this is not a subject properly within the scope of the enabling legislation or the Code, both of which speak of "substances." (As noted in footnote 1, above, the act, as amended by L. 1967, c. 106, § 5, now speaks of "air contaminants" instead of "substances.") Defendant relies upon Verona v. Shalit, 92 N. J. Super. 65, 222 A. 2d 145 (1966), a County Court case where it was said that the Code "does not contain any prohibition against odors." On appeal, however, the Appellate Division expressly refrained from dealing with this issue, resting its affirmance on other grounds. See Verona v. Shalit, 96 N. J. Super. 20, 25, 232 A. 2d 431 (1967). In any event, we consider defendant's conclusion a mistaken one.

In the first place, the County Court decision itself refutes defendant's claim when it says that the "substances" prohibited from being emitted by the Code "may include smoke, flying ash, air contaminants, consisting of 'coarse and fine solid particles, liquid particles, vapors or gases which are discharged into the outdoor atmosphere.'"

An odor is a substance of gaseous character or a quid of high vaporizing quality. The odor of perfume, or example, is an emission of vapor into the air, aused by evaporation of the liquid vehicle carrying e odoriferous element. The familiar odor of rotten ggs is the gas hydrogen sulphide. The odor of formaldehyde or acetone is the air-borne vapor of these hemicals. All are clearly "substances" within the efinition of the word. Thus, in prohibiting emission f noxious substances the obvious legislative purpose as to include odors. Defendant would hardly contend at the Legislature did not intend to prohibit the rease into the air of high concentrations of the odor of hlorine or hydrogen cyanide, both of them deadly ases. Furthermore, odors may amount to a nuisance produced in unreasonable quantities, and their production could therefore be proscribed under the act.

Under the new definition of "air pollution" contained n the 1967 amendment, an odor is clearly an "air ontaminant." By this amendment the Legislature made explicit what it meant by "substances."

XI

It is claimed that the hearing officer improperly xcluded defendant's offer of proof that other sources—pecifically, the exhaust from motor vehicles—were esponsible for the complaints registered by the Department's witnesses. The hearing officer found the roffered evidence "too remote" to be relevant on the ssue of defendant's pollution of the atmosphere. We annot say this was error, even under rules of evidence which need not be strictly enforced in a Department earing held under the Air Pollution Control Act. See . J. S. A. 26:2C–16. As we said in D'Amico v. Blanck, 5 N. J. Super. 297, 303, 204 A. 2d 609 (1964), certification denied 43 N. J. 448, 205 A. 2d 443 (1964), "the hoice of accepting or rejecting the testimony of witnesses rests with the administrative agency, and here such choice is reasonably made, it is conclusive on appeal." Absent a showing that the exclusion of e proffered evidence was inconsistent with substanal justice, we will not disturb the administrative etermination. R. R. 1:5–3(b). Defendant has not made such a showing.

XII

Defendant's final argument is that the doctrine of "unavoidable necessity" dictates that the Commissioner's order may not be sustained.

As the State correctly points out, the applicability of the doctrine turns upon the reasonableness of the statute or regulation under review and of the proscription imposed. Assuredly, it is not unreasonable for the State, in the interest of the public health and welfare, to seek to control air pollution. Even if this means the shutting down of an operation harmful to health or unreasonably interfering with life or property, the statute must prevail. But no such drastic measure was called for in this case.

Upon analysis, defendant's argument based on "unavoidable necessity" is that since no known equipment exists which could solve the situation, no unreasonable interference with the comfortable enjoyment of life or property can be asserted against it. The record does not support that claim. The best that can be said is that no method yet found and used by Owens-Corning is totally effective. However, steps that will substantially improve the air pollution condition are available. The proofs are that when Owens-Corning used certain equipment on its U-1 line, there was a diminution of pollution. The company, as shown by the Briley letter of June 21, 1966, is not entirely satisfied with the result achieved on the U–1 line and does not intend to install similar equipment on its other lines. It represents that it is presently engaged in a crash research program to develop major changes in its basic manufacturing processes. Two very promising changes have already been developed and are being tested.

The Commissioner has ordered that certain steps be taken which he considers will curb the too-noxious emissions from the Barrington plant. Defendant must, for the moment, comply with the order. If the steps prescribed do not wholly accomplish the desired result, other or supplemental steps may be taken. In short, the situation is subject to the continuing jurisdiction of the Department. We hold that the doctrine of unavoidable necessity is not available to defendant and is not viable in the context of the Air Pollution Code.

The amended order is accordingly affirmed in all respects.

FOOTNOTE

1. Effective June 15, 1967 this section of the Code was amended by L. 1967, c. 106, § 5 to read:
"'Air pollution' as used in this act shall mean the presence in the outdoor atmosphere of one or more air contaminants in such quantities and duration as are, or tend to be, injurious to human health or welfare, animal or plant life or property, or would unreasonably interfere with the enjoyment of life or property throughout the State and in such territories of the State as shall be affected thereby and excludes all aspects of employer-employee relationship as to health and safety hazards."

Most communities of any substantial size in the United States have an ordinance designed to control air pollution. These ordinances are of three sorts, each categorized by its "target." The three are Basic, or smoke control; Emission Control; and Air Quality Control.

local ordinances: three types

Basic ordinances attempt to control smoke emission, generally by required reference to a Ringelmann Chart, which gives a visual comparison to determine smoke density in daylight. Often certain smoke-producing activities are prohibited, such as open burning. Fuels also may be regulated.

Comprehensive emission control ordinances usually encompass the requirements of basic ordinances, but regulate emissions in addition to smoke. The controls may be more restrictive than the Federal or state program, or cover other types of emissions. Generally polluters are required to obtain a permit. It is not infrequent that the provisions are inconsistent, creating headaches for all concerned. This type of ordinance nevertheless is the basic model for all present serious efforts to control air pollution at the local level, and its characteristics are discussed subsequently in this chapter with reference to the Cleveland Code.

Ambient air quality ordinances base control on achieving a given atmospheric quality. It is based on the philosophy found in the 1967 Federal Act and still partially alive in the Clean Air Act as amended. In some cases enforcement is based on a required showing that an emission reduces atmospheric air quality. These ordinances are generally passed by industry-dominated groups. The complexity of the legal and scientific jargon obscures its unenforceability. The only pollution-control use is when very large and well-funded air pollution control agencies are created, which then make emission requirements that can be enforced independently of any showing of atmospheric quality.

emission standards

To be effective, an emission control ordinance must meet a variety of legal requirements. Some of the major considerations are:

1. Does the ordinance fall within the subject matter and scope of authority granted by the State?
2. Does the enforcement agency meet the requirements of the city charter and/or home rule powers?
3. Does the enforcement agency meet any applicable administrative procedure act requirements; are appeals and judicial review properly provided?
4. Does the act have enforceable sanctions, and are realistic penalties provided?
5. Does the complexity of the act match the size and funding of the agency?
6. Does the act make sense from a technical point of view—are the goals attainable yet not too lenient?
7. Does the act mesh with regional, county, state, and Federal activities?

the Cleveland Code: an example

The Cleveland Code which follows is an example of a comprehensive emission control ordinance. It is selected to represent a strong local ordinance in a state which gives very strong home rule powers to cities. The New Jersey material which follows deals with a state in which local authority over pollution control has been largely assumed by the state. Since the Cleveland Code was in part written by the author its background and provisions can be explained based on personal experience.

The first draft of the ordinance was made early in 1969 by the engineering staff of what was then the National Air Pollution Control Administration (now a part of the Environmental Protection Agency), which provides Federal assistance to local governments. This first draft followed the standard model ordinances, and was similar to that of several Midwestern cities.

The usual industry-versus-citizens disagreements arose. This writer produced a second draft of the ordinance for a coalition of citizen groups, while industry had a study prepared for it by a Pittsburgh law firm that argued for an ordinance based on atmospheric air quality.

Citizen pressure for a strong ordinance was considerable. A third draft prepared by this writer was taken by the City's law department and adopted almost completely as the City's ensuing draft. Political pressure by industry was intense, although citizen groups dominated the public aspects of the city council's committee hearings. During the summer several weakening provisions were inserted in the draft ordinance.

Citizen groups once again exerted pressure. A meeting was held by representatives of the mayor, enforcement personnel, and several members of the city council, plus this writer. The final draft was written at this meeting, primarily by this author, with technical advice from enforcement officials. The law department put the draft in final form for the city council, which approved it in October of 1969 after a last-minute effort by industry failed to weaken it.

This brief account has been from the point of view of the drafter of an ordinance, but obviously many other factors than the precise provisions and wording were of immense importance. Many persons actively sought Federal money for the project, while others concentrated on developing city council interest and adequate press coverage. Public officials needed the courage to buck considerable pressure from polluters who were to be forced to spend many millions of dollars. All of these aspects were of great importance to passage of the ordinance in a useful form.

Cleveland Code

At the time the code was being considered, Cleveland already had an emission code with a staff to enforce it. The code had many glaring weaknesses, but an enforcement agency existed, though it too needed to be strengthened. A new deputy commissioner was provided for, though he actually joined the staff prior to the passage of the act. The staff of about thirty-five and budget of about $300,000 was substantial in 1968 terms. This meant that a comprehensive emission code when backed by a larger staff and budget could handle the work that would be involved. There is sometimes a tendency to regard laws as self-executing. Such is the opposite of reality. A law, good or bad, is one part, and not the most important part, of a control program. It is probably better to have a strong public nuisance ordinance for a very small organization than an emission-based ordinance that requires personnel and skills that are unavailable. It must be remembered that any meaningful code, applicable to a large urban area, will require the inspection and control of thousands of emission sources.

This ordinance was also designed to be used as part of any regional implementation plan that developed. Cleveland's program covered only a part of the Cleveland Region, which in turn was one of five regions in the State. Nevertheless, since Cleveland's program was about three times the size of the State's program, it was clear that Cleveland would play a key part in any enforcement effort.

SECTION ANALYSIS

The first part of the ordinance deals with **definitions.** The usual definitions of air contaminant and air pollution are provided, except that the words "are, or may be injurious" strengthen the act substantially and prevent challenges based on the limitations of our scientific knowledge. The usual exception for uncombined water vapor was included. Several months after the ordinance was passed, an unusual cold wave caused the emissions of unconsolidated water vapor to fall to the ground, creating a severe localized icing condition. The ordinance states that such water is not a contaminant (4.0302). However, emergencies dealt with in 4.1905 give the Commission the power to abate emissions from an air contaminant source.

The water vapor was an emission and it was from an air contaminant source, and under this section it did not have to be an air contaminant. This writer wishes he could claim such felicitous language was due to his perception.

Chapter 5 of the Code deals with administration. It was intended to give the Commission many different ways to abate pollution. The abatement order provision for a 90-day plus 60-day time limit is very short, but was insisted upon by the city council. For the installation of major equipment such a provision is unenforceable.

Notice that while a person can get five months to abate, he must appeal within ten days. That provision is to prevent a pollutor from waiting five months and then getting a further delay by appealing. The appeals board is one major weakness of the Code. Appeals go to the Board of Building Standards and Building Appeals. This is required by the city charter. An attempt to change the city charter and create a board of air pollution appeals was voted down in 1970.

Chapter 7 of the Code requires a permit for any construction or modification of equipment that produces air pollution. Such a provision gives the Commissioner some control over air pollution prior to its development. The secret process provision is not as favorable to public disclosure as it should be, but the discretion is in the hands of the Commission and is not based on a claim made by the pollution emitter.

Chapter 9 requires a certificate of operation in order to discharge air pollutants. This is the heart of an emission code. Note the variance provisions. They are very rigorous, and if interpreted literally, would result in no variances being granted. Note also an exemption for small homes from certificates of operations (4.0910). The permit fees cover much of the operating costs of the department.

Chapter 11 deals with visible emissions and odors. The visible emissions are based on the Ringelmann Chart. Nearly everyone agrees that the technical and scientific deficiencies of this system are great. Nevertheless it is a good provision to have in an act. The tests for violation need not be done from the premises of the pollutor, and an inspector with no technical background can be trained in a few hours. No one is likely to be successfully prosecuted unless his actions are clearly in the prohibited zone, and in those cases the preparation and prosecution of such actions is relatively easy. Expert witnesses are not needed. There is a long judicial history upholding the validity of these tests. The odor provision is interesting and should be read carefully.

Chapter 13 deals with particulate emissions. The requirements when passed were considered very strict for a steel industry town, and that they would be very difficult to meet. Such emission limitation, however, is probably too lenient to meet Federal Air Quality Standards.

Chapter 15 has several miscellaneous provisions. The first case tried under the act involved open burning. A rather substantial burning of construction waste material was involved. The city tried the case on the basis that all fires were prohibited. They won the case, but got a lot of bad publicity as the defense was that the fire was in a barrel and used to warm the hands of workers. The newspapers gave attention to this aspect of the case, and the control officials were made to appear interested only in prosecuting the little man.

The sulfur limitation of two percent on existing equipment is not the nation's strictest. But Ohio is a major producer of coal, much of it high in sulfur. This and the particulate limitations were the most contested aspects of the Code.

The nuisance provisions are useful to add to any code. Note the definition of nuisance. Section 4.1505 allows other contaminants to be covered by regulations.

Chapter 17 deals with testing. It was drafted to give very broad powers to the Commissioner. Note under 4.1702(B) he can test for anything.

Chapter 19 deals with penalties. The most powerful penalty is sealing, which puts a person out of business. Three violations of the code can lead to a sealing. For fines, each day's violation is a separate offense.

The major area not covered by the Code is the provision for citizen suits and citizen participation in rulemaking such as that found in the Illinois Act (see Chapter One).

Automobiles were not covered because the cost to do anything meaningful would be prohibitive, and it would be difficult to control out-of-city automobiles. It was desired to amend the ordinance to cover aircraft, but the 1970 Federal amendments would prohibit this unless this point is successfully challenged (See proceeding sub-section of pollution from aircraft).

Cleveland Air Pollution Code

TABLE OF CONTENTS

THE CLEVELAND AIR POLLUTION CODE

The complete text of the code is published here. The graphs in the appendices, however, have been omitted.

CHAPTER 1 — TITLE

§4.0103. Title and Distribution.

This part of the Codified Ordinances of the City of Cleveland shall be known as the "Air Pollution Code of the City of Cleveland" and may be separately printed and distributed. The term "this code" wherever used in this ordinance means the Air Pollution Code of the City of Cleveland.

CHAPTER 3 — DEFINITIONS

§4.0301. Air Cleaning Equipment.

Air cleaning equipment is any control equipment which removes, reduces, or renders less noxious air contaminants discharged into the atmosphere.

§4.0302. Air Contaminant.

Air contaminant is any solid, liquid, or gas, or any combination thereof except uncombined water, discharged into the atmosphere.

§4.0303. Air Pollution.

Air pollution is the presence in the atmosphere of one or more air contaminants in such quantities for such period of time that they are, or may be, injurious to human, plant or animal life, or to property, or that they interfere with the comfortable enjoyment of life or property or the conduct of business.

§4.0304. A. S. M. E.

A. S. M. E. is the American Society of Mechanical Engineers.

§4.0305. A. S. T. M.

A. S. T. M. is the American Society for Testing Materials.

§4.0306. Atmosphere.

Atmosphere is the air that envelops or surrounds the earth.

§4.0307. B. T. U.

B. T. U. or British Thermal Unit is the amount of heat required to raise 1 pound of water 1 degree Fahrenheit.

§4.0308. Control Equipment.

Control equipment is any equipment designed to regulate the release of contaminants from process, fuel-burning or refuse-burning equipment by reducing the creation of air contaminants or the emission of air contaminants into the atmosphere, or both.

§4.0309. Emission.

Emission is the act of releasing air contaminants into the atmosphere or the material so passed into the atmosphere.

§4.0310. Fuel.

Fuel is any form of combustible matter—solid, liquid, or gas but does not include refuse.

§4.0311. Fuel-Burning Equipment.

Fuel-burning equipment is any furnace, boiler apparatus, stack and all appurtenances thereto used in the process of burning fuel for the primary purpose of producing heat or power.

§4.0312. Odor.

Odor is that property of an air contaminant which affects the sense of smell.

§4.0313. Opacity.

Opacity is the state of a substance which renders it partially or wholly impervious to the rays of light. Opacity as used in this ordinance refers to the obscuration of an observer's view.

§4.0314. Open Fire.

Open Fire is a fire from which the products of combustion are emitted directly into the open air without passing through a stack or chimney.

§4.0315. Particulate Matter.

Particulate matter is material other than uncombined water, which is suspended in or discharged into the atmosphere in a finely divided form as a liquid or solid, at standard conditions.

§4.0316. Person.

Person means any individual, partnership, partner, firm, company, corporation, association, joint stock company, trust, estate, governmental entity, or any other legal entity, or their legal representatives, agents, or assigns.

§4.0317. Process Equipment.

Process equipment is any equipment, device, or contrivance for changing any materials whatever or for storing or handling of any materials, and all appurtenances thereto, including ducts and stack, the use of which may cause discharge of an air contaminant into the atmosphere, but not including that equipment specifically defined in this ordinance as fuel-burning equipment or refuse-burning equipment.

§4.0318. Process Weight.

Process weight is the total weight of all material introduced into a unit operation or unit process, including solid fuels, but excluding liquid fuels and gaseous fuels when these are used solely as fuels and excluding air introduced for purposes of combustion.

§4.0319. Process Weight Per Hour.

Process weight per hour is a rate established as follows:

(a) For continuous or long-run steady-state unit operation or unit process, the total process weight for the entire period of continuous operation or for a typical portion thereof, divided by the number of hours of such period or portion thereof.

(b) For cyclical or batch unit operation or batch process, the total process weight for a period that covers a complete operation or an integral number of cycles, divided by the hours of actual process operation during such period.

Where the nature of any process or operation or the design of any equipment is such as to permit more than one interpretation of this definition, the interpretation that results in the minimum value for allowable emission shall apply.

§4.0320. Refuse-Burning Equipment.

Refuse-burning equipment is any incinerator, equipment, device, or contrivance used for the destruction of garbage or other combustible wastes by burning, and all appurtenances thereto.

§4.0321. Ringelmann Chart.

Ringelmann Chart is the chart published and described in the U. S. Bureau of Mines Information Circular 8333, and on which are illustrated graduated shades of grey to black for use in estimating the light obscuring capacity of smoke.

§4.0322. Seal for Sealing Equipment or Premises.

Seal is any device, tag, or marking installed or affixed by the Commissioner of Air Pollution Control or by his agents or representatives so as to prevent use of the process, fuel-burning, refuse-burning, or control equipment or premises causing a violation, or from which violations of this ordinance originate.

§4.0323. Smoke.

Smoke is small gas-borne particles resulting from incomplete combustion, consisting predominantly, but not exclusively, of carbon, ash, and other combustible material.

§4.0324. Stack.

Stack is a duct, chimney, flue, conduit, vent or opening designed or arranged for the emission into the atmosphere of air contaminants.

§4.0325. Standard Conditions.

The term "standard conditions" means a gas temperature of 60 degrees Fahrenheit and a gas pressure of 14.7 pounds per square inch absolute dry air.

§4.0326. Unit Operation.

The term "unit operation" means methods where raw materials undergo physical change, or methods by which raw materials may be altered into different states, such as vapor, liquid or solid without changing into a new substance with different properties or composition.

§4.0327. Unit Process.

The term "unit process" means reactions where raw materials undergo chemical change or where one or more raw materials are combined and changed into a new substance with different properties or composition.

§4.0328. Appeals Board.

The term "appeals board" wherever used in this ordinance means the Board of Building Standards and Building Appeals or such other successor appeals board as shall be established by ordinance and vested with jurisdiction in matters relating to air pollution.

CHAPTER 5 — ADMINISTRATIVE

§4.0501. Air Pollution Personnel.

The Division of Air Pollution Control shall employ and qualify such personnel as is needed to insure the successful administration of this code. Such personnel of the Division shall carry out the directions of the Commissioner of Air Pollution Control in all matters, consistent with duties of their respective job descriptions, qualifications and assignments, relating to enforcement of this code, including the signing of affidavits for warrants sought for violations, and shall aid and assist the Commissioner in the efficient discharge of his duties.

No person employed in the Division shall be directly or indirectly interested in sales of services or goods, or in any matter in conflict with his employment.

§4.0502. Duties of Commissioner.

The Commissioner of Air Pollution Control under the supervision and direction of the Director of Public Health and Welfare shall:

A. Supervise the execution of all laws, rules and regulations pertaining to air pollution as provided in this ordinance;

B. Institute complaints against all violators of any provisions of this ordinance and institute necessary legal proceedings, either personally or through his representatives;

C. Issue and have served upon violators orders requiring the repair of equipment or abatement of conditions not in compliance with this code;

D. Compel the prevention and abatement of air pollution or odors or nuisances arising therefrom;

E. Examine and approve or disapprove the plans for fuel-burning, refuse-burning, process, and control equipment to be installed, constructed, reconstructed, altered or added to;

F. Make inspections and tests of existing and newly installed equipment subject to this ordinance to determine whether such equipment complies with this code;

G. Investigate complaints of violations of the provisions of this code and make inspections and observations of air pollution conditions. Records shall be maintained of all such investigations, complaints, inspections and observations;

H. Approve or reject applications for permits and administer the issuance of certificates of operation, notices, waiver citations, permits and other documents required under the provisions of this code;

I. Prepare and place before the Director of Public Health and Welfare for his consideration proposals for additions or revisions to this ordinance, or other rules and regulations pertaining to air pollution;

J. Encourage voluntary cooperation by persons or affected groups in the preservation and restoration of the purity of the outdoor atmosphere;

K. Collect and remit to appropriate officials of the City of Cleveland fees collected for certificates of operation or examination of permits;

L. Work with other city agencies for the purpose of coordinating activities for the common municipal good;

M. Conduct tests and make studies of air contaminants whether or not controlled by specific limitations of this code;

N. Do any and all acts which may be necessary for the successful prosecution of the purposes of this ordinance and such other acts as may be specifically enumerated herein.

§4.0503. Rules and Regulations.

The Commissioner of Air Pollution Control, under the supervision and direction of the Director of Public Health and Welfare, may adopt, amend or alter written rules and regulations of this code. Such rules and regulations shall not conflict with nor waive any provisions of this code nor any other of the Codified Ordinances of the City of Cleveland, nor shall these rules and regulations be the basis for criminal prosecutions for violations of this code. Such rules and regulations and amendments thereto and alterations thereof shall become effective after two successive publications in the City Record.

§4.0504. Abatement Orders.

Whenever any equipment is found upon inspection to be operated in violation of this code or in such condition or so installed that it cannot be operated in conformity with this code, the Commissioner shall issue a written order to the person owning, operating or in control of such equipment, requiring the abatement of all violations of this code and the correction of any condition which may result in a violation of this code within the time limit set forth in such order such time limit not to exceed ninety (90) days. Should the person to whom such order is issued fail to act upon such order within the time limit set forth therein or within a time limit extension granted by the Commissioner not to exceed sixty (60) days, the Commissioner shall revoke any existing certificate of operation or seal such equipment for failure to comply with such order.

§4.0505. Appeals.

(A) Appeals of a person adversely affected by any order, requirement, decision or determination of the Commissioner of Air Pollution Control shall be heard and decided by the appeals board. Such appeal shall stay the enforcement of an order or the sealing of the equipment unless the Commissioner determines that there is an immediate danger to human life, health, safety, welfare, or comfort.

(B) Any appeal from an abatement order under Section 4.0504 must be filed within ten (10) days after receipt of a written abatement order.

(C) Any person affected by a decision of the appeals board may obtain judicial relief as provided by law.

CHAPTER 7 — PERMITS

§4.0701. Application Required.

No person shall construct, install, reconstruct, or alter any process, fuel-burning, or refuse-burning equipment, or control equipment pertaining thereto, that may be a source of air contaminant, for use within the City of Cleveland until an application, including not less than two sets of properly prepared plans and specifications of the process, fuel-burning, refuse-burning, or control equipment and structures or buildings used in connection therewith have been filed by the person or his agent in the office of, and have been approved by, the Commissioner of Air Pollution Control, and until an installation permit has been issued by the Commissioner for such construction, installation, reconstruction, or alteration except as stated in Section 4.0702. Such plans and specifications shall show the form and dimensions of the process, fuel-burning, refuse-burning, or control equipment, together with the description and dimensions of the building or part thereof in which such equipment is to be located, including the means provided for admitting the air for combustion processes; the character and composition of the fuel to be used; the maximum quantity of such fuel to be burned per hour; the kind and amount of raw materials processed; the expected air contaminant emission rate; the operating requirements; the use to be made of such process, fuel-burning, refuse-burning, or control equipment; contaminant concentration, gas volume, and gas temperature at the emission point; physical characteristics of particulates emitted; the location and elevation of the emission point relative to nearby structures and window openings; a flow diagram showing the equipment under consideration and its relationship to other processes, if any, and a general description of these processes; and any other reasonable and pertinent information that may be required by the Commissioner. The Commissioner shall issue a permit only if he determines from the plans and specifications that the proposed installation will not create a condition of air pollution. Failure to comply with any requests for information made by the Commissioner shall be cause for rejection of an application.

§4.0702. Emergency Repairs.

An emergency repair may be made prior to the application for an installation permit if serious air pollution consequences may result if the repair were deferred. When such repair is made, the person concerned shall notify the Commissioner of Air Pollution Control on the first business day after the emergency occurred and file an application for installation permit if directed to do so by the Commissioner.

§4.0703. Action on Permit Applications.

An application shall be acted upon within thirty calendar days after it is filed in the office of the Commissioner of Air Pollution Control. Approval of the application for a permit may, at the discretion of the Commissioner, include a condition requiring emission tests to be made upon completion of installation for which the permit has been issued, to establish compliance with the emission limitations of this ordinance. The Commissioner shall notify the person applying for the permit of the approval or reasons for rejection of the application in writing. Upon the approval of the application and upon the payment of the prescribed fees, the Commissioner shall issue a permit for the construction, reconstruction, installation, or alteration of such process, fuel-burning, refuse-burning, or control equipment.

§4.0704. Alternate Action on Permit Application.

In the event the plans, specifications, and information submitted to the Commissioner of Air Pollution Control pursuant to Section 4.0701 of this ordinance, reveal a proposal to construct, install, reconstruct or alter any process, fuel-burning, refuse--burning, or control equipment of complex design, involving technological ingenuity or advances of considerable magnitude, the Commissioner may, at his option, and in lieu of issuing an installation permit, require the applicant to file with the Commissioner a statement certifying that the proposed equipment or installation will comply with all of the applicable provisions and limitations set forth in this code. Upon filing of such certificate of compliance, the applicant may proceed with the proposed installation, subject, however, to all of the provisions of this code.

§4.0705. Applicability of the Permit.

No construction, installation, reconstruction or alteration shall be made which is not in accordance with the plans, specifications, and other pertinent information upon which the installation permit was issued without the written approval of the Commissioner of Air Pollution Control.

§4.0706. Permit Violation.

Violation of the installation permit shall be sufficient cause for the Commissioner of Air Pollution Control to stop all work in connection with said permit, and he is hereby authorized to seal the installation without notice. No further work shall be done until the Commissioner is assured that the condition in question will be corrected and that the work will proceed in accordance with the installation permit.

§4.0707. Time Limit on Permits.

If construction, reconstruction, installation, or alteration is not begun within six months nor completed within one year from the date of the issuance of the permit, such permit shall automatically become void and all fees paid shall be forfeited unless an extension of time is granted by the Commissioner of Air Pollution Control.

§4.0708. Registration of Contractors.

No permit required by the provisions of the air pollution code of the City of Cleveland shall be issued for work to be undertaken by contract except to a registered contractor, as authorized by Section 5.9735 of The Codified Ordinances of the City of Cleveland.

§4.0709. Secret Process.

Any records or other information furnished to the Division of Air Pollution Control concerning one or more air contaminant sources, which records or information, as certified by the Commissioner of Air Pollution Control, relating to processes or production unique to the owner or operator, or which tend to affect adversely the competitive position of such owner or operator, shall be only for the confidential use of the Division of Air Pollution Control in the administration of this ordinance, unless such owner or operator shall expressly agree to their publication or availability to the general public or unless the disclosure of such information is required for the prosecution of a violation of this ordinance. Nothing herein shall be construed to prevent use of such records or information by the Division in compiling or publishing analyses or summaries relating to the general condition of the ambient atmosphere, provided that such analyses or summaries do not identify any owner or operator or reveal any information otherwise confidential under this section.

CHAPTER 9—

CERTIFICATE OF OPERATION

§4.0901. Certificate of Operation.

No person shall operate or cause to be operated, any process, fuel-burning, refuse-burning, or control equipment or any equipment pertaining thereto for which an installation permit was required or was issued under this code until an inspection has been made by the Commissioner of Air Pollution Control or his representative. The person responsible for the installation, construction, reconstruction, or alteration of any process, fuel-burning, refuse-burning, or control equipment for which an installation permit is required shall notify the Commissioner when the work is completed and ready for final inspection. No equipment shall be operated for any other purpose or in any other manner than that for which the installation permit was approved and for which a certificate of operation has been issued unless otherwise authorized in writing by the Commissioner. After the installation permit has been issued and it is demonstrated to the satisfaction of the Commissioner that the process, fuel-burning, refuse-burning, or control equipment can be operated in compliance with this Code, an initial certificate of operation shall be issued by the Commissioner. Emission tests may be required by the Commissioner before the issuing of an initial certificate of operation. Said certificate of operation shall be kept posted on or near the installation for which it was issued.

The issuance of a certificate of operation shall not operate as a guarantee of immunity from prosecution or other legal action for violations occurring during the period covered by the certificate. Failure to operate under test within the limitations and requirements of this code shall constitute sufficient grounds for ordering changes in the process, fuel-burning, refuse-burning, or control equipment or appurtenances thereto before an initial certificate of operation can be granted. When the Commissioner refuses to issue a certificate of operation, the Commissioner is authorized to seal the process, fuel-burning, refuse-burning, or control equipment until the person required to procure the certificate of operation has complied with the provisions of this ordinance.

The Commissioner may, by rule or regulation, require periodic inspection of designated classes of equipment. No period of time between inspections shall exceed two (2) years.

4.0902. Renewal of Certificate of Operation.

The Commissioner of Air Pollution Control shall require:

(1) The renewal of certificates of operation on all installations for which an installation permit was obtained;

(2) Application for certificates of operation on equipment existing prior to the adoption of this code and for which no certificate of operation has been issued;

(3) Payment of appropriate fees for such certificates.

Certificates shall be renewed according to the schedule for periodic inspections.

4.0903. Denial or Revocation of Certificates of Operation.

A certificate of operation may be denied or, once granted, may be revoked:

(1) Incident to any discontinue and seal order;

(2) In an emergency where operation of the subject equipment may be dangerous to persons or property;

(3) Where no air pollution control equipment or modification, if required, has been installed to permit operation in conformity with the provisions of this code.

(4) Where equipment is of such condition or so installed that it cannot be or is not being operated in conformity with the provisions of this code.

(5) Upon failure or refusal of the person responsible to submit information required by this code.

(6) Upon failure or refusal of the person

responsible to comply with an abatement order issued under the provisions of Section 4.0504 of this code.

Notice in writing must be sent by the Commissioner of Air Pollution Control to persons in violation of paragraphs (1), (4) and (5) of this section, unless excepted pursuant to Section 4.1901, demanding compliance within a time limit set forth therein, or within a time limit extension granted by the Commissioner prior to the revocation of an existing certificate.

Denial or revocation of a certificate of operation shall not be a bar to prosecution for violation of any of the provisions of this code.

§4.0904. Prima Facie Evidence of Unlawful Emission.

In any hearing of the municipal court or any court of competent jurisdiction, the fact of operation without a valid certificate of operation, together with testimony as to ownership or responsibility from the records of the Division of Air Pollution Control shall be prima facie evidence of unlawful emissions and that the equipment for which the certificate of operation is not in effect is being operated in violation of the provisions of this ordinance.

§4.0905. Data Registration.

The Commissioner of Air Pollution Control may require periodic data registration and shall prepare appropriate forms for such purpose. The data to be registered shall include plans and specifications for equipment, and the submission required under this section is in addition to the submission of plans and specifications under Section 4.0701. The Commissioner may use such information to prepare emission inventories.

Plans and specifications for process, refuse--burning, and fuel-burning equipment shall show type of installation, the form and dimension of such equipment, the location of sources or emissions, dimensions of the building or part thereof in which equipment is located, amount of work to be accomplished by such equipment, type of fuel used, means of limiting emissions to conform to limitations set forth in this ordinance, and written evidence to substantiate information required, such as test data, calculated values, material balance, maximum quantity of fuel to be burned per hour, operating requirements, purpose and use of equipment, means of ventilating room in which equipment is located, raw material used, products produced, operating schedules, and such other information as may be required by the Commissioner of Air Pollution Control.

§4.0906. Issuance of Permits-Other Departments.

No permit for the erection, construction, reconstruction, or alteration of any building, plant, or structure, related in any manner to fuel-burning equipment, refuse-burning equipment, or process equipment which may be a source of air contaminants, shall be issued by the Commissioner of Building or by any other department, bureau, division, officer, or employee of the city until the Commissioner of Air Pollution Control has issued an installation permit covering the equipment under his jurisdiction to be used in the building, plant, or structure as provided by this code.

§4.0907. Coordination of Departments.

It shall be the duty of the various departments, bureaus, divisions, officers, and employees of the City of Cleveland, having charge of the inspection of the premises upon which such equipment is located, to cooperate with the Commissioner of Air Pollution Control to determine that the execution of work so authorized by said permit shall be done in conformity with plans and specifications approved by the Commissioner of Air Pollution Control.

§4.0908. Breakdown of Equipment.

Emissions exceeding any of the limits established under this code as a direct result of the breakdown of any such equipment, shall not be deemed to be in violation of such limits provided the owner or operator by telephone, messenger or in person immediately advises the Commissioner of Air Pollution Control of the circumstances and outlines a corrective program acceptable to the Commissioner, and confirms to the Commissioner such program in writing by registered or certified mail within five days after the occurrence of such breakdown and provided further that the Commissioner shall give written approval of the proffered corrective program.

If under this section the number of breakdowns of any piece of equipment exceed three (3) in any one year period, the Commissioner may require an owner or operator to submit a satisfactory maintenance program for such equipment. Failure to maintain equipment in accordance with such a maintenance program shall be grounds for revocation of a certificate of operation.

§4.0909. Variances.

(A) Any person who owns or is in control of any plant, building, structure, process or equipment may apply to the appeals board for a variance from provisions of this ordinance. The appeals board may grant such variance upon satisfactory proof by the applicant that:

(1) The emissions occurring or proposed to occur do not endanger or will not tend to endanger human health, safety, or welfare; and in addition that

(2) (a) Compliance with the provisions of codified ordinances from which variance is sought would produce serious hardship without equal or greater benefits to the public, or

(b) No practicable means are known or available for the adequate prevention, abatement, or control of the air pollution involved; or

(c) Compliance with the particular requirements from which variance is sought will necessitate the taking of measures which because of their extent or cost, must be spread over a considerable period of time. A variance granted upon a finding involving this paragraph (c) shall contain a time table for the taking of action in an expeditious manner and shall be conditioned on adherence to such time table.

(B) No variance shall be granted pursuant to this section except after public hearing on reasonable notice and until the appeals board has considered the relative interests of the applicant, other owners of property likely to be affected by the discharges or emissions, and the general public. Notice of such hearing shall be given to the parties affected and to the Clerk of Council.

(C) If a variance is granted, it shall be for not more than one year. Any variance may be renewed on terms and conditions and for periods of one year. If complaint is made to the appeals board on account of the variance no renewal thereof shall be granted unless following public hearing on the complaint the appeals board finds that renewal is justified. No renewal shall be granted except on application therefor. Any such application shall be made at least sixty days prior to the expiration date of the variance. Immediately upon receipt of an application for renewal the appeals board shall give public notice of such application in accordance with rules and regulations of the board.

(D) A variance or renewal shall not be a right of the applicant or holder thereof but shall be in the discretion of the appeals board, as provided in paragraph (A) of this section. Any person adversely affected by a variance or renewal granted by the board may obtain judicial relief thereof.

(E) Nothing in this section and no variance or renewal granted pursuant hereto shall be construed to prevent or limit the application of the emergency provisions and procedures of this code to any person or his property.

§4.0910.

The provisions of this code shall not apply to any combustion device erected, constructed, altered, or installed in any single or two-family house not used for commercial purpose or retail business; or any single or two-family dwelling that has not more than one retail establishment attached thereto or included therein, said retail establishment being the secondary or incidental function of the building or serving not more than two dwelling units, nor shall the provisions of this code apply to the erection, construction, alteration, installation or inspection of any warm air furnace, any unit heater, direct fired unit heater or ceiling type unit heater provided, however, that if the operation of such equipment violates Chapter 11 of this Code and a complaint is received, the Division of Air Pollution Control shall abate the violation.

§4.0911. Fees.

(A) Fees for the examination of plans and applications for the issuance of permits, and for the original inspection and certificate of operation for the construction, installation, reconstruction, or alteration of any process, fuel-burning, refuse-burning or control equipment, within the jurisdiction of this code, and renewal of certificates of operation shall be as follows:

	Permit and Initial Certificate	Renewal Certificate
PROCESS AND FUEL-BURNING EQUIPMENT FOR EACH UNIT		
1. Of a rated input capacity of less than 500,000 BTU/HR	$ 10.00	$ 5.00
2. Of a rated input capacity of 500,000 BTU/HR and less than 2,500,000 BTU/HR	25.00	10.00
3. Of a rated input capacity of 2,500,000 BTU/HR and less than 10,000,000 BTU/HR	50.00	15.00
4. Of a rated input capacity of 10,000,000 BTU/HR and less than 100,000,000 BTU/HR	100.00	25.00
5. Of a rated input capacity of 100,000,000 BTU/HR or more	200.00	50.00
REFUSE-BURNING EQUIPMENT FOR EACH UNIT		
1. Having a primary furnace volume of 6 cubic feet or less	5.00	5.00
2. Having a primary furnace volume over 6 cubic feet but less than 50 cubic feet	20.00	10.00
3. Having a primary furnace volume over 50 cubic feet but less than 100 cubic feet	40.00	15.00
4. Having a primary furnace volume of 100 cubic feet or more	60.00	25.00
PROCESS EQUIPMENT		
a. Process equipment requiring control by exhaust air ventilation in order to comply with Chapters on Prohibited Emissions.		
1. Up to 500 scfm maximum	$ 10.00	$ 5.00
2. 501-5,000 scfm maximum	15.00	5.00
3. 5,001-10,000 scfm maximum	30.00	10.00
4. 10,001-25,000 scfm maximum	45.00	15.00
5. 25,001-50,000 scfm maximum	60.00	20.00
6. Over 50,000 scfm maximum	75.00	25.00
b. Process equipment requiring control other than by exhaust air ventilation in order to comply with Chapters on Prohibited Emissions.		
1. Each piece of process equipment	15.00	5.00
2. Total fees for all pieces of process equipment in this category in each work room shall not exceed	75.00	25.00

AIR CLEANING EQUIPMENT AND APPURTENANCES

A separate permit shall be required and shall carry the same fees as the process equipment for which it is installed (see above a, 1 to 6).

ANY OTHER PROCESS EQUIPMENT

	Permit and Initial Certificate	Renewal Certificate
Any other process equipment and not included in the above schedule	15.00	5.00

(B) The provisions of this code shall apply within the City of Cleveland to all governmental units unless the imposition and collection of fees are prohibited by law.

§4.0912. Schools and Churches.

No fee shall be demanded or collected under the provisions of this code for the required inspection of combustion devices installed or to be installed in any public or parochial school or any churches in the City of Cleveland.

CHAPTER 11 — VISIBLE EMISSIONS—ODORS

§4.1101. Visible Emissions—Smoke and Equivalent Opacity.

(A) No person shall discharge or cause to be discharged, into the atmosphere from any new source of process equipment or fuel-burning equipment, approved for installation after the effective date of this code, emission of any air contaminant whatsoever which is:

(1) Of a shade or density darker than that designated as a No. 1 on the Ringelmann Chart, or

(2) Of such opacity as to obscure an observer's view to a degree greater than does smoke described in subsection (A) 1 above, or

(3) Of a shade or density darker than that designated as No. 2 on the Ringlemann Chart for a period or periods aggregating more than 3 minutes in any one hour, but not to exceed 9 minutes in any 8 hour period, or

(4) Of such opacity as to obscure an observer's view to a degree greater than does smoke described in subsection (A) 3 above for a period or periods aggregating more than 3 minutes in any 1 hour, or 9 minutes in any 8 hour period.

(B) No person shall discharge, or cause to be discharged, into the atmosphere from existing sources of process equipment, fuel-burning equipment or open fire, approved in accordance with Section 4.1501, emission of any air contaminant whatsoever, which is

(1) Of a shade or density equal to or darker than that designated as a No. 2 on the Ringelmann Chart, or

(2) Of such opacity as to obscure an observer's view to a degree greater than does smoke described in subsection (B) 1 above, or

(3) Of a shade or density equal to or darker than that designated as a No. 3 on the Ringelmann Chart for a period or periods aggregating more than 5 minutes in any 1 hour, but not to exceed 15 minutes in any 8 hour period, or

(4) Of such opacity as to obscure an observer's view to a degree greater than does smoke described in subsection B (3) above for a period or periods aggregating more than 5 minutes in any 1 hour, or 15 minutes in any 8 hour period.

(C) No person shall discharge or cause to be discharged into the atmosphere from any refuse burning equipment emissions of any air contaminant which is darker in shade or density than that designated as No. 1 on the Ringelmann Chart or of such opacity as to obscure an observer's view to a degree greater than that designated as No. 1 on the Ringelmann Chart for smoke.

(D) No person shall discharge or cause to be discharged into the atmosphere from any diesel locomotive or diesel driven steamship emissions of any air contaminant which is darker in shade or density than that designated as No. 1 on the Ringelmann Chart or of such opacity as to obscure an observer's view to a degree greater than that designated as No. 1 on the Ringelmann Chart for smoke, or of a shade or density equal to or darker than that designated as No. 3 on the Ringelmann Chart or equivalent opacity for a period or periods aggregating more than thirty (30) seconds in any three (3) consecutive minutes or four (4) minutes in fifteen (15) consecutive minutes.

(E) Exceptions and Special Provisions.

(1) The limitations on visible emissions established by paragraphs (A), (B), and (C) of this section shall not apply to fire started for the purpose of training or research, when approved by the Commissioner of Air Pollution Control.

(2) Where the presence of uncombined water is the only reason for the failure of an emission to meet the limitations established by paragraphs (A), (B), and (C) of this section, the limitations set forth in such paragraph shall not apply.

(F) All process equipment or fuel-burning equipment existing prior to the effective date of this code must be in compliance with the limits in paragraph (A) by December 31, 1971.

§4.1102. Emission of Odors into the Atmosphere.

(A) No owner, occupant or person in charge, by himself, his agent or employee, shall cause, suffer or allow the emission of odorous matter into the atmosphere such as to cause an objectional odor, as determined by the Commissioner or his duly authorized representative:

(1) On or adjacent to residential, recreational, institutional, retail sales, hotel or educational premises;

(2) On or adjacent to industrial premises when air containing such odorous matter is diluted with 20 or more volumes of odor-free air;

(3) On or adjacent to premises other than those in paragraphs (1) and (2) when air containing such odorous matter is diluted with four or more volumes of odor-free air.

(B) An odor shall also be deemed objectionable when thirty percent or more of a sample of the people exposed to it believe it to be objectionable in usual places of occupancy, the sample size to be at least twenty people or seventy-five percent of those exposed if fewer than twenty people are exposed.

(C) After an odor is deemed objectionable as provided in paragraph (B) of this section or by the Commissioner of Air Pollution Control or his duly authorized representative under paragraph (A) of this section, the Commissioner shall issue an order for abatement as provided in Section 4.0504.

§4.1103. Odors—Rendering Plants.

(A) As used in this section the term "rendering plant" includes the land, buildings, machinery, apparatus and fixtures employed in a process by which, through the use of heat or other methods, unsalable, spoiled, or contaminated animal, poultry, or fish matter is treated so as to convert it into fats and oils, food for poultry, livestock or pets, fertilizer or other products.

(B) No person shall operate or cause to be operated a rendering plant unless:

(1) All vents to the atmosphere from such rendering plant are substantially free of any odor causing air pollution;

(2) Appropriate and suitable air cleaning equipment is so placed and operated and air pollution control measures are so instituted that air contaminants are removed or re-cycled to the process in such manner that the effluent air will not create air pollution;

(3) Odor producing materials are confined and handled in such a manner that odors produced within or outside the rendering plant from this source can be controlled;

(4) Excessive accumulations of odor producing materials resulting from spillage or escape do not occur;

(5) Air contaminant emissions arising from unit operations or unit processes, as well as from the handling of general materials, are confined at the point of origin;

(6) All finished products, by-products and waste materials are either odor free or so treated as to eliminate or prevent air pollution.

(C) No person in charge, by himself, his agent or employee shall cause, suffer or allow the violation of any of the provisions of paragraph (B) of this section so as to cause a nuisance. Such nuisance may be the subject of an order for abatement, as provided in Section 4.0504.

CHAPTER 13—PARTICULATE LIMITATIONS, PROCESS, FUEL-BURNING AND REFUSE BURNING EQUIPMENT

§4.1301. Emission of Particulate Matter from Fuel Burning Equipment.

(A) No person shall cause or allow to be emitted into the atmosphere from any fuel-burning equipment or premises, or to pass a convenient measuring point near the stack outlet, particulate matter in the gases to exceed 0.60 lb. per 1,000,000 BTU heat input for installations using less than 10,000,000 BTU per hour total input. Figure I and Table I shall be used to determine the allowable particulate emission limitation for sources with a rated heat input equal to or greater than 10,000,000 BTU per hour.

(B) The burning of refuse in fuel-burning equipment is hereafter prohibited.

(C) All fuel-burning equipment existing prior to the effective date of this code must be in compliance with the limits in paragraph (A) by December 31, 1971.

§4.1302. Emission of Particulate Matter from Refuse-Burning Equipment.

(A) No person shall cause or allow to be emitted into the atmosphere from any refuse-burning equipment or premises, or to pass at a convenient measuring point near the stack outlet, particulate matter in the gases to exceed 0.40 lb. per hour for installations charging equal to or less than 175 pounds per hour of total refuse. For installations charging greater than 175 pounds per hour of total refuse, Figure II and Table II shall be used to determine the allowable particulate emission limitation.

(B) All refuse-burning equipment existing prior to the effective date of this code must be in compliance with the limits in paragraph (A) by December 31, 1971.

§4.1303. Emission of Particulate Matter from Process Equipment.

(A) No person shall cause or allow the emission of any particulate matter from any process equipment whatsoever in excess of the permitted emission as provided for in Figure III and Table III.

To use the table, find the process weight per hour in the table, and note the allowable rate of emissions in pounds per hour for said process weight per hour. If two or more process units connect to a single stack or chimney, each unit shall for the purpose of computing the maximum allowable emission rate be considered a separate entity with the allowable emission rate for the stack or chimney being the sum of the individual computations. A more severe limitation may be imposed depending upon the quantity and the degree of toxicity of individual components of the particulate emission.

(B) All process equipment existing prior to the effective date of this code shall be in compliance with the limits in paragraph (A) by December 31, 1971.

§4.1304. Conformance to Interim Standards.

(A) No person required to comply with the provisions of Chapter 13 by December 31, 1971 shall fail to comply with emission standards established by this section and figures IV, V, and VI for the period beginning with the enactment of this code and ending on December 31, 1971.

(B) No person shall cause or allow the emission of any particulate matter from fuel-burning equipment or premises for the period of time established by paragraph (A) of this section in excess of the permitted emission rate provided for in Figure IV.

(C) No person shall cause or allow the emission of particulate matter from refuse-burning equipment, metallurgical fume or dust for the period of time established by paragraph (A) of this section in excess of the permitted emission rate provided in Figure V.

(D) No person shall cause or allow the emission of particulate matter in flue gas from ferrous foundries for the period of time established by paragraph (A) of this section in excess of the permitted emission rate provided by Figure VI.

All penalties for violation of this code shall apply to violations of this section.

CHAPTER 15—MISCELLANEOUS LIMITATIONS

§4.1501. Open Fires.

(A) No person shall cause or allow the burning of paper, wood, leaves, or other combustible matter, waste material, or a motor vehicle or any part thereof within the corporate limits of the City of Cleveland in any open fire without prior written approval of the Commissioner of Air Pollution Control.

§4.1502. Emission of Sulfur Oxides.

(A) Except as provided in Section 4.1504 of the Codified Ordinances of the City of Cleveland, no person shall cause or allow the emission of gas containing sulfur oxides in excess of 2,000 ppm (volume) from any existing process equipment or in excess of 500 ppm (volume) from any new process equipment.

(B) No person shall cause or allow the use of fuel containing two percent or more of sulfur by weight in existing fuel-burning equipment or fuel containing one percent or more of sulfur by weight in new fuel-burning equipment.

(C) Nothing in paragraph (B) of this Section shall prohibit the use of fuel in fuel-burning equipment with a sulfur content greater than the maximum amount permitted by this Section, provided that the fuel-burning equipment is equipped with such control apparatus as to continually prevent the emission of any sulfur oxides in amounts greater than those that would be emitted from the burning in the same fuel-burning equipment without such control apparatus of fuel containing the maximum amount of sulfur by weight that is permitted in paragraph (B) of this Section.

(D) The percentage by weight of sulfur in the fuel shall be determined in accordance with the methods of the American Society for Testing Materials (ASTM).

(E) For the purpose of this Section all emissions of sulfur oxides shall be expressed as concentrations of sulfur dioxide.

(F) All process equipment and fuel-burning equipment existing prior to the effective date of this code must be in compliance with the limits in paragraphs (A), (B) and (C) by December 31, 1971.

§4.1503. Emission of Particulate Matter from Transporting and Material Handling in Open Air.

No person shall cause or allow the handling, processing, transporting, or storage of any material on any premises in a manner which allows or may allow particulate matter to become air-borne which exceeds either of the following standards: (1) Ringelmann No. 1 or its equivalent opacity (2) a suspended particulate matter value of 500 micrograms per cubic meter at or beyond the property line measured at normally occupied levels for a sampling period of one hour or more.

§4.1504. Nuisance.

(A) No owner, occupant or person in charge, by himself, his agent or employee, shall cause, suffer or allow the emission of air contaminants into the atmosphere so as to cause a nuisance as determined by the Commissioner of Air Pollution Control or his duly authorized representative.

(B) An emission shall also be deemed a nuisance when thirty percent or more of a sample of the people exposed to it believe it to be objectionable in usual places of occupancy, the sample size to be at least twenty people or seventy-five percent of those exposed if fewer than twenty people are exposed.

(C) After an emission is deemed a nuisance as provided in paragraph (B) of this section or by the Commissioner or his duly authorized representative under paragraph (A) of this section, the Commissioner shall issue an order for abatement as provided in Section 4.0504 of this code.

§4.1505. Other Emissions.

Air contaminants not specifically covered by provisions of this code may be the subject of tests, studies and orders for abatement by the Commissioner of Air Pollution Control.

§4.1506. Submission of Reports.

The person in charge of equipment operated prior to the enactment of this code and not conforming to Chapters 13 and 15 thereof until December 31, 1971 shall submit within six months of the enactment of this code to the Commissioner of Air Pollution Control for his approval a program for ultimate conformance to Chapters 13 and 15 of this code. Semiannually thereafter such person shall submit reports indicating progress towards ultimate conformance to Chapters 13 and 15 of this code.

CHAPTER 17—TESTING.

§4.1701. Emission Test Methods.

Emission tests shall be undertaken by generally recognized standards or methods of measurement. Methods found in the ASME Test Code for Determining Dust Concentrations in Gas Streams PTC 27-1957, the Los Angeles County Source Testing Manual or recommended procedures of the National Air Pollution Control Administration shall be used, but these may be modified or adjusted by the Commissioner of Air Pollution Control to suit specific sampling conditions or needs based upon good practice, judgment and experience. Updating of these standards and modifications thereof shall be published in rules and regulations of the Commissioner of Air Pollution Control.

§4.1702. Sampling and Testing.

(A) The Commissioner of Air Pollution Control is hereby authorized to conduct, or cause to be conducted, any test or tests of any new or existing process, fuel-burning, refuse-burning, or control equipment the operation of which in his judgment may result in emissions in excess of the limitations contained in this ordinance or when the emissions from any such equipment may exceed the limits of emissions provided for herein. All tests shall be conducted in a manner determined by the Commissioner and a complete detailed test report of such test or tests shall be submitted to him. When tests are taken by the owner or independent testers employed by the owner, the Commissioner shall require that the said tests be conducted by reputable, qualified personnel and shall stipulate that a qualified representative or representatives of the Division of Air Pollution Control be present during the conduct of such tests. The Commissioner may stipulate a reasonable time limit for the completion of such test and the submission of test reports.

(B) Nothing in this section concerning tests conducted by and paid for by any person or his authorized agent shall be deemed to abridge the rights of the Commissioner or his representatives to conduct separate or additional tests of any process, fuel--burning, refuse-burning, or control equipment on behalf of the City of Cleveland, whether or not such tests relate to emissions controlled by specific limitations under this code.

§4.1703. Test Facilities and Access.

(A) It shall be the responsibility of the owner or operator of the equipment tested to provide, at his expense, utilities, facilities and reasonable and necessary openings in the system or stack, and safe and easy access thereto, to permit samples and measurements to be taken. All new sources of air contaminants created after the effective date of this ordinance may be required by the Commissioner of Air Pollution Control to provide utilities, facilities and adequate openings in the system or stack, and safe and easy access thereto, to permit measurements and samples to be taken.

(B) When any process equipment, fuel-burning equipment or refuse-burning equipment has caused an air pollution nuisance, as determined by the Commissioner, or has violated a provision of Chapter 11, 13 or 15 of this code, the Commissioner may, at his discretion require that said equipment be equipped with an air contaminant recording device with an audible alarm set so as to become activated upon reaching prohibited levels of emission, which device shall be maintained in proper operating conditions at all times. Records from such recording device shall be made available to the Commissioner for periods up to one year.

§4.1704. Test Costs.

If emission tests conducted as a result of the action of the Commissioner of Air Pollution Control substantiate that a violation exists, the person or persons responsible for the violation shall be responsible for paying all attendant costs for conducting said tests. If said tests do not show that a violation exists, then the City shall be responsible for paying all costs for conducting the said test. In no event shall the city assume costs of providing facilities, utilities and access for such testing. When the person responsible elects to conduct his own stack emission tests, then the person so electing shall pay for the test or tests notwithstanding other provisions of this section, and irrespective of the result. The costs of emission tests required by the Commissioner on newly installed equipment for the issuance of the initial permit to install and the issuance of the initial certificate of operation shall not be at the expense of the City of Cleveland regardless of results. The tests for existing sources relating to contaminants not specifically controlled by this code shall be at the expense of the City of Cleveland except for facilities, utilities and access required to be provided by this Chapter.

§4.1705. Circumvention and Right of Entry.

(A) No person shall build, erect, install, or use any article, machine, equipment, or other contrivance, the sole purpose of which is to dilute or conceal an emission without resulting in a reduction in the total release of air contaminants to the atmosphere nor shall a person do any thing nor commit any act with the intent to distort stack test emission results.

(B) Any person who in any manner hinders, obstructs, delays, resists, prevents, or in any manner interferes or attempts to interfere with the Commissioner or his representatives in the performance of any duty enjoined, or shall refuse to permit the Commissioner or such representatives to perform their duty by refusing them, or either of them, entrance at reasonable hours to any premises in which the provisions of this ordinance are being violated, or are suspected of being violated, or refuse to permit testing, or permit the inspection or examination of such premises for the purpose of the enforcement of this ordinance shall be subject to cancellation of the certificate of operation, or such other action as may be provided at law or by provisions of this code.

CHAPTER 19—PENALTIES.

§4.1901. Sealing.

(A) Any person who has been found to have violated the provisions of this ordinance three or more times within a twelve month period, shall be notified by registered or certified mail to show cause before the Commissioner of Air Pollution Control within ten days why the offending equipment may not be sealed. The notice shall be directed to the last address of the person to be notified, or if the person or his whereabouts is unknown, then the notice shall be posted on or near the premises at which the violations have occurred. If upon the hearing, at which the violator or his agent or attorney may appear and be heard, the Commissioner finds that adequate corrective measures have not been taken, he may seal the equipment until such time as corrective measures have been taken.

(B) Sealing may also be ordered by the Commissioner and effected after reasonable notice:

(1) On any equipment being operated without a valid, unexpired certificate of operation as required by this ordinance;

(2) Where necessary repairs or alterations are not accomplished within the time limit specified and not appealed;

(3) In cases of emergency the equipment may be sealed without notice where operation of the equipment is or may reasonably be dangerous to health or safety;

(4) Where the control equipment has been installed in order to enable an operation or process to meet the conditions of the issuance of a permit or certificate of operation, but is not being operated;

(5) Where test facilities and access required under Chapter 17 are not provided;

(6) Where process equipment, fuel-burning equipment, refuse-burning equipment or control equipment has been installed without permits, the equipment may be sealed without notice.

Pursuant to Section 4.0904 of this ordinance, a prima facie evidence of violation will support the action of the Commissioner in sealing certain equipment, as provided therein.

Sealing of equipment shall not be a bar to other legal action against the owner or operator thereof.

It shall be unlawful to break or remove a seal or to operate equipment sealed by the Commissioner, unless such breaking, removal, or use is authorized in writing by the Commissioner.

§4.1902. On Site or Vicinity Citation by Waiver Ticket.

(A) Violations of the provisions of Section 4.1101 of this ordinance involving readings of the Ringelmann Chart or equivalent opacity as well as violations of Section 4.1501 which violations are determined by visual observations and violations of Sections 4.1102 and 4.1103 may be cited at the time and place of observation of violations or vicinity thereof by Air Pollution Control personnel, trained to make such observations. Upon failure of the person cited to accept such waiver ticket, the air pollution representative shall note such refusal on record and proceed as in other violations to cause an affidavit and warrant to issue.

(B) No waiver citations shall be permitted to a person who has been cited two or more times previously in a twelve month period.

§4.1903. Waivers.

(A) Notwithstanding the provisions of Section 4.1904, any person who has violated the provisions of Sections 4.1101, 4.1102, or 4.1103 of this code, upon executing before and filing with the Clerk of the Municipal Court, Criminal Branch, an instrument waiving the formal issuance of an affidavit and warrant, together with the reading of such affidavit, and the right to be present personally at the trial of such action, further waiving the right of appeal and error, authorizing a plea of guilty to be entered and submitting himself to the mercy of the Court and upon depositing within forty-eight (48) hours after citation, with said Clerk the sum of Three Hundred Fifty Dollars ($350.00) and costs of Court, or depositing within seventy-two hours after citation with said Clerk the sum of Five Hundred Dollars ($500.00) shall be fined said respective amounts by the Court.

(B) Notwithstanding the provisions of Section 4.1904, any person who has violated as a first offense the provisions of Section 4.1501 of this code, upon executing and filing with the Clerk the instrument described in paragraph (A) of this section and depositing with such instrument the sum of Twenty-Five Dollars ($25.00), shall be fined such amount by the Court.

§4.1904. Penalties.

(A) No person shall violate any of the provisions of this Code nor participate in the violation of its provisions.

(B) Whoever violates Section 4.1501 of this code or participates in the violation of its provisions shall be punished by a fine of not less than Twenty-Five Dollars ($25.00) nor more than Five Hundred Dollars ($500.00).

(C) Whoever violates or participates in the violation of Section 4.1101, 4.1301, 4.1302, 4.1303,

4.1304, 4.1502, or 4.1503 or paragraph (C) of Section 4.1901 shall be punished by a fine of not less than Five Hundred Dollars ($500.00) nor more than One Thousand Dollars ($1000.00) or imprisonment of not more than ninety days or both, for a first offense, and for each subsequent offense shall be punished by a fine of One Thousand Dollars ($1000.00) and imprisonment of ninety days.

Each day's violation shall constitute a separate offense and shall be subject to the penalties set forth in this section.

§4.1905. Emergencies.

(A) Notwithstanding other provisions of law and in addition thereto, if the Commissioner of Air Pollution Control finds that a generalized condition of air pollution exists in the city or in any part of the city and that it creates an emergency requiring immediate action to protect human health or safety he shall, with the concurrence of the Director of Public Health and Welfare and the Mayor, and upon their direction, order persons causing or contributing to the air pollution to reduce or discontinue immediately the emission of air contaminants.

(B) In the absence of a generalized condition of air pollution referred to in paragraph (A) of this section, if the Commissioner finds the emissions from the operation of one or more air contaminant sources is causing imminent danger to human health or safety, he may order the person, persons, or firms responsible for the operation or operations in question to reduce or discontinue emissions immediately, without regard to the provisions of Chapters 11, 13, and 15 of this code.

(C) Nothing in this section shall be construed to limit any power which the Mayor of the City of Cleveland may have to declare an emergency and act on the basis of such declaration, if such power is conferred by statute, ordinance, constitutional provision or inherent in the office.

CHAPTER 21—CONSTITUTIONALITY

§4.2101. Severability.

If any clause, sentence, paragraph or part of this ordinance, or the application thereof to any person, or circumstances shall for any reason be adjudged by a Court of competent jurisdiction to be unconstitutional or invalid, said judgment shall not affect, impair or invalidate the remainder of this ordinance and the application of such provisions to other persons or circumstances, but shall be confined in its operation to the controversy in which such judgment shall have been rendered and to the person, firm, corporation or circumstances involved. It is hereby declared to be the legislative intent of this body that this ordinance would have been adopted had such invalid provisions not been included.

Effective October 27, 1969.

APPENDIX A — TABLE I

Maximum Allowable Particulate Emissions from Fuel Burning Equipment

Total Input/Hr Millions of Btu.	Maximum Rate of Emissions Pounds of Particulate/Million Btu.
1 to 10	0.60
15	0.57
30	0.49
50	0.45
70	0.42
100	0.39
500	0.28
1,000	0.24
2,000	0.21
5,000	0.18
10,000 and over	0.15

Interpolation of the data in this table for values between 10 and 10,000 millions of BTU not given shall be accomplished by use of the equation $E = 0.953H^{-0.201}$, where E = Maximum allowable particulate matter emission rate ($\#/10^6$Btu) and H = Total heat input in millions (10^6) Btu/hr.

APPENDIX B — TABLE II

Maximum Allowable Particulate Emissions from Refuse Burning Equipment

Total Refuse Charged Pounds per Hour	Allowable Emissions Pounds per Hour
175 or less	0.40
200	0.45
250	0.56
300	0.67
400	0.88
500	1.10
750	1.61
1,000	2.14
2,500	5.20
5,000	10.15
7,500	15.10
10,000	19.50
20,000	39.00
50,000	95.05
100,000	186.20

Interpolation of the data in this table for refuse burning equipment over 175 pounds per hour capacity shall be accomplished by use of the equation $E = 0.00263\ R^{0.97}$, where E is the rate of emission in pounds per hour and R represents refuse charged in pounds per hour.

APPENDIX C — TABLE III

Allowable Rate of Emission Based on Process Weight Rate

Process Weight Rate Lb/Hr	Process Weight Rate Tons/Hr	Rate of Emission Lb/Hr	Process Weight Rate Lb/Hr	Process Weight Rate Tons/Hr	Rate of Emission Lb/Hr
100	0.05	0.551	16,000	8.00	16.5
200	0.10	0.877	18,000	9.00	17.9
400	0.20	1.40	20,000	10.	19.2
600	0.30	1.83	30,000	15.	25.2
800	0.40	2.22	40,000	20.	30.5
1,000	0.50	2.58	50,000	25.	35.4
1,500	0.75	3.38	60,000	30.	40.0
2,000	1.00	4.10	70,000	35.	41.3
2,500	1.25	4.76	80,000	40.	42.5
3,000	1.50	5.38	90,000	45.	43.6
3,500	1.75	5.96	100,000	50.	44.6
4,000	2.00	6.52	120,000	60.	46.3
5,000	2.50	7.58	140,000	70.	47.8
6,000	3.00	8.56	160,000	80.	49.0
7,000	3.50	9.49	200,000	100	51.2
8,000	4.00	10.4	1,000,000	500.	69.0
9,000	4.50	11.2	2,000,000	1,000.	77.6
10,000	5.00	12.0	6,000,000	3,000	92.7
12,000	6.00	13.6			

Interpolation of the data in this table for process weight rates up to 60,000 lb/hr shall be accomplished by use of the equation $E = 4.10\ P^{0.67}$ and interpolation and extrapolation of the data for process weight rates in excess of 60,000 lb/hr shall be accomplished by use of the equation: $E = 55.0P^{0.11} - 40$, where E = rate of emission in lb/hr and P = process weight rate in tons/hr.

home rule differences

The Cleveland Code was promulgated in a state where home rule powers are broad and where until very recently state efforts were virtually non-existent. Most, but not all, states fall into the Ohio pattern. New Jersey is an example where the State program has for some years completely dominated the pollution control field.

In New Jersey local governments can adopt more stringent codes than the State's, but approval of the State government is required. The Federal required implementation plan meant increased participation by municipal government, and thus in 1969 the State created a local program coordinator. Codes promulgated by the New Jersey Department of Environmental Protection are generally not enforceable by local government unless adopted as a local ordinance. Air pollution from private residences are normally controlled only by local ordinances. To assist local communities and provide uniformity, the state prepared a model ordinance. The state also assists the local government when problems are beyond its technical capability and helps in control efforts. Coordination with State requirements concerning construction and installation permits, and certificates of operation, is necessary.

Regional agencies are encouraged by the Federal government and are provided for by N.J.S.A. 26:3-83. Regional agencies must develop programs consistent with the Federal "guidelines for Approval of Local Ordinances and Applications for Federal Grants for Air Pollution Control." In addition, the activities must be in accord with the New Jersey Air Quality Control Region Implementation Plan required by the Air Quality Act of 1967. Financing of these regional agencies is from local, state and federal funds. Regional air pollution agencies have violations prosecuted in the local municipal court by the municipal attorney. The maximum fine is $500 though some local air pollution codes provide jail sentences of up to 90 days for a second conviction in a twelve-month period. Thus chronic violations may also be referred to the N.J. Department of Environmental Protection for prosecution. State laws provide for a maximum penalty of $2,500 per day and/or injunctive relief.

REFERENCES

Pluta and Tozzi, Development of Local Air Pollution Control Programs in New Jersey, 64th Annual Meeting of the Air Pollution Control Association, June 27–July 2, 1971.

Goldshare and Tozzi, The State's role in the development of local air pollution control programs, 21 J. Air. Poll. Control Assoc. 115 (March 1971)

Local Regulation of Air Pollution, Washington University L. Q., 1968

Mix, The Misdemeanor Approach to Pollution Control, 10 Arizona L. Rev. 90 (1968)

SELECTED BIBLIOGRAPHY

MULCHAY, CAMARA and SEE: "A Constitutional Problem with Effect on Air Pollution Control," 10 *Arizona L. Rev.* 120 1968

POLLACK, "Legal Boundaries of Air Pollution Control—State and Local Legislative Purpose and Techniques," 33 *Law and Contemporary Problems* 331, Spring 1969

HENZ, "The Ringelmann Number as an Irreputable Presumption of Guilt, An Outdated Concept," 3 *Nat. Res. Law* 232, May 1970

EDELMAN, "The Law of Air Pollution Control," 1970

LANDAU and RHEINGOLD, *The Environmental Law Handbook*, 1971

Los Angeles County Air Pollution Control District *Profile of air pollution control in Los Angeles County*, Los Angeles, 1969

DEGLER, Stanley E., *State Air Pollution Control Laws*, Washington, BNA Books, 1969

LEWIS, S. F., GORDON, A. H., and HARTELIUS, C. J., "Law and the Municipal Ecology, Air, Water, Noise, Over-Population," *Nimlo Research Report* 156, 1970

APPENDIX—Chapter Three

FEDERAL REGISTER, VOL. 36, NO. 84
FRIDAY, APRIL 30, 1971

Title 42—PUBLIC HEALTH

Chapter IV—Environmental Protection Agency

PART 410—NATIONAL PRIMARY AND SECONDARY AMBIENT AIR QUALITY STANDARDS

AUTHORITY: The provisions of this Part 410 issued under sec. 4, Public Law 91–604, Stat. 1679.

A new Part 410 is added to Chapter IV, Title 42, Code of Federal Regulations as follows:

§ 410.1 Definitions.

(a) As used in this part, all terms not defined herein shall have the meaning given them by the Act.

(b) "Act" means the Clean Air Act, as amended (Public Law 91–604; 84 Stat. 1676).

(c) "Agency" means the Environmental Protection Agency.

(d) "Administrator" means the Administrator of the Environmental Protection Agency.

(e) "Ambient air" means that portion of the atmosphere, external to buildings, to which the general public has access.

(f) "Reference method" means a method of sampling and analyzing for an air pollutant, as described in an appendix to this part.

(g) "Equivalent method" means any method of sampling and analyzing for an air pollutant which can be demonstrated to the Administrator's satisfaction to have a consistent relationship to the reference method.

§ 410.2 Scope.

(a) National primary and secondary ambient air quality standards under section 109 of the Act are set forth in this part.

(b) National primary ambient air quality standards define levels of air quality which the Administrator judges are necessary, with an adequate margin of safety, to protect the public health. National secondary ambient air quality standards define levels of air quality which the Administrator judges necessary to protect the public welfare from any known or anticipated adverse effects of a pollutant. Such standards are subject to revision, and additional primary and secondary standards may be promulgated as the Administrator deems necessary to protect the public health and welfare.

(c) The promulgation of national primary and secondary ambient air quality standards shall not be considered in any manner to allow significant deterioration of existing air quality in any portion of any State.

(d) The proposal, promulgation, or revision of national primary and secondary ambient air quality standards shall not prohibit any State from establishing ambient air quality standards for that State or any portion thereof which are more stringent than the national standards.

§ 410.3 Reference conditions.

All measurements of air quality are corrected to a reference temperature of 25° C. and to a reference pressure of 760 millimeters of mercury (1,013.2 millibars).

§ 410.4 National primary ambient air quality standards for sulfur oxides (sulfur dioxide).

The national primary ambient air quality standards for sulfur oxides, measured as sulfur dioxide by the reference method described in Appendix A to this part, or by an equivalent method, are:

(a) 80 micrograms per cubic meter (0.03 p.p.m.)—annual arithmetic mean.

(b) 365 micrograms per cubic meter (0.14 p.p.m.)—Maximum 24-hour concentration not to be exceeded more than once per year.

§ 410.5 National secondary ambient air quality standards for sulfur oxides (sulfur dioxide).

The national secondary ambient air quality standards for sulfur oxides, measured as sulfur dioxide by the reference method described in Appendix A to this part, or by an equivalent method, are:

(a) 60 micrograms per cubic meter (0.02 p.p.m.)—annual arithmetic mean.

(b) 260 micrograms per cubic meter (0.1. p.p.m.)—maximum 24-hour concentration not to be exceeded more than once per year, as a guide to be used in assessing implementation plans to achieve the annual standard.

(c) 1,300 micrograms per cuibc meter (0.5 p.p.m.)—maximum 3-hour concentration not to be exceeded more than once per year.

§ 410.6 National primary ambient air quality standards for particulate matter.

The national primary ambient air quality standards for particulate matter, measured by the reference method described in Appendix B to this part, or by an equivalent method, are:

(a) 75 micrograms per cubic meter—annual geometric mean.

(b) 260 micrograms per cubic meter—maximum 24-hour concentration not to be exceeded more than once per year.

§ 410.7 National secondary ambient air quality standards for particulate matter.

The national secondary ambient air quality standards for particulate matter, measured by the reference method described in Appendix B to this part, or by an equivalent method, are:

(a) 60 micrograms per cubic meter—annual geometric mean, as a guide to be used in assessing implementation plans to achieve the 24-hour standard.

(b) 150 micrograms per cubic meter—maximum 24-hour concentration not to be exceeded more than once per year.

§ 410.8 National primary and secondary ambient air quality standards for carbon monoxide.

The national primary and secondary ambient air quality standards for carbon monoxide, measured by the reference method described in Appendix C to this part, or by an equivalent method, are:

(a) 10 milligrams per cubic meter (9 p.p.m.)—maximum 8-hour concentration not to be exceeded more than once per year.

(b) 40 milligrams per cubic meter (35 p.p.m.)—maximum 1-hour concentration not to be exceeded more than once per year.

§ 410.9 National primary and secondary ambient air quality standards for photochemical oxidants.

The national primary and secondary ambient air quality standard for photochemical oxidants, measured and corrected for interferences due to nitrogen oxides and sulfur dioxide by the reference method described in Appendix D to this part, or by an equivalent method, is: 160 micrograms per cubic meter (0.08 p.p.m.)—maximum 1-hour concentration not to be exceeded more than once per year.

§ 410.10 National primary and secondary ambient air quality standard for hydrocarbons.

The hydrocarbons standard is for use as a guide in devising implementation plans to achieve oxidant standards.

The national primary and secondary ambient air quality standard for hydrocarbons, measured and corrected for methane by the reference method described in Appendix E to this part, or by an equivalent method, is: 160 micrograms per cubic meter (0.24 p.p.m.)—maximum 3-hour concentration (6 to 9 a.m.) not to be exceeded more than once per year.

§ 410.11 National primary and secondary ambient air quality standard for nitrogen dioxide.

The national primary and secondary ambient air quality standard for nitrogen dioxide, measured by the reference method described in Appendix F to this part, or by an equivalent method, is: 100 micrograms per cubic meter (0.05 p.p.m.)—annual arithmetic mean.

NOTE: The extensive and very technical appendices listed below are omitted. They may be found in the Federal Register as cited.

Appendix A—Reference Method for the Determination of Sulfur Dioxide in the Atmosphere (Pararosaniline Method).

Appendix B—Reference Method for the Determination of Suspended Particulates in the Atmosphere (High Volume Method).

Appendix C—Reference Method for the Continuous Measurement of Carbon monoxide in the Atmosphere (Non-dispersive Infrared Spectrometry).

Appendix D—Reference Method for the Measurement of Photochemical Oxidants Corrected for Interferences Due to Nitrogen Oxide and Sulfur Dioxide.

Appendix E—Reference Method for the Determination of Hydrocarbons Corrected for Methane.

Appendix F—Reference Method for the Determination of Nitrogen Dioxide (24-Hour Sampling Method).

Executive Order 11602, Providing for Administration of the Clean Air Act with Respect to Federal Contracts, Grants, or Loans — June 30, 1971

By virtue of the authority vested in me by the provisions of the Clean Air Act, as amended (42 U.S.C. 1857 et seq.), and particularly section 306 of that Act as added by the Clean Air Amendments of 1970 (Public Law 91–604, approved December 31, 1970), it is hereby ordered as follows:

SECTION 1. *Policy.* It is the policy of the Federal Government to improve and enhance environmental quality. In furtherance of that policy, the program prescribed in this Order is instituted to assure that each Federal agency empowered to enter into contracts for the procurement of goods, materials, or services and each Federal agency empowered to extend Federal assistance by way of grant, loan, or contract shall undertake such procurement and assistance activities in a manner that will result in effective enforcement of the Clean Air Act (hereinafter referred to as "the Act").

SEC. 2. *Designation of Facilities.* (a) The Administrator of the Environmental Protection Agency (hereinafter referred to as "the Administrator") shall be responsible for the attainment of the purposes and objectives of this Order.

(b) In carrying out his responsibilities under this Order, the Administrator shall, in conformity with all applicable requirements of law, designate facilities which have given rise to a conviction for an offense under section 113(c)(1) of the Act. The Administrator shall, from time to time, publish and circulate to all Federal agencies lists of those facilities, together with the names and addresses of the persons who have been convicted of such offenses. Whenever the Administrator determines that the condition which gave rise to a conviction has been corrected, he shall promptly remove the facility and the name and address of the person concerned from the list.

SEC. 3. *Contracts, Grants, or Loans.* (a) Except as provided in section 8 of this Order, no Federal agency shall enter into any contract for the procurement of goods, materials, or services which is to be performed in whole or in part in a facility then designated by the Administrator pursuant to section 2.

(b) Except as provided in section 8 of this Order, no Federal agency authorized to extend Federal assistance by way of grant, loan, or contract shall extend such assistance in any case in which it is to be used to support any activity or program involving the use of a facility then designated by the Administrator pursuant to section 2.

SEC. 4. *Procurement, Grant, and Loan Regulations.* The Federal Procurement Regulations, the Armed Services Procurement Regulations, and, to the extent necessary, any supplemental or comparable regulations issued by any agency of the Executive Branch shall, following consultation with the Administrator, be amended to require, as a condition of entering into, renewing, or extending any contract for the procurement of goods, materials, or services or extending any assistance by way of grant, loan, or contract, inclusion of a provision requiring compliance with the Act and standards issued pursuant thereto in the facilities in which the contract is to be performed, or which are involved in the activity or program to receive assistance.

Sec. 5. *Rules and Regulations.* The Administrator shall issue such rules, regulations, standards, and guidelines as he may deem necessary or appropriate to carry out the purpose of this Order.

Sec. 6. *Cooperation and Assistance.* The head of each Federal agency shall take such steps as may be necessary to insure that all officers and employees of his agency whose duties entail compliance or comparable functions with respect to contracts, grants, and loans are familiar with the provisions of this Order. In addition to any other appropriate action, such officers and employees shall report promptly any condition in a facility which may involve noncompliance with the Act or any rules, regulations, standards, or guidelines issued pursuant to this Order to the head of the agency, who shall transmit such report to the Administrator.

Sec. 7. *Enforcement.* The Administrator may recommend to the Department of Justice or other appropriate agency that legal proceedings be brought or other appropriate action be taken whenever he becomes aware of a breach of any provision required, under the amendments issued pursuant to section 4 of this Order, to be included in a contract or other agreement.

Sec. 8. *Exemptions—Reports to Congress.* (a) Upon a determination that the paramount interest of the United States so requires—

(1) The head of a Federal agency may exempt any contract, grant, or loan, and, following consultation with the Administrator, any class of contracts, grants or loans from the provisions of this Order. In any such case, the head of the Federal agency granting such exemption shall (A) promptly notify the Administrator of such exemption and the justification therefor; (B) review the necessity for each such exemption annually; and (C) report to the Administrator annually all such exemptions in effect. Exemptions granted pursuant to this section shall be for a period not to exceed one year. Additional exemptions may be granted for periods not to exceed one year upon the making of a new determination by the head of the Federal agency concerned.

(2) The Administrator may, by rule or regulation, exempt any or all Federal agencies from any or all of the provisions of this Order with respect to any class or classes of contracts, grants, or loans which (A) involve less than specified dollar amounts, or (B) have a minimal potential impact upon the environment, or (C) involve persons who are not prime contractors or direct recipients of Federal assistance by way of contracts, grants, or loans.

(b) Federal agencies shall reconsider any exemption granted under subsection (a) whenever requested to do so by the Administrator.

(c) The Administrator shall annually notify the President and the Congress of all exemptions granted, or in effect, under this Order during the preceding year.

Sec. 9. *Related Actions.* The imposition of any sanction or penalty under or pursuant to this Order shall not relieve any person of any legal duty to comply with any provision of the Act.

Sec. 10. *Applicability.* This Order shall not apply to contracts, grants, or loans involving the use of facilities located outside the United States.

Richard Nixon.

Urban air pollution problems

The following is excerpted from the Report to the Administrator of the Environmental Protection Agency on *Our Urban Environment and Our Most Endangered People* (1971):

Air Pollution In Urban Areas

Air Pollution Levels, Low In the Country, High In the City—Over every urban area, on a typical day, one finds a dome of polluted air. The 1971 Annual Report of the Council on Environmental Quality contains data describing the air pollution gradient as it increases from remote to urban areas. The data show central city residents breathing air containing five times (500 percent) more suspended particulate matter than air being breathed by people in remote areas. The difference in the lead content of polluted city air and clean rural air is even more striking—50 times, (5,000 percent) more lead in the city air.

The Polluted Urban Air—The pollution content of the air varies not only from time to time and place to place, within a given city, but also from city to city. Thus, the air pollution problem of Washington, D.C., which is primarily caused by motor vehicles, differs considerably from the problem of an industrial city, such as Gary, Indiana. Generally, the same pollutants are found in the air of every city, only the relative concentrations of each pollutant vary from city to city. For example, there is more particulate matter in the air over Gary, Indiana than over Washington, D.C., but in Washington the photochemical oxidants resulting from automobile emissions are likely to be more of a problem than in Gary, Indiana.

Air Pollutants and Their Effects, Especially on the Poor—Air pollution dosage can be appreciated best with a knowledge of the various pollutants and their effects on people.

Air Pollutants at the dosage levels found in inner cities are injurious to man, animals, vegetation, metals, and building materials and fabrics and property in general. Such levels cause man discomfort, eye irritation, and difficulty in breathing. Pollution levels restrict his enjoyment of the environment by reducing visibility and violating his aesthetic values. Of all these effects, the most pressing is the destruction of man's health. Each pollutant adds its burden to urban man's health problems.

Particulates—Particulates is a general term for particles of solid matter which are found in the air of all industrialized cities and towns. Particulate matter may be composed of one substance or a combination of substances. The following is an analysis of particulate matter composition.

TABLE 1

Suspended particulates—102 micrograms (millionth of a gram) per cubic meter (micrograms/m^3) average

Analyzed fractions	micrograms/m^3
Benzene soluble organics	6.9
Benzo (a) pyrene	.002
Ammonium	0.06
Nitrate salts	2.9
Sulfate salts	10.7
16 metals—at highest measured levels in U.S.	18.33
Total known	39.432 micrograms/m^3

Ambient air quality standards to protect the public's health have been set for particulate matter at 75 micrograms per cubic meter for an annual average, and at 260 micrograms/m^3 maximum, for 24 hours, not to be exceeded more than once a year.

Most major cities have particulate concentrations which exceed the national standards. In many cities the standards are exceeded by a factor of two. For example, in the "Critical Areas" report the following annual average suspended particulate concentrations were given:

TABLE 2

	micrograms/ m^3
Chattanooga	181
Gary	151
Indianapolis	158
Los Angeles	145
New York	189
Washington	104

effects of soot

Particulates (soot is a common particulate) have subtle but significant effects on health. Particulates are of concern for several reasons:

1. Some particles are so small they elude the human respiratory system's ability to remove them and they therefore remain in the lung.

2. Particulates are often composed of toxic substances. Some are carcinogenic (cancer-causing) substances.

3. Some particulates increase the harmful effects of other pollutants which are present in inhaled air.

4. Particulate matter can react in the atmosphere to increase the amount of harmful pollution—sulfur dioxide is converted to more toxic sulfur trioxide in the presence of some mineral particles.

Particulates are often a severe pollution problem in the inner city because factories, power plants, and incinerators built many years ago are not equipped with modern emission control equipment. The urban poor are often housed near such heavy sources of pollution.

Sulfur Oxides—Sulfur Oxides is a generic term for another class of pollutants which includes sulfur dioxide, sulfur trioxide and their acids and acid salts. These pollutants result from the combustion of fuels containing sulfur.

The ambient air standard for sulfur oxides is 80 micrograms/ m^3 or (0.03 ppm), annual arithmetic average. Sulfur oxides concentrations vary considerably from city to city because the fuels used in different cities have different sulfur contents. Thus, while Los Angeles has ambient concentrations of 65 micrograms/ m^3, approaching the standard, Chicago has sulfur oxides levels of 372 micrograms/ m^3, or more than three times the level considered protective of the public's health. The sulfur oxides attack the sensitive tissues of the lungs and are believed to be a contributing factor in the development of emphysema and other respiratory diseases.

Oxidants—Oxidants are a major class of chemical compounds found in photochemical smog. An ambient air quality standard to protect the public's health has been set by EPA at 125 micrograms/ m^3 or 0.06 ppm for one (1) hour not be exceeded more than once a year. Oxidants, ozone being the most common oxident, result primarily from the interaction of automobile exhaust gases (hydrocarbons and oxides of nitrogen) under the influence of sunlight. Ozone causes irritation of the respiratory system and causes difficulty in breathing.

In Los Angeles, to protect their health, children are restricted from active play on high smog days. The urban poor of Los Angeles live in Watts, which is located in one of the worst smog areas of the L.A. basin. The adverse health effects of smog are not the most pressing problems of the people of Watts, but they are a real though unappreciated part of the oppressive burden they carry.

Oxides of Nitrogen—Oxides of Nitrogen is a term which refers to the family of compounds of oxygen and nitrogen which are formed when combustion occurs. The ambient air quality standard for nitrogen dioxide (the most toxic of the nitrogen oxides) has recently been set by the Administrator at 100 micrograms/m³ or 0.05 ppm for annual average. In Washington, D.C., the continuous Air Monitoring Program (CAMP) station recorded an annual average of 0.05 ppm in 1968 (the last year of data presented in the criteria document for nitrogen oxides). In most major cities yearly average nitrogen dioxide levels are approaching levels known to be harmful to health. On high pollution days concentrations of 0.05 ppm are often exceeded by a factor of 4.

Nitrogen dioxide is the compound of most concern since its toxicity is even greater than the toxicity of an equal amount of carbon monoxide.

Carbon Monoxide—Ambient air quality standards to protect the public's health have been set for carbon monoxide at 10 micrograms/m³ (9 ppm) for an 8 hour maximum, not to be exceeded more than once a year. This value was exceeded 70 percent of the time at the Chicago CAMP station between 1962-1967. On the city streets where the urban poor live, traffic frequently creates carbon monoxide levels on the order of 100 ppm. Traffic jams create levels of several hundred parts per million (ppm) carbon monoxide.

The toxicity of carbon monoxide is a result of its chemical characteristic of attacking the blood's oxygen carrying capacity. Carbon monoxide reacts with the red blood cells 200 times faster than oxygen. The ambient levels of carbon monoxide commonly found in city air (around 10 ppm) result in individuals living day in and day out, deprived of 2 percent of their blood's oxygen carrying capacity. The urban poor who live and play on city streets are deprived of even more of their blood's oxygen carrying capacity. Ambient carbon monoxide levels may poison as much as 5 percent of the blood. Lest one erroneously conclude 2 to 5 percent to be an insignificant deprivation of oxygen, one must remember certain points:

1. Thirty percent of the body's oxygen is used by just one physiological organ - the brain.
2. Dizziness and headache result with over 5 percent deprivation.
3. Above 50 percent deprivation death occurs.
4. The rule of thumb, often used by air pollution control officials to relate effects with ambient concentrations is:
   10 ppm—Dullness (of thought process)
   100 ppm—Dizziness
   1,000 ppm—Death

Inner city residents continually carry a heavy carbon monoxide poisoning burden. Their other environmental burdens: noise, rats, malnutrition, undernourishment, pesticides, and all the other air pollutants magnify the significance of the carbon monoxide burden. This is especially true for those urban poor with heriditary traits, such as sickle cell anemia, and the G6PD deficiency, which make them particularly vulnerable to the effects of carbon monoxide.

For example, the National Academy of Sciences Report on "The Effects of Chronic Exposure to Low Levels of Carbon Monoxide on Human Health, Behavior and Performance" devotes a chapter to the effect of carbon monoxide in the presence of abnormal hemoglobin. In this chapter concern is expressed that people with anemia or other abnormal hematological conditions will suffer magnified adverse effects when exposed to carbon monoxide.

> "Carboxyhemoglobin in theory can affect the physical-chemical equilibria and reaction velocities of abnormal hemoglobins to a different extent from those of normal hemoglobin A. However, the loss of oxygen-transport capacity and shift of the dissociation curve for oxygen to the left, as mentioned earlier (*) for normal Hb, are often exaggerated by anemia and complicate it."

*"A second, more subtle disadvantage is that the effective O_2Hb dissociation curve is shifted to the left and becomes relatively more hyperbolic. Although the affinity for oxygen is increased, the tissue cells are in jeopardy, because the local pO_2 must be reduced to remove a given amount of oxygen from the Hb."

effects of lead

Lead—Lead air pollution occurs in two forms: inorganic solid lead particles so tiny as to be invisible to the naked eye, and organic lead in vapor form.

Lead vapors last only briefly in the atmosphere, they quickly convert from the vapor to the solid particle form. But lead vapors are of concern because they are estimated to be ten times more toxic than lead particles. Automobiles emit most of the lead found in urban air, (roughly 90 percent). Lead emissions from tailpipes are a by-product of the combustion of leaded gasoline.

Lead Air Standards—Recently, California adopted an ambient air quality standard for lead of 1.5 micrograms/m³ over a 30 day averaging time. Yet this level is often exceeded in urban areas and that urban lead levels have increased during the 1960's.

Lead Air Standards Exceeded—Every day millions of U.S. citizens are breathing air which is contaminated to levels beyond these standards. Residents of urban areas breathe air with annual average concentrations of lead ranging from 1 micrograms/m³ to 3 micrograms/m³. In a current report, Colucci, Begeman and Kulmar recorded an annual average of 7.9 micrograms/m³ at Herald Square, New York City. Recent NASN data show 11 cities exceeding California's 1.5 micrograms/m³ level 30 day standard all year long as follows:

11 Cities	*Annual Average Lead micrograms per cubic meter*
Phoenix	2.00
San Francisco	2.00
Oakland	2.07
Burlington	2.08
Fairbanks, Alaska	2.12
Detroit	2.42
Scranton	2.50
Long Beach	2.60
Glendale	2.80
Omaha, Nebraska	2.80
Los Angeles	3.10

Data on localized in-traffic or near-freeway conditions reveal much greater exposure to atmospheric lead. In a review of this data, Landau, Smith, and Lynn reported "Lead concentrations measured in traffic have been about an order of magnitude higher than those measured at off the road sampling cities . . . in a 1967 study designed to determine the levels of lead in cars in rush hour traffic, ½ hour averages in the 5-25 micrograms/m³ range were found."

Dr. Goldsmith testified that monthly average values in excess of 5 micrograms/m³ have been recorded in Los Angeles and individual samples obtained near heavily traveled roadways contained concentrations in excess of 50 micrograms/m³.

A rough picture of urban air masses which seems to be forming shows far out surburban levels of 0.1 micrograms/m³ and urban levels of 1.0 micrograms/m³. This gradient can also be seen in blood lead levels of the exposed populations. A composite figure for the blood and lead level of the rural American male is 16 micrograms/100g while the composite figure for the urban American male is 21/100g, more than 30 percent higher. For females the figures are 10 micrograms/100g rural, and 16 micrograms/100g urban, or a 60 percent increase with exposure.

Health Effects of Lead—Historically lead has been known to be toxic to humans for over 2000 years. Its effects on the human organism seem to be diverse, diffuse, and many. Inorganic lead is thoroughly implicated as a causative agent in decreased hemoglobin synthesis, liver and kidney damage, mental retardation in children and in abnormalities of fertility and pregnancy.

Any discussion of the health effects of lead must be set in proper perspective. The following quote from a classical medical text on lead toxicology does this:

"One of the most dangerous features of lead poisoning is the

> insidiousness of its development. Absorption, excretion and storage of excessive quantities of lead may continue for many years without significant manifestation of intoxication."

The body's long term, delayed response to lead can be seen from this excerpt from a report on a lead experiment.

> "The daily absorbed dose for the first dosage level was about 0.50 mg; this produced a noticeable decrease in red blood cell count and hemoglobin count *within two months,* while urine coproporphyrin rose sharply *within two weeks.*"

Lead also is absorbed rapidly by bone and apparently is released at a slow rate over extended periods of time. Lead workers, removed several years from exposure, still have shown high levels of porphyrin in their blood. Presumably, sufficient lead was released slowly from accumulated reserves to interfere with porphyrin metabolism.

Children are much more susceptible to lead intoxication than adults. Encephalopathy and mental deterioration in lead-poisoned children have been well documented. One study disclosed that 200 normal children had blood lead levels of 14 to 30 micrograms per 100 grams of blood while 100 mentally defective children showed 40 to 80 micrograms per 100 grams of blood. Aminolevulinic acid levels in the blood of these latter children were also high. It has been stated that an upper limit for blood lead in children should be 40 micrograms per 100 grams of blood. This figure already borders on the lower value found in affected children, though general population studies of children have not been done.

burden on poor

Longer Exposure—High air pollution levels found in city areas have long been a cause for concern. These high levels have a greater impact on the urban poor than the average urban dweller.

Urban poor tend to live, work, and play in the inner city, thus they spend twenty-four hours a day, nearly everyday, breathing higher air pollution levels. The middle class, on the other hand, lives, works, and/or plays much of the time in the areas where the air is cleaner. They have the financial means to live in the suburbs, or cleaner parts of town, take day trips through the country-side nearby, spend summers at the lake, etc. At the end of a year's time the urban poor have spent considerably more time breathing polluted air than their more affluent suburban counterparts.

Urban poor tend to live in row or tenemant housing close to street traffic. They breathe the high pollution levels produced by traffic coming into the city in the morning and leaving in the evening. This type of living is in sharp contrast to suburban residential living which is typified by houses, surrounded by grass and shrubbery, and set back from tree lined streets over which pass occasional cars.

Typically higher traffic counts on inner city streets cause high peak pollution levels. These peak levels are often 10 to 30 times higher than average ambient levels. An example of higher traffic counts can be seen from Table 5 below:

TABLE 5

ESTIMATED VEHICLE COUNTS BY LAND USE CATEGORY

GARY, Indiana — 1968

TYPE	COUNT, VEHICLES/DAY
Major streets	17,000
Industrial	14,000
Commercial	10,000
Residential —	
Single dwelling	500
Multiple dwelling	1,000
Other	1,000

People in the inner city experience high pollution levels caused by higher traffic counts and more frequent traffic jams. The road in front of an average suburban home carries traffic typified by a car cruising at 25 mph—the lowest pollution traffic mode. The street in front of an average city house carries high traffic counts typified by frequent stops with long idle periods, accelerations and decelerations—all high pollution traffic modes.

In the inner city, houses are not the only things found in a dilapidated condition. Factories built in the early 1900's are now surrounded by low income housing. These factories are often equipped with outdated, inadequate, dilapidated or poorly maintained air pollution controls (sometimes no emission controls).

The Result of Higher Pollution Levels and Greater Exposure—Air Pollution Poisoning—The net effect of these conditions is to expose inner city residents, especially urban poor, to more pollution than suburbanites and far more than rural residents. The results of such greater exposure can be seen in the following simmary of a study of the blood lead content of residents of the Philadelphia area:

> Blood specimens of three groups of persons in the Philadelphia area were taken to determine the amount of lead in their systems. The groups were divided into those who had lived and worked in the down-town area, and those who lived in the same neighborhood as the suburban commuter, but also worked in the suburbs. For both men and women, lead was significantly highest in the city dwellers. The suburbanites who worked in the city showed higher lead concentrations than those who lived and worked in the suburbs.

These results demonstrate the greater dosage of pollution received by inner city residents. The dosage received by any given individual is determined by the level of pollution to which the individual is exposed and the length of time such exposure continues.

A graph from the California Department of Public Health shows the effects of higher lead dosage received by inner city residents—the higher the dosage of lead breathed, the higher the levels of lead found in the blood. Thus the dosage received in the inner city environment is far greater than received in the less hostile environment of the suburbs. The hostility of the inner city environment has often been credited with contributing to the "flee to the suburbs" both because it enabled people to move out of the city away from mass transit systems and because it helped convert the city into a hostile environment. In fact it has been conjectured by cynics that the automobile industry has a positive incentive to design cars that continue to pollute city air.

It is maintained that the automobile industry's historic opposition to stringent emission control standards and mass transit is rooted in their interest in furthering the "flee to the suburb" syndrome, because, suburbanites are totally dependent upon the automobile for their transportation needs.

Lead Poisoning of the Urban Poor

Lead in gasoline contributes to the dangerously high blood lead levels found in inner city children. Some 400,000 inner city children are believed to be suffering from high blood lead levels. The street dirt found in the inner city, containing high levels of lead from the tailpipes of automobiles burning leaded gasoline, adds to the lead burden of inner city children.

While airborne lead is of concern to the 130 million inhabitants of urban America, it is of a special concern to the inner city poor, especially the children because the children are:

a. very sensitive to lead.
b. exposed to the highest concentrations of lead.
c. ingesting lead from both the street air and street dirt in which they play.

d. ingesting lead from lead based paints found in dilapidated housing.
e. carrying dangerously high blood lead levels (an estimated 400,000 of them)
f. undernourished and malnourished, with diminished ability to ward off the effects of environmental lead assault which include mental retardation and death.
g. have a high prevalence of anemia. The National Pre-School Nutrition Survey found 48% of the children tested from low-income families suffering from iron deficiency.
Hemoglobin deficiency was found in 34% of Blacks tested in the National Nutrition Survey.
h. carry heriditary traits of sicke cell and G6PD deficiency which are believed to make them even more vulnerable to the adverse effects of lead.
i. breathe other air pollutants, especially carbon monoxide and nitrogen oxides which attack the circulatory system (blood) as does lead and thus add to the harmful effects of lead.

SPECIFIC PROGRAM RECOMMENDATIONS

Air

1. Promulgate by January 1972 a regulation requiring all gasoline to be lead-free by 1977.

2. Pursue voluntary compliance from automobile and oil industries to accelerate use of lead-free gasoline as an interim measure.

3. Adopt by January 1972 an ambient air quality standard for lead.

4. Promulgate by December 31, 1971, a regulation requiring automobile manufacturers to label vehicles with consumer information, such as octane and lead content of gasoline to be used.

5. Conduct public education programs to encourage lead-free gasoline usage, car tune-ups, low-pollution driving habits.

6. Take leadership role in encouraging "clean street" and "green city" projects.

7. Staff the Urban Advisory Council with two air pollution experts to assure State and local air quality implementation policies are responsive to the needs of the urban poor.

End, selection from Our Urban Environment and Our Most Endangered People.

ADDITIONAL REFERENCE

For a detailed analysis of the economic impact of removing lead from gasoline, *see* Bonner and Moore Associates, Inc., *An Economic Analysis of Proposed Schedules for Removal of Lead Additives from Gasoline,* National Technical Information Service, U.S. Dept. of Commerce, Springfield, Va., June 25, 1971.

Implementation plans under Federal Air law — a summary

The summation below of the implementation plan system under the Clean Air Act is from *A Citizen's Guide to Clean Air,* which was prepared by the Conservation Foundation under contract with the Environmental Protection Agency. This summation will serve as a useful review for those studying the Act in depth, and as a aid to understanding by those using this work primarily as a reference tool.

The national ambient air quality standards represent goals that must be achieved and maintained; they do not, in themselves, clean up the air. The mechanism for achieving the standards is the state implementation plan. Section 110 of the Act requires that, within nine months of the establishment of any national ambient air quality standard, the states submit for EPA's approval a plan which provides for the "implementation, maintenance and enforcement" of that standard. These implementation plans (to be referred to in this chapter simply as "plans") must provide for the attainment of each primary standard within three years and for the attainment of each secondary standard within a "reasonable time."

On August 14, 1971, EPA published a set of regulations entitled "Requirements for Preparation, Adoption, and Submittal of Implementation Plans." These regulations spell out the required basic components of a plan. This chapter describes the major points of the Act and of the EPA regulations.

REGIONAL CLASSIFICATIONS

The units for which the standards are designed are called air quality control regions. The country is now divided into about 250 such control regions. Thus, large states often contain several regions, among which are widely varying pollution levels and problems. One state (Hawaii) itself comprises a single control region. And the boundaries of some control regions encompass parts of two or more states. Obviously, different control measures will be needed from region to region, depending on their location, the nature of the pollution, and the degree of urbanization.

To accommodate these differences in the implementation process, EPA has devised a classification system. Its purpose is, in EPA's words, to ensure that "the time and resources to be expended in developing the plan for that region, as well as the substantive content of the plan, will be commensurate with the complexity of the air pollution problem."

The classification system works like this. Each control region is graded by EPA as Priority I, Priority II, or Priority III, on the basis of the known or estimated levels of the six pollutants presently covered by national standards. Hence, the most heavily polluted regions are Priority I; regions with less pollution are Priority II; and those with pollution levels below or just above standard levels are Priority III.

Moreover, a given control region may have different classifications for different pollutants. It could be classified as Priority I for sulfur oxides and Priority III for carbon monoxide. And some regions, where precise air quality data are lacking, may be classified according to population—for example, any region with an urban concentration exceeding 200,000 people will generally be classified as Priority I. If several regions within one state share the same classification for a given pollutant, the state may develop one plan for that pollutant with provisions applicable to all of those control regions.

Citizens in Priority III regions should be alert to the possibility that their state plan may permit some deterioration of the air quality in their control regions. This would be true when a state plan does not protect the air quality from being polluted up to the standard level. Such deterioration in air quality is a matter of choice among the citizens of the control region and the state. But the Senate Public Works Committee had this to say in its report on the 1970 Amendments:

> ... Once ... national goals are established, deterioration of air quality should not be permitted except under circumstances where there is no available alternative. Given the various alternative means of preventing and controlling air pollution—including the use of the best available control technology, industrial processes, and operating practices—and care in the selection of sites for new sources, land use planning and traffic controls—deterioration need not occur.*

Later, EPA, in issuing the first six national ambient standards on April 30, 1971, stated that:

> The promulgation of national primary and secondary ambient air quality standards shall not be considered in any manner to allow significant deterioration of existing air quality in any portion of any State.**

Further, the Act allows states to adopt standards for individual control regions that are more stringent than the national ones. Citizens in unpolluted regions should take a hard look at this. They may want to urge their state agency officials, their governor, and their state legislators to protect the quality of the air in their region against deterioration by setting such stricter standards. Ideally, the best way to do this is by having the state agency hold a separate hearing to consider such standards—prior to hearings on an implementation plan. But since lack of time may foreclose this opportunity, an alternative would be to testify in favor of such standards at hearings on the implementation plan itself.

ELEMENTS OF A PLAN

In order to meet EPA requirements, an implementation plan must include provisions for the following major components:

1. Legal authority
2. Control strategy
3. Compliance schedules
4. Emergency episodes
5. Surveillance systems
6. Review of new sources
7. Resources
8. Interstate cooperation.

Each of these is discussed in order on the following pages.

Legal Authority

First, the federal government must be satisfied that the state has the necessary authority to produce and execute an implementation plan. Each plan must contain evidence of that authority. Basically, there must be legal authority to:

1. Adopt emission standards and any other measures necessary to attain and maintain national standards;

---

* U.S. Senate Public Works Committee Report No. 91-1196, page 11.

** Section 410.2(c) Code of Federal Regulations, *Federal Register,* April 30, 1971.

2. Enforce all applicable laws and regulations and, when necessary, seek injunctive relief (i.e., a court order to a polluter to cease violating an applicable law or regulation);

3. Take emergency action to abate pollution which substantially endangers human health;

4. Prevent the construction, modification, or operation of any stationary source at any location where its emissions will prevent the attainment or maintenance of a national standard;

5. Obtain any information needed to determine whether sources are in compliance with applicable laws. This includes authority to inspect sources, to conduct tests, and to require sources to keep emission records or any other specified records; and

6. Require stationary sources to install, maintain, and use emission monitoring devices and to periodically report on the nature and amounts of such emissions. Such monitoring data and reports must be correlated with applicable emission limitations. (The state must make the emission data and the correlations available to the public.)

Most states do have the authority to set and enforce control standards. Many, however, do not have the requisite authority specified in Nos. 5 and 6 above. Consequently, EPA has ruled that the similar federal powers (under Section 114 of the Act) may be delegated to the states so that they will be able to satisfy these requirements.

There is one other exception. If an implementation plan calls for state regulation of motor-vehicle emissions or for land-use controls, the state does not have to show that it already has the power to carry out such programs through existing laws. But it must include a timetable for acquiring such power (if it does not yet have it).

Control Strategy

Each plan must contain a control strategy—defined by EPA as "a combination of measures designed to achieve the aggregate reduction of emissions necessary for attainment and maintenance of a national standard." It is this "strategy" which tells, in effect, what steps the state intends to take.

EPA's regulations contain the following list of acceptable control-strategy measures:

1. Emission limitations;

2. Federal or state emission charges, or taxes, or other economic incentives;

3. Closing or relocation of residential, commercial, or industrial facilities;

4. Changes in schedules or methods of operating commercial or industrial facilities or transportation systems;

5. Periodic inspection and testing of motor vehicle emission control systems;

6. Emission control measures applicable to in-use motor vehicles, including mandatory maintenance, installation of emission control devices, and fuel conversion to gaseous fuels;

7. Measures to reduce motor vehicle traffic, including commuter taxes, gasoline rationing, parking restrictions, or staggered working hours;

8. Expansion or promotion of mass transportation facilities by increasing the frequency, convenience, and passenger-carrying capacity of mass transportation systems, or by providing for special bus lanes on major streets and highways;

9. Any other land-use or transportation control measures; and

10. Any variation of, or alternative to, any of these measures.

EPA made it clear that this list was not to be considered comprehensive; in other words, states are free to devise control methods that do not appear on EPA's list.

The plan for each primary and secondary standard must show that the strategy adopted (i.e., the combination of all control measures) will result in the achievement of the standard within the required time.

The strategy must also be sufficient to maintain each standard in the face of "emission increases that can reasonably be expected to result from projected growth of population, industrial activity, motor vehicle traffic, or other factors that may cause or contribute to increased emissions."

Citizens will want to examine carefully the strategy proposed for their control region. Substantial reliance on only one method, such as emission limitations, may be insufficient even to maintain current levels of air quality. In such cases, citizens may want to insist that the plan contain provisions calling for additional measures, such as land-use and transportation controls. Later, of course, they will have to work with their state legislators to get these measures approved, but their inclusion in the plan is an important first step.

Compliance Schedules

Each major source of pollution within a control region must prepare and follow a detailed, step-by-step schedule of measures it will take to bring it into accord with the implementation plan. Such individual timetables are called compliance schedules. EPA requires the states to negotiate compliance schedules with all major sources of pollution. Once negotiated, such schedules become legally enforceable and are a part of the state's implementation plan. However, since such individual negotiations are bound to be slow, EPA did not require the inclusion of compliance schedules in the implementation plans due in January, 1972. Instead, EPA allowed the states an additional six months for the preparation of compliance schedules. By the end of that period, they must be submitted to EPA, together with the first semi-annual progress report that states are required to prepare. (See page 37.)

EPA further requires that any compliance schedule extending for 18 or more months contain provisions "for periodic increments of progress toward compliance." Citizens may want to urge state agencies to adopt similar regulations for compliance schedules covering lesser time periods. "Increments of progress" can take such forms as deciding upon abatement methods, letting bids for equipment or construction, signing contracts, or beginning installation of control equipment.

State agencies are prohibited from granting any variance or exemption from a compliance schedule if such a variance would prevent the attainment of any national standard by the required deadline. In our view, any request for a variance from a compliance schedule should be the subject of a public hearing if its granting could result in a continuing or significant degradation of a region's air. (See page 78 for suggestions regarding variances.)

Emergency Episode Procedures

In heavily polluted areas, consideration must be given to the emergency measures needed when the pollution level threatens to reach or exceed the danger point. Such occurrences are referred to euphemistically as "episodes," and they happen with some frequency in heavily urbanized or industrialized areas—usually as a result of heavy pollution and persistent climatic conditions. Without an effective procedure to contain or reverse an episode, it has within it the potential to produce severe health effects. Consequently, EPA regulations require that each Priority I control region formulate a contingency plan covering the emergency measures to be taken when there is a likelihood that pollution will reach levels that constitute "imminent and substantial endangerment to the health of persons." These danger levels were described in the *Federal Register* of October 23, 1971.

EPA's regulations include a suggested model plan for emergency episodes based on air quality data and meteorological factors. The first, or "alert", stage occurs when adverse meteorological conditions and pollutant concentrations approach levels at which preventive action becomes necessary. The second, or "warning", stage would be reached if the situation continues to deteriorate. The third stage—the "emergency" stage—occurs when air quality continues to "degrade toward a level of significant harm to the health of persons," thus requiring the fullest possible curtailment of contributing sources.

Each contingency plan is to specify the control measures to be taken at each stage, including legally enforceable control programs to be required of each stationary source emitting more than 100 tons of pollutants annually. Such control programs for individual sources must be submitted to EPA within one year after submission of a state's implementation plan. Moreover, the control measures must be aimed at curtailing in advance any single source that could trigger any stage of an emergency episode.

Depending upon the types of pollutants involved, such measures may include prohibitions or restrictions on motor vehicle traffic; curtailment of retail, commercial, manufacturing, or industrial activities; prohibitions and limitations on the use of incinerators, combustion of fuels, and burning of materials; and limitations on any other activity which may contribute to atmospheric pollution. In any state plan, the emphasis should be placed on *preventing* the occurrence of high pollutant concentrations, rather than on remedial actions. In other words, the reduction strategies applied during the early stages should be designed to prevent the occurrence of the next level. They should comprise an *action,* rather than a *reaction,* plan.

The contingency plans for emergency episodes must also include provisions for:

1. Acquisition of daily forecasts of atmospheric conditions during episodes;
2. Inspection of sources to ensure compliance with individual control requirements; and
3. Communication procedures for contacting public officials, major sources, and news media.

EPA does not require that contingency plans for Priority II regions be as detailed as the emergency episode contingency plan described above. But plans for Priority II regions must provide for at least a two-stage alert and warning system and for any necessary control measures (although curtailment programs for all major individual sources are not required).

Surveillance Systems

Both the Act and the EPA regulations require that state plans include two different surveillance systems—one for monitoring pollution levels in the ambient air, the other for monitoring emissions from individual sources, e.g., from each stack in a factory.

The *ambient surveillance system* must be fully completed and operating within two years of EPA's approval of a plan. EPA has established minimum requirements for such a system. For details, see the *Federal Register* of August 14, 1971.

EPA also requires that at least one sampling site in each control region be located in the area of estimated maximum concentration for each pollutant, that sampling schedules be described in the plan (along with the methods of data handling and analysis), and that the plan include a timetable for the installation of equipment to complete the system.

Citizens may want to inform themselves about the number and location of the sampling stations in their control region. Many state agencies have maps available that show these locations.

The *surveillance system for individual sources* has two components. First, EPA requires that all owners or operators of stationary sources maintain records and periodically report to the responsible state or local agency on the nature and amounts of their emissions. Second, the state agency must establish an inspection system to check on compliance by individual sources.

Obviously, since the requirement placed on the individual operator is essentially one for self-monitoring and reporting, it is imperative that the state set up a creditable system of inspection. State regulations usually specify the inspection procedures and tests to be used. In our view, these regulations should also require that owners or operators of sources permit access to any authorized official at reasonable hours for inspecting any facilities, equipment, or records. "Reasonable hours" should be defined as any time during operating hours. Inspections should be made with some frequency, and should be unannounced, with no published schedule. Records of each inspection and the findings, including raw emission data, should be available to the public.

Citizens might want to consider pressing for provisions that would require the control agency or the source to retain surveillance data (both ambient and emission source) for a minimum of three years.

We believe that state regulations should require sources to report promptly any significant breakdown, shutdown, or other failure of monitoring or control equipment. In the case of continuous or prolonged failure, the agency should have authority to require cutbacks, shutdowns, or other control measures.

Review of New Sources

EPA requires that each plan contain legally enforceable procedures that will enable the state agency to prevent the construction or modification of any stationary source that would interfere with attainment or maintenance of a national standard. EPA also requires that construction or modification be prevented if it will result in violations of any portion of an applicable control strategy. For instance, if a control strategy calls for reduction of sulfur oxides by all means possible, the state agency should be able to prohibit the construction of a new fossil-fuel power plant that would bring additional sulfur oxide pollution.

In addition, EPA requires that anyone who proposes to construct or modify a stationary source submit to the state agency information on the nature and amounts of expected emissions, the location, design, construction, and operations of such source, and any other information the agency may require in deciding whether to allow the proposed construction or modification.

Beyond this, EPA has left it to the states to work out their own procedures for controlling new or modified source emissions. In fact, there is no requirement that all control responsibilities rest with the state air pollution control agency. Citizens would therefore be well advised to scrutinize carefully any delegation of air pollution control authority to other state agencies. The delegated agency may find itself faced with a potential conflict of interest between the program it is routinely charged with advancing and the state's air quality program. For example, a public utilities commission may have difficulty giving much weight to the effect of a new power plant on air quality.

Neither the Act nor EPA requires states to have a formal permit system to control new sources. (For a brief discussion of permit systems, see page 46.)

Resources

Each plan must include a description of the manpower and funds needed to carry out the plan for five years. The description must include what is currently available, as well as projections of the additional resources needed at one-, three-, and five-year intervals.

Manpower needs include administrative, engineering, technical, and enforcement services. In a small agency, several of these roles may be filled by one person. Depending on the structure of the state institutions responsible for environmental services, some enforcement and management functions may be assigned to persons in other agencies, such as lawyers in the state attorney general's office. (See page 76 for further discussion of state government structures, and pages 73-76 for discussion of funding.)

Interstate Cooperation

Each plan must provide for the exchange of all necessary information among the responsible agencies in each control region whose boundaries lie in more than one state. All data on emissions, air quality, and control strategy development must be furnished upon request from one state to another. In addition, each state must provide for exchange of information on such factors as construction of new industrial plants, which may significantly affect air quality in any portion of another state or region.

When more than one state has jurisdiction over a given control region, EPA regulations require that each state involved give notice to the other affected states of any public hearings it is going to hold on implementation plans for that region.

And when agencies other than the state control agency are to have responsibility for carrying out any part of a plan, these agencies and the extent of their duties must be described in the state plan.

PUBLIC PARTICIPATION

Within the process of designing, adopting, and implementing a plan, there are important opportunities for the public to participate. These opportunities are specified within the Act, and the language of the Act, as well as its legislative history, make it clear that Congress intended the citizen to have an influential role in the air quality control process. Hearings held by the Senate Subcommittee on Air and Water Pollution, which drafted the bulk of the legislation, as well as public statements by subcommittee members, have emphasized the need for citizen involvement—not only because public support is necessary for good control programs, but because the determination of the nation's air quality is properly the right and responsibility of its citizens.

Public Hearings

The Act declares that public hearings *must* be held in each state before the state adopts an implementation plan and sends it on to EPA for approval. EPA's regulations require that each state:

1. Provide at least 30 days' notice of a hearing through "prominent advertisement" of the hearing's date, time, and place;
2. Make available for public inspection, in at least one location in each control region, the principal portions of the proposed plan for that region;
3. Make available for inspection all rules and regulations proposed for inclusion in the plan; and,
4. Keep hearing records that will contain, at a minimum, the list of those testifying, together with the text of each presentation.

A public hearing does not have to be held in each region covered by a proposed state plan. Hearings could be held, for instance, only in the state capital. Persons wishing to testify would have to travel to the capital or submit written testimony for the hearing record, in accordance with applicable state regulations. You may wish to press your state control officials and your governor to hold a public hearing in each control region. In addition, you may want to urge the agency control officials to adopt their own rules to make it easier for citizens to take part in the process. (See page 72 for suggestions.)

Each state may also choose to hold separate hearings on primary and secondary standards. But unless a separate hearing is provided, implementation plans for primary and secondary standards must be considered at the same hearing.

States may choose to hold more than one hearing on the plan. They may, for example, hold separate hearings on different portions of the plan: one on regulations pertaining to sulfur oxides, one on those for particulate matter, one on emergency episode procedures, and so on. While it is easier to concentrate on one portion of a plan at a time, it is often difficult to attend a succession of hearings. In order to enable citizens to deal with the total plan as an integrated entity, however, you may want to urge your state to hold at least one hearing on the plan in its entirety.

Public Reporting

The Act recognizes the right of citizens to know what the air quality situation is in their respective regions. To this end, the Act and EPA require that states gather emission data from individual sources, correlate them with the standards established under the Act, and make all of this available to the public.

EPA also requires each state to submit quarterly reports on air quality and semi-annual reports on implementation progress. EPA does not require that the states make these reports available. But many state agencies already treat such reports as public information. Citizens in other states may want to press their state agencies to make such reports available—or at least summaries of such reports, if the reports themselves are lengthy and technical.

In developing portions of their plans, such as the control strategies and "emergency episode" procedures, state agencies are required to collect and analyze data on emissions from point sources and area sources.* EPA requires that such data and analyses be retained for its inspection, although it does not specify that such information must be made public. However, citizens may find this information valuable in evaluating state plans and may want to request that the state agency make it available.

PLAN APPROVAL

The state has nine months from the time EPA issues national ambient standards in which to devise and submit its implementation plan for EPA's approval. For the first six national standards, the process has already begun, and states have until January 30, 1972, in which to submit their respective plans.

At the conclusion of the nine-month period, EPA has four additional months (until May 30, 1972) to approve or disapprove each plan or any portion of it. To be approved, a plan must satisfy all the requirements of the Act, as well as the EPA regulations described in this chapter.

Under some circumstances, EPA is required to propose its own plan (or portion of one). This occurs when:

1. Any state fails to submit its own plan;
2. A submitted plan is judged by EPA to be inadequate; or when
3. A state fails to revise a plan satisfactorily within 60 days of notification to do so.

Within six months of proposing its own plan for a state, EPA must hold a public hearing and promulgate a final plan for that state. The plan then becomes effective for that state.

* "Point sources" are stationary sources emitting pollutants in amounts above specified levels (such as 25 tons per year), depending on their location and the processes used. "Area sources" are small, diffused individual pollutant sources such as automobiles, home or commercial heating units, and small home incinerators.

A record of the public hearing on the state implementation plan must accompany the state's submission to EPA. EPA is expected to review it, giving careful consideration to the public testimony. One thing citizens might do is ask the state to notify them of any changes made in an implementation plan after the hearing and before submission to EPA. Some states will provide written explanations of all such changes and make available to the public copies of the submitted plan, its justifications, and the hearing record.

If changes in a plan are made but not explained, or if the explanation appears to be unjustifiable, citizens can protest in writing to the EPA Administrator, citing relevant passages in the hearing record and other necessary arguments to support their protests. If EPA approves the plan, citizens may challenge the approval in the courts under the citizen-suit provisions of the Act. (See Chapter Seven.)

A state may ask EPA to determine the adequacy of a plan prior to final submission. When this happens, EPA's evaluation will be made available to the public upon request.

A more detailed description of the Act's provisions regarding implementation plans is included in the Natural Resources Defense Council's publication, *Action for Clean Air.* (See bibliography on page 92.)

REVISIONS AND EXTENSIONS OF THE PLAN

Even after EPA approval, an implementation plan is still subject to change. No air quality region is static. Each community grows or changes. And so, consequently, does the quality of its air. Also, new things are constantly being learned about the chemical composition of air pollution and its detrimental effects. As this new knowledge emerges, the national ambient standards may need revision, and new standards will require changes in the plans and procedures for implementation.

Revisions

There are three particular circumstances provided for in the Act under which an implementation plan must be revised:

1. To reflect changes in the national standards whenever these occur;
2. To take into account the availability of improved methods of achieving such standards (for instance, improvements in technology or applications of new control methods, such as emission taxes); and,
3. Whenever EPA finds that the plan is "substantially inadequate to attain or maintain the national standard which it implements."

The main initiative for revision lies with EPA, which must notify the state of any need to revise. Upon such notice, the state generally has 60 days to comply. However, EPA may extend the time after consultation with the state.

On the other hand, there is nothing to prevent a state from proposing its own revisions. Citizens may want to urge their state to include provisions in the plan for such state-inspired changes. Any such provision should be carefully worded to protect against a possible weakening of the plan's intent or effectiveness. All revisions, whether initiated by the state or by EPA, are subject to a public hearing, and all must have the final approval of EPA.

Extensions

The Act allows EPA to grant to the states three types of deadline extensions:

1. *Extension of a Primary Standard Deadline.* At the time a state submits its implementation plan to EPA for approval, the governor of that state may request EPA's permission to extend from three years to five the deadline for achieving the primary standards in control regions classified as Priority I. If the control region is an interstate area, the request is supposed to be submitted jointly with requests of the other governors who share responsibility for the region; if other governors do not intend to request such an extension, they must at least be notified of the request.

Any such request must be accompanied by a plan that will provide for the attainment of the standard within the extended period. The request must show that the necessary technology or other control measures required by the plan will not be available soon enough to permit attainment of the standard within the established three-year period. All sources which will be unable to comply must be clearly identified. All assumptions made about the time at which the controls will be available must also be identified and justified. Moreover, the plan must identify any alternative means of attaining the standard which were considered but rejected. Finally, the plan must require that all sources able to comply do so within the established three years and that the identified non-complying sources adopt specified reasonable interim control measures.

There is no specific requirement for a public hearing on a request for extension of the deadline for achieving a primary standard. Conceivably, a state could prepare and hold a hearing on a three-year plan, then propose to revise it to extend over five years —without a second hearing on the extension request.

2. *Postponement of Source Compliance.* The Act allows the governor of a state to request a one-year postponement in applying those parts of a plan that cover any stationary source or class of moving sources.* Such a request cannot be made until one year before those parts are scheduled to take effect. The request must include evidence that:

1. Efforts have been made, in good faith, to comply with such requirements as originally scheduled;
2. The source or class of sources is unable to comply because necessary technology or alternative measures are not yet available;
3. Available alternative measures have been or will be applied to reduce the impact of source emissions on health; and
4. The continued operation of the source is essential to national security or to public health and welfare.

A public hearing on such a request must be held before the proper EPA official. In interstate control regions, requirements for notifying the governors of other affected states are the same as those described on page 39.

But if postponement of an applicable portion of a plan will not prevent the attainment or maintenance of a national standard, the state does not have to make a formal request for extension under these provisions. In such a case, the postponement will be considered a plan revision and, as such, is subject to public hearing.

3. *Extension for Secondary Standard Plans.* If a state finds it difficult to prepare plans simultaneously for both primary and secondary standards, it may ask EPA for an 18-month extension of the deadline for submitting a plan to implement a secondary standard —but only for regions classified as Priority I or II. Any such request must show that attaining the secondary standard will require emission reductions beyond those which can be achieved through the "application of reasonably available control technology." In other words, the state must show that, given the present technology, there is no "reasonable" way of reaching the goal set by the secondary standards. In interstate regions, requirements for noti-

* This differs from a variance. A variance is usually requested by a source, whereas a postponement is requested by the government on behalf of a source or sources.

fying the governors of other affected states are the same as those on page 39. Finally, any such request must be made early enough to permit the development of a plan in time to meet the established deadline in case EPA refuses to grant the extension.

Citizens should ask their state agency to announce any intent to seek such an extension. If it does plan to seek an extension, its justification should be examined, with particular attention to its discussion of "reasonably available control technology." Has the agency, for instance, accepted without verification protests by pollution sources that technology is not available? What independent sources of information have been asked to evaluate such claims? Is applicable technology in use anywhere else? If so, why is it "reasonably available" there but not here?

If citizens feel that a state agency is seeking an extension that is not justified, they can write to the EPA Administrator, urging that the request be denied and explaining why.

If EPA grants such an extension, it means that only the timing is affected—not the standard. The plan must still provide for achievement of the national standard within a time specified by the state and accepted as "reasonable" by EPA.

End, excerpt from *A Citizen's Guide to Clean Air.*

Timetable for ambient air standards and plans

Action	Time Ceiling
(a) Administrator publishes [and shall from time to time thereafter revise] *list* of pollutants for which criteria are to be issued	30 Jan. 1972
(b) Administrator issues *criteria*	30 Jan. 1973
(c) Administrator issues *proposed* primary and secondary ambient standards	30 Jan. 1973
(d) Written comments submitted on proposed national ambient standards	(No date specified)
(e) Administrator *promulgates* primary and secondary ambient standards	30 April 1973
(f) States hold public hearings on plans to implement national ambient standards	(No date specified)
(g) Submission of state plans for *implementing* primary and secondary standards	30 Jan. 1974 (Administrator may postpone submission of plan for secondary standards to 30 July 1974)
(h) Governors may seek 2 year extension of time for compliance with primary standards	30 Jan. 1974
(i) Governors may seek 1 year postponement of time for compliance with primary or secondary standard	before 30 May 1977 (primary) within a "reasonable time" (secondary)
(j) President may grant 1 year (renewable) exemption	Anytime
(k) Administrator approves or disapproves state implementation plans	30 May 1974
(l) *All states must achieve primary standards*	30 May 1971 (or later if (i), (j), or (k) is granted
(m) *All states must achieve secondary standards*	Within a "reasonable time" or later if (j) or (k) is granted

SIERRA CLUB v. RUCKELSHAUS
344 F.Supp. 253 (D.C.D. June 2, 1972)

MEMORANDUM OPINION

Prat, J.:

Initially, this matter came before the Court on plaintiffs' motion for temporary restraining order wherein they sought to enjoin the Administrator of the Environmental Protection Agency from approving certain portions of state air pollution control plans—implementing the national primary and secondary standards—which had been submitted to the Administrator pursuant to Section 110 of the Clean Air Act of 1970. 42 U.S.C. §1857c-5(1970). Having been informed that the Administrator would not be approving the plans until May 31, 1972, we denied the motion for temporary restraining order and scheduled a hearing on the preliminary injunction for May 30. At the conclusion of the May 30 hearing, having considered the pleadings and memoranda and the arguments of counsel, we announced our findings and conclusions and granted plaintiffs' motion for preliminary injunction. We now set down those findings and conclusions in memorandum form.

Standing

Although the Administrator does not question plaintiffs' standing to bring this action, it is clear to us that under the allegations of the complaint each of the four environmental groups who are parties-plaintiff has the requisite standing, even under the limitation expressed in the most recent Supreme Court case on the subject, *Sierra Club v. Morton,* ___U.S.___, 92 S.Ct. 1361 (1972).

Jurisdiction

The Administrator challenges the jurisdiction of this Court to hear this case on the theory that the plaintiffs should wait until the Administrator approves the plans and then appeal the approval under 42 U.S.C. §1857h-5. We disagree. It is our judgment that plaintiffs have the right to bring the action in this Court at this juncture under 42 U.S.C. §1857h-2(a) which provides in pertinent part that

> "any person may commence a civil action on his own behalf—
>
> * * *
>
> (2) against the Administrator where there is alleged a failure of the Administrator to perform any act or duty under this chapter which is not discretionary with the Administrator.
>
> The district courts shall have jurisdiction, without regard to the amount in controversy or the citizenship of the parties, . . . to order the Administrator to perform such act or duty, as the case may be."

The Administrator, in recent testimony before Congress, indicated that he had declined to require state implementation plans to provide against significant deterioration of the existing clean air areas—i.e., areas with levels of pollution lower than the secondary standard—because he believed that he lacked the power to act otherwise. Unpublished transcript of Hearings Before the Subcomm. on Public Health and the Environment of the House Comm. on Interstate and Foreign Commerce, 92d Cong., 2d Sess. at 351-52 (remarks delivered on Jan. 27–28, 1972).

Previously, the Administrator had promulgated a regulation permitting states to submit plans which would allow clean air areas to be degraded, so long as the plans were merely "adequate to prevent such ambient pollution levels from exceeding such secondary standard." 40 C.F.R. §51.12(b) (1972).

Plaintiffs' claim that the Administrator's interpretation of the extent of his authority is clearly erroneous and that his declination to assert his authority, evidenced in his remarks before Congress and his promulgation of a regulation that is contrary to the Clean Air Act, amounts to a failure to perform a non-discretionary act or duty.

It would appear that such an allegation is precisely the type of claim which Congress, through 52 U.S.C. §1857h-2(a), intended interested citizens to raise in the district courts. In view of this clear jurisdictional grant, the Administrator's assertion that plaintiffs should await his approval of the state plans (formulated, in part, pursuant to his allegedly illegal regulation) and then proceed to appeal his approval under 42 U.S.C. §1857h-5 is, in our opinion, untenable.

In discussing the merits of the present action—i.e., the extent of the Administrator's authority and the validity of the questioned regulation—we turn to the stated purpose of the Clean Air Act of 1970, the available legislative history of the Act and its predecessor, and the administrative interpretation of the Act.

Purpose of the Act

In Section 101(b) of the Clean Air Act, Congress states four basic purposes of the Act, the first of which is

> "to protect and enhance the quality of the Nation's air resources so as to promote the public health and welfare and the productive capacity of its population." 42 U.S.C. §1857(b)(1).

On its face, this language would appear to declare Congress' intent to improve the quality of the nation's air and to prevent deterioration of that air quality, no matter how presently pure that quality in some sections of the country happens to be.

Legislative History

The "protect and enhance" language of the Clean Air Act of 1970 stems directly from the predecessor Air Quality Act of 1967, 81 Stat. 485. The Senate Report underlying the 1967 Act makes it clear that all areas of the country were to come under the protection of the Act. S. Rep. No. 403, 90th Cong., 1st Sess. 2–3 (1967).

The administrative guidelines promulgated by the National Air Pollution Control Administration (NAPCA) of the Department of Health, Education and Welfare (HEW), which at that time had the responsibility of carrying out the directives of the Air Quality Act of 1967, point up the significance of the "protect and enhance" language as follows:

> "[A]n explicit purpose of the Act is 'to *protect* and *enhance* the quality of the Nation's air resources' (emphasis added). Air quality standards which, even if fully implemented, would result in significant deterioration of air quality in any substantial portion of an air quality region clearly would conflict with this expressed purpose of the law." National Air Pollution Control Administration, U.S. Dept. of HEW, *Guidelines for the Development of Air Quality Standards and Implementation Plans,* Part I§1.51, p. 7 (1969).

Turning now to the legislative history of the 1970 Act, we note at the outset that both Secretary Finch and Under Secretary Veneman of HEW testified before Congress that neither the 1967 Act nor the proposed Act would permit the quality of air to be degraded. Hearings on Air Pollution Before the Subcomm. on Air and Water Pollution of the Senate Public Works Comm., 91st Cong., 2d Sess., at 132-33, 143 (1970); Hearings on Air Pollution and Solid Waste Recycling Before the Subcomm. on Public Health and Welfare of the House Interstate and Foreign Commerce Comm., 91st Cong., 2d Sess., at 280, 287 (1970).

More important, of course, is the language of the Senate Report accompanying the bill which became the Clean Air Act of 1970. The Senate Report, in pertinent part, states:

> "In areas where current air pollution levels are already equal to or better than the air quality goals, the Secretary shall not approve any implementation plan which does not provide, to the maximum extent practicable, for the continued maintenance of such ambient air quality." S. Rep. No. 1196, 91st Cong., 2d Sess., at 2 (1970).

The House Report, although not as clear, does not appear to contradict the Senate Report. *See* H. Rep. No. 1146, 91st Cong., 2d Sess., at 1, 2 and 5 (1970).

Administrative Interpretation

As we noted under our discussion of the legislative history of the 1967 Act, the 1969 guidelines promulgated by HEW's NAPCA emphasized that significant deterioration of air quality in any region would subvert the "protect and enhance" language of the 1967 Act. We also pointed out that Secretary Finch and Under Secretary Veneman applied this same administrative interpretation to the very same language found in the proposed 1970 Act.

On the other hand, the present Administrator, in remarks made in January and February of 1972 before certain House and Senate Subcommittees, has taken the position that the 1970 Act allows degradation of clean air areas. Several Congressional leaders voiced their strong disagreement with the Administrator's interpretation. Unpublished transcript of Hearings Before the Subcomm. on Public Health and the Environment of the House Comm. on Interstate and Foreign Commerce, 92d Cong., 2d Sess., at 352 (remarks of Congressman Paul Rogers, Chairman of the Subcommittee); Unpublished transcript of Hearings Before the Subcomm. on Air and Water Pollution of the Senate Comm. on Public Works, 92d Cong., 2d Sess. at 33-34, 260 *et seq.* (remarks of Senator Thomas Eagleton, Vice-Chairman of the Subcommittee, presiding over the hearings at the time).

Sierra Club v. Ruckelshaus

The Administrator's interpretation of the 1970 Act, as disclosed in his current regulations, appears to be self-contradictory. On the one hand, 40 C.F.R. §50.2(c) (1970) provides:

> "The promulgation of national primary and secondary air quality standards shall not be considered in any manner to allow significant deterioration of existing air quality in any portion of any State."

Yet, in 40 C.F.R. §51.12(b), he states:

> "In any region where measured or estimated ambient levels of a pollutant are below the levels specified by an applicable secondary standard, the State implementation plan shall set forth a control strategy which shall be adequate to prevent such ambient pollution levels from exceeding such secondary standard."

The former regulation appears to reflect a policy of nondegradation of clean air but the latter mirrors the Administrator's doubts as to his authority to impose such a policy upon the states in their implementation plans. In our view, these regulations are irreconcilable and they demonstrate the weakness of the Administrator's position in this case.

Initial Conclusions

Having considered the stated purpose of the Clean Air Act of 1970, the legislative history of the Act and its predecessor, and the past and present administrative interpretation of the Acts, it is our judgment that the Clean Air Act of 1970 is based in important part on a policy of non-degradation of existing clean air and that 40 C.F.R. §51.12(b), in permitting the states to submit plans which allow pollution levels of clean air to rise to the secondary standard level of pollution, is contrary to the legislative policy of the Act and is, therefore, invalid. Accordingly, we hold that plaintiffs have made out a claim for relief.

Injunctive Relief

Whether this Court may properly grant injunctive relief depends on whether the plaintiffs have met the four criteria set forth in *Virginia Petroleum Jobbers Ass'n. v. Federal Power Commission,* 104 U.S. App. D.C. 106, 259 F.2d 921 (1958) and such later authorities as *A Quaker Action Group v. Hickel,* 137 U.S. App. D.C. 176, 421 F.2d 111 (1969).

First, have the plaintiffs made a strong showing that they are likely to prevail on the merits? It appears to us, from our foregoing discussion, that the plaintiffs have made such a showing in this case.

Second, have the plaintiffs shown that without such relief they would suffer irreparable injury? In view of the nature and extent of the air pollution problem, once degradation is permitted the range of resulting damages could well have irreversable effects. Thus, we hold that plaintiffs have made the requisite showing of irreparable injury.

Third, will the issuance of a stay cause any significant harm or inconvenience to the Administrator or other parties interested in the proceedings? We are persuaded that no substantial harm or inconvenience will result from our order granting the preliminary injunction. The order is a very limited one. It was submitted by plaintiffs' counsel after consultation with counsel for the Administrator and, in our view, it provides the Administrator with sufficient time and flexibility so that he may exercise his expertise and carry out his duties under the Act with as little inconvenience as possible.

Fourth, and finally, where lies the public interest? It seems to us that the public interest in this case strongly supports the legislative policy of clean air and the non-degradation of areas in which clean air exists.

Conclusion

Having separately considered the four criteria for injunctive relief, and having found that plaintiffs have met each of these criteria, we conclude that we can and should grant the requested relief. The order effecting such relief is attached hereto.

PRELIMINARY INJUNCTION

It appearing to the Court that a Preliminary Injunction pending hearing and determination of plaintiffs' request for a permanent injunction and other relief should be issued because, unless defendant is enjoined from approving portions of state implementation plans permitting significant deterioration of air quality, plaintiffs may suffer immediate and irreparable injury, loss and damage before the determination of this case on the merits,

NOW, THEREFORE, IT IS ORDERED, that defendant, his agents, officers, servants, employees, and attorneys, and any persons in active concert or participation with him, be and they are, hereby enjoined until plaintiffs' request for a permanent injunction and other relief has been determined by this Court from, directly or indirectly, approving any state implementation plan under 42 U.S.C. 1857c-5 unless he approves the state plan subject to subsequent review by him to insure that it does not permit significant deterioration of existing air quality in any portion of any state where the existing air quality is better than one or more of the secondary standards promulgated by the Administrator. The Administrator shall complete this review of all the state plans within four months of this order. The Administrator, shall, within this four-month period, approve any portion of a state plan which effectively prevents the significant deterioration of existing air quality in any portion of any state, and disapprove any portion of a state plan which fails to effectively prevent the significant deterioration of existing air quality in any portion of any state.

The Administrator shall prepare and publish proposed regulations, pursuant to 42 U.S.C. 1857 c-5(c) as to any state plan which he finds, on the basis of his review, either permits the significant deterioration of existing air quality in any portion of any state or fails to take the measures necessary to prevent such significant deterioration. Such regulations shall be promulgated within six months of this order.

NATURAL RESOURCES DEFENSE COUNCIL, INC., v. RUCKELSHAUS
___F.Supp.___(D.C.D. May 5, 1972)

Giebell, J.:

MEMORANDUM OPINION AND ORDER

Plaintiffs claim that the Administrator of the Environmental Protection Agency promulgated hydrocarbon emission standards for model year 1975 automobiles which were not authorized under section 202 of the Clean Air Act, 42 U.S.C. §1857f-1 and thus failed to perform duties mandated by that Act. A declaratory judgment and affirmative relief are sought.

Plaintiffs are nonprofit corporations established, respectively, for the purposes of promoting and protecting environmental quality and assuring access of the citizenry to scientific expertise to promote the general welfare.

Plaintiffs allege that the hydrocarbon emission standard of 0.41 grams per vehicle mile (g/mi) promulgated by the Administrator on July 2, 1971, (36 Fed. Reg. 12658, §1201.21, 40 C.F.R. 85.21), fails to achieve a reduction of 90 percent from emissions allowable for model year 1970 and fails to assure the attainment of the Primary Ambient Air Quality Standards for hydrocarbons as contemplated by §?02 of the Clean Air Act. Defendant contends that, in fact, the required 90 percent reduction is achieved by the challenged regulations. The matter is now before the Court on defendant's motion to dismiss. The issue has been fully briefed and argued.

The Court has jurisdiction under section 304 of the Act since, as will appear, the Administrator has in his discretion adopted new test procedures in developing regulations designed to accomplish the congressional purpose.

In the early stages of consideration of the Clean Air Amendments of 1970, P.L. 91-604, certain test procedures then in effect measured emissions of hydrocarbon from 1970-model cars at 2.2 g/mi. Section 202 (b) (1) (A), which was added by the Amendments, requires that model 1975 cars shall reduce such emissions by at least 90 percent.* The Administrator over a period of time developed two more sophisticated tests for measuring emissions, a 1972 Procedure and a 1975 Procedure. He then applied these new tests to the 1970-model cars, finding that the same hydrocarbon emissions of such models came to 4.6 g/mi as measured by the 1972 Procedure and 4.1 g/mi as measured by the 1975 Procedure. The Administrator then utilized the 1975 Procedure to calculate the required 90 percent reduction. On this basis, ten percent of the 1970 model year car emissions of 4.1 g/mi, (as measured on the 1975 Procedure), or .41 g/mi, was set as the hydrocarbon standard for 1975 models to be measured on the 1975 Procedure.

All the Administrator did, in effect, was translate the 1970 emissions figures from the original test procedure into a more accurate procedure and calculate the 90 percent reduction according to the latter. This appears to be a reasonable exercise of the discretion necessary to corrolate a fixed directive of the statute with evolving test procedures in a new technological area of governmental regulation. The Administrator has thus complied with the requirements of section 202 (b) (1) (A) of the Act.

A further aspect of the controversy concerns whether or not the standard calculated for the 1975 models will enable the Administrator to

*Section 202 (b) (1) (A) provides that regulations prescribed by the Administrator "shall contain standards which require a reduction of at least 90 per centum from emissions of carbon monoxide and hydrocarbons allowable under the standards under this section applicable to light duty vehicles and engines manufactured in model year 1970." 42 U.S.C. §1857f-1 (b) (1) (A).

achieve expected Ambient Air Quality Standards for the country as a whole provided for in Title I of the Act. Many factors contribute to these goals. Motor vehicles are not the only source of carbon monoxide and hydrocarbons and vary in intensity in different localities. Other provisions of the Clean Air Act enable various levels of federal and state governments to move against other sources of these same emissions. Therefore, it is unnecessary for the Court to resolve the technical complexities involved in determining whether the 90 percent reduction for motor vehicles, as finally calculated, specifically complies with the Ambient Air Quality Standards.

Finally, plaintiffs urge that the 90 percent reduction as calculated will not achieve certain reduction targets established in November, 1969, by the Secretary of Health, Education, and Welfare, for the auto industry to reach by 1980. This argument appears to be without merit since, after the passage of the Act with its specific guidelines, the 1980 goal was not binding on the Administrator, and since, in addition, it appears that the 1980 goals of .46 g/mi was met by the 1975 reduction goal of .41 g/mi (both measured by the 1975 test procedure).

The Administrator has acted in a reasonable and proper manner in interpreting his duties under the Act. The complaint is without merit and the defendant's motion to dismiss is granted. So ordered.

KENNECOTT COPPER CORP. v. E.P.A.

___F.2d___(D.C. Cir. Feb. 18, 1972)

Before WRIGHT, TAMM and LEVENTHAL, *Circuit Judges.*

LEVENTHAL, *Circuit Judge*: In this appeal, Kennecott Copper Corporation attacks the "national secondary ambient air quality standards" for sulfur oxides, promulgated by the Environmental Protection Agency on April 30, 1971.[1] It raises as objections that the standards (1) were not "based on" the underlying "air quality criteria" issued by the Government, as required by Section 109 of the Clean Air Act (Act), as amended in 1970;[2] (2) were not accompanied by a "concise general statement of their basis and purpose" as required by § 4(c) of the Administrative Procedure Act,[3] and in any event (3) were not adequately supported by a statement of their basis necessary to insure adequate judicial review.

---

[1] As part of the National Primary and Secondary Ambient Air Quality Standards, 36 Fed. Reg. 8186. The Notice of Proposed Rule-making was published on January 30, 1971, see 36 Fed. Reg. 1502.

[2] Clean Air Amendments of 1970, 84 Stat. 1676, P.L. 91-604, § 4, 42 U.S.C. § 1857c-4(b).

[3] 5 U.S.C. § 553(c).

The Act provides for the establishment of national primary and secondary ambient air quality standards, to prescribe maximum concentrations of pollutants that will be permitted in the air of our country. Primary standards are those "requisite to protect the public health," while secondary standards are those "requisite to protect the public welfare," which is defined[4] as including, but not limited to, "effects on soil, water, crops, vegetation, man made materials, animals, wild life, weather, visibility and climate, damage to and deterioration of property, and hazards to transportation, as well as effects on economic values and on personal comfort and well-being."

This appeal involves the non-health-related "secondary" standards for sulfur oxides, which are more stringent than the "primary" standards, though greater time flexibility is provided for attaining secondary standards.[5] In particular, this appeal has come to focus on the requirement in the secondary air quality standard limiting the annual arithmetic mean amount of sulfur oxides (sulfur dioxide) to: "60 micrograms per cubic meter—annual arithmetic mean."

Sections 108 and 109 of the Act,[6] reprinted in the Appendix, are the key sections for present purposes. The statute requires air quality criteria, if not issued prior to the 1970 amendments, to be issued by the Administrator within 12 months after the listing of an air pollutant. The Administrator is required to publish and revise a list which includes each pollutant present in the ambient air, from numerous or diverse mobile or stationary sources, which in the judgment of the Administrator "has an adverse effect on public health or welfare."[7]

Section 108 makes clear that the term "air quality criteria" is not used in the law with the conventional meaning of "criterion," as referring to a standard. What the term refers to is a document which "shall accurately reflect the latest scientific knowledge useful in indicating the kind and extent of all identifiable effects on public health or welfare which may be expected from the presence of such pollutant in the ambient air in varying qualities."[8]

Section 109 of the Act provides for expeditious issuance of air quality standards "based on" the criteria. They were

---

[4] 42 U.S.C. § 1857h(h).

[5] By Section 110 of the Act, 42 U.S.C. § 1857c-5, and in particular subsections (a) (2) (A) (ii) and (b).

[6] 42 U.S.C. §§ 1857c-3, 1857-4.

[7] Section 108(a) (1) (A) of the Act, 42 U.S.C. § 1857c-3 (a) (1) (A).

[8] 42 U.S.C. § 1857c-3(a) (2). By implication this provision is applicable to criteria issued prior to the 1970 Amendments on which standards issued subsequent to those amendments are based.

required within 30 days after the 1970 enactment of P.L. 91-604, for each air pollutant for which air quality criteria had been issued prior to such enactment. As for criteria issued subsequent to the 1970 law, the Administrator is required, simultaneously, to publish proposed national air quality standards. In either event the air quality standards prescribe a level of air quality "the attainment and maintenance of which in the judgment of the Administrator, based on such criteria" is requisite to protect the public interest—in the case of primary standards, "requisite to protect the public health;" in the case of secondary standards, "requisite to protect the public welfare from any known or anticipated adverse effects associated with the presence of such air pollutant in the ambient air."

Congress provided for informal rule-making, for proposed standards, written comments thereon, without any general necessity for evidentiary submissions, culminating in promulgation by regulation of standards based on the criteria.

In the case before us the air quality criteria were published in January 1969, prior to the 1970 law, by the Department of Health, Education and Welfare.[9] No contention is made that they were not adequate to serve the function contemplated of criteria under the 1970 law, of reflecting pertinent scientific knowledge concerning effects that may be expected from the presence of the pollutant. The complaint is that there is no adequate indication of the basis of the 1971 standard of 60 micrograms per cubic meter. It is particularly stressed that the summarizing "Resume" paragraph, reproduced in the footnote,[10] of the 1969 Criteria refer to no effects at a level below 85 micrograms per cubic meter. While the statement of the purpose and nature of the regulation set forth the basis for the

---

[9] *Air Quality Criteria For Sulfur Oxides,* published in January 1969 by the United States Department of Health, Education, and Welfare, Public Health Service, Consumer Protection and Environmental Health Service, National Air Pollution Control Administration.

[10] *C. RESUME*

In addition to health considerations, the economic and aesthetic benefits to be obtained from low ambient concentrations of sulfur oxides as related to visibility soiling, corrosion, and other effects should be considered by organizations responsible for promulgating ambient air quality standards. Under the conditions prevailing in areas where the studies were conducted, adverse health effects were noted when 24-hour average levels of sulfur dioxide exceeded 300 ug/m^3 (0.11 ppm) for 3 to 4 days. Adverse health effects were also noted when the annual mean level of sulfur dioxide exceeded 115 ug/m^3 (0.04 ppm). Visibility reduction to about 5 miles was observed at 285 ug/m^3 (0.10 ppm); adverse effects on materials were observed at an annual mean of 345 $ug/^3$ (0.12 ppm); and adverse effects on vegetation were observed at an annual mean of 85 ug/m^3 (0.03 ppm). It is reasonable

primary standards, simultaneously adopted, in some detail, as to secondary standards the Administrator said only:

> National secondary ambient air quality standards are those which, in the judgment of the Administrator, based on the air quality criteria, are requisite to protect the public welfare from any known or anticipated adverse effects associated with the presence of air pollutants in the ambient air.

In support of the EPA's annual standard of 60 micrograms per cubic meter, the Government and intervenor, National Resources Defense Council,[11] refer to lower figures in the material in the body of the Criteria, saying that the Resume is not conclusive. In the alternative they argue that the 85 figure in the Resume supports a 60 standard, on the basis of the Administrator's judgment as to anticipated effects and a margin necessary to avoid the adverse effects noted at the 85 level.

We do not undertake to rule on these particular matters. This court has been assigned special responsibility for determining challenges to EPA's air quality standards.[12] This judicial review rests on the premise that agency and court "together constitute a 'partnership' in furtherance of the public interest, and are 'collaborative instrumentalities of justice.' The court is in a real sense part of the total administrative process." Greater Boston Television Corp. v. FCC, —— U.S.App.D.C. ——, 444 F.2d 841, 851-52, *cert. denied,* —— U.S. —— (1971). Inherent in the responsibility entrusted to this court is a requirement that we be given sufficient indication of the basis on which the Administrator reached the 60 figure so that we may consider whether it embodies an abuse of discretion or error of law.[13]

Kennecott Copper Corp. v. E.P.A.

---

and prudent to conclude that, when promulgating ambient air quality standards, consideration should be given to requirements for margins of safety which take into account long-term effects on health, vegetation, and materials occurring below the above levels.

[11] This intervention will be permitted to stand for purposes of the Council's presentation, on a basis different from that of the Government, of materials and argument in support of the annual standard. We do not find it necessary to rule at this juncture on any other aspect of the intervenor's standing.

[12] 42 U.S.C. § 1857h-5(b)(1).

[13] As to any agency approach based on "margin of error," the appellant concedes some latitude for a figure below the 85 level which was identified as in the criteria as producing harm to vegetation. But appellant contends that a figure as low as 60 is inconsistent with the law's failure to include, as to secondary standards, the phrase "margin of safety" set forth in § 109(b) for primary standards. We intimate no view on this contention. We point it out to identify the kind of legal issue that cannot meaningfully be disposed of without some awareness of the basis of the Administrator's action.

The provision for statutory judicial review contemplates some disclosure of the basis of the agency's action. Citizens to Preserve Overton Park v. Volpe, 401 U.S. 402, 416, 420 (1971); Securities and Exchange Commission v. Chenery Corp., 318 U.S. 80, 94 (1943). We are not to be taken as specifying that the agency must provide the same articulation as is required for orders or regulations issued after evidentiary hearings. Greater Boston Television Corp. v. FCC, *supra,* 444 F.2d at 851. We are keenly aware of the need to avoid procedural strait jackets that would seriously hinder this new agency in the discharge of the novel, sensitive and formidable, tasks entrusted to it by Congress. This concern is emphasized by the fact that in the 1970 Amendments Congress was significantly concerned with expedition [14] and avoidance of previous cumbersome and time-consuming procedures in effect under prior law.[15]

---

[14] H. Rept. No. 91-1146, 91st Cong., 2d sess., pp. 1, 5 (1970):

"The purpose of the legislation reported unanimously by your committee is to speed up, expand, and intensify the war against air pollution * * *. While a start has been made in controlling air pollution since the enactment of the Air Quality Act of 1967, progress has been regrettably slow. This has been due to a number of factors: (1) cumbersome and time-consuming procedures called for under the 1967 act * * *. Therefore, it is urgent that Congress adopt new clean air legislation which will make possible the more expeditious imposition of specific emission standards * * * and the effective enforcement of such standards by both State and Federal agencies." See also Sen. Muskie, 116 Cong. Rec. 32901(9-21-70): "* * * we have learned that the air pollution problem is more severe, more pervasive, and growing faster than we had thought. Unless we recognize the crisis and generate a sense of urgency from that recognition, lead times may melt away without any chance at all for a rational solution to the air pollution problem."

[15] The President's proposal for national standards served to shorten the time period for controlling air pollution. Hearings in each region prior to adoption of regional air quality standards were to be eliminated. No longer could each State propose different sets of standards. No longer would the Government have to review 50 different sets of standards. Time would not have to be devoted to selecting regional boundaries; instead, States could concentrate on developing effective, enforceable implementation plans.

Congress not only was in accord, but further accelerated pollution control efforts. First, specific deadlines for proposal and promulgation of national ambient air quality standards (for pollutants, such as sulfur oxides, for which criteria had previously been issues) were written into the legislation. Second, a time limit for approval or disapproval of state implementation plans was established. Third, specific time limits were established by which the implementation plans had to achieve the national primary ambient air quality standards. Finally, to assure that the adoption of effective national ambient air quality standards would not be needlessly delayed by litigation in the courts, Congress required those who wished to contest the standards to do so within 30 days

The provision by Congress of only informal rule-making, as a preliminary to the issuance of standards,[16] and the contemplation of expedition, yield as reasonable corrollaries some latitude in the requirement for delineation of approach. While the provision in § 4 of the APA for a "concise general statement" of the basis and purpose of regulations is not to be interpreted over-literally, the regulation before us contains sufficient exposition of the purpose and basis of the regulation as a whole to satisfy this legislative minimum.[17] Particularly as applied to environmental regulations, produced under the tension of need for reasonable expedition and need for resolution of a host of nagging problems, we are loath to stretch the requirement of a "general statement" into a mandate for reference to all the specific issues raised in comments.

There are contexts, however, contexts of fact, statutory framework and nature of action, in which the minimum requirements of the Administrative Procedure Act may not be sufficient.[18] In the interest of justice, *cf.* 28 U.S.C. § 2106, and in aid of the judicial function, centralized in this court, of expeditious disposition of challenges to standards, the record is remanded for the Administrator to supply an implementing statement that will enlighten the court as to the basis on which he reached the 60 standard from the material in the Criteria. It is contemplated that the Administrator may and should proceed with all

Kennecott Copper Corp. v. E.P.A.

---

after their promulgation. Moreover, jurisdiction to review the standards was placed in this Court alone to avoid conflicting holdings by various federal courts of appeals and thus to assure a prompt and uniform determination on the validity of the standards.

[16] No public hearings are required to be held on proposed national ambient air quality standards under the Clean Air Act. Public hearings are required, however, prior to state adoption of implementation plans to meet and maintain the national standards. Sections 110(a)(1) and (c) of the Act, 42 U.S.C. sec. 1857c-5(a)(1) and (c). The legislative history of the "Clean Air Amendments of 1970" (Pub. L. 91-604) makes it clear that Congress felt public hearings on the national standards were unnecessary in light of the implementation plan hearings and would unduly delay achievement of air quality protective of the public health and welfare. See, for example, Hearings on S. 3229, S. 3466, S. 3546, before the Subcomm. on Air and Water Pollution of the Senate Comm. on Public Works, 91st Cong., 2d sess., Pt. 1, at pp. 152, 154-155, 157-158, 163-164 (1970).

[17] Automotive Parts & Accessories Ass'n v. Boyd, 132 U.S. App.D.C. 200, 407 F.2d 330 (1968).

[18] Compare Holm v. Hardin, —— U.S.App.D.C. ——, 449 F.2d 1009 (1971); American Airlines, Inc. v. CAB, 123 U.S. App.D.C. 310, 359 F.2d 624 (en banc), *cert denied*, 385 U.S. 843 (1966). These precedents establish that in a particular case fairness may require more than the APA minimum, but are not to be taken as suggesting in any way that the court considers the kind of problems involved in environment regulations to require more than the written submissions specified by Congress.

Kennecott Copper Corp. v. E.P.A.

reasonable expedition, just as the court has expedited the hearing of argument and issuance of this remand, in conformance to the legislative judgment as to need for reasonable expedition in achieving this important national goal.[19] It is further contemplated that this remand will not halt or delay the on-going proceedings for state adoption of implementation plans to meet and maintain the national standards. To avoid any misunderstanding we state expressly that the Administrator has freedom to revise the criteria on the basis of material in hand without any requirement of additional submissions.[20] Furthermore, our remand is not to be considered as limiting the Administrator's discretion to enlarge the administrative process as part of his further consideration. Compare FCC v. Pottsville Broadcasting Co., 309 U.S. 134 (1940). The Administrator may also provide for receipt of additional material, and even, if he be so advised, may revise the standards without being limited to the procedure of presenting such revisions in the form of recommendations to this court.[21]

The record will be remanded to the Administrator for further action not inconsistent with this opinion.

So ordered.

---

[19] The EPA has notified the court that it has taken steps, to avoid any possible confusion on the part of the state officials responsible for air pollution control, by notifying them directly that the 24 hour standard is intended to serve as a non-enforceable guideline rather than a mandatory requirement such as the annual standard. Because the states' implementation plans were due on January 30, 1972, only a short time after the problem of possible confusion became apparent, states will upon request be given an "adequate period" during which to revise their implementation plans in light of the clarification.

While we do not say this is mandatory, we think it desirable to use the facilities of the Federal Register, available for interpretative rulings, to assure widespread notice of administrative steps taken in the interest of clarification.

[20] At oral argument, counsel for petitioner conceded that the criteria may be amended, on the basis of the record in hand, including comments, without providing for further comments on the amendments. We think that is an appropriate construction of § 108 in the context of this case.

[21] The secondary standards promulgated April 30, 1971, remain in effect pending amplification of basis on remand and further review by this court. Following remand proceedings petitioner may supplement its petition to review without filing a new petition to review. In specifying that the Administrator may revise the standards, following the remand, without leave of court we do not speak to the procedures that may be requisite for issuance of revised standards, *cf.* § 109 (b) (2), 42 U.S.C. § 1857(c)-4.

SAMPLE COMPLAINT

The author is indebted to Mr. Bernard S. Cohen, Esq. of Cohen and Rosenblum, in Alexandria, Virginia, for having supplied the complaint reproduced below. As explained in Chapter Five, the attorney representing the plaintiff in environmental litigation must insure that the court will hear his case on the merits. The following complaints illustrate the best way to accomplish this goal. Include all bases for relief (common law causes of action, modern tort concepts, Federal and state statutes, Constitutional claims, etc.), including requests for declaratory judgment and injunctive relief wherever appropriate.

IN THE UNITED STATES DISTRICT COURT
FOR THE EASTERN DISTRICT OF VIRGINIA
Alexandria Division

DR. F. D. CUSTER
P. O. Box 27
Oakland, Maryland 21550 **Plaintiff**

vs.

CIVIL ACTION NO. 311-71-A

VIRGINIA ELECTRIC AND
POWER COMPANY
Serve: Linwood G. Parrish
Registered Agent
700 East Franklin St.
Richmond, Virginia **Defendant**

COMPLAINT

1. Plaintiff is a citizen of the State of Maryland and defendant, Virginia Electric and Power Company (hereinafter VEPCO) is a corporation incorporated under the laws of the State of Virginia having its principal place of business in a state other than the State of Maryland. The matter in controversy, exclusive of interest and costs, exceeds the sum of Ten Thousand Dollars ($10,000.00).

2. Plaintiff, F. D. Custer, D.V.M., owns and operates the Mountain Top Tree Farms, Oakland, Maryland. On his farms in Garrett County, Maryland and Grant County, West Virginia, plaintiff grows Christmas trees and nursery stock. Plaintiff also provides custom shearing, planting, harvesting and management for a number of other plantations.

3. Garrett County, Maryland and Grant County, West Virginia are sparsely settled areas with little industrial development.

4. VEPCO owns and operates the Mt. Storm Power Station in Grant County, West Virginia.

5. The Mt. Storm Power Station has two units fully operational and a third unit is currently under construction and is expected to be in operation within the near future. Each unit of this station is capable of burning 5,000 tons of coal per twenty-four (24) hours.

6. The stacks on the two units of the Mt. Storm Power Station are 350 feet high and are equipped with electro-static filters. These filters have never operated at full efficiency.

7. The Mt. Storm Power Station has used high sulfur content coal in its operation and to this day uses such low quality coal.

8. The operations of the Mt. Storm Power Station result in tons of particulates and harmful and noxious emissions being daily emitted into the ambient air.

9. The Mt. Storm Power Station is the largest source of air pollution in the Grant County, West Virginia and Garrett County, Maryland area.

10. Plaintiff's Christmas trees and nursery stock have been damaged by air pollution created by defendant's Mt. Storm Power Station.

FIRST CLAIM FOR RELIEF—NUISANCE

The plaintiff hereby incorporates by reference all of the allegations of Paragraphs 1 through 10 as if they were here fully set out and further states as follows:

COUNT I—Relating to plaintiff's Christmas tree plantations in Grant County, West Virginia.

11. Defendant VEPCO, in violation of its duty owed to the plaintiff, has operated its Mt. Storm Power Station in such a manner as to create a continuing nuisance.

12. As a direct and proximate result of the defendant's creation of a continuing nuisance, the plaintiff has suffered and will continue to suffer extensive damage to his property and to his Christmas tree business, including damage to his Christmas trees, his nursery stock and to the use and enjoyment of his property.

13. The continuing nuisance created by the defendant's power station has made it impossible for the plaintiff to operate his business.

COUNT II—Relating to plaintiff's Christmas tree plantations in Garrett County, Maryland.

14. Defendant VEPCO, in violation of its duty owed to the plaintiff, has operated its Mt. Storm Power Station in such a manner as to create a continuing nuisance.

15. As a direct and proximate result of the defendant's creation of a continuing nuisance, the plaintiff has suffered and will continue to suffer extensive damage to his property and to his Christmas tree business including damage to his Christmas trees, his nursery stock and to the use and enjoyment of his property.

16. The continuing nuisance created by the defendant's power station has made it impossible for the plaintiff to operate his business.

SECOND CLAIM FOR RELIEF—TRESPASS

Plaintiff hereby incorporates by reference all of the allegations of Paragraphs 1 through 10 as if they were here fully set out and further states as follows:

COUNT I—Relating to plaintiff's Christmas tree plantations in Grant County, West Virginia.

17. Defendant VEPCO, in violation of its duty owed to the plaintiff, has operated its Mt. Storm Power Station in such a manner as to create a trespass in that the property of the plaintiff has been frequently invaded by particulates and harmful and noxious emissions.

18. As a direct and proximate result of the defendant's commission of a trespass and continuing trespasses, the plaintiff has suffered and will continue to suffer extensive damage to his property and to his Christmas tree business including damage to his Christmas trees, his nursery stock and to the use and enjoyment of his property.

19. The trespasses committed by the defendant VEPCO have made it impossible for the plaintiff to operate his business.

COUNT II—Relating to plaintiff's Christmas tree plantations in Garret County, Maryland.

20. Defendant VEPCO, in violation of its duty owed to the plaintiff, has operated its Mt. Storm Power Station in such a manner as to create a trespass in that the property of the plaintiff has been frequently invaded by particulates and harmful and noxious emissions.

21. As a direct and proximate result of the defendant's commission of a trespass and continuing trespasses, the plaintiff has suffered and will continue to suffer extensive damage to his property and to his Christmas tree business including damage to his Christmas trees, his nursery stock and to the use and enjoyment of his property.

22. The trespasses committed by the defendant VEPCO have made it impossible for the plaintiff to operate his business.

THIRD CLAIM FOR RELIEF-NEGLIGENCE

Plaintiff hereby incorporates by reference all of the allegations of Paragraphs 1 through 10 as if they were here fully set out and further states as follows:

COUNT I—Relating to plaintiff's Christmas tree plantations in Grant County, West Virginia.

23. Defendant VEPCO, in violation of its duty owed to the plaintiff, did negligently operate its Mt. Storm Power Station in such a manner as to create extensive air pollution.

24. As a direct and proximate result of the negligent operation of defendant's Mt. Storm Power Station, plaintiff suffered extensive damage to his property and to his Christmas tree business including damage to his Christmas trees, his nursery stock and to the use and enjoyment of his property.

25. The negligent operation of defendant's power station has made it impossible for the plaintiff to operate his business.

COUNT II—Relating to plaintiff's Christmas tree plantations in Garrett County, Maryland.

26. Defendant VEPCO, in violation of its duty owed to the plaintiff, did negligently operate its Mt. Storm Power Station in such a manner as to create extensive air pollution.

27. As a direct and proximate result of the negligent operation of defendant's Mt. Storm Power Station, plaintiff suffered extensive damage to his property and to his Christmas tree business including damage to his Christmas trees, his nursery stock and to the use and enjoyment of his property.

28. The negligent operation of defendant's power station has made it impossible for the plaintiff to operate his business.

sample complaint

FOURTH CLAIM FOR RELIEF—STRICT LIABILITY

Plaintiff hereby incorporates by reference all of the allegations of Paragraphs 1 through 10 as if they were here fully set out and further states as follows:

COUNT I—Relating to plaintiff's Christmas tree plantation in Grant County, West Virginia.

29. Defendant VEPCO, in violation of its duty owed to the plaintiff, has operated its Mt. Storm Power Station in such a manner as to create an unreasonably dangerous and harmful situation.

30. As a direct and proximate result of the defendant's creation of this unreasonably dangerous and harmful situation, plaintiff has suffered extensive damage to his property and to his Christmas tree business including damage to his Christmas trees, his nursery stock and to the use and enjoyment of his property.

31. The operation of defendant's power station so as to create an unreasonably dangerous and harmful situation has made it impossible for the plaintiff to operate his business.

COUNT II—Relating to plaintiff's Christmas tree plantations in Garrett County, Maryland.

32. Defendant VEPCO, in violation of its duty owed to the plaintiff, has operated its Mt. Storm Power Station in such a manner as to create an unreasonably dangerous and harmful situation.

33. As a direct and proximate result of the defendant's creation of this unreasonably dangerous and harmful situation, plaintiff has suffered extensive damage to his property and to his Christmas tree business including damage to his Christmas trees, his nursery stock and to the use and enjoyment of his property.

34. The operation of defendant's power station so as to create an unreasonably dangerous and harmful situation has made it impossible for the plaintiff to operate his business.

WHEREFORE, plaintiff demands judgment in the amount of TWO AND A HALF MILLION DOLLARS ($2,500,000.00) damages and his costs expended plus interest.

DR. F. D. CUSTER

By Counsel

COHEN AND ROSENBLUM
110 North Royal Street
P. O. Box 1079
Alexandria, Virginia 22313
836-2121

By ________________________
BERNARD S. COHEN

SUB-CHAPTER THREE-B: Noise

Noise as a pollutant with serious consequences is often overlooked in a survey of environmental problems. Unlike the tangible pollutants of the air, water and land, noise is a waste product in pure energy form. Together with other energy pollutants such as heat, it is only beginning to be recognized as a widespread environmental problem. Perhaps because noise is a transient phenomenon it is most often tolerated rather than regulated. Added to its transient nature is the subjective character of human perception of noise. Sound with social value to one person may be noise—sound without value—to another.

Noise can seriously affect living organisms. In humans sound is detected by the 1½-inch organ of corti located in the inner ear. Here some 17,000 irreplaceable hair cells detect the air pressure fluctuations and, through the fibers of the auditory nerves, send impulses to the brain. Excessive noise, both high intensity for short periods, and lower intensity over an extended period, causes destruction of these hair cells. The result is a impairment of hearing ability which can range from very slight reductions in sensitivity, sometimes in only certain frequency ranges, to total deafness. Aside from the auditory effects of noise, there are other physiological, psychological, and sociological effects.

Because of this harm, the basis for regulation exists. Rational regulatory efforts, owing to the potential subjective differences of opinion on the acceptability of any particular noise, require a relatively precise objective measure of noise in order to introduce an element of predictability and rationality into regulatory efforts.

Noise pollution may be limited by a wide range of governmental activities. Control of noise requires the direction of attention to the noise source, the environment and path through which it travels, and the immediate environment of the individual recipient of the noise. Regulatory schemes have been directed at all three control areas. Generally the simple anti-noise ordinance has a limited effectiveness.

Source Control

Source controls have been imposed by several levels of government. Such laws have required reductions of the amount of noise produced, but many times the law has been ineffective because of non-enforcement. The range of sources covered extends from aircraft through machines and tools and automobiles and other vehicles to amplification devices when used commercially and even privately. Noise standards have not been imposed on small appliances and tools for private consumption for the most part. Required disclosure of noise levels produced by consumer products, as has been suggested in recent legislation proposals, would allow consumers to evaluate this additional factor in product selection; perhaps this would offset the tendancy to design for increased noise levels so as to impress customers with the apparent power of the product.

Path Control

In the area of aircraft noise regulation, the techniques of night-time curfews, alteration in flight paths, thrust cutbacks, and selection of runways to avoid noise-sensitive areas are being used. Zoning around airports for noise-insensitive uses has recently been instituted in certain areas. Zoning regulations, parks, and greenbelts are being used in highway noise minimization. The technique benefits those living adjacent to the highway, not those using the highway. Perhaps the most prevalent noise path control is the housing code provision requiring certain amounts of acoustical insulation.

Receiver Shields

The principal area in which noise reduction has been attempted at the receiver is the area of occupational noise. All three levels of government have acted here to reduce impact from industrial noise in the working environment by shielding workers' ears with plugs or muffs to prevent auditory impacts.

Increasingly, at the base of all these control strategies is an objective measurement of noise. Sound pressure levels, power levels, or intensity can be measured by comparison to a minimum reference level, usually the lowest level sound perceivable by the average human ear. Because the range of detectable sounds is so extensive, measurements are done on a logarithmic scale. The standard unit is the decibel (dB). All other units in use derive from this basic starting point. The other units were developed to suit particular problems.

Measurement

A decibel is a logarithmic measure of sound. Because it is logarithmic, linear comparisons of decibel levels cannot be made. For example, a noise pressure level of 130 decibels is 10 times as great as one of 120 decibels and 100 times as great as a noise pressure level of 110 decibels. It is widely accepted that steady exposure to about 90 decibels can cause permanent hearing loss.

The most important modification is the weighted decibel. Response to sound is a function of frequency, the human ear being more sensitive in the middle as opposed to the high and low tones. To approximate the frequency response of the human ear the A-weighted decibel (dBA) was developed. It is in wide use today in regulatory schemes. Measurements in dB, dBA and dBC (bass tone weighted) can be taken with small meters.

But measurements of sound levels to prove compliance or non-compliance with an applicable law must be coupled with a determination of the distance from the meter to the noise source, and a characterization of the source as a line or point source. A sound wave is produced by a compression of a transmitting medium for a single energy release. As the wave propogates it dissipates as a function of the distance squared. Thus, a 50 dBA reading, without knowledge of the distance from the source to the receptor, is meaningless. The lack of a measurement distance exists in many regulatory schemes, making them useless.

There are other single event noise measurements; these include Perceived Noise Level (in PNdB), and Effective Perceived Noise Level (EPNdB), developing an entirely new unit in each case, although still based on the decibel. We also are beginning to see the use of dBA and dB in criteria under different names, such as California's Single Event Noise Equivalence Level (SENEL). These units were all conceived specifically for measuring single-aircraft noise levels. PNdB is in use by the Port of New York Authority, and EPNdB is used by the Federal Aviation Administration.

Long ago it was recognized that there is a cumulative effective of a repetitious series of noises which exceeds the summed effect of the individual events. Special units have been developed, again for the aviation context, to measure the noise impact of the entire operation of an airport. These units are based on standard noise characteristics for each type of plane operating from the airport, the number of daily operations of each type of aircraft, and the time of day or night for each operation. Night operations are given as much as ten times more weight than day operations to account for the impact of noise on the sleeping community. The determination of these values is a complex matter generally left to computers. The results are plotted on a map of the airport vicinity as contour lines of noise exposure. California uses the community noise equivalent level (CNEL) based on dBA measurements. The other major units are Composite Noise Rating (CNR) based on PNdB, and Noise Exposure Forecast (NEF) based on EPNdB readings.

Such noise measurements are valuable for land use planning in the area of airports (and are being used by HUD and certain states such as Minnesota for this purpose), but have limited value in regulatory attempts to control noise from the airport. California has devised a scheme to require the shrinking of noise impact on the surrounding community by putting the burden on the airport operator to shrink the CNEL value on a contour which originally measured CNEL = 80, but this regulatory technique is the exception rather than the rule.

A whole second class of units is in use, though not really to measure noise, but to measure the performance of insulation techniques. The primary criteria in use is Sound Transmission Class (STC), which measures the *loss* in decibels of a sound level resulting from the introduction of insulating walls and partitions. Other units in use are Noise Reduction Coefficient (NRC), Noise Isolation Class (NIC), Impact Insulation Class (IIC) and Absorption Coefficient. A special group of units is used to assess the environment in terms of acceptability for working conditions and ease of

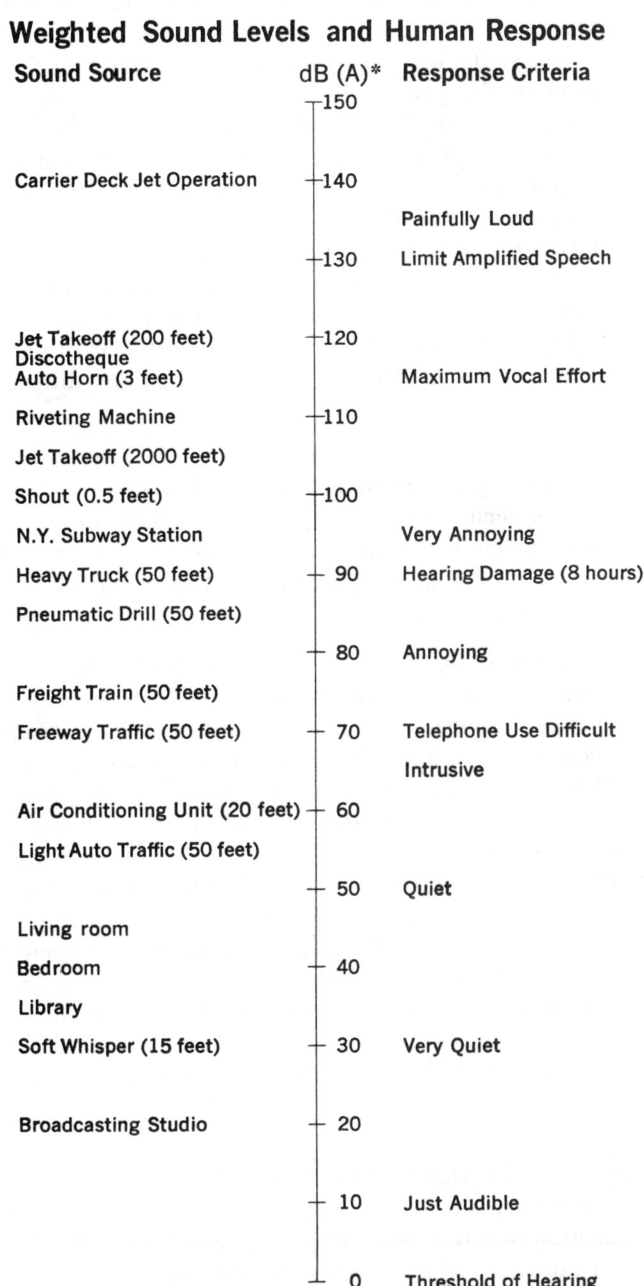

*Typical A—Weighted sound levels taken with a sound-level meter and expressed as decibels on the scale. The "A" scale approximates the frequency response of the human ear.

Source: Department of Transportation.

communications. These units are Speech Interference Level (SIL) using dB, Noise Criterion (NC) based in dB, dBC, dBA, and Articulation Index (AI) which ranges from 0.0 to 1.0 with high speech intelligibility ranging from 0.6 up.

At the base of all the complex special function criteria is the dB scale. The most commonly used unit is dBA, since it most nearly reflects the acoustic response of the human ear over the audible frequency spectrum. For a basic feel of the meaning of a certain dBA level the accompanying chart, weighted sound levels and human response, is quite helpful.

Effects

A recent EPA study, *Report to the President and Congress on Noise* (Dec. 31, 1971), identifies four broad areas of harmful effects on humans resulting from noise exposure—auditory, physiological, psychological and sociological effects. Interestingly this report also recognizes that noise adversely affects non-human animal life. Auditory effects range from a slight handicap to total deafness. These classifications are based on shifts in the hearing threshold—the minimum sound pressure level the individual can detect. Such shifts are measured in dB difference from a baseline examination of the person. It is generally only in the industrial work environment that such shifts are detected. Primarily through labor union pressures, some industrial health programs include initial and periodic hearing examinations. (see also statutory materials in this chapter on occupational noise control.)

Besides hearing damage, noise also causes adverse auditory effects in terms of masking desired sounds. Such masking can impair speech communications to the detriment of educational, occupational and social activities. The accompanying chart gives an indication of the range of noise associated with varying degrees of communications difficulty. As EPA's report notes,

> Interference with speech communication by noise is among the most significant adverse effects of noise on people. Free and easy speech communication is probably essential for full development of individuals and social relations, and freedom of speech is but an empty phrase if one cannot be heard or understood because of noise.

Of particular significance is the deleterious masking effect of noise on warning signals such as train whistles, emergency vehicle sirens, and motor vehicle horns. Here again, noise has a particularly harmful effect in a work environment where such warning signals are crucial to operational safety.

There is considerable dispute regarding the possible range of physiological effects. Rather than speculate on the veracity of some of the more tenuous physiological consequences of noise, the following is presented as the conclusions of the highly professional group participating in the recent Environmental Protection Agency study, *Report to the President and Congress on Noise* (1971). This massive report was the basic source for virtually all of this subchapter until the section on litigation. Large sections of this report are quoted directly, while other sections were edited, excerpted, and in general "boiled down". Occasional bits of material in no way derived from the reort are set off by brackets. The report:

GENERAL PHYSIOLOGICAL EFFECTS

There are general physiological responses to transient noise, and it has been proposed that there may be general physiological responses to persistent noise. It has also been proposed that noise can be a significant source of stress and can in this way increase the incidence of health problems. Each of these topics is discussed below.

Transient Physiological Response to Noise

There are three classes of transient general physiological responses to sound:

1. Fast responses of the voluntary musculature that are mediated by the somatic nervous system.
2. The slightly slower responses of the smooth muscles and glands that are mediated by the visceral nervous system.
3. The even slower responses of the neuro-endocrine system.

Responses of the Voluntary Musculature

Muscular responses to sound can be studied by visual observation of bodily movements or by electrical measurements of muscular activity. By these techniques it has been shown that people are equipped with an elaborate set of auditory-muscular reflexes that serve the basic functions of orienting the head and eyes toward a source of sound and of preparing for action appropriate to an object or event signalled by sound. These reflexes operate at low levels of sound, where they can be detected by sophisticated electrical measurements, as well as at high levels of sound. Such auditory-muscular reflexes underlie muscular responses to sound that range from rhythmic movements and dance to the body's startle response to impulsive sounds such as gunshots or sonic booms.

The body's startle response to impulsive sounds can interfere with human performance and is one of the factors that underlie the annoyance produced by sudden noises. The startle response has been studied in detail and includes an eyeblink, a typical facial grimace, bending of the knees, and, in general, flexion (inward and forward) as opposed to extension of bodily parts. The startle response to a nearby gunshot, even when expected, may undergo various degrees of diminution with repetition, depending upon the individual, the rate of repitition, and the predictability of the impulse sound. Some individuals show little diminution of the response with repetition, others show marked reduction. The eyeblink and head movement persist even in experienced marksmen when shooting their own guns.

Auditory-muscular reflexes can have more subtle effects on human activity than those of the startle response. Interestingly, the greater the tension in a muscle, the greater its reflex response to sound. Therefore, the influence of auditory-muscular reflexes on the performance of a given task depends on posture and the pattern of muscular tension as well as on the movements required by the given task. For example, when a given task requires a movement of flexion and the resting posture heightens tension in the flexor muscles, then a burst of sound at an appropriate time can speed the required movement. Under other conditions, the burst of sound can greatly interfere with this movement.

In summary, the ebb and flow of muscular activity is closely linked to and influenced by the rise and fall of sound. The obvious effects of the startle response and other auditory-muscular reflexes often diminish with repetition of the sound stimulus. However, even after many repetitions these reflexes may continue to operate in a subtle manner, and their effects will depend on the details of posture and resting muscular tension, on the details of the task at hand, and on the physical properties of the sound stimulus.

Responses of the Smooth Muscles and Glands

In response to brief sounds, there is general constriction in the peripheral blood vessels, with a reduction in peripheral blood flow. There may be acceleration or deceleration of heart rate, changes in resistance of skin to electrical current (an indication of activation of the peripheral visceral nervous system), changes in breathing pattern, changes in the motility of the gastrointestinal tract, and changes in the secretion of saliva and gastric juice. These responses are obvious when the noise level exceeds 70 dBA. For sounds below this intensity level, it is doubtful that the recording techniques have been sufficiently sensitive to decide whether or not these responses occur. In any case, they are either small or nonexistent.

Some aspects of these responses diminish and seem to disappear with predictable repetition of the sounds, while others may not.

Some of these responses to sound are part of a pattern of response known as the orienting reflex or "what is it?" response. The orienting reflex disappears rapidly as the stimulus becomes known or predictable. Others of these responses to sound are probably part of a response known as the defense reflex, which prepares an organism to escape or accept injury or discomfort. Defense reflexes occur in response to warnings of painful stimuli, to painful stimuli themselves, or in response to very intense stimulation of any sense organ. Responses that are part of the defense reflex disappear more slowly with stimulus repetition than do those of the orienting reflex. Sometimes they may never completely disappear.

Neuro-endocrine Responses

Loud sounds as well as other intense stimuli, such as forced immobilization, forced exercise, cold, pain, and injuries, can activate a complicated series of changes in the endocrine system. These changes, in turn, can cause changes in hormone levels, blood composition, and a whole complex of other biochemical and physiological changes.

Possible Persistent Physiological Responses to Noise

It has been proposed that frequent repetition of the transient physiological responses to noise can lead to persistent, pathological changes in nonauditory bodily functions. Also, it has been proposed that such repetition of these transient physiological responses to sounds are often useful because they help to protect people from potentially harmful events. It is also appropriate that these responses diminish when repetition of the noise signifies that particular noises do not represent a threatening condition. The crux of the question is whether man is so designed as to adapt to nonthreatening noises that are also quite intense or whether the modern environment presents such ever changing noises that the transient physiological responses are chronically maintained.

At least some of the transient physiological responses to noise do appear to be chronically maintained. Furthermore, there is some evidence that workers exposed to high levels of noise have a higher incidence of cardiovascular disease, ear-nose-and-throat disorders, and equilibrium disorders than do workers exposed to lower levels of noise. However, it is also possible to explain these observations in terms of non-noise factors such as age, dust levels, occupational danger, or life habits.

Also, there is evidence from animal research that high sound levels can interfere with sexual-reproductive functions, can interfere with resistance to viral disease, and can also produce other pathological effects. These experiments, however, have often not been well controlled; i.e., fear, animal handling conditions, and so on have not been equated between noise-exposed and non-noise-exposed groups. Further, rodents were used as experimental subjects, and these animals are known to have special susceptibility to the effects of certain sounds. Finally, the sound levels were well above those encountered by most people.

The evidence taken as a whole hints that chronic exposure to sufficiently variable or intense noise may contribute to nonauditory physiological and anatomical pathology. However, the case is far from proven and merits further research and investigation.

Stress Theory

The neuro-endocrine responses previously mentioned seem similar to the responses to stress. Responses to stress have general characteristics that appear in response to all stressors and special characteristics that are linked to specific stressors.

The response to stress, called the general adaptation syndrome, consists of three stages: an alarm reaction, a stage of resistance, and a stage of exhaustion. If a stressor is severe and is maintained for prolonged periods of time, an organism passes in succession through the stages of the alarm reaction, of resistance, and of exhaustion. In the extreme case, the end result is a breakdown of bodily function and death. Even in the less severe case, a price may be paid for continued stress during a prolonged stage of resistance. This price may include increased susceptibility to infection and, perhaps, specific diseases known as the diseases of adaptation. Such diseases may include, among others, some types of gastrointestinal ulcers, some types of high blood pressure, and some types of arthritis. Many medical authorities do not accept the theory that there are diseases of adaptation. Rather, they theorize that each disease has its own special set of causes.

Stress theory, even as presented by its strongest advocates, is complicated. These advocates speak of interactions between conditioning factors that set the scene for disease, specific reactions to particular stressors, and general reactions to non-specific stressors.

GENERAL PSYCHOLOGICAL AND SOCIOLOGICAL EFFECTS

Noise not only has direct auditory effects but also produces behavioral effects of a more general nature. Noise can interfere with sleep. Further, it can be a source of annoyance and can lead to community actions against those producing noise or those responsible for its regulation. Noise may interfere with the performance of tasks, plays a role in privacy, and is sometimes associated with psychological distress.

Interference with Sleep

Sleep is not a single state but consists of a series of stages that can be graded from light to deep. Physiological measurements allow one to identify the stage of sleep.

Everyday observations suggest that noise can and does interfere with sleep, and research, both in the laboratory and the field, confirms these observations. Messages from the sense organs reach the highest centers of the brain even during the deepest sleep. Whether a sleeping person is aroused by a stimulus depends on a variety of factors. Arousal can be recognized by brief changes in physiological functions, by shifts from deep to lighter stages of sleep, or by behavioral evidence of awakening.

During normal sleep, arousal by noise depends upon the following factors: the intensity level of the noise, the fluctuation of the intensity level of the noise, the motivation of the person to be aroused by particular sounds as established while awake, the depth of sleep, the amount of accumulated sleep, previous sleep deprivation, and the person's age and sex. Other factors such as drugs and psychological disorders can also affect the ability of a person to sleep through noise.

The greater the intensity of a brief noise, the greater are the chances that noise will arouse a sleeping person. In a quiet bedroom, noise levels below 30 dBA do not ordinarily have any arousal effect. As the noise level increases from 30 to 100 dBA, the chances of awakening increase. Brief noises with levels of 100 to 120 dBA awaken nearly everyone.

Sources

Noise is perhaps the most pervasive pollutant we experience. Any sound in an unwanted context is a noise. The more common sources of noise can be broadly classified as industrial noise, construction noise, engine noise from non-transportation devices, and domestic noise. Collectively these noises combine to produce community background noise.

Transportation Systems

One of the most significant byproducts of our increasing population and economic growth is the increasing demand for improved modes of transportation [a subject that will be treated at length in Volume Two.] In 1970, the transportation industry represented, in total, approximately 14.5 percent of the gross national product, and employed approximately 13.3

percent of the total labor force. This major section of the nation's economy includes the:

- aviation industry
- highway vehicle industry
- railroad and urban mass transit industry
- recreational vehicle industry

While there are many important sources of intrusive noise, transportation vehicle noise tends to dominate most residential areas, and thus is largely responsible for the current general concern with noise. The relative portions and activity of the various transportation industries are shown below.

aviation

The increase in air travel during the last decade (10.7 million U.S. commercial operations in 1970) is closely related to the introduction and growth of the commercial jet aircraft fleet. The advantages of jet-powered passenger airplanes have led to a gradual phasing out of the older propeller-driven commercial aircraft.

There is still a substantial propeller aircraft fleet in operation, both commercial and private. Noise from both piston and turboprop aircraft is produced primarily by the propellers. Depending on the blade shape and operating conditions, the frequency of the noise ranges from 50 to 250 Hz (fundamental frequency) with noise at higher frequencies consisting of harmonics and discrete frequency noise from the engine parts and the exhaust mixing.

The helicopter is distinguished in terms of noise impact because of its capability of operating from urban centers, and its ability to hover. Of the 3,260 non-military helicopters registered in the United States in mid-1972, 1,900 were based in urban areas. [In the city of Washington, it is rare, at least at night, to be out of hearing range of a municipal police helicopter, though during the day the sound is often masked by other noise. The sleep of high-rise dwellers near the residential core of the city is frequently disturbed.]

The helicopter's noise signature, a distinctive low-frequency, throbbing sound, is noticeably different from all other common noise generators. It is extremely difficult to control noise intrusion into the passenger cabin (90 to 110 dBA), or into buildings, because sound-insulation methods are markedly inefficient in the low-frequency range. This problem is further complicated by the fact that low-frequency sound travels through the atmosphere more readily than high-frequency sound. Thus, helicopter noise can be distinguished at greater distances than can most other sources of equal noise level.

Early turbojet engines produce high noise levels from the turbulent mixing of jet exhaust with the surrounding air. Sound power increases with increasing jet velocity. The turbofan, with a lower jet velocity, produces lower jet noise levels. However, the enlarged fan size and power add a second significant noise source more noticeable on approach. Thus turbofan jet aircraft takeoffs are characterized by low frequency jet noise and landings by high frequency fan noise. Multi-engine jet aircraft have reduced this noise somewhat. The new Jumbo jets use high bypass ratio engines so that takeoff and approach produce nearly equal noise levels. Still, discrete frequency fan whine is the persistent noise reduction obstacle. The respective average noise levels of these craft appear in the accompanying chart.

Unlike propeller aircraft, jet cabin noise is produced primarily by high speed causing turbulent mixing in the boundary layer between the fuselage and the surrounding air. Remaining noise components, as all cabin noise in propeller aircraft, are from the engine operations. The jet interior noise levels during cruise typically range from 79 to 88 dBA, depending on the seat location, with a typical value of 82 dBA. During takeoff and landing operations, the noise levels are up to 12 dBA higher.

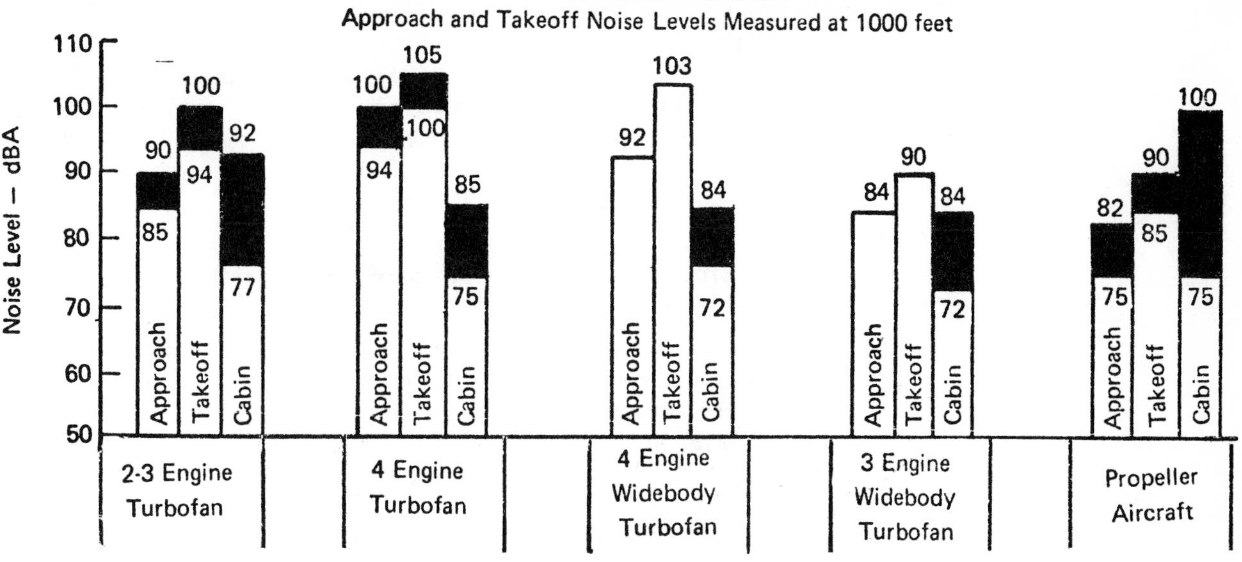
Typical Noise Levels
Approach and Takeoff Noise Levels Measured at 1000 feet
Noise Level – dBA
110
100
90
80
70
60
50
Approach
Takeoff
Cabin
2-3 Engine Turbofan
90
85
100
94
92
77
4 Engine Turbofan
100
94
105
100
85
75
4 Engine Widebody Turbofan
92
103
84
72
3 Engine Widebody Turbofan
84
90
84
72
Propeller Aircraft
82
75
90
85
100
75

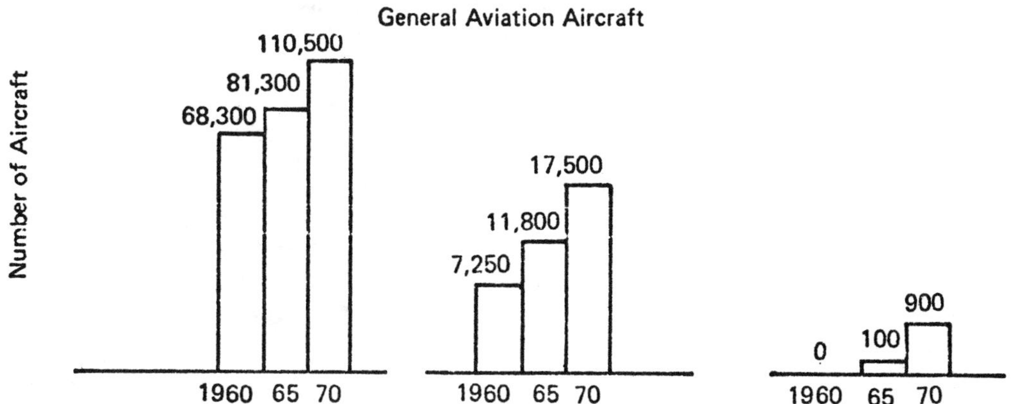
General Aviation Aircraft
Number of Aircraft
68,300
81,300
110,500
7,250
11,800
17,500
0
100
900
1960
65
70

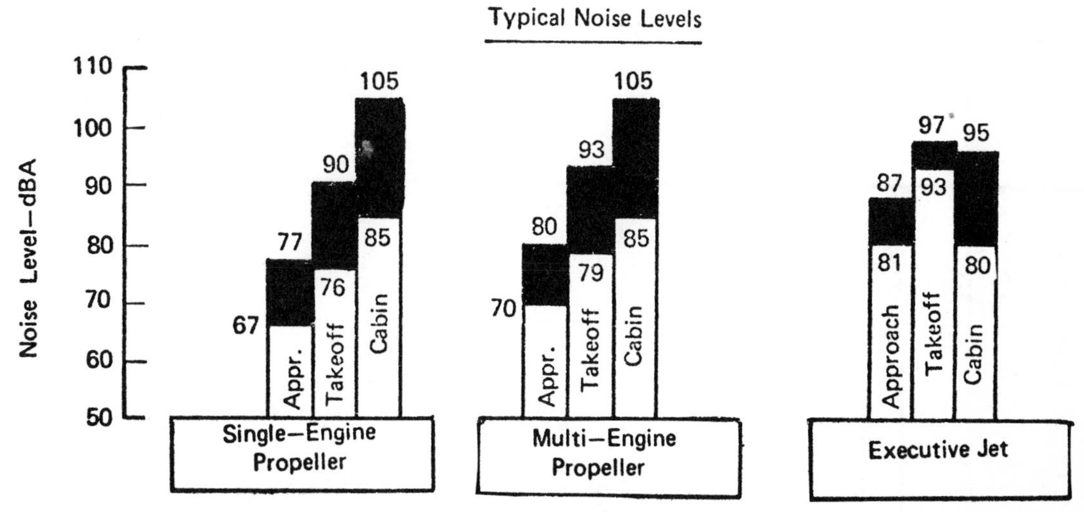
Typical Noise Levels
Noise Level–dBA
110
100
90
80
70
60
50
Single–Engine Propeller
67
77
76
90
85
105
Appr.
Takeoff
Cabin
Multi–Engine Propeller
70
80
79
93
85
105
Executive Jet
87
81
97
93
95
80
Approach

roads

Highway Vehicles

For the purposes of this discussion, highway vehicles include automobiles, trucks, buses, and maintenance and utility vehicles. Motorcycles are treated in the discussion of recreation vehicles. For each 1,000 persons in the United States, 1,600 to 2,300 automobile trips, and 200 to 400 truck trips are made daily. Urban travel represents about 52 percent of the estimated 3 billion highway-vehicle-miles traveled in 1970.

The noise levels produced by highway vehicles are a function of speed and can be attributed to three major causes:

- rolling stock: tires and gearing
- propulsion system: engine and related accessories
- aerodynamic and body noise.

At truck speeds below 45 mph, and automobile speeds below 35 mph, engine noise is dominant. It is generated at the exhaust and intake openings and directly at the casing (engine vibration).

Above 50 mph, tire noise is dominant in both trucks and automobiles, with the larger, differently designed, truck tires being generally noisier. Tire noise increases with speed and can vary at constant speed up to 20 dB as a function of road surface, axle loading, tread design, or wear condition. For instance, one common truck tire is known as "Singing Sam." This tire, most often a retread, has a suction cup texture surface. It is 10 to 20 dB noisier than other truck tire designs. Other noise sources are aerodynamic turbulence and the rattling of loose parts.

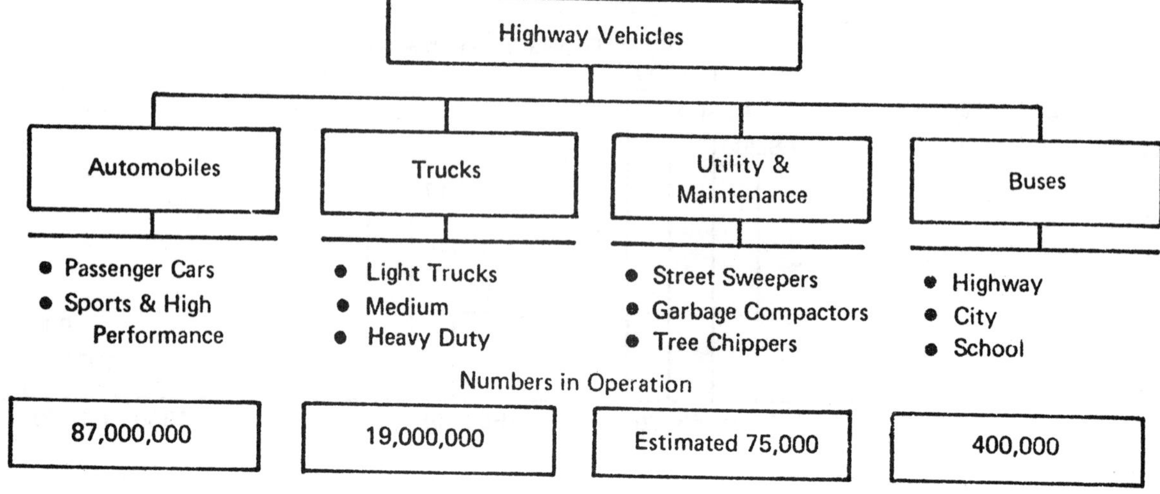

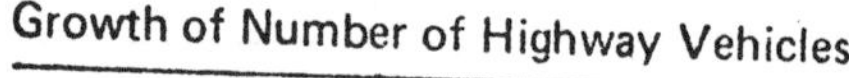

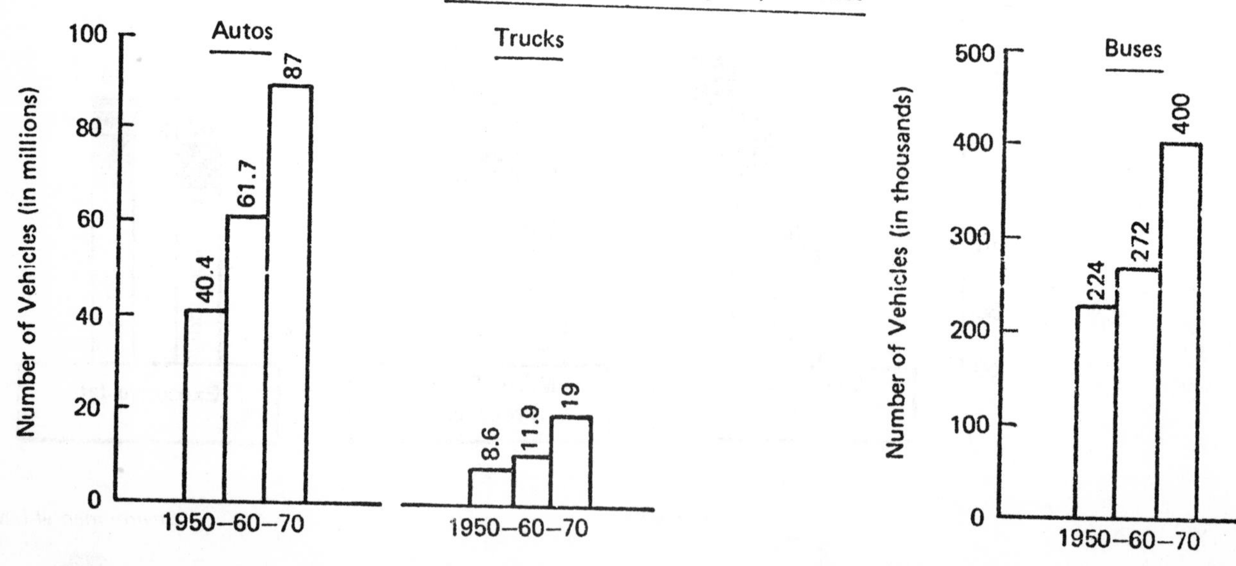

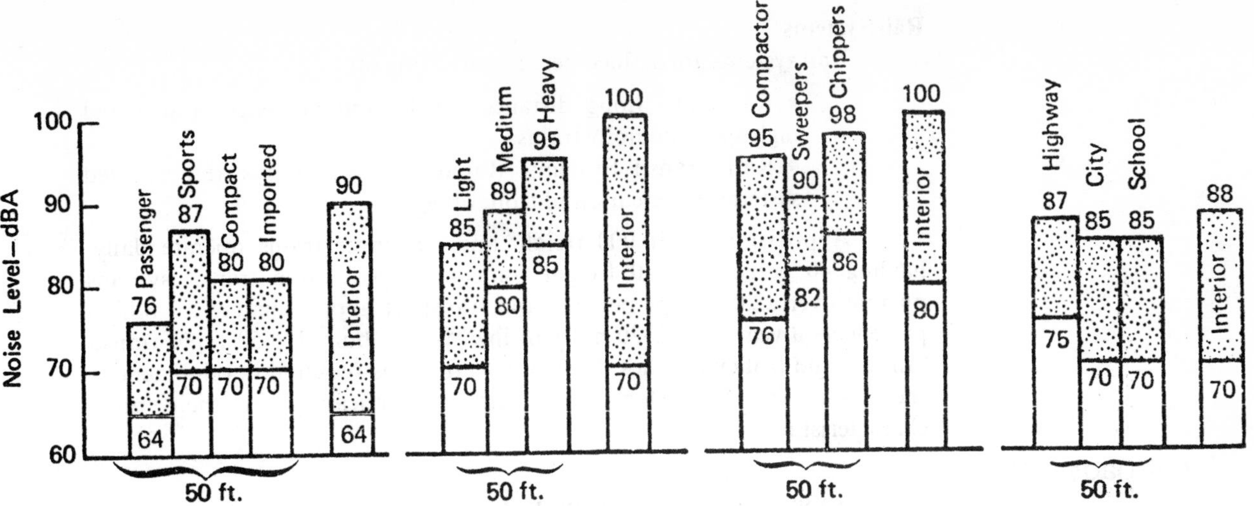

In addition to the information on the proceeding graphs it can generally be said that of the 19 million operating trucks, the 2 to 3 percent that are diesel-powered are 8 to 10 dB noisier than gasoline-powered models. Buses tend to be quieter than trucks, owing to large mufflers and a more enclosed compartment. Special trucks such as garbage and utility trucks produce additional noise from the auxilliary functions performed.

Automobiles are significant noise sources because of the abundance of these vehicles—an estimated 91 million in use in the U.S. in 1972. Interior noise levels in larger American cars range from 65 to 70 dBA (windows closed). Economy and sports cars have interior noise in the 70 to 82 dBA range because there is less buffer material and distance between source and receptor. There still exists a marketing philosophy, and perhaps considerable buyer attitude, that more noise equates with more power. This reasoning is particularly prevalent in the "high-performance" car market. In the luxury car market, we now see a definite equation of elegance and comfort with silence.

Highway Vehicle Noise in the Community

Vehicular traffic generally establishes the residual noise levels in most urban and suburban communities. This residual noise level varies throughout the day, based on the average density of noise sources in a given community. However, in the immediate vicinity of a major arterial highway or freeway, the noise level is much higher. Its actual value is dependent upon traffic flow rate, average vehicle speed, distance to the traffic lane, and the ratio of trucks to automobiles on the highway. For a typical eight-lane freeway, average daytime traffic flow rates can be on the order of 6,000 to 10,000 vehicles per hour. For this condition, the median noise level beyond 100 feet from the flowing traffic is equivalent to that from a continuous line of noise sources. Typical median traffic noise levels near a major freeway are about 75 to 80 dBA at 100 feet from the roadway and about 65 dBA at 1000 feet.

Superimposed on this median traffic noise level are the intrusive or single-event noises from individual trucks, cars, and motorcycles that are normally 15 to 25 dBA above the residual noise levels on neighborhood streets. However, at the high traffic flow rates typical for freeways, these individual single events are less distinguishable from the overall roar of the total traffic flow.

Rail Systems

Rail systems are defined here as consisting of:

- Railroads. Long distance freight and passenger trains and high speed intercity trains.
- Rail Transit Systems. Rapid transit subways and elevated systems, streetcars, and trolley lines.

Approximately 10,000 freight and passenger trains operate daily, hauling 40 percent of all freight tonnage. Urban rapid transit systems operate over 22,000 trips per day and transport approximately 2.3 billion passengers a year over 1,070 miles of line, using about 11,650 rapid transit rail cars and trolley coaches. Each application has required development of specialized vehicle systems that differ significantly in their noise characteristics.

railroads

Noise in railroad systems is made up of the contributions from locomotives and the train vehicles that the locomotives haul.

Locomotives. Ninety-nine percent of the 27,000 locomotives in service in the United States in 1971 were diesel-electric, and the majority of the remainder were electric. Approximately one-half of the locomotives are used for main line hauling. The remainder are lower powered locomotives used for short-hauls and as switchers in railroad yards.

The sources of noise in a moving diesel-electric locomotive are, in approximate order of contribution to the overall noise level:

- Diesel exhaust muffler.
- Diesel engine and surrounding casing, including the air intake and turbo-charger (if any)
- Cooling fans.
- Wheel/rail interaction.
- Electrical generator.

An additional source of noise is the siren or horn, which produces noise levels 10 to 20 dBA greater than that from the other sources. This is not a continuously operated source (30 times per hour on a typical run), however, and is a necessary operational safety feature and is therefore excluded from the above list. The electrical locomotive draws electrical power from an overhead line and, except for noise generated during braking operations, is considerably quieter than its diesel-electric counterpart.

Train vehicles. Since freight and passenger cars have no propulsion system of their own, the exterior noise produced is due mainly to the interaction between the wheels and the rails. The magnitude of the noise depends heavily on the condition of the wheels and track, on whether or not the track is welded, and on the type of vehicle suspension. Modern passenger vehicles with auxiliary hydraulic suspension systems in addition to the normal springs can be about 10 dBA quieter than the older vehicles and most freight cars, which have only springs.

The interior noise of passenger vehicles is partly due to structurally-borne noise from the wheel/rail interaction and the passing of the wheels over rail joints. Another source is airborne noise passing through the car body and windows, which becomes more important when the train is passing through cuttings and tunnels. Welded track, present on only about 10 percent of the nation's railroad track mileage, materially reduces interior noise levels, but the amount of welded track is being increased at the rate of only 3000 miles per year (or less than 1 percent per year) as the older sectional type requires replacement. In addition to the track noise, interior passenger car noise levels are produced by the air conditioning system.

In suburban areas, many commuter trains consist of multiple-unit electric cars that operate from the lead car. Many of these systems utilize modern, high-speed equipment with low track noise levels. The interior noise level, then is dependent upon the air conditioning system.

One other major source of noise from railroads is braking operations in retarder yards, which produce a high-pitched sound at a level that can exceed 120 dBA at 50 feet.

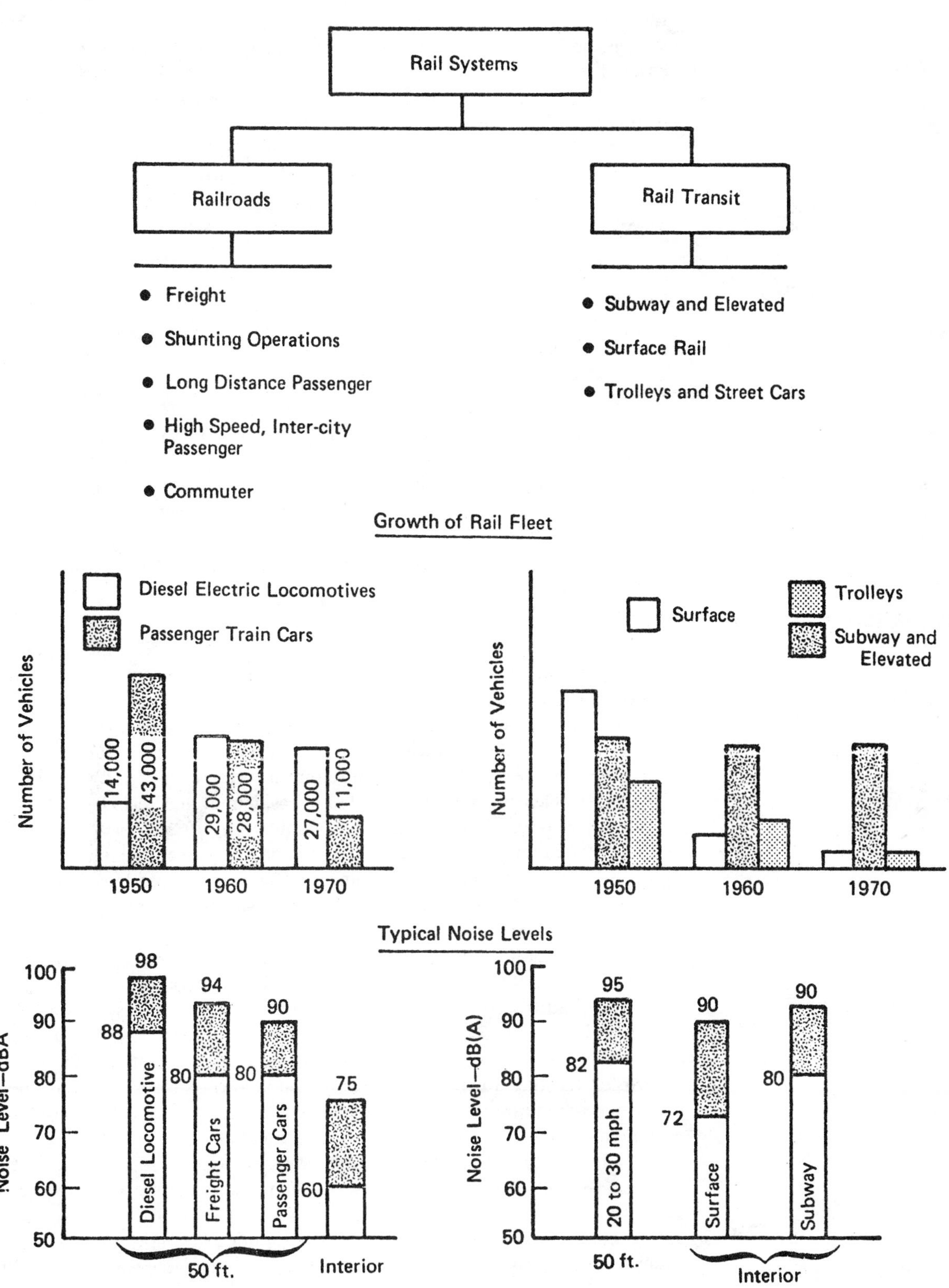

Characteristics of Rail Systems

rapid transit

All the rapid transit/rail systems use electric multiple-unit rail cars, designed with many exit doors for rapid handling of passengers, large windows for good visibility, and lightweight structure to reduce the overall load. The result is that these vehicles have lower noise insulation than railroad passenger cars. Suspension systems universally contain steel springs, additional cushioning being provided by either rubber pads or air cushioning systems.

There is presently a wide range in the age of the operational vehicles of this type. The newer vehicles have better suspension systems than the older types, and there is also a current requirement to use air conditioned vehicles that allow all windows to be permanently sealed. Both the new suspension systems and the sealed windows serve to provide substantially lower noise levels inside the new transit cars.

The main source of noise is the interaction between the wheels and rails. This is more serious in rapid transit systems than in rail systems because the tracks are subject to a much higher rate of wear. Other sources of noise are the propulsion system and the auxiliary equipment. Rapid transit system noise is complicated by other elements not totally connected with the vehicles, including the reverberant effect of tunnels on noise in subway systems, the increased vibration-induced noise from elevated systems, and the higher reflectivity of concrete roadbeds used for some rapid transit lines.

Street and trolley cars still operate in Boston, San Francisco, Philadelphia, and other cities. In some cases they operate in conjunction with subway systems. External noise levels vary for streetcars between the old and the new types of cars, the levels ranging from approximately 68 to 80 dBA at 50 feet under varying operating conditions.

recreational vehicles

Recreational vehicles, as defined here, include all types of motorcycles, snow-mobiles, all-terrain vehicles, and pleasure boats. There has been a remarkable growth in the number of these vehicles in the last 10 to 20 years, which is a reflection of the greater amount of leisure time and of the availability of these vehicles at attractive prices.

Over 90 percent of the 2.6 million motorcycles in the United States are used for pleasure and are operated in residential and recreational areas. This number is expected to increase to 9 million by 1985. Nearly 80 percent of the 1.6 million snow-mobiles in use today are operated primarily for pleasure by families in rural communities. Boating, enjoyed by an estimated 44 million persons in 1970, presents the most widely employed form of recreational travel.

The noise output of recreational vehicles, although dependent upon speed, is primarily a function of their mode of operation. For example, many off-road motorcycles and snowmobiles are capable of speeds of 80 to 100 mph but are most often operated at low speed in the lower gears, with medium to high engine power output. thus, except when cruising at constant speeds or coasting downhill, they are operated at high throttle settings near their maximum noise output. This high noise level is frequently considered synonymous with high power by the recreational user.

The major contributing source of noise from these vehicles is the exhaust system. This exhaust noise is often increased by operators who modify or remove their exhaust muffler in a misguided attempt to produce more engine power. Of secondary, but significant, importance in these vehicles is the noise radiated from their intakes and engine walls. Generally, intakes are not silenced and engines are either partially or totally unshielded. As a result of this lack of silencing, some of these vehicles create noise levels as high as 100 to 110 dBA at 50 feet. Pending state legislation to regulate the noise produced by off-road machines has caused manufacturers to reduce the maximum noise levels of vehicles in current production to 92 dBA.

The type of pleasure vehicle that currently reflects the most significant noise reduction technology in its basic engineering design is the outboard-powered pleasure boat. The power plants on most of these boats represents the most effectively silenced application of the widely used two-stroke internal combustion engine.

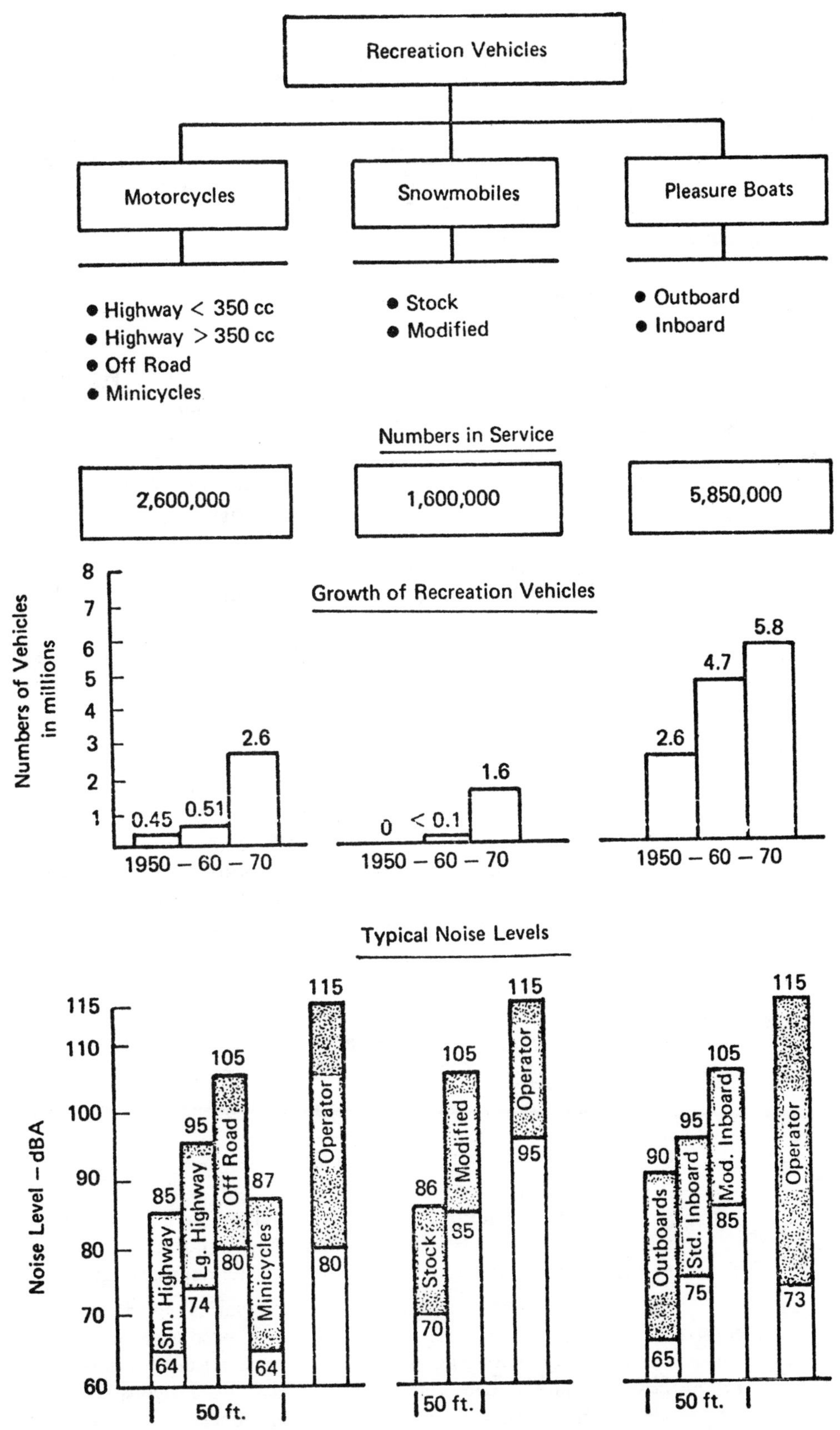

Characteristics of Recreation Vehicles

Motorcycles

The noise levels produced by many motorcycles increase rapidly with cruising speed. Typical noise levels at 50 feet range from 59 to 69 dBA at 20 mph to 78 to 86 dBA at 60 mph. Typical noise exposure levels at the operators ear range from 85 to 90 dBA for the quiet highway cycles to 110 dBA for the large off-the-road motorcycles and modified large highway motorcycles.

Snowmobiles

The noise levels produced by snowmobiles are largely dependent upon their age, because of a trend to improved designs. Current production models are generally in the range of 77 to 86 dBA, measured at 50 feet, under maximum noise conditions. The noise level of older or poorly muffled machines ranges from 90 to 95 dBA, with racing machines generating levels as high as 105 to 110 dBA at this same distance. The noise from new machines normally ranges from 95 to 115 dBA at the operator position but can be higher on racing machines.

Pleasure Boats

The maximum noise levels measured in a recent survey of a large number of pleasure boats (both inboard- and outboard-powered) ranged from 65 to 105 dBA at a distance of 50 feet. The lower limits of this range are created by small craft (with 6 to 10-horsepower engines). The highest levels, exceeding 105 dBA at 50 feet, were produced by inboard-powered ski boats with unmuffled exhausts.

Engine exhausts are the main source of noise for the boats exhibiting the highest noise levels. On the ski boats, which have large exposed engines, intake and engine mechanical noise also provide a significant contribution. The noise levels of smaller inboard engines are typically lower; but the exhaust, even though released under water, is still the major noise source. In the medium and smaller outboard engine sizes, the engine and intake, though acoustically shielded, produce almost as much noise as the exhaust.

The typical noise exposures for operators of outboard boats are also high. These exposures range from 84 dBA for 6-horsepower units to 98 to 105 dBA for 125-horsepower units measured at the driver position under accelerating conditions. At cruising speeds, operator levels on all boat types (inboard and outboard) range from 73 to 96 dBA.

Dune Buggies, All-Terrain Vehicles and Other Off-Road Vehicles

The major source of noise output in the remainder of those vehicles considered under the recreation classification is predominantly exhaust. Because of the unregulated nature of these vehicles and their use, the owners tend to attempt the achievement of maximum power output through the use of tuned and unmuffled exhaust systems.

construction

Construction Site Noise

There are four major site categories which have significant noise impacts. These are:

- Domestic housing—including residences for one to several families.
- Nonresidential buildings—including offices, public buildings, hotels, hospitals, schools.
- Industrial—including industrial buildings, religious and recreational centers, stores, service and repair facilities.
- Public works—including roads, streets, water mains, sewers.

The type of activity at any given site varies considerably as construction progresses. Further, since the noise produced on the site depends on the equipment being used, it exhibits a great deal of variability. For purposes of characterizing this noise, one may consider construction at a given site in terms of the following five consecutive phases:

1. Ground clearing—including demolition and removal of prior structures, trees, rocks.

2. Excavation.
3. Placing foundations—including reconditioning old roadbeds, compacting trench floors.
4. Erection—including framing, placing of walls, floors, windows, pipe installation.
5. Finishing—including filling, paving, cleanup.

Characterization of Site Noise

To totally describe construction site noise, the five described phases for each of four different types of sites must be considered. However, there is an additional complication. Since the intrusion produced by any noise depends on the residual noise,the residual noise levels that exist at a site location in the absence of any construction activity must be taken into account. For comparison purposes, it is enough to consider only the two cases of urban (relativity noisy) and suburban (relatively quiet) environments.

For purposes of these site noise characterizations, a model was developed in which the equipment producing the highest A-weighted noise levels was taken to be located 50 feet from an observer (at the boundary of the site), and all other equipment was considered as being located at 2000 feet from the observer. The noise contributions of the various equipment items were calculated for representative duty cycles. Although this construction site noise model may not be entirely realistic, it still may be expected to yield at least a relative measure of the noise annoyance potential of each type of site and construction phase.

The energy equivalent noise levels (L_{eq}) for each construction phase at each site are shown in Table 2-15. For each phase/construction type element, a range of levels is given; reflecting different mixes of construction equipment that might be used for the same kind of process. The range encompasses maximum (I) and minimum (II) concentrations of equipment.

TYPICAL RANGES OF ENERGY EQUIVALENT NOISE LEVELS, L_{eq} IN dBA, AT CONSTRUCTION SITES

Table 2-15

	Domestic Housing		Office Building, Hotel, Hospital, School, Public Works		Industrial Parking Garage, Religious Amusement & Recreations, Store, Service Station		Public Works Roads & Highways, Sewers, and Trenches	
	I	II	I	II	I	II	I	II
Ground Clearing	83	83	84	84	84	83	84	84
Excavation	88	75	89	79	89	71	88	78
Foundations	81	81	78	78	77	77	88	88
Erection	81	65	87	75	84	72	79	78
Finishing	88	72	89	75	89	74	84	84

I – All pertinent equipment present at site.

II – Minimum required equipment present at site.

The maximum levels range from 77 to 89dBA for all categories and have an average value of approximately 85 dBA. The minimum values for all categories have a wider range, extending from 65 to 88 dBA, and have an average value of 78 dBA. The table also shows that the initial ground clearing and excavation phases generally are the noisiest, that the intermediate foundation placement and erection phases are somewhat quieter, and that the final finishing phase tends to produce considerable noise annoyance.

Construction Equipment Noise

Although there is a great variety in the types and sizes of available construction equipment, similarities in the dominant noise sources and operational characteristics of commonly used equipment items permit noise characterization of all equipment in terms of only a few categories.

Equipment Powered by Internal Combustion Engines

Engine-powered equipment may be characterized according to its mobility and operating characteristics as:

- Earthmoving equipment, including excavating machinery (such as bulldozers, shovels, backhoes, front loaders) and highway building equipment (such as scrapers, graders, compactors).
- Materials handling equipment, such as cranes, derricks, concrete mixers, and concrete pumps.
- Stationary equipment, such as pumps, electric power generators, and air compressors.

Earthmoving equipment employs internal combustion engines (primarily of the diesel type) rated from about 50 hp to above 600 hp, both for propulsion and power for working mechanisms. Materials handling equipment, for which locomotion does not constitute a part of the major work cycle, employs internal combustion engines for powering working parts. In stationary equipment, of course, engines are used for the desired power generation.

In virtually all engine-powered equipment, the engine constitutes the primary noise source. Engine noise is produced at the intake and exhaust and equipment-cooling fans, with noise from mechanical or hydraulic power transmission or actuation systems generally of secondary importance. In earthmoving equipment, the tracks often contribute noticeable noise.

For all engine-powered equipment, the greatest noise reductions may be obtained by quieting the engines. Significant amounts of noise reduction may often be readily achieved by the use of better exhaust mufflers, intake silencers, and redesigned cooling fans. Use of acoustic enclosures for stationary equipment also appears to be readily implemented, and is a useful noise reduction approach (which has already been employed by some air compressor manufacturers). Practical, long term abatement on the order of 15 to 20 dBA can probably be achieved by basic engine design changes with greater noise reduction requiring a substitution of power source or elimination of the equipment all together.

Impact Equipment and Tools

Pile drivers and pneumatic tools accomplish their functions by causing a “hammer” to strike against a work piece. The resulting impact constitutes one of the major noise sources associated with such equipment, and because this impact is essential to operation of the equipment, its control generally cannot be accomplished practically.

In steam-driven pile drivers, noise is also produced by the boiler and by release of steam at the head; in diesel drivers, noise is also produced by the combustion explosion that actuates the hammer. Impact noise is absent in the so-called sonic pile drivers, which have no drop hammer since they use engine-driven eccentric weights to vibrate the driven pile at resonance. For such drivers, the engines are the primary noise sources. Unfortunately,

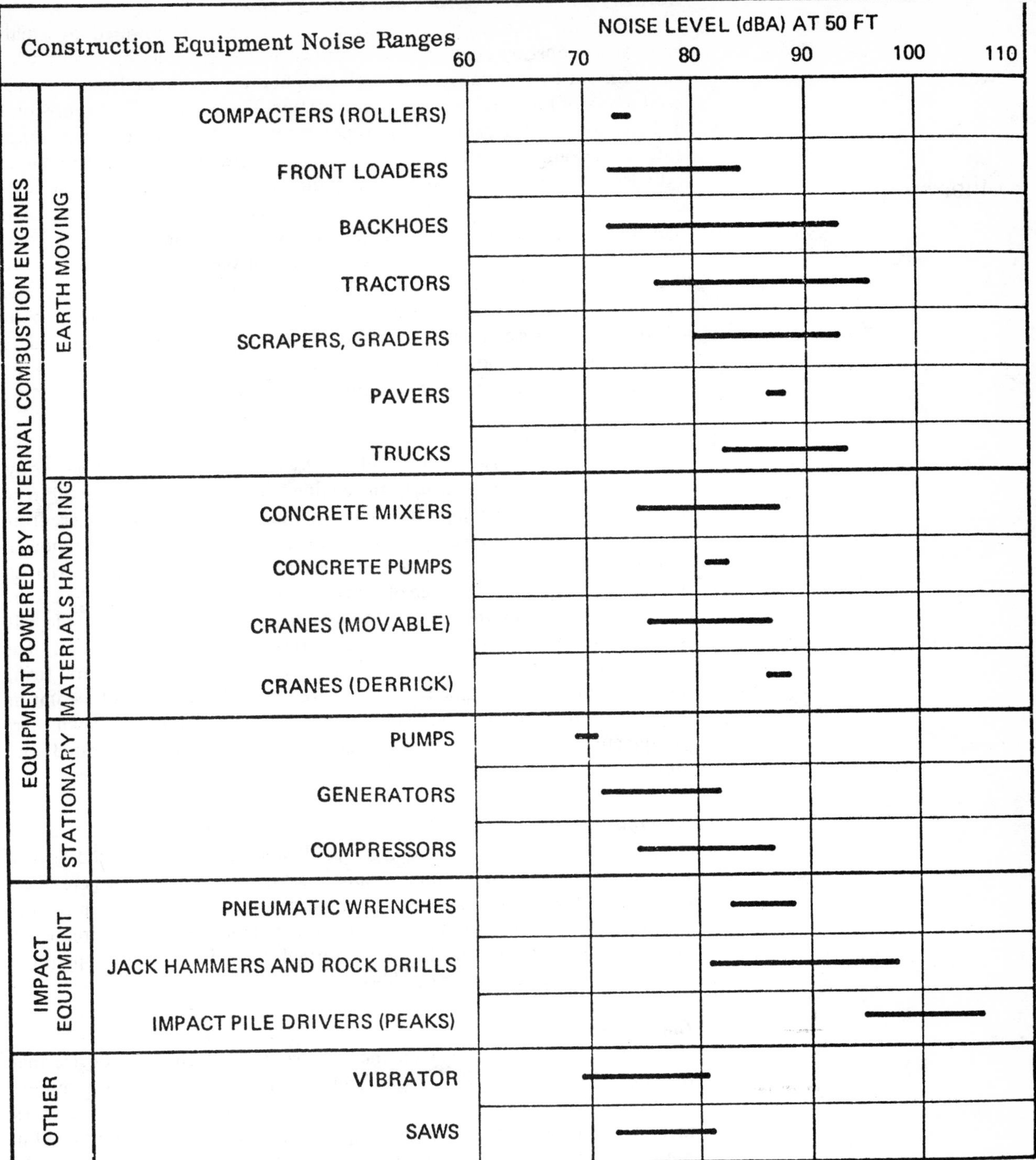

Note: Based on Limited Available Data Samples

the use of these pile drivers is not widespread, owing in part to codes for pile load- bearing assessment based on impact response.

Most impact tools, such as pavement breakers and rock drills, are pneumatically powered. The same is true of such hand-held tools as impact wrenches. In such tools, noise is produced primarily by the high pressure exhaust and by the working impact. This pneumatic exhaust noise does not occur in hydraulically or electrically powered tools.

The use of tools that do not involve impacts appears to be the best means for coping with impact noise. Where such replacement is not possible, use of enclosures may be required, although these tend to be cumbersome, costly, and of limited benefit. Exhaust noise from pneumatic tools (or from steam or diesel pile drivers) can be reduced effectively by mufflers, but the size and weight limitations on workman-handled tools limit the size and effectiveness of mufflers for such tools.

other motors

Devices Powered by Internal Combustion Engines

The noise emanating from lawn care equipment powered by small internal combustion engines is well known to the millions of people who maintain gardens or lawns and their neighbors. The total United States production of these engines was about 10.9 million units in 1969. This total includes all engines below 11 horsepower except those used for boating, automotive, and aircraft applications. Over 95 percent of these are single cylinder, air cooled engines. The vast majority are four cycle, while the two-cycle version of the same size dominates the remaining market. More than half of the single cylinder engines power the estimated 17 million lawnmowers in use today, while the majority of the remaining engines are used in other lawn and garden equipment such as leaf blowers, mulchers, tillers, edge trimmers, garden tractors, and snowblowers. In addition, about 750,000 chain saws and 100,000 engines for equipment such as small loaders and tractors, were produced in 1970, while agricultural and industrial usage together accounted for another 1.5 million engines.

Lawn Care Equipment

The characteristic noise produced by lawn care equipment has a low frequency peak corresponding to the engine firing frequency (about 50 to 60 cycles per second) and a high frequency maximum occurring anywhere from two to three octaves above the firing frequency. In the case of a lawnmower, much of the energy in the high frequency noise peak is from the exhaust, which has only a minor degree of muffling. Additional high noise levels are radiated by the rotating blade. Equipment without a rotating blade will generally have other machinery noise of the same approximate level. The modulation of the high frequency engine noise by the engine firing frequency makes the engine noise more audible than the noise of a rotating blade or other machinery. Thus, even heavy muffling on lawn care equipment cannot totally eliminate the characteristic noise associated with this modulation.

Generators

Of the 100,000 generators sets sold each year in the United States, most are used in mobile homes, campers, and large boats, where their electrical power output is used for air conditioning, lighting, and other equipment. Their noise output is generally dominated by high frequency exhaust noise, which can be well muffled to achieve quiet operation acceptable to users and their neighbors.

Chain Saws

The typical chain saw engine is a two-cycle, high-speed device that operates with a firing frequency of about 150 times per second. A minimum muffler is usually a part of the configuration and is equipped with a spark arrestor to prevent fire. The high firing frequency and light muffler result in noise levels as high as 115 dBA at the operator position, with levels of 83 dBA common at a 50-foot distance.

industrial noise

A study of industrial plants as sources of community noise must begin with the individual noise sources within the plant. Industrial plant noise sources can be generally classified into five major categories.

- *Impact:* punch presses, stamping hammers
- *Mechanical:* machinery imbalance, gears, bearings
- *Fluid Flow:* fans, blowers, compressors, valves
- *Combustion:* furnaces, flare sticks
- *Electromechanical:* motors, generators, transformers

Typical noise levels from these sources are given in the accompanying chart.

RANGE OF INDUSTRIAL MACHINERY, EQUIPMENT, AND PROCESS NOISE LEVELS*

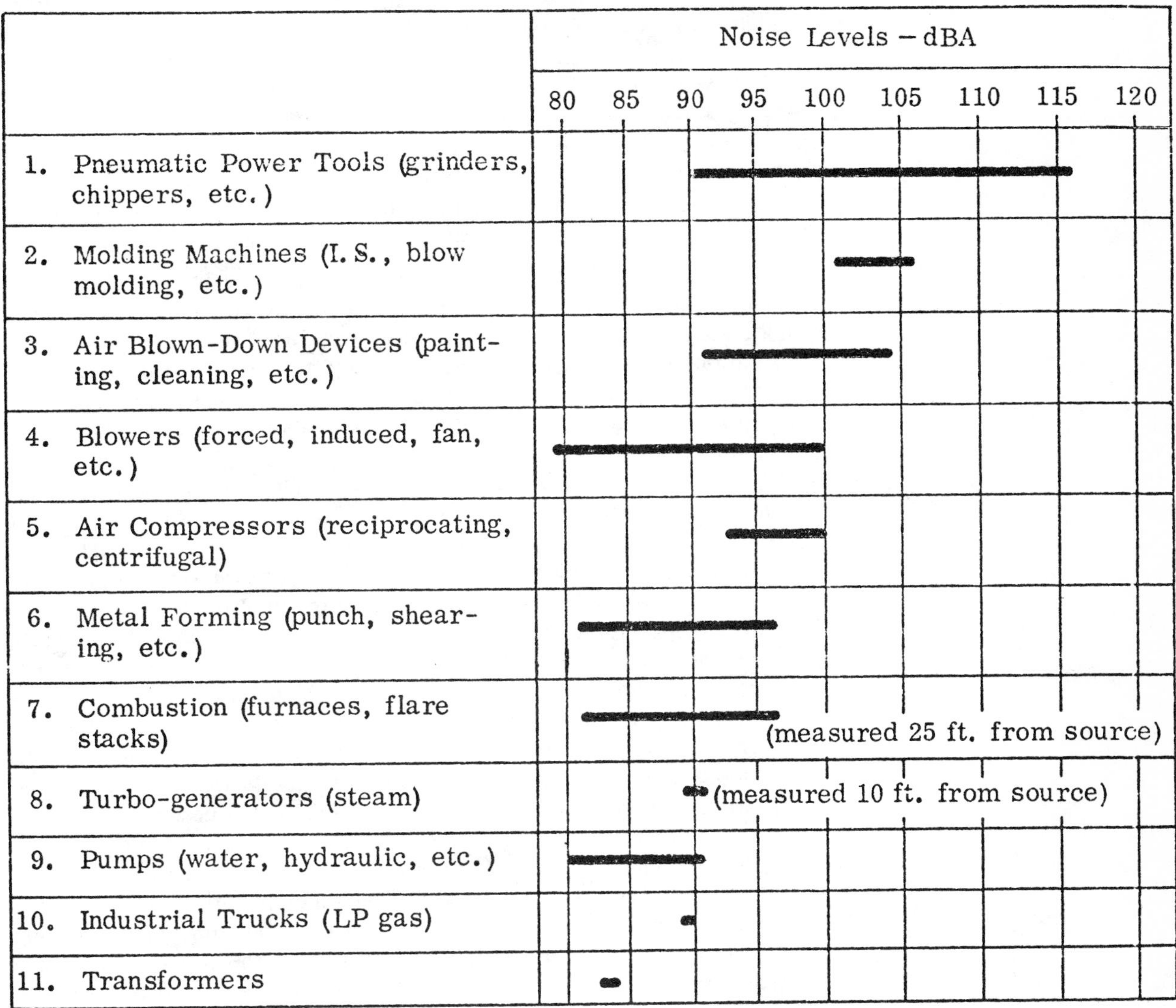

*Measured at operator positions, except for 7 and 8.

Persons exposed to industrial noise can be separated into those who work within the plant and those who inhabit the surrounding community. Noise levels within the plant in most heavy industries are relatively high—so high in fact, that finally there are Federal statutes and regulations to augment the existing state and (infrequently) local laws to limit the exposure of such workers although the standards established have been criticized as being too high to provide any meaningful protection.

The surrounding community may still feel the noise impact from the plant. Although building insulation and intervening property reduces the noise levels, annoying noise may well penetrate the surrounding community. Most often the impact is greatest with heavy industry operating on a 24-hour-day, 7-day-week basis, thus interfering with sleep and weekend leisure-time activities.

The adverse impact of industrial noise is not easily measurable in terms of adverse community response (a technique sometimes used to evaluate the effects of aircraft noise). Several factors combine to account for this:

1. Many times the potential complaintant is also an employee of the

noisy industry, thereby creating a feeling of necessity for the noise, or at least fear of losing employment if a complaint is lodged.

2. Often people believe it is futile to complain.

3. People may not object to fairly high noise levels, choosing rather to adopt their own life styles, when the noise;

- is continuous
- does not interfere with speech communication
- is devoid of pure tones
- is relatively steady in intensity and frequency
- does not interfere with sleep
- and does not instill fear for life and limb due to its character or the character of the operation producing the noise.

A final factor which must be considered when discussing industrial noise is that industrial activity is most often intimately connected with other noise sources which constitute a necessary component of the industrial operation. Primary among these is transportation noise associated with bringing raw materials to the plant and distributing finished products from the plant. This adds to the overall community impact of the industrial operation.

Industrial noise is one type of noise which can be eliminated, in the community impact sense. What is required is proper land use control so that residential communities are not permitted to border on industrial areas. [See also Volume Two] Siting of industries near airports, railroad yards and truck depots, while decidely beneficial from the industry point of view for ready transportation access, can fulfill the dual pusrpose of buffering residential areas from aircraft noise and locating industry in an environment where surrounding areas already are subject to high noise levels.

While this will free other land for residential uses, it must be remembered that this technique involves an environmental tradeoff; with industry and airport now sited away from all residential areas, use of the airport and provision of employees at the plants will necessitate a major transportation network with attendant traffic congestion and air pollution. Further, the concentration of many industries in one area under present [inadequate] laws will create a substantial water pollution problem if the plants require substantial amounts of water for processing. By introducing many effluents at one point in a river or lake, the natural assimilative capacity of the waters may be overwhelmed, creating extended impacts in other regions of the body of water. Therefore great care is needed in making such decisions in regard to land use.

household and building

Home Appliances In general, motors, fans, knives (or other cutting blades), and air flow are the most frequent sources of noise from home appliances. Noise radiated from the casing or panels of the appliances and noise radiated from walls, floors, cabinets, sinks (set into vibration by solid structural connections) are also of major importance. Some of the more annoying noise sources are:

Room Air Conditioners The major sources of noise are the motor, the blower (evaporator fan), the propeller fan (condenser fan), the compressor, and the air flow across the evaporator coils. In addition, panels of the housing radiate noise, as does the structure to which the air conditioning unit is mounted.

Food Waste Disposers The primary noise sources include the motor, the grind wheel, the sloshing of water and waste against the housing of the chamber, and resonances in the sink.

Dishwashers Noise generating sources in a dishwasher , in addition to the impingement of water against the sides and top of the tub, are the motor, the pump, the excitation of panel casings, the structural connections to water supply, water drain and cabinet, and the blower.

Vacuum Cleaners The primary noise sources in vacuum cleaners are the motor, blower, resonances of the unit structure, and, in upright vacuum cleaners, a mechanism (either vibrating agitators or rolling brushes) that beats the carpet to bring dirt to the surface.

Toilets The important parameters in toilet noise are the type (tank vs valve) and the mounting (floor vs wall). In each type of toilet, noise is attributed to valves and water flow.

Heating, cooling and building services equipment

The majority of electrical and mechanical equipment in buildings is used to supply the building occupants with a suitable quantity of air at a comfortable temperature and moisture content. In addition, fluid pumping and piping systems and elevators, escalators and other conveyances are used for moving people and materials. Much of this equipment is hidden in mechanical equipment rooms, above ceilings, in walls, or behind cabinet-type exterior enclosures.

Overall assessment of impact

The impact of noise has been discussed for each of the major non-occupational noise source categories. These impact assessments have been developed from various points of view, which are pertinent to the noise and use characteristics of each source category. Together with the presentation of the detailed noise characteristics of the sources and the community, they provide the basic data for an assessment of the total environmental impact of noise. This assessment is made relative to interference with speech, community reaction, and noise that may produce potential hearing damage. The impact assessments are based upon criteria specified elsewhere in this report and the data presented earlier in this chapter.

It should be kept in mind that the noise environment is primarily a product of man and his machines and consists of an all-pervasive and nonspecific residual noise, to which is added both constant and intermittent intrusive noises. The residual noise level in urban residential communities is generally the integrated result of the noise from traffic on streets and highways but does vary widely with the type of community.

Interference with Speech

Residual noise levels in suburban and rural areas do not appear to interfere with speech communication at distances compatible with normal use of patios and backyards. However, some interference with outdoor speech is found in urban residential communities, and considerable continuous interference is found in the very noisy urban and downtown city areas. Thus, the use of outdoor spaces for relaxed conversation is effectively denied to an estimated 5 to 10 million people who reside in very noise urban areas.

The backyards, patios, and balconies facing an urban freeway are similarly rendered useless on a continuous basis, except when traffic is light in the early morning hours. Although windows are kept closed in many dwelling units adjacent to freeways to keep out the noise, the noise level inside the dwelling may still be too high for relaxed conversation. An estimated 2.5 to 5 million people living near freeways are significantly affected by such intrusive noise. Probably, another 7 to 14 million people are affected to a lesser degree by the noise from traffic on the 96,000 miles of major arterial roads in urban communities.

Construction in urban areas is characterized by a relatively high continuous intrusive noise level, plus intermittent higher level noise events. It is estimated that, during daylight and early evening hours, the ability of 21 million people to enjoy outdoor conversation is severly impaired, particularly during the higher level noise events. In many of these cases, the ability to converse indoors is also impaired. The tolerance of people to construction noise appears to be higher than to other intruding noises because of the expectation that the construction activity will soon cease. However, in many larger cities where there appears to be almost continuous construction activity near apartment dwellings, intolerance of construction noise may be expected to be similar to that of other forms of noise intrusion.

Table 2-21 APPROXIMATE NUMBER OF OPERATORS OR PASSENGERS IN NON-OCCUPATIONAL SITUATIONS EXPOSED TO POTENTIALLY* HAZARDOUS NOISE FROM VARIOUS SIGNIFICANT SOURCES

Source	Noise Level in dBA		Approximate Number of People Exposed (In Millions)***
	Average**	Maximum	
Snowmobiles	108	112	1.60
Chain Saws	100	110	2.50
Motorcycles	95	110	3.00
Motorboats (over 45 HP)	95	105	8.80
Light Utility Helicopters	94	100	0.05
General Aviation Aircraft	90	103	0.30
Commercial Propeller Aircraft	88	100	5.00
Internal Combustion Lawnmowers and other Noisy Lawn Care Equipment	87	95	23.00
Trucks (Personal Use)	85	100	5.00
Home Shop Tools	85	98	13.00
Highway Buses	82	90	2.00
Subways	80	93	2.15

*Although average use of any one of these devices by itself may not produce permanent hearing impairment, exposure to this noise in combination, or together with occupational noise will increase the risk of incurring permanent hearing impairment.

**Average refers to the average noise level for devices of various manufacture and model type.

***Single-event exposures. Many individuals may receive multiple exposures. For example an individual may be exposed during the week to noise from any or all of the above sources.

Thus, the combination of continuous daytime noise caused by traffic on city streets, major arterial streets, and freeways impairs the utility of the patios, porches, and yards of approximately 7 to 15 percent of the total population, while at any one time the noise from construction similarly affects another 10 percent.

The noise from many home appliances and other equipment makes it difficult for the operator and others in the home environment to converse or hear a child's cry. The noisier items in this category include lawnmowers, homeshop tools, food disposers and blenders, sewing machines, electric shavers, and vacuum cleaners, and it is estimated that at least 66 million people operate one or more of these devices. Together with an estimated 115 million dwelling occupants, they experience a severe reduction in speech intelligibility whenever such devices are used.

There is a long history of occupational noise causing various degrees of hearing impairment in some of the working population. The legal structure for the protection of workers now exists through the provisions of the Occupational Health and Safety Act, and also the Coal Mine Safety and Health Act.

However, there are also many occasions when people may be exposed to potentially hazardous noise in non-occupational environments. The more significant of these potential hazardous noise exposures are summarized in Table 2-21. These data include only those people directly affected by the noise sources, that is, operators and passengers rather than bystanders. Although those who are only occasionally exposed to such noises will not necessarily suffer permanent hearing impairment, frequent exposure to the noise from any one or several of such sources, or occasional exposure in combination with industrial noise, will increase the risk of incurring such damage. In addition, the proliferation and use of such noise sources further increase the risk of hearing impairment for a substantial percentage of the general population.

summation

This data shows that approximately 22 to 44 million people have lost part of the utility of their dwellings and yards to noise from traffic and aircraft on a continuous basis, and another 21 million at any one time are similarly affected by noise from construction activity. Further, many people are exposed to potentially hazardous noise when operating noisy devices. Although the number exposed to potentially hazardous noise cannot be accurately assessed (since the people referred to in Table 2-21 are not additive), a total of 40 million people might be reasonable.

Thus, not including the contribution of appliances, noise appears to affect at least 80 million people, or 40 percent of the population. Roughly one-half of the total impact of noise represents a potential health hazard (in terms of hearing impairment potential alone), and the remaining half represents an infringement on the ability to converse in the home. Such impact estimates clearly show the need to reduce the number of devices that emit potentially hazardous noise levels and to reduce the outdoor noises that interfere with the quality of life.

risk of hearing damage

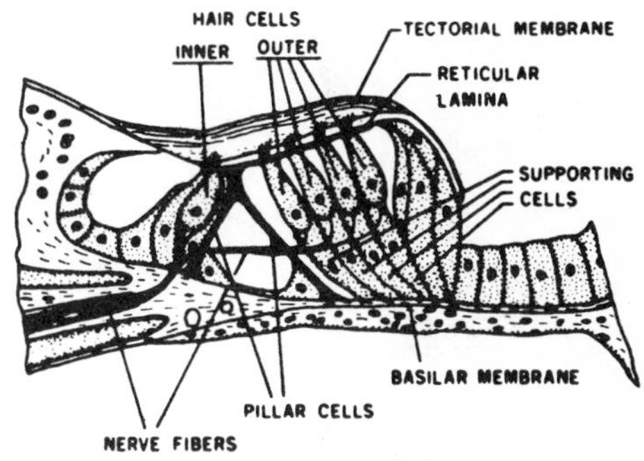

(A) NORMAL ORGAN OF CORTI

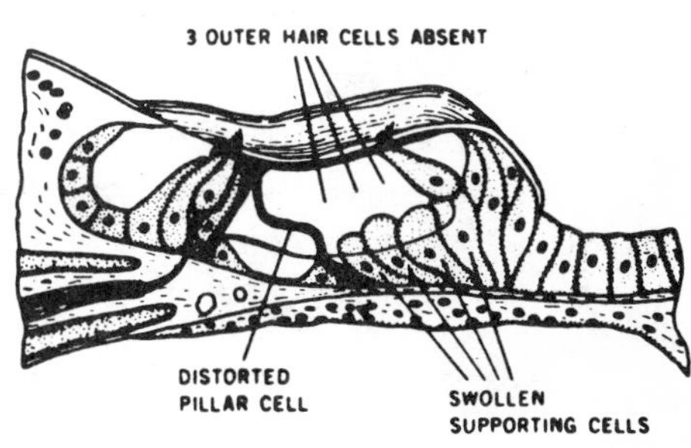

(B) PARTIAL INJURY

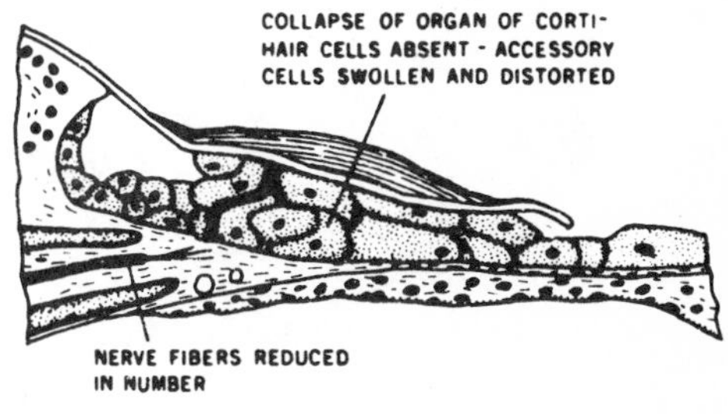

(C) SEVERE INJURY

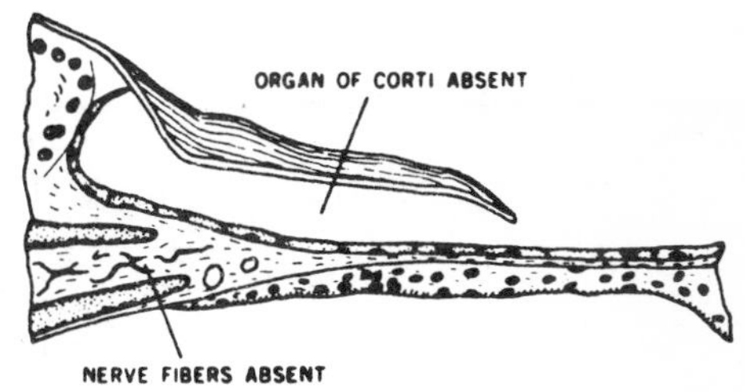

(D) TOTAL DEGENERATION

Four views of the inner ear

Statutory noise abatement techniques

Legislative interest and action in the area of environmental noise abatement and control is increasing as the magnitude of the general problem becomes more obvious. Despite this increased awareness, regulatory schemes on all levels of government are not fully successful. Generally, the problem can be attributed to two factors, acting separately or in combination:

1. Poorly written laws that do not provide the needed authority or incentive to alleviate the problem and that are technically deficient regarding acoustics and noise measurements.

2. Poor enforcement of existing laws due to lack of available personnel and to the lack of knowledge on the part of enforcement officers as to sound measurement equipment and techniques.

The following discussion provides an overview of the entire legal structure regarding noise abatement and control.

Federal level

General Policy. The Noise Pollution and Abatement Act of 1970 was the first legislation to provide a central focus for overall environmental noise abatement at the Federal level. This Act required that an Office of Noise Abatement and Control be established in the Environmental Protection Agency (EPA) to carry on research and investigations into environmental noise. The act further directed, in Section 402(c) that, following a determination by the Administrator of EPA that noise related to a Federal agency's activity or its sponsored activities is a public nuisance or is otherwise objectionable, the Federal department or agency sponsoring such activity must consult with the Administrator of EPA to determine possible ways of abating such noise. Previous Federal legislation had been directed to noise abatement with respect to specific noise sources (such as aircraft noise) or in regard to special environmental situations (such as occupational exposure or transportation planning).

Further, the National Environmental Policy Act of 1969 has required, since 1 January 1970, that Federal agencies use an interdisciplinary approach to integrate the "environmental design arts" into the decision making process (Section 102(2) (C) on all "Federal actions" significantly affecting the human environment. Such statements should, therefore, include consideration of environmental noise. Sections 102(2) (A&B) are intended to bring about the synthesis of an environmental awareness within Federal agency decision making processes.

With respect to construction contracts for Federal buildings, the Occupational Safety and Health Act (OSHA) noise standards have been applied by the Department of Labor pursuant to the Construction Safety Act of 1969. However, there may be a question as to whether OSHA standards can be applied to construction noise in view of fundamental differences in physical environment between an open, multistory construction site and a closed factory work place. In a closed factory environment, one can assume that the factory owner has control of the entire noise exposure of his workers. However, on an open construction site, the contractor cannot control many of the noises that affect his workers. Thus, the engineering controls open to him are limited, if not nonexistent. There is no reason that hearing protection devices could not be used, however, to reduce the noise impact to meet the exposure standards. A pilot project is underway, via a GSA contract, to develop baseline data to these and other questions concerning the applicability of the regulations.

As pointed out earlier in this discussion, the military and internal Federal noise control operations provide an excellent overview of the noise problems encountered by the Federal government, as well as other governmental levels. These external Federal control measures will not be considered in terms of the general category of the particular noise source.

Transportation Noise Abatement and Control

Federal efforts to bring about transportation noise abatement are directed at aircraft and highway noise, with the former receiving the greater attention. But concern and action in the highway noise area are also significant and increasing.

Aircraft Noise. The Department of Transportation (DOT) Act of 1966 was the first statutory authority relevant to aircraft noise. Section 4(a) of the Act directed the Secretary of Transportation to "promote and undertake research and development relating to transportation, including noise abatement, with particular attention to aircraft noise." Although some efforts were undertaken by the Federal Aviation Administration (FAA) as early as 1960, it was not until the 1968 enactment of Section 611 (PL 90-411), relating to Control of Aircraft Noise and Sonic Boom, as an amendment to the Federal Aviation Act of 1958, that the Federal government undertook an active program of civil aircraft noise abatement. Considerable impetus to the enactment of this legislation resulted from the Office of Science and Technology study on jet aircraft noise near airports, completed in 1966. Implementation of this effort to abate noise at the source began 1 December 1969, with regulations made applicable to new subsonic aircraft. Regulations with respect to retrofit, sonic boom, SST type certification, and STOL/VTOL type certification are still in the development stages.

In the Airport and Airways Development Act of 1970, the FAA has a valuable tool that could be used to abate noise with respect to airports, since the Act declares the "national policy that airport development projects authorized pursuant to this part shall provide for the protection and enhancement of the natural resources and the quality of environment of the Nation." The airport certification provisions of Section 51(b) (1) direct the Administrator of the FAA to set minimum operational safety standards for airports served by Civil Aeronautics Board (CAB)-certified air carriers, but do not apply to the regulation of airport noise levels. The Act is applicable to all projects involving new airports and runways or extension of existing runways; thus, relatively few airport developments that might create additional noise escape consideration. State and local governments gain two leverage mechanisms with respect to such projects: first, the community acceptance provision of the Act requires that the project be accepted by communities around the airport before DOT may give its approval; second, under the state air and water quality certification section, the governor of the state in which the airport is located must certify that there is "reasonable assurance that the project . . . will comply with applicable air and water quality standards" before Federal approval. Since some states have included noise as an air contaminant, the noise standards of these states will figure in the development of airports via this provision of the Act. Unfortunately, the more sophisticated state noise laws are not generally under such an air quality framework, but, rather, are given separate consideration. Thus, these states do not have the input potential provided under the Act.

Highway Noise. Beginning in 1965, the Secretary of Commerce (duties transferred to the Secretary of Transportation since 1966) was required to "cooperate with the States . . . in the development of long range highway plans . . . which are formulated with due consideration to their probable effect on the future development of urban areas of more than fifty thousand population." The first active consideration of highway noise at the Federal level was Policy and Procedures Memorandum 20-8 of the Bureau of Public Roads, issued January 14, 1969. Environmental effects, which must be considered by the state or local sponsor seeking Federal aid, are defined to include "noise, air, and water pollution." Pursuant to a 1970 amendment to the Federal-aid Highway Act (PL 91-605), the Secretary of Transportation is directed "to assure that possible adverse economic, social, and environmental effects have been considered in developing . . . [all Federally aided highway] projects . . ." Further, he is to "develop and promulgate standards for highway noise levels compatible with different land uses after July 1, 1972."

Occupational Noise Abatement and Control

Following the lead provided under Federal supply and construction contracts, discussed earlier, by the Department of Labor regulations under the Walsh-Healey Public Contracts Act and the Construction Safety Act, the Secretary of Labor carried over these regulations under OSHA. The standards under all three acts are the same. While the Walsh-Healey regulations carry only a potential penalty of removal of the contractor from the eligible bidder list for 3 years, the Occupational Safety and Health Act provides for both civil and criminal penalties.

An interesting feature of the new Act is that a state may take over regulation of a particular matter through a program of application and acceptance by the Secretary of Labor. This may provide a technique deserving broader application to the noise abatement area, to avoid potential preemption problems.

The Atomic Energy Commission (AEC), in AEC Manual 0550-01 OS, 25 February 1970, and the Department of Interior, pursuant to the Coal Mine Health and Safety Act of 1969, have also adopted the OSHA standards for occupational noise programs. The AEC program is intended, ". . . for the protection of AEC and AEC contractor employees, the general public, and the environment. . . ." The Department of Interior, through the Bureau of Mines, applies the standards to some 1,900 licensed underground coal mines.

Construction Noise Abatement and Control

Construction Site Noise. The only Federal activity directed toward noise abatement at construction sites has been considered under the discussion of the Federal military and in-house government activities. Construction site noises are covered by the Occupational Safety and Health Act as being a business affecting interstate commerce, and the standards adopted for noise exposure by the Department of Labor under that Act apply to construction sites. Construction activities are enforced in the Occupational Safety and Health Administration.

Acoustical Characteristics of Buildings. Regarding acoustical characteristics of buildings, the Department of Housing and Urban Development (HUD) has issued Policy Circular 1390.2, 4 August 1971, concerning acoustical acceptability of new sites and existing buildings to be aided by HUD monies. This circular applies noise standards to programs where none existed previously and replaces the standards of the Federal Housing Administration (FHA), which is under HUD, to the extent that programs, ". . . have less demanding noise exposure requirements." The existing noise abatement programs of FHA now must be reviewed concerning their continued applicability. These programs relate to:

1. Mortgage underwriting in noisy areas near airports (FHA Manual, Vol. VII, Book 1, §71453 — new development not be considered for mortgage underwriting, if site within NEF-40 contour, pro and con evaluation for NEF-35, site approved without further consideration for NEF-30 or less.

2. Minimum property standards for multifamily dwellings for which FHA financial assistance is sought (FHA #2600, reissued February 1971, setting sound transmission standards and impact noise standards for partitions and floors/ceilings for developments of multifamily residences supported by FHA money).

Other Noise Sources Controlled at the Federal Level

The Federal Power Commission, acting under the authority of the Natural Gas Act of 1938 (15 U.S.C. §717), has directed in 18 C.F.R. §2.69, 1971 (first appearing on 16 July 1970 in 35 Fed. Reg. 11389) that compressors, when used above ground in connection with gas pipelines, must be located and treated so as to reduce the noise impact on the environment.

SUMMARY OF FEDERAL LAWS

Atomic Energy Commission (AEC)

Occupational and Aircraft Noise

AEC Manual 0550-01 (February 25, 1970) (adopts Walsh-Healey Occupational Noise standards and Federal Aviation Administration Part 36 standards)

Air Force

Occupational Noise

AFR 160-3 (29 October 1956) as amended,
AFR 160-3A (27 June 1960), and
AFR 160-3B (7 February 1967)

Aircraft Noise

AFM 86-5, TM 5-365, NAVDOCKS P-98 (10 October 1964)
A.F. Reg. 55-34 (5 February 1971)
MIL-N-93155A (USAF) (25 March 1970, amended 2 September 1970)
MIL-S-008806B (USAF)

Army

Aircraft Noise

TM 5-365, AFM 86-5, NAVDOCKS P-98 (10 October 1964)

Construction Noise (both acoustical characteristics of buildings and construction site noise)
Corps. of Engineers, U.S. Army, EM 385-1-1, *Safety: General Requirements,* §32, "Noise Control" at 27 (1 November 1967)

Corps. of Engineers, CE-1300 (May 1970) ETL 1110-3-141 (30 November 1970)

Department of Defense

General

MIL-STD-1472A (acts concurrently with other military regulations)

Department of Interior

Occupational Noise

30 U.S.C. §846 (Supp. V, 1970)
28 C.F.R. §70-504.1, now appearing at 36 Fed. Reg. 12740 (July 7, 1971)

Department of Labor

Occupational Noise

41 U.S.C. §35(e) (1964)
41 C.F.R. §50-204.1 and .10 (1971)
29 U.S.C.A. §651, *et seq.* (1971)
29 C.F.R. §1910.1 and .95 (May 29, 1971)

Construction Noise

40 U.S.C.A. §333 (1971)
29 C.F.R. §1518.52, now appearing at 36 Fed. Reg. 7348 (April 17, 1971)

Department of Transportation

General Transportation Noise

49 U.S.C. §1653(a) (Supp. IV, 1969)
DOT Order 1100.37, 2 September 1969
DOT Order 1100.23 Chg. 2, 8 May 1968

Aircraft

49 U.S.C. §1653(a) (Supp. IV, 1969)
see generally Federal Aviation Administration

Highway-Related Noise

23 U.S.C. §101, *et seq.* (1964), particularly the Federal-Aid Highway Act of 1970, §136, amending 23 U.S.C. §109 (g), 84 Stat. 1713

Environmental Protection Agency
General
Title IV of the Clean Air Amendments of 1970, Pub. L. No. 91-604

Federal Aviation Administration
Aircraft
Generally provisions of 49 U.S.C. §1301, *et seq.* (1964) but particularly 49 U.S.C. §1431 (Supp. IV, 1969)
14 C.F.R. §36 and 21 (1971)
49 U.S.C.A. §1701, *et seq.* (Supp. 1971)

Federal Highway Administration
Highway-Related Noise
23 U.S.C.A. §101.109 (Supp. 1971)
Bureau of Public Roads, PPM 20-8 "Public Hearing and Location Approval" (January 14, 1969)

Federal Housing Administration
Construction (Acoustical Characteristics of Buildings)
FHA Manual, Vol. VII, Book 1, Underwriting-Home Mortgages, §71453
FHA #2600, Minimum Property Standards for Multifamily Housing, §M405 (February 1971)
(See HUD)

Federal Power Commission
Industrial (Internal Combustion Engine)
15 U.S.C. §717, *et seq.* (1964)
18 C.F.R. §*2.69 (1971)*

General Services Administration
Construction Noise (Acoustical Characteristics of Buildings and Site Noise)
GSA Handbook: PBS P 3410.5 Chg. 1 (September 2, 1969) and PBS P 3460.1C

Public Building Service:Guide Specifications, PBS 4-0950 (May 1968)
PBS 4-1031 (February 1968), and
PBS 4-515-71 (April 1970)

Also see trial clause in government construction contract at Contract GSA-Washington, D.C. 71-8378, "United States Courthouse and Federal Office Building, Philadelphia, Pennsylvania," Cl. 35.6 at 2-14

Department of Health, Education, and Welfare
Occupational Noise
Review authority under the Coal Mines Health and Safety Act of 30 U.S.C.A. §846 (Supp. V, 1970)

Department of Housing and Urban Development
Construction Noise (Acoustical Characteristics of Buildings)
HUD Policy Circular 1390.2 (July 16, 1971)

Navy
Occupational Noise
BUMEDINST 6260.6B (5 March 1970) BuMedNote 6260.732 (28 April, 1971)
NAVAIRINST 6260.1 (24 February 1971)
OPNAVINST 5100.14 (11 August 1970)
Aircraft Noise
NAVDOCKS P-98, AFM 86-5, TM 5-365 (10 October 1964)

State level

Many states are entering the noise control field in earnest, as demonstrated by the large number of recently enacted state laws in this area (nine during the first half of 1971 alone). It is increasingly common for states to establish environmental departments to deal with noise and other pollutants, and the number of noise sources being regulated by any single state is growing. The states are also becoming more sophisticated in the writing of noise laws and are beginning to substitute specific decibel limits for subjective standards such as "unnecessary" and "unreasonable," although such standards have by no means disappeared. A growing number of states are also setting standards for noise from new vehicles and equipment, forbidding the sale of any that fail to conform to the standards.

Five states (Florida, Hawaii, Illinois, New York, and North Dakota) have delegated, to departments dealing with environmental affairs, the power to set standards for the limitation of noise from many sources. All of these states are currently preparing for or conducting hearings on standards, many of which will probably be promulgated in late 1971 or during 1972. California and Illinois have declared their policy to be to reduce noise, and both require environmental reports from state agencies. Illinois has declared it unlawful to create unreasonable and unnecessary noise on one's property, while Colorado has established decibel limits on noise permitted to emanate from any premises.

Following development and adoption of standards in late 1971 and early 1972, the state programs to combat noise will enter a new phase. The success of these programs will be determined by the ability of the states to enforce their new laws.

Transportation

California has developed a complex regulatory scheme for controlling airport noise. The law requires airport operators to monitor takeoff and landing noise and to establish a noise impact boundary around the airport, with noise at this boundary to be reduced over the next 15 years. Also, the airport operator must set noise limits on single takeoffs and landings and must report violations to county enforcement officials. Those airports failing to come within the noise limits may lose their licenses or face other state sanctions. The legal basis for the law is the state's licensing power over airports and the asserted proprietary rights of airports vis-a-vis the scheduled airlines and other users. Discussions of the legality of this law and the problem of Federal preemption are presented elsewhere in this chapter.

The states have long provided statutory restrictions on noise from motor vehicles, with 43 states requiring mufflers on vehicles and 15 restricting noise from horns. Five states set limits on the total vehicle noise, based on subjective standards. Connecticut has recently empowered its Commissioner of Motor Vehicles to set noise limits not to exceed 90 dBA, and New York and Idaho set decibel limits on the operation of vehicles. California sets standards on noise from the operation of vehicles as well as noise limits on new vehicles. Colorado and Minnesota have recently enacted legislation patterned closely after the California law. Of these laws, the Idaho law specifies a limit of 92 dBA measured at 20 feet, while the others provide limits in the range of 88 to 92 dBA measured at 50 feet. California, Colorado, and Minnesota have provisions for lower limits to take effect in several years.

Five states specifically require mufflers on motorcycles, while California, Colorado, and Minnesota set overall noise limits on these vehicles. As with automobiles and trucks, the standards will become stricter over time.

Five states require mufflers on boats. Wisconsin delegates to its communities the power to regulate motorboars.

Snowmobiles have been given increased attention by the states. Maine and Wisconsin require mufflers, while Colorado, Massachusetts, Montana, and New York set limits on new snowmobiles. Colorado and Massachusetts also regulate noise from the operation of snowmobiles.

Occupational Noise

Twenty five states have reported existing occupational noise standards of some kind. These reports were made to the Secretary of Labor pursuant to the Occupational Safety & Health Act of 1970 and its program for state substitution for the Federal regulatory framework under the Act. California, as an example of these state frameworks, has adopted the same standard as that promulgated by the Secretary of Labor under the Walsh-Healey Public Contracts Act. Responses have yet to be received by the Secretary from 12 states (nine of which plan to exercise their takeover option and three of which have decided not to enter into temporary agreements with the Department of Labor to continue enforcement on the state level during the takeover period.

Construction Site Noise

Colorado alone sets decibel limits on noise from construction sites, namely 80 dBA measured at 25 feet from the source from 7:00 a.m. to 7:00 p.m. and 75 dBA measured at 25 feet between 7:00 p.m. and 7:00 a.m.

Acoustical Treatment of Buildings

The small amount of state regulation in the construction field is directed primarily toward shielding individuals from noise rather than toward restricting noise at its source. The New York State building code sets standards for sound retardation in new apartment buildings. Hawaii requires school officials to acoustically treat schools so as to insulate students from the effects of transportation noise. California forbids new freeways that increase the noise in existing schools, although state officials may acoustically treat the schools so as to prevent an increase in the noise experienced by students.

Other Noise Sources

Noise that disturbs the peace is specifically prohibited in 20 states, with 14 delegating this authority to municipalities. The states provide penalties for violations to a greater degree in this area than any other. A few states regulate commercial noise in some way. Mississippi, New Jersey, and Nevada delegate this power to localities, while Delaware and Texas restrict noise from businesses dealing in alcoholic beverages.

Trends and Gaps in State Legislation

More states are entering the field of noise regulation. The number of sources restricted by any one state is also expanding. The trend in the area of state regulation is toward more sophisticated, objective laws enforced by environmental agencies. States tend to adopt laws that set progressively stricter standards over specified time periods and often direct their laws at the manufactrers.

Despite these encouraging signs, there are still gaps in state regulation. Aircraft noise is not restricted except in California. Colorado has taken the steps only in the direction of control of railroad and construction site noise, and industrial and commercial noise is hardly regulated on the state level. This is also true of household noise.

With some exceptions, states have not been experimenting with new methods of regulating noise. In particular, there has been noticeable failure to employ land use policies to limit the effects of noise. The single exception of this appears to be the Minnesota statute, which provides for state control over zoning around new state-owned airports. This type of implementation technique could be used to a much greater degree by state governments.

Noise Sources Regulated at the Regional Level

The only significant regional regulation of noise sources is the limit on aircraft takeoff noise imposed by the Port of New York Authority, which operates Kennedy, La Guardia, Newark, and Teterboro Airports in the New York City vicinity. Takeoffs are not permitted if atmospheric conditions and operating procedures would cause a limit of 112 PNdB to be exceeded at certain measuring points near the airpot.

SUMMARY OF STATE LAWS

Alabama

Title 36, Sec. 36 Horns
Sec. 39 Mufflers

Alaska

Title 11, Sec. 11.45.030 Disorderly Conduct

Arizona

Title 13, Art. 15, Sec. 13-371 Disturbing the Peace
Title 28, Sec. 28-954 Horns
Sec. 28-955 Mufflers

Arkansas

Title 75, Sec. 725 Horns
Sec. 726 Mufflers

California

Title 7, Chap. 1.5 Office of Planning and Research
Title 11, Sec. 415 Disturbing the Peace
Public Utilities Code, Chap. 5 Powerplant Sites Sec. 21669-21669.4 Airports
Public Resources Code, Div. 13, Sec. 21000-21150, Environmental Quality Act
Motor Vehicle Code, Sec. 23130, Sec. 23160, Motor Vehicle Noise Limits
Streets and Highways Codes, Sec. 216

Colorado

Chap. 13, Sec. 5-104 Horns
Sec. 5-105 Mufflers
Chap. 66, Art. 35 Noise Abatement
Chap. 132, Sec. 1-9-1-10 Environmental Quality

Connecticut

Title 7, Sec. 194 Municipal Powers
Title 14, Sec. 14-80(e) Motor Vehicle Noise
Public Act No. 762-Maximum Vehicle Noise Levels

Delaware

Title 4, Sec. 543 Grounds for Refusal of License to Sell Alcoholic Beverages
Sec. 561 Grounds for Cancellation or Suspension of License
Chap. 43, Sec. 4311 Mufflers

Florida

Sec. 317.631 Mufflers
Sec. 403.031, 403.061 Air and Water Pollution Control-Noise

Georgia

Title 68, Sec. 1716 Horns
Sec. 1717 Mufflers

Hawaii

Chap. 103, Sec. 103 Noise Control in Schools
Chap. 322, Excessive Noise
Sec. 267-1 Common Nuisances
Sec. 311-24 Mufflers on Motor Scooters

Idaho

Sec. 49-835 Mufflers

Illinois

Vehicle Code, Sec. 12-121 Mufflers
Sec. 314-3 Mufflers on Boats
Sec. 11-5-2 Municipal Powers
Chap. 111½ Environmental Protection Act

Indiana
Sec. 47-2230 Mufflers
Sec. 48-1401 Municipal Corporations Powers

Iowa
Chap. 138, Sec. 138.1 Migrant Labor Camps
Sec. 321.436 Mufflers
Sec. 368.7 Powers of Cities and Towns

Kansas
Chap. 8, Sec. 8-5, 102 Horns
Sec. 8-5, 103 Mufflers
Chap. 21. 21-950 Disturbance of the Peace
Sec. 21-4101 Disorderly Conduct
Chap. 82a, Sec. 82a-809 Motorboat Mufflers

Kentucky
Sec. 82.220 Powers of Local Units
Sec.85.180 Powers of Local Units
Sec. 85-190 Powers of Local Units
Sec. 189.020 Vehicle Equipment
Sec. 189.140 Mufflers

Louisana
R.S. 14, Sec. 103 Disturbing the Peace
R.S. 32, 352 Mufflers

Maine
Title 12, Chap. 304 Snowmobiles
Title 20, Sec. 3771 Disturbing Schools
Title 29, Sec. 1362 Motor Vehicle Noise
Sec. 1364 Mufflers

Maryland
Art. 66½, Sec. 11-1117 Excessive Vehicle Noise
Sec. 11-1409 Muffler Cutouts
Sec. 12-401 Horns
Sec. 12-401.1 Bells on Ice Cream Sales Vehicles
Sec. 12-402 Mufflers

Massachusetts
Chap. 90, Sec. 16 Motor Vehicle Noise
Chap. 90B, Sec. 24 Restrictions on Noise of Snow Vehicles
Chap. 272, Sec. 41 Disturbance of Libraries

Michigan
Sec. 5.1740 General Powers of City Corporation
Sec. 9.2406 Horns
Sec. 9.2407 Mufflers

Minnesota
Chapt. 169, Sec. 169.69 Mufflers
Sec. 169.691 Motor Vehicle Noise Limits
Chap. 412, Sec. 412.191 Village Council Powers
Chap. 360, Sec. 360.063 Airport Zoning
360.075 Advertising Noise from Aircraft

Mississippi
Title 11, Sec. 2088 Disturbance of Family
Sec. 2090.5 Disturbance in Public Place
Title 16, Sec. 3374-124 Power of Municipalities
Title 30, Sec. 8251 Mufflers

Missouri
Sec. 304.560 Horns, Mufflers
Sec. 562.240 Disturbing the Peace

Montana
Sec. 32-31-146 Mufflers

Fish and Game Laws (Supp. 1971), p. 174 (Senate Bill 54, Sec. 9)—Snowmobiles

Nebraska

Sec. 14-102 Powers of Cities of Metropolitan Class
Sec. 16-227 Powers of Cities of the First Class to Prevent Noises
Sec. 16-228 Powers of Cities of the First Class to Prevent Disorderly Conduct
Sec. 17-556 Powers of Cities of Second Class to Prevent Noises
Sec. 32-466 Disturbing Elections
Sec. 39-777 Mufflers
Sec. 81-815.09 Mufflers on Boats

Nevada

Sec. 486.100 Mufflers on Power Cycles
Sec. 266.360 Power of City Councils to Regulate Business Noise

New Hampshire

Sec. 263.46 Mufflers

New Jersey

Chap. 418, Public Laws of 1971 (1/24/72) Noise Control Act of 1971
Title 40, Sec. 40:175-10 Powers of Local Boards
Title 39, Sec. 39:3-70 Mufflers
Sec. 39:4-78 Carrying Metals

New Mexico

64-20-44 Mufflers

New York

Conservation Law Sec. 8-0305 Snowmobiles
General Business Law, Sec. 7 Sports and Shows on Sunday
Sec. 14 Parades on Sundays
Penal Law, Sec. 240.20 Disorderly Conduct
Sec. 240.21 Disturbance of Religious Service
Navigation Law Sec. 44 Mufflers on Boats
Multiple Dwelling Law, Sec. 84 Construction Standards for Control of Noise
Town Law Sec. 130 Powers of Town Boards
Vehicle and Traffic Law Sec. 375 (31) Mufflers
Sec. 381 Motorcycle Equipment
Sec. 386 Motor Vehicle Noise Limit
Environmental Conservation Law

North Carolina

Sec. 20-128 Mufflers

North Dakota

Sec. 23-01-17 Noise Harmful to Health and Safety
Sec. 39-21-37 Mufflers

Ohio

Sec. 2923.41 Disturbance of the Peace
Sec. 4513.22 Mufflers

Oklahoma

Title 11, Sec. 655 Powers of Local Councils to Prohibit Noises
Title 21, Sec. 1321.8 Riots
Title 47, Sec. 12-402 Mufflers

Oregon

Sec. 483.446 (3) Horns
Sec. 483.448 Mufflers

Pennsylvania

Title 34 Sec. 1311.704 (g) Hunting Sounds

Title 53 Sec. 46202 (20) Powers of Boroughs to Regulate Disturbance of the Peace
Title 55 Sec. 411 Mufflers on Boats
Sec. 485F Mufflers on Motorboats
Title 71 Sec. 510-517 Abatement of Nuisances
Title 75 Sec. 828 Mufflers

Puerto Rico
Title 9 Sec. 1302 Mufflers

Rhode Island
Sec. 12-2-4 Power of R.R. Police to Arrest Disorderly Person
Sec. 12-2-5 Power of Steamboat Police to Arrest Disorderly Person
Sec. 31-23-13 Mufflers

South Carolina
Sec. 46-601 Mufflers

South Dakota
Sec. 32-15-10 Horns
Sec. 32-15-11 Sirens
Sec. 32-15-17 Mufflers

Tennessee
Sec. 39-1204 Disturbing Religious, Educational, Literacy or Temperance Assemblies
Sec. 38-1213 Disturbance of Peace
Sec. 59-901 (a) Horns
Sec. 59-902 Mufflers

Texas
Title 28, Art. 1015 Powers of Governing Bodies of Cities, Towns and Villages
Title 9, Art. 281 Disturbing Congregation
Art. 451 Disturbing Families
Art. 465 Disturbing Residences
Art. 474 Disturbing the Peace
Title 11, Art. 666-12 Cancellation or suspension of Permit to Sell Alcoholic Beverages
Title 13, Art. 796 Horns
Art. 797 Devices to Prevent Unusual Noise

Utah
Sec. 10-8-47 Powers of Cities and Towns to Prevent Noises
Sec. 10-8-50 Powers of Cities and Towns to Punish for Disturbing the Peace
Sec. 76-52-9 Disturbing Neighborhood Quiet
Sec. 76-55-3 Disturbing Assembly for Religious Worship
Sec. 41-6-147 Mufflers

Vermont
Title 13, Sec. 1022 Noises in the Nighttime
Sec. 1023 Disturbing Meetings and Schools
Sec. 1051 Breach of the Peace
Title 23, Sec. 1097 Mufflers Cutouts

Virginia
Sec. 46.1-301 Vehicle Exhaust
Sec. 46.1-302 Muffler Cutout Illegal

Virgin Islands
Title 14 Sec. 622 Disturbing the Peace
Sec. 624 Disturbing Meetings
Title 20 Sec. 464 Horns and Mufflers
Title 20 Sec. 465 Motorcycle Mufflers

Washington
Title 9, Sec. 9.76.010 Sabbath Breaking

Sec. 9.76.050 Disturbing Religious Meeting
Title 35, Sec. 35.22.280 (36) Power of First Class Cities to Provide for Disorderly Conduct
Sec. 35.23.440 (10) Power of Second Class Cities to Prevent Disturbance of the Peace
Title 46, Sec. 46.37.390 Mufflers

West Virginia
Sec. 17C-15-34(a) Mufflers

Wisconsin
Chap. 22, Sec. 22.40 (11) (12) Auto Races on State Fair Grounds
Chap. 60, Sec. 60.29 (35) Power of Town Boards to Regulate Motorboats
Vehicle Code, Title 44, Sec. 347.39 Mufflers
Sec. 350-10 Provisions for Snowmobile Operation
Criminal Code, Title 45, Sec. 947.01 Disorderly Conduct

Wyoming
Sec. 6-112 Disturbing Meetings, Generally
Sec. 6-114 Breach of the Peace
Sec. 6-173 Disturbing Religious Worship
Sec. 31-204 Horns
Sec. 31-205 Mufflers

Noise sources regulated on the local level

The information in this portion of the report is based on data gathered from 83 local governments. Many large cities are represented, as well as smaller communities.

General Noise Laws

Better than two-thirds (69 percent) of the 83 cities examined have either no noise laws whatever or have only general laws covering noise from any source. The most popular type of general law is that patterned after the Model Ordinance Prohibiting Unnecessary Noises, issued by the National Institute of Municipal Law Officers (NIMLO). Over one-third of the cities examined have laws similar to this model ordinance. The model employs subjective criteria and prohibits loud, unnecessary, and unusual noise. Three cities have ordinances that differ from the NIMLO model but that apply similar subjective standards. Two other cities set a limit of 80 dBA at 20 feet, or 20 feet from the property line of the noise source. A number of cities combat noise through the use of public nuisance laws that label excessive noise as a public nuisance and provide for its abatement.

One of the most popular methods of noise control on the local level is the zoning ordinance, which sets limits on noise in designated residential, commercial, or industrial zones. Cities often include quantitative noise level standards in their zoning ordinances.

Transportation Noise

Aircraft Noise. Six of the cities in this survey place some restriction on noise from aircraft. These ordinances are of two types:

1. Those that undertake to limit nonflight activity.
2. Those that purport to limit operating noise from aircraft in flight.

In the first category, Denver restricts noise not necessary to flight, while Salt Lake City regulates noise in ground runup areas. In the second category, Santa Barbara, California, limits noise on takeoffs and landings as well as noise from runup areas and sonic booms. Scottsbluff, Nebraska, forbids any flight below 2000 feet. Park Ridge, Illinois, prohibits noise over 95 dBC in designated areas extending from the runways of O'Hare Airport. Portland, Oregon, limits noise from helicopters.

Motor Vehicle Noise. Thirty-three municipalities examined require mufflers on motor vehicles, while 22 restrict horn noise and 12 cities set subjective limits, such as "unnecessary," on the total noise from vehicles. Three cities set objective limits in the 90- to 95-dBA range measured at 20 or 25 feet. Chicago and Minneapolis, in recently enacted legislation, set stricter noise limits on vehicle operation, as well as noise emission standards for new vehicles.

Specific provisions concerning noise from motorcycles were made by four of the cities examined. Missoula, Montana, and Detroit set subjective limits, while the new Chicago and Minneapolis laws restrict noise from operation and set a limit on noise from new motorcycles.

Other Transportation Noise Sources. Chicago regulates noise from boats in its new law, and Detroit restricts noise from whistles of steamers using its harbor. Generally cities have been slow to respond to snowmobiles as new noise sources. Chicago sets objective limits on these vehicles, while Dillon, Colorado, allows them only on marked trails—of which there are none.

Commercial Noise

Noise from commercial establishments or individuals acting in business capacities is widely regulated at the local level. The nonadvertising regulation in this area can be divided into five categories:

1. Regulation of business establishments (either all business or particular businesses).
2. Regulation of some particular accessory or device used by the business (such as noisy air-conditioning equipment) or some noisy aspect of the commercial operation (such as loading or unloading materials).
3. Regulation of musicians.
4. Regulation of music-producing machines.
5. Regulation of sound equipment.

Noise from advertising, especially the use of sound-producing or sound-amplifying equipment, is heavily regulated on the local level. Itinerant peddlars calling their wares, stationary sound equipment, and sound equipment mounted on vehicles and aircraft are either prohibited or subject to strict controls.

Occupational Noise

Two cities have objective decibel limits on the amount of noise to which workers may be subjected. The Detroit standards are identical to the Walsh-Healey limits previously discussed. Philadelphia has adopted standards that are less strict than the old Walsh-Healey limits, with the exception of the maximum limit placed on impact noise.

Construction Noise

Many cities regulate noise from construction sites, using curfews and zoning restrictions. Minneapolis sets a noise limit on the entire construction operation, while Chicago specifies noise limits on most types of construction equipment.

Acoustical Treatment of Buildings

Several cities have requirements concerning the acoustical treatment of buildings. The new New York City law on multifamily residential buildings sets limits on the noise that can be allowed to travel between two apartments and between apartments and public areas of the building. These objective limits are based on measurement standards adopted by various associations, such as the United States of American Standards Institute. Before a permit is issued approving the opening of the building to occupants, the Department of Buildings must be satisfied, as a result of either its tests or those of an independent firm, that the new building conforms to the limits.

Other Noise Sources Controlled at the Local Level

Disturbing the peace is heavily regulated on the local level. Some cities simply prohibit such behavior, while others impose curfew and zoning regulations. Domestic noise is beginning to come under regulation at the local level. The recent Chicago noise laws cover noise from various home products such as lawnmowers, power tools, and snowblowers by setting decibel limits for new products. Minneapolis sets a curfew on this equipment if noise from it causes the noise level at property lines to exceed specified standards. Sound equipment used for noncommercial activities is also heavily regulated. Some cities ban its use, while others require permits or set curfew and zoning restrictions. There are also local ordinances pertaining to noisy animals.

As with the states, more cities are developing programs to cope with excessive noise. Some have established noise abatement offices with special noise monitoring teams. City noise laws are becoming more sophisticated, substituting decibel limits for the former subjective standards. These laws also provide for tougher standards over time. As is true for the states, the success of city antinoise programs will depend upon enforcement of the new laws. Unfortunately, enforcement strains the already overburdened budgets of many of the nation's cities.

Trends and Gaps in Local Legislation

Noise has traditionally been regulated more often at the local level. However, with the increase in the general environmental noise levels of American cities in recent years, local governments have begun to adopt new laws to deal with this phenomenon. Like the states, cities have developed more sophisticated laws covering more noise sources. These laws are tending to include tougher standards over time and are often directed at manufacturers. Although the major noise sources are regulated at the local level, any one city does not have laws governing noise from every type of noise source. More cities must expand the number of regulated noise sources if local control of noise is to be more effective.

Common law remedies

Attempts to achieve noise reduction through common law actions have generally been unsuccessful. This is most often attributable to the inflexibility of the common law actions to fit the modern context of a noise impact. Actions that have been argued include trespass, constitutional taking and inverse condemnation, and public and private nuisance. Although such actions have been brought with respect to the full range of noise sources the most common suit is one against aircraft noise.

Trespass

Trespass actions have succeeded when the source of the noise intrudes upon complainants property, but such actions are infrequent because of elements of the cause of action. A direct physical invasion onto the plaintiff's land is required for a trespass. Rather ingeniously in *Causby v. United States,* 328 U.S. 256 (1946), the plaintiff argued a trespass occured when aircraft flew through the airspace above the plaintiff's land, basing the invation on the *ad coelum* theory of ownership of the column of air extending forever upward from the boundary of plaintiff's land. The Supreme Court essentially dismissed the trespass question as an antiquated concept but instead considered that the fly-overs, but not fly-bys, affected the land below to the extent of constituting a constitutional taking compensable under the Fifth Amendment.

Nuisance

Nuisances are either private or public and the common law elements of these two actions differ substantially. Both will allow relief in the form of damages or injunctive relief.

Private nuisances are connected with an interference with the use and enjoyment of real property. This includes certain personal rights such as mental and physical well being and undisturbed enjoyment of the land as an integral component of the property interest. The interference must be substantial and unreasonable when considered in the context of persons of ordinary sensibilities. Thus the questions essentially cannot be subjected to a standard measure; reasonableness is a question of fact which must consider such factors as the surrounding conditions, and most important the social benefits deriving from the noise-producing activities measured against the private cost which the plaintiff pays as a result.

Public nuisance actions will lie when the noise affects an interest common to the general public. Relatively local conditions can constitute a public nuisance if persons coming in contact with the noise conditions in the exercise of a public right experience interference with those rights.

But the individual plaintiff, seeking a judicial determination that some activity is a public nuisance, must show that he suffers unique damage differing in kind from that suffered by the general public. Ordinarily personal damages to health or property are sufficiently unique to fulfill this requirement. However, the balancing of social benefit against private harm can give the courts just enough latitude to dispose of many complaints as public inconveniences which all must suffer. See for example *Mathewson v. New York State Thruway Authority,* 174 N.E.2d 754 (1961). Many times it appears that the courts are justifying such suits when the damages are merely different in degree and not in kind and such instances illustrate judicial sympathy with those who have suffered harm.

nuisance actions

Legislatures become involved in nuisance law in two ways; 1) specific activities are often labelled public nuisances *per se;* 2) certain noise producing activities are often specifically permitted and encouraged by statute and then exempted from nuisance actions by a general providion such as, "Nothing which is done or maintained under the express authority of a statute can be deemed a nuisance." Generally public nuisance *per se* statutes do not address noise since these often were enacted prior to any noise problem. As to the legislative authority to conduct an activity which would otherwise constitute a nuisance, this is limited to minor interferences with the property. But there is real power hidden in such legislative authority even when the plaintiff is also fulfilling important social need. Consider this passage from *Deaconess Hospital v. Washington State Highway Commission:*

> The freeway is to be built not only under general statutory authority of the highway statutes, but also pursuant to specific enactment of the legislature establishing the highway as state primary highway No. 2. . . . No claim is made that the highway derives its nuisance qualities from faulty design or negligence in construction or that it will be improperly maintained. The fact of nuisance found to exist in future by the court comes directly from the consequences of proximity. Deaconess Hospital wishes to enjoin the highway — not generally as a nuisance but specifically within 300 feet of its buildings. Our legislature seems to have anticipated this very situation, for in 1881 . . . it re-enacted the following: "Nothing which is done or maintained under the express authority of a statute, can be deemed a nuisance."

Id. at 71-72. Under other circumstances, however, a hospital has been successful in maintaining an action for nuisance against noise-making sources. In *Clinit & Hospital v. McConnell* 236 S.W.2d 384 (1951) (23 ALR 2d 1278) the plaintiff sought to enjoin the operation of a loud speaker in the front window of a music store diagonally across the street from which music was continuously broadcast, sometimes until 11:00 p.m. The hospital was established long before the music store. The sound was clearly audible in the hospital above ambient street noise. Evidence showed that the sound had an injurious effect on some patients. The court considered interference with the operation of the hospital to be "relatively serious" and determined that the defendants should be perpetually enjoined. The general principle was stated by the court as follows:

> (A) business which is lawful in itself may become a nuisance where it is not operated in a fair and reasonable way with regard

to the rights of others in the use and enjoyment of their property. . . . [T]he question is one of reasonableness. What is . . . an unreasonable invasion of another's use and enjoyment of his property cannot be determined by exact rules, but must necessarily depend upon the circumstances of each case, such as locality and the character of the surroundings, the nature, utility and social value of the use, the extent and nature of the harm involved, the nature, utility and social value of the use or enjoyment invaded, and the like. See *Restatement of Torts,* Vol. IV, §822 and §831, at 214 (23 ALR 2d 1287).

For discussion of particular noise sources as a nuisance see:

Annot., 2 ALR 3d 1372 (Truck Terminal)
Annot., 4 ALR 3d 902 (Power Plant)
Annot., 5 ALR 3d 989 (Tavern)
Annot., 26 ALR 3d 661 (Shooting Range)
Annot., 18 ALR 2d 1035 (Stockyard)
Annot., 39 ALR 2d 1007 (Undertaker)
Annot., 44 ALR 2d 1394 (Dance Hall)
Annot., 26 ALR 2d 653 (Auto Wrecking Yard)
Annot., 44 ALR 2d 1322 (Oil Refinery)
Annot., 91 ALR 2d 575 (Drive-In Restaurant)
Annot., 92 ALR 2d 977 (Dairy and Creamery)
Annot., 93 ALR 2d 1171 (Drive-In Movie)
Annot., 23 ALR 2d 1289 (Business Premises)

Also see recent cases:

common law doctrines in the courts

Davoust v. Mitchell, 257 N.E. 2d 332 (Ind. 1970) (Dog Pen)
Johnson v. Mount Ogden Enterprises, Inc., 23 Utah 2d 169, 460 P. 2d 333 (1969) (Drive-In Theater)
Severt v. Beckkley Coals, Inc., 170 S.E. 2d 577 (Sp. Ct. W.Va. 1969) (Coal Mine)
Corporation of the Presiding Bishop of the Church of the Latter Day Saints v. Ashton, 92 Idaho 571, 448 P. 2d 185 (1968) (Church Activities, Baseball Games)
Smith v. Western Wayne County Conservation Association, 380 Mich 526, 158 N.W. 2d 463 (1968) (Gun Club)
Kasala v. Kalispell Pee Wee Baseball League, 151 Mont. 109, 439 P. 2d 65 (1968) (Baseball Game)
City of Fredericktown v. Osborne, 429 S.W. 2d 17 (Mo. App. 1968) (Keeping Dogs)
Bates v. Quality Ready Mix, Inc., 261 Ia 696, 154 N.W. 2d 852 (1967) (Cement Factory)
Sanders v. Roselawn Memorial Gardens, 152 W.Va. 91, 159 S.E. 2d 784 (1968) (Cemetery).

The noise producer must exercise due care and regard for private and public interests. If the interference is major and is created by governmental action, then we move into the area of condemnation and just compensation involved with constitutional "taking" theories.

Constitutional Taking; Eminent Domain and Inverse Condemnation

The common situation involving property condemnation and noise is not an eminent domain action but rather the inverse situation where the property owner claims the condemnation of his property, inverse condemnation. Naturally such actions are limited to those defendants who can exercise the right of eminent domain, normally governments and specifically authorized private concerns serving a public need. The *Aaron* case, set out below, contains a good discussion of inverse condemnation suits and eliminates the artificial distinction between fly-over noise and fly-by noise mentioned earlier under trespass.

For years states and local governments have attempted to abate noise by statutory schemes, discussed earlier in this chapter. While the effectiveness of these schemes is questionable, (see discussion on effectiveness, *infra*) in the area of aircraft noise regulation, the constitutionality of these statutes and ordinances is doubtful at best. These lower-level statutes generally run afoul of the supremacy clause of Article IV of the United States Constitution. The argument hinges on the Federal Aviation Act of 1958, (49 U.S.C. §1301 *et seq.*) and its preemption of the field of regulation of air commerce in the United States. This argument was successfully used by the airlines in invalidating a local ordinance which prohibited flights over the village of Cedarhurst, New York at less than 1,000 feet. Cedarhurst is adjacent to and under the flight path to John F. Kennedy International Airport in New York City. *Alleghany Airlines, et al. v. Cedarhurst,* 258 F.2d 812 (2d Cir. 1956).

However other local ordinances have been upheld, at least in state courts. For instance a night time curfew prohibiting the takeoff or launching of jet aircraft between the hours of 11 P.M. and 7 A.M. at Santa Monica Municipal Airport in California was found not to conflict with the Federal scheme. *Stagg v. Municipal Court of Santa Monica,* 81 Cal. Rptr. 578 (Cal. Ct. App. 1969). The ordinance was upheld as a valid exercise both of the municipality's police power and its proprietary rights of ownership of the airport. In dismissing the argument of Federal preemption, the court relied on *Loma Portal Civic Club v. American Airlines,* 39 Cal. Rptr. 708, 394 P.2d 548, (1964). This latter case was a nuisance action brought by owners of property located under the flight path to Lindbergh Field in San Diego. The prayer was for injunctive relief. That being the situation, the court felt that the complaint must be dismissed on a balancing of the interests of the plaintiffs against the interests of the general public in the services provided by the commercial airlines, all of whom operated under FAA certificates to provide service in the public interest to San Diego.

Having thus decided the case in favor of the defendant airlines, the court went on to dismiss the defendant's arguments of Federal preemption. But particularly significant is the fact that this was a common law action and not an action based on a state statute or local ordinance. As a common law action, the court noted that the Federal Aviation Act provides at 49 U.S.C. §1506,

> Nothing contained in this chapter shall in any way abridge or alter the remedies now existing at common law or by statute, but the provisions of this chapter are in addition to such remedies.

While noting that, "It is clear that the Federal legislation was not intended to be exclusive," (39 Cal. Rptr. 715) the court draws a fine distinction between preemption by Federal law and conflict with Federal law in stating,

> To be sure, the supremacy clause precludes the enforcement of state law which conflicts with Federal law, e.g., we could not enjoin a pilot from flying in the landing pattern that he was ordered to follow by the control tower, and it is for this reason, not preemption, that a state may not prohibit that which federal authority directs. (39 Cal. Rptr. 714).

This last question was then not at issue in *Loma Portal Civic Club* and was essentially dismissed off-handedly in *Stag,* perhaps because the ordinance only burdened private jet aircraft operations for only the low flight density portion of the night.

Lockheed Air Terminal v. Burbank [___ F.2d ___ (9th Cir. March 22, 1972), 3 ERC 1938] held an aircraft curfew ordinance to be prohibited by Federal pre-emption. The court, however, emphasized the ordinance in question was an exercise of the police power, not the act of a governmental proprietor of an airport.

AARON v. LOS ANGELES

Calif. Superior Ct., Los Angeles County, (Feb. 5, 1970), 3 ERC 1779

Partial Text of Opinion

Jefferson, J.:

This is an action for damages for inverse condemnation. There are approximately one thousand five hundred plaintiffs who allege that they are the owners of real property in the neighborhood of Los Angeles International Airport, sometimes hereafter referred to as the Airport, and that the City of Los Angeles, the only defendant in this action, has permitted and caused an increasing number of jet airplane flights over and in the immediate vicinity of the plaintiffs' properties, so that the noise, smoke, virbrations and fumes from the aircraft have damages these properties.

Besides denying the allegations set forth in the complaint, the defendant City asserts a number of affirmative defenses. The defenses raised by the defendant are as follows: (1) that the complaint fails to state a cause of action; (2) that the cause of action is barred by the statute of limitations as set forth in sections 312, 318 and 319 of the Code of Civil Procedure; (3) that the action is barred by the statute of limitations as set forth in section 338, subdivision 2, of the Code of Civil Procedure; (4) that the Federal Aviation Act of 1958, as amended, has preempted control of airspace navigation; (5) that the defendant City has acquired by prescription an easement in the airspace involved because of more than five years' adverse use by defendant City; (6) that public convenience and necessity require that defendant City use the airspace involved in this action, and that the City is entitled to an easement for continued use of this airspace.

The basic theory of liability which plaintiffs advance is that the noise from jet aircraft flying over and near the residential properties of plaintiffs has resulted in a substantial diminution in the market value of these properties, which thus constitutes a "taking or damaging" of these properties within the purview of Article I, section 14, of the California Constitution.

It is conceded that the Los Angeles International Airport was in existence at its present location prior to the acquisition by the plaintiffs of their residential properties.

Before the year 1959, planes flying into, and departing from, the Los Angeles International Airport were of the propeller type. The first jet airplanes started using this Airport in 1959, and, since 1959, there has been a gradual, yearly increase in the number of jet aircraft arriving and departing from this Airport. Apparently, there has been little or no complaint from property owners with respect to noise emanating from the propeller-type airplanes. The noise problem developed only with the advent of jet aircraft.

[T]he essence of the claimed reductions in market values of property affected is related solely to the noise from the jet planes as the responsible cause.

What plaintiffs seek in this action are money damages measured by the extent to which the market value of the respective parcels of property has been reduced because of noise from jet aircraft flying over and near these parcels located within and near the landing and takeoff patterns.

One of the crucial issues involved in this litigation is whether noise from jet aircraft presents a proper case for inverse condemnation. It is the contention of the defendant City that the law does not sanction any recovery for noise against a government entity, even assuming that such noise has caused a diminution in property values. The trial courts must chart the theories of recovery or nonrecovery, and, ultimately, the California Supreme Court will be asked to determine this aspect of the law of inverse condemnation upon appeals from judgments of the trial courts.

Under the federal cases, an injury to property without displacement or ouster of the owner is not compensable.

In United States v. Causby, 328 U.S. 256 (1946), the United States Supreme Court held that flights on takeoff and landing at low level over an owner's property could be considered a "taking" in the nature of an easement of flight, and rendered the Government liable for the decreased value of the owner's property. [T]his decision was limited to permitting recovery by a property owner over whose land the planes took off, and could not be considered as a holding to protect nearby owners. The nearby owners are considered to have suffered incidental damage for which no recovery is allowed.

A second view would permit recovery in inverse condemnation by property owners who suffer substantial diminution in market value from jet aircraft noise, regardless of whether the planes fly directly over the owner's property or not. This was the holding in Thornburg v. Port of Portland, 233 Ore. 178, 376 P.2d 100 (1962). The Oregon court adopted a nuisance theory, which permits recovery for damages so long as there is proof of real injury, whether resulting from noise coming from flyover or flyby aircraft.

A third view is a further extension of the Oregon rule, and permits recovery for any damage, whether substantial or not, which results to the property owner from aircraft noise, regardless of whether the noise comes from flyover or flyby aircraft. This view is espoused by the State of Washington. Martinez v. Port of Seattle, 64 Wash.2d 324, 391 P.2d 540 (1964). [P]laintiffs were property owners near the Seattle-Tacoma International Airport, owned and operated by the Port of Seattle, a municipal corporation. Some of the plaintiffs were located underneath the flight patterns, while others were not directly underneath but were near the flight patterns, and all claimed a decrease in property values from the jet noise. The Washington court held that plaintiffs' complaint stated a cause of action, [...and] rejected the view that less-than-substantial damage would be considered noncompensable as incidental damage, holding that any diminution of property values, however slight, should be compensable.

We now turn to the law of California to determine if California has embraced a particular theory for recovery in airport noise cases. We start with a consideration of the street or freeway noise cases. To date, California has taken the view that a property owner whose property has not been taken for freeway or street purposes, but whose property has been decreased in value from the vehicular noise of a freeway or street, may not recover from the governmental entity any damages for such decrease in property values. This was the holding in People ex rel. Dept. of Public Works v. Symons, 54 Cal.2d 855 (1960).

A more recent case in point is Lombardi v. Peter Kiewit Sons, 266 Cal.App.2d 599 (1968), where it was held that a complaint did not state a cause of action in inverse condemnation. The complaint alleged that the plaintiffs were property owners next to a freeway, and that the building and operation of a freeway resulted in fumes, noise, dust, shocks and vibrations, causing mental, physical and emotional distress to the plaintiffs and damage to the real property. The court held that this complaint did not state a cause of action in inverse condemnation because no recovery may be had unless damage in a substantial amount to the property itself has been sustained. Lombardi cites as authority for its holding the cases of Albers v. County of Los Angeles, 62 Cal.2d 250 (1960); and Frustuck v. City of Fairfax, 212 Cal.App.2d 345 (1963).

If there can be recovery for physical damage to realty without any actual trespass upon or physical invasion of the landowner's property by the governmental entity, it would seem to follow that an invasion of the air surface above the land by aircraft overflights would be sufficient to permit recovery in inverse condemnation, so long as there has been a loss in market value resulting from such aircraft overflight noise. It should be immaterial whether a loss of market value from aircraft overflight noise is looked upon as a "taking" or "damaging" of private property, since the California Constitution provides for eminent domain compensation where there is a "taking" or "damaging" (See California Constitution, Article I, section 14.)

A more serious question, however, is whether the California cases, such as Albers, Lombardi and Symons, restrict recovery in inverse condemnation in the aircraft noise situation to those cases in which the market value of private property has been diminished by noise from aircraft flyovers.

There is every reason to believe that the citadel of Symons must crumble and fall in the face of changing conditions created by the advent of jet aircraft. The Symons rule must be restricted in its application to the narrow factual situation presented in that and similar cases.

Furthermore, there is a significant difference between the noise emanating from jet aircraft and that coming from automobiles and trucks on a street or freeway. This difference is so pronounced that the legal consequences of jet noise should not be the same as the legal consequences of a street and freeway noise of cars and trucks as enunciated by cases such as Albers, Lombardi and Symons. Scientific studies demonstrate that jet aircraft noise creates a severe disturbance to the comfort, enjoyment and use of residential property by the owners affected. The sounds emanating from cars and trucks on streets and freeways are simply minor contrasted with the irritating and offensive sounds emanating from jet aircraft. Scientific evaluation of sound and noise establishes a significant difference between the two types of sounds and noises and their effects upon human beings. Studies made by acoustical scientists and experts establish that the comparative offensiveness of different sounds is capable of measurement by accepted standards of numerical ratings.

Noise is simply one type of sound. Noise is commonly considered as unwanted sound because of the ear's reception and reaction to different kinds of sounds. In dealing with noise, whether it be from automobiles or aircraft, we are concerned with its annoyance and offensive effect upon people, and whether such noise results in a substantial interference with the comfort, enjoyment or use of one's home.

The hue and cry over aircraft noise did not develop until the coming of jet aircraft. The explanation is that propeller aircraft creates sounds that are predominantly in the low frequency range, and low frequency sounds are not as disturbing to the ear as are high frequency sounds. Likewise, the sounds from automobiles and trucks traversing the streets and freeways are predominantly low frequency or low pitch sounds, and hence do not begin to have the annoyance and offensive consequence to the human ear as the high frequency sounds made by jet aircraft. Tests conducted by acoustical experts indicate that if the average person hears two sounds of the same intensity or loudness and one is a high frequency sound and the other a low frequency sound, such person will believe that the high frequency sound is louder than the low frequency sound.

Acoustical experts have developed the term "Effective Perceived Noise Level," abbreviated EPNL. Effective Perceived Noise Level represents a noise scale which provides a means for comparing the relative noise content of sounds on the basis of the two components, intensity and frequency. The EPNL rating of noise sounds represents the annoyance or offensive value which hearers place on the noise spectrum.

The physical factors which go into the calculations to arrive at an EPNL rating are obtained in part from field tests, which record by means of instruments and cameras the jet noise from flyover and flyby aircraft at various land points in the takeoff and landing patterns. The EPNL value determined at a particular land location takes into consideration factors such as the altitude of the aircraft and its distance from the land location as it approaches and leaves the specific location on its flight, the duration of the sound, the type of sound produced by different types of aircraft and the number of flights of different types of aircraft per day and night.

The reason that the number of operations per day of jet aircraft is important in a determination of the EPNL rating in jet aircraft noise is that if the noise of a single aircraft is such that it interferes with normal communication in a home, an increase in the number of flights thereby increases the chances of an interference with normal communication, and hence increases the annoyance effect of jets. Thus, several flights a day of jet aircraft may constitute little interference with normal communication. But if there are hundreds of flights per day, the interference with normal communication obviously becomes substantial.

An expert in applied acoustics and aircraft and vehicle noise sound measurements testified for the plaintiffs. This expert was the co-author of a study made by the firm of Bolt, Beranek and Newman, Inc., for the Federal Aviation Administration. The study was made to determine Noise Exposure Forecast areas resulting from aircraft takeoff and landing operations at the Los Angeles International Airport for the year 1965.

The Noise Exposure Forecast areas, hereafter referred to as NEF areas or contours, were determined and based upon aircraft noise measured numerically in terms of Effective Perceived Noise Levels, and which thus took into consideration factors such as the number of jet flights per day as compared to the number at night, the various types of jet aircraft, operating conditions, such as takeoff and landing thrusts and performance and the altitudes of aircraft at various locations in the takeoff and landing patterns.

The NEF areas delineated as a result of the study constitute a measuring of the noise environment surrounding the Los Angeles International Airport, using the PENL standard of measurement. The study resulted in the designation of three NEF areas or zones. An inner zone, designated NEF Area "C," constitutes a zone of the highest noise level, in which jet aircraft would have the greatest impact on people living within that area. An outer area, designated NEF Area "A," was the zone of the lowest noise level, in which it was determined that there should be no annoyance from aircraft noise to the persons living in that zone. In between these two NEF areas was a third zone, designated NEF Area "B." The middle zone was one in which it was concluded that it would be difficult to predict to what extent persons living in that area would be affected by jet aircraft noise.

So far as noise levels are concerned, the expert witness indicated that there was a 15 decibel difference in noise level rating resulting from jet aircraft between NEF Area "A" and NEF Area "C." In other words, in NEF Area "C," where jet aircraft noise had its greatest annoyance value to residents, the EPNL rating was 15 decibels higher than the noise level in NEF Area "A," where there should be no substantial effect upon residential living. The three NEF areas depict, therefore, areas of significant difference in terms of the deleterious effects of aircraft noise. The 15 decibel difference between an area seriously affected by jet aircraft noise and an area not materially affected has significance because of the accepted principle that an increase of 10 decibels in the Effective Perceived Noise Level rating corresponds to a doubling of the annoyance effect upon persons subjected to a noise level increase of 10 decibels.

The NEF areas recognize that persons to the side of aircraft flying at an altitude of two hundred feet, for example, may be affected by the jet noise to an even greater degree than one whose land is immediately under a flight path at an altitude of five hundred feet.

The development of the NEF contour areas provides a good means of drawing a reasonable line between those landowners who may establish a cause of action for inverse condemnation and those who may not. All landowners who suffer from substantially the same noise level are treated on an equal basis. Thus, all landowners located in NEF Area "C" are subjected to noise from jet aircraft which substantially interferes with residential comfort, enjoyment and use of their property.

[T]he Effective Perceived Noise Level rating scale offers a practical means for comparing noise environments. Conditions which occur immediately below the line of flight appear also at lateral points along the surface. The Effective Perceived Noise Level scales permit the making of practical noise estimations and depicting this situation by contour maps of the surface. This has been done through the development and delineation of NEF Areas "A," "B" and "C" with respect to land adjacent to and near the LosAngeles International Airport.

The view of this Court that landowners who are damaged by noise from flyover or flyby aircraft should have a cause of action for inverse condemnation receives support from legislation enacted by the California Legislature. Section 1239.3 was added to the Code of Civil Procedures in 1965. This section provides that a condemning agency, such as a city or airport district, may acquire airspace or an air easement in the airspace above the surface of property in the vicinity of an airport in which excessive noise, vibration, discomfort, inconvenience or interference with the use and enjoyment of real property produces a reduction in the market value of real property and occurs because of the operation of aircraft to and from an airport.

The view of many courts, regardless of the theory of recovery, is that property owners must suffer substantial damage from jet noise in order to recover for inverse condemnation. This was the view enunciated in the Oregon court in the first appeal in Thornburg, which adopted a nuisance theory and permitted recovery by property owners who suffered damage from jet aircraft noise, whether the noise cam from flyover aircraft or flyby aircraft. How is substantial damage to be defined? The cases dealing with the law of nuisance do not indicate any clear concept of what is meant by substantial damage. A reasonable view is one which holds that damage is substantial if it is measurable as contrasted with that which is merely nominal. Under this view, no particular dollar amount or percentage of reduction in the market value of property from jet noise is required for proof of substantial damage. Evidence that the market value of real property has been reduced by jet noise to an extent which is reasonably measurable satisfies the requirement of substantial damage.

One of the defenses raised by the defendant City is that the Federal Aviation Act of 1958 has preempted for the federal government the control and regulation of the use of navigable airspace. The Federal Aviation Act of 1958, as amended, declares that there exists in behalf of the citizens of the United States a public right of freedom of transit through the navigable airspace of the United States. This act defines "navigable airspace" to be the "airspace above the minimum altidues of flight prescribed by regulations issued under this chapter, and shall include airspace needed to insure safety in take-off and landing of aircraft." (48 U.S.C. §1301 (24).) Defendant City correctly points out that it has no control over setting the altitudes at which aircraft may fly in takeoffs or in landings. However, the fact that the federal government establishes the altitudes of flight does not answer the question of whether state law may impose liability for damage caused by jet aircraft noise. In Aaron v. United States, 311 F.2d 798 (Ct. Cl. 1963), the federal court indicated that a right of recovery for damage from aircraft flyover noise was limited to flights below the navigable airspace designated by Congress. The theory that there can be no taking of private property and hence no liability for noise ; from aircraft within the designated airspace was considered to be derived from the precedents existing for highways. Every citizen is entitled to use the highways, regardless of the noise made by his automobile. Similarly, it was said that citizens should be entitled to fly in the navigable airspace without liability. It is obvious that airplanes must fly at low altitudes for a certain distance adjacent to the runways upon making a landing and upon takeoff. If we accept the defendant City's contention, it would mean that the only liability for aircraft noise, regardless of the amount of damage in terms of diminution in market value, would come from aircraft which flew at lower altitudes than those designated. In Aaron, although the federal court accepted the preemption theory generally, it rejected the contention of immunity for flights within the navigable airspace at least to the extent of stating that a property owner's constitutional rights would have to be considered if it could be shown that a property owner suffered substantial impairment of his property rights from aircraft flights within the designated navigable airspace. With respect to state law imposition of liability, it could be reasonably asserted that if an owner's property is destroyed or damaged by aircraft noise, any immunity granted by Congress would be null and void because it would constitute a taking or damaging of private property without due process of law guaranteed by the Fourteenth Amendment to the United States Constitution.

State courts have rejected this theory of federal preemption for aircraft flying within the navigable airspace. In Thornburg, the Oregon court rejected the doctrine of federal preemption creating an immunity from liability on the ground that such immunity is predicated on the view that there can be no trespass from planes flying in the navigable airspace, and, without a trespass, there can be no damage to the landowner. Since the Oregon court rejected the trespass and taking theory and relied upon a nuisance theory for recovery, it concluded that the nuisance theory would permit recovery for damage to property from aircraft noise even if flights are within the navigable airspace designated pursuant to congressional legislation. In Anderson v. Souza, 38 Cal.2d 825, 839 (1952), it was stated that the federal declaration with respect to navigable airspace was "not intended to and do not divest owners of the surface of the soil of their lawful rights incident to ownership."

In Loma Portal Civic Club v. American Airlines, Inc., 61 Cal. 2d 582 (1964), the California Supreme Court again rejected the contention of federal preemption. The Loma Portal Civic Club case determined that Congress had not indicated any intent to establish a federal preemption policy so that state action would be precluded because of an extensive pattern of federal regulation in the field. The court said that Congress had not indicated such a federal preemption because the Federal Aviation Act contained an express declaration that nothing therein contained should, in any way, abridge or alter remedies existing at common law or by statute. The court also reached the conclusion that there was no federal preemption by applying the test of whether the enforcement of state law would conflict with the purposes of the federal legislation, whether by frustrating an affirmative purpose or by interfering with a matter left intentionally unregulated by Congress. The court concluded that only a compelling federal interest, as where a state-created liability would clearly frustrate federal purposes, would justify inferring an intent on the part of Congress to nullify rights normally considered in the state-law sphere. The definition and adjustment of property rights and the protection of health and welfare are matters primarily of state law. Thus, state courts may entertain wrongful death actions against airlines (Porter v. Southeastern Aviation Inc., 191 F.Supp. 42 [M.D. Tenn. 1961]).

Closely allied with the defense of federal preemption is the contention of defendant City that it cannot be held liable for damage to property owners from jet aircraft noise because it has no control over the airlines' choise of aircraft engines or the flight altitudes on the glide paths to and from the Airport. Although these are matters regulated by the Federal Aviation Administration, they offer no valid defense to the defendant City. The United States Supreme Court rejected such a defense in Griggs v. Allegheny County, 369 U.S. 84 [1 ERC 1058] (1962). There it was held that Allegheny County, which owned and operated the Greater Pittsburgh Airport, was bound under the Fourteenth Amendment to the United States Constitution to compensate a property owner who was damaged as a result of aircraft flights over his land. The fact that approach patterns were within the navigable airspace declared by Congress did not preclude the holding that there had been a "taking" of private property by the governmental owner and operator of the airport. The reasoning of the Supreme Court was that the County exercised the sole discretion to place the airport in the specific location, and that had it not so located the airport, there would have been no federal licensing of airplanes or fixing of navigable airspace to and from the specific location. Thus, in the case at bench, the City of Los Angeles made the decision to locate the Los Angeles International Airport where it now stands, and, as a result of that decision, must compensate those who own property adjacent to and near the Airport and who can establish that they have been damaged as a result of noise from jet aircraft.

One of the defenses asserted by the defendant City is that the defendant has acquired an easement by prescription because aircraft has used the airspace above plaintiffs' properties for more than five years preceding the filing of the complaint, and that the use of this airspace has been open and notorious and adverse to any interests claimed or asserted by plaintiffs. There is a serious question of whether it is legally possible for an operator and owner of an airport to obtain an easement by prescription with respect to aircraft flights over an owner's land. It is generally held that an easement in the air may not be obtained by prescription. See Hinman v. Pacific Air Transport, 84 F.2d 755 (9 Cir. 1936). However, defendant City offered no evidence to support this defense, and the matter requires no further consideration.

Another defense urged by defendant City is that public convenience and necessity for more than five years preceding the filing of the complaint required, and still requires, the use of the airspace over and adjacent to the properties of plaintiffs for public aviation purposes. We all recognize that jet aircraft is a modern necessity and convenience for public travel. Some inconvenience, discomfort and annoyance from the noise of such aircraft must be borne and tolerated by citizens as a part of urban living. There is a limit, however, to the annoyance and damage from aircraft noise which residents must tolerate and bear without compensation. This limit is reached as to those property owners located in the vicinity of the flight paths of the landing and takeoff aircraft who suffer from jet aircraft noise out of proportion to other residents of the community who are inconvenienced and annoyed by jet aircraft noise. Public convenience and necessity cannot be permitted to justify the damaging, without compensation, of the property of persons living in close proximity to the landing and takeoff aircraft patterns. However, because of the great public convenience and necessity for jet aircraft and air travel, the public in general who benefit from the existence of jet aircraft and air travel must pay for this convenience and necessity through the compensation allowed to the few who are damaged by virtue of the chance selection of their place of abode.

It is the position of the defendant City that an award of compensation should carry with it the grant of an easement to the defendant City for jet aircraft flights as flyovers or flybys with respect to the particular parcel of real property. This result is dictated by the legislative recognition of such an easement found in section 1239.3 of the Code of Civil Procedure.

The question is raised, however, of whether such a flight easement in airspace is permanent so far as the damage to the property so affected is concerned. If the City is granted an easement as a result of compensation awarded to property owners, is there any recourse if the number of jet flights are increased or the character of the jet engines is changed so that the Effective Perceived Noise Level is increased, resulting in a further reduction in the market value of property over and above that found to exist by virtue of the judgment. The general law of easements would seem to have application in this situation. So long as the burden of the easement upon the property owner is not increased, there would be no basis for additional relief. However, if the property owner is able to establish that subsequent increases in the number of jet flights using the airspace or the character of the noise has changed so that there is a substantial increase in the Effective Perceived Noise Level, with a resulting further diminution in the market value of the affected property, the property owner should be entitled to recover the additional damage in such a case. The burden of proof would be upon the property owner to establish that there has been such an increase in the number of flights or a change in the character of the noise from factors in addition to, or separate from, the number of flights to justify a cause of action for additional damage. In this case, the award of compensation and the corresponding easement are determined for conditions existing in the year 1963.

AUTHOR'S NOTE

The U.S. Supreme Court held in *Laird v. Nelms* ___ U.S. ___ 92 S.Ct. 1899 (1972) that sonic boom damage caused by military aircraft was not actionable under the Federal Tort Claims Act where no negligence, misfeasance, or nonfeasance on the part of the Government was shown. Nor does a high-altitude flight constitute trespass.

VIRGINIANS FOR DULLES v. VOLPE
___F.Supp___(E.D.Vir. May, 26, 1972), 4 erc 1232
appeal pending

This suit is an action for injunctive and declaratory relief against a number of named defendants, but is basically against the Federal Aviation Administration (FAA) as operator of the Washington National Airport (WNA) and against the commercial airlines which operate jet aircraft at that airport. It involves alleged pollution from aircraft emissions and aircraft noise. Originally the complaint contained a request for damages and allegations of conspiracy and violation of the anti-trust laws. These have been withdrawn.

The complaint is prolix and it is difficult to determine upon just what theories plaintiffs rely; however, during pretrial proceedings and at trial the following surfaced as the main theories:

(1) That the actions of the FAA have been arbitrary, capricious and constitute an abuse of discretion and therefore relief is warranted under 5 U.S.C. §701, et seq. (Administrative Procedure Act).

(2) That the actions of the FAA violate both the procedural and substantive provisions of the National Environmental Policy Act of 1969, 42 U.S.C. §4321, et seq.

(3) That the actions of the FAA, acting through the defendant airlines, constitute a nuisance, depriving the plaintiffs of rights under the Fifth and Ninth Amendments to the United States Constitution.

Pursuant to the pretrial conference, the parties entered into a stipulation, which is attached to the original hereof and adopted as part of the Court's findings of fact. Also, by stipulation, affidavits of some experts and many lay witnesses for both plaintiffs and defendants were accepted in lieu of their live testimony. The direct testimony of nearly all expert witnesses was presented by written report, furnished in advance to opposing counsel, and those witnesses were then made available for cross-examination.

The suit was instituted as a class action. No formal determination has been made that it may be so maintained. The allegations of the class at the beginning of the complaint are immensely broad. The action cannot be maintained for such a class. It became apparent during trial that there are a number of persons defined as some of the named plaintiffs and as those persons whose affidavits were presented on behalf of the plaintiffs, who live or work in the vicinity of the WNA and the flight paths of jet aircraft approaching and departing therefrom, and who present a claim that activities at the airport annoy, inconvenience and disturb them to the point of interfering with the comfortable enjoyment of their life and property. To the extent that the complaint undertakes to state a class action on behalf of persons other than that group, the Court cannot say that the named parties are representative of the class, since in the opinion of the Court this is basically a private nuisance action in which specific injury must be shown. Obviously many members of the larger class originally alleged make no complaint of injury or are not injured. There are substantial questions of fact not common to a class broader than the named plaintiffs and affiants. Allowing intervention by the affiants is more feasible than proceeding as a class. Although the action must be stripped of its character as a class action, enough of the named plaintiffs have presented their claims to enable the Court to decide the issues presented. Those named plaintiffs individually present a justiciable claim so that the standing of other named plaintiffs is immaterial.

The complaint requests the ultimate and prompt phasing out of all jet aircraft operations from the airport; however, at trial the thrust of plaintiffs' claim was to so reduce such operations so that they would no longer interfere with their comfortable enjoyment of their life and property. This was to be accomplished by diversion of air traffic elsewhere, particularly to Dulles International Airport (Dulles) or Friendship

International Airport (Friendship), or both.

Evidence was adduced by the plaintiffs tending to show an evaluation of the airport in terms of a zone of environmental influence around WNA; adverse effects of noise on health; adverse effect of WNA on property values; measurements of noise at different locations on the ground; the advantages of expanding use at Dulles over modernization of WNA; under-utilization of Dulles at the expense of WNA; numerous violations of the voluntary curfew between 10:00 p.m. and 7:00 a.m.; the scheduling by the airlines of many flights (15 to 21) within a minute of 10:00 p.m., making it physically impossible to complete operations before the 10:00 p.m. curfew; numerous violations of the noise abatement procedures; futility of complaints to the FAA; interference with cultural, civic and personal use of property; and extreme annoyance and disturbance resulting from the noise of frequent and low flying jet aircraft.

From that evidence and the evidence of defendants the Court finds as follows:

A. That the NEF is a useful tool in planning, but is too imprecise for measuring, or even predicting with any degree of accuracy, the environmental impact on the community of aircraft noise or community response to that noise; that even using the NEF concept, the number of people within the NEF 30 contour around WNA is less than 3,000 and around Dulles more than 20,000;

B. That the evidence does not establish that noise from aircraft at WNA has any direct affect on the health of persons on the ground, health being defined as the absence of disease or infirmity;

C. That the evidence does not establish that noise from aircraft at WNA has an adverse effect on property values in the vicinity of the airport and the flight paths;

D. That the measurements conducted on the ground by Waters and Magrab are inconclusive, the samplings are unrepresentative, and in most instances the sounds measured were below the "threshold of annoyance" of 80 dBA;

E. That there has been adopted at WNA the following five limitations:

1. A noise abatement procedure which under normal conditions requires that jet aircraft departing WNA maintain takeoff power until an altitude of 1500 feet is reached, at which point aircraft flap settings are held constant and thrust reduced to a setting computed for hot day conditions at maximum cross takeoff weight to give approximately a 500 feet per minute climb. Unless otherwise directed by departure control the aircraft must follow the Potomac River. When landing and weather conditions permit the aircraft are directed to follow the natural flyways of the Potomac River and to remain at 3,000 feet or higher as long as possible;

2. A high density rule limiting the number of carrier operations (40 per hour) and the number of operations by general aviation (20 per hour);

3. A voluntary agreement between FAA and the defendant airlines forbidding the use of WNA by jet aircraft from 10:00 p.m. to 7:00 a.m.;

4. A perimeter restriction prohibiting scheduled non-stop service to and from points greater than 640 miles from Washington with the exception of seven grandfather cities;

5. Equipment restrictions applicable to jet aircraft using WNA;

F. That the violations *by the defendant airlines* of the voluntary curfew are the exception rather than the rule and are caused by scheduling practices, many of which are not completely within the control of the airlines but are dictated by customer preference, interrelation with schedules at other airports, weather and emergency conditions, and requirements of the U.S. Postal Service;

G. That violations of noise abatement procedures are minimal and are often caused by emergency or weather conditions; that operations to the south of the airport are guided in part by the necessity of avoiding Andrews Air Force base air traffic;

H. That there has been a good faith effort on the part of the airlines to comply with the above mentioned five limitations;

I. That community complaints, while often unsatisfactorily answered, have resulted in sincere efforts on behalf of the defendants to reduce noise levels emanating from the airport, specifically as represented by the above five limitations;

J. That noise from the airport has interfered with the use of the property of, and caused extreme annoyance and disturbance to, some of the named plaintiffs and those persons who have filed affidavits on behalf of the plaintiffs;

K. That, except for the 40 flight per hour density rule, these limitations are voluntary on the part of the airlines;

L. That there is a strong preference by the traveling public for WNA over Dulles; that there is a public interest to be served in having a short-haul airport convenient to downtown Washington, the Nation's Capital as well as a city of substantial size and business activity;

M. That scheduling is a complex matter which must accommodate competing interests such as impact on the community, economics of operation by the airlines, schedules at other airports, and convenience of the traveling public;

N. That any substantial diversion of jet aircraft from WNA would result in a severe economic setback to the region surrounding WNA;

O. That WNA is part of a national system of air transportation as well as a regional system involving Dulles and Friendship, and any substantial alteration of schedules or diversion of commercial jet aircraft would have a serious impact on both systems;

P. That Dulles will in the near future reach its planned capacity and will then be incapable of absorbing any major diversion of jet aircraft from WNA without expansion of its facilities;

Q. That the aircraft industry as a whole is working to reduce aircraft noise; that marked advancement in noise reduction had been achieved in the last few years, some of which are presently in use; and that technology resulting in substantially lower noise levels without appreciable adverse effects on nearby residents will be available in 1977 or 1978;

R. That there are persons, represented by affidavits presented on behalf of the defendants, living in the vicinity of WNA or under its flight paths whose enjoyment of life and property is not interfered with or disturbed by operations at WNA.

Plaintiffs put on their evidence on noise pollution first. When they undertook to offer evidence on the subject of pollution from air emissions, the defendants objected on the ground that federal regulations and laws have preempted the field of federal common law of nuisance from air emissions. 42 U.S.C. §§1857f-9 to 1857f-12. *Washington v. General Motors Corp.,* 40 U.S. L.W. 4437 (U.S. April 24, 1972); *Illinois v. City of Milwaukee,* 40 U.S. L.W. 4439 (U.S. April 24, 1972). Feeling that nuisance was the only real basis of relief for the plaintiffs, the Court sustained the objections.

Plantiffs' three theories will be treated in order:

(1) *Relief under the Administrative Procedure Act (APA).* The question to be determined here is whether there has been an abuse of discretion by the FAA or that its actions are arbitrary or capricious. While sensing a certain timidity on the part of the FAA in enforcing operational guidelines for the airlines at the airport, (the evidence shows not a single instance of a pilot being disciplined for violation of a voluntary or regulatory limitation) the evidence does establish that in setting those guidelines the agency based its action or inaction on a consideration of the relevant factors of the traveling public's convenience, fostering growth of aviation, transportation needs, environmental impact on the community and safety. WNA is envisaged as a short-haul airport; Dulles a long-haul

airport; and Friendship as a combination long-haul and short-haul airport. Whether or not the Court agrees with the agency actions in acquiescing in or not requiring more stringent rules than the five limitations enumerated above, the Court cannot say such action is a clear error of judgment warranting judicial relief under the APA. To enter this field would, in the Court's opinion, constitute a substitution of the Court's judgment for that of the agency, a substitution for which the Court has neither the expertise, the inclination, nor the right. On the question of the pervasiveness of federal regulation in the area of the 40 flight per hour density rule see *Lockheed Air Terminal, Inc. v. City of Burbank,* ___ F.2d ___ (9th Cir., March 22, 1972).

Accordingly, relief under the APA is denied.

(2) *The National Environmental Policy Act (NEPA).* The principal argument of the plaintiffs here is that the ongoing and future activities at WNA violate the declared public policy of the act that federal agencies minimize adverse effects upon the national environment and protect and preserve the same "to the fullest extent possible." More specifically plaintiffs say that introduction of the Boeing 727-200 jets, the so-called "stretch" jets, at WNA in 1968 was a "major action" requiring an environmental impact statement under §102 (2) (C) of the Act.

Insofar as the ongoing and future activities are concerned, the Court feels, at this stage certainly, they are outside the requirements of NEPA. The airport has certainly reached that stage of completion that "the costs already incurred" in adopting and using it as a commercial jet airport "so outweigh the benefits of altering or abandoning" it as such that "no feasible and prudent alternative to the use" would exist. *Arlington Coalition v. Volpe,* ___ F.2d ___ (4th Cir., April 4, 1972). No case has yet held that NEPA's requirements apply to such an ongoing project, and this Court is unwilling to so hold. Moreover, I do not interpret §101 of the Act as creating any substantive private right.

Virginians for Dulles v. Volpe

The Court concludes that the introduction of the "stretch" jets into WNA in 1968 was not a "major action" as that term is used in §102 (2) (c). It bases this conclusion on its findings that the difference between the 727-200 (stretch jet) and 727-100 (the stretch jet's predecessor) is minimal insofar as "affecting the quality of human environment" is concerned. While it is fifteen to twenty feet longer and can carry 120 passengers as opposed to 98 for the 727-100, it is quieter, safer and rarely if ever loaded to a gross maximum weight greater than that of the 727-100. Moreover, the testimony establishes that a bigger aircraft does not, of itself, create more passenger traffic.

(3) *Fifth and Ninth Amendment right violations and nuisance.* These are treated together by the plaintiffs. They argue that injury to health (in violation of due process clause of Fifth Amendment) and the right or privacy and right not to be personally injured (Ninth Amendment) are involved here, as distinguished from the nuisance cases where only injury to property is at issue, and that consequently the doctrine of balancing of equities is inapplicable. Plantiffs apply the proscription of these Amendments to the airlines because, they say, the airlines are the instrumentality by which the FAA creates a nuisance; and the airlines, through strict regulation by the FAA and civil Aeronautics Board, have become, in effect, instrumentalities of the United States.

Plaintiffs would ideally define health in the euphoric terms of the World Health Organization - "A state of complete physical, mental, and social well-being, and not merely the absence of disease or infirmity." Realistically, however, they offered evidence of physical disease and infirmity being causally connected to the noise from WNA. This evidence, *insofar as it relates to the type of noise here perceived,* i.e., *on-the-ground noise from aircraft over-flights,* falls far short of a preponderance and does not persuade the Court. The noise is annoying, however. Even discounting to an extent some of the testimony because of possible oversensitivity of some witnesses, it is extremely annoying to and genuinely interferes with the comfortable enjoyment of the property of that segment of the population represented by some of the named plaintiffs and by those who have filed affidavits and who live in the vicinity of WNA and its flight paths.

The Court does not find that property values in those areas have declined as a result of airport operations. The expert on this subject, Gill, gave completely conclusory testimony in this regard, without any supporting facts or testimony showing comparisons with other areas uninfluenced by an airport. The lay witness, Madison, had actually made a profit on the sale of her home of approximately $4,720 within ten months.

Testimony was presented by the plaintiffs, through Dr. Dorn McGrath, a land use planner, concerning a zone of environmental influence surrounding WNA. He undertook to measure this by means of a standard called Noise Exposure Forecast (NEF), a computerized area arrived at after input of such things as frequency of flights, trip lengths, angles of descent and take-off, and time of day of flights. Within certain contour areas he testified certain community response could be predicted. While the NEF may be useful as a planning tool, there are too many variables left out of the input to make it sufficiently accurate for use in a court of law as a predictor of community response to noise.

The testimony that Dulles is under-utilized at this time may well have merit, although the testimony indicates that it is near its capacity at which time it will be unable to absorb any major diversion from WNA. This avenue of solving any problem at WNA, however, merely transfers the problem to somebody else's back yard. Forecasts indicate that in the near future the area around Dulles will be as impacted as that around WNA, and without the benefit of being partially surrounded by water as is the case at WNA. The area occupied by water around WNA is an area which might well be occupied by residences.

Virginians for Dulles v. Volpe

Plaintiffs presented no case of specific personal injury causally related to noise from WNA. Absent this and absent a finding of generalized injury to health or property from such noise, no Fifth or Ninth Amendment claim is, in the opinion of the Court, present. Plaintiffs concede that this would be the first court to sustain the contention that the Ninth Amendment (right of privacy or right to be free from injury) protects persons from noise. This circuit has declined the invitation to elevate to constitutional level the concerns for protection of the environment. *Ely v. Velde,* 451 F.2d 1130, 1139 (4th Cir., 1971).

Contrary to plaintiffs' position, the Court feels this is a case where balancing of the equities is applicable. Taking into account what the Court feels to be the relevant factors of traveling public convenience and service; economic impact on the community and on the airlines; the position of WNA in the whole scheme of national transportation; the environmental impact on the community; safety; and the position of aviation as a means of public transportation, relief must be denied the plaintiffs. Burdensome as it may be, plaintiffs must submit to the great annoyance in the public interest, an annoyance which is no more than that felt by that segment of the public which lives adjacent to other methods of public transportation, such as the heavily traveled interstate highway or frequently-used railroad track.

Moreover, there are other obstacles to relief for the plaintiffs. If, as the Supreme Court has said, albeit by dicta, in *Washington v. General Motors Corp., supra,* and *Illinois v. City of Milwaukee, supra,* federal regulations and laws have preempted the federal common law of nuisance so far as *emissions* from airplanes are concerned, the regulations and laws are at least as pervasive in the field of aircraft *noise.* 49 U.S.C. §1431, 14 CFR Part 36. Surely the Administrator under that law will consider frequency of flights and duration of noise as well as noise levels themselves. In addition, it is extremely doubtful whether, under the doctrine announced in *Larson v. Domestic & Foreign Commerce Corp.,* 337 U.S. 682 (1949), and *Ferris v. Wilbur,* 27 F.2d 262 (4th Cir., 1928), an injunction can be awarded against the FAA in the exercise of what is here its discretionary functions.

The Complaint is dismissed; and it is so ordered.

SMITH v. PETERSON

230 Pacif Rptr. 2d 522 (4th Dist. Ct. of Appeal, Calif. 1955)

GRIFFIN, Justice. **[Edited]**

This proceeding involves the constitutionality of sections 673 and 684 of the Vehicle Code in reference to the prevention of excessive or unusual noises from mufflers on automobiles. These sections read in part as follows:

> §673. Every motor vehicle subject to registration and operated on a highway shall at all times be equipped with an adequate muffler in constant operation and properly maintained to prevent any excessive or unusual noise and no such muffler or exhaust system shall be equipped with a cut-out, by-pass, or similar device. No person shall modify the exhaust system of a motor vehicle in a manner which will amplify or increase the noise emitted by the motor of such vehicle above that emitted by the muffler originally installed on the vehicle and such original muffler shall comply with all of the requirements of this section * * *"
>
> "§684. It shall be unlawful for any person to sell, lease, install or replace, either for himself or as the agent or employee of another, or through such agent or employee, any * * * muffler, exhaust, * * * for use in any vehicle, * * * that is not in conformity with the provisions of this code or the regulations made thereunder."

Plaintiffs, Robert D. Smith, transacting business as Advance Muffler Company, and Forrest W. Ricks, its agent operating in Fresno, allege that the California Highway Patrol Commissioner, and other officers, periodically and frequently arrested them and their customers for installing, selling and replacing mufflers upon various motor vehicles in violation of these sections; that plantiffs were so arrested on a complaint filed in Fresno Municipal Court on December 18, 1952, charging them with the "sale or installation of unlawful equipment * * * mufflers"; that they have suffered great detriment and expense in defending said actions, posting bail, etc.; and that the trial of the above mentioned action was continued for trial at a later date. A restraining order was sought restraining the officers from enforcing or attempting to enforce the provisions of these sections.

It is also alleged that plaintiffs, for approximately 13 years, have been engaged in the business of manufacturing and installing mufflers, etc., particularly their "Advance Steel Pack muffler", and that they have been manufactured, sold and installed on cars throughout the state. It is then claimed that these mufflers do not make any excessive or unusual noise, do not annoy the public, and that it is impossible for plaintiffs to know whether these exhaust pipes will amplify or increase the noise emitted by the motors of the vehicles upon which they are installed above that emitted by the mufflers originally installed thereon, and that accordingly these sections violate the Constitution of the United States and of California in the following particulars, i.e., that these sections are discriminatory and violate plaintiffs' right of equal protection of the laws and deprive them of their property and their liberty without due process of law, and their right to follow a lawful occupation; that these sections are uncertain, indefinite and vague in that no reasonable standard is set up; that they interfere with the rights of plaintiffs to dispose of their property in a lawful manner and to make a lawful contract; that they tend to create a monopoly for the benefit of the manufacturer of mufflers originally installed on vehicles; that they are arbitrary, capricious, unreasonable and confiscatory; that the acts alleged in these sections are made criminal acts of the plaintiffs although such acts are performed by other persons; and that under the provisions of said sections, if plaintiffs installed such mufflers in compliance with said sections they could be held guilty even though the operator of said vehicle otherwise created excessive or unusual noises by the *operation* of said vehicle.

Section 673, as reasonably construed, fixes a standard of all originally installed mufflers in this, that they must "comply with all of the requirements of this section". This section requires that they must be "effective in reducing noise" and be "an adequate muffler" so as to "prevent any excessive or unusual noise", and not be equipped with a cut-out, by-pass, or similar device. It thus provides that every motor vehicle operated on the highway shall, at all times, be so equipped and maintained in constant operation. It then provides that no person shall modify the *exhaust system* (which includes placing a muffler thereon) in a manner which will amplify or increase the noise emitted by such vehicle above that emitted by the muffler originally installed on the vehicle. In fixing the original standard it must be presumed that at the time of the original installation of the muffler there was a compliance with the law in its installation, and that the vehicle was equipped with an adequate muffler so as to prevent any "excessive or unusual noise". Section 684 then makes it unlawful for a person, either for himself or as agent for another, to sell, lease, install or replace any muffler or exhaust that is not in conformity with the provisions of that section. We see no justification for the conclusion that plaintiff might be criminally liable for the operation of a vehicle by another with a defective muffler if plaintiffs installed or replaced a muffler that complied with said section 673.

It was the conclusion of the trial court, expressed in the memorandum opinion, that by the descriptive words "excessive" or "unusual" noise, the noise emitting from such muffler may appear to be excessive or unusual to one and may not be excessive or unusual to another; that accordingly the only standard fixed would be the opinion of the law-enforcing officer; and that a more definite and better standard than that fixed in the section, as to noise, should be employed such as the standard of measuring sound or noise in decibels. It concluded that the provisions of section 684, supra, insofar as it attempts to provide enforcement of section 673 of the Vehicle Code, are unconstitutional and unenforceable, and accordingly restrained defendants from enforcing them against plaintiffs.

It is defendant's position here [is] that these sections are not vague, indefinite or uncertain and that at the time of their enactment they provided for the only reasonable standard upon which they could operate fairly and without discrimination.

It is well settled that a criminal statute which is so indefinite, vague and uncertain that the definition of the crime or standard of conduct cannot be ascertained therefrom, is unconstitutional and void. However, there is a uniformity of opinion among the authorities that a statute will not be held void for uncertainty if any reasonable and practical construction can be given to its language. Nor does the fact that its meaning is difficult to ascertain or susceptible of different interpretations render the statute void. All presumptions and intendments favor the validity of a statute and mere doubt does not afford sufficient reason for a judicial declaration of invalidity. Statutes must be upheld unless their unconstitutionality clearly, positively and unmistkably appears. Doubts as to its construction will not justify us in disregarding it. In determining whether a penal statute is sufficiently explicit to inform those who are subject to it what is required of them the courts must endeavor, if possible, to view the statute from the standpoint of the reasonable man who might be subject to its terms. It is not required that a statute, to be valid, have that degree of exactness which inheres in a mathematical theorem. It is not necessary that a statute furnish detailed plans and specifications of the acts or conduct prohibited. The requirement of reasonable certainty does not preclude the use of ordinary terms to express ideas which find adequate interpretation in common usage and understanding.

The case of Department of Public Safety v. Buck, Tex. Civ. App., 1953, 256 S.W.2d 642, is directly in point on this question and the statute there involved is quite identical to the California statute. It provided that "Every motor vehicle must have devices in good working order which shall at all times be in constant operation to prevent excessive or unusual noises

* * *. Every motor vehicle shall at all times be equipped with a muffler in good working order and in constant operation to prevent excessive or unusual noise and annoying smoke * * *." Vernon's Ann. P.C. art. 797, Vernon's Ann. Civ.St. art. 6701d, §134(a). The constitutionality of that statute was attacked on the ground that the use of the words "excessive" or "unusual" was vague and uncertain and did not set forth an adequate standard of conduct. The trial court there, as here, issued an injunction on that ground. In reversing the judgment of the trial court it said: "We think any ordinary and interested person would have no difficulty in determining whether or not an excessive and unusual noise or offensive or excessive exhaust fumes accompanied the operation of a motor vehicle." It held that the meaning of the term "excessive" is to be determined in the light of, and with reference to, the cause of action asserted, and, as applied to the operators of motor vehicles, it is to be interpreted as descriptive " 'of the evil or mischief intended to be prohibited'." It then cites Webster's New International Dictionary, Second Edition, as giving the full definition of the word "excessive", i.e., " 'Characterized by, or exhibiting excess, as: a. Exceeding what is usual or proper; over much. b. Greater than the usual amount or degree; exceptional, very great.' The word 'unusual' simply means not usual, uncommon." It cites Omaechevarria v. State of Idaho, 246 U.S. 343, 38 S.Ct. 323, 62 L.Ed. 763, for the general statement that men familiar with actual conditions and desirous of observing the law will have little difficulty in determining what is prohibited.

Smith v. Peterson

In Kovacs v. Cooper, 336 U.S. 77, 69 S.Ct. 448, 449, 93 L.Ed. 513, 10 A.L.R. 2d 608, cited and discussed in Haggerty v. Associated Farmers of California, Inc., 44 Cal.2d ___, 279 P.2d 734, 735, the court upheld an ordinance which declared it unlawful for any person to use or operate on the public streets any device which emits "loud and raucous" noises. The objection centered around the use of the words "loud and raucous". The court said while these are abstract words, they have, through daily use, acquired a content that conveys to any interested person a sufficiently accurate concept of what is forbidden; that every motor vehicle, when in normal operation, necessarily makes some noise, makes some smoke, and permits gas or steam to escape to some extent; that they are in constant operation on our streets and highways; and even in the sparsely settled areas of our state they are in constant operation in view of the citizens.

The Haggerty case, supra, involved an anti-noise ordinance making unlawful the emission or transmission of " 'any loud and raucous' " noise upon a public highway, etc. It then endeavored to define " 'loud and raucous' " noise as any noise made by the motor of a vehicle " 'not reasonably required in the operation thereof * * *' " including " 'backfiring, motor racing' " etc., and the human voice " 'when amplified by any device * * * to such an extent as to cause it to carry on to private property or to be heard by others using the public highways' " and any sound of such volume " 'as to tend to interfere with the peace and quiet of persons' " thereon. The majority court cited the Kovacs case, supra, where it is said that "this ordinance", involving the emission of sound from a truck by means of a sound amplifier or any instrument which emits " 'loud and raucous noises' " is an exercise of the authority granted to the state of New Jersey " 'to prevent disturbing noises * * * nuisances well within the municipality's power to control.' " It then held that the ordinance was a proper regulation of the conduct of all persons seeking to use such devices and that the restrictions are uniformly applicable; that it was a reasonable one; that the term loud and raucous noise was not so vague and indefinite as to establish no ascertainable standard of guilt; and approved the ordinance in the Kovacs case in this respect and the statement that "while these are abstract words, they have, through daily use acquired a content that conveys to any interested person a sufficiently accurate concept of what is forbidden".

Attack was similarly made in the Haggerty case upon clause one which included noise "of 'the motor * * * *not reasonably required* in the operation thereof under the circumstances,'" was too vague and indefinite a standard of guilt. Many cases are there cited which our Supreme Court discussed and said:

> "These cases, however, involve loose definitions in fields where generally there may be great differences of opinion as to what conduct may be reasonable. A restriction upon the operation of motor vehicles so as to eliminate unreasonable noises operated in an area where a determination as to what is necessary and reasonable may be made more precisely and has a content of fairly fixed meaning to operators of such vehicles. More nearly in point are prohibitions against 'unreasonable and unsafe speed' * * * and the use of horns emitting 'an unreasonably loud or harsh sound'." Citing vehicle Code sec. 671.

Smith v. Peterson

The terms of the ordinance defining noises which "interfere" and "tend to interfere" with the "peace and quiet" of persons were also similarly challenged. This was held to be a sufficient standard of definiteness.

It appears to us that the requirement that a motor vehicle be equipped with a muffler in constant operation so as to prevent any excessive or unusual noise seems as certain as any rule which could be practically enforced. Motor vehicles have been used so long and have become so common, and mufflers so uniformly used to minimize the noise from their exhaust that what is usual has become a matter of common knowledge, and anything in excess of that is excessive and unusual, and usually capable of ascertainment as such. It may be that physicists have established definite standards of loudness of sound and means for measuring it, but this does not mean that such laboratory operations must be carried out by traffic officers on the highway where violators of this statute must be found and the evidence against them obtained. The tendency of the recent decisions is toward a more liberal construction of the rule requiring certainty. The sections here involved have been on the statute books in substantially the same form since 1913. The standard there defined has since been applied. The mere fact that there may have been some new scientific instrument capable of measuring noise more scientifically would not make the statute unconstitutional.

We conclude that the words "excessive" or "unusual", when viewed in the context in which they are used are sufficiently certain to inform persons of ordinary intelligence of the nature of the offense which is prohibited, and are therefore sufficient to establish a standard of conduct which is ascertainable by persons familiar with the operation of automobiles.

In view of the conclusions here reached and from the decisions cited, the other claimed reasons advanced why the sections are unconstitutional are equally untenable.

Order reversed.

BARNARD, P. J., and MUSSELL, J., concur.
Hearing denied; CARTER, J., dissenting.

Pending Federal legislation

Much of the problem in the aircraft noise area and increasingly in other areas of growing Federal activity such as highway noise and industrial noise stems from the lack of a Federal abatement scheme based on noise limit standards enforceable by Federal officials and, ideally, also by private citizen actions.

At publication time in July of 1972 such legislation was pending, having been approved by the Senate Public Works Subcommittee and the House (H.R. 11021). Under the House version the Administrator of EPA would promulgate, within two years of enactment of the Act, noise emission standards applicable over the useful life of the product for each new product which is:

1) identified by the Administrator as "a major source of noise" (based on reports and studies during the first 18 months of the Act) and

2) falls into one of the following categories:

a) construction equipment
b) transportation equipment
c) any motor or engine
d) electric or electronic equipment.

These standards would be enforceable by the Federal government or by any person after he has notified the Federal government of the violation and given it 60 days to commence its own action. Intervention as a matter of right is reserved to both. Citizen suits in Federal court are not constrained by the diversity of citizenship or the amount in controversy requirements of the present U.S. Code under the proposed legislation. The Administrator of EPA would be able to access fines of up to $25,000 for each violation of the noise emissions standards and enforce these fines through civil actions. Wilful violations can lead to criminal penalties of $25,000 per day of violation and or imprisonment for up to one year.

The legislation preempts state and local noise abatement via the emissions standard technique when the Administrator has prescribed a standard covering the product in question but reserves to states and local governments the authority to control, regulate or restrict the use, operation, or movement of any product. This presently remains a very confusing area and many feel that there is considerable overlap between emissions standards and control of use, operation, or movement of noise sources.

The Senate version includes new sections on emergency situations, judicial review, federal procurement, railroad emission standards, and motor carrier emission standards, See *Environment Reporter,* "Current Developments," Vol. 3 No. 8, June 23, 1972 at 243.

NOTE ON ADDITIONAL SOURCES OF INFORMATION

For further technical information, see FRANKEN, Peter, and PAGE, Daniel, "Noise in the Environment," Environmental Science & Technology, Vol. 6, No. 2, February 1972.

For studies on acoustics and the indoor environment, see Architectural & Engineering News, Vol. 12, No. 2, February 1970. The entire issue is devoted to the subject. Of special interest to lawyers is the article by Kenneth C. STEWART at 40 discussing safety and health noise standards that apply to industries with contracts of more than $10,000 with the Federal Government. (Walsh-Healey Act as amended)

For a discussion of the use of plants to absorb noise, see Forest Service Research Bulletin No. 246, GPO.

See also The Economic Impact of Noise, a report for the Environmental Protection Agency, Dec. 31, 1971, GPO. Noise Assessment Guidelines, HEW, Aug. 1971, GPO.

ORDER-OF-MAGNITUDE ESTIMATES OF EXPOSURE TO HOME APPLIANCE AND BUILDING EQUIPMENT NOISE EXPRESSED IN MILLIONS OF PERSON-HOURS PER WEEK

Noise Source	Speech Interference*		Sleep Interference*		Hearing Damage Risk	
	Moderate	Severe	Slight	Moderate	Slight	Moderate
Group I: Quiet Major Equipment and Appliances						
Fans	1200		0		0	
Air Conditioner	242		121		0	
Clothes Dryer	94		10		0	
Humidifier	10		15		0	
Freezer	0		0		0	
Refrigerator	0		0		0	
Group II: Quiet Equipment and and Small Appliances						
Plumbing (Faucets, Toilets)		535	267		0	
Dishwasher		461	4		0	
Vacuum Cleaner		280	0.5		0	
Electric Food Mixer		222	1		0	
Clothes Washer		215	0.5		0	
Electric Can Opener		117	0.2		0	
Electric Knife		1	0.1		0	
Group III: Noisy Small Appliances						
Sewing Machine		19		0.5	9	
Electric Shaver		6		1	5	
Food Blender		2		0.2	0.5	
Electric Lawn Mower		1		1	0.3	
Food Disposer		0.5		0.5	0.5	
Group IV: Noisy Electric Tools						
Home Shop Tools		5		2		1
Electric Yard Care Tools		1.5		1		0.4

*These figures are not directly interpretable in terms of person-hours of lost sleep or speech interference (see text).

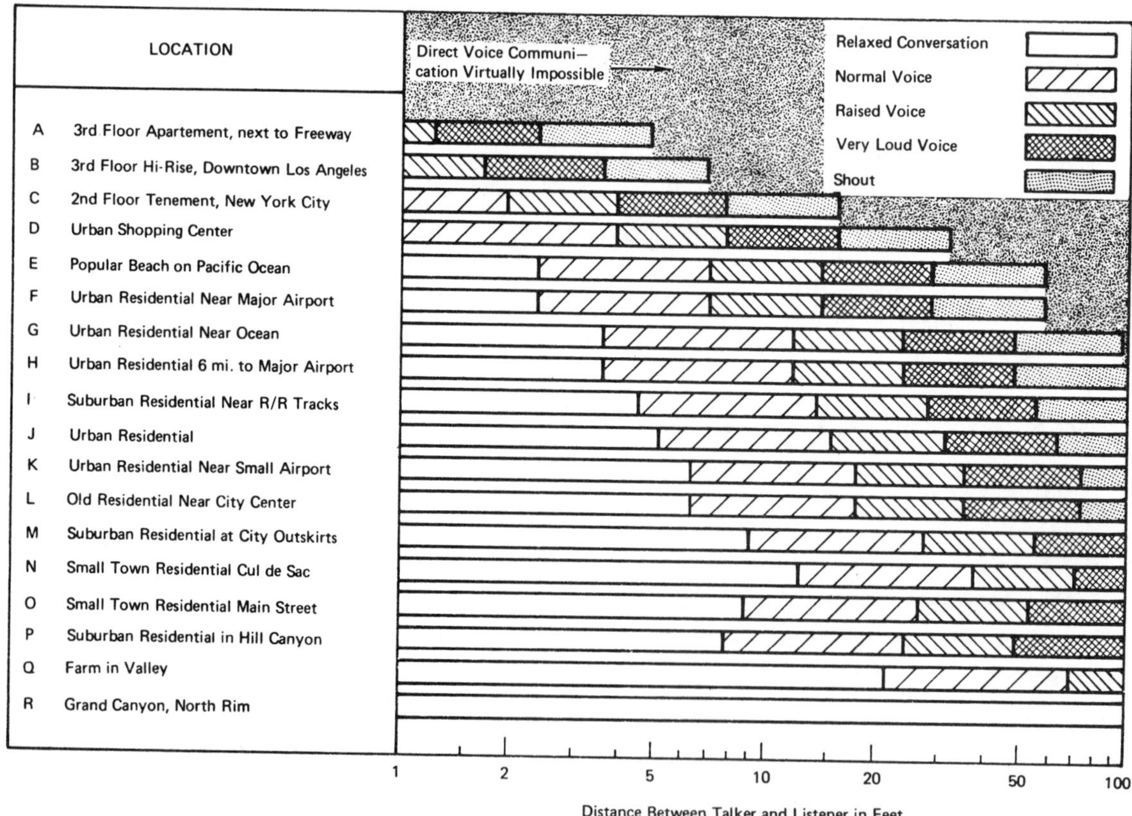

Estimated Maximum Distances Between Talker and Listener That Permit Intelligible Conversation and Those That Enable Relaxed Conversation When the Outdoor Noise Level Equals the Daytime Median Noise Level.

SOURCE: Report to the President and Congress on Noise, GPO, 1972.

APPENDIX—Chapter Three-B

SAMPLE COMPLAINT

IN THE UNITED STATES DISTRICT COURT
FOR THE DISTRICT OF COLUMBIA

CIVIL ACTION NO. ________

VIRGINIANS FOR DULLES
By Clive L. Duval, 2d, Chairman
P. O. Box 7081
Arlington, Virginia 22207 **Plaintiff**
vs.

JOHN VOLPE, Individually and as
Secretary of Transportation
Washington, D. C.
and
JOHN SHAFFER, Individually and as
Administrator, Federal Aviation
Administration
Washington, D. C. **Defendants**

NOTE: This complaint is not that of the case immediately preceding this, although the subject matter is related.

COMPLAINT
FOR INJUNCTIVE RELIEF

JURISDICTION

1. This action arises under Title 42, United States Code, §4321 *et seq.* (Public Law 91-190, 83 Stat. 852, known as the National Environmental Policy Act of 1969):

> The purposes of this Act are: To declare a national policy which will encourage productive enjoyable harmony between man and his environment; to promote efforts which will prevent or eliminate damage to the environment and biosphere and stimulate the health and welfare of man; to enrich the understanding of the ecological systems and natural resources important to the nation; and to establish a council on environmental quality.

2. Jurisdiction of this Court is invoked under Title 23, United States Code, §1361:

> The district courts shall have original jurisdiction of any action in the nature of mandamus to compel an officer or employee of the United States or any agency thereof to perform a duty owed to the plaintiff.

3. Jurisdiction of this Court is also invoked under Title 28, United States Code, §1331:

> The district courts shall have original jurisdiction of all civil actions wherein the matter in controversy exceeds the sum or value of $10,000, exclusive of interest and costs, and arises under the Constitution, laws, or treaties of the United States.

4. Jurisdiction of this Court is also invoked under the Administrative Procedures Act, Title 5, United States Code, §§551-576, §§701-706.

5. This action also arises under Executive Order No. 11514, "Protection and Enhancement of Environmental Quality," March 5, 1970.

PARTIES

6. Virginians for Dulles was organized in 1967 and has been in the forefront of the efforts to promote a rational use of the airports in the Washington/Baltimore area. It is composed of hundreds of residents of Northern Virginia living in an area stretching from Mount Vernon to Great Falls. Membership is drawn from fifty different neighborhoods.

7. John Volpe is the Secretary of the Department of Transportation.

8. John Shaffer is the Administrator of the Federal Aviation Administration, Department of Transportation. The Federal Government owns National and Dulles and the FAA is charged with the responsibility of operating them. These two airports are the only airports in the country run by the FAA and not owned by the local community.

FACTS

9. Washington National Airport (hereinafter National) is owned by the Federal Government and operated by the Federal Aviation Administration (hereinafter FAA). It opened in 1941 on its present site, a 761 acre enclave on the west bank of the Potomac, located in the midst of a densely populated area. Surrounded on three sides by water, National is severely restricted as to ground access. Access is possible by only two highways (George Washington Memorial Parkway and Jefferson Davis Highway), both of which are presently clogged by non-airport traffic during the hours of principal demand for air travel.

10. Dulles International Airport (hereinafter Dulles) is owned by the Federal Government and operated by the FAA. It opened November 19, 1962, as a 10,000 acre facility designated, situated, zoned and built to accommodate all varieties of jet aircraft with the minimum of disturbance to the surrounding population and environment. It is located in Loudoun and Fairfax Counties in the State of Virginia, 26 miles from the District of Columbia.

11. As landlord of National, the FAA has the authority to determine the number and type of aircraft that use the airport and the hours during which planes may arrive and depart National.

12. The FAA had limited the hours during which jet aircraft could land and take off from National to between 7:00 a.m. and 10:00 p.m. The FAA had granted the airlines a one hour grace period whereby flights scheduled to land and take off at National before 10:00 p.m. were allowed to do so until 11:00 p.m. Before the air traffic controllers "sick out" of March–April, 1970, planes were diverted to other airports if they were unable to land at National before 11:00 p.m.

13. During the air traffic controllers "sick-out" the Administrator of the FAA, without any public hearing or notice, relaxed this 11:00 p.m. deadline and allowed flights to land at National throughout the night.

14. The Administrator of the FAA has continued this policy and gives every indication that it will continue in the future.

15. Each airline using National signs a lease agreement with the FAA. This lease agreement provides that the Director of the Bureau of National Capital Airports (hereinafter BNCA) (formerly the branch of the FAA that operated National) could limit ". . . the number and types of aircraft operations . . ." using National, taking into account in making this decision ". . . the adequacy and suitability of the aircraft and passenger handling facilities at the Airport, and the availability and suitability of other air carrier airports serving the Washington metropolitan area."

16. Because of National's limited facilities and its peculiarly sensitive location, the FAA has prohibited the airlines from using four (4) engine jets at National.

17. The FAA also had prohibited the Boeing 727-200 (frequently called a "stretch jet") from operating at National. The Boeing 727-200 is a longer, heavier aircraft capable of carrying more passengers than the Boeing 727.

18. Since 1966 representatives of the FAA have made numerous public pronouncements that the Boeing 727-200 would not be allowed into National.

19. In private correspondence and in testimony before Congressional committees, both the Director of the BNCA and the Administrator of the FAA have repeatedly assured members of Congress that the Boeing 727-200 would not be allowed into National.

20. On April 9, 1970, during the air traffic controllers "sick-out" the Administrator of the FAA did allow the Boeing 727-200 into National.

21. The FAA allowed the introduction of the Boeing 727-200 into National without notifying the public or soliciting the comments of other Federal agencies as they are required to do by §102(2)(C) of the National Environmental Policy Act of 1969 (hereinafter NEPA). NEPA requires the filing of an environmental impact statement (frequently called a §102 Statement) before a Federal agency takes "any major federal action significantly affecting the human environment."

22. The FAA allowed the Boeing 727-200 into National despite warnings of members of Congress that their introduction would have deleterious environmental effects.

23. Studies by FAA and BNCA experts as well as a study prepared by the National Capital Planning Commission advised against the decision to introduce the Boeing 727-200 into National.

24. The FAA did not prepare an environmental impact statement on the effects of the introduction of the Boeing 727-200 into National as they were required to do by §102(2)(C) of NEPA nor have they today prepared such a statement.

25. In February 1971, the FAA released a report prepared by FAA personnel entitled "Analysis of Boeing 727-200 Operations at Washington National Airport." The FAA did not indicate that this report was in lieu of an environmental impact statement nor did the report meet the requirements of an environmental impact statement.

26. *Executive Order 11514:* In Executive Order 11514 dated March 5, 1970, the President directed that Federal agencies ". . . shall initiate measures needed to direct their policies, plans and programs so as to meet national environmental goals." Section 2 directed that Federal agencies shall ". . . develop programs and measures to protect and enhance environmental quality . . ."

27. *Interim Guidelines of Council on Environmental Quality:* On April 30, 1970, the Council of Environmental Quality (hereinafter CEQ) issued Interim Guidelines which Federal departments and agencies were to be guided by in the preparation of environmental statements on ". . . major Federal actions significantly affecting the quality of the human environment as required by Section 102(2)(C) of the National Environmental Policy Act . . . ."

28. Section 5(b) of the Interim Guidelines provides: "Proposed actions the environmental impact of which is likely to be highly controversial should be covered in all cases."

29. Numerous citizens in the Washington, D.C. area had for years complained about the noise and disturbance of late jet flights into National. The Administrator of the FAA was aware that allowing planes to land at National past the 11:00 p.m. deadline would disturb local citizens and result in a loud public outcry.

sample complaint

30. In failing to prepare an environmental impact statement on (1) the effects of the introduction of the Boeing 727-200 into National and (2) the relaxing of the 11:00 p.m. deadline, the FAA has violated NEPA and CEQ's Interim Guidelines.

31. *Department of Transportation Order 5610.1:* Department of Transportation (hereinafter DOT) Order 5610.1 dated October 7, 1970, ". . . outlines procedures for the Department of Transportation regarding the preparation of detailed environmental statements on proposals for legislation and other major Federal actions significantly affecting the quality of the human environment, as required by Section 102(2)(C) of the National Environmental Policy Act of 1969 (P.L. 91-190) . . . ."

32. Section 2b of the Order provides: "Section 102(2)(C) of the National Environmental Policy Act is designed to ensure that environmental considerations are given careful attention and appropriate weight in all decisions of the Federal Government." The FAA in its decision to introduce the Boeing 727-200 and to relax the 11:00 p.m. deadline did not give adequate consideration to environmental factors.

33. Section 1 of the Definitional Guidelines of DOT Order 5610.1 provides: "When there is doubt whether or not to prepare a statement it should be prepared. Where the environmental consequences of a proposed action are unclear but potentially significant, a statement should be prepared."

34. The environmental consequences of the introduction of the Boeing 727-200 and the relaxing of the 11:00 p.m. deadline are "potentially significant."

35. "Federal Actions" as defined under the Order include: a. "Direct Federal programs, projects and administrative activities, such as: (3) construction of and operation of Federal facilities."

36. National Airport is a federal facility established by an Act of Congress and operated by a federal agency.

37. Section 4(a) lists those actions which ". . . should be considered significant and a statement should be prepared:"

> d(a)(1) "any action that is likely to be highly controversial on environmental grounds"

38. The environmental impact and effects of the introduction of the Boeing 727-200 into National and a relaxation of the 11:00 p.m. deadline had been highly controversial for several years.

39. Section 4(b) lists these actions which are likely to be significant:

> 4(b)(1) lead to a noticeable change in the ambient noise level for a substantial number of people

4(b)(3) divide or disrupt an established community . . .

4(b)(4) lead to significantly increased air or water pollution in a given area

The introduction of the Boeing 727-200 into National and the relaxation of the deadline have had effects similar to those described in sections 4(b)(1), 4(b)(3), and 4(b)(4).

40. *Final Guidelines of Council on Environmental Quality:* On April 23, 1971, CEQ issued Final Guidelines to aid Federal agencies in the preparation of environmental impact statements.

41. Section 3 of CEQ's Final Guidelines refers to Section 2(f) of Executive Order 11514 which directs heads of Federal agencies to proceed with measures required by section 102(2)(C) of the Act. CEQ has directed Federal agencies in consultation with CEQ to establish by July 1, 1971, those formal procedures which will allow them to meet the requirements of NEPA.

42. The FAA in their operation of National and Dulles has not established procedures to be followed in meeting the requirements of NEPA.

43. Section 5 of the Final Guidelines lists the criteria to be employed ". . . by agencies in deciding whether proposed action requires the preparation of an environmental statement." "Actions" include but are not limited to: (ii) Projects and continuing activities directly undertaken by Federal agencies . . ."

sample complaint

44. Section 4 included the requirement as did the Interim Guidelines that proposed projects with a controversial environmental impact should always be covered by an environmental statement.

45. Despite the FAA's awareness of the intense public controversy over the effects of the introduction of the Boeing 727-200 and the relaxation of the deadline it failed to prepare an environmental statement.

46. In failing to prepare an environmental statement on the effects of the introduction of the Boeing 727-200 and relaxation of the deadline, the FAA has failed to comply with NEPA and CEQ's Final Guidelines.

REQUEST FOR RELIEF

The plaintiff asks that the Court issue an Order:

1. Ordering the FAA to establish formal procedures which pertain specifically to the operations of National and Dulles airports, as directed by §2(f) of Executive Order 11514 and CEQ's Final Guidelines in order to meet the requirements of NEPA.

2. Ordering the FAA to immediately prohibit the Boeing 727-200 from landing at National until it shall have filed a final statement as required by §102(2)(C) of NEPA as to the environmental impact of the introduction of the Boeing 727-200 into National.

3. Ordering the FAA to immediately prohibit jet planes from arriving and departing National after 11:00 p.m. until it shall have filed a statement as required by §102(2)(C) of NEPA as to the environmental impact of the relaxation of the 11:00 p.m. deadline at National.

4. Ordering such further relief which equity requires.

VIRGINIANS FOR DULLES
By Clive L. Duval, 2d, Chairman

By Counsel

Counsel for Plaintiff

COHEN AND ROSENBLUM
110 North Royal Street
P. O. Box 1079
Alexandria, Virginia 22313
336-2121

By ____________________
BERNARD S. COHEN

CHAPTER FOUR: Water Pollution

a. History & background

Human pollution of water has occurred for thousands of years, and has been responsible periodically for decimating the populations of both urban and rural areas.

Typhoid fever and cholera are two of the diseases borne by polluted water that killed hundreds of thousands, particularly the poor compacted in cities. Seventy-two thousand persons died in England in the 1848 cholera epidemic. In the United States, cholera epidemics occurred in 1832, 1849 and 1865. In New York City, more than 5,000 persons died from this disease in 1849. In 1866, faced with the prospect of another epidemic, the city removed some 160,000 tons of excrement from vacant lots. This and other sanitation measures helped limited the death toll to 591, although the city had greatly increased in population since 1832.

In the cities of the past, a vast number of the inhabitants lived in overly odorous and unhealthful conditions. Human wastes and refuse were dumped into streets and lots. Swine and chickens ate the garbage. Filth was a way of life. Local waterways received this waste, and were used for drinking water.

Today water pollution still kills humans, but the victims are more often inhabitants of rural areas without plumbing. Thus in Mexico it is well known among newsmen that deaths due to water-borne diseases must be described as deaths "due to the heat," when heat actually was a factor only in that it lowered the water table, making wells and water holes stagnant. The reason for these falsified statistics is simple: heat deaths are "acts of God"; deaths due to water pollution are avoidable—though obviously the cause must be recognized.

When the connection between disease and water contamination was discovered, there were some limited efforts made to dispose of wastes in a non-polluting manner. Early efforts included the collection of sewage and piping it for land irrigation. This technique has recently been revived, and will be discussed later in this chapter. But early attempts with this method failed because transportation was difficult, and the available land was too limited. The concept of diluting sewage with clean water was developed. Using rivers and streams up to their assimilative capacity became the theory of waste management, an approach still advocated by many pollutors when faced with the cost of controlling their effluents.

It was not until the end of the nineteenth century that mechanical technology began to be applied to sewage treatment. In 1886 the Massachusetts Board of Health was given control over inland water pollution. This led to the establishment of the Lawrence Experiment Station to study and develop sewage control techniques. In England, France, and Germany the study of sanitary engineering was beginning.

By the turn of the century the trickling filter had been developed, a system for secondary treatment used today by many of America's smaller communities. It provides better treatment than most waste in this country receives. By 1910, the activated sludge treatment had been developed. This system for secondary treatment is the most commonly used today, for it requires much less space than the trickling filter. Thus by 1910 we had developed the technology that with very little change remains the basis of our present sewage treatment.

Our society knew how to treat sewage to prevent the spread of disease, but in general it did nothing. In part this was because those with power did not care, and in part because to treat sewage cost money, which would have raised taxes.

evolution of the problem

Another factor was the introduction in the United States in about 1912 of chlorine as a killer of harmful living matter in drinking water. This, together with filtration, allowed for considerable protection of public health at a much lower cost than that incurred in avoiding pollution by treating wastes prior to their being dumped into waterways.

The result was a steady deterioration in water quality, but one that could be temporarily ignored if the healthfulness of home water supplies was the only consideration. But by the 1930's, the population increase and its compaction in cities meant that drinking water treatment alone could not protect our health from the dangers of unsanitary waterways, the ruination of which for other uses had become sufficiently intolerable to move the government into taking some limited steps to achieve cleaner flowing waters.

The governments' (Federal, state and local) actions logically included some controls on industrial waste. For since the industrial revolution, a nearly endless array of poisons have flowed from factories into the public waters. Many of these wastes are affected by neither the natural water environment nor the water treatment given at municipal facilities. Thus these poisons become a part of our drinking water and a part of the sea. Industrial wastes from 300,000 water-using factories in the United States discharge three- to four-times as much oxygen-demanding wastes as the entire sewered population of the nation. In addition, many of these wastes are toxic. And the volume of industrial wastes is growing several times faster than the volume of conventional sewage from homes, offices, etc. More than half the volume discharge to water comes from four major industry groups: paper, organic chemicals, petroleum, and steel.

Recognizing these factors, the federal government has developed a program to sue a few pollutors each year and to spend nearly a billion dollars a year to install early nineteenth century pollution control equipment in municipalities throughout the nation. Special emphasis has been given to politically equitable distributions of these funds, particularly to small towns and cities, with little regard for pollution control effectiveness. The porkbarrel description cannot be avoided.

references

DAVIES, *The Politics of Pollution,* New York, Western Pub. Co. 1970

MURPHY, *Water Purity,* Madison, The University of Wisconsin Press, 1961

ROSENBERG, *The Cholera Years,* Chicago, The University of Chicago Press, 1962

RIDGEWAY, *The Politics of Ecology,,* New York, E. P. Dutton & Co., Inc., 1970

Environmental Quality, The First Annual Report of the Council on Environmental Quality, Aug. 1970 at 32

b. Pollutants: what & where

The following is excerpted from *A Primer on Waste Water Treatment,* by the Environmental Protection Agency's Water Quality Office, Washington, March, 1971:

Present-day problems that must be met by sewage treatment plants can be summed up in the eight types of pollutants affecting our waters.

The eight general categories are: common sewage and other oxygen-demanding wastes; disease-causing agents; plant nutrients; synthetic organic chemicals; inorganic chemicals and other mineral substances; sediment; radioactive substances; and heat.

Oxygen-demanding wastes—These are the traditional organic wastes and ammonia contributed by domestic sewage and industrial wastes of plant and animal origin. Besides human sewage, such wastes result from food processing, paper mill production, tanning, and other manufacturing processes. These wastes are usually destroyed by bacteria if there is sufficient oxygen present in the water. Since fish and other aquatic life depend on oxygen for life, the oxygen-demanding wastes must be controlled, or the fish die.

Disease-causing agents—This category includes infectious organisms which are carried into surface and ground water by sewage from cities and institutions, and by certain kinds of industrial wastes, such as tanning and meat packing plants. Man or animals come in contact with these microbes either by drinking the water or through swimming, fishing, or other activities. Although modern disinfection techniques have greatly reduced the danger of this type of pollutant, the problem must be watched constantly.

Plant nutrients—These are the substances in the food chain of aquatic life, such as algae and water weeds, which support and stimulate their growth. Carbon, nitrogen and phosphorus are the three chief nutrients present in natural water. Large amounts of these nutrients are produced by sewage, certain industrial wastes, and drainage from fertilized lands. Biological waste treatment processes do not remove the phosphorus and nitrogen to any substantial extent—in fact, they convert the organic forms of these substances into mineral form, making them more usable by plant life. The problem starts when an excess of these nutrients over-stimulates the growth of water plants which cause unsightly conditions, interfere with treatment processes, and cause unpleasant and disagreeable tastes and odors in the water.

Synthetic organic chemicals—Included in this category are detergents and other household aids, all the new synthetic organic pesticides, synthetic industrial chemicals, and the wastes from their manufacture. Many of these substances are toxic to fish and aquatic life and possibly harmful to humans. They cause taste and odor problems, and resist conventional waste treatment. Some are known to be highly poisonous at very low concentrations. What the long-term effects of small doses of toxic substances may be is not yet known.

Inorganic chemicals and mineral substances—A vast array of metal salts, acids, solid matter, and many other chemical compounds are included in this group. They reach our waters from mining and manufacturing processes, oil field operations, agricultural practices, and natural sources. Water used in irrigation picks up large amounts of minerals as it filters down through the soil on its way to the nearest stream. Acids of a wide variety are discharged as wastes by industry, but the largest single source of acid in our water comes from mining operations and mines that have been abandoned.

Many of these types of chemicals are being created each year. They interfere with natural stream purification; destroy fish and other aquatic life; cause excessive hardness of water supplies; corrode expensive water treatment equipment; increase commercial and recreational boat maintenance costs; and boost the cost of waste treatment.

Sediments—These are the particles of soils, sands, and minerals washed from the land and paved areas of communities into the water. Construction projects are often large sediment producers. While not as insidious as some other types of pollution, sediments are a major problem because of the sheer magnitude of the amount reaching our waterways. Sediments fill stream channels and harbors, requiring expensive dredging, and they fill reservoirs, reducing their capacities and useful life. They erode power turbines and pumping equipment, and reduce fish and shellfish populations by blanketing fish nests and food supplies.

types of pollutants

More importantly, sediments reduce the amount of sunlight penetrating the water. The sunlight is required by green aquatic plants which produce the oxygen necessary to normal stream balance. Sediments greatly increase the treatment costs for municipal and industrial water supply and for sewage treatment where combined sewers are in use.

Radioactive substances—Radioactive pollution results from the mining and processing of radioactive ores; from the use of refined radioactive materials in power reactors and for industrial, medical, and research purposes; and from fallout following nuclear weapons testing. Increased use of these substances poses a potential public health problem. Since radiation accumulates in humans, control of this type of pollution must take into consideration total exposure in the human environment—water, air, food, occupation, and medical treatment.

Heat—Heat reduces the capacity of water to absorb oxygen. Tremendous volumes of water are used by power plants and industry for cooling. Most of the water, with the added heat, is returned to streams, raising their temperatures. With less oxygen, the water is not as efficient in assimilating oxygen-consuming wastes and in supporting fish and aquatic life. Unchecked waste heat discharges can seriously alter the ecology of a lake, a stream, or even part of the sea.

Water in lakes or stored in impoundments can be greatly affected by heat. Summer temperatures heat up the surfaces, causing the water to form into layers, with the cooler water forming the deeper layers. Decomposing vegetative matter from natural and man-made pollutants deplete the oxygen from these cooler lower layers with harmful effects on the aquatic life. When the oxygen-deficient water is discharged from the lower gates of a dam, it may have serious effects on downstream fish life and reduce the ability of the stream to assimilate downstream pollution.

To complicate matters, most of our wastes are a mixture of the eight types of pollution, making the problems of treatment and control that much more difficult.

Municipal wastes usually contain oxygen-consuming pollutants, synthetic organic chemicals such as detergents, sediments, and other types of pollutants. The same is true of many industrial wastes which may contain, in addition, substantial amounts of heat from cooling processes. Water that drains off the land usually contains great amounts of organic matter in addition to sediment. Also, land drainage may contain radioactive substances and pollutants washed from the sky, vegetation, buildings, and streets during rainfall.

End, selection from *A Primer on Waste Water Treatment.*

prevalence and sources of pollution

The following is digested from *Cost of Clean Water, Volume II, Cost Effectiveness and Clean Water,* by the Environment Protection Agency's Water Quality Office, March, 1971:

The proposed substantial expansion of Federal grants for construction of waste treatment works places the nation at the threshold of an enormous investment program. Current plans call for at least a 50% expansion within the next five years of the value of waste treatment capital put in place during the twentieth century.

Paradoxically, this massive spending program is being undertaken at a time when only about five percent of the sewered population of the nation is not served by waste treatment, and when the degree of waste reduction accomplished by treatment is greater than it has ever been before for the population of the U. S.

There is little question that the money can be spent. Indeed, public comment on the question of funding tends to be directed exclusively to the possibility of deficiencies in the proposed level of spending. And if the public's tendency to question the adequacy of municipal waste treatment funding may be thought to arise more from an awareness of water pollution problems and from urgency with respect to their abatement than from knowledge of the causes of pollution or the status of municipal waste treatment, it is sophisticated analysis of the rate of growth of waste loadings, the shift of industrial waste treatment

Disposition of increases in two major pollutants, 1964–68

	Change, 1964-68 Millions of Pounds	Annual Rate
Disposition of Net Increase in BOD		
Public sewers, populations	+ 900	+2.8%
Public sewers, factory connections	+1570	+8.4%
Separately discharging factories	+5640	+6.9%
Net Discharge of BOD	-2410	-4.3%
From public systems	- 610	-3.3%
From separately discharging factories	-1800	-4.6%
Net Increase in Phosphorus	+122.3	+5.9%

responsibilities to the public sector, the pressures of upgrading and replacement, and the effects of inflation and technological modification that is responsible for the enlarged investment targets.

There is some question, however, whether the money will be spent effectively. And here the record of the past is not reassuring. The data indicate that cost-effectiveness may be low in the conduct of public waste disposal services.Without significant changes in existing practice, there is slim hope that the rate of environmental improvement will be proportionate to the rate of spending.

A substantial portion of American waterways is characterized by FWQA assessors to be persistently polluted. Of 233 second order drainage systems in the forty-eight contiguous States, FWQA could define only 19 in which no greater than 5% of stream miles were continually or recurrently in violation of established physical, chemical, or bacteriological criteria--and 16 of those 19 are found in one area, the region distinguished here as the Southeast. Even with the relatively low prevalence of pollution in the Southeastern U. S., we find that the median and modal incidence of pollution for the nation occurs at over 30% of stream miles (cf. Table 18). More than a third of total stream miles are defined to be polluted in every region of the U. S. except the Southeast.

The incidence of pollution, as it is defined by the FWQA national assesment, fits none of the accepted patterns of cause. The conventional wisdom offers no ready explanations for the phenomenon. The fact that the Northeastern States have the highest indicated prevalance of pollution is almost comforting, in that it fits all of the preconceptions. The area is characterized by large and highly concentrated population, massive manufacturing capacity, a relative deficiency in waste treatment.

NATIONAL WATER QUALITY ASSESSMENT:

PREVALENCE OF POLLUTION IN SECOND ORDER DRAINAGE SYSTEMS

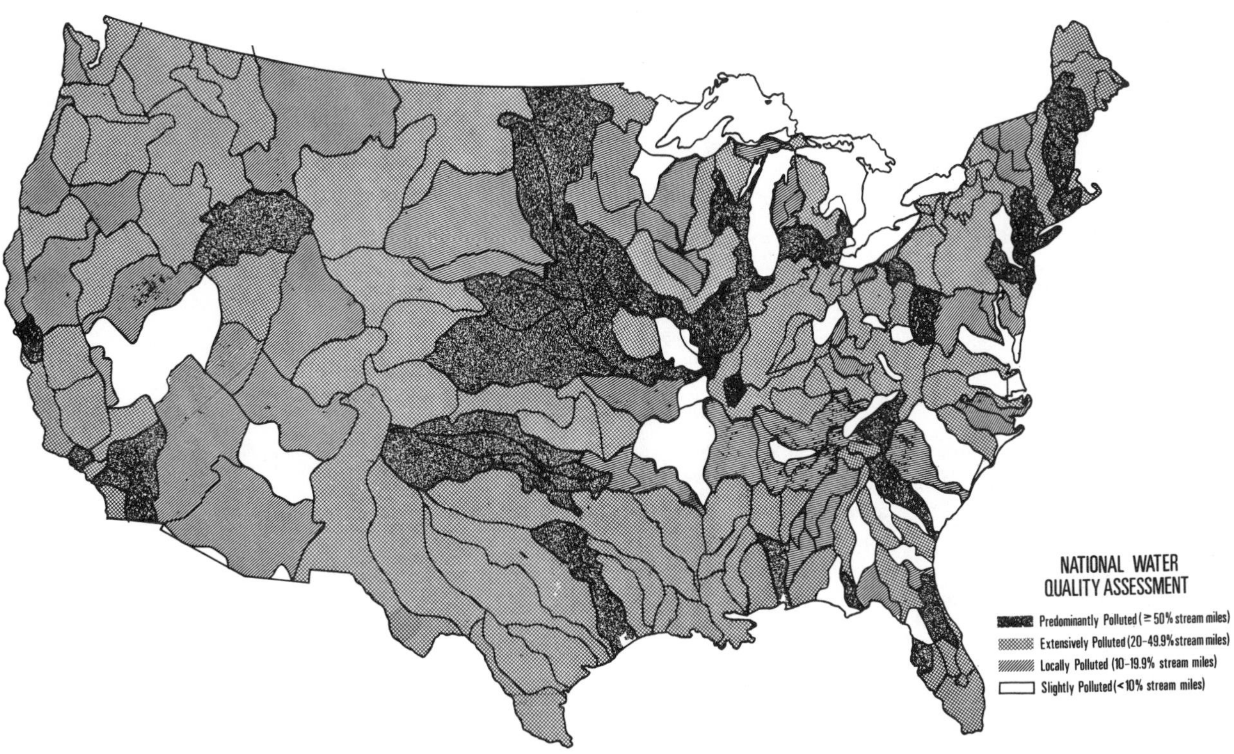

SOURCE: Cost of Clean Water, Volume II, EPA, 1971

Generalized prevalence of water pollution, 1970

Region	Percent of Stream Miles Polluted	Percent of Watersheds In Pollution Status: Predominantly Polluted 1/	Extensively Polluted 2/	Locally Polluted 3/	Slightly Polluted 4/
Pacific Coast	33.9	14.8	59.3	22.2	3.7
Northern Plains	40.0	37.5	33.3	25.0	4.2
Southern Plains	38.8	27.3	51.5	18.2	6.1
Southeast	23.3	14.3	41.1	16.1	28.6
Central	36.6	23.2	51.8	21.4	3.6
Northeast	43.9	36.1	55.6	5.6	2.8
E. of Mississippi R.	31.6	23.0	48.7	15.5	12.8
W. of Mississippi R.	35.5	24.1	47.1	20.7	4.6
U. S.	32.6	23.7	48.5	17.7	9.9

1/ Predominantly Polluted : ≥ - 50% of Stream Miles Polluted

2/ Extensively Polluted: 20 - 49.9% of Stream Miles Polluted

3/ Locally Polluted: 10 - 19.9% of Stream Miles Polluted

4/ Slightly Polluted: < 10% of Stream Miles Polluted

Aspects of regional sewage services, 1968

	U.S.	Pacific Coast	Northern Plains	Southern Plains	South East	Central	North East
1. Population, 1968							
Total (Millions)	198.0	25.7	14.8	23.5	39.9	45.7	48.3
Annual Increase, 1962-68 (Percent)	1.2	2.1	0.4	1.2	1.4	1.3	0.8
Percent Metropolitan	68.6	83.6	53.4	59.6	46.4	74.8	82.4
2. Sewering, 1968							
Percent of SMSA pop.	79.5	85.1	72.4	84.7	59.9	82.3	82.9
Percent of Non-SMSA	45.9	53.8	48.6	59.8	37.4	36.2	58.7
Percent Annual Increase, 1962-68 SMSA	2.7	5.4	1.1	4.6	2.4	1.8	1.5
Percent Annual Increase, 1962-68 Non-SMSA	2.9	2.5	1.6	3.3	3.3	1.2	4.2
3. 1968 Waste Treatment							
Percent Untreated Discharge	7.3	0.7	13.2	2.0	15.0	1.9	11.9
Percent Primary Treatment	26.6	46.0	22.6	4.6	24.5	22.7	33.5
Percent Intermediate & Lagoons	8.6	7.5	16.7	12.8	7.7	6.0	8.6
Percent Secondary Treatment	56.7	44.7	43.7	80.1	52.4	69.0	45.4
Percent Greater than Secondary Treatment	0.7	1.6	3.7	0.5	0.6	0.2	0.5

The region should, according to the conventional scenario, have a great number of polluted stream miles. But the Northern Plains States stand second to the Northeast in the average prevalance of pollution, and exceed the Northeast in the relative number of watersheds in the most polluted category.
That the sparsely populated Dakotas, almost completely unindustrialized, where every small town has its secondary waste treatment plant, should have relatively more polluted stream miles than New York State is unsettling. And to find that the nation's best water quality--in terms of compliance with water quality standards--is to be found in the region with the lowest incidence of waste treatment does additional violence to any complacency about the direction of existing pollution abatement programs.

Not even the most ancient of our conceptions of sources of water quality degradation, deficiency of streamflow, holds up entirely. While eastern streams, in total, are judged to be less extensively polluted than western streams, the better showing traces entirely to the waters of the Southeastern States. Pacific Coast States provide a consistently better record of compliance with water quality standards than either the Central or the Northeastern States; and even the most arid of the six regions, the Southern Plains, compares quite favorably with the Northeast and not unfavorably with the Central States.

We are left, then, with only a single certainty. A very large portion of all U. S. waters consistently demonstrates quality characteristics that violate established criteria. These violations occur in densely populated and sparsely populated areas, in humid and arid climates, in industrialized, in agricultural, and in forested regions, and apparently without reference to either the prevalance or the intensity of waste treatment. The lack of a pattern makes it impossible to judge whether conditions are improving or deteriorating; but the consistency of the pattern of pollution suggests that there may be inefficiencies in current approaches to pollution abatement.

categories of water pollution

The apparently erratic geographic distribution of water pollution may be explained in part by a review of apparent causes. The national assessment of the prevalence of water pollution included an evaluation for each second order watershed of the indicated causes of pollution, in terms of relative weight.

Causes of pollution were classified according to their association with categories of human activity. Natural causes of poor water quality were not considered, on the basis that water quality standards are, at least in theory, developed in terms of water uses that are possible within the framework of natural conditions. Recognized sources of pollution for the assessment were eight:

1) Municipal Wastes include all wastes that are collected and transmitted through community systems of sanitary sewers. Both commercial and domestic sanitary wastes, and the wastes discharged by manufacturing plants to public sewer systems, fall into the category.

2) Other Urban Wastes include the waterborne residues of urban activity that do not routinely enter the system of sanitary sewers. Direct runoff from urban areas, overflows and bypasses of waste treatment plants caused by combined storm and sanitary sewers, and the unassimilated drainage of septic tanks comprise the major elements of the category.

Prime causes of stream pollution by extent of pollution

Prime Causes, In Descending Rank	Percent of Stream Pollution Attributed to Prime Causes						
	U. S.	Pacific Coast	Northern Plains	Southern Plains	Southeast	Central	Northeas
Industrial Wastes	23.7	12.7	21.0	9.2	34.7	21.5	33.5
Municipal	21.8	13.0	15.6	14.2	21.2	28.5	27.1
Agriculture	11.2	19.1	28.8	27.6	1.3	5.8	0.5
Other	3.7	11.8	0.6	16.6	1.7	0.4	-
Mining	2.8	2.4	2.6	12.6	0.3	4.9	2.6
Other Urban Wastes	0.9	-	-	0.1	0.7	1.9	1.3
Power Generation	0.4	1.5	-	-	0.6	0.6	0.1
Spills	0.1	-	-	-	-	0.2	-
Total Prime Causes	64.6	60.5	68.6	70.3	60.5	63.8	65.1

Prime causes of stream pollution in all U.S. second-order watersheds

Prime Causes and (Rank)	Percent of Pollution Attributed to Prime Causes				
	All Streams	Predominantly Polluted	Extensively Polluted	Locally Polluted	Slightly polluted
Industrial Wastes (1)	23.7	24.9	24.0	14.9	20.8
East of Miss. R. (1)	28.9	31.0	28.3	19.6	18.2
West of Miss. R. (2)	14.6	14.8	15.7	8.4	12.4
Municipal Wastes (2)	21.8	23.2	19.6	23.7	27.2
East of Miss. R. (2)	26.0	26.5	25.0	29.4	34.5
West of Miss. R. (3)	14.4	17.8	9.9	15.7	34.3
Agriculture (3)	11.2	10.5	10.8	18.9	5.5
East of Miss. R. (4)	2.9	1.4	3.0	14.0	5.4
West of Miss. R. (1)	25.8	25.5	26.5	25.7	19.1
Other (4)	3.7	3.1	4.6	3.2	0.4
East of Miss. R. (7)	0.6	-	1.2	1.3	-
West of Miss. R. (4)	9.3	8.2	11.4	5.7	4.8
Mining (5)	2.8	3.0	2.3	2.5	5.8
East of Miss. R. (3)	2.9	3.9	2.2	-	7.1
West of Miss. R. (5)	2.5	1.5	3.0	6.0	9.5
Other Urban Wastes (6)	0.9	1.0	0.9	0.2	-
East of Miss. R. (5)	1.4	1.6	1.4	-	-
West of Miss. R. (7)	-	-	-	0.4	-
Power Generation (7)	0.4	0.3	0.6	-	0.9
East of Miss. R. (6)	0.5	0.6	0.4	-	1.2
West of Miss. R. (6)	0.4	-	0.9	-	-
Spills (8)	0.1	-	0.1	-	-
East of Miss. R. (8)	0.1	-	0.2	-	-
West of Miss. R. (8)	-	-	-	-	-

Reitze

3) Industrial Wastes include the separately discharged wastes of manufacturing. Both process waters and manufacturers' cooling waters fall under this heading.

4) Electrical generating was defined to include the discharge of heated cooling waters of thermal power generating stations, the presence of radioactivity from nuclear fueled power plants, and the particulate fallout and acidity associated with fossil fueled power plants. In several watersheds, however, the disruption of the natural hyrologic regimen associated with generation of hydroelectric power was included by assessors under this category rather than the general category of "other" which was intended to include all water management activities.

5) Agriculture, as a source of water pollution, includes the effects of runoff on siltation of streams, organic and nutrient loadings originating with livestock, concentrations of pesticides and herbicides from the runoff of agricultural lands, and salinity that occurs with leaching and evapotranspiration in the irrigation process.

6) Mining's effects on water quality include siltation from scarred lands, acid drainage from reaction of water with exposed mineral seams, and pumping of brine deposits.

7) Spills, which receive a great deal of attention because of their often catastrophic nature, include the deposit in water of any polluting or toxic material as the result of accident.

8) Other sources of water pollution are, obviously, unlimited in concept, since they include any human event or activity not considered under one of the other seven categories of polluting activity. In practice, however, the "other" category resolves into three principal classes: water management in the highly regulated streams of the west, the promotion of sedimentation by construction, and the effects of transportation--principally navigation--including stream dredging.

pollution causes and resource allocation

Industrial wastes, which account for almost 80% of sewered oxygen demand and for 34% of estimated stream pollution, have been the source of about half a billion dollars a year of investment and several millions a year of operation costs over the last three years. Current targets call for investment to be increased to over $600 million a year.

Municipal wastes, which account for a little over 20% of sewered oxygen demand, and are presumed to be the principal source of nutrient phosphorous, are estimated to be responsible for a third of all stream pollution. Investments, about a billion dollars a year over the last three years, will step up significantly as a result of increased Federal financial assistance. Operating costs that currently approach $300 million a year, should come close to half a billion by the middle of the current decade. A very minor part of the added financial burden will be directed toward alleviating the nutrient problem, believed to be the principal mechanism by which sanitary sewage causes water pollution today.

Agriculture, estimated to cause almost 20% of all stream pollution, makes almost no direct investment for pollution control purposes. Costs of remedial procedures--including erosion control, limitation of use of some pesticides, locational practices for feed lots and dairies--may amount to several tens of millions of dollars each year, with the benefits experienced in such areas as nuisance alleviation, increased productivity, and land resettlement alternatives as much as in water pollution control.

Other activities producing pollution--water management practices, construction, navigation, and recreation--are estimated to cause slightly more than 6% of stream pollution, most of it west of the Mississippi. Again, control measures can amount to no more than tens of millions, occurring principally in the form of higher construction costs.

Mining is estimated to account for about 5% of stream pollution, concentrated largely in the Appalachian coal mining region. The petroleum industry has indicated that its expenditures for pollution control consequences of production exceed $100 million a year. While no estimates of costs have been presented for other mining sectors, it is considered improbable that their total would approach half of that claimed for petroleum extraction.

Other urban wastes, estimated to account for a little over 1% of stream pollution, are approached almost entirely as a function of the system of storm and sanitary sewers that currently sustains an annual investment of about $600 million. It is uncertain to what extent the sewering program serves to alleviate water pollution due to urban drainage--indeed, there is some concern that the net effect of such programs is negative with respect to water quality.

Power generation is estimated to be directly responsible for less than 1% of stream pollution. Current investment in cooling water recycling facilities by the steam power industry is in the area of $200 million a year. Air pollution control investments are approximately equal; and these have collateral water pollution control benefits in some cases, a function of reduction in fallout of particulate matter.

Spills are accorded responsibility for almost no recurrent water pollution, though intermittent spill damages have proved in some cases to be locally catastrophic. It is impossible to estimate costs of spill control measures. End of excerpts from *Cost of Clean Water, Volume II.*

For a discussion of water pollution relating to **thermal** and **radiation** problems, see the electric power section in Volume Two. See also, for other water pollution problems, the sections in Volume Two on **pesticides** and **oil spills.**

c. Collection and treatment of wastes

Once again, we quote from *A Primer on Waste Water Treatment,* by the Environmental Protection Agency's Water Quality Office, 1971:

The most common form of pollution control in the United States consists of a system of sewers and waste treatment plants. The sewers collect the waste water from homes, businesses, and many industries and deliver it to the plants for treatment to make it fit for discharge into streams or for reuse.

There are two kinds of sewer systems—combined and separate. Combined sewers carry away both water polluted by human use and water polluted as it drains off homes, streets, or land during a storm.

In a separated system, one system of sewers, usually called sanitary, carries only sewage. Another system of storm sewers takes care of the large volumes of water from rain or melting snow.

Each home has a sewer or pipe which connects to the common or lateral sewer beneath a nearby street. Lateral sewers connect with larger sewers called trunk or main sewers. In a combined sewer system, these trunk or main sewers discharge into a larger sewer called an interceptor. The interceptor is designed to carry several times the dry-weather flow of the system feeding into it.

During dry weather when the sewers are handling only the normal amount of waste water, all of it is carried to the waste treatment plant. During a storm when the amount of water in the sewer system is much greater, part of the water, including varying amounts of raw sewage, is allowed to bypass directly into the receiving streams. The rest of the wastes are sent to the treatment plant. If part of the increased load of water were not diverted, the waste treatment plant would be overloaded and the purifying processes would not function properly. (A research, development and demonstration program is being conducted to solve this urban run-off pollution problem. The aim is to develop technology that will control and/or treat combined sewer overflows, storm water discharges and general washoff of rainwater polluted by dirt or other contaminants on the land.)

Interceptor sewers are also used in sanitary sewer systems as collectors of flow from main sewers and trunks, but do not normally include provisions for bypassing.

A waste treatment plant's basic function is to speed up the natural processes by which water purifies itself. In many cases, nature's treatment process in streams and lakes was adequate before our population and industry grew to their present size.

When the sewage of previous years was dumped into waterways, the natural process of purification began. First, the sheer volume of clean water in the stream diluted the small amount of wastes. Bacteria and other small organisms in the water consumed the sewage or other organic matter, turning it into new bacterial cells, carbon dioxide, and other products.

But the bacteria normally present in water must have oxygen to do their part in breaking down the sewage. Water acquires this all-important oxygen by absorbing it from the air and from plants that grow in the water itself. These plants use sunlight to turn the carbon dioxide present in water into oxygen.

The life and death of any body of water depend mainly upon its ability to maintain a certain amount of dissolved oxygen. This dissolved oxygen—or DO—is what fish breathe. Without it they suffocate. If only a small amount of sewage is dumped into a stream, fish are not affected and the bacteria can do their work and the stream can quickly restore its oxygen loss from the atmosphere and from plants. Trouble begins when the sewage load is excessive. The sewage will decay and the water will begin to give off odors. If carried to the extreme, the water could lose all of its oxygen, resulting in the death of fish and beneficial plant life.

Since dissolved oxygen is the key element in the life of water, the demands on it are used as a measure in telling how well a sewage treatment plant is working. This measuring device is called biochemical oxygen demand, or BOD. If the effluent or the end-product from a treatment plant has a high content of organic pollutants, the effluent will have a high BOD. In other words, it will demand more oxygen from the water to break down the sewage and consequently will leave the water with less oxygen (and also dirtier).

PRIMARY TREATMENT

At present, there are two basic ways of treating wastes. They are called primary and secondary. In primary treatment, solids are allowed to settle and are removed from the water. Secondary treatment, a further step in purifying waste water, uses biological processes.

As sewage enters a plant for primary treatment, it flows through a screen. The screen removes large floating objects such as rags and sticks that may clog pumps and small pipes. The screens vary from coarse to fine—from those with parallel steel or iron bars with openings of about half an inch or more to screens with much smaller openings.

Screens are generally placed in a chamber or channel in an inclined position to the flow of the sewage to make cleaning easier. The debris caught on the upstream surface of the screen can be raked off manually or mechanically.

Some plants use a device known as a comminutor which combines the functions of a screen and a grinder. These devices catch and then cut or shred the heavy solid material. In the process, the pulverized matter remains in the sewage flow to be removed in a settling tank.

After the sewage has been screened, it passes into what is called a grit chamber where sand, grit, cinders, and small stones are allowed to settle to the bottom. A grit chamber is highly important for cities with combined sewer systems because it will remove the grit or gravel that washes off streets or land during a storm and ends up at treatment plants.

The unwanted grit or gravel from this process is usually disposed of by filling land near a treatment plant.

In some plants, another screen is placed after the grit chamber to remove any further material that might damage equipment or interfere with later processes.

With the screening completed and the grit removed, the sewage still contains dissolved organic and inorganic matter along with suspended solids. The latter consist of minute particles of matter that can be removed from the sewage by treatment in a sedimentation tank. When the speed of the flow of sewage through one of these tanks is reduced, the suspended solids will gradually sink to the bottom. This mass of solids is called raw sludge.

Various methods have been devised for removing sludge from the tanks.

In older plants, sludge removal was done by hand. After a tank had been in service for several days or weeks, the sewage flow was diverted to another tank. The sludge in the bottom of the out-of-service tank was pushed or flushed with water to a pit near the tank, and then removed, usually by pumping, for further treatment or disposal.

Almost all plants built within the past 30 years have had a mechanical means for removing the sludge from sedimentation tanks. Some plants remove it continuously while others remove it at intervals.

To complete the primary treatment, the effluent from the sedimentation tank is chlorinated before being discharged into a stream or river. Chlorine gas is fed into the water to kill and reduce the number of disease-causing bacteria. Chlorination also helps to reduce objectionable odors.

Although 30 percent of the municipalities in the United States give only primary treatment to their sewage, this process by itself is considered entirely inadequate for most needs.

Today's cities and industry, faced with increased amounts of wastes and wastes that are more difficult to remove from water, have turned to secondary and even advanced waste treatment.

SECONDARY TREATMENT

Secondary treatment removes up to 90 percent of the organic matter in sewage by making use of the bacteria in it. The two principal types of secondary treatment are trickling filters and the activated-sludge process.

The trickling filter process or the activated sludge process is used mostly today. After the effluent leaves the sedimentation tank in the primary stage of treatment, it flows or is pumped to a facility using one or the other of these processes. A trickling filter is simply a bed of stones from three to ten feet deep through which the sewage passes. Bacteria gather and multiply on these stones until they can consume most of the organic matter in the sewage. The cleaner water trickles out through pipes in the bottom of the filter for further treatment.

The sewage is applied to the bed of stones in two principal ways. One method consists of distributing the effluent intermittently through a network of pipes laid on or beneath the surface of the stones. Attached to these pipes are smaller, vertical pipes which spray the sewage over the stones.

Another much-used method consists of a vertical pipe in the center of the filter connected to rotating horizontal pipes which spray the sewage continuously upon the stones.

The trend today is toward the use of the activated sludge process instead of trickling filters. This process speeds up the work of the bacteria by bringing air and sludge heavily laden with bacteria into close contact with the sewage.

After the sewage leaves the settling tank in primary treatment, it is pumped to an aeration tank where it is mixed with air and sludge loaded with bacteria and allowed to remain for several hours. During this time, the bacteria break down the organic matter.

From the aeration tank, the sewage, now called mixed liquor, flows to another sedimentation tank to remove the solids. Chlorination of the effluent completes the basic secondary treatment.

The sludge, now activated with additional millions of bacteria and other tiny organisms, can be used again by returning it to an aeration tank for mixing with new sewage and ample amounts of air.

The activated sludge process, like most other techniques, has advantages and limitations. The size of the units necessary for this treatment is small, thereby requiring less land space and the process is free of flies and odors. But it is more costly to operate than the trickling filter, and the activated sludge process sometimes loses its effectiveness when faced with difficult industrial wastes.

An adequate supply of oxygen is necessary for the activated sludge process to be effective. Air is mixed with sewage and biologically active sludge in the aeration tanks by three different methods.

The first, mechanical aeration, is accomplished by drawing the sewage from the bottom of the tank and spraying it over the surface, thus causing the sewage to absorb large amounts of oxygen from the atmosphere.

In the second method, large amounts of air under pressure are piped down into the sewage and forced out through openings in the pipe. The third method is a combination of mechanical aeration and the forced air method.

The final phase of the secondary treatment consists of the addition of chlorine, as the most common method of disinfection, to the effluent coming from the trickling filter or the activated sludge process. Chlorine is usually purchased in liquid form, converted to a gas, and injected into the effluent 15 to 30 minutes before the treated water is discharged into a watercourse. If done properly, chlorination will kill more than 99 percent of the harmful bacteria in an effluent.

LAGOONS AND SEPTIC TANKS

There are many well-populated areas in the United States that are not served by any sewer systems or waste treatment plants. Lagoons and septic tanks may act as less than satisfactory alternatives at such locations.

A septic tank is simply a tank buried in the ground to treat the sewage from an individual home. Waste water from the home flows into the tank where bacteria in the sewage may break down the organic matter and the cleaner water flows out of the tank into the ground through sub-surface drains. Periodically the sludge or solid matter in the bottom of the tank must be removed and disposed of.

In a rural setting, with the right kind of soil and the proper location, the septic tank may be a reasonable and temporary means of disposing of strictly domestic wastes. Septic tanks should always be located so that none of the effluent can seep into sources used for drinking.

Lagoons, or as they are sometimes called, stabilization or oxidation ponds also have several advantages when used correctly.

They can give sewage primary and secondary treatment or they can be used to supplement other processes.

A lagoon is a scientifically constructed pond, usually three to five feet deep, in which sunlight, algae, and oxygen interact to restore water to a quality that is often equal to or better than effluent from secondary treatment. Changes in the weather may change the effectiveness of lagoons.

When used with other waste treatment processes, lagoons can be very effective. A good example of this is the Santee, California, water reclamation project. After conventional primary and secondary treatment by activated sludge, the town's waste water is kept in a lagoon for 30 days. Then the effluent, after chlorination, is pumped to land immediately above a series of lakes and allowed to trickle down through sandy soil into the lakes. The resulting water is of such good quality, the residents of the area can swim, boat, and fish in the lake water.

need for further treatment of wastes

In the past, pollution control was concerned primarily with problems caused by domestic and the simpler wastes of industry. Control was aimed principally towards protecting downstream public water supplies and stopping or preventing nuisance conditions.

Pollution problems were principally local in extent and their control a local matter.

This is no longer true. National growth and change have altered this picture. Progress in abating pollution has been outdistanced by population growth, the speed of industrial progress and technological developments, changing land practices, and many other factors.

The increased production of goods has greatly increased the amounts of common industrial wastes. New processes in manufacturing are producing new, complex wastes that sometimes defy present pollution control technology. The increased application of commercial fertilizers and the development and widespread use of a vast array of new pesticides are resulting in a host of new pollution problems from water draining off land.

The growth of the nuclear energy field and the use of radioactive materials foreshadow still another complicating and potentially serious water pollution situation.

Long stretches of both interstate and intrastate streams are subjected to pollution which ruins or reduces the use of the water for many purposes. Conventional biological waste treatment processes are hard-pressed to hold the pollution line, and for a growing number of our larger cities, these processes are no longer adequate.

Our growing population not only is packing our central cities but spreading out farther and farther into suburbia and exurbia. Across the country, new satellite communities are being born almost daily. The construction or extension of sewer lines has not matched either the growth rate or its movements. Sea water intrusion is a growing problem in coastal areas. It is usually caused by the excessive pumping of fresh water from the ground which lowers the water level, allowing salt water to flow into the ground water area.

These new problems of a modern society have placed additional burdens upon our waste treatment systems. Today's pollutants are more difficult to remove from the water. And increased demands upon our water supply aggravate the problem. During the dry season, the flow of rivers decreases to such an extent that they have difficulty in assimilating the effluent from waste treatment plants.

In the future, these problems will be met through better and more complete methods of removing pollutants from water and better means for preventing some wastes from even reaching our streams in the first place.

advanced treatment techniques

The best immediate answer to these problems is the widespread application of existing waste treatment methods. Many cities that have only primary treatment need secondary treatment. Many other cities need enlarged or modernized primary and secondary systems.

But this is only a temporary solution. The discharge of oxygen-consuming wastes will increase despite the universal application of the most efficient waste treatment processes now available. And these are the simplest wastes to dispose of. Conventional treatment processes are already losing the battle against the modern-day, tougher wastes.

The increasing need to reuse water now calls for better and better waste treatment. Every use of water—whether in home, in the factory, or on the farm—results in some change in its quality.

To return water of more usable quality to receiving lakes and streams, new methods for removing pollutants are being developed. The advanced waste treatment techniques under investigation range from extensions of biological treatment capable of removing nitrogen and phosphorus nutrients to physical-chemical separation techniques such as adsorption, distillation, and reverse osmosis.

These new processes can achieve any degree of pollution control desired and, as waste effluents are purified to higher and higher degrees by such treatment, the point is reached where effluents become "too good to throw away."

Such water can be deliberately and directly reused for agricultural, industrial, recreational, or even drinking water supplies. This complete water renovation will mean complete pollution control and at the same time more water for the Nation.

COAGULATION—SEDIMENTATION

The application of advanced techniques for waste treatment, at least in the next several years, will most likely take up where primary and secondary treatment leave off. Ultimately, entirely new systems will no doubt replace the modern facilities of today.

The process known as coagulation-sedimentation may be used to increase the removal of solids from effluent after primary and secondary treatment. Besides removing essentially all of the settleable solids, this method can, with proper control and sufficient addition of chemicals, reduce the concentration of phosphate by over 95 percent.

In this process, alum, lime, or iron salts are added to effluent as it comes from the secondary treatment. The flow then passes through flocculation tanks where the chemicals cause the smaller particles to floc or bunch together into large masses.

The larger masses of particles or lumps will settle faster when the effluent reaches the next step—the sedimentation tank.

Although used for years in the treatment of industrial wastes and in water treatment, coagulation-sedimentation is classified as an advanced process because it is not usually applied to the treatment of municipal wastes. In many cases, the process is a necessary pre-treatment for some of the other advanced techniques.

ADSORPTION

Technology has also been developed to effect the removal of refractory organic materials. These materials are the stubborn organic matter which persists in water and resists normal biological treatment.

The effects of the organics are not completely understood, but taste and odor problems in water, tainting of fish flesh, foaming of water, and fish kills have been attributed to such materials.

Adsorption consists of passing the effluent through a bed of activated carbon granules which will remove more than 98 percent of the organics. To cut down the cost of the procedure, the carbon granules can be cleaned by heat and used again.

An alternative system utilizing powdered carbon is under study. Rather than pass the effluent through a bed of granules, the powdered carbon is put directly into the stream. The organics stick to the carbon and then the carbon is removed from the effluent by using coagulating chemicals and allowing the coagulated carbon particles to settle in a tank.

The use of this finely ground carbon will improve the rate at which the refractory organics are removed. The potential widespread use of powdered carbon adsorption depends largely on the effectiveness of regenerating the carbon for use again.

Except for the salts added during the use of water, municipal waste water that has gone through the previous advanced processes will be restored to a chemical quality almost the same as before it was used.

When talking of salts in water, salt is not limited to the common kind that is used in the home for seasoning food. In waste treatment language, salts mean the many minerals dissolved by water as it passes through the air as rainfall, as it trickles through the soil and over rocks, and as it is used in the home and factory.

ELECTRODIALYSIS

Electrodialysis is a rather complicated process by which electricity and membranes are used to remove salts from an effluent. A membrane is usually made of chemically treated plastic. The salts are forced out of the water by the action of an electric field. When a mineral salt is placed in water it has a tendency to break down into ions. An ion is an atom or a small group of atoms having an electrical charge.

As an example, the two parts of common table salt are sodium and chlorine. When these two elements separate as salt dissolves in water, the sodium and chlorine particles are called ions. Sodium ions have a positive charge while chlorine ions have a negative charge.

When the effluent passes through the electrodialysis cell, the positive sodium ions are attracted through a membrane to a pole or electrode that is negatively charged. The negatively charged chlorine ions are pulled out of the water through another membrane toward an electrode with a positive charge.

With the salts removed by the action of the two electrodes, the clean water flows out of the electrodialysis cell for reuse or discharge into a river or stream.

As a city uses its water, the amount of salts in the water increases by 300-400 milligrams per liter. Fortunately, electrodialysis can remove this buildup of salts.

In other words, this process returns the salt content of the water back to where it was or even better than when the city first received the water.

THE BLENDING OF TREATED WATER

Properly designed and applied, the methods that have been explained will be able to supply any quality of water for any reuse.

But none of these processes will stand alone. They must be used in a series or a parallel plan. In a series, all the sewage passes through all the processes, one after another, each process making a particular contribution toward improving the water. For example, the conventional primary treatment removes the material that will readily settle or float; the secondary biological step takes care of the decomposable impurities; coagulation-sedimentation, the third step, eliminates the suspended solids; carbon adsorption removes the remaining dissolved organic matter; electrodialysis returns the level of the salts to what it was before the water was used; and, finally, chlorination provides the health safety barrier against disease carriers.

advanced treatment techniques

Basically the same result can be achieved by separating the effluent into two streams. In this instance, all of the waste receives the primary and secondary treatment and then passes through the coagulation-sedimentation and adsorption processes which remove the organic matter. Half of the sewage is then treated by evaporation and adsorption to remove all impurities including the minerals. This effluent, when blended with the other half, can provide water with the desired level of minerals. After chlorination, the water can be reused.

Almost any degree of water quality can be achieved by varying the flow of the two streams. This technique reduces the treatment cost, since only a fraction of the flow requires treatment with the more expensive unit processes, such as distillation.

Distillation or evaporation basically consists of bringing the effluent to the boiling point. The steam or vapor produced is piped to another chamber where it is cooled, changing it back to a liquid. Most of the unwanted polluting impurities remain in the original chamber. However, some volatile substances may distill along with the water and carry along foreign materials that contribute objectionable taste.

As most people have discovered, distilled water has a flat, disagreeable taste caused by the absence of minerals and air. But by blending this pure water with water that still contains some minerals, a clean, better tasting water results. And just as importantly, the more expensive distillation process is used on only part of the effluent, and the rest of the waste water is treated by the less costly procedures.

advanced treatment techniques

So far, the most readily available processes that will solve most current pollution problems have been covered. But the future holds many new challenges. Scientists are still looking for the ultimate system that will do the complete job of cleaning up water, simply and at a reasonable cost.

One such possible process under study is reverse osmosis. When liquids with different concentrations of mineral salts are separated by a membrane, molecules of pure water tend to pass by osmosis from the more concentrated to the less concentrated side until both liquids have the same mineral content.

Scientists are now exploring ways to take advantage of the natural phenomena of osmosis, but in reverse. When pressure is exerted on the side with the most minerals, this natural force reverses itself, causing the molecules of pure water to flow out of the compartment containing a high salt concentration.

This means that perfectly pure water is being taken out of the waste, rather than taking pollutants out of water as is the traditional way. And this process takes clean water away from everything—bacteria, detergents, nitrates.

Tests have shown that the theory works well, resulting in water good enough to drink. Efforts are now under way to develop large membranes with long life. Also, the process and equipment need to be tested on a large scale.

Many other techniques to improve waste treatment are under development in laboratories and in the field.

For example, special microscopic organisms are being tested for removing nitrates from waste water by reducing the nitrates to elemental nitrogen.

CHEMICAL OXIDATION

Municipal waste waters contain many organic materials only partially removed by the conventional treatment methods. Oxidants such as ozone and chlorine have been used for many years to improve the taste and odor qualities or to disinfect municipal drinking water. They improve the quality of water by destroying or altering the structure of the chemicals in the water.

However, the concentration of the organic materials in drinking water supplies is much less than it is in the waste-bearing waters reaching treatment plants. Until recently, the cost of the oxidants has prevented the use of this process in the treating of wastes. Now, improvements in the production and application of ozone and pure oxygen may reduce costs sufficiently to make their use practicable. When operated in conjunction with other processes, oxidation could become an effective weapon in eliminating wastes resistant to other processes.

POLYMERS AND POLLUTION

In discussing the coagulation-sedimentation process, mention was made of the use of alum or lime to force suspended solids into larger masses. The clumping together helps speed up one of the key steps in waste treatment—the separation of solids and liquids.

During the past 10 to 15 years, the chemical industry has been working on synthetic organic chemicals, known as polyelectrolytes or polymers, to further improve the separation step.

Formerly, polymers have proved effective when used at a later stage of treatment—the sludge disposal step. Sludge must be dewatered so that it can be more easily disposed of. By introducing polymers into the sludge, the physical and chemical bonds between the solids are tightened. When this happens, the water can be extracted more rapidly.

Wider use of polymers is now being investigated. By putting polymers into streams or rivers, it may be possible to capture silt at specified locations so that it can be removed in quantity.

If polymers are put into raw sewage, waste treatment plants may be able to combine a chemical process with the standard primary and secondary stages. And this method of removing solids can be applied immediately without lengthy and expensive addition of buildings or new facilities.

The chemicals also hold promise as a means of speeding the flow of waste waters through sewer systems, thus, in effect, increasing the capacity of existing systems.

---

the problem of sludge

No matter how good the treatment of wastes, there is always something left over. It may be the rags and sticks that were caught on the screens at the very beginning of the primary treatment. It could be brine or it could be sludge—that part of the sewage that settles to the bottom in sedimentation tanks. Whatever it is, there is always something that must be burned, buried, or disposed of in some manner.

It is a twofold problem. The sludge or other matter must be disposed of to complete a city's or industry's waste treatment. And it must be disposed of in a manner not to add to or upset the rest of the environment.

If it is burned, it must be done in a way not to add to the pollution of the atmosphere. This would only create an additional burden for our already overburdened air to cope with. And air pollutants by the action of rain and wind have a habit of returning to the water, complicating the waste treatment problem rather than helping it.

There are many methods and processes for dealing with the disposal problem, which is sometimes referred to as the problem of ultimate disposal. The most common method for disposing of sludge and other waste concentrates consists of digestion followed by filtration and incineration.

The digestion of sludge takes place in heated tanks where the material can decompose naturally and the odors can be controlled. As digested sludge consists of 90 to 95 percent water, the next step in disposal must be the removal of as much of the water as possible.

Water can be removed from sludge by use of a rotating filter drum and suction. As the drum rotates in the sludge, the water is pulled through the filter and the residues are peeled off for disposal. For more effective dewatering, the sludge can be first treated with a coagulant chemical such as lime or ferric chloride to produce larger solids before the sludge reaches the filter.

Drying beds which are usually made of layers of sand and gravel can be used to remove water from sludge. The sludge is spread over the bed and allowed to dry. After a week or two of drying, the residue will be reduced in volume and, consequently, will be easier to dispose.

Incineration consists of burning the dried sludge to reduce the residues to a safe, non-burnable ash. The ash can be disposed of by filling unused land or by dumping it well out into the ocean. Since most of the pollutants have been removed by the burning, the ash should cause very little change in the quality of the ocean waters.

A very promising new method of sludge disposal gets rid of the unwanted sludge and helps restore a ravaged countryside. In many areas of the country, tops of hills and mountains were sliced away to get at the coal beneath. This strip mining left ugly gashes and scars in otherwise beautiful valleys of many States. It would take nature many years to restore the denuded areas.

With the new disposal idea, digested sludge in semi-liquid form is piped to the spoiled areas. The slurry, containing many nutrients from the wastes, is spread over the land to give nature a hand in returning grass, trees, and flowers to the barren hilltops.

Restoration of the countryside will also help in the control of acids that drain from mines into streams and rivers, endangering the fish and other aquatic life and adding to the difficulty in reusing the water. Acids are formed when pyrite containing iron and sulfur is exposed to the air.

Slugde or other waste concentrates are not always costly burdens. By drying and other processes, some cities have produced fertilizers that are sold to help pay for part of the cost of treating wastes. If not sold to the public, some municipalities use the soil enrichers on parks, road parkways, and other public areas.

End, selection from the EPA's *A Primer on Waste Water Treatment.* See also the section in Chapter Two—Solid Wastes, concerning disposal of sewage sludge. The material above deals with the control of organic pollution, primarily from municipal sources. For information concerning control devices aimed at the wide variety of industrial pollutants, see the materials cited in the bibliography.

recycling of organics

A problem that is becoming of some concern is that the volume of wastes generated is so large that the return of even completely treated sewage containing only water and carbon dioxide (the end product of biological decomposition) may be sufficient to encourage eutrophication—a subject to be discussed in the next section. However, very few municipalities treat their wastes so completely, and virtually all municipal wastes contain phosphorous compounds that serve as nutrients to fertilize our waters. Furthermore, the present agricultural processes themselves threaten to destroy the fertility of the land while also damaging our waters. Recycling of organic wastes back to our lands may be the only proper direction for a waste treatment program to take.

This approach was used in the 19th century in England and is extensively used in Asia. A carefully monitored use of this technique has been carried on since the early 1960's at Pennsylvania State University under the direction of Louis T. Kardos. See also pp. Two-28 through Two-31.

REFERENCES AND SELECTED BIBLIOGRAPHY

See: KARDOS, "A New Prospect," 12 Environment No. 2, March 1970 at 10

COMMONER, "Soil and Freshwater: Damaged Global Fabric," 12 Environment No. 2, March, 1970 at 4

LAW and KERR, *Agricultural Utilization of Sewage Effluent and Sludge—an annotated bibliography,* FWPCA, U.S. Dept. of Interior, Jan. 1968 (obtainable from EPA)

Estimated increases in gross production of BOD^5 during 1957–68

Millions of Pounds of BOD_5 Per Year

Waste Source	1957	1964	1968	Increase 1957-64	Increase 1964-68
Food Processing	3400	4300	4600	900	300
Textile Mill Products	660	890	1100	230	210
Paper & Allied Products	4300	5900	7800	1600	1900
Chemical & Allied Products	5500	9700	14200	4200	4500
Petroleum & Coal	410	500	550	90	50
Rubber & Plastics	20	40	60	20	20
Primary Metals	350	480	550	130	70
Machinery	100	130	180	30	50
Transportation Equipment	50	120	160	70	40
All Other	300	390	470	90	80
Manufacturing Total	15,090	22,460	29,670	7370	7220
Sewered Population	5,700	7,600	8,500	2100	900
TOTAL	20,790	30,060	38,170	9470	8120
Annual Rate				5.4%	6.2%
Reduced by Treatment	8,090	14,090	24,610	6000	10,520
Annual Rate				8.2%	15.0%
Discharged	12,700	15,970	13,560	3270	-2410
Annual Rate				5.9%	-4.2%
Aggregate Treatment Efficiency	39%	47%	64%	21%	36%
Ratio of Domestic to Industrial BOD	1:2.6	1:2.9	1:3.5	1:3.9	1:8.0

d. The Costs of pollution

The following is excerpted from the second annual report of the Council on Environmental Quality, August, 1971:

damages from water pollution

The costs of water pollution damage are even less well documented than the costs of air pollution. The prices that industries and water users pay for treating polluted water for use, although relatively small, are measurable in dollars. Further, there are clear economic losses in contaminated fish and in lost fishery resources. Costs of lost amenities and recreational opportunities are less tangible but are no less real economic costs.

The losses of ocean and coastal fisheries and shellfish production by pollution of estuarine areas are substantial. Over one-fifth of the Nation's shellfish beds have been closed because of pollution. Before 1935, between 100,000 and 300,000 pounds of soft shell crabs were commercially harvested annually in San Francisco Bay. The industry is virtually nonexistent today, largely because of pollution. Similarly, the annual commercial harvest of shrimp from coastal areas dropped from over 6.3 million pounds before 1936 to only 10,000 pounds in 1965.

Increased salinity, due chiefly to man's use of water for irrigation, imposes costs on other users. Housewives must use more detergents in order to overcome water hardness. Industries must treat or dilute river water in order to meet boiler feed or cooling water requirements. Farmers may suffer decreased yields because of water salinity. The total of these damages in the Lower Colorado River Basin and Southern California Water Service area was estimated at $16 million annually in 1970. With the expected growth in these regions and the expected increase in salinity, these damages are estimated to climb to $28 million annually in 1980, and to over $50 million by 2010.

The value of cleaner water for recreation alone is roughly indicated by the results of a 1966 study of water quality in the Delaware estuary. Water degradation causes an estimated loss in the present value of recreational opportunities of up to $350 million. This estimate suggests that water pollution may cause recreational losses extending into many billions of dollars nationwide.

The possibility of large recreational losses is supported by recent studies of the value of outdoor recreational opportunities in a series of California reservoirs, where water quality permitted a range of recreational activities. Annual benefits from water sports ranged up to over $2 million per lake—values that would be lost with the level of deterioration that is now found in many of the Nation's water bodies. The rapidly increasing demands for recreation and scenic amenities will raise the value of losses from pollution.

Once again we quote from the second annual CEQ report.

water pollution costs

Current data for water pollution control expenditures are primarily for municipal and industrial waste treatment. Data on such "nonpoint" sources as agricultural runoff and acid mine drainage are considerably less reliable.

public treatment costs

public treatment costs—During 1970, municipal waste treatment facilities serviced about 95 percent of the sewered population (70 percent of the total population). These municipal operations also provided waste treatment for most small non-water-intensive industries; for some heavy industry; and nearly all commercial, institutional and financial establishments. Over 60 percent of the total sewered population is receiving at least secondary (biological) treatment, and 35 percent is receiving only primary (settling) treatment. Only 5 percent of the sewered population is receiving no treatment at all.

The current replacement value of municipal treatment plants amounts to about $6.1 billion. Interceptor sewers, pumping stations, and outfalls associated with the waste treatment plants add a replacement value of approximately $7.6 billion, for a total of $13.7 billion. These figures do not include

public treatment costs

the estimated value of sanitary, storm, or combined sewers which feed into municipal systems—about $12 billion additional capital.

Much of this treatment plant investment has been made in recent years. Annual costs to operate, maintain, service, and replace this growing system have been rising steadily. In 1970, they were close to $1.6 billion, compared to $800 to $900 million in 1965.

In spite of the sharp rise in the levels of investment and their magnitude, far more capital will be required to keep municipal treatment in step with national water quality objectives. Estimates indicate that slightly more than $4 billion will be required to eliminate deficiencies in existing treatment facilities. Another $8 billion will be necessary between 1971 and 1974 to meet replacement and population growth needs.

This EPA estimate of $12 billion total is for treatment and related facilities, eligible for Federal grants. The National League of Cities/U.S. Conference of Mayors made another estimate of municipal waste treatment needs of between $33 and $37 billion. That estimate was calculated from responses from its member cities. However, when costs ineligible for funds under the Federal grant program are deducted and double counting eliminated, the National League of Cities/U.S. Conference of Mayors estimate becomes about $11 billion on a comparable basis with EPA estimates.

Based on 1968 data, additional costs have been estimated for capital investment needed to alleviate the problems of overflows from combined sewers. The American Public Works Association calculates that it will cost between $15 billion and $48 billion to remedy overflows from combined sewers. The $15 billion figure would cover a variety of alternatives short of complete separation, and the $48 billion would finance complete separation of combined sewers—$30 billion in public costs and $18 billion in private costs.

The accumulated investment in treatment systems by 1974 will be accompanied by substantially increased costs of operation. The 1974 annualized costs of municipal water treatment are projected at $3.2 billion. Table A–1 compares these municipal annual investments, cumulative investments, and annualized expenditures for 1970 and 1974. Costs will continue to increase even after 1974, but at less dramatic rates.

These annual expenditures can be compared with expenditures for other municipal services. The annual costs for municipal waste treatment will amount to about $20 to $22 per person served, compared to 1969 municipal per capita expenditures of $22 for police, $34 for education, and $18 for public welfare.

private treatment costs

private treatment costs—The Bureau of the Census reports that of the 240,000 manufacturing establishments in the U.S. in 1968, fewer than 10,000 used 20 million or more gallons of water. Ninety-one percent of the 35.7 trillion gallons of water used by major manufacturers in 1968 was used by 5,000 food, pulp and paper, chemicals, petroleum, and primary metals firms. Their

Table A–1

Current and Projected Expenditures for Public Waste Water Treatment Systems, 1970 and 1974

(In millions of dollars)

Type of expenditure	1970	1974
Cumulative investment		
Waste treatment	$ 6,100	$ 9,400
Waste transmission	7,600	14,000
Total	13,700	23,400
Annual investment		
Replacement of existing facilities	400	800
New investment	800	3,200
Total	1,200	4,000
Annualized costs		
Operation	310	900
Replacement	410	760
Interest [1]	840	1,520
Total	1,560	3,180

[1] Expressed as an opportunity cost of carrying replacement value at average 1970 rate for high-grade local government bond, 6.51 percent.

waste water discharge was several times the amount discharged by the sewered population of the United States. The bio-chemical oxygen demand (BOD)—a measure of oxygen needed to decompose the wastes—was roughly four to five times that of total domestic liquid wastes.

The waste loads of many of the smaller manufacturers do not significantly differ from other sources of municipal waste loads. The overwhelming number of these companies discharge directly to municipal systems. Yet because they are relatively small water users, they account for only about 10 percent of all manufacturing waste water discharges.

There are significant differences in the economics of pollution abatement for municipal and industrial operations. Industrial investment is usually far smaller to achieve the same level of treatment. In most cases, a manufacturer does not incur the collection and intercepting sewer costs which represent a majority of municipal costs. In addition, the more concentrated nature and greater volume of their wastes result in lower unit investment costs for treatment. However, industrial operating costs are higher than municipal operating costs—averaging twice as much per unit of invested capacity.

Another difference between municipal and industrial abatement costs is the wider range of alternatives available to industry. Unlike municipalities, industries can reduce waste discharges through process changes and better internal management as well as through treatment. Industrial expenditures for process changes that reduce pollution often result in more efficient production. Accordingly, it is often difficult—and sometimes impossible—to allocate costs between pollution abatement and increased production.

private treatment costs

Nationwide, an estimated 50 percent of the wastes treated in municipal plants are from industrial sources, although the percentage of municipal capacity so used varies greatly from plant to plant. The costs of such capacity are included within the estimates of capital and operating costs for municipal waste treatment plants.

Most existing industrial waste treatment facilities have probably been built over the last decade. As estimated by McGraw-Hill, investments by manufacturing plants were about $870 million in 1970 and $600 million in 1969—compared with less than $200 million in 1960. Industries other than manufacturing—mining, electric utilities, commercial establishments, etc.—estimate their 1970 investment for water pollution control at $287 million. The total 1970 investment, then, is approximately $1.2 billion. The McGraw-Hill survey indicated that industry planned to spend $1.6 billion for water pollution control investments in 1971. A breakdown of 1970 investments by industry is shown in Table A–2. Although most of this investment is for treating process wastes, it also includes the costs for electric utilities to reduce thermal pollution. These figures do not include investment in municipal systems specifically for treating industrial wastes.

This large investment in treatment facilities requires significant expenditures for operation and maintenance. EPA estimates that the annualized costs—which include both capital and operation and maintenance costs—of manufacturing related water pollution treatment may amount to slightly over $1 billion for 1970 alone. About $575 million of it was operation and maintenance costs, and about $475 million was annualized capital costs. These figures do not include the user charges paid by many smaller firms for waste treatment by municipal systems. Nor do they include the operating costs

Table A–2

Total Investment for Water Pollution Control, 1970

(In millions of dollars)

Industry	Investments
Food and kindred products	$46
Textiles	9
Paper	94
Chemicals	90
Petroleum	185
Rubber	18
Primary metals	140
Machinery	66
Transportation	31
Other manufacturing	193
Total manufacturing	872
Mining	42
Electric utilities	149
Other business	96
All business	1,159

Source: McGraw-Hill Publications Co.

associated with electric power generation, mining and a number of small industries.

EPA estimates that manufacturers' investments for waste treatment equipment should average about $1 billion per year between 1971 and 1974—$3.1 billion for new waste treatment facilities and another $1 billion for capital replacement. Annualized costs of control in 1974 would also substantially increase, to over $1.8 billion.

EPA estimates that up to $2 billion additional investment will be needed to control thermal pollution from electric power plants. This estimate assumes complete use of recirculation or closed systems for cooling water.

Table A–3 contrasts current manufacturing expenditures with those required by 1974 water quality standards. As the table indicates, four industries—paper, food, chemicals, and primary metals—spent two-thirds of the money in 1970. By 1974, they will account for almost 80 percent of the total.

miscellaneous pollution costs

other water pollution control costs—Although erosion contributes more pollutants by weight than any other source, estimated control costs are unavailable, incomplete or rudimentary. Costs for erosion control on farms are unknown. EPA estimates of highway erosion control costs range from $130 million up to $7 billion. Increased costs for erosion control at urban construction projects has been esimated at between $140 million and $1.4 billion a year. Sediment control for 300,000 miles of stream banks is estimated at between $200 million and $3 billion.

Estimates of costs to curb pollution from mining also vary widely. One study estimated that to curtail acid mine drainage from the most severe cases of unreclaimed surface mines may cost upwards of $300 million. To reclaim the total 2 million acres of unreclaimed or inadequately reclaimed lands would cost an estimated $750 million. To upgrade these lands further to farming, grazing, and recreational quality levels might bring total costs to at least $1.2 billion. But even these estimates may be too low. For example, to control acid mine drainage in Appalachia alone—from both surface and underground sources—is estimated in another study to cost over $5 billion, which might raise the national bill to $7 billion.

Costs for control of vessel pollution have also been estimated. In 1971, EPA estimated that the initial costs of meeting marine secondary waste treatment standards would range between $1.1 and $2.3 billion.

These various estimates do not cover the costs of water pollution control from a number of other sources. For example, there are no reliable estimates of the costs of controlling feedlot or other animal wastes or oil spills and intentional discharges of oil.

Table A–3

Estimated Costs of Industrial Waste Treatment, 1970 and 1974 [1]

(Dollars in millions)

Industry	1970 [2]		1974		
	Annual costs	Percent of total	Annual costs	Percent of total	Percent increase 1970–74
Primary metals	239.3	23	426.0	23	78
Chemicals	187.2	18	421.4	23	125
Food and kindred products	158.4	15	260.0	14	.64
Paper	116.9	11	325.9	18	179
Transportation equipment	107.9	10	115.4	6	7
Petroleum	95.5	9	110.2	6	15
Machinery	60.1	5	42.3	2	(30)
Textiles	50.2	5	79.9	4	59
Rubber and plastics	8.9	1	23.5	1	164
All other manufacturing	29.2	3	57.2	3	96
Total	1,053.6	100	1,861.8	100	77

[1] Interest costs based on average 1970 rate of Aaa + Bbb corporate, or 7.42 percent.
[2] Assumes 1954–70 rate of increase in output and 1954–68 shift in water use per unit of output.

Source: Environmental Protection Agency.

The following is also from the Council on Environmental Quality's second annual report:

impact on industries

impact on industries

To say that environmental controls will hurt business and industry is to confuse the interests of existing firms with the health of commerce as a whole. Some companies—particularly those that must absorb large pollution costs—will be hard hit. But many firms will benefit, and new firms and industries will emerge in response to changing environmental demands.

A few major industries account for most industrial water use and most industrial water pollution. They will bear a much bigger share of the total burden, but as Table 6 shows, in most cases their water pollution control costs will probably fall substantially below 1 percent of the value of their products shipped. These estimates are for annualized costs of control in 1974—assuming secondary treatment by all manufacturers. However, the value of shipments is for 1967; hence the percentage of pollution control costs to value of shipments is overstated. The 5 percent increase in total payroll shown in Table 6 indicates that the costs of water pollution control are generally less than historic wage increases. And once the pollution control equipment is installed, the costs of operating it will probably not rise nearly as fast as labor costs.

These estimates may, however, understate the impact on some individual industries, given the large number of different products and processes within the manufacturing categories indicated. For example, the food and kindred products category in Table 6 includes everything from bakeries—with almost no problems of water pollution—to dairy and cannery operations, which must control huge amounts of waste water effluents. Consequently, average costs for broadly defined groups overstate costs for some and seriously understate costs for others.

Table 6

Impact of Waste Water Treatment Costs on Selected Industries, 1974

(Dollars in millions)

Industry	1967 value of shipments	Total annual control costs	5 percent increase in wages	Control costs as percent of 1967 value of shipments	5 percent increase in wages as percent of 1967 value of shipments
Food and kindred products	$84,062	$260	$506	0.3	0.6
Textiles	19,733	80	218	.4	1.1
Paper	20,740	326	221	1.6	1.1
Chemicals	42,470	421	325	1.0	.8
Petroleum	22,042	110	61	.5	.3
Rubber and plastics	12,789	24	165	.2	1.3
Primary metals	46,550	396	492	.9	1.1
Machinery, excluding electrical	48,357	42	708	.1	1.5
Transportation equipment	68,238	115	752	.2	1.1

Source: Based on U.S. Department of Commerce, Bureau of the Census, and Environmental Protection Agency data.

potential for control

new applications of technology—A promising example of recent innovation in technological experimentation by State governments and their subdivisions is the Muskegon County Wastewater Management System. With more than $2 million from EPA, the Michigan county has initiated a demonstration project using partially treated municipal sewage, which contains soil conditioners and nutrients, to reclaim barren land for agricultural use. When waste water is sprayed on the land, the soil will remove nutrients and absorb heavy metals, both of which are used by plants. The project is designed, however, to prevent overloading of heavy metals in the soil. A drainage network of tiles and wells will return clean water to the county's aquifers, lakes, and rivers—to augment water supply or stream flows. The concept is not new, but the large-scale application of it is.

A bold project that required the cooperative commitment of the county, the State, the Federal Government, and 13 units of local government, the Muskegon County experiment is an ex-potential for control

ample of increasing and needed efforts to reuse waterborne wastes rather than simply collecting them for unproductive and costly disposal. If the project proves viable for widespread application, it will provide an alternative to the conventional municipal waste treatment plant. Preliminary evaluation suggests the project will be less costly than expensive tertiary treatment that would still result in wastes being discharged into Lake Michigan.

In a related, subsequent development, the Army Corps of Engineers and the Environmental Protection Agency announced a joint program to develop regional waste water management systems for five of the Nation's largest urban centers. In these areas—Boston (Merrimack Basin), Chicago, Cleveland, Detroit, and San Francisco—the two agencies will jointly study alternative waste water management posibilities in close cooperation with State and local governments. Based on the premise that pollutants are potential resources out of place, these studies will consider alternatives such as the Muskegon County system. Only alternatives capable of achieving established water quality standards and compliance schedules will be considered.

End, quote from CEQ report.

REFERENCES AND SELECTED BIBLIOGRAPHY

Report to the Congress, Controlling Industrial Water Pollution—Progress and Problems, Federal Water Quality Administration, Department of the Interior, Dec. 2, 1970

Environmental Health Series, *Symposium on Streamflow Regulation for Quality Control,* U.S. Department of Health, Education, and Welfare, Public Health Service, June 1965

LUND, Herbert F., ed., *Industrial Pollution Control Handbook,* McGraw-Hill: 1971

HOLDEN, W.S., ed., *Water Treatment and Examination,* Williams and Wilkines Co.: 1970

VELZ, Clarence J., *Applied Stream Sanitation,* Wiley-Interscience: 1970

BRYAN, E. H., "Water Supply & Pollution Control Aspects of Urbanization," 30 *Law & Contemporary Problems* 176 (Winter 1965)

CARMICHAEL, D. M., "Forty Years of Water Pollution Control in Wisconsin: A Case Study," 1967 *Wisc. L. Rev.* 350 (Sept. 1967)

"Cold Facts on Hot Water: Legal Aspects of Thermal Pollution," 1969 *Wisc. L. Rev.,* 253 (1969)

EDWARDS, M.N., "The Legislative Approach to Air & Water Quality," 1 *Nat. Res. Law* 58 (Jan. 1968)

KRODELL, J.D., "Liability for Pollution of Surface & Underground Waters," 12 *Rocky Mt. ML Institute* 1 (1967)

NEBOLSINE, R., "Today's Problems of Industrial Waste Water Pollution Abatement," 1 *Nat. Res. Law* 39 (Jan. 1968)

HINES, "Controlling Industrial Water Pollution: Color the Problem Green," 9 *Boston Col. Ind. & Comm. L. Rev.* No. 3 (Spring 1968)

"Agriculture: The Unseen Foe in the War on Pollution," 55 *Cornell L. Rev.* 740 (1970)

DEGLER, Stanley E., *Federal Pollution Control Programs; Water, Air and Solid Wastes,* Washington, BNA Books, 1969

National Research Council Committee on Pollution, *Waste Management and Control,* Washington, National Academy of Sciences, National Research Council, 1966

WILLRICH, Ted L. and HINES, N. Williams, eds., *Water Pollution Control and Abatement* Ames, Iowa State University Press, 1967

MURPHY, Earl F., *Water Purity: a Study in Legal Control of Natural Resources,* Madison, The University of Wisconsin Press, 1961

American Public Health Association, *Standard Methods for the Examination of Water and Wastewater.* 12th ed. New York, American Public Health Assn. 1967

BABBITTand BAUMANN, *Sewerage and Sewage Treatment,* 8th ed. New York, John Wiley Sons, Inc. 1958

CARR, Donald E., *Death of the Sweet Waters,* New York, W.W. Norton & Co., Inc., 1966.

COHN, Morris M., *Sewers for Growing America,* Ambler Certain Teed Products Corp. 1966

ECKENFELDER, William Wesley, *Industrial Water Pollution Control,* New York, McGraw-Hill, 1966

EHLERS, Victor Marcus, *Municipal and Rural Sanitation*, 6th ed. New York, McGraw-Hill, 1965

Federal Water Pollution Control Administration, U.S. Department of the Interior, by the American Public Works Association, *Problems of Combined Sewer Facilities and Overflows*, December, 1967

GOLDMAN, Marshall I., ed., *Controlling Pollution, The Economics of a Cleaner America* Englewood Cliffs, N. J., Prentice-Hall, Inc. 1967

GRAHAM, Frank, Jr., *Disaster by Default: Politics and Water Pollution*, New York, M. Evans and Company, Inc., 1966

Cleaning Our Environment, The Chemical Basis for Action, American Chemical Society, Washington, 1969 paper

U.S. Dept. of the Interior, FWPCA *The Practice of Water Pollution Biology*, Washington, D.C. G.P.O., 1969 paper

BESSELIEVRE, Edmund B., *The Treatment of Industrial Wastes*, New York, McGraw-Hill Book Co., 1969

GAVIS, Jerome, *Waste Water Reuse*, National Technical Information Service Publication No. TB201 535 (July 1971)

e. Eutrophication

Eutrophication, from the Greek for "well-fed," is the process of giving a lake a belly ache.

In more dignified language, it is the process of a body of water becoming overloaded with algae. The algae, although giving off oxygen while alive, become so numerous that they no longer have sufficient light and carbon dioxide to live. Then they die in vast numbers, and in decomposing, oxygen is used. Considerable additional oxygen is used after the biological breakdown in the breakdown of the forms of nitrogen that were in the algae.

It is common in euthrophic waters for the layers near the surface to be tolerably well oxygenated, while lower levels are almost devoid of oxygen. The layers are largely prevented from mixing because warmer water is less dense, and floats above colder water.

The decomposition of algae releases the nutrients (principally phosphates) to feed yet more algae. Lakes thus are first enriched biologically, then turn into swamps, and finally fill-in to become dry land

the problem of phosphates

Man-added plant nutrients assist this process. Plant nutrients are primarily nitrogen and phosphorus compounds. They can enter the water by run-off, particularly from agriculture areas, where inorganic chemical fertilizers have been applied to the land. However, most phosphorus entering our waters comes from municipal waste. The most serious source of phosphate nutrients are detergents which passed through municipal treatment plants with very little reduction in quantity. Nitrates are another nutrient, and until lately had been ignored, both because of technical difficulties in their removal, and because of the vast supply of nitrogen already available from the air. But lately some experiments have been made at removing nitrates in sewage treatment plants.

The biological response produced by natural eutrophication is extremely slow. On the other hand, the inputs of man-derived nutrients into a lake can produce in a few decades a biological response similar to that which under natural conditions would take tens of thousands of years.

Increased population, industrialization, intensified agricultural practices and the use of phosphorus-based detergents since the late 1940's have greatly increased the rate of eutrophication of lakes in many parts of the world. Dense nuisance growths of algae and aquatic weeds degrade water quality. *Cladophora,* and attached algae, piles up on the beaches when dislodged by wave action. Blue-green algae accumulate, creating unsightly odorous scums.

These eutrophic conditions inhibit many of the legitimate uses of the lake. Algae growths interfere with domestic and industrial water supplies by causing taste and odor problems and by clogging filters; contribute to the dramatic decrease in the number of valuable species of fish; restrict the use of prime recreational areas such as beaches; degrade shoreline properties; and spoil aesthetic values.

The most publicized eutrophication problem has been Lake Erie. The phosphorus entering Lake Erie amounts to 137,000 pounds per day. Municipal wastes make up 72 percent, rural water run-off 17 percent, industrial wastes 4 percent, and urban water run-off 7 percent. In municipal wastes, 66 percent of the phosphorus comes from detergents. Most of the remainder comes from human wastes.

The aid to algae growth given by detergents brings the danger that the Lake will reach such a state of eutrophication whereby, in spite of eliminating all waste inputs, the bottom sediments become such that the cycle is indefinitely perpetuated. The algae blooms and low oxygen levels already found in the Lake lend credence to this fear. In 1964, a 2,600 square mile area in the central basin was found practically devoid of oxygen beneath the thermocline. Nearly one-fourth of the lake area now becomes nearly devoid of oxygen in bottom water during summer thermal stratification, and this situation is increasing both in extent and duration of occurrence.

the problem of phosphates

The immediate effects of these algae are the eyesores created at beaches when this material is washed ashore and the ecological change in the Lake that is destroying commercial fishing. The highest commercial fish yield of record, 1915, was 76 million pounds. This had declined to an average of 52 million pounds in 1960-64, and in 1967, fish production was down to 49.4 million pounds.

Even more important, the commercial value of the catch has substantially declined as the more desirable species have been replaced by scavenger fish. Carp accounted for nearly half the catch reported in the Michigan waters of Lake Erie in 1966. Whitefish and pike have virtually disappeared; biological as well as commercial extinction is imminent. Blue pike production in 1956 was nearly seven million pounds, worth $1,316,000. By 1963, production was down to 200 pounds, worth $120. In 1964 it was but 136 pounds. To reverse this trend, salmon and trout plantings were made in 1968. The introduction of Coho salmon into Lake Erie is a pilot program carried out under the Anadromous Fish Act. Such a program after apparent success in Lake Michigan was set back by the discovery of large amounts of pesticides in the fish. Time will tell whether these fish take to other lakes.

Nutritional over-enrichment of Lake Erie presents the greatest threat to its future. Yet little has been done to stop it. One approach would be to change the composition of detergents so as to end the use of plant nutrients as an ingredient of detergents. Detergents have been changed once under pressure of society. Until late 1964, alkylbenzene sulfonate (ABS) was a major ingredient of detergents. This was not biodegradable (decomposable organically), and the result was detergent foam which appeared in drinking water and complicated all sewage treatment. Between 1961 and 1964, hearings held by federal and state legislative bodies "encouraged" the detergent industry to develop "soft" or biodegradable products. Linear alkylate sulfonate (LAS) was developed. In late 1964, substitution of this raw material in widely used products began, and by July 1965, all washing and cleaning products manufactured for household and industrial use were biodegradable.

Thus, the soap and detergent industry solved one technical problem, but phosphates continue to be used in the manufacture of detergents. The industry claims an acceptable substitute for phosphate is not available. This is true, but as is so often the case, the rate at which such technical knowledge will be developed is primarily in the hands of those who would be regulated.

The soap and detergent representatives acknowledge that phosphates affect the nutrient balance of waters, but believe that the exact role of algal growth and eutrophication have not been clearly defined. They pointed out that in 1958, 70 percent of the elemental phosphorous sold went into fertilizers and 13 percent became constituents of detergents. For several years they argued that we did not really know what caused eutrophication. This was and continues to be true—a problem that raises philosophical questions as to who should bear the risk and expense of partially understood technological developments. With the development of substitutes, the industry position continues to emphasize the lack of knowledge while both using and pointing to the dangers of substitutes. A joint government-industry task force to investigate control of eutrophication was formed. Its mandate was to develop a standardized procedure to determine algae growth potential (AGP) of various chemicals and waters. The problem, of course, does need more study, for the scientific relationship between nutrients and algae growth is far from being understood. But the major efforts of the task force seems to have been to delay government regulation. Recently the International Joint Commission's publications indicate that this organization is convinced that phosphate is the most serious nutrient pollution. Canada is moving to ban this substance. In the United States the feeling in Congress seems to be that they are willing to legislate on the subject if someone can propose an intelligent solution. No one seems able to do so. The cause of eutrophication is not completely understood. Phosphates need to be used in detergents until an acceptable substitute is found; no consensus of experts has yet agreed on a substitute either less harmful or potentially harmful.

the problem of phosphates

The detergent industry encourages the consideration of phosphate removal in the sewage treatment plant. This achieves the desired result and shifts the removal cost away from the industry. Phosphate removal has now progressed so that it is technically possible to remove the substance. A variety of substances can be added in the activated sludge process to create a removable insoluble precipitate. Aluminum plus calcium or sodium seems to give the best results. The use of pulverized coal as a filter and adsorbent also offers interesting possibilities, since after use it can be burned as a fuel, eliminating the usual disposal problem. This process, in contrast to conventional bio-oxidation systems, does not produce nitrates from nitrogen compounds, so the concentration of nitrates in the effluent from this process is very low. Phosphate removal will prevent the phosphates from passing through the sewage treatment facility and into a lake, but the process can be expected to increase treatment costs, perhaps substantially.

The above subject is treated at much greater depth in this author's article, "Wastes, Water, and Wishful Thinking: The Battle for Lake Erie," *Case Western Reserve Law Review*, Vol. 20, No. 5, of November, 1968.

To deal with the eutrophication problem requires an understanding of the role of detergents in American life and their composition.

A detergent does five things:

1. It wets the surface to be cleaned;
2. Wets the dirt;
3. Emulsifies the oily dirt;
4. Removes dirt;
5. Keeps the dirt suspended in the water.

The first four requirements are necessary for cleaning. The last requirement is necessary to the proper functioning of modern washing machines.

A typical detergent, until the anti-phosphate movement, would have contained approximately: 20 percent surface-active agents; 35–50 percent polyphosphates; 5 percent sodium silicate (a corrosion inhibitor); 1 percent sodium carboxymethylcellulose (CMC) (a soil suspender); optical brighteners; coloring matter; perfume bleach; enzymes; and some chemical impurities in small amounts. Fillers of inert ingredients make up the remainder. Sodium sulfate and sodium carbonate are the most common.

The surface-active ingredient reduces the surface tension of wash water, permits the fabric to be wetted properly and removes dirt. This ingredient had not been biodegradable prior to 1965. Since 1965, it is, though problems can still occur when insufficient oxygen is present.

determining phosphorous content

The present eutrophication problem is caused by polyphosphates. Sodium tripolyphosphate is the most common, but other polyphosphates containing different percentages of phosphorous are used. Thus, "X percent of polyphosphates" means nothing, since this alone does not tell the percentage of phosphorous, which is the factor of importance.

However, by knowing the specific polyphosphate used and its percentage, it is possible to calculate the percentage of phosphorous by multiplying the percentage of the specific polyphosphate by the figures indicated in the following table:

STPP	by	0.2526
TSPP	by	0.2332
TKPP	by	0.1937
TSP	by	0.1892
ClTSP	by	0.0813
Octadecene	by	0.093

Key to Phosphate Abreviations

STPP	Pentasodium Tripolyphosphate ($Na_5P_3O_{10}$)
TSPP	Tetrasodium Pyrophosphate ($Na_4P_2O_7$)
TKPP	Tetrapotassium Pyrophosphate ($K_4P_2O_7$)
TSP	Trisodium Orthophosphate (Na_3PO_4)
ClTSP	Chlorinated Trisodium Orthophosphate Hydrate
Octadecene	Phosphonated Octadecene

See *Phosphates and Phosphate Substitutes in Detergents: Government Action and Public Confusion*, Ninth Report by the Committee on Government Operations, 92d Cong., 2d Sess., House Report No. 92-918, March 15, 1972.

In New York State boxes of detergent must be labeled as a percent of trisodium phosphate regardless of the polyphosphate actually used. Canadian law expresses phosphate as percentages of phosphorus pentoxide (P^2O^5). Water pollution legislation aimed at removal efficiency often expresses phosphorus in other ways.

The summary of water quality standards-phosphate criteria was issued by the EPA, Office of Water Programs, on March 1, 1972. *See* BNA 621:0701.

role of detergents

The phosphate is necessary to:

1. Soften water by sequestering hardness ions;
2. Increase the efficiency of the surface active agent;
3. Furnish alkalinity necessary for cleaning.

Substitutes Soap manufacturing is dependent on a source of fatty acids as a raw material. If everyone changed to soap, under present conditions it is doubtful that there is a sufficient supply of animal fat to meet demands. Further there is a major odor pollution output from fat rendering plants. Expanded use of palm oil from coconut palms as a fatty acid source may provide a feasible substitute to animal fat. This would have a definite impact on the economies of many underdeveloped and developing nations of the world. (*See,* Barry Commoner, *The Closing Circle* [1971] at 153).

Colgate-Palmolive has begun marketing carbonate-based (soda ash) detergents in three areas that have banned phosphates. These are Eire County, N.Y.; Dade County (Miami), Florida, and Cook County (Chicago), Illinois. *See*, "Colgate Detergents Without Phosphates To Be Sold in 3 Areas," *The Wall Street Journal,* June 6, 1972 at 24.

Washing soda added to soap acts as a water softener. Washing soda creates a precipitate which can form soap curd, a fact which may make use in home washers difficult. They can, however, redeposit the dirt plus curd in the laundry which at least gives some people the impression that they are getting soft laundry.

Don't wash could be a useful technique from an environmental point of view, though moderation would be required to avoid localized air pollution. In this vein one wonders about the social utility of large advertising campaigns to encourage greater consumption of a product that is very likely harmful. Careful design of washing machines to use a minimal amount of detergent should be encouraged. Carefully tailoring detergents to use the minimal amount of polyphosphate necessary for water conditions in the local area should be encouraged. Driving phosphate below this level could result in increased use of detergent. Allowing the purchaser to obtain detergent with phosphate levels as low as possible for the use intended could be beneficial.

No such labelling requirement currently exists, but it is quite possible that such a law will be passed at the federal level.

substitutes for phosphates

In order to abate the problems created by detergent phosphate, many manufacturers began to substitute nitrilotriacetic acid (NTA) for at least part of the phosphate component of detergents. Shortly after this substitution began, eminent scientists such as Dr. Samuel Epstein began to question the safety of NTA. (*Environment*, Sept. 1970 at 3) Test data indicated that substantial potential for harm was possible from NTA. To increase exposure to several billion pounds a year would, in the words of Dr. Epstein, be "jumping from an ecological frying pan into a toxicological fire." Criticism from the scientific community continued, and by December of 1970, under intense government pressure, industry agreed not to use NTA as a constituent of detergents.

dangers of substitutes

Another substitute might be organic polyelectrolytes. Dr. I. A. Eldib, president of Eldib Engineering and Research, of Newark, N.J., a firm which produces polyelectrolyte detergents, has impressive figures on their use. He has testified repeatedly as to their efficacy, but they do not seem to have been adopted.

The question then remains, what will be used as a substitute for phosphate that is not more harmful? What substances are used in the detergents now on the market that are advertised as not containing phosphates?

Good Housekeeping magazine of January 1971 has some naive advice:

"But it is already known that some of these products contain high amounts of such ingredients as sodium chloride (salt), sodium metasilicate, sodium carbonate and borax, none of which has cleaning power equivalent to phosphates. In addition to being light on soil-removing ingredients, some products may be extremely caustic and therefore prove corrosive to equipment and hazardous in use. However, phosphate-free products are arriving on the scene almost daily and we suggest that would-be users read labels carefully and perhaps request data regarding safety from the manufacturer."

The labels of some of the new "pollution-free" detergents read:

"CAUTION: Contains alkaline silicates. Avoid contact with eyes. In case of eye contact flush with plenty of water. If swallowed, give water or milk and follow with citrus fruit juice or diluted vinegar. Call a physician immediately. KEEP OUT OF REACH OF CHILDREN"

This can legally be sold and is being sold. If everyone adopts this pollution-free detergent, several billion pounds will go into America's water supply. In Connecticut, an infant was killed by breathing the dust of a detergent (*New Republic*, Oct. 9, 1971 at 13). On September 23, 1971, a Federal Trade Commission complaint (File No. 7123679) alleged that Ecolo-G detergent falsely advertised that it was safe and not hazardous.

NOTE: The National Health Institute of Environmental Health Sciences reportedly has found that all of several detergents tested can irritate eyes, and that some of these can cause blindness. A soap tested (Ivory Snow) was the least dangerous of the cleaning powders tested. Worst of those tested was one with metasilicate (Ecolo-G), followed by those with carbonates (Sears and Arm and Hammer). See: "Eye Peril Seen in Some Detergents," an Associated Press story printed in the Washington, D. C., Evening Star July 5, 1972 at A-10 and in many other papers in the nation.

The following three paragraphs are quoted from the Council on Environmental Quality's second annual report, at p. 44:

restrictions on phosphates

Phosphates—At both the State and local levels, one of the most publicized regulatory activities in the past year was enactment of restrictions on phosphate content of detergents. Cities and counties in Florida, Illinois, Maine, Maryland, Michigan, New York, Ohio and Wisconsin have acted to limit phosphates in detergents. Several of these laws have been challenged in court by detergent manufacturers.

Among the States, Connecticut, Florida, Indiana, Maine, Minnesota, and New York have enacted legislation to regulate the phosphate content of detergents.* In New York and Connecticut phosphates will be banned from detergents after January 1 and June 30, 1973, respectively. In Indiana, phosphates will be limited to 3 percent by weight on January 1, 1973. These three States have also authorized or required interim reductions. In Maine, phosphates in detergents are limited to 8.7 percent (phosphorus) as of June 1, 1972. Florida provides that after January 1, 1973, no detergent may contain additives—including but not limited to phosphates—found by the State pollution control agency to be harmful to health or the environment. Minnesota legislation authorizes the State pollution control agency to regulate maximum permissible concentrations of any nutrients, such as phosphorus. Many other States and communities are considering phosphates legislation.

End excerpt from CEQ report.

phosphate bans in court

Courts are not interfering with those states which have passed laws limiting the phosphate content of detergent. The recent case of the *Soap and Detergent Association v. A.C. Offutt*, __F.Supp.__, 3 ERC 1117, S.D. Ind., Indianapolis Div. (August 31, 1971), saw a federal court uphold Indiana's law restricting detergent phosphate content to 3 per cent after January 1, 1973 as non-violative of the Due Process or Equal Protection Clauses of the Fourteenth Amendment.

Speaking for the three-judge panel, Judge Stevens, in a uniquely phrased opinion, found (3 ERC at 1118, 1120):

> [U]ltimately what is being requested is that a three-Judge Federal Court enjoin the operation of a statute enacted by the legislature of Indiana.
>
> * * * *
>
> The impact of the Statute, insofar as the evidence discloses, seems to be on the people of Indiana primarily who will be deprived of what may well be a very desirable product, phosphate detergents, and who may have to pay more because of the added cost these large companies will have to incur to distribute in Indiana, but that is a cost and sacrifice the people of Indiana will have to suffer. We do not find in the evidence any significant showing of adverse impact on out-of-State consumers or on out-of-State manufacturers, except of course, there may be additional cost on Defendants. We don't think the economies of scale which are involved to a certain extent here really rise to the dignity of a constitutionally protected right.
>
> * * * *
>
> In other words, to put it more directly, if the people of Indiana prefer to wear gray shirts and have a little hardness distilled on their glasses, so forth and so on, as a price for obtaining cleaner water, or for obtaining a chance of having lesser phosphate content which in turn may produce or may not produce, we don't know, lesser amounts of algae, that is a choice which we feel the people of Indiana should make through the Indiana Legislature.

*Public Act No. 248 [1971], Conn. Laws; Public Act No. 71-355 [1971], Fla. Laws; H. Bill No. 1551 [1971], Ind. Laws; Ch. 323 [1971], Me. Laws; Ch. 896 [1971], Minn. Laws; Ass. Bill No. 6963-A [1971], New York Laws.

In another case, the three major phosphate detergent manufacturers —Lever Bros.,Colgate-Palmolive, and Procter & Gamble—sought a preliminary injunction to prevent a Florida no-phosphate law from going into effect. They lost. [*Soap and Detergent Association v. Clark* (S.D. Florida, Sept. 8, 1971) 3 ERC 1075]. They did not appeal, but are going the political route. They hired the firm of former U.S. Senator George Smathers and two firms in which former county attorneys are members. [Carper, "Industry Fights Detergent Ban In Miami Area," The *Washington Post,* Oct. 30, 1971 at A4. See also *Lever Bros. v. FTC,* ___F.2d.___(1st Cir. 1971) [2 ERC 1651] (Dismissal for lack of ripeness affirmed), and *Soap & Detergent Assn. v. City of Akron,* No. 287406 (Ohio C. P. Summit County 1971) for a case in a state with unusually broad home-rule powers. Forces seeking to preserve the phosphate content of detergents are aided by the press releases issued in mid-September, 1971, by the U.S. Surgeon General, which criticize the phosphateless detergents.

To prevent the destruction of lake ecosystems the Canadian government and American state and local governments are moving to ban phosphate. The federal government was moving in this direction until about 1970 and since then has been marking time because of the fear that a phosphate ban could create an even more serious environmental and/or public health problem. Also in the background lies the possibility that phosphate is not the critical substance in causing eutrophication, or if it is no longer dumped a different species of algae will grow (one more nitrogen dependent).

REFERENCES AND SELECTED BIBLIOGRAPHY

FERGUSON, "A Nonmyopic Approach to the Problem of Excess Algal Growths," *Environmental Science and Technology,* March 1968 at 188

EDMONDSON, "Water-Quality Management and Lake Eutrophication: The Lake Washington Case," in *Water Resources Management and Public Policy,* ed. Cambell & Sylvester, 1968, at 139

MACKENTHUN, *Nitrogen and Phosphorous in Water,* an annotated selected bibliography of their biological effects, U.S. Dept. of H.E.W., Public Health Service, 1965

Pollution of Lake Erie, Lake Ontario and the International Section of the St. Lawrence River, Report to the International Joint Commission, Vol. 1-Summary, 1969

Pollution of Lake Erie, Lake Ontario and the International Section of the St. Lawrence River, Report to the International Joint Commission, Vol. 2-Lake Erie, 1969

Hearings, Subcommittee of the Committee on Government Operations, House of Representatives, 91st Cong., 1st Sess., Dec. 15 and 16, 1969. *Phosphates in Detergents and the Eutrophication of America's Waters,* 1970

Committee on Government Operations, *Phosphates in Detergents and the Eutrophication of America's Waters,* 91st Cong. 2d Sess., House Report No. 91-1004, April 14, 1970

REESE, "Detergent debate: Are worksavers helping to ruin our waters?," 1 *Smithsonian* No. 5, August 1970 at 25

REITZE, "Wastes, Water, and Wishful Thinking: The Battle of Lake Erie," 20 *Case Wes. Res. L. Rev.* 5 (Nov. 1968)

U.S. Dept. of the Interior, FWPCA, *Lake Erie Report,* (Aug. 1968)

Special Report on Potential Oil Pollution, Eutrophication, and Pollution from Watercraft, International Joint Commission, April 1970.

"No-Phosphate Detergents: Do They Work?" *Consumer Reports,* Oct. 1971

f. Public water supplies

Our water supply is something we take for granted. Very little law exists on the subject, for most environmental water law is aimed at the control of waste discharges. While water supplies are drawn from our polluted waterways, they are filtered and disinfected by public agencies and then ignored as an environmental problem. The United States Public Health Service provides guidelines, but has nearly no regulatory authority. State and local governments have some health laws dealing with the subject, but rarely is attention focused on these laws. The material below indicates the assumption of pure water in our municipal systems may not be justified.

The following is excerpted from the Environmental Protection Agency-Council on Environmental Quality *Issue Paper on Water Supply,* May 11, 1971, which summarized many aspects of the problem and outlined alternate solutions and legislative options. Briefly, these were the major problems according to the study:

> A. A number of communities—particularly communities of less than 5,000 population—are delivering *potentially dangerous* water. Based on extrapolation of the findings of the Community Water Supply Study, the phenomenon affects approximately 5.4% of the 160 million persons served by public water supply. Problems are generally related to bacterial contamination and/or harmful quantities of toxic or hazardous constituents.

impurities in water for drinking

> B. Nearly 25% of the 160 million persons served by community water supply systems are using water which *exceeds recommended* drinking water limits for one or more parameters. Although consumption of such water is not considered to represent an immediate threat to health, aesthetic (related to taste and odor), economic and convenience (related to excessive mineralization) problems exist, and such water supply systems may not provide adequate protection over the longer term.
>
> C. Most community water supply systems, including some large systems but most prevalent with smaller community systems, evidence *deficiencies* relating to construction, operation, maintenance and surveillance which may inhibit the ability of the suppliers to deliver water of an acceptable quality on a continuing basis.

Some 274,000 persons (or 3.3% of the 82 million people served by interstate carrier systems) are consuming water now prohibited under interstate quarantine regulations.

During the ten-year period 1961–1970, there were 128 known outbreaks of disease or poisoning attributed to drinking water. Of these, 35 outbreaks involving 39,810 cases of illness were attributed to drinking water from public water supply systems. Nearly half of these outbreaks were caused by contamination of distribution systems, and the causes of most of the remaining outbreaks were evenly distributed between inadequate treatment facilities and improper control of treatment processes. About one waterborne outbreak that we know about occurs per month with something over 100 persons becoming ill. Some of the illness is quite severe and about two deaths per year are attributed to waterborne outbreaks.

End, excerpt from EPA-CEQ Issue Paper.

The following is from the *Congressional Record,* Proceedings & Debates of the 91st Congress, Second Session, Vol. 116, No. 189, Wednesday, November 25, 1970, p. H10843, National Water Hygiene Act of 1970:

[Edited]

(Mr. Rogers of Florida)

A national survey conducted by the Department of Health, Education, and Welfare's Bureau of Water Hygiene, Environmental Health Service, and U.S. Public Health Service has caused grave concern in this Nation about the quality of our drinking water. This survey of 969 public water systems, known as the "Community Water Supply Study" in its July 1970 published form, is a systematic, sample analysis of the raw water sources, public water supply systems, and water distribution systems in various States and communities of our Nation. Some of the major findings of this survey are summarized as follows:

First, 41 percent of the 969 public water systems surveyed were delivering waters of inferior quality to 2.5 million people. In fact, 360,000 persons in the study population were being served by waters of a potentially dangerous quality.

water-borne diseases

The fact that waterborne diseases persist today was evidenced by the epidemic at Riverside, Calif., in 1965 which affected 18,000 people.

Under existing law the Public Health Service has only general authority to regulate interstate water carrier supplies, and then only relating to the control of communicable diseases caused by bacteriological contaminants in the water of some 709 systems in the Nation which supply only 82 million people with water. There is no authority over the water systems supplying the remaining 118 million people in our nation, and what little authority the public service has, is limited to biological contaminants, and not radiological, or chemical contaminants. For example, there is authority to protect only about 40 percent of the people in the United States from bacterially caused diarrhea, however, under law, chemically caused diarrhea induced by magnesium sulfate cannot be required to conform to minimum national hygiene standards. [*sic*] Since there are some 12,000 toxic chemical compounds in industrial use today, and more than 500 new chemicals are developed each year, we must move to correct this void in the law. We need mandatory minimum national standards for such dangerous chemicals or substances as arsenic, mercury, lead, selenium, organic carcinogens, nitrates, cyanide, and others, which under present law are only recommended.

End, passage quoted from the *Congressional Record.*

Pending legislation (S. 1478) would spread Federal authority on drinking water to all public utilities. The EPA's advisory Committee on Revision and application of Drinking Water Standards in 1972 was preparing new regulations that would be used under existing law or for the proposed comprehensive new water pollution control law.

A combination of ultraviolet and ultrasonic waves are used in a water decontaminator that reportedly is far superior in some ways to other systems. *See, The New York Times,* July 1, 1972 at C27.

The Environmental Protection Agency, in a news release Sept. 29, 1971, announced that the drinking water of Gulfport, Miss., had been prohibited for use on vessels calling at the piers or U.S. Coast Guard station there. Mentioned as other cities whose water supplies had recently been placed on the prohibited list were Asheville, N.C.; Pottsville, Pa.; Fall River, Mass., and Pascagoula, Miss.

A special water supply problem has been created in states such as California where groundwater is used for public drinking water supplies. Nitrate contamination is occurring because of agricultural irrigation practices. See report, "Poisoning the Wells," 11 *Environment* No. 1, Jan.-Feb. 1969 at 16

Stead, "Desalting California," 11 *Environment,* No. 5, June 1969 at 2

Regulations for making and processing loans and grants to rural communities and other associations for central domestic water and water disposal systems were issued by the Farmers Home Administration June 17, 1972 (*Federal Register* Vol. 37, 12036).

references

BALBE, Nelson M., *Water for the Cities: A History of the Urban Water Supply Problem in the United States,* New York, Syracuse Univ. Press, 1956

BEHRMAN, A.S., *Water is Everybody's Business,* Garden City, N.Y., Doubleday & Co., Inc., 1968 paper

WOLMAN, Abel (Selected Papers), WHITE, Gilbert F., ed. *Water, Health and Society,* Bloomington, Indiana Univ. Press, 1969

Public Health Service Drnking Water Standards, Revised 1962, U.S. Department of Health, Education and Welfare, Pub. No. 956

g. History of Federal water pollution control

The federal government has two major statutory programs for water pollution control. The first is based on the Rivers and Harbors Act of 1899, which gives the Army Corps of Engineers control over the pollution discharged into navigable waterways. It was originally designed to protect navigability but the language of the Act has been interpreted so that pollution more broadly defined can be controlled. For many years the use of the Act to control water pollution was minimal. The few cases prosecuted were usually aimed at the occasional or one-time discharge. Injunctive relief was, therefore, not a common remedy; only a small fine was imposed. Pollution, particularly when part of normal industrial operations, was usually considered to be a state responsibility, unless navigability was threatened. This act would have remained unimportant but for three developments. First, beginning in 1956, the Federal government entered the water pollution control field with a series of acts that created public acceptance of federal responsibility in this area. Second, the new acts were designed to be unenforceable (Industry doesn't want control, the public does. Compromise! Pollution control laws for the public, unenforceability for industry.) Third, the public's environmental concern, growing into a demand for action by 1969, caused a search for usable existing legislation, resulting in the rejuvenation of the 1899 Act. Recent regulatory changes have made this act in combination with the more recent legislation a major part of the Federal government's pollution control efforts.

The second program is based on the Federal Water Pollution Control Act, as amended.

This program can be traced back as far as 1912 when the Public Health Service was authorized to investigate pollution. However, except for waste treatment construction grants, during the 30's, the Federal efforts did not amount to much.

During this period, industrial lobbyists had firm control over the direction of the Federal effort. Alben Barkley, the Democratic senator from Kentucky and later vice president, was a key opponent of a strong Federal pollution program. Along with Fred Vinson of Kentucky in the House, he successfully protected the coal and industrial interests in the Ohio valley by pressing for legislation that would limit Federal efforts to investigations and sewer grants to municipal governments. Even this approach was not enacted into law until 1948, but for some twelve years was used as a device to kill more meaningful legislation, including the 1936 bill by Connecticut's Senator Lonergan to give the Federal government injunctive powers, and the 1940 bill by Senator Mundt to give the Corps of Engineers power to clean-up pollution. Finally in 1948, Senator Barkley cosponsored with Senator Robert A. Taft the bill that became the Water Pollution Control Act of 1948. It required the U.S. Public Health Service to provide technical information to the states and a Water Pollution Control Division was established in the Public Health Service. It also made a very small amount of money available for building sewers though even these sums required appropriation which declined from $3 million in 1950 to less than $1 million in 1955. The Act was to have expired in 1953 but it was continued until 1956.

The basic water pollution act was passed July 9, 1956 (P.L. 84-660). This act was in large part the result of efforts made by Congressman John Blatnik of Minnesota but its passage had been blocked by Senator Robert Kerr of Oklahoma.

This Act provided for studying pollution problems and for matching grants for local sewage disposal plants. Half the money was to go to cities under 125,000 people. A very weak conference procedure for interstate pollution abatement was provided. Even this limited Act was never used to its capacity as President Eisenhower opposed Federal involvement in pollution abatement. He also opposed sewer grants and vetoed the granting of money for this purpose. When President Kennedy took office little

Reitze

change took place. The enforcement conference was used to a very limited extent in the early 1960's. In 1961, amendments to the Federal Water Pollution Control Act (P.L. 87–88) authorized seven laboratories for water pollution studies, three to be located in the districts of key Congressmen.

By 1963, key Congressmen who opposed pollution control legislation had died and Senators Edmund Muskie of Maine and Caleb Boggs of Delaware, were able to get legislation through the Senate. In the House, Congressman Blatnik's subcommittee blocked the legislation for nearly two years because representatives from Louisiana and Florida under oil industry pressure would not allow a bill out of committee.

The major start toward a serious Federal Program came with the Water Quality Act of 1965 (P.L. 89–234). This act took water pollution control out of the Public Health Service and created the Federal Water Pollution Control Administration (FWPCA) in HEW. Five months later, on February 28, 1966, Reorganization Plan No. 2 transferred the FWPCA to the Department of the Interior. The 1965 Act authorized larger appropriations and higher ceilings on construction grants but more important was the entry of the federal government into the water quality control field. States were directed to prepare stream quality standards by June 30, 1967 and plans to meet them. This program will be examined in detail in the next section. In 1966, the Clean Water Restoration Act was passed (P.L. 89–753). This act expanded federal grant funds, authorized various studies, aided demonstration programs, and provided federal matching money under a bonus system for states that participated in financing the construction of treatment plants and imposed state-wide water quality standards. The concept of including water pollution abatement activities in river basin planning was encouraged, which brought the FWPCA into the planning activities of the Corps of Engineers, and the Departments of Interior, H.E.W., and Agriculture under the coordination of the Water Resources Council. These activities, however, have not done much for the water quality improvement program. During the period following the act, the FWPCA became a large dispenser of federal money to the states for sewage treatment construction. About ninety percent of the FWPCA budget was for these grants. The other 10 percent supported their administration and the programs for enforcement, research and development, planning, training, and technical assistance. Thus the well-publicized increase in funding for water pollution control has been almost entirely for the municipal sewage treatment construction grant program.

In 1970 the Water Quality Improvement Act (P.L. 91–224) strengthened the act in numerous areas. Oil pollution, wastes from water craft, and other pollutants were subjected to better control. However, the basic weak Federal-State program of control of interstate waters remained. The F.W.P.C.A. became the Federal Water Quality Administration. Only a short time later the F.W.Q.A. became part of the new Environmental Protection Agency under Reorganization Plan No. 3 of 1970. Because no meaningful enforcement program existed under this Act, the Act of 1899 became important. In 1971 plans developed, through regulation, to require a permit from all who discharge into navigable waterways. Such a permit would be granted if the discharge didn't violate the Federal Water Pollution Control Act as amended. Thus the 1899 Act would become in effect another amendment to the Federal Water Pollution Control Act.

REFERENCES AND SELECTED BIBLIOGRAPHY

DAVIES, The Politics of Pollution, New York, Western Pub. Co., 1970

RIDGEWAY, The Politics of Ecology, New York, E.P. Dutton & Co. Inc., 1970

"The Water Pollution Control Act of 1948: the dilemma of economic compulsion versus social restraint," *Technical Information for Congress,* Committee on Science and Astronautics, U.S. House of Representatives, 92 Cong., revised April 15, 1971 at 327.

h. Pending Federal legislation

In July of 1972, as this book goes to press, the most important thing to say about Federal water pollution law is that nearly all of it may be meaningless within a few months. This is because both houses of Congress, after more than two years of preparatory work, have passed comprehensive water pollution control bills that would take the place of both the present Federal Water Pollution Control Act and the "Refuse Act" of 1899. Each of these laws is discussed in detail in the material which follows.

The engrossed bills (i.e.—bills which have passed one House of Congress) are S. 2770 (passed November 2, 1971) and H.R. 11896 (passed March 29, 1972). Both bills are immense (the Senate bill was 190 pages) and based in general on emission control laws such as the Clean Air Act Amendments of 1970. (The present comprehensive law is based on water quality standards—a fact that makes it virtually unenforceable.) Both bills provide for sewage treatment grants, pollution control methods, and administration. But the two bills differ substantially on at least a dozen points.

The conference committee which was to iron out the differences met in May and June of 1972 and, as this book goes to press, had adjourned for several weeks for the July political conventions. Although closed to the public, it was related that the bills' major differences had still not been resolved—though how much this was due to election-year politics and how much was due to genuine differences of opinion was impossible to say.

The overriding differences were being described as three: *money* (i.e., the amount of total authorization and for the sewage treatment grant program); *time* (i.e., whether an end to polluting discharges should be required by 1985 (Senate), or whether this was an impossibility best left stated in non-mandatory language), and *who* (i.e., who will have the various responsibilities for enforcement).

There was mention (e.g., *Conservation Report,* June 9, 1972 at 206) of controversy concerning citizen suit and thermal discharge provisions.

Conveniently, Congress has published a side-by-side comparison of the two lengthy bills in House Report 92-91, 92d Cong., 2d Sess., 173-390 (1972).

If these bills are finally resolved and a version becomes law, the author and this publisher intend to publish a supplement to this book with the bill and historical materials already prepared by Alexander W. Whitaker, J.D., George Washington University, June, 1972. The following is Mr. Whitaker's analysis of the key differences between the Senate and House bills:

1. The total authorization in S. 2770 would be increased by about $7 billion to a total of $27 billion in H.R. 11896;
2. S. 2770 authorizes $14 billion for the construction of waste treatment works, and H.R. 11896 would raise the amount to $20 billion;
3. Construction grants are allotted on the basis of population in S. 2770, but in H.R. 11896, grants are allotted on the basis of the needs of the States;
4. S. 2770 authorizes a maximum Federal share of waste treatment plant costs of 70 percent, whereas H.R. 11896 authorizes a maximum of 75 percent;
5. Unlike S. 2770, H.R. 11896 makes sewage collection systems eligible for Federal grants;
6. The policy, goals, and the schedules in both bills are essentially the same; however, H.R. 11896 does not contain the mandatory language of no discharge by 1985, as is found in S 2770;
7. H.R. 11896 would integrate planning more closely with existing planning authorities in River Basins of the Nation; (e.g., $200,000,000 for the Water Resources Council to complete the comprehensive water and land resources planning by 1981);
8. H.R. 11896 establishes in Section 302 (effluent limits established by the Administration) "fair and equitable methods" in assuring that the views of the environmental, economic and scientific advisors of the President will be given proper consideration;
9. H.R. 11896 additionally requires that in the consideration of factors making up the "best practical technology" and "the best available

technology" that consideration be given to foreign competition in addition to those factors in S. 2770;

10. H.R. 11896 contains a provision requiring the National Academys of Sciences and Engineering to study total social and economic affects of achieving or failing to achieve the limits and goals set for 1981;

11. H.R. 11896 authorizes a study of the relationships between various national goals being set by statutes and otherwise, and requests recommendations as to how these should be reconciled; and

12. H.R. 11896 authorizes environmental financing at a level $100 million in order to provide assistance to local communities who are in need of financing these programs.

Suffice it to say, that the Federal Water Pollution Control Act Amendments of 1972 are forthcoming, probably before the end of 1972.

The following is from the Report of the Committee on Public Works of the United States Senate on Federal Water Pollution Control Amendments of 1971.

The legislation recommended by the Committee proposes a major change in the enforcement mechanism of the Federal water pollution control program from water quality standards to effluent limits.

The Committee recommends the change to effluent limits as the best available mechanism to control water pollution.

It is the Committee's intent to restore the balance of Federal-State effort in the program as contemplated by the 1965 and 1966 Acts. The Committee is particularly concerned that there should be a balanced effort in the discharge permit system initiated under section 13 of the 1899 Refuse Act.

The permit system, as restated by this legislation, prohibits the discharge of pollutants into the navigable waters.

In order to carry out the objective of this legislation, a two-phase program for applying effluent limits is created; the first based on best practicable technology, the second based on best available technology.

In Phase I, to be implemented by 1976, all industrial pollution sources must apply the best practicable technology. Communities will be required to have secondary treatment construction programs by June 30, 1974.

In Phase II, to be implemented by 1981, communities and industries will be required to apply, where the goal of no-discharge cannot be attained, the best available technology.

To assist States and localities, the bill proposes a 4-year program of Federal grants for construction of sewage treatment plants. The Federal matching funds total $14 billion through fiscal year 1975.

The minimum Federal grant is set at 60 percent of project cost. If a State contributes as much as 10 percent of project cost, the Federal grant is increased by a matching 10 percent. A locality's share thus becomes 20 percent of project cost.

The bill also provides reimbursement for sewage treatment plants built without Federal assistance during earlier stages of the Federal program. Plants begun between fiscal year 1956 and fiscal year 1966 are eligible for grants equal to 30 percent of project cost. Plants begun after June 30, 1966 are eligible for grants equal to 50 percent of project cost. A total of $2.4 billion is authorized for this purpose.

The task of enforcing provisions of the bill is assigned to the Administrator. He is authorized to enforce permit violations immediately, or if a State fails to act within 30 days after receipt of a notice of violation, the Administrator may issue an order to comply or go to court against the violator.

Civil and criminal penalties are provided. A second conviction shall be punished by a fine of not more than $50,000 per day of violation, two years in prison, or both.

Under the bill, citizens themselves may go to United States District Courts against those who violate effluent standards or compliance orders. Citizens may also go to court against the Administrator for failure to carry out non-discretionary duties under the law.

End quote from committee report.

i. FEDERAL WATER POLLUTION CONTROL ACT[1]

text and commentary

DECLARATION OF POLICY

FWPCA
Sec. 1:
purpose

SECTION. 1. (a) The purpose of this Act is to enhance the quality and value of our water resources and to establish a national policy for the prevention, control, and abatement of water pollution.[2]

(b) In connection with the exercise of jurisdiction over the waterways of the Nation and in consequence of the benefits resulting to the public health and welfare by the prevention and control of water pollution, it is hereby declared to be the policy of Congress to recognize, preserve, and protect the primary responsibilities and rights of the States in preventing and controlling water pollution, to support and aid technical research relating to the prevention and control of water pollution, and to provide Federal technical services and financial aid to State and interstate agencies and to municipalities in connection with the prevention and control of water pollution. The Secretary of the Interior (hereinafter in this Act called "Secretary") shall administer this Act through the Administration created by section 2 of this Act, and with the assistance of an Assistant Secretary of the Interior designated by him, shall supervise and direct the head of such Administration in administering this Act. Such Assistant Secretary shall perform such additional functions as the Secretary may prescribe.

(c) Nothing in this Act shall be construed as impairing or in any manner affecting any right or jurisdiction of the States with respect to the waters (including boundary waters) of such States.

COMMENTARY

Note that Congress recognizes the basic role of the States in implementing and enforcing water pollution control regulations while asserting broad federal regulatory authority to back up the States. This Federal authority has continuously increased since the original Federal Water Pollution Control Act, 62 Stat. 1155 (1948). In part this can be attributed to the interstate and national scope of the pollution problem as well as the failure of most states to act with sufficient vigor to begin to solve the problem.

Section 1(c) contains a disavowal of any attempt at Federal preemption.

FWPCA
Sec. 2:
administrative
agency

FEDERAL WATER QUALITY ADMINISTRATION

SEC. 2. Effective ninety days after the date of enactment of this section[3] there is created within the Department of the Interior a Federal Water Quality Administration[4] (hereinafter in this Act referred to as the "Administration"). The head of the Administration shall be appointed, and his compensation fixed, by the Secretary. The head of the Administration may, in addition to regular staff of the Administration, which shall be initially provided from the personnel of the Department, obtain, from within the Department or otherwise as authorized by law, such professional, technical, and clerical assistance as may be necessary to discharge the Administration's functions and may for that purpose use funds available for carrying out such functions; and he may delegate any of his functions to, or otherwise authorize their performance by, an officer or employee of, or assigned or detailed to, the Administration.

COMMENTARY

The FWQA is now a part of the EPA as part of the Reorganization Plan No. 3 of 1970 (See chapter one, page 135 for text of plan.) It is now called the Federal Water Program Office, Environmental Protection Agency.

[1] Basic Act (Public Law 84-660), approved July 9, 1956, amended by the Federal Water Pollution Control Act Amendments of 1961 (Public Law 87-88), approved July 20, 1961, by the Water Quality Act of 1965 (Public Law 89-234), approved October 2, 1965, by the Clean Water Restoration Act of 1966 (Public Law 89-753), approved November 3, 1966, and by the Water Quality Improvement Act of 1970 (Public Law 91-224), approved April 3, 1970.

[2] This subsection added by sec. 1, P.L. 87-88.

[3] This section added by sec. 2, Public Law 89-234, approved October 2, 1965.

[4] This name added by sec. 110 Public Law 91-224.

FWPCA
Sec. 3:
plan making

SEC. 3. (a) The Secretary shall, after careful investigation, and in cooperation with other Federal agencies, with State water pollution control agencies and interstate agencies, and with the municipalities and industries involved, prepare or develop comprehensive programs for eliminating or reducing the pollution of interstate waters and tributaries thereof and improving the sanitary condition of surface and underground waters. In the development of such comprehensive programs due regard shall be given to the improvements which are necessary to conserve such waters for public water supplies, propagation of fish and aquatic life and wildlife, recreational purposes, and agricultural, industrial, and other legitimate uses. For the purpose of this section, the Secretary is authorized to make joint investigations with any such agencies of the condition of any waters in any State or States, and of the discharges of any sewage, industrial wastes, or substance which may adversely affect such waters.

(b)[5](1) In the survey or planning of any reservoir by the Corps of Engineers, Bureau of Reclamation, or other Federal agency, consideration shall be given to inclusion of storage for regulation of streamflow for the purpose of water quality control, except that any such storage and water releases shall not be provided as a substitute for adequate treatment or other methods of controlling waste at the source.

(2) The need for and the value of storage for this purpose shall be determined by these agencies, with the advice of the Secretary, and his views on these matters shall be set forth in any report or presentation to the Congress proposing authorization or construction of any reservoir including such storage.

(3) The value of such storage shall be taken into account in determining the economic value of the entire project of which it is a part, and costs shall be allocated to the purpose of water quality control in a manner which will insure that all project purposes share equitably in the benefits of multiple-purpose construction.

(4) Costs of water quality control features incorporated in any Federal reservoir or other impoundment under the provisions of this Act shall be determined and the beneficiaries identified and if the benefits are widespread or national in scope, the costs of such features shall be nonreimbursable.

(c)[6](1) The Secretary shall, at the request of the Governor of a State, or a majority of the governors when more than one State is involved, make a grant to pay not to exceed 50 per centum of the administrative expenses of a planning agency for a period not to exceed 3 years, if such agency provides for adequate representation of appropriate State, interstate, local, or (when appropriate) international, interests in the basin or portion thereof involved and is capable of developing an effective, comprehensive water quality control and abatement plan for a basin.

(2) Each planning agency receiving a grant under this subsection shall develop a comprehensive pollution control and abatement plan for the basin which—

(A) is consistent with any applicable water quality standards established pursuant to current law within the basin;

(B) recommends such treatment works and sewer systems as will provide the most effective and economical means of collection, storage, treatment, and purification of wastes and recommends means to encourage both municipal and industrial use of such works and systems; and

(C) recommends maintenance and improvement of water quality standards within the basin or portion thereof and recommends methods of adequately financing those facilities as may be necessary to implement the plan.

(3) For the purposes of this subsection the term "basin" includes, but is not limited to, rivers and their tributaries, streams, coastal waters, sounds, estuaries, bays, lakes, and portions thereof, as well as the lands drained thereby.

COMMENTARY

For regulations governing water pollution control programs, see 18 CFR Chap. V, Part 601.1-601.8

See also: *Guidelines, Water Quality Management Planning*, EPA, January 1971.

[5] This subsection added by sec. 2, Public Law 87-88.

[6] This subsection added by sec. 101, Public Law 89-753.

FWPCA Sec. 4: interstate compacts

SEC. 4. (a) The Secretary shall encourage cooperative activities by the States for the prevention and control of water pollution; encourage the enactment of improved and, so far as practicable, uniform State laws relating to the prevention and control of water pollution; and encourage compacts between States for the prevention and control of water pollution.

(b) The consent of the Congress is hereby given to two or more States to negotiate and enter into agreements or compacts, not in conflict with any law or treaty of the United States, for (1) cooperative effort and mutual assistance for the prevention and control of water pollution and the enforcement of their respective laws relating thereto, and (2) the establishment of such agencies, joint or otherwise, as they may deem desirable for making effective such agreements and compacts. No such agreement or compact shall be binding or obligatory upon any State a party thereto unless and until it has been approved by the Congress.

COMMENTARY

Sec. 4(a) is interesting because it has so little impact. There seems to be some attempt to create uniform standards among various states in a river basin, but this is on an informal basis. There have been no regulations under this section, nor do reports of EPA mention the section.

Interstate compacts have a long history but the control of pollution through interstate compact organizations has been of minor importance. Pollution control authority was given in the New England Interstate Water Pollution Compact of 1947; the New York Harbor Interstate Sanitation Compact of 1935; the Ohio River Valley Water Sanitation Compact of 1948; and the Potomac River Basin Compact of 1939. These compacts resulted in some achievement, particularly in the early years of the Ohio compact (ORSANCO), but the powers and financing provided in these compacts was so limited that only very limited benefits could be achieved.

In recent years a few interstate compacts have developed in which the Federal government is a party. The Delaware River Basin Compact of 1961 and the Susquehanna River Basin Compact of 1970 are the two examples. [More detailed information on this subject is found in Volume Two of this work under Estuaries.

Several reasons exist to explain why so few interstate compacts have been created. First the process is very cumbersome and time-consuming. But more important is the attitude of Congress in refusing to approve compacts that are meaningless. Since most states are not willing to give up power or to finance properly such organizations, they do not come into existence.

River basin planning, however, is becoming a normal part of dealing with water resources. Such planning includes water pollution control planning. This aspect of river basin planning is usually minor, though occasionally pollution control is an excuse used to justify environmentally or economically unsound projects. [See for example Sec. 3(b) of the FWPCA.]

REFERENCES AND SELECTED BIBLIOGRAPHY

MUYS, Jerome, *Interstate Water Compacts,* National Water Commission, NTIS PB 202 998, 1971.

TRELEASE, Frank, *Federal-State Relations in Water Law,* NTIS PB 203 600, 1971.

FRANKFURTER and LANDIS, "The Compact Clause of the Constitution," 34 *Yale L.J.* 685 (1925)

HINES, "Nor Any Drop to Drink: Public Regulation of Water Quality, Part II: Interstate Arrangements for Pollution Control," 52 *Iowa Law Review* 432 (1966)

CLEARY, *The ORSANCO Story,* 1967

MARTIN, *River Basin Administration and the Delaware,* 1960

National Estuary Study, Vol. 6, U.S. Dept. of the Interior, Bureau of Sport Fisheries and Wildlife & Bureau of Commercial Fisheries, 91st Cong., 2d. Sess., House Document No. 91-286 (1970).

RESEARCH, INVESTIGATIONS, TRAINING, AND INFORMATION

SEC. 5. (a) The Secretary shall conduct in the Department of the Interior and encourage, cooperate with, and render assistance to other appropriate public (whether Federal, State, interstate, or local) authorities, agencies, and institutions, private agencies and institutions, and individuals in the conduct of, and promote the coordination of, research, investigations, experiments, demonstrations, and studies relating to the causes, control, and prevention of water pollution. In carrying out the foregoing, the Secretary is authorized to—

(1) collect and make available, through publications and other appropriate means, the results of and other information as to research, investigations, and demonstrations relating to the prevention and control of water pollution, including appropriate recommendations in connection therewith;

(2) make grants-in-aid to public or private agencies and institutions and to individuals for research or training projects and for demonstrations, and provide for the conduct of research, training, and demonstrations by contract with public or private agencies and institutions and with individuals without regard to sections 3648 and 3709 of the Revised Statutes;

(3) secure, from time to time and for such periods as he deems advisable, the assistance and advice of experts, scholars, and consultants as authorized by section 15 of the Administrative Expenses Act of 1946 (5 U.S.C. 55a);

(4) establish and maintain research fellowships in the Department of the Interior with such stipends and allowances, including traveling and subsistence expenses, as he may deem necessary to procure the assistance of the most promising research fellowships: *Provided*, That the Secretary shall report annually to the appropriate committees of Congress on his operations under this paragraph [7]; and

(5) provide training in technical matters relating to the causes, prevention, and control of water pollution to personnel of public agencies and other persons with suitable qualifications.

(b) The Secretary may, upon request of any State water pollution control agency, or interstate agency, conduct investigations and research and make surveys concerning any specific problem of water pollution confronting any State, interstate agency, community, municipality, or industrial plant, with a view of recommending a solution of such problem.

(c) The Secretary shall, in cooperation with other Federal, State, and local agencies having related responsibilities, collect and disseminate basic data on chemical, physical, and biological water quality and other information insofar as such data or other information relate to water pollution and the prevention and control thereof.

(d)[8] In carrying out the provisions of this section the Secretary shall develop and demonstrate under varied conditions (including conducting such basic and applied research, studies, and experiments as may be necessary):

(A) Practicable means of treating municipal sewage and other waterborne wastes to remove the maximum possible amounts of physical, chemical, and biological pollutants in order to restore and maintain the maximum amount of the Nation's water at a quality suitable for repeated reuse;

(B) Improved methods and procedures to identify and measure the effects of pollutants on water uses, including those pollutants created by new technological developments; and

(C) Methods and procedures for evaluating the effects on water quality and water uses of augmented streamflows to control water pollution not susceptible to other means of abatement.

(e)[9] The Secretary shall establish, equip, and maintain field laboratory and research facilities, including, but not limited to, one to be located in the northeastern area of the United States, one in the Middle Atlantic area, one in the southeastern area, one in the midwestern area, one in the southwestern area, one in the Pacific Northwest, and one in

[7] This proviso added by sec. 3, Public Law 87–88.

[8] Sec. 3(b), Public Law 87–88, was amended by sec. 201(c), Public Law 89–753. Amendment strikes out "(1)" before remaining language of subsection, and strikes out this provision: "(2) for the purposes of this subsection there is authorized to be appropriated not more than $5,000,000 for any fiscal year, and the total sum appropriated for such purposes shall not exceed $25,000,000."

[9] This subsection added by sec. 3, Public Law 87–88.

the State of Alaska, for the conduct of research, investigations, experiments, field demonstrations and studies, and training relating to the prevention and control of water pollution. Insofar as practicable, each such facility shall be located near institutions of higher learning in which graduate training in such research might be carried out.

(f)[9] The Secretary shall conduct research and technical development work, and make studies, with respect to the quality of the waters of the Great Lakes, including an analysis of the present and projected future water quality of the Great Lakes under varying conditions of waste treatment and disposal, an evaluation of the water quality needs of those to be served by such waters, an evaluation of municipal, industrial, and vessel waste treatment and disposal practices with respect to such waters, and a study of alternate means of solving water pollution problems (including additional waste treatment measures) with respect to such waters.

(g)[10](1) For the purpose of providing an adequate supply of trained personnel to operate and maintain existing and future treatment works and related activities, and for the purpose of enhancing substantially the proficiency of those engaged in such activities, the Secretary shall finance a pilot program, in cooperation with State and interstate agencies, municipalities, educational institutions, and other organizations and individuals, of manpower development and training and retraining of persons in, on entering into, the field of operation and maintenance of treatment works and related activities. Such program and any funds expended for such a program shall supplement, not supplant, other manpower and training programs and funds available for the purposes of this paragraph. The Secretary is authorized, under such terms and conditions as he deems appropriate, to enter into agreements with one or more States, acting jointly or severally, or with other public or private agencies or institutions for the development and implementation of such a program.

FWPCA Sec. 5: training

(2) The Secretary is authorized to enter into agreements with public and private agencies and institutions, and individuals to develop and maintain an effective system for forecasting the supply of, and demand for, various professional and other occupational categories needed for the prevention, control, and abatement of water pollution in each region, State, or area of the United States and, from time to time, to publish the results of such forecasts.

(3) In furtherance of the purposes of this Act, the Secretary is authorized to—

"(A) make grants to public or private agencies and institutions and to individuals for training projects, and provide for the conduct of training by contract with public or private agencies and institutions and with individuals without regard to sections 3648 and 3709 of the Revised Statutes;

"(B) establish and maintain research fellowships in the Department of the Interior with such stipends and allowances, including traveling and subsistence expenses, as he may deem necessary to procure the assistance of the most promising research fellowships; and

"(C) provide, in addition to the program established under paragraph (1) of this subsection, training in technical matters relating to the causes, prevention, and control of water pollution for personnel of public agencies and other persons with suitable qualifications."

(4) The Secretary shall submit, through the President, a report to the Congress within eighteen months from the date of enactment of this subsection, summarizing the actions taken under this subsection and the effectiveness of such actions, and setting forth the number of persons trained, the occupational categories for which training was provided, the effectiveness of other Federal, State, and local training programs in this field, together with estimates of future needs, recommendations on improving training programs, and such other information and recommendations, including legislative recommendations, as he deems appropriate.

(h) The Secretary is authorized to enter into contracts with, or make grants to, public or private agencies and organizations and individuals for (A) the purpose of developing and demonstrating new or improved methods for the prevention, removal, and control of

[10] This subsection added by sec. 105, Public Law 91-224.

natural or manmade pollution in lakes, including the undesirable effects of nutrients and vegetation, and (B) the construction of publicly owned research facilities for such purpose.[7]

(i) The Secretary shall—

"(A) engage in such research, studies, experiments, and demonstrations as he deems appropriate, relative to the removal of oil from any waters and to the prevention and control of oil pollution;

"(B) publish from time to time the results of such activities; and

"(C) from time to time, develop and publish in the Federal Register specifications and other technical information on the various chemical compounds used as dispersants or emulsifiers in the control of oil spills."

In carrying out this subsection, the Secretary may enter into contracts with, or make grants to, public or private agencies and organizations and individuals.[11]

FWPCA Sec. 5: research

(j) The Secretary shall engage in such research, studies, experiments, and demonstrations as he deems appropriate relative to equipment which is to be installed on board a vessel and is designed to receive, retain, treat, or discharge human body wastes and the wastes from toilets and other receptacles intended to receive or retain body wastes with particular emphasis on equipment to be installed on small recreational vessels. The Secretary shall report to Congress the results of such research, studies, experiments, and demonstrations prior to the effective date of any standards established under section 13 of this Act. In carrying out this subsection the Secretary may enter into contracts with, or make grants to, public or private organizations and individuals.[11]

(k) In carrying out the provisions of this section relating to the conduct by the Secretary of demonstration projects and the development of field laboratories and research facilities, the Secretary may acquire land and interests therein by purchase, with appropriated or donated funds, by donation, or by exchange for acquired or public lands under his jurisdiction which he classifies as suitable for disposition. The values of the properties so exchanged either shall be approximately equal, or if they are not approximately equal, the values shall be equalized by the payment of cash to the grantor or to the Secretary as the circumstances require.[11]

(l)(1) The Secretary shall, after consultation with appropriate local, State, and Federal agencies, public and private organizations, and interested individuals, as soon as practicable but not later than two years after the effective date of this subsection, develop and issue to the States for the purpose of adopting standards pursuant to section 10(c) the latest scientific knowledge available in indicating the kind and extent of effects on health and welfare which may be expected from the presence of pesticides in the water in varying quantities. He shall revise and add to such information whenever necessary to reflect developing scientific knowledge.

(2) For the purpose of assuring effective implementation of standards adopted pursuant to paragraph (1) the President shall, in consultation with appropriate local, State, and Federal agencies, public and private organizations, and interested individuals, conduct a study and investigation of methods to control the release of pesticides into the environment which study shall include examination of the persistency of pesticides in the water environment and alternatives thereto. The President shall submit a report on such investigation to Congress together with his recommendations for any necessary legislation within two years after the effective date of this subsection.[11]

(m)(1) The Secretary shall, in cooperation with the Secretary of the Army, the Secretary of Agriculture, the Water Resources Council, and with other appropriate Federal, State, interstate, or local public bodies and private organizations, institutions, and individuals, conduct and promote, and encourage contributions to, a comprehensive study of the effects of pollution, including sedimentation, in the estuaries and estuarine zones of the United States on fish and wildlife, on sport and commercial fishing, on recreation, on water supply and water power, and on other beneficial purposes. Such study shall also consider the

[11] These subsections added by sec. 105, Public Law 91–224.

effect of demographic trends, the exploitation of mineral resources and fossil fuels, land and industrial development, navigation, flood and erosion control, and other uses of estuaries and estuarine zones upon the pollution of the waters therein.

(2) In conducting the above study, the Secretary shall assemble, coordinate, and organize all existing pertinent information on the Nation's estuaries and estuarine zones; carry out a program of investigations and surveys to supplement existing information in representative estuaries and estuarine zones; and identify the problems and areas where further research and study are required.

FWPCA Sec. 5: reports

(3) The Secretary shall submit to the Congress a final report of the study authorized by this subsection not later than three years after the date of enactment of this subsection. Copies of the report shall be made available to all interested parties, public and private. The report shall include, but not be limited to—

(A) an analysis of the importance of estuaries to the economic and social well-being of the people of the United States and of the effects of pollution upon the use and enjoyment of such estuaries;

(B) a discussion of the major economic, social, and ecological trends occurring in the estuarine zones of the Nation;

(C) recommendations for a comprehensive national program for the preservation, study, use, and development of estuaries of the Nation, and the respective responsibilities which should be assumed by Federal, State, and local governments and by public and private interests.

(4) There is authorized to be appropriated the sum of $1,000,000 per fiscal year for the fiscal years ending June 30, 1967, June 30, 1968, June 30, 1969, June 30, 1970, and June 30, 1971 to carry out the purposes of this subsection.[12]

(5) For the purpose of this subsection, the term "estuarine zones" means an environmental system consisting of an estuary and those transitional areas which are consistently influenced or affected by water from an estuary such as, but not limited to, salt marshes, coastal and intertidal areas, bays, harbors, lagoons, inshore waters, and channels, and the term "estuary" means all or part of the mouth of a navigable or interstate river or stream or other body of water having unimpaired natural connection with open sea and within which the sea water is measurably diluted with fresh water derived from land drainage.[13]

(n) There is authorized to be appropriated to carry out this section, other than subsection (g) (1) and (2), not to exceed $65,000,000 per fiscal year for each of the fiscal years ending June 30, 1969, June 30, 1970, and June 30, 1971. There is authorized to be appropriated to carry out subsection (g) (1) of this section $5,000,000 for the fiscal year ending June 30, 1970, and $7,500,000 for the fiscal year ending June 30, 1971. There is authorized to be appropriated to carry out subsection (g) (2) of this section $2,500,000 per fiscal year for each of the fiscal years ending June 30, 1970, and June 30, 1971.[14]

COMMENTARY

With the expansion and increased numbers and complexity of waste water treatment plants throughout the nation, the demand for technically trained persons to run them has mounted considerably. According to some estimates, 32,000 jobs in this field will have to be filled in the next 10 years. At present, many technical schools and colleges offer some courses in this field, but only one, Charles County Community College, in La Plata, Maryland, specializes in training environmental water sciences technicians. About 400 of the Charles County College's 1,200 students are enrolled in two-year programs leading to certification either in waste water treatment technology or in estuarine studies technology. (*Washington Post,* Nov. 18, 1971 at F1)

---

[12] Extension added by sec. 105, Public Law 91–224.

[13] This subsection added by sec. 201(b), Public Law 89–753, renumbered by sec. 105, Public Law 91–224.

[14] This subsection originally added by sec. 201(d), Public Law 89–753, amended by sec. 105, Public Law 91–224.

The following commentary is excerpted from *Clean Water for the 1970's, A Status Report,* by U.S. Department of the Interior, June 1970 at 55. Federal Water Quality Administration, Research, Development, and Demonstration Programs are discussed:

The mechanisms utilized in carrying out this program are three-fold:

(1) In-house research and development at eight laboratory locations and a number of associated field sites.

(2) Contract projects, primarily with industry.

(3) Grant projects with universities, industries, States and municipalities.

Contract projects are funded entirely with Federal dollars and are utilized primarily for laboratory investigations and pilot-scale research projects which involve a high degree of uncertainty and which are primarily aimed at determination of feasibility and development of design requirements. These are not the types of projects that municipalities and private corporations will readily sponsor with matching funds because of the large degree of risk involved. The work performed under contracts often requires highly-specialized personnel, equipment and facilities, having a high value over a short period of time, but limited value in the long term.

Grant projects require some level of matching support from the grantee. Grants are employed in meeting objectives where it is desirable to utilize State, municipal, academic or industrial talents and expertise in carrying out research, development and, often, demonstration efforts on a cost-sharing basis to the mutual benefit of both the Federal government and the grantee.

FWQA's in-house activity forms the real foundation of an effective overall program. In-house researchers must establish objectives and plans of attack; they must review and evaluate the many, many project proposals received by this Agency; and they must be the ones to integrate the results of these efforts into a usable and applicable form.

In addition to the in-house efforts carried on at agency laboratories, FWQA is also involved in a number of joint efforts with the Bureau of Reclamation, Atomic Energy Commission, Office of Saline Water, Office of Water Resources Research, Public Health Service, and Tennessee Valley Authority.

Notable in the research, development and demonstration program are the special authorities to support both pilot-scale and full-scale demonstration projects on storm and combined sewer discharges, advanced waste treatment and wastewater renovation, and industrial waste treatment and control. These projects are particularly significant in permitting FWQA to carry on research and development findings into the demonstration phase, thereby literally showing what can be accomplished through the use of new technology and at what cost.

In order to effectively manage this program, communicate the results to users, and respond to special Administration, Congressional and public requests, a computerized management information system was instituted. As a result, up-to-date information is readily available on nearly 2,000 projects, on future needs, on priorities, on work plans, and on necessary planning, programming and budgeting data to effectively direct future efforts.

A supplementary project reports system has been established for the acquisition, filing, indexing and, most importantly, dissemination of research results. The final results in the form of reports and publications are indexed into a technical library, distributed, and made known to a wide range of users both inside and outside FWQA. In Executive Order 11514, President Nixon directed that the results of Federal research programs be made available for widespread use. FWQA will continue to emphasize this important aspect of the research, development and demonstration program.

Municipal Pollution Control Technology

Municipal wastes, as indicated earlier, are a major source of pollution in the United States. Although a technology to treat these wastes has already been developed and is being applied, FWQA is continuing the search for better and more efficient ways of treating municipal wastes in conventional systems. For example, significant improvement and upgrading of treatment in overloaded plants has been demonstrated using synthetic organic polyelectrolytes.

Another major concern is research on methods to control the more complex municipal problems, such as combined sewer and urban sediment control. Combined sewers carry both sanitary sewage and urban runoff. During storms, the volumes in these sewers are often too much for local treatment plants and wastes are discharged untreated. Yet control of these discharges has largely been neglected until recent years because the only method of solving the problem was separation of combined sewers, a costly and disruptive process. Through the efforts of FWQA's research program, a new technology for control of sewer discharges is being developed.

One of the alternatives being demonstrated is storage of excessive flows until they can be released to the treatment plants. Full-scale storage facilities under construction in Boston, Massachusetts; Milwaukee, Wisconsin; Dallas, Texas; and Shelbyville, Illinois, have determined the design criteria necessary for such facilities. Cost-effectiveness evaluation will allow other communities to economically design similar combined sewer pollution abatement facilities.

Another major alternative is treatment. Existing municipal and industrial treatment processes cannot be utilized for combined sewer overflow treatment because of the intermittent, widely fluctuating high-flow rates and the dynamic quality changes of combined sewer overflows. Screening and dissolved air flotation are two treatment methods which are amenable to the above constraints.

The demonstration of a novel, rotating collar, vibratory base screening treatment unit for combined sewer overflows was carried out in Portland, Oregon, in 1969. The unit provided primary treatment to normally bypassed sewage at a cost only slightly higher than the equivalent conventional treatment. The space utilization of the screens is one-tenth that of settling tanks.

Through these studies, a combination of control methods is being developed which will be applicable to the different combined and stormwater sewer problems throughout the country. Although determinations of the cost of controlling these discharges by the new methods being demonstrated are very preliminary, the total job may cost only about one-third of the earlier estimates based on separation.

Of great importance is FWQA's research on joint treatment of municipal and industrial wastes. As has been pointed out, the benefits of joint treatment are considerable. Industry, while paying operating costs, is spared the burden of the capital costs; and regionalization of waste treatment and economies of scale help communities achieve more effective pollution control.

With the expansion of both the population and the industrial sector and the corresponding needs for water, conservation of water is becoming increasingly important. Much of today's research is directed toward finding easy-to-treat and re-use water effluents. A project with the Johns-Manville Products Corporation in Defiance, Ohio, demonstrates that a wastewater treatment system using diatomite filtration can effectively treat a waste stream, containing glass fibers, caustic and phenols, to a quality suitable for process reuse. The treatment facilities are operating on a 72,000 gallon-per-day basis with effective pollution control a demonstrated success.

Agricultural Pollution Control Technology

The most difficult sources of wastes to control are those that do not come out of pipes. Agricultural pollution is a good example of such "diffuse" wastes. Major forms of pollution associated with agriculture have already been identified as problems in earlier sections of the report. They include: nutrients; pesticides; salts and other materials in irrigation return flows; animal feedlot wastes; and silt and other solids from logging operations. Most of these wastes are not collectible and, therefore, cannot be treated in a conventional fashion. New and imaginative solutions are being sought for these problems.

Projects with Cornell University, South Carolina State, and South Dakota University are aimed at studying the addition of nutrients to streams from cropping practices as related to their respective geoagranomic areas. This is a precursor to the development of criteria for new management concepts that include considerations for waste management.

The quality of irrigation return flows is a major problem in the arid sections of the country, primarily because of nutrients, silt, and salts. Treatment of such flows has long been considered impractical. A development program at Firebaugh, California, has developed two techniques for removing nitrates from irrigation return waters. These will be demonstrated on an engineering scale to obtain more definitive operating and cost data that will be applicable to a complete treatment system for the entire San Luis Drain.

Work is also under way with the Bureau of Reclamation to demonstrate a technique of forecasting the effects of irrigation practices on the quality of underground aquifers and surface streams before lands are irrigated. This method will enable us to make better provision for avoiding water quality damage in planning and developing new irrigation projects.

The tremendous load of animal wastes discharged from a rapidly growing number of animal feedlots is an area of particular concern in FWQA's research program. Projects have been initiated to demonstrate available techniques for treating runoff from animal feeding operations and for preventing its discharge to receiving waters. These include activated sludge, oxidation ditch, anaerobic-aerobic lagooning and management changes to control and collect the runoff. Cooperative projects with the Department of Agriculture have also been initiated to determine the quantity and pathways of nitrate addition to surface streams and underground water formations from excreta in beef feeding operations.

The federal efforts are also directed toward the control of mine acid, wastes from watercraft, oil pollution, salt water intrusion, and many other technical problems.

Water Quality Control Technology

This part of the research program includes all research, development and demonstration directed toward: the prevention and control of accelerated eutrophication and thermal pollution; the control of pollution by means other than waste treatment (e.g. industrial manufacturing process change to eliminate a waste); the socio-economic, legal and institutional aspects of pollution; the assessment and control of pollution in extremely cold climates; and the identification, source and fate of pollutants in surface, ground and coastal waters.

Waste Treatment and Ultimate Disposal Technology

Waste treatment and ultimate disposal technology focuses on the development and demonstration of new processes and process modifications to control pollution from any source.

There are actually two corollary objectives to be attained through improved waste treatment technology. The obvious one is the alleviation of the Nation's increasing water pollution problems through removal of pollutants from waste effluents; the other is the renovation of wastewaters for deliberate reuse as industrial, agricultural, recreational, or, in some cases, even municipal supplies. These two objectives cannot really be separated, for as our ability to cleanse wastewaters increases, the resulting product water approaches closer and closer to, and may even exceed, the quality of a water supply. This concept, perhaps startling to the average citizen, will nonetheless play a larger and larger role in water resource management, especially in water-short areas.

Far too little is known about the effects of pollution. The drastic effects, such as the massive fish kill, can be easily recognized, but quite often the true cause of such events cannot be defined even with extensive investigation. To look ahead and to predict the occurrence of such events is, unfortunately, well beyond our current capability for any but the simplest stream systems under the least complicated set of environmental conditions and pollution loads. There is also the challenge of detecting, understanding and preventing the more subtle, long-term effects of pollution, which could, even now, be robbing us of valuable water resources. Such effects, as yet unknown, may be just as severe as the sudden fish kill, the unpalatable water supply or the condemned bathing beach. Because these problems are difficult to solve and the starting baseline inadequate, a rapidly accelerated program has been initiated.

Extensive, background data has been acquired and new test methods have been developed to better and more rapidly define the process employs a greater use of chemicals than current processes, and pure oxygen, instead of air, is used in the biological phase of the treatment. The new process appears capable of removing nearly 100 percent of the biological impurities, 96 percent of the phosphates and 85 percent of the nitrogen in wastewater.

The results of this program have provided the necessary technology to reduce the pollution from municipal sources to essentially zero. The present cost is within economic feasibility, but further efforts are needed to optimize both processes and economics. This breakthrough will mean the development of effective, safe and economical wastewater systems, which, in effect, will amount to the same thing as creating a new water supply.

Water Quality Requirements Research

This program provides information on the effect of pollution needed to provide an improved scientific basis for determining the water quality necessary for municipal, industrial, agricultural, and recreational uses and for the propagation of fish and other aquatic life. This information is essential to the establishment and refinement of the Nation's water quality standards. Because of the tremendous number of new chemical compounds being synthesized and finding their way into our environment each year, intensive research investigations must be conducted to develop a predictive capability that will allow us to predict the potential pollutional impact of these compounds in advance.

End quote.

NOTE: Many of these topics are treated at much greater depth in Vol. Two of this work.

Sec. 6, Grants for Research and Development; **Sec. 7,** Grants for Water Pollution Control Programs; and **Sec. 8,** Grants for Construction, are discussed subsequently. Regulations for this program are found in 18 CFR Chapter V, Part 601.

FWPCA Sec. 6: research grants

GRANTS FOR RESEARCH AND DEVELOPMENT

SEC. 6.[15] (a) The Secretary is authorized to make grants to any State, municipality, or intermunicipal or interstate agency for the purpose of—

(1) assisting in the development of any project which will demonstrate a new or improved method of controlling the discharge into any waters of untreated or inadequately treated sewage or other wastes from sewers which carry storm water or both storm water and sewage or other wastes, or

(2) assisting in the development of any project which will demonstrate advanced waste treatment and water purification methods (including the temporary use of new or improved chemical additives which provide substantial immediate improvement to existing treatment processes) or new or improved methods of joint treatment systems for municipal and industrial wastes,

and for the purpose of reports, plans, and specifications in connection therewith.

(b) The Secretary is authorized to make grants to persons for research and demonstration projects for prevention of pollution of waters by industry including, but not limited to, treatment of industrial waste.

(c) Federal grants under subsection (a) of this section shall be subject to the following limitations:

(1) No grant shall be made for any project pursuant to this section unless such project shall have been approved by the appropriate State water pollution control agency or agencies and by the Secretary;

(2) No grant shall be made for any project in an amount exceeding 75 per centum of the estimated reasonable cost thereof as determined by the Secretary; and

(3) No grant shall be made for any project under this section unless the Secretary determines that such project will serve as a useful demonstration for the purpose set forth in clause (1) or (2) of subsection (a).

(d) Federal grants under subsection (b) of this section shall be subject to the following limitations:

(1) No grant shall be made under this section in excess of $1,000,000;

(2) No grant shall be made for more than 70 per centum of the cost of the project; and

(3) No grant shall be made for any project unless the Secretary determines that such project will serve a useful purpose in the development or demonstration of a new or improved method of treating industrial wastes or otherwise preventing pollution of waters by industry, which method shall have industry-wide application.

(e) For the purposes of this section there are authorized to be appropriated—

(1) for the fiscal year ending June 30, 1966, and for each of the next five succeeding fiscal years, the sum of $20,000,000 per fiscal year for the purposes set forth in subsections (a) and (b) of this section, including contracts pursuant to such subsections for such purposes;

(2) for the fiscal year ending June 30, 1967, and for each of the next four succeeding fiscal years, the sum of $20,000,000 per fiscal year for the purpose set forth in clause (2) of subsection (a); and

(3) for the fiscal year ending June 30, 1967, and for each of the next four succeeding fiscal years, the sum of $20,000,000 per fiscal year for the purpose set forth in subsection (b).[16]

---

[15] This subsection originally added by sec. 4, Public Law 89–234, amended by sec. 201 (a), Public Law 89–753.

[16] This subsection amendesd by sec. 106, Public Law 91–224, approved April 3, 1970.

SEC. 7. (a) [17] There are hereby authorized to be appropriated for the fiscal year ending June 30, 1957, and for each succeeding fiscal year to and including the fiscal year ending June 30, 1961, $3,000,000, for each succeeding fiscal year to and including the fiscal year ending June 30, 1967, $5,000,000, and for each succeeding fiscal year to and including the fiscal year ending June 30, 1971, $10,000,000 for grants to States and to interstate agencies to assist them in meeting the costs of establishing and maintaining adequate measures for the prevention and control of water pollution, including the training of personnel of public agencies.

(b) The portion of the sums appropriated pursuant to subsection (a) for a fiscal year which shall be available for grants to interstate agencies and the portion thereof which shall be available for grants to States shall be specified in the Act appropriating such sums.

(c) From the sums available therefor for any fiscal year the Secretary shall from time to time make allotments to the several States, in accordance with regulations, on the basis of (1) the population, (2) the extent of the water pollution problem, and (3) the financial need of the respective States.

(d) From each State's allotment under subsection (c) for any fiscal year the Secretary shall pay to such State an amount equal to its Federal share (as determined under subsection (h)) of the cost of carrying out its State plan approved under subsection (f), including the cost of training personnel for State and local water pollution control work and including the cost of administering the State plan.

(e) From the sums available therefor for any fiscal year the Secretary shall from time to time make allotments to interstate agencies, in accordance with regulations, on such basis as the Secretary finds reasonable and equitable. He shall from time to time pay to each such agency, from its allotment, an amount equal to such portion of the cost of carrying out its plan approved under subsection (f) as may be determined in accordance with regulations, including the cost of training personnel for water pollution control work and including the cost of administering the interstate agency's plan. The regulations relating to the portion of the cost of carrying out the interstate agency's plan which shall be borne by the United States shall be designed to place such agencies, so far as practicable, on a basis similar to that of the States.

(f) The Secretary shall approve any plan for the prevention and control of water pollution which is submitted by the State water pollution control agency or, in the case of an interstate agency, by such agency, if such plan—

(1) provides for administration or for the supervision of administration of the plan by the State water pollution control agency or, in the case of a plan submitted by an interstate agency, by such interstate agency;

(2) provides that such agency will make such reports, in such form and containing such information, as the Secretary may from time to time reasonably require to carry out his functions under this Act;

(3) sets forth the plans, policies, and methods to be followed in carrying out the State (or interstate) plan and in its administration;

(4) provides for extension or improvement of the State or interstate program for prevention and control of water pollution;

(5) provides such accounting, budgeting, and other fiscal methods and procedures as are necessary for the proper and efficient administration of the plan; and

(6) sets forth the criteria used by the State in determining priority of projects as provided in section 8(b)(4).[18]

The Secretary shall not disapprove any plan without first giving reasonable notice and opportunity for hearing to the State water pollution control agency or interstate agency which has submitted such plan.

(g)(1) Whenever the Secretary, after reasonable notice and oppor-

[17] This subsection amended by sec. 202, Public Law 89–753.

[18] Added by sec. 4(b), Public Law 87–88.

tunity for hearing to a State water pollution control agency or interstate agency finds that—

(A) the plan submitted by such agency and approved under this section has been so changed that it no longer complies with a requirement of subsection (f) of this section; or

(B) in the administration of the plan there is a failure to comply substantially with such a requirement,

the Secretary shall notify such agency that no further payments will be made to the State or to the interstate agency, as the case may be, under this section (or in his discretion that further payments will not be made to the State, or to the interstate agency, for projects under or parts of the plan affected by such failure) until he is satisfied that there will no longer be any such failure. Until he is so satisfied, the Secretary shall make no further payments to such State, or to such interstate agency, as the case may be, under this section (or shall limit payments to projects under or parts of the plan in which there is no such failure).

(2) If any State or any interstate agency is dissatisfied with the Secretary's action with respect to it under this subsection, it may appeal to the United States court of appeals for the circuit in which such State (or any of the member States, in the case of an interstate agency) is located. The summons and notice of appeal may be served at any place in the United States. The findings of fact by the Secretary, unless contrary to the weight of the evidence, shall be conclusive; but the court, for good cause shown, may remand the case to the Secretary to take further evidence, and the Secretary may thereupon make new or modified findings of fact and may modify his previous action. Such new or modified findings of fact shall likewise be conclusive unless contrary to the weight of the evidence. The court shall have jurisdiction to affirm the action of the Secretary or to set it aside, in whole or in part. The judgment of the court shall be subject to review by the Supreme Court of the United States upon certiorari or certification as provided in title 28, United States Code, section 1254.

FWPCA Sec. 7: control grants

(h)[19] (1) The "Federal share" for any State shall be 100 per centum less that percentage which bears the same ratio to 50 per centum as the per capita income of such State bears to the per capita income of the United States, except that (A) the Federal share shall in no case be more than 66⅔ per centum or less than 33⅓ per centum, and (B) the Federal share for Puerto Rico and the Virgin Islands shall be 66⅔ per centum.

(2) The "Federal shares" shall be promulgated by the Secretary between July 1 and September 30 of each even-numbered year, on the basis of the average of the per capita incomes of the States and of the continental United States for the three most recent consecutive years for which satisfactory data are available from the Department of Commerce.

(3) As used in this subsection, the term "United States" means the fifty States and the District of Columbia.

(4) Promulgations made before satisfactory data are available from the Department of Commerce for a full year on the per capita income of Alaska shall prescribe a Federal share for Alaska of 50 per centum and, for purposes of such promulgations, Alaska shall not be included as part of the "United States". Promulgations made thereafter but before per capita income data for Alaska for a full three-year period are available for the Department of Commerce shall be based on satisfactory data available therefrom for Alaska for such one full year or, when such data are available for a two-year period, for such two years.

(i) The population of the several States shall be determined on the basis of the latest figures furnished by the Department of Commerce.

(j) The method of computing and paying amounts pursuant to subsection (d) or (e) shall be as follows:

(1) The Secretary shall, prior to the beginning of each calendar quarter or other period prescribed by him, estimate the amount to be paid to each State (or to each interstate agency in the case of subsection (e)) under the provisions of such subsection for such period, such estimate to be based on such records of the State (or the interstate agency) and information furnished by it, and such other investigation, as the Secretary may find necessary.

[19] Amended by sec. 23, Public Law 86–624.

(2) The Secretary shall pay to the State (or to the interstate agency), from the allotment available therefor, the amount so estimated by him for any period, reduced or increased, as the case may be, by any sum (not previously adjusted under this paragraph) by which he finds that his estimate of the amount to be paid such State (or such interstate agency) for any prior period under such subsection was greater or less than the amount which should have been paid to such State (or such agency) for such prior period under such subsection. Such payments shall be made through the disbursing facilities of the Treasury Department, in such installments as the Secretary may determine.

FWPCA Sec. 8: grants for construction

GRANTS FOR CONSTRUCTION

SEC. 8. (a) The Secretary is authorized to make grants to any State, municipality, or intermunicipal or interstate agency for the construction of necessary treatment works to prevent the discharge of untreated or inadequately treated sewage or other waste into any waters and for the purpose of reports, plans, and specifications in connection therewith.

(b) Federal grants under this section shall be subject to the following limitations: (1) No grant shall be made for any project pursuant to this section unless such project shall have been approved by the appropriate State water pollution control agency or agencies and by the Secretary and unless such project is included in a comprehensive program developed pursuant to this Act; (2) no grant shall be made for any project in an amount exceeding 30 per centum of the estimated reasonable cost thereof as determined by the Secretary; (3) no grant shall be made unless the grantee agrees to pay the remaining cost; (4) no grant shall be made for any project under this section until the applicant has made provision satisfactory to the Secretary for assuring proper and efficient operation and maintenance of the treatment works after completion of the construction thereof; and (5) no grant shall be made for any project under this section unless such project is in conformity with the State water pollution control plan submitted pursuant to the provisions of section 7 and has been certified by the appropriate State water pollution control agency as entitled to priority over other eligible projects on the basis of financial as well as water pollution control needs; (6) the percentage limitation of 30 per centum imposed by clause (2) of this subsection shall be increased to a maximum of 40 per centum in the case of grants made under this section from funds allocated for a fiscal year to a State under subsection (c) of this section if the State agrees to pay not less than 30 per centum of the estimated reasonable cost (as determined by the Secretary) of all projects for which Federal grants are to be made under this section from such allocation; (7) the percentage limitations imposed by clause (2) of this subsection shall be increased to a maximum of 50 per centum in the case of grants made under this section from funds allocated for a fiscal year to a State under subsection (c) of this section if the State agrees to pay not less than 25 per centum of the estimated reasonable costs (as determined by the Secretary) of all projects for which Federal grants are to be made under this section from such allocation and if enforceable water quality standards have been established for the waters into which the project discharges, in accordance with section 10(c) of this Act in the case of interstate waters, and under State law in the case of intrastate waters.[20]

(c) In determining the desirability of projects for treatment works and of approving Federal financial aid in connection therewith, consideration shall be given by the Secretary to the public benefits to be derived by the construction and the propriety of Federal aid in such construction, the relation of the ultimate cost of constructing and maintaining the works to the public interest and to the public necessity for the works, and the adequacy of the provisions made or proposed by the applicant for such Federal financial aid for assuring proper and efficient operation and maintenance of the treatment works after completion of the construction thereof. The sums appropriated pursuant to subsections (d) for each fiscal year ending on or before June 30, 1965, and the first $100,000,000 appropriated pursuant to subsection (d) for each fiscal year beginning on or after July 1, 1965,[21] shall be allotted by the Secretary from time to time, in accordance with regulations, as follows: (1) 50 per centum of such sums in the ratio that the population of each State bears to the population of all the States, and (2) 50

FWPCA Sec. 8: grants for construction

per centum of such sums in the ratio that the quotient obtained by dividing the per capita income of the United States by the per capita income of each State bears to the sum of such quotients for all the States. All sums in excess of $100,000,000 appropriated pursuant to subsection (d) for each fiscal year beginning on or after July 1, 1965, shall be allotted by the Secretary from time to time, in accordance with regulations, in the ratio that the population of each State bears to the population of all States. Sums allotted to a State under the two preceding sentences which are not obligated within six months following the end of the fiscal year for which they were allotted because of a lack of projects which have been approved by the State water pollution control agency under subsection (b)(1) of this section and certified as entitled to priority under subsection (b)(4) of this section, shall be reallotted by the Secretary, on such basis as he determines to be reasonable and equitable and in accordance with regulations promulgated by him, to States having projects approved under this section for which grants have not been made because of lack of funds including States having projects eligible for reimbursement pursuant to the sixth and seventh sentence of this subsection:[22] Provided, however, that whenever a State has funds subject to reallocation and the Secretary finds that the need for a project in a community in such State is due in part to any Federal institution or Federal construction activity, he may, prior to such reallocation, make an additional grant with respect to such project which will in his judgment reflect an equitable contribution for the need caused by such Federal institution or activity. Any sum made available to a State by reallotment under the preceding sentence shall be in addition to any funds otherwise allotted to such State under this Act. The allotments of a State under the second, third, and fourth sentences of this subsection shall be available, in accordance with the provisions of this section, for payments with respect to projects in such State which have been approved under this section, except[23] that in the case of any project on which construction was initiated in such State after June 30, 1966, which was approved by the appropriate State water pollution control agency and which the Secretary finds meets the requirements of this section but was constructed without such assistance, such allotments for any fiscal year ending prior to July 1, 1971, shall also be available for payments in reimbursement of State or local funds used for such project prior to July 1, 1971, to the extent that assistance could have been provided under this section if such project had been approved pursuant to this section and adequate funds had been available. In the case of any project on which construction was initiated in such State after June 30, 1966, and which was constructed with assistance pursuant to this section but the amount of such assistance was a lesser per centum of the cost of construction than was allowable pursuant to this section, such allotments shall also be available for payments in reimbursement of State or local funds used for such project prior to July 1, 1971, to the extent that assistance could have been provided under this section if adequate funds had been available. Neither a findings by the Secretary that a project meets the requirements of this subsection, nor any other provision of this subsection, shall be construed to constitute a commitment or obligation of the United States to provide funds to make or pay any grant for such project. For purposes of this section, population shall be determined on the basis of the latest decennial census for which figures are available, as certified by the Secretary of Commerce, and per capita income for each State and for the United States shall be determined on the basis of the average of the per capita incomes of the States and of the continental United States for the three most recent consecutive years for which satisfactory data are available from the Department of Commerce.

(d)[24] There are hereby authorized to be appropriated for each fiscal year through and including the fiscal year ending June 30, 1961, the sum of $50,000,000 per fiscal year for the purpose of making grants under this section. There are hereby authorized to be appropriated, for the purpose of making grants under this section, $80,000,000 for

---

[20] Subsection 8(b) amended by section 203, P.L. 89–753.
[21] Added by sec. 4, Public Law 89–234.
[22] Added by sec 111, Public Law 91–224.
[23] Reimbursement provision added by sec. 204, Public Law 89–753.
[24] This subsection amended by sec. 205, Public Law 89–753.

the fiscal year ending June 30, 1962, $90,000,000 for the fiscal year ending June 30, 1963, $100,000,000 for the fiscal year ending June 30, 1964, $100,000,000 for the fiscal year ending June 30, 1965, $150,000,000 for the fiscal year ending June 30, 1966, $150,000,000 for the fiscal year ending June 30, 1967; $450,000,000 for the fiscal year ending June 30, 1968; $700,000,000 for the fiscal year ending June 30, 1969; $1,000,000,000 for the fiscal year ending June 30, 1970; and $1,250,000,000 for the fiscal year ending June 30, 1971. Sums so appropriated shall remain available until expended. At least 50 per centum of the funds so appropriated for each fiscal year ending on or before June 30, 1965, and at least 50 per centum of the first $100,000,000 so appropriated for each fiscal year beginning on or after July 1, 1965, shall be used for grants for the construction of treatment works servicing municipalities of one hundred and twenty-five thousand population or under.

(e) The Secretary shall make payments under this section through the disbursing facilities of the Department of the Treasury. Funds so paid shall be used exclusively to meet the cost of construction of the project for which the amount was paid. As used in this section the term "construction" includes preliminary planning to determine the economic and engineering feasibility of treatment works, the engineering, architectural, legal, fiscal, and economic investigations and studies, surveys, designs, plans, working drawings, specifications, procedures, and other action necessary to the construction of treatment works; and the erection, building, acquisition, alteration, remodeling, improvement, or extension of treatment works; and the inspection and supervision of the construction of treatment works.

FWPCA Sec. 8: grants for construction

(f) Notwithstanding any other provisions of this section, the Secretary may increase the amount of a grant made under subsection (b) of this section by an additional 10 per centum of the amount of such grant for any project which has been certified to him by an official State, metropolitan, or regional planning agency empowered under State or local laws or interstate compact to perform metropolitan or regional planning for a metropolitan area within which the assistance is to be used, or other agency or instrumentality designated for such purposes by the Governor (or Governors in the case of interstate planning) as being in conformity with the comprehensive plan developed or in process of development for such metropolitan area. For the purposes of this subsection, the term "metropolitan area" means either (1) a standard metropolitan statistical area as defined by the Bureau of the Budget, except as may be determined by the President as not being appropriate for the purposes hereof, or (2) any urban area, including those surrounding areas that form an economic and socially related region, taking into consideration such factors as present and future population trends and patterns of urban growth, location of transportation facilities and systems, and distribution of industrial, commercial, residential, governmental, institutional, and other activities, which in the opinion of the President lends itself as being appropriate for the purposes hereof.[25]

(g) The Secretary shall take such action as may be necessary to insure that all laborers and mechanics employed by contractors or subcontractors on projects for which grants are made under this section shall be paid wages at rates not less than those prevailing for the same type of work on similar construction in the immediate locality, as determined by the Secretary of Labor, in accordance with the Act of March 3, 1931, as amended, known as the Davis-Bacon Act (46 Stat. 1494; 40 U.S.V., secs. 276a through 276a–5). The Secretary of Labor shall have, with respect to the labor standards specified in this subsection, the authority and functions set forth in Reorganization Plan Numbered 14 of 1950 (15 F.R. 3176; 64 Stat. 1267; 5 U.S.C. 133z–15) and section 2 of the Act of June 13, 1934, as amended (48 Stat. 948; 40 U.S.C. 276c).[26]

---

[25] Added by sec. 4, Public Law 89–234.
[26] Added by sec. 4, Public Law 89–234.

WASTE TREATMENT GRANTS

Federal grants program funding

The federal effort for water pollution control is primarily channeled into the waste treatment grants program. It is the one area of environmental activity that has had its funding increased dramatically in the past few years. The water pollution budget excluding grants and buildings and facilities, has increased very modestly. The waste treatment grant program, however, was $874 million in 1970, $214 million in 1969, $203 million in 1968, $150 million in 1967, $121 million in 1966, and $90 million in 1965, 1964 and 1963. In 1962 it was $80.1 million.

The increase is expected to continue, so as to assist the states and localities in reducing the backlog of treatment facilities needs. The budget authority for 1971 is an estimated $1,108 million and for 1972 is estimated at $2,089 million. Actual outlays will continue at about half of the budget authority for several years.

In addition to several grant programs for water and sewer grants administered by the Federal Water Quality Administration, there are other acts authorizing such grants. Other than the requirement to use a common preliminary application form from localities seeking assistance (to meet Office of Management and Budget desires) there is little coordination between programs.

The Environmental Protection Agency's General Grant Regulations and Procedures, State and Local Assistance [Interim Regulations] may be found in the *Federal Register,* Vol. 37, No. 112, June 19, 1972 at 11649. These grants concern state and local water quality, solid waste, and air pollution programs.

Monies available under Sections 6, 7, and 8 apply to urban areas as described in the following excerpt from, *Our Urban Environment,* A Report to the Administrator of EPA by the Task Force on Environmental Problems of the Inner City, (September 1971).

Training and Manpower Development

Development of Wastewater Treatment Plant Operator Training—This program includes: (a) a pilot State training grants program for water pollution control operator training; (b) an intensive technical training program for supervisory treatment plant and public works department personnel; and (c) an instructor training program .

Professional Training—Professional training grants are awarded to educational institutions for graduate training programs. Office of Water Programs (EPA) encourages institutions to develop specialized water pollution control courses within multidisciplinary curricula and to consider total environment needs which may cross and combine a number of traditional disciplines. During 1972, 88 training grants to academic institutions will be supported and these will provide traineeships for about 930 students.

Research and Development

Research/demonstration grants and contracts are awarded to assist in supporting basic and applied research projects and to develop and demonstrate the feasibility of new methods related to the causes, control, and prevention of water pollution. They support projects in the field of water pollution control which are directed toward the discovery and application of new information and technology in the chemical, physical biological and social sciences, in engineering, and in administrative aspects related to water pollution in urban and rural areas, including the inner city environment. These grants and contracts may be awarded to States, municipalities, intermunicipal agencies, public and private agencies, institutions, and individuals.

Construction Grants and Wastewater Treatment Works

Grants are provided to assist and serve as an incentive in the construction of waste treatment works and major interceptor sewers to prevent the discharge of untreated or inadequately treated sewage or other wastes into any waters. Basic grants cover 30 percent of the cost of a project; may be increased to 50 percent if the State pays at least 25 percent of the cost.

Municipalities (including the inner city areas), States, and interstate agencies having jurisdiction over the disposal of wastes are eligible.

The proposed $12 billion program is designed to meet municipal needs as identified in water quality standards. Approval of grants is based on conformance with basin/metro plans, approved cost effective guidelines, EPA (OWP) design, operation, and maintenance guidelines, and State approval.

Water Quality Planning

EPA's planning programs include three general kinds of activities:

a. financial assistance to regional, State and local planning agencies.

b. the administration of the grants used to provide this financial assistance; and,

c. direct performance of broad scope planning in cooperation with states and other federal agencies.

EPA-OEP requirements necessitate the development of metropolitan, basin or regional plans, including urban areas, and that these plans incorporate adequate sewage treatment facilities in compliance with water quality standards.

Federal Planning and Technical Assistance—This includes interagency water resources planning program; joint Federal-State river basin planning program (development of mathematical models of the 100 most critical and complex basins); and direct assistance and review program, to increase aid to State, regional, and metropolitan water quality planning agencies to ensure effective plans and conformance of construction grant applications with those plans.

Interagency Relationships—Water Quality Planning is conducted at all governmental levels, and such planning together with construction of wastewater collection and treatment systems is supported by grants from EPA Wastewater Treatment Works Construction Grant Program and River Basin Grants. HUD provides grants from Water and Sewer Facilities Grant Programs and 701 Planning Assistant Program. However, fundamental responsibility for water pollution control is at the State and local level.

Comprehensive planning by the States, with the assistance of Federal agencies, develops fundamental water quality goals and objectives, guides development, and provides a framework for regional, metropolitan, and local water quality management planning. Planning will be done by areawide planning organizations recognized by EPA, HUD, and the Governor of each State. On or after October 1, 1971, area and organizational, comprehensive planning, and water/sewer planning and programming certifications are required by both EPA and HUD prior to grant awards.

EPA regional staff are available for establishing coordination with State, local and regional agency officials.

End, excerpt from *Our Urban Environment*.

Because of criticism of the sewage grant program by Congress, the FWQA has been tightening its administration of the grant program. [*Need For Improved Operation and Maintenance of Municipal Waste Treatment Plants,* Report to the Congress by the Comptroller General of the United States, Sept. 1, 1970; *Examination Into the Effectiveness of the Construction Grant Program for Abating, Controlling, and Preventing Water Pollution,* Report to the Congress by the Comptroller General of the United States, Nov. 3, 1969.] In addition to the statute, regulations, and guidelines found in these materials, the FWQA has issued Federal Guidelines—Design, Operation and Maintenance of Waste Water Treatment Facilities, September 1970.

See also *Equitable Recovery of Industrial Waste Treatment Costs in Municipal Systems,* available from the Environmental Protection Agency's Office of Water Programs (October, 1971).

For an internal critique of the inefficiency in the use of capital provided for pollution control, see, *Cost of Clean Water, Vol. II, Cost Effectiveness and Clean Water,* EPA, March 1971.

For statistical data see *Municipal Waste Facilities in the United States,* U.S. Dept. of the Interior, FWQA, 1968 (available from EPA).

grants program guidelines

Federal funds for water pollution control and abatement include not only the construction grant program but a wide variety of other programs. These are research, development, and demonstration programs; manpower development and training programs; and various available planning grants.

Because of the number of programs and the variety of agencies involved, a listing of these programs is almost immediately out of date. The reader is therefore directed to the *Catalog of Federal Domestic Assistance* compiled for the Executive Office of the President by the Office of Economic Opportunity—April 1970. It is in looseleaf form and hopefully will be kept up to date. The *Environment Reporter* (BNA) also has a section on federal programs which may be a helpful starting point.

In order to assist an applicant in properly applying for a grant, the Environmental Protection Agency has issued a booklet, *Guidelines, Water Quality Management Planning,* January 1971. These are interim guidelines covering both EPA and HUD programs. Final guidelines eventually will be issued, but with pending legislation that would affect this program, it is likely that regulatory changes will take place on a regular basis.

The Environmental Protection Agency's General Grant Regulations and Procedures, State and Local Assistance [Interim Regulations] may be found in the *Federal Register,* Vol. 37, No. 112, June 19, 1972 at 11649. These grants concern state and local water quality, solid waste, and air pollution.

references

Research, Development, and Demonstration Projects, 1970 Grant and Contract Awards, EPA.

Sewage Facilities Construction 1969, U.S. Dept. of the Interior, FWQA (available from EPA)

Water Pollution Control Training Grants, U.S. Department of the Interior, FWPCA, 1969, (available from EPA)

EPA also publishes booklets of training courses available in the various environmental fields.

ROWLAND, Howard S., *The New York Times Guide to Federal Aid For Cities and Towns.* Quadrangle Books, New York, 1972.

WATER POLLUTION CONTROL ADVISORY BOARD

FWPCA Sec. 9: advisers

Sec. 9. (a) (1) There is hereby established in the Department of the Interior a Water Pollution Control Advisory Board, composed of the Secretary or his designee, who shall be chairman [27] and nine members appointed by the President, none of whom shall be Federal officers or employees. The appointed members, having due regard for the purposes of this Act, shall be selected from among representatives of various State, interstate and local governmental agencies, of public or private interests contributing to, affected by, or concerned with water pollution, and of other public and private agencies, organizations, or groups demonstrating an active interest in the field of water pollution prevention and control, as well as other individuals who are expert in this field.

(2) (A) Each member appointed by the President shall hold office for a term of three years, except that (i) any member appointed to fill a vacancy occurring prior to the expiration of the term for which his predecessor was appointed shall be appointed for the remainder of such term, and (ii) the terms of office of the members first taking office after June 30, 1956, shall expire as follows: three at the end of one year after such date, three at the end of two years after such date, and three at the end of three years after such date, as designated by the President at the time of appointment, and (iii) the term of any member under the preceding provisions shall be extended until the date on which his successor's appointment is effective. None of the members appointed by the President shall be eligible for reappointment within one year after the end of his preceding term but terms commencing prior to the enact-

[27] Reorganization Plan No. 2 of 1966 provided that the Secretary of Health, Education, and Welfare shall be an additional member of the Board.

ment of the Water Pollution Control Act Amendments of 1956 shall not be deemed "preceding terms" for purposes of this sentence.

(B) The members of the Board who are not officers or employees of the United States, while attending conferences or meetings of the Board or while otherwise serving at the request of the Secretary, shall be entitled to receive compensation at a rate to be fixed by the Secretary, but not exceeding $50 per diem, including travel time, and while away from their homes or regular places of business they may be allowed travel expenses, including per diem in lieu of subsistence, as authorized by law (5 U.S.C. 73b–2) for persons in the Government service employed intermittently.

(b) The Board shall advise, consult with, and make recommendations to the Secretary on matters of policy relating to the activities and functions of the Secretary under this Act.

(c) Such clerical and technical assistance as may be necessary to discharge the duties of the Board shall be provided from the personnel of the Department of the Interior. [now EPA]

COMMENTARY

The President's Water Pollution Control Advisory Board meets periodically. The minutes of these meetings are public documents. The Board's primary characteristic seemingly is that it does not have much influence or effect of any kind on the operations of the Federal government.

THE PRESIDENT'S WATER POLLUTION CONTROL ADVISORY BOARD

Chairman
Honorable William D. Ruckelshaus
Administrator
Environmental Protection Agency
Washington, D.C. 20460

Executive Secretary
Mr. Alan Levin
Office of Media Programs
Environmental Protection Agency
Washington, D.C. 20460

COMMENTARY

The major Federal regulatory program for water pollution control is carried out under **Sec. 10** of the Act:

FWPCA Sec. 10: enforcement

ENFORCEMENT MEASURES AGAINST POLLUTION OF INTERSTATE OR NAVIGABLE WATERS

SEC. 10. (a) The pollution of interstate or navigable [28] waters in or adjacent to any State or States (whether the matter causing or contributing to such pollution is discharged directly into such waters or reaches such waters after discharge into a tributary of such waters), which endangers the health or welfare of any persons [28] shall be subject to abatement as provided in this Act.

(b) Consistent with the policy declaration of this Act, State and interstate action to abate pollution of interstate or navigable waters [28] shall be encouraged and shall not, except as otherwise provided by or pursuant to court order under subsection (h), be displaced by Federal enforcement action.

(c) (1) If the Governor of a State or a State water pollution control agency files, within one year after the date of enactment of this subsection,[29] a letter of intent that such State, after public hearings, will before June 30, 1967, adopt (A) water quality criteria applicable to interstate waters or portions thereof within such State, and (B) a plan for the implementation and enforcement of the water quality criteria adopted, and if such criteria and plan are established in accordance with the letter of intent, and if the Secretary determines that such State criteria and plan are consistent with paragraph (3) of this subsection, such State criteria and plan shall thereafter be the water quality standards applicable to such interstate waters or portions thereof.

(2) If a State does not (A) file a letter of intent or (B) establish water quality standards in accordance with paragraph (1) of this subsection, or if the Secretary or the Governor of any State affected by water quality standards established pursuant to this subsection desires

[28] Phrase added by sec. 7, Public Law 87–88.

[29] This subsection added by sec. 5(a), Public Law 89–234, approved October 2, 1965.

a revision in such standards, the Secretary may, after reasonable notice and a conference of representatives of appropriate Federal departments and agencies, interstate agencies, States, municipalities and industries involved, prepare regulations setting forth standards of water quality to be applicable to interstate waters or portions thereof. If, within six months from the date the Secretary publishes such regulations, the State has not adopted water quality standards found by the Secretary to be consistent with paragraph (3) of this subsection, or a petition for public hearing has not been filed under paragraph (4) of this subsection, the Secretary shall promulgate such standards.

(3) Standards of quality established pursuant to this subsection shall be such as to protect the public health or welfare, enhance the quality of water and serve the purposes of this Act. In establishing such standards the Secretary, the Hearing Board, or the appropriate State authority shall take into consideration their use and value for public water supplies, propagation of fish and wildlife, recreational purposes, and agricultural, industrial, and other legitimate uses. In establishing such standards the Secretary, the Hearing Board, or the appropriate State authority shall take into consideration their use and value for navigation.[30]

(4) If at any time prior to 30 days after standards have been promulgated under paragraph (2) of this subsection, the Governor of any State affected by such standards petitions the Secretary for a hearing, the Secretary shall call a public hearing, to be held in or near one or more of the places where the water quality standards will take effect, before a Hearing Board of five or more persons appointed by the Secretary. Each State which would be affected by such standards shall be given an opportunity to select one member of the Hearing Board. The Department of Commerce and other affected Federal departments and agencies shall each be given an opportunity to select a member of the Hearing Board [31] and not less than a majority of the Hearing Board shall be persons other than officers or employees of the Department of the Interior. The members of the Board who are not officers or employees of the United States, while participating in the hearing conducted by such Hearing Board or otherwise engaged on the work of such Hearing Board, shall be entitled to receive compensation at a rate fixed by the Secretary, but not exceeding $100 per diem, including travel time, and while away from their homes or regular places of business they may be allowed travel expenses, including per diem in lieu of subsistence, as authorized by law (5 U.S.C. 73b–2) for persons in the Government service employed intermittently. Notice of such hearing shall be published in the Federal Register and given to the State water pollution control agencies, interstate agencies and municipalities involved at least 30 days prior to the date of such hearing. On the basis of the evidence presented at such hearing, the Hearing Board shall make findings as to whether the standards published or promulgated by the Secretary should be approved or modified and transmit its findings to the Secretary. If the Hearing Board approves the standards as published or promulgated by the Secretary, the standards shall take effect on receipt by the Secretary of the Hearing Board's recommendations. If the Hearing Board recommends modifications in the Standards as published or promulgated by the Secretary, the Secretary shall promulgate revised regulations setting forth standards of water quality in accordance with the Hearing Board's recommendations which will become effective immediately upon promulgation.

FWPCA
Sec. 10:
enforcement

(5) The discharge of matter into such interstate waters or portions thereof, which reduces the quality of such waters below the water quality standards established under this subsection (whether the matter causing or contributing to such reduction is discharged directly into such waters or reaches such waters after discharge into tributaries of such waters), is subject to abatement in accordance with the provisions of paragraph (1) or (2) of subsection (g) of this section, except that at least 180 days before any abatement action is initiated under either paragraph (1) or (2) of subsection (g) as authorized by this subsection, the Secretary shall notify the violators and other inter-

---

[30] Last sentence added by sec. 112, Public Law 90–224.

[31] Reorganization Plan No. 2 of 1966 provided that the Secretary of the Interior shall give the Secretary of Health, Education, and Welfare an opportunity to select a member of the Hearing Board.

ested parties of the violation of such standards. In any suit brought under the provisions of this subsection the court shall receive in evidence a transcript of the proceedings of the conference and hearing provided for in this subsection, together with the recommendations of the conference and Hearing Board and the recommendations and standards promulgated by the Secretary, and such additional evidence, including that relating to the alleged violation of the standards, as it deems necessary to a complete review of the standards and to a determination of all other issues relating to the alleged violation. The court, giving due consideration to the practicability and to the physical and economic feasibility of complying with such standards, shall have jurisdiction to enter such judgment and orders enforcing such judgment as the public interest and the equities of the case may require.

(6) Nothing in this subsection shall (A) prevent the application of this section to any case to which subsection (a) of this section would otherwise be applicable, or (B) extend Federal jurisdiction over water not otherwise authorized by this Act.

(7) In connection with any hearings under this section no witness or any other person shall be required to divulge trade secrets or secret processes.

(d) (1)[32] Whenever requested by the Governor of any State or State water pollution control agency, or (with the concurrence of the Governor and of the State water pollution control agency for the State in which the municipality is situated) the governing body of any municipality, the Secretary shall, if such request refers to pollution of waters which is endangering the health or welfare of persons in a State other than that in which the discharge or discharges (causing or contributing to such pollution) originates, give formal notification thereof to the water pollution control agency and interstate agency, if any, of the State or States where such discharge or discharges originate and shall call promptly a conference of such agency or agencies and of the State water pollution control agency and interstate agency, if any, of the State or States, if any, which may be adversely affected by such pollution. Whenever requested by the Governor of any State, the Secretary shall, if such request refers to pollution of interstate or navigable waters which is endangering the health or welfare of persons only in the requesting State in which the discharge or discharges (causing or contributing to such pollution) originate, give formal notification thereof to the water pollution control agency and interstate agency, if any, of such State and shall promptly call a conference of such agency or agencies, unless, in the judgment of the Secretary, the effect of such pollution on the legitimate uses of the waters is not of sufficient significance to warrant exercise of Federal jurisdiction under this section. The Secretary shall also call such a conference whenever, on the basis of reports, surveys, or studies, he has reason to believe that any pollution referred to in subsection (a) and endangering the health or welfare of persons in a State other than that in which the discharge or discharges originate is occurring[33] or he finds that substantial economic injury results from the inability to market shellfish or shellfish products in interstate commerce because of pollution referred to in subsection (a) and action of Federal, State, or local authorities.

(2)[34] Whenever the Secretary, upon receipt of reports, surveys, or studies from any duly constituted international agency, has reason to believe that any pollution referred to in subsection (a) of this section which endangers the health or welfare of persons in a foreign country is occurring, and the Secretary of State requests him to abate such pollution, he shall give formal notification thereof to the State water pollution control agency of the State in which such discharge or discharges originate and to the interstate water pollution control agency, if any, and shall call promptly a conference of such agency or agencies, if he believes that such pollution is occurring in sufficient quantity to warrant such action. The Secretary, through the Secretary of State, shall invite the foreign country which may be adversely affected by the pollution to attend and participate in the conference, and the representative of such country shall, for the purpose of the conference

FWPCA Sec. 10: enforcement

[32] Amended by sec. 7, Public Law 87–88.
[33] Remainder of sentence added by sec. 5(b), Public Law 89–234.
[34] This paragraph added by sec. 206, Public Law 89–753.

and any further proceeding resulting from such conference, have all the rights of a State water pollution control agency. This paragraph shall apply only to a foreign country which the Secretary determines has given the United States essentially the same rights with respect to the prevention and control of water pollution occurring in that country as is given that country by this paragraph. Nothing in this paragraph shall be construed to modify, amend, repeal, or otherwise affect the provisions of the 1909 Boundary Waters Treaty between Canada and the United States or the Water Utilization Treaty of 1944 between Mexico and the United States (59 Stat. 1219), relative to the control and abatement of water pollution in waters covered by those treaties.

(3) The agencies called to attend such conference may bring such persons as they desire to the conference. In addition,[35] it shall be the responsibility of the chairman of the conference to give every person contributing to the alleged pollution or affected by it an opportunity to make a full statement of his views to the conference. Not less than three weeks' prior notice of the conference date shall be given to such agencies.

(4) Following this conference, the Secretary shall prepare and forward to all the water pollution control agencies attending the conference a summary of conference discussions including (A) occurrence of pollution of interstate or navigable waters subject to abatement under this Act; (B) adequacy of measures taken toward abatement of the pollution; and (C) nature of delays, if any, being encountered in abating the pollution.

FWPCA Sec. 10: enforcement

(e) If the Secretary believes, upon the conclusion of the conference or thereafter, that effective progress toward abatement of such pollution is not being made and that the health or welfare of any persons is being endangered, he shall recommend to the appropriate State water pollution control agency that it take necessary remedial action. The Secretary shall allow at least six months from the date he makes such recommendations for the taking of such recommended action.[36]

(f)(1) If, at the conclusion of the period so allowed, such remedial action has not been taken or action which in the judgment of the Secretary is reasonably calculated to secure abatement of such pollution has not been taken, the Secretary shall call a public hearing, to be held in or near one or more of the places where the discharge or discharges causing or contributing to such pollution originated, before a Hearing Board of five or more persons appointed by the Secretary. Each State in which any discharge causing or contributing to such pollution originates and each State claiming to be adversely affected by such pollution shall be given an opportunity to select one member of the Hearing Board [37] and at least one member shall be a representative of the Department of Commerce, and not less than a majority of the Hearing Board shall be persons other than officers or employees of the Department of the Interior. At least three weeks' prior notice of such hearing shall be given to the State water pollution control agencies and interstate agencies, if any, called to attend the aforesaid hearing and the alleged polluter or polluters. It shall be [38] the responsibility of the Hearing Board to give every person contributing to the alleged pollution or affected by it an opportunity to make a full statement of his views to the Hearing Board. On the basis of the evidence presented at such hearing, the Hearing Board shall make findings as to whether pollution referred to in subsection (a) is occurring and whether effective progress toward abatement thereof is being made. If the Hearing Board finds such pollution is occurring and effective progress toward abatement thereof is not being made it shall make recommendations to the Secretary concerning the measures, if any, which it finds to be reasonable and equitable to secure abatement of such pollution. The Secretary shall send such findings and recommendations to the person or persons discharging any matter causing or contributing to such pollution, together with a notice specifying a reasonable time (not less than six months) to secure abatement of such pollution, and shall also send such findings and recommendations and

[35] This sentence added by sec. 207, Public Law 89–753.
[36] Amended by sec. 7, Public Law 87–88.
[37] Reorganization Plan No. 2 of 1966 provided that the Secretary of the Interior shall give the Secretary of Health, Education, and Welfare an opportunity to select a member of the Hearing Board.
[38] This sentence added by sec. 208(b), Public Law 89–753.

such notice to the State water pollution control agency and to the interstate agency, if any, of the State or States where such discharge or discharges originate.

(2)[39] In connection with any hearing called under this section the Secretary is authorized to require any person whose alleged activities result in discharges causing or contributing to water pollution to file with him, in such form as he may prescribe, a report based on existing data, furnishing such information as may reasonably be required as to the character, kind, and quantity of such discharges and the use of facilities or other means to prevent or reduce such discharges by the person filing such a report. Such report shall be made under oath or otherwise, as the Secretary may prescribe, and shall be filed with the Secretary within such reasonable period as the Secretary may prescribe, unless additional time be granted by the Secretary. No person shall be required in such report to divulge trade secrets or secret processes, and all information reported shall be considered confidential for the purposes of section 1905 of title 18 of the United States Code.

(3)[40] If any person required to file any report under paragraph (2) of this subsection shall fail to do so within the time fixed by the Secretary for filing the same, and such failure shall continue for thirty days after notice of such default, such person shall forfeit to the United States the sum of $100 for each and every day of the continuance of such failure, which forfeiture shall be payable into the Treasury of the United States, and shall be recoverable in a civil suit in the name of the United States brought in the district where such person has his principal office or in any district in which he does business. The Secretary may upon application therefor remit or mitigate any forfeiture provided for under this paragraph and he shall have authority to determine the facts upon all such applications.

FWPCA Sec. 10: enforcement

(4)[40] It shall be the duty of the various United States attorneys, under the direction of the Attorney General of the United States, to prosecute for the recovery of such forfeitures.

(g)[41] If action reasonably calculated to secure abatement of the pollution within the time specified in the notice following the public hearing is not taken, the Secretary—

(1) in the case of pollution of waters which is endangering the health or welfare of persons in a State other than that in which the discharge or discharges (causing or contributing to such pollution) originate, may request the Attorney General to bring a suit on behalf of the United States to secure abatement of pollution, and

(2) in the case of pollution of waters which is endangering the health or welfare of persons only in the State in which the discharge or discharges (causing or contributing to such pollution) originate, may, with the written consent of the Governor of such State, request the Attorney General to bring a suit on behalf of the United States to secure abatement of the pollution.

(h) The court shall receive in evidence in any such suit a transcript of the proceedings before the Board and a copy of the Board's recommendations and shall receive such further evidence as the court in its discretion deems proper. The court, giving due consideration to the practicability and to the physical and economic feasibility of securing abatement of any pollution proved, shall have jurisdiction to enter such judgment, and orders enforcing such judgment, as the public interest and the equities of the case may require.

(i) Members of any Hearing Board appointed pursuant to subsection (f) who are not regular full-time officers or employees of the United States shall, while participating in the hearing conducted by such Board or otherwise engaged on the work of such Board, be entitled to receive compensation at a rate fixed by the Secretary, but not exceeding $100 per diem, including travel time, and while away from their homes or regular places of business they may be allowed travel expenses, including per diem in lieu of subsistence, as authorized by law (5 U.S.C. 73b–2) for persons in the Government service employed intermittently.[42]

(j) As used in this section the term—

(1) "person" includes an individual, corporation, partnership,

[39] This paragraph added by sec. 208(b), Public Law 89–753.
[40] Subparagraphs added by sec 208(b), Public Law 89–753.
[41] Amended by sec. 7, Public Law 87–88.

FWPCA Sec. 10: enforcement

association, State, municipality, and political subdivision of a State, and

(2) "municipality" means a city, town, borough, county, parish, district, or other public body created by or pursuant to State law.[42]

(k)[43](1) At the request of a majority of the conferees in any conference called under this section the Secretary is authorized to request any person whose alleged activities result in discharges causing or contributing to water pollution, to file with him a report (in such form as may be prescribed in regulations promulgated by him) based on existing data, furnishing such information as may reasonably be requested as to the character, kind, and quantity of such discharges and the use of facilities or other means to prevent or reduce such discharges by the person filing such a report. No person shall be required in such report to divulge trade secrets or secret processes, and all information reported shall be considered confidential for the purposes of section 1905 of title 18 of the United States Code.

(2) If any person required to file any report under this subsection shall fail to do so within the time fixed by regulations for filing the same, and such failure shall continue for thirty days after notice of such default, such person may, by order of a majority of the conferees, be subject to a forfeiture of $100 for each and every day of the continuance of such failure which forfeiture shall be payable into the Treasury of the United States and shall be recoverable in a civil suit in the name of the United States brought in the district where such person has his principal office or in any district in which he does business. The Secretary may upon application therefor remit or mitigate any forfeiture provided for under this subsection and he shall have authority to determine the facts upon all such applications.

(3) It shall be the duty of the various United States attorneys, under the direction of the Attorney General of the United States, to prosecute for the recovery of such forfeitures.

COMMENTARY

Major responsibility for the Federal water pollution program has been given to the Federal Water Program Office. This organization, formerly called the Federal Water Quality Administration, and still earlier the Federal Water Pollution Control Administration, was created by **Sec. 2** of the Water Quality Act of 1965, and was transferred from HEW to the Department of Interior and under Reorganization Plan No. 3 of 1970 was transferred to the Environmental Protection Agency.

The majority of the EPA Water Quality employees are in field offices. Of the 1970 FWQA staff of 2,538 permanent and temporary employees, 1,946 were assigned to the then nine regions. Under EPA there are 10 regions designated by numbers and headquartered in Boston, New York, Philadelphia, Atlanta, Chicago, Dallas, Kansas City, Denver, San Francisco, and Seattle. (See chapter one, pp. 139–40 for further organizational information). The budget for water pollution control for fiscal year 1971 is $1,552 million. Of this sum $1,256 million is for construction grants for waste treatment works. The other major recipient of funds is research, development and demonstration programs. EPA spends most of this money obligated for water pollution control.

[42] Amended by sec. 7, Public Law 87–88.

enforcement methods

Under the procedure set forth in **Sec. 10(c)(1)** of the Act, the governor or the state water pollution control agency of each state must file a letter of intent indicating that the state will hold public hearings and, before June 30, 1967, they were to have adopted water quality criteria applicable to interstate waters within the state, as well as a plan for the implementation and enforcement of the criteria. All of the states filed such letters . Most states also moved to regulate intrastate waters.

The state's water quality criteria and implementation plan were then to be submitted to the Secretary, who determined whether such state criteria and plan are consistent with **Sec. 10(c)(3)** of the Act. That section provides that the standards adopted under the Act must "protect the public health or welfare, enhance the quality of water, and serve the purposes of this Act," and that in establishing such standards, the use and value of the stream in question for public water supplies, propagation of fish and wildlife, recreational purposes, and agricultural, industrial and other legitimate uses must be considered.

If the Secretary approves the state criteria and plan, they become the water quality standards applicable to the interstate waters in question under both state and Federal law. All States, three Territories, and the District of Columbia, have submitted standards. As of May, 1972, 46 states, territories and the District of Columbia had been approved by EPA. In the final process are Tennessee, Georgia, and Mississippi; still in earlier stages are Illinois, Louisiana, Michigan and Ohio. On March 11, 1972 EPA published proposed water quality standards for Alabama under the authority of Sec. 10(c) (2) of the Federal Water Pollution Control Act. (37 Fed. Reg. 5260, March 11, 1972). Six months are allowed for comment on these standards after which time EPA will promulgate standards for the state.

See also 40 CFR 120; 36 Fed. Reg. 22489, Nov. 25, 1971, as amended by 37 Fed. Reg. 6087, March 24, 1972.

A substantial number of EPA objections have been based upon the state's failure to include either (1) a requirement of secondary treatment or (2) a nondegradation provision, under which waters whose existing quality were better than the established standards on the effective date must be maintained at their existing high quality. Another basic area of disagreement involves the temperature and dissolved oxygen requirements.

Under **Sec. 10(c),** each state must apply specific quality categories to each interstate stream. This requirement is normally expanded to include intrastate streams. Streams are zoned, based on possible uses, so that specific scientific tests are applied to each section of a stream. Sometimes categories such as "A", "B", "C" and "D" are used, and sometimes more descriptive categories, such as those of Ohio, are used. These stream standards become goals of water quality which are to be reached over a several-year period by controlling effluent. The effluent from municipal and industrial sources is affected through regulations aimed at controlling waste coming from discharge pipes. Normally this is accomplished through a permit system to meet the implementation plan requirement of **Sec. 10(c)(1)(b).** The stream quality tests are applied to the stream, not to the waste discharges. The strength and toxicity of effluent discharged into streams is controlled by regulations, often under a state permit system called the industrial waste code. Further regulations are promulgated to control municipal facilities. While most states have a permit system, these permit programs differ substantially. California is a large state without a permit system. California has waste discharge requirements which include a monitoring program and quarterly monitoring reports. Many states that have permit requirements do not have the manpower to make the system work. It should be understood that the compliance with **Sec. 10** requires two sets of regulatory materials—one controls streams and is expressed as a water quality *goal;* the other regulates waste discharges.

Since the passage of the Water Quality Act of 1965, the states have taken many different approaches in developing criteria to judge water quality. This has frequently resulted in delay in establishing enforceable standards. As an example of stream quality criteria, those of the Ohio Water Pollution Board, as adopted April 14, 1970, are reprinted below:

water quality criteria

MINIMUM CONDITIONS APPLICABLE TO ALL WATERS AT ALL PLACES AND AT ALL TIMES

1. Free from substances attributable to municipal, industrial or other discharges, or agricultural practices that will settle to form putrescent or otherwise objectionable sludge deposits.
2. Free from floating debris, oil, scum and other floating materials attributable to municipal, industrial or other discharges, or agricultural practices in amounts sufficient to be unsightly or deleterious.
3. Free from materials attributable to municipal, industrial or other discharges, or agricultural practices producing color, odor or other conditions in such degree as to create a nuisance.
4. Free from substances attributable to municipal, industrial or other discharges, or agricultural practices in concentrations or combinations which are toxic or harmful to human, animal, plant or aquatic life.

PROTECTION OF HIGH QUALITY WATERS

Waters whose existing quality is better than the established standards as of the date on which such standards become effective will be maintained at their existing high quality, pursuant to the Ohio water pollution control statutes, so as not to interfere with or become injurious to any assigned uses made of, or presently possible, in such waters. This will require that any industrial, public or private project or development which would constitute a new source of pollution or an increased source of pollution to high quality waters will be required, as part of the initial project design, to provide the most effective waste treatment available under existing technology. The Ohio Water Pollution Control Board will cooperate with other agencies of the state, agencies of other states, interstate agencies and the Federal Government in the enforcement of this policy.

WATER QUALITY DESIGN FLOW

Where applicable for the determination of treatment requirements the water quality design flow shall be the minimum seven consecutive day average that is exceeded in 90 percent of the years.

STREAM-QUALITY CRITERIA

FOR PUBLIC WATER SUPPLY

The following criteria are for evaluation of stream quality at the point at which water is withdrawn for treatment and distribution as a potable supply:

1. Bacteria: Coliform group not to exceed 5,000 per 100 ml as a monthly average value (either MPN or MF count); nor exceed this number in more than 20 percent of the samples examined during any month; nor exceed 20,000 per 100 ml in more than five percent of such samples.
2. Threshold-odor Number: Not to exceed 24 (at 60 deg. C.) as a daily average.
3. Radioactivity: Gross beta activity not to exceed 1,000 picocuries per liter (pCi/l), nor shall activity from dissolved strontium-90 exceed 10 pCi/l, nor shall activity from dissolved alpha emitters exceed 3 pCi/l.
5. Chemical constituents: Not to exceed the following specified concentrations at any time.

Constituent	Concentration (mg/l)
Arsenic	0.05
Barium	1.0
Cadmium	0.01
Chromium (hexavalent)	0.05
Cyanide	0.025
Fluoride	1.0
Lead	0.05
Selenium	0.01
Silver	0.05

FOR INDUSTRIAL WATER SUPPLY

The following criteria are applicable to stream water at the point at which the water is withdrawn for use (either with or without treatment) for industrial cooling and processing:

1. Dissolved oxygen: Not less than 2.0 mg/l as a daily-average value, nor less than 1.0 mg/l at any time.
2. pH: Not less than 5.0 nor greater than 9.0 at any time.
3. Temperature: Not to exceed 95 deg. F. at any time.
4. Dissolved solids: Not to exceed 750 mg/l as a monthly average value, nor exceed 1,000 mg/l at any time.

FOR AQUATIC LIFE A

The following criteria are for evaluation of conditions for the maintenance of a well-balanced, warm-water fish population. They are applicable at any point in the stream except for areas necessary for the admixture of waste effluents with stream water:

1. Dissolved oxygen: Not less than an average of 5.0 mg/l per calendar day and not less than 4.0 mg/l at any time.
2. pH:
   A. No values below 6.0 nor above 8.5.
   B. Daily fluctuations which exceed the range of pH 6.0 to pH 8.5 and are correlated with photosynthetic activity may be tolerated.

3. Temperature:
   A. No abnormal temperature changes that may affect aquatic life unless caused by natural conditions.
   B. The normal daily and seasonal temperature fluctuations that existed before the addition of heat due to other than natural causes shall be maintained.
   C. Maximum temperature rise at any time or place above natural temperatures shall not exceed 5 deg. F. In addition, the water temperature shall not exceed the maximum limits indicated in the following table.

WATERS	Maximum Temperature in Deg. F. During Month											
	Jan.	Feb.	Mar.	Apr.	May	June	July	Aug.	Sept.	Oct.	Nov.	Dec.
All waters except Ohio River	50	50	60	70	80	90	90	90	90	78	70	57
Main Stem-Ohio River	50	50	60	70	80	87	89	89	87	78	70	57

4. Toxic substances: Not to exceed one-tenth of the 48-hour median tolerance limit, except that other limiting concentrations may be used in specific cases when justified on the basis of available evidence and approved by the appropriate regulatory agency.

FOR AQUATIC LIFE B

The following criteria are for evaluation of conditions for the maintenance of desirable biological growths and, in limited stretches of a stream, for permitting the passage of fish through the water, except for areas necessary for admixture of effluents with stream water:

1. Dissolved oxygen: Not less than 3.0 mg/l as a daily-average value, nor less than 2.0 mg/l at any time.
2. pH: Not less than 6.0 nor greater than 8.5 at any time.
3. Temperature: Not to exceed 95 deg. F. at any time.
4. Toxic substances: Not to exceed one-tenth of the 48-hour median tolerance limit, except that other limiting concentrations may be used in specific cases when justified on the basis of available evidence and approved by the appropriate regulatory agency.

FOR RECREATION

The following criterion is for evaluation of conditions at any point in waters designated to be used for recreational purposes, including such water-contact activities as swimming and water skiing:

Bacteria: The fecal coliform content (either MPN or MF count) not to exceed 200 per 100 ML as a monthly geometric mean based not less than five samples per month; nor exceed 400 per 100 ML in more than ten percent of all samples taken during a month.

FOR AGRICULTURAL USE AND STOCK WATERING

The following criteria are applicable for the evaluation of stream quality at places where water is withdrawn for agricultural use or stock-watering purposes:

1. Free from substances attributable to municipal, industrial or other discharges, or agricultural practices that will settle to form putrescent or otherwise objectionable sludge deposits.
2. Free from floating debris, oil, scum and other floating materials attributable to municipal, industrial or other discharges, or agricultural practices in amounts sufficient to be unsightly or deleterious.
3. Free from materials attributable to municipal, industrial or other discharges, or agricultural practices producing color, odor or other conditions in such degree as to create a nuisance.
4. Free from substances attributable to municipal, industrial or other discharges or agricultural practices in concentrations or combinations which are toxic or harmful to human, animal, plant or aquatic life.

End, text of Ohio Water Quality Board's water quality criteria.

As the previous material shows, the State of Ohio, like many states, has adopted water quality criteria for various water uses. These criteria include minimum standards applicable to all waters; a non-degradation clause; a paragraph explaining that the treatment to be required will not have to be good enough to meet the chosen quality standards on those occasions every decade or so when water flow is at its lowest; and the standards which water must meet to qualify for various uses. As the tests for the various uses are of different types, it is possible to require that the same section of the same stream meet more than one set of tests to qualify for more than one use.

The next step is to assign an inventory of intended water use to each section of each stream. Then an inventory of effluents is studied to determine what improvements are needed to permit the stream to meet the relevant criteria. A timetable for changes in effluent discharges is then drawn up.

It is, of course, possible to require that one set of criteria be met by one date, and an additional set of criteria be met by a more distant date.

Political or economic pressures may of course enter into this theoretical clean-up process at any point to sabotage or assist the effort.

As an example of an effluent control timetable, the following is excerpted from one promulgated by the Ohio Water Quality Board under water quality criteria in use up to adoption of those printed above.

CUYAHOGA RIVER BASIN		Completion Dates		
		Report & Gen.Plan	Detail Plans	Constr.
(1) Municipalities				
Akron	Enlarg.of prim.& second. treat.facils.	-	9-15-69	12-15-70
	Advanced waste treat. facils.	1-15-72	7-15-73	1-1-75

		Completion Dates		
		Report & Gen.Plan	Detail Plans	Constr.
(2) County Sewer Districts				
Cuyahoga County Brecksville SD 13	Enlarg.of treat.facils.	8-15-69	8-15-70	12-15-71
(3) State Park				
Punderson State Park Geauga Co.	Imprvts to exist.treat. facilities.	2-15-70	2-15-71	2-15-72
(4) Industries				
Diamond Crystal Salt Company Akron	Complete program to reduce chlorides.	-	-	6-1-69
Firestone Tire & Rubber Company Akron	Addtnl treat.facils or disch.of pretreated wastes to Akron sew.syst.	-	12-31-69	12-31-70
Middlefield Swiss Cheese Co-op. Middlefield	Elimin.of whey from IW discharge.	-	3-1-69	9-1-69
Ohio Edison Co. Gorge Plant Akron	Reduct.of effects of thermal load.	-	1-1-71	1-1-72
Republic Steel Corp., Cleveland				
Bolt & Nut Div.	Acid Iron: Removal of strong acids evaluat. of effects of rinse waters pretreat.of plating wastes with disch.to city sewers.	-	Apprvd	12-31-69
Cleveland Dist.	Acid Iron: Evaluat.of effects of rinse water disch.	-	-	12-31-69
	Blast Furn.: Imprvd solids removal.	-	Apprvd	12-31-69
	Mill Scale: Imprvd oil and solids removal.	-	4-1-69	12-31-69
U.S.Steel Corp. Tubular Opns. Central Furnaces Cleveland	Blast Furn.: Improved solids removal.	-	-	12-31-69
Weather-Tite Div. Pacific Coast Co. Walton Hills	Elimin.of storm water from wastewater treat. facilities.	-	6-1-69	12-31-69

COMMENTARY

the failure of jawboning

The standards set by the states and the implementation plan to achieve those standards form the basic framework of the Federal-state water pollution program. To have credibility, an act must provide for enforcement and sanctions for those who do not comply.

It is in this area that the Section 10 program is most deficient.

The first line of enforcement is via the state program to enforce standards which are usually also state law. In this situation the quality of the water within a state, to the extent the condition was created in that state, is going to be dependent upon state zeal directed toward pollution control. This can vary substantially.

The following is from the second annual report of the council on environmental quality, August, 1971 at 12:

> **other enforcement**—The present FWPCA provides two limited and cumbersome enforcement mechanisms for pollution abatement by the Federal Government. The first is a three-step procedure consisting of a conference of Federal, State, and interstate water quality agency representatives; a public hearing; and finally, court action.
>
> The conference may be called at State or Federal initiative. However, there must be a State request if the pollution causes only intrastate effects unless the pollution causes economic injury to shellfish producers. The enforcement conference is a mechanism for bringing to light complex and longstanding pollution situations.
>
> Two new enforcement conferences have been called since EPA was established. The first covered the interstate waters of Long Island Sound in Connecticut and New York, and the second covered the navigable waters of Galveston Bay and its tributaries in Texas.
>
> EPA has reconvened five conferences, two of which received wide attention. The four-State Lake Michigan conference, first convened in 1968, focused on the need to protect Lake Michigan from waste heat discharges. The EPA Administrator recommended strict temperature standards for the Lake. After considering proposals of the State and Federal conferees, the Administrator issued a conference summary recommending closed cycle cooling systems for new waste heat discharges and deadlines for plants now in operation to install abatement facilities. In the Lake Superior enforcement conference, first convened in 1969, the remaining difficult issue is the discharge of taconite tailings into the Lake from a Reserve Mining Co. facility in Minnesota.
>
> The second enforcement procedure under the FWPCA, also applicable primarily to interstate pollution, calls for notification both to the violator of water quality standards and to interested parties, followed by court action if necessary. Under the present law, 180 days must elapse after a notice of violation is issued before court action may be initiated. This gives violators the opportunity to comply voluntarily. EPA recently issued a violation notice to Reserve Mining Co. because of its failure to present an acceptable abatement plan to the Lake Superior enforcement conference.
>
> One of the EPA Administrator's first official acts was to issue violation notices to three major cities—Atlanta, Cleveland, and Detroit. By the end of the 180-day period, EPA announced agreements with each of the three cities and with the States involved for joint Federal-State-local financing of the needed waste treatment facilities construction. Of the total estimated cost of $1.2 billion, more than $1 billion will go to reducing pollution of Lake Erie by Cleveland and Detroit.

End quote from CEQ report.

While the Federal government touts the effectiveness of the conference procedure the quality of water in America's rivers refutes its sanguineness. Only one case has ever gone to court. That case stemmed from the Conference on Pollution of Interstate Waters of the Missouri River—St. Joseph, Missouri Area, in June of 1957. In 1960 the U.S. government, after conferences failed, filed suit [*United States v. St. Joseph,* W.D.Mo. No. 1077, Complaint filed Sept. 29, 1960]. The proceeding took place on March 27, 1967, and an order was made on March 16, 1970. However, although within two years the city then constructed a sewage treatment plant, the plant treated only half of the city's sewage. Daily, 5 million tons of raw sewage continued to be dumped into the river.

The time-consuming conference procedure has been used a little over 50 times since 1956. By reconvening many enforcement actions, they can drag on for years. Under the three-step conference procedure, four conferences have moved to hearings, and there has been a court action. There will probably be at least one more court action in the next fifteen years.

The 1965 Act providing for a two-step conference allows a suit 180 days after notice has been given that a discharge reduces water quality below that which has been established by standards. It applies only to interstate waters, while the three-step conference applies to interstate or navigable waters. [**Sec. 13(e)** defines interstate waters.]

The time required to complete such actions is not the only reason for the failure to use the enforcement devices. Political pressure by industry and municipal poverty have played a part. Important also is the requirement for proof that the discharge endangers health, followed by complete judicial review. This review allows both the admission of new evidence and challenges to the standards imposed. The court also applies a new test of "practicability and physical and economic feasibility."

It is not surprising that the government is in no hurry to try cases under this Act.

fast talk and diplomacy

An example of the great speed typical of the conference technique can be seen in the following EPA press release of August 2, 1971:

William D. Ruckelshaus, Administrator of the Environmental Protection Agency, announced that he is reconvening a Federal-State conference to consider further steps to halt acid mine drainage and other pollution problems in the Monongahela River [Northwestern West Virginia to Pittsburgh, Pa.] and its tributaries.

At the first session of the conference, held in December 1963, at the direction of the Secretary of Health, Education, and Welfare, the conferees unanimously agreed to a recommendation to establish a technical committee to explore means of abating pollution caused by coal mine drainage. The committee was directed to locate, sample, and describe the sources of mine drainage. The committee began its field studies in January, 1965 and continued them through May, 1968.

Ruckelshaus said, "Since the committee has now analyzed its data and prepared a report, I am asking that the conference be reconvened to examine its findings." He added that the conference will enable West Virginia, Pennsylvania, and Maryland—the three States which have active or inactive mines contributing to Monongahela River pollution—to adopt a specific abatement program to deal with the problem.

Ruckelshaus said that the studies made by the conference technical committee show that the total net acid load from all coal mining in the Monongahela River Basin amounts to approximately 1.2 million pounds per day, and the iron load totals more than 300,000 pounds per day.

The conference technical committee has recommended that a remedial project committee for the Monongahela Basin be established to direct and coordinate the abatement programs recommended by the conferees. Specific Federal recommendations for abatement action are being developed for the consideration of the conferees.

Ruckelshaus has designated Murray Stein, chief enforcement officer of EPA's Water Quality Office, as chairman of the conference. The State water pollution control agencies of Pennsylvania, Maryland, and West Virginia, the Ohio River Valley Sanitation Commission, and EPA are parties to the conference.

End, text of EPA press release.

REFERENCES AND SELECTED BIBLIOGRAPHY

For a criticism of the conference process, see:

ZWICK, Ed., *Water Wasteland, Nader Task Force Report on Water Pollution, Washington, D.C., Center for Study of Responsive Law, 1971*

RIDGEWAY, The Politics of Ecology, New York, E. P. Dutton & Co., Inc. 1970

For further information on the Federal-State program see:

PITTS, "The Interaction of the Federal and State Systems: The Experience in the Central U.S.," 3 *Nat. Res. Lawyer* 26 (Jan. 1970)

FWPCA, U.S. Dept. of the Interior, *Federal Water Pollution Enforcement Actions,* Feb. 1970

DUNKELBERGER, "The Federal Government's Role in Regulating Water Pollution Under the Federal Water Quality Act of 1965," 3 *Nat. Res. Lawyer* 6, Jan. 1970

STEIN, "Regulatory Aspects of Federal Water Pollution Control," 45 *Denver L.J.* 267 (1968)

REITZE, "Wastes, Water, and Wishful Thinking: The Battle of Lake Erie," 20 *Case Wes. Res. L. Rev.* 5 (1968)

KLINE, "Intergovernmental Relations in the Control of Water Pollution," 4 *Nat. Res. Lawyer* 505, July 1971

FWPCA
Sec. 11:
oil pollution

CONTROL OF POLLUTION BY OIL [44]

SEC. 11. (a) For the purpose of this section, the term—

(1) "oil" means oil of any kind or in any form, including, but not limited to, petroleum, fuel oil, sludge, oil refuse, and oil mixed with wastes other than dredged spoil;

(2) "discharge" includes, but is not limited to, any spilling, leaking, pumping, pouring, emitting, emptying or dumping;

(3) "vessel" means every description of watercraft or other artificial contrivance used, or capable of being used, as a means of transportation on water other than a public vessel;

(4) "public vessel" means a vessel owned or bare-boat chartered and operated by the United States, or by a State or political subdivision thereof, or by a foreign nation, except when such vessel is engaged in commerce;

(5) "United States" means the States, the District of Columbia, the Commonwealth of Puerto Rico, the Canal Zone, Guam, American Samoa, the Virgin Islands, and the Trust Territory of the Pacific Islands;

(6) "owner or operator" means (A) in the case of a vessel, any person owning, operating, or chartering by demise, such vessel, and (B) in the case of an onshore facility, and an offshore facility,

[43] This subsection added by sec. 208(a), Public Law 89–753.
[44] Added by sec. 102, Public Law 91–224.

any person owning or operating such onshore facility or offshore facility, and (C) in the case of any abandoned offshore facility, the person who owned or operated such facility immediately prior to such abandonment;

(7) "person" includes an individual, firm, corporation, association, and a partnership;

(8) "remove" or "removal" refers to removal of the oil from the water and shorelines or the taking of such other actions as may be necessary to minimize or mitigate damage to the public health or welfare, including, but not limited to, fish, shellfish, wildlife, and public and private property, shorelines, and beaches;

(9) "contiguous zone" means the entire zone established or to be established by the United States under article 24 of the Convention on the Territorial Sea and the Contiguous Zone;

(10) "onshore facility" means any facility (including, but not limited to, motor vehicles and rolling stock) of any kind located in, on, or under, any land within the United States other than submerged land;

(11) "offshore facility" means any facility of any kind located in, on, or under, any of the navigable waters of the United States other than a vessel or a public vessel;

(12) "act of God" means an act occasioned by an unanticipated grave natural disaster;

(13) "barrel" means 42 United States gallons at 60 degrees Fahrenheit.

FWPCA
Sec. 11:
oil pollution

(b)(1) The Congress hereby declares that it is the policy of the United States that there should be no discharges of oil into or upon the navigable waters of the United States, adjoining shorelines, or into or upon the waters of the contiguous zone.

(2) The discharge of oil into or upon the navigable waters of the United States, adjoining shorelines, or into or upon the waters of the contiguous zone in harmful quantities as determined by the President under paragraph (3) of this subsection, is prohibited, except (A) in the case of such discharges into the waters of the contiguous zone, where permitted under article IV of the International Convention for the Prevention of Pollution of the Sea by Oil, 1954, as amended, and (B) where permitted in quantities and at times and locations or under such circumstances or conditions as the President may, by regulation, determine not to be harmful. Any regulations issued under this subsection shall be consistent with maritime safety and with marine and navigation laws and regulations and applicable water quality standards.

(3) The President shall by regulation, to be issued as soon as possible after the date of enactment of this paragraph, determine for the purposes of this section, those quantities of oil the discharge of which, at such times, locations, circumstances, and conditions, will be harmful to the public health or welfare of the United States, including, but not limited to, fish, shellfish, wildlife, and public and private property, shorelines, and beaches except that in the case of the discharge of oil into or upon the waters of the contiguous zone, only those discharges which threaten the fishery resources of the contiguous zone or threaten to pollute or contribute to the pollution of the territory or the territorial sea of the United States may be determined to be harmful.

(4) Any person in charge of a vessel or of an onshore facility or an offshore facility shall, as soon as he has knowledge of any discharge of oil from such vessel or facility in violation of paragraph (2) of this subsection, immediately notify the appropriate agency of the United States Government of such discharge. Any such person who fails to notify immediately such agency of such discharge shall, upon conviction, be fined not more than $10,000, or imprisoned for not more than one year, or both. Notification received pursuant to this paragraph or information obtained by the exploitation of such notification shall not be used against any such person in any criminal case, except a prosecution for perjury or for giving a false statement.

(5) Any owner or operator of any vessel, onshore facility, or offshore facility from which oil is knowingly discharged in violation of paragraph (2) of this subsection shall be assessed a civil penalty by the Secretary of the department in which the Coast Guard is operating of not more than $10,000 for each offense. No penalty shall be assessed unless the owner or operator charged shall have been given notice and

opportunity for a hearing on such charge. Each violation is a separate offense. Any such civil penalty may be compromised by such Secretary. In determining the amount of the penalty, or the amount agreed upon in compromise, the appropriateness of such penalty to the size of the business of the owner or operator charged, the effect on the owner or operator's ability to continue in business, and the gravity of the violation, shall be considered by such Secretary. The Secretary of the Treasury shall withhold at the request of such Secretary the clearance required by section 4197 of the Revised Statutes of the United States, as amended (46 U.S.C. 91), of any vessel the owner or operator of which is subject to the foregoing penalty. Clearance may be granted in such cases upon the filing of a bond or other surety satisfactory to such Secretary.

(c) (1) Whenever any oil is discharged, into or upon the navigable waters of the United States, adjoining shorelines, or into or upon the waters of the contiguous zone, the President is authorized to act to remove or arrange for the removal of such oil at any time, unless he determines such removal will be done properly by the owner or operator of the vessel, onshore facility, or offshore facility from which the discharge occurs.

(2) Within sixty days after the effective date of this section, the President shall prepare and publish a National Contingency Plan for removal of oil pursuant to this subsection. Such National contingency Plan shall provide for efficient, coordinated, and effective action to minimize damage from oil discharges, including containment, dispersal, and removal of oil, and shall include, but not be limited to—

FWPCA Sec. 11: oil pollution

(A) assignment of duties and responsibilities among Federal departments and agencies in coordination with State and local agencies, including, but not limited to, water pollution control, conservation, and port authorities;

(B) identification, procurement, maintenance, and storage of equipment and supplies;

(C) establishment or designation of a strike force consisting of personnel who shall be trained, prepared, and available to provide necessary services to carry out the Plan, including the establishment at major ports, to be determined by the President, of emergency task forces of trained personnel, adequate oil pollution control equipment and material, and a detailed oil pollution prevention and removal plan;

(D) a system of surveillance and notice designed to insure earliest possible notice of discharges of oil to the appropriate Federal agency;

(E) establishment of a national center to provide coordination and direction for operations in carrying out the Plan;

(F) procedures and techniques to be employed in identifying, containing, dispersing, and removing oil; and

(G) a schedule, prepared in cooperation with the States, identifying (i) dispersants and other chemicals, if any, that may be used in carrying out the Plan, (ii) the waters in which such dispersants and chemicals may be used, and (iii) the quantities of such dispersant or chemical which can be used safely in such waters, which schedule shall provide in the case of any dispersant, chemical, or waters not specifically identified in such schedule that the President, or his delegate, may, on a case-by-case basis, identify the dispersants and other chemicals which may be used, the waters in which they may be used, and the quantities which can be used safely in such waters.

The President may, from time to time, as he deems advisable, revise or otherwise amend the National Contingency Plan. After publication of the National Contingency Plan, the removal of oil and actions to minimize damage from oil discharges shall, to the greatest extent possible, be in accordance with the National Contingency Plan.

(d) Whenever a marine disaster in or upon the navigable waters of the United States has created a substantial threat of a pollution hazard to the public health or welfare of the United States, including, but not limited to, fish, shellfish, and wildlife and the public and private shorelines and beaches of the United States, because of a discharge, or an imminent discharge, of large quantities of oil from a vessel the United States may (A) coordinate and direct all public and private efforts directed at the removal or elimination of such threat; and (B) summarily remove, and, if necessary, destroy such vessel by whatever means are available without regard to any provision of law governing the employment of personnel or the expenditure of appropriated funds. Any expense incurred under this subsection shall be a cost incurred by the United States Government for the purposes of subsection (f) in the removal of oil.

(e) In addition to any other action taken by a State or local government, when the President determines there as an imminent and substantial threat to the public health or welfare of the United States, including, but not limited to, fish, shellfish, and wildlife and public and private property, shorelines, and beaches within the United States, because of an actual or threatened discharge of oil into or upon the navigable waters of the United States from an onshore or offshore facility, the President may require the United States attorney of the district in which the threat occurs to secure such relief as may be necessary to abate such threat, and the district courts of the United States shall have jurisdiction to grant such relief as the public interest and the equities of the case may require.

FWPCA
Sec. 11:
oil pollution

(f) (1) Except where an owner or operator can prove that a discharge was caused solely by (A) an act of God, (B) an act of war, (C) negligence on the part of the United States Government, or (D) an act or omission of a third party without regard to whether any such act or omission was or was not negligent, or any combination of the foregoing clauses, such owner or operator of any vessel from which oil is discharged in violation of subsection (b) (2) of this section shall, notwithstanding any other provision of law, be liable to the United States Government for the actual costs incurred under subsection (c) for the removal of such oil by the United States Government in an amount not to exceed $100 per gross ton of such vessel or $14,000,000, whichever is lesser, except that where the United States can show that such discharge was the result of willful negligence or willful misconduct within the privity and knowledge of the owner, such owner or operator shall be liable to the United States Government for the full amount of such costs. Such costs shall constitute a maritime lien on such vessel which may be recovered in an action in rem in the district court of the United States for any district within which any vessel may be found. The United States may also bring an action against the owner or operator of such vessel in any court of competent jurisdiction to recover such costs.

(2) Except where an owner or operator of an onshore facility can prove that a discharge was caused solely by (A) an act of God, (B) an act of war, (C) negligence on the part of the United States Government, or (D) an act or omission of a third party without regard to whether any such act or omission was or was not negligent, or any combination of the foregoing clauses, such owner or operator of any such facility from which oil is discharged in violation of subsection (b) (2) of this section shall be liable to the United States Government for the actual costs incurred under subsection (c) for the removal of such oil by the United States Government in an amount not to exceed $8,000,000, except that where the United States can show that such discharge was the result of willful negligence or willful misconduct within the privity and knowledge of the owner, such owner or operator shall be liable to the United States Government for the full amount of such costs. The United States may bring an action against the owner or operator of such facility in any court of competent jurisdiction to recover such costs. The Secretary is authorized, by regulation, after consultation with the Secretary of Commerce and the Small Business Administration, to establish reasonable and equitable classifications of those onshore facilities having a total fixed storage capacity of 1,000 barrels or less which he determines because of size, type, and location do not present a substantial risk of the discharge of oil in violation of subsection (b) (2) of this section, and apply with respect to such classifications differing limits of liability which may be less than the amount contained in this paragraph.

(3) Except where an owner or operator of an offshore facility can prove that a discharge was caused solely by (A) an act of God, (B) an act of war, (C) negligence on the part of the United States Government, or (D) an act or omission of a third party without regard to whether any such act or omission was or was not negligent, or any combination of the foregoing clauses, such owner or operator of any

such facility from which oil is discharged in violation of subsection (b)(2) of this section shall, notwithstanding any other provision of law, be liable to the United States Government for the actual costs incurred under subsection (c) for the removal of such oil by the United States Government in an amount not to exceed $8,000,000, except that where the United States can show that such discharge was the result of willful negligence or willful misconduct within the privity and knowledge of the owner, such owner or operatior shall be liable to the United States Government for the full amount of such costs. The United States may bring an action against the owner or operator of such a facility in any court of competent jurisdiction to recover such costs.

(g) In any case where an owner or operator of a vessel, of an onshore facility, or of an offshore facility, from which oil is discharged in violation of subsection (b)(2) of this section proves that such discharge of oil was caused solely by an act or omission of a third party, or was caused solely by such an act or omission in combination with an act of God, an act of war, or negligence on the part of the United States Government, such third party shall, notwithstanding any other provision of law, be liable to the United States Government for the actual costs incurred under subsection (c) for removal of such oil by the United States Government, except where such third party can prove that such discharge was caused solely by (A) an act of God, (B) an act of war, (C) negligence on the part of the United States Government, or (D) an act or omission of another party without regard to whether such act or omission was or was not negligent, or any combination of the foregoing clauses. If such third party was the owner or operator of a vessel which caused the discharge of oil in violation of subsection (b)(2) of this section, the liability of such third party under this subsection shall not exceed $100 per gross ton of such vessel or $14,000,000, whichever is the lesser. In any other case the liability of such third party shall not exceed the limitation which would have been applicable to the owner or operator of the vessel or the onshore or offshore facility from which the discharge actually occurred, if such owner or operator were liable. If the United States can show that the discharge of oil in violation of subsection (b)(2) of this section was the result of willful negligence or willful misconduct within the privity and knowledge of such third party, such third party shall be liable to the United States Government for the full amount of such removal costs. The United States may bring an action against the third party in any court of competent jurisdiction to recover such removal costs.

FWPCA
Sec. 11:
oil pollution

(h) The liabilities established by this section shall in no way affect any rights which (1) the owner or operator of a vessel or of an onshore facility or an offshore facility may have against any third party whose acts may in any way have caused or contributed to such discharge, or (2) the United States Government may have against any third party whose actions may in any way have caused or contributed to the discharge of oil.

(i)(1) In any case where an owner or operator of a vessel or an onshore facility or an offshore facility from which oil is discharged in violation of subsection (b)(2) of this section acts to remove such oil in accordance with regulations promulgated pursuant to this section, such owner or operator shall be entitled to recover the reasonable costs incurred in such removal upon establishing, in a suit which may be brought against the United States Government in the United States Court of Claims, that such discharge was caused solely by (A) an act of God, (B) an act of war, (C) negligence on the part of the United States Government, or (D) an act or omission of a third party without regard to whether such act or omission was or was not negligent, or of any combination of the foregoing causes.

(2) The provisions of this subsection shall not apply in any case where liability is established pursuant to the Outer Continental Shelf Lands Act.

(3) Any amount paid in accordance with a judgment of the United States Court of Claims pursuant to this section shall be paid from the fund established pursuant to subsection (k).

(j)(1) Consistent with the National Contingency Plan required by subsection (c)(2) of this section, as soon as practicable after the effective date of this section, and from time to time thereafter, the President shall issue regulations consistent with maritime safety and with marine and navigation laws (A) establishing methods and procedures for removal of discharged oil, (B) establishing criteria for the development and implementation of local and regional oil removal contingency plans, (C) establishing procedures, methods, and requirements for equipment to prevent discharges of oil from vessels and from onshore facilities and offshore facilities, and (D) governing the inspection of vessels carrying cargoes of oil and the inspection of such cargoes in order to reduce the likelihood of discharges of oil from such vessels in violation of this section.

(2) Any owner or operator of a vessel or an onshore facility or an offshore facility and any other person subject to any regulation issued under paragraph (1) of this subsection who fails or refuses to comply with the provisions of any such regulation, shall be liable to a civil penalty of not more than $5,000 for each such violation. Each violation shall be a separate offense. The President may assess and compromise such penalty. No penalty shall be assessed until the owner, operator, or other person charged shall have been given notice and an opportunity for a hearing on such charge. In determining the amount of the penalty, or the amount agreed upon in compromise, the gravity of the violation, and the demonstrated good faith of the owner, operator, or other person charged in attempting to achieve rapid compliance, after notification of a violation, shall be considered by the President.

(k) There is hereby authorized to be appropriated to a revolving fund to be established in the Treasury not to exceed $35,000,000 to carry out the provisions of subsections (c), (i), and (l) of this section and section 12 of this Act. Any other funds received by the United States under this section shall also be deposited in said fund for such purposes. All sums appropriated to, or deposited in, said fund shall remain available until expended.

(l) The President is authorized to delegate the administration of this section to the heads of those Federal departments, agencies, and instrumentalities which he determines to be appropriate. Any moneys in the fund established by subsection (k) of this section shall be available to such Federal departments, agencies, and instrumentalities to carry out the provisions of subsections (c) and (i) of this section and section 12 of this Act. Each such department, agency, and instrumentality, in order to avoid duplication of effort, shall, whenever appropriate, utilize the personnel, services, and facilities of other Federal departments, agencies, and instrumentalities.

(m) Anyone authorized by the President to enforce the provisions of this section may, except as to public vessels, (A) board and inspect any vessel upon the navigable waters of the United States or the waters of the contiguous zone, (B) with or without a warrant arrest any person who violates the provisions of this section or any regulation issued thereunder in his presence or view, and (C) execute any warrant or other process issued by an officer or court of competent jurisdiction.

(n) The several district courts of the United States are invested with jurisdiction for any actions, other than actions pursuant to subsection (i)(1), arising under this section. In the case of Guam, such actions may be brought in the district court of Guam, and in the case of the Virgin Islands such actions may be brought in the district court of the Virgin Islands. In the case of American Samoa and the Trust Territory of the Pacific Islands, such actions may be brought in the District Court of the United States for the District of Hawaii and such court shall have jurisdiction of such actions. In the case of the Canal Zone, such actions may be brought in the United States District Court for the District of the Canal Zone.

(o)(1) Nothing in this section shall affect or modify in any way the obligations of any owner or operator of any vessel, or of any owner or operator of any onshore facility or offshore facility to any person or agency under any provision of law for damages to any publicly-owned or privately-owned property resulting from a discharge of any oil or from the removal of any such oil.

(2) Nothing in this section shall be construed as preempting any State or political subdivision thereof from imposing any requirement or liability with respect to the discharge of oil into any waters within such State.

(3) Nothing in this section shall be construed as affecting or modifying any other existing authority of any Federal department, agency, or instrumentality, relative to onshore or offshore facilities under this Act or any other provsion of law, or to affect any State or local law not in conflict with this section.

(p) (1) Any vessel over three hundred gross tons, including any barge of equivalent size, using any port or place in the United States or the navigable waters of the United States for any purpose shall establish and maintain under regulations to be prescribed from time to time by the President, evidence of financial responsibility of $100 per gross ton, or $14,000,000 whichever is the lesser, to meet the liability to the United States which such vessel could be subjected under this section. In cases where an owner or operator owns, operates, or charters more than one such vessel, financial responsibility need only be established to meet the maximum liability to which the largest of such vessels could be subjected. Financial responsibility may be established by any one of, or a combination of, the following methods acceptable to the President: (A) evidence of insurance, (B) surety bonds, (C) qualification as a self-insurer, or (D) other evidence of financial responsibility. Any bond filed shall be issued by a bonding company authorized to do business in the United States.

(2) The provisions of paragraph (1) of this subsection shall be effective one year after the effective date of this section. The President shall delegate the responsibility to carry out the provisions of this subsection to the appropriate agency head within sixty days after the date of enactment of this section. Regulations necessary to implement this subsection shall be issued within six months after the date of enactment of this section.

(3) Any claim for costs incurred by such vessel may be brought directly against the insurer or any other person providing evidence of financial responsibility as required under this subsection. In the case of any action pursuant to this subsection such insurer or other person shall be entitled to invoke all rights and defenses which would have been available to the owner or operator if an action had been brought against him by the claimant, and which would have been available to him if an action had been brought against him by the owner or operator.

(4) The Secretary of Transportation, in consultation with the Secretaries of Interior, State, Commerce, and other interested Federal agencies, representatives of the merchant marine, oil companies, insurance companies, and other interested individuals and organizations, and taking into account the results of the application of paragraph (1) of this subsection, shall conduct a study of the need for and, to the extent determined necessary.

(A) other measures to provide financial responsibility and limitation of liability with respect to vessels using the navigable waters of the United States;

(B) measures to provide financial responsibility for all onshore and offshore facilities; and

(C) other measures for limitation of liability of such facilities;

for the cost of removing discharged oil and paying all damages resulting from the discharge of such oil. The Secretary of Transportation shall submit a report, together with any legislative recommendations, to Congress and the President by January 1, 1971.

COMMENTARY

control of oil pollution

President Nixon, on July 20, 1970, by **Executive Order 11548** (Fed. Reg. Doc. 70-9493) delegated responsibilities for control of oil under **Sec. 11** of the Federal Water Pollution Control Act, as amended.

FINANCIAL RESPONSIBILITY AND INSURANCE is delegated to the Federal Maritime Commission.

PREPARATION AND PUBLICATION OF THE NATIONAL CONTINGENCY PLAN is delegated to the Council on Environmental Quality.

NOTICE OF DISCHARGE OF OIL must be given to the Coast Guard. Procedures and equipment for prevention of discharge of oil from ships is the responsibility of the Secretary of Transportation.

MOST OF THE OTHER FUNCTIONS are exercised by EPA in Consultation with the Secretary of Transportation. Most of the Secretary's responsibilities have been further delegated to the Coast Guard.

The major treatment of oil pollution in this work appears in Volume Two. However, for the benefit of those who may have access only to this volume, the following summary of the problem is reprinted, in edited form, from Clean Water for the 1970's, A Status Report, by the Federal Water Quality Administration, June, 1970:

Control of Oil Pollution

With the grounding of the TORREY CANYON in 1967, the breakup of the OCEAN EAGLE in Puerto Rican waters in 1968, and the Santa Barbara offshore oil well leak in 1969, oil pollution has become recognized as a serious national and worldwide problem. These incidents were spectacular in terms of the damages they caused, the control and clean-up efforts and expenditures they necessitated, and the public concern they generated. Of even greater significance, however, is the fact that these major disasters are matched by the aggregate of large and small incidents that occur every day throughout the Nation's coastal and inland waters.

It is estimated that there are annually over 10,000 spills of polluting materials into our Nation's waters. About three-fourths of these spills are oil; the remainder are other hazardous materials, such as chlorine and anhydrous ammonia. The sources of these incidents are vessels, pipelines, rail and highway carriers, land- and water-based storage tanks, refining and other manufacturing operations, the jettisoning of fuel tanks by aircraft, on and offshore petroleum loading and unloading terminals, on and offshore petroleum drilling and production operations, and various other facilities and activities. The problem of accidental spills of oil is further compounded by discharges of oily ballast waters from tankers and other vessels. Pollution from oil and hazardous materials is an everyday occurrence and affects all our waters.

Oil pollution may come from several different sources. Gasoline service stations dispose annually of 350 million gallons of used oil. Two hundred thousand miles of pipelines carry more than a billion tons of oil and hazardous substances. The pipelines cross waterways and reservoirs and are subject to cracks, punctures, corrosion, and other causes of leakage. Offshore oil and gas exploration and production occur mainly in the Gulf of Mexico, Southern California coastal waters, Cook Inlet in Alaska, the Great Lakes, and the East Coast. The blowout of wells, the dumping of drilling muds and oil-soaked wastes, and the demolition of offshore drilling rigs by storms and vessel collisions are significant potential pollution sources. In 1969 a massive oil spill occurred off Santa Barbara, California, with severe damage to the coastline, waterfowl and beaches. More recently a fire and subsequent oil blowout on an offshore production well in the Louisiana Gulf presented a serious threat to our marine environment.

Dumping and accidental spilling of oil and other hazardous materials continue to increase each year and constitute major pollution threats to the water resources of the Nation. Pollution by oil and other hazardous substances may occur in any of our waterways and coastal areas, or on the high seas as a result of deliberate dumping, accidental spills, leaks in pipelines, drilling rigs and storage facilities, or the breakup of transportation equipment.

Vessel casualties, too, are a prime source of oil pollution, and the damage can be extensive when several million gallons of oil enter the water at one time. The largest spill to date was over 30 million gallons in 1967 from the TORREY CANYON. England, alone, spent $8 million on clean-up following this casualty. In Tampa Bay on February 13, 1970, the tanker DELIAN APOLLON ran aground and spilled over ten thousand gallons of fuel oil into the bay, and some 100 square miles of area were contaminated as a result. Discharge of either oily ballast water or "slop oil" recently occurred offshore of Alaska, causing extensive waterfowl mortalities and contamination of fur seals and sea lions.

Damages caused by oil pollution are both significant and diverse. Such pollution can destroy or limit marine life, ruin wildlife habitat, kill birds, limit or destroy the recreational value of beach areas, contaminate water supplies, and create fire hazards. Damages caused by other

Birds suffered most from the more than 200,000 gallons of crude oil that escaped from this ruptured Santa Barbara well.

hazardous substances can be just as significant and diverse as those caused by oil pollution. The sheer volume of oil transported or used, however, makes oil the largest single source of pollution of this type.

The majority of oil spills exceeding 100 barrels involve discharge from vessels. Approximately one-third of the incidents involve pipelines, oil terminals, bulk storage facilities, etc.

Reported Oil Spills in U.S. Waters (Over 100 barrels)

	1968	1969
Vessels	347	532
Shore facilities	295	331
Unidentified	72	144
Total	714	1007

Of particular significance are the potentially large and damaging oil spill accidents that might easily result from the increase in shipping and pipeline transport of oil. The emergence of supertankers as the prime oceanic movers of crude oil imports, the construction of a large pipeline, such as the Trans-Alaska Pipeline System from the new Alaska North Slope oil fields, and the greater development of offshore oil are all contributing factors to the oil spill problem. This rapid increase of oil traffic and the expansion of the offshore production of oil only intensifies the possibility of more frequent and larger accidents and of significantly greater damage to the environment.

Presently, the technology for coping with oil and hazardous materials spills is woefully inadequate. Prevention of accidents is the only sure way of protecting the environment. The Santa Barbara incident and subsequent similar spill situations have shown conclusively that no completely effective techniques are available to control oil spills in the open ocean or lake waters. Wind and wave actions neutralize the effectiveness of oil spill containment devices, such as floating booms. Vacuum or scoop equipment to remove floating oils from the water does not accomplish the job, being effective only in rarely occurring calm seas. Chemical dispersants, sinking agents, and other materials are often ineffective and frequently very toxic to marine and wildlife. Common straw, which soaks up oil so that it can be removed, is still the standard material for fighting and cleaning up oil spills.

Compounding these technological shortcomings, the legal and institutional devices available for handling oil and hazardous material spills have been less than adequate. The Oil Pollution Act of 1924, as amended—the principal Federal legislation in this area of pollution control —prohibited and provided penalties for only the "grossly negligent and willful" spilling or discharging of oils and oily materials. This restrictive legal language essentially precluded enforcement of the Act. This has been rectified by passsage of the Water Quality Improvement Act of 1970, which repeals the 1924 Act and greatly increases the regulatory controls for oil pollution incidents. Many State and local governments, however, are still lacking in oil pollution control authority.

In addition to lack of adequate legal tools, well-organized and well-equipped governmental forces have not always been available to respond in a timely manner to oil pollution incidents. Many of the smaller incidents go undiscovered or ignored by local, State, and Federal agencies; only the larger incidents generally receive the type of response necessary to assure adequate control and clean-up. The usual procedure is to encourage or require the party responsible for the spill to procure the equipment, materials and personnel and to bear the expense of control and clean-up. In some cases, these resources may not be available in the local area, adding yet another problem.

In the area of research and development, the Federal agencies have divided among themselves the work necessary to find new and improved technology to deal with oil and hazardous materials pollution. FWQA has taken on the primary tasks pertaining to prevention, containment and clean-up in sheltered and inland waters, the fate and ecological effects in these waters, and the technology for cleaning oil contaminated beaches. The Departments of Transportation, Defense and Health, Education and Welfare, as well as other agencies of the Department of the Interior, are assuming primary responsibility for other pertinent areas of research, including the combating of oil pollution in open waters.

Although a considerable amount of attention is devoted to reporting and response activities, a significant effort has been and is directed to other program activities. These include contingency planning; evaluation of potential pollution situations and impacts, including those associated with offshore oil drilling and production; testing of hazardous materials and the neutralizing or combating agents needed to deal with them when a spill occurs; participation in international meetings on oil spill prevention; and technical assistance to State and local agencies and other groups.

Along these lines, several significant actions were undertaken in 1969. The bunker oil from the grounded motorship, NORDMEER, which threatened to rupture and spill its contents into Lake Huron, was removed to prevent a serious incident. This was the first effort of its kind by FWQA.

End, excerpts from Clean Water for the 1970's.

Petroleum transportation may be subject to the Transportation of Explosives and Other Dangerous Articles Act, also known as the Hazardous Materials Act, 18 U.S.C.A. 831 et seq.

COMMENTARY

The Council on Environmental Quality has prepared a National Contingency Plan to coordinate the response of various Federal agencies to whatever spills of oil or other hazardous materials that occur. This plan was published in the *Federal Register* of June 2, 1970 (Vol. 35, p. 8508). However, the subsequent activities at spills in the Gulf of Mexico, San Francisco Bay, and elsewhere, demonstrate that disaster plans are not a very effective way to keep the environment unsullied.

For definitions and further information, see the guidelines concerning Discharge of Oil, Code of Federal Regulations Title 18, Chapter V, Part 610, F.R. Doc 70-12180, filed Sept. 10, 1970, *Environment Reporter,* Federal Laws 71:5177.

For the Coast Guard Regulations on Oil Spills, see Code of Federal Regulations Title 33, Chapter 1, Subchapter O—Pollution, Part 153—Control of Pollution by Oil and Hazardous Substances, Discharge Removal, *Environment Report,* Federal Laws 71:5171.

The regulations concerning financial responsibility for oil pollution cleanup are found in the Code of Federal Regulations, Title 46, Chapter IV, Part 542.

See also Keener, "Federal Water Pollution Legislation and Regulations with Particular Reference to the Oil Industry," 4 Nat. Res. Lawyer 484 (July 1971)

There are an almost unlimited number of articles on oil pollution. Two articles stand out as being the definitive works on the subject. They are:

BALDWIN, "Public Policy on Oil—An Ecological Perspective," 1 *Ecology L. Quart.* No. 2, Spring 1971 at 245

BLUMER, "Scientific Aspects of the Oil Spill Problem," 1 *Environmental Affairs 54 (April 1971)*

There is a useful government report by the Secretary of the Interior and the Secretary of Transportation entitled, Oil Pollution A Report on Pollution of the Nation's Waters by Oil and Other Hazardous Substances, Feb. 1968.

A bibliography on marine oil pollution listing more than 800 documents is—

CHRISTOL, *Oil Pollution of the Marine Environment—A Legal Bibliography,* Public Works Committee Print, 92nd Cong., 1st Sess., (Jan. 1971).

NOTE: The problems of oil pollution are discussed in greater detail in the materials on ocean environments in Volume Two.

FWPCA Sec. 12: hazardous substances

CONTROL OF HAZARDOUS POLLUTING SUBSTANCES [45]

SEC. 12. (a) The President shall, in accordance with subsection (b) of this section, develop, promulgate, and revise as may be appropriate, regulations (1) designating as hazardous substances, other than oil as defined in section 11 of this Act, such elements and compounds which, when discharged in any quantity into or upon the navigable waters of the United States or adjoining shorelines or the waters of the contiguous zone, present an imminent and substantial danger to the public health or welfare, including, but not limited to, fish, shellfish, wildlife, shorelines, and beaches; and (2) establishing, if appropriate, recommended methods and means for the removal of such substances.

(b) Sections 551 through 559, inclusive (other than section 553(c)), and 701 through 706, inclusive, of title 5, United States Code, shall apply to regulations issued under authority of this section.

(c) In order to facilitate the removal, if appropriate, of any hazardous substance any person in charge of a vessel or of an onshore or offshore facility of any kind shall, as soon as he has knowledge of any discharge of such substance from such vessel or facility, immediately notify the appropriate agency of the United States of such discharge.

[45] Added by sec. 102, Public Law 91-224.

(d) Whenever any hazardous substance is discharged into or upon the navigable waters of the United States or adjoining shorelines or the waters of the contiguous zone, unless removal is immediately undertaken by the owner or operator of the vessel or onshore or offshore facility from which the discharge occurs or which caused the discharge, pursuant to the regulations promulgated under this section, the President, if appropriate, shall remove or arrange for the removal thereof in accordance with such regulations. Nothing in this subsection shall be construed to restrict the authority of the President to act to remove or arrange for the removal of such hazardous substance at any time.

(e) Nothing in this section shall affect or modify in any way the obligations of any owner or operator of any vessel, onshore or offshore facility to any person or agency under any provision of law for damages to any publicly- or privately-owned property resulting from a discharge of any hazardous substance or from the removal of any such substance.

(f)(1) For the purpose of this section the definitions in subsection (a) of section 11 of this Act shall be applicable to the provisions of this section, except as provided in paragraph (2) of this subsection:

(2) For the purpose of this section, the term—

(A) "remove" or "removal" refers to removal of the hazardous substances from the water and shorelines or the taking of such other actions as may be necessary to minimize or mitigate damage to the public health or welfare, including, but not limited to, fish, shellfish, wildlife, and public and private property, shorelines, and beaches;

(B) "owner or operator" means any person owning, operating, chartering by demise, or otherwise controlling the operations of, a vessel, or any person owning, operating, or otherwise controlling the operations of an onshore or offshore facility; and

(C) "offshore or onshore facility" means any facility of any kind and related appurtenances thereto which is located in, on, or under the surface of any land, or permanently or temporarily affixed to any land, including lands beneath the navigable waters of the United States and which is used or capable of use for the purpose of processing, transporting, producing, storing, or transferring for commercial purposes any hazardous substance designated under this section.

FWPCA Sec. 12: hazardous substances

(g) The President shall submit a report to the Congress, together with his recommendations, not later than November 1, 1970, on the need for, and desirability of, enacting legislation to impose liability for the cost of removal of hazardous substances discharged from vessels and onshore and offshore facilities subject to this section including financial responsibility requirements. In preparing this report, the President shall conduct an accelerated study which shall include, but not be limited to, the method and measures for controlling hazardous substances to prevent this discharge, and the most appropriate measures for (1) enforcement (including the imposition of civil and criminal penalties for discharges and for failure to notify) and (2) recovery of costs incurred by the United States if removal is undertaken by the United States. In carrying out this study, the President shall consult with the interested representatives of the various public and private groups that would be affected by such legislation as well as other interested persons.

(h) Any moneys in the funds established by section 11 of this Act shall be available to the President to carry out the purposes of this section. In carrying out this section the President shall utilize the personnel, services, and facilities of Federal departments, agencies, and instrumentalities in such manner as will avoid duplication of effort.

COMMENTARY

In 1970 section 12 was added to the Act. Little experience has been developed under the act. Regulation was proposed in January 1971. There is little question that control is needed. Thousands of new substances are developed each year, many of which are toxic. They are extremely difficult to discover, monitor, or remove after entering a water course. They can "disappear" into the life fabric of the water ecosystem or bottom sediments and not be discovered during routine testing. Often these substances are toxic in quantities that are measured in parts per million or even parts per billion. They can be cumulative—that is, stored in the body until a harmful level is reached, and the harm they cause may take years to manifest itself. The harm may also affect man's genetic structure and thus not be discovered for generations. The many kinds of materials absorbed may interact to produce harm. The almost unlimited range of chemical combinations make knowledge of this problem very difficult to obtain.

A category of toxic pollutants which has recently become the subject of much attention includes such health-impairing metals as lead, mercury, cadmium, beryllium, nickel, vanadium. Unlike most other pollutants, these are natural substances. For many years, man has been extracting these metals from stable minerals found in nature, distributing them in forms that can be harmful. The flow of metallic pollutants into the environment has accelerated in recent years to such an extent that now the general public may be threatened by substances formerly considered health hazards only inside mines or factories.

control of hazardous substances

Americans learned about the toxicity and persistence of these contaminants with the "mercury scare" of 1970. At about the same time, lead additives in gasoline came under an intensifying attack More and more metallic pollutants are becoming subjects of concern. Beryllium, emitted mainly by processing plants, can damage the respiratory system as can nickel, which is entering our air from metallurgical plants, from the burning of coal and oil, and as an unburned fuel additive. Cadmium gets into the air through the refining of associated metals such as zinc, lead, and copper. Particles of cadmium are picked up from galvanized water mains and pipes, and thus enters our drinking water too. Medical evidence indicates that cadmium can cause high blood pressure or lead to respiratory ailments and kidney damage. Vanadium, released by certain types of fuel oil and by refining and alloying processes, inhibits the synthesis of cholesterol, even in relatively small concentrations. People are now accustomed to think of cholesterol as undesirable, but in small amounts it is essential in metabolism.

This, of course, is far from a complete list. There are twenty or so other metals that bear watching. The special difficulty with all metallic pollutants is their persistence. Most organic substances are degradable by natural processes; no metal is degradable.

It would be unrealistic, however, to suppose that a complete ban on any of these metals is in the making. They are too essential, too ingrained in our life, too abundant in the natural environment. Still, the economic damage from the coming restrictions may prove to be substantial. It may become unprofitable to mine certain ore deposits, for example. And we can expect increasing use of expensive substitute materials where metals might present a health hazard.

The search for sound data about metallic pollutants and their effects encounters a peculiar complication in that metals have been part of the human environment, and the human body, for as long as man has existed. No fewer than 51 metals, from aluminum to zirconium, are known to be present in the body in varying amounts. Without some of them, in trace amounts, no plant or animal could live. Iron, magnesium, manganese, molybdenum, calcium, chromium, cobalt, copper, and zinc are known to be essential to life, and vanadium, nickel, and tin are thought to be. Metals, often incorporated into proteins, serve as catalysts that initiate or assist in biological reactions. Each of the four iron atoms in a hemoglobin molecule, for instance, is a "handle" to which oxygen molecules become attached, to be carried throughout the body in the red pigment of the blood. In plants, an atom of magnesium serves as the structural hub of every molecule of chlorophyll.

Over the millennia, organisms developed delicate balancing, or homeostatic, mechanisms to regulate the rate at which essential trace metals are incorporated into their tissues. But in general, organisms, including man, failed to develop comparable defenses against the heavier metals that perform no beneficial biological function. These metals are toxic in their elemental form, especially if they are absorbed as small particles. They become even more hazardous in organic compounds; these are more rapidly absorbed into the body and tend to concentrate in nerve tissue. A notable example is methyl mercury, which is far more dangerous than mercury in its familiar metallic form. Another is tetraethyl lead, which is readily soluble in fats and is particularly damaging to nerve centers and to the brain.

Toxic wastes, of course, include many substances in addition to heavy metals. Today we produce and transport more than 1200 products described by the Department of Transportation as "dangerous articles" (49 C.F.R. 172.5), of which more than 300 are considered extra-hazardous commodities by the ICC because they could destroy life or property in catastrophic proportion. Not all of these materials are toxic but the number gives some idea of the variety of dangerous products that flow through the arteries of commerce. These products range from cyanide and arsenic, whose toxicity is well known, to polychlorinated biphenyls, about which little is known. Lead and mercury have been known to be deadly for hundreds of years, yet have only recently been recognized as major environmental hazards. Other products such as chlorinated hydrocarbon pesticides were known to be extremely toxic, yet were thought to be safe if used properly.

control of hazardous substances

Some of the other kinds of materials that pollute our environment that are toxic are: radioactive wastes, pesticides, food additives, asbestos, antibiotics and hormones fed to animals that remain as an involuntary food additive, and an almost unlimited number of chemicals that are discharged into our waters and air as industrial waste.

references

An excellent handbook on this subject is Sax, Dangerous Properties of Industrial Materials, 1968. This book provides hazard-analysis information on more than 12,000 industrial and laboratory materials. Of course since 1968 hundreds of new toxic substances have been developed and released into the atmosphere.

Radioactive wastes and pesticides are treated separately in volume II for they are subject to a separate body of regulatory law. Whether the law functions to protect the public from radiation hazards is questionable. The law clearly does not protect us from pesticides injury. The legal and administrative protection for our food supply is minimal.

The discussion of the remaining categories of toxic waste will center on their major characteristic—the absence of any body of law to protect the public. Toxic wastes, despite their danger, are controlled only by the general water pollution laws applicable to all pollutants. Even the body of law applicable to pesticides makes little attempt to keep such substances out of our water supply. While you can't legally sell Coho salmon with 19 ppm of D.D.T., such concentrations in the water you swim in would be subject to the same government rules applicable to other water pollutants. Under current Federal law, the penalty for dumping a Sunday newspaper into a navigable waterway is the same as for dumping 1000 pounds of mercury. Stronger state regulations to make mercury dumping a serious offense are unlikely, and little credence can be given to the existing and usually unenforced state laws.

The following is excerpted from the booklet, ***Toxic Substances***, by the Council on Environmental Quality, GPO, April, 1971:

EXISTING LEGAL CONTROLS

Existing law does not entirely ignore the types of substances dealt with in this study. Toxic substances are specifically dealt with in the Hazardous Substances Act (15 U.S.C. 1261–1273), section 12 of the Federal Water Pollution Control Act (33 U.S.C. 1162), the recent amendments to the Clean Air Act, and the authorities of the Department of Transportation relating to transportation of hazardous substances.

The Hazardous Substances Act covers household products and toys—but not the raw materials from which they are manufactured. Thus the law authorizes the Secretary of Health, Education, and Welfare only to require how a product should be labeled. Although the Act does allow extremely hazardous products to be banned from interstate commerce, the definition of a "hazardous substance" is quite restrictive, stating that a substance may be banned only if special labeling or packaging is found ineffective in preventing a hazard. Only three household products have been banned.

Section 12 of the Federal Water Pollution Control Act authorizes the President to designate hazardous substances and to recommend methods and means for their removal from water. Under the section (33 U.S.C. 1162(a)), "hazardous substances" is limited to "such elements and compounds which, when discharged in any quantity into or upon the navigable waters of the United States or adjoining shorelines or the waters of the contiguous zone, present an imminent and substantial danger to the public health or welfare . . ." The section is generally aimed at accidental discharges of such substances into water and thus does not cover either continuous discharges into water or release of hazardous substances into other media.

The Clean Air Amendments of 1970 contain a section directed specifically at hazardous substances and also authorize the Administrator of EPA to regulate the use of fuel additives. Section 112 requires the EPA Administrator to publish a list of air pollutants which are not covered by air quality standards and which "may cause, or contribute to, an increase in mortality or an increase in serious irreversible, or incapacitating reversible, illness."

The Department of Transportation (DOT) regulates interstate transportation of hazardous substances under several authorities, including the Department of Transportation Act (49 U.S.C. 1651 et seq.), the Transportation of Explosives Act (18 U.S.C. 831–837), and the Hazardous Cargo Act (46 U.S.C. 170). DOT has defined several classes of hazardous materials (49 C.F.R. Parts 170–179), and its Hazardous Materials Regulations Board plans further classification based upon health hazard (35 Fed. Reg. 8831, June 6, 1970). Although some testing for effects of hazardous substances is involved in the implementation of these regulations, substances are classified primarily from the perspective of hazards involved in their transportation and possible spills from accidents. Most of the problems of toxic substances discussed in this report relate to aspects of their use rather than to transportation and spills.

It is clear that current laws are inadequate to control the actual and potential dangers of toxic substances comprehensively or systematically. The controls over manufacture and distribution pertain to only a small percentage of the chemical substances which find their way into the environment.

Both controls over production and controls over effluents suffer from the limited focus of their authority. For example, the Food and Drug Administration carefully examines food containers for their effect on food but does not address the environmental and health effects of incinerating the containers. With the exception of radioactive materials, disposal is not a consideration in any programs controlling manufacture.

But the problems of focus are broader than specific examples. Setting rational standards for many pollutants under existing legislation is almost impossible. The key factors involved in setting standards are the *total* human exposure to a substance and its *total* effect on the environment. The focus must be on a particular pollutant and all the pathways by which it travels through the ecosystem. Controls over distribution approach this perspective, but most fail to consider important environmental factors adequately.

The obvious limitation of controls over effluents is that they generally deal with a problem only *after* it is manifest. They do not provide for obtaining information on potential pollutants before widespread damage has occurred.

More subtle but more serious limitations of effluent controls arise from their focusing on the media—air or water—in which the pollution occurs. This approach has several consequences: First, it leads to concern with those substances found in air or water in the greatest quantities. For example, the Air Pollution Control Office uses the gross weight of air pollutants as one indicator of the severity of air pollution. Gross weight is a valid indicator, but it disregards the degrees of danger of the various pollutants. Small amounts of some substances can cause severe damage, but media-oriented programs tend to overlook the importance of such substances. Another consequence of the media approach is that it cannot deal effectively with the fact that many, perhaps most, toxic substances find their way into the environment through several media. They cannot be characterized strictly as water pollutants or as air pollutants, for they are found in air, in water, and often in soil, food, and other parts of the environment.

TECHNOLOGICAL METHODS OF CONTROL

Several control strategies exist for almost all the substances included in this study because each enters the environment in numerous ways. The strategies are of two general types: control of a product and its uses, including total prohibition of the product, and control of the effluents.

From a materials balance analysis, reducing the amount of a contaminant that is initially used ultimately reduces the amount that can enter the environment from effluents, regardless of the number or complexity of intermediate steps.

For example, fuel oils contain varying concentrations of metals. In the future we may have to look to fuels with low concentrations of highly toxic metals, just as we look to low–sulfur fuels today. Fuel oil combustion is chiefly responsible for vanadium concentrations in the atmosphere. Residual oil imported from Venezuela has up to 63 percent vanadium pentoxide in ash, compared with 14 to 38.5 percent for oil from Iran and 0.4 percent, 1.4 percent, and 5.1 percent for oil from Kansas, Texas, and California, respectively. (*35*) Changing to low-vanadium fuel is a control that could be used to reduce atmospheric vanadium concentrations if such reduction were necessary.

Changing end products or prohibiting their production is an important control technique because man is directly affected by these products and by their disposal—through interaction with the environment and through further interaction with man. Simply changing an ingredient can also effect a desired change. For example, lead has been used in paint to accelerate drying; its harmful effects can be eliminated by removing it from the product formulation and substituting another less toxic or nontoxic material.

Changes in production processes may, in some cases, significantly reduce the quantities of contaminants that are discharged as effluents or that become intermediate or final products. For example, improving the efficiency of synthetic organics production can reduce the volume of toxic or potentially toxic effluents. Yields of organic products are rarely, if ever, 100 percent. Remaining chemical constitutents are usually wastes, which may be recovered, treated, or released to the environment. Hence, to the degree that production is made more efficient and more of the raw material is utilized, wastes released to the environment are reduced.

Most sewage treatment plants are not capable of removing many of the toxic substances found in waste water. Secondary sewage treatment is capable of removing a large portion of the metals, but many synthetic organic chemicals are unaffected by the biological treatment processes employed by municipalities. Even if the toxic substances are removed by treatment, their presence in sewage sludge may still pose a problem.

About 10 percent of all municipal solid wastes are incinerated. During combustion, organic and metallic materials are converted into a multitude of compounds. Some are partially oxidized or reduced and their structure and properties substantially changed. Some remain unaltered chemically, changing only physically, as from a solid to a gas. Some gaseous or particulate products of combustion are drawn off through the stacks; those that are not removed by stack gas cleaning reach the atmosphere. The solid residue from combustion is often quenched with water, which then enters the general environment. Eventually most airborne emissions return to earth and are deposited on land and in water.

Materials disposed of at some landfills also can present a problem. At landfills the volume of wastes is frequently reduced by open burning. The resultant particulate and gaseous emissions can cause the same pollution problems encountered in incineration. Even when the wastes are buried, leaching of toxic metals or organic compounds is possible, causing contamination of ground or surface water.

METALS AND THEIR COMPOUNDS

Singly or in combination, the 105 known elements form the basis of all matter. Of these, 77 are metals. Simply stated, metals are elements generally characterized by ductility, malleability, luster, and conductance of heat and electricity. Of the 77 elemental metals, 52 can be considered "economic metals," that is, they are in sufficient industrial and commercial usage to warrant collection of statistical production data. The quantities used vary from millions of tons for iron and manganese to only thousands of ounces for iridium.

Serious adverse environmental and/or health effects, actual and potential, have been observed or indicated for roughly one-fourth of the metals in common economic usage today. Many of the troublesome metals are the so-called "heavy metals," of which lead and mercury are the most common examples. Table 1 shows the estimated U.S. consumption of selected metals for which adverse human effects have been documented. Not included in these estimates are data for production and release of metals from processes other than those used to produce the metals for consumption. For example, Table 1 does not include the amounts of vanadium released to the atmosphere from oil combustion or of mercury released from coal combustion.

After originally extracting metals from the earth, man reintroduces them into the environment directly in elemental form or in a wide variety of compounds. The compounds may have quite different effects from their elemental forms; some metals are more toxic as compounds.

TABLE 1.—*Estimated U.S. Consumption of Selected Metals, 1948 and 1968 (44, 45)*

Metal	Total estimated consumption[1] (in tons)		Percent increase 1948–1968
	1948	1968	
Arsenic (AS_2O_3)	24,000	◇25,000	◇4
Barium (barite)	894,309	1,590,000	78
Beryllium (beryl)	1,438	8,719	507
Cadmium	3,909	6,664	70
Chromium (chromite)	875,033	1,316,000	50
Copper	1,214,000	1,576,000	30
Lead	1,133,895	1,328,790	17
Manganese (ores, 35% or more Mn)	1,538,398	2,228,412	45
Mercury	1,758	2,866	63
Nickel	93,558	159,306	70
Selenium	419	762	82
Silver[2]	3,611	4,983	38
Vanadium	[3] N.A.	5,495	----------
Zinc	◇1,200,000	1,728,400	44

[1] Includes stocks released to the open market by the Federal Government and imports; does not include exports.

[2] Consumption by industry and arts; monetary consumption not included because much was stockpiled.

[3] Figures not available between 1946 and 1955; consumption in 1946 was about 748 tons, in 1955 about 1,700 tons.

The compounds of metals appear in larger number than do the metals themselves as intermediate and consumer products. For example, at least 40 lead compounds and more than 45 cadmium compounds are currently in commercial use. The total number of variants for just two of these metals is thus more than five times the total number of metals for which adverse effects have been identified. Most of the other metals are also used in a wide array of compounds.

Numerous manufacturing processes and products employ metals and their compounds. Arsenic, for example, is used in the manufacture of glass, pigments, textiles, paper, metal adhesives, ceramics, linoleum, and mirrors. Its compounds are used in wood preservatives and paints, insecticides and herbicides, and electrical semiconductors. Beryllium is used in several of the above manufacturing operations as well as in electroplating and as a catalyst in organic chemical manufacture. Barium is used in paper manufacturing, fabric printing and dyeing, embalming, synthetic rubber production, and animal and vegetable oil refining. It is a component of fireproofing compounds, x-ray screens, water softening chemicals, enamels, lubricants, and photographic supplies.

These products exemplify the diversity of uses of metals and the almost unending list of products in which they may be present. When metals are used in the manufacture of products, effluents from the operations often contain metallic compounds, which may contaminate the environment. When metals are present in final products, direct human contact or environmental exposure is possible during use or after disposal.

A survey of eight heavy metals in U.S. waters showed that these metals were distributed in low concentrations. Their level in drinking water generally did not exceed standards but did indicate potential problems in some areas.

Examples of the toxic effects of metals are readily found. Compounds of nickel and beryllium, which accumulate in the lungs, may cause fatal diseases. If inhaled, barium can cause respiratory disease, or if ingested in sufficient quantities, it causes heart, intestinal, and nervous system disorders.

Some laboratory experiments indicate that exposure to metals may interfere with vital chemical reactions. In a study of rats and mice living in a carefully controlled environment relatively free from metal contamination, the sample group lived 20 to 25 percent longer than the control group in its usual contaminated environment. In addition, laboratory breeding mice exposed to concentrations of cadmium, lead, or selenium produced abnormal offspring. Long periods of arsenic and molybdenum exposure changed the sex ratios of mice and rat offspring. Antimony, in low doses, shortened the lifespan of rats.

Lead—Lead is one of the oldest known pollutants. In the second century B.C., the wealthy class of Rome was decimated by sterility, child mortality, and permanent mental impairment. According to one theory, this decline can be traced to lead poisoning from wine and food vessels. The lower classes survived because they could not afford lead utensils.

Today lead is absorbed by humans in a more democratic way, because all social classes are exposed to lead in the atmosphere. Lead particles in the air eventually settle to land and water, mixing with other sources of the metal and following complex pathways in the environment. The increase in lead pollution is now global in scope. For example, between 1904 and 1964, lead concentrations in Greenland snow increased 16-fold.

A variety of industrial and mining effluents, disposal of consumer products such as automobile batteries, and various food products all contribute to both environmental and human accumulation of lead. However, these sources are small contributors to lead pollution compared with combustion of leaded gasoline. In 1968 alone, 180,000 tons of lead were emitted from leaded-gasoline combustion—14 percent of all lead consumed in the United States that year.

Vanadium—Very little research has been done on the toxicity of environmental concentrations of vanadium. When the route of exposure is the respiratory tract, vanadium may accumulate in the lungs. High concentrations of the metal may damage human gastrointestinal and respiratory tracts. Exposure to lower concentrations has resulted in inhibition of cholesterol synthesis in man.

Trace amounts of vanadium are natural to all humans, but it is probably a recent addition to the atmosphere. There is no evidence that ambient levels of vanadium are toxic. But these levels have been increasing in recent years due to the burning of fuel oils containing vanadium and to increased industrial use of vanadium compounds. Eighteen compounds of vanadium are now used in a wide variety of commerical processes.

Cadmium—Like most metals, cadmium is stable and does not degrade in the environment. Thus, as increasing amounts of cadmium are refined, more and more of it is circulated in the environment, and increasing amounts may reach man.

Only a fraction of the cadmium taken into the body is actually absorbed by the body. The cadmium which is absorbed accumulates in the kidneys and the liver, and because there appears to be an inefficient excretory mechanism in humans, accumulation tends to increase with increased absorption.

The effects of such accumulation vary according to the amount and time period of exposure. Some preliminary studies indicate that exposure to low levels of cadmium from sources present in the everyday environment may lead to hypertension and heart disease and perhaps to cancer.

Many sources contribute to the accumulation of cadmium in humans. The metal is found in concentrations of 50 to 170 parts per million in superphosphate fertilizers, and it is also used in some pesticides. Cadmium becomes an air and water pollutant through a variety of industrial processes, and it is being used in increasing amounts by the storage battery, plastics, plating, and petroleum industries. Additional amounts are introduced into the home by the pipes which carry drinking water. Food is another major source of cadmium—it has been found in a variety of products, from dry cereal to vermouth.

Mercury—Although poisoning from mercury has been recognized as an occupational hazard for years, concern with mercury as a general environmental contaminant in the United States is quite recent.

Metallic mercury was long thought environmentally inert. When discharged into a river, for example, it was believed to settle to the bottom and remain there. Then in 1960, it was reported that 111 persons had died or suffered serious neurological damage near Minamata, Japan, as a result of eating fish and shellfish which had been contaminated by mercury discharged into Minamata Bay by a plastics manufacturing plant. In 1965, another poisoning incident was reported in Niigata, Japan, and in 1966, Swedish studies indicated that many species of birds were being poisoned by mercury. Other Swedish studies pinpointed the critical facts that metallic mercury, previously thought inert, can be changed by bacteria into methylmercury—a compound that is far more toxic than metallic mercury—and that methylmercury can enter the food cycle through uptake by aquatic plants, algae, lower forms of animal life, and fish. Even more significantly, the studies showed that the concentration factor in the fish could be 3,000 or more to 1. Thus, harmless levels of mercury in water can be concentrated to hazardous levels in fish.

In 1967, large amounts of methylmercury were reported in fresh-water fish in Sweden. A study submitted in the same year to the U.S. Public Health Service concluded: "From our review of mercury as an environmental chemical contaminant, it is obvious that a considerable amount of mercury has been cycled through our environment. . . . We have little or no information as to where the mercury that is being cycled through our environment is going." The report recommended expanded monitoring and study of the health effects of mercury.

Finally, in the spring of 1970, high levels of mercury were discovered in fish in Lake St. Clair, on the Canada–U.S. border. Canada banned the sale of fish from the Lake, and 10 days later Michigan followed suit.

The concern over mercury is well-founded. Some organic mercury compounds are accumulated in humans, concentrating in the brain, the kidney, the liver, and the fetus. They can destroy the cells of the brain, cause tremors and mouth ulcers, and produce birth defects because of chromosome breakage.

The sources of mercury are numerous. It is used in a number of industrial processes and appears in such varied products as paints, electrical apparatus, thermometers and other instruments, and cosmetics. Primary concern has focused on mercury as a water pollutant, largely because it is now known to reach the food chain by water, but the metal is also present in soil and in air. End quote.

REFERENCES AND SELECTED BIBLIOGRAPHY

See, Mercury Pollution and Enforcement of the Refuse Act of 1899, Hearings before a Subcommittee of the Committee on Government Operations, U.S. House of Representatives, Parts I and II, October 21 and November 5, 1971.

The Senate hearings held in 1970 demonstrate both the failure of the agencies charged with protecting the nation's waterways to recognize the disastrous environmental effects of the unrestrained dumping of one of the most dangerous of poisons, and show industry's pious declarations in defense of these acts as well as their failure to devote research efforts to discover the hazards involved.

See, *Effects of Mercury on Man and the Environment, Hearings before the Subcommittee on Energy, Natural Resources, and the Environment of the Committee on Commerce, United States Senate,* Serial 91-73, May 8, 1970. Especially pp. 6 to 37.

See also, COMMONER, "A Current Problem in the Environmental Crisis, Mercury Pollution and Its Legal Implications." 4 *Nat. Res. Lawyer* No. 1, Jan. 1971 at 139.

GRANT, "Mercury in Man; STAFF, "Mercury in the Air," 13 *Environment* No. 4, May 1971 at 2, 16, 28.

Report of the Advisory Boards on Control of Pollution of the Boundary Waters and the International Great Lakes Water Pollution Boards on Mercury Pollution in the Lower Great Lakes, August 1970.

DURUM, Hem, & Heidel, *Reconnaissance of Selected Minor Elements in Surface Waters of the United States,* October 1970, Geological Survey Circular 643 (1971).

BROWN, "Probing the Law and Beyond: A Quest for Public Protection from Hazardous Product Catastrophies," 38 *The Geo. Wash. L. Rev.* 431 (1970).

For a fine short discussion from the technical side, *see*: DEAN, John Q., BOSQUI, Frank L., and LANOUETTE, Kenneth H., "Removing Heavy Metals From Waste Water," *Environmental Science & Technology,* Vol. 6, No. 6, June 1972 at 519.

For an excellent summation of the problem of lead in our environment, *see,* HALL, Stephen K., "Pollution and Poisoning." *Environmental Science & Technology,* Vol. 6, No. 1, January 1972 at 31.

SYNTHETIC ORGANIC COMPOUNDS

The Chemical Abstracts Service Registry Number System has registered some 1.8 million chemical compounds, and the list is growing by the addition of 250,000 chemicals each year. Approximately 300 to 500 new chemical compounds are introduced annually into commercial use. Of those which are or may be used commercially, synthetic (manmade) organic chemicals are of special concern because frequently they are alien to the natural environment, and in some instances their modification, redistribution, or persistence have already had some dangerous effects.

Approximately 9,000 synthetic organic compounds were in commercial use by 1968. As shown in Table 2, production is increasing rapidly, from over 103 billion pounds in 1967 to nearly 120 billion pounds in 1968, an increase of about 15 percent. Compared to the 1957–1959 annual average of 46 billion pounds, production increased 161 percent in approximately 10 years. With changes in industrial needs and technological knowledge, new and more complex compounds with new and different uses are constantly being developed.

The synthetic organic chemicals shown by classes in Table 2 are obtained from coal, crude petroleum, natural gas, wood, vegetable oils, fats, resin, and grains. Products are formed by such processes as thermal decomposition, synthesis, catalytic cracking, distillation, absorption, or fermentation. Intermediate products are sometimes consumed directly or may be further processed. The category of intermediates in Table 2 refers to those that are consumed directly.

TABLE 2.—*U.S. Production of Synthetic Organic Chemicals, 1968* [1]

Chemical	1968 Production (in millions of pounds)	Percent increase over 1967
Intermediates	25,014	20.3
Colorants:		
Dyes	226	9.7
Pigments	54	1.9
Flavors and perfumes	117	4.5
Plastic products:		
Plastics and resins	16,360	18.6
Plasticizers	1,331	5.4
Rubber products:		
Processing chemicals	313	18.6
Elastomers	4,268	11.6
Surface active agents	3,739	7.5
Miscellaneous	67,525	13.1
Total	118,947	15

[1] Includes data on production measured at several successive steps in the manufacturing process and therefore reflects some duplication.

Public disclosure is not permitted by the data-collecting agency when only one manufacturer produces a chemical. When production of an item was below 1,000 pounds, or sales below $1,000, a product is not included. Further, medicinals and pesticides are not included.

Organic chemicals can be tailored in structure and properties to fit almost any imaginable need. During 1968, production of chemicals in the miscellaneous category shown in Table 2 totaled 67,525 million pounds, over half of all synthetic organic chemicals produced. Examples of chemicals in this category are some of the halogenated hydrocarbons, which are used as solvents in dry cleaning and refrigerants, and aerosol propellants for hair sprays, paints, and deodorants. Alcohols, nitrogen compounds, acids and anhydrides, aldehydes, and ketones are also included in this category.

A vast number of synthetic organic chemicals is being introduced into the environment, and many of these chemicals have not been identified. A study prepared for the Water Quality Office of the Environmental Protection Agency reported that 496 organic chemicals were found or suspected in fresh water, but the chemical composition of only 66 of these was identified. (*22*) The disparity between the number recorded and the number identified indicates the need for better monitoring and analytical techniques. It also shows the difficulty of dealing with such substances once they have entered the environment.

Some organic compounds have been identified as tumor–producing in experimental animals. A smaller number have been singled out as capable of causing cancer in humans. Research on teratogenic effects has been limited, but a few chemicals have been shown to be teratogenic in humans in doses corresponding to those which might be expected in the environment. So little testing has been conducted on the mutagenic effects of synthetic organic chemicals that almost nothing is known about such effects.

Discussed below are three example of synthetic organic chemicals which have posed some hazard to human health or the environment.

PCB's (Polychlorinated Biphenyls)—The molecules of plastics are generally inert and nonreactive. Problems arise because of certain types of plasticizers, dyes, oxidation retardants, and various stabilizers which are added to plastics. These additives are not always chemically bound to the plastic molecules and thus may be released into the environment. PCB's, also known as Aroclors, are such a group of additives.

PCB's are among the more persistent organic chemicals—they degrade very slowly in the environment. In addition to their use as plasticizers, they have also been used in paint, electrical transformers, and lacquer resins and as lubricants, heat transfer fluids, and "carriers" for some insecticides. Structurally, PCB's resemble DDT, and like DDT, they are not soluble in water but are fat soluble and therefore can be absorbed by human tissue. The resemblance to DDT goes further. PCB residues have been found in fish and wildlife around the world. Normally used analytical methods find it difficult to differentiate between DDT and PCB's.

Tests with PCB's have shown that 0.1 parts per million were fatal to juvenile pink shrimp after a 48-hour exposure.

PCB's have also been found in Great Lakes fish and in human fatty tissue. A study of human tissue samples showed concentrations of from less than 1.0 parts per million to as high as 250 parts per million. Fifteen percent of the samples exceeded 1.0 parts per million PCB's. Another study showed that over half the urban residents examined had traces of PCB in their blood.

ONCB (Orthonitrochlorobenzene) *(26)*—ONCB is an unusable byproduct in the manufacture of paranitrochlorobenzene, a chemical in wide commercial use. In 1958, this unique and persistent chemical was found at levels of .021 parts per million in water samples taken at monitoring stations between St. Louis and New Orleans. Concentrations of 0.03 parts per million of ONCB were found in treated drinking water, indicating that ONCB survived normal potable water treatment procedures. Few studies have been done on the effects of ONCB, but it was calculated that 5 to 50 parts per million would be lethal to humans and that 0.5 to 5 parts per million would cause clinical symptoms.

NTA (Nitrilotriacetic Acid)—NTA recently came into extensive use as a substitute for phosphates in detergents. Until a couple of years ago, almost no NTA was used. NTA, a substance with which the consumer has suddenly come into direct contact, may enter the general aquatic environment in large quantities through flushing into sewers and septic tanks. If NTA proved safe, an estimated 600 million pounds would have been used annually in detergents by 1973. Because of its concern with water pollution caused by detergents, the Federal Government studied the health and environmental effects of NTA and other phosphate substitutes. Preliminary results indicated that NTA may combine with cadmium, mercury, and other metals to enhance the toxicity of these metals. Therefore, the major detergent manufacturers recently agreed not to use NTA until completion of testing now underway.

INTERACTIONS WITHIN THE ENVIRONMENT

After substances enter the environment, they may be diluted or concentrated by physical forces, and they may undergo chemical changes, including combination with other chemicals, that affect their toxicity. The substances may be picked up by living organisms which may further change and either store or eliminate them.

The results of the interaction between living organisms and chemical substances are often unpredictable, but such interaction may produce materials that are more dangerous than the initial pollutants. One example is inorganic mercury, which was thought to settle safely into the bottom sediments when discharged into water. Anaerobic bacteria are now known to convert inorganic mercury into very toxic and soluble organic mercury compounds, such as methylmercury, which pass through the food chain by aquatic algae and by fish, eventually reaching man.

DDT, another example, is nearly insoluble in water. It occurs in high concentrations among some fish-eating birds as a result of two factors: DDT's solubility in fats is much higher than in water, and plankton, shellfish, and fish generally pass successively higher concentrations of DDT on to the organism next in the food chain. Polychlorinated biphenyls (PCB's), which are chemically similar to DDT, have been found in similar association with marine food chains. Oysters exposed to one type of PCB for 96 hours accumulated the substance to a level 3,300 times that of the ambient water.

Synergism is another complicating interaction. Two or more compounds acting together may have an effect on organisms greater than the sum of their separate effects. For example, the toxic effects of mercuric salts are accentuated by the presence of trace amounts of copper. Cadmium acts as a synergist with zinc and cyanide in the aquatic environment to increase toxicity. Conversely, sometimes the presence of one substance lessens the effect of another substance on an organism. Arsenic, a toxic substance itself, counteracts the toxicity of selenium and has been added to poultry and cattle feed in areas where animal feeds are naturally high in selenium.

FWPCA
Sec. 13:
sewage from
watercraft

CONTROL OF SEWAGE FROM VESSELS [46]

SEC. 13. (a) For the purpose of this section, the term—

(1) "new vessel" includes every description of watercraft or other artificial contrivance used, or capable of being used, as a means of transportation on the navigable waters of the United States, the construction of which is initiated after promulgation of standards and regulations under this section;

(2) "existing vessel" includes every description of watercraft or other artificial contrivance used, or capable of being used, as a means of transportation on the navigable waters of the United States, the construction of which is initiated before promulgation of standards and regulations under this section;

(3) "public vessel" means a vessel owned or bareboat chartered and operated by the United States, by a State or political subdivision thereof, or by a foreign nation, except when such vessel is engaged in commerce;

(4) "United States" includes the States, the District of Columbia, the Commonwealth of Puerto Rico, the Virgin Islands, Guam, American Samoa, the Canal Zone, and the Trust Territory of the Pacific Islands;

(5) "marine sanitation device" includes any equipment for installation on board a vessel which is designed to receive, retain, treat, or discharge sewage, and any process to treat such sewage;

(6) "sewage" means human body wastes and the wastes from toilets and other receptacles intended to receive or retain body wastes;

(7) "manufacturer" means any person engaged in the manufacturing, assembling, or importation of marine sanitation devices or of vessels subject to standards and regulations promulgated under this section;

(8) "person" means an individual, partnership, firm, corporation, or association, but does not include an individual on board a public vessel;

(9) "discharge" includes, but is not limited to, any spilling, leaking, pumping, pouring, emitting, emptying, or dumping.

(b) (1) As soon as possible, after the enactment of this section and subject to the provisions of section 5(j) of this Act, the Secretary, after consultation with the Secretary of the department in which the Coast Guard is operating, after giving appropriate consideration to the economic costs involved, and within the limits of available technology, shall promulgate Federal standards of performance for marine sanitation devices (hereafter in this section referred to as "standards") which shall be designed to prevent the discharge of untreated or inadequately treated sewage into or upon the navigable waters of the United States from new vessels and existing vessels, except vessels not equipped with installed toilet facilities. Such standards shall be consistent with maritime safety and the marine and navigation laws and regulations and shall be coordinated with the regulations issued under this subsection by the Secretary of the department in which the Coast Guard is operating. The Secretary of the department in which the Coast Guard is operating shall promulgate regulations, which are consistent with standards promulgated under this subsection and with maritime safety and the marine and navigation laws and regulations, governing the design, construction, installation, and operation of any marine sanitation device on board such vessels.

(2) Any existing vessel equipped with a marine sanitation device on the date of promulgation of initial standards and regulations under this section, which device is in compliance with such initial standards and regulations, shall be deemed in compliance with this section until such time as the device is replaced or is found not to be in compliance with such initial standards and regulations.

(c) (1) Initial standards and regulations under this section shall become effective for new vessels two years after promulgation; and for existing vessels five years after promulgation. Revisions of standards and regulations shall be effective upon promulgation, unless another effective date is specified, except that no revision shall take effect before the effective date of the standard or regulation being revised.

---

[46] Added by sec. 102, Public Law 91-224.

(2) The Secretary of the department in which the Coast Guard is operating with regard to his regulatory authority established by this section, after consultation with the Secretary, may distinguish among classes, types, and sizes of vessels as well as between new and existing vessels, and may waive applicability of standards and regulations as necessary or appropriate for such classes, types, and sizes of vessels (including existing vessels equipped with marine sanitation devices on the date of promulgation of the initial standards required by this section), and, upon application, for individual vessels.

(d) The provisions of this section and the standards and regulations promulgated hereunder apply to vessels owned and operated by the United States unless the Secretary of Defense finds that compliance would not be in the interest of national security. With respect to vessels owned and operated by the Department of Defense, regulations under the last sentence of subsection (b)(1) and certifications under subsection (g)(2) of this section shall be promulgated and issued by the Secretary of Defense.

(e) Before the standards and regulations under this section are promulgated, the Secretary and the Secretary of the department in which the Coast Guard is operating shall consult with the Secretary of State; the Secretary of Health, Education, and Welfare; the Secretary of Defense; the Secretary of the Treasury; the Secretary of Commerce; other interested Federal agencies; and the States and industries interested; and otherwise comply with the requirements of section 553 of title 5 of the United States Code.

FWPCA
Sec. 13:
sewage from
watercraft

(f) After the effective date of the initial standards and regulations promulgated under this section, no State or political subdivision thereof shall adopt or enforce any statute or regulation of such State or political subdivision with respect to the design, manufacture, or installation or use of any marine sanitation device on any vessel subject to the provisions of this section. Upon application by a State, and where the Secretary determines that any applicable water quality standards require such a prohibition, he shall by regulation completely prohibit the discharge from a vessel of any sewage (whether treated or not) into those waters of such State which are the subject of the application and to which such standards apply.

(g)(1) No manufacturer of a marine sanitation device shall sell, offer for sale, or introduce or deliver for introduction in interstate commerce, or import into the United States for sale or resale any marine sanitation device manufactured after the effective date of the standards and regulations promulgated under this section unless such device is in all material respects substantially the same as a test device certified under this subsection.

(2) Upon application of the manufacturer, the Secretary of the department in which the Coast Guard is operating shall so certify a marine sanitation device if he determines, in accordance with the provisions of this paragraph, that it meets the appropriate standards and regulations promulgated under this section. The Secretary of the department in which the Coast Guard is operating shall test or require such testing of the device in accordance with procedures set forth by the Secretary as to standards of performance and for such other purposes as may be appropriate. If the Secretary of the department in which the Coast Guard is operating determines that the device is satisfactory from the standpoint of safety and any other requirements of maritime law or regulation, and after consideration of the design, installation, operation, material, or other appropriate factors, he shall certify the device. Any device manufactured by such manufacturer which is in all material respects substantially the same as the certified test device shall be deemed to be in conformity with the appropriate standards and regulations established under this section.

(3) Every manufacturer shall establish and maintain such records, make such reports, and provide such information as the Secretary or the Secretary of the department in which the Coast Guard is operating may reasonably require to enable him to determine whether such manufacturer has acted or is acting in compliance with this section and regulations issued thereunder and shall, upon request of an officer or employee duly designated by the Secretary or the Secretary of the department in which the Coast Guard is operating, permit such officer or employee at reasonable times to have access to and copy such records. All information reported to or otherwise obtained by, the Secretary or the Secretary of the department in which the Coast Guard is operating

or their representatives pursuant to this subsection which contains or relates to a trade secret or other matter referred to in section 1905 of title 18 of the United States Code shall be considered confidential for the purpose of that section, except that such information may be disclosed to other officers or employees concerned with carrying out this section. This paragraph shall not apply in the case of the construction of a vessel by an individual for his own use.

(h) After the effective date of standards and regulations promulgated under this section, it shall be unlawful—

(1) for the manufacturer of any vessel subject to such standards and regulations to manufacture for sale, to sell or offer for sale, or to distribute for sale or resale any such vessel unless it is equipped with a marine sanitation device which is in all material respects substantially the same as the appropriate test device certified pursuant to this section;

(2) for any person, prior to the sale or delivery of a vessel subject to such standards and regulations to the ultimate purchaser, wrongfully to remove or render inoperative any certified marine sanitation device or element of design of such device installed in such vessel;

(3) for any person to fail or refuse to permit access to or copying of records or to fail to make reports or provide information required under this section; and

(4) for a vessel subject to such standards and regulations to operate on the navigable waters of the United States, if such vessel is not equipped with an operable marine sanitation device certified pursuant to this section.

FWPCA Sec. 13: sewage from watercraft

(i) The district courts of the United States shall have jurisdictions to restrain violations of subsection (g)(1) and subsections (h)(1) through (3) of this section. Actions to restrain such violations shall be brought by, and in, the name of the United States. In case of contumacy or refusal to obey a subpena served upon any person under this subsection, the district court of the United States for any district in which such person is found or resides or transacts business, upon application by the United States and after notice to such person, shall have jurisdiction to issue an order requiring such person to appear and give testimony or to appear and produce documents, and any failure to obey such order of the court may be punished by such court as a contempt thereof.

(j) Any person who violates subsection (g)(1) or clause (1) or (2) of subsection (h) of this section shall be liable to a civil penalty of not more than $5,000 for each violation. Any person who violates clause (4) of subsection (h) of this section or any regulation issued pursuant to this section shall be liable to a civil penalty of not more than $2,000 for each violation. Each violation shall be a separate offense. The Secretary of the department in which the Coard Guard is operating may assess and compromise any such penalty. No penalty shall be assessed until the person charged shall have been given notice and an opportunity for a hearing on such charge. In determining the amount of the penalty, or the amount agreed upon in compromise, the gravity of the violation, and the demonstrated good faith of the person charged in attempting to achieve rapid compliance, after notification of a violation, shall be considered by said Secretary.

(k) The provisions of this section shall be enforced by the Secretary of the department in which the Coast Guard is operating and he may utilize by agreement, with or without reimbursement, law enforcement officers or other personnel and facilities of the Secretary, other Federal agencies, or the States to carry out the provisions of this section.

(l) Anyone authorized by the Secretary of the department in which the Coast Guard is operating to enforce the provisions of this section may, except as to public vessels, (1) board and inspect any vessel upon the navigable waters of the United States and (2) execute any warrant or other process issued by an officer or court of competent jurisdiction.

(m) In the case of Guam, actions arising under this section may be brought in the district court of Guam, and in the case of the Virgin Islands such actions may be brought in the district court of the Virgin Islands. In the case of American Samoa and the Trust Territory of the Pacific Islands, such actions may be brought in the District Court of the United States for the District of Hawaii and such court shall have jurisdiction of such actions. In the case of the Canal Zone, such actions may be brought in the District Court for the District of the Canal Zone.

sewage from watercraft

As an unsewered population, yachtsmen cause bacterial pollution in water. Sometimes they create a trash problem as well. But probably of greater importance is the petroleum pollution caused by the notoriously inefficient boat engines. Jacques-Yves Cousteau, the famous oceanographer, estimates that a spectacular disaster such as the *Torrey Canyon* wreck contributes only about 3 percent as much oil to the earth's waters as do private yachts each year (interview in the 1970 *National Fisherman* yearbook). See also, *Wastes from Watercraft,* U.S. Dept. of the Interior, S.Doc.No. 48, 90th Cong., 1st Sess. 3 (1967), and *Special Report on Potential Oil Pollution, Eutrophication, and Pollution from Watercraft, Third Interim Report on Pollution of Lake Erie, Lake Ontario and the International Section of the St. Lawrence River,* by the International Joint Commission, April 1970.

For a case upholding a state's right to require sanitary facilities on boats, see *Aiple Towing v. Voight,* ___ F.Supp. ___ [2 ERC 1690] (W.D.Wisc. April 5, 1971).

In *Lake Carriers' Association v. Ralph A. MacMullan,* ___ U.S. ___, 92 S. Ct. 1749, May 30, 1972, the Court ruled that State requirements on discharge of sewage will be preempted when initial Federal standards promulgated under the Water Quality Improvement Act, §13 (f), 33 U.S.C.A. §1163 (f), become effective.

If a state so requests, the Environmental Protection Agency will issue a total ban on the discharge of sewage (treated or untreated) from vessels into any or all navigable interstate waters within the state. *See, Federal Register,* Vol. 37, No. 122, June 23, 1972 at 12391.

Again we quote from *Clean Water for the 1970's,* by the Federal Water Quality Administration, June, 1970:

Control of Vessel Wastes

The Water Quality Improvement Act of 1970 provides for the establishment of performance or effluent standards for the sanitary waste discharges from all classes of watercraft. These standards are to be set by the Secretary of the Interior. The amendment further provides for the establishment and enforcement of regulations to implement these standards by the Secretary of Transportation, under whose administration the Coast Guard comes. This Federal statute applies to new and existing vessels and provides for penalties for the failure of vessel owners and manufacturers to provide adequate shipboard treatment or control of sanitary wastes. Importantly, this new legislation provides for uniform, nationwide regulation of watercraft waste discharges. This will promote a comprehensive attack on vessel pollution problems by FWQA and the Coast Guard, who will join in carrying out this task.

In June 1969, FWQA completed a report of its San Diego Bay Vessel Pollution Study Project following intensive field and laboratory activity. The purpose of this project was to determine the magnitude, extent and kinds of pollutional effects to be expected from the discharges of shipboard sanitary wastes and the pollution abatement measures required to reduce or eliminate these discharges. The findings were illustrative of this problem: vessel waste discharges were found to cause serious bacterial pollution, to be responsible for bottom sludge deposits and floating waste material and to cause violations of the water quality standards established for San Diego Bay. The pollution was directly attributable to the high numbers of military, commercial and pleasure vessels using the Bay.

Investigations by State agencies and FWQA have discovered similar conditions in other bodies of water across the United States.

It will not be an easy task to remedy vessel waste pollution. The weight and volume of waste treatment devices or waste handling tanks cause considerable installation problems, particularly on existing vessels, especially if they are military. The expense of control devices, particularly to pleasure craft owners, is also a factor. A considerable amount of research and development is underway by Federal agencies including FWQA, the Navy and the Coast Guard to find adequate and adaptable control systems.

Within recent years, many of the States have enacted or strengthened their legislation or regulations pertaining to the control of vessel wastes. Unfortunately, the non-uniformity of the waste treatment and control requirements imposed by these States has presented some significant compliance problems for vessels which travel between States. Also, in many cases the State regulations do not apply to or are ineffective in their coverage of interstate and international carriers and Federal vessels.

AREA ACID AND OTHER MINE WATER POLLUTION CONTROL DEMONSTRATIONS [47]

SEC. 14. (a) The Secretary in cooperation with other Federal departments, agencies, and instrumentalities is authorized to enter into agreements with any State or interstate agency to carry out one or more projects to demonstrate methods for the elimination or control, within all or part of a watershed, of acid or other mine water pollution resulting from active or abandoned mines. Such projects shall demonstrate the engineering and economic feasibility and practicality of various abatement techniques which will contribute substantially to effective and practical methods of acid or other mine water pollution elimination or control.

(b) The Secretary, in selecting watersheds for the purposes of this section, shall (1) require such feasibility studies as he deems appropriate, (2) give preference to areas which have the greatest present or potential value for public use for recreation, fish and wildlife, water supply, and other public uses, and (3) be satisfied that the project area will not be affected adversely by the influx of acid or other mine water pollution from nearby sources.

(c) Federal participation in such projects shall be subject to the conditions—

(1) that the State or interstate agency shall pay not less than 25 percentum of the actual project costs which payment may be in any form, including, but not limited to, land or interests therein that is needed for the project, or personal property or services, the value of which shall be determined by the Secretary; and

(2) that the State or interstate agency shall provide legal and practical protection to the project area to insure against any activities which will cause future acid or other mine water pollution.

(d) There is authorized to be appropriated $15,000,000 to carry out the provisions of this section, which sum shall be available until expended. No more than 25 percentum of the total funds available under this section in any one year shall be granted to any one State.

COMMENTARY

Sec. 14 provides money for demonstration projects concerned with the control of acid mine drainage. No serious regulatory effort exists at the federal level. Federal research in this area is conducted by the Bureau of Mines and the Appalachian Regional Commission. (See especially, *Acid Mine Drainage in Appalachia,* a report by the Appalachian Regional Commission, 1969.) This subject is dealt with in detail in Volume Two of the work you are reading. However, as a compromise for those who have only volume one, the following very brief survey of the problem is excerpted from *Clean Water for the 1970's, A Status Report,* Federal Water Quality Administration, 1970:

Mine Drainage

Mine drainage, one of the most significant causes of water quality degradation and destruction of water uses in Appalachia and the Ohio Basin States, as well as in some other mining areas of the United States, degrades water primarily by chemical pollution and sedimentation. Acid formation occurs when water and air react with the sulfur-bearing minerals in the mines or refuse piles to form sulfuric acid and iron compounds. The acid and iron compounds then drain into ponds and streams. About 60 percent of the mine drainage pollution problem is caused by mines which have been worked and then abandoned. Coal mines idle for 30 to 50 years may still discharge large quantities of acid waters.

Although acid pollution is usually limited to coal field areas, suspended solids and sedimentation damage can extend much further downstream. Mine drainage pollution may degrade municipal and industrial water supplies; reduce recreational uses of waters; lower the aesthetic quality of waterbodies and corrode boats, piers and other structures. During 1967, over a million fish were reported killed by mine discharges, ranking mine drainage as one of the primary causes of fish kills in the United States.

Total unneutralized acid drainage from both active and unused coal mines in the United States is estimated to amount to over 4 million tons of sulfuric acid equivalent annually. Although about twice this amount of acid is actually produced, roughly one-half is neutralized by natural alkalinity in mines and streams. In Appalachia alone, where an estimated 75 percent of the coal mine drainage problem occurs,

[47] Added by sec. 102, Public Law 91–224.

approximately 10,500 miles of streams are reduced below desirable levels of quality by acid mine drainage. About 6,700 miles of these streams are continuously degraded; the remainder are degraded some of the time. Acid mine drainage problems also occur from other types of mining throughout the Nation, such as phosphate, sand and gravel, clay, iron, gold, copper and aluminum mines.

It is estimated that 3.2 million acres of land in the United States had been disturbed by surface (strip and auger) mine operations prior to January 1, 1965. Of these 3.2 million acres, approximately 2 million acres are either unreclaimed or only partially reclaimed. An additional 153,000 acres have since been disturbed each year, only part of which are reclaimed annually. In addition to contributing to the acid pollution problem, surface mines also contribute large quantities of sediment to the Nation's streams.

Sediment yields from strip-mined areas average nearly 30,000 tons per square mile annually—10 to 60 times the amount of sedimentation from agricultural lands. At this rate, the 2 million acres of strip-mined land in need of reclamation could be the source of 94 million tons of sediment a year.

In addition to mine drainage, refuse piles, tailings ponds and washery preparation residues are also important indirect sources of pollution from mining. For many minerals, such as phosphate, the pollution from processing operations exceeds that resulting directly from the mining operation. The pollution from coal mines in Indiana and Illinois, for example, stems primarily from refuse piles, tailings ponds and preparation plants. No national estimates are available, however, which show the volume or relative importance of pollution from these sources.

End, quote .

FWPCA Sec. 15: Great Lakes

POLLUTION CONTROL IN GREAT LAKES [48]

Sec. 15. (a) The Secretary, in cooperation with other Federal departments, agencies, and instrumentalities is authorized to enter into agreements with any State, political subdivision, interstate agency, or other public agency, or combination thereof, to carry out one or more projects to demonstrate new methods and techniques and to develop preliminary plans for the elimination or control of pollution, within all or any part of the watersheds of the Great Lakes. Such projects shall demonstrate the engineering and economic feasibility and practicality of removal of pollutants and prevention of any polluting matter from entering into the Great Lakes in the future and other abatement and remedial techniques which will contribute substantially to effective and practical methods of water pollution elimination or control.

(b) Federal participation in such projects shall be subject to the condition that the State, political subdivision, interstate agency, or other public agency, or combination thereof, shall pay not less than 25 per centum of the actual project costs, which payment may be in any form, including, but not limited to, land or interests therein that is needed for the project, and personal property or services the value of which shall be determined by the Secretary.

(c) There is authorized to be appropriated $20,000,000 to carry out the provisions of this section, which sum shall be available until expended.

Secs. 16, 17, 18, 19, and **20** as printed below are edited versions, and not the full texts.

FWPCA Sec. 16: training grants

TRAINING GRANTS AND CONTRACTS [48]

[Edited]

Sec. 16. The Secretary is authorized to make grants to or contracts with institutions of higher education, or combinations of such institutions, to assist them in planning, developing, strengthening, improving, or carrying out programs or projects for the preparation of undergraduate students to enter an occupation which involves the design, operation, and maintenance of treatment works, and other facilities whose purpose is water quality control.

FWPCA Sec. 17: applying for training grants

APPLICATION FOR TRAINING GRANT OR CONTRACT; ALLOCATION OF GRANTS OR CONTRACTS [49] **[Edited]**

Sec. 17. (1) A grant or contract authorized by section 16 may be made only upon application to the Secretary at such time or times and containing such information as he may prescribe

[48] Sections added by sec. 102, Public Law 91-224.

[49] Sections added by sec. 102, Public Law 91-224.

AWARD OF SCHOLARSHIPS [49]
[Edited]

SEC. 18. (1) The Secretary is authorized to award scholarships in accordance with the provisions of this section for undergraduate study by persons who plan to enter an occupation involving the operation and maintenance of treatment works.

FWPCA Sec. 18: Scholarships

(3) The Secretary shall approve a program of an institution of higher education for the purposes of this section only upon application by the institution and only upon his finding—

(A) that such program has as a principal objective the education and training of persons in the operation and maintenance of treatment works

DEFINITIONS AND AUTHORIZATIONS [50]
[Edited]

FWPCA Sec. 19: definitions & authorizations

SEC. 19. (1) As used in sections 16 through 19 of this Act—

(A) The term "State" includes the District of Columbia, Puerto Rico, the Canal Zone, Guam, the Virgin Islands, American Samoa, and the Trust Territory of the Pacific Islands.

ALASKA VILLAGE DEMONSTRATION PROJECTS [51]
[Edited]

FWPCA Sec. 20: Alaskan villages

SEC. 20. (a) The Secretary is authorized to enter into agreements with the State of Alaska to carry out one or more projects to demonstrate methods to provide for central community facilities for safe water and elimination or control of water pollution in those native villages of Alaska without such facilities. Such project shall include provisions for community safe water supply systems, toilets, bathing and laundry facilities, sewage disposal facilities, and other similar facilities, and educational and informational facilities and programs relating to health and hygiene. Such demonstration projects shall be for the further purpose of developing preliminary plans for providing such safe water and such elimination or control of water pollution for all native villages in such State.

COOPERATION BY ALL FEDERAL AGENCIES IN THE CONTROL OF POLLUTION [52]

FWPCA Sec. 21: inter-agency cooperation

SEC. 21. (a) Each Federal agency (which term is used in this section includes Federal departments, agencies, and instrumentalities) having jurisdiction over any real property or facility, or engaged in any Federal public works activity of any kind, shall, consistent with the paramount interest of the United States as determined by the President, insure compliance with applicable water quality standards and the purposes of this Act in the administration of such property, facility, or activity. In his summary of any conference pursuant to section 10(d)(4) of this Act, the Secretary shall include references to any discharges allegedly contributing to pollution from any such Federal property, facility, or activity, and shall transmit a copy of such summary to the head of the Federal agency having jurisdiction of such property, facility, or activity. Notice of any hearing pursuant to section 10(f) of this Act involving any pollution alleged to be effected by any such discharges shall also be given to the Federal agency having jurisdiction over the property, facility, or activity involved, and the findings and recommendations of the hearing board conducting such hearing shall include references to any such discharges which are contributing to the pollution found by such board.

(b)(1) Any applicant for a Federal license or permit to conduct any activity including, but not limited to, the construction or operation of facilities which may result in any discharge into the navigable waters of the United States, shall provide the licensing or permitting agency a certification from the State in which the discharge originates or will originate, or, if appropriate, from the interstate water pollution control agency having jurisdiction over the navigable waters at the point where the discharge originates or will originate, that there is reasonable assurance, as determined by the State or interstate agency that such activity will be conducted in a manner which will not violate applicable water quality standards. Such state or interstate agency

---

[51] Added by sec. 102, Public Law 91–224.

[52] Amended by sec. 103, Public Law 91–224.

[50] Added by sec. 102, Public Law 91–224.

FWPCA Sec. 21: inter-agency cooperation

shall establish procedures for public notice in the case of all applications for certification by it, and to the extent it deems appropriate, procedures for public hearings in connection with specific applications. In any case where such standards have been promulgated by the Secretary pursuant to section 10(c) of this Act, or where a State or interstate agency has no authority to give such a certification, such certification shall be from the Secretary. If the State, interstate agency, or Secretary, as the case may be, fails or refuses to act on a request for certification, within a reasonable period of time (which shall not exceed one year) after receipt of such request, the certification requirements of this subsection shall be waived with respect to such Federal application. No license or permit shall be granted until the certification required by this section has been obtained or has been waived as provided in the preceding sentence. No license or permit shall be granted if certification has been denied by the State, interstate agency, or the Secretary, as the case may be.

(2) Upon receipt of such application and certification the licensing or permitting agency shall immediately notify the Secretary of such application and certification. Whenever such a discharge may affect, as determined by the Secretary, the quality of the waters of any other State, the Secretary within thirty days of the date of notice of application for such Federal license or permit shall so notify such other State, the licensing or permitting agency, and the applicant. If, within sixty days after receipt of such notification, such other State determines that such discharge will affect the quality of its waters so as to violate its water quality standards, and within such sixty-day period notifies the Secretary and the licensing of permitting agency in writing of its objection to the issuance of such license or permit and requests a public hearing on such objection, the licensing or permitting agency shall hold such a hearing. The Secretary shall at such hearing submit his evaluation and recommendations with respect to any such objection to the licensing or permitting agency. Such agency, based upon the recommendations of such State, the Secretary, and upon any additional evidence, if any, presented to the agency at the hearing, shall condition such license or permit in such manner as may be necessary to insure compliance with applicable water quality standards. If the imposition of conditions cannot insure such compliance such agency shall not issue such license or permit.

(3) The certification obtained pursuant to paragraph (1) of this subsection with respect to the construction of any facility shall fulfill the requirements of this subsection with respect to certification in connection with any other Federal license or permit required for the operation of such facility unless, after notice to the certifying State, agency, or Secretary, as the case may be, which shall be given by the Federal agency to whom application is made for such operating license or permit, the State, or if appropriate, the interstate agency or the Secretary, notifies such agency within sixty days after receipt of such notice that there is no longer reasonable assurance that there will be compliance with applicable water quality standards because of changes since the construction license or permit certification was issued in (A) the construction or operation of the facility, (B) the characteristics of the waters into which such discharge is made, or (C) the water quality standards applicable to such waters. This paragraph shall be inapplicable in any case where the applicant for such operating license or permit has failed to provide the certifying State, or if appropriate, the interstate agency or the Secretary, with notice of any proposed changes in the construction or operation of the facility with respect to which a construction license or permit has been granted which changes may result in violation of applicable water quality standards.

(4) Prior to the initial operation of any federally licensed or permitted facility or activity which may result in any discharge into the navigable waters of the United States and with respect to which a certification has been obtained pursuant to paragraph (1) of this subsection, which facility or activity is not subject to a Federal operating license or permit, the licensee or permittee shall provide an opportunity for such certifying State, or if appropriate, the interstate agency or the Secretary to review the manner in which the facility or activity shall be operated or conducted for the purposes of assuring that applicable water quality standards will not be violated. Upon notification by the certifying State, or if appropriate, the interstate agency or the Secretary that the operation of any such federally licensed or permitted

facility or activity will violate applicable water quality standards, such Federal agency may, after public hearing, suspend such license or permit. If such license or permit is suspended, it shall remain suspended until notification is received from the certifying State, agency, or Secretary, as the case may be, that there is reasonable assurance that such facility or activity will not violate applicable water quality standards.

(5) Any Federal license or permit with respect to which a certification has been obtained under paragraph (1) of this subsection may be suspended or revoked by the Federal agency issuing such license or permit upon the entering of a judgment under section 10(h) of this Act that such facility or activity has been operated in violation of applicable water quality standards.

(6) No Federal agency shall be deemed to be an applicant for the purposes of this subsection.

(7) In any case where actual construction of a facility has been lawfully commenced prior to the date of enactment of the Water Quality Improvement Act of 1970, no certification shall be required under this subsection for a license or permit issued after the date of enactment of such Act of 1970 to operate such facility, except that any such license or permit issued without certification shall terminate at the end of the three-year period beginning on the date of enactment of such Act of 1970 unless prior to such termination date the person having such license or permit submits to the Federal agency which issued such license or permit a certification and otherwise meets the requirements of this subsection.

FWPCA Sec. 21: inter-agency cooperation

(8) Except as provided in paragraph (7), any application for a license or permit (A) that is pending on the date of enactment of the Water Quality Improvement Act of 1970 and (B) that is issued within one year following such date of enactment shall not require certification pursuant to this subsection for one year following the issuance of such license or permit, except that any such license or permit issued shall terminate at the end of one year unless prior to that time the licensee or permittee submits to the Federal agency that issued such license or permit a certification and otherwise meets the requirements of this subsection.

(9)(A) In the case of any activity which will affect water quality but for which there are no applicable water quality standards, no certification shall be required under this subsection, except that the licensing or permitting agency shall impose, as a condition of any license or permit, a requirement that the licensee or permittee shall comply with the purposes of this Act.

(B) Upon notice from the State in which the discharge originates or, as appropriate, the interstate agency or the Secretary, that such licensee or permittee has been notified of the adoption of water quality standards applicable to such activity and has failed, after reasonable notice, of not less than six months, to comply with such standards, the license or permit shall be suspended until notification is received from such State or interstate agency or the Secretary that there is reasonable assurance that such activity will comply with applicable water quality standards.

(c) Nothing in this section shall be construed to limit the authority of any department or agency pursuant to any other provision of law to require compliance with applicable water quality standards. The Secretary shall, upon the request of any Federal department or agency, or State or interstate agency, or applicant, provide, for the purpose of this section, any relevant information on applicable water quality standards, and shall, when requested by any such department or agency or State or interstate agency, or applicant, comment on any methods to comply with such standards.

(d) In order to implement the provisions of this section, the Secretary of the Army, acting through the Chief of Engineers, is authorized, if he deems it to be in the public interest, to permit the use of spoil disposal areas under his jurisdiction by Federal licensees or permittees, and to make an appropriate charge for such use. Moneys received from such licensees or permittees shall be deposited in the Treasury as miscellaneous receipts.

COMMENTARY

Sec. 21 of the Federal Water Pollution Control Act, is concerned with the abatement of pollution from Federal facilities. Among the laws and regulations also applicable generally to this are the National

Environmental Policy Act of 1969 (p. One-87), the Environmental Quality Improvement Act of 1970 (p. One 91), Executive Order 11514 (p. One-93), and Executive Order 11507, the text of which follows. E.O. 11507 replaced E.O. 11288, which had been signed by President Johnson on July 2, 1966. The replaced order was similar to the newer one, although it was weaker in the compliance requirements. The earlier order had been ignored by many Federal agencies. A point worth noting is that under the Clean Air Act Amendments of 1970, Federal facilities must meet State and local requirements. *See, Scenic Hudson Preservation Conference v. Diamond* at Four-105.

Note that both the Executive Order and Section 21 of the Federal Water Pollution Control Act must be met. The National Environmental Policy Act will also be applicable.

EXECUTIVE ORDER No. 11507, February 4, 1970

executive order on pollution control at federal facilities

By virtue of the authority vested in me as President of the United States and in furtherance of the purpose and policy of the Clean Air Act, as amended (42 U.S.C. 1857), the Federal Water Pollution Control Act, as amended (33 U.S.C. 466), and the National Environmental Policy Act of 1969 (Public Law No. 91–190, approved January 1, 1970), it is ordered as follows:

SECTION 1. *Policy.* It is the intent of this order that the Federal Government in the design, operation, and maintenance of its facilities shall provide leadership in the nationwide effort to protect and enhance the quality of our air and water resources.

SEC. 2. *Definitions.* As used in this order:

(a) The term "respective Secretary" shall mean the Secretary of Health, Education, and Welfare in matters pertaining to air pollution control and the Secretary of the Interior in matters pertaining to water pollution control.

(b) The term "agencies" shall mean the departments, agencies, and establishments of the executive branch.

(c) The term "facilities" shall mean the buildings, installations, structures, public works, equipment, aircraft, vessels, and other vehicles and property, owned by or constructed or manufactured for the purpose of leasing to the Federal Government.

(d) The term "air and water quality standards" shall mean respectively the quality standards and related plans of implementation, including emission standards, adopted pursuant to the Clean Air Act, as amended, and the Federal Water Pollution Control Act, as amended, or as prescribed pursuant to section 4(b) of this order.

(e) The term "performance specifications" shall mean permissible limits of emissions, discharges, or other values applicable to a particular Federal facility that would, as a minimum, provide for conformance with air and water quality standards as defined herein.

(f) The term "United States" shall mean the fifty States, the District of Columbia, the Commonwealth of Puerto Rico, the Virgin Islands, and Guam.

SEC. 3. *Responsibilities.* (a) Heads of agencies shall, with regard to all facilities under their jurisdiction:

(1) Maintain review and surveillance to ensure that the standards set forth in section 4 of this order are met on a continuing basis.

(2) Direct particular attention to identifyinig potential air and water quality problems associated with the use and production of new materials and make provisions for their prevention and control.

(3) Consult with the respective Secretary concerning the best techniques and methods available for the protection and enhancement of air and water quality.

(4) Develop and publish procedures, within six months of the date of this order, to ensure that the facilities under their jurisdiction are in conformity with this order. In the preparation of such procedures there shall be timely and appropriate consultation with the respective Secretary.

(b) The respective Secretary shall provide leadership in implementing this order, including the provision of technical advice and assistance to the heads of agencies in connection with their duties and responsibilities under this order.

(c) The Council on Environmental Quality shall maintain continuing review of the implementation of this order and shall, from time to time, report to the President thereon.

Sec. 4. *Standards.* (a) Heads of agencies shall ensure that all facilities under their jurisdiction are designed, operated, and maintained so as to meet the following requirements:

(1) Facilities shall conform to air and water quality standards as defined in section 2(d) of this order. In those cases where no such air or water quality standards are in force for a particular geographical area, Federal facilities in that area shall conform to the standards established pursuant to subsection (b) of this section. Federal facilities shall also conform to the performance specifications provided for in this order.

(2) Actions shall be taken to avoid or minimize wastes created through the complete cycle of operations of each facility.

(3) The use of municipal or regional waste collection or disposal systems shall be the preferred method of disposal of wastes from Federal facilities. Whenever use of such a system is not feasible or appropriate, the heads of agencies concerned shall take necessary measures for the satisfactory disposal of such wastes, including:

(A) When appropriate, the installation and operation of their own waste treatment and disposal facilities in a manner consistent with this section.

(B) The provision of trained manpower, laboratory and other supporting facilities as appropriate to meet the requirements of this section.

(C) The establishment of requirements that operators of Federal pollution control facilities meet levels of proficiency consistent with the operator certification requirements of the State in which the facility is located. In the absence of such State requirements the respective Secretary may issue guidelines, pertaining to operator qualifications and performance, for the use of heads of agencies.

(4) The use, storage, and handling of all materials, including but not limited to, solid fuels, ashes, petroleum products, and other chemical and biological agents, shall be carried out so as to avoid or minimize the possibilities for water and air pollution. When appropriate, preventive measures shall be taken to entrap spillage or discharge or otherwise to prevent accidental pollution. Each agency, in consultation with the respective Secretary, shall establish appropriate emergency plans and procedures for dealing with accidental pollution.

(5) No waste shall be disposed of or discharged in such a manner as could result in the pollution of ground water which would endanger the health or welfare of the public.

(6) Discharges of radioactivity shall be in accordance with the applicable rules, regulations, or requirements of the Atomic Energy Commission and with the policies and guidance of the Federal Radiation Council as published in the Federal Register.

(b) In those cases where there are no air or water quality standards as defined in section 2(d) of this order in force for a particular geographic area or in those cases where more stringent requirements are deemed advisable for Federal facilities, the respective Secretary, in consultation with appropriate Federal, State, interstate, and local agencies, may issue regulations establishing air or water quality standards for the purpose of this order, including related schedules for implementation.

(c) The heads of agencies, in consultation with the respective Secretary, may from time to time identify facilities or uses thereof which are to be exempted, including temporary relief, from provisions of this order in the interest of national security or in extraordinary cases where it is in the national interest. Such exemptions shall be reviewed periodically by the respective Secretary and the heads of the agencies concerned. A report on exemptions granted shall be submitted to the Council on Environmental Quality periodically.

SEC. 5. *Procedures for abatement of air and water pollution at existing Federal facilities.* (a) Actions necessary to meet the requirements of subsections (a)(1) and (b) of section 4 of this order pertaining to air and water pollution at existing facilities are to be completed or under way no later than December 31, 1972. In cases where an enforcement conference called pursuant to law or air and water quality standards require earlier actions, the earlier date shall be applicable.

(b) In order to ensure full compliance with the requirements of section 5(a) and to facilitate budgeting for necessary corrective and preventive measures, heads of agencies shall present to the Director of the Bureau of the Budget by June 30, 1970, a plan to provide for such improvements as may be necessary to meet the required date. Subsequent revisions needed to keep any such plan up-to-date shall be promptly submitted to the Director of the Bureau of the Budget.

(c) Heads of agencies shall notify the respective Secretary as to the performance specifications proposed for each facility to meet the requirements of subsections (a) (1) and (b) of section 4 of this order. Where the respective Secretary finds that such performance specifications are not adequate to meet such requirements, he shall consult with the agency head and the latter shall thereupon develop adequate performance specifications.

(d) As may be found necessary, heads of agencies may submit requests to the Director of the Bureau of the Budget for extensions of time for a project beyond the time specified in section 5(a). The Director, in consultation with the respective Secretary, may approve such request if the Director deems that such project is not technically feasible or immediately necessary to meet the requirements of subsections 4 (a) and (b). Full justification as to the extraordinary circumstances necessitating any such extension shall be required.

(e) Heads of agencies shall not use for any other purpose any of the amounts appropriated and apportioned for corrective and preventive measures necessary to meet the requirements of subsection

(a) for the fiscal year ending June 30, 1971, and for any subsequent fiscal year.

Sec. 6. *Procedures for new Federal facilities.* (a) Heads of agencies shall ensure that the requirements of section 4 of this order are considered at the earliest possible stage of planning for new facilities.

(b) A request for funds to defray the cost of designing and constructing new facilities in the United States shall be included in the annual budget estimates of an agency only if such request includes funds to defray the costs of such measures as may be necessary to assure that the new facility will meet the requirements of section 4 of this order.

(c) Heads of agencies shall notify the respective Secretary as to the performance specifications proposed for each facility when action is necessary to meet the requirements of subsections (a)(1) and (b) of section 4 of this order. Where the respective Secretary finds that such performance specifications are not adequate to meet such requirements he shall consult with the agency head and the latter shall thereupon develop adequate performance specifications.

(d) Heads of agencies shall give due consideration to the quality of air and water resources when facilities are constructed or operated outside the United States.

Sec. 7. *Procedures for Federal water resources projects.* (a) All water resources projects of the Departments of Agriculture, the Interior, and the Army, the Tennessee Valley Authority, and the United States Section of the International Boundary and Water Commission shall be consistent with the requirements of section 4 of this order. In addition, all such projects shall be presented for the consideration of the Secretary of the Interior at the earliest feasible stage if they involve proposals or recommendations with respect to the authorization or construction of any Federal water resources project in the United States. The Secretary of the Interior shall review plans and supporting data for all such projects relating to water quality, and shall prepare a report to the head of the responsible agency describing the potential impact of the project on water quality, including recommendations concerning any changes or other measures with respect thereto which he considers to be necessary in connection with the design, construction, and operation of the project.

(b) The report of the Secretary of the Interior shall accompany at the earliest practicable stage any report proposing authorization or construction, or a request for funding, of such a water resource project. In any case in which the Secretary of the Interior fails to submit a report within 90 days after receipt of project plans, the head of the agency concerned may propose authorization, construction, or funding of the project without such an accompanying report. In such a case, the head of the agency concerned shall explicitly state in his request or report concerning the project that the Secretary of the Interior has not reported on the potential impact of the project on water quality.

Sec. 8. *Saving provisions.* Except to the extent that they are inconsistent with this order, all outstanding rules, regulations, orders, delegations, or other forms of administrative action issued, made, or otherwise taken under the orders superseded by section 9 hereof or relating to the subject of this order shall remain in full force and effect until amended, modified, or terminated by proper authority.

Sec. 9. *Orders superseded.* Executive Order No. 11282 of May 26, 1966, and Executive Order No. 11288 of July 2, 1966, are hereby superseded.

cleaning up
U.S. property

Once again we quote from *Clean Waters for the 1970's, A Status Report,* by the Federal Water Quality Administration, June, 1970. References to the Department of the Interior and its Secretary should now be read as to the Environmental Protection Agency and its Administrator.

Control of Pollution from Federal Activities

The Federal government is involved in many activities which have an impact on the quality of our Nation's waters. These operations include the maintenance of Federal facilities, such as military bases, lighthouses and post offices; management of Federal lands; and diverse activities, such as dredging, nuclear energy development, and pest control. Today, in the United States, there are approximately 20,000 Federal real properties, many of which have an impact on the environment. In addition, Federal lands comprise one-third of the United States, and the use of these lands has a bearing on progress in achieving national goals of clean water and a quality environment.

Correction of conventional municipal and industrial waste problems from Federal facilities is only a part of the job in ensuring that the wide-ranging activities of the Federal establishment have a minimum impact on the environment. New opportunities for pollution abatement are continually being brought to the attention of other agencies. As the wastes from conventional point sources are brought under control or eliminated, the wastes from nonpoint sources come to the forefront as significant problems.

One such area receiving recent attention was related to management practices on Federal lands. In the past year FWQA chaired a Department of the Interior task force established to assess the effect of Federal land management practices on water quality. A pilot review study conducted in Oregon showed a major need and opportunity to reduce water pollution associated with Federal land management practices and conservation measures. The report, *Federal Land Management Practices and Water Quality Control,* found serious damage to the environment stemming from long-established practices, as well as from more recent practices involving pesticides, fertilizers, and other chemical applications. The report specifically identified 12 kinds of land management practices and 22 conservation measures having an impact on water quality. These would be reviewed by agencies and altered whenever necessary to conform with national environmental goals.

Operation Plowshare, the Atomic Energy Commission's program to develop peaceful uses of atomic energy, represents another activity which must be carefully monitored and controlled to avoid unwanted effects on the environment. This program has and will involve nuclear explosions designed to stimulate gas production in oil and gas bearing formations, to fracture mineral formations to enable extraction by leaching, to develop storage for water or other materials. To assure that the program, as planned, provides adequate safeguards for water quality, FWQA provides review and advice to the Commission concerning these experiments. Careful planning of the program, as well as pre- and post-detonation surveillance, is essential because of the potentially great hazards involved.

The Corps of Engineers' dredging activities in the Great Lakes and elsewhere are yet another cause for concern. For more than 100 years the Corps of Engineers has been dredging material from the harbors of the Great Lakes and depositing most of the dredged material in designated dumping areas in the open waters. Growing concern over the resulting effect on the Lakes led to completion last year of a Corps of Engineers' pilot program related to dredging and water quality problems in the Great Lakes. Among the conclusions of the Corps' study were that heavily polluted sediments when transported to the open waters must be considered presumptively undesirable because of their possible long-term effects on the ecology of the Great Lakes, as evidenced by bio-assays of the effects on bottom organisms and plankton, and that disposal in diked areas would be the least costly effective method of withholding pollutants associated with dredgings from the Lakes.

We also must be increasingly alert to the environmental impact of such diverse activities as Forest Service timber sales in Alaska, use of persistent pesticides for quarantine control at Federal airports, and proposed development of oil shale lands in Colorado, Wyoming, and Utah.

Control of Pollution from Federally Licensed and Supported Activities

Closely related to pollution resulting from direct Federal activities, is the environmental impact of the various functions conducted under loans, grants, contracts, leases and permits from the Federal government. These diverse activities range from the nuclear power plants receiving licenses from the Atomic Energy Commission to urban renewal projects financed by the Department of Housing and Urban Development. Combined, these Federally supported and licensed activites constitute a real and potential threat to the environment, which cuts across the full spectrum of the Nation's economic life. They also reflect an unusual opportunity for the Federal government to extend the exercise of its responsibilities for pollution control.

Recent enactment of the Water Quality Improvement Act of 1970 gave further impetus to this trend. The Act provides that any applicant for a Federal permit or license to construct or operate any facility which may result in any discharge into the navigable waters of the United States shall provide certification from the State in which the discharge originates that such facilities or related activities can be expected to comply with applicable water quality standards. The Act further provides that no license or permit shall be granted without such certification and such conditions as the State may reasonably require, including but not limited to provision for suspension or termination of any issued license or permit for failure to be in compliance with applicable water quality standards.

The legislation is clear in its intent that the States are to exercise primary responsibility for the administration of the water quality standards for their waters and for the assurance that State-Federal water quality standards are met by anyone who uses these waters, and that FWQA is to cooperate with other Federal agencies, with State and interstate agencies, and with water users in assuring that appropriate control measures are applied to meet the water quality standards. The legislation provides that the Secretary of the Interior shall provide, upon the request of any Federal department or agency, or State or interstate agency or applicant, any relevant information on applicable water quality standards and comment on any methods of complying with such standards.

FWPCA
Sec. 21(b)

Sec. 21(b) is important, for it may strengthen controls by federal agencies over pollution-causing activities subject to state controls. The AEC, for example, will require compliance with state thermal pollution limitations as a prerequisite to obtaining a permit for the construction of a nuclear power plant.

For regulations concerning state certification of activities requiring a Federal license see 18 C.F.R., Chapter V, Part 615.

For further information concerning state certification see the material in this chapter on the permit system under the Refuse Act of 1899 and the material on state regulation of water pollution.

Sec. 21 (b) is a significant weapon in the arsenal of the environmental lawyer. A recent decision in the Albany County New York Supreme Court is a most enlightening example. The Scenic Hudson Preservation Conference, a conglomeration of citizen groups and local governments, expended seven years in the Federal agency review process and the Federal courts, but eventually lost its battle to prevent Federal approval of a pump storage electric power plant on Storm King Mountain, New York. Final defeat seemed to have come on October 22, 1971 when the Second Circuit Court of Appeals held that the Federal Power Commission's issuance of construction and operation permits to Consolidated Edison Company was based on substantial evidence. This evidence was in the form of a second hearing record over 1900 pages in length, the first hearings having been found inadequate in earlier court actions. (1 ERC 1084) (*See Scenic Hudson Preservation Conference v. Federal Power Commission,* 3 ERC 1132 [2d Cir. 1971] and the materials in Volume Two).

The U.S. Supreme Court on June 20, 1972 refused 8-1, (Justice Douglas dissenting) to review the Court of Appeals' decision. But, in a flanking movement, the environmentalists' attorney's brought Sec. 21 (b) into play.

SCENIC HUDSON PRESERVATION CONFERENCE v. DIAMOND

New York Supreme Court, Albany County, 3 ERC 1903

PITT, J.

Consolidated Edison Company of New York, Inc., sought a Federal license for the construction and operation of facilities known as the Cornwall Project to be constructed on the west bank of the Hudson River in the Village and Towns of Cornwall and Highlands in Orange County, New York. The project is described as a pumped storage hydroelectric generating facility. The purpose of the project is stated to be to supply electricity to the Metropolitan New York Region and the New York Power Pool during periods of peaked demand and during periods of emergency. In its operation the facility, to be the largest in the world, would pump water from the Hudson River at night and on weekends to a storage reservoir and then discharge the water back into the River when generating electicity.

Section 21(b) of the Federal Water Pollution Control Act (33 U.S.C.A. § 1171[b]) provides that an applicant for a federal license to construct or operate facilities which will result in discharge into navigable waters shall provide the licensing agency [The Federal Power Commission in this instance] with a certification from the State that there is "reasonable assurance *** that such activity will be conducted in a manner which will not violate applicable water qualities standards." The noted section continues, "Such State *** shall establish procedures for public notice in the case of all applications for certification by it and to the extent it deems appropriate procedures for public hearings in connection with the specific applications. *** No license *** shall be granted until the certification required by this section has been obtained or has been waived *** No license *** shall be granted if certification has been denied by the State ***."

Thus, reserved to the State by this Federal legislation is the opportunity to consider water qualities standards of the navigable water within its boundaries. This opportunity became an obligation of the Respondent, Commissioner, under Section 15(10)(13) of the Environmental Conservation Law and Section 1210 of the Public Health Law. Pursuant to these sections the Commissioner gave notice of the application pending before him as well as an opportunity for objections to the same to be filed. Apparently, finding that a public hearing was necessary to assist him in his determination the Commissioner, pursuant to discretionary authority contained in Rules and Regulations promulgated by him, ordered that a public hearing be held. (6 NYCRR 611.16[b][I][i][ii] and [2].)

The issues before this Court narrow to a consideration of what questions were to be properly considered by the Respondent, Commissioner, in determining the application before him, and whether or not he erred in granting the noted certificate.

Casting aside certain aesthetic considerations urged by the petitioners the Court finds that properly before the Commissioner were questions of salt water contamination, potential damage to the Catskill Aqueduct, thermal pollution of the waters of the Hudson, as well as the effect of the project upon the fish population of the Hudson and of certain salt water species which spawn in its waters. It is to this Court's mind of no moment that some of these questions may well have been considered at the federal licensing level. These questions clearly concern water quality standards. The Commissioner was then obligated to examine into these questions to determine whether or not the proposed project would in any manner violate existing water quality control standards. He is called upon by statute to certify that there is reasonable assurance that the project would not violate such standards.

It is urged that the Commissioner acted in excess of his jurisdiction and in violation of law. This argument is sound. The report of the Commissioner's Hearing Officer noted that there exists a complete absence of studies concerning salt water contamination. It admitted, also, a lack of assurance that the waters would not be thermally polluted. It recognized that the fish would be killed. The aqueduct problem received no consideration. In short the report to the Commissioner and the Commissioner's determination itself reflected a lack of the "reasonable assurance" that he was thereafter to certify existed. Indeed, and notwithstanding the fact that the noted § 21(b) called for the present existence of reasonable assurance, the Respondent, Commissioner, attempted to provide for the future assurance of the same. This was done by attaching to his certification conditions. In effect these conditions would require Consolidated Edison immediately to terminate the operation of its project upon evidence of "violations or contravention of the water qualities standards assigned to the Hudson River," and specifically noted as areas of concern thermal pollution and salt water intrusion." The monitoring of the project to assure that these conditions were fulfilled was delegated to Consolidated Edison.

It is argued that this delegation of authority by a public agency to a private entity is unlawful. It is also urged that in operation the conditions are impractical to the point of being ridiculous in the light of human experience. Consolidated Edison is by these conditions called upon to police itself and if it finds itself violative of the Commissioner's conditions to abandon immediately its multi-million dollar project. This Court hearing no sound contrary argument and failing to imagine any concludes the conditions to be meaningless in law and in fact.

Certainly, the conditions reflect the lack of the existence of present reasonable assurance. What factual presentation would constitute reasonable assurance may and must be left to the sound determination of the Commissioner. But, this state of assurance must be founded upon something factual. The Commissioner has effectively demonstrated that he did not possess this assurance at the time he issued his certificate. His act, therefore, was in excess of his authority and in violation of law.

The above renders unnecessary specific treatment of other issues and of the Objections in Point of Law seeking dismissal.

Submit accordingly.

As this book went to press, the Appellate Division of New York's Supreme Court reportedly had reversed this decision (June 30, 1972), but an appeal was underway. See, Environment Reporter, Vol. 3, No. 10, July 7, 1972.

COMMENTARY

Secs. 22, 23, 24, 25 and **26** as printed below are edited versions, and not the full texts.

ADMINISTRATION
[Edited]

FWPCA Sec. 22: administration

SEC. 22. (a) The Secretary is authorized to prescribe such regulations as are necessary to carry out his functions under this Act.

(b) The Secretary, with the consent of the head of any other agency of the United States, may utilize such officers and employees of such agency as may be found necessary to assist in carrying out the purposes of this Act.

DEFINITIONS
[Edited]

FWPCA Sec. 23: definitions

SEC. 23. When used in this Act:

(a) The term "State water pollution control agency" means the State health authority, except that, in the case of any State in which there is a single State agency, other than the State health authority, charged with responsibility for enforcing State laws relating to the abatement of water pollution, it means such other State agency.

OTHER AUTHORITY NOT AFFECTED **[Edited]**

FWPCA Sec. 24: other authority not affected

SEC. 24. This Act shall not be construed as (1) superseding or limiting the functions, under any other law, of the Surgeon General or of the Public Health Service, or of any other officer or agency of the United States, relating to water pollution, or (2) affecting or impairing the provisions of sections 13 through 17 of the Act entitled "An Act making appropriations for the construction, repair, and preservation of certain public works on rivers and harbors and for other purposes", approved March 3, 1899, as amended, or (3) affecting or impairing the provisions of any treaty of the United States.

SEPARABILITY **[Edited]**

FWPCA Sec. 25: separability

SEC. 25. If any provision of this Act, or the application of any provision of this Act to any person or circumstance, is held invalid, the application of such provision to other persons or circumstances, and the remainder of this Act, shall not be affected thereby.

FWPCA Sec. 26: information

SEC. 26. (a) In order to provide the basis for evaluating programs authorized by this Act, the development of new programs, and to furnish the Congress with the information necessary for authorization of appropriations for fiscal years beginning after June 30, 1968.

SHORT TITLE

FWPCA Sec. 27: short title

SEC. 27. This Act may be cited as the "Federal Water Pollution Control Act".

j. The Rivers and Harbors Act of 1899

NOTE: As this book goes to press in July of 1972, the enforcement of this Act was in serious doubt due to two recent court decisions concerning a complex permit program for industrial discharges. This is discussed beginning on page Four-118. The reader should also be aware that proposed legislation could alter or supersede all or part of this Act. <u>See</u> Four-36,37.

The Rivers and Harbors Act has in recent years become a major piece of environmental litigation. This is due in part to court interpretations that have made this statute the most stringent Federal water pollution law. At the same time the other major water pollution statute, the Federal Water Quality Act, has been of limited value. Its enforcement procedure requires years to complete. The absence of penalties renders the Water Quality Act nearly useless. When a serious water pollution problem such as industrial dumping of mercury is discovered, the venerable 1899 Act is the most effective tool that the government possesses.

The key section is **407,** which, with Secs. **411** and **413,** is often referred to as the **1899 Refuse Act.** This section forbids the dumping of refuse into any navigable water or tributary of any navigable water. It also forbids the depositing of material on the bank of a navigable waterway where it can be washed into the water and impede navigation. The Act prohibits all pollution discharges except liquid waste from streets and sewers, and activities carried out by the United States as public works.

In *U.S. v. Genoa,* ____ F.2d ____ , W.D. Wisc., 4 ERC 1040 (January 6, 1972), the §407 statutory exception of refuse matter "flowing from streets and sewers and passing therefrom in a liquid state into any navigable water" was found to apply only to municipal sewage and not to industrial waste, even if industrial waste is in liquid form.

Dumping is permissible under conditions specified in a permit issued by the Secretary of the Army (Corps of Engineers). As of early July, 1972, virtually no one had such permits, though a major campaign to place pollutors under the permit system began early in 1971. The failure to have a permit renders the pollutor liable to the penalty provisions of **Sec. 411.**

Other provisions of the Rivers and Harbors Act of 1899 can also be used to protect the environment. Any type of dredge or fill activity or construction in a navigable waterway requires a permit under **Sec. 403.** For an example of the use of this section, see *U.S. v. Moretti,* 331 F.Supp. 151 (S.D.Fla. 1971). The failure to have such a permit can require the removal of the obstruction under Sec. 406. Such a penalty could be very costly. Needless to say, this provision is also applicable to bays, inlets, and estuaries. It is important to recognize that the Corps responsibilities for issuing these permits includes a consideration for environmental values because of the Fish and Wildlife Coordination Act of 1934 as amended (16 U.S.C.A. 661 *et seq*) and the National Environmental Policy Act of 1969.

The **Fish and Wildlife Coordination Act** requires federal agencies proposing water resources projects to consult with the Fish and Wildlife Service of the Department of Interior to protect wildlife. One of the more significant decisions implementing the Act is *Zabel v. Tabb,* 430 F.2d 199, (5th Cir. 1970), 1 ERC 1449. A reading of this case is recommended to the student who will not be studying the Fish and Wildlife Coordination Act with other materials. Wildlife conservation is treated in Volume Two of this work.

Sec. 401 requires governmental approval before a bridge, dam, dike, or causeway can be constructed over navigable water. This provision has been used by environmental groups to attack a proposed highway. See *Citizen's Committee for the Hudson Valley v. Volpe* [302 F.Supp. 1083 (S.D.N.Y. 1969), aff'd 425 F.2d 97 (2d Cir. 1970)].

Sec. 401 has been modified by subsequent legislation to require various people or groups to approve proposed construction. This has resulted in strange inconsistencies in the kinds of approval needed for the different projects.

Bridges must be approved by the Chief of Engineers acting under the Secretary of the Army, as well as the Secretary of Transportation. Specific Congressional consent has not been required since the enactment of the General Bridge Act of 1946 [33 U.S.C. 525].

Dams require the approval of the Chief of Engineers and the Secretary of the Army and the consent of Congress.

Dikes require the approval of the Chief of Engineers and the Secretary of the Army and Congress.

Causeways require the approval of the Secretary of Transportation since the Department of Transportation Act of 1966 [49 U.S.C. 1651 et. seq.] and the consent of Congress.

The authority of the Corps of Engineers to control construction was extended to include the Outer Continental Shelf lands in 1964. [43 U.S.C. 1331-1343].

THE RIVERS AND HARBORS APPROPRIATIONS ACT OF 1899[1]

(Sections 408, 409, 410 and 412 have been omitted.)

§ 401. Construction of bridges, causeways, dams or dikes generally

It shall not be lawful to construct or commence the construction of any bridge, dam, dike, or causeway over or in any port, roadstead, haven, harbor, canal, navigable river, or other navigable water of the United States until the consent of Congress to the building of such structures shall have been obtained and until the plans for the same shall have been submitted to and approved by the Chief of Engineers and by the Secretary of the Army:[2] *Provided,* That such structures may be built under authority of the legislature of a State across rivers and other waterways the navigable portions of which lie wholly within the limits of a single State, provided the location and plans thereof are submitted to and approved by the Chief of Engineers and by the Secretary of the Army before construction is commenced: *And provided further,* That when plans for any bridge or other structure have been approved by the Chief of Engineers and by the Secretary of the Army, it shall not be lawful to deviate from such plans either before or after completion of the structure unless the modification of said plans has previously been submitted to and received the approval of the Chief of Engineers and of the Secretary of the Army.

§ 403. Obstruction of navigable waters generally; wharves; piers, etc.; excavations and filling in

The creation of any obstruction not affirmatively authorized by Congress, to the navigable capacity of any of the waters of the United States is prohibited; and it shall not be lawful to build or commence the building of any wharf, pier, dolphin, boom, weir, breakwater, bulkhead, jetty, or other structures in any port, roadstead, haven, harbor, canal, navigable river, or other water of the United States, outside established harbor lines, or where no harbor lines have been established, except on plans recommended by the Chief of Engineers and authorized by the Secretary of the Army; and it shall not be lawful to excavate or fill, or in any manner to alter or modify the course, location, condition, or capacity of, any port, roadstead, haven, harbor, canal, lake, harbor of refuge, or inclosure within the limits of any breakwater, or of the channel of any navigable water of the United States, unless the work has been recommended by the Chief of Engineers and authorized by the Secretary of the Army prior to beginning the same.

1. 33 U.S.C. §§ 401, 403-4,406-9, 411-15 (1970) (originally enacted as Act of March 3, 1899, ch. 425, 30 Stat. 1151); as amended by Act of February 20, 1900, ch. 23 §§ 243, 31 Stat. 32; Act of March 3, 1911, ch. 231, § 291, 36 Stat. 1167; Act of June 25, 1948, ch. 646, § 1, 62 Stat. 909; Act of June 13, 1902, ch. 1079, § 12, 32 Stat. 375, 33 U.S.C. §§ 407a (1970) (Act of August 5, 1886, ch. 929, § 2, 24 Stat. 329); 33 U.S.C. § 410 (1970) (Act of May 9, 1900, ch. 387 §§ 1-3, 31 Stat. 172).

2. Duties of the Secretary of the Army in regard to location and clearances of bridges and causeways on navigable waterways were transferred to the Secretary of Transportation by P.L. 89-670, Oct. 15, 1966, 80 Stat. 931.

§ 404. Establishment of harbor lines; conditions to grants for extension of piers, etc.

Where it is made manifest to the Secretary of the Army that the establishment of harbor lines is essential to the preservation and protection of harbors he may, and is, authorized to cause such lines to be established, beyond which no piers, wharves, bulkheads, or other works shall be extended or deposits made, except under such regulations as may be prescribed from time to time by him: *Provided*, That whenever the Secretary of the Army grants to any person or persons permission to extend piers, wharves, bulkheads, or other works, or to make deposits in any tidal harbor or river of the United States beyond any harbor lines established under authority of the United States, he shall cause to be ascertained the amount of tidewater displaced by any such structure or by any such deposits, and he shall, if he deem it necessary, require the parties to whom the permission is given to make compensation for such displacement either by excavating in some part of the harbor, including tidewater channels between high and low water mark, to such an extent as to create a basin for as much tidewater as may be displaced by such structure or by such deposits, or in any other mode that may be satisfactory to him.

§ 406. Penalty for wrongful construction of bridges, piers, etc.; removal of structures

Every person and every corporation that shall violate any of the provisions of sections 401, 403, and 404 of this title or any rule or regulation made by the Secretary of the Army in pursuance of the provisions of section 404 of this title shall be deemed guilty of a misdemeanor, and on conviction thereof shall be punished by a fine not exceeding $2,500 nor less than $500, or by imprisonment (in the case of a natural person) not exceeding one year, or by both such punishments, in the discretion of the court. And further, the removal of any structures or parts of structures erected in violation of the provisions of the said sections may be enforced by the injunction of any district court exercising jurisdiction in any district in which such structures may exist, and proper proceedings to this end may be instituted under the direction of the Attorney General of the United States.

§ 407. Deposit of refuse in navigable waters generally

It shall not be lawful to throw, discharge, or deposit, or cause, suffer, or procure to be thrown, discharged, or deposited either from or out of any ship, barge, or other floating craft of any kind, or from the shore, wharf, manufacturing establishment, or mill of any kind, any refuse matter of any kind or description whatever other than that flowing from streets and sewers and passing therefrom in a liquid state, into any navigable water of the United States, or into any tributary of any navigable water from which the same shall float or be washed into such navigable water; and it shall not be lawful to deposit, or cause, suffer, or procure to be deposited material of any kind in any place on the bank of any navigable water, or on the bank of any tributary of any navigable water, where the same shall be liable to be washed into such navigable water, either by ordinary or high tides, or by storms or floods, or otherwise, whereby navigation shall or may be impeded or obstructed: *Provided*, That nothing herein contained shall extend to, apply to, or prohibit the operations in connection with the improvement of navigable waters or construction of public works, considered necessary and proper by the United States officers supervising such improvement or public work: *And provided further*, That the Secretary of the Army, whenever in the judgment of the Chief of Engineers anchorage and navigation will not be injured thereby, may permit the deposit of any material above mentioned in navigable waters, within limits to be defined and under conditions to be prescribed by him, provided application is made to him prior to depositing such material; and whenever any permit is so granted the conditions thereof shall be strictly complied with, and any violation thereof shall be unlawful.

§ 407a. Deposit of debris of mines and stamp works

In places where harbor-lines have not been established, and where deposits of debris of mines or stamp works can be made without injury to navigation, within lines to be established by the Secretary of the Army, said officer may, and is authorized to, cause such lines to be established; and within such lines such deposits may be made, under regulations to be from time to time prescribed by him. **Aug. 5,** 1886, c. 929, § 2, 24 Stat. 329.

§ 411. Penalty for wrongful deposit of refuse; use of or injury to harbor improvements, and obstruction of navigable waters generally

Every person and every corporation that shall violate, or that shall knowingly aid, abet, authorize, or instigate a violation of the provisions of sections 407, 408, and 409 of this title shall be guilty of a misdemeanor, and on conviction thereof shall be punished by a fine not exceeding $2,500 nor less than $500, or by imprisonment (in the case of a natural person) for not less than thirty days nor more than one year, or by both such fine and imprisonment, in the discretion of the court, one-half of said fine to be paid to the person or persons giving information which shall lead to conviction.

§ 413. Duty of United States attorneys and other Federal officers in enforcement of provisions; arrest of offenders

The Department of Justice shall conduct the legal proceedings necessary to enforce the provisions of sections 401, 403, 404, 406, 407, 408, 409, 411, 549, 686, and 687 of this title; and it shall be the duty of United States attorneys to vigorously prosecute all offenders against the same whenever requested to do so by the Secretary of the Army or by any of the officials hereinafter designated, and it shall furthermore be the duty of said United States attorneys to report to the Attorney General of the United States the action taken by him against offenders so reported, and a transcript of such reports shall be transmitted to the Secretary of the Army by the Attorney General; and for the better enforcement of the said provisions and to facilitate the detection and bringing to punishment of such offenders, the officers and agents of the United States in charge of river and harbor improvements, and the assistant engineers and inspectors employed under them by authority of the Secretary of the Army, and the United States collectors of customs and other revenue officers shall have power and authority to swear out process, and to arrest and take into custody, with or without process, any person or persons who may commit any of the acts or offenses prohibited by the said sections, or who may violate any of the provisions of the same: *Provided,* That no person shall be arrested without process for any offense not committed in the presence of some one of the aforesaid officials: *And provided further,* That whenever any arrest is made under such sections, the person so arrested shall be brought forthwith before a commissioner, judge, or court of the United States for examination of the offenses alleged against him; and such commissioner, judge, or court shall proceed in respect thereto as authorized by law in case of crimes against the United States.

NOTE: Several other statutes provide protection for specific harbors. See for example: 33 U.S.C. 441 and 451-454 which applies to New York, Baltimore, and Hampton Roads, (Act of June 29, 1888 25 Stat. 209); 33 U.S.C. 421 which applies to Lake Michigan near Chicago.

UNITED STATES v. STANDARD OIL CO.

No. 384 U.S. Supreme Court,
decided May 23, 1966

[Edited]

MR. JUSTICE DOUGLAS delivered the opinion of the Court.

The question presented for decision is whether the statutory ban on depositing "any refuse matter of any kind or description" [1] in a navigable water covers the discharge of commercially valuable aviation gasoline.

The indictment charged appellee, Standard Oil (Kentucky), with violating § 13 by allowing to be discharged into the St. Johns River "refuse matter" consisting of 100-octane aviation gasoline. Appellee moved to dismiss the indictment, and, for the purposes of the motion, the parties entered into a stipulation of fact. It states that the gasoline was commercially valuable and that it was discharged into the St. Johns only because a shut-off valve at dockside had been "accidentally" left open.

From an examination of these statutes, several points are clear. *First,* the 1894 Act and its antecedent, the 1888 Act applicable to the New York Harbor,[4] drew on their face no distinction between valuable and valueless substances. *Second,* of the enumerated substances, some may well have had commercial or industrial value prior to discharge into the covered waterways. To be more specific, ashes and acids were banned whether or not they had any remaining commercial or industrial value. *Third,* these Acts applied not only to the enumerated substances but also to the discharge of "any other matter of any kind." Since the enumerated substances included those with a pre-discharge value, the rule of *ejusdem generis* does not require limiting this latter category to substances lacking a pre-discharge value. *Fourth,* the coverage of these Acts was not diminished by the codification of 1899. The use of the term "refuse" in the codification serves in the place of the lengthy list of enumerated substances found in the earlier Acts and the catch-all provision found in the Act of 1890. The legislative history demonstrates without contradiction that Congress intended to codify without substantive change the earlier Acts.

The philosophy of those antecedent laws seems to us to be clearly embodied in the present law. It is plain from its legislative history that the "serious injury" to our watercourses (S. Rep. No. 224, 50th Cong., 1st Sess., p. 2) sought to be remedied was caused in part by obstacles that impeded navigation and in part by pollution—"the discharge of sawmill waste into streams" (*ibid.*) and the injury of channels by "deposits of ballast, steam-boat ashes, oysters, and rubbish from passing vessels." *Ibid.* The list is obviously not an exhaustive list of pollutants. The words of the Act are broad and inclusive: "any refuse matter of any kind or description whatever." Only one exception is stated: "other than that flowing from streets and sewers and passing therefrom in a liquid state, into any navigable water of the United States." More comprehensive language would be difficult to select. The word "refuse" does not stand alone; the "refuse" banned is "of any kind or description whatever," apart from the one exception noted. And, for the reasons already stated, the meaning we must give the term "refuse" must reflect the present codification's statutory antecedents.

That seems to us to be the common sense of the matter. The word "refuse" includes all foreign substances and pollutants apart from those "flowing from streets and sewers and passing therefrom in a liquid state" into the watercourse.

We pass only on the quality of the pollutant, not on the quantity of proof necessary to support a conviction nor on the question as to what *scienter* requirement the Act imposes, as those questions are not before us in this restricted appeal.[6]

Reversed.

MR. JUSTICE HARLAN, whom MR. JUSTICE BLACK and MR. JUSTICE STEWART join, dissenting.

The best that can be said for the Government's case is that the reach of the provision of § 13 of the Rivers and Harbors Act of 1899, 30 Stat. 1152,

[4] The codification did not include the Acts of 1886 and 1888 which pertained only to New York. These remain in effect and are found at 33 U. S. C. §§ 441–451 (1964 ed.). The New York Harbor statute has been held to apply not only to waste oil which was unintentionally discharged (*The Albania,* 30 F. 2d 727) but also to valuable oil negligently discharged. *The Colombo,* 42 F. 2d 211.

[6] "Having dealt with the construction placed by the court below upon the Sherman Act, our jurisdiction on this appeal is exhausted. We are not at liberty to consider other objections to the indictment or questions which may arise upon the trial with respect to the merits of the charge. For it is well settled that where the District Court has based its decision on a particular construction of the underlying statute, the review here under the Criminal Appeals Act is confined to the question of the propriety of that construction." *United States v. Borden Co.,* 308 U. S. 188, 206–207.

33 U. S. C. § 407 (1964 ed.), under which this indictment is laid, is uncertain. This calls into play the traditional rule that penal statutes are to be strictly construed. In my opinion application of that rule requires a dismissal of the indictment.

Whatever might be said about how properly to interpret the 1890 and, more especially, the 1894 statutes, it is the 1899 Act that has been on the books for the last 67 years, and its purposes and language must guide the determination of this case. To the extent that there were some differences in scope between the 1890 and 1894 Acts, these were necessarily resolved in the 1899 codification, which, while embodying the essential thrust of both prior statutes, appears from its plain language to have favored the more restrictive coverage of the 1890 Act. Moreover, it is questionable to what extent the Court's speculation as to the meaning of a phrase in one of the prior statutes is relevant at all when the language of the present statute, which is penal in nature, is in itself explicit and unambiguous.

The purpose of § 13 was essentially to eliminate obstructions to navigation and interference with public works projects. This 1899 enactment, like the two preexisting statutes which it was intended to codify, was a minor section attached to a major appropriation act together with other measures dealing with sunken wrecks,[1] trespassing at public works sites,[2] and obstructions caused by improperly constructed bridges, piers, and other structures.[3] These statutes were rendered necessary primarily because navigable rivers, which the Congress was appropriating funds to improve, were being obstructed by depositing of waste materials by factories and ships.[4] It is of course true, as the Court observes, that "oil is oil," *ante,* p. 226, and that the accidental spillage of valuable oil may have substantially the same "deleterious effect on waterways" as the wholesale depositing of waste oil. But the relevant inquiry is not the admittedly important concerns of pollution control, but Congress' purpose in enacting this anti-obstruction Act, and that appears quite plainly to be a desire to halt through the imposition of criminal penalties the depositing of obstructing refuse matter in rivers and harbors.

The Court's construction eschews the everyday meaning of "refuse matter"—waste, rubbish, trash, debris, garbage, see Webster's New International Dictionary, 3d ed.—and adopts instead an approach that either reads "refuse" out of the Act altogether, or gives to it a tortured meaning.

A more important contemporary purpose of the notion of strict construction is to give notice of what the law is, in order to guide people in their everyday activities. Again, however, it is difficult to justify a narrow reading of § 13 on this basis. The spilling of oil of any type into rivers is not something one would be likely to do whether or not it is legally proscribed by a federal statute. A broad construction would hardly raise dangers of penalizing people who have been innocently pouring valuable oil into navigable waters, for such conduct in Florida is unlawful whatever the effect of § 13. A Florida statute penalizing as a misdemeanor the depositing into waters within the State of "any rubbish, filth, or poisonous or deleterious substance or substances, liable to affect the health of persons, fish, or live stock . . . ," Fla. Stat. Ann., § 387.08 (1960 ed.), quite evidently reaches the dumping of commercial oil. And Florida's nuisance law would likewise seem to make this conduct actionable in equity.

Justice Holmes declared that "Although it is not likely that a criminal will carefully consider the text of the law before he murders or steals, it is reasonable that a fair warning should be given to the world in language that the common world will understand, of what the law intends to do if a certain line is passed." 283 U. S., at 27. The policy thus expressed is based primarily on a notion of fair play: in a civilized state the least that can be expected of government is that it express its rules in language all can reasonably be expected to understand. Moreover, this requirement of clear expression is essential in a practical sense to confine the discretion of prosecuting authorities, particularly important under a statute such as § 13 which imposes criminal penalties with a minimal, if any, *scienter* requirement.

In an area in which state or local law has traditionally regulated primary activity, there is good reason to restrict federal penal legislation within the confines of its language. If the Federal Government finds that there is sufficient obstruction or pollution of navigable waters caused by the introduction of commercial oil or other nonrefuse material, it is an easy matter to enact appropriate regulatory or penal legislation. Such legislation can be directed at specific types of pollution, and the remedies devised carefully to ensure compliance. Indeed, such a statute was enacted in 1924 to deal with oil pollution in coastal waters caused by vessels, 43 Stat. 605, 33 U. S. C. §§ 433, 434 (1964 ed.).

To conclude that this attempted prosecution cannot stand is not to be oblivious to the importance of preserving the beauties and utility of the country's rivers. It is simply to take the statute as we find it. I would affirm the judgment of the District Court.

---

[1] Rivers and Harbors Act of 1899, § 15, 30 Stat. 1152, 33 U. S. C. 409 (1964 ed.).

[2] Rivers and Harbors Act of 1899, § 14, 30 Stat. 1152, 33 U. S. C. 408 (1964 ed.).

[3] Rivers and Harbors Act of 1899, § 12, 30 Stat. 1151, 33 U. S. C. 406 (1964 ed.).

[4] Congress was presented, when considering one of the predecessors the 1899 Act, with the representations of the Office of the Chief Army Engineers that there had been "serious injury to navigable aters by the discharge of sawmill waste into streams . . . . In ir-ways of harbors, channels are injured from deposits of ballast, eam-boat ashes, oysters, and rubbish from passing vessels." S. Rep. o. 224, 50th Cong., 1st Sess., 2 (1888). See also H. R. Rep. No. 26, 55th Cong., 3d Sess., 3–4 (1899). There is no support for the oposition that these statutes were directed at "pollution" independently of "obstruction."

U.S. v. ESSO

375 F.2d 621 (3rd Cir. March 27, 1967)

[Edited]

Staley, Chief Judge.

Esso Standard Oil Company of Puerto Rico (hereinafter "Esso") was convicted on two charges of the offense of discharging refuse into navigable waters in violation of §13 of the Rivers and Harbors Act, 33 U.S.C.A. §407 (1957), and was fined $1,000 for each violation. The trial judge, sitting without a jury, found that on two occasions, Esso had caused liquid petroleum products to be spilled upon its land, that these products flowed over the ground into the ocean, and that such conduct violated §13, and that there was insufficient evidence before the trial judge to support the convictio

During the latter part of December, 1964, some of the persons living along the coast near Esso's tank farm complained to the Coast Guard that Esso was causing petroleum pollution in the adjoining coastal waters. On December 23, 1964, one of the neighbors, Admiral John H Schultz (Ret.) called the Coast Guard to complain of renewed pollution, and asked that one of the Coast Guardsmen meet him at the Esso tank farm. Then Admiral Schultz and Mr. Theodore Smejkal, operator of a nearby resort, went over to Esso's establishment.

At the trial, both Admiral Schultz and Mr. Smejkal testified that they observed and photographed heavy spillage of a clear, irridescent petroleum product at the Esso tank farm. Their pictures, introduced into evidence, show this spillage running from the area where Esso's pumps are located, across the road in front of Esso's establishment, down the side of the distillery's apron, and through a hole cut in the curbing of the apron and thence to the rocks below and the sea. The oil remaining on the road, the apron and in pools between the rocks below the apron was described as clear. Admiral Schultz testified that when he said to the Esso attendant that the attendant had spilled kerosene, the attendant replied, "No, it is diesel oil."

A member of the Coast Guard testified that he had responded to the various complaints, and had visited the Esso tank farm pursuant thereto to try to correct the problem. While the Coast Guardsman was not able to verify the pollution of the 23rd of December because he arrived too late in the day, he did testify that there was evidence of pollution about the premises and the shore when he visited the tank farm on the 29th of December.

On the basis of the testimony before him, the district judge denied Esso's motions for acquittal and found Esso guilty on both counts. A motion for a new trial was denied, and sentences were imposed.

Esso argued in the district court and on appeal that it could not have violated §13 of the Rivers and Harbors Act as a matter of law.

Esso urges that the remoteness of its activities from the shoreline isolates it from liability under the Act. As Esso points out, §13 creates two separate offenses: (1) the discharge of refuse into any navigable water, and (2) the deposit of material on the bank of navigable water where it is likely that the material will be washed into the water and impede or obstruct navigation. Both Esso and the United States agreed here that Esso did not violate the second clause because there is no suggestion that navigation was impeded or obstructed. Esso further argues that the first clause of §13 contemplates only "direct" discharges of refuse into navigable water, and that therefore the evidence showing the remote spillage of a liquid petroleum peoduct and the flow of this liquid over a road and another company's property and into the sea does not establish a violation of the first clause of §13.

We cannot agree with Esso's construction of §13. Just last year the Supreme Court, holding that 100-octane gasoline was refuse within §13, announced that §13 must not be given a "narrow, cramped reading" to defeat its purposes.

It seems clear to us that the first clause of §13 does reach "indirect" deposits of refuse in navigable water. This first clause expressly proscribes the deposit of refuse into non-navigable water where the refuse will in turn wash into navigable water. That other "indirect" deposits are within the contemplation of the first clause is clearly implied by the express exemption of one type of indirect deposit--the collection and discharge of sewage, i.e., "refuse *** flowing from streets and sewers and passing therefrom in a liquid state, into any navigable water *** or tributary of any navigable water **." United States v. Republic Steel Corp., 362 U.S. at 490-491, 80 S.Ct. 884. Here, though Esso did not run a pipe to the water's edge and discharge petroleum products directly into the sea. Esso's discharge of the oil was in such close proximity to the sea that the oil flowed there by gravity alone. While there may be cases where the defense of remoteness would be available, this is not such a case. To accept the construction urged upon us by Esso would indeed constitute the adoption of a technical or "cramped" reading of the section contrary to the mandate of the Supreme Court, supra.

Esso also argues that the Government's evidence was insufficient to support a criminal conviction. The findings of fact by the trial judge are supported by adequate testimony and we will not interfere with them on appeal. Government of the Virgin Islands v. Du Boyce, 4 V.I. 107, 267 F.2d 512 (C.A.3, 1959).

The judgment of the district court will be affirmed.

U.S. v. INTERLAKE STEEL CORP.

329 F.Supp. 339 (N.D. Ill. March 27, 1969) 1 ERC 1045
[Edited]

MEMORANDUM AND ORDER ON DEFENDANT'S MOTION TO DISMISS THE INFORMATION

The information in this criminal prosecution charges the defendant, Interlake Steel Corporation, with discharging iron particles and an oily substance into the Little Calumet River on June 3, 1968, in violation of Section 13 of the Rivers and Harbors Act of 1899. 33 U.S.C. §407. The defendant has moved this court to dismiss the information on three grounds. For the reasons set forth below, this court is of the opinion that the motion should be denied.

The defendant first contends that the information is fatally defective because it fails to allege that this prosecution was undertaken at the request of the Secretary of the Army, the United States Corps of Engineers, or any other officer authorized to do so under the provision of Section 17 of the Act. 33 U.S.C. §413. Section 17 directs the United States Attorney to vigorously prosecute violators of the Act whenever requested to do so by certain named federal officials and agencies whose responsibility it is to enforce the Act. The defendant contends that the United States Attorney is powerless to enforce the criminal sanctions of the Act absent a request by one of the officials or agencies enumerated in Section 17.

The court notes that in its response, the Government indicates that the information leading to this prosecution was furnished by the United States Coast Guard, a federal agency vested with the duty of protecting the navigable waters of the United States. Although the Coast Guard is not among those agencies fixed with the responsibility of enforcing the Rivers and Harbors Act by Section 17, enforceability of the Act clearly should not rest upon the fortuity of which particular federal agency, with jurisdiction over the navigable waters of the United States, detects a violation and reports it to the United States Attorney. Furthermore, it appears that in at least one recent successful prosecution under Section 13, detection and prosecutorial information was provided by the Coast Guard. United States v. Esso Standard Oil Company of Puerto Rico, 375 F.2d 621 (3rd Cir. 1967). For these reasons, this court finds that the information alleges the requisite elements and essential facts of a violation of Section 11 of the Rivers and Harbors Act of 1899. Rule 7(c), Federal Rules of Criminal Procedure.

Secondly, it is asserted that the information is fatally defective because it fails to allege that the defendant violated the Act willfully, intentionally, knowingly or negligently. Section 16 does not require any element of *scienter* be shown for conviction of a substantive Section 13 offense, although knowledge is a required element of an aiding and abetting offense. Depositing refuse in navigable waters is the <u>malum prohibitum</u> [3] constituting a violation of Section 13. Even indirect discharges of refuse into navigable waters have been held to violate the Act.

The Regulations invoked here by the defendant state that it is the long-standing and established policy of the Corps of Engineers not to take any action where the alleged violation is "minor, unintentional or accidental" and, "as a general rule," not to recommend prosecution where the alleged violation is "trivial, apparently unpremeditated and results in no material public injury." Prosecution is recommended "in all cases of willful or intentional violations." 33 C.F.R. §§209.395 and 209.400. These policy statements are not conclusively binding on the Corps of Engineers in their own administrative proceedings, and certainly do not establish a basis for requiring the Government to allege in its information that the violation was not "minor, unintentional, nor accidental." For these reasons, this court concludes that the information is not fatally defective because it does not contain an allegation regarding <u>scienter</u>.

As the third and final ground for dismissing this prosecution, the defendant asserts that the information fails to state an offense against the United States. The defendant contends that Section 13 of the Rivers and Harbors Act is superceded and modified by the provisions of the Water Quality Act of 1965. 33 U.S.C.A. §466 <u>et seq</u>. The latter statute provides that the Secretary of the Interior shall set water quality criteria for the interstate waters of the nation either by approving water quality standards submitted by a State or by his own regulation. 33 U.S.C.A. §466g. The defendant's interpretation of this statute, which this court cannot accept, would relax the prohibitions against discharging refuse into the nation's waters as proscribed by the Rivers and Harbors Act, by invoking legislation clearly intended to secure <u>higher</u> water quality standards. The statute itself negates such an interpretation. Standards set by a state agency must be consistent with any applicable water quality standards established pursuant to current law within a given river, lake, etc. 33 U.S.C.A. §466b(c)(2)(A). Discharge of matter prohibited by the Rivers and Harbors Act cannot be condoned under the standards set by a state agency pursuant to the Water Quality Act.

It is the defendant's position that "the Water Quality Act is meaningless if one arm of the federal government can commence criminal proceedings and get a conviction while the defendant is all the while in compliance with the modern, up-to-date standards for water pollution control set by another arm of government." This court observes, without so ruling, that the conduct complained

---

3 "***[A]n act which is not inherently immoral, but becomes so because its commission is expressly forbidden by positive law... Contrasted with <u>malum in se</u>." Black's Law Dictionary 1112 (4th ed. 1957.)

of by the United States Attorney appears to also be in violation with the announced quality standards of the Illinois State Water Board. In order to "accommodate" the defendant, this court would be required to repeal an Act of Congress and reverse a decision of the Supreme Court. Nowhere in the Water Quality Act and its legislative history can this court find any congressional intent to repeal or modify the Rivers and Harbors Act. To the contrary, the Water Pollution Control Act of 1956, to which the Water Quality Act of 1965 is an amendment, states that 33 U.S.C. §§ 466-466k shall not be construed "as affecting or impairing the provisions of...§407...of this title," i.e., Section 13 of the Rivers and Harbors Act. 33 U.S.C. §466k. For these reasons, this court finds that the information states an offense against the United States.

It is therefore ordered that the motion to dismiss the information be, and it is hereby denied.

Note For other cases supporting this decision see:
U.S. v. Maplewood Poultry, ___F.Supp.___ (N. Div. Maine 1971) 2 ERC 16
U.S. v. U.S. Steel, ___F.Supp.___ (N. Dist. Ind. 1970) 2 ERC 1700
U.S. v. Vulcan Materials, ___F.Supp.___ (D.C.N.J. 1970) 2 ERC 1145
U.S. v. Armco Steel, ___F.Supp.___ (S.D.Tex. 1971) 3 ERC 1067

U.S. permits program

The Refuse Act is simple and nearly all inclusive. Virtually any discharge into any water is a violation of the Act and subjects the pollutor to civil and criminal penalties. The way to avoid these sanctions is to obtain a permit under section 13 of the Act (33 U.S.C. 407) from the Secretary of the Army, acting through the Corps of Engineers.

This permit authority has long been neglected. In the period beginning with the passage of the Act in 1899 and ending in May of 1971, only 415 permits were granted. Half of these permits had expired and were never renewed. In 22 states no permits had ever been issued.*

In December of 1970 President Nixon called for the initiation of a permit program. In April of 1971 regulations governing this program were issued. The following is from President Nixon's "Statement on the Army Corps of Engineer's Permit Program Under the Refuse Act for Water Quality Enforcement Purposes," December 23, 1970:

> I have today directed the establishment of a Federal permit program covering facilities which discharge waste into navigable waters and their tributaries in the United States. * * * To deal with those who are disregarding our pollution control laws, a swift and comprehensive enforcement mechanism is provided by this authority. * * * I wish to make clear that although the Refuse Act generally does not apply to municipal discharges, we will continue to vigorously employ other authorities for dealing with violations of water quality standards by municipalities.

End Quote.

The following is from *The Wall Street Journal,* June 5, 1972 at 13:

> . . .after 15 years of negotiations, hearings and conferences, the Environmental Protection Agency is asking the Justice Department to take Kansas City, Kan., to court. It would be only the second time that Uncle Sam has sued a municipality over water pollution.

End quote. The reader should be aware that proposed Federal legislation would supersede all or parts of these laws. *See* pp. Four-36-37.

*The New Republic, Comment, *Water Pollution,* p. 8 (March 27, 1971).

As of October 30, 1971, the Corps reported that 20,000 applications for industrial waste permits had been received, and that about 8,300 had been processed and sent on to EPA and the state agencies for processing there. [*Environment Reporter,* Current Developments, at 795] Industry is complaining about the amount and nature of the data required and is questioning its relevance. Estimates of the number of permit applications to be received run as high as 300,000.

The Corps is confident that these applications can be processed expeditiously, but this seems unlikely. The numerous agencies that must comment on the applications, the expected lack of cooperation from many states, and the possible public hearings, will combine to result in a processing time that could run as long as four years. For these reasons a new program is likely to be created. Senate Bill S.2770 which was passed by the Senate on November 2, 1971 would create effluent controls. The permit system would be run by EPA but would delegate authority to the States as long as the program met the requirements of the Federal Act.

Nevertheless, at the present time, permits are unavailable; processing of applications was continuing, but approval was being postponed. The only aspect of this program that is certain is that it will continue to change. For information on the status of the permit program, the reader is advised to consult the Army Corps of Engineers in Washington (*see* p. Introduction-87) or at one of the regional offices. The Corps has been publishing detailed forms and instructions concerning permits. but the changes have been so rapid as to make their publication here foolish.

An excerpt from a U.S. district court decision currently under appeal, *Kalur v. Resor,* is given below. Other aspects of this case are treated elsewhere in this book. Be sure to read the materials following this case.

KALUR v. RESOR

___F.Supp.___(D.C.D. Dec. 16, 1971), 3 ERC 1456

[Edited]

This is an action brought by plaintiffs for declaratory judgment and injunctive relief under the provisions of 28 U.S.C. Sections 2201, 2202. This jurisdiction of this Court is invoked under 28 U.S.C. Section 1331, and 5 U.S.C. Sections 702, 706. Plaintiffs Jerome S. Kalur and Donald Large are consistent users of the Grand River in Northeastern Ohio. They use the river for numerous conservational and recreational activities. This suit is brought by them on behalf of all persons and conservation groups that are similarly situated. Defendants Resor, Ruckelshaus, and Clark are duly appointed United States Government employees and are respectively, Secretary of the Army, Administrator of the Environmental Protective Agency, and Chief of Engineers for the Army Corps of Engineers.

The suit requires the interpretation of The Rivers and Harbors Act of 1899, Section 13 (Refuse Act). This section prohibits the discharge of refuse into any navigable water, or tributary of any navigable water. The same section provides that the Secretary of the Army may permit the deposit of "refuse" in navigable waters. In 1971, pursuant to Executive Order Number 11574, the Corps of Engineers, Department of the Army, promulgated regulations covering the issuance of these permits. These regulations included the power to issue permits to dump "refuse" into navigable waters of the United States and into any tributary where its flow would reach a navigable water.

Plaintiffs aver that the defendants have exceeded their statutory authority, and continue to do so, in issuing permits under the terms of these regulations. Plaintiffs claim that the defendants have absolutely no authority or right to order the issuance of permits to deposit "refuse" matter into non-navigable waterways of the United States and the Grand River of Ohio in particular.

In addition to the above, plaintiffs complaint alleges a further violation of environmental laws on the part of defendants. The National Environmental Policy Act states that all agencies of the federal government shall . . . "include in every recommendation or report on proposals for legislation and other major Federal actions significantly affecting the quality of the human environment, a detailed statement by the responsible official" on the environmental impact of the proposed action, any adverse environmental effects which cannot be avoided should the proposal be implemeted, alternatives to the proposed action, the relationship between local short-term use of man's environment and the maintenance and enhancement of long-term productivity, and any irreversible and irretrievable commitments of resources that would be involved in the proposed action should it be implemented. This Act, the plaintiffs state, is subverted and violated by the regulations issued by the Corps of Army Engineers wherein they exempt the Corps from making such a detailed statement in all cases where the question is solely one of water quality.

The defendants deny that they have acted in excess of their statutory authority or in violation of the National Environmental Policy Act. There being no questions of fact in dispute the parties have briefed the issues of law. These issues are now before this Court for determination on cross motions for Summary Judgment. It is the finding of this Court that the defendants have acted in excess of their statutory authority and also, in violation of the National Environmental Policy Act. [For portions of this decision relating to the National Environmental Policy Act, *see* pp. Appendix One-34-37.]

Defendants next allege the lack of a case or controversy. In deciding whether a case or controversy exists, one must look to the rigorous set of rules as to what constitutes a justifiable case or controversy as laid down by the Supreme Court. The judicial power of this Court extends to all cases and controversies as designated under our Constitution. Cases, however, are not to be decided in a vacuum. The judicial power may be applied only in those instances where questions arise in a case or controversy. A "controversy" in the constitutional sense must be one that is appropriate for judicial determination. A justifiable controversy is thus distinguished from a difference or dispute of a hypothetical or abstract character; from one that is academic or moot. The controversy must be definite and concrete, touching legal relations of parties having adverse legal interests. Controversies must be real and substantial, admitting of specific relief through a decree of a conclusive character. This distinguishes them from advisory opinion on what the law would be upon a hypothetical state of facts. Courts must limit their decisions to concrete cases where questions are precisely framed in clashes of genuine adversary argument that explores the penumbra of every issue. Focusing on the key elements, it is imperative that Courts look to the nature of the case before them, the interests of the parties involved, and the relief sought by them in determining whether they may extend their judicial power to the case. All three factors are inexorably intertwined in the decision.

As examined above, the legal interests involved in this case are sufficient to meet the standards of a "case and controversy." The government argues that this is not a situation meeting the requirements for a "case and controversy." They point to alleged vagueness of the facts and lack of injury to the plaintiffs. The defendants note that the public issues are of such importance and complexity that they should not be decided on speculative facts as an abstract question.

Further, defendants state that no permits have been issued under the regulations in dispute, and no dumping of refuse has occurred due to such permits that would injure the plaintiffs' interests. The defendants call for judicial restraint to await the developments of the permit program. They aver that plaintiffs may bring any objections to the permit program before the Corps of Engineers when they hold hearing on the issuance of particular permits.

Defendants' arguments are without merit. It remains unchallenged that the regulations have been promulgated. There is contemplated no further action by the Corps of Engineers as to their content or expense. The Supreme Court, in *Abbott Laboratories* v. *Gardner*, upheld the availability of pre-enforcement judicial review of a regulation challenged as promulgated in excess of a government agent's authority under the law. There the Supreme Court rejected the same arguments forwarded here by defendants, and held that the issues were appropriate for judicial resolution because the issues were solely legal, and no further administrative rulemaking procedures were contemplated. Unless there is a showing of clear and convincing evidence that Congress did not want judicial review of this question, then aggrieved persons may obtain review of administrative decisions. The fact that hearings are to be held upon some individual applications for permits does not aid the person who desires to challenge the authority of the agency to issue those permits initially.

In *Toilet Goods Association* v. *Gardner*, the Supreme Court set out two conditions that need be met to determine reviewability. First, are the tendered issues appropriate for judicial review? Second, what is the hardship to the parties should review be denied? Here, *Abbott Labs* dictates the answer to the first condition. The issues are appropriate for review. The hardship to the parties, if review should be denied, is explicitly suggested by the revelation that twelve corporations have either submitted applications for permits to dump refuse into the Grand River, or have noted their intent to do so. If permits to dump are issued, the aesthetic and environmental interests recognized by the Courts as protectable would be infringed by water pollution. The hardship that would be caused by delay at this juncture clearly outweighs any of the contentions put forth by the defendants.

The issue presented to this Court is purely a legal one. The regulations constitute final agency action. An administrative agency's regulations may have the force of law both before and after their sanctions are invoked. As evidenced by the briefs presented here, the validity of the regulations themselves is a question that brings these adverse parties before the Court. The regulations herein challenged authorize the Corps of Engineers to issue permits for the Grand River in Ohio and other non-navigable waterways. Plaintiffs claim this is beyond their statutory power under the Rivers and Harbors Act and the National Environmental Policy Act. These are the legal questions needing no further factual context in which to be decided. There is no indication of Congressional intent that would prevent judicial review of the regulations at this or any other time. Moreover, this controversy is definite, concrete, and touching on the legal relations of the parties who have adverse legal interests. Specific relief is available to the plaintiffs. Furthermore, this is not based upon a hypothetical state of facts or presented in an abstract form. Defendants readily admit that twelve companies have or intend to ask for permits to dump in the very river that plaintiffs seek to protect. The imminence of harm that flows from implementation of these regulations permits this Court to conclude that a "case and controversy" exists.

Kalur v. Resor

III

Defendants request that this suit be dismissed as it is an unconsented suit against the United States. They state that if the relief sought would expend itself on the public treasury or require affirmative action or inaction by the Federal officers in the performance of their official duties, the suit is in effect a suit against the sovereign. They note that since defendants are asked to account for their actions performed in their official capacities the relief sought would operate directly against the United States.

In the present case plaintiffs claim that the various named government officials have acted outside of and in excess of any statutory authority conferred upon them. Such a claim clearly takes this action outside the scope of sovereign immunity, for if the plaintiffs' claim proves true, the actions of the defendants must be considered individual rather than soverign acts. The defendants readily admit that sovereign immunity does not apply if the exercise or power in a particular case by a government official is constitutionally void. The defendants state, however, that this exception to the rule does not apply here, as they can find no showing in the complaint that any of the alleged actions of the defendants are beyond the scope of statutory powers or unconstitutional by virtue of being done under an unconstitutional statute. The clear reading of the complaint establishes beyond a reasonable doubt that this is the very allegation being made by the plaintiffs. This is the exact question to be reached on the merits of this case. Have these federal officers acted outside their statutory powers, or if acting within those powers, have they exercised those powers in this case in a constitutionally void manner? Sovereign immunity is not a bar to this action.

Defendants allege that this is an injunction suit against the Federal Government, and as such, the Court has no jurisdiction over it, as there is no jurisdiction to maintain an injunction suit against the United States. This claim, like the claim for sovereign immunity, goes to the merits of the complaint's allegations. Is this a suit against the United States, or is it a suit against these defendant individuals for acting in excess of their statutory authority? Where government officials act in excess of their authority injunctive relief is authorized. The cases are legion permitting this injunctive relief in "environmental" contexts, where it has been determined that government officials have acted in excess of their bounds.

V

The Rivers and Harbors Act (Refuse Act) provides the following prohibition:

> It shall not be lawful to throw, discharge, or deposit, or cause, suffer, or procure to be thrown, discharged, or deposited either from or out of any ship, barge, or other floating craft . . . or from the shore, . . . manufacturing establishment, . . . any refuse matter of any kind or description whatever . . ., *into any navigable water of the United States, or into any tributary of any navigable water* from which the same shall float or be washed into such navigable water. . . .
>
> (P)rovided further, That the Secretary of the Army . . ., may permit the deposit of any material above mentioned in *navigable waters*. . . . (emphasis added)

The proviso clause of this Act was never fully implemented until the President signed Executive Order 11574 on December 23, 1970. This Order established a permit program under the Act to regulate discharges of pollutants and other refuse matter into the navigable waters of the United States.

On April 7, 1971, the Secretary of the Army published the challenged regulations. These regulations prescribe the policy, practice and procedure to be followed by all Corps of Engineers installations and activities in connection with applications for permits authorizing discharges or deposits in navigable waters of the United States or into any tributary from which such discharged or deposited matter shall float or be washed into a navigable water.

The plaintiffs allege that the regulations, as promulgated, extend beyond statutory authorization the Corps of Engineer's permit authority in that it includes as areas subject to permit issuance, tributaries of navigable waterways where discharge into those waters would float or be washed into a navigable waterway. The defendants proffer that the authority to issue permits for the discharge of refuse matter is as broad as the scope of the prohibition from dumping refuse into waterways in the statute; therefore, the Chief of Engineers may lawfully issue permits to persons desiring to discharge refuse into tributaries of navigable waters.

Pointing to past cases interpreting this Act, defendants insist that the purpose underlying the enactment of the Refuse Act precludes a narrow reading of the statute. The cases cited, however, merely discuss the term "refuse" as defined within the Act. "Refuse" has been held to have broad dimensions. This does not lend support for the defendants reading of the permit clause of the Act. The reason for the broad reading given to the word "refuse" is abundantly clear. The purpose of the Act required that the prohibition against dumping "refuse" into our waters be as broad as possible. Nowhere in the cases is there any discussion of limiting this broad prohibition other than as specifically stated within the Act. None of the cases cited to this Court remotely discuss the permit clause and its scope.

Defendants argue further, that although deposits into non-navigable tributaries that wash into navigable streams are prohibited, there is no indication in the legislative history that Congress meant the prohibition on discharges into tributaries to be any more absolute than the prohibition on discharges into the navigable waters themselves. Defendants posit that when refuse is discharged into a non-navigable tributary, and that refuse floats into a navigable stream, that at that point the Corps of Engineers may issue a permit for the deposit. From this, they argue, that considerations would not differ for the issuance of a permit at either juncture, therefore the Refuse Act Permit Program should be construed broadly to allow the issuance of permits for the dumping of refuse into both navigable and non-navigable waters. Without this power to issue permits to Companies located on non-navigable waters the defendants state that industrial plants would find themselves in a position of being in violation of the Act without ability to bring themselves into compliance short of closing. This would be true even if the plant's discharges were in no manner violating the other standards of water quality.

We are dealing here with the statutory grant of authority given to the Secretary of the Army to issue permits for the dumping of "refuse" into non-navigable waterways that eventually lead into navigable waters. The law is clear. The Secretary of the Army does not have that power under the Refuse Act. The regulations, therefore, insofar as they purport to vest in the Corps of Engineers and the Secretary of Army such authority are hereby declared *ultra vires* and of no effect.

An examination of the statute indicates that it is divided into two parts, the first part setting forth the prohibition against the "discharge . . . of refuse matter", and the second part providing an exception for permits for such discharges by the Chief of Engineers. The first part, or prohibition, applies by its terms to "any navigable water, *or . . . any tributary of any navigable water* . . ." (emphasis added). Discharges of "refuse" matter are clearly prohibited in both navigable waters and in non-navigable tributaries of navigable waters.

The second part of the section, pertaining to the permits provision, is more limited in scope. The Secretary of the Army "may permit the deposit of any material above mentioned in *navigable waters. . . .*" (emphasis added). This separate proviso makes no mention of tributaries in contrast to the specific language in the prohibition part of the section. The conclusion that is drawn from this language is that the Corps of Engineers has no authority to authorize deposits of refuse matter in non-navigable tributaries of navigable waterways. The prohibition part of this section is plainly larger than the exception for permits. Had Congress intended that the language of the exception be read to include tributaries it had only to use the precise language that it used in describing the scope of the prohibition against discharging refuse. As the Supreme Court often has stated, the legislative history of a statute cannot radically affect the Court's interpretation if the language of the statute is clear.

Kalur v. Resor

Defendants desire that this Act be construed broadly to effectuate its remedial purpose. They cite cases to this effect. Indeed, these cases are the principal reason why the Refuse Act is today in the effort to control environmental destruction of waterways. The definition of "refuse" is of broad scope. The samples of refuse into a waterway covered by this Act is violation, and as such is subject to the usual rules regarding street construction. Statutes cannot be construed broadly to create criminal violations out of wholecloth. A clearly established criminal prohibition, however, such as this section, cannot be administered out of existence by the defendants' attempt to exceed their clearly defined statutory authority. In *United States* v. *Republic Steel Corporation* the Supreme Court declined an invitation to expand the exception for the dumping of "refuse" in stating: "We follow the line Congress has drawn and cannot accept the invitation to broaden the exception in Section 13 because other matters "in a liquid state" might logically have been treated as favorably as sewage is treated." This Court similarly declines defendants invitation to expand a clearly drawn exception in Section 13. Once a polluter has received a permit from the Corps of Engineers to dump "refuse" into a non-navigable waterway, the polluter is shielded from prosecution so long as he stays within the permit's terms. Shields from prosecution for otherwise criminal offenses should not be broadly distributed. The clear language of the section delimits those areas where permits may be issued.

The cases cited by defendant make the Rivers and Harbors Act an effective weapon in the attempt to improve the quality of the nation's waterways. Until recently, no permits were ever issued under the Act. Every person depositing refuse into the nation's waters was and is in violation of this Act. This fact, coupled with the United States Attorneys' power to obtain injunctive relief, makes the Act simple and effective. There can be no remorse for those companies who have since 1899 violated the criminal law who now find themselves in the position of being unable to comply with the law. Defendants' permit program only hinder the effectiveness of Congress' intent to keep our waterways clean for both navigation and environmental reasons. Congress did not want non-navigable waters to be subjected to the dumping of "refuse." It is of little effect that any "refuse" illegally dumped in a non-navigable water could be legally dumped in a navigable waterway if a permit were issued.

The statutory prohibition against dumping protects non-navigable tributaries. The United States Attorney's office, therefore, has authority under this Act to prosecute violators who dump "refuse" into non-navigable waterways where such discharge would find its way into a navigable waterway. The regulations in issue here act to undermine this authority and instead of serving a remedial purpose, they are in fact, aiding to perpetuate and cloak the already mass obviation of the Refuse Act by corporate entities. There are many clean and still unspoiled rivers, streams, and lakes that do not fall within the expanding definition of "navigable." Many of these are suitable for canoeing, fishing, swimming and other recreational pursuits. Such pure streams can be preserved as the Act absolutely prohibits deposits of refuse matter into them. Defendants may not go beyond their legal authority to issue permits that shield polluters and potential polluters where Congress has specifically prohibited such activity.

ORDER

Upon consideration of the cross motions for summary judgment, and upon consideration of both supporting and opposing memoranda, and for the reasons set forth in an opinion filed herewith, it is, on this 15th day of December, 1971.

ORDERED, that Plaintiffs' motion for summary judgment be and hereby is *granted*, and further,

ORDERED, that the regulations noted at 33 C.F.R. Section 209.131, insofar as they purport to allow the issuance of permits to discharge refuse matter into non-navigable waterways, is *ultra vires*, and of no effect; and further, defendants are permanently enjoined from issuing permits to discharge refuse matter into non-navigable waterways; and further,

ORDERED, that these same regulations, insofar as they exempt the defendants and applicants from the requirements of filing detailed environmental impact statements, is declared *ultra vires* as being in excess of and beyond the defendants' authority, and thereof of no effect; and defendants are further enjoined permanently from issuance of said permits pursuant to the provisions of 33 C.F.R. Section 209.131 until such time as the defendants amend said regulation to require environmental impact statements as specified by Section 102(2)(C) of the National Environmental Policy Act of 1969, 42 U.S.C. Section 332(2)(C) (1971).

AUBREY E. ROBINSON, JR.,
U.S. District Judge.

permits to pollute: a warning

After the *Kalur* decision, the government did not vigorously press appeal of the injunction, and seemed prepared to write off the permit program. The Corps of Engineers stopped issuance of permit public notices, and a new water pollution control act was expected shortly from Congress which would contain provisions for a new permit program.

However, in early 1972 the Corps position changed. EPA proposed changes in the new water legislation that would cure the defects in the Refuse Act Permit Program. At the same time, EPA suggested that the permit program be extended for an entire year beyond enactment of the new legislation. On January 21, the Corps resumed issuing public notices. Meanwhile EPA announced that it was expediting permit application review in the coming months, with the 3,000 most serious polluters receiving top priority.

Uninformed of these developments, and believing the permit program to be dead, the public has been ignoring the 30-day public comment period, although ten-to-fifteen public notices are being issued daily. Unless the public takes a much more active role, five-year discharge permits to major polluters may be issued without any public scrutiny at all.

However, as noted on page Four-119, approval of permits was in suspension as this book went to press.

On May 30, 1972, the other shoe fell in regard to enforcement of the Refuse Act. On that day, the U.S. Court of Appeals for the Third Circuit decided *United States v. Pennsylvania Chemical Corp.* (4 ERC 1241) In this case, the court held that the company had been "convicted of a crime which Congress has never created." The court reasoned that while the Refuse Act clearly authorizes the conviction of one who discharges without a permit, it does not authorize conviction of one who discharges when no permit is available. The discharge in question occurred in August of 1970, four months prior to initiation of the permit program.

A contributing factor in the reversal of the conviction, according to Judge Arlin M. Adams, was that the Army Corps of Engineers "affirmatively mislead" the company by telling it that the Refuse Act "would be inapplicable to discharges of wastes that didn't impede navigation."

But the more important fact about this case was that, because of the on-again, off-again operation of the permit program, the Refuse Act, like the present Federal Water Pollution Control Act, might prove virtually unenforceable.

John R. Quarles, general counsel of the Environmental Protection Agency, proclaimed that the *Pennsylvania Chemical* decision "could stop us dead in our tracks" by bringing "a ban on present prosecutions" for water pollution. He added that the permit program had become a "bureaucratic nightmare." [This last comes as no surprise to those many environmentalists who warned that the permit program was designed from its inception to prevent enforcement of the Refuse Act, regardless of how many honest men and women tried to get it to function.]

The EPA, Quarles said, was requesting the Justice Department to seek a new hearing in the *Pennsylvania Chemical* case, and an expedited appeal of the *Kalur* case. *See:* "EPA Battles for Pollution Curb," *The Washington Post* at A10, and "Clean Water Battle Near Drowning, Key Agency Fears," *The Wall Street Journal* at 10, both June 13, 1972.

In November 1971 the Senate passed S.2770, entitled the Federal Water Pollution Control Act Amendments of 1971. The bill, if enacted, would terminate the present permit program. The EPA would administer a permit program, but States with the capacity to administer the program within their boundaries would take over EPA's activity. The enforcement of the remainder of the Rivers and Harbors Act of 1899 would continue to be primarily the responsibility of the Corps of Engineers.

effluent inventories

One major benefit of such a permit system is that an inventory of industrial waste water will be developed. While we have had water pollution legislation for a number of years, we still do not know what wastes are being discharged into our nation's waterways. The major reason for this lack of knowledge is that the Bureau of the Budget (now the OMB) would not allow such an inventory to be taken unless it was limited to one river basin and the data was kept confidential. Thus for years the President's office protected industry from any need to provide effluent discharge data. The public could not learn the details of who was responsible for pollution, and public administrators were hampered in developing abatement programs.

See:

The Establishment of a National Industrial Wastes Inventory, Committee on Government Operations, 91st Cong., 2d Sess., House Report No. 91-1717, December 10, 1970.

"Industrial waste water: FWQA inventory underway at last," 5 Environmental Science and Technology No. 1, January 1971 at 20.

"When you wish to produce a result by means of an instrument, do not allow yourself to complicate it by introducing many subsidiary parts, but follow the briefest way possible, and do not act as those who when they do not know how to express a thing. . .proceed by a method of circumlocution and with great prolixity and confusion.

—Leonardo da Vinci

enforcement

Unlike the almost useless Federal Water Pollution Control Act previously discussed, the Refuse Act is a very simple act. Its current implementation is very complex. As an example, we would like to have reproduced a copy of the Department of the Army's flow chart dated April 7, 1971, for processing Refuse Act permit violations. But we found the chart would have to occupy two full pages even with the smallest readable type, and really wouldn't be very useful. This Byzantine document, which covers only the role of the Army Corps of Engineers in the process, and not the roles also required of the Environmental Protection Agency and State agencies, starts with "receipt of application," and ends, after 50 boxes, in one marked "final disposition will be in accordance with instructions from higher authority."

Refuse Act penalties

The Refuse Act is a criminal statute that prohibits the discharge of refuse into navigable waters of the United States. Upon conviction, the penalty is a fine not to exceed $2,500 and not less than $500, or imprisonment for not less than 30 days nor more than a year, or both fine and imprisonment.

But in the Act's long history, it had seldom been enforced, and when it was, until very recently fines were minimal and criminal penalties were not imposed. Toward the end of 1971, however, there were some signs that the Refuse Act was occasionally being prosecuted with vigor. We quote from the *Environmental Action,* Nov. 13, 1971, at 11:

> After years of frustration in dealing with water polluters, the federal government is beginning to take a hard-line attitude with the most recalcitrant of its corporate foes. Although no policy directive has come down from Washington, a number of aggressive United States Attorneys around the country are beefing up their attacks by filing criminal charges against companies.
>
> At present, the presidents of a woolen company and a ceramics concern in Massachusetts, the manager of a U.S. Steel plant in Chicago, and the president of an automobile cleansing plant in Baltimore are under criminal indictment under the 1899 Refuse Act.
>
> These actions, and others which are emerging in New York and elsewhere, constitute a major change in government policy. In the past, the government has relied upon civil actions which levy only fines against companies. Under criminal actions, both fines and jail sentences can be handed down.
>
> J.J. O'Donnell, president of J.J. O'Donnell Woolens of Grafton, Mass., has received what is believed the first criminal conviction in the U.S. because of his company's pollution. The company has been under investigation since 1962 for discharging soaps and dyes into the Blackstone River. O'Donnell could receive a sentence of up to a $12,500 fine and five years in jail.
>
> Although the Justice Department has not been eager to use criminal actions in water pollution cases, there appears to be a good deal of latitude as to how aggressively each U.S. Attorney can pursue cases. Apparently, criminal charges will be filed more often now, although only in cases of extreme recalcitrance on the part of polluting industries.
>
> In Chicago, Charles M. Kay, manager of U.S. Steel's South Works, will face a federal trial on a criminal count of aiding the discharge of iron oxides and other solid wastes into Lake Michigan in 1969. U.S. Steel, which has battled with various branches of the federal government over pollution recently, stated that it was "astonished" at the criminal indictment of Kay.
>
> In Baltimore, a grand jury handed down a 100-count indictment against James Byrne, president of Baltimore Imported Car Service and Storage, Inc., for dumping cosmoline and kerosine into tne city's harbor. The company removes cosmoline, a petroleum residue, from imported autos.

Between 1964 and 1969, an average of 43 criminal prosecutions per year were initiated. In fiscal year 1970, the number increased to 129, and during the first 11 months of FY 1971 approximately 159 criminal actions were initiated. Fines have also increase, since each discharge or each day can be a separate offense. In November, 1971, a U.S. district court fined Anaconda Wire and Cable Co. $200,000 for discharging copper wastes into the Hudson River just north of New York City. The fine was imposed after the company pleaded guilty to 100 violations of the Refuse Act between January 4 and May 24, 1971. The fine was the largest yet imposed under the Refuse Act. [*Environment Reporter,* Current Developments, Vol. 2, No. 29 at 850]

The definition of a "separate violation" has not yet been authoritatively settled. A Federal district court has held that a ship which discharged wastes three times at intervals of a few hours had committed three spearate violations. See *U.S. v. S.S. Mormasaga,* 204 F.Supp. 701 (D.C.Pa. 1958).

Until early in 1970, the statute was administered in the Department of Justice as a criminal statute. Since that time the Refuse Act has been used as a civil statute to secure injunctive relief from pollution. Actions for injunctive relief are not expressly authorized in the statute, but are deemed to be authorized by implication. [See *United States v. Republic Steel Corp.,* 362 U.S. 482 (1960) and *Wyandotte Transportation Co. v. United States,* 389 U.S. 191 (1967)].

The first civil injunction ever initiated under the Refuse Act was filed in 1970 against Florida Light and Power Co. to abate the discharge of heated water into Biscayne Bay, Florida. As of the summer of 1971, there were pending about 50 major civil actions for injunctive relief. During FY 1971, 14 civil actions were concluded by court-approved settlements. The Act was also used against mercury pollutors to reduce the discharge from 139 pounds to two pounds per day, with interim stipulations for further reductions expected.

The Federal Government takes the position that heat is a pollutant under the Refuse Act based on the decisions in the case of *United States v. Florida Power and Light Company* (S.D. Florida). The case, however, was decided against the government, for they failed to prove irreparable harm.

After numerous procedural moves, the case was settled in December of 1971, with the company agreeing to meet water pollution (including thermal) standards. For the documents involved in this suit see Landau, N., and Rheingold, P., *The Environmental Law Handbook,* 1971 at 218.

One continuous source of controversy has been the issue of whether a pollutor discharging on a continuous basis should be prosecuted rather than simply being made subject to the Water Quality Act. The Nixon administration opposed the use of the Refuse Act. As a result, Assistant Attorney General Kashiwa, then head of the Lands and Natural Resources Division, issued a memorandum prohibiting U.S. attorneys from bringing civil or criminal actions against manufacturing plants which continuously discharge refuse into navigable waters. Intense protests from conservation organizations followed. The enforcement policies were modified, and at the same time the Justice Department litigation guidelines were ignored by some of the U.S. attorneys. Nevertheless, the issue has been made somewhat moot by the major effort to put continuous pollutors under the permit program. Law suits are not being brought against those who are considered to be cooperating with the federal permit effort.

On September 24, 1971, EPA Administrator William D. Ruckelshaus announced that the Justice Department had been asked to prosecute 35 industrial firms for failure to apply for discharge permits. However, the list consisted mainly of inconsequential pollutors such as the

Menominee Enterprises, Inc., a very small Wisconsin Indian business. In addition, the nearly complete lack of evidence gathered makes it clear that the announcement was primarily a government public relations ploy. One substantial pollutor, U.S. Steel, is being sued, but this action seems to be the result of a direct challenge to the government by this corporation.

For background information see "Federal Enforcement Under the Refuse Act of 1899" by James T.B. TRIPP and Richard M. HALL, 35 Albany Law Review 60 (1970).

See also:

"The Refuse Act: Its Role Within the Scheme of Federal Water Quality Legislation," 46 *N.Y.U.L.Rev.* 304 (April 1971)

EAMES, "The Refuse Act of 1899: Its Scope And Role in Control of Water Pollution." 1 *Ecology Law Quart.* 173 (1971)

fees for informers

The Administration's position, expressed earlier in the Justice Department litigation guidelines, has been to limit the use of the Refuse Act in cases where the Federal Water Quality Act was applicable. Local pressure on U.S. Attorneys, however, has resulted in a reversal of the official position, so that the Justice Department now is increasingly bringing Refuse Act suits and criminal actions, and has even issued guidelines, for citizens' investigations.

This is one of the few federal criminal statutes where citizens have on a regular basis gathered the facts and evidence necessary for prosecution and presented the evidence to the U.S. Attorneys. [For an interesting case history of the efforts to stop Interlake, Inc., from polluting Lake Michigan see POLIKOFF, "The Inter-lake Affair," *The Washington Monthly,* Vol. 3, No. 1, March 1971.

The Act in 33 U.S.C. §411 provides that half of any fine imposed against pollutors may be given to the person or persons supplying information which leads to a conviction.

A New York District Court so interpreted this provision, to the $12,500 profit of the two informers, in the following case, *U.S. v. Transit Mix:*

UNITED STATES v. TRANSIT-MIX

___F.Supp.___ (S.D.N.Y. Dec. 11, 1970) 2 ERC 1074

[Full text]

WYATT, District Judge:

This is a motion for judgment by Gwen B. Zeichner and her son, Steven Zeichner, acting for themselves and without counsel, for payment to them of "one half (or some portion thereof)" of the fines involved.

In the situation here, while the government had information about discharges of defendant before the Zeichners gave information, no "proceedings [had] been commenced in pursuance of that information".

The decision here must be made on the specific fact pattern present and on the specific statute applicable.

I conclude that although the Zeichners did not give all (or even a great part of) the information on which the conviction was obtained; and although the government had information about discharges of defendant before that given by the Zeichners, nevertheless the information that they gave and the fact that they gave it did, under the circumstances here, "lead to conviction" of defendant.

Under the statute as I read it, payment to a qualified informer is "in the discretion of the court" but if discretion be exercised in favor of payment, the amount of the payment must be one half. While the wisdom of the inflexible one-half requirement might be questioned, so the statute appears to read.

It may reasonably be felt that one-half of the fine is too much to award to the Zeichners but as between paying the Zeichners nothing and paying them one-half, I feel that they should be paid one-half of the $25,000 in fines imposed.

It is accordingly ordered that the sum of $12,500, constituting one-half of the fines imposed herein be paid over jointly to Gwen B. Zeichner and Steven Zeichner pursuant to the provisions of Section 411 of Title 33 of the United States Code.

End, Transit-Mix case.

In 1972 the District Court for the Southern District of New York spoke again on the informer's fee in *U.S. v. Anaconda Wire & Cable* [— F.Supp. — (May 22, 1972), 4 ERC 1135] they held that the court has the discretion to award less than one half of the fine if a lesser amount is more appropriate.

In *Miller v. United States,* 445 F.2d 833 (S.D. W.Vir. 1971, 3 ERC 1129, the court held that persons who reported a violation of the Refuse Act (for which they might receive a portion of the fine) had a procedural due process right to notice that their claim was being adjudicated, to confront and cross-examine adverse witnesses, to participate in proceedings by counsel, and adduce relevant evidence in their own behalf.

In another case the informer's fee was held not to apply when the government brought in *a rem* action against an offending vessel. *U.S. v. T/B* NMS No. 40, 330 F.Supp. 781 (D.C. Tex. 1971)

Qui tam citizen suits

As indicated earlier, the Refuse Act provides that citizen informers shall receive part of the fine imposed upon pollutor's conviction.

Those citizens whose prime concern was the enforcement of pollution laws found that U.S. Attorneys ignored them when presented with information pertaining to Refuse Act violations. Legal theorists began to ask whether the provision didn't actually amount to authority for the citizen to bring a civil suit on his own behalf to recover one-half of the statutory penalty.

Such action was encouraged by a very influential document published by Congressman Reuss' House Subcommittee on Conservation and Natural Resources, entitled "*Qui tam* Actions and the 1899 Refuse Act: Citizen Lawsuits Against Pollutors of the Nation's Waterways" (September 1970). Citizens and conservation organizations around the country responded by filing many of these *qui tam* actions.

Bouvier's Law Dictionary (3d ed.) defines "*qui tam*" to mean:

> An action under a statute which imposes a penalty for the doing or not doing an act, and gives that penalty in part to whomsoever will sue for the same, and the other part to the commonwealth, or some charitable, literary, or other institution, and makes it recoverable by action. The plaintiff describes himself as suing *as well* for the commonwealth * * * as for himself * * *. [Emphasis in original.]

This *qui tam* theory, however, has not been accepted by the courts, as they have refused to construe the Refuse Act to allow citizen enforcement. The *Bass Angler v. Scholze Tannery* case which follows drives yet another coffin nail into this legal theory, dropping qui tam's district court won-lost record to 0-12.*

It should be recognized, however, that these cases did serve a valuable purpose. They pointed out the almost total lack of enforcement of the Nation's water pollution laws, and emphasized the Justice Department's disinterest in suing the large pollutors. The resulting pressure has helped career Justice Department lawyers in their efforts to bring suits, and has helped to create the political pressure now leading to a meaningful permit program.

**Bass Anglers v. U.S. Steel* (N.D.Ala. Feb. 8, 1971) 324 F.Supp. 412 [2 ERC 1204];
Bass Anglers v. U.S. Plywood (S.D.Tex. Feb. 10, 1971) — F.Supp. — [2 ERC 1298];
Bass Anglers v. Scholtze Tannery (E.D.Tenn. May 17, 1971) 329 F.Supp. 339 [2 ERC 1771];
Bass Anglers v. Koppers (5th Cir. Sept. 10, 1971) — F.Supp. — [3 ERC 1065];
Connecticut Action Now v. Roberts Plating (D.Conn. June 21, 1971) — F.Supp. — ;
Durning v. ITT Rayonier (W.D.Wash. Oct. 5, 1970) — F.Supp. — [2 ERC 1170];
Enquist v. Quaker Oats (D.Neb. May 6, 1971) — F.Supp. — [2 ERC 1601];
Gerbing v. ITT Rayonier (M.D.Fla. July 21, 1971) — F.Supp. — ;
Matthews v. Florida Vanderbilt (D.Neb. May 6, 1971) — F.Supp. — [2 ERC 1601];
Mattson v. Northwest Paper (D.Minn. Apr. 16, 1971) — F.Supp. — [2 ERC 1566];
Reuss v. Moss American and *Reuss v. Peter Cooper Corp.* (E.D.Wis. Feb. 23, 1971) — F.Supp. — [2 ERC 1259].

BASS ANGLERS SPORTSMAN'S SOCIETY v. SCHOLZE TANNERY

___F.Supp.___ (E.D. Tenn., S. Div. May 17, 1971) 2 ERC 1771

[Edited]

WILSON, J.:

This civil suit for penalties and injunctive relief arises out of alleged violations of 33 U.S.C. §§407 and 411 (the Rivers and Harbors Act of 1899).

The legal theory of the plaintiffs in the instant case appears identical to the theory of the plaintiffs in the case entitled Bass Anglers Sportsman's Society of America, et al v. U.S. Plywood-Champion Papers, Inc., et al," ___F.Supp.___[2 ERC 1298] (D.C.S.D. Texas 1971, Docket #70-H-1004). Judge Seals there defined the plaintiff's theory in the following terms:

> The legal theory of the plaintiffs in the present suit is that they have the right to prosecute a qui tam action pursuant to Sections 407 and 411 of Title 33, U.S.C., to obtain an injunction prohibiting the industrial defendants from dumping refuse into Texas waterways without a permit in violation of §407, to obtain penalties provided by §411 for each such violation of §407, and to obtain an injunction requiring defendant Stanley R. Resor, Secretary of the Army, and defendant, Frederick J. Clark, Chief of Engineers, United States Army Corps of Engineers, to establish standards for the issuing of permits allowing the dumping of refuse into navigable waterways and tributaries of navigable waterways in the State of Texas and to apply these standards, once formulated, to anyone deserving to dump refuse into those navigable Texas waterways protected by 33 U.S.C. §§407 and 411. The plaintiffs have stated their cause of action no broader than §§407 and 411 of Title 33, U.S.C. Thus, plaintiffs must establish that they may, by this civil action, sue to enforce sections 407 and 411, or else the action must be dismissed for failure to state a claim upon which relief can be granted.

The plaintiffs maintain that they should be permitted to proceed with this suit under §407 and §411 as a qui tam action. A qui tam action is "an action brought by an informer, under a statute which establishes a penalty for the commission of a certain act, and provides that the same shall be recoverable in a civil action, part of the penalty to go to any person who will bring such action and the remainder to the state or some other institution." Black's Law Dictionary, p. 1414. Judge Pollock in Williams v. Wells Fargo & Co. Express, 177 F. 352 (8th Cir. 1910) described the qui tam action as follows:

> It would seem at the common law actions to recover panalties prescribed by law were often prosecuted by what was known as "common informers." Blackstone's Commentaries, Book 3 [Coolidge Ed.] 160, and when a portion to the sovereign, the action was styled a "qui tam action."

Judge Pollock also observed that:

> While it has been held there must be either express statutory authority authorizing an informer to prosecute in his own name, or such right must be given by necessary implication (cases cited), yet on the contrary, it has been ruled where a statute gives a portion of the recovery to an informer who prosecutes for the same...such statute contains sufficient implied authority to support a prosecution by an informer in his own name. Adams, Qui Tam v. Woods, 2 Cranch 336, 2 L.Ed. 297;...

This observation was further considered in U.S. ex rel Marcus v. Hess, 317 U.S. 537, 87 L.Ed. 443 (1943), where Justice Black noted in footnote 4 that: "Statutes providing for a reward to informers which do not specifically either authorize or forbid the informer to institute the action are construed to authorize him to sue. Adams v. Woods, 2 Cranch (U.S.) 336, 2 L.Ed. 297." Adams v. Woods, supra, was an action of debt brought to recover a penalty imposed by an act entitled "An Act to prohibit the carrying on the salve trade from the United States to any foreign place or country." The Court applying rules of statutory construction concluded that: "In this particular case, the statute which creates the forfeiture does not prescribe the mode of demanding it; consequently, either debt or information would lie."

Turning to the circumstances of the instant case, each of the District Courts that have had occasion to consider Justice Black's comments, have rejected his analysis of the law.

[As stated in Bass Anglers Sportsman's Society v. U.S.Plywood-Champion Papers, Inc.:]

> There must be statutory authority, either express or implied, for the informer to bring the qui tam action. When the statute is silent as to whether the qui tam action is authorized, and nothing can be gleaned concerning congressional intent from the circumstances surrounding the passage of the statute then perhaps Justice Black's construction in favor of the qui tam action may be justified in many instances. But Black's construction obviously is inappropriate whenever the statute's language by necessary implication precludes such a conclusion.

An examination and analysis of §411 shows clearly that the criticism of Justice Black's dictum is well taken. First of all, §411 provides that every person or corporation violating §407:

> ...(S)hall be guilty of a misdemeanor, and <u>on conviction</u> thereof shall be punished by a fine... <u>or</u> by imprisonment...,<u>or</u> by both such fine and imprisonment, <u>in the discretion of the court</u>, one-half of said fine to be paid to the person or persons giving information <u>which shall lead to conviction</u>. (Emphasis added)

Accordingly, the informer's rights depend upon three prerequisites:

1) A criminal proceeding being instituted under §411;

2) A conviction obtained in the criminal proceeding; and

3) The imposition of a fine as punishment.

The informer's rights are dependent entirely upon the successful prosecution of a criminal action.

Viewed in this light, several additional observations are in order. First, criminal statutes cannot be enforced by civil proceedings.

Second and more important, case law indicates that alleged violations of criminal statutes may be enforced only by the proper prosecuting authorities and not by private parties.

Moreover, mandamus will not lie to control the exercise of this discretion nor may the courts or private citizens otherwise interfere with the free exercise of the discretionary powers of the Attorney General and his representatives in their consideration, investigation and prosecution of criminal violations.

Accordingly under the circumstances of the instant case and the applicable law the Court is of the opinion that the plaintiffs have no standing to maintain this action pursuant to Secs. 407 and 411 nor to recover the penalty provided by Sec. 411 short of a successful criminal prosecution. These statutes create and define crimes which may not be prosecuted by private civil action. The designation of the action as a <u>qui tam</u> action does not circumvent the conclusions reached for Sec. 413 provides explicitly that the power to enforce the provisions of Secs. 407 and 411 lies exclusively in the Department of Justice, thereby precluding any private civil action for the recovery of the informer's morety.

End, text of case.

[The Court also refused to provide injunctive relief.]

NOTE

The Army Corps of Engineers' Procedures on Investigation of Refuse Act Violations, including the text of a Memorandum of Understanding between the Administrator of the Environmental Protection Agency and the Secretary of the Army, appeared as *Federal Register Document* 71-2134, dated January 12, 1971, and filed with the *Federal Register* on February 16, 1971. The document may also be found in the BNA *Environment Reporter,* as can the Justice Department's Guidelines for Investigations of Violations of the 1899 Refuse Act.

k. State and local water pollution control

legal history

Local laws concerning sewage date back to colonial times. In the 19th century laws were passed to protect the navigability of streams. In the 1870's and 1880's state and local boards of health were created to enforce water purification requirements and to prevent pollution. The impetus seemed to be largely due to the control of cholera in 1866, by the newly created New York City health board. The attempts to protect water supplies were somewhat more successful than the pollution control efforts though typhoid fever and other waterborne diseases were common. After the relationship between contagious diseases and water contamination became known it was still not unusual to have health laws unenforced or water purification bonds voted down—occasionally even during typhoid outbreaks. State and local efforts in providing sewage treatment, except for the Depression years of the 1930's, never kept pace with the need, and thus much of our effort to control water pollution from municipal sources consists of trying to remedy past deficiences. The technology of controlling pollution from this source has evolved so slowly that our expenditures today are often for the installation of equipment and facilities that were available in the 30's.

State programs were found in every state by 1948, usually in the health department. During the following twenty years independent boards of pollution control became common in about half the states, often attached to the natural resource program or department. The difference was somewhat regional with Health Department control more common in the West and Midwest.

state control

STATE CONTROL OF WATER POLLUTION

When the 1965 Water Quality Act was passed the Federal government obtained substantial power to shape state water pollution law. The states were required to follow Federal guidelines and develop stream quality standards. Interstate streams, rivers, and lakes were classified into categories. Specific scientific criteria were developed for each category based on such measurements as pH, temperatures, dissolved solids, bacteria count, etc. The states were then required to develop implementation plans to control the effluent discharged into these waters in order to reach the stream quality goals expressed as Standards. The Federal pressure has resulted in substantial similarity in the approach to stream standards among the states. The implementation plan, however, has not been the subject of specific Federal requirements and therefore state programs differ. [The Federal Program and an example of the regulations for stream standards are found in the discussion of Section 10 of the Federal Water Pollution Control Act. The material on Section 21(b) should also be reviewed].

Every state has a water pollution control agency, either an independent agency or a subdivision of an executive department. The responsibility of these agencies includes the meeting of federally imposed standards as well as developing and enforcing the state law applicable to waters that are not interstate, and therefore are not subject to the Federal section 10 program. Usually, but not always, the agency issues permits for discharges of wastes. These are usually conditional and can be revoked if the requirements are not met. The board may have the power to issue compliance orders, and apply penalties not only for pollution but for failure to obey an order. Enforcement can be based on fines, criminal penalties, injunctive remedies, or closure for violating orders. Except for the last named penalty, the provisions of most statutes are so weak and/or unenforced that they are nearly meaningless.

In most states the enforcement procedure requires an investigation, followed by an informal or formal hearing, issuance of a cease and desist order, and formal hearing, if not previously held. The cease and desist order may be a final order allowing for appeal or it may be subject to modification after the formal hearing. When the order is final an appeal may be taken by the pollutor to either the agency head or to the courts, depending on the state government structure. The government usually enforces the order by literally asking the state attorney general to bring a law suit to abate the pollution when his schedule permits. States which have more expeditious procedures and/or give more power to the administrative agencies are the exception. At any step in a contested proceeding, a ruling in favor of the pollutor gives no appeal to the public. In pollution law, due process means due process for the pollutors—poison for the people.

Some states, in addition to the administrative programs set up to comply with the Federal Water Pollution Control Act, have a variety of statutes that are applicable to water pollution. It is not uncommon for their enforcement to rest in other agencies. Statutes may make water pollution a public nuisance. The fish and game code may protect fish and provide penalties for pollution kills. The health code may have pollution statutes relating to such subjects as septic tank practices, well water, etc. The constitutionality of such laws, so long as they meet a general reasonableness test, will not be successfully challenged.

State Water Quality Program Elements, May 1971

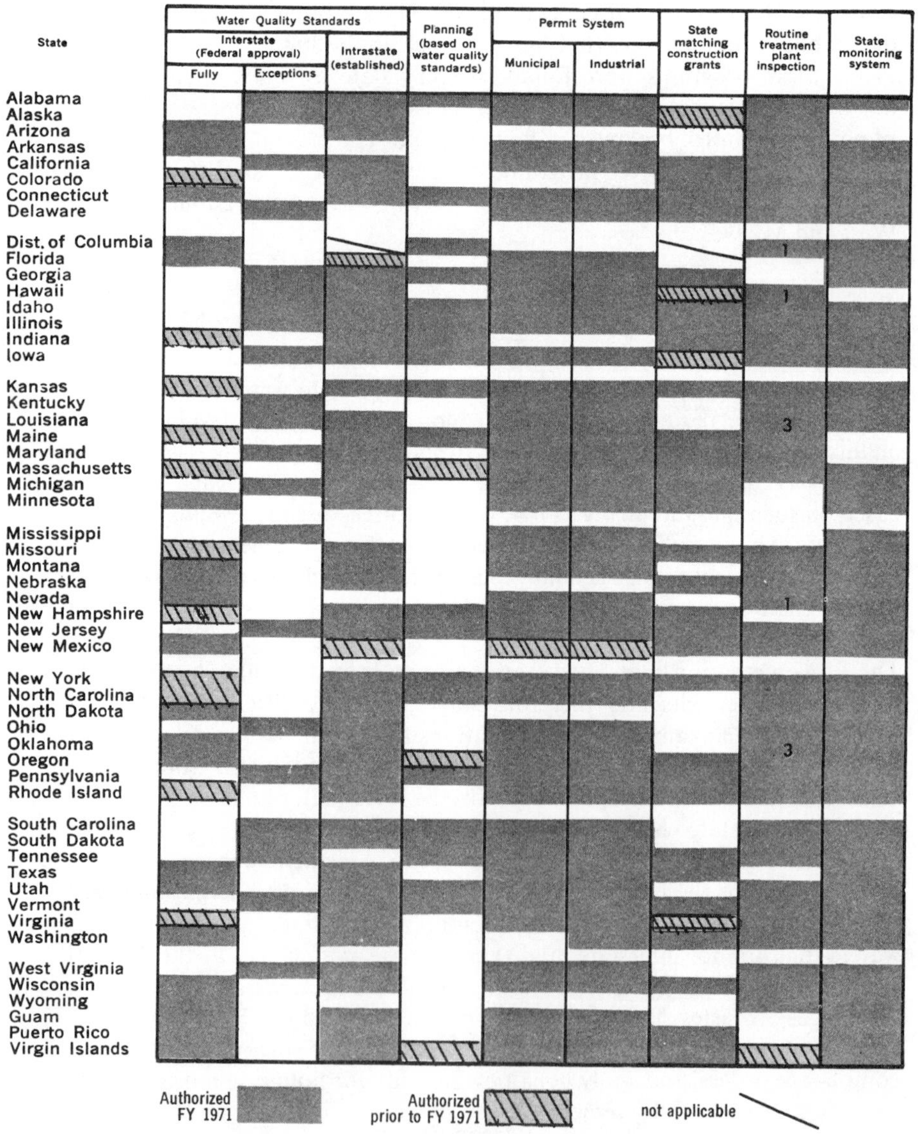

Source: Environmental Protection Agency, Office of Water Programs.
[1] Municipal only.
[2] Federal only.
[3] Municipal and State only.

Printed below is an example of an application for a water pollution discharge permit from the State of Ohio. On the reverse of this page are reprinted two blank "licenses to pollute" from the same state.

Application No. ______________________

Date Received ______________________

Permit No. ______________________

Date of Board Action ______________________

WATER POLLUTION CONTROL BOARD

DEPARTMENT OF HEALTH
STATE OF OHIO

APPLICATION FOR PERMIT TO DISCHARGE SEWAGE, INDUSTRIAL WASTES, OR OTHER WASTES INTO WATERS OF THE STATE

Please read carefully instructions on reverse side of this application before filling out.

1. Name ______________________
2. Location ______________________
3. Type of Establishment *(if not a political subdivision)* ______________________
4. Type of Discharge ______________________
5. Body of Water Receiving Discharge ______________________
   (a) Next larger receiving tributary ______________________
6. Is Discharge Treated? Yes ________ No ________
7. Relevant information with respect to characteristics of discharge is submitted in attached report entitled ______________________

Any supplemental information submitted in connection with this application will be treated as confidential by the Board.

Submission of this application does not constitute a waiver by the applicant of any rights or exemptions provided by law.

In accordance with the provisions of the Water Pollution Control Act, Sections 6111.01 – 6111.08 of the Revised Code of Ohio, and with the rules and regulations adopted by the Water Pollution Control Board in pursuance thereto, application hereby is made for a permit to discharge into the waters of the state sewage, industrial wastes, or other wastes, as described above, and in supplemental information hereto attached, all of which is made a part of this application.

Signature of authorized official ______________________

Title ______________________

Post Office Address ______________________

VERIFICATION

______________________, being first duly sworn, says that he is the officer or person duly authorized to execute the foregoing application, and that the statements made and answers given therein, written or printed, are true as he verily believes.

Signature of Applicant ______________________

Sworn to and subscribed in my presence this ____________ day of ____________, 19 ____,

at ____________, County of ____________ and State of ____________.

Signature of Officer ______________________

Official Title ______________________

four-136

STATE OF OHIO

Date Issued

Permit No.

DEPARTMENT  OF HEALTH

WATER POLLUTION CONTROL BOARD

COLUMBUS

This certifies that

____

____

____

has been granted permission to discharge industrial wastes (acid mine-drainage) from the above designated mine into waters of the state under authority of the Ohio Water Pollution Control Act, Sections 6111.01 to 6111.08 Revised Code of Ohio, until such time as this permit may be revoked or the operation of said mine is terminated (including the period permitted by law for reclamation) by the operator to whom this permit is issued.

STATE OF OHIO

Permit No.

DEPARTMENT OF HEALTH

Date Issued

Expiration Date

WATER POLLUTION CONTROL BOARD

COLUMBUS

This certifies that

____

____

has been granted permission to discharge ________________________________

into ______________________________ under authority of the Ohio Water Pollution Control Act, Sections 6111.01 to 6111.08 Revised Code of Ohio, until the expiration date indicated hereon. Renewal of this permit is subject to the conditions prescribed by the Water Pollution Control Board as contained in the letter transmitting this permit.

This permit is subject to modification or revocation.

Application for renewal, re-issuance or extension of this permit shall be made not less than 30 days prior to the expiration date.

WATER POLLUTION CONTROL BOARD

____

CHAIRMAN

Reitze

state pollution control boards

One of the major impediments to effective pollution control has been the control of the state agencies by the major pollutors. Policies, standards, implementation plans, permit requirements and enforcement are directed by part-time pollution control boards made up of gubernatorial appointees who represent the pollutors. The situation in pollution control could be compared to a criminal law system in which the trial judges were selected by the inmates of the Federal prisons from among their numbers. An investigation by Gladwin Hill of the *New York Times* and reprinted in 36 *Izaak Walton Magazine* No. 1, January 1971 at 1 details this problem.

It should be emphasized that advisory boards made up of members of the regulated class are a normal part of our administrative process—and they serve a useful purpose. In addition, government agencies often use boards of technical experts from the private sector to help solve technical problems. Furthermore, many agencies have been charged with being captives of the regulated industries. But in pollution control, industry representatives, paid by industry, have regulatory and enforcement powers over the groups that employ them. Only seven states were found in the *Times* inquiry to have boards without members whose business or professional ties posed possible conflicts of interest. Eight states including New York and New Jersey get along without such boards.

Many boards have allocated seats for categories such as agriculture, industry, and municipalities. In addition, states such as Missouri, Utah, and Ohio require that certain pollution board seats be split between the Republicans and Democrats. Often the head of State agencies such as Commerce, Natural Resources, etc., sit on such part-time boards because of their government job, but these government appointments are usually made to provide representation for commercial and economic interests. Rarely is more than a tiny minority of the board made up of representatives of the broader public interest.

State boards, ranging in size from five to fifteen members, usually include in their number several state officials, representatives of the various economic interests (industry, agriculture), municipal governments, and the public.

The steel industry is a major pollutor. United States Steel Company executives sit on the air pollution boards of Alabama and Utah. Bethlehem Steel employees are members of the air pollution boards of Indiana and Erie County, N.Y. A National Steel employee is on the Indiana water pollution board. The Anaconda Company has an executive on Kentucky's air pollution board. One of their lawyers is on Utah's water pollution board, and a former high executive is chairman of Montana's Water Pollution Control Council. A Reynolds Metal employee is on the Alabama Water Commission. An Alcoa employee sits on the North Carolina Pollution Board, while an Alcoa staff doctor chairs Iowa's Air Pollution Control Commission.

The chemical industry is equally well represented. Hundreds of the members of state boards are employees of other industries. The result of this representation can be judged by the polluted condition of our waters. Successful abatement actions in most states can be counted on the fingers of one hand. Nearly four years after the statutory deadlines, 17 states have not adopted water quality standards satisfactory to the Federal government.

Because water has so many uses, state activities relating to water quality, including those which lower water quality were spread among dozens of organizations. The tendency in the past several years has been to reverse this trend and create environmental protection agencies with broad power over environmental matters. In order to be effective these agencies must be adequately staffed and financed, for with a few notable exceptions (California, Illinois, and New Jersey), state "environmental protection agencies" have moved to control pollution only as the Federal government prods them. For a comprehensive study of recent state efforts in this area, see Elizabeth Haskell et al, *Managing the Environment: Nine States Look for New Answers* (Washington, D.C., 1971). The Federal government has taken over the control of the State program in air pollution—using the state as their enforcement and monitoring arm. Similar legislation concerning water pollution could be enacted within a year.

For an example of the difficulties encountered by a state in attempting to force a corporation to abate its polluting discharge, see *GAF Corp. v. EPA* (Illinois),' No. PCB 71-11 before the Illinois Pollution Control Board [2 ERC 1458] April 19, 1971.

For a similar case with a more favorable decision for the industry see *Diamond v. Mobile Oil,* 2 ERC 1228 [N.Y. Sup. Ct. Erie County (1970)].

REFERENCES AND SELECTED BIBLIOGRAPHY

FALLOWS, James, *The Water Lords,* (Georgia), Grossman Pub., New York 1971

DASMANN, Raymond, *The Destruction of California,* MacMillian, New York, 1966

VAN NESS, "A Survey of Washington Law," in *Water Resources Management and Public Policy,* ed. by CAMPBELL and SYLVESTER, U. of Wash. Press 1968

National Capital Region, Water and Waste Management Report, Environmental Protection Agency, April, 1971

CARMICHAEL, "Forty Years of Water Pollution Control in Wisconsin," 1967 *Wis. L.Rev.* 350

HALLORAN, "Water Pollution Control in New York," 31 *Albany L. Rev.* 50 (1967)

POWE, "Water Pollution Control in Washington," 43 *Wash. L.Rev.* 425 (1967)

REITZE, "Wastes, Water, and Wishful Thinking, the Battle of Lake Eire," 20 *Case Western Reserve L.Rev.* 5(1968)

"Current Problems Project: Water Pollution Control in Texas, "48 *Tex. L.Rev.* 1029 (1970)

The following is from the second annual report of the Council on Environmental Quality, August, 1971:

reorganization

States, like the Federal Government, have reorganized themselves to cope with the environment. The trend toward consolidation of State pollution control programs began in the late 1960's. And it has taken a variety of forms. The examples discussed are representative although not necessarily typical.

Prior to the reorganizations discussed below, environmental programs in most States were—and in many other States still are—scattered among several agencies, boards, and commissions. Boards and commissions, manned by government agency representatives, citizens, special interest groups, or all of these, usually wielded considerable influence in setting pollution control policy. Often these entities exercised powers independent of the Governor, and special interest groups sometimes dominated them.

state programs

new york—By a statute enacted on Earth Day 1970, and effective July 1, 1970, New York State transferred most of its pollution control and resource management programs—the air, water, and pesticides control programs and the water resource, forest, fish and wildlife, and marine and mineral management programs—to a new Department of Environmental Conservation (DEC).[36] Solid waste disposal regulation, land use planning, and noise pollution control were also put under the Department's general purview, and it is expected that DEC will seek more specific statutory authority in these areas.

DEC is empowered to develop a statewide environmental plan and a statement of goals and strategies, to review all State agency programs affecting the environment, and to formulate guidelines for measuring the environmental values and relationships involved.

washington—The State of Washington enacted legislation in 1970—less extensive in scope than the New York law—which consolidates environmental protection programs under a Department of Ecology (DOE).[37] Created on July 1, 1970, DOE resulted from an across-the-board effort in the State to overhaul government structures and make them more responsive to the Governor, the legislature, and the public.

DOE consolidates the water and air quality, solid waste management, and water resource programs. In contrast to New York's DEC, DOE does not incorporate other resource management programs. Although the Department is basically a pollution control agency, programs such as pesticide control and drinking water quality remain with the Agriculture and Social and Health Services Departments, respectively.

Preexisting citizen or interagency boards such as the Water Resources Advisory Council and the Air Pollution Control Board gave way to an Ecological Commission to advise the DOE director. All nonprocedural rules and regulations proposed by the Director of DOE are reviewed by the Commission. The Commission has veto power over such proposals if five of its seven members disapprove.

The third element in Washington's new pollution control structure is a three-member quasi-judicial Pollution Control Hearings Board. It hears appeals from decisions of the DOE and of local air pollution control authorities.

One of the most significant aspects of DOE is its internal structure. It is structured according to functions, such as standard setting and planning. There is no separate air quality, water quality, water resource, or solid waste component. Instead, there are two functional branches—one for administration and planning and one for public services

illinois—Probably the most innovative State reorganization program was adopted in Illinois. The Illinois Environmental Protection Act of 1970[38] transferred preexisting authorities and programs and added some new ones to three new functional entities. Resource management programs were not affected. The Pollution Control Board (PCB) sets standards and adjudicates enforcement proceedings. The State Environmental Protection Agency (EPA) identifies and prosecutes alleged violators before the Board, issues permits, and gives technical assistance. The Institute for Environmental Quality (IEQ) conducts long-range policy planning and applied research.

Pollution control programs—air quality, water quality, radiation control, and "land pollution control" (solid wastes)—thus were divided in the reorganization among three organizations. This is an atypical response to common problems that have led various other states to reorganize.

The Illinois reorganizers saw many problems. The State Department of Public Health (DPH) overadvised and overconsulted with polluters instead of regulating and prosecuting them. Part-time standard-setting boards—such as the Air Pollution Control Board and the Sanitary Water Board—were ineffective; they met infrequently, and some members were associated with polluting constituencies. The air and water quality boards were separate. Finally, the pollution control units within DPH had to compete with other important DPH interests for money.

The framers of the Illinois reorganization plan were guided by principles in large measure different from those followed by other States. First, rather than eliminating or reducing the role of the policymaking board, Illinois professionalized it by giving it a full-time membership with staff. It also gave the board sharply defined, final authority for standard setting and policy development.

Second, Illinois acted upon the theory that some functions, such as prosecution and adjudication, conflict, or at least compete unfavorably, if administered by a single agency. The State also felt that long-range research and planning inevitably suffered when forced to compete for funds within an agency that must respond primarily to immediate crises and pressures. Hence, it created the independent IEQ.

Third, the Illinois approach is grounded in the belief that some duplication of responsibilities promotes a healthy competition that will maximize action against pollution. It assumes that interacting and overlapping organizations, with an involved citizenry, will "check and balance" inadequate or arbitrary action by any one organization. The Illinois Environmental Protection Agency, the Attorney General, and any private citizen all have authority to initiate enforcement proceedings. And citizens as well as the State EPA and IEQ may initiate standard-setting proceedings.

state financing

waste management and its financing—Three States, Maryland, New York, and Ohio, have public corporations empowered to engage in a traditionally local function: financing, constructing, and operating municipal sewage treatment and solid waste disposal facilities. The Maryland and Ohio corporations have similar authority with respect to some industrial facilities, and the New York and Ohio corporations have responsibility for water supply facilities.

maryland—The most recent of these three innovative institutions is the Maryland Environmental Service (MES), created in 1970.[43] MES may finance, design, construct, operate, and maintain solid and liquid waste disposal facilities. It provides research, technical assistance, and planning services on a regional basis. MES may contract with municipalities, other government entities, and private parties to provide these services. When directed to do so by State pollution control officials, it must install or operate abatement facilities for a municipality, firm, or individual that has failed to comply with an order issued by such officials. Recipients of MES services bear the costs.

MES is expected to effect economies of scale through regionalization of waste treatment and disposal, better financing opportunities than those available to most local jurisdictions (MES is authorized to issue its own bonds), and stricter compliance with water quality standards and solid waste disposal regulations.

MES will draft and seek to implement 5-year plans for the regions that it designates. However, the MES legislation requires approval by local governing bodies in a designated region as a precondition to adoption and implementation of a plan. Only the State General Assembly can override a local veto. Moreover, local governments can veto the location of waste disposal sites and continue to set fees for sewer and refuse services. Once a plan is adopted, an MES district will be established to acquire or construct the necessary facilities.

Some skeptics suggest that the local veto provision will hamstring MES and force it merely to implement local priorities instead of pursuing regional objectives. However, it is quite possible that MES can at least move toward regional waste management by persuading local officials that it will be cheaper and more effective to think regionally. MES must sell itself.

End quote.

43. Md. Ann. Code art. 33B, §1 *et seq.*

Funding and Manpower from State Water Quality Agencies, 1970–71[1]

State	Fiscal year 1970 funding			Fiscal year 1971 budgeted			Fiscal year 1970 man-years	Fiscal year 1971 man-years
	Federal	State	Total	Federal	State	Total		
Alabama	185,012	58,068	243,080	190,500	158,750	349,250	21.90	22.20
Alaska	20,100	56,280	76,380	20,000	114,700	134,700	8.20	15.00
Arizona	69,377	59,003	128,380	75,500	88,117	163,617	12.75	11.00
Arkansas	118,169	182,401	300,570	115,700	275,000	390,700	27.30	35.00
California	662,460	2,314,066	2,976,526	661,100	2,801,270	3,462,370	239.00	192.30
Colorado	84,970	141,463	226,433	88,000	220,485	308,485	20.00	21.00
Connecticut	169,811	324,787	494,598	167,400	503,905	671,305	50.80	64.00
Delaware	86,267	217,312	303,579	85,900	202,200	288,100	36.33	33.20
District of Columbia	89,055	271,515	360,570	87,800	579,744	667,544	51.70	63.80
Florida	267,440	462,300	729,740	266,300	658,519	924,819	68.50	72.00
Georgia	223,337	412,894	636,231	218,700	535,544	754,244	38.00	50.00
Hawaii	65,100	114,781	179,881	71,100	184,900	256,000	24.20	31.00
Idaho	42,957	173,467	216,424	44,100	214,000	258,100	9.75	20.30
Illinois	379,097	645,359	1,024,456	428,000	2,327,340	2,755,340	95.00	188.00
Indiana	229,696	346,732	576,428	230,000	484,358	714,358	66.03	56.80
Iowa	123,699	121,309	245,008	121,200	124,580	245,780	15.25	22.75
Kansas	98,724	321,285	420,009	97,600	426,400	524,000	37.75	49.61
Kentucky	171,210	218,059	389,269	165,000	327,546	492,546	33.00	45.80
Louisiana	187,743	266,887	454,630	184,100	331,502	515,602	40.00	49.00
Maine	64,122	371,023	435,145	63,000	397,093	460,093	24.00	29.00
Maryland	183,480	1,135,869	1,319,349	181,300	1,369,830	1,551,130	69.20	82.60
Massachusetts	224,604	413,490	638,094	264,600	457,598	722,198	58.00	58.00
Michigan	358,803	659,392	1,018,195	357,800	992,200	1,350,000	91.00	95.50
Minnesota	156,651	561,030	717,681	155,400	661,955	817,355	60.40	60.00
Mississippi	149,000	123,235	272,235	145,100	72,550	217,650	25.75	25.00
Missouri	199,368	224,456	423,824	196,700	230,534	427,234	31.50	31.50
Montana	39,896	69,117	109,013	39,000	68,664	107,664	7.00	7.00
Nebraska	66,404	77,909	144,313	66,400	117,021	183,421	12.20	11.90
Nevada	21,485	32,682	54,167	23,787	34,213	58,000	5.50	5.71
New Hampshire	63,488	300,544	364,032	63,500	517,326	580,826	55.00	66.00
New Jersey	313,742	856,408	1,170,150	311,900	726,204	1,038,104	77.90	88.90
New Mexico	52,875	34,943	87,818	52,300	113,000	165,300	11.30	14.60
New York	671,175	4,349,545	5,020,720	650,400	4,564,632	5,215,032	328.00	300.00
North Carolina	269,764	438,219	707,983	264,600	509,930	774,530	58.50	57.00
North Dakota	34,398	30,454	64,852	37,200	27,700	64,900	6.00	5.85
Ohio	445,000	495,549	940,549	447,300	819,875	1,267,175	51.10	60.00
Oklahoma	119,156	138,437	257,593	117,600	181,098	298,698	19.00	31.90
Oregon	97,121	497,780	594,901	96,900	468,835	565,735	38.50	41.80
Pennsylvania	496,504	1,779,523	2,276,027	488,300	2,085,978	2,574,278	206.00	170.81
Rhode Island	110,443	163,827	274,270	111,000	187,200	298,200	29.65	32.60
South Carolina	159,749	200,631	360,380	157,400	365,474	522,874	36.50	43.00
South Dakota	41,165	58,683	99,848	38,500	66,500	105,000	11.70	8.70
Tennessee	212,537	188,780	401,317	208,200	329,320	537,520	31.50	37.50
Texas	436,951	1,796,201	2,233,152	427,000	1,771 339	2,198,339	133.00	145.00
Utah	54,592	62,455	117,047	55,400	92,052	147,452	11.15	12.67
Vermont	43,999	216,078	260,077	43,700	239,820	283,520	21.60	23.00
Virginia	212,858	625,220	838,078	210,500	1,065,740	1,276,240	78.50	100.00
Washington	131,037	997,205	1,128,242	131,037	1,025,803	1,156,840	73.50	73.50
West Virginia	111,682	173,790	285,472	111,682	233,870	345,552	28.50	28.50
Wisconsin	196,393	959,602	1,155,995	193,000	1,402,000	1,595,000	75.00	83.00
Wyoming	23,786	31,302	55,088	23,600	39,400	63,000	2.50	3.00
Guam	46,719	43,105	89,824	75,000	39,469	114,469	7.80	10.60
Puerto Rico	198,900	106,234	305,134	195,000	182,813	377,813	26.50	36.95
Virgin Islands	52,725	35,325	88,050	70,300	35,150	105,450	10.40	10.90
Total	**9,334,796**	**24,956,011**	**34,290,807**	**9,392,406**	**32,051,045**	**[2] 41,443,451**	**2709.11**	**[3] 2934.75**

[1] Data represent activities of water quality agencies, not expenditures for pollution control facilities. Fiscal year refers to the Federal July–June fiscal year.
[2] 20.86 percent increase over 1970 expenditures.
[3] 8.3 percent increase over 1970 level.

Source: Environmental Protection Agency, Office of Water Programs.

local regulation

LOCAL REGULATION

The first step in any analysis of local water pollution law is to determine whether the local government has authority over this subject. Even if authority exists it may be very limited. The entry of the state into the water pollution control field since 1965 may have substantially reduced local government powers over this subject.

Water pollution control by local government is generally not very significant. What cases are brought are usually based on the common law remedies discussed in Chapter 5.

People v. Choate, [1 ERC 1697] (Buffalo City Court, September 14, 1970)

Mikoll, Associate Judge:

The defendant stands charged under separate counts of a violation of Chapter IX. section 22 of the Buffalo City Ordinances.

On behalf of the defendant, a motion was made before the Court attacking the constitutionality of the ordinance on the ground that the ordinance and the matters it attempts to deal with have been preempted by the State and upon the further ground that the ordinance is in conflict with the State Statutes dealing with the same regulations.

The State has entered the field of pollution control of water by virtue of Article 12 of the Public Health Law. It is obvious from a reading of Article 12 and the state regulations adopted to implement Article 12, that the City Ordinance prohibits more than the State Statute.

There is then a conflict between the State and City enactments. The latter are more prohibitive.

It has been held that local laws which are in conflict with State Law are unconstitutional and must fall.

WHEREFORE, I find that the complaints must be dismissed.

So ordered.

End, text of case.

Cities may have ordinances protecting their water supply. They may also have health ordinances relating to the dumping of wastes. Sometimes a state statute allows the enforcement of ordinances outside the city limits. See *City of Durham v. Eno Cotton Mills* [141 N.C. 615, 54 S.E. 453 (1906)]. The zoning power can be used to prohibit activities that affect either health or the municipal water supply. The city may also have rights based on the property concepts of water law. These appropriation, riparian, or statutory rights have often been modified by statutes and/or court decisions so that municipal governments have greater rights than private holders of water rights. Public nuisance ordinances exist which either generally or specifically include pollution. Common law remedies, discussed in Chapter 5, may also be applicable.

If the municipality or some type of larger unit such as a sewer district has a more complex organization with responsibilities that stem from the Federal Water Pollution Control Act, their responsibilities are similar to those discussed under State laws and in the material in Chapter 3 on municipal air pollution control.

REFERENCES AND SELECTED BIBLIOGRAPHY

LEWIN, GORDON, and HARTELIUS, *Law and the Municipal Ecology—Air, Water, Noise, Over-Population,* Nimlo Research Report 1971 at 156.

WOLMAN, Abel (Selected Papers), WHITE, Gilbert F., ed., *Water, Health and Society,* Bloomington, Indiana Univ. Press, 1969

HIRSHLEIFER, Jack, DeHAVEN, James C., and MILLIMAN, Jerome W., *Water Supply—Economics, Technology, and Policy,* Chicago, The Univ. of Chicago Press, 1960

BALBE, Nelson M., *Water for the Cities: A History of the Urban Water Supply Problem in the United States,* New York, Syracuse Univ. Press, 1956

Deep-well injection of liquid wastes

by Charles W. Shipley

Current efforts to control pollution are mostly aimed at the air, water and surface lands—the visible environment. However, there is a fourth, unseen, dimension of great importance: the earth's crust. This crust is an extremely complicated and heterogeneous milieu, as compared with the atmosphere or surface land and water, and we know far less about the crust than of the other dimensions of our environment.

The crustal environment is polluted from many activities ranging from leachate drainage of landfills to subsurface storage of radioactive wastes. This paper will concentrate on the activity which seems to be the most environmentally hazardous, due to its widespread and rapidly increasing use: deep-well disposal of liquid wastes, introducing the technical, environmental, and legal problems arising from this practice.

An important point which must be understood before further discussion is that when liquid wastes are injected into subsurface strata, the result is *storage* of that waste—not treatment, and not disposal—since it will be there in its original toxic state for the foreseeable future. This is due to the lack of oxygen and the reduced quantity of microorganisms needed to decompose organic wastes, and to the lack of sufficient liquid medium to dilute inorganic wastes. Thus, deep-well disposal at very best is merely a temporary holding action until better treatment facilities are developed. We are merely storing our problems for future generations to deal with rather than accepting and dealing with them ourselves.

Technical and Environmental Aspects

In 1960, there were only thirty known deep injection wells used for industrial wastes. The official figure had reached 150 by 1969, and was expected to double in 1971.[1] However, some observers have estimated that the number of clandestine disposal operations puts the present total number in the thousands.[2]

At present, refineries, chemical plants, and steel mills use approximately 82 percent of the industrial liquid waste disposal wells in the United States. Approximately 63 percent of the deep wells use disposal zones 1,000 to 4,000 feet below the surface; 87 percent of these wells have injection rates less than 400 gallons per minute, and 84 percent have injection pressures less than 700 pounds per square inch at the surface.[3]

Virtually all types of industrial waste waters are now being pumped underground in significant quantities. They include alkalies, acids, chromates, nitrates, phosphates, sulfites, alcohols, ketones, phenols, cyanides and chlorinated hydrocarbons, as well as radioactive wastes.[4]

As a matter of perspective, it should be noted that the injection of liquids in subsurface strata is not a new concept. This technique has been employed for half a century by the petroleum industry for two purposes: to increase crude oil production by water-flooding or re-pressuring of oil strata; and as a means for returning to the underground the salt water normally associated with oil extraction. What is new, relatively, is the

1. National Academy of Engineering, Committee on Engineering Aspects of Environmental Quality, "Proposal for a Planning Grant with Regard to Utilization and Preservation of the Continental Crust," March 10, 1971. (Unpublished).

2. Evan, David, & Bradford, Albert, "Under the Rug," *Environment* p. 11 (October, 1969).

3. National Industrial Pollution Control Council, *Waste Disposal in Deep Wells,* February 1971, p. 9.

4. Warner, Don. L., "Deep-wells for Industrial Waste Injection in the United States—Summary of Data," *Bull.* WP - 20 - 10, Dept. of Interior, FWPCA, Cincinnati, Ohio. November 1967, pp. 3-4.

application of injection-well technology to underground storage of a variety of industrial waste-waters. The distinction to be made is this: when salt water is injected into the stratigraphic zone from which it originated, the process merely returns to the subsurface a liquid that had been long accommodated and confined there. This condition of course, does not apply to injection of extraneous wastewaters.[5] In the latter case, the physical and chemical properties of a waste can cause plugging of the pores (of the injection horizon) with suspended solids or entrained gas in the injected liquid, by reactions between injected fluid and aquifer minerals, or by reactions between the injected and interstitial fluids. Plugging of the pores results in loss of permeability and reduction in well intake rate and well life. The extent and ramifications of the chemical reactions between the wastes and the storage medium are not fully understood.[6] Consequently, citing oil-field brine disposal experience as the precedent to justify extension of underground injection for other liquid wastes is not altogether relevant.

feasibility

The feasibility of a deep-well is in large part dependent upon the geologic and hydrologic characteristics of the proposed disposal site. The geologic characteristics which Winer considers necessary for waste injection wells are:

> 1. The injection horizon should have sufficient porosity, permeability, and areal extent to act as a liquid storage reservoir at safe injection pressures.
>
> 2. The injection horizon should be vertically below the level of fresh water and should be separated vertically from fresh water and other natural resources by rocks that are, for practical purposes, impermeable to waste.[7]

An analysis of the geologic characteristics of a proposed disposal site requires a consideration of such factors as rock properties, stratigraphy, structure and hydrodynamics.[8]

Under favorable conditions, almost any type of rock will accept injected wastes. However, naturally fractured or unfractured marine sedimentary rocks such as sandstones, limestones, and shale are the most likely to have the requisite characteristics of porosity and permeability. The pores of most sedimentary rocks will be filled with water of varying temperature and salinity. Other resources such as oil, gas and coal may be intermixed with the sedimentary deposit.

Stratigraphy refers to the arrangements or rocks in layers or strata. Stratigraphic data will provide information on the depth of fresh water zones, the sequence of geologic formations and the thickness of the various strata. The stratum into which the waste will be injected must be confined by impermeable rock of sufficient thickness to prevent wastes from migrating vertically to contaminate resources in other strata.

Structurally, sedimentary strata are characterized by faults and folds. A fault is a discontinuity in the various strata of rock, so that strata on one side of the fault line do not correspond with strata on the other side. A waste injection stratum could be directly connected along a fault line with other strata containing valuable natural resources. In addition, wastes can migrate along fault lines to contaminate other strata or possibly cause earthquakes.

There are two types of folds: in relation to the surface, anticlinal folds are convex, while synclinal folds are concave. Wastes with a density lower

5. Cleary, E.J. and Warner, D.C., *Perspective on the Regulation of Underground Injection of Waste-waters,* p. A-2, December 1969. An appraisal sponsored by the Ohio River Valley Water Sanitation Commission.

6. Warner, D.C., "Deep Well Waste Injection—Reaction with Aquifer Water," *Journal of the Sanitary Engineering Division, American Society of Civil Engineers,* p. 45-6, August, 1966.

7. Winer, "The Disposal of Wastewater Underground," *Industrial Engineering,* p. 21, March, 1967.

8. See Generally, Piper, A.M., *Disposal of Liquid Wastes by Injection Underground—Neither Myth or Millennium,* Geological Survey Circular 631, (1969).

than the water in the pores of the sedimentary rock should be injected into an anticline. The low density wastes will rise to the top of the anticline and be trapped. High density wastes should be injected into a syncline, where the waste will settle to the bottom.

Anticlinal and synclinal waste entrapment may not occur, however, if a hydrodynamic gradient exists in the waste injection stratum. Hydrodynamics is a branch of physics dealing with the movement of water. Where a hydrodynamic gradient exists, the fluids in a stratum will circulate and move laterally within the stratum. Other effects of hydrodynamics were pointed out recently by United States Geological Survey research hydrologists:

> In deep saline aquifers, natural pressure, and geothermal heat (from the interior of the earth) can induce convective ground water movements from the bottom to the top of an aquifer—somewhat akin to the circulation that can be observed in a teapot being warmed on a stove.[9]

Thus, the rate and direction of fluid movement within the injection stratum should be a determining factor in the suitability of a proposed disposal site. Some wastes may be rendered harmless after an appropriate detention time so that some limited fluid movement may be permissible. Other wastes may not be degradable, and will require an infinite detention time under static conditions. However, researchers have recently reminded us that "ground-water reservoirs" (aquifers, subsurface water-bearing rocks) are not static environments, but are systems which will undergo changes when a new stress is applied. Such a new stress is the pressure used to inject wastes into deep aquifers. Although the waste itself may move slowly away from the injection point, the pressure increase is propagated rapidly outward, and may displace brine, for example, into a fresh-water aquifer a great distance from the injection site.[10] Piper has criticized the general neglect of hydrodynamics:

knowledge inadequate

> Unfortunately, in a large fraction of the relevant current literature, effects of injection have been assessed only in terms of hydrostatics and of injection wells under hydraulic equilibrium. As a result, the assessment has not always been adequate.[11]

The operating life of an injection well is determined by the cumulative volume of wastes which can be stored. The volume of wastes which can be injected is limited by the area of the stratum and by the injection pressure. The injection pressure can be limited by law, by equipment design, or by critical pressures.

Experience in the petroleum industry has shown that as the injection pressure increases, the rate of waste injection increases proportionately until, at a so-called critical pressure, the rate of waste injection suddenly increases anomalously.[12] At the critical pressure, it is generally believed that *hydrofracturing* (rupturing) takes place. Hydrofracturing increases the permeability of the stratum and causes the anomalous increase in the rate of injection. Though increased permeability in the disposal stratum may be desirable, it is feared that at the critical pressure, hydrofracturing of the impermeable confining strata may also occur. This raises the possibility that contaminating wastes will escape to overlying formations. For this reason, the critical pressure has been accepted in practice as the maximum safe injection pressure.

Warner and Piper appear somewhat skeptical about whether hydrofracturing actually takes place at the critical pressure. Warner lists the

9. Department of Interior, news release for November 30, 1971, "Underground Waste Injection Problems Drawing Increasing Attention." p. 2.

10. Id.

11. Supra note 8, at 9.

12. Supra note 8, at 10.

following occurrences that could also result in an anomalous increase in the injection rate at the critical pressure:

1. Horizontal parting between adjacent vertical strata.
2. Opening of pre-existing cracks or joints.
3. Compaction of shales adjacent to or in the recovery formation.
4. Yielding of backers.[13]

Piper makes reference to waste injection wells which are operating at injection pressures much higher than those considered to be safe, but with no reports of hydrofracturing.[14] In some cases, Piper suggests, substantial benefits could be derived from the hydrofracturing of stratum at pressures *exceeding* the critical pressure. In contrast, Piper notes that the maximum safe pressure in potential earthquake zones may be much *less* than the critical pressure, and so blind reliance upon the rule of thumb that the critical pressure is the safe pressure might result in earthquake hazards.[15]

injection pressure

At issue is the determination of the safe injection pressure which, as Piper suggests, may be higher or lower than the critical pressure, depending on the circumstances.[16] Piper suggests the need for new safe injection pressure criteria,[17] and Warner states:

> Although it is unlikely that hydraulic fracturing results in damage to confining beds, it would seem prudent to consider the pressure at which hydraulic fracturing occurs as being the maximum safe injection pressure until the question is resolved, particularly in cases where confining strata are relatively thin and vertical confinement is essential.[18]

Warner seems to neglect the earthquake hazards that may exist at injection pressures much less than the critical pressure, but his statement was published before the correlation between injection wells and earthquakes received widespread publication. It does point up, however, the inability of experts to predict all possible effects of deep-well injection of wastes.

The foremost example of this prediction failure is the series of earthquakes that apparently have been set off by such injection in several places across the country. The most documented of these occurred at the United States Army Chemical Corps' Rocky Mountain Arsenal near Denver, Colorado. Initially, the Arsenal attempted to dispose of its wastes in unlined reservoirs, which allowed them to seep into and contaminate surrounding groundwater supplies. The Federal government paid $74,000 in crop damages to the adjacent irrigation farmers.[19]

After an unsuccessful attempt to dispose of the wastes by solar evaporation from lined reservoirs, the deep injection well was constructed. It is the deepest injection well in the United States—bottoming out at 12,045 feet in a fractured granite gneiss—a metamorphic rock. In March, 1962, wastes were first injected into the well. In the next month the first Denver earthquakes since 1882 occurred.

Waste injections continued intermittently until February, 1966, when the well was permanently shut down. Numerous investigators, the first being a geologist, David M. Evans, have verified a correlation between the frequency of earthquakes and the volume of wastes injected month by

13. Warner, D.L., *Deep-Well Injection of Liquid Wastes,* Public Health Service, U.S. Dept. of Health, Education, and Welfare (April, 1965).

14. Supra note 8, at 10.

15. Id.

16. Id.

17. Id.

18. Supra Note 13, at 13.

19. Gahr, "Contamination of Groundwater Vicinity of Denver", *The Sanitarian* p. 328, (May—June, 1962).

month.[20] Since April, 1962, the Denver area has experienced more than 1500 earthquakes. It has been determined that these earthquakes are centered in the vacinity of the Arsenal.

Since the injection well has been shut down, the earthquakes have continued. The most severe quake occurred on August 9, 1967,[21] and the most recent on May 23, 1970.[22] Damage from these quakes have been relatively minor. The most severe quake caused cracked plaster, broken windows and other minor breakage. Commercial establishments such as super markets and liquor stores experienced the most extensive damage due to broken bottles and overturned shelves.

Although there is still some doubt, the general consensus of the scientific community is that the quakes were caused by the injection of wastes in the Arsenal well.[23] The fluid pressure of the injected wastes caused the fractured rock of the injection stratum to separate, permitting the wastes to flow through the fractures. The wastes acted as a lubricant, reducing friction between rock layers, and permitting the rock to shift, causing earthquakes.

earthquakes

The reason that the earthquakes continued even though the injections were stopped is that the previously injected wastes continued to percolate through the fractured rock zone.[24]

Suggestions that the Arsenal well might be pumped out to avoid possibilities of continuing quakes or a catastrophic one might have been countered by the argument that such action might precipitate exactly the event sought to be avoided.[25] This again illustrates how little certainty there is about what can happen underground—even among experts. A second, and very important, point to be noted is that once something unfavorable does happen underground, it is very difficult, if not impossible to reverse the process.

According to the United States Geological Survey's National Center for Earthquake Research, earthquakes in the Rangely oil field in northwestern Colorado, as well as the Arsenal earthquakes, have been "clearly linked" to high pressure subsurface fluid injection.[26] Also, the Center proclaimed, "there is presently no way to determine before drilling whether an injection at a given rate will produce earthquakes."[27] Other earthquakes in Texas and Utah have been related to deep-well liquid injections.[28]

Operational risks are illuminated by the failure of an injection well at the Hammermill Paper Co. on the shore of Lake Erie. Here, a 1,610 foot deep-well was drilled in 1964 to dispose of some 2.5 thousand gallons per day of spent sulfite liquor along with other waste residues. Utilizing pressures up to 1,300 pounds per square inch, the liquids were pumped into a dolomite formation. On April 14, 1968, the top of the well blew off with such force that equipment was thrown thirty feet into the air. The gusher of waste liquids that followed poured into Lake Erie at the rate of 200 gallons per minute for several days before the well could be capped. This failure was attributed to corrosion of a joint in the injection tube. As a result, the

20. Evans, "Man-Made Earthquakes in Denver," *Geotimes,* p. 11 (May—June, 1966).

Evans, "Man-Made Earthquakes—A Progress Report," *Geotimes,* p. 19 (July—August, 1967).

Healy, "The Denver Earthquakes," *Science,* p. 1301 (Sept. 27, 1968).

21. *Denver Post,* Aug. 9, 1967, p. 1, Col. 4.

22. *Denver Post,* May 23, 1970, p. 1, Col. 4.

23. Supra Note 8, at 5.

24. Supra note 20, Evans—"A Progress Report", at 19.

25. Supra Note 5, at A-5.

26. Supra Note 9, at 3.

27. Id.

28. Congressional Record—House, p. 4094, May 18, 1971.

pressurized liquid stored beneath the ground gained entry into the annulus (area surrounding the injection tube) of the well, and thus escaped to the surface. A spokesman for the company attributed this series of events to "technological shortcomings."[29]

It must also be remembered that once the wastes are injected into a subsurface strata, it is unrealistic to regard them as being sealed in a leak-proof container. As mentioned before, lateral migration of the wastes can result in escape to overlying strata. Vertical migration can occur along geologic faults or fractures, or as the result of a rupturing of the confining strata by excessive injection pressures.[30]

The possibility of the confining strata being fractured by natural earthquakes must also be considered—especially in areas with a history of seismic disturbances. Recent research points out that clay beds which have been considered to be an effective capping seal for underground liquid waste storage may, under certain conditions, behave as "natural semi-permeable membranes."[31] It is also possible that the confining strata may collapse as loadbearing material dissolves, due to the chemical reaction between the waste injected and the receiving rock.[32]

reasons for caution

From the viewpoint of natural resources stewardship, there are compelling reasons to exhibit caution in countenancing subsurface storage of contaminated liquids. Proliferation of the use of the underground for wastewater injection could imperil potable groundwater resources as well as limit, if not foreclose, future opportunities for: (a) the extraction of minerals; (b) the development of subsurface reservoirs for purposes such as freshwater or natural gas storage; and (3) the potential utilization of brackish groundwaters.[33]

The need to be concerned about precluding future uses of the crustal environment is perhaps best illustrated by the emerging reasons for conserving our saline ground water. The United States Geological Survey points out that saline groundwater can be found under nearly two-thirds of the United States, and suggests that it may be one of the Nation's valuable resources of the future—in spite of the fact that today it is regarded as worse than useless since it is a "misery" to well drillers.[34] In a recent article it was pointed out that:

> Much of the monitoring that is currently being done is to check the safety of freshwater reservoirs underground. Disposal engineers are careful to point out that poisonous wastes will only be injected into disposal zones containing salt water, and that freshwater resources will be carefully avoided. However, geologist William C. Finch of Houston, Texas, who is an authority on desalting, explains the folly of this course of action. "To begin with," he says, "there are three kinds of water—freshwater that has less than 1,000 parts per million of dissolved salts; brackish water that contains less salt than seawater and more than freshwater; salt or seawater (or over 35,000 parts per million dissolved salts.)" The so-called salt water in most potential disposal wells is in reality brackish water. There is hundreds of times more brackish water underground than freshwater. Brackish water can be desalted at about one-fourth of the cost of desalting seawater and is likely to be our next big source of freshwater as human and industrial demands

29. Sheldrick, M.G., "Deep-Well Disposal: are Safeguards Being Ignored?", *Chemical Engineering,* April 7, 1969, p. 74.

30. Supra Note 8, at 10.

31. Supra Note 9, at 5.

32. Supra Note 9, at 4.

33. Supra Note 5, at A-7.

34. Anon. "Salty Groundwater Has Vast Potential," *Clean Air and Water News,* May 29, 1969, p. 2, Commerce Clearing House, Inc., Chicago.

rise. It is an irreplaceable natural resource, and Finch contends it would be the wildest kind of folly to contaminate it with industrial waste.

We can desalt brackish water with 2,500 parts per million salts for 25 cents a thousand gallons, against 98 cents a thousand gallons for seawater," Finch says, "Brackish water is located where it will soon be needed—beneath the deserts of Arizona and Nevada and the plains of west Texas and eastern Colorado, for example.[35]

The rational advanced by proponents of expanded use of the underground for waste disposal is that it provides a safe means of disposing of untreatable wastes. As has been pointed out above, there is little safety in such method; there is no assurance that the wastes will stay where they are put; and it is primarily storage, not disposal, of the wastes.

Another point in rebuttal of that rational is that nearly all waste materials are treatable—at a cost.[36] Therefore, it is evident that the primary motivating force toward deepwell disposal is economic. The costs of conventional industrial waste treatment are increasing as industry is being forced by public regulation and public anti-pollution sentiment to account for its surface polluting activities. Profit-oriented industries seeking to minimize costs will welcome deep-well disposal as a least cost alternative. For example:

minimizing costs

> The Chemstrand Company operates the world's largest wholly unified nylon plant at Pensacola, Florida. To combat increasing waste disposal costs, a deep-well was constructed. It was found that capital and operating costs of the deep-well were approximately one-tenth that of a conventional treatment system.[37]
>
> Inland Steel Company of East Chicago, Indiana, had been disposing of 158,000 gallons per day of "pickle liquor" acid into Lake Michigan. When water pollution regulations prohibited such discharges, the company constructed a deep-well to a depth of 4,300 feet where the wastes are being injected into a sandstone formation. The costof the well was $32,500,000.[38]
>
> The Holland-Suco Color Company of Holland, Michigan, produces 36,000 gallons per day of color pigment wastes. A 5,896 foot deep-well was constructed into a sandstone formation at a cost of $100,000. The deep-well eliminated the need for an expensive waste neutralization process.[39]

A 1968 study by the Interstate Oil Compact Commission concluded: "A majority of the decisions leading to the approval of a disposal program (speaking of industrial waste injection) are based on opinion rather than fact."[40] A leading authority in waste injection says:

> ...the United States appears to verge on accepting deep injection of wastes as a certain cure for all the ills of water pollution. Uncritical acceptance would be ill advised. It is fostered by a technical and commercial literature which, to a distressing degree, describes capabilities of injection in terms so highly

35. Supra Note 2, at p. 9.

36. Supra Note 5, at p. A-11.

37. Batz, "Deep Well Disposal of Nylon Waste Water," *Chemical Engineering Progress,* p. 85, October, 1964.

38. Anon., "Injection Well Incorporates Many Safeguards" *Groundwater Age,* p. 34, June 1968.

39. Anon. *Civil Engineering,* p. 92 May, 1966.

40. *Subsurface Disposal of Industrial Wastes,* p. 68, 1968, Interstate Oil Compact Commission, Oklahoma City, Oklahoma.

generalized as to be all but meaningless in relation to a specific waste in a particular environment.[41]

legal and regulatory aspects

A significant body of statutory and case law has developed to protect public and private rights from the detrimental effects of waste disposal. Primarily this law has been the result of experiences involving the re-injection of brine from oilfield operations, but another body of law is developing with respect to the rights and liabilities associated with underground stoage of natural gas.[42]

The following two cases from Kansas will illustrate how the judicial process has handled claims of damage from deep-well disposal. By statute in Kansas, it is the duty of oil and gas well operators to keep salt water brines safely confined and to prevent their escape.[43] Knowing or willful breach of this duty is made a misdemeanor punishable by fine or imprisonment.[44] Both of the following cases deal with a breach of this duty.

In the 1936 case of *Alliston v. Shell Petroleum Corporation,*[45] the plaintiff sought damages for permanent injury to a fresh water stratum underlying his land. It was claimed that the damage was negligently and unlawfully caused by the escape of salt water brines from defendant's oil well operations. The defendant had drilled a disposal well to a depth of 2,936 feet. Although the stratigraphic log of the well did not reveal a suitable injection stratum, the defendant nevertheless decided to use the well for salt water disposal. His decision was based on the log of a nearby dry well which revealed a suitable disposal formation. Defendant injected wastes under pressure for more than two years. The well was then shut down, interestingly enough, because the defendant had acquired a pipeline to dispose of the wastes into the Arkansas River.

The plaintiff owned a 440-acre farm with several fresh water wells (the deepest being 72 feet) used for domestic and livestock water supply. During the period in which defendant was using the disposal well, plaintiff's water supply became increasingly polluted, until it was conceded at the trial that the fresh water wells were totally unusable.

In the trial court the defendant entered a general denial and a plea of a two-year statute of limitations. The defendant alleged that its deep-well operations had been in accord with the latest recognized methods, and that other oil well operators had caused the pollution. The jury awarded the plaintiff a general verdict of $11,000 damages which amounted to the difference in the market value of plaintiff's property before and after the pollution. The property had decreased in value from seventy-five to fifty dollars per acre. The defendant appealed, claiming among other things that the verdict was not supported by the evidence.

In upholding the verdict, the court relied heavily upon the testimony of two expert witnesses who had testified on behalf of the plaintiff. One expert was a chemist who had analyzed a mixture composed of the salt water wastes found in defendant's disposal well and the fresh water found in plaintiff's water supply wells. He concluded that this mixture would result in the chemical composition of the polluted water found in plaintiff's wells.

The other expert was an engineer with a long history of experience in oil well operations. He testified that defendant's disposal well did not have a sufficiently porous injection formation. As a result, the injected waste migrated under pressure to the stratum of least resistance, which happened to be plaintiff's fresh water aquifer.

41. Supra Note 8, at 2.

42. 94 A.L.R. 2d 543.

43. 55 Kan. Stat. Ann. 121.

44. 55 Kan. Stat. Ann. 122.

45. 55 P. 2d 396 (1936).

The court proficiently analyzed the technical evidence to eliminate all of the possible sources of pollution except that of the defendant. For example, other oil well operators in the vicinity had been disposing of salt water in unlined earthen storage ponds. Seepage from these ponds could have polluted plaintiff's fresh water aquifer at a depth of 72 feet. The court found, however, that there were fresh water aquifers underlying the seepage ponds but overlying the plaintiff's aquifer that had not been polluted. Since it was impossible for the wastes to contaminate plaintiff's aquifer without contaminating these other aquifers as well, the court concluded that seepage from the ponds was not the cause of plaintiff's polluted wells.

The 1968 case of *Augustine v. Hinnen*[46] is similar in that the court relied upon a mass of technical evidence and expert testimony. The defendant had constructed and operated a salt brine disposal well under a permit granted by the Kansas State Corporation Commission. The plaintiff claimed that the salt brine had escaped from a hole in the casing of the well and polluted the groundwater aquifer from which he took his fresh water supply. The interesting part of this case is that the jury awarded the plaintiff $12,651.25 in actual damages and $18,000 in punitive damages. On appeal, the court upheld the actual damage award but reversed the punitive damage award. The court stated that punitive damages are imposed

damages awarded

> ...by way of punishing a defendant for malicious, vindictive or a willful and wanton invasion of a plaintiff's rights—the purpose being to restrain him and deter others from the commission of like wrongs.[47]

The court reasoned that even though the defendant may have been subject to criminal prosecution for allowing the salt brine to escape, this alone was not sufficient to justify an award of punitive damages. The court failed to find in the evidence the requisite additional element of maliciousness or reckless indifference to the rights of others.

A strong dissenting opinion noted that the defendant had failed to take remedial action even though salt water had been flowing from an open well in the vicinity of the defentant's disposal well for a sufficient length of time to permit a pool of water to form, and to warrant an investigation by the State Board of Health. This was a strong enough breach of duty to convince the dissenting judge that punitive damages should have been awarded.

The most recent case which treats the deep-well injection issue is *United States v. Armco Steel Corporation,* 333 F.Supp. 1073 (1971). The United States District Court for the Southern District of Texas, Houston Division, found Armco guilty of violating §13 of the Rivers and Harbors Act of 1899 (also known as the Refuse Act) by dumping its industrial effluent, containing high concentrations of toxic cyanide, phenols, ammonia, and sulfides, into the Houston Ship Channel.

The court, under the doctrine of pendent jurisdiction, also chose to consider the ecological question raised by the Texas Water Quality Board's order to Armco to dispose of its toxic wastes by means of an injection well system. Judge Hannay, however, never explained his finding of a "related state claim" requisite for the application of the pendent jurisdiction doctrine. The court enjoined the Texas Water Quality Board from enforcing its order until certain recommendations of the Federal Environment Protection Agency regarding the plugging of abandoned wells in the area had been complied with. [333 F.Supp. at 1083, 1084.] Though this decision is questionable procedurally, it does indicate at least one Federal court's willingness to deal with the complex environmental issues raised by deep-well waste injection.

It can be expected, however, that as cases arise involving the hazards of deep-well technology, the courts will probably continue to react in a

46. 443 P. 2d 354. (1968).

47. Id. at 357.

rather traditional fashion, even though the Armco Steel case just discussed seems to portend an opposite conclusion.

The inadequacies of the judicial system to deal effectively with the problems of pollution have been outlined in several sources.[48] The inadequacies cited by the National Academy of Sciences are briefly summarized as follows:

1. Lack of technical staffs for courts.
2. Courts cannot initiate actions; they must wait for cases to arise.
3. Courts are generally restricted to narrow rather than comprehensive considerations.
4. Burden of proof requirements may be excessively costly for plaintiffs. (This could be particularly true in deep-well cases.)
5. Vague legalisms such as "reasonableness" and "substantial" create uncertainty as to legal relations.[49]

summation

A declaration of deep-well disposal of wastes as an "ultrahazardous activity" would help to solve some of the problems in burden of proof in establishing negligence, and would help to eliminate the legal hurdles of "reasonableness" and "substantial." This use of deep-wells certainly fits the definition of "ultrahazardous activities" set out in a recent case. In *McLane v. Northwest Natural Gas Co.,*[50] the court held the surface storage of pressurized liquid petroleum gas to be "ultrahazardous," defining it to be, "an activity in which abnormal risks are inherent."[51] However, rather than wait for the courts to so declare it, a better approach is to include in the regulatory statute a provision declaring such use of deep-wells to be ultrahazardous—notwithstanding its permit to operate from the regulatory agency. This has the advantage of putting the operators on notice of their strict liability from the initiation of any such activity.

As with any highly complicated activity which requires regulation, the foundation of that regulation must lie in an agency which has the statutory authority and technical expertise to handle the situation. As yet no Federal laws cover the subject of deep-well disposal, although two bills have been introduced in the U.S. Congress to put the activity under the Environmental Protection Agency's control.[52]

Also in the bill which passed the Senate in late 1971 which would amend the Federal Water Pollution laws,[53] the administrator of the Environmental Protection Agency is directed to advise the states as to what they must do to set up an effective regulatory system including, inter alia, water pollution from "the disposal of materials in wells or subsurface excavations.[54]

Two Surveys published in 1968,[55] and one of which has been up-dated with a 1970 supplement,[56] show the extent of the use in each state of deep-well disposal of wastes, and the state's regulatory approach, if any, to such activity. The following is a synopsis of those reports. No state is known

48. National Academy of Sciencies, National Research Council, *Waste Management and Control,* p. 232 (1966); Kneese and Bower *Managing Water Quality:* Economics, *Technology, Institutions,* p. 86 (1968); Hines, "Nor Any Drop to Drink: Public Regulation of Water Quality," 52 Iowa L.R. 799 (1967).

49. National Academy of Sciences, Supra note 48.

50. 467 P 2d 635 (1970).

51. Id at 637.

52. H.R. 8532, 92nd Cong., 1st Sess., May 18, 1971; H.R. 10800, 92nd Cong., 1st Sess., September 22, 1971.

53. S. 2770, 92nd Cong., 1st Sess., November 21, 1971.

54. Id. at Section 304 (e) (z) (d).

55. Interstate Oil Compact Commission, Supra note 40; Walker, W.R., and Stewart, R.C., "Deep-Well Disposal of Wastes," *Sanitary Engineering Journal.* p. 945-966, October, 1968.

56. Interstate Oil Compact Commission, Supra Note 40, Supplement, January, 1970.

to have legislation that denies the installation of waste water injection systems. However, nine states subscribe to a policy of either rejecting applications (Arizona, Idaho, New Jersey and Wisconsin) or discouraging them (Alaska, South Carolina, South Dakota and New York). New York, for example, recently declared that its policy will be one of regarding liquid-waste injection as a "last resort" after all other methods have been evaluated.

Present policy in the remaining states (among which information from five is not available) is to permit the practice of subsurface disposal. However, only three states—Ohio, West Virginia and Texas—have specific legislation pertaining to the regulation of industrial wastewater injection. Regulations applied in other states apparently stem from a patchwork of legislation, some of which relates to the protection of groundwater aquifers or to the installation of salt water injection wells.

The regulatory procedures in the states are simply not adequate. Among the major deficiencies cited are: (a) inadequacy of legislative guidelines and technological criteria; (b) poorly defined jurisdictional linkage among agencies traditionally involved with underground resources and those concerned with pollution control; and (c) staff unfamiliarity with the complex and often novel aspects of subsurface injection practice.[57] Another inadequacy in most states' regulatory approach is a specific requirement that the agencies insist upon an alternative system of disposal in case of failure of the deep-well. Kentucky has such a requirement.[58]

A recent project in Oklahoma illustrates the scope and cost of the exploration and research which is appropriate before decisions regarding underground waste disposal can be made.[59] Reichhold Chemicals, Inc., under the supervision of the Alabama Geological Survey, will drill a 5,500-foot test well at its Tuscaloosa plant to develop data on the porosity, confinement potentialities, compatibility characteristics and other conditions that may be relevant to environmentally safe waste injection. The company allocated $675,000 for this research project, and the Alabama Geological Survey received a $314,000 grant from the Federal Water Pollution Control Administration to enable their participation in the project.

Lack of money and expertise on the part of the states suggests that most of the money and expertise should come from those proposing to use the deep-wells. This must be coupled with the proponents carrying the burden of proving the safety of their operation and design, as well as being unconditionally liable for any damages caused by their operations. The agency must bear in mind its long-range stewardship of the total environment; New York's policy of allowing deep-well storage of wastes only as a "last resort" should be the credo of all the states.

EDITOR'S POSTNOTE: Although it has been mentioned above, it should be doubly stressed that at the time this book went to press in July of 1972, Federal legislation was pending regarding the control of deep-well injection. This was in one of the versions of a general water pollution control bill being considered by a House-Senate conference committee. If that bill becomes law, North American International plans a supplement to this book.

There is already some Federal regulation of subsurface storage of gases on Federal lands. These storage rights are sold or rented under the Mineral Leasing Act (30 U.S.C. 181 *et seq.*), according to the U.S. Geological Survey. General Federal policy toward deep-well

57. Supra, Note 5 at A-8.

58. Supra Note 40, at 22.

59. "Research Drilling Project for Waste Disposal," *Clean Air and Water News,* pp 14-15, November 21, 1969, Commerce Clearing House, Inc., Chicago, Ill.

injection is that it is to be discouraged if the wastes can be treated, but permitted if the wastes cannot be treated, providing that such disposal will not harm "present or potential subsurface water supplies . . . or otherwise damage the environment." This policy is based on a 2-page document of October, 1970 (before EPA existed) that remains current EPA policy, according to Assistant Administrator Stanley Greenfield (6 *Environmental Science & Technology* 2, February, 1972 at 121). Lacking, of course, are effective enforcement provisions.

No part of the country—or, indeed, the world—is completely safe from the destruction of its subsurface waters. According to the U.S. Geological Survey's D.A. Goodsby, Monsanto Corporation has inserted "more than 4 billion gallons of acidic industrial waste into a limestone aquifer" near Pensacola, Florida. Simply because this problem is currently little-known is no reason to ignore it.

A recent bibliography on the subject of deep-well injection is available from the U.S. Government Printing Office: *Water Supply Paper No. 2020,* U.S. Geological Survey, $1.50.

APPENDIX—Chapter Four

SAMPLE COMPLAINT

IN THE UNITED STATES DISTRICT COURT FOR THE DISTRICT OF NEW JERSEY (Camden Division)

CIVIL ACTION NO. ________

CAPE MAY COUNTY CHAPTER, INC., IZAAK WALTON LEAGUE OF AMERICA By JONATHAN SAYRE, President
R.D. No. 1, Box 36
Cape May, New Jersey 08204

Plaintiffs

On its own behalf and on behalf of all those people whose beneficial rights and interests in subaqueous lands, tidal marshes, tidal waters and related natural resources are being irreparably diminished, permanently damaged and destroyed by indiscriminate dredging and filling and other deleterious activities in and around Cape May County, New Jersey; and on behalf of all those people who are entitled to the full benefit, use and enjoyment of their environment free from damage caused by the failure of certain Federal, State and local government agencies to prohibit the filling, dredging and other activities adversely affecting the subaqueous lands, tidal marshes, tidal waters and related natural resources of the Middle Atlantic ecosystem; and on behalf of all those entitled to the full benefit, use and enjoyment of the unique natural resources of the United States and the Middle Atlantic ecosystem in which plaintiffs reside; and on behalf of all those people similarly situated.

v.

TITO MACCHIA
ANTONIETTA MACCHIA
JAMES A. RUETSCHLIN
KATHRYN M. RUETSCHLIN
Avalon, New Jersey

and

JOHN DOE, INC., #1 and #2
(Fictitious Names for Corporations owned by Tito Macchia, Antonietta Macchia, and/or James H. Ruetschlin, Kathryn M. Ruetschlin)

and

STANLEY A. RESOR, Individually and as Secretary of the Army
Washington, D.C.

and

COLONEL JAMES A. JOHNSON, Individually and as District Engineer, U. S. Army Corps of Engineers
Custom House
2nd and Chestnut Streets
Philadelphia, Pennsylvania 19106

and

RICHARD J. SULLIVAN, Commissioner
State of New Jersey
Department of Environmental Protection
Trenton, New Jersey 08609

and

JERRY H. MAY, JR., MAYOR
Township of Middle
County of Cape May
Cape May C. H., New Jersey 08210

Defendants

VERIFIED COMPLAINT FOR DECLARATORY AND INJUNCTIVE RELIEF AND FOR DAMAGES

Jurisdiction

1. The jurisdiction of this court is invoked under Title 28, United States Code, §1331(a) (Federal question); and, under Title 28, United States Code, §§1343(3), 1343(4):

> The district courts shall have original jurisdiction of any civil action authorized by law to be commenced by any person:
>
> (3) To redress the deprivation, under color of any state law, statute, ordinance, regulation, custom or usage, of any right, privilege, or immunity secured by the Constitution of the United States or by any Act of Congress providing for equal rights of citizens or of all persons within the jurisdiction of the United States;

> (4) To recover damages or to secure equitable or other relief under any Act of Congress providing for the protection of civil rights . . . .

and, under Title 42, United States Code, §1983:

> Every person who under color of any statute, ordinance, regulation, custom, or usage of any state or territory, subjects or causes to be subjected, any citizen of the United States or other person within the jurisdiction thereof to the deprivation of any rights, privileges or immunities secured by the Constitution and laws, shall be liable to the party injured in an action at law, suit in equity, or other proceeding for redress.

and, under Title 28. United States Code, §1337:

> The district courts shall have original jurisdiction of any civil action or proceeding arising under any Act of Congress regulating commerce or protecting trade and commerce against restraints and monopolies.

2. This action also arises under Article VI, Section 2, of the Constitution of the United States:

> This Constitution, and the Laws of the United States which shall be made in Pursuance thereof; and all Treaties made, or which shall be made, under the Authority of the United States, shall be the supreme Law of the Land; and the Judges in every state shall be bound thereby; any Thing in the Constitution of Laws of any State to the Contrary notwithstanding.

and involves the declaration and interpretation of the rights of the plaintiff and all the People of the United States secured by the Ninth Amendment of the Constitution of the United States:

> The enumeration in the Constitution of certain rights, shall not be construed to deny or disparage others retained by the people.

and under the *due process clause* of the Fifth Amendment to the Constitution of the United States:

> . . . nor shall any person . . . be deprived of life, liberty or property, without due process of law . . .

and under the *due process, equal protection,* and *rights, privileges and immunities clauses* of the Fourteenth Amendment of the Constitution of the United States:

> . . . no State shall make or enforce any law which shall abridge the privileges or immunities of citizens of the United States; nor shall any state deprive any person of life, liberty or property, without due process of law; nor deny to any person within its jurisdiction the equal protection of the laws.

and under the *commerce clause,* Article I, Section 8, of the Constitution of the United States.

3. This action also arises under the following Federal statutes:

The National Environmental Policy Act of 1969, 42 U.S.C.A. §4331-47:

> The purposes of this act are: To declare a national policy which will encourage productive enjoyable harmony between man and his environment; to promote efforts which will prevent or eliminate damage to the environment and biosphere and stimulate the health and welfare of man; to enrich the understanding of the ecological systems and natural resources important to the nation; and to establish a council on environmental quality.

And, under the Fish and Wildlife Coordination Act, 16 U.S.C.A. §661, *et seq.:*

> Except as hereafter stated in subsection (h) of this section [not applicable], whenever the waters of any stream or other body of water are proposed or authorized to be impounded, diverted, the channel deepened, or the stream or other body of water otherwise controlled or modified for any purpose whatever, including navigation and drainage, by any department or agency of the United States, or by any public or private agency under federal permit or license, such department or agency first shall consult with the United States Fish and Wildlife Service, Department of the Interior, and with the head of the agency exercising administration over the wildlife resources of the particular state wherein the impoundment, diversion, or other control facility is to be constructed, with a view of the conservation of wildlife resources by preventing loss of and damage to such resources as well as providing for the development and improvement thereof in connection with such water-resource development. (§662(a)).

And, under the Rivers and Harbors Act of 1899, Title 33, United States Code, §403:

> The creation of any obstruction not affirmatively authorized by Congress, to the navigable capacity of any of the waters of the United States is prohibited; and it shall not be lawful to build or commence the building of any wharf, pier, dolphin, boom, weir, breakwater, bulkhead, jetty, or other structures in any port, roadstead, haven, harbor, canal, navigable river, or other water of the United States, outside established harbor lines, or where no harbor lines have been established, except on plans recommended by the Chief of Engineers and authorized by the Secretary of the Army; and it shall not be lawful to excavate or fill, or in any manner to alter or modify the course, location, condition, or capacity of, any port, roadstead, haven, harbor, canal, lake, harbor of refuge, or inclosure within the limits of any breakwater, or of the channel of any navigable water of the United States, unless the work has been recommended by the Chief of Engineers and authorized by the Secretary of the Army prior to beginning the same.

And, under the Refuse Act of 1899, Title 33, United States Code, Section 407:

> It shall not be lawful to throw, discharge, or deposit, or cause, suffer, or procure to be thrown, discharged, or deposited either from or out of any ship, barge, or other floating craft of any kind, or from the shore, wharf, manufacturing establishment, or mill of any kind, any refuse matter of any kind or description whatever other than that flowing from streets and sewers and passing therefrom in a liquid state, into any navigable water of the United States, or into any tributary of any navigable water from which the same shall float or be washed into such navigable water; and it shall not be lawful to deposit, or cause, suffer, or procure to be deposited material of any kind in any place on the bank of any navigable water, or on the bank of any tributary of any navigable water, where the same shall be liable to be washed into such navigable water, either by ordinary or high tides, or by storms or floods, or otherwise, whereby navigation shall or may be impeded or obstructed: *Provided,* That nothing herein contained shall extend to, apply to, or prohibit the operations in connection with the improvement of navigable waters or construction of public works, considered necessary and proper by the United States officers supervising such improvement or public work: *And provided further,* That the Secretary of the Army, whenever in the judgement of the Chief of Engineers anchorage and navigation will not be injured thereby, may permit the deposit of any material above mentioned in navigable waters, within limits to be defined and under conditions to be prescribed by him, provided application is made to him prior to depositing such material; and whenever any permit is so granted the conditions thereof shall be strictly complied with, and any violation thereof shall be unlawful.

sample complaint

And, under the Water Quality Improvement Act of 1970, Public Law 91-224, Section 21:

> Any applicant for a Federal license or permit to conduct any activity including, but not limited to, the construction or operation of facilities, which may result in any discharge into the navigable waters of the United States, shall provide the licensing or permitting agency a certification from the State in which the discharge originates or will originate . . . that there is reasonable assurance . . . that such activity will be conducted in a manner which will not violate applicable water quality standards . . . (§21(b)(1))

Request for Declaratory Relief

4. Plaintiff seeks a declaration of rights under 28 U.S.C. §2201 and §2202.

Class Action

5. The members of the class are so numerous as to make it impracticable to bring them all before this Court. There are substantial questions of law and fact common to the class and common relief on behalf of all members of the class is sought.

6. This action is brought by the plaintiff, CAPE MAY COUNTY CHAPTER, INC., IZAAK WALTON LEAGUE OF AMERICA on its own behalf and on behalf of all those people whose beneficial rights and interests in subaqueous lands, tidal marshes, tidal waters and related natural resources are being irreparably diminished, permanently damaged and destroyed by indiscriminate dredging and filling and other deleterious activities in and around Cape May County, New Jersey; and on behalf of all those people who are entitled to the full benefit, use and enjoyment of their environment free from damage caused by the failure of certain Federal, State and local government agencies to prohibit the filling, dredging and other activities adversely affecting the subaqueous lands, tidal marshes, tidal waters and related natural resources of the Middle Atlantic ecosystem; and on behalf of all those

entitled to the full benefit, use and enjoyment of the unique natural resources of the United States and the Middle Atlantic ecosystem in which plaintiffs reside; and on behalf of all those people similarly situated, not only of this generation, but of generations yet unborn.

7. The claims of the representative being typical of the claims of the members of the class, and the defendants' actions having substantial effect upon all members of the class thereby making appropriate final injunctive and corresponding declaratory relief with respect to the class as a whole, this action is a proper class action under Rule 23(b)(2), Federal Rules of Civil Procedure.

8. The prosecution of separate actions by individual members of the class would create a risk of inconsistent or varying adjudications with respect to individual members of the class which would establish incompatible standards of conduct for the defendants, so that this action is a proper class action under Rule 23(b)(1)(A).

9. Adjudications with respect to individual members of the class would, as a practical matter, be dispositive of the interests of the other members of the class not party to this litigation so that this action is a proper class action under Rule 23(b)(1)(B).

10. The members of the class are fairly and adequately represented by this plaintiff and the plaintiff has no interest adverse to that of any individual who might be entitled to the relief sought herein.

Parties

11. Cape May County Chapter, Inc., Izaak Walton League of America, is a non-profit organization of citizens incorporated in the State of New Jersey and dedicated to the preservation and restoration of the environment. As a local component of the Izaak Walton League of America, an Illinois Corporation, the Chapter has been chartered among other educational functions to foster public appreciation of marine and marine-related resources, and to engage in action programs for their protection. The League has a long history of activity in conservation matters and natural resource preservation. It has been active for many years in urging Congressional and other legislative action and has participated before as a plaintiff in class actions involving environmental litigation.

12. John Doe, Inc., #1 and #2 are fictitious names for corporations in which Macchia, et al have a controlling interest. The plaintiff believes that Macchia, et al may have applied for various permits from the Department of Environmental Protection, State of New Jersey, under the name of unknown corporation of which Macchia, et al have a controlling interest. Some of the allegations applying to Macchia, et al may apply to other corporations and plaintiff intends to name the corporations upon their discovery.

13. Defendant Colonel James A. Johnson is Director Engineer of U.S. Army Corp of Engineers, Custom House, Philadelphia, Pennsylvania and is charged with the responsibility of issuing permits for all dredging activities in U.S. navigable waters and with the enforcement of the Rivers and Harbors Act of 1899 and the Refuse Act of 1899 within the Philadelphia District, Corp of Engineers.

14. Defendant Stanley Resor is Secretary of the Army and has under his control and jurisdiction the activities of the U.S. Army Corp of Engineers.

15. Defendant Richard J. Sullivan is Commissioner of the Department of Environmental Protection, State of New Jersey. He is charged with the responsibility of protecting New Jersey's wetlands and the State's natural resources.

16. Defendants Tito Macchia, Antonietta Macchia, James H. Ruetschlin, and Kathryn M. Ruetschlin are real estate partners having an interest in the lands which are the subject of this suit. In addition, they may be involved in other corporations, at this time unknown, which have an interest in the above lands.

17. Defendant Jerry H. May, Jr., is Mayor of Township of Middle from whom Macchia, et al secured a zoning variance allowing them to "store sand" on twenty acres within the dyked area on the southern end of Gravens Island.

Facts

18. Since August 28, 1965, Tito Macchia, Antonietta Macchia, James A. Ruetschlin, and Kathryn M. Ruetschlin (hereinafter referred to as Macchia, et) with the knowledge, and on occasion with the consent, of the U. S. Army Corps of Engineers, the State of New Jersey, and the Township of Middle, Cape May County, New Jersey, has undertaken a series of dredge and fill operations which are now resulting in the destruction of Gravens Island and the subaqueous lands, tidal marshes, tidal waters and related natural resources thereof.

19. Gravens Island now consists of approximately 110 acres of filled land and 250 acres of tidal marsh, located in the Township of Middle, Cape May County, New Jersey (Tax Map D5-Block 121, Lot 1.) It is bounded on the west and north by Ingram Thorofare, on the east by Gravens Thorofare and on the south by Long Reach. These waters are the tributaries of Great Sound and are in fact and in law the navigable waters of the United States.

20. The entire 360 acres of Gravens Island are, or at one time were, laced with minor and unnamed tributaries which are, or at one time were, in fact and in law "navigable," and subject to the ebb and flow of the ordinary mean high tide.

21. Free-flowing tidal action makes the Island highly productive for finfish, shellfish, and other marine life as well as habitat, nursery, and feeding grounds essential to the fisheries of the Continental Shelf of the Atlantic Ocean which is in close proximity to it and essential to the food chain of the Middle Atlantic ecosystem.

22. On May 22, 1953, through the Submerged Lands Act (Public Law 31, 83rd Congress) Chapter 65, the Federal Government confirmed the title of the State of New Jersey in the subaqueous lands of Gravens Island which were for the most part "permanently or periodically" covered by the mean high tide.

sample complaint

Count I

(Relates to Portion of Gravens Island North of Avalon Boulevard)

23. Plaintiff incorporates by reference paragraphs 18 to 22.

24. On August 28, 1965, Macchia, et al held, by virtue of riparian ownership, certain limited interest in and to portions of Gravens Island and conveyed the same to the Cape May County Bridge Commission, Cape May Court House, New Jersey for the sum of ONE DOLLAR ($1.00). (Deed Book No. 1133, page 679.) The conveyance to the Commission, for the purpose of constructing "new" Avalon Boulevard, was made "Under and subject to the rights of the State of New Jersey, the United States, and the public in any part of the premises in question lying below the ordinary high water line of Ingram Thorofare, Gravens Thorofare or any other tide waters crossing or bounding the premises in question . . . Also under and subject to rights, if any, of the State of New Jersey, in and to that part of the premises in question now or formerly flowed by tide water."

25. The conveyance of the deed was also subject to a reservation by Macchia, et al of the right to construct one intersection across Avalon Boulevard, a distance of 70 feet from curb to curb, so that he, his heirs and assigns would have access to and from the lands and waters of Gravens Island north and south of Avalon Boulevard.

26. In 1966, the Department of Conservation and Economic Development, State of New Jersey, granted a permit (No. 66-301) to Macchia, et al to dyke off and fill 65 acres of Gravens Island north of the then newly constructed Avalon Boulevard.

27. Macchia, et al, exceeding the terms of the permit, dyked and filled more than 90 acres, completely obliterating the tidal character of the northern portion of the Island, including several small, unnamed tributaries which were in fact and in law navigable and subject to the ebb and flow of the ordinary mean high tide. The action of Macchia, et al caused irreparable damage to publicly-owned marine and marine-related resources which depended on that portion of the Island for their existence, and over which the State of New Jersey exercised a fiduciary obligation for the public benefit.

28. On information and belief, plaintiff avers that the dyking material was obtained from construction of Avalon Boulevard and from dredgings in the navigable waters of the United States adjacent to the Island.

29. On information and belief, plaintiff avers that the permit by the Corps of Engineers to Macchia, et al, if any, to dredge such material and deposit it on the northern portion of Gravens Island was a clear violation of the Fish and Wildlife Coordination Act, the Refuse Act and the Rivers and Harbors Act.

30. On information and belief, plaintiff avers that Macchia, et al has applied for a riparian grant from the State of New Jersey for title to the filled acreage of Gravens Island north of Avalon Boulevard, which application is still pending.

31. The plaintiff asserts that the granting of such title by the State of New Jersey to Macchia, et al would further violate the public trust and result in further damage to the ecology and resources of Gravens Island and the adjacent environment of Cape May County.

Count II

(Relates to Portion of Gravens Island South of Avalon Boulevard)

32. Plaintiff incorporates by reference paragraphs 18 to 22.

33. On May 17, 1967, Macchia, et al applied to the Resources Development Council of the State of New Jersey for a riparian grant of a strip of land 600 feet wide, south of and parallel to Avalon Boulevard, stretching from Ingram Thorofare to Gravens Thorofare. Macchia, et al submitted a surveyors report stating that the entire area named in the application was .4 to 1.0 feet above the mean high tide, thereby implying that the State of New Jersey had no further interest in and to said lands.

34. On or about May 17, 1967, the Resources Development Council granted this land to Macchia, et al. To plaintiff's knowledge and belief, the application is still pending and has not been approved by the Commissioner, Department of Conservation and Economic Development, nor by his successor, the Commissioner of the newly constituted Department of Environmental Protection.

35. On information and belief, plaintiff asserts that only a portion of said 600 feet wide strip had been filled as a consequence of the construction of Avalon Boulevard.

36. Plaintiff asserts that a riparian grant of this land to Macchia, et al would result in further damage to the ecology and resources of Gravens Island and to the adjacent environment of Cape May County.

Count III

(Relates to Illegal Dyking and Filling of Portions of Gravens Island South of Avalon Boulevard)

37. Plaintiff incorporates by reference paragraphs 18 to 22.

38. Prior to April 11, 1967, Macchia, et al, without a permit from the State of New Jersey or the United States Army Corps of Engineers, dyked off approximately 200 acres of Gravens Island marshland south of Avalon Boulevard for the purpose of filling said marshland and eventually constructing a housing development thereon.

39. The dyking of this southerly portion of Gravens Island obstructed the flow of tidal waters, damaging the publicly owned marine and marine-related resources thereof and jeopardizing the adjacent environment of Cape May County and the fisheries of the Middle Atlantic ecosystem.

40. On April 11, 1967, the Commissioner of the Department of Conservation and Economic Development ordered defendants Macchia, et al to cease further dyking.

41. Plaintiff asserts that it is feasible to remove these dykes, which are still in existence, so as to aid in the restoration of the southern portion of Gravens Island and the public resources thereof.

42. On information and belief, plaintiff avers that the dyking material was obtained from dredgings in the navigable waters of the United States adjacent to Gravens Island.

43. On information and belief, plaintiff avers that the permit by the Corps of Engineers to Macchia, et al, if any, to dredge such material and deposit it on the southern portion of Gravens Island was a clear violation of the Fish and Wildlife Coordination Act, the Refuse Act and the Rivers and Harbors Act.

44. Prior to December 4, 1969, defendants Macchia, et al began filling in the extreme southern portion of the dyked area with material dredged from Long Reach, a navigable waterway of the United States. By December 4, 1969, approximately 5 acres had been filled.

45. On or about January, 1970, the Township of Middle halted the filling as a violation of Zoning Ordinance No. 236-69, Article 7, Section 2, under which the southern portion of Gravens Island had been designated for its highest and best use as a wetlands district.

46. On April 16, 1970, the Township of Middle, on recommendation from the Township Zoning Board, granted a variance to said ordinance #236-69 to Macchia, et al for the purpose of "storing sand," in that portion of Gravens Island inside of the dykes which Macchia, et al had already begun filling.

47. Plaintiff asserts that the variance was a subterfuge to permit Macchia, et al to continue their illegal filling for the purpose of eventually constructing a housing subdivision thereon.

48. Plaintiff asserts that at the present date approximately 20 acres of the southern portion of Gravens Island have been filled from dredge material obtained from Long Reach, a navigable waterway of the United States.

49. Plaintiff asserts that a permit from the U. S. Army Corps of Engineers, if any, to Macchia, et al to dredge such material for the purpose of filling the southern portion of Gravens Island was a violation of the Fish and Wildlife Coordination Act, the Refuse Act of 1899 and the Rivers and Harbors Act of 1899.

50. Plaintiff asserts that any permits issued to Macchia, et al by the Department of Environmental Protection for the purpose of continuing the dredging and filling and other related activities on the southern portion of Gravens Island will lead to destruction of Gravens Island and the publicly-owned marine and marine-related resources thereof over which the State of New Jersey has a fiduciary obligation; and plaintiff further asserts that any such permits will result in irreparable damage to the environment of Cape May County and to the Middle Atlantic ecosystem.

sample complaint

51. Plaintiff asserts that any further permits issued to Macchia, et al by the United States Army Corps of Engineers for the purpose of continuing the dredging and filling and other related activities on or near the southern portion of Gravens Island will lead to the destruction of Gravens Island and the navigable waters and related marine resources thereof, and will be in violation of the Fish and Wildlife Coordination Act, the Rivers and Harbors Act, the Refuse Act, the National Environmental Policy Act, and the Water Quality Improvement Act.

Count IV

52. Plaintiff incorporates by reference paragraphs 18 to 22.

53. On June 11, 1970, Macchia, et al applied to the Department of Environmental Protection, Division of Water Policy and Supply of the State of New Jersey, to divert up to 500,000 gallons per day of fresh water from wells in the Township of Middle, Cape May County (Application No. 1525) to serve the proposed development of Gravens Island in said Township.

54. Plaintiff asserts that issuance of such permit by the Department of Environmental Protection, Division of Water Policy and Supply, will contribute to the permanent destruction of Gravens Island and the publicly-owned marine and marine-related resources thereof as well as to the irreparable damage to the environment of Cape May County and to the Middle Atlantic ecosystem.

Request for Declaratory and Injunctive Relief and for Damages

WHEREFORE, the plaintiff respectfully requests:

1. A declaration of the rights of the people of the United States and of the State of New Jersey, in particular, to the protection of their environment and of the natural resources of the Middle Atlantic ecosystem which are held in public trust for the full benefit, use and enjoyment of the people by the State of New Jersey, the several States, and the United States.

2. A declaration of the rights of the people of the United States and of the State of New Jersey, in particular, to the full benefit, use and enjoyment of the environment and natural resources of the middle Atlantic ecosystem without degradation from the indiscriminate dredging, filling and other related activities in the navigable waters of the United States and their tributaries in and adjacent to Cape May County, New Jersey.

3. A declaration of the rights of the people of the United States and of the State of New Jersey, in particular, to the protection of the subaqueous lands, tidal marshes, tidal waters and related natural resources of Cape May County in the Middle Atlantic ecosystem, all of which public property is held in public trust for the full benefit, use and enjoyment of the people of this and future generations.

4. A declaration that the continued failure of defendant Federal, State and local authorities to protect the ecological and commercial value of subaqueous lands held in trust for the public is in violation of the rights of the people of the United States guaranteed under the Ninth Amendment of the Constitution of the United States and protected by the *due process clause* of the Fifth Amendment of the Constitution of the United States, by the *due process, equal protection,* and *rights, privileges and immunities clauses* of the Fourteenth Amendment of the Constitution of the United States, by the *commerce clause* of the Constitution of the United States, and by the Rivers and Harbors Act of 1899, by the Refuse Act of 1899, by the Fish and Wildlife Coordination Act, by the National Environmental Policy Act of 1969, and by the Water Quality Improvement Act of 1970.

5. That the United States Army Corps of Engineers be enjoined and ordered to revoke and suspend any and all permits issued to Macchia, et al for the purpose of dredging and filling Gravens Island.

6. That the United States Army Corps of Engineers be enjoined and ordered from issuing any further permits to defendants Macchia, et al for the purpose of dredging and filling Gravens Island.

7. That the State of New Jersey, Department of Environmental Protection, be enjoined and ordered from making any grants of subaqueous lands, or lands which were at one time subaqueous, of and adjacent to Gravens Island.

sample complaint

8. That the State of New Jersey, Department of Environmental Protection, be enjoined and ordered from issuing any permits to dredge and fill additional subaqueous lands; of Gravens Island.

9. That the State of New Jersey, Department of Environmental Protection, Division of Water Policy and Supply, be enjoined and ordered from issuing any permit to defendants Macchia, et al for the purpose of diverting well water to supply and serve the proposed development on Gravens Island.

10. That the Township of Middle, Cape May County, New Jersey, be enjoined and ordered to repeal any variance to Zoning Ordinance No. 236-69 granted to defendants Macchia, et al for the purpose of "storing sand" on Gravens Island.

11. That defendants Macchia, et al be enjoined and ordered to remove all dykes and other impediments to the tides and navigable waters on and around Gravens Island.

12. That defendants Macchia, et al be enjoined and ordered to pay any costs associated with necessary and practicable measures, as determined by the New Jersey Division of Fish and Game, Department of Environmental Protection, to restore that portion of Gravens Island south of Avalon Boulevard to its original condition.

13. That the defendants Macchia, et al be enjoined and ordered from developing for any purpose that portion of Gravens Island north of Avalon Boulevard.

14. That the Court award judgement in the amount of FIVE HUNDRED THOUSAND DOLLARS ($500,000) for compensatory damages, and judgement in the amount of ONE MILLION DOLLARS ($1,000,000) for punitive damages for the malicious, willful, and illegal dredging and filling of Gravens Island by defendants Tito Macchia, Antonietta Macchia, James A. Ruetschlin, Kathryn M. Ruetschlin, and John Doe, Inc., #1 and #2; such compensatory and punitive damages to be placed into a special trust fund, administered by the State of New Jersey, Department of Environmental Protection, and by the Bureau of Sport Fisheries and Wildlife, United States Department of the Interior, with accounting to the court, for the purpose of aiding the protection and restoration of the marine and marine-related resources of Cape May County and the Middle Atlantic ecosystem.

15. That the Court award reasonable costs and attorneys' fees.

16. That the Court award such other relief as shall be just and proper under the circumstances.

U.S. v. ASBURY PARK

___F.Supp.___(D.N.J. 1972) 3 ERC 1714

BARLOW, J.:

Plaintiff, the United States of America, brings this action for a preliminary and permanent injunction to restrain the discharge of sewage sludge by sixteen of the named defendants herein. The Government contends that the practice of discharging sludge into the Atlantic Ocean is in violation of 33 U.S.C. §407. Jurisdiction is conferred on this Court pursuant to 28 U.S.C. §1345.

All defendants operate primary sewage treatment plants in Monmouth and Ocean Counties, New Jersey. The defendants receive raw sewage and separate it into two components—sludge, which consists of the solids which settle out of the sewage, and liquid effluent. Both the effluent and the sludge are pumped into the Atlantic Ocean through outfall pipes. The point of entry into the ocean is approximately 1000 feet eastward from the beach.

The effluent is chlorinated and customarily pumped into the ocean continuously throughout the year. The sludge, which is composed of water, organic matter and inorganic matter, in varying percentages, is retained in holding tanks during the year and is pumped into the ocean during the three-month period between December 15th and March 15th. The pumping process is facilitated by diluting the sludge with liquid effluent and/or water. This essentially two-step process of municipal waste disposal has been practiced on the New Jersey coast for nearly forty years.

When this suit was instituted, on January 14th, 1972, the defendants had not yet pumped the sludge contained in their holding tanks into the Atlantic Ocean. On that date, this Court issued a temporary restraining order preventing the defendants from pumping sludge into the ocean for ten days. On January 21st, 1972, the restraint was continued for an additional ten-day period. On February 3rd, 1972, the restraint was continued until further order of the Court.

During December, 1971, and January, 1972, representatives of the Government studied the sludge discharge procedures employed by the Borough of Belmar, which is not a party here. Samplings of Belmar's retained sludge were taken and the effect of its sludge and effluent discharge into the Atlantic Ocean was observed. Belmar's procedures were described as being representative of the defendants herein in that its system was essentially the same primary sewage treatment, septic tank facility employed by the defendants.

FACTS AS TO THE APPLICABILITY OF THE ACT

The defendants' primary sewage treatment plants fall into three categories:

A. *SEPTIC TANK* (See Exhibit G-37)

> Bradley Beach, Avon, Neptune City, Neptune Township, Spring Lake Plant No. 2, Spring Lake Heights, Sea Girt, Manasquan, Point Pleasant Beach and Lavallette all have septic tank systems. A septic tank is basically a rectangular tank with a sloping bottom. As raw sewage enters the tank, those suspended solids with a specific gravity greater than water are pulled by gravity to the bottom of the tank. The suspended solids are both separated from raw sewage and permitted to decompose in the same tank. Decomposition of these removed solids (sludge) is known as anaerobic digestion; that is, the oxidation of organic

material, with gases as the byproduct.[1] As gasification takes place, the specific gravity of the sludge changes and some of the sludge changes and some of the sludge will rise to the surface and form a "scum blanket" on the top of the tank. The scum blanket will be made up of hair particles and fibrous materials, as well as some of the organic material. Thus, there are two layers of sludge build-up, residue at the bottom and the scum blanket on the top, that must be removed.

High pressure hoses, using city water, are customarily used to break up sludge so that it can be pumped. Sludge is generally pumped by positive displacement pumps, rather than by centrifugal pumps which are used for sewage, because sludge is heavier than sewage. It takes approximately five days to break up and pump all the accumulated sludge into the ocean.

B. *IMHOFF TANK* (See Exhibit G-38)

Seaside Park has an Imhoff tank and Seaside Heights has a more modern version of it, known as a Clari-Gestor. The Imhoff tank is divided into two compartments. Raw sewage is admitted into the upper chamber, or settling compartment, and gravity pulls the solid particles to the bottom. Rather than the solids remaining in the tank, as in the septic tank, they pass through the hopper bottom into the lower compartment. Anaerobic digestion of sludge occurs in this lower compartment, and as gasification takes place a scum blanket will form.

C. *PRIMARY CLARIFIER* (See Exhibit G-39)

Raw sewage enters the tank and solids, as in the other systems, fall to the bottom by the force of gravity. As the solids settle, rather than building up, they are continuously dragged by a moving chain mechanism to one end of the tank. The accumulated sludge is then pumped to digesters or other sludge treatment facilities. Asbury Park, Spring Lake Plant No. 1, Bay Head and Long Beach Township all use the primary clarifier, and the physical differences among the plants are slight. Anaerobic digestion occurs in these digesters or holding tanks.

Samples of sludge were taken by representatives of the Environmental Protection Agency (EPA) from the defendants' plants. The physical descriptions of sludge varied, depending, in large measure, on which plant was being described. In terms of color, most witnesses described sludge in varying shades of brown, black and gray. The physical consistency was also described as varying from "bone dry" to "99% water". For example, when the EPA took a sludge sample from a sludge pump at Seaside Heights, they found it too watery to transfer into a plastic bag. When, however, a sample was taken from the outfall line at Belmar, the spigot became clogged and a wire had to be inserted to clear the line. Other witnesses testified to the sludge's clogging funnels and pipettes; to its inability to pass through screens of varying dimensions; to its clogging of pumps, and to its clogging of the EPA's water-sampling boat's cooling system strainers to the point of causing that boat's system to fail.

Sludge, generally, is composed of human excretion, household waste from food preparation, laundry waste, commercial waste, dirt, etc. Items such as corn kernels, tomato seeds and prophylactics, sanitary napkins, pieces of orange peel, sand, shaving brushes, toothbrushes, plastic diaper liners, plastic toys and filter-tip cigarettes are some of the items frequently found in primary sludge. Further, sludge is not homogeneous; that is, unless it is mixed, the lighter materials will rise to the surface, with the heavier particles falling to the bottom.

1. The process of decomposition, or digestion, reduces the removed solids to about 50% of its original content. The remaining solids are not easily degraded biologically; that is, further chemical breakdown is very slow.

Experts for all parties defined and characterized sludge in a number of ways: a thin suspension of solids; a slurry of solids in a water vehicle — "slurry" being defined as a mixture of insoluble material in water (gasoline was offered as an example of a pure liquid or fluid); sludge is a plastic solid because it has rigidity and shearing force; sludge is a fluid because it will flow where a shearing force is applied — "shearing force" being defined as a force applied tangentially; sludge is definitely a liquid if its solids content is less than 15%; sludge is a liquid because it flows; sludge is a liquor — that is, it contains two states, a solid state and a liquid state.

Total solids tests were performed by the EPA on sludge samples taken from sewage treatment plants of the defendants and others. Most of the plants tested showed total solids concentrations of between 6% and 20%; that is, a range of 60,000 to 200,000 solid parts per million.

If sludge has a solids content of 14% or more it cannot be pumped without being diluted, as noted heretofore. The defendants add water and effluent to dilute their sludge. In Point Pleasant Beach, water and effluent is added to sludge at the rate of 10 to 1; in Sea Girt the dilution is 18 to 1; in Bay Head the dilution is 13 to 1, exclusive of the water needed to break up the sludge crust; in Long Beach Township the dilution is between 6 and 8 to 1. If these dilutions are used in conjunction with the EPA's figures for the total solids found in these municipalities' sludge tanks, the total solids to be found in diluted sludge as it passes into the ocean can be reasonably estimated. These results are found in Government Exhibit G-53, and are summarized below:

U.S. v. Asbury Park

MUNICIPALITY	TOTAL SOLIDS IN SLUDGE % BY		TOTAL SOLIDS OF DILUTED SLUDGE IN STORAGE TANK		TOTAL SOLIDS OF DILUTED SLUDGE AND EFFLUENT MIXTURE	
	Weight	*ppm*	*Dilution Ratio*[7]	*ppm*	*Dilution Ratio*	*ppm*
POINT PLEASANT BEACH	18	180,000			10:1	18,000
SEA GIRT	9	90,000	9:1	10,000	18:1	5,000
BAY HEAD	7	70,000	3:1	23,300	13:1	5,400
SEASIDE HGTS.	1	10,000				
ASBURY PARK	1	10,000			0:1	10,000
LONG BEACH TWP.	19	190,000	4:1	47,500	7:1	27,100

The above data indicate that the lowest concentration of solids in sludge pumped by the illustrative defendants into the ocean is 5,000 parts per million.

Raw sewage, by definition, is the water supply of a community after it has been fouled by various uses. From the standpoint of source, it is a combination of the liquid or water-carried wastes from residences and business and industry, together with ground water, surface water and storm water. It also is composed of suspended solids and dissolved solids, including human fecal material. Primary sewage treatment, such as employed by the municipalities herein, only removes the suspended solids. Suspended solids are visible and make up about 50% of the total solids, which are defined as that material which is retained on a .045 micron filter. The dissolved solids must be removed by secondary sewage treatment.

Raw sewage, sludge and sea water can also be defined in terms of solid parts per million. The experts uniformly define normal raw sewage as 200 parts per million, or .02% solids. Put another way, it consists of 99.98% water. It was clear, however, from the testimony, that the solids concentration in sewage can vary markedly, depending on the amount of rainfall and other water which enters the sewers. "Strong" raw sewage can contain as much as 1000 solid parts per million, or, as stated in another fashion, it consists of 99.9% water.

Theoretically, sludge can be diluted to the point where it has the same or even a lesser solids concentration (by weight) than raw sewage. This does not ensure, however, that the individual solid particles can be reduced to the size in which they are found in raw sewage.

Drinking water normally contains no more than two or three solid parts per million. The United States Public Health Service allows up to 500 solid parts per million in soft drinking water, and in some sections of the Southwest drinking water can exceed 2,500 solid parts per million.

The total solids in sea water is at least 1.79%, or 17,900 parts per million. Most sea water, however, has between 30,000 and 35,000 solid parts per million, but the concentration of suspended solids may be only 10 parts per million.

At the time Belmar discharged its sludge into the Atlantic Ocean, the Government, as we have noted, by prearrangement, observed that process and the Environmental Protection Agency (EPA) made video tapes both of the sludge and effluent discharge duging the months of December, 1971, and January, 1972. The tapes disclosed that when the treatment plant was pumping, a "boil" was observed at the end of the outfall line. Further, the "plume" of the discharge would move in various directions, depending on current and wind conditions. Dye was added to the effluent discharge in order to trace the plume's movement. When sludge was pumped in addition to the normal discharge of effluent, dye was not used. Observers testified that the sludge plume was visible for 1 to 1½ miles from the point of discharge. The discharge was described as being "dark brown" and observers noted surface scum up to ½ mile from the point of discharge. The scum was described as consisting of small white particles, and there was also observed high turbidity in the water outside of the discharge bubble. Observers on the EPA water-sampling vessel also saw large amounts of suspended solids and surface solids at the point of the outfall during the time that sludge was being pumped. These same persons also noticed that sea gulls swooped down when sludge was being pumped, but not when effluent alone was discharged. Scum was not observed when effluent alone was pumped.

CONCLUSIONS OF LAW AS TO THE APPLICABILITY OF THE ACT

The Government contends that the practice of sludge-dumping in the Atlantic Ocean by the defendants herein is in violation of §13 of the Rivers and Harbors Act of 1899, 33 U.S.C. §407 (hereinafter sometimes referred to as the "Refuse Act" or "Act"). The Government further seeks injunctive relief to prevent future discharges of sludge into the Atlantic Ocean.

The defendants contend, first, that the Rivers and Harbors Act is applicable only to rivers and harbors and not to the Atlantic Ocean, or, put another way, that the Atlantic Ocean is not navigable water within the intendment of the Act. Secondly, the defendants urge that the sludge currently being discharged into the Atlantic Ocean by the defendants falls within the exception set forth in the Act in that it is a by-product of sewage and, when discharged into the ocean is flowing in a liquid state. Lastly, the defendants insist that the Government has not established — as they are required to do — that to continue the discharge of sludge would occasion immediate and irreparable harm, and that the Government is, accordingly, not entitled to the injunctive relief it seeks.

The defendants initial argument that the Atlantic Ocean is not a navigable water of the United States within the purview of the Rivers and Harbors Act of 1899 is without merit. It has long been established that the authority of the United States to regulate its navigable waters is derived from the Constitution. *U.S. Const.*, art. I, §8, subsec. 3 (the Commerce Clause), and *U.S. Const.*, art. III, §2, subsec. 1 (the Admiralty Clause); *United States v. Appalachian Electric Power Co.*, 311 U.S. 377 (1941); *Economy Light and Power Company v. United States,* 256 U.S. 113 (1921); *Leovy v. United States,* 177 U.S. 621 (1900); *Egan v. Hart,* 165 U.S. 188 (1897); *United States v. Rodgers,* 150 U.S. 249 (1911); *The Montello,* 87 U.S. 430 (1874);

The Daniel Ball, 77 U.S. 557 (1871); *Imbrovek v. Hamburg-American Steam Packet Co.*, 190 F.229 (D.C. Md., 1911); *United States v. Banister Realty Co.,* 155 F.583 (E.D. N.Y., 1907).

There can be no question that the Atlantic Ocean is a navigable water of the United States within the meaning of the Rivers and Harbors Act of 1899. The authority of the United States to regulate its navigable waters, including the Atlantic Ocean, is clearly implicit under any test defining the navigable waters of the United States as those capable of supporting commerce or those to which the admiralty jurisdiction of the United States extends. Clearly, it would seem any statute which attempts to regulate the navigable waters of the United States must — unless limited in some specific fashion — include all of the waters of the United States. No such limiting words appear in §13 of the Rivers and Harbors Act of 1899 (33 U.S.C. §407).[2]

While it has occasionally been argued that the principal legislative purpose of the Refuse Act was the protection of navigation — and that argument is made tangentially here — it is clear that the scope of the Act is not limited merely to the protection of navigability upon United States waters, but has been interpreted to prohibit pollution of those waters, and is in no sense limited to those forms of pollution which may be said to impede or affect navigation.

In *United States v. Standard Oil Co.,* 384 U.S. 224, 86 S.Ct. 1427, 16 L.Ed.2d 492 [1 ERC 1033] (1966), the Supreme Court, after an examination of the history of the Act, concluded: "It is plain from its legislative history that the 'serious injury' to our water courses * * * sought to be remedied was caused in part by obstacles which impeded navigation *and in part by pollution.*" 384 U.S., at 228-29. (Emphasis supplied.) See, also, *United States v. Standard Oil Co.,* supra; *United States v. Esso Standard Oil Co., of Puerto Rico,* 375 F.2d 621, 623 [1 ERC 1038] (3d Cir., 1967). See *United States v. Ballard Oil Co., of Hartford,* 195 F.2d 269, 371 (2d Cir., 1952); *La Merced,* 84 F.2d 444, 446 (9th Cir., 1936); *United States v. Maplewood Poultry Co.,* 327 F.Supp. 686, 688 [2 ERC 1646] (D. Me., 1971); *United States of America v. U.S. Steel Corporation,* 328 F.Supp. 354 [2 ERC 1700] (N.D. Ind., 1970), supra.[3]

U.S. v. Asbury Park

It is clear, then, that the Government may not be precluded from maintaining this action for lack of statutory authority unless the discharge of sludge, in the circumstances here, falls within the exception expressed in the statute, removing from the reach of the statute refuse "* * * flowing from streets and sewers and passing therefrom in a liquid state * * *."

In *United States v. Standard Oil Co.,* supra, Justice Douglas undertook to review the legislative history of §13 of the Rivers and Harbors Act, and he concluded that that section codified certain pre-existing statutes,[4] including the 1894 Act (28 Stat. 363), which prohibited, in substance, depositing in harbors and rivers for which Congress had appropriated money for improvements, "ballast, refuse, dirt, ashes, cinders, mud, sand, dredgings, *sludge*, acid, or any other matter of any kind other than that flowing from streets, sewers, and passing therefrom in a liquid state". (Emphasis supplied) Justice Douglas further concluded that "* * * the use of the term 'refuse' in the codification serves in the place of the lengthy list of enumerated

2. Dilution ratio represents the amount of water added to sludge so that it can be pumped.

3. *United States v. Esso Standard Oil Co. of Puerto Rico,* 375 F.2d 621 [1 ERC 1038] (3d Cir., 1967), involved the prosecution of the defendant under §13 of the Rivers and Harbors Act, 33 U.S.C. §407. Although the argument advanced by the defendants here apparently was not made there, the facts of that case disclose that the defendants were convicted of a violation of the statute for permitting liquid petroleum products to flow directly into the coastal waters surrounding Puerto Rico.

4. The Court in *United States v. Ballard Oil Co. of Hartford,* supra, held that 33 U.S.C. §407 established two separate, though related, offenses, and that the statutory language "whereby navigation shall or may be impeded or obstructed" qualifies only the offenses set forth in the second clause of the statute and has no application to a violation of the first clause, to which the present action is addressed. See, also, *United States of America v. U.S. Steel Corporation,* supra.

substances found in the earlier Acts * * *. The legislative history demonstrates that Congress intended to codify, without substantive change, the earlier Acts". Accordingly, the term "refuse", as currently employed in §13, includes sludge, and sludge, of course, is not limited to the by-product of a sewage disposal system, but applies equally to other industrial and commercial procedures which separate particulate matter from water.[5]

In *United States v. Republic Steel Corporation,* supra [1 ERC 1022], which involved an attempt by the Government to enjoin several steel companies from discharging industrial wastes into the Calumet River under §§10 and 13 of the Refuse Act, Justice Douglas, analyzing the nature of the exception, observed that:

> "* * *The materials carried here are 'industrial solids,' as the District Court found. The particles creating the present obstruction were in suspension, not in solution. Articles in suspension, such as organic matter in sewage, may undergo chemical change. Others settle out. All matter in suspension is not saved by the exception clause in §13. *Refuse flowing from 'sewers' in a 'liquid state' means to us 'sewage.'* . . . The fact that discharges from streets and sewers may contain some articles in suspension that settle out and potentially impair navigability is no reason for us to enlarge the group to include these industrial discharges." (362 U.S., at 490-91.) (Emphasis supplied.)

The central question here, then, is, simply stated: Is "sludge" sewage or, being a by-product of or derived from sewage, is it to be considered as being within the exception contained in the Act?[6] It is our view that sludge is not sewage or its equivalent and is not, therefore, within the exception of the Act.

It is apparent from the evidence produced here that in terms of the relative solid-liquid ratio of sludge, the proportion varies markedly among the defendants' sewage plants, as well as within the individual plants themselves. In some instances the samples taken from the retaining tanks were described as "bone dry" and in other cases as being almost entirely water. In general, however, the Court is satisfied that sludge, being the accumulated and thereby concentrated residue of raw sewage, is much more viscous and varies substantially and demonstrably from the consistency of raw sewage. Raw sewage consists, as we have seen, of approximately 99.98% water. It is clear that sludge cannot meet this definition, even after it is diluted for pumping by water or by the addition of liquid effluent, as the data compiled in Exhibit G-58 reveals. While sludge is in the retaining tanks of the various defendants' sewage systems, it must be regarded more as a solid than a liquid, even though it can be found in both states. Adding water or liquid effluent in order that it be diluted sufficiently to pump it to sea does not reconstitute it as raw sewage. Moreover, in support of the Government's claim that sludge was more solid or "heavier" or more viscous than sewage, the witnesses generally agreed that positive displacement pumps were required to pump sludge because it is heavier than sewage, and not centrifugal pumps, which are customarily used for the pumping of sewage. In short, sludge is essentially a solid when compared to raw sewage, and is not made any less so when water or liquid effluent is added to it in order that it may be diluted sufficiently to be pumped into the sea.

Further, the Court is satisfied that the circumstantial evidence indicates that while the consistency of sludge may vary amongst the plants of the various defendants — and, indeed, in the plants themselves — the

5. An 1886 Act (24 Stat. 329); an 1888 Act (25 Stat. 209); an 1890 Act (26 Stat. 453).

6. In 1899, sludge, as a by-product of sewage treatment, was probably not unknown, although the term at that time must have been designed to include "sludge" from other industrial and commercial procedures, for in *United States v. Republic Steel Corporation,* supra, at p. 506, n. 27 [1 ERC 1022], Justice Harlan, in his dissent, noted that: "In 1900, only 4% of the urban population having sewage facilities provided any treatment at all for domestic and trade wastes. *Modern Sewage Disposal* (1938, p. 13), Fed. of Sewage Works Assns.; Langdon Pearse, Editor, Anniversary Book, Lanc. Press., Inc.)"

characteristics of sludge in all of the defendants' plants are essentially the same. Sludge, then, is not sewage and is not, by composition, its equivalent. Accordingly, sludge is not "refuse * * * flowing from streets and sewers and passing therefrom in a liquid state * * *", within the exception contained in the Act.

FACTS AND CONCLUSIONS OF LAW AS TO INJUNCTIVE RELIEF

The EPA, during December, 1971, and January, 1972, collected a series of sludge samples both from the defendants' retaining tanks and from the sea water at the time of the sludge discharge procedures at Belmar.

Tests of these samples were made to determine the viral content thereof; the presence of heavy metals; the presence of bacteria, and the chemical oxygen demand of these samples.

VIRAL CONTENT

Viruses were isolated in the liquid portion of some sea water samples, and in the sludge which was filtered-out. More viruses were found in the sludge than in the liquid. Types of paralytic polio virus were identified. Although the tests were capable of recovering only a very small percentage of the viruses which can occur in human feces, it was established that if one pathogen (disease-producing organism) is found, there is a high scientific probability that many others are also present.

U.S. v. Asbury Park

The viruses found were of the type which multiply in or near the gastrointestinal tract of man, and are excreted by infected people in their feces. The viruses are thus found in raw sewage, and in sludge. Viruses will not multiply outside a living host, and will gradually die-off if stored in a sewage treatment plant holding tank. Although the viral population will decrease when stored, its virulence[7] can only be changed by passing the virus through another living host. Virulence is also affected by the phenomenon known as the "reversion factor"; that is, when polio vaccine is ingested for immunization purposes, some virus excreted in the recipient's feces will assume a more virulent form. In any event, the polio virus excreted cannot be less virulent than the virus found in vaccine.

These viruses can survive for many months in cold water.[8] The addition of effluent enables them to survive longer in the ocean.[9] If sludge was dumped now, it is probably that some viruses would survive into the summer months.

The testimony established that if a person took a large dose of virus, he would probably become sick, and he could infect his family.[10] All viruses are pathogenic; that is, they can cause disease or infection. The viruses found in sludge are capable of producing a wide range of disease; for example, poliomyelitis, aseptic meningitis, herpangina, pleurodynia, myocarditis, rash diseases, diarrheal diseases, and respiratory diseases. Hepatitis is transmitted by virus found in human feces, and enters the ocean through sewage and sludge. The virus becomes concentrated in the flesh of shellfish, and thus may enter the human food chain.

The testimony also established that the dumping of sludge is a health hazard, and the dumping of virus-containing material in any place where it might contact humans is dangerous and hazardous. Although the testimony was inconclusive as to whether sludge has caused or will cause harm to marine life and animals, it was asserted that, in general, the pollution of water with viruses results in the transmission of disease.

Virtually no destruction of viruses occurs in chlorinated sewage effluents with a residual chlorine level of 2 parts per million; 30 parts per million are necessary to destroy viruses. The sewage treatment plants tested by the EPA used residual chlorine levels of 2-3 parts per million.

7. Virulence is a measure of a virus' disease or infection capability.

8. In fact, viruses survive longer in a cold than in a warm environment.

9. Although salt water destroys viruses more quickly than fresh water.

10. Virulence tests were not performed on EPA samples.

BACTERIAL CONTENT

The evidence discloses that sludge has a high organic content, and is a source of nutrients for bacteria and other microorganisms; that sludge will tend to accumulate and settle-out in water, thus providing an environment in which bacteria will multiply. The survival capability of fecal coliform bacteria in a permanent resident population, as found in ocean bottom sediments, is significantly greater than in the water. These bacteria may eventually be released to the surrounding waters. There is a high probability that some bacteria in ocean bottom sediments could exist for two months, although a few days after the sludge is dumped in the ocean the coliform count[11] in the water might be low. Daily effluent pumping tends to increase the survival of fecal coliform.

The EPA tested for total coliform bacteria, which are found in the feces of warm-blooded animals, and for fecal coliform, which is that portion of the total coliform found only in the gut and feces of warm-blooded animals. The coliform count is used to determine the presence of pathogens. Referring to G-54 (bacteriological results of sludge taken from defendants' plants), the testimony revealed that the samples showed very high levels of fecal bacteria and a high level of disease-producing micro-organisms, especially since salmonella bacteria was isolated, it was concluded that these levels were much higher than usually found in recreational beach areas. The EPA also took sea water samples off Belmar in December, 1971, before Belmar discharged sludge, and in January, 1972, after the sludge had been pumped. These tests showed that in December, 1971, the bacterial content of the sea water was below the State standard and no salmonella was isolated; but in January, 1972, the fecal coliform count exceeded acceptable limits[12] and salmonella was found in sea water. Although the defendants offered ocean sampling tests taken June 28, 1971, November 17, 1971, and January 21, 1972, to prove that the total coliform and fecal coliform counts were within acceptable levels, it appeared, however, that for these tests to be accurate and more representative, sampling should have been done more frequently, as water quality varies from moment to moment. The testimony further established by a defense witness that the practice of discharging sludge and primary-treated effluent violates New Jersey's water quality standards. Moreover, the State of New Jersey directed the defendant-municipalities to phase-out the current plants, and in 1967 each of the defendants was directed to upgrade its plant, which has not yet been accomplished.

The evidence further revealed that fecal pollution is one of the worst types of water pollutants in terms of containing disease-producing bacteria; that is, salmonella, shigella, brucella, mycobacterium, and vibrio. Salmonella[13] produces gastroenteritis; shigella produces bacterial dysentary; vibrio produces cholera; mycobacterium produces tuberculosis; brucella produces brucellosis.

Twenty-five percent (25%) of New Jersey's shellfish harvesting area is closed because it does not meet state-federal water quality standards; that is, the total coliform median cannot exceed 80 mpn in 100 milliliters, and no more than 10% of the samples can have a 230 mpn reading. It was further stated that shellfish from an area where there is a high total coliform count (greater than 70 mpn per 100 milliliters) pose a health threat if eaten.

11. The generally accepted measure of bacterial quality in water is the total coliform test.

12. The fecal coliform standard for Coastal Waters-1 [waters of the Atlantic Ocean up to roughly 1500 feet from shore] shall not exceed 50 mpn per 100 milliliters.

13. Salmonella, however, dies very quickly in salt water. In a few days, 90% will die, and only 10% will persist up to 30 days. Although the salmonella findings were negative in most instances, these results do not prove the absence of salmonella since the testing method is crude and its sensitivity is low. A positive reading, however, implies a high number of salmonella present. There is also a high scientific probability that if one pathogen is found, others are present.

HEAVY METALS CONTENT

The EPA tests detected the presence of heavy metals in sludge samples and, further, the testimony indicated that diluting sludge has no effect on the toxicity of the heavy metals found therein; that is, the presence of 50 parts of mercury per billion of diluted sludge would inhibit and almost arrest algae growth, and would adversely affect photosynthesis. The deleterious effect on photosynthesis also harms marine life by reducing the amount of dissolved oxygen present in the ocean.

Copper was described as a notorious agent for destroying algae and inhibiting its growth—2 or 3 parts per million would be sufficient (See Exhibit G-42, heavy metals concentrations in defendants' sludge tanks). Copper also reacts with other metals in a phenomenon called "synergism", where the effect on a living organism is toxicity greater than either metal imparts alone.

The results disclosed by Exhibit G-61 indicated that the mercury, copper, lead, chromium and aluminum concentrations are in excess of between 40 to 2000 times the concentrations in which they are usually found in the ocean. This increase in heavy metals concentrations means greater toxicity, which can affect the growth of or even kill organisms living in the ocean. By reducing the number of organisms which are available as food for the next higher organism, the entire food web is affected.

CHEMICAL OXYGEN DEMAND (COD) TESTS

The chemical oxygen demand, stated simply, is the oxygen needed to satisfy the requirements of an organism. Sewage has a large COD; if sludge has 2000 times as many solid parts per million as sewage (20% sludge compared with normal raw sewage of 200 parts per million), it will have a COD 2000 times that of sewage.

The high COD of sludge reduces the amount of oxygen available for microorganisms, and thus reduces the number of microorganisms that can survive. This, in turn, makes survival for higher level organisms which feed on microorganisms (e.g., fish) more difficult. Carried to its extreme, this process reduces the quantity of marine life available for man's consumption. The testimony disclosed that if the sludge found in in Exhibit G-42 were dumped into the ocean, the oxygen concentration in the water would be reduced, thus affecting the algal population and its ability to produce oxygen. In addition, the sludge would stimulate the growth of bacteria not normally present in high concentrations in marine systems, would contribute to the turbidity of the system, and would decrease the amount of sunlight available to all marine organisms.

CONCLUSION

The basis of injunctive relief in the Federal Courts has historically been predicated upon a finding of irreparable harm and the inadequacy of legal remedies (*Beacon Theaters v. Westover,* 359 U.S. 500, 506; 3 L.Ed.2d 988; 79 S.Ct. 948 (1959).

The evidence presented here by the Government satisfies both of these tests. The discharge of sludge into the Atlantic Ocean, in the circumstances here, constitutes immediate and irreparable harm and produces a destructive impact upon marine life and upon the environment generally. More importantly, the sludge disposal practice of the defendants here presents a dangerous health hazard, that is both immediate and continuing, to those many thousands of human beings who utilize the coastal waters along the New Jersey beaches for year-round recreation.

Accordingly, it is ORDERED that the defendants herein be and hereby are permanently enjoined from discharging or depositing all sludge accumulations currently retained by them into the waters of the Atlantic Ocean, and are, further, permanently enjoined from all future deposits or discharges of sludge into the waters of the Atlantic Ocean.

U.S. v. VULCAN MATERIALS
___F.Supp.___(D.N.J. 1970), 2 ERC 1145

WHIPPLE, District Judge:

Defendants, Verona Corporation (hereinafter Verona) and Vulcan Materials Company (hereinafter Vulcan) are corporations operating manufacturing plants on the Kill Van Kull and Newark Bay. For several years the defendant corporations have been discharging waste acid, alkaline and oil into these waters which constitute a part of the New York Harbor. Criminal proceedings have been previously brought against Verona for specific violations prohibiting pollution which resulted in a conviction in December 1967. Failure on the part of these defendants to cease polluting the harbor waters prompted the filing of criminal informations for offenses committed in the past year. Specifically, the three informations charge that on thirteen separate occasions these defendants discharged into the waters of New York Harbor acid, alkaline and oil waste and refuse in violation of 33 U.S.C. §441. This statute provides:

> "The placing, discharging, or depositing, by any process or in any manner, of refuse, dirt, ashes, cinders, mud, sand, dredgings, sludge, acid, or any other matter of any kind, other than that flowing from streets, sewers, and passing therefrom in a liquid state, in the tidal waters of the harbor of New York *** is strictly forbidden ****."

The defendants have moved to dismiss the informations on various grounds:

(1) It is contended that the informations fail to state an offense. Defendants urge that their discharges were within the statute's proviso language, i.e., all of the substances discharged were liquids and entered the water by way of a piped sewer line, and that such discharges are expressly permitted by the proviso language of the statute. Secondly, the defendants urge that their discharges are not within the prohibitions of the statute since the legislative history of the act indicates that Congress was concerned with deposits of bulky and insoluble substances in the harbor and that the harbor would become obstructed with shoals of refuse materials which would present a hazard to navigation. While defendants admit that their discharges may be polluting the waters of New York Harbor, they contend that 33 U.S.C. §441 was not designed as an anti-pollution statute, but on the contrary, was meant to be a navigational obstruction statute. They urge that concern for the problems of pollution cannot be permitted to override the intent of Congress in enacting the statute. Congress' concern, they argue, was with disruptions of shipping and harbor activity by the shoaling of refuse. They contend that substances which would not obstruct navigation were of no concern to Congress and therefore, Congress authorized an exemption for fluid waste from streets and sewers. On these grounds the defendants urge that the government has failed to state a violation of the New York Harbor Act and therefore, the informations should be dismissed.

The government contends that the word "sewer," has been defined by the courts and does not have the broad connotation the defendants place on it. The Supreme Court in United States v. Republic Steel Corp., 362 U.S. 482 [1 ERC 1022] (1960) held that "refuse flowing from sewers in a liquid state" means sewage which essentially involves organic matter, which will eventually decompose. However, the acid, alkaline and oil waste and refuse, as in the case at bar, do not decompose and are not sewage. The government also points out that while water pollution was not a paramount concern of Congress in 1888 when §441 was originally enacted, Congress, through a 1958 amendment, made it clear that §441 should be used to alleviate the devastating effect of water pollution on our environment. The Senate Report which accompanied the amendment referred to oil pollution as being a principal problem and dangerous to navigation and an interference with the beaches normally used for recreational purposes. There is no doubt that the discharge of acid, alkaline and oil waste and refuse, in addition to polluting the harbor, has a highly injurious effect upon ships and docks as well as on the fish and animal life therein. The action of the defendants, if continued, would only add to the deterioration of the harbor facilities and would certainly diminish and obstruct the usefulness of the New York Harbor. Finally, it should be noted, the discharging of oil into New York Harbor has consistently been held to be a violation of 33 U.S.C. §441. The Albania, 30 F.2d 727 (S.D. N.Y. 1928); The Columbo, 42 F.2d 211 (2d Cir. 1930); The S.S. Nea Hellis, 116 F.2d 803 (2d Cir. 1941).

(2) The defendants urge the dismissal of the informations contending that the statute under which they are being prosecuted (New York Harbor Act) has been impliedly repealed by the Federal Water Pollution Control Act, 33 U.S.C. §466, et seq. They contend that Congress has developed a comprehensive legislative plan for dealing with the problems of pollution and has enacted this and other similar acts to this end. Any direct application of the New York Harbor Act to pollution, according to the defendants, has been superseded by the newer legislation.

The Federal Water Pollution Control Act of 1956 authorized technical assistance, grants for state programs and construction subsidies by the Federal Government for municipal and state facilities. This Act does not provide for the criminal prosecution of polluters. Only abatement procedures are established and formulated under the terms and provisions of the Act. Thus, it becomes inconceivable that Congress intended to repeal the New York Harbor Act, a criminal statute, by implication, with a civil statute, as is urged by the defendants. Furthermore, it is noted, that the Federal Water Pollution Control Act specifically states that it "shall not be construed as (1) superseding or limiting the functions, under any other law, *** of any other officer or agency of the United States, relating to water pollution." It follows, therefore, that the contentions of the defendant in support of this ground are lacking in merit.

(3) The contention of the defendants is that if the New York Harbor Act is to be applied to water pollution, there will be an overlap and conflict with the more recent Federal Water Pollution Control Act of 1956, as amended. They urge that the New York Harbor Act be harmonized with the declared purposes of the more recent Act. This they contend would require the policies and purposes of the Federal Water Pollution Control Act being read in conjunction with the New York Harbor Act.

The Acts are completely separate and distinguishable. The

intent and purpose of each statute is diametrically opposed to the other. One is civil, the other is criminal. One has given to the states, with the assistance of the Federal Government, control of waterways within the states. The other concerns a particular body of water, the Harbor of New York, under the exclusive control of the Federal Government and its agencies.

The defendants also argue that it is procedurally unfair for the government to prosecute them criminally for the specific violations charged in the informations inasmuch as the State of New Jersey has also instituted civil proceedings against them and has extended the time for complying. The local civil proceedings instituted by the State have no bearing on the several separate and distinct criminal violations committed by the defendants and charged in these criminal informations.

Defendants assert that they have expended "millions to cure the problems at its plant by constructing a new facility in another area." This action on their part is not relevant to the pending criminal charges. That defendants have agreed with the State of New Jersey to move their plant to another state is no reason why criminal sanctions should not follow if criminal acts have been committed in this jurisdiction.

Defendants' final argument is that his criminal prosecution is unfair inasmuch as they have planned and are taking appropriate steps to remedy the water pollution problems that confront them. What the defendants plan on doing is, at best, speculative. Criminal prosecutions are predicated upon statutory violations and not on after-the-fact assurances of future good conduct. This argument is not persuasive.

The defendants' motion to dismiss the several criminal informations, being without merit, is denied. Let an order in conformity with the foregoing opinion be submitted.

NOTE: Section 441 [Act of June 29, 1888, c. 496, §1, 25 State. 209] of 33 U.S.C. provides the same protection for the harbors of New York, Baltimore and Hampton Roads that section 407 does for all navigable waters, including the waters of those three harbors.

NOTE ON ADDITIONAL CASES

Several additional cases on various aspects of water pollution control law are listed below. They are suggested for instructors who prefer to teach with a greater stress on case law, and for students who wish additional reading in this field.

United States v. Republic Steel Corp., 362 U.S. 482 (1960)
(Refuse Act: definition of sewage)

U.S. v. Maplewood Poultry, ____F. Supp.____(D. Me. June 10, 1971)
2 ERC 1646 (Refuse Act application, relation to FWPCA)

U.S. v. U.S. Steel, ____F. Supp. ____(N. D. Ind. Nov. 10, 1970), 2 ERC 1700 (Refuse Act: willfulness, obstruction, FWPCA)

Aiple Towing v. Voight, ____F. Supp. ____(W. D. Wis. April 5, 1971)
2 ERC 1690 (state statute on boat discharges; FWPCA)

Lake Carriers v. MacMullan, ____F. Supp. ____(E. D. Mich. July 12, 1971), 2 ERC 1837 (same as above; both deal with possible conflicts with Federal law)

CHAPTER FIVE: Private Remedies

The judicial process is expensive, often slow, and does not always bring satisfactory results. Therefore, every effort should be made to eliminate the cause of an environmental grievance without litigation. However, if you must litigate, do it well.

This chapter is concerned with how to prepare for the formalities of litigation. It is comprised of seven principal sections, each with a topic treated primarily in its relation to litigation for environmental protection: a. Selection of a court; b. Requirements for standing; c. The doctrine of sovereign immunity; d. Jurisdiction and procedure of administrative bodies; e. Private remedies—old, new, and suggested; f. Obtaining information from governmental bodies, and, g. the Fairness Doctrine of broadcasting.

a. Selection of a court

Picking a court is the first step. Very often the attorney has a choice between a federal and a state court, or among courts of the same sort in different localities.

The choice should depend on a thorough study of relevant court rulings in each potential forum. Possible obstacles to the effective presentation of evidence, such as relative unavailability of witnesses,[1] should be foreseen and weighed.

state level

The common presumption by state courts of subject jurisdiction permits filing of most environmental protection law suits. A party challenging the application of this presumption must show a constitutional provision, statute, or rule which denies jurisdiction.[2]

Of course, if a state has more than one inferior court, a selection based on subject matter is necessary. But this usually is quite simple.

federal level

Many subjects allow for jurisdiction by both state and federal courts, although there are some subjects over which the federal courts have exclusive jurisdiction. Apart from these subjects, it is perfectly possible for a state court to decide actions based entirely on federal claims.[3]

In a suit against a federal officer, the problems of jurisdiction are reduced somewhat by statutory provisions,[4] although care must be taken if each of the defendants is not an officer or agency of the United States government.

1 *See, e.g.*, Sive, *Securing, Examining, and Cross-Examining Expert Witnesses in Environmental Cases*, 68 MICH. L. REV. 1175 (1970).

2 C. WRIGHT, HANDBOOK OF THE LAW OF FEDERAL COURTS, § 7 (2d. ed. 1970) (hereinafter referred to as WRIGHT). *See also* Hart, *The Relations Between State and Federal Law*, 54 COLUM. L. REV. 489 (1954).

3 WRIGHT § 45.

4 *See* 28 U.S.C.A. § 1391 (1967) which provides:

(a) A civil action wherein jurisdiction is founded only on diversity of citizenship may, except as otherwise provided by law, be brought only in the judicial district where all plaintiffs or all defendants reside, or in which the claim arose.

(b) A civil action wherein jurisdiction is not founded solely on diversity of citizenship may be brought only in the judicial district where all defendants reside, or in which the claim arose, except as otherwise provided by law.

(c) A corporation may be sued in any judicial district in which it is incorporated or licensed to do business or is doing business, and such judicial district shall be regarded as the residence of such corporation for venue purposes.

(d) An alien may be sued in any district.

Most subjects which come before the federal courts involve concurrent jurisdiction of state and federal courts, but if a state action is involved, a litigant must normally exhaust state statutory or administrative remedies before challenging state action in a federal court.[5]

Also of importance is selection of venue—that is, of a locality in which judicial power over a defendant may be exercised by the selected court branch. That power usually exists where the service of process properly can be made.

Both venue and jurisdiction must be considered in bringing a law suit, but the concepts are legally distinct. If venue is improper, a party may nevertheless consent to be sued there. But parties cannot alter jurisdiction by consent, for jurisdiction can be conferred only by law.[6]

Within the federal system, original jurisdiction is exercised by the district courts. These districts comprise entire states, portions of states, the District of Columbia, Puerto Rico, the Virgin Islands, and Guam.[7]

Federal question

Federal courts, however, are courts of limited jurisdiction in the sense that they have only the jurisdiction which Congress expressly confers upon them.[8] Therefore, the moving party in a federal court must affirmatively show the requisite jurisdictional authority.

In environmental litigation the district court would probably be used only where injunctive relief was sought in order to restrain the enforcement of a state statute or order claimed to be contrary to the federal constitution, or where injunctive relief was sought against acts of Congress claimed to be unconstitutional.[9] Other than these situtations, the most likely forum would be that of the state courts. However, in most instances when a federal district court is used, jurisdiction is usually founded upon a general federal question or upon the diversity of citizenship of the parties.

The "federal question" jurisdiction is based on 28 U.S.C. section 1331(a) which states:

> The district courts shall have *original jurisdiction* of all civil actions wherein the matter in controversy exceeds the sum or value of $10,000 exclusive of interest and costs, and arises under the Constitution, laws, or treaties of the United States. (Emphasis supplied.)

However, the jurisdictional amount of $10,000 is not required if jurisdiction is based on one of the many federal statutes passed

(e) A civil action in which each defendant is an officer or employee of the United States or any agency thereof acting in his official capacity or under color of legal authority, or an agency of the United States, any, except as otherwise provided by law, be brought in any judicial district in which: (1) a defendant in the action resides, or (2) the cause of action arose, or (3) any real property involved in the action is situated, or (4) the plaintiff resides if no real property is involved in the action.

The summons and complaint in such an action shall be served as provided by the Federal Rules of Civil Procedure except that the delivery of the summons and complaint to the officer or agency as required by the rules may be made by certified mail beyond the territorial limits of the district in which the action is brought.

5 WRIGHT § 49.

6 WRIGHT § 42.

7 WRIGHT § 2.

8 U.S. CONST. art. III, § 1.

9 WRIGHT § 50.

subsequently which do not require a minimum dollar figure.[10] Although federal jurisdiction may be based on either the Constitution, a statute of the United States, or a treaty, court decisions require a substantial claim to be founded directly upon federal law. Determining what constitutes a substantial federal question requires careful analysis of many confusing decisions.[11] This problem is further exacerbated by the fact that the courts will focus exclusively on the pleadings to see if the required federal question is present.[12] Therefore, the environmental attorney should carefully review the applicable federal statutes and plead a claim based on *all* relevant statutes, including the Environmental Policy Act of 1969[13] if it can be considered applicable. Such a technique decreases the possibility of failing to meet the jurisdictional requirements. Today many federal acts, particularly those governing administrative agency actions,[14] provide for judicial review. These statutes, if applicable, solve the substantial federal question problem and usually obviate the need to consider the jurisdictional amount requirement.

The United States can sue in a federal court, and approximately one third of the civil cases in the district courts have the United States as a party. Jurisdiction over most environmental subjects is concurrent with state courts except for suits involving seizures, or recovery of fines, penalties, or forfeitures incurred under any Act of Congress where the federal district courts have exclusive jurisdiction.[15] Usually, a suit against the United States will take place in the federal district court. However, most claims for damages which do not sound in tort, go to the Court of Claims, unless the claim is less than $10,000, in which case the district court has jurisdiction. Moreover, most negligence claims are usually brought under the Federal Tort Claims Act,[16] whereby the federal district courts have exclusive jurisdiction to entertain such suits. Under many situations involving the United States government, consent to be sued has been granted by statute and this procedure should be followed[17] when commencing an action in which the United States government is a party.

diversity of citizenship

The federal courts have jurisdiction over diversity cases involving a controversy between citizens of a different state or between a citizen of a state and an alien if, in both situations, a sum of at least $10,000 is in controversy. Since this basis for jurisdiction has little logical support, there have been many technical rules concerning jurisdiction based on diversity claims.[18] Diversity of citizenship requires that there be diversity between each plaintiff and all defendants to the action. If an indispensible party destroys the diversity requirement the action must be dismissed.[19]

10 *See e.g.*, 33 U.S.C. § 466 g-1 (1964).

11 WRIGHT § 17.

12 WRIGHT § 18.

13 42 U.S.C.A. § 4321 (Supp. 1971).

14 *See, e.g.*, FCC, 47 U.S.C. § 402 (1964); NLRB, 29 U.S.C. § 160(f) (1964).

15 28 U.S.C. §§ 1355, 1356 (1964).

16 28 U.S.C. § 1291 (1964).

17 WRIGHT § 22. *See generally* D. SCHWARTZ & S. JACOBY, LITIGATION WITH THE FEDERAL GOVERNMENT (ALI-ABA 1970).

18 WRIGHT §§ 23, 25.

19 WRIGHT §§ 24, 29.

Therefore, in order to determine citizenship for purposes of diversity, a person usually is considered to be a citizen of the state in which he resides with the intention of making that state his home indefinitely. But since this test is based on "domicile," which in turn is based on a person's intent, mere residency is not controlling.[20] A corporation has dual citizenship for purposes of diversity in the state in which it has been incorporated and in the state where it has its principal place of business.[21] Unquestionably, determining what constitutes the principal place of business is not always an easy task.[22]

jurisdictional amount

In cases involving "diversity of citizenship" or a "federal question," the amount in controversy, exclusive of interest and costs, must exceed $10,000. However, in nearly all areas involving a general federal question, a special statute has been enacted governing the procedure which removes the requirement of a minimum dollar value. For example, the Mandamus and Venue Act of 1962[23] has explicitly authorized all federal district courts to take original jurisdiction of any action in the nature of mandamus to compel an officer or employee of the United States to perform a duty owed to the plaintiff. The only federal question cases of significance that are still subject to the jurisdictional amount are those which come under the Jones Act[24] or those where challenges to the constitutionality of state statutes are involved, although Professor Wright feels that the jurisdictional amount requirement is even more narrowly applied.[25] However, the jurisdictional amount continues to be applicable in diversity cases.

When confronted with actions which require $10,000 to be in controversy, the court will make its jurisdictional decision from the pleadings, and if the plaintiff recovers less than $10,000 the court may refuse to allow costs or may impose costs against him.[26]

equitable remedies

Many environmental cases seek equitable remedies such as injunctions which create additional problems in determining whether the requirement for $10,000 in controversy has been met. Whether the value is considered by looking at the point of view of the plaintiff, or the defendant, or the party seeking to invoke federal jurisdiction can be important. The first test seems to be one accepted rather inconclusively by the Supreme Court; the other tests have been used by some district courts and have not been rejected by the Supreme Court.[27] If claims are aggregated or counterclaims are involved, jurisdictional amount determinations are even further complicated.[28]

Supreme Court's original jurisdiction

The U.S. Supreme Court under Article III, §2 of the Constitution, has original jurisdiction, "In all Cases affecting Ambassadors, other public Ministers and Consuls, and those in which a State shall be a party." Suits by one state against another are within the original and exclusive jurisdiction of the Supreme

20 WRIGHT § 26.

21 28 U.S.C. § 1332(c) (1964).

22 WRIGHT § 27.

23 28 U.S.C. § 1361 (1964).

24 46 U.S.C.A. § 883 (Supp. 1971).

25 WRIGHT § 32.

26 28 U.S.C. §§ 1331(b), 1332(b) (1964). *See* WRIGHT § 33.

27 WRIGHT § 34.

28 WRIGHT §§ 36, 37.

Court. [Wright §109] Many such cases have been brought to resolve water rights. [CLARK, Robert ed., *Waters and Water Rights,* 1967, Vol. 2 at 321]

The case of *Ohio v. Wyandotte Chemicals Corp.,* 91 S.Ct. 1005 [2 ERC 1331] (1971), illustrates the Supreme Court's determination to employ increasingly strict standards before it will allow its original jurisdiction to be invoked in environmental cases. The State of Ohio had asked the Court to enjoin several chemical companies from dumping mercury into Lake Erie, an exercise of original jurisdiction Ohio claimed was necessitated by Supreme Court decisions in previous interstate pollution cases. In an 8–1 decision, the Court denied Ohio's request, holding essentially that it lacked the technical expertise to hear such a case; that the complaint involved state and not federal issues, which would more appropriately be decided by state courts; and that the seriousness of the interstate pollution alleged could not justify the Court's diverting its attention from its more important federal appellate duties.

Justice Douglas disagreed, feeling that the Court was presented with a "classic type of case [to abate a public nuisance] congenial to our original jurisdiction . . . that the appointment of a Special Master or panel or scientific advisors would solve the court's expertise problem," and that he could "think of no case of more transcending importance than this one." 91 S.Ct. at 1013, 1016-17 [2 ERC 1336, 1338].

This case is already the subject of at least one critical article (Woods and Reed, "The Supreme Court and Interstate Environmental Quality: Some Notes on the *Wyandotte* Case," 12 Arizona Law Review 691, Winter 1970). However, *Ohio v. Wyandotte Chemicals* did not completely close the Supreme Court's original jurisdiction door on interstate pollution cases, for the majority observed that the hearing of such cases, which it considered to be "a serious intrusion on society's interest in our most deliberate and considerate performance of our paramount role as the supreme federal appellate court, could . . . be justified only by the *strictest necessity.*" 91 S.Ct. at 1013 [2 ERC at 1336] (emphasis supplied). Considering tne widely-reported deleterious effects of ingested mercury on human and other organisms, a subject discussed at length in conjunction with Sec. 12 of the Water Pollution Control Act, as amended, Chapter 4, it becomes difficult to believe that this "strictest necessity" test was not satisfied in *Ohio v. Wyandotte Chemical Corp.* However, the political overtones of the case, and the fact that the Governor and Attorney General were "lame ducks," as well as the fact that the problem was effectively being dealt with under the Refuse Act, may have influenced the Court.

The new Ohio Attorney General reinstuted the case on March 22, 1972 *(State of Ohio v. BSAF Wyandotte Chemicals, et al)* in Cuyahoga County Common Pleas Court (#904571). Note the state can represent the public as parens patriae. *See Hawaii v. Standard Oil Company of California,* 92 S.Ct. 885 (1972).

The Supreme Court recently granted leave to the State of Vermont to file a complaint invoking the Court's original jurisdiction against the State of New York, *Vermont v. New York,* __U.S.__, 40 U.S.L.W. 4466 (April 24, 1972), Vermont alleging that New York had failed to stop a New York paper company from dumping sludge onto Vermont's portion of the Lake Champlain lakebed. Two cases decided the same day probably revolutionized the role of the federal judiciary in interstate pollution cases. *Washington v. General Motors Corp.,* __U.S.__, 40 U.S.L.W. 4437, and *Illinois v. Milwaukee,* __U.S.__, 40 U.S.L.W. 4439, both decided on April 24, 1972, The Supreme Court found that ". . . When we deal with air or water in their ambient or interstate aspects, there is a federal common law . . . ." *Illinois v. Milwaukee,* 40 U.S.L.W. at 4443. Both cases appear at the end of this chapter.

transfer of cases

Another technique being used by the government to win environmental lawsuits through procedural strategies is to move them out of Washington where the public interest groups are located. This increases the cost of litigation, and since the Justice Department can use the taxpayer's money, such a strategy is an effective way of "winning" for the government.

The government recently succeeded in transferring the environmental law suits involving the Four Corners power plants in the Southwest from the U.S. District for the District of Columbia to that of Arizona. Two of these cases, *National Wildlife Federation, v. Morton,* Civ. No. 1090 and *Jicarilla Apache Tribe of Indians v. Morton* Civ. No. 1089, were consolidated and transferred on August 24, 1971. A Third case, *Yazzie v. Morton,* Civ. No. 938, also was transferred to the Arizona District Court on August 30, 1971. *Environmental Action* of August 21, 1971 reports:

> U.S. District Court Judge George L. Hart has rejected a motion by the Nixon Administration to transfer the Alaska pipeline case from Washington, D.C. to Alaskan federal courts.
>
> The move by Hart seemed to be a victory for environmentalists, who fear that federal judges closer to the scene of environmental problems will be more oriented to industrial and pro-development philosophies. But Hart indicated that "most" such cases "should be tried at the site."
>
> And this appears to be the trend. Another Washington judge recently gave up jurisdiction over a suit to prevent the Glen Canyon Dam from flooding parts of Rainbow Bridge National Monument in southern Utah.
>
> The cross-Florida Barge Canal case was removed from a judge who had already ordered a temporary halt to construction and transferred to U.S. District Court in Florida.

b. Standing

In order to meet the constitutional requirements of Article III of the federal constitution a "case or controversy" must exist thereby bringing the litigation within the judicial power of the courts. Jurisdiction requires a real controversy, not one which is hypothetical, or moot, or academic.[29] However, the category of interests which permit a law suit to be maintained has been narrowed by requiring that the court-imposed doctrine of standing be met. In order to assure the proper prosecution of an adversary proceeding, a plaintiff must have sufficient injury to forcefully press his claim.[30]

state level

In most state courts the question of standing does not present a problem, since few cases exist, and most of the existing decisions broadly interpret the requirements to find proper standing. Furthermore, a taxpayer suit to enjoin the spending of public money is permissible in most states. Often in state courts, the action need not even involve a governmental expenditure. For example, in *Nickols v. Commissioners of Middlesex County,*[31] the court held that taxpayers have standing as citizens to enforce a public duty by mandamus to prevent injuries to the shores and woodlands of Walden Pond. State standing requirements may be eased still further by new statutes such as the Michigan Environmental Protection Act of 1970[32] and similar legislation in other states.[33]

federal level

In federal courts, however, the question of standing has been the subject of much litigation. For many years an economic injury was a general prerequisite for such standing. However, today this narrow

29 WRIGHT § 12.

30 WRIGHT § 12. L. JAFFE & N. NATHANSON, ADMINISTRATIVE LAW: CASES AND MATERIALS ch. 2 C (3d ed. 1968). For a discussion of current tests of standing *see* Note, *Standing to Challenge Admin. Action: The Concept of Personal Stake*, 39 GEO. WASH. L. REV. 570.

31 341 Mass. 13, 166 N.E.2d 911 (1960). However, standing can be denied in state courts *see* Kerpelman v. Board of Public Work, Maryland Court of Appeals, 2 E.R.C. 1473 (April 1971), *see also* 2 Cooper, State Admin. Law § 35 (1965).

32 MICH. COMP. LAWS §§ 691-1201-1207 (1970).

33 *See, e.g.,* Illinois Environmental Protection Act, H.B. 3788, Laws of 1970; Washington Environmental Quality Reorganization Act of 1970, S.B. 1, ch. 62, Laws of 1970.

view is no longer the law within the federal forum. *Scenic Hudson Preservation Conference v. Federal Power Commission*,[34] was a case, brought by an unincorporated association of conservation organizations, which challenged orders of the Federal Power Commission granting a license to Consolidated Edison Company of New York to construct a pumped storage hydroelectric project on the Hudson River at Storm King Mountain. The court, in finding that the plaintiffs had standing, stated:

> In order to insure that the Federal Power Commission will adequately protect the public interest in the aesthetic, conservational, and recreational aspects of power development, *those who by their activities and conduct have exhibited a special interest in such areas, must be held to be included in the class of "aggrieved" parties . . . .*[35] (Emphasis supplied.)

The historic *Scenic Hudson* decision on standing made the legal battle for Storm King Mountain an historic one. But much more was involved, and the outcome was still in doubt in the Summer of 1972. The FPC approved the project a second time, and was upheld by the Court of Appeals, Second Circuit, on October 22, 1971. The U.S. Supreme Court on June 20, 1972 refused 8-1 to review that decision. But the project was challenged on a a water quality certificate issued by the state concerning the effect on the Hudson River. See *Scenic Hudson v. Diamond* in the Appendix to Chapter Four.

standing: federal level

While the *Scenic Hudson* case expanded the class of people deemed to have sufficient legal interest to bring a law suit, it did not open the doors of the courthouse to everyone who desired to litigate. *Scenic Hudson* was a licensing case, a type of administrative action in which the public has had broad rights to intervene in the governmental process. It was also significant that the plaintiffs could point to a federal statute, the Federal Power Act,[36] which by calling for the consideration of public uses including recreation provided a lever for showing their legal interest.

Since 1965, many cases have been decided which have expanded the class of people considered to have legal standing. Several cases have been particularly important to this evolving area of the law. *Office of Communication of the United Church of Christ v. Federal Communications Commission*[37] was a case in which it was found that responsible representatives of the listening public had standing as "parties of interest" to appear before the FCC to contest the renewal of a broadcast license. The court found that economic injury was not a prerequisite to recovery.

Another change occurred with the expanding use of taxpayer actions, which prior to 1968 had rather limited use in federal courts. *Flast v. Cohen*[38] involved an action by federal taxpayers to enjoin the expenditure of federal funds for the purchase of text books for use in parochial schools. The claim was that the expenditure was prohibited by the First Amendment of the United States Constitution. The court upheld the taxpayers' claim saying that they had standing to raise issues about "specific" clauses of the Constitution. Even this expansion of standing was criticized as being illogical and too limited.[39]

[34] 354 F.2d 608 (2d Cir. 1965), *cert. denied*, 384 U.S. 941 (1966).
[35] 354 F.2d at 616.
[36] 16 U.S.C. §§ 791 *et seq.* (1964).
[37] 359 F.2d 994 (D.C. Cir. 1966).
[38] 392 U.S. 83 (1968).
[39] Davis, *Standing, Taxpayers and Others*, 35 U. Chi. L. Rev. 601 (1968).

On March 3, 1970, the Supreme Court of the United States spoke again on the subject, expanding the class of people having standing within the federal court system by introducing some new tests to further confuse the determination of what constitutes standing. In two companion cases, *Association of Data Processing Service Organizations, Inc. v. Camp*[40] and *Barlow v. Collins*[41] the Court required that two tests be met. The first required that at least the constitutionally required "case" or "controversy" be present. The second test required that there must be an injury in fact, economic or otherwise. Such a test required that the interest sought to be protected by the complainant must arguably be within the zone of interests to be protected or regulated by the statute or constitutional guarantee in question. Such required interest, at times, may reflect aesthetic, conservation, and recreational as well as economic values. These tests encourage the attorney representing environmental litigants to bring his action under as many federal statutes as possible, in order to meet the standing requirements. The concept of standing has been broadened to such a degree that almost anyone should be able to comply therewith.

standing: federal level

However, although the concept of standing has been expanded considerably during the past decade, care must still be exercised by the environmental attorney when he seeks to satisfy the standing requirements for his client. In *Sierra Club v. Hickel*[42] the court found that the Sierra Club failed to sufficiently allege that it was "aggrieved" or "adversely affected" within the meaning of the rules of standing. Actions "personally displeasing or distasteful" to a group were found to be insuffiicent for the conferring of standing; therefore, this decision makes it important to include as party plaintiffs a local organization of local area residents affected by the administrative action for which judicial relief is sought.[43] In January

40 397 U.S. 150 (1970).

41 397 U.S. 159 (1970. *See* Hardin, "Conservationist's Standing to Challenge the Actions of Federal Agencies," 1 Ecology Law Quarterly 305 (Spring 1971), in which the author, after analyzing *Association of Data Processing* and *Barlow* and their likely usefulness to conservationists, concludes at 329 that:

> "the political process on the federal level is not meaningfully responsive to a citizen or a small, poorly funded organization of citizens . . .[I]t is appropriate for the courts to correct concrete illegality, even if the motivation for the litigation is ideological. The staffing and the functions of the courts must be expanded to meet pressing public needs."

But *see* Student Note, "Standing to Challenge Administrative Actions: The Concept of Personal Stake," 39 Geo. Wash. L. Rev. 570 (March 1971), in which the author takes a more restrictive view of standing and the judicial role.

42 433 F.2d 24 (9th Cir. 1970).

43 *See* "The Concept of Personal Stake," *supra* note 41, in which the note writer predicts that the Supreme Court will reject the appeal in *Sierra Club v. Hickel.* The author contends that the Ninth Circuit properly denied standing in finding that the Sierra Club had neither established a personal interest nor demonstrated a personal stake in the controversy (at 606), and adds that, because amicus curiae briefs had been filed supporting the defendants by certain ski associations and by the County in which the project was sited,

> ". . . the Court would have had to assume the role of a legislative body in identifying the public interest because of the competing interests involved." At 607.

of 1971, the *Sierra Club* decision was reinforced by a holding that a California conservation organization did not have standing to sue a salt company to stop the filling of San Francisco Bay though named property owners had standing.[44]

The conflict between the Ninth Circuit and other U.S. Courts of Appeals on the issue of standing was resolved in a Supreme Court decision April 19, 1972 on this case, which had been restyled, Sierra Club v. Morton. In this decision, the Court held that the Sierra Club itself did not have standing, but that individuals whose rights were impared would have standing; hence the club's members were encouraged to bring the suit again styled differently, and they have done so. The decision, although on its face unfavorable to the conservationist movement, actually was not a serious setback, and in fact may have helped by fixing the tests for standing in a less ambiguous manner. The text of this case is printed at Appendix Five-8. Additional discussion is contained in the section on the National Environmental Policy Act of 1969 at page One-17.

standing: federal level

In *Crowther v. Seaborg,*[46] two of the three parties succeeded in establishing their standing to challenge an Atomic Energy Commission nuclear test in Colorado by sufficiently alleging a direct threat to their health, welfare, and safety. Those of the first party owned property close to the test site; the second party was a public benefit corporation bringing a class action suit on behalf of the state's citizens. The court found their allegations sufficient to constitute a substantial assertion of a personal stake in the controversy. However, the court denied standing to the third party, the district attorney for the Ninth Judicial District, because he confined his complaint to trespass, nuisance, and action in excess of authority granted by the Atomic Energy Act. Since he alleged neither property ownership in the test site vicinity nor an official obligation to protect public health, the court found that he had "failed to establish . . . [an] interest . . . adequate to present a justiciable controversy sufficient to provide the adversary setting necessary for the operation of the judicial machinery."[47] Again, a more careful pleading of the district attorney's official responsibilities to protect health and safety, etc., could probably have shown the necessary interest to meet the standing requirements.

The material on standing has grown substantially, but the problems found within this area have tended to mask the real issue. The ability to get into court is not sufficient; the environmental

44 Alameda Conservation v. California, 2 Environment Reporter: Decisions (hereinafter referred to as E.R.C.) 1175 (9th Cir. 1971).

45 Sierra Club v. Morton, 39 U.S.L.W. 3359 (U.S. Feb. 23, 1971).

46 312 F. Supp. 1205 (D. Colo. 1970).

47 *Id.* at 1218. Although this challenge to the conduct of the AEC test failed because plaintiffs failed to prove the "unreasonableness" of the AEC's decision, the court did retain jurisdiction over the subject matter and required the AEC to make available to the public complete test data.

litigant must win on the merits. Among many environmental organizations, the preoccupation with satisfying the standing requirement has caused these organizations to ignore the fact that standing is only one of many procedural obstacles that must be overcome before a victory can be had on the merits.[48] Further expansion of the standing concept will not materially aid the environmental litigant. In 1965, the conservationists won the *Scenic Hudson* case. The result was a remand to the FPC. On August 19, 1970, the FPC once again ruled against Scenic Hudson.[49] The case continues while the costs to the litigants mount astronomically. In the meantime, the delay in construction for Consolidated Edison has required them to move to expand fossil fuel plants in New York City which will increase the city's air pollution. Nevertheless the case continued, and on October 22, 1971, the U.S. Court of Appeals for the Second Circuit (3 ERC 1232) upheld the FPC,viewing their review as being limited to determining whether the Commission considered all relevant factors and whether the findings were supported by substantial evidence. Standing must, therefore, be considered in the context of the *total strategy necessary to achieve an environmental goal.* In particular, the administrative agencies which have responsibilities for environmental protection must be forced to do a better job. Expanded standing must be coupled with a more complete judicial review based on the *reasonableness* of administrative action.

c. Sovereign immunity

Environmental litigation is often directed against an agency of government or a government employee. Sometimes such a suit is prohibited by the doctrine of sovereign immunity. This doctrine has its historical roots in the concept "the King can do no wrong." In more recent times such a doctrine was based on the thought that suits against the government were inconsistent with the idea of supreme executive power. Today the doctrine has been substantially eroded, but sufficient problems still exist to make it necessary to consider the possible impact of such a doctrine.

The United States may not be sued without its consent. The most common expression of consent is found in the statutes governing the agency or having the action in controversy subject to the Administrative Procedure Act [5 U.S.C. 701]. Claims for money based on contract may be brought under the Tucker Act [28 U.S.C.A. 1346, 1481]. Negligence actions against the government are governed by the Federal Tort Claims Act of 1946 [28 U.S.C.A. 1346 and numerous other sections in this title].

[48] Berger, *Standing to Sue in Public Actions: Is it a Constitutional Requirement?*, 78 YALE L.J. 816 (1969); Davis, *Standing to Challenge Governmental Action*, 39 MINN. L. REV. 353 (1955); JAFFE, STANDING TO SUE IN CONSERVATION SUITS, LAW AND THE ENVIRONMENT 123 (1970); Jaffe, *The Citizen as a Litigant in Public Actions: The Non-Hohfeldia·· or Ideological Plaintiff*, 116 U. PA. L. REV. 1033 (1968); Jaffe, *Standing to Secure Judicial Revue: Private Actions*, 75 HARV. L. REV. 255 (1961); Rogers, *The Need for Meaningful Control in the Management of Federally Owned Timberlands*, 4 U. WYOMING LAND & WATER L. REV. 121; Willner, *Who Has Standing in Oregon to Defend the Environment*, 1 ENVIRONMENTAL LAW 44 (Lewis & Clark College 1970); Comment, *The Congressional Intent to Protect Test: A Judicial Lowering of the Standard Barrier*, 41 U. COLO. L. REV. 96 (1969); Comment, *Expansion of "Public Interest" Standing*, 45 N.C. L. REV. 998 (1967); Comment, *Standing to Challenge Administrative Actions—Anyone Arguably Protected by Statute May Sue*, 23 VAND. L. REV. 814 (1970).

[49] Opinion No. 584, Project No. 2338 (Aug. 19, 1970).

The difficulties arise when no statute can be found to deal with the problem and the plaintiff seeks nonstatutory review in the nature of injunction, mandamus, habeas corpus, or other common-law remedies. The law on this subject has become exceedingly complex. *Larson v. Domestic and Foreign Commerce Corporation* [337 U.S. 682 (1949)] is a leading case. That case held that a suit against a government officer may be brought only if he acted "unconstitutionally" or "ultra vires" his authority. Furthermore, relief could be granted only if the court can order cessation of the conduct rather than requiring affirmative action of the sovereign. This case and the subsequent cases following its reasoning have been criticized by most writers. See Byse, "Proposed Reforms in Federal 'Nonstatutory' Judicial Review: Sovereign Immunity, Indispensible Parties, Mandamus," 75 *Harv. L. Rev.* 1479 (1962); Davis, "Suing the Government by Falsely Pretending to Sue an Officer." 29 *U. Chi. L. Rev.* 435 (1962); Jaffe, "Suits Against Governments and Officers," 77 *Harv. L. Rev.* 1, 209 (1963).

sovereign immunity: federal level

In 1962 a statutory change eased the suing of an employee of the United States for mandamus, 28 U.S.C. 1361. Wright, *Law of Federal Courts* §22 (1970). In 1963 the case of *Dugan v. Rank* [372 U.S. 609 (1963)] continued the *Larson* approach. Suits against an officer continued to be barred if the decree would operate against the sovereign.[See also *Hawaii v. Gordon,* 373 U.S. 57 (1963)]. In a suit against a Forest Service officer the court held that an officer may not be sued for property wrongfully taken unless such action is outside his statutory powers, or the exercise of their powers was unconstitutional. [*Malone v. Bowdoin,* 369 U.S. 643 (1962)]. This has been limited somewhat by *State of Washington v. Udall,* 417 F.2d 1310 (9th Cir. 1969).

The doctrine continues to be used but also continues to be criticized. [See Crampton, "Nonstatutory Review of Federal Administrative Action: The Need for Statutory Reform of Sovereign Immunity, Subject Matter Jurisdiction, and Parties Defendant," 68 *Mich. L. Rev.* 387 (1971); Davis, *Administrative Law Treatise,* 1970 Supplement, Chapter 27.]

In the past several years the courts have made the use of the sovereign immunity doctrine more difficult to invoke by finding a statutory basis for such a review. The National Environmental Policy Act, discussed in chapter one, is a much-used statute. See, *Izaak Walton League v. St. Claire* 313 F.Supp. 1312 (D.Minn. 1970).

The case of *Abbott Laboratories v. Gardner* [387 U.S. 136 (1967)] holds that there is a presumption of judicial review of agency action to be restricted by clear, convincing evidence of contrary legislative intent. Other cases continue to seek a broad interpretation of statutes to allow for court review. [See*Tooahnippah v. Hickel,* 397 U.S. 598 (1970); *City of Chicago v. United States,* 396 U.S. 162 (1969); *Coalition for United Community Action v. Romney,* 316 F.Supp. 742 (N.D. Ill. 1970); *United States v. District Court for Eagle County,* 91 SCt. 998 (1971)].

Thus, while the Federal government continues to use the defense of sovereign immunity, it usually loses. The wide range of statutory permission to sue the government can usually be used to overcome this defense.

See generally, Scalia, "Sovereign Immunity and Nonstatutory Review of Federal Administrative Action: Some Conclusions From the Public Lands Cases," 68 Mich.L.Rev. 867 (1970).

sovereign immunity: state level

State governments have also enjoyed immunity from law suits for their actions. In all states, this doctrine has been modified to allow some actions to be brought. However, often such actions are limited to those based on contract claims or tort. State special purpose districts, agencies and subdivisions are often easier to sue than the state. The statutes governing the subject matter and the state administrative procedure act should be examined. Court interpretations of the doctrine often favor the state in addition to limiting liability for the acts of agents and employees. The variation in the application of this doctrine among the states makes it mandatory to research the law of the specific jurisdiction of concern. [See Prosser, *Law of Torts* 1971 §131].

sovereign immunity: municipal level:

Municipal corporations are more amenable to law suits than state governments.

Often a distinction is made between proprietary functions, *i.e.,* operating a golf course, providing electricity, etc., which are more likely to bring liability than acts committed as part of the governmental function. Governmental functions are those that can be performed adequately only by government, the character of the activity being determined more by historical accident and court decisions than by logic. Thus, there is usually no liability for acts of police officers, garbage collectors, etc. Even a governmental function, however, may create liability if the municipality has created or maintains a nuisance. Furthermore, statutes in many states have changed the court-created law; some statutes expand liability, some restrict it, and some limit the amount of recovery. Whether a public official can be sued individually is based on another series of unsatisfactory distinctions. Generally only lower administrative officers acting in administrative or ministerial capacity are liable, though often a showing of the existence of improper motives is necessary. See, Prosser, *Law of Torts,* 1971 at § 131.

d. Administrative agencies

primary jurisdiction

Both federal and state administrative agencies exist with responsibilities over most environmental matters. Air and water pollution agencies, public health authorities, agriculture, recreation, and forestry agencies are a few of the kinds of agencies found in most states. A basic determination must be made of whether it is possible to sue in a court if the agency has been entrusted with the responsibility for a particular area of regulation. If the subject matter is peculiarly within the competence of an administrative agency or if it requires the resolution of issues that have been placed within the special competence of an administrative body, the court will probably refuse to accept jurisdiction and refer the matter to the administrative agency. The defendants or the court may raise the defense of primary jurisdiction and since the subsequent judicial review of agency action is often very limited, the invocation of the primary jurisdiction doctrine can effectively preclude judicial review.[54]

It is difficult to predict when the doctrine will be invoked, for courts have substantial discretion.[55] The more forceful and more

[53] The leading case, Abbott Laboratories v. Gardner, 387 U.S. 136 (1967) held:

> [J]udicial review of a final agency action by an aggrieved person will not be cut off unless there is persuasive reason to believe that such was the . . . purpose of Congress . . . . Early cases . . . have been reinforced by the enactment of the Administrative Procedure Act, which embodies the basic presumption of judicial review to one "suffering legal wrong because of agency action, or adversely affected or aggrieved by agency action within the meaning of a relevant statute," 5 U.S.C. § 702, so long as no statute precludes such relief or the action is not one committed by law to agency discretion, 5 U.S.C. § 701(a). The Administrative Procedure Act provides specifically not only for review of "[a]gency action made reviewable by statute" but also for review of "final agency action for which there is no other adequate remedy in a court," 5 U.S.C. § 704. [t]he Administrative Procedure Act's "generous review provisions" must be given a hospitable interpretation. . . . [O]nly upon a showing of "clear and convincing evidence" of a contrary legislative intent should the courts restrict access to judicial review.

Id. at 140. *See* Tooahnippah v. Hickel, 397 U.S. 598 (1970); City of Chicago v. United States, 396 U.S. 162 (1969); Coalition for United Community Action v. Romney, 316 F. Supp. 742. (N.D. Ill. 1970).

[54] *See* L. Jaffe & N. Nathanson, *supra* note 30, ch. 5.

[55] *See* Best v. Humbolt Placer Mining Co., 371 U.S. 334 (1963) (natural resource case where imposition of primary jurisdiction doctrine denied); United States v. Western Pacific Railroad Co., 352 U.S. 59 (1956) (court found primary jurisdiction doctrine applicable); Coalition for United Community Action v. Romney, 316 F. Supp. 742 (N.D. Ill. 1970) (primary jurisdiction rejected to court review).

convincing the presentation by the attorney of the agency's inability to handle the matter, the greater the likelihood that the courts will entertain the case. The environmental attorney should also emphasize the fact that expert consideration of a matter solely within the competency of the agency is *not* involved; that uniformity of decision is not of primary importance; and that the decision has limited effect on broad agency policy.[55a]

If the doctrine of primary jurisdiction is invoked, then the case must first be acted upon by the administrative agency. However, the opportunity to have decisions of administrative agencies judicially reviewed is not totally lacking in our legal system since most statutes governing federal administrative agencies provide that appeals for review of the actions of the agency go to the Federal Court of Appeals. The exception to this rule occurs with appeals from the Interstate Commerce Commission and from certain orders of the Secretary of Agriculture, which go to a three-judge district court.[56] There is also available a nonstatutory review of the officer or agency's action, brought by a suit in the federal district court.[57]

Generally, judicial review will be based on section 10(e) of the Federal Administrative Procedure Act,[58] although there are enough exceptions to necessitate a review of each agency's procedures prior to appeal. However, the review will be based on the record made by the agency, and will be affirmed if supported by tests under section 10(e) of the Act.

judicial review

Under the Federal Administrative Procedure Act, a court will set aside an agency's actions if they are arbitrary, capricious, and abuse of discretion, contrary to the Constitution, in excess of statutory jurisdiction or unsupported by substantial evidence.[58a] It is not easy to meet these tests. Since the administrative agency usually has the ability to shape the development of the record, it is very difficult to attack them in court and show that they have violated their legal duty.

If such evidence is not found, the case will often be remanded to the agency for rehearing. Therefore, judicial review gives very limited protection to the plaintiffs.

Another problem is created by the rules concerning the burden of proof, which often place an impossible burden on the litigant seeking protection of the environment.[59] Yet another problem arises when section 10(a) renders the APA inapplicable because the action in question was committed to agency discretion by law. The better view would allow a limited judicial review to determine whether the agency has exercised its discretion within permissible bounds, but another point of view, exposited by Professor Davis and adopted by some courts, is that no review is permissible when discretion is so assigned by law.[59a]

[55a] *See also* Jaffe, *Primary Jurisdiction*, 77 HARV. L. REV. 1037 (1964).

[56] WRIGHT § 103.

[57] Byse, *Proposed Reforms in Federal "Nonstatutory" Judicial Review*: Sovereign Immunity, Indispensible Parties, Mandamus, 75 HARV. L. REV. 1479 (1962).

[58] 5 U.S.C.A. § 706 (1967).

[58a] 5 U.S.C.A. § 706 (1967). The substantial evidence test is limited to agency actions which take place after an adjudicatory hearing. Other agency actions will be overturned only if they fail the other tests.

For the substantial evidence test defined, see Scenic Hudson Preservation Conference v. FPC, __F.2d__ (2nd Cir. 1971) 3 ERC 1232

[59] Krier, *Environmental Litigation and the Burden of Proof, Law and the Environment*, 105 (Baldwin & Pope ed. 1970).

[59a] For a discussion of this problem see Littell v. Morton, No. 15,208 (4th Cir. July 14, 1971).

See generally, "The Conservationists and the Public Lands: Administrative and Judicial Remedies Relating to the Use and Disposition of the Public Lands Administered by the Department of the Interior," 68 Mich.L.Rev. 1200 (1970). For cases challenging the traditional scope of review given to the actions of administrative agencies, see *Environmental Defense Fund v. Ruckelshaus,* 439 F.2d 584 (D.C.Cir. 1971), and *Citizens to Preserve Overton Park v. Volpe,* 401 U.S. 402 (1971).

Review by state courts of state administrative agencies is often controlled by statute. Statutes governing agency action may refer to administrative procedure acts which in turn provide for review. In the absence of such statutory review, the traditional common law prerogative of employing writs of prohibition, mandamus, and certiorari are used. Since each state has different laws, the requirement of the state to which an appeal may be directed must be determined and met.[60]

For a variety of reasons the potential plaintiff may find that the matter of interest to him requires his participation in proceedings of an administrative agency. This is often because the potential environmental harm will be due to the activities of an agency that should be protecting the public interest.

becoming a party

The first difficulty arises in obtaining notice of proposed administrative actions. While governmental agencies usually follow the prescribed legal requirements, the attorney who depends on such processes for notice will either fail to receive actual notice or will have insufficient time to properly respond. There is no substitute for continuous personal contact with the agency whose activities are of concern to such attorney.

If possible, the potential litigant should formally participate in agency activities as early as possible. This helps to show the interest necessary to obtain standing while enabling the participants to shape the record which will be the basis, and often the only basis, for any future court review. The procedure to be followed for such intervention will usually be found in the statute providing the agency's authority or the regulations promulgated under the statute. For example, while the standing requirements of the Atomic Energy Commission are very easy to meet, the procedure set forth in the regulations governing the AEC must be closely followed. Any person desiring to contest the granting of a construction permit for a nuclear power plant should become a party by following the rules for official intervention.[63] Once involved in the administrative process, both standing and the right to seek judicial review of agency action are protected.[64] However, before one can obtain judicial review of an agency decision, one must anticipate and avoid several defenses to review by a court.

ripeness

A case must be ripe for review. This judge-made doctrine expands upon the Article III "case" or "controversy" requirement of the Constitution to avoid having the courts provide advisory opinions. It is questionable what it adds to the doctrine of "standing" and "exhaustion of administrative remedies," but courts reject cases for

60 L. Jaffe & Nathanson, *supra* note 30. ch. 2.

63 10 C.F.R. § 2.714 (1970).

64 Crowther v. Seaborg, 312 F. Supp. 1205 (D. Colo. 1970) (The Project Rulison Case); Citizens Committee for the Hudson Valley v. Volpe, 302 F. Supp. 283 (S.D. N.Y. 1969).

lack of ripeness.[65] One ripeness problem can be created by the agency which never exercises its discretionary authority. If such discretion is not exercised by the administrative agency, the case may never be "ripe for review" and so judicial review will not be possible. However, a recent case, ***Environmental Defense Fund v. Hardin,***[66] held that the Secretary of Agriculture's failure to take action promptly was tantamount to an order denying the request, and therefore made the case ripe for review.

exhaustion

Closely related to the required ripeness is the requirement that all administrative remedies be exhausted before going to court unless such action would be futile. What is considered futile depends upon the relevant court decisions applicable to the specific problem.[67] The exhaustion requirements are usually based on the Federal Administrative Procedure Act.[68] Section 10(a) provides:

> A person suffering legal wrong because of agency action, or adversely affected or aggrieved by agency action within the meaning of a relevant statute, is entitled to judicial review thereof.[69]

Section 10(c) also provides review from a final agency action for which there is no other adequate remedy in a court.[70] It is difficult to meet either of these requirements unless the agency has completed its work and promulgated an order.[71]

Similar requirements for the exhaustion of state administrative remedies are found in the statutes of most states. Typical is the procedure provided in the Model State Administrative Procedure Act: "A person who has exhausted all administrative remedies available within the agency and who is aggrieved by a final decision in a contested case is entitled to judicial review under this Act."[72] The problem faced by attorneys attempting to obtain judicial review of an agency's action is that the administrative process can consume a great deal of time and money; thus exhaustion of administrative remedies can be synonymous with exhaustion of the litigants who are attempting to represent the public interest.[73]

More serious is the extremely limited review provided by judicial review.

remand

The Administrative Procedure Act should be changed or courts should begin to interpret the substantial evidence requirement to make judicial review meaningful. The record should be open to attack if the agency has failed to exercise, in a positive manner, its responsibility to forcefully advocate and protect the public interest. If a court finds that the agency has failed in its responsibility, it

[65] L. JAFFE & N. NATHANSON, *supra* note 30, ch. 20; K. DAVIS, ADMINISTRATIVE LAW TREATISE ch. 21 (1958).

[66] 428 F.2d 1093 (D.C. Cir. 1970).

[67] L. JAFFE & N. NATHANSON, *supra* note 30, ch. 2E; K. DAVIS, *supra* note 64, ch. 20.

[68] 5 U.S.C.A. § 702 (1967).

[69] *Id.*

[70] *Id.* § 704.

[71] Crowther v. Seaborg, 312 F. Supp. 1205 (D. Colo. 1970) and Road Review League v. Boyd, 270 F. Supp. 650 (S.D. N.Y. 1967) are recent environmental cases reviewed under the APA which also raised many of the other procedural issues of standing, sovereign immunity, choice of defendant, etc.

[72] MODEL STATE ADMINISTRATIVE PROCEDURE ACT § 15(a) (1961).

[73] A fact of life in environmental litigation is that defendants are usually financed by the public, either from the treasury or from rates paid to utilities, or at least their expenses are tax deductible so that the public pays roughly half the cost.

should attempt to avoid remanding the case to the agency, since this merely builds a better record while avoiding the intent of the remand.[75] Occasionally courts do this, but all too often judicial review, even if successful, does not provide a meaningful remedy. It is becoming quite commonplace for major environmental litigation to linger for many years as courts remand cases to agencies which then work to maintain their original decision.[76] While orderly use of the administrative process requires that a presumption of propriety be given to an agency's action, the present interpretation of section 10 of the Administrative Procedure Act is an abrogation of judicial responsibility. However, two recent cases may presage a greater willingness on behalf of the courts to expand both the ripeness doctrine and the scope of judicial review. In *Environmental Defense Fund v. Ruckelshaus*,[77] the court declared that the "denial of a suspension order must be reviewable as a final order where . . . the denial subjects the public to an imminent hazard [of irreparable injury]."[78] The court further stated:

scope of review

> We stand on the threshhold of a new era in the history of the long and fruitful collaboration of administrative agencies and reviewing courts . . . . [Where] courts [once] regularly upheld agency action, with a nod in the direction of the "substantial evidence" test, and a bow to the mysteries of administrative expertise . . . [they now frequently set aside agency actions and require] that administrators articulate the factors on which they base their decisions.
>
> . . . .
>
> . . . Judicial review must operate to ensure that the administrative process itself will confine and control the exercise of discretion. Courts should require administrative officers to articulate the standards and principles that govern their discretionary decisions in as much detail as possible.[79]

[75] *See* Citizens to Preserve Overton Park v. Volpe, 39 U.S.L.W. 4287 (U.S. March 2, 1971) (upon reversal of the Secretary's decision, the case was remanded to the federal district court in lieu of the administrative agency).

The recent *Cassius Clay aka Muhammad Ali* case [39 Law Week 4873, U.S. (June 28, 1971)] is one of a limited number of occasions in which the court has reversed an administrative agency's ruling for failure to support its decision by the hearing record. The Supreme Court found that the Department of Justice had overruled its own hearing officer's report in recommending to Ali's state appeal board that his conscientious objector claim should be denied.

In reversing Ali's conviction for draft evasion, the Court stated:

"Since the Appeal Board gave no reasons for its denial of [Ali's] claim, there is absolutely no way of knowing . . . the grounds [for the denial]. . . . [I]t is indisputably clear . . . that the Department was simply wrong as a matter of law in advising that [Ali's] beliefs were not religiously based. . . . [A] long established rule of law embodied in . . . settled precedents [that an error of law by the Department in so advising an Appeal Board 'must vitiate the entire proceedings . . .] thus clearly requires that the judgment . . . be reversed."

[76] For examples of time consuming cases *see* Scenic Hudson Preservation Conference v. FPC, 354 F.2d 608 (2d Cir. 1965), and the cases involving the Three Sisters Bridge Project in Washington D.C., District of Columbia Federation of Civic Ass'ns v. Volpe, 316 F. Supp. 754 (D.D.C. 1970); 308 F. Supp. 423 (D.D.C. 1970).

[77] 2 E.R.C. 1114 (D.C. Cir. 1971). This case was the successor to EDF v. Hardin, 428 F.2d 1093 (D.C. Cir. 1970) discussed at Five-15.

[78] 2 E.R.C. at 1116 n.8. Oddly enough the granting of such a suspension order to environmentalists may "lack the finality" prerequisite to allow the polluter judicial review. In Nor-Am Agricultural Products, Inc. v. Hardin, 2 E.R.C. 1016 (7th Cir. 1970), the petitioner fungicide manufacturers were denied review of the order suspending the sale of their fungicide products, the court reasoning that such an order was not ripe for review because administrative proceedings would inevitably follow the order.

[79] 2 E.R.C. at 1122.

In a companion case, *Wellford v. Ruckelshaus*,[80] the court recognized "an obligation to ensure that the administrator has made a reasoned decision, which conforms to the legislative language and purpose. And close scrutiny of administrative action is particularly appropriate when the interests at stake are not merely economic interest in a license or a rate structure, but personal interest in life and health."[81]

scope of review

While the very limited review by courts is the general rule, it must be emphasized that each administrative agency has its own statutory structure and applicable court interpretations. A careful legal analysis of the agency's power is necessary before going to court. There can be excessive review as well as too little review. A prime example lies in the Federal Water Quality Act. This Act has so many review stages (and no legal sanctions prior to obtaining a court order[82]) that it is nearly impossible to halt a polluter. A result is that the Federal government has chosen to go to court using this statute only once in the past five years.

The frustration attached to the review process applicable to most administrative agencies has resulted in proposed legislation, usually to expand standing but often granting additional rights. (This will be discussed subsequently under statutory remedies.) Before concluding the discussion of procedure, two special types of law suits that have received attention in relation to environmental litigation should be mentioned; they are class actions and shareholder actions.

class actions

When a wrong is being committed against a group so numerous that it is impracticable to bring them all before the court, a class action can be used. Such an action is provided for under Rule 23 of the Federal Rules of Civil Procedure which states:

> If persons constituting a class are so numerous as to make it impracticable to bring them all before the court, such of them, one or more, as will fairly insure the adequate representation of all may, on behalf of all, sue or be sued, when the character of the right sought to be enforced for or against the class is
>
> (1) joint, or common, or secondary in the sense that the owner of a primary right refuses to enforce that right and a member of the class thereby becomes entitled to enforce it;
>
> (2) several, and the object of the action is the adjudication of claims which do or may affect specific property involved in the action; or
>
> (3) several, and there is a common question of law or fact affecting the several rights and common relief is sought.

It must, however, be possible to identify in some manner what parties comprise the class. This problem has been the subject of much litigation.[83] In addition, the class action cannot be maintained where the interests of the plaintiffs are antagonistic to and not wholly compatible with the interests of those whom they purport to represent.[84]

80 2 E.R.C. 1123 (D.C. Cir. Jan. 7, 1971).

81 *Id.* at 1124.

82 33 U.S.C.A. § 1151 (1970).

83 *See* WRIGHT § 72.

84 Hansburg v. Lee, 311 U.S. 32 (1940); Kentucky Home Mutual Life Ins. Co. v. Duling, 190 F.2d 797 (6th Cir. 1951).

One recent successful class action to abate air pollution was *Biechele v. Norfolk and Western Railway Co.* [309 F.Supp. 354 (N.D. Ohio 1969)]. This case covers the class action problem so well that it is worth setting out the procedural portion of the opinion in full:

class actions

YOUNG, J: This action was originally commenced in the Court of Common Pleas of Erie County, Ohio, and was removed to this Court by defendant on the ground of diversity of citizenship. The action was intended as a class action, and seeks damages and an injunction because of an alleged nuisance created by defendant in the operation of its coal storage and shipping facilities in Sandusky.

After some preliminary skirmishing the Court concluded that this was properly maintainable as a class action and that a representative class was present. Federal Rules of Civil Procedure 23 (a). Actually, there are two separate and distinct class actions involved. The first and principal action is that for injunctive relief. The action is founded upon Rule 23(b) (1) and (2) of the Federal Rules of Civil Procedure. Jurisdiction for this action is based upon diversity, 28 U.S.C. § 1332, the amount in controversy being the value of the right involved. *Hulsenbusch v. Davidson Rubber Co.,* 344 F.2d 730 (8th Cir. 1965); *Pennsylvania R.R. Co. v. City of Girard,* 210 F.2d 437 (6th Cir. 1954); *John B. Kelly, Inc. v. Lehigh Nav. Coal Co.,* 151 F.2d 734 (3rd Cir. 1945); *Wisconsin Electric Co. v. Dumore Co.,* 35 F.2d 555 (6th Cir. 1929). It appears to the Court that the right of each member of the class to live in an environment free from excessive coal dust and conversely, the right of defendant to operate its coal loading facility are both in excess of $10,000.00.

The second action is one for damages resulting from the action of defendant. This action has predominating factual questions in common with the injunctive action and requiring the same evidence as presented in that action. The damage action is properly maintainable as a class action under Rule 23 (b) (3) of the Federal Rules of Civil Procedure, common questions of fact predominating. Although diversity of citizenship exists between the parties, the Court does not believe that any of the claims exceed $10,000.00. These claims cannot be aggregated to achieve the jurisdictional amount. *Snyder v. Harris,* 37 L.W. 4262 (U.S. Sup. Ct. March 25, 1969)

Jurisdiction properly lies in this Court under 28 U.S.C. § 1441 (c). The claims are sufficiently separate to allow removal of the injunctive action alone. Therefore this Court, in the interest of judicial efficiency, will assume jurisdiction over the entire controversy. *Climax Chemical Co. v. C.F. Braun & Co.,* 370 F.2d 616 (10th Cir. 1966); *Moosburgger v. McGraw-Edison Co.,* 215 F.Supp. 486 (D.Minn. 1963).

Delineation of the class in the damage action through the establishment of geographical boundaries was undertaken. Evidence taken at a hearing for a temporary restraining order before Senior District Judge Kloeb as to the extent and locations of the complaints together with a knowledge of the prevailing winds was employed in ascertaining the geographical boundries to be employed. Without such geographical delineation any person who felt that he had been aggrieved by defendant's operation of its coal dock, regardless of the geographical remoteness of his claim, would have had the right to gain redress in this Court. Through this limitation the Court is able to give attention to the vast body of claims for which a reasonably plausible geographical basis can be determined, avoid placing great strain on its docket with numerous actions with only nuisance value, and preserve to the truly aggrieved individual whose claim is geographically remote his right of action (since he, not being a member of the class, is not bound by the judgment).

In furtherance of the policy of the 1966 amendment to Rule 23 to prevent one way intervention and to prevent as much as possible the solicitation of claims as well as to provide the court and the parties with some idea of the real magnitude of the controversy, the Court entered an order requiring all those desiring to present damage claims to enter an appearance in the case on or before November 8, 1968. Such orders are not unknown. *Iowa v. Union Asphalt & Roadoils, Inc.*, 281 F.Supp. 391 (S.D. Iowa 1968); *Philadelphia Electric Co. v. Anaconda American Brass*, 43 F.R.D. 452 (E.D. Pa. 1968); *Harris v. Jones, 41 F.R.D. 70 (D. Utah 1966).*

No list of the potential members of the class in the damage suit was available nor could one have been compiled. Therefore the Court determined that the best possible service would be by publication of its orders delineating the class and requiring the presentation of claims together with the notice required by Rule 23(c) (2) of the Federal Rules of Civil Procedure. It was, however, determined that the publication in the Sandusky Registrar would not be a standard legal notice, but would be prominently placed so that the class members would better have the attention drawn to it. See, *Booth v. General Dynamics Corp.*, 265 F.Supp. 465 (N.D.Ill. 1965). As a result of this notice, seven hundred thirty-one (731) persons joined the damage action as plaintiffs, five hundred thirty-two (532) filed declinations to participate and several thousand others took no action.

class actions

Promptly thereafter, by agreement of the parties, the case was submitted to the Court upon evidence and written argument for a determination of the question of whether or not there was an actionable nuisance, and, if there was, whether plaintiffs were entitled to an injunction, to damages, or to both.

End, text of decision.

The class action is becoming a useful tool in the fight for a decent environment. A large part of our environmental destruction is created by the economic influences present when a pollutor can shift the pollution to the general public and avoid the substantial costs of control. Since no member of the public is injured sufficiently to afford expensive litigation, the pollutor profits from his socially reprehensible conduct. Therefore, the use of class actions may help to restore the legal system's balance to allow the adversary system to work. If a pollutor saves a million dollars in abatement costs by inflicting a few dollars of damage on each of a million citizens, the class action can redress their grievance. Perhaps the next step will be to combine class actions with new tort concepts that would allow all pollutors in an area where the concentration of pollutants was sufficient to cause harm to be sued as joint tortfeasors. The levels of air pollution causing harm could be determined from the National Air Pollution Control Administration's Air Quality Criteria.[85]

Class actions, however, have their weaknesses, both from procedural and philosophic points of view.

If the defense challenges the make-up of the class, attorney for the plaintiffs may almost have to try the case twice, since he must first prove that a proper class exists.

85 *See* 36 Fed. Reg. 1515 (1971). *See also* Pub. L. No. 91-604, § 108 (Dec. 31, 1970).

There are also deeply disturbing philosophical objections to class actions, based on the fact that the attorney who files a class action binds and represents a class, and the results of his wisdom or stupidity, honesty or charlatanry, affect many persons, possibly tens of thousands, who may not even be aware a portion of their fate is at stake. A class action settles the rights of all members of a class.

class actions

As to the stakes involved, two clippings from the same day's *Washington Post* (Nov. 26, 1971) may be instructive. On page A21, an Associated Press story reported that the Nevada Cement Co. had been ordered to pay $2 million in damages for what District Court Judge Richard Waters termed the "deliberate, wanton destruction of the property of others." The judge added that the company "knew that for every day of full operation, 27,000 pounds of dust and dirt were being expelled over the area. Yet never once did it shut down or offer to shut down the monstrous excretion it was spewing forth." On page A24 it was reported that the four petroleum firms sharing the oil drilling platform that caused the Santa Barbara (Calif.) oil spill in January of 1969 had agreed to pay 1,560 beachfront property owners a total of $4.5 million in damages. It was added that the lawyers and their clients were disputing whether the lawyers' fee was 33-1/3 or 27-1/2 percent.

The size of the possible verdict in the appropriate class action suits staggers the mind as has been evidenced by several grandiose actions commenced. One suit involved a thirty-nine billion dollar claim against virtually all the industry and all municipal corporations in Los Angeles County, but was dismissed on the court's motion.[86] Another suit involved the continuation of the antitrust conspiracy suit against the automotive industry after the Justice Department allowed a consent decree.[87] Two Chicago aldermen continued the claim with a class action suit seeking $3 billion.[88]

shareholder actions

The shareholder action or stockholders' derivative action is a special type of class action provided for in Rule 23(b).[89] Separate claims cannot be aggregated by shareholder claimants in a class action to reach the $10,000 required for diversity jurisdiction (Snyder v. Harris, 394 U.S. 332 (1969).

In an action against a corporation, a shareholder may have more rights than an ordinary member of the public. Suits for improper management of the corporation, or for information, or for recovery of money for the corporation (fines paid by management for intentional violation of the law) are a possibility. Such suits are not easy to maintain, particularly when the nearly limitless assets of the corporation can be used for defense, but they are possible and should not be discounted.[90] Other more imaginative uses of the security laws offer the interesting possibility of public intervention to change corporate policies or goals.[91]

86 Diamond v. General Motors, No. 947, 429 (Calif.Sup.Ct.). The plaintiff appealed and lost again: C.A. 3d Cir. 374 [3 ERC 1227] (1971). *See* Farrell, *Let the Pollutor Beware*, Case & Comment, 6 (Sept-Oct. 1970).

See also, Zahn v. International Paper Co., __F.Supp.__(D.Vt. 1971) 3 ERC 1191.

87 United States v. Auto Mfrs., No. 69-75-JWC (S.D. Calif.).

In Chicago v. General Motors, 2 ERC 1711, No. 70 C 1904, N.D. Ill., June 25, 1971, the court dismissed the class action suit, holding that a case brought by the City of Chicago to abate motor vehicle pollution involved a class too complex to be represented adequately by Chicago.

88 Kean v. General Motors, No. 69 c1900 (N.D. Ill.).

89 Fed. R. Civ. P. 23(b). *See* Wright § 73.

90 Hetherington, *Fact and Legal Theory: Shareholders, Managers, and Corporation Social Responsibility*, 21 Stan. L. Rev. 248 (1969); Dykstra, *Revival of the Derivative Suit*, 116 U. Pa. L. Rev. 74 (1967).

e. Remedies

After the potential plaintiff has resolved the procedural difficulties that were previously discussed he must plead a claim for which the court has the power to provide relief. The claim may be based on common law causes of action, more modern tort concepts, property law concepts, state or federal statutes, or constitutional claims. The plaintiff may seek to obtain money damages and/or equitable remedies, such as, an injunction ordering a person to cease an activity or mandamus to force a public official into action.

common law remedies

Common law remedies are those remedies recognized and developed by court decisions promulgated by English and American courts over the centuries. The doctrines traditionally recognized are nuisance, trespass, and negligence. These venerable doctrines have evolved through court decisions, but today the successful prosecution of such suits requires careful consideration of applicable statutory material. A statute or ordinance may define the tort, such as an air pollution ordinance that defines a nuisance to include odors that adversely affect a given percentage of those exposed to it.[92] A statute or a regulation promulgated under the statute may set standards with the violation of such a statute or regulation being proof of negligence, or at least evidence of negligence. An example of the aforementioned would be the situtation where aircraft landings are violating noise levels set by regulations of a U.S. government agency.[93] Statutes may also determine the amount of proof that must be presented, who has the burden of proof, and which defenses can be used.[94]

In some situtations, such as some suits against the government, a common law remedy has been replaced by a statutory tort.[95] In this type of situation, a procedural limitation then becomes the substantive law on the subject because it defines what is the legal wrong for which a remedy has been provided.

private nuisance

A cause of action for the abatement of an environmental nuisance is not new as evidenced by the decision in 1611 in *William Aldred's Case*[96] wherein it was found that the odor from the defendant's hog sty was a nuisance.[97]

A nuisance may be either a public or a private nuisance, but the legal basis for each is quite distinct. A private nuisance is a civil wrong based on the interference with a property right, while a public nuisance is a catch-all criminal offense involving interference with the rights of the community at large, which may give rise to a

91 One organization pursuing this approach is The Project On Corporate Responsibility (Campaign GM), 1609 Connecticut Avenue, N.W., Washington, D.C. 20009. See also, LANDAU & RHEINGOLD, *The Environmental Law Handbook*, 1971 at 36, for a discussion of Mrs. Abigail Avery's suit against Florida Power and Light Co.

92 *See, e.g., Cleveland, Ohio*, § 4.1504, Air Pollution Ordinance 1659-A-69.

93 *See generally* Hildebrand, *Noise Pollution: An Introduction to the Problem and an Outline for Future Legal Research*, 70 COLUM. L. REV. 652 (1970); *Aircraft Noise Unrelenting, Unremitting, Intolerable*, 1 ENVIRONMENTAL SCIENCE & TECHNOLOGY 976 (Dec. 1967); Alekshun, *Aircraft Noise Law: A Technical Perspective*, 55 A.B.A.J. 740 (1969).

94 *See generally* KEETON & SHAPO, PRODUCTS AND THE CONSUMER: DEFECTIVE AND DANGEROUS PRODUCTS, (1970).

95 Jaffe, *Suits Against Governments and Officers: Sovereign Immunity*, 77 HARV. L. REV. 1 (1963); Jaffe, *Suits Against Governments and Officers: Damage Actions*, 77 HARV. L. REV. 209 (1963).

96 77 Eng Rep. 816 (K.B. 1611).

97 *See* Comment, *A History of Federal Air Pollution Control*, 30 OHIO ST. L.J. 516, 517 (1969).

98 W. PROSSER, HANDBOOK OF THE LAW OF TORT § 87 (3d. ed. 1964)

tort action that can be maintained by a private individual.[98] Because the conduct of a defendant may create both a private and a public nuisance, lawyers often plead both causes of action in the alternative as well as other tortious wrongs.[99] These confused pleadings are followed by court decisions that can charitably be described as fuzzy. This leaves the subject intellectually muddled and the successful attorney may take advantage of such confusion in his own pleading of multiple causes of action in the alternative. However, such an approach is possible because of sloppy defense work on behalf of counsel for the defendant. The intelligent defense attorney should move to dismiss each cause of action for which the necessary elements are not alleged or proved.

A private nuisance is an interference with rights in land. The Restatement of Torts, section 822 has attempted to set out the elements of nuisance stating:

private nuisance

> The actor is liable in an action for damages for a non-trespassory invasion of another's interest in the private use and enjoyment of land if,
>
> (a) the other has property rights and privileges in respect to the use or enjoyment interfered with; and
> (b) the invasion is substantial; and
> (d) the actor's conduct is a legal cause of the invasion; and
> (c) the invasion is either
> (i) intentional and unreasonable; or
> (ii) unintentional and otherwise actionable under the rules governing liability for negligent, reckless or ultra-hazardous conduct.

Only those whose property rights have been denied can bring an action. In addition, the invasion of the property rights in question must be substantial.[100] If the particular conduct in question involved a physical effect on land, the showing of a substantial interference is not difficult to prove. But, if the interference involves aesthetics, inconvenience, or some other subjective annoyance, the showing of a substantial interference is more difficult to prove. In these cases, the interpretation of what constitutes a "substantial" invasion is based upon the values within the community of what constitutes a use of property in a normal manner. Interference with either an idiosyncratic or hypersensitive plaintiff or with unusual property use is not substantial interference.[101]

The required substantial interference requirement is related to the balancing of interests carried out by the court in a private nuisance action. Each property owner may use his property as he wishes as long as he does not interfere with the rights of other property owners to do likewise. However, most uses will have some impact on neighboring properties. Property owners are, therefore, required to use their property reasonably, and this is determined by a court's balancing of the equities. One of the landmark cases is *Madison v. Ducktown Sulphur, Copper & Iron Company*.[102] This case involved an action by farmers for property damage from a mining processing enterprise. The court recognized that in order to prevent harming farms of little value it would be necessary to close

99 WRIGHT §§ 66-69.
100 PROSSER § 89.
101 PROSSER § 90.
102 113 Tenn. 331, 83 S.W. 658 (1904).
103 161 Cal. 239, 118 P. 928 (1911).

down the plant, thus making this manufacturing property nearly worthless; in addition this closing would destroy nearly half of the county's tax base and create massive unemployment. Under such circumstances the court refused to issue an injunction, but rather it sought to rectify the wrong by permitting the defendant to make payment of money damages to the plaintiff.

The weakness of this balancing doctrine is apparent. The powerful polluter will never be stopped unless he injures an equally large economic interest. The contrary approach, recognizing the court's obligation to protect the weak, was articulated in *Hulbert v. California Portland Cement Company*,[103] in which an injunction was granted to protect citrus fruit growers from cement dust, in spite of the ensuing economic injury to the defendant. This approach, however, does not represent the attitude of the majority of courts, and the reader of nuisance cases finds, with depressing repetition, the toleration of substantial environmental damage because the destruction was slight when weighed against the business interest involved. However, the attorney contemplating such a suit should not be unduly discouraged by the body of old case law that accepted pollution as unavoidable for "progress." Many older cases involved "either/or" propositions. A community that wished industry had to accept pollution. This attitude still presents a problem with some businesses that are environmental abusers, particularly when their operations are so marginally profitable that they cannot afford pollution controls. However, the vast majority of pollution problems can be cured if the companies expend the funds necessary for such corrective measures. The cries of technological impossibility and cost limitations should be anticipated by the attorney bringing a nuisance case and refuted. If a defendant is to go out of business because of his inability to be a good neighbor, the court should recognize that it need not be that way, *i.e.*, it is the *polluter's* choice.

private nuisance

The attorney bringing a nuisance suit against an air polluter should realize that virtually all air pollution, except perhaps the emission from coke ovens, can be controlled by existing technology. This does not mean that the problems created by the lack of money, lack of space, and obsolete physical plants found when dealing with specific problems can always be handled satisfactorily; not all problems are subject to a satisfactory technological answer. Nevertheless, the plaintiff's attorney should begin with the assumption that the problem can be controlled and be prepared to rebut arguments to the contrary. If the suit involves common air contaminants, the Environmental Protection Agency (which includes, *inter alia*, what was formerly the National Air Pollution Control Administration) has publications available on control techniques.[104] There are ample sources relevant to other types of pollution as well, so that preparation by an attorney in a pollution suit is not too difficult.

While preparation is important for the attorney, a societal change that benefits the plaintiffs in a nuisance action is the general recognition of the harm to health and property caused by pollution and other environmental abuses. Courts are no longer viewing these cases as a balancing of economic interests against aesthetic values.

104 *See, e.g.*, U.S. Dept. of Health, Education, and Welfare, Control Techniques for Particulate Air Pollutants (January 1969, Pub. AP-51) and Control Techniques for Sulphur Oxide Air Pollutants (January 1969, Pub. AP-52).

105 100 N.J. Super. 366, 242 A.2d 21 (1968).

106 *Id.* at 394, 242 A.2d at 35.

An example of this new attitude is found in *Department of Health v. Owens-Corning Fiberglass*,[105] in which the court held, "it is not unreasonable for the State, in the interest of the public health and welfare, to seek to control air pollution. Even if this means the shutting down of an operation harmful to health or unreasonably interfering with life or property, the statute must prevail."[106] The present court interest in environmental consideration can be further enhanced by a careful showing by the plaintiff's attorney of the various harms caused by environmental abuses, particularly the damage to health. The result of the change in community attitudes is that courts will balance the equities and find for the plaintiff even though the law of nuisance has not changed.[107]

While the balancing test is the one on which most plaintiffs lose their case, there are other elements of the doctrine of nuisance that can create problems for the plaintiff. In some courts, the doctrine of nuisance must include the recurrence or continuance of the harm over a period of time. This however, is not a universal requirement.[108] Another problem in nuisance is that the balancing of the equities forces the court to become judicial zoners. Thus, a use which will be considered unreasonable in one area may not be unreasonable in another. Heavy industrial uses in an industrial area would be tolerable, though courts would find them intolerable if such activity took place in an exclusive residential area. This, in turn, means that an individual who moves into an area in which pollution activities are already taking place is in a weak position to challenge the industrial activities as being a nuisance. Since the nuisance theory is a property concept, the individual creating the nuisance may obtain a prescriptive right to continue his nuisance if he has been carrying out the activity for the period of time necessary to acquire a prescriptive right under the law of the state. Thus, pollution carried out for a long period of time may give the polluter a legal right to continue such actions.

public nuisance

Public nuisance developed historically as an omnibus criminal offense which allowed the government to prevent an interference with the rights of the community. The two concepts, public nuisance and private nuisance, have little relationship, except that the conduct which interferes with the private use of property may also be the conduct which interferes with the well-being of the community. Public nuisance cases represent a wide variety of activities deemed to be improper. These include interference with public morals as with houses of prostitution, illegal gambling houses, or illegal bars. It also includes such activities as those involving the creation of odors, air pollution, noise, parking problems, or danger to the public safety.[109] The first requirement of a public nuisance is that it affects an interest of the general public as opposed to that of only a few individuals. In the United States, there are statutes in each state making a public nuisance a statutory crime and punishable as

[107] *See, e.g.*, Biechele v. Norfolk & Western R.R., 309 F. Supp. 354 (N.D. Ohio 1969); Richards v. Village of Edinburg, 97 Ill. App. 2d 36, 239 N.E.2d 479 (1968); Maryland v. Galaxy Chem., 1 E.R.C. 1660 (Md. Cir. Ct. 1970); Nelson v. C&C Plywood Corp., 154 Mont. 414, 465 P.2d 314 (1970); Jost v. Dairyland Power Cooperative, 45 Wis. 2d 164, 172 N.W.2d 647 (1969). *See also* Juergensmeyer, *Control of Air Pollution Through the Assertion of Private Rights*, 1967 DUKE L.J. 1126; Kennedy & Porter, *Air Pollution: Its Control and Abatement*, 8 VAND. L. REV. 854 (1955); Lewin, Gordon, & Hartelius, *Law and the Municipal Ecology*, NIMLO RESEARCH REPORT 156, 184 (1970).

[108] PROSSER § 88.

[109] PROSSER § 89.

such.[110]

While a public nuisance is considered an injury to the public, the law has for hundreds of years recognized the right of an individual plaintiff to bring a tort action for a public nuisance. However, the plaintiff must show that he has suffered special damages over and above the ordinary damage caused to the public at large. He must show not only that he has been injured but that his injury is different in kind, rather than in degree, from that of the general public. Thus, when a polluter injures an entire community it is difficult, if not impossible, for any single individual or small group of individuals to prove that they have been injured differently in kind rather than in degree from the injury to the rest of the community. Once it is shown that an injury different from that of the general public has been suffered it must be shown that this injury is caused by a violation of a legally protected right. Whether the injury is caused by the negligence, intentional conduct, or the breach of an absolute duty by the defendant is not important. It is the invasion of a legal interest that is protected. But since the plaintiff cannot represent the general public interest, his legally protected interest must be different from that of the general community. The easiest way of showing particular injury is to be able to prove that the plaintiff suffered physical injury because of the public nuisance. While physical injury may in fact occur to a large number of the public, the courts seem not to regard this as a bar to action by a plaintiff who can prove injury. Thus, public nuisance as a doctrine has its best use in physical injury cases.

public nuisance

Another ground for successful use of a public nuisance doctrine is found when the plaintiff has suffered a pecuniary loss that was not inflicted upon the community as a whole. A business interference, common to a small group within the community, is the type of monetary loss for which public nuisance can provide a remedy. If the loss affects the whole community, the doctrine cannot be used. However, loss to an individual of money because of delay or inconvenience caused by the defendant's conduct will probably not support an action in public nuisance. Needless to say, there is a substantial gray area between specific pecuniary loss to a business, general loss to a business and general loss due to inconvenience or delay.

Interference with the use of land also constitutes a special type of damage for which public nuisance actions will lie. These actions include those to secure the access to land. Complete deprivation of access to land is not necessary if there is substantial cut-off from the access to the land. Interference with the public right of passage, however, is not a public nuisance; a detour will not support an action, while deprivation of access to land will. Thus, while a public nuisance case can be prosecuted without the balancing problems of a private nuisance case, the factual context in which the cases arise require that the courts make a type of balancing decision when deciding questions as to whether the interference was substantial or whether the plaintiff was injured in a manner different from that of the rest of the community. The major difficulty in the public nuisance suit continues to be the requirement of proving injury to the individual in a manner different from that to the community at large.[111] Cases in this area are somewhat confused by the fact that a physical injury would also usually give a right to a private nuisance cause of action. Since attorneys normally plead both causes of action and courts decide the case as to whether a nuisance has

110 *Id.*

been presented, it is sometimes difficult to tell whether the case is being prosecuted and/or decided as a private or public nuisance case. Several elements of proof necessary in suits for private nuisance, however, may be easier to meet in a public nuisance case. In private nuisance a recurring injury may be required, while a single occurrence has allowed recovery for a public nuisance.[112] There may be less balancing in public nuisance actions, particularly if the public nuisance is defined by statute. Finally, the defense that the polluter's discharge has ripened into a prescriptive right is not available.[113]

relief available

The remedies for nuisance are three.[114] The plaintiff can seek money damages, equitable relief by injunction, or abate the nuisance by self help. The receipt of money damages for a nuisance is no different from that of other tort actions. For a temporary nuisance the amount of money damage that will be payable is the value of the use of the property or the loss of the rental of the property for the period of time that the nuisance existed. If the nuisance is permanent, the measure of damages will be the permanent loss in value of the property. If you cannot evaluate the loss of value of the property, you can capitalize the loss of income from the property to determine the value lost. One measurement technique is to use the value multiplied by the interest rate applicable to the risk to find the rental value; alternatively, the net income, if that is known, divided by the appropriate interest rate will equal the value. This type of valuation problem is common in property taxation and any general work on property tax or an assessment manual can be used. If there has been personal injury or personal discomfort, there may be further money damages awarded as with any other tort action.

The use of money damages by the court, however, can be used to allow a nuisance to continue. If an individual cannot abate his nuisance, the court may grant money damages to the plaintiffs and in return allow the individual whose conduct is causing this harm to continue his operations. Many of the cases mentioned earlier involved that kind of damage settlement. Sometimes money damages can be forced on the plaintiff by the failure of the defendant to react; he would rather absorb the money damages, and the court cooperates.

In *Spur Industries v. Del E. Webb Development,* Arizona Sup.Ct., 4 ERC 1052 (March 17, 1972), a private developer sued to enjoin the operation of a cattle feeding lot. Although the court found both a private [special injury in loss of sales] and public nuisance [odors, flies] were created by the feed lot and issued a permanent injunction on the operation of the feed lot, the developer was held to be liable to Spur Industries [feed lot operator], ". . . for a reasonable amount of the cost of moving or shutting down. It should be noted that this relief to Spur is limited to a case wherein a developer has, with foreseeability, brought into a previously agricultural or industrial area, the population which makes necessary the granting of an injunction against a lawful business and for which the business has no adequate relief."

In the case of *Cox v. Schlachter,*[115] a commercial mouse-breeding establishment was producing a nuisance. The defendant

[112] Juergensmeyer, *supra* note 106, at 1142.

[113] Prosser, *Private Action for Public Nuisance,* 52 VA. L. REV. 997 (1966) (the definitive work on this subject).

[114] PROSSER § 91.

[115] 1 E.R.C. 1681 (Ind. App. 1970).

[116] Boomer v. Atlantic Cement Co., 26 N.Y.2d 219, 257 N.E.2d 870, 309 N.Y.S.2d 312 (1970).

refused to respond to a court order to abate the nuisance. The court then entered judgment that this nuisance was unabatable. Therefore, damages were assessed against the defendant measured by the difference in value of the plaintiff's land before and after the commission of such nuisance. In another case,[116] a cement plant valued at 45 million dollars and employing over 300 persons was found to be a nuisance, but an injunction was denied. New York State's highest court decided that permanent damages of $185,000 rather than an injunction should be granted.[117] Thus, a large polluter can force individuals with limited resources to an extended legal fight, and the result, even if the polluter loses, is only the required payment of money sufficient to pay for a diminution of a portion of the plaintiff's property value. This type of damage payment can also be the result of suing a community or other government body.[118]

damages

This type of measurement is often unfair, for the diminution in property value may only be tangentially related to the injury caused to the plaintiff by a disagreeable odor or other nuisance. The market value for property is determined by many factors, and the value of a piece of real estate with a very desirable location may be unaffected by almost any conceivable nuisance, short of one causing immediate physical harm. Limiting the plaintiff's recovery is unfair; a better test would be to allow a jury to also consider the loss of value from the point of view of the plaintiff, based on his life style.

Occasionally, punitive damages will be allowed. Though such damages are not "favored in the law," whenever there is evidence that an intentional act was committed with knowledge that it would cause harm to a particular person or persons, punitive damages will be allowed.[119]

Since the award of money damages is not a satisfactory remedy for environmental torts, the equity court's power to enjoin the nuisance should be exercised. In theory, since land is unique, money damages are not sufficient where the use of land is seriously impaired. However, the cases cited show that the theory is not consistently used by the courts. Since the remedy is discretionary, the attorney for the plaintiff can assist the court by showing the court the action which could be taken to end the nuisance and yet protect the public interest in having continued employment and useful economic activity. The more unreasonable the conduct of the defendant under the circumstances of the case, the better the opportunity will be to obtain an equitable remedy. A careful demonstration of the abatement steps that could be taken should result in an increase in the granting of equitable remedies. Another advantage of the equity power is that it can be exercised to prevent a threatened harm which has not yet materialized. If the defendant's action makes the creation of a nuisance highly probable, it can be enjoined.[120]

Abatement through self-help is an old remedy. This remedy exists only for a short time after knowledge of the nuisance is acquired. The doctrine is limited. Only the minimum abatement necessary to protect the individual from special damage is allowed. The use of

117 *Id.* at 228, 257 N.E.2d at 875, 309 N.Y.S.2d at 319.

118 *See, e.g.*, Richards v. Village of Edinburg, 97 Ill. App. 2d 36, 239 N.E.2d 479 (1968).

119 *See, e.g.*, McElwain v. Georgia—Pacific Corp., 245 Ore. 247, 421 P.2d 957 (1966) (punitive damages allowed for pollution from a paper mill).

120 W. DE FUNIAK, HANDBOOK OF MODERN EQUITY § 34, at 62-64 (2d ed. 1956).

this method must be reasonable, for the user is likely to have to justify his conduct to a court. What is reasonable depends upon all the circumstances, but it should normally be used only when an emergency does not allow resort to the usual process and delay in abatement would create danger of serious harm. Unless the emergency is so immediate that there is no time, most courts require notice and a demand for abatement to be given to the creator of the nuisance prior to exercising a self-help remedy.[121]

trespass

Trespass is a venerable legal doctrine that has been little used in environmental litigation. The distinction between trespass and nuisance lies in the fact that trespass is an invasion of the right to exclusive possession of land, a direct interference, while nuisance is an invasion of the right to use and enjoy land, an indirect interference.[122] One interference such as air pollution can, therefore, often be both a trespass and a nuisance. However, from an evidentiary point of view, the trespass doctrine provides fewer problems of proof. Actual damages need not be shown, for the right to be free from a trespass is absolute,[123] but only in theory, for if no actual damages are shown the recovery will be limited to minimal money damages and equitable relief will be denied. Even though the balancing argument is not an element of trespass, and therefore, is not necessarily specifically articulated by courts, the rule of reason requires its use.[124] The doctrine of "coming to the nuisance" and the special injury required in a public nuisance case is avoided but the creation of a prescriptive right is still a defense.[125] The fact that a trespass may be committed above or below the surface of the land[126] allows its use in air pollution and aircraft interference cases.[127]

Perhaps the most useful distinction is that the statute of limitations usually runs for a longer period of time for a trespass; the statute begins when the invasion commences, and for a continuing trespass, continues to begin anew. The cause of action for nuisance, however, begins when the interference causes substantial harm.[128]

The most important air pollution cases based on the trespass theory are the series of fluoride cases from the states of Washington and Oregon.[129] It should be pointed out that the direct invasion involved in these cases was particulates carried by the air and that in one case,[130] the court awarded punitive damages for not acting in good faith. An unreported Ohio case also employed this doctrine suc-

121 RESTATEMENT OF TORTS § 201 (1934).

122 PROSSER § 90.

123 RESTATEMENT OF TORTS §§ 158, 163 (1934).

124 PROSSER § 13.

125 *Id.*

126 RESTATEMENT OF TORTS § 519 (1934).

127 PROSSER § 13.

128 PROSSER § 52.

129 Reynold Metals v. Lampert, 316 F.2d 272, *rev'd*, 324 F.2d 465 (9th Cir. 1963), *cert. denied*, 376 U.S. 910 (1964); Arvidson v. Reynolds Metals Co., 236 F.2d 224 (9th Cir. 1956), *cert. denied*, 352 U.S. 968 (1957); Fairview Farms v. Reynolds Metals Co., 176 F. Supp. 178 (D. Ore. 1959); Martin v. Reynolds Metals Co., 342 P.2d 790 (Ore. 1959), *cert. denied*, 362 U.S. 918 (1960).

130 Reynolds Metals Co. v. Lampert, 316 F.2d 272, *rev'd*, 324 F.2d 465 (9th Cir. 1963), *cert. denied*, 376 U.S. 910 (1964).

cessfully in an air pollution action.[131] Therefore, although a traditional doctrine within American jurisprudence, it is being applied in a novel fashion in environmental litigation.

negligence

Negligence is defined by the Restatement of Torts as conduct which falls below the standard established by law for the protection of others against unreasonable risk of harm.[132] The elements of negligence necessary to impose liability are: (a) an interest protected against unintentional invasion, (b) negligent conduct of the actor, (c) conduct which is a legal cause of the invasion, and (d) the injured party has not been contributorily negligent thereby disabling himself from bringing an action.[133] Professor Prosser divides negligence into four elements: a duty recognized by law requiring conformity to a standard of conduct to protect others from unreasonable risks; a failure to conform to the standard required; a close causal connection between the conduct and the injury (proximate cause); and actual loss or damage.[134]

The difficult problem is proving that some applicable standard of conduct has been breached,[135] and that this breach has been the cause of the harm to the plaintiff.[136] The result is that this doctrine has been of value primarily where a single polluter has acted so as to cause specific demonstrable injury to a plaintiff.[137] Negligence cases have been made easier by some of the modifications to the negligence doctrine discussed subsequently under new environmental remedies. The main problem for the plaintiff lies in proving an extremely difficult causal relation when scientific knowledge is very limited and the harm caused by pollution is diffuse, slow to manifest itself, and often the result of exposure to a wide variety of pollutants and/or from a wide variety of sources.[138] In addition the standard defenses of assumption of the risk and contributory negligence are available to the defendants.[139] Smoking, for example, may be considered contributory negligence in an air pollution suit for lung damage.[140] In most states, if a plaintiff in a negligence action is even one percent negligent, he cannot recover from a defendant who is ninety-nine percent negligent.[141] The harshness of this doctrine is ameliorated by the unwillingness of judges and juries to find contributory negligence if it is minor.[142] Such harshness is further

131 Reliable Oldsmobile Inc. v. Grabler Manufacturing Co., No. 838749 (Guy County C.P. Dec. 12, 1968).

132 Restatement of Torts § 282 (1934).

133 *Id.* § 281.

134 Prosser § 30.

135 Prosser chs. 5 & 10.

136 Prosser ch. 7.

137 *See, e.g.*, Greyhound Corp. v. Blakely, 262 F.2d 401 (9th Cir. 1958); Hagy v. Allied Chem. & Dye Corp., 122 Cal. 2d 361, 265 P.2d 86 (1954).

138 *See generally* Miller & Borchers, *Private Lawsuits and Air Pollution Control*, 56 A.B.A.J. 465 (1970).

139 Prosser § 64, 67.

140 Rheingold, *Civil Cause of Action for Lung Damage Due to Pollution of Urban Atmosphere*, 33 Brooklyn L. Rev. 17 (1966).

141 Prosser § 64.

142 Prosser §§ 64-65.

ameliorated by the doctrine of comparative negligence, though it is presently recognized in only a few states.[143]

The use of contemporary negligence approaches occasionally allows plaintiffs to obtain awards. As a legal theory, however, negligence is of marginal value for prosecuting broader public interest cases; equitable remedies are not available, and usually it is not possible to combine sufficient individual claims to achieve a public interest goal. The costs of preparing negligence cases and the difficulty of proving causation has limited the value and the number of law suits pursued under this theory. This has meant that for most pollution programs the cost to defendants of defending and paying numerous claims has not been sufficient to create a change in their conduct, literally to take the profit out of pollution. Class actions, however, may offer some possibility of meaningfully using this doctrine.

See also postscript to Galaxy Chemical Co. case at Five-49.

new remedies in environmental actions

The traditional tort remedies have been of limited value in protecting injured plaintiffs from the damages of a society with a complex technology which has the propensity for a wide variety of injuries. However, negligence doctrines as modified by modern statutes and court interpretations have made recovery much easier. A combination of court decisions and statutory enactments have provided recovery under such doctrines as warranty, absolute liability in tort, and nuisance *per se*.[144] Other changes include the shifting of the burden of proof under a variety of doctrines. The general thesis is that if injury can be proven to be caused by the actions of the defendant the legal theories will be adjusted to fit the facts. In particular, injuries to health, if proven, will be compensable.[145]

Several other trends are also discernible, though recovery is dependent upon the law of the particular state in question and the skill with which the case is handled. One approach is to join multiple defendants making them jointly liable for atmospheric contamination. Perhaps courts will accept the idea that injury can be proven to be the result of the combined effects of pollution. There are many weaknesses in this approach, but given the synergistic reaction of pollutants, the alternative is to deny recovery to injured plaintiffs. Another trend is to base the required standard of care on the use of the highest level of available control technology. Failure to have such equipment would be negligence or the basis for finding a nuisance.[146] As with other legal concepts, the courts have been able to adapt their thinking to allow recovery for personal injuries created by life in a complex technological society. The problem now is to prompt the courts to use the same kind of creative legal theorizing to protect the broader public interest needed for environmental protection.

A variation of the shareholder action is the citizen suit to enjoin the sale of revenue bonds where the proceeds would be used to finance an environmentally destructive project. Such suits have a tendency to frighten off bidders. The same result can occur if governmental agencies threaten legal actions over environmental issues. *See, The Wall Street Journal,* April 28 and May 5, 1972 both at 23.

143 **PROSSER § 66.**

144 PROSSER ch. 14.

145 *See* Bellis, *Kolsky, & Wolf, Legal Approach to Industrial Pollution, Trial* at 29 (June/July 1968).

146 *Id.*

147 Basic Water Law texts are: J. SAX, WATER LAW, PLANNING & POLICY (1968); TRELEASE, WATER LAW (1967).

See also, MEYERS & TARLOCK, *Water Resources Management* (1971), and Davis, Theories of Water Pollution Litigation, 1971 *Wis. L. Rev.* No. 3 at 738.

water rights

Water pollution may be attacked by the legal doctrines of water law. These may be riparian rights, appropriation rights, or statutory rights modifying either of the first two basic doctrines.[147] There may also be other remedies available under more sophisticated provisions of water management organizations, such as irrigation districts or interstate water management agencies. Riparian rights are recognized by the humid states of the eastern half of our nation, and by the Pacific Coast states which have a complex combination of both riparian and appropriation law. Riparian rights are water rights that belong to the owners of land contiguous to a water course. Such riparian owners have the right to use the water as it flows past their property. Most states today define this right to be limited to the right of reasonable use. Since other owners have correlative rights, a use should not unreasonably affect either the quality or the quantity of the stream. What is a reasonable use is determined by the court decisions of the state involved. These decisions are few and create little if any substantive right that cannot be considered to exist under nuisance theories. If necessary, they may provide a longer statute of limitations. The riparian doctrine has been an ineffective means of pollution control, but if it is possible to use the doctrine it should be pleaded as an additional cause of action. It might provide benefits through stricter new interpretations of what is reasonable use, as opposed to past judicial court interpretations of the other common law doctrines.[148]

Appropriation law is used in arid areas and gives the water right holder, who is not required to own any land along the water course, the right to a specific amount of water as long as it is used beneficially. Often the water must be returned after use to the watercourse to satisfy the needs of other holders of appropriation rights. If it is returned so polluted that it cannot be used the other appropriators would have a cause of action based on their water rights.[149]

inverse condemnation

Inverse condemnation is action that can be prosecuted against a government defendant for the value of property that has been taken, in effect, even though there has been neither formal taking through the power of eminent domain nor physical occupancy. The two major actions from which these cases arise are damage to property from nearby highway construction which materially limits the use of the property, and therefore its value, and damage caused by the noise from low flying aircraft which likewise materially diminishes

148 *See generally* R. CLARK, WATER AND WATER RIGHTS (1967). For pollution cases involving an interference with riparian rights *see, e.g.*, American Cynamid Co. v. Sparto, 267 F.2d 425 (5th Cir. 1959); Borough of Westville v. Whitney Home Builders, 40 N.J. Super. 62, 122 A.2d 233 (1956). For material on the measure and elements of damages for pollution of a stream *see* 49 A.L.R.2d 253 (1956).

For recent cases see Cape May County Chapter, Inc., Izaak Walton League of America v. Macchia, 329 F. Supp. 504 (1971); and Ratzlaff v. Franz Foods of Arkansas, 468 S.W. 2d 239 (1971).

149 *See supra* p. 811. For cases applying the appropriation doctrine to limit the right to pollute *see, e.g.*, Antioch v. Williams Irr. Dist., 188 Cal. 451, 205 P. 688 (1922); Phoenix Water Co. v. Fletcher, 23 Cal. 481 (1863); Suffolk Gold Mining & Milling Co. v. San Miguel Consol., 9 Colo. App. 407, P. 828 (1897).

146Brown, Probing the Law and Beyond: A Quest for Public Protection from Hazardous Product Catastrophes, 38 *Geo. Wash. L. Rev.* 431 (1970.

See also, Rheingold, Handling Environmental Litigation—From the Plaintiff's Viewpoint, 21 Fed. of Ins. Counsel No. 4 (1971) at 81.

the value of the property.[150] This cause of action circumvents some of the sovereign immunity problems present when attempting to sue government agencies.[151]

public trust doctrine

The public trust doctrine holds that the government has a duty to all citizens to protect the Nation's natural resources for them as their trustee. If the government does not act to protect these resources as a trustee a court action may be instituted by a citizen. Old case law in this country uses this doctrine to prevent the government from giving away rights to public lands and waters without adequately protecting the public interest.[152] At the risk of dangerously oversimplifying the legal concept of these cases, one can state that the common legal basis for successful litigation is that certain public lands and waters are inalienable. Perhaps the most famous of these cases is *Illinois v. Illinois Central Railroad,*[153] where the State of Illinois, suing to prevent the city of Chicago from giving away most of the harbor of the city to the Illinois Railroad, prevented this transfer as a breach of public trust.

It is not easy to use the public trust doctrine to prevent the disposal of public lands or waters. Case law is confused, for many of the transfers that came before the courts were made during a period when the prevailing sentiment was that anything the government could give to business was a good thing to do. The conflict with basic property rights of private owners further complicated the use of the doctrine. For example, in water law, the Federal Government has a navigational interest in water that will be legally protected, but the riparian owner and the State also have legal interests in the same body of water. Asserting one interest can diminish the other interest, and thus, evaluation (both factually and legally) is complicated for it is often at the expense of some recognized legal interest that other legal interests are protected.

Some states, such as Wisconsin and Massachusetts, have acted to define more clearly what rights are protected by the public trust doctrine through statutory and constitutional enactments. In Wisconsin, the court in *City of Milwaukee v. State*[154] held that a transfer of public land could be accomplished if it was necessary for the promotion of the public trust benefits. Another useful case is the 1969 Massachusetts decision of *Robbins v. Department of Public Works.*[155] The primary requirement in these cases is that the transfer must be necessary. The public trust doctrine has been applied

150 United States v. Causby, 328 U.S. 256 (1946); Thomburg v. Port of Portland, 233 Ore. 178, 376 P.2d 100 (1962).

151 *See generally* D. Mandelker, Managing Our Urban Environment 519-26 (1966). For other material consult O. Gray, Cases and Materials on Environmental Law ch. 3H (1970); Ross, *Inverse Condemnation Absent Overflight,* 8 Nat. Res. J. 561 (1968).

See also Joslin v. Marin Municipal Water District, Calif. Sup. Ct. 67C. 2d 132, 60 Cal.Rptr. 377, 429 P2d 889 (1969)

152 These cases have been very throughly evaluated by Professor Joseph Sax in *The Public Trust Doctrine in Natural Resource Law* 68 Mich. L. Rev. 471 (1970).

153 146 U.S. 387 (1892).

154 193 Wis. 423, 214 N.W. 820 (1927).

155 355 Mass. 328, 244 N.E.2d 577, (1969).

not only to public lands and waters but also to cases involving wildlife protection and public roads. Whether this doctrine can be further extended to protect public rights to pure air and water and to an undefiled environment will depend upon the actions of those willing to litigate.[156]

statutory rights

Statutes may be used in two ways by a private citizen seeking to redress an environmentally related grievance. The statute itself may provide a cause of action, by creating a new legal right through legislative action. A wide range of statutory material modifying traditional tort law has developed—particularly in the product liability area.[157] Much more common is a statute that may provide a standard which can be used to show a right to recover under the previously discussed common law doctrines.[158]

The most publicized statutory enactment giving new rights is the National Environmental Policy Act of 1969.[159] This Act in section 102 requires a report to be made to the Council of Environmental Quality for every federal action significantly affecting the human environment. Sufficient time has not yet passed to know what interpretation will be given to many of the Act's provisions, but citizen action to force the required governmental consideration of environmental considerations has been successful. As of September, 1970, there have been at least twenty-two lawsuits filed that were based, at least in part, on the Act.

The most significant case is probably the *Wilderness Society v. Hickel*[160] which restrained the construction of the Trans-Alaska Pipeline System. The Act has expanded citizens' rights, and given Federal Government agencies new responsibilities. Time will show whether this is the beginning of an Environmental Bill of Rights.[161] At present the Act seems primarily useful in requiring consideration of environmental values. Furthermore, the ability of citizens to intervene increases the channels of communication and assists citizens in showing the required interest necessary to have standing.[162]

More powerful citizen rights could be granted by legislation proposed in 1970. The Clean Air Act of 1970,[163] and the Hart-

156 The author has used ideas found in Cohen, "The Constitution, The Public Trust Doctrine and the Environment," Vol. 1970, No. 3. Utah L.Rev. 388 (June 1970).

See also:

BERLIN, ROISMAN & KESSLER, LAW IN ACTION: THE TRUST DOCTRINE, LAW AND THE ENVIRONMENT 166 (Baldwin & Page ed. 1970).

157 *See generally* KEETON & SHAPIRO, PRODUCTS AND THE CONSUMER: DEFECTIVE AND DANGEROUS PRODUCTS (1970).

158 PROSSER, § 35.

159 42 U.S.C.A. §§ 432 *et seq.* (Supp. 1971).

160 325 F.Supp. 422 (E.D.Ark. 1970) 1 ERC 1335.

161 *An Environmental Bill of Rights: The Citizen Suit and the National Environmental Policy Act of 1969*, 24 RUTGERS L. REV. 230 (1970). However, a court has held, that the Act creates no substantive rights. EDF v. Corps of Engineers, 2 E.R.C. 1260 (E.D. Ark. 1970).

See also section in Chapter One dealing with NEPA, particularly the discussion of the Calvert Cliffs case.

162 *See* Peterson, *Title I of the National Environmental Policy Act of 1969*, ENVIRON. L. REP. 50035 (1971). Yannacone, *National EPA of 1969* , 1 ENVIRONMENTAL LAW 8 (1970) (Lewis & Clark College).

163 Pub. L. No. 91-604 (Dec. 31, 1970).

McGovern Bill,[164] both provide statutory authority for citizen suits. In addition, by providing the right to sue to stop unreasonable pollution as in the Hart Bill,[165] unreasonable pollution becomes a legal wrong, created by statute, and subject to definition through judicial decisions. The Clean Air Act would create a legal wrong when any one of a number of administrative requirements were not met.[166] Procedural rights which have the effect of creating new substantive rights have already been granted by the Michigan Environmental Protection Act of 1970,[167] a creation primarily of Professor Joseph Sax of the University of Michigan Law School. Other states considering similar legislations include New York, Massachusetts, Colorado, Tennessee, and Pennsylvania.

Another federal act of current interest is the 1899 Refuse Act.[168] This prohibits the dumping of refuse of any kind into navigable waters, except municipal liquid waste from sewers, unless a permit from the Corps of Engineers has been obtained. Very few permits have been granted, although the Corps plans a massive program to put the industrial users of water throughout the Nation under permit. Criminal fines for dumping are provided[169] and court interpretations have ruled that even small amounts of oil and other wastes dumped only once are prohibited by the Act.[170] The Act provides for one-half of the fine to go to the person providing information leading to a conviction.[171] A person having such information should give it to the local United States Attorney. It might also be useful to send a copy to the Lands and Natural Resources Division of the Department of Justice in Washington, D.C. It would also be useful to consult the procedures governing the Corps of Engineers, the Environmental Protection Agency, and the Justice Department. The question of whether a person can bring suit under the Act is unresolved, but, as mentioned in the chapter on Water Pollution, a substantial number of lower courts have ruled against these private actions.[172] See the discussion in Chapter Four.

Statutes that provide for court actions by private citizens are, as the preceding material demonstrates, limited. However, a wide range of statutory material creating obligations to the public can provide

[164] S.3575. This Bill was intended to be the Environmental Policy Act of 1970, but it failed to pass.

[165] *Id.* § 2.

[166] Pub. L. No. 91-604, § 304 (Dec. 31, 1970).

[167] Mich. Comp. Laws §§ 691. 1201-1207 (1970).

See also, Commonwealth v. National Gettysburg Battlefield Tower (Pa.Ct. Common Pleas) 3 ERC 1270 (1971)

[168] 33 U.S.C. 407 (1964).

[169] *Id.* § 411.

[170] United States v. Republic Steel Corp., 362 U.S. 482 (1960); United States v. Interlake Steel Corp., 297 F. Supp. 912 (N.D. Ill. 1969). *See also* Trip & Hall, *Federal Enforcement Under the Refuse Act of 1899*, 35 Albany L. Rev. 60 (1970).

[171] 33 U.S.C. § 411 (1964); *see* United States v. Transit-Mix, 2 E.R.C. 1074 (S.D.N.Y. 1970).

[172] Bass Angler v. U.S. Steel, 2 E.R.C. 1204 (D. Ala. 1971); Reuss v. Moss-American, Inc., 2 E.R.C. 1259 (E.D. Wis. 1971); Durning v. ITT Rayonier, 2 E.R.C. 1171 (N.D. Wash. 1970). For material on the use of this Act and the possibility of private court actions see the pamphlet *Qui Tam Actions and the 1899 Refuse Act: Citizen Lawsuits Against Polluters of the Nation's Waterways* (Comm. on Government Operations, Sept. 1970).

the yardstick necessary to show a violation of the standard of care or a violation of the duty that is imposed by society on the polluter. For example, the attorney in the *Maryland v. Galaxy Chemical*[173] case used state air quality limitations applicable to air inside a factory in successfully demonstrating that the defendant's air pollution was a public nuisance.[174] Federal, state, and local health and safety laws can similarly be used to show a standard necessary to protect the public. It may be possible to use the Federal Water Quality Standards for private purposes.[175] The use of statutory standards in air pollution suits is not unusual.[176] The coverage of environmental activities by statutes is so pervasive that few suits can be brought without considering the effect of statutes and administrative regulations. A zoning ordinance can be used to prevent water pollution,[177] and the complex regulations governing public lands may be used to protect public rights relating to federally-owned lands.[178] The use of such material is limited only by the imagination of the attorney.

Constitutional rights

The desire to protect our environment and the realization of how our system of government encourages environmental destruction has led in recent times to an outpouring of feeling that there is a constitutional right to a decent environment, and if there is none, there should be one.[179]

While few conservationists would argue against further legal protection, the environmental attorney seeks existing law which can, if necessary, be creatively interpreted to provide needed environmental protection. Unfortunately, most of the discussion takes place in journals, and courts do not seem willing to accept the idea that any constitutional right to an undefiled environment exists. The Ninth Amendment, it is argued, can be used to protect the environment.[180] The Ninth Amendment of the United States Constitution states:

173 1 E.R.C. 1660 (M.D. Cir. Ct. 1970).

174 The "winners" in this particular battle continue to lose the war, however. Declining to declare the Galaxy plant a health hazard, which probably would have forced its closing, the court judged it to be a nuisance, and in giving it six months to remove its obnoxious odors, appointed Galaxy's former chief engineer to report on its progress. Meanwhile, more than 50 of Galaxy's neighbors continue to vomit and suffer from severe headaches, aching joints and chest pains, while the plant's owners cry "Conspiracy!" The National Observer, Jan. 18, 1971 at 1, col. 1, *id.* at 20, col. 5.

175 *See, Water Quality Standards in Private Nuisance Actions*, 79 Yale L.J. 102 (1967).

176 *See* Miller & Borchers, *supra* note 138; Rheingold, *supra* note 140.

177 City of Corpus Christi v. Lone Star Fish & Oyster Co., 335 S.W.2d 621 (Tex. 1960).

178 Comment, *The Conservationist and the Public Land: Administrative and Judicial Remedies Relating to the Use and Disposition of the Public Lands Administered by the Department of the Interior*, 68 Mich. L. Rev. 1200 (1970).

179 A recent example of the "should be" type of advocacy is, Platt, *Toward Constitutional Recognition of the Environment*, 56 A.B.A.J. 1061 (Nov. 1970). *See also* Roberts, *The Right to a Decent Environment: Progress Along a Constitutional Avenue*, Law and Environment 134 (Baldwin & Page ed. 1970).

180 *See, e.g.*, Roberts, *An Environmental Lawyer Urges: Plead the Ninth Amendment*, LXXIX Natural History No. 7, at 18 (Aug.-Sept. 1970).

The enumeration in the constitution, of certain rights, shall not be construed to deny or disparage others, retained by the people.

Only time will tell whether this can be made into a sword for environmental protection, and there is little evidence that augurs for success. The one successful Ninth Amendment case, *Griswold v. Connecticut*,[181] involved the right to provide birth control information and was decided primarily on the basis of a right to privacy—a basis that is of limited value to environmentalists. The Ninth Amendment argument was rejected in *EDF v. Hoerner Waldorf*,[182] an air pollution case directed against a kraft process pulp and paper mill in Montana, because of the absence of "state action." The court held:

Constitutional rights

So it seems to me that each of us is constitutionally protected in our natural and personal state of life and health. But the constitutional protection is against governmental action either federal or state.

The Fifth Amendment protects against federal action and the Fourteenth against state action. It seems clear also, though the point has never been decided by the Supreme Court, that the Ninth Amendment is a limitation upon the powers and conduct of the federal government and by the Fourteenth Amendment such limitation is extended to the power of the state.

. . . .

There are no allegations of federal action which would bring the Fifth Amendment or Ninth Amendment into play, so far as the federal government is concerned, but plaintiff contends that there was the requisite state action in that the City of Missoula, through its Mayor, extended an invitation to defendant to become "a part of our (Missoula's) growing economy . . . ." The plaintiff further relies on state action in licensing defendant and that the failure of the state to abate the alleged pollution establishes the requisite state action.

None of the actions alleged here partake of those affirmative or permissive actions which are designed to violate constitutional rights. . . . [T]o support a Ninth or Fourteenth Amendment suit, the action of the state must be unconstitutional or the proximate cause of unconstitutional action, and the court can find no such unconstitutional action from the allegations made here.[183]

Whether the dictum recognizing the constitutional right will be recognized by other courts remains in doubt.[184]

[181] 381 U.S. 479 (1965). See also Symposium on the Griswold Case and the Right of Privacy, 64 Mich.L.Rev.No. 2. (Dec. 1965)

[182] 1 E.R.C. 1640 (D. Mont. 1970).

[183] *Id.* at 1641-42.

[184] EDF v. Corps of Engineers, 2 E.R.C. 1260 (E.D. Ark. 1971) (the claim of ninth amendment rights was raised again and rejected by the court); Ely v. Velde, 1 Environ. L. Rep. 20082 (E.D. Va. Jan. 22, 1971) (claim of ninth amendment rejected).

[185] *See* Adamson v. California, 332 U.S. 46 (1947); Munn v. Illinois, 94 U.S. 113 (1876).

[186] *See* Griggs v. Allegheny County, 369 U.S. 84 (1962); United States v. Causby, 328 U.S. 256 (1946).

[187] *See* Shapiro v. Thompson, 394 U.S. 618 (1969); Williams v. Rhodes, 393 U.S. 23 (1968).

[188] *See* Shapo, *Constitutional Tort: Monroe v. Pape, and the Frontiers Beyond*, 60 N.Y.U.L. Rev. 227 (1965).

[189] *See* York v. Story, 324 F.2d 450 (9th Cir. 1963); Travers v. Paton, 261 F. Supp. 110 (D. Conn. 1966).

The civil rights argument is also rejected in Guthrie v. Alabama By-Products Co., 328 F.Supp. 1140 (N.D.Ala. Sept. 20, 1971).

Other legal theories abound. These include the charge that the action is a violation of due process under the Fifth and Fourteenth Amendments of the Constitution,[185] or is a taking of property under the Fifth and Fourteenth Amendments.[186] Another theory involves the concept that fundamental rights are involved,[187] and still another theory is that environmental rights are civil rights and bring 42 U.S.C. section 1983 into action:

Constitutional rights

> Every person who, under color of a statute, ordinance, regulation, custom, or usage, of any State or Territory, subjects, or causes to be subjected, any citizen of the United States or other person within the jurisdiction thereof to the deprivation of any rights, privileges, or immunities secured by the Constitution and laws, shall be liable to the party injured in an action at law, suit in equity, or other proper proceeding for redress.[188]

Though the concept of civil rights has broadened,[189] the previously-mentioned *EDF v. Hoerner Waldorf* case rejected the civil rights argument.

While these doctrines are alive, it is important to note that no environmental case has yet enunciated them. Whether a court of any significance will expand the constitutional arguments to provide environmental protection is difficult to prognosticate. Nevertheless, it is safe to conclude that environmental litigation based on these constitutional arguments will be costly, time-consuming, and will have little chance for success.

Many other aspects of the relationship between Constitutional rights and environmental protection are discussed in Chapter One of this book—particularly at One-12 through One-16, and One-50 through One-55.

cases

On the pages which follow there are the edited texts of decisions in four environmental lawsuits which were selected to illustrate the use of common law concepts. The first, *Folmar v. Elliot Coal Co.,* illustrates the trespass doctrine. The others, *Peyton v. Hammer, Wales Trucking v. Stallcup, and Maryland v. Galaxy Chemical Corp.,* all illustrate various aspects of nuisance.

SEE ALSO the cases in the appendix to this chapter, and the sample complaints and cases in the appendicies to chapters One, Two, Three, Four, and subchapter Three-B.

FOLMAR v. ELLIOTT COAL CO., Penn. Supreme Ct. Nos. 210 and 211, 2 ERC 1183, Jan. 25, 1971

Pomeroy, Judge:

These are suits in trespass to recover damages for injury to plaintiff's property allegedly caused by air pollution attributable to defendant's operation of its coal-cleaning plant. 1/ The trial court by its verdict found for the defendant in both cases and, as provided by Supreme Court Rule 1048, supported its verdict with findings of fact and conclusions of law. Plaintiffs' exceptions to the findings and conclusions were overruled, and these appeals followed. 2/

---

1. The present suits were commenced as equity actions for the abatement of a nuisance and for damages limited to the cost of restoring and cleaning the plaintiffs' properties. After trial before the chancellor but before a decree was rendered, this Court's decision in Commonwealth v. Glen Alden Corp., 418 Pa. 57, 210 A.2d 256 (1965) was entered. In that case the Court held, construing the Air Pollution Act of 1960, that equity was without jurisdiction where the provisions of that act were applicable. It was then stipulated by the parties to the present cases that they should be certified to the law side of the court and proceeded with as actions in trespass to be heard by the court without a jury. The testimony already taken was deemed applicable to the law actions, and additional evidence was also received. Before judgment the legislature, responding to Glen Alden, supra, amended the Air Pollution Control Act so as to preserve equitable jurisdiction to abate private or public nuisances. Act of June 12, 1968, P.L.______, No. 92 §8, 35 P.S. §4012.1 (Supp. 1970). The lower court nevertheless, and without objection, continued to treat the cases "as an alleged trespassory invasion seeking damages in law."

2. The parties stipulated, with the approval of the lower court, that they accept all of the trial judge's findings of fact as correct and supported by the evidence. The transcript of testimony has therefore not been submitted for our review. We did, however, remand for supplementation of the record in several respects, including a certificate of the amount in controversy prepared in conformity with our Rule 61. This supplementary material was furnished on October 1, 1970.

The findings of fact, broadly stated, were as follows: The two appellants purchased their homes in 1931 and 1959, respectively. Both properties are located within 1500 feet of appellee's coal processing plant, which consists of crushers, conveyors, vibrating equipment, screens and picking tables. The plant has been operated by the appellee and its predecessor since 1948, and the appellants realized at the times of their respective purchases that the properties were located in an area generally used for industrial and coal mining purposes. As a result of complaints, appellee installed in 1962 an air cleaner, thermodryer and coal washing unit, and soon thereafter a dust collector and covered coal conveyor. Notwithstanding these measures, the appellee's coal cleaning operation has contributed to air pollution affecting the properties of appellants from 1962 to the time of trial. 3/ The appellee has employed specialists in the field of fuel and combustion air pollution who have conducted numerous tests. They have recommended the installation of a certain type of wet scrubber on the thermodryer as a means of reducing emission of dust from that source. This equipment will cost $20,000 to $30,000. The appellee has adopted the recommendation and "intends to either discontinue using the thermodryer or install the wet scrubber." "With the installation of the wet scrubber, defendant company will have done everything now known and economically feasible to eliminate any source of air pollution." The cleaning plant is not in default in compliance with any requirements of the Air Pollution Control Commission.

The trial court concluded, as a matter of law, that the invasion of appellants' properties by coal dust from appellee's plant has not been substantial, 4/ nor was it intentional or unreasonable; neither has the appellee been negligent in conducting its operations. 5/

---

3. Finding of fact number 27 noted that one other factor contributing to appellants' pollution problem is the coal dropped by passing trucks, which coal is subsequently pulverized by passing traffic.

4. The finding as to substantiality, though below labeled a conclusion of law, is perhaps technically a finding of fact, since it is solely concerned with the quantity and quality of precipitation. The court did find as a fact that the invasion reduced the pleasant use and enjoyment of appellants' properties, and this is probably the "discomfort and annoyance" not amounting to substantial invasion which the court notes in its conclusions of law. Appellee deduces that these findings coalesce to produce a finding of fact that the invasion was not substantial. Based upon the abbreviated record presented and without opportunity to review the complete testimony, this seems to be a reasonable reading of the adjudication. In any event, the appellants are not bound by the lower court's finding of nonsubstantiality, since they have excepted to it as a conclusion of law.

5. The appellant did not except to the lower court's conclusion that the appellee had not been negligent in conducting its operations and does not contest that conclusion on this appeal.

Both the lower court and the parties have accepted §822 of the Restatement of Torts as the law governing this case. Our Court adopted that section in Waschak v. Moffat, 379 Pa. 441, 109 A.2d 310 (1954) and it is reproduced in full in the margin. 6/ In essence, it provides that the owner of private property is entitled to damages due to injury occurring from a non-trespassory invasion of his premises if the defendant's conduct is the legal cuase of the invasion and the invasion is (a) substantial, and (b) intentional and unreasonable, or unintentional, negligent, reckless or ultra-hazardous conduct. The appellants have not been able to satisfy the requirements of that section of the Restatement.

The primary question, as we view it, is whether the trial court was correct in concluding that the invasion of appellants' properties was not unreasonable when the condition could be cured by the installation of equipment which had not, at the time of trial, been installed. An actor's conduct is unreasonable under §822 of the Restatement, unless the utility of his conduct outweighs the gravity of the harm. Restatement of Torts, §826 (1939). Our Court has stated that the actor's conduct lacks utility if it is economically and technically possible to correct the harm and such steps are not taken. Burr v. Eidemiller, 386 Pa. 416, 126 A.2d 403 (1956); see Herring v. H. W. Walker Co., 409 Pa. 126, 133, 185 A.2d 565 (1962). The limited record before us does not disclose when the recommendations as to the wet scrubber were made or when this device became technically and economically feasible, or, how long before trial the appellee had decided that it would either make the installation or discontinue its thermodryer. Since such facts are requisite to show an invasion was unreasonable and they have not been proven on the record, it can only be concluded that the appellants did not carry their burden of proof. It is clear, however, that the learned trial judge had before him sufficient facts to justify the legal conclusion that the invasion was not unreasonable: the major improvements in 1962, and the continuing attention to the problem thereafter, culminating in a decision to employ apparatus whereby the appellee "will have done everything now known and economically feasible to eliminate any source of air pollution."

---

6. Section 822 of the Restatement of Torts provides:

The actor is liable in an action for damages for a non-trespassory invasion of another's interest in the private use and enjoyment of land if,

(a) the other has property rights and privileges in respect to the use or enjoyment interfered with; and
(b) the invasion is substantial; and
(c) the actor's conduct is a legal cuase of the invasion; and
(d) the invasion is either
(i) intentional and unreasonable; or
(ii) unintentional and otherwise actionable under the rules governing liability for negligent, reckless or ultrahazardous conduct. (Emphasis ours.)

Since, as indicated above, the posture of this case at the time of decision was an action at law for damages tried without a jury, the court was obligated to render a verdict for either the plaintiffs or defendant; the injunctive or conditional forms of equity decrees were not available. It is clear that the verdict for the appellee was based in part, at least, on its announced intention at trial to install a wet scrubber or abandon the thermodryer. Because the verdict was based in part on an expectation, however, the judgment thereon is not to be considered res judicata as to any damage subsequent to the date of the verdict in the event the appellee has not subsequently fulfilled that expectation or discontinued what otherwise might be considered an unreasonable invasion of the appellants' property.

Judgment affirmed.

Jones, J., did not participate in the consideration or decision of this case.

Cohen, J., did not participate in the decision of this case.

PEYTON v. HAMMER, 269 N.E. 136, Ct. of Common Pleas of Ohio, Clinton County, No. 21518, Dec. 14, 1970

DECISION, ENTRY AND ORDER.

Swaim, Judge:

Plaintiff owns land in Blanchester, this County, through which a small branch or run flows, and asks for an injuntion against Defendants, restraining them from draining offensive waters, such as sewage, wash waters and the like, into this small waterway. Defendants claim a prescriptive right to use such small stream for their drainage, as same has been so used for more than 21 years.

The evidence showed that Defendants did empty their wastes such as sewage, wash water and the like into this stream, that the same was offensive, particularly in warm weather, that dead tadpoles and minnows had been seen in this stream, when in the opinion of witness, they could have survived in clear water. Also, that this small stream had been so used since the early 1940's when the houses now owned by Defendants were built.

The waters of this small branch flow into Second Creek, in or near Blanchester, and this Creek flows into Todds Fork (of the Little Miami River) southeasterly from Morrow, Warren County, and this Fork flows into the Little Miami River in Morrow, and this River flows into the Ohio River on the easterly side of Cincinnati.

The waters of this little branch, (or run, or brook, or rivulet) are governed by the provisions of Chapter 6111. Revised Code, styled "Water Pollution Control", of which several sections are pertinent here.

"6111.01. Definitions: As used in sections 6111.01 to 6111.08, inclusive, and sections 6111.31 to 6111.38, of the Revised Code:

"(A) "Pollution" means the placing of any noxious or deleterious substances in any waters of the state or affecting the properties of any waters of the state in a manner which renders such waters harmful or inimical to the public health, or to animal or aquatic life, or to the use of such waters for domestic water supply, or industrial or agricultural purposes, or for recreation.

"(B) "Sewage" means any substance that, contains any of the waste products or excrementitious or other discharge from the bodies of human beings or animals, which pollutes the waters of the state.

"(D) "Other wastes" means garbage, refuse, decayed wood, sawdust, shavings, bark, and other wood debris, lime (except hydrated or dehydrated lime), sand, ashes, offal, night soil, tar, coal dust, or silt, and other substances which are not included within the definitions of sewage and industrial waste set forth in this section, which pollute the waters of the state.

"(H) "Waters of the state" means all streams, lakes, ponds, marshes, water-courses, waterways, wells, springs, irrigation systems, drainage systems, and all other bodies or accumulations of water, surface and underground, natural or artificial, which are situated wholly or partly within, or border upon, this state, or are within its jurisdiction, except those private waters which do not combine or effect a junction with natural surface or underground waters.

"(I) "Person" means the state, any municipal corporation, notwithstanding section 6111.11 of the Revised Code, political subdivision, public or private corporation, individual, partnership, or other entity."

"6111.04. Acts of pollution prohibited; exceptions.

"No person shall cause pollution as defined in division (A) of section 6111.01 of the Revised Code of any waters of the state, or place or cause to be placed any sewage, industrial waste, or other wastes in a location where they cause pollution of any waters of the state. Any such action is hereby declared to be a public nuisance, except in such cases where the water pollution control board has issued a valid and unexpired permit, or renewal thereof, as provided in sections 6111.01 to 6111.08 inclusive, of the Revised Code.

* * * * * * * * * *

"No person who is discharging or causing the discharge of any sewage, industrial waste, or other wastes into the waters of the state shall continue or cause the continuation of such discharge after September 27, 1952, without first obtaining a permit therefor issued by the board, pursuant to rules and regulations to be prescribed by it."

"6111.08. Equity and common law rights unaffected.

"Sections 6111.01 to 6111.08, inclusive, of the Revised Code do not abridge rights of action or remedies in equity or under the common law, nor do such sections, estop the state, or any municipal corporation or person, as riparian owners or otherwise, in the exercise of their rights in equity or under the common law to suppress nuisances or to abate pollution."

These sections were first enacted in 1951, as part of the "Water Pollution Control Act of Ohio", 124 Ohio Laws 855. Of that Act, Section 1261.1b, General Code, as amended is now Section 6111.01, Revised Code: Section 1261-1e, General Code, as amended is now Section 6111.04, Revised Code; and Section 1261-1i, General Code, as amended is now Section 6111.03, Revised Code.

The Defendants rely upon Cleveland v. Standard Bag & Paper Company, (1905), 72 Ohio St. 324, 74 N. E. 206, for support of their theory of prescriptive right for their pollution of this small stream:

The law therein was no longer law in Ohio, prior to the enactment of the Water Pollution Control Act of Ohio in 1951, as is seen by Vian v. Sheffield Building & Development Co., (1948), 85 Ohio App. 191, 40 Ohio Ops. 144, 88 N. E. 2d 410, of which the syllabus is:

"1. One may not obtain by prescription, or otherwise than by purchase, a right to cast sewage upon the lands of another without his consent.

2. The discharge of effluent, from a disposal system, into a public water-course, from which, through natural and artificial means, it finds its way onto the lands of another, and the permitting of overflow from a sewage wet well to drain onto the lands of another, may be enjoined."

This case is no longer law in Ohio, except as to the enjoining of pollution of waters of this state.

Modern thinking upon the pollution of waters is in Board of Commissioners of Lake County v. Mentor Lagoons, Inc., (1965), 6 Ohio Misc. 126, 35 Ohio Ops. 2d 244, 216 N. E. 2d 643, in which the question was alleged pollution of Lake Erie.

No claim was made by the Defendants that there had been a valid permit issued to any of them by the Water Pollution Control Board after September 27, 1952, for their wastes to go into this small stream, and therefore their such acts have been illegal since September 27, 1952, and are now illegal.

The Court finds that there is pollution of this small stream, that it comes from the wastes from the properties of the Defendants, who have no prescriptive right to allow such wastes, causing the pollution, to enter this small stream, and further finds that the Plaintiff, through whose land this small stream flows, has a right of action to enjoin these Defendants from polluting this small stream in any way.

The Court finds that the prayer of the Plaintiff must be granted and an injunction ordered herein against the three Defendants, each of them, from causing any pollution of this small stream.

The Court therefore enjoins each Defendant from allowing any wastes of any kind, coming within the description of "sewage" (Section 6111.01(B), Revised Code), and "other wastes" (Section 6111.01(D), Revised Code), to enter this small stream, which is one of the "waters of the state" (Section 6111.01(H), Revised Code), which would result in "pollution" (Section 6111.01(A), Revised Code.)

And the Court orders that the defendants, each of them, to so treat these wastes from their property so that the waters of this small stream, after the wastes enter it, are not "Harmful or inimical to the public health, or to animal or aquatic life, or to the use of such waters for domestic water supply, or industrial or agricultural purposes, or for recreation" (Section 6111.01 (A), Revised Code).

As the Defendants will need some time to change the plans of disposal of their wastes that now flow into this small stream, the above order of injunction against each defendant shall be suspended for a period of 120 days, within which each Defendant shall so change his waste disposal system so that can be no pollution of this small stream from his own waste disposal system, and the three Defendants shall jointly so change the joint system, so that there can be no pollution of this small stream from the joint waste outlet into the small stream.

The Defendants to pay the costs herein.

The Clerk of Courts shall issue a Certified Copy of this Decision, Entry and Order, for each Defendant.

WALES TRUCKING v. STALLCUP, Texas Ct. of Civil Appeals, 2d Dist., No. 17165, 2 ERC 1382, March 5, 1971

[EDITED]

Langdon, J.:

Louis Stallcup and wife initiated this suit against the Wales Trucking Company, a Texas corporation, for dust damages sustained by them as the result of an alleged nuisance created and maintained by Wales through its unreasonable use of the unimproved public county road which runs in front of their rural home. Based on a jury verdict, judgment was rendered for the Stallcups for damages in the amount of $5,000.00. Wales has appealed.

Wales was engaged in hauling heavy concrete water pipe from the Gifford-Hill plant located in the Fort Worth-Dallas area to the site of the right-of-way of the water pipeline being constructed to bring water from Lake Arrowhead in Clay County to the City of Wichita Falls. The limit of Wales' responsibility was was to haul the water pipe. For a period of about four (4) months between April 15 to September 1 of 1968, Wales made commercial use of the roadway in front of the Stallcup home seven days per week by transporting about 825 truck loads of pipe over such road and returning an equal number of empty trucks over the same route. (Approximately 1650 truck trips during the 4 month period.) The center of the roadway was 75 feet from the front wall of the Stallcup home. A majority of the loaded trucks weighed 58,000 pounds. A few grossed 72,000 pounds. The loaded trucks traveled 25 to 30 miles per hour. Because of weather conditions or the production schedule of the water pipe the deliveries thereof varied between zero and 20 during any one day. Wales' commercial use of the roadway, as above indicated, was extensive and for the period of approximately four months converted the seldom used country road in front of the Stallcup home to a heavily traveled thoroughfare. ". . . they (Wales) were just beating the road up and it just got like ashes." Dust from the dirt and graveled surface drifted onto the Stallcups' premises and into their home causing discomfort and irritation.

In the case at bar the jury in answering Special Issues 1 through 8, respectively, found: (1) Wales' use of the roadway caused substantial amounts of dust to be deposited on Stallcup's property; (2) such depositing of dust was the result of a nuisance, i. e., the unreasonable and excessive use of the roadway; (3) as a proximate cause of such nuisance the Stallcups suffered damage for (a) the temporary loss of enjoyment of their dwelling house and (b) for temporary physical discomfort; (4) $2,500.00 in damages was awarded for (a) temporary loss of enjoyment and

$2,500.00 for (b) temporary physical discomfort; (5) Wales had notice of damage resulting to the Stallcups from such nuisance; and (6) continued the nuisance after having such notice. (The matters involved in Special Issues 5 and 6 relating to notice were indisputed.)

The seven points of error presented, briefed and argued by Wales on this appeal are singly and collectively based upon the sole proposition that there can be no right of recovery against it in the absence of pleadings, proof and findings of either negligent or unlawful conduct on its part. Wales in its reply brief says: "The primary issues on appeal as highlighted by the two prior opposing briefs are whether either negligence or unlawful use must be plead and proven in establishing as a nuisance the use of a public roadway.

"Appellant contends that one or both of these elements must be present. Appellee contends that it is sufficient to establish that use of the roadway was 'unreasonable'."

Wales makes it clear that its no evidence and insufficient evidence points are based solely on the proposition that there is no evidence or that the evidence is insufficient to establish that it was guilty of either negligent or unlawful conduct and that therefore as a matter of law its conduct did not constitute a nuisance.

The Stallcups contend that an abutting property owner who sustains damage caused by a nuisance which is created by a member of the public in making an unreasonable use of a public road is liable to such abutting property owner for the damages caused by such nuisance.

We have concluded from our analysis of Wales' briefs that it in effect admits that at common law and therefore in Texas that an abutting property owner does have a cause of action such as is described in the preceding paragraph. The only difference in the contentions of the parties to this appeal is that Wales contends that a showing of conduct of an unlawful or negligent nature is an essential element of such a cause of action.

Stallcups take the position that the elements of negligence and unlawful conduct are not essential elements of their cause of action.

"As a general rule, proof of negligence is not essential to imposition of liability for the creation or maintenance of a nuisance. This is so though the nuisance complained of may be the consequence of negligence. A nuisance does not rest on the degree of care used, but on the degree of danger or annoyance existing even with the best of care. Consequently, if a nuisance exists, the fact that the due care was exercised against its becoming a danger or annoyance is no excuse. However, where the act or condition in question can become a nuisance only by reason of the negligent manner in which it is performed or permitted, no right of recovery is shown independently of the existence of negligence." 41 Tex. Jur. 2d 591, § 17.

While there is no agreement as to the facts in the present case, it is accurate to state that the elments above referred to in the King case are present here and are undisputed. We submit that regardless of whether or not Wales' vehicles were property licensed, did not exceed load limits, had proper permits from the Railroad Commission and were operated within permissive speed limits would not have altered the damages sustained by the Stallcups.

The law "does no allow anyone, whatever his circumstances or condition may be, to be driven from his home, or to be compelled to live in it in positive discomfort, although caused by a lawful and useful business carried on in his vicinity."

In applying the above stated general rules of law to the facts of this case we find and hold that pleadings and proof of either negligent or unlawful conduct or both are not necessary or essential elements of the cause of action here involved.

"Every person has the right to have the air diffused over his premises, whether located in the city or the country, in its natural state and free from artificial impurities. However, by air in its natural state and free from artificial impurities is meant pure air consistent with the locality and character of the community. The pollution of the air so far as is reasonably necessary to the enjoyment of life and indispensable to the progress of society is not actionable, But this right of pollution must not be exercised in an unreasonable manner so as to inflict injury on another unnecessarily. Any business, though in itself lawful, that necessarily impregnates large volumes of the atmosphere with disagreeable, unwholesome, or offensive matter may become a nuisance to those occupying adjacent property, in case it is so near and the atmosphere is so contaminated as to substantially impare the comfort or enjoyment of adjacent occupants. Thus smoke, dust, noxious fumes or gases, or stenches or smells may constitute a nuisance under some circumstances." 41 Tex. Jur. 2d 608, sec. 33, and pocket parts.

The dust caused by the operators of the trucks created a nuisance regardless of the care exercised by such operators and regardless of the lawful manner in which the trucks were operated. Thus it was unnecessary to plead and prove negligence or unlawful conduct on the part of such operators.

We have examined the entire record in this case. We have concluded the evidence was sufficient to support the answers of the jury to each of the special issues submitted to it.

All points of error are overruled. The judgment of the trial court is affirmed.

MARYLAND v. GALAXY CHEMICAL CO., Maryland Circuit Ct. for Cecil County, 1 ERC 1660, Sept. 16, 1970

OPINION

This is an action by the Air Quality Control Division of the Maryland State Department of Health to enjoin the Galaxy Chemical Company from emitting into the air beyond its property line gases, vapors and odors which are or may be predicted by reasonable certainty to be injurious to human, plant or animal life or property or which unreasonably intereferes with the proper enjoyment of property of others or maintaining a public nuisance which endangers the health, safety and general welfare of the people of the State of Mayland. It has taken eight days for the State to present its testimony and six days for the Company to respond.

a. Testimony of the Health Department

The relevant testimony for the State may be summarized as follows. The Galaxy Chemical Company plant is located in the Providence Valley along the Little Elk Creek five miles north of Elkton, Maryland. Dr. Elmer E. Hackman, III, an environmental specialist, tested the ambient air in the Providence area on May 8, June 2, June 9 and June 12, 1970. The upper levels permissible in a factory (known as threshold limit values and referred to as TLVs) are 25 parts of benzene per million parts of air, 500 parts of methylene chloride (MeCl) and 200 parts of methyl ethyl ketone (MEK). There are no established permissible levels for the general population outside of the factory but everyone agrees that the levels must be lower in order to be safe. The significant concentrations found in the four days of testing were on May 8 when a few hundred yards from the plant property lines a concentration of 23 parts of benzene, 16 parts of methylene chloride and 94 parts of methyl ethyl ketone were discovered. As can be seen, only the benzene level approached the upper levels permissible in factories.

Dr. Edgar Folk, Board certified to practice internal medicine, diagnosed eight residents of the Galaxy area. Marlene Evans had abdominal pain and tenderness and an elevated lipase level. Upon leaving the area she improved rapidly. Diagnosis was pancreatitis probably due to toxicity. George Johnson was diagnosed as having a peptic ulcer. Two other patients were not evaluated for toxicity. Pietro Capurro is discussed as a patient below as his testimony is summarized. Fred Spencer, Dale Spencer and Thomas Evans were also examined by Dr. Kailin (see below) and Dr. Folk's diagnosis will be included below.

This doctor sees 20 to 30 patients a year at the Veterans Administration Hospital at Perry Point suffering from pancreatitis caused by virus or alcohol or debilitating disease. One may have mild pancreatitis or hepatitis with symptoms that wouldn't necessarily send him to a doctor. Even physical examination may be negative in mild cases.

Specific laboratory tests for pancreatitis are the amylase test (above 250 is abnormal) and the lipase test (readings above 1.0 are abnormal). A good ancillary test is the glucose tolerance level (readings above 105 are abnormal). The barium test is another ancillary test. Fecal analysis is of limited value. The starch tolerance test is for chronic pancreatitis where other tests do not indicate the trouble. The necrosis test is not indicated unless there is large scarring of the pancreas. Classic symptoms for pancreatitis are upper abdominal pain, nausea, vomiting, diarrhea and, if chronic, a weight loss.

Laboratory tests for hepatitis are protein, albumin, globulin, enzyme (SGOT and SGPT) and the alkaline phosphatase test. The classic symptom of hepatitis is an enlarged and tender liver.

The next witness was Dr. Pietro Capurro appearing as a fact witness as well as an expert witness. He is Chief of Pathology, Union Hospital, Elkton, Maryland. As a fact witness this party has been very zealous from December 1967 in seeking corrective action of what he believes to be a nuisance and health problem. In his zeal he has called the President of the United States, written repeatedly to various officials, has sought to communicate with this member of the Court and when unsuccessful filed a suit for damages in proper person in an effort to get direct access to the Court.

Dr. Capurro related these facts. Since moving to the area in November 1967 he has been made ill many times from Galaxy fumes. He becomes weak, dizzy, sleepy and suffers upper abdominal pain, headache and leg pains. His mind becomes confused. He passes blood in his urine. He is so shaky he cannot draw blood from the arm of patients. The Little Elk Creek which flows by his home one mile south of the Galaxy plant is black and stinking. Once upon smelling a water sample from this Creek he collapsed. Five other times he has collapsed in his home. He thinks his pancreas is permanently damaged. From September 13, 1969 to March 29, 1970 he lived in a motel to escape the Galaxy fumes.

With this history he admitted himself to Union Hospital as a patient six times during the year ending January 1970. While a patient Dr. Capurro continued to work in his pathology laboratory. Dr. Folk, with his permission, was shown as the admitting physician and in fact examined, made laboratory tests and diagnosed Dr. Capurro as having pancreatitis and possible hepatitis caused by toxic fumes. In so doing he ruled out other causes such as virus and alcohol. He noted that the laboratory tests quickly returned to normal readings and that symptoms were lacking when the patient was out of the area for awhile and that there was a recurrence when the patient returned to the area. The established fact that Dr. Capurro was subjected to high concentrations of toluene, chloroform and xylene six to ten years ago in the opinion of Dr. Folk would not make any difference except that it makes him more susceptible to these subsequent exposures at Galaxy.

Dr. Capurro qualified as a medical expert in pathology and toxicology. He testified laboratory testing at Union Hospital was done by technicians without his active intervention, that they follow standard procedures, i.e., for the lipase test see Plaintiff's Exhibit 10. By virtue of their combination in the air trichlorethylene and benzene, for example, in his opinion increase five to six times in toxicity and danger. TLVs for the general population should be 500 to 1000 times lower than factory levels because the general is not as healthy, is exposed longer and is exposed continuously. Concentrations of 94 MEK and 23 benzene parts discovered by Dr. Hackman are dangerous to the general population. He cited a textual report that even in the factory 100 parts of MEK caused a slight throat irritation. The upper limit of benzene in the ambient air should be 0.2 parts. As for toluene, he cited textual authority that 0–50 parts produces dorwsiness and a headache, 50–100 parts, fatigue and sleepiness, and 100–200 parts, paresthesia, nausea, insomnia, incoordination and confusion. As for methyl isobutyl ketone (MIBK) 100 parts in a factory caused headache and nausea which largely disappeared upon installation of a fan which reduced the level to 20 parts MIBK. Regarding pancreatitis, allergy is a rare initiating factor. One can have pancreatitis without symptoms and without knowledge.

The doctor then described the history, symptoms, laboratory tests and diagnoses of nine resident patients, most of whom were examined also by Dr. Kailin and will be discussed below.

Dr. Eloise Kailin, the fourth witness, is a medical doctor qualified as an expert in allergy and environmental medicine. The doctor divides her time between private practice and research. She agrees that the TLVs for factory workers are much higher than those which are safe for the general population. For sulphur dioxide, for example, she believes that the level should be 100 times lower. For carbon monoxide the TLV is 50 but in Washington, D.C. for the general population they have adopted a figure of 20 parts per million. She confirms that by the principles of synergism and potentiation chemicals combining in the open air can produce much greater toxic effects than can exposure to any one chemical alone.

When the State Health Department requested she investigate this matter she read the background on the chemicals involved, examined the records and the patients. She also toured the area with Mr. York, a chemical engineer with the State Health Department. She was in Cecil County on four different days. She concluded by certain "double blind" tests that the illnesses were real, not suggested. She noticed statistically that lipase levels were elevated to 3.0 or above in 5% of 78 general hospital patients tested at random while similarly elevated in 40% of 10 Providence Valley residents tested. Likewise, the glucose tolerance level was up in 66% of general hospital patients but in 92% of the 12 Valley residents tested. Statistically speaking, a representative of the National Institute of Health indicates the odds against these differences are 100–1 under normal conditions. It was her opinion that the operations of Galaxy Chemical Company were adversely affecting the health of the Valley residents. This opinion was based upon several being sick at the same time in the nature of an epidemic and the laboratory abnormalities when present in the Valley which upon leaving became normal again as the patient felt better and improved generally. She also stated that one can have pancreatitis without knowing it and without symptoms.

Dr. Kailin examined 13 patients. Dr. Capurro and Dr. Folk examined many of the same patients and where there is anything additional that either doctor had to add to the findings of Dr. Kailin it will be stated.

Fred Spencer, age 46, complained of abdominal pain, indigestion, headache and stuffy nose. The lipase test, glucose tolerance test, ethanol test and insulin curve test were all abnormal. A pancreatic scan was abnormal. The diagnosis was indigestion and possible pancreatitis. Etiology was an over exposure to Galaxy fumes. Dr. Folk did not assess a cause.

Dale Spencer, age 12, was uncommunicative and complained of abdominal pain and a stuffy nose. The lipase, glucose tolerance, ethanol and insulin curve tests were all abnormal. The diagnosis was sinusitis although chronic pancreatitis was also indicated. Dr. Kailin did not state the cause. Dr. Capurro, upon his examination, noted this patient to be tired and with headache, to have an abnormal PH and an abnormal amylase test. On this basis his diagnosis was toxic pancreatitis but without permanent damage to the pancreas. Dr. Folk's diagnosis had been mild pancreatitis.

Goldie Evans, age 40, an epileptic, complained of nausea and difficulty in thinking. Initial diagnosis was epilepsy which might be triggered by Galaxy fumes; also, a possible chemical pneumonitis caused by Galaxy fumes. She had no abnormal laboratory tests. Apparently none were done.

Robert Mahaffey, age 31, suffered from headache, irritability, and had an abnormal glucose tolerance test and ethanol test. The diagnosis was cerebral irritation and possible pancreatitis coincident with Galaxy fumes. Dr. Capurro had found abdominal pain, leg pain, tiredness, indigestion, and an abnormal ICD. He did not take a hstory and did not check the pancreas. His diagnosis was toxic hepatitis.

Gloria Mahaffey, age 28, complained of nausea, abdominal pain, leg pain, headache, dizziness and, according to Dr. Kailin, problems with vision. The patient later denied problems with vision. Her lipase test, glucose tolerance test, insulin curve SGOT and ICD were all abnormal. Diagnosis was cerebral malfunction and pancreatitis caused by Galaxy fumes. Dr. Capurro's diagnosis was toxic pancreatitis caused by Galaxy fumes.

Thomas Evans, age 42, was the most severely affected patient. He was chronically tired, complained of abdominal pain, nausea, dizziness, leg pain, arm pain, irritability, indigestion, forgetfulness and bronchitis. His lipase, amylase, glucose tolerance and insulin curve tests were repeatedly abnormal. The pancreas, upon scan, was twice the normal size. He improved upon leaving the Providence Valley for a short while. The diagnosis was pancreatitis with permanent damage to the pancreas, hepatitis and cerebral malfunction due to the Galaxy fumes.

David Evans, age 12, complained of abdominal and leg pain, nausea but no tenderness upon physical examination. His glucose tolerance and ethanol tests were abnormal. He improved rapidly upon leaving the Valley. The diagnosis was initially peripheral neuritis and possible hepato-pancreatitis. Dr. Kailin stated in testimony a diagnosis of pancreatitis closely related to Galaxy fumes.

Ann Evans, age 54, complained of nausea and headache but no abdominal pain or tenderness. The ethanol test was abnormal. Diagnosis was migraine headaches caused by Galaxy fumes.

Rosemary Mitchell, age 15, complained of headache, nausea and weight loss. Upon examination, the liver was enlarged and tender and the abdomen was tender. She improved rapidly upon leaving the Valley. Her lipase, glucose tolerance, ethanol and insulin curve tests were all abnormal. The diagnosis was hepatitis and possible pancreatitis related to Galaxy fumes. Dr. Capurro also found abnormal LDH and protein tests. His diagnosis was mild toxic pancreatitis.

Sharon Logan, age 13, complained of nasal irritation which improved upon leaving the Valley. There were no laboratory tests. The diagnosis was rhinitis historically related to Galaxy fumes.

Dorothy Logan, age 48, complained of nasal irritation, headache, nausea, leg ache, arm tingling, dizziness and palpatation. Her ethanol test was abnormal. She was diagnosed as having possible hepatitis historically related to Galaxy fumes.

Ruby Mitchell, age 52, complained of leg and abdominal pain and had lost 20 pounds in a period of six months. Her lipase, glucose and insulin curve tests were abnormal. Diagnosis was pancreatitis from an unknown cause, probably Galaxy fumes. Dr. Capurro's diagnosis was the same. He noted additionally complaints of tiredness, dizziness, headache, nausea and an inability to smell.

William Mitchell, age 56, complained of headaches, abdominal pain which went away when he left the Valley to go to work in Delaware. His liver was slightly enlarged. Diagnosis was possible mild pancreatitis, the cause being unknown.

Dr. Capurro thought the four worst cases were himself, Fred Spencer, Thomas Evans and Ruby Mitchell.

Carl York, the fifth witness, qualified as an expert chemical engineer and toxic chemical handler. He testified that Galaxy handles 23 named chemicals which collectively produce the symptoms of nausea and others described by the foregoing residents of the Valley. Twelve of these 23 chemicals either by skin absorption, inhalation or ingestion may cause death or permanent injury after very short exposure to small quantities. Four others of these chemicals have an unknown toxic hazard rating since there is not enough information on humans to rate them. These 23 chemicals were processed by Galaxy during the period January 1968 to date of trial.

In handling, processing, maintaining equipment and disposing of wastes odors escape from the Galaxy plant. Mr. York suggests that an odorous chemical such as MEK be processed through the system to pinpoint where odor is escaping. Then he believes that the installation of a process of incineration or adsorption in activated charcoal which will take at the most seven months to install and which Galaxy can afford would prevent the escape of most of the odors.

Mr. York testified that he smelled odors different in type and strength on at least ten occasions from January to May 1969. On June 1, 1969 a bottom pit, a source of odor, was removed which was a major improvement. But even since June 1, 1969 on at least 36 occasions through June 1970 Mr. York smelled odors beyond the Galaxy property line. These 46 investigations were in response to complaints of people in the Valley.

Fourteen (14) persons testified affirmatively that the odors which could have no source other than Galaxy seriously interfered with the use and enjoyment of the property they owned and the air they breathe producing in many cases serious physical discomfort and illness. Thomas Evans testified that Dr. Lanzi advised him to move out of the area (Dr. Lanzi confirmed this.). This concluded the State's case.

b. Defendant's testimony

The following testimony was offered by the Galaxy Chemical Company.Paul Mraz, age 42, received a bachelor degree with honors in chemical enginering in 1952. After eight years employment in this field he and one James Waters formed Galaxy Chemical Company and started operating in the Village of Providence on the site of an abandoned paper mill. They each own 50% of the business but it is Mraz who operates the business. Liquid by-products are purchased from the chemical industry in the east coast area. Delivery is made in 6,000 gallon tank trucks. By a process of vaporizing and condensing valuable parts are separated from the bad parts and marketed. The bad parts are put in 55 gallon drums or other containers and hauled away to a landfill near Elkton. The valuable parts are hauled to market in the 6,000 gallon tank trucks. Under present operating conditions it is undisputed that many opportunities exist for fumes to escape into the air. Mr. Mraz does dispute the Health Department contention that the fumes go very far, last very long or smell very bad.

Galaxy employs 15 persons including Mr. Mraz, a technician, a secretary, two truck drivers and probably five workers in "F" area and five workers in "H" area. They operate around the clock. Only one worker is present in each area from 4:00 P.M. to 8:00 A.M. daily. The technician has been with the company five years. Almost all of the workers are relatively new employees.

The Company's daily operating records show the chemicals being processed at any given hour (Galaxy Exhibit 26). When Dr. Hackman measured pollutant concentrations in the neighborhood on May 8, June 2, June 9 and June 12, 1970 (State's Exhibit 3) Galaxy was processing, loading or unloading on those dates the pollutants discovered except for benzene. When 23 parts per million of benzene were discovered in the ambient air on May 8, 1970 a few hundred yards west of the plant property line tetra hydro foran (THF) containing 40% benzene was lying in the evaporating lagoon on the plant property. THF had been processed May 6th and May 7th. Also, the Company was processing toluene which contains an unstated percentage of benzene.

Mr. Mraz testified that in the autumn of 1967 he knew there was a problem but he did not determine until January 1969 whether it was the emissions from the plant or the imagination of the complaining neighbor, Dr. Pietro Capurro. But at least four neighbors complained to Mr. Mraz about the Galaxy odors before Dr. Capurro entered the scene. The attack on Galaxy is of major proportions in Mr. Mraz' view and he has been "at battle readiness" for three years. He admits personally detecting some odors beyond the Galaxy property lines. By April 3, 1969 he had an "increased sensitivity" to the problem.

He does not subscribe to either the adsorption or incineration process recommended by the State Health Department as a feasible solution *if* an odor problem exists. He believes incineration particularly would be complex, expensive and dangerous. To prevent unreasonable emission of odors Mr. Mraz enumerated seven other steps that might be taken which have not been taken to date. One step is to install conservation vents at 24 needed points. They cost $70. each. To date only seven have been installed although Mr. Mraz has been aware of their value since at least 1960.

Galaxy transfers chemicals from tank trucks to storage tanks at the rate of 150 gallons of liquid per minute. It is imperative that an equal volume of air be vented from the tank into the ambient air. This vented air could consist of up to 25% fumes of the chemical being transferred. But Mr. Mraz does not believe the rapid filling is a potential odor source. In fact the plan is to speed up filling because he observes, undoubtedly correctly, that Galaxy does not make money by slowing the fill.

Dr. Peter Stavrakis testified that he had tended George Johnson, Dorothy Logan and Sharon Logan over recent years and did not relate their problems to Galaxy fumes. Only in the case of Dorothy Logan, however, and this only on September 4, 1969 did the possibility of fume etiology appear to come within the ambit of consideration by the doctor.

Dr. Edward T. Radford, a medical doctor with emphasis on environmental medicine and toxicology, was asked to investigate the Galaxy situation by the Air Quality Control Division of the State Health Department. In November 1969 he interviewed Dr. Capurro, and five other complaining witnesses. He detected an acetone odor 50 yards from the plant upon a visit. In some people such odors will produce nausea, vomiting and headache, *inter alia. Response to odors is a highly individualized thing,* the doctor testified. There were four pieces of record "evidence": (1) The death certificate of Mr. Morgan (not otherwise mentioned in 15 days of testimony); (2) The clinical record of Dianne Logan, deceased (she died of leukemia); (3) A summary by a public health nurse; and, (4) Hospital records which Dr. Capurro brought to him and shoved at him in a very disorganized state. Dr. Radford's conclusion was that the Galaxy operation was *a nuisance justifying this suit* but that there was insufficient evidence presented to him to conclude that it was a health problem.

Mr. William Bradley, not a medical doctor but an expert industrial toxicologist, testified that the proposed TLVs for the general population vary but are always lower than the factory values. Twenty years ago a level ten times lower was felt to be safe but today, at least for sulphur compounds, he thinks that even lower TLVs are required for the general population. Mr. Bradley visited the plant and suggested things Galaxy could to to eliminate the odors. He favors a vapor condensation system over incineration (danger of explosion) or adsorption (unwieldy).

Sixty-three neighbors and eight employees of Galaxy testified they had not detected any significant odor over the past year identifiable as coming from Galaxy. As evidence of their objectivity practically all of the neighbors denied any acquaintance with Mr. Mraz or Mr. Waters. Almost all these persons signed a petition prepared and solicited by Mr. Mraz that the odors from Galaxy had not affected their health. Leonard Madison, a supervisor for Galaxy, stated he did not smell anything unless he stuck his head in the storage tank. Charles Ginegar, a Galaxy truck driver is able to smell the chemicals when one foot from them and he gets a light headache when he sticks his head inside the tank. Shirley Kiebler's children play ten feet from the plant and she believes they smell nothing. But several of these witnesses had detected some odors. Betty Shellender last experienced a slight odor from Galaxy two weeks ago. When it is cloudy and humid Ronald Spratt smells odors from Galaxy. Dorothy Bender has smelled an occasional odor over the past year. William T. Hilaman and his wife, Dorothy, have both smelled odors from Galaxy within the past year. Mrs. William Mueller stated that in May 1970 a very potent unpleasant odor awakened her. She lives one mile south of the Galaxy plant. Two of this group of witnesses had signed petitions complaining of Galaxy as late as June 1969. Robert King signed three such petitions. Leonard Spratt signed one petition. He stated the purpose of signing was "to clear up the creek." Charlotte King testified Mr. Mraz had her sign the petition on the basis that the odors had not injured her health, that she lives a few hundred yards south of the plant and the odor is "pretty bad" inside and outside; that "just one night last week" whe had to close all the windows to keep odors out. Her husband, Owen King, said the odor only bothers him once in a while. Manure odors from a mushroom house do not bother him.

Dr. Franz Goldstein, a Board certified gastroenterologist, testified pancreatitis is an uncommon disease; and, that toxic inhalation is an uncommon cause. Symptoms are weight loss, pain, vomiting, shock, fever, indigestion and diarrhea. The specific laboratory tests for pancreatitis are the amylase and lipase tests (elevations are highly suggestive of pancreatitis). The secretin test, seldom used in acute cases, is the best test for chronic cases. The glucose tolerance test and the insulin curve test have no place in diagnosing acute pancreatitis. The former may indicate the severity of chronic pancreatitis. Some chemicals, i.e., carbon tetrachloride and benzene inhaled in large doses can cause hepatitis.

Dr. Goldstein studied the hospital records of twelve persons, (1) Gloria Mahaffey: A single lipase elevation was insufficient evidence upon which to diagnose pancreatitis as Drs. Kailin and Capurro had done. They stated they also found nausea, abdominal and leg pain, headache, dizziness and tiredness as well as an abnormal SGOT, ICD, glucose tolerance level and insulin curve. (2) Robert Mahaffey: No evidence of other than a pulmonary problem. Dr. Kailin based on headaches diagnosed a cerebral irritation and possible pancreatitis. Dr. Capurro, on the basis of abdominal pain, leg pain, tiredness, indigestion and an abnormal ICD diagnosed a toxic hepatitis. (3) Odas Mahaffey: A liver disfunction. Dr. Capurro diagnosed toxic hepatitis. (4) Wilbur Smith: Emphysema. No one disagrees. (5) Marlene Evans: Upper respiratory infection. Dr. Folk had found, in addition to an elevated lipase, abdominal pain and tenderness, all which improved rapidly upon leaving the Galaxy area. His diagnosis was pancreatitis probably due to toxicity. (6) Rosemary Mitchell: Possible infectious mononucleosis. Dr. Goldstein found several symptoms of hepatitis too. Dr. Kailin noted an elevated lipase, glucose tolerance and insulin curve plus headache, nausea, abdominal tenderness, liver enlarged and tender and a weight loss. The patient improved upon leaving home. Her diagnosis was hepatitis and possible pancreatitis. (7) Dale Spencer: Pancreatitis. No one disagreed although Dr. Kailin only indicated same, did not diagnose it. (8) Goldie Evans: Epileptic. No one disagrees. (9) Fred Spencer: Urethral stricutre. Dr. Kailin found an abnormal lipase, glucose tolerance, insulin curve and an abnormal pancreatic scan plus abdominal pain, headache and indigestion. Her diagnosis was indigestion and possible pancreatitis. (10) Thomas Evans: Pancreatitis and diabetes. No one disagrees. Dr. Kailin also diagnosed hepatitis. (11) George Johnson: An ulcer. No one disagrees. (12) Pietro Capurro: Diabetes and pancreatitis. No one disagrees. Dr. Kailin also diagnosed hepatitis but Dr. Goldstein says there is insufficient evidence to do so.

Dr. Goldstein stated he sees 30–40 patients a year with pancreatitis. A damaged pancreas can lead to diabetes. One can have pancreatitis without symptoms and without knowledge (confirming previous expert testimony).

Dr. Goldstein agrees with the diagnoses of Health Department doctors in six of the twelve cases above (numbers 4, 7, 8, 10 and 12 above). There is room for possible agreement as to hepatitis in two others (numbers 3 and 6). As for numbers 1, 2, 5 and 9 above there is not agreement. Dr. Goldstein conceded that he was at a significant disadvantage in not seeing the patient, in seeing only the hospital records.

Dr. Joseph Lanzi is the company doctor for Galaxy. He testified Thomas Evans had been his patient since October 1959 and might have then had pancreatitis. He had at that time recurrent abdominal pain of an unidentified etiology. He now definitely diagnoses diabetes and pancreatitis. When the lipase highly elevated (5.9), he advised him and his family to move out of the Galaxy area. They did. A few days later lipase was 2.7 (normal is 1.0 or below). A week later it was 0.7. Then he moved back home and within 10 days the lipase level was back up to 2.2.

Marlene Evans' lipase level upon hospital admission was 0.0, the next day 0.6 and the next day 1.8 which Dr. Lanzi discounts as an inaccurate reading.

This concluded the testimony of the Galaxy Chemical Company. The Health Department had no rebuttal.

c. Findings of Fact

The Court finds the following facts after due consideration of the credibility of all the evidence.

(1) From at least January 1968 to the date of trial Galaxy Chemical Company has regularly processed at least 23 different chemicals. Twelve, by skin absorption, inhalation or ingestion, may cause death or permanent injury after very short exposure to small quantities. Four have an unknown toxic hazard rating since there is not enough information on humans to rate them. (Joint Exhibit Number 1).

(2) Chemical fumes escape from Galaxy Chemical Company and travel significant distances beyond the Galaxy property. Present operating conditions present many opportunities for this. To the date of trial the emissions have been frequent.

(3) The escaping fumes have an odor which interferes with the use and enjoyment of *some* properties and causes discomfort and illness of *some* people.

(4) Response to odors is a highly individualized thing (Dr. Edward T. Radford, an expert witness for Galaxy Chemical Company). Odors affect different people in different ways, some remarkably and some not at all. Thus sixty-three (63) neighbors had not smelled any odors which they could attribute to Galaxy over the past year. (The Court knows many of these neighbors personally and would vouch for their complete integrity even if they had not been sworn to tell the truth.)

(5) The emission of odors can be prevented whether it be by incineration or adsorption (rejected by Galaxy) or by vapor condensation (recommended by Mr. Bradley, a Galaxy expert witness) or by steps suggested by Mr. Mraz or some combination of these or possibly other methods. The prevention of the emission of odors is economically feasible for Galaxy Chemical Company. The methods mentioned appear to be practical and standard in the industry.

(6) A factory employee works eight hours at a time, then has 16 hours away from the factory every day, 64 hours away on weekends. He is likely to be in better health than the average member of the general population. A resident where a chemical factory emits fumes into the neighborhood 24 hours a day, while not likely to be as healthy, is exposed to escaping fumes over four times as long as the factory worker. This resident is also exposed, not eight hours at a time but continuously, thus if prolonged exposure to chemicals has any cumulative physiological effect he is subject to it. Clearly the concentrations of chemical fumes in the ambient air upon which this resident depends for life must be lower than in the factory. Dr. Capurro testified the concentration should be 500 times lower. Dr. Kailin said 100 times for sulphur and 2½ times for carbon monoxide. The Galaxy witness, Mr. Bradley, testified over 10 times lower. Thus, if only 25 benzene, 500 MeCl and 200 MEK parts are permissible in the factory, then using Mr. Bradley's "10 times" formula, 2.5 benzene, 50 MeCl and 20 MEK would be the permissible exposure for the general population. Thus the 23 benzene and 94 MEK parts per million of air discovered by Dr. Hackman May 8, 1970 in the Providence area (well beyond the Galaxy property lines) substantially exceeds permissible exposure for the Providence general population.

(7) (a) If certain chemicals combine in the ambient air the physiological effect in combination is more than twice as great as if exposed to each separately. (b) With repeated exposure to many chemicals the ability to tolerate them decreases. (c) With repeated exposure to many chemicals one is less aware of their presence.

(8) Exposure to toxic chemicals is one of several causes, an uncommon cause, of pancreatitis. Specific laboratory tests are the lipase and amylase tests and, if chronic, the secretin test. Ancillary tests are glucose tolerance and barium tests. Classic symptoms of pancreatitis are upper abdominal pain, nausea, vomiting, diarrhea and, if chronic, weight loss.

(9) The Court records 18 Providence residents examined, 10 by a single Health Department witness (Dr. Folk or Capurro or Kailin), 5 by two doctors and 3 by all three doctors. Thirteen of the eighteen were found to have classic symptoms and abnormal tests suggestive of pancreatitis or hepatitis. There were eight diagnoses of pancreatitis, four of possible pancreatitis, one with hepatitis and five with neither pancreatitis or hepatitis. Some who were said to have pancreatitis primarily were said to have hepatitis secondarily. Where more than one doctor examined, diagnoses were essentially the same. Dr. Franz Goldstein, an expert witness for Galaxy, examined the hospital records of twelve of these residents. In six cases he agreed with the Health Department diagnoses; in two other cases there was a lot of agreement as to symptoms of hepatitis and in the four other cases Dr. Goldstein could not agree. He never saw the patients and conceded this to place him at a decided disadvantage in diagnosing. In most of the positive diagnoses the cause attributed by the examining doctor was exposure to toxic fumes from Galaxy Chemical Company.

(10) Statistically the evidence of lipase abnormalities pointing to pancreatitis in the area of Galaxy Chemical Company was eight times higher than among a random group of hospital patients.

(11) Since one may have pancreatitis without symptons and without knowledge a lay person cannot know whether or not he has pancreatitis.

(12) The conclusions and opinions of testifying medical experts is summarized as follows. On threshold limit values, see (6) *supra.* Dr. Kailin concluded the illnesses of the residents she examined were real, not the result of suggestion. She opined that the operation of Galaxy Chemical Company adversely affects the health of the neighbors. Drs. Folk, Capurro and Kailin and the Galaxy witness, Dr. Goldstein, agreed one might have pancreatitis without symptoms and without knowledge. Dr. Radford, a witness for Galaxy Chemical Company, concluded the Company operations constitute a nuisance justifying this suit by the Health Deaprtment but he stated insufficient evidence was presented to him for him to conclude that the operations pose a helath problem. Dr. Goldstein saw only hospital records, and, aside from holding toxic fumes to be an uncommon cause of pancreatitis and hepatitis, did not speculate as to etiology. As to the extent of his agreement with diagnoses of other doctors, see (9) *supra.*

(13) Management of Galaxy Chemical Company is very capable, very self confident and naturally very anxious to be successful. It appears to believe that it has been subjected to a major attack for the past three years; this suit is the culmination of that attack; that attack has forced Galaxy to maintain a position of "battle readiness"; that attack is without merit or justification; and, no substantial corrective action is needed.

d. Conclusions

Many smelled fumes. Many others did not.

It is the law that positive evidence ordinarily is entitled to greater weight than negative evidence and the positive testimony of one credible witness as to a fact in issue must outweigh a dozen equally credible witnesses whose testimony is merely negative, *M.L.E. Evidence, Section 326.* In this case we have many credible witnesses who smelled the fumes from Galaxy Chemical Company (positive evidence) and many more credible witnesses who did not smell anything at all or if they did detect odors they could not be sure they were from Galaxy (negative evidence). Note that this latter group of witnesses did not state that there were no odors. They merely stated they did not smell odors. Under the law as quoted above the Court is required to rely on the positive evidence over the negative evidence. Therefore, the Court concludes that noxious odors from Galaxy Chemical Company were present in the neighborhood although a considerable number of neighbors did not smell them.

The legal definition of a nuisance is anything that unlawfully annoys or does damage to another, and it includes everything that endangers life or health, gives offense to the senses, violates the laws of decency, or obstructs the reasonable and comfortable use of property. Traditionally, it is a thing or condition on premises or adjacent thereto, offensive or harmful to those who are off the premises, *M.L.E. Nuisances, Section 1.*

Upon the foregoing facts the Court concludes that the present method of operation of Galaxy Chemical Company constitutes a nuisance. The Court specifically concludes that the operation gives offense to the senses; and, that it obstructs or interferes with the reasonable and comfortable use of property. Without concluding positively that the present method of operating is a hazard to health, the Court concludes that it may be a hazard to health. In any case correction is imperative. Accordingly, the Court will sign a decree upon presentation enjoining Galaxy Chemical Company, its agents, servants or employees from emitting into the air beyond its property lines gases, vapors and odors which are or may be predicted by reasonable certainty to be injurious to human, plant or animal life or property, or which unreasonably interferes with the proper enjoyment of property of others and from maintaining a public nuisance which endangers the health, safety or general welfare of any person or persons. Since the Court views this as a correctible nuisance, the Court shall permit six (6) months from the date of this decree for completion of corrective action and full compliance with the terms of this injunction or else the factory is to cease operating. Counsel will please submit an appropriate decree.

DATED: September 8, 1970

H. Kenneth Mackey
Judge

ORDER

The testimony of the parties in the above captioned case having been heard and considered and an opinion and finding of fact having been filed herein on the 8th day of September, 1970, for the reasons stated therein, it is this 16th day of September, 1970:

ORDERED that the defendant, the Galaxy Chemical Co., Inc., its agents, servants and employees, is hereby enjoined from emitting into the ambient air beyond its property line, gases, vapors and odors which are or may be predicted with reasonable certainty to be injurious to human, plant or animal life or which unreasonably interfere with the enjoyment of the property of others; and,

IT IS FURTHER ORDERED that the Galaxy Chemical Co., Inc., its agents, servants and employees shall cease and desist from the maintenance of a public nuisance which endangers the health, safety and general welfare of any persons; and,

IT IS FURTHER ORDERED that the effect of this injunction shall be stayed for a period of six (6) months from the date of this order under the following terms and conditions:

(1) That the Company commence corrective action immediately;

(2) That the Maryland State Department of Health, its agents, servants, employees and designees be permitted free, unscheduled and unannounced access to the premises of the Company for the purpose of determining the specific progress of corrective action; and,

(3) That the said Department of Health report to this Court on October 20, 1970, December 5, 1970, January 20, 1971 and March 1971 the corrective action progress by the Company.

IT IS FURTHER ORDERED that all the foregoing shall be subject to such additional orders of the Court as in the judgment of the Court may be warranted by the circumstances.

H. Kenneth Mackey
Judge

MARYLAND v. GALAXY CHEMICAL CO., Maryland Circuit Ct. for Cecil County, 2 ERC 1199, Jan. 26, 1971

OPINION AND ORDER

The Court finds as a fact based upon periodic reports of the Maryland State Department of Health and Mental Hygiene which were placed in evidence today, and the testimony offered at the hearing today, that at least as early as August 1968 the health authorities requested the Defendant to take corrective action regarding odor emissions, that the corrective action progress of Galaxy Chemical Co., Inc. ordered September 16, 1970 has not progressed satisfactorily, that there has been no substantial abatement of the nuisance and possible health hazard, that in the opinion of the Maryland State Department of Health and Mental Hygiene corrective action could not be completed by March 16, 1971, the end of the six month period prescribed in the injunction order of September 16, 1970, and thus the conditions requisite for a stay of the injunction ordered September 16, 1970 have not been met by the Galaxy Chemical Co., Inc.

The Court, by its Order dated September 16, 1970, having retained jurisdiction to issue such additional Orders as in its judgment may be warranted by the circumstances, it is this 25th day of January, 1971, upon the recommendation of the Maryland State Department of Health and Mental Hygiene.

ORDERED that the Defendant, Galaxy Chemical Co., Inc., its officers, agents, servants and employees, and its successors and assigns, as of midnight Friday, January 29, 1971, cease all manufacturing and processing operations at the Defendant's chemical solvent recovery plant located in Providence, Maryland until such time as it shall demonstrate to the satisfaction of the Court that the operation of the plant will not continue to be a public nuisance and will not continue to cause emissions into the ambient air beyond its property lines of gases, vapors and odors which are or may be predicted with reasonable certainty to be injurious to human, plant or animal life or which unreasonably interfere with the enjoyment of the property of others.

FURTHER ORDERED that the Galaxy Chemical Co., Inc. may, with the written consent of the Maryland State Department of Health and Mental Hygiene, Division of Air Quality Control, for periods not to exceed 48 consecutive hours in any week operate its plant for the purpose of diagnosing or testing methods to control the emissions resulting from the Company's processes.

FURTHER ORDERED that all the foregoing shall be subject to such additional Orders of the Court as in the judgment of the Court may be warranted by the circumstances.

H. Kenneth Mackey
Judge

POSTSCRIPT TO THE GALAXY CASE

As of October 26, 1971, when the situation after several years of litigation was checked for this book, the Galaxy Chemical Co. plant was still in operation, albeit under the theoretical restrictions placed on it by the court. Nevertheless, neighbors continued to complain about the odors, and some were hospitalized with ailments attributed to those fumes from Galaxy (Washington Post, May 11, 1971 at C2). A damage suit by nine of Galaxy's neighbors had finally been set for trial after numerous continuances at the company's request. It is perhaps ironical that Galaxy is engaged in an environmentally beneficial task: that of recycling used chemicals. It employs about a dozen persons.

On June 6, 1972, according to an article of that same date in the Washington Post at C1, ten neighbors of Galaxy were awarded damages of $34,932 (more than half of it to pay for medical expenses and "loss of enjoyment of their properties".) More than half the total went to one family living 500 feet from the plant. The award was made by Caroline County Circuit Court Judge James A. Wise; an appeal was considered possible.

The public frustration concerning the Galaxy case is at least in part due to the court's use of the traditional "solution" of remanding a dispute to the responsible administrative agency. Such frustration is not confined to the Galaxy case; rather, it is a too-frequent phenomenon. Environmental Defense Fund v. Ruckelshaus,— F.2d—(D.C.Cir. Jan. 7, 1971) is an outstanding example (this is the DDT dispute).

Recently, some courts have taken an alternate approach, giving detailed clean-up instructions to offenders. A fine example of this is Wayne County v. Chrysler Corp., 2 ERC 1708 (Mich. Cir. Ct. Wayne Cy., June 18, 1971). Another excellent example is Pennsylvania v. U. S. Steel, 2 ERC 1714, Penn. Ct. of Common Pleas, Butler Cy. No. 2 of Equity, June 8, 1971.

f. Freedom of information

A recurring problem for environmental lawyers is that of obtaining information concerning the actions of government agencies. Much of the work of such agencies is carried on in secret. The substantial area of administrative discretion and the inadequate judicial review mechanisms when combined with this secrecy, permits the use and abuse of public resources with little opportunity for public participation. This secrecy benefits those who profit from the destruction of our environment, for many of the exploiters have means of access to the governmental processes not enjoyed by the public at large. Trade associations, well-financed professional lobbyists, advisory councils made up of environmental abusers, the use of administrative law firms, and large campaign contributions frequently bring preferential treatment for the environmental destroyers. At Federal, state and local levels it is common to place representatives of the regulated industries on the regulatory boards.

federal level

In an attempt to make the activities of the Federal government more open to citizen scrutiny, the Freedom of Information Act [5 U.S.C. 552] was passed effective July 4, 1967. Like much legislation, this act promises more benefits than are really available, but a knowledge of its use is important.

The Act is difficult to interpret, and this problem is exacerbated by the legislative history. The Senate Committee Report follows essentially the words of the Act. The House Committee report, written after the Senate passed the bill, attempts to change the meaning of the Act's words, usually in favor of nondisclosure.

The Attorney General, during 1967, released the Attorney General's Memorandum on the Public Information Section of the Administrative Procedure Act. The Memorandum guides the agency practices, but relies on the House Committee report and favors a restrictive interpretation of the Act. Two court decisions have favored the Senate Report: *Benson v. General Services Administration,* 289 F.Supp. 590; affirmed on other grounds, 415 F.2d 878 (4th Cir. 1969); and *Consumers Union of the United States v. Veterans Administration,* 301 F.Supp. 796 (S.D.N.Y. 1969). The result is that governmental practices often are more restrictive than those approved by Congress or the courts, but no remedy is available for the bulk of restrictive practices which citizens cannot afford to take to the courts. The intimidation of agency personnel, and the government's frequent efforts to deny knowledge of the existence of documents, further limits the literal language of the statute. See Fellmeth, "The Freedom of Information Act and the Federal Trade Commission: A Study in Malfeasance," 4 *Harv. Civ. Rights L. Rev.,* 345, Spring 1969.

The Act is further restricted by the use of the doctrine of executive privilege, and by other statutes that may restrict disclosure.

However, the basic thrust of the Act is to require disclosure to all persons without the balancing of the interest of the party desiring information. The identity of the person seeking the information need not be revealed to the agency. The Act in subsection 4(b) includes nine categories of information that need not be provided. For a discussion of the interpretations given to these exceptions see Davis, *Administrative Law Treatise,* 1970 Supplement, chapter 3A.

A well-known example of virtually all of these governmental sins was the sequestering of the Garwin Committee report on the feasibility of the Supersonic Transport plane. The committee came to an unfavorable conclusion regarding continued governmental involvement in the SST project, primarily on economic grounds, the very grounds cited by the Nixon Administration most frequently in its strenuous fight to continue the project. Despite efforts by Congressmen, the President kept secret from the people the report their money paid for. A year-long legal battle had a Pyrrhic triumph in the U.S. Court of Appeals for the District of Columbia when the court ruled April 13, 1971 that the report fell under the Freedom of Information Act unless it met nine categories of exemptions. The case was remanded to the district court, where it faced imminent trial. However, the Executive Branch at this point released the report, now that it was without significance (Aug. 21, 1971). Thus the Freedom of Information Act has served so far largely to help historians.

The Garwin Report case was *Soucie v. David*, 448 F.2d 1067 (D.C. Cir. April 13, 1971), 2 ERC 1626. This case is a key one in the field. Another important case is *Bristol-Meyers v. Federal Trade Commission*, 424 F.2d 935 (D.C. Cir. March 26, 1970).

The trans-Alaska pipeline case involves similar suppression of public documents, as did the dispute over the Amchitka, Alaska, hydrogen bomb test. Documents highly relevant to the environmental effects in question were illegally kept secret by the Presidency until a day before the blast took place, despite a long and strenuous court fight that had resulted in a court order weeks previous to make public the unclassified documents intended for the public. (*Mink v. Environmental Protection Agency*, ___ F.2d ___ (D.C. Cir. Oct. 25, 1971), 3 ERC 1166.

The documents in the *Mink* cases (brought by Rep. Patsy T. Mink and 32 other members of Congress, and so given special priority under 5 U.S.C. 552(a)(3)(1970)) were held secret under the exasperating "staple technique"—i.e., non-secret documents withheld on "national defense" grounds by being placed in the same file with a secret document. The court saw this ruse for what it was, and so perhaps ended this long-favored tricky practice.

SEE ALSO the section on use of the National Environmental Policy Act of 1969 to obtain information, One-42, and the series of related cases beginning at Appendix One-47.

The recent decision of the U.S. District Court for the District of Columbia, *Moss v. Laird*, Civ. No. 1254-71, ___ F.Supp. ___ (December 7, 1971), involving an attempt to make public portions of the Pentagon Papers, illustrates a failure of the judiciary to apply the Freedom of Information Act as Congress intended.

In order to make the Freedom of Information Act work as Congress intended, several reforms are needed:

(1) Judicial review of FOI cases must be given the highest priority, and the government's time to answer the initial complaint should be reduced from the current maximum of 60 days;

(2) Courts must be allowed to judge the reasonableness of any exemptions claimed under the Act, including those now required by Executive Order to be kept secret "in the interest of the national defense or foreign policy."

(3) Administrative remedies should be streamlined. Agency denials of requests for information under FOI should be made promptly, specifying the reasons for denial. Final action on appeals from such denials should be taken as soon as practicable (i.e., within 20 working days) after the appeal has been filed.

(4) Reasonable attorney's fees should be awarded for those who successfully obtain information under the Act.

A memorandum in support of similar recommendations has been prepared by Donald A. Giannella, Professor of Law, Villanova University. Edmund Muskie in 1972 introduced a bill (S. 2965) which could provide attorney's fee's for those successfully using the Freedom of Information Act to obtain blocked information.

REFERENCES AND SELECTED BIBLIOGRAPHY

references

See generally, "The People's Right to Know," a series of eight articles in *Trial* magazine beginning Vol. 8, No. 2 (March/April, 1972).

See also:

NADER, R. Freedom of Information: The Act and Agencies, 5 *Harvard Civil Rights L.R.* (1970)

JOHNSTONE, J., The Freedom of Information Act and the FDA, 25 *Food Drug, and Cosmetic Law J.* 296 (June 1970)

CARON, A.J., Federal Procurement and the Freedom of Information Act, 28 *Federal Bar J.* 761 (summer, 1967)

KATZ, J., The Games Bureaucrats Play: Hide and Seek under the Freedom of Information Act, 48 *Texas L.R.* 1261 (November 1970)

FREEDOM OF INFORMATION ACT, 5 U.S.C. Sec. 552

§ 552. Public information; agency rules, opinions, orders, records, and proceedings.

(a) Each agency shall make available to the public information as follows:

(1) Each agency shall separately state and currently publish in the Federal Register for the guidance of the public—

(A) descriptions of its central and field organization and the established places at which, the employees (and in the case of a uniformed service, the members) from whom, and the methods whereby, the public may obtain information, make submittals or requests, or obtain decisions;

(B) statements of the general course and method by which its functions are channeled and determined, including the nature and requirements of all formal and informal procedures available;

(C) rules of procedure, descriptions of forms available or the places at which forms may be obtained, and instructions as to the scope and contents of all papers, reports, or examinations;

(D) substantive rules of general applicability adopted as authorized by law, and statements of general policy or interpretations of general applicability formulated and adopted by the agency; and

(E) each amendment, revision, or repeal of the foregoing.

Except to the extent that a person has actual and timely notice of the terms thereof, a person may not in any manner be required to resort to, or be adversely affected by, a matter required to be published in the Federal Register and not so published. For the purpose of this paragraph, matter reasonably available to the class of persons affected thereby is deemed published in the Federal Register when incorporated by reference therein with the approval of the Director of the Federal Register.

(2) Each agency, in accordance with published rules, shall make available for public inspection and copying—

(A) final opinions, including concurring and dissenting opinions, as well as orders, made in the adjudication of cases;

(B) those statements of policy and interpretations which have been adopted by the agency and are not published in the Federal Register; and

(C) administrative staff manuals and instructions to staff that affect a member of the public;

unless the materials are promptly published and copies offered for sale. To the extent required to prevent a clearly unwarranted invasion of personal privacy, an agency may delete identifying details when it makes available or publishes an opinion, statement of policy, interpretation, or staff manual or instruction. However, in each case the justification for the deletion shall be explained fully in writing. Each agency also shall maintain and make available for public inspection and copying a current index providing identifying information for the public as to any matter issued, adopted, or promulgated after July 4, 1967, and required by this paragraph to be made available or published. A final order, opinion, statement of policy, interpretation, or staff manual or instruction that affects a member of the public may be relied on, used, or cited as precedent by an agency against a party other than an agency only if—

(i) it has been indexed and either made available or published as provided by this paragraph; or

(ii) the party has actual and timely notice of the terms thereof.

(3) Except with respect to the records made available under paragraphs (1) and (2) of this subsection, each agency, on request for identifiable records made in accordance with published rules stating the time, place, fees to the extent authorized by statute, and procedure to be followed, shall make the records promptly available to any person. On complaint, the district court of the United States in the district in which the complainant resides, or has his principal place of business, or in which the agency records are situated, has jurisdiction to enjoin the agency from withholding agency records and to order the production of any agency records improperly withheld from the complaint. In such a case the court shall determine the matter de novo and the burden is on the agency to sustain its action. In the event of noncompliance with the order of the court, the district court may punish for contempt the responsible employee, and in the case of a uniformed service, the responsible member. Except as to causes the court considers of greater importance, proceedings before the district court, as authorized by this paragraph, take precedence on the docket over all other causes and shall be assigned for hearing and trial at the earliest practicable date and expedited in every way.

(4) Each agency having more than one member shall maintain and make available for public inspection a record of the final votes of each member in every agency proceeding.

(b) This section does not apply to matters that are—

(1) specifically required by Executive order to be kept secret in the interest of the national defense or foreign policy;

(2) related solely to the internal personnel rules and practices of an agency;

(3) specifically exempted from disclosure by statute;

(4) trade secrets and commercial or financial information obtained from a person and privileged or confidential;

(5) inter-agency or intra-agency memorandums or letters which would not be available by law to a party other than an agency in litigation with the agency;

(6) personnel and medical files and similar files the disclosure of which would constitute a clearly unwarranted invasion of personal privacy;

(7) investigatory files compiled for law enforcement purposes except to the extent available by law to a party other than an agency;

(8) contained in or related to examination, operating, or condition reports prepared by, on behalf of, or for the use of an agency responsible for the regulation or supervision of financial institutions; or

(9) geological and geophysical information and data, including maps, concerning wells.

(c) This section does not authorize withholding of information or limit the availability of records to the public, except as specifically stated in this section. This section is not authority to withhold information from Congress. (Pub. L. 89–554, Sept. 6, 1966, 80 Stat. 383, amended Pub. L. 90–23, § 1, June 5, 1967, 81 Stat. 54.)

Freedom of information state and local

Under the common law, members of the public have access to public records if they can establish an interest and a legitimate purpose. Sometimes that interest can be established by taxpayer status alone, but 48 of the 50 states have given some statutory support to that right, in most cases simplifying requirements for standing and sometimes broadening the scope of information previously held to be open for public inspection.

The key sources for compiled information on this subject are the publications of the Freedom of Information Center at the University of Missouri, Box 858, Columbia, Mo. 65201. Their booklets include "State Access Statutes" (no. 202), "Access Problems on the Local Level" (no. 25) and "Access Laws: Interpretations" (no. 88) and "Access Laws: Defeats" (no. 89). Also of considerable interest is a booklet entitled "The Damned Information," published by the Washington Institute of Quality Education, 300 M Street S. W., Washington, D.C. This contains sample complaints as well as a fairly comprehensive listing of relevant state laws and court decisions.

The following state-by-state listing of relevant state laws is culled largely from the sources just mentioned.

See also:

LANE, M.T., Acquisition of State Documents, 63 *Law Library J.* 92 (February 1970)

ALABAMA Code of Ala. title 41, §§ 145-47 (1945).

ALASKA Alaska Stats. title 9, ch. 25, §§ 110 and 120 (1962).

ARIZONA Ariz. Rev. Stats. title 39, § 121 (1956).

ARKANSAS Ark. Stats. title 12, ch. 28, § 01-07.

CALIFORNIA West's Annotated Government Code §§ 6250-6260 (supp. 1971).

COLORADO Colo. Rev. Stats. ch. 123, art. 33, § 2(2) (perm. supp. 1965).

CONNECTICUT Conn. Gen. Stats. Ann. title 1, ch. 3. § 7-20.

DELAWARE Del. Code Ann. title 29, § 3327 (d) (1953).

FLORIDA Fla. Stats. Ann. ch. 119, title 10, § 01 (1959) and §§ .011, .21, .31, .41, .05-.10 (supp. 1971).

GEORGIA Code of Ga. Ann. title 40, ch. 27, §§ 01-03 (supp. 1970).

HAWAII Hawaii Rev. Stats. title 8, ch. 92, §§ 1-6, 21 (1968).

IDAHO Idaho Code title 59, ch. 10, §§ 1009-10011 (1947).

ILLINOIS Ill. Stats. ch. 116, §§ 43.4-43.6 (Smith-Hurd supp. 1971).

INDIANA Burns Ann. Ind. Stats. titles 57 and 601-09 (supp. 1970).

IOWA Ia. Code. Ann. ch. 622, § 622.46 as amended Ia. Laws of Session ch. 106 §§ 1-12 (1967).

KANSAS Kan. Stats. Ann. ch. 45, §§ 201-203 (1957).

KENTUCKY Ky. Rev. Stats. ch. 171, §§ 410-990 (1969) as amended by Ky. Acts ch. 92, §§ 32, 46, 48 (1970).

LOUISIANA La. Rev. Stats. title 44, ch. 1, §§ 1-9, 31-41 (supp. 1971).

MAINE Me. Rev. Stats. Ann. title 1, ch. 13, §§ 401-02 and 404-06 (1964).

MARYLAND Ann. Code of Md. article 76A, §§ 1-5 (supp. 1970).

MASSACHUSETTS Mass. Gen. Laws Ann. title 1, ch. 4, § 7(26) (supp. 1971).

MICHIGAN Mich. Comp. Laws Ann. ch. 750, § 491 (1964) and § 492 as amended (supp. 1970).

MISSISSIPPI Miss. Code 1942 Ann. title 7, ch. 2, § 878 (supp. 1970).

MISSOURI Ann. Mo. Stats. ch. 109. §§ 180 amd 190 (Vernon's 1966).

MONTANA Rev. Codes of Mont., 1947, Ann. title 16, ch. 9, § 906 (Repl. Vol. 1967).

NEBRASKA Rev. Stats. of Neb. ch. 25, § 1280 (1964).

NEVADA Nev. Rev. Stats. title 19, ch. 239, § 010 (1967).

NEW HAMPSHIRE N.H. Rev. Stats. Ann. ch. 91-A, §§ 1-7 (supp. 1970).

NEW JERSEY N.J. Stats. Ann. title 47, § 47:1A1,2,3,4 (West supp. 1970).

NEW MEXICO N.M. Stat. 1953 Ann. ch. 71, article 5, §§ 1-3 (repl. vol. 1961).

NEW YORK N.Y. Judiciary Law § 225 (McKinney 1965).

NORTH CAROLINA Gen Stats. N.C. ch. 132, §§ 1-9 (1964).

NORTH DAKOTA N.D. Century Code Ann. title 44, ch. 44-04, §§ 18, 19 (1960).

OHIO Ohio Rev. Code Ann. title 1, §§ 149.40-149.99 (Page's 1969).

OKLAHOMA Okla. Stats. Ann title 51, ch. 1, § 24 (1962).

OREGON Ore. Rev. Stats. title 19, § 192.005-192.220 (1969).

PENNSYLVANIA Purdon's Pa. Stats. title 65, ch. 3, § 66.1-66.3 (1959); § 66.4 as amended 17 Pa. Stats. § 211.508 (a) (90) (supp. 1971).

RHODE ISLAND No statutory authority, but common law remedies available, see *Nolan v. McCoy,* 77 R.I. 96, 73 A.2d 693 (1950) and *Bilodeau v. Dolan,* 85 R.I. 348, 350 (1957).

SOUTH CAROLINA Code of Law of S.C. title 9, §§ 2-14 (Cumulative supp. 1970).

SOUTH DAKOTA S.D. Comp. Laws. Ann. title 1, ch. 1-25, §§ 1-25-1 to 1-25-4 (1967).

TENNESSEE Tenn. Code Ann. title 15, §§ 304-07 (Cumulative supp. 1970).

TEXAS Rev. Civil Stats. of State of Tex. Ann. title 89, article 5441a, § 1 (Vernon's 1970).

UTAH Utah Code Ann. title 78, ch. 26, §§ 78-26-1 to 78-26-3 (1953).

VERMONT Vt. Stats. Ann. title 1, §§ 311 and 314 (1958).

VIRGINIA Code of Vir. Ann. title 2.1, ch. 21, §§ 2.1-340 to 2.1-346 (supp. 1970).

WASHINGTON Rev. Code of Wash. Ann. title 40, § 40.14.10 (1961).

WEST VIRGINIA No Statutory authority, but traditional limited common law rights were upheld in two cases, *West Virginia v. Harrison,* 130 W. Vir. 246, 43 S.E. 2d 214 (1947) and *Charleston Mail Association v. Kelly,* 149 W. Vir. 766, 143 S.E. 2d 139 (1965).

WISCONSIN Wisc. Stats. Ann. §§ 19.21 and 19.22 (West's 1970).

WYOMING Wyo. Stats. 1957 Ann. title 9, ch. 7.1, §§ 9-692.5 (supp. 1969).

g. Fairness Doctrine

Our first amendment rights today are of limited value unless they include the ability to communicate opposing views to the entire nation. The traditional values and philosophies of the nation's commercial interests are expressed daily through an unrelenting bombardment over the mass media, with both advertising and the entire tenor of programming designed not to challenge the sacrosanct opinions of those interests who control the media.

The ability to gain access to the media to present opposing views is a prerequisite for meaningful environmental as well as any other social change. The basic thrust of this movement for change has occurred through attempts to use the FCC's Fairness Doctrine.

Briefly, the Fairness Doctrine requires that when a broadcaster undertakes to present programming dealing with controversial issues of public importance, he must make reasonable efforts to present conflicting viewpoints on such issues. This may mean a round-table discussion, where various views are presented. Or it may be satisfied by a later program produced by the station which undertakes to air an opposing view. Finally, it may require that the station allow members of the public, representing different viewpoints, to present and explain their views over the air.

The Fairness Doctrine should be distinguished from its cousin, the statutory provision for "equal opportunities," which requires that when any legally qualified candidate for public office is permitted to use a station's broadcast facilities, all other candidates for the same office must be offered equal broadcast time. The "equal time" requirement is much more specific, applying only to candidates, and much more rigid, with its requirement of "equal" time, than the Fairness Doctrine, which applies to any controversial issue of public importance and requires only "reasonable time" for presentation of conflicting views.

However, the ideological basis of both policies is the same. Each rests on the concept that the people of the nation, acting through Congress, have paramount rights to the airwaves, simply granting licensees a temporary privilege to broadcast. The licensee is therefore not free to monopolize the air for its own purposes, but remains a trustee impressed with the duty of preserving the airwaves as a medium of free expression and fair presentation for all.

Federal regulation of broadcast radio began with the Radio Act of 1912, [37 Stat. 1162] which for the first time required a license from the Secretary of Commerce for the operation of radio apparatus. Electrical interference, not program content, was the sole criterion in issuing these early licenses. After World War I, however, broadcast stations mushroomed, and the Secretary of Commerce attempted to find room for everybody by limiting the stations' power and hours of operation, so that several could share the same channel. Regulation, however, was struck down in 1926 when the Acting United States Attorney General ruled that the Radio Act gave the Secretary no power to restrict frequency, power, or hours of radio station operation.

To combat the ensuing chaos, Congress enacted the Radio Act of 1927, which created the Federal Radio Commission and endowed it with a wide range of regulatory and licensing powers. The act established the new doctrine that access to the airwaves should be limited to private licensees who, while free to determine the content and format of program material, were required to operate in the "public interest, convenience, or necessity," a statutory standard which was nowhere defined.

The Radio Commission's first major task was a reallocation of frequencies and hours of operation among the stations. In so doing the Commission was faced with many, often mutually exclusive, applications. In choosing among competing applicants, the Commission began to pour specific policy goals into the vague statutory "public interest" standard. The primary concept to develop, which was to form the ideological basis for the Fairness Doctrine, was that since the licensee's access to the air was only a temporary privilege, granted by the government representing the people, the licensee could not use his station merely as an outlet for the presentation of a single set of views. [Chicago Federation of Labor v. Fed. Radio Comm'n.. 41 F.2d 422, 423 (D.C.Cir. 1930)].

In 1934 the Radio Act was replaced by the Communications Act of 1934. The new law continued provision for equal time for candidates but omitted such protection for discussion of "public questions". The standard of "public interest, convenience, or necessity" remained the only regulatory guide.

The Federal Communications Commission, in *Mayflower Broadcasting Corp.* [8 F.C.C. 333 (1940)] held that instead of simply operating a "propaganda station," the licensee must present varied viewpoints.

However, at the same time, the Commission banned all editorializing.

This ban on editorials lasted until 1949 when the Commission issued a position paper, "Editorializing by Broadcast Licensees," the first detailed enunciation of the Fairness Doctrine as formal Commission policy. The Editorializing Report, which is still the keystone of the Doctrine today, made two basic points. The licensee has an affirmative responsibility to devote a reasonable portion of broadcast time to the presentation of public issues, and, such programming must be designed so that listeners have an opportunity to hear conflicting positions on the public issues of interest in the community. Since the licensee still retains discretion over the format used to achieve these goals, he is free, if he wishes, to employ clearly identified editorials as one means of presenting the issues, so long as he also makes his facilities available for the presentation of opposing views.

In 1959 Congress, for the first time, provided explicit statutory underpinnings for the long-standing administrative interpretation. It amended 47 U.S.C. § 315(a), the "equal time" provision for candidates, to add:

"Nothing in the foregoing sentence shall be construed as relieving broadcasters, in connection with the presentation of newscasts, news interviews, news documentaries, and on-the-spot coverage of news events, from the obligation imposed upon them under this chapter to operate in the public interest and to afford reasonable opportunity for the discussion of conflicting views on issues of public importance."

The newest addition to the Fairness Doctrine is a regulation, promulgated by the FCC in 1967, to cover personal attacks and political editorials, the only two aspects of the Doctrine to be thus explicitly defined. The doctrine, including the new regulation, was considered by the U.S. Supreme Court for the first time in June of 1969 in the case of *Red Lion Broadcasting Co. v. Federal Communications Commission.* The doctrine and regulation were upheld by a unanimous Court as a "legitimate exercise of congressionally delegated authority. [395 U.S. 367 (1969)].

complaining

When a listener wants to complain about a violation of the Fairness Doctrine, he should notify the FCC of the station involved, controversial issue discussed, the date and time of the program, the basis for his claim that the station presented only one side of the issue, and whether the station has presented or intends to present dissenting views. If the Commission believes that a substantial issue is raised, it advises the licensee of the complaint and requests the station's comments. Unless further information is required from either side, the Commission proceeds to decide whether a violation has occurred, and if so, what action is appropriate.

The Commission's usual procedure is to issue informal rulings by letter or telegram at the time of the incident, and then to consider the matter more fully at license renewal time. The purpose of the immediate consideration is to give the public an opportunity to hear the opposing views while the particular issue is still controversial. If the FCC finds a Fairness Doctrine violation and orders the licensee to present dissenting viewpoints, the order is subject to immediate judicial review under 47 U.S.C. § 402(a).

Although stricter penalties are available, there is no evidence that they are ever used for Fairness violations because of their severity and administrative awkwardness. 47 U.S.C. § 503(b) provides for forfeitures of up to $1,000 per day for willful or repeated failure to observe the Commission's rules or to operate according to license, but § 504(a)'s proviso that forfeitures are recoverable only in a civil suit with trial de novo discourages its use. Under 47 U.S.C. § 312, the Commission may issue a cease and desist order or even revoke the offending party's license for the causes set forth in § 503; here again, however, a full hearing is required, with the burden of proof on the Commission, and appeal is permitted to the Court of Appeals for the District of Columbia under 47 U.S.C. § 402(b).

The Commission's final opportunity to penalize a broadcaster for Fairness violations is at the end of the three-year term, when a license renewal is sought. At this point, the licensee is required to make a detailed showing of its compliance with the Fairness Doctrine, with the burden on the station rather than on the Commission. However, the FCC has never denied a license renewal solely because of the station's failure to broadcast all sides of a particular issue. Moreover the FCC's record demonstrates almost a cavalier disregard of the public interest in favor of commercial interests. For a demonstration of this, see *United Church of Christ v. F.C.C.,* 359 F.2d 994 (1966) and In re *Complaint by Alan F. Neckritz* et al *concerning Standard Oil of California's F-310 Gasoline Advertising,* before FCC, docket no. 63075, FCC 71-526 (May 12, 1971).

recent applications.

On September 23, 1971, the FCC ruled 6-1 that the National Broadcasting Company had fulfilled its obligation under the Fairness Doctrine in its coverage of the Alaskan pipeline proposal. The Wilderness Society and Friends of the Earth had asked air time to balance a series of paid advertisements by the Standard Oil Co. of New Jersey (ESSO) that, without mentioning the proposed pipeline, sought to encourage a favorable view of oil exploration and production in the North of Alaska and Canada.

The Commission had ruled in June of 1971 that the Fairness Doctrine was applicable to the situation and that balancing comment was required by NBC. Ruled as adequate balancing comment was NBC's total of 21 minutes and 15 seconds of views opposing the pipeline compared with 10 minutes and 52 seconds favoring the pipeline. These figures exclude the 28 minutes of the relevant ESSO commercials.

But the FCC decision was accompanied by considerable expression of unhappiness from the Commission members themselves. The lone dissenter, Nicholas Johnson, stated that the spot advertisements may be more powerful than the remaining coverage, since the broadcast is "without interruptions, cuts...and the proponent is asked no questions...either before, during or after his spot." Johnson added that he found it "curious that when a case is difficult or impossible to resolve, this commission usually disposes of it by concluding that the broadcaster wins" (Washington *Evening Star,* Sept. 23, 1971 at B6).

FCC Chairman Dean Burch concurred with the majority but with "a sense of frustration and disenchantment" because of the difficulties of determining what is fair under the Fairness Doctrine. He added that after 20 years of interpreting that doctrine, there were no clear precedents to guide the agency. He summed up his position with: "Bluntly, the situation we face is a chaotic mess." *(ibid).*

what's "fair"

Mention was also made that the time of day and setting were important factors, that the "stop watch" theory was badly flawed, and, if practiced on every issue, was completely unworkable.

The Federal Communications Commission first applied the Fairness Doctrine to product advertising in *Banzhaf v. F.C.C.* 132 U.S. App. D.C. 14, 405 F.2d 1082 (19681. In affirming, the Court of Appeals for the District of Columbia found that the statutory mandate of section 315 of the Communications Act, that broadcast licensees "operate in the public interest . . . to afford [a] reasonable opportunity for the discussion of conflicting views on issues of public importance," required the presentation of anti-smoking messages.

Several recent F.C.C. decisions, however, appeared to deal serious blows to those who would further expand the Fairness Doctrine. *Business Executives' Move for Vietnam Peace,* 25 F.C.C.2d 242 (1970), and *Democratic National Committee,* 25 F.C.C.2d 216 (1970) held that broadcast licensees could, as a general policy, refuse to sell any of their advertising time to groups or individuals wishing to speak out on controversial public issues. And in *Friends of the Earth,* 24 F.C.C.2d 743 (1970), the Commission specifically held that *Banzhaf* did not apply to automobile and gasoline commercials, a holding echoed in the *Chevron F-310 Gasoline Advertising* case, No. 63705, FCC 71-526 (May 12, 1971) [2 ERC 1824].

court reverses FCC

Fortunately for environmentalists, the Court of Appeals has reversed the Commission's Fairness Doctrine holdings in both *Business Executives' Move* and *Democratic National Committee,* Nos. 24,492 and 24,537 (D.C. Cir., August 3, 1971) and in *Friends of the Earth,* No. 24,556 (D.C. Cir., August 16, 1971). In the former cases, Circuit Judge Wright held that "a flat ban on paid public issue announcements is in violation of the First Amendment, at least when other sorts of paid announcements are accepted." *B.E.M./D.N.C.,* slip opinion at 4. And in the latter case, Circuit Judge McGowan held that the Commission had improperly distinguished the cigarette commercials in *Banzhaf* from those for automobiles and gasoline in *Friends of the Earth. F.O.E.,* slip opinion at 14. Interestingly enough, the Commission itself acted as precursor to these events when it ruled that the Fairness Doctrine applied to Standard Oil of New Jersey (ESSO) commercials relating to the development of oil reserves on Alaska's North Slope, *In re National Broadcasting Company,* No. 63804, FCC 71-704 (June 30, 1971) [2 ERC 1716]—a holding quoted extensively by the court in *Friends of the Earth.* It thus appears likely that the court of appeals will continue to expand the Fairness Doctrine's applicability to product commercials by reversing the Commission's dismissal order in the *Chevron F-310 Gasoline* appeal, App. No. 71-1392 (D.C.C.A., filed May 24, 1971).

Despite the decision in *Business Executives' Move for Vietnam Peace v. Federal Communications Commission,* ___ F.2d ___ (D.C. Cir. Aug. 3, 1971), the policies of the television networks had not changed almost a year later. All three commercial networks continue a policy of not selling time to anyone for discussion of controversial issues that do not involve the sale of a product. In June of 1972, Sen Harold Hughes of Iowa and 13 other members of Congress complained to the FCC that they were refused the right to buy television broadcasting time to offer their views on the President's war policies. (Washington, D.C., *Evening Star,* June, 14, 1972 at A-4.) This occurred despite the explicit recognition by the court of appeals in the above case that speed of action was of great importance.

counter-commercials

On January 6, 1972, the Federal Trade Commission submitted a statement to the FCC supporting the concept of "counter-advertising," i.e., the right of access to the broadcast media for the purpose of expressing views and positions on controversial issues raised by commercial advertising. *In re The Handling of Public Issues Under the Fairness Doctrine and the Public Interest Standards of the Communications Act,* Part III, FCC Dkt. No. 19260 (January 6, 1972) (mimeograph). Portions of this statement follow:

> 1. *Advertising asserting claims of product performance of characteristics that explicitly raise controversial issues of current public importance.*" E.g., claims that products contribute to the solution of ecological problems, or that their companies are making special efforts to improve the environment generally.
>
> The FCC has recognized the Fairness Doctrine's applicability to this category of advertising. *See In re Complaint of the Wilderness Society, Friends of the Earth, et al,* (esso), 31 F.C.C. 2d 729 (September 23, 1971). 3 ERC 1292.

2. *Advertising stressing broad recurrent themes, affecting the purchase decision in a manner that implicitly raises controversial issues of current public importance.*" E.g., detergent ads which may be viewed as contributing to water pollution, or central themes associated by advertising with various product categories which some persons or groups may consider to be contributing factors to social and economic problems. *See Friends of the Earth v. FCC,* Dkt. 24, 566 (D.C. Cir., Aug. 16, 1971) 2 ERC 1900, in which the FCC found the Fairness Doctrine applicable to commercials insinuating that greater human personality fulfillment accrues to the owner of the large, powerful car.

3. *Advertising claims that rest upon or rely upon scientific premises which are currently subject to controversy within the scientific community.*" E.g., products advertised as being beneficial for the prevention or cure of common problems, or as being useful for particular purposes because of special properties with regard to performance, safety and efficacy.

4. *Advertising that is silent about negative aspects of the advertised product.*" E.g., contrasting the claims of small car advertisers emphasizing low cost and economy with those who view such cars as considerably less safe than larger cars, or countering the large car claims emphasizing safety and comfort with ads concerning the greater pollution arguably generated by such cars.

recommendations

The FTC then urged that "the following points be embodied in any final plan:

1. Adoption of rules that incorporate the guidelines expressed above, permitting effective access to the broadcast media for counter-advertisements. These rules should impose upon licensees an affirmative obligation to promote effective use of this expanded right of access.

2. Open availability of one hundred percent of commercial time for anyone willing to pay the specified rates, regardless of whether the party seeking to buy the time wishes to advertise or 'counter' advertise. Given the great importance of product information, product sellers should not possess monopolistic control by licensees over the dissemination of such information, and licensees should not be permitted to discriminate against counter-advertisers willing to pay, solely on account of the content of their ideas.

3. Provision by licensees of a substantial amount of time, at no charge, for persons and groups that wish to respond to advertising like that described above but lack the funds to purchase available time slots. In light of the above discussion, it seems manifest that licensees should not limit access, for discussions of issues raised by product commercials, to those capable of meeting a price determined by the profitability of presenting one side of the issues involved. Providing such free access would greatly enhance the probability that advertising, a process largely made possible by licensees themselves, would fully and fairly contribute to a healthy American marketplace.

But although counter-commercials have been the subject of considerable publicity in the printed media (*e.g., Newsweek,* June 5, 1972 at 65), and have gained some very limited local acceptance, they remain simply a suggestion on which the FCC has yet to react comprehensively.

The counter-commercial idea is based basically at combating untruths, yet with curious innocence, lobbyists and television industry executives alike proclaim that their branch of communications media could not survive the shock of truth. See the statements of former White House counsel Theodore Sorensen of the Television Bureau of Advertising, and Julian Goodman, president of the National Broadcasting Company, *Newsweek, supra.* Under present conditions, of course, they may be right: this author would not be the first to note that the amount of advertising seems to vary almost inversely with the real worth of a product. *See also,* "Administration Hits FTC Counter-Advertising Plan," *Washington Post,* Feb. 20, 1972 at K1.

REFERENCES AND SELECTED BIBLIOGRAPHY

Note, "The Fairness Doctrine and the Alaska Pipeline," 51 *B.U.L. Rev.* 698 (1971).

Note, "Friends of the Earth and the Fairness Doctrine," 36 *Albany L. Rev.* 216 (1971).

LEVENTHAL, Caution: Cigarette Commercials May Be Hazardous to Your License—the New Aspect of Fairness, 22 *Fed. Com. B.J.* 55 (1968)

F.C.C., Applicability of the Fairness Doctrine in the Handling of Controversial Issues of Public Importance, 29 *Fed. Reg.* no. 145, Pt. II, July 25, 1964 at 10415.

references

"The tuned-out, turned-off FCC," *Consumer Reports,* Oct. 1968 at 532

"Making FCC's Mission Impossible," *Consumer Reports,* February 1970 at 109

Two recent law review articles which are highly critical of the FCC's earlier holdings are the Editorial Note, "A Fair Break for Controversial Speakers: Limitations of the Fairness Doctrine and the Need for Individual Access," 39 *George Washington Law Review* 532 (March 1971), and Barr, "Using the FCC's Fairness Doctrine to Effect Environmental Reform," 1 *Environmental Affairs* (Boston College Environmental Law Society) 367 (June 1971).

Two organizations which represent the public interest in fights with the FCC and which have publications are:

Office of Communication, United Church of Christ, How To Protect Citizen Rights in Television and Radio, 289 Park Ave. South, New York, N.Y. 10010.

National Citizens Committee for Broadcasting, 609 Fifth Ave., New York, N.Y. 10017.

47 U.S.C. Sec. 315

(basis for candidates' equal time and fairness doctrines)

Sec. 315. Candidates for public office; facilities; rules

(a) If any licensee shall permit any person who is a legally qualified candidate for any public office to use a broadcasting station, he shall afford equal opportunities to all other such candidates for that office in the use of such broadcasting station: Provided, That such licensee shall have no power of censorship over the material broadcast under the provisions of this section. No obligation is imposed upon any licensee to allow the use of its station by any such candidate. Appearance by a legally qualified candidate on any—

(1) bona fide newscast

(2) bona fide news interview,

(3) bona fide news documentary (if the appearance of the candidate is incidental to the presentation of the subject or subjects covered by the news documentary), or

(4) on-the-spot coverage of bona fide news events (including but not limited to political conventions and activities incidental thereto),

shall not be deemed to be use of a broadcasting station within the meaning of this subsection. Nothing in the foregoing sentence shall be construed as relieving broadcasters, in connection with the presentation of newscasts, news interviews, news documentaries, and on-the-spot coverage of news events, from the obligation imposed upon them under this chapter to operate in the public interest and to afford reasonable opportunity for the discussion of conflicting views on issues of public importance.

(b) The charges made for the use of any broadcasting station for any of the purposes set forth in this section shall not exceed the charges made for comparable use of such station for other purposes.

APPENDIX—Chapter Five

STATE OF ILLINOIS v. CITY OF MILWAUKEE

U.S. Supreme Ct., April 24, 1972

MR. JUSTICE DOUGLAS delivered the opinion of the Court.

This is a motion by Illinois to file a complaint under our original jurisdiction against four cities of Wisconsin, the Sewerage Commission of the City of Milwaukee, and the Metropolitan Sewerage Commission of the County of Milwaukee. The cause of action alleged is pollution by the defendants of Lake Michigan, a body of interstate water. According to plaintiff, some 200 million gallons of raw or inadequately treated sewage and other waste materials are discharged daily into the lake in the Milwuakee area alone. Plaintiff alleges that it and its subdivisions prohibit and prevent such discharges, but that the defendants do not take such actions. Plaintiff asks that we abate this public nuisance.

I

Article III, § 2, cl. 2, of the Constitution provides: "In all Cases . . . in which a State shall be a party, the Supreme Court shall have original jurisdiction." Congress has provided in 28 U. S. C. § 1251 (a)(1) that "The Supreme Court shall have original and exclusive jurisdiction of: All controversies between two or more States . . . ."

It has long been this Court's philosophy that "our original jurisdiction should be invoked sparingly." *Utah* v. *United States,* 394 U. S. 89, 95. We construe 28 U. S. C. § 1251 (a)(1), as we do Art. III, § 2, cl. 2, to honor our original jurisdiction but to make it obligatory only in appropriate cases. And the question of what is appropriate concerns of course the seriousness and dignity of the claim; yet beyond that it necessarily involves the availability of another forum where there is jurisdiction over the named parties, where the issues tendered may be litigated, and where appropriate relief may be had. We incline to a sparing use of our original jurisdiction so that our increasing duties with the appellate docket will not suffer. *Washington* v. *General Motors Corp., post,* —.

Illinois presses its request for leave to file saying that the agencies named as defendants are instrumentalities of Wisconsin and therefore that this is a suit against Wisconsin which could not be brought in any other forum.

Under our decisions there is no doubt that the actions of public entities might, under appropriate pleadings, be attributed to a State so as to warrant a joinder of the State as party defendant.

In *Missouri* v. *Illinois,* 180 U. S. 208, Missouri invoked our original jurisdiction by an action against the State of Illinois and the Sanitary District of the City of Chicago, seeking an injunction to restrain the discharge of raw sewage into the Mississippi River. On a demurrer to the motion for leave to file a complaint, Illinois argued that the Sanitary District was the proper defendant and that Illinois should not have been made a party. That was rejected:

> "The contention . . . seems to be that, because the matters complained of in the bill proceed and will continue to proceed from the acts of the Sanitary District of Chicago, a corporation of the State of Illinois, it therefore follows that the State, as such, is not interested in the question, and is improperly made a party.
>
> "We are unable to see the force of this suggestion. The bill does not allege that the Sanitary District is acting without or in excess of lawful authority. The averment and the conceded facts are that the corporation is an agency of the State to do the very things which, according to the theory of the complainant's case, will result in the mischief to be apprehended. It is state action and its results that are complained of,—thus distinguishing this case from that of *Louisiana* v. *Texas* [176 U. S. 1], where the acts sought to be restrained were alleged to be those of officers or functionaries proceeding in a wrongful and malevolent misapplication of the quarantine laws of Texas. The Sanitary District of Chicago is not a private corporation, formed for purposes of private gain, but a public corporation, whose existence and operation are wholly within the control of the State.
>
> "The object of the bill is to subject this public work to judicial supervision, upon the allegation that the method of its construction and maintenance will create a continuing nuisance, dangerous to the health of a neighboring State and its inhabitants. Surely, in such a case, the State of Illinois would have a right to appear and traverse the allegations of the bill, and, having such a right, might properly be made a party defendant." 180 U. S., at 242.

In *New York* v. *New Jersey,* 256 U. S. 296, the State of New York brought an original action against the State of New Jersey and the Passaic Valley Sewerage Commissioners, seeking an injunction against the discharge of sewage in the Upper New York Bay. The question was whether the actions of the sewage agency could be attributed to New Jersey so as to make that State responsible for them. The Court said:

> "Also, for the purpose of showing the responsibility of the State of New Jersey for the proposed action of the defendant, the Passaic Valley Sewerage Commissioners, the bill sets out, with much detail, the acts of the legislature of that State authorizing and directing such action on their part.
>
> "Of this it is sufficient to say that the averments of the bill, quite undenied, show that the defendant sewerage commissioners constitute such a statutory, corporate agency of the State that their action, actual

or intended, must be treated as that of the State itself, and we shall so regard it." 256 U. S., at 302.

The most recent case is *New Jersey* v. *New York,* 345 U. S. 369. The action was originally brought by the State of New Jersey against the City and State of New York for injunctive relief against the diversion of waters from Delaware River tributaries lying within New York State. Pennsylvania was subsequently allowed to intervene. The question presented by this decision was the right of the City of Philadelphia also to intervene in the proceedings as a party plaintiff. The issues raised were broad:

"All of the present parties to the litigation have formally opposed the motion to intervene on grounds (1) that the intervention would permit a suit against a state by a citizen of another state in contravention of the Eleventh Amendment; (2) that the Commonwealth of Pennsylvania has the exclusive right to represent the interest of Philadelphia as *parens patriae;* and (3) that intervention should be denied, in any event, as a matter of sound discretion." 345 U. S., at 372.

We denied the City of Philadelphia's motion to intervene, saying:

"The City of Philadelphia represents only a part of the citizens of Pennsylvania who reside in the watershed area of the Delaware River and its tributaries and depend upon those waters. If we undertook to evaluate all the separate interests within Pennsylvania, we could, in effect, be drawn into an intramural dispute over the distribution of water within the Commonwealth. . . .

"Our original jurisdiction should not be thus expanded to the dimensions of ordinary class actions. An intervenor whose state is already a party should have the burden of showing some compelling interest in his own right, apart from his interest in a class with all other citizens and creatures of the state, which interest is not properly represented by the state." 345 U. S., at 373.

We added:

"The presence of New York City in this litigation is urged as a reason for permitting Philadelphia to intervene. But the argument misconstrues New York City's position in the case. New York City was not admitted into this litigation as a matter of discretion at her request. She was forcibly joined as a defendant to the original action since she was the authorized agent for the execution of the sovereign policy which threatened injury to the citizens of New Jersey. Because of this position as a defendant, subordinate to the parent state as primary defendant, New York City's position in the case raises no problems under the Eleventh Amendment." 345 U. S., at 374–375.

We conclude that while under appropriate pleadings, Wisconsin could be joined as a defendant in the present controversy, it is not mandatory that it be made one.

It is well settled that for the purposes of diversity of citizenship, political subdivisions are citizens of their respective States.[1] *Bullard* v. *City of Cisco,* 290 U. S. 179; *Cowles* v. *Mercer County,* 7 Wall. 118, 122. If a political subdivision is a citizen for diversity purposes, then it would make no jurisdictional difference whether it was the plaintiff or defendant in such an action. That being the case, a political subdivision in one State would be able to bring an action founded upon diversity jurisdiction against a political subdivision of another State.

We therefore conclude that the term "States" as used in 28 U. S. C. § 1251 (a)(1) should not be read to include their political subdivisions. That, of course, does not mean that political subdivisions of a State may not be sued under the head of our original jurisdiction, for 28 U. S. C. § 1251 (b)(3) provides that "The Supreme Court shall have original but not exclusive jurisdiction of . . . All actions or proceedings by a State against the citizens of another State . . . ."

If the named public entities of Wisconsin may, however, be sued by Illinois in a federal district court, our original jurisdiction is not mandatory.

It is to that aspect of the case that we now turn.

II

28 U. S. C. § 1331 (a) provides that "The district courts shall have original jurisdiction of all civil actions wherein the matter in controversy exceeds the sum or value of $10,000, exclusive of interest and costs, and arising under the Constitution, laws, or treaties of the United States."

The considerable interests involved in the purity of interstate waters would seem to put beyond question the jurisdictional amount provided in § 1331 (a). See *Glenwood Light & Water Co.* v. *Mutual Light, Heat & Power Co.,* 239 U. S. 121; *Mississippi & Missouri R.* v. *Ward,* 2 Black 485, 492; *Ronzio* v. *Denver & R. G. W. R.,* 116 F. 2d 604, 606; C. Wright, The Law of Federal Courts 117–119 (2d ed. 1970); Note, 73 Harv. L. Rev. 1369. The question is whether pollution of interstate or navigable waters creates actions arising under the "laws" of the United States within the meaning of § 1331(a). We hold that it does; and we also hold that § 1331 (a) includes suits brought by a State.

Mr. Justice Brennan, speaking for the four members of this Court in *Romero* v. *International Terminal Operating Co.,* 358 U. S. 354, 393, who reached the issue, concluded that "laws," within the meaning of § 1331 (a), embraced claims founded on federal common law:

"The contention cannot be accepted that since petitioner's rights are judicially defined, they are not created by 'the laws . . . of the United States' within the meaning of § 1331 . . . . In another context, that of state law, this Court has recognized that the statutory word 'laws' includes court

[1] It is equally well settled that a suit between a State and a citizen of another State is not a suit between citizens of different States for the purposes of diversity of citizenship jurisdiction. *Postal Telegraph Cable Co.* v. *Alabama,* 155 U. S. 482, 487.

decisions. The converse situation is presented here in that federal courts have an extensive responsibility of fashioning rules of substantive law . . . . These rules are as fully 'laws' of the United States as if they had been enacted by Congress." (Citations omitted.)

Lower courts have reached the same conclusion. See, *e. g., Murphy* v. *Colonial Federal Savings & Loan Assn.*, 388 F. 2d 609, 611–612 (CA2 1967); *Stokes* v. *Adair,* 265 F. 2d 662 (CA4 1959); *Mater* v. *Holley,* 200 F. 2d 123 (CA5 1952); ALI, Study of the Division of Jurisdiction Between State and Federal Courts 180–182 (1969).

Judge Harvey M. Johnsen in *Texas* v. *Pankey,* 441 F. 2d 236, 240, stated the controlling principle:

> "As the field of federal common law has been given necessary expansion into matters of federal concern and relationship (where no applicable federal statute exists, as there does not here), the ecological rights of a State in the improper impairment of them from sources outside the State's own territory, now would and should, we think, be held to be a matter having basis and standard in federal common law and so directly constituting a question arising under the laws of the United States."

Chief Judge Lumbard, speaking for the panel in *Ivy Broadcasting Co.* v. *American Tel. & Tel. Co.,* 391 F. 2d 486, 492, expressed the same view as follows:

> "We believe that a cause of action similarly 'arises under' federal law if the dispositive issues stated in the complaint require the application of federal common law . . . . The word 'laws' in § 1331 should be construed to include laws created by federal judicial decisions as well as by congressional legislation. The rationale of the 1875 grant of federal question jurisdiction—to insure the availability of a forum designed to minimize the danger of hostility toward, and specially suited to the vindication of, federally created rights—is as applicable to judicially created rights as to rights created by statute." (Citations omitted.)

We see no reason not to give "laws" its natural meaning, see *Romero* v. *International Terminal Operating Co., supra,* at 393 n. 5 (BRENNAN, J., dissenting), and therefore conclude that § 1331 jurisdiction will support claims founded upon federal common law as well as those of a statutory origin.

As respects the power of a State to bring an action under § 1331 (a), *Ames* v. *Kansas,* 111 U. S. 449, 470–472, is controlling. There Kansas had sued a number of corporations in its own courts and, since federal rights were involved, the defendants had the cases removed to the federal court. Kansas resisted saying that the federal court lacked jurisdiction because of Art. III, § 2, cl. 2 of the Constitution which gives this Court "original jurisdiction" in "all cases . . . in which a State shall be a party." The Court held that, where a State is suing parties who are not other States, the original jurisdiction of this Court is not exclusive (*Id.,* at 470) and that those suits "may now be brought in or removed to the Circuit Courts [now the District Courts] without regard to the character of the parties." [2] *Ibid.* We adhere to that ruling.

III

Congress has enacted numerous laws touching interstate waters. In 1899 it established some surveillance by the Corps of Engineers over industrial pollution, not including sewage, Rivers and Harbors Act of March 3, 1899, c. 425, 30 Stat. 1121, a grant of power which we construed in *United States* v. *Republic Steel Corp.,* 362 U. S. 482, and in *United States* v. *Standard Oil Co.,* 384 U. S. 224.

The 1899 Act has been reinforced and broadened by a complex of laws recently enacted. The Federal Water Pollution Control Act, 33 U. S. C. § 1151, tightens control over discharges into navigable waters so as not to lower applicable water quality standards. By the National Environmental Policy Act of 1969, 42 U. S. C. § 4321, Congress "authorizes and directs" that "the policies, regulations, and public laws of the United States shall be interpreted and administered in accordance with the policies set forth in this Act" and that "all agencies of the Federal Government shall . . . identify and develop methods and procedures . . . which will insure that presently unquantified environmental amenities and values may be given appropriate consideration in decision-making along with economic and technical considerations." Congress has evinced increasing concern with the quality of the aquatic environment as it affects the conservation and safeguarding of fish and wildlife resources. See, *e. g.,* Fish and Wild Life Act of 1956, 16 U. S. C. § 742a; the Migratory Marine Game Fish Act, 16 U. S. C. § 760c; and the Fish and Wildlife Coordination Act, 16 U. S. C. § 661.

Buttressed by these new and expanding policies, the Corps of Engineers has issued new Rules and Regulations governing permits for discharges or deposits into navigable waters. 36 Fed. Reg. 6564 *et seq.*

The Federal Water Pollution Control Act in § 1 (b) declares that it is federal policy "to recognize, preserve, and protect the primary responsibilities and rights of the States in preventing and controlling water pollution." But the Act makes clear that it is federal, not state, law that in the end controls the pollution of interstate or navigable waters.[3] While the States are given time to establish water quality standards, § 10 (c)(1), if a State fails to do so the federal administrator [4] promulgates

[2] See also H. R. Rep. No. 308, 80th Cong., 1st Sess., A 104 (1947): "The original jurisdiction conferred on the Supreme Court by Article 3, section 2, of the Constitution is not exclusive by virtue of that provision alone. Congress may provide for or deny exclusiveness."

[3] The contrary indication in *Ohio* v. *Wyandotte Chemicals Corp.,* 401 U. S. 493, 498, n. 3, was based on the preoccupation of that litigation with public nuisance under Ohio law, not the federal common law which we now hold is ample basis for federal jurisdiction under 28 U. S. C. § 1331 (a).

[4] The powers granted the Secretary of the Interior under the Federal Water Quality Act were assigned by the President to the Administrator of the Environmental Protection Agency pursuant to Reorganization Plan No. 3 of 1970. See 35 Fed. Reg. 15623.

one. § 10 (c)(2). Section 10 (a) makes pollution of interstate or navigable waters subject "to abatement" when it "endangers the health or welfare of any persons." The abatement that is authorized follows a long, drawn-out procedure unnecessary to relate here. It uses the conference procedure, hoping for amicable settlements. But if none is reached, the federal administrator may request the Attorney General to bring suit on behalf of the United States for abatement of the pollution. § 10 (g).

The remedy sought by Illinois is not within the precise scope of remedies prescribed by Congress. Yet the remedies which Congress provides are not necessarily the only federal remedies available. "It is not uncommon for federal courts to fashion federal law where federal rights are concerned." *Textile Workers* v. *Lincoln Mills*, 353 U. S. 448, 457. When we deal with air or water in their ambient or interstate aspects, there is a federal common law,[5] as *Texas* v. *Pankey*, 441 F. 2d 236, recently held.

The application of federal common law to abate a public nuisance in interstate or navigable waters is not inconsistent with the Water Pollution Control Act. Congress provided in § 10 (b) of that Act that, save as a court may decree otherwise in an enforcement action, "State and interstate action to abate pollution of interstate and navigable waters shall be encouraged and shall not . . . be displaced by federal enforcement action."

The leading air case is *Georgia* v. *Tennessee Copper Co.*, 206 U. S. 230, where Georgia filed an original suit in this Court against a Tennessee company whose noxious gases were causing a wholesale destruction of forests, orchards, and crops in Georgia. The Court said:

> "The caution with which demands of this sort, on the part of a State, for relief from injuries analogous to torts, must be examined, is dwelt upon in *Missouri* v. *Illinois*, 200 U. S. 496, 520, 521. But it is plain that some such demands must be recognized, if the grounds alleged are proved. When the States by their union made the forcible abatement of outside nuisances impossible to each, they did not thereby agree to submit to whatever might be done. They did not renounce the possibility of making reasonable demands on the ground of their still remaining *quasi*-sovereign interests; and the alternative to force is a suit in this court. *Missouri* v. *Illinois*, 180 U. S. 208, 241." 206 U. S., at 237.

The nature of the nuisance was described as follows:

> "It is a fair and reasonable demand on the part of a sovereign that the air over its territory should not be polluted on a great scale by sulphurous acid gas, that the forests on its mountains, be they better or worse, and whatever domestic destruction they have suffered, should not be further destroyed or threatened by the act of persons beyond its control, that the crops and orchards on its hills should not be endangered from the same source. If any such demand is to be enforced this must be, notwithstanding the hesitation that we might feel if the suit were between private parties, and the doubt whether for the injuries which they might be suffering to their property they should not be left to an action at law." *Id.*, at 238.

Our decisions concerning interstate waters contain the same theme. Rights in interstate streams, like questions of boundaries, "have been recognized as presenting federal questions."[6] *Hinderlider* v. *LaPlata Co.*, 304 U. S. 92, 110. The question of apportionment of interstate waters is a question of "federal common law" upon which state statutes or decisions are not conclusive.[7] *Ibid.*

In speaking of the problem of apportioning the waters of an interstate stream, the Court said in *Kansas* v. *Colorado*, 206 U. S. 46, 98, that "through these successive disputes and decisions this Court is practically building up what may not improperly be called interstate common law." And see *Texas* v. *New Jersey*, 379 U. S. 674 (escheat of intangible personal property), *Texas* v. *Florida*, 306 U. S. 398, 405 (suit by bill in the nature of interpleader to determine the true domicile of a decedent as the basis of death taxes).

---

[5] While the various federal environmental protection statutes will not necessarily mark the outer bounds of the federal common law, they may provide useful guidelines in fashioning such rules of decision. What we said in another connection in *Textile Workers* v. *Lincoln Mills*, 353 U. S. 448, 456–457, is relevent here:

"The question then is, what is the substantive law to be applied in suits brought under § 301 (a)? We conclude that the substantive law to apply in suits under § 301 (a) is federal law, which the courts must fashion from the policy of our national labor laws. The Labor Management Relations Act expressly furnishes some substantive law. It points out what the parties may or may not do in certain situations. Other problems will lie in the penumbra of express statutory mandates. Some will lack express statutory sanction but will be solved by looking at the policy of the legislation and fashioning a remedy that will effectuate that policy. The range of judicial inventiveness will be determined by the nature of the problem. Federal interpretation of the federal law will govern, not state law. But state law, if compatible with the purpose of § 301, may be resorted to in order to find the rule that will best effectuate the federal policy. Any state law applied, however, will be absorbed as federal law and will not be an independent source of private rights." (Citations omitted.) See also Woods & Reed, The Supreme Court and Interstate Environmental Quality: Some Notes on the Wyandotte Case, 12 Ariz. L. Rev. 691, 713–714; Note, 56 Va. L. Rev. 458.

[6] Thus, it is not only the character of the parties which requires us to apply federal law. See *Georgia* v. *Tennessee Copper Co.*, 206 U. S. 230, 237; cf. *Wisconsin* v. *Pelican Ins. Co.*, 127 U. S. 265, 269; The Federalist No. 80 (A. Hamilton). As Mr. Justice Harlan indicated for the Court in *Banco Nacional de Cuba* v. *Sabbatino*, 376 U. S. 398, 421–427, where there is an overriding federal interest in the need for a uniform rule of decision or where the controversy touches basic interests of federalism, we have fashioned federal common law. See also *Clearfield Trust Co.* v. *United States*, 318 U. S. 363; *D'Oench, Duhme & Co.* v. *Federal Deposit Ins. Corp.*, 315 U. S. 447; C. Wright, The Law of Federal Courts 249 (2d ed. 1970); Woods & Reed, The Supreme Court and Interstate Environmental Quality: Some Notes on the Wyandotte Case, 12 Ariz. L. Rev. 691, 703–713; Note, 50 Texas L. Rev. 183. Certainly these same demands for applying federal law are present in the pollution of a body of water such as Lake Michigan bounded, as it is, by four States.

[7] Those who maintain that state law governs overlook the fact that the *Hinderlider* case was authored by Mr. Justice Brandeis who also wrote for the Court in *Erie R. Co.* v. *Tompkins*, 304 U. S. 64, the two cases being decided the same day.

Equitable apportionment of the waters of an interstate stream has often been made under the head of our original jurisdiction. *Nebraska* v. *Wyoming,* 325 U. S. 589; *Kansas* v. *Colorado,* 206 U. S. 469; cf. *Arizona* v. *California,* 373 U. S. 546, 562. The applicable federal common law depends on the facts peculiar to the particular case.

> "Priority of appropriation is the guiding principle. But physical and climatic conditions, the consumptive use of water in the several sections of the river, the character and rate of return flows, the extent of established uses, the availability of storage water, the practical effect of wasteful uses on downstream areas, the damage to upstream areas as compared to the benefits to downstream areas if a limitation is imposed on the former—these are all relevant factors. They are merely an illustrative, not an exhaustive catalogue. They indicate the nature of the problem of apportionment and the delicate adjustment of interests which must be made." 325 U. S., at 618.

When it comes to water pollution this Court has spoken in terms of "a public nuisance," [8] *New York* v. *New Jersey,* 256 U. S. 296, 313; *New Jersey* v. *New York City,* 283 U. S. 473, 481, 482. In *Missouri* v. *Illinois,* 200 U. S. 496, 520–521, the Court said, "It may be imagined that a nuisance might be created by a State upon a navigable river like the Danube, which would amount to a *casus belli* for a State lower down, unless removed. If such a nuisance were created by a State upon the Mississippi the controversy would be resolved by the more peaceful means of a suit in this Court."

It may happen that new federal laws and new federal regulations may in time pre-empt the field of federal common law of nuisance. But until that comes to pass, federal courts will be empowered to appraise the equities of the suits alleging creation of a public nuisance by water pollution. While federal law governs,[9] consideration of state standards may be relevant. Cf. *Connecticut* v. *Massachusetts,* 282 U. S. 660, 670; *Kansas* v. *Colorado,* 185 U. S. 125, 146–147. Thus a State with high water quality standards may well ask that its strict standards be honored and that it not be compelled to lower itself to the more degrading standards of a neighbor. There are no fixed rules that govern; these will be equity suits in which the informed judgment of the chancellor will largely govern.

We deny, without prejudice, the motion for leave to file. While this original suit normally might be the appropriate vehicle for resolving this controversy, we exercise our discretion to remit the parties to an appropriate District Court [10] whose powers are adequate to resolve the issues.

So ordered.

---

[8] In *North Dakota* v. *Minnesota,* 263 U. S. 365, 374, the Court said:

"... where one State, by a change in its method of draining water from lands within its border, increases the flow into an interstate stream, so that its natural capacity is greatly exceeded and the water is thrown upon the farms of another State, the latter State has such an interest as quasi-sovereign in the comfort, health and prosperity of its farm owners that resort may be had to this Court for relief. It is the creation of a public nuisance of simple type for which a State may properly ask an injunction."

[9] "Federal common law and not the varying common law of the individual States is, we think, entitled and necessary to be recognized as a basis for dealing in uniform standard with the environmental rights of a State against improper impairment by sources outsides its domain. The more would this seem to be imperative in the present era of growing concern on the part of a State about its ecological conditions and impairments of them. In the outside sources of such impairment, more conflicting disputes, increasing assertions and proliferating contentions would seem to be inevitable. Until the field has been made the subject of comprehensive legislation or authorized administrative standards, only a federal common law basis can provide an adequate means for dealing with such claims as alleged federal rights. And the logic and practicality of regarding such claims as being entitled to be asserted within the federal-question jurisdiction of § 1331 (a) would seem to be self-evident." *Texas* v. *Pankey, supra,* 241–242.

[10] The rule of decision being federal, the "action . . . may be brought only in the judicial district where all defendants reside, or in which the claim arose," 28 U. S. C. § 1391 (b), thereby giving flexibility to the choice of venue. See also 28 U. S. C. § 1407.

Whatever may be a municipality's sovereign immunity in actions for damages, see Van Alstyne, Governmental Tort Liability: A Decade of Change, 1966 Ill. L. F. 919, 944–948; Note, 4 Suffolk L. Rev. 832 (1969), actions seeking injunctive relief stand on a different footing. The cases are virtually unanimous in holding that municipalities are subject to injunctions to abate nuisances. See cases collected in 17 McQuillin, The Law of Municipal Corporations § 49.51 *et seq.* (3d rev. ed. 1968). See also Wis. Stat. Ann. § 5996 (6)(b) (1957) as respects the suability of metropolitan sewage commissions.

While the kind of equitable relief to be accorded lies in the discretion of the chancellor (*City of Harrisonville* v. *Dickey Clay Mfg. Co.,* 289 U. S. 334), a State that causes a public nuisance is suable in this Court and any of its public entities is suable in a federal district court having jurisdiction:

"... it is generally held that a municipality, like a private individual, may be enjoined from maintaining a nuisance. Thus in a proper case a municipal corporation will be restrained by injunction from creating a nuisance on private property, as by the discharge of sewage or poisonous gases thereon, or, in some jurisdictions, by the obstruction of drainage of waters, or by discharging sewage or filth into a stream and polluting the water to the damage of lower riparian owners, or by dumping garbage or refuse, or by other acts. Likewise, a municipality may be enjoined from creating or operating a nuisance, whether the municipality is acting in a governmental or proprietary capacity, impairing property rights. And, if a nuisance is established causing irreparable injury for which there is no adequate remedy at law it may be enjoined irrespective of the resulting damage or injury in the municipality." 17 McQuillin, *supra,* § 49.55.

STATE OF WASHINGTON v. GENERAL MOTORS CORP.
U.S. Supreme Ct., April 24, 1972

MR. JUSTICE DOUGLAS delivered the opinion of the Court.

Plaintiffs are 18 States who, by this motion for leave to file a complaint, seek to invoke this Court's original jurisdiction under Art. III, § 2, cl. 2 of the Constitution.[1] Named as defendants are the Nation's four major automobile manufacturers and their trade association.

Plaintiffs allege a conspiracy among the defendants to restrain the development of motor vehicle air pollution control equipment. They allege that the conspiracy began as early as 1953 but was concealed until January 1969. Count I of the proposed complaint charges a violation of the federal antitrust laws. Count II charges a common-law conspiracy in restraint of trade independent of the Sherman and Clayton Acts.[2] In their prayer for relief, plaintiffs seek an injunction requiring the defendants to undertake "an accelerated program of spending, research and development designed to produce a fully effective pollution control device or devices and/or pollution free engine at the earliest feasible date" and also ordering defendants to install effective pollution control devices in all motor vehicles they manufactured during the conspiracy and as standard equipment in all future motor vehicles which they manufacture. Other prophylactic relief is also sought.

The proposed complaint plainly presents important questions of vital national importance. See, *e. g.*, Hearings before the Subcommittee on Air and Water Pollution of the Senate Committee on Public Works, 90th Cong., 1st Sess. (1967). Our jurisdiction over the controversy cannot be disputed. *Georgia* v. *Pennsylvania R. Co.*, 324 U. S. 439; *Georgia* v. *Tennessee Copper Co.*, 206 U. S. 230. For reasons which will appear, however, we deny leave to file the complaint.

The gravamen of plaintiffs' allegations is a horizontal conspiracy among the major automobile manufacturers to impede the research and development of automotive air pollution control devices. See generally L. Jaffe & L. Tribe, Environmental Protection 141–180 (1971). It is argued that the facts alleged in support of the statutory and common-law claims are identical and that they could be elicited as well by a Special Master appointed by this Court as by a federal district court judge, and that resort to a Special Master would not place a burden on this Court's time and resources substantially greater than when we hear an antitrust case on direct appeal from a district court under the Expediting Act, 15 U. S. C. § 29. And it is argued that the sheer number of States that seek to invoke our original jurisdiction in this motion is reason enough for us to grant leave to file.[3]

The breadth of the constitutional grant of this Court's original jurisdiction dictates that we be able to exercise discretion over the cases we hear under this jurisdictional head, lest our ability to administer our appellate docket be impaired. *Massachusetts* v. *Missouri,* 308 U. S. 1, 19; *Ohio* v. *Wyandotte Chemicals Corp.,* 401 U. S. 493, 497–499; H. Hart & H. Wechsler, The Federal Courts and the Federal System 258–260 (1953); Woods & Reed, The Supreme Court and Interstate Environmental Quality: Some Notes on the Wyandotte Case, 12 Ariz. L. Rev. 691; Note, 11 Stanford L. Rev. 665, 694–700. In *Massachusetts* v. *Missouri, supra,* at 18–19, where Massachusetts sought to invoke our original jurisdiction in order to collect a tax claim, we said:

> "In the exercise of our original jurisdiction so as truly to fulfill the constitutional purpose we not only must look to the nature of the interest of the complaining State—the essential quality of the right asserted—but we must also inquire whether recourse to that jurisdiction . . . is necessary for the State's protection. . . . To open this Court to actions by States to recover taxes claimed to be payable by citizens of other States, in the absence of facts showing the necessity for such intervention, would be to assume a burden which the grant of original jurisdiction cannot be regarded as compelling this Court to assume and which might seriously interfere with the discharge by this Court of its duty in deciding the cases and controversies appropriately brought before it."

By the same token, we conclude that the availability of the Federal District Court as an alternative forum and the nature of the relief requested suggest we remit the parties to the resolution of their controversies in the customary forum. The nature of the remedy which may

[1] Fifteen States originally moved for leave to file a complaint. We subsequently granted leave to the State of Idaho to intervene as plaintiff. 403 U. S. 949. By today's decision we also grant leave to the States of North Dakota and West Virginia to be joined as parties plaintiff.

[2] A third count of plaintiffs' proposed complaint also charged "a public nuisance contrary to the public policy of the Plaintiff States . . . [and] the federal government." Motion for Leave to File Complaint, at 12. In a memorandum filed with this Court February 19, 1972, however, plaintiffs struck this count from their proposed complaint; but Idaho, the intervenor, did not join in that motion. In light of our disposition of Counts I and II of the complaint, Idaho's motion for leave to file a bill of complaint solely for Count III should be denied *a fortiori.* Should any of the plaintiffs desire to renew the public nuisance count of the complaint in the District Court, they are free to do so under our decision today in *Illinois* v. *City of Milwaukee, ante,* at —.

[3] In addition to the 18 States who are plaintiffs, 16 other States and the City of New York have filed a brief as *amicus curiae* supporting plaintiffs' motion for leave to file a complaint.

be necessary, if a case for relief is made out, also argues against taking original jurisdiction.

Air pollution is, of course, one of the most notorious types of public nuisance in modern experience. Congress has not, however, found a uniform, nationwide solution to all aspects of this problem and, indeed, has declared "that the prevention and control of air pollution at its source is the primary responsibility of States and local governments." 42 U. S. C. § 1857a (3). To be sure, Congress has largely pre-empted the field with regard to "emissions from new motor vehicles," 42 U. S. C. § 1857–6a (a); 31 Fed. Reg. 5170 (1966); and motor vehicle fuels and fuel additives. 42 U. S. C. §§ 1857f–6c (c)(4). See Currie, Motor Vehicle Air Pollution: State Authority and Federal Pre-emption, 68 Mich. L. Rev. 1083 (1970); Hill, The Politics of Air Pollution: Public Interest and Pressure Groups, 10 Ariz. L. Rev. 37, 44–45 (1968); Stevens, Air Pollution and the Federal System: Responses to Felt Necessities, 22 Hastings L. J. 661, 674–676 (1971). It has also pre-empted the field so far as emissions from airplanes are concerned. 42 U. S. C. §§ 1857f–9 to 1857f–12. So far as factories, incinerators, and other stationary devices are implicated, the States have broad control to an extent not necessary to relate here.[4] See Stevens, *supra, passim;* Comment, 58 Calif. L. Rev. 1474 (1970). But in certain instances, as for example, where federal primary and secondary ambient air quality standards have been established,[5] 42 U. S. C. §§ 1857c–4 and 1857c–5, or where "hazardous air pollutants" have been defined, 42 U. S. C. § 1857c–7, there may be federal pre-emption. See 42 U. S. C. § 1857c–8 *et seq.* Moreover, geophysical characteristics which define local and regional airsheds are often significant considerations in determining the steps necessary to abate air pollution. See Hearings before the Subcommittee on Air and Water Pollution of the Senate Committee on Public Works, 90th Cong., 1st Sess., at 130 (1967); Coons, Air Pollution and Government Structure, 10 Ariz. L. Rev. 48, 60–64 (1968). Thus, measures which might be adequate to deal with pollution in a city such as San Francisco, might be grossly inadequate in a city such as Phoenix, where geographical and meteorological conditions trap aerosols and particulates.

As a matter of law as well as practical necessity corrective remedies for air pollution, therefore, necessarily must be considered in the context of localized situations.[6] We conclude that the causes should be heard in the appropriate federal district courts.[7]

The motions of the States of North Dakota and West Virginia to be joined as parties plaintiff are granted. The motion for leave to file a complaint is denied and the parties are remitted without prejudice to the other federal forum.

It is so ordered.

MR. JUSTICE POWELL took no part in the consideration or decision of these motions.

---

[4] Because federal motor vehicle emission control standards apply only to new motor vehicles, States also retain broad residual power over used motor vehicles. Moreover, citizens, States, and local governments may initiate actions to enforce compliance with federal standards and to enforce other statutory and common law rights. 42 U. S. C. § 1857h–2.

[5] National primary ambient air quality standards are those "which in the judgment of the Administrator [of the Environmental Protection Agency] . . . are requisite to protect the public health . . . ." 42 U. S. C. § 1857c–4 (b)(1). Secondary ambient air quality standards are those "requisite to protect the public welfare," 42 U. S. C. § 1857c–4 (b)(2), which "includes, but is not limited to, effects on soils, water, crops, vegetation, manmade materials, animals, wildlife, weather, visibility and climate damage to and deterioration of property, and hazards to transportation, as well as effects on economic values and on personal comfort and well-being." 42 U. S. C. § 1857h (h). For implementation plans for primary and secondary ambient air quality standards, see 42 U. S. C. § 1857c–5.

[6] It was in recognition of this fact that Congress directed the Administrator of the Environmental Protection Agency to "designate as an air quality control region any interstate area or major intrastate area which he deems necessary or appropriate for the attainment and maintenance of ambient air quality standards." 42 U. S. C. § 1857c–2 (c).

[7] Multi-district litigation apparently involving the same factual claims as are presented here has been consolidated in the District Court for the Central District of California and pretrial proceedings are already underway. See *In re Motor Vehicle Air Pollution Control Equipment,* 311 F. Supp. 1349 (J. P. M. L. 1970).

SIERRA CLUB v. MORTON

U.S. Supreme Ct., April 19, 1972

MR. JUSTICE STEWART delivered the opinion of the Court.

I

The Mineral King Valley is an area of great natural beauty nestled in the Sierra Nevada Mountains in Tulare County, California, adjacent to Sequoia National Park. It has been part of the Sequoia National Forest since 1926, and is designated as a National Game Refuge by special Act of Congress.[1] Though once the site of extensive mining activity, Mineral King is now used almost exclusively for recreational purposes. Its relative inaccessibility and lack of development have limited the number of visitors each year, and at the same time have preserved the valley's quality as a quasi-wilderness area largely uncluttered by the products of civilization.

The United States Forest Service, which is entrusted with the maintenance and administration of national forests, began in the late 1940's to give consideration to Mineral King as a potential site for recreational development. Prodded by a rapidly increasing demand for skiing facilities, the Forest Service published a prospectus in 1965, inviting bids from private developers for the construction and operation of a ski resort that would also serve as a summer recreation area. The proposal of Walt Disney Enterprises, Inc., was chosen from those of six bidders, and Disney received a three-year permit to conduct surveys and explorations in the valley in connection with its preparation of a complete master plan for the resort.

The final Disney plan, approved by the Forest Service in January, 1969, outlines a $35 million complex of motels, restaurants, swimming pools, parking lots, and other structures designed to accommodate 14,000 visitors daily. This complex is to be constructed on 80 acres of the valley floor under a 30-year use permit from the Forest Service. Other facilities, including ski lifts, ski trails, a cog-assisted railway, and utility installations, are to be constructed on the mountain slopes and in other parts of the valley under a revocable special use permit. To provide access to the resort, the State of California proposes to construct a highway 20 miles in length. A section of this road would traverse Sequoia National Park, as would a proposed high-voltage power line needed to provide electricity for the resort. Both the highway and the power line require the approval of the Department of the Interior, which is entrusted with the preservation and maintenance of the national parks.

Representatives of the Sierra Club, who favor maintaining Mineral King largely in its present state, followed the progress of recreational planning for the valley with close attention and increasing dismay. They unsuccessfully sought a public hearing on the proposed development in 1965, and in subsequent correspondence with officials of the Forest Service and the Department of the Interior, they expressed the Club's objections to Disney's plan as a whole and to particular features included in it. In June of 1969 the Club filed the present suit in the United States District Court for the Northern District of California, seeking a declaratory judgment that various aspects of the proposed development contravene federal laws and regulations governing the preservation of national parks, forests, and game refuges,[2] and also seeking preliminary and permanent injunctions restraining the federal officials involved from granting their approval or issuing permits in connection with the Mineral King project. The petitioner Sierra Club sued as a membership corporation with "a special interest in the conservation and sound maintenance of the national parks, game refuges, and forests of the country," and invoked the judicial review provisions of the Administrative Procedure Act, 5 U. S. C. § 701 *et seq.*

After two days of hearings, the District Court granted the requested preliminary injunction. It rejected the respondents' challenge to the Sierra Club's standing to sue, and determined that the hearing had raised questions "concerning possible excess of statutory authority, sufficiently substantial and serious to justify a preliminary injunction . . . ." The respondents appealed, and the Court of Appeals for the Ninth Circuit reversed. 433 F. 2d 24. With respect to the petitioner's standing, the court noted that there was "no allegation in the complaint that members of the Sierra Club would be affected by the actions of [the respondents] other than the fact that the actions are personally displeasing or distasteful to them," *id.*, at 33, and concluded:

> "We do not believe such club concern without a showing of more direct interest can constitute

[1] Act of July 3, 1926, 44 Stat. 821, 16 U. S. C. § 688.

[2] As analyzed by the District Court, the complaint alleged violations of law falling into four categories. First, it claimed that the special use permit for construction of the resort exceeded the maximum acreage limitation placed upon such permits by 16 U. S. C. § 497, and that issuance of a "revocable" use permit was beyond the authority of the Forest Service. Second, it challenged the proposed permit for the highway through Sequoia National Park on the grounds that the highway would not serve any of the purposes of the park in alleged violation of 16 U. S. C. § 1, and that it would destroy timber and other natural resources protected by 16 U. S. C. §§ 41 and 43. Third, it claimed that the Forest Service and the Department of the Interior had violated their own regulations by failing to hold adequate public hearings on the proposed project. Finally, the complaint asserted that 16 U. S. C. § 45 (c) requires specific congressional authorization of a permit for construction of a power transmission line within the limits of a national park.

standing in the legal sense sufficient to challenge the exercise of responsibilities on behalf of all the citizens by two cabinet level officials of the government acting under Congressional and Constitutional authority." *Id.*, at 30.

Alternatively, the Court of Appeals held that the Sierra Club had not made an adequate showing of irreparable injury and likelihood of success on the merits to justify issuance of a preliminary injunction. The court thus vacated the injunction. The Sierra Club filed a petition for a writ of certiorari which we granted, 401 U. S. 907, to review the questions of federal law presented.

II

The first question presented is whether the Sierra Club has alleged facts that entitle it to obtain judicial review of the challenged action. Whether a party has a sufficient stake in an otherwise justiciable controversy to obtain judicial resolution of that controversy is what has traditionally been referred to as the question of standing to sue. Where the party does not rely on any specific statute authorizing invocation of the judicial process, the question of standing depends upon whether the party has alleged such a "personal stake in the outcome of the controversy," *Baker* v. *Carr*, 369 U. S. 186, 204, as to ensure that "the dispute sought to be adjudicated will be presented in an adversary context and in a form historically viewed as capable of judicial resolution." *Flast* v. *Cohen*, 392 U. S. 83, 101. Where, however, Congress has authorized public officials to perform certain functions according to law, and has provided by statute for judicial review of those actions under certain circumstances, the inquiry as to standing must begin with a determination of whether the statute in question authorizes review at the behest of the plaintiff.[3]

The Sierra Club relies upon § 10 of the Administrative Procedure Act (APA), 80 Stat. 392, 5 U. S. C. § 702, which provides:

> "A person suffering legal wrong because of agency action, or adversely affected or aggrieved by agency action within the meaning of a relevant statute, is entitled to judicial review thereof."

Early decisions under this statute interpreted the language as adopting the various formulations of "legal interest" and "legal wrong" then prevailing as constitutional requirements of standing.[4] But, in *Association of Data Processing Service Organizations, Inc.* v. *Camp*, 397 U. S. 150, and *Barlow* v. *Collins*, 397 U. S. 157, decided the same day, we held more broadly that persons had standing to obtain judicial review of federal agency action under § 10 of the APA where they had alleged that the challenged action had caused them "injury in fact," and where the alleged injury was to an interest "arguably within the zone of interests to be protected or regulated" by the statutes that the agencies were claimed to have violated.[5]

In *Data Processing*, the injury claimed by the petitioners consisted of harm to their competitive position in the computer servicing market through a ruling by the Comptroller of the Currency that national banks might perform data processing services for their customers. In *Barlow*, the petitioners were tenant farmers who claimed that certain regulations of the Secretary of Agriculture adversely affected their economic position *vis-à-vis* their landlords. These palpable economic injuries have long been recognized as sufficient to lay the basis for standing, with or without a specific statutory provision for judicial review.[6] Thus, neither *Data Processing* nor *Barlow* addressed itself to the question, which has arisen with increasing frequency in federal courts in recent years, as to what must be alleged by persons who claim injury of a noneconomic nature to interests that are widely shared.[7] That question is presented in this case.

III

The injury alleged by the Sierra Club will be incurred entirely by reason of the change in the uses to which Mineral King will be put, and the attendant change in the aesthetics and ecology of the area. Thus, in referring to the road to be built through Sequoia National Park, the complaint alleged that the development "would destroy or otherwise affect the scenery, natural and historic objects and wildlife of the park and would impair the enjoyment of the park for future generations." We do not question that this type of harm may amount to an "injury in fact" sufficient to

[3] Congress may not confer jurisdiction on Art. III federal courts to render advisory opinions, *Muskrat* v. *United States*, 219 U. S. 346, or to entertain "friendly" suits, *United States* v. *Johnson*, 319 U. S. 302, or to resolve "political questions," *Luther* v. *Borden*, 7 How. 1, because suits of this character are inconsistent with the judicial function under Art. III. But where a dispute is otherwise justiciable, the question whether the litigant is a "proper party to request an adjudication of a particular issue," *Flast* v. *Cohen*, 392 U. S. 83, 100, is one within the power of Congress to determine. Cf. *FCC* v. *Sanders Bros. Radio Station*, 309 U. S. 470, 477; *Flast* v. *Cohen*, 392 U. S. 83, 120 (Harlan, J., dissenting); *Associated Industries* v. *Ickes*, 134 F. 2d 694, 704. See generally Berger, Standing to Sue in Public Actions: Is it a Constitutional Requirement?, 78 Yale L. J. 816, 837 ff. (1969); Jaffe, The Citizen as Litigant in Public Actions: The Non-Hohfeldian or Ideological Plaintiff, 116 U. Pa. L. Rev. 1033 (1968).

[4] See, *e. g.*, *Kansas City Power & Light Co.* v. *McKay*, 225 F. 2d 924, 932; *Ove Gustavsson Contracting Co.* v. *Floete*, 278 F. 2d 912, 914; *Duba* v. *Schuetzle*, 303 F. 2d 570, 574. The theory of a "legal interest" is expressed in its extreme form in *Alabama Power Co.* v. *Ickes*, 302 U. S. 464, 479–481. See also *Tennessee Electric Power Co.* v. *TVA*, 306 U. S. 118, 137–139.

[5] In deciding this case we do not reach any questions concerning the meaning of the "zone of interests" test or its possible application to the facts here presented.

[6] See, *e. g.*, *Hardin* v. *Kentucky Utilities Co.*, 390 U. S. 1, 7; *Chicago* v. *Atchison, T. & S. F. R. Co.*, 357 U. S. 77, 83; *FCC* v. *Sanders Bros. Radio Station*, 309 U. S. 470, 477.

[7] No question of standing was raised in *Citizens to Preserve Overton Park, Inc.* v. *Volpe*, 401 U. S. 402. The complaint in that case alleged that the organizational plaintiff represented members who were "residents of Memphis, Tennessee who use Overton Park as a park land and recreation area and who have been active since 1964 in efforts to preserve and protect Overton Park as a park land and recreation area."

lay the basis for standing under § 10 of the APA. Aesthetic and environmental well-being, like economic well-being, are important ingredients of the quality of life in our society, and the fact that particular environmental interests are shared by the many rather than the few does not make them less deserving of legal protection through the judicial process. But the "injury in fact" test requires more than an injury to a cognizable interest. It requires that the party seeking review be himself among the injured.

The impact of the proposed changes in the environment of Mineral King will not fall indiscriminately upon every citizen. The alleged injury will be felt directly only by those who use Mineral King and Sequoia National Park, and for whom the aesthetic and recreational values of the area will be lessened by the highway and ski resort. The Sierra Club failed to allege that it or its members would be affected in any of their activities or pastimes by the Disney development. Nowhere in the pleadings or affidavits did the Club state that its members use Mineral King for any purpose, much less that they use it in any way that would be significantly affected by the proposed actions of the respondents.[8]

The Club apparently regarded any allegations of individualized injury as superfluous, on the theory that this was a "public" action involving questions as to the use of natural resources, and that the Club's longstanding concern with and expertise in such matters were sufficient to give it standing as a "representative of the public."[9] This theory reflects a misunderstanding of our cases involving so-called "public actions" in the area of administrative law.

The origin of the theory advanced by the Sierra Club may be traced to a dictum in *Scripps-Howard Radio, Inc.* v. *FCC*, 316 U. S. 4, in which the licensee of a radio station in Cincinnati, Ohio, sought a stay of an order of the FCC allowing another radio station in a nearby city to change its frequency and increase its range. In discussing its power to grant a stay, the Court noted that "these private litigants have standing only as representatives of the public interest." *Id.*, at 14. But that observation did not describe the basis upon which the appellant was allowed to obtain judicial review as a "person aggrieved" within the meaning of the statute involved in that case,[10] since Scripps-Howard was clearly "aggrieved" by reason of the economic injury that it would suffer as a result of the Commission's action.[11] The Court's statement was rather directed to the theory upon which Congress had authorized judicial review of the Commission's actions. That theory had been described earlier in *FCC* v. *Sanders Bros. Radio Station*, 309 U. S. 470, 477, as follows:

> "Congress had some purpose in enacting § 402 (b)(2). It may have been of opinion that one likely to be financially injured by the issue of a license would be the only person having a sufficient interest to bring to the attention of the appellate court errors of law in the action of the Commission in granting the license. It is within the power of Congress to confer such standing to prosecute an appeal."

Taken together, *Sanders* and *Scripps-Howard* thus established a dual proposition: the fact of economic injury is what gives a person standing to seek judicial review under the statute, but once review is properly invoked, that person may argue the public interest in support of his claim that the agency has failed to comply with its statutory mandate.[12] It was in the latter sense that the "standing" of the appellant in *Scripps-Howard* existed only as a "representative of the public interest." It is in a similar sense that we have used the phrase "private attorney general" to describe the function performed by persons upon whom Congress has conferred the right to seek judicial re-

[8] The only reference in the pleadings to the Sierra Club's interest in the dispute is contained in paragraph 3 of the complaint, which reads in its entirety as follows:

"Plaintiff Sierra Club is a non-profit corporation organized and operating under the laws of the State of California, with its principal place of business in San Francisco, California since 1892. Membership of the Club is approximately 78,000 nationally, with approximately 27,000 members residing in the San Francisco Bay area. For many years the Sierra Club by its activities and conduct has exhibited a special interest in the conservation and sound maintenance of the national parks, game refuges and forests of the country, regularly serving as a responsible representative of persons similarly interested. One of the principal purposes of the Sierra Club is to protect and conserve the national resources of the Sierra Nevada Mountains. Its interests would be vitally affected by the acts hereinafter described and would be aggrieved by those acts of the defendants as hereinafter more fully appears."

In an *amici curiae* brief filed in this Court by the Wilderness Society and others, it is asserted that the Sierra Club has conducted regular camping trips into the Mineral King area, and that various members of the Club have used and continue to use the area for recreational purposes. These allegations were not contained in the pleadings, nor were they brought to the attention of the Court of Appeals. Moreover, the Sierra Club in its reply brief specifically declines to rely on its individualized interest, as a basis for standing. See n. 15, *infra*. Our decision does not, of course, bar the Sierra Club from seeking in the District Court to amend its complaint by a motion under Rule 15, Federal Rules of Civil Procedure.

[9] This approach to the question of standing was adopted by the Court of Appeals for the Second Circuit in *Citizens Committee for the Hudson Valley* v. *Volpe*, 425 F. 2d 97, 105:

"We hold, therefore, that the public interest in environmental resources—an interest created by statutes affecting the issuance of this permit—is a legally protected interest affording these plaintiffs, as responsible representatives of the public, standing to obtain judicial review of agency action alleged to be in contravention of that public interest."

[10] The statute involved was § 402 (b)(2) of the Communications Act of 1934, 48 Stat. 1064, 1093.

[11] This much is clear from the *Scripps-Howard* Court's citation of *FCC* v. *Sanders Bros. Radio Station*, 309 U. S. 470, in which the basis for standing was the competitive injury that the appellee would have suffered by the licensing of another radio station in its listening area.

[12] The distinction between standing to initiate a review proceeding, and standing to assert the rights of the public or of third persons once the proceeding is properly initiated, is discussed in 3 Davis, Administrative Law Treatise, §§ 22.05–22.07 (1958).

view of agency action. See *Data Processing, supra,* at 154.

The trend of cases arising under the APA and other statutes authorizing judicial review of federal agency action has been towards recognizing that injuries other than economic harm are sufficient to bring a person within the meaning of the statutory language, and towards discarding the notion that an injury that is widely shared is *ipso facto* not an injury sufficient to provide the basis for judicial review.[13] We noted this development with approval in *Data Processing, supra,* at 154, in saying that the interest alleged to have been injured "may reflect 'aesthetic, conservational, and recreational' as well as economic values." But broadening the categories of injury that may be alleged in support of standing is a different matter from abandoning the requirement that the party seeking review must have himself suffered an injury.

Some courts have indicated a willingness to take this latter step by conferring standing upon organizations that have demonstrated "an organizational interest in the problem" of environmental or consumer protection. *Environmental Defense Fund, Inc.* v. *Hardin,* 428 F. 2d 1093, 1097.[14] It is clear that an organization whose members are injured may represent those members in a proceeding for judicial review. See, *e. g., NAACP* v. *Button,* 371 U. S. 415, 428. But a mere "interest in a problem," no matter how longstanding the interest and no matter how qualified the organization is in evaluating the problem, is not sufficient by itself to render the organization "adversely affected" or "aggrieved" within the meaning of the APA. The Sierra Club is a large and long-established organization, with an historic commitment to the cause of protecting our Nation's natural heritage from man's depredations. But if a "special interest" in this subject were enough to entitle the Sierra Club to commence this litigation, there would appear to be no objective basis upon which to disallow a suit by any other bona fide "special interest" organization, however small or short-lived. And if any group with a bona fide "special interest" could initiate such litigation, it is difficult to perceive why any individual citizen with the same bona fide special interest would not also be entitled to do so.

The requirement that a party seeking review must allege facts showing that he is himself adversely affected does not insulate executive action from judicial review, nor does it prevent any public interests from being protected through the judicial process.[15] It does serve as at least a rough attempt to put the decision as to whether review will be sought in the hands of those who have a direct stake in the outcome. That goal would be undermined were we to construe the APA to authorize judicial review at the behest of organizations or individuals who seek to do no more than vindicate their own value preferences through the judicial process.[16] The principle that the Sierra Club would have us establish in this case would do just that.

As we conclude that the Court of Appeals was correct in its holding that the Sierra Club lacked standing to maintain this action, we do not reach any other questions presented in the petition, and we intimate no view on the merits of the complaint. The judgment is

Affirmed.

MR. JUSTICE POWELL and MR. JUSTICE REHNQUIST took no part in the consideration or decision of this case.

---

[13] See, *e. g., Environmental Defense Fund, Inc.* v. *Hardin,* 428 F. 2d 1093, 1097 (interest in health affected by decision of Secretary of Agriculture refusing to suspend registration of certain pesticides containing DDT); *Office of Communication of the United Church of Christ* v. *FCC,* 359 F. 2d 994, 1005 (interest of television viewers in the programming of a local station licensed by the FCC); *Scenic Hudson Preservation Conf.* v. *FPC,* 354 F. 2d 608, 615–616 (interests in aesthetics, recreation, and orderly community planning affected by FPC licensing of a hydroelectric project); *Reade* v. *Ewing,* 205 F. 2d 630, 631–632 (interest of consumers of oleomargarine in fair labeling of product regulated by Federal Security Administration); *Crowther* v. *Seaborg,* 312 F. Supp. 1205, 1212 (interest in health and safety of persons residing near the site of a proposed atomic blast).

[14] See *Citizens Committee for the Hudson Valley* v. *Volpe,* n. 8, *supra; Environmental Defense Fund, Inc.* v. *Corps of Engineers,* 325 F. Supp. 728, 734–736; *Izaac Walton League* v. *St. Clair,* 313 F. Supp. 1312, 1317. See also *Scenic Hudson Preservation Conf.* v. *FPC, supra,* at 616:

"In order to ensure that the Federal Power Commission will adequately protect the public interest in the aesthetic, conservational, and recreational aspects of power development, those who by their activities and conduct have exhibited a special interest in such areas, must be held to be included in the class of 'aggrieved' parties under § 313 (b) [of the Federal Power Act]."

In most, if not all of these cases, at least one party to the proceeding did assert an individualized injury either to himself or, in the case of an organization, to its members.

[15] In its reply brief, after noting the fact that it might have chosen to assert individualized injury to itself or to its members as a basis for standing, the Sierra Club states:

"The Government seeks to create a 'heads I win, tails you lose' situation in which either the courthouse door is barred for lack of assertion of a private, unique injury or a preliminary injunction is denied on the ground that the litigant has advanced private injury which does not warrant an injunction adverse to a competing public interest. Counsel have shaped their case to avoid this trap."

The short answer to this contention is that the "trap" does not exist. The test of injury in fact goes only to the question of standing to obtain judicial review. Once this standing is established, the party may assert the interests of the general public in support of his claims for equitable relief. See n. 12 and accompanying text, *supra.*

[16] Every schoolboy may be familiar with de Tocqueville's famous observation, written in the 1830's, that "Scarcely any political question arises in the United States that is not resolved, sooner or later, into a judicial question." 1 Democracy in America 280 (Alfred A. Knopf, 1945). Less familiar, however, is de Tocqueville's further observation that judicial review is effective largely because it is not available simply at the behest of a partisan faction, but is exercised only to remedy a particular, concrete injury.

"It will be seen, also, that by leaving it to private interest to censure the law, and by intimately uniting the trial of the law with the trial of an individual, legislation is protected from wanton assaults and from the daily aggressions of party spirit. The errors of the legislator are exposed only to meet a real want; and it is always a positive and appreciable fact that must serve as the basis for a prosecution." *Id.,* at 102.

Dissent in Sierra Club v. Morton

MR. JUSTICE DOUGLAS, dissenting.

I share the views of my Brother BLACKMUN and would reverse the judgment below.

The critical question of "standing"[1] would be simplified and also put neatly in focus if we fashioned a federal rule that allowed environmental issues to be litigated before federal agencies or federal courts in the name of the inanimate object about to be dispoiled, defaced, or invaded by roads and bulldozers and where injury is the subject of public outrage. Contemporary public concern for protecting nature's ecological equilibrium should lead to the conferral of standing upon environmental objects to sue for their own preservation. See Stone, Should Trees Have Standing? Toward Legal Rights for Natural Objects, 45 S. Cal. L. Rev. 450 (1972). This suit would therefore be more properly labeled as *Mineral King* v. *Morton.*

Inanimate objects are sometimes parties in litigation. A ship has a legal personality, a fiction found useful for maritime purposes.[2] The corporation sole—a creature of ecclesiastical law—is an acceptable adversary and large fortunes ride on its cases.[3] The ordinary corporation is a "person" for purposes of the adjudicatory processes, whether it represents proprietary, spiritual, aesthetic, or charitable causes.[4]

So it should be as respects valleys, alpine meadows, rivers, lakes, estuaries, beaches, ridges, groves of trees, swampland, or even air that feels the destructive pressures of modern technology and modern life. The river, for example, is the living symbol of all the life it sustains or nourishes—fish, aquatic insects, water ouzels, otter, fisher, deer, elk, bear, and all other animals, including man, who are dependent on it or who enjoy it for its sight, its sound, or its life. The river as plaintiff speaks for the ecological unit of life that is part of it. Those people who have a meaningful relation to that body of water—whether it be a fisherman, a canoeist, a zoologist, or a logger—must be able to speak for the values which the river represents and which are threatened with destruction.

I do not know Mineral King. I have never seen it nor travelled it, though I have seen articles describing its proposed "development"[5] notably Hano, *Protec-*

---

[1] See generally *Data Processing Service* v. *Camp,* 397 U. S. 150 (1970); *Barlow* v. *Collins,* 397 U. S. 159 (1970); *Flast* v. *Cohen,* 392 U. S. 83 (1968). See also MR. JUSTICE BRENNAN's concurring opinion in *Barlow* v. *Collins, supra,* at 167. The issue of statutory standing aside, no doubt exists that "injury in fact" to "aesthetic" and "conservational" interests is here sufficiently threatened to satisfy the case or controversy clause. *Data Processing Service* v. *Camp, supra,* at 154.

[2] *In rem* actions brought to adjudicate libellants' interests in vessels are well known in admiralty. Gilmore & Black, The Law of Admiralty 31 (1957). But admiralty also permits a salvage action to be brought in the name of the rescuing vessel. *The Comanche,* 75 U. S. (8 Wall.) 449, 476 (1869). And, in collision litigation, the first-libelled ship may counterclaim in its own name. *The Gylfe* v. *The Trujillo,* 209 F. 2d 386 (CA2 1954). Our case law has personified vessels:

"A ship is born when she is launched, and lives so long as her identity is preserved. Prior to her launching she is a mere congeries of wood and iron. . . . In the baptism of launching she receives her name, and from the moment her keel touches the water she is transformed. . . . She acquires a personality of her own." *Tucker* v. *Alexandroff,* 183 U. S. 424, 438

[3] At common law, an office holder, such as a priest or the King, and his successors constituted a corporation sole, a legal entity distinct from the personality which managed it. Rights and duties were deemed to adhere to this device rather than to the office holder in order to provide continuity after the latter retired. The notion is occasionally revived by American courts. *E. g., Reid* v. *Barry,* 93 Fla. 849, 112 So. 846 (1927), discussed in Note, 12 Minn. L. Rev. 295 (1928), and in Note, 26 Mich. L. Rev. 545 (1928); see generally 1 Fletcher Cyclopedia Corporation, §§ 50–53; P. Potter, Law of Corporation 27 (1881).

[4] Early jurists considered the conventional corporation to be a highly artificial entity. Lord Coke opined that a corporation's creation "rests only in intendment and consideration of the law." The Case of Suttons Hospital, 77 Eng. Rep. 937, 973 (K. B. 1613). Mr. Chief Justice Marshall added that the device is "an artificial being, invisible, intangible, and existing only in contemplation of law." *Trustees of Dartmouth College* v. *Woodward,* 17 U. S. (4 Wheat.) 518, 636 (1819). Today suits in the names of corporations are taken for granted.

[5] Although in the past Mineral King Valley has annually supplied about 70,000 visitor-days of simpler and more rustic forms of recreation—hiking, camping and skiing (without lifts)—the Forest Service in 1949 and again in 1965 invited developers to submit proposals to "improve" the Valley for resort use. Walt Disney Productions won the competition and transformed the Service's idea into a mammoth project 10 times its originally proposed dimensions. For example, while the Forest Service prospectus called for an investment of at least $3 million and a sleeping capacity of at least 100, Disney will spend $35.3 million and will bed down 3300 persons by 1978. Disney also plans a nine-level parking structure with two supplemental lots for automobiles, 10 restaurants and 20 ski lifts. The Service's annual license revenue is hitched to Disney's profits. Under Disneys' projections, the Valley will be forced to accommodate a tourist population twice as dense as that in Yosemite Valley on a busy day. And, although Disney has bought up much of the private land near the project, another commercial firm plans to transform an adjoining 160-acre parcel into a "piggyback" resort complex, further adding to the volume of human activity the Valley must endure. See generally; Note, Mineral King Valley: Who Shall Watch the Watchman?, 25 Rutgers L. Rev. 103, 107 (1970); Thar's Gold in Those Hills, 206 The Nation 260 (1968). For a general critique of mass recreation enclaves in national forests see Christian Science Monitor, Nov. 22, 1965, at 5, col. 1. Michael Frome cautions that the national forests are "fragile" and "deteriorate rapidly with excessive recreation use" because "(t)he trampling effect alone eliminates vegatative growth, creating erosion and water runoff problems. The concentration of people, particularly in horse parties, on excessively steep slopes that follow old Indian or cattle routes, has torn up the landscape of the High Sierras in California and sent tons of wilderness soil washing downstream each year." M. Frome, The Forest Service 69 (1971).

tionists v. *Recreationists*—the Battle of Mineral King, N. Y. Times Mag., Aug. 17, 1969; and Browning, Mickey Mouse in the Mountains, Harper's, March 1972, p. 65. The Sierra Club in its complaint alleges that "One of the principal purposes of the Sierra Club is to protect and conserve the national resources of the Sierra Nevada Mountains." The District Court held that this uncontested allegation made the Sierra Club "sufficiently aggrieved" to have "standing" to sue on behalf of Mineral King.

Mineral King is doubtless like other wonders of the Sierra Nevada such as Tuolumne Meadows and the John Muir Trail. Those who hike it, fish it, hunt it, camp in it, or frequent it, or visit it merely to sit in solitude and wonderment are legitimate spokesmen for it, whether they may be a few or many. Those who have that intimate relation with the inanimate object about to be injured, polluted, or otherwise despoiled are its legitimate spokesmen.

The Solicitor General, whose views on this subject are in the Appendix to this opinion, takes a wholly different approach. He considers the problem in terms of "government by the Judiciary." With all respect, the problem is to make certain that the inanimate objects, which are the very core of America's beauty, have spokesmen before they are destroyed. It is, of course, true that most of them are under the control of a federal or state agency. The standards given those agencies are usually expressed in terms of the "public interest." Yet "public interest" has so many differing shades of meaning as to be quite meaningless on the environmental front. Congress accordingly has adopted ecological standards in the National Environmental Policy Act of 1969, Pub. L. 91-90, 83 Stat. 852, 42 U. S. C. § 4321, *et seq.*, and guidelines for agency action have been provided by the Council on Environmental Quality of which Russell E. Train is Chairman. See 36 Fed. Reg. 7724.

Yet the pressures on agencies for favorable action one way or the other are enormous. The suggestion that Congress can stop action which is undesirable is true in theory; yet even Congress is too remote to give meaningful direction and its machinery is too ponderous to use very often. The federal agencies of which I speak are not venal or corrupt. But they are notoriously under the control of powerful interests who manipulate them through advisory committees, or friendly working relations, or who have that natural affinity with the agency which in time develops between the regulator and the regulated.[6] As early as 1894, Attorney General Olney predicted that regulatory agencies might become "industry-minded," as illustrated by his forecast concerning the Interstate Commerce Commission:

> "The Commission is or can be made of great use to the railroads. It satisfies the public clamor for supervision of the railroads, at the same time that supervision is almost entirely nominal. Moreover, the older the Commission gets to be, the more likely it is to take a business and railroad view of things." M. Josephson, The Politicos 526 (1938).

Years later a court of appeals observed, "the recurring question which has plagued public regulation of industry [is] whether the regulatory agency is unduly oriented toward the interests of the industry it is designed to regulate, rather than the public interest it is supposed to protect." *Moss* v. *CAB*, 430 F. 2d 891, 893 (CADC 1970). See also *Office of Communication of the United Church of Christ* v. *FCC*, 359 F. 2d 994, 1003-1004; *Udall* v. *FPC*, 387 U. S. 428; *Calvert Cliffs' Coordinating Committee, Inc.* v. *AEC*, 449 F. 2d 1109; *Environmental Defense Fund, Inc.* v. *Ruckelshaus*, 439 F. 2d 584; *Environmental Defense Fund, Inc.* v. *HEW*, 428 F. 2d 1083; *Scenic Hudson Preservation Conf.* v. *FPC*, 354 F. 2d 608, 620. But see Jaffe, The Federal Regulatory Agencies In a Perspective: Administrative Limitation In A Political Setting, 11 Bos. C. I. & C. Rev. 565 (1970) (labels "industry-mindedness" as "devil" theory).

The Forest Service—one of the federal agencies behind the scheme to despoil Mineral King—has been notorious for its alignment with lumber companies, although its mandate from Congress directs it to consider

[6] The federal budget annually includes about $75 million for underwriting about 1,500 advisory committees attached to various regulatory agencies. These groups are almost exclusively composed of industry representatives appointed by the President or by Cabinet members. Although public members may be on these committees, they are rarely asked to serve. Senator Lee Metcalf warns: "Industry advisory committees exist inside most important federal agencies, and even have offices in some. Legally, their function is purely as kibitzer, but in practice many have become internal lobbies—printing industry handouts in the Government Printing Office with taxpayers' money, and even influencing policies. Industry committees perform the dual function of stopping government from finding out about corporations while at the same time helping corporations get inside information about what government is doing. Sometimes, the same company that sits on an advisory council that obstructs or turns down a government questionnaire is precisely the company which is withholding information the government needs in order to enforce a law." Metcalf, The Vested Oracles: How Industry Regulates Government, 3 The Washington Monthly 45 (1971). For proceedings conducted by Senator Metcalf exposing these relationships, see Hearings on S. 3067 before the Subcommittee on Intergovernmental Relations of the Senate Committee on Government Operations, 91st Cong., 2d Sess. (1970); Hearings on S. 1737, S. 1964, and S. 2064 before the Subcommittee on Intergovernmental Relations of the Senate Committee on Government Operations, 92d Cong., 1st Sess. (1971).

The web spun about administrative agencies by industry representatives does not depend, of course, solely upon advisory committees for effectiveness. See Elman, Administrative Reform of the Federal Trade Commission, 59 Geo. L. J. 777, 788 (1971); Johnson, A New Fidelity to the Regulatory Ideal, 59 Geo. L. J. 869, 874, 906 (1971); R. Berkman & K. Viscusi, Damming The West, The Ralph Nadar Study Group Report On The Bureau of Reclamation 155 (1971); R. Fellmeth, The Interstate Commerce Omission, Ralph Nader Study Group on the Interstate Commerce Commission and Transportation 15-39 and *passim* (1970); J. Turner, The Chemical Feast, The Ralph Nader Study Group on Food Protection and the Food and Drug Administration *passism* (1970); Massel, The Regulatory Process, 26 Law and Contemporary Problems 181, 189 (1961); J. Landis, Report on Regulatory Agencies to the President-Elect 13, 69 (1960).

the various aspects of multiple use in its supervision of the national forests.[7]

The voice of the inanimate object, therefore, should not be stilled. That does not mean that the judiciary takes over the managerial functions from the federal agency. It merely means that before these priceless bits of Americana (such as a valley, an alpine meadow, a river, or a lake) are forever lost or are so transformed as to be reduced to the eventual rubble of our urban environment, [the voice of the existing beneficiaries of these environmental wonders should be heard.[8]]

[7] The Forest Reserve Act of 1897, 30 Stat. 34, 16 U. S. C. § 551, imposed upon the Secretary of the Interior the duty to "preserve the [national] forests . . . from destruction" by regulating their "occupancy and use." In 1905 these duties and powers were transferred to the Forest Service created within the Department of Agriculture by the Act of Feb. 1, 1905, 33 Stat. 628, 16 U. S. C. § 472. The phrase "occupancy and use" has been the cornerstone for the concept of "multiple use" of national forests, that is, the policy that uses other than logging were also to be taken into consideration in managing our 154 national forests. This policy was made more explicit by the 1960 Multiple Use and Sustained Yield Act, 74 Stat. 215, 43 U. S. C. § 315, which provides that competing considerations should include outdoor recreation, range, timber, watershed, wildlife and fish purposes. The Forest Service, influenced by powerful logging interests, has, however, paid only lip service to its multiple use mandate and has auctioned away millions of timberland acres without considering environmental or conservational interests. The importance of national forests to the construction and logging industries results from the type of lumber grown therein which is well suited to builders' needs. For example, Western acreage produces douglas fir (structural support) and ponderosa pine (plywood lamination). In order to preserve the total acreage and so-called "maturity" of timber, the annual size of a Forest Service harvest is supposedly equated with expected yearly reforestation. Nonetheless, yearly cuts have increased from 5.6 billion board feet in 1950 to 13.74 billion in 1971. Forestry professionals challenge the Service's explanation that this 240% harvest increase is not really overcutting but instead has resulted from its improved management of timberlands. "Improved management" answer the critics is only a euphemism for exaggerated regrowth forecasts by the Service. N. Y. Times, Nov. 15, 1971, at 48, col. 1. Recent rises in lumber prices have caused a new round of industry pressure to auction more federally owned timber. See Wagner, Resources Report/Lumbermen, conservationists head for new battle over government timber, 3 Nat. J. 657 (1971).

Aside from the issue of how much timber should be cut annually, another crucial question is *how* lumber should be harvested. Despite much criticism the Forest Service had adhered to a policy of permitting logging companies to "clearcut" tracts of auctioned acreage. "Clearcutting," somewhat analogous to strip mining, is the indiscriminate and complete shaving from the earth of all trees—regardless of size or age—often across hundreds of contiguous acres.

Of clearcutting Senator Gale McGee, a leading antagonist of Forest Service policy, complains: "The Forest Service's management policies are wreaking havoc with the environment. Soil is eroding, reforestation is neglected, if not ignored, streams are silting, and clearcutting remains a basic practice." N. Y. Times, Nov. 14, 1971, at 60, col. 2. He adds "In Wyoming . . . the Forest Service is very much nursemaid . . . to the lumber industry . . . ." Hearings on Management Practice on the Public Lands before the Subcommittee on Public Lands of the Senate Committee on Interior and Insular Affairs, pt. 1, at 7 (1971).

Senator Jennings Randolph offers a similar criticism of the leveling by lumber companies of large portions of the Monongahela National Forest in West Virginia. *Id.*, 9. See also 116 Cong. Rec. 36971 (1970) (reprinted speech of Sen. Jennings Randolph concerning Forest Service policy in Monongahela National Forest). To investigate similar controversy surrounding the Service's management of the Bitterroot National Forest in Montana, Senator Lee Metcalf recently asked forestry professionals at the University of Montana to study local harvesting practices. The faculty group concluded that public dissatisfaction had arisen from the Forest Service's "overriding concern for sawtimber production" and its "insensitivity to the related forest uses . . . and the public interest in environmental values." S. Doc. 91–115, 91st Cong., 2d Sess., 14 (1970). See also Behan, Timber Mining: Accusation or Prospect? 77 American Forests 4 (1971) (additional comments of faculty participant); Reich, The Public and the Nation's Forests, 50 Cal. L. Rev. 381–400 (1962).

Former Secretary of the Interior Walter Hickel similarly faulted clearcutting as excusable only as a money-saving harvesting practice for large lumber corporations. W. Hickel, Who Owns America? 130 (1971). See also Risser, the U. S. Forest Service; Smokey's Strip Miners, 3 The Washington Monthly 16 (1971). And at least one Forest Service study team shares some of these criticisms of clearcutting. U. S. Dept. of Agriculture, Forest Management in Wyoming 12 (1971). See also Public Land Law Review Comm'n, Report to the President and to the Congress 44 (1970); Chapman, Effects of Logging upon Fish Resources of the West Coast, 60 J. of For. 533 (1962).

A third category of criticism results from the Service's huge backlog of delayed reforestation projects. It is true that Congress has underfunded replanting programs of the Service but it is also true that the Service and lumber companies have regularly ensured that Congress fully fund budgets requested for the Forest Service's "timber sales and management." Frome, The Environment and Timber Resources, What's Ahead for Our Public Lands? 24 (A. Pyles ed. 1970).

[[8] Permitting a court to appoint a representative of an inanimate object would not be significantly different from customary judicial appointments of guardians *ad litem*, executors, conservators, receivers, or counsel for indigents.]

The values that ride on decisions such as the present one are often not appreciated even by the so-called experts.

"A teaspoon of living earth contains 5 million bacteria, 20 million fungi, one million protozoa, and 200,000 algae. No living human can predict what vital miracles may be locked in this dab of life, this stupendous reservoir of genetic materials that have evolved continuously since the dawn of the earth. For example, molds have existed on earth for about 2 billion years. But only in this century did we unlock the secret of the penicillins, tetracyclines, and other antibiotics from the lowly molds, and thus fashion the most powerful and effective medicines ever discovered by man. [Medical scientists still wince at the thought that we might have inadvertently wiped out the rhesus monkey, medically, the most important research animal on earth.] And who knows what revelations might lie in the cells of the blackback gorilla nesting in his eyrie this moment in the Virunga Mountains of Rwanda? And what might we have learned from the European lion, the first species formally noted (in 80 A. D.) as extinct by the Romans?

["When a species is gone, it is gone forever. Nature's genetic chain, billions of years in the making, is broken for all time."] 13 Conserv. 4 (Nov. 1971).

Aldo Leopold wrote in Round River (1953) p. 147:

"In Germany there is a mountain called the Spessart. Its south slope bears the most magnificent oaks in the world. American cabinetmakers, when they want the last word in quality, use Spessart oak. The north slope, which should be better, bears an indifferent stand of Scotch pine. Why? Both slopes are part of the same state forest; both have been managed with equally scrupulous care for two centuries. Why the difference?

"Kick up the litter under the oaks and you will see that the leaves rot almost as fast as they fall. Under the pines, though, the needles pile up as a thick duff; decay is much slower. Why? Because in the Middle Ages the south slope was preserved as a deer forest by a hunting bishop; the north slope was pastured, plowed, and cut by

Perhaps they will not win. Perhaps the bulldozers of "progress" will plow under all the aesthetic wonders of this beautiful land. That is not the present question. The sole question is, who has standing to be heard?

Those who hike the Appalachian Trail into Sunfish Pond, New Jersey, and camp or sleep there, or run the Allagash in Maine, or climb the Guadalupes in West Texas, or who canoe and portage the Quetico Superior in Minnesota, certainly should have standing to defend those natural wonders before courts or agencies, though they live 3,000 miles away. Those who merely are caught up in environmental news or propaganda and flock to defend these waters or areas may be treated differently. That is why these environmental issues should be tendered by the inanimate object itself. Then there will be assurances that all of the forms of life [9] which it represents will stand before the court—the pileated woodpecker as well as the coyote and bear, the lemmings as well as the trout in the streams. Those inarticulate members of the ecological group cannot speak. But those people who have so frequented the place as to know its values and wonders will be able to speak for the entire ecological community.

Ecology reflects the land ethic; and Aldo Leopold wrote in A Sand County Almanac 204 (1949), "The land ethic simply enlarges the boundaries of the community to include soils, waters, plants, and animals, or collectively, the land."

That, as I see it, is the issue of "standing" in the present case and controversy.

APPENDIX TO OPINION OF DOUGLAS, J.

Statement of the Solicitor-General:

. . . . .

"As far as I know, no case has yet been decided which holds that a plaintiff which merely asserts that, to quote from the complaint here, its interest would be widely affected, and that 'it would be aggrieved,' by the acts of the defendant, has standing to raise legal questions in court.

"But why not? Do not the courts exist to decide legal questions? And are they not the most impartial and learned agencies we have in our governmental system? Are there not many questions which must be decided by courts? Why should not the courts decide any question which any citizen wants to raise? As the tenor of my argument indicates, this raises, I think, a true question, perhaps a somewhat novel question, in the separation of powers. . . .

"Ours is not a government by the Judiciary. It is a government of three branches, each of which was intended to have broad and effective powers subject to checks and balances. In litigable cases, the courts have great authority. But the Founders also intended that the Congress should have wide powers, and that the executive branch should have wide powers. All these officers have great responsibilities. They are no less sworn than are the members of this Court to uphold the Constitution of the United States.

"This, I submit, is what really lies behind the standing doctrine, embodied in those cryptic words 'case' and 'controversy' in Article III of the Constitution. Analytically, one could have a system of government in which every legal question arising in the course of government would be decided by the courts. It would not be, I submit, a good system. More important, it is not the system which was ordained and established in our Constitution, as it has been understood for nearly 200 years.

"Over the past 20 or 25 years there has been a great shift in the decision of legal questions in our governmental operations into the courts. This has been the result of continuous whittling away of the numerous doctrines which have been established over the years, designed to minimize the number of governmental questions which it was the responsibility of the courts to consider.

"I have already mentioned the most ancient of all, case or controversy, which was early relied on to prevent the presentation of feigned issues to the court. But there are many other doctrines, which I cannot go into in detail: reviewability, justiciability, sovereign immunity, mootness in various aspects, statutes of limitations and laches, jursdictional amount, real party in interest and various questions in relation to joinder. Under all of these headings, limitations which previously existed to minimize the number of questions decided in courts have broken down in varying degrees. I might also mention the explosive development of class actions which has thrown more and more issues into the courts. . . .

"If there is standing in this case, I find it very difficult to think of any legal issue arising in government which will not have to await one or more decisions of the court before the administrator sworn to uphold the law, can take any action. I'm not sure that this is good for the government. I'm not sure that it is good for the courts. I do find myself more and more sure that it is not the kind of allocation of governmental power in our tripartite constitutional system that was contemplated by the Founders. . . .

"I do not suggest that administrators can act at their whim and without any check at all. On the contrary, in this area they are subject to continuous check by the Congress. Congress can stop this development any time it wants to."

---

settlers, just as we do with our woodlots in Wisconsin and Iowa today. Only after this period of abuse something happened to the microscopic flora and fauna of the soil. The number of species was greatly reduced, *i. e.*, the digestive apparatus of the soil lost some of its parts. Two centuries of conservation have not sufficed to restore these losses. It required the modern microscope, and a century of research in soil science, to discover the existence of these 'small cogs and wheels' which determine harmony or disharmony between men and land in the Spessart."

[9] Senator Cranston has introduced a bill to establish a 35,000 acre Pupfish National Monument to honor the pupfish which are one inch long and are useless to man. S. 2141, 92d Cong., 1st Sess. They are too small to eat and unfit for a home aquarium. But as Michael Frome has said:

"Still, I agree with Senator Cranston that saving the pupfish would symbolize our appreciation of diversity in God's tired old biosphere, the qualities which hold it together and the interaction of life forms. When fishermen rise up united to save the pupfish they can save the world as well." Field & Stream, December 1971, p. 74.

MR. JUSTICE BRENNAN, dissenting.

I agree that the Sierra Club has standing for the reasons stated by my Brother BLACKMUN in Alternative No. 2 of his dissent. I therefore would reach the merits. Since the Court does not do so, however, I simply note agreement with my Brother BLACKMUN that the merits are substantial.

MR. JUSTICE BLACKMUN, dissenting.

The Court's opinion is a practical one espousing and adhering to traditional notions of standing as somewhat modernized by *Association of Data Processing Service Organizations, Inc.* v. *Camp,* 397 U. S. 150 (1970); *Barlow* v. *Collins,* 397 U. S. 159 (1970); and *Flast* v. *Cohen,* 392 U. S. 83 (1968). If this were an ordinary case, I would join the opinion and the Court's judgment and be quite content.

But this is not ordinary, run-of-the-mill litigation. The case poses—if only we choose to acknowledge and reach them—significant aspects of a wide, growing and disturbing problem, that is, the Nation's and the world's deteriorating environment with its resulting ecological disturbances. Must our law be so rigid and our procedural concepts so inflexible that we render ourselves helpless when the existing methods and the traditional concepts do not quite fit and do not prove to be entirely adequate for new issues?

The ultimate result of the Court's decision today, I fear, and sadly so, is that the 35.3-million-dollar complex, over 10 times greater than the Forest Service's suggested minimum, will now hastily proceed to completion; that serious opposition to it will recede in discouragement; and that Mineral King, the "area of great natural beauty nestled in the Sierra Nevada Mountains," to use the Court's words, will become defaced, at least in part, and, like so many other areas, will cease to be "uncluttered by the products of civilization."

I believe this will come about because: (1) The District Court, although it accepted standing for the Sierra Club and granted preliminary injunctive relief, was reversed by the Court of Appeals, and this Court now upholds that reversal. (2) With the reversal, interim relief by the District Court is now out of the question and a permanent injunction becomes most unlikely. (3) The Sierra Club may not choose to amend its complaint or, if it does desire to do so, may not, at this late date, be granted permission. (4) The ever-present pressure to get the project underway will mount. (5) Once underway, any prospect of bringing it to a halt will grow dim. Reasons, most of them economic, for not stopping the project will have a tendency to multiply. And the irreparable harm will be largely inflicted in the earlier stages of construction and development.

Rather than pursue the course the Court has chosen to take by its affirmance of the judgment of the Court of Appeals, I would adopt one of two alternatives:

1. I would reverse that judgment and, instead, approve the judgment of the District Court which recognized standing in the Sierra Club and granted preliminary relief. I would be willing to do this on condition that the Sierra Club forthwith amend its complaint to meet the specifications the Court prescribes for standing. If Sierra Club fails or refuses to take that step, so be it; the case will then collapse. But if it does amend, the merits will be before the trial court once again. As the Court's footnote 2, *ante*, p. 3, so clearly reveals, the issues on the merits are substantial and deserve resolution. They assay new ground. They are crucial to the future of Mineral King. They raise important ramifications for the quality of the country's public land management. They pose the propriety of the "dual permit" device as a means of avoiding the 80-acre "recreation and resort" limitation imposed by Congress in 16 U. S. C. § 497, an issue that apparently has never been litigated, and is clearly substantial in light of the congressional expansion of the limitation in 1956 arguably to put teeth into the old, unrealistic five-acre limitation. In fact, they concern the propriety of the 80-acre permit itself and the consistency of the entire, enormous development with the statutory purposes of the Sequoia Game Refuge, of which the Valley is a part. In the context of this particular development, substantial questions are raised about the use of National Park area for Disney purposes for a new high speed road and a 66,000-volt power line to serve the complex. Lack of compliance with existing administrative regulations is also charged. These issues are not shallow or perfunctory.

2. Alternatively, I would permit an imaginative expansion of our traditional concepts of standing in order to enable an organization such as the Sierra Club, possessed, as it is, of pertinent, bona fide and well-recognized attributes and purposes in the area of environment, to litigate environmental issues. This incursion upon tradition need not be very extensive. Certainly, it should be no cause for alarm. It is no more progressive than was the decision in *Data Processing* itself. It need only recognize the interest of one who has a provable, sincere, dedicated, and established status. We need not fear that Pandora's box will be opened or that there will be no limit to the number of those who desire to participate in environmental litigation. The courts will exercise appropriate restraints just as they have exercised them in the past. Who would have suspected 20 years ago that the concepts of standing enunciated in *Data Processing* and *Barlow* would be the measure for today? And MR. JUSTICE DOUGLAS, in his eloquent opinion, has imaginatively suggested another means and one, in its own way, with obvious, appropriate and self-imposed limitations as to standing. As I read what he has written, he makes only one addition to the customary criteria (the existence of a genuine dispute; the assurance of adversariness; and a conviction that the party whose standing is challenged will adequately represent the interests he asserts), that is, that the litigant be one who speaks knowingly for the environmental values he asserts.

I make two passing references:

1. The first relates to the Disney figures presented to us. The complex, the Court notes, will accommodate

14,000 visitors *a day* (3,100 overnight; some 800 employees; 10 restaurants; 20 ski lifts). The State of California has proposed to build a new road from Hammond to Mineral King. That road, to the extent of 9.2 miles, is to traverse Sierra National Park. It will have only two lanes, with occasional passing areas, but it will be capable, it is said, of accommodating 700–800 vehicles per hour and a peak of 1,200 per hour. We are told that the State has agreed not to seek any further improvement in road access through the park.

If we assume that the 14,000 daily visitors come by automobile (rather than by helicopter or bus or other known or unknown means) and that each visiting automobile carries four passengers (an assumption, I am sure, that is far too optimistic), those 14,000 visitors will move in 3,500 vehicles. If we confine their movement (as I think we properly may for this mountain area) to 12 hours out of the daily 24, the 3,500 automobiles will pass any given point on the two-lane road at the rate of about 300 per hour. This amounts to five vehicles per minute, or an average of one every 12 seconds. This frequency is further increased to one every six seconds when the necessary return traffic along that same two-lane road is considered. And this does not include service vehicles and employees' cars. Is this the way we perpetuate the wilderness and its beauty, solitude and quiet?

2. The second relates to the fairly obvious fact that any resident of the Mineral King area—the real "user"—is an unlikely adversary for this Disney-governmental project. He naturally will be inclined to regard the situation as one that should benefit him economically. His fishing or camping or guiding or handyman or general outdoor prowess perhaps will find an early and ready market among the visitors. But that glow of anticipation will be short-lived at best. If he is a true lover of the wilderness—as is likely, or he would not be near Mineral King in the first place—it will not be long before he yearns for the good old days when masses of people—that 14,000 influx per day—and their thus far uncontrollable waste were unknown to Mineral King.

Do we need any further indication and proof that all this means that the area will no longer be one "of great natural beauty" and one "uncluttered by the products of civilization?" Are we to be rendered helpless to consider and evaluate allegations and challenges of this kind because of procedural limitations rooted in traditional concepts of standing? I suspect that this may be the result of today's holding. As the Court points out, *ante*, pp. 11–12, other federal tribunals have not felt themselves so confined.[1] I would join those progressive holdings.

The Court chooses to conclude its opinion with a footnote reference to De Tocqueville. In this environmental context I personally prefer the older and particularly pertinent observation and warning of John Donne.[2]

[1] *Environmental Defense Fund, Inc.* v. *Hardin*, 428 F. 1093, 1096–1097 (CADC 1970); *Citizens for the Hudson Valley* v. *Volpe*, 425 F. 2d 97, 101–105 (CA2 1970), cert. denied, 400 U. S. 949; *Scenic Hudson Preservation Conference* v. *FPC*, 354 F. 2d 608, 615–617 (CA2 1965); *Izaak Walton League* v. *St. Clair*, 313 F. Supp. 1312, 1316–1317 (Minn. 1970); *Environmenal Defense Fund, Inc.* v. *Corps of Engineers*, 324 F. Supp. 878, 879–880 (DC 1971); *Environmental Defense Fund, Inc.* v. *Corps of Engineers*, 325 F. Supp. 728, 734–736 (ED Ark. 1971); *Sierra Club* v. *Hardin*, 325 F. Supp. 99, 107–112 (Alas. 1971); *Upper Pecos Association* v. *Stans*, 328 F. Supp. 332, 333–334 (N. Mex. 1971); *Cape May County Chapter, Inc., Izaak Walton League* v. *Macchia*, 329 F. Supp. 504, 510–514 (N. J. 1971).

See *National Automatic Laundry & Cleaning Council* v. *Schultz*, 443 F. 2d 689, 693–694 (CADC 1971); *West Virginia Highlands Conservancy* v. *Island Creek Coal Co.*, 441 F. 2d 232, 234–235 (CA4 1971); *Environmental Defense Fund, Inc.* v. *HEW*, 428 F. 2d 1083, 1085 n. 2 (CADC 1970); *Honchok* v. *Hardin*, 326 F. Supp. 988, 991 (Md. 1971).

[2] "No man is an Iland, intire of itselfe; every man is a peece of the Continent, a part of the maine; if a Clod bee washed away by the Sea, Europe is the lesse, as well as if a Promontorie were, as well as if a Mannor of thy friends or of thine owne were; any man's death diminishes me, because I am involved in Mankinde; And therefore never send to know for whom the bell tolls; it tolls for thee." Devotions XVII.

DIAMOND v. GENERAL MOTORS

Calif. Ct. of Appeals, 2d Dist. Div. 4 (Sept. 30, 1971), 3 ERC 1227

[Edited]

Files, P. J.:

This is an action brought by plaintiff "on behalf of himself and all other possessors of real property in, and residents of, the County of Los Angeles," as a class numbering 7,119,184 persons. The named defendants are 293 industrial corporations and municipalities who are alleged to have polluted the atmosphere of the county. Additional defendants, whose names are unknown to plaintiff, are also sued under the fictitious name of "Doe 1 through Doe 1,000." The complaint seeks billions of dollars in compensatory and punitive damages, 1/ and "an injunction permanently restraining defendants from emitting and discharging pollutants into the atmosphere of the County of Los Angeles." As against those defendants which are engaged in the manufacture and distribution of automobiles, the complaint also seeks "an injunction restraining the sale and registration in the County of Los Angeles of motor vehicles manufactured and produced by defendants which pollute the atmosphere" and the appointment of a special administrator to administer the retrofitting of each motor vehicle registered in the County of Los Angeles and produced and manufactured by the defendants," the cost of such retrofitting to be assessed against the defendant manufacturers.

A number of defendants appeared and demurred to the first amended complaint. All demurrers were sustained without leave to amend upon the grounds of (1) misjoinder of parties plaintiff, and (2) failure to state facts sufficient to constitute a cause of action. In a memorandum the trial judge explained his opinion that (1) this is not a class action, (2) a private person may not maintain an action for the abatement of a public nuisance without pleading special injury to himself, (3) the court lacks facilities or competency to undertake the problem of abating air pollution within the Los Angeles Basin, and (4) the complaint fails to state a cause of action in favor of plaintiff as an individual.

In substance, the automobile manufacturers are charged with negligently producing and distributing machines which are defective in that they emit harmful substances into the atmosphere; petroleum refiners are charged with manufacturing and distributing motor fuel which, in its intended use, pollutes the atmosphere; owners of industrial plants, steam generating plants, gasoline filling stations and airports are charged with unnecessarily discharging harmful substances and odors into the air. The conduct of the defendants is characterized as wilful, malicious and oppressive.

1/ The total amount of damages prayed is uncertain, depending upon whether the damages alleged in the several counts are read as cumulative or redundant.

The complaint is plainly an attempt to deal with the problem of air pollution in Los Angeles County as a whole, as between all of the individuals in the county constituting a class of plaintiffs, and the industries which plaintiff believes to be responsible for the problem, as defendants.

As we shall explain, we believe the trial court properly concluded that the class action which plaintiff is attempting may not be maintained. This is a case where (1) there are significantly disparate interests within the alleged class; (2) the right of each member to recover (as well as the amount of his recovery) will depend upon substantial issues which must be litigated as between individual plaintiffs and defendants; and (3) the number of parties, the diversity of their interests, and the multiplicity of issues all in a single action would make the proceeding unmanageable.

The Class Suit As an Action for Damages

The substance of the factual allegations of the damage claims (other than the defective products counts against the automobile and oil industries) is that the defendants are maintaining a continuing public nuisance.

Ordinarily the abatement of such a condition is the business of the sovereign, acting through its law officers (See Civ. Code, §§3491, 3494; California Oregon Power Co. v. Superior Court (1955) 45 Cal. 2d 858, 871 [291 P.2d 455]; People v. McCue (1907) 150 Cal. 195 [88 P. 899].) Civil Code section 3493 provides: "A private person may maintain an action for a public nuisance, if it is specially injurious to himself, but not otherwise." Plaintiff here attempts to bring his complaint within that statute by alleging that each member of the class has suffered special injury in that each "is prevented from enjoying his own unique property." No particulars of these special injuries are set forth.

Plaintiff relies upon such cases as Fisher v. Zumwalt (1900) 128 Cal. 493 [61 P. 82] for the proposition that a single plaintiff who is specially damaged by a public nuisance may have relief in the form of damages and injunction; and plaintiff argues that he is simply combining here all of the special damage claims of the persons he proposes to represent. This means that plaintiff is trying to allege, in a single cause of action, 7,119,184 claims for unliquidated damages arising out of 7,119,184 special injuries.

Requiring plaintiff to state separately the seven million causes of action, and to plead factually the damage as to each, would in and of itself constitute a practical bar to this action. If we were to ignore the pleading problem and allow plaintiff to come into court with a single general allegation, the trial court's problems would be only beginning. Whether an individual has been specially injured in his person will depend largely upon proof relating to him alone--going to such matters as his general health, his occupation, place of residence, and activities. Whether a parcel of real property has been damaged will depend upon its unique characteristics, such as its location, physical features and use.

The problem of trying a case of this kind is compounded by the joinder of a large number of defendants who are not alleged to have acted jointly. Nor has plaintiff alleged, or suggested that he could allege, any facts which would make one defendant vicariously liable for the acts of others. Thus the critical fact of injury would have to be litigated on distinct facts by each of the seven million residents against each of the defendants.

In addition to the counts of the complaint which allege nuisance, there are two counts which add allegations that the described conditions constitute trespasses; and there are four counts which seek damages from the automobile and oil industries upon theories of negligent manufacture and strict liability for defective design. Every one of these counts, whether stated in the language of trespass, negligence, or strict liability, presents the same basic problem of trial and proof. Each is an aggregation of tort claims for unliquidated damages; each requires a determination of the fact of injury (as well as the amount of damage) separately as to each resident as against each defendant.

The Class Suit for Injunctive Relief

In aggregating the claims of seven million residents for an injunction against air pollution, plaintiff presents a superficially attractive question of common interest. Everyone is interested in clean air. But an analysis which takes into account matters of common knowledge, as well as the state of the existing statutory law upon the subject, will disclose that the issue is not that simple.

We recognize, as did the trial court, that an excessive demand for relief does not make a complaint vulnerable to general demurrer so long as the complaint does state facts entitling the plaintiff to some relief.

But in deciding whether the complaint states a cause of action on behalf of a class, the claimed efficacy of the group relief must be considered, since an important function of the class action is to provide an economical and effective group remedy. (See Vasquez v. Superior Court (1971) 4 Cal. 3d 800, 807 [94 Cal. Rptr. 796, 484 P.2d 964].)

Once it is acknowledged that a superior court cannot, by decree, abolish air pollution, it is appropriate to face some demonstrable realities of the problem which plaintiff is asking the court to solve. We do not deal with a simple dispute between those who breathe the air and those who contaminate it. The need for controls is not in question. The issue is not "shall we," but "what kind, how much, how soon."

Plaintiff's brief makes it clear that his case is not based upon violation of any existing air pollution control law or regulation. His position is that the present system of statutes and administrative rules is inadequate, and that the enforcement machinery is ineffective. Plaintiff is simply asking the court to do what the elected representatives of the people have not done: adopt stricter standards over the discharge of air contaminants in this county, and enforce them with the contempt power of the court.

We assume, for the purposes of this decision, that notwithstanding the existing administrative machinery, anyone claiming to have sustained personal injury or property damage caused by an unreasonable discharge of contaminants into the atmosphere by one or more of the defendants could state a cause of action for his damages and for injunctive relief. But the class action attempted by plaintiff, as the purported representative of every resident of the county, is a wholly different kind of suit. The objective, which plaintiff envisions to justify his class action, is judicial regulation of the processes, products and volume of business of the major industries of the county.

It was entirely reasonable for the trial court to conclude from the face of the pleading that such an undertaking was beyond its effective capability. The plaintiff has paid the court an extravagant compliment in asking it to supersede the legislative and administrative regulation in this critical area, but the trial judge showed the greater wisdom in declining the tender.

The judgment is affirmed.

MARKS v. WHITNEY

Calif. Supreme Ct. (Dec. 9, 1971) 3 ERC 1437

[Edited]

McComb, J.:

This is a quiet title action to settle a boundary line dispute caused by overlapping and defective surveys and to enjoin defendants (herein "Whitney") from asserting any claim or right in or to the property of plaintiff Marks. The unique feature here is that a part of Marks' property is tidelands acquired under an 1874 patent issued pursuant to the Act of March 28, 1968 (Stats. 1867-68, c. 415, p. 507); a small portion of these tidelands adjoins almost the entire shoreline of Whitney's upland property. Marks asserted complete ownership of the tidelands and the right to fill and develop them. Whitney opposed on the ground that this would cut off his rights as a littoral owner and as a member of the public in these tidelands and the navigable waters covering them. He requested a declaration in the decree that Marks' title was burdened with a public trust easement; also that it was burdened with certain prescriptive rights claimed by Whitney.

The trial court settled the common boundary line to the satisfaction of the parties. However, it held that Whitney had no "standing" to raise the public trust issue and it refused to make a finding as to whether the tidelands are so burdened. It did find in Whitney's favor as to a prescriptive easement across the tidelands to maintain and use an existing seven-foot wide wharf but with the limitation that "Such rights shall be subject to the right of Marks to use, to fill and to develop" the tidelands and the seven-foot wide easement area so long as the Whitney "rights of access and ingress and egress to and from the deep waters of the Bay shall be preserved" over this strip.

Questions: First. Are these tidelands subject to the public trust; if so, should the judgment so declare?

Yes. Regardless of the issue of Whitney's standing to raise this issue the court may take judicial notice of public trust burdens in quieting title to tidelands. This matter is of great public importance, particularly in view of population pressures, demands for recreational property, and the increasing development of seashore and waterfront property. A present declaration that the title of Marks in these tidelands is burdened with a public easement may avoid needless future litigation.

Tidelands are properly those lands lying between the lines of mean high and low tide covered and uncovered successively by the ebb and flow thereof.

The trial court found that the portion of Marks lands here under consideration constitutes a part of the Tidelands of Tomales Bay, that at all times it has been, and now is, subject to the daily ebb and flow of the tides in Tomales Bay, that the ordinary high tides in the bay overflow and submerge this portion of his lands, and that Tomales Bay is a navigable body of water and an arm of the Pacific Ocean.

This land was patented as tidelands to Marks' predecessor in title. Prior to the issuance of this patent it was held that a patent to tidelands conveyed no title (Kimball v. MacPherson (1873) 46 Cal. 104; People ex rel. Pierce v. Morrill (1864) 26 Cal. 336); or a voidable title (Taylor v. Underhill (1871) 40 Cal. 471). It was not until 1913 that this court decided in People v. California Fish Co., 166 Cal. 576, 596, that "The only practicable theory is to hold that all tide land is included, but that the public right was not intended to be divested or affected by a sale of tide lands under these general laws relating alike both to swamp land and tide lands. Our opinion is that. . .the buyer of land under these statutes receives the title to the soil, the jus privatum, subject to the public right of navigation, and in subordination to the right of the state to take possession and use and (improve) it for that purpose, as it may deem necessary. In this way the public right will be preserved and the private right of the purchaser will be given as full effect as the public interests will permit."

Public trust easements are traditionally defined in terms of navigation, commerce and fisheries. They have been held to include the right to fish, hunt, bathe, swim, to use for boating and general recreation purposes the navigable waters of the state, and to use the bottom of the navigable waters for anchoring, standing, or other purposes. (See Bohn v. Albertson (1951) 107 Cal. App. 2d 738; Forestier v. Johnson, supra, 164 Cal. 24; Munninghoff v. Wisconsin Conservation Comm'n. (1949) 255 Wis. 252; Jackvony v. Powel (1941) 67 RI 218; Nelson v. DeLong (1942) 213 Minn. 425; Proctor v. Wells (1869) 103 Mass 216.) The public has the same rights in and to tidelands.

The public uses to which tidelands are subject are sufficiently flexible to encompass changing public needs. In administering the trust the state is not burdened with an outmoded classification favoring one mode of utilization over another (Colberg, Inc. v. State, 67 Cal. 2d 408, 421-422.) There is a growing public recognition that one of the most important public uses of the tidelands—a use encompassed within the tidelands trust—is the preservation of those lands in their natural state, so that they may serve as ecological units for scientific study, as open space, and as environments which provide food and habitat for birds and marine life, and which favorably affect the scenery and climate of the area.

The power of the state to control, regulate and utilize its navigable waterways and the lands lying beneath them, when acting within the terms of the trust, is absolute except as limited by the paramount supervisory power of the federal government over navigable waters (Colberg, Inc. v. State, supra, 67 Cal. 2d 416-422).

We are confronted with the issue, however, whether the trial court may restrain or bar a private party, namely, Whitney, "from claiming or asserting any estate, right, title, interest in or claim or lien upon" the tidelands quieted in Marks. The injunction so made, without any limitation expressing the public servitude, is broad enough to prohibit Whitney from asserting or in any way exercising public trust uses in these tidelands and the navigable waters covering them in his capacity as a member of the public. This is beyond the jurisdiction of the court. In the absence of state or federal action the court may not bar members of the public from lawfully asserting or exercising public trust rights on this privately owned tidelands.

There is absolutely no merit in Marks' contention that as the owner of the jus privatum under this patent he may fill and develop his property, whether for navigational purposes or not; nor in his contention that his past and present plan for development of these tidelands as a marina have caused the extinguishment of the public easement. Reclamation with or without prior authorization from the state does not ipso facto terminate the public trust nor render the issue moot. (Newcomb v. City of Newport Beach, 1936, 7 Cal. 2d 393, 402; Atwood v. Hammond (1935) 4 Cal. 2d 31, 40-41.)

Second: <u>Does Whitney have "standing to request the court to recognize and declare the public trust easement on Marks' tidelands?</u>

<u>Yes</u>. The relief sought by Marks resulted in taking away from Whitney rights to which he is entitled as a member of the general public. It is immaterial that Marks asserted he was not seeking to enjoin the public. The decree as rendered does enjoin a member of the public.

Members of the public have been permitted <u>to bring</u> an action to enforce a public right to use a beach access route (Dietz v. King (1970) 3 Cal. 3d 29); <u>to bring</u> an action to quiet title to private and public easements in a public beach (Morse v. E. A. Robey and Co., Inc. (1963) 214 Cal. App. 2d 464); and <u>to bring</u> an action to restrain improper filling of a bay and secure a general declaration of the rights of the people to the waterways and wildlife areas of the bay (Alameda Conservation Association v. State of Cal. (1971) 437 F.2d 1087, 1095-1098) [2 ERC 1175]. Members of the public have been allowed <u>to defend</u> a quiet title action by asserting the right to use a public right of way through private property (The Diamond Match Co. v. Savercool (1933) 218 Cal. 665). They have been allowed to assert the public trust easement for hunting, fishing and navigation in privately owned tidelands <u>as a defense</u> in an action to enjoin such use (Forestier v. Johnson, supra, 164 Cal. 24), and to navigate on shallow navigable waters in small boats (Bohn v. Alberston (1951) 107 Cal. App. 2d 738).

Whitney had standing to raise this issue. The court could have raised this issue on its own. "It is now well settled that the court may finally determine as between the parties in a quiet title action all of the conflicting claims regarding any estate or interest in the property." (Hendershoot v. Shipman (1951) 37 Cal. 2d 190, 194.) Where the interest concerned is one that, as here, constitutes a public burden upon land to which title is quieted, and affects the defendant as a member of the public, that servitude should be explicitly declared.

NATIONAL HELIUM CORP. v. MORTON

___F.2d___ (10th Cir. 1971), 3 ERC 1129

DOYLE, Circuit Judge.

The Secretary of the Interior in this case has appealed the decision of the United States District Court for the District of Kansas in which an injunction was entered prohibiting the termination by the Secretary of a contract for the purchase of helium from appellee companies. It presents jurisdictional and procedural problems, but the decisive question is primarily one of substance. It is whether the Secretary could summarily terminate the purchase contract without carrying out the requirements of the National Environmental Policy Act, 1/ which section provides that federal agencies shall, in connection with major actions affecting the quality of the human environment, consider and make a statement as to the environmental impact of the proposed act and other environmental consequences. The District Court in granting the injunction held that it had jurisdiction and that the statement of the Secretary in terminating the contract contained no reference to consideration by the Secretary of the application of the NEPA. The court also held that the NEPA applies to the Helium Act and that, absent the injunction, helium would be lost in the atmosphere.

Under the terms of the Helium Act 2/ the Secretary of the Interior is authorized to enter contracts of no more than 25 years' duration for the "acquisition, processing, transportation, or conservation of helium." 3/ The objects of this Act as shown by §167m are first, to develop a helium producing industry in the private sector and, secondly, to assure a steady supply of helium for "essential Government activities." 4/ The meaning of "essential Government activities" as shown by the legislative history of the Act is the needs principally of the Atomic Energy Commission, the Department of Defense and the National Aeronautics and Space Administration. 5/ The sponsors of the Act predicted that 70 percent of all helium produced would be used by government agencies and

---

1. 42 U.S.C. §4321 et seq. (hereinafter referred to as the NEPA).
2. 50 U.S.C. §167 et seq., as amended in 1960.
3. 50 U.S.C. §167(a)(2).
4. This section so provides:

   > It is the sense of the Congress that it is in the national interest to foster and encourage individual enterprise in the development and distribution of supplies of helium, and at the same time provide, within economic limits, through the administration of this chapter, a sustained supply of helium which, together with supplies available or expected to become available otherwise, will be sufficient to provide for essential Government activities. 50 U.S.C. §167m.

5. 106 Cong. Rec. 18544 (1960) (remarks of Senator Allott).

another 20 percent by government contractors, whereas only 10 percent would be used by private industry. 6/

Under the Act the Secretary is not required to purchase any helium. The entire matter is left to his discretion. 7/ In deciding to terminate the contract 8/ the Secretary stated that the basic purposes of the Act had been fulfilled, that is that the 25-year purchase program envisioned by the Act was unnecessary because as of the time of termination his estimates showed that there was enough helium in storage to fulfill government requirements through 1995. The Secretary notified the companies on January 26, 1971, that the contracts would be terminated effective March 27, 1971. In his letter he stated that there had been a diminution in the requirements of helium for essential governmental activities, and that there had been new discoveries since the execution of the contract, which discoveries had provided large sources of available helium if more of the gas "is required for essential government activities than is now in storage or will be recovered in government plants."

In its complaint the plaintiff, National Helium Corporation, joined by intervenors, Cities Service Helex, Inc. and Phillips Petroleum Company, has alleged that the Secretary's action was procedurally defective because he failed to hold public hearings in accordance with the Helium Act and the Administrative Procedure Act, and in that he had failed to consult the Council on Environmental Quality. The prayer of each contractor was for preliminary injunction preventing termination of the contract. In anticipation of the Secretary's raising jurisdictional questions as to standing, the companies alleged that they were seeking to protect not only their own financial interests, but were also appearing as private attorneys general in order to protect the public interest in the helium program. In this latter connection they have alleged that if the helium is not extracted by them from the natural gas before the natural gas is delivered to the consumer, the helium would be vented into the atmosphere and lost when the natural gas was consumed as fuel.

In our judgment the District Court had jurisdiction to entertain the suit and did not act properly in issuing injunctive relief in view of the Secretary's failure to observe the requirements of

---

6. Id. at 18544, 18546 (remarks of Senator Allott).

7. Id. at 18545, 18608 (remarks of Senators Allott and Carroll).

8. The termination clause under which the Secretary acted reads as follows:

> Buyer may, at its option, terminate this contract at any time if, (1) in the opinion of the Secretary of the Interior, the discovery of large new helium resources or a substantial diminution in helium requirements or any circumstance of similar nature should occur which would make the continued operation of Seller's plant and the continued purchase of helium-gas mixture extracted therein unnecessary to accomplish the purposes of the Act or any amendment thereto, or (2) a material circumstance of force majeure making it impracticable of impossible for either Buyer or Seller to carry out its obligations under this contract which circumstance cannot be remedied with reasonable dispatch.

the NEPA prior to termination. Apart from this one aspect, we view the termination as action which is entirely within the discretion of the Secretary, involving as it does a contract which was entered into in the first instance solely on the basis of the Secretary's decision.

II

The government's claim is that the District Court lacked jurisdiction to review the action of the Secretary because the subject matter involved a government contract in which the amount in controversy exceeds $10,000, and that the sole remedy available is an action in the Court of Claims under the Tucker Act, 28 U.S.C. §1346. The government further maintains that the plaintiffs lack standing because they do not qualify as private attorneys general purporting to act in the public interest since the magnitude of their own private interests are manifestly opposed to the interests of the public.

The District Court thought that it was "passing strange" to see the giants of the oil and gas industry representing the public interest, but concluded that they were not per se disqualified to occupy this role and concluded that §10 of the Administrative Procedure Act gives standing to government contractors seeking review of administrative action challenged as arbitrary and capricious, abusive of discretion, or otherwise illegal.

We are of the opinion that the contention that this was not an agency action within the meaning of §702 of the Administrative Procedure Act is untenable since the termination is not merely a contract termination but the termination of an extensive program authorized by act of Congress. The Administrative Procedure Act defines agency action as "an agency rule, order, license, sanction, relief, or the equivalent or denial thereof, or failure to act." We must therefore hold that the termination of a program as extensive as this which also poses substantial environmental problems qualifies under the mentioned definition. It cannot be denied that the companies have a genuine substantial financial interest in the termination of the contract. But it is their asserted representation of the public interest - which from their personal standpoint is admittedly less important than their private financial stake - which in final analysis justifies their seeking judicial review. It is the Secretary's violation of or failure to comply with the mandate of the Environmental Protection Act which furnishes a jurisdictional basis. If the contracting parties were not invoking NEPA, the problem of federal question jurisdiction would be perhaps somewhat tenuous. Their remedy under the Tucker Act in the Court of Claims could arguably at least be adequate. At the same time, this Court of Claims remedy is not preemptive merely because it sounds in contract.

III

The Secretary next argues that he is protected from suit here by the doctrine of sovereign immunity because 1) the United States is the real litigant; 2) there is no statute authorizing injunctive interference with the termination of a government contract; and 3) the Administrative Procedure Act does not remove the bar to suits of this nature. However, as previously noted, we are of the view that the conservation and environmental issue makes the difference. It serves to distinguish this case from Wells v. Roper, 246 U.S. 335 (1918) and Larson v. Domestic and Foreign Commerce Corp., 337 U.S. 682 (1949). The fact that the Secretary was compelled by law to act in accordance with the NEPA and failed to do so brings this case within the exception noted in Dugan v. Rank, 372 U.S. 609 (1963), i.e. it is action which is contrary to law; and cf. Pankey Land & Cattle Company v. Hardin, 427 F.2d 43 (10th Cir. 1970), which involved the mere exercise of discretion by the Secretary of Agriculture. As we heretofore have noted, the Administrative Procedure Act authorized review of agency action in cases such as this one.

It would be repetitious to discuss at length the further argument of the Secretary that the plaintiffs lack standing. We are unable to say that the companies are motivated solely by protection of their own pecuniary interest and that the public interest aspect is so infinitesimal that it ought to be disregarded altogether. It is not part of our function to weigh or proportion these conflicting interests. Nor are we called upon to determine whether persons seeking to advance the public interest are indeed conscientious and sincere in their efforts. True, the plaintiffs are not primarily devoted to ecological improvement, but they are not on this account disqualified from seeking to advance such an interest. No group has a monopoly on working for the public good.

IV

The declared purpose of the NEPA is to encourage productive and enjoyable harmony between man and his environment; to promote efforts which will prevent or eliminate damage to the environment; to stimulate the health and welfare of man; to enrich the understanding of the ecological systems and natural resources important to the nation; and to establish a Council on Environmental Quality. It is further stated in subsection (b), 42 U.S.C. §4331 et seq. that its purpose is to improve and coordinate federal plans, functions, programs and resources to the end that the nation may.

> (5) achieve a balance between population and resource use which will permit high standards of living and a wide sharing of life's amenities; and
> (6) enhance the quality of renewable resources and approach the maximum attainable recycling of depletable resources. 42 U.S.C. §4331 (emphasis added.)

(The court here quotes from Sec. 102(2)(c) of the National Environmental Policy Act of 1969. The full text of this Act is published in Chapter One.)

It is undeniable that the Act compels the Department to comply with its provisions when action is being taken having to do with a depletable resource. Here also there is evidence of "new and expanding technological advances" directly related to the need for an application of this resource.

It is undisputed that the Secretary has not considered the environmental impact and has not taken any steps to fulfill the requirements of the NEPA. Indeed the Secretary has not even followed the regulations of his own Interior Department purporting to implement the statute. The NEPA also establishes a Council (in 42 U.S.C. §4344). In order to carry out the mandate of the statute the Council must be apprised of agency actions having environmental consequences. It does not appear from the statute that the agency action must await any responsive comments from the Council. Instead, the apparent purpose of the Council is to review federal programs and activities so as to keep the President informed on the extent to which these activities may affect the policies set forth in the Act. Thus, the Council's function is in no way regulatory. Its purpose is to take information and to coordinate the reporting of governmental activities so as to aid the policy makers.

The mandatory nature of the NEPA is emphasized in recent decisions. See, for example, Calvert Cliffs' Coordinating Committee v. U.S. Atomic Energy Commission, _____F.2d_____ (D.C. Cir. July 23, 1971 #24,839). The decisions are also clear that the mandates of the NEPA pertain to procedure and do not undertake to control decision making within the departments.

As we view it then the purposes of the NEPA are realized by requiring the agencies to assess environmental consequences in formulating policies, and by insuring that the governmental agencies shall pay heed to environmental considerations by compelling them to follow out NEPA procedures.

The Secretary in the instant case proposes to take an action which has environmental consequences, namely rapid depletion of the helium resources of the country. Whether the Secretary's proposed action has significant long range consequences, or whether the environmental effects are insignificant in relationship to the countervailing government interests, are decisions which are left to the Secretary. The important thing is that he must consider the problem. As was said by the D.C. Circuit in Calvert Cliffs', supra:

> The sweep of NEPA is extraordinarily broad, compelling consideration of any and all types of environmental impact of federal action.

In oral arguments the appellees have expressed a desire for extensive administrative proceedings. We do not see any such requirement. This is an intra-departmental matter in which the Secretary fulfills his obligation by following the mandate of the NEPA. Neither the APA nor the NEPA compels him to appoint an examiner and conduct hearings. Indeed the Department has NEPA procedures in its manual. He ought to at least follow these. There is no indication that Congress in enacting the NEPA intended to impose extensive procedural impediments to Department action.

Having concluded that the court had jurisdiction in this cause and that the NEPA fully applies to the action here involved, it follows that the District Court acted properly in enjoining the termination program, at least pending the compliance by the Secretary with the NEPA.

We agree with the Secretary that the matter here involved is urgent and should be expedited in every possible way.

The judgment is affirmed.

AUTHOR'S POSTSCRIPT

The following paragraph is a recommendation from the Committee on Resources and Man of the National Academy of Sciences-National Research Council, which was submitted with testimony before the Subcommittee on Conservation and Natural Resources of the House Committee on Government Operation, Sept. 15-16, 1969:

> *That the present Helium Conservation Program of the Department of the Interior be reevaluated.*—Helium is unique in its combination of unusual properties and critical uses. It is essential for cryogenics, superconductivity, cooling of nuclear reactors, exploration of the seabed, and the space program. According to available estimates it is in short supply, yet it continues to be wasted in the combustion of natural gases. Its recovery from these gases and conservation for the future is feasible and is already being done on a limited scale. The Helium Conservation Program should be carefully reevaluated to determine if it can meet helium needs beyond the early part of the 21st century. If such evaluation leaves any question at all about the adequacy of the program, the program should be extended without delay to apply to lower concentrations of helium and more natural gas fields.

GENERAL INDEX
Volume One

includes cases printed in this volume